Educational Psychology
windows on classrooms

5TH EDITION

Paul Eggen

University of North Florida

Don Kauchak

University of Utah

Merrill
Prentice Hall

Upper Saddle River, New Jersey
Columbus, Ohio

Library of Congress Cataloging in Publication Data

Eggen, Paul D.
    Educational psychology : windows on classrooms / Paul Eggen, Don Kauchak.—5th ed.
      p.   cm.
    Includes bibliographical references and index.
    ISBN 0-13-017176-X (pbk.)
      1. Educational psychology—Study and teaching (Higher)—United States. 2. Learning,
Psychology of—Case studies.   I. Kauchak, Donald P.   II. Title.
    LB051.E463   2001
    370.15—dc21   00-026983

370.15
.E466
2001

Vice President and Publisher: Jeffery W. Johnston
Executive Editor: Kevin Davis
Editorial Assistant: Christina Kalisch
Development Editor: Hope Madden
Production Editor: Sheryl Glicker Langner
Design Coordinator: Karrie Converse-Jones
Photo Coordinator: Nancy Harre Ritz
Cover Designer: Ceri Fitzgerald
Cover photo: Suzie Fitzhugh
Production Manager: Laura Messerly
Electronic Text Management: Marilyn Wilson Phelps, Melanie Ortega, Karen Bretz
Director of Marketing: Kevin Flanagan
Marketing Manager: Amy June
Marketing Services Manager: Krista Groshong

This book was set in Garamond by Prentice Hall. It was printed and bound by R. R. Donnelley & Sons Company. The cover was printed by Phoenix Color Corp.

Photo Credits: p. 2 by Tom Tracy/Photophile; pp. 6, 21, 22, 31, 58, 86, 144, 147, 151, 168, 189, 192, 204, 237, 263, 278, 363, 367(top), 373, 422, 430, 435, 449, 470, 563, 613, 615, 624 by Scott Cunningham/Merrill; p. 11 by Will Hart/PhotoEdit; pp. 17, 177(lt), 322, 566, 610 by James L. Shaffer; p. 28 by Richard Hutchings/PhotoEdit; pp. 40, 490, 596 by Mary Kate Denny/PhotoEdit; pp. 41, 240, 300, 379, 562 by Anthony Magnacca/Merrill; p. 45 by Bill Bachmann/The Image Works; pp. 48, 296 by Bill Bachmann/Photo Researchers, Inc.; p. 70 by Anne Vega/Merrill; p. 80 by Bob Daemmrich/Uniphoto Picture Agency; pp. 88, 95, 130, 212, 358, 390, 408, 579 by David Young-Wolff/PhotoEdit; p. 94 by Gale Zucker Photography; p. 101 by Blair Seitz/Photo Researchers, Inc.; pp. 103, 254 by Bill Aaron/PhotoEdit; pp. 107, 260, 287, 367(bottom), 500, 519, 581, 635 by Tom Watson/Merrill; p. 116 by Dennis MacDonald/PhotoEdit; p. 122 by Lawrence Migdale/Pix; pp. 127, 177(rt), 191, 217, 218, 339, 345 by Todd Yarrington/Merrill; pp. 138, 315, 413, 497 by KS Studios/Merrill; pp. 155, 201, 202, 272 by Paul Conklin/PhotoEdit; p. 162 by Arthur Tilley/FPG International LLC; pp. 173, 534 by Will & Deni McIntyre/Photo Researchers, Inc.; p. 181 by Rhoda Sidney/PhotoEdit; p. 184 by Linda Peterson/Merrill; p. 215 by Michelle Bridwell/PhotoEdit; p. 222 by Jeff Greenberg/Omni-Photo Communications, Inc.; pp. 229, 396, 445, 462, 542 by Michael Newman/PhotoEdit; pp. 231, 569 by Larry Hamill/Merrill; p. 248 by Barbara Schwartz/Merrill; p. 258 by Lloyd Lemmerman/Merrill; p. 293 by Bonnie Kamin/PhotoEdit; p. 308 by Robert Houser/Comstock; p. 327 by Steve Skjold/PhotoEdit; p. 333 by Jeff Greenberg/Visuals Unlimited; p. 336 by Randall Hyman; p. 388 by Kevin Horan/Tony Stone Images; p. 402 by Dana White/PhotoEdit; p. 423 by Blair Seitz; p. 450 by James D. Wilson/Liaison Agency, Inc.; p. 474 by Bob Daemmrich/The Image Works; p. 478 David Young-Wolff/Tony Stone Images; p. 484 by Laima Druskis/PH College; p. 486 by Robert Finken; p. 514 by Charles Gupton/Uniphoto Picture Agency; p. 523 by David Napravnik/Merrill; p. 525 by Robert Finken/Index Stock Imagery, Inc.; p. 527 by Pearson Learning; p. 550 by Jose Pelaez Photography/The Stock Market; p. 555 by Silver Burdett Ginn; p. 573 by Tony Freeman/PhotoEdit; p. 592 by Russell D. Curtis/Photo Researchers, Inc.

Additional Credits: "Family Circus" cartoons on pp. 14 and 17 reprinted with special permission of King Features Syndicate.

10 9 8 7 6 5 4 3 2 1
ISBN 0-13-017176-X

This book is dedicated to Clifton Eggen and Martin Kauchak.
They gave us their best.

Preface

Educational psychology continues to rapidly change and evolve, and we have written the fifth edition to reflect this progress. At the same time, however, we remain true to our original goals in writing this book: to provide you, our readers, with a text that effectively applies educational psychology to the real world. The implications of educational psychology has learning and teaching remain the core of our text. The subtitle "Windows on Classrooms" refers to our active portrayal of true classroom scenarios, which continue to be essential. We liberally use case studies and vignettes taken from actual classrooms to make the content of the text concrete and understandable. This practice is grounded in learning theory and is consistent with the latest learning and motivation research.

We introduce each chapter with a detailed classroom case to provide an applied framework for the chapter content. Frequent references to the case, including specific portions of dialogue, illustrate chapter topics and emphasize application in classroom settings. In this way, our case studies—both written and video—are integrated with each topic presented.

Application alone isn't sufficient, of course. Theory and research are at the heart of educational psychology. In preparing this edition we continually looked to research to inform our writing, and added many new topics, including a close, applied look at technology in education, to focus the book on the cutting edge of theory and research.

New and Revised Sections

- **Increased Coverage of Theory.** This edition increases its coverage of recent theoretical advances, including cognitive load theory, dual-processing theory, dual-coding theory, and increased emphasis on cognitive motivation theory.
- **Increased Emphasis on Social Constructivism.** Social constructivism is increasingly emphasized as a framework for guiding instruction, and this edition includes expanded discussions of its implications for teaching.
- **Revised and Expanded Discussion of Motivation.** This edition includes an expanded discussion of the influence of learner beliefs on motivation, increased emphasis on making learners responsible for their own motivation, and a revised and expanded discussion of the role of autonomy and relatedness in learner motivation.
- **Revised and Expanded Discussion of Cognitive and Social Development.** Principles of development provide a framework for discussion, of research on brain growth and possible implications for instruction, as well as expanded coverage of social development, perspective taking, and social problem solving.
- **Increased Coverage of Language Development.** The discussion of language development and language diversity has been revised and expanded for this edition.
- **Understanding and Applying Educational Research.** Professional educators need to understand the research that influences their practice. A new section in Chapter 1 introduces the reader to descriptive, correlational, and experimental research, the relationships between research and theory, and how research and theory are applied to classroom practice.

▌ **Increased Coverage of Learner Differences**. Recent research on gender differences, cultural diversity, as well as revisions in provisions for learners with exceptionalities are reflected in this edition.
▌ **Alternative Assessment**. This discussion of alternative assessment with emphasis on the use of portfolios as assessment tools is expanded for this edition.
▌ **Technology and Learning**. To capitalize on the rapidly increasing influence of technology in our lives, this edition now includes a "Technology and Learning" section in every chapter. Each section focuses on the implications of technology for learning and teaching.

New Companion Pieces

"Concepts in Classrooms" Video Segments

The success of the third edition's **integrated** cases and the fourth edition's **insights into learning** video cases prompted the development of video segments that illustrate specific concepts in educational psychology. The 10 episodes, each 8–12 minutes long, provide specific, real-world illustrations of some of educational psychology's most important topics, including **cognitive development, constructing understanding, transfer of learning, essential teaching abilities,** and **discovery learning**.

Interactive CD-ROM for Students

An interactive CD-ROM accompanies this text and is integrated into four chapters, allowing the reader to use technology to investigate and explore the following topics in greater depth: cognitive development, schema theory and background knowledge, conceptual change, and moral development.

Expanded Companion Website

The Companion Website for this edition has been expanded to include a **Student Self-Assessment** section including case-based essay questions, which provides students with additional practice in applying the content to the real world; an **Online Casebook**, which presents cases for discussion and analysis, including feedback for students and instructors; and a **Message Board**, which includes discussion topics and questions.

Features of This Text

In addition to the elements that are new for this edition, the text retains many of the features that have proven to be valuable for helping educational psychology students learn about and understand the topics presented in the book.

Integrated Video Case Studies

To truly integrate topics presented in the text with real-world applications, seven classroom video case studies are used—including the three **Insights-into-Learning** cases that introduce topics in Chapters 7, 8, and 13. By examining learners' thinking in both classroom learning activities and follow-up interviews, these videos provide insights into learning by illustrating learners' thinking and demonstrating the complexities of learning and the sophistication of teaching required to promote that learning. The three, hour-long videos include the actual lesson, an interview with four students, and an interview with the teacher. The focus in each case is on learning and learners' thinking. These three Insights-into-Learning videos, plus the end-of-chapter video cases in Chapters 2, 7, 8, and 13, exist in both written and video formats. These cases illustrate actual classroom life—real learners and real teachers involved in learning and teaching in authentic classroom contexts.

Additional Case Studies

In addition to these integrated video case studies, the text includes more than 50 additional written cases—all taken from actual classroom experiences—that illustrate the content of the chapters. Each chapter begins with a case study that provides an anchor for the chapter. The case study is then woven into the chapter to illustrate the topics being discussed.

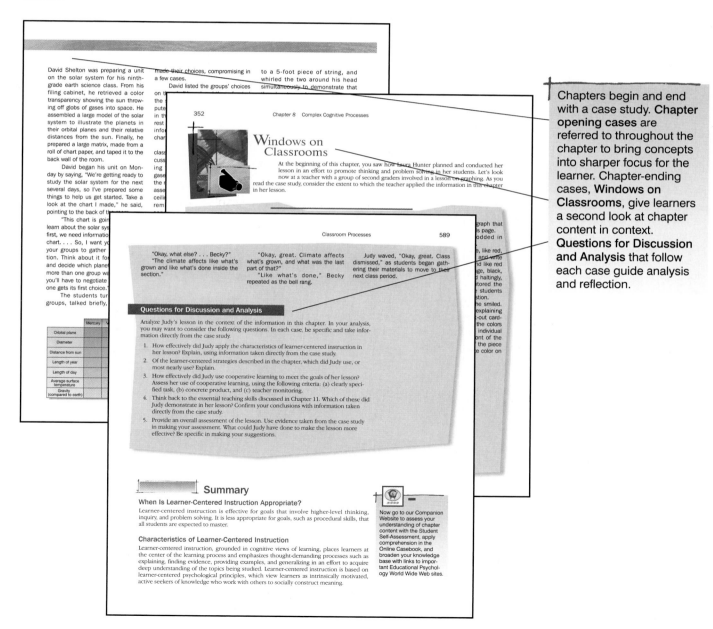

Chapters begin and end with a case study. **Chapter opening cases** are referred to throughout the chapter to bring concepts into sharper focus for the learner. Chapter-ending cases, **Windows on Classrooms**, give learners a second look at chapter content in context. **Questions for Discussion and Analysis** that follow each case guide analysis and reflection.

Windows on Classrooms

Each chapter also ends with a case. This feature, called **Windows on Classrooms**, illustrates applications of the chapter content. Each "Windows on Classrooms" case is followed by a series of "Questions for Discussion and Analysis" that encourage you to assess the learning and teaching in the case and to reflect on your own knowledge and beliefs as your understanding of learning and teaching develops.

Theory into Perspective

Teachers are faced with a number of alternate theories that attempt to describe and explain learning. Assessing the appropriateness of these theories for specific learning situations can be a daunting task. **Theory into Perspective** sections at the end of each major learning theory analyze the strengths and weaknesses of these theories and their value in different learning contexts.

Classroom Connections

As in earlier editions, we have included sections throughout each chapter that offer suggestions for applying the content to specific learning and teaching situations. **Classroom Connections** describe successful teaching practices in classrooms, from all grade levels and content areas, to illustrate a variety of effective applications.

Each chapter contains at least three **Classroom Connections**, which review practical strategies for improving the learning of diverse student populations. Aimed at helping you see the application of teaching in real classrooms with real learners they provide practical suggestions for implementing the content by making connections to classroom learning.

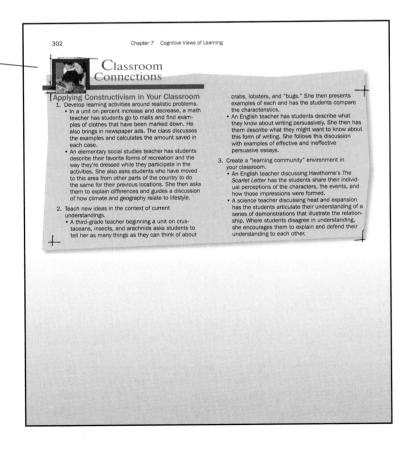

302   Chapter 7   Cognitive Views of Learning

Classroom Connections

Applying Constructivism in Your Classroom

1. Develop learning activities around realistic problems.
   - In a unit on percent increase and decrease, a math teacher has students go to malls and find examples of clothes that have been marked down. He also brings in newspaper ads. The class discusses the examples and calculates the amount saved in each case.
   - An elementary social studies teacher has students describe their favorite forms of recreation and the way they're dressed while they participate in the activities. She also asks students who have moved to this area from other parts of the country to do the same for their previous locations. She then asks them to explain differences and guides a discussion of how climate and geography relate to lifestyle.

2. Teach new ideas in the context of current understandings.
   - A third-grade teacher beginning a unit on crustaceans, insects, and arachnids asks students to tell her as many things as they can think of about

crabs, lobsters, and "bugs." She then presents examples of each and has the students compare the characteristics.
   - An English teacher has students describe what they know about writing persuasively. She then has them describe what they might want to know about this form of writing. She follows this discussion with examples of effective and ineffective persuasive essays.

3. Create a "learning community" environment in your classroom.
   - An English teacher discussing Hawthorne's *The Scarlet Letter* has the students share their individual perceptions of the characters, the events, and how those impressions were formed.
   - A science teacher discussing heat and expansion has the students articulate their understanding of a series of demonstrations that illustrate the relationship. Where students disagree in understanding, she encourages them to explain and defend their understanding to each other.

Learner Diversity

To respond to the increasingly diverse student populations that we as teachers will encounter, it is critical that we capitalize on the richness that this diversity can bring to learning and teaching environments. To reflect this emphasis, learner diversity is a theme for this text. Each chapter contains a section on diversity, with its own set of Classroom Connections, and Chapter 4 is devoted to this topic.

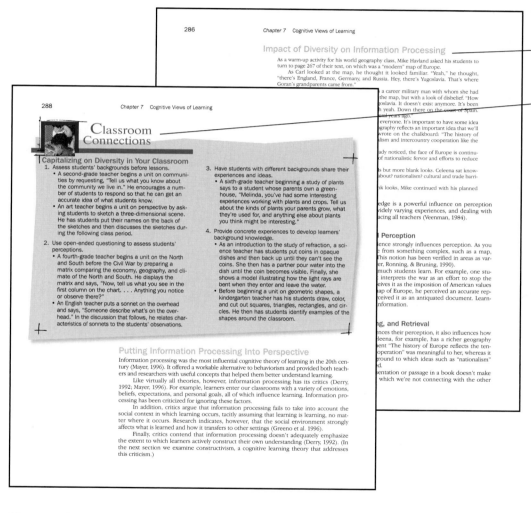

Every chapter contains a section that examines issues relevant to diversity. And at least one **Classroom Connections** feature in every chapter offers learners practical suggestions and applications for implementing strategies that foster the learning of all students.

Margin Questions

Research indicates that learning is enhanced when students are actively involved in the learning process. To place you in an active learning role, we use margin questions that ask you to do one of three things: explain a specific aspect of the content on the basis of theory and/or research, relate the immediate topic to one you've studied in an earlier chapter, or relate a topic to a real-life experience. In this regard, the margin questions are intended to help you reflect on the content, further apply your understanding of educational psychology to classrooms, integrate topics, and make the content more personal by applying it to your everyday experiences.

Technology Coverage

Technology and its implications for student learning are explored and utilized, first in a regular chapter feature that looks closely at the way technology can be and is used in K–12 classrooms, and again in chapters 2, 3, 7, and 9 as we ask you to utilize the information on the accompanying CD-ROM to better ground your own understanding of educational psychology concepts.

Every chapter contains a section on **Technology and Learning**, which examines the influence of technology in today's classrooms, offering useful information and practical examples concerning technology and education.

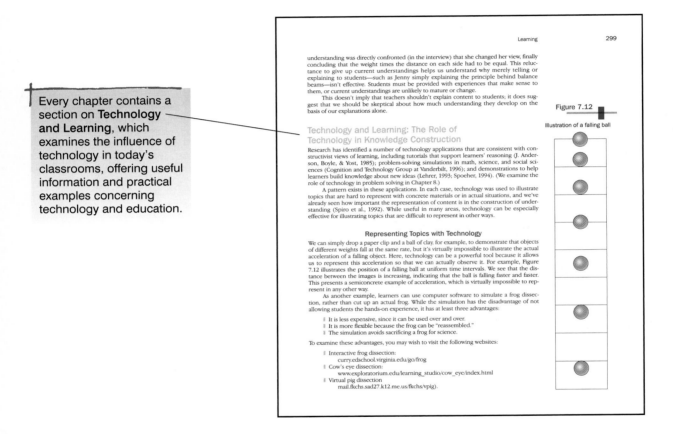

Important Concepts

Important concepts in this book are identified in the body of the text with bold-faced type followed by an italicized definition. This allows you to identify these in context as you read and study the text. These important concepts also appear at the end of each chapter, identified by page number.

Figures, Tables, and Outlines

Learning is more efficient when information is organized so that connections and relationships are apparent, rather than presented in isolated segments. Figures, tables, and outlines are used frequently to summarize important information and give you additional examples of each chapter's topics.

Chapter Endings

We know that learning is enhanced by summaries and reviews of important topics. For this reason we close each chapter with a Summary that succinctly describes significant ideas in the chapter. Each summary is organized using major chapter headings and is intended to further help you integrate the ideas you've studied in earlier chapters.

End of Text

A Reference list provides bibliographic information for all the sources we cite. Detailed author and subject indexes allow quick access to specific topics.

Text Supplements

To further aid your learning and development as a teacher, several supplements have been provided for you and your instructor's use. To maximize the opportunities for learning, the entire package—text, video cases, and supplements—is thoroughly integrated. In our attempt to provide you and your instructor with the most complete educational psychology package that exists, we have written our own supplements, making every effort to ensure that all the components complement each other.

Student Study Guide

Organized by chapter, the Student Study Guide includes chapter outlines, chapter overviews, chapter objectives, and application exercises. These exercises put you in an active role as you apply concepts to authentic classroom situations. Feedback is provided for the application exercises.

Each chapter also includes a self-help quiz, using the same format as the items in the test bank that accompanies the text, answers to the self-help quiz, and suggested responses to the margin questions in the chapters.

In addition to the chapter-by-chapter materials, the Student Study Guide includes suggestions and guidelines to enable you to better understand how to effectively use case studies in your coursework.

Companion Website

The expanded Companion Website includes a Student Self-Assessment section; an Online Casebook; annotated, content-related web links; and a chat area and message board.

Transparencies

A transparency package is available for your instructor's use. As with the figures and tables that appear throughout the text, the transparencies help organize the information you're studying to deepen and broaden your understanding of text content. Electronic versions of the transparencies are also available on the CD-ROM for Instructors.

Video Library

In Chapter 1, we discuss the work of experts who suggest that teachers should think critically, practically, and artistically. They believe that teachers should carefully examine research, their own work, and the work of other teachers. To help you develop your critical thinking, you will have the opportunity to study videotaped segments that focus on cognitive development, classroom management, cooperative learning, metacognition, whole language, and diversity. Some episodes represent "slices of classroom life" that can serve as focal points for analysis and discussion. Questions such as "What are the major strengths and weaknesses of this lesson?" and "How could this have been taught more effectively?" encourage reflection. This process of analysis will help cultivate your ability to critically examine your own work, complementing the written and video Windows on Classrooms cases that we've already described.

Test Bank

Research consistently indicates that learning is enhanced when teachers have high expectations for their students and when they ask them to think critically and analytically about the content they are learning. In line with these findings, many of the test items you'll encounter on quizzes will be case studies that require you to analyze information taken from classrooms and to make decisions based on evidence. Instead of memorizing strings of words, you'll apply what you have learned to new situations. This is a challenging and rewarding experience and, with practice, your ability to think critically and analytically will improve.

The *Self-Help Quizzes* in the **Student Study Guide** and the *Student Self-Assessment* on the **Companion Website** will help you develop your analytical skills with practice items similar to those you'll encounter on quizzes and tests.

A printed test bank and computerized versions in Windows® or Macintosh software are available to your professor.

Instructor's Manual

In addition to the supplements we've already described, the Instructor's Manual contains suggestions for learning activities, groupwork, and out-of-class assignments. While you won't encounter the content of the Instructor's Manual directly, it is an integral part of this overall package.

CD-ROM for Instructors

A flexible and user-friendly CD-ROM is also available to your instructor. Features of the printed supplements can be accessed on the CD-ROM and printed out. In addition, for professors who teach using an LDS screen or some other electronic display, all print materials, including the transparencies, will be accessible for editing and creating customized presentations.

All of the components in this text and the supplements are designed to be consistent with what we know about learning and motivation. We believe they reflect a realistic view of learning and teaching today and as we move into the new millennium. We wish you the best of luck in your study. We hope that you find it both exciting and meaningful.

Acknowledgments

Every book reflects the work of a team that includes the authors, the staff of editors, and the reviewers. We appreciate the input we've received from professors and students who have used previous editions of the book, and gratefully acknowledge the contributions of the reviewers who offered us constructive feedback to guide us in this new edition: Jerrell C. Cassady, Ball State University; Jennifer Fager, Western Michigan University; Anthony J. Gabriele, University of Northern Iowa; Newell T. Gill, Florida Atlantic University; Glenda Griffin, Texas A & M University; Jane Marie Litwak, Kutztown University; Marian R. Plant,

Northern Illinois University; Zola Richie, Chicago State University; Robert J. Stevens, Pennsylvania State University; and Atilano Valencia, California State University, Fresno.

In addition, we acknowledge with our thanks, the reviewers of our previous editions. They are: Kay S. Bull, Oklahoma State University; Thomas G. Fetsco, Northern Arizona University; Newell T. Gill, Florida Atlantic University; Dov Liberman, University of Houston; Hermine H. Marshall, San Francisco State University; Luanna H. Meyer, Massey University–New Zealand; Nancy Perry, University of British Columbia; Jay Samuels, University of Minnesota; Gregory Schraw, University of Nebraska–Lincoln; Dale H. Schunk, Purdue University; Rozanne Sparks, Pittsburg State University; Karen M. Zabrucky, Georgia State University; Patricia Barbetta, Florida International University; David Bergin, University of Toledo; Scott W. Brown, University of Connecticut; Barbara Collamer, Western Washington University; Betty M. Davenport, Campbell University; Charles W. Good, West Chester University; Tes Mehring, Emporia State University; Evan Powell, University of Georgia; Robert J. Stevens, Pennsylvania State University; and Julianne C. Turner, Notre Dame University.

Special thanks go to Catherine Crain-Thoreson of Western Washington University for her efforts in helping us improve the test bank, and to Royal Van Horn of the University of North Florida for helping us develop the technology and learning sections of each chapter. Their contributions to this edition were invaluable.

In addition to the reviewers who guided our revisions, our team of editors gave us support in many ways. Kevin Davis, our Executive Editor, continues to guide us with his intelligence, insight, and finger on the pulse of the field. Hope Madden, our development editor, helped us make the book more accessible to our readers, and her good humor was appreciated when the pressure was on. A very special thanks to Sheryl Langner for her conscientiousness and diligence in producing the book under an incredibly tight time schedule. She has been with us for three editions; in each she has been supportive and flexible, and the professionalism and commitment to excellence that she consistently demonstrates are appreciated more than we can say. Sheryl, stay with us; we need you.

Our appreciation goes to all these fine people who have taken our words and given them shape. We hope that all our efforts will result in increased learning for students and more rewarding teaching for instructors.

Finally, we would sincerely appreciate any comments or questions about anything that appears in the book or any of its supplements. Please feel free to contact either of us at any time. Our e-mail addresses are: peggen@unf.edu and kauchak@gse.utah.edu.

Good luck.

Paul Eggen
Don Kauchak

Our Website

Discover the Companion Website
Accompanying This Book

The Prentice Hall Companion Website: A Virtual Learning Environment

Technology is a constantly growing and changing aspect of our field that is creating a need for content and resources. To address this emerging need, Prentice Hall has developed an online learning environment for students and professors alike—A Companion Website—to support this textbook.

In creating this Companion Website, our goal is to build on and enhance what *Educational Psychology: Windows on Classrooms* already offers. For this reason, the content for this user-friendly website, prepared by Paul Eggen and Don Kauchak specifically for the web environment, is organized by chapter and provides the professor and student with a variety of meaningful resources. Features of this Companion Website include:

For the Professor—

Our Companion Website integrates **Syllabus Manager**™, an online syllabus creation and management utility.

- **Syllabus Manager**™ provides you, the instructor, with an easy, step-by-step process to create and revise syllabi, with direct links into Companion Website and other online content without having to learn HTML.
- Students may logon to your syllabus during any study session. All they need to know is the web address for the Companion Website and the password you've assigned to your syllabus.
- After you have created a syllabus using **Syllabus Manager**™, students may enter the syllabus for their course section from any point in the Companion Website.
- Class dates are highlighted in white and assignment due dates appear in blue. Clicking on a date, the student is shown the list of activities for the assignment. The activities for each assignment are linked directly to actual content, saving time for students.
- Adding assignments consists of clicking on the desired due date, then filling in the details of the assignment—name of the assignment, instructions, and whether or not it is a one-time or repeating assignment.
- In addition, links to other activities can be created easily. If the activity is online, a URL can be entered in the space provided, and it will be linked automatically in the final syllabus.
- Your completed syllabus is hosted on our servers, allowing convenient updates from any computer on the Internet. Changes you make to your syllabus are immediately available to your students at their next logon.

For the Student—

- **Chapter Objectives and Summaries** — outline key concepts from the text
- **Interactive Self-Quizzes** — both multiple choice and essay, complete with feedback and automatic grading that provide immediate feedback for students

After students submit their answers for the interactive self-quizzes, the Companion Website **Results Reporter** computes a percentage grade, provides a graphic representation of how many questions were answered correctly and incorrectly, and gives a question by question analysis of the quiz. Students are given the option to send their quiz to up to four email addresses (professor, teaching assistant, study partner, etc.).

- **Message Board** — complete with author supplied discussion topics, serves as a virtual bulletin board to post—or respond to—questions or comments to/from a national audience
- **Web Destinations** — offer specific, annotated links to meaningful, chapter content related www sites
- **Online Casebook** — provides experience in applying educational psychology concepts and theories to genuine classroom scenarios, including questions for analysis, feedback, and citations to appropriate textbook chapters for background research

To take advantage of these and other resources, please visit the *Educational Psychology: Windows on Classrooms* Companion Website at

www.prenhall.com/eggen

Brief Contents

Contents

▌ Chapter 3
Personal, Social, and Emotional Development   80

▌ Chapter 4
Learner Differences   122

Part III: Classroom Processes

▌Chapter 10

Increasing Learner Motivation   408

▌Chapter 11

Creating Productive Learning Environments   462

▌Chapter 12

Teacher-Centered Approaches to Instruction   514

▌ Chapter 13

Learner-Centered Approaches to Instruction   550

▌ Chapter 14

Assessing Classroom Learning   592

NOTE: Every effort has been made to provide accurate and current Internet information in this book. However, the Internet and information posted on it are constantly changing, so it is inevitable that some of the Internet addresses listed in this textbook will change.

Part I

The Classroom

The Learner

Teaching in the Real World

1

"Good morning, Keith." Jan Davis, a sixth-grade math teacher greeted Keith Jackson, a first-year teacher and colleague at Lake Park Middle School. "How're you doing? You look beat—or deep in thought. What's up?"

"I was just thinking about my last-period math class. Sometimes I'm not sure what I'm doing. I think about it quite a bit, and then I get a little confused—well, not exactly confused—maybe uneasy, I think."

Reacting to the questioning look on Jan's face, Keith continued. "The students are fine when we do the plain old mechanics. They do their work, seem to understand what they're doing, and even act like they sort of like it. Then . . . we get to word problems. Ugh! It's the exact opposite. I know we're supposed to try to teach the students to solve problems. So . . . I try it. They hate it. That makes me ask myself what I'm doing. They act as if this is the first time they've ever had to solve word problems. . . . I understand why word problems are important, but I just hate cramming them down their throats. They always try to take the easiest way out. They memorize a formula and work like robots. If the next problem is written even the tee-niest bit differently, they can't do it.

"Then," he continued, "some of them just blow the whole thing off. They just sit like bumps on logs and barely try. . . . I thought I was going to be so great when I got here. I have a really good math background, and I love math. I just knew the students would love it too. I'm not so sure any-more. No one prepared me for this.

"And then there's Kelly," Keith went on with a resigned shrug. "She disrupts everything I do. I can't get her to keep her mouth shut. I've tried everything. I thought maybe she was trying to get attention, so I ignored her talking. I've given her referrals, put her in detention, tried to 'catch her being good.' Nothing has worked. She's not really a bad student. . . . I even took her aside after school and simply leveled with her. I asked her straight out why she was giving me such a hard time. Actually, I think she's a bit better lately.

"I know that I'm in my first year and that you've been here forever," Keith continued, "but don't you ever get frustrated? Maybe I'm just having a bad day."

"I'll just ignore that 'forever' remark," Jan replied, "but yes, I get frustrated. I think everybody does.

"You're actually in the process of becoming a real teacher," she continued. "You're looking at problems for which there are no easy answers, and for the most part, the solutions—to the extent that they exist—must come from you. Very little in teaching is cut-and-dried . . . but then, that's also part of the fun of it," she added, smiling.

"Think about Kelly," she continued. "She's not actually a rotten kid. You said it seemed to help when you took her aside. Make it a point to talk with her one-on-one every now and then about her behavior and continue to be straight with her. I don't think she has another adult she can talk to, and she may need some-one to be interested in her. We all have personal and emotional needs, and they take precedent over academic ones."

"I guess I'll stay with it," Keith shrugged.

"And the quiet ones in the back of the classroom—every class has them. They just don't seem to care, and that can be discouraging. Let me tell you what works for me. First, I move them right up to the front of the room. I tell them why: 'I want you to learn, and I want you up close where I can work with you.' Then I make it a point to call on all of them, and I do it randomly. It's one of the most impor-tant ideas I learned in the classes I've taken. I had an instructor that kept talking about research saying that all the kids need to be called on equally. At first, they complain that they didn't have their hands up, but after I explain that I'm trying to get everyone to participate, they actually like it. It really makes a difference."

"Hmm. . . . Do you have any suggestions about the math part?" Keith asked. "I've tried explaining the stuff until I'm blue in the face."

"As it happens, I'm taking another course to upgrade my certifi-cate, and I wasn't too crazy about it at first, but I've really learned a lot. The course is based on the NCTM stan-dards . . . National Council of Teach-ers of Mathematics," Jan added, see-ing the uncertain look on Keith's face, "and in a way, they're talking about exactly the stuff you're struggling with, like problem solving. I actually thought I didn't have that much to learn. I've been around *forever* as you say, but this course and these new standards have opened my eyes. They're making a big deal of trying to focus more on the student—shifting emphasis. We read these research articles for class that talk about putting the student in the center of the process, and then we're learning how to apply it with our own students.

"I was really skeptical at first, but I said, 'What the heck; I'll give it my best shot,' and interestingly, the students really got into it. Let me give you an example.

"We've been reviewing decimals, and, just as you're saying, the students don't get it and they don't like it all that well. So I went into class, and just as class started, I put a shopping bag on my desk and said, 'You all drink soft drinks. Do you know which is the best buy in terms of size and number?' Then I took out a single 12-ounce can, a 16-ounce bottle, a liter bottle, a 6-pack, a 12-pack, and a 24-can pack.

"'Which is the best buy?' I challenged them. We had a lively discussion, and most agreed that bigger is better, but the skeptical ones asked how much better and is it worth the hassle?

"Then I put price tags on each of the containers, starting with the single can from the vending machine and broke the students into small groups. Some of the groups struggled for a while trying to figure out whether they should do price per can or price per ounce and what to do about liters. At the end of the class, we agreed to use a common format for a table, and the next day the groups computed their answers, and we compared them as a whole-class activity. The bottom line is that they have to see how math relates to them and their lives.

"Maybe even more important," she continued, "although I had to guide them, a lot of what we did came from them, and it got me thinking about some things. I'll do parts of it differently next time. At times I think I jumped in too soon when they could have figured it out for themselves, and at other times I think I let them stumble around too long, and they wasted more time than necessary. But overall, I feel good about it, and I'm definitely going to do more of it."

"I hate to admit this," Keith said almost sheepishly, "but some of my courses at the university suggested just what you did. It was fun, but I didn't think it was 'real' teaching."

"Maybe you couldn't relate to it at that time," Jan returned. "You didn't have a real class with real students who 'didn't get it.'

"My compliments to you, and I mean that," she continued. "The fact that you're thinking about it means you really care about what you're doing. That's what we need in teaching. If you hadn't brought it up, we probably wouldn't have had this talk. For a rookie, you're okay," she added, bantering again.

Keith peered at Jan, impressed with her fervor. "Why aren't you burned out? I thought all 'old' teachers burned out."

"Watch it, kid," Jan replied in a mock threat. "I have my days. I get tired, and the students sometimes bother me, but I try to leave it here, go home, get a little exercise, let off some steam, and return the next day."

W elcome! You're beginning what we hope will be an interesting and fascinating study; interesting, because this is a book about *learning* and *teaching* and the things that influence them, and fascinating, because even though we focus particularly on school-age children, you might see yourself in many of the experiences described. In some cases, you might even find that ideas you've held about people, learning, and teaching aren't valid.

As you examine the *ways we learn, how we develop intellectually, emotionally, and socially, what makes each person an individual and different, why we're motivated by some experiences but not others, and how teaching can increase the amount students learn,* you'll be studying the content of **educational psychology**.

This is a book about educational psychology, and as you study it, remember that the focus in educational psychology is on learning and teaching and the factors that influence them.

After you've completed your study of this chapter, you should be able to meet the following objectives:

▎ Identify the different types of knowledge required in learning to teach.
▎ Explain how research leads to knowledge that can be applied to classroom practice.
▎ Describe the relationships between research and theory.
▎ Explain how professional decision making affects teaching.
▎ Explain how reflective teaching uses educational psychology to improve professional decision making.

Educational Psychology:
Teaching in the Real World

This is a book about learning, what influences it, and how we as teachers can increase it. Our ability to teach effectively depends on our knowledge, knowledge that occurs in a variety of forms (Borko & Putnam, 1996). Our goal in studying educational psychology is to increase the amount we know, so we're equipped to make the most effective professional decisions possible.

To begin, please complete the following "Learning and Teaching Inventory." It provides a brief introduction to the kinds of knowledge we need to best understand our students, ourselves, and the way learning works. Read the following items and mark them true or false:

Learning and Teaching Inventory

1. The thinking of children in elementary schools tends to be limited to the concrete and tangible, whereas the thinking of junior high and high school students tends to be abstract.
2. Students have a generally clear understanding of how much they know about a topic.
3. Experts in the area of intelligence view knowledge of facts, such as "On what continent is Brazil?" as one indicator of intelligence.
4. Effective teaching is essentially a process of presenting information to students in succinct and organized ways.
5. Preservice teachers who major in a content area are much more successful than nonmajors in providing clear examples of the ideas they teach.
6. Students doing individual work at their seats may react negatively when a teacher comes by and offers them help.
7. To increase students' motivation to learn, teachers should use as much praise as possible.
8. Teachers who are the most successful at creating and maintaining orderly classrooms are those who can quickly stop disruptions when they occur.
9. Preservice teachers generally believe they will be more effective than teachers who are now out in the field.
10. Teachers primarily learn by teaching; in general, experience is all that is necessary in learning to teach.
11. Testing usually detracts from learning, because students who are tested frequently develop negative attitudes and usually learn less than those who are tested less often.

Let's see how you did. The answer and an explanation for each item are outlined in the following paragraphs. As you read the explanations, remember that they describe students or other people *in general*, and exceptions will exist.

1. *The thinking of children in elementary schools tends to be limited to the concrete and tangible, whereas the thinking of junior high and high school students tends to be abstract.*

   False: Research indicates that junior high, high school, and even university students can think effectively in the abstract *only when they are studying areas in which they have considerable experience and expertise* (Lawson & Snitgren, 1982; Pulos & Linn, 1981; Thornton & Fuller, 1981). When we examine development of students' thinking in Chapter 2, you'll understand why and the implications for teaching.

2. *Students have a generally clear understanding of how much they know about a topic.*

   False: Contrary to what we might think, learners in general, and young children in particular, often cannot accurately assess what they know (Schommer, 1994). Students' awareness of the ways they learn, and the amount they already know, strongly influence student understanding, and cognitive learning theory helps us understand why. (We discuss cognitive learning theory in Chapters 7 to 9.)

3. *Experts in the area of intelligence view knowledge of facts, such as "On what continent is Brazil?" as an indicator of intelligence.*

   True: The *Wechsler Intelligence Scale for Children—Third Edition* (WISC—III, Wechsler, 1991), the most popular intelligence test in use today, has several items very similar to the example. Is this an effective way to measure intelligence? Theories of intelligence, which are analyzed in Chapter 4, examine this and other issues related to learner ability.

4. *Effective teaching is essentially a process of presenting information to students in succinct and organized ways.*

   False: As we better understand learning, we find that simply explaining information to students often isn't effective in promoting understanding (Bransford, 1993; Greeno, Collins, & Resnick, 1996). Learners develop their own understanding based on what they already know, and their emotions, beliefs, and expectations all influence the process (Bruning, Schraw, & Ronning,

---

1.1 ▬
Many of you probably responded by saying, "True," to statement 4 that teaching is a process of transmitting knowledge to learners. Why do many preservice and beginning teachers believe this?

Concepts learned in educational psychology help teachers understand the complex events occurring in classrooms.

1999; Mayer, 1998, 1999). Educational psychology helps us understand each of these factors and what we can do to promote as much learning as possible. (We examine the processes involved in constructing understanding in Chapters 2 and 7.)

5. *Preservice teachers who major in a content area are much more successful than nonmajors in providing clear examples of the ideas they teach.*

    False: One of the most pervasive myths in teaching is that knowledge of subject matter is all that is necessary to teach effectively. In a study of teacher candidates, math majors were no more capable than nonmajors in effectively illustrating and representing math concepts in ways that learners could understand (National Center for Research on Teacher Learning, 1993). While knowledge of content is critical, of course, understanding how to make that content meaningful to students requires an additional kind of knowledge, knowledge that educational psychology helps us acquire. (We discuss in detail ways of making knowledge accessible to learners in Chapters 2 and 7 to 9.)

6. *Students doing individual work at their seats may react negatively when a teacher comes by and offers them help.*

    True: Being perceived as being intelligent and capable is very important to students, and researchers have found that children as young as 6 rated students who were offered unsolicited help lower in ability than others offered no help (Graham & Barker, 1990). Further, when offered unsolicited help, learners themselves often perceive the offer as an indication that the teacher believes they have low ability (Meyer, 1982). Theories of motivation, which are examined in Chapter 10, help us understand why learners react this way.

7. *To increase students' motivation to learn, teachers should use as much praise as possible.*

    False: While appropriate use of praise is certainly important, overuse detracts from its credibility. This is particularly true for older students, who discount praise they perceive as unwarranted or invalid and interpret praise given for easy tasks as indicating that the teacher thinks they have low ability (Emmer, 1988; Good, 1987a). Your study of motivation in Chapter 10 will help you understand this and other factors influencing students' desires to learn.

8. *Teachers who are the most successful at creating and maintaining orderly classrooms are those who can quickly stop disruptions when they occur.*

    False: Classroom management is one of the greatest concerns of preservice and beginning teachers (Borko & Putnam, 1996). Research indicates that teachers who are most effective at creating and maintaining orderly classrooms are those who can prevent management problems *before* they occur (W. Doyle, 1986; Evertson, Emmer, Clements, & Worsham, 2000; Kounin, 1970). (Classroom management is discussed in detail in Chapter 11.)

9. *Preservice teachers generally believe they will be more effective than teachers who are now out in the field.*

    True: Preservice teachers (like yourself) are optimistic and idealistic. They believe they'll be very effective with young people, and they generally believe they'll be better than teachers now in the field (Borko & Putnam, 1996). They're also sometimes "shocked" when they begin work and face the challenge of teaching completely on their own for the first time (Veenman, 1984). Keith's comment "I thought I was going to be so great when I got here. I have a really good math background, and I love math. I just knew the students would love it too. I'm not so sure anymore. No one prepared

1.2

What is the most likely reason that math majors were no more successful than nonmajors in effectively illustrating math topics?

me for this" illustrates the experience of many beginning teachers. The more knowledge you have about teaching, learning, and learners, the better prepared you'll be to cope with the realities of your first job. Keith's discussion with Jan helped him acquire some of that knowledge. Their discussion focused on topics that you'll study in educational psychology.

10. *Teachers primarily learn by teaching; in general, experience is all that is necessary in learning to teach.*

    False: While experience is essential in learning to teach, it isn't sufficient by itself. In many cases, experience can result in repeating the same procedures and techniques year after year, regardless of their effectiveness (Putnam, Heaton, Prawat, & Remillard, 1992). Knowledge of learners and learning, combined with experience, however, can lead to high levels of teaching expertise (Cochran & Jones, 1998).

11. *Testing usually detracts from learning, because students who are tested frequently develop negative attitudes and usually learn less than those who are tested less often.*

    False: In a comprehensive review of the literature on assessment, Crooks (1988) concluded that frequent, thorough assessment is one of the most powerful influences on learning. (We discuss assessment and the role it plays in learning in Chapter 14.)

The items you've just examined give you a brief sampling of the different kinds of knowledge teachers need to help students learn as much as possible. Educational psychology helps teachers acquire this knowledge, and this is our goal in writing this book. Let's examine this knowledge.

 # Knowledge and Learning to Teach

About the middle of the 20th century, educational psychology experienced a major shift, moving away from viewing learning as acquiring specific, observable behaviors and toward seeing it as an internal, mental process (Mayer, 1998). This shift, commonly described as the "cognitive revolution," has resulted in a much greater emphasis on teachers' knowledge and thinking in the process of learning to teach.

Studies of expertise in a variety of fields confirm the importance of knowledge in the development of expert performance (Bruning et al., 1999), and this is true for teaching as well.

> The accumulation of richly structured and accessible bodies of knowledge allows individuals to engage in expert thinking and action. In studies of teaching, this understanding of expertise has led researchers to devote increased attention to teachers' knowledge and its organization (Borko & Putnam, 1996, p. 674).

Research indicates that at least four different kinds of knowledge are essential for effective teaching:

- Knowledge of content
- Pedagogical content knowledge
- General pedagogical knowledge
- Knowledge of learners and learning (Peterson, 1988; Shulman, 1987)

Knowledge of Content

We can't teach what we don't understand. This simple statement is self-evident, and it is well documented by research examining the relationships between what teachers know and how they teach (Shulman, 1986; Wilson, Shulman, & Richert, 1987). To effectively teach about the American Revolutionary War, for example, a social studies teacher must know not only basic facts about the War but also how it relates to other aspects of history, such as the French and Indian War, our relationship with England before the Revolution, and the characteristics of the colonies. The same is true for any topic in any content area.

Pedagogical Content Knowledge

Pedagogical content knowledge is *an understanding of "ways of representing . . . the subject that make it comprehensible to others"* and *"an understanding of what makes the learning of specific topics easy or difficult"* (Shulman, 1986, p. 9, emphasis added). Pedagogical content knowledge depends on an understanding of a particular topic, such as understanding the factors leading to the American Revolution, but it goes beyond this understanding and includes knowing how to represent these factors so they make sense to students.

Teachers who possess pedagogical content knowledge also recognize when topics are hard to understand and illustrate these difficult-to-teach ideas with concrete experiences that make them meaningful. To illustrate this process, do the following activity. Take a piece of plain 8½ × 11 paper, fold it into thirds, and cross-hatch one ⅓ of the paper so it appears as follows:

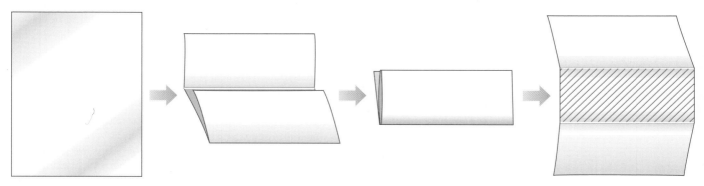

Your cross-hatched portion is now ⅓ of the sheet of paper. Refold your paper so that ⅓ is exposed, as follows:

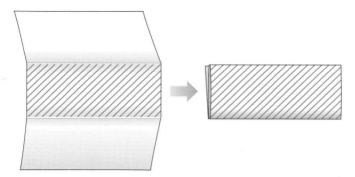

Now, fold the ⅓ of the paper in half, and fold the half in half again, so you have ¼ of your ⅓, and cross-hatch it the opposite way of your original cross-hatching. Then unfold it, so it appears as follows:

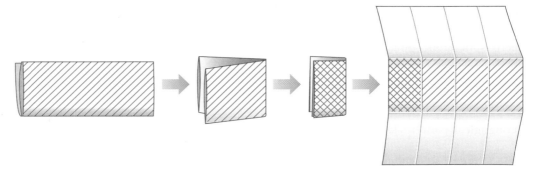

You have created a concrete example of the process of multiplying fractions. In this case, you demonstrated that ¼ × ⅓ = ½12. The "subject" was multiplying fractions, and the representation was your folded piece of paper.

Concrete representations of topics like multiplying fractions are important because they make abstract ideas clear and meaningful, which allows students to apply their understanding in a variety of real-world settings (Mayer & Wittrock, 1996). Intuitively, it doesn't make sense that multiplying two numbers results in a smaller number; so, many students mechanically perform the operation with little understanding. This is why teachers' abilities to create effective representations are so essential. Without the examples, students grasp what they can and memorize as much as possible, and little understanding develops.

Representations of content exist in a variety of forms. Some include the following:

- *Examples.*   A math teacher uses your folded piece of paper to illustrate the multiplication of fractions. An eighth–grade physical science teacher, Karen Johnson (see case study in Chapter 2), compresses the cotton in a drink cup to illustrate the concept *density.*
- *Demonstrations.*   A first-grade teacher, Jenny Newhall, demonstrates that air takes up space and exerts pressure (see case study in Chapter 2). A ninth-grade earth science teacher, David Shelton, demonstrates that planets revolve around the sun in the same direction and in the same plane by swinging socks tied to strings (see case study in Chapter 7).
- *Case studies.*   The case studies like the one at the beginning of this chapter are used throughout this text to demonstrate the different topics being discussed.
- *Metaphors.*   A world history teacher uses her students' loyalty to their school, their ways of talking, and their weekend activities as a metaphor for the concept *nationalism.* A high school history teacher, Kathy Brewster, uses the class's "crusade" for extracurricular activities as a metaphor for the actual Crusades (see case study in Chapter 10).
- *Simulations.*   An American government teacher creates a mock trial to simulate the workings of our country's judicial system, or a history teacher has students role play delegates in a simulated Continental Congress.
- *Models.*   A science teacher uses the model of an atom to help students visualize the organization of the nucleus and electrons. The model in Figure 7.1 helps us think about the ways we take in and store information in memory.

1.3
Which form of representation best describes what Jan Davis did in her lesson on decimals and "best buys"? Explain.

From the preceding examples, we can see why Item 5 on the "Learning and Teaching Inventory" is false. Majoring in math doesn't ensure that a teacher will be able to create examples like the one involving the multiplication of fractions, and majoring in history does not ensure that a social studies teacher will think of using the students' school activities as a metaphor for the Crusades. The ability to do so requires both a clear understanding of content and pedagogical content knowledge. If either is lacking, teachers commonly paraphrase information in learners' textbooks or provide abstract explanations that aren't meaningful to their students. Your study of educational psychology will help you develop pedagogical content knowledge by increasing your understanding of the ways students learn and the kinds of examples and representations that make topics meaningful for them.

> **1.4** ▬
> Identify a statement Keith Jackson made that best indicates that he lacks pedagogical content knowledge in trying to teach problem solving with his students. Explain why the statement indicates that he lacks this knowledge.

General Pedagogical Knowledge

Knowledge of content and pedagogical content knowledge are domain specific; that is, they depend on knowledge of a particular topic or content area, such as multiplying fractions, density, the Crusades, or our judicial system. In comparison, **general pedagogical knowledge** *involves an understanding of instruction and management that transcends individual topics or subject matter areas* (Borko & Putnam, 1996). Your study of educational psychology will help you understand how instructional strategies promote learning and how classroom management contributes to a productive learning environment.

Instructional Strategies

Instruction is at the center of teaching. Teachers must understand different ways of involving students in learning activities, techniques for checking their understanding, and strategies for keeping lessons running smoothly (Leinhardt & Greeno, 1986). Questioning is an important example. Regardless of the content or topic, teachers must ask questions that engage all students as equally as possible (McDougall & Granby, 1996), give them time to think about their responses (Rowe, 1986), and provide prompts and cues when they're unable to answer (Shuell, 1996). Teachers must also be able to provide students with feedback about their understanding of a topic, identifying areas that need additional work. In this text we'll examine these strategies and see how they increase learning.

Pedagogical content knowledge helps teachers represent difficult-to-learn concepts in meaningful ways.

Classroom Management

Regardless of the content area or topic being taught, teachers must also know how to create classroom environments that are orderly and focused on learning (W. Doyle, 1986). Understanding how to keep 20 to 35 or more students actively engaged and working together in learning activities requires that teachers know how to plan, implement, and monitor rules and procedures, organize groups, deliver meaningful lessons, and react to misbehavior. The complexities of these processes helps us see why Item 8 in the "Learning and Teaching Inventory" is false. It is virtually impossible to maintain an orderly, learning-focused classroom if we wait for misbehavior to occur. Classroom environments must be designed to prevent, rather than stop, disruptions.

Knowledge of Learners and Learning

Knowledge of learners and learning is essential, "arguably the most important knowledge a teacher can have" (Borko & Putnam, 1996, p. 675). Let's see how this knowledge can influence the way we teach.

Knowledge of Learners

Items 1, 2, 6, and 7 in the "Learning and Teaching Inventory" all involve knowledge of learners, and each has important implications for the way we teach and interact with our students. For instance, we found in Item 1 that most students need abstract ideas illustrated with examples. This means that—even for older students—the more concretely we're able to represent our topics, the more meaningful they'll be. Chapter 2, which focuses on cognitive development, describes how understanding learners increases our pedagogical content knowledge and helps us provide meaningful representations, such as in the example of multiplying fractions.

Item 2 suggests that learners often aren't good judges of either how much they know or the ways they learn. Chapter 7, which discusses the development of metacognition, helps us understand how to help our students become more strategic in their study, and the more strategic they become, the more they learn (Bruning et al., 1999).

Items 6 and 7 have implications for the ways we interact with our students. Intuitively, it seems that offering help and providing as much praise as possible would be a positive and effective way to work with students. However, both research and theories of motivation, important topics in educational psychology (Chapter 10), help us understand why this isn't always the case.

Knowledge of Learning

As we better understand the ways people learn, we better understand why Item 4 on the "Learning and Teaching Inventory" was false. For example, evidence overwhelmingly indicates that people don't behave like tape recorders; they don't simply record what they hear or read. Rather, they interpret information in an effort to make sense of it (Marshall, 1998; Mayer, 1998). In the process, meaning can be distorted, sometimes profoundly. For instance, look at the following statements actually made by students:

- "The phases of the moon are caused by clouds blocking out the unseen parts."
- "Coats keep us warm by generating heat, like a fire."
- "*Trousers* is an uncommon noun, because it is singular at the top and plural at the bottom."
- "A triangle which has an angle of 135° is called an obscene triangle."

Obviously, students didn't acquire these ideas from a teacher's explanation. Rather, the students interpreted what they heard, experienced, or read, related it to what they already knew, and attempted to make sense of both.

These examples help us see why "wisdom can't be told" (Bransford, 1993, p. 6), and they help us understand why simply explaining "the stuff until I'm blue in the face," as Keith said to Jan, often doesn't work very well. Effective teaching is much more complex than simply explaining, and expert teachers have a thorough understanding of the way learning occurs. (We examine learning in detail in Chapters 6 to 9.)

We now see why Item 10 was false. Experience is essential in learning to teach, and no one would argue that it isn't necessary. However, from our discussion to this point, we can already see that teachers won't acquire all the knowledge needed to be effective from experience alone. This is the reason you're studying educational psychology. The knowledge you acquire from it, combined with your experience, will start you on your way to becoming an expert teacher.

> **1.5**
> A life science teacher holds up a sheet of bubble wrap and then places a second sheet of bubble wrap on top of the first to help her students visualize the way that cells are organized into tissue. What kind of knowledge does the teacher's demonstration indicate? Explain.

The Role of Research in Acquiring Knowledge

In the last section, we considered the different kinds of knowledge teachers need to help their students learn. Where did this knowledge originate, how does it accumulate, and how can we acquire it?

One answer is experience, sometimes called "the wisdom of practice" (Berliner, 1988; Leinhardt & Greeno, 1986). Effective teacher education programs integrate clinical experiences in schools with theoretical knowledge. A second is **research**, which is *the process of systematically gathering information for the purpose of answering one or more questions*. Jan referred to research in her conversation with Keith, saying, "I had an instructor that kept talking about research saying that all the kids need to be called on equally," and "We read these research articles for class that talk about putting the student in the center of the process." Jan is a veteran with considerable experience, but she is growing professionally because her knowledge is increasing, and research contributes to that knowledge.

Research is the process all professions use to develop a body of knowledge. For example, research examining students' writing indicates that students who practice writing with computers compose better quality essays than those who don't, but only if they have well-developed word processing skills (Jerry & Ballator, 1999; Roblyer & Edwards, 2000). Educators are trying to understand why this occurs and what benefits technology might have in the process of learning to write. Without systematically gathering information, we wouldn't be able to answer these questions.

Research exists in several forms. In this chapter we consider three:

▌ Descriptive research
▌ Correlational research
▌ Experimental research

Descriptive Research

Descriptive research, as the term implies, *uses surveys, interviews,* or *observations to describe opinions, attitudes,* or *events*. For instance, periodic surveys of parents and teachers are conducted to determine their attitudes toward public schools. In answering the question, "What are schools' biggest problems?" researchers found that teachers most commonly cited lack of parental support (Langdon, 1996), whereas parents cited classroom management and student discipline (Rose & Gallup, 1999). These studies simply *describe* teachers' and parents' attitudes, and as we've just seen, the researchers used a *survey*.

Descriptive research also uses interviews as a technique for gathering information. For example, researchers interviewed students to describe their perceptions of caring teachers:

Nichole:	It's more an attitude, and they do say it. Like Ms. G. She's like . . . she never says it, but you know, she's just there and she just wants to teach, but she doesn't want to explain the whole deal.
Interviewer:	How do you know that?
Nichole:	I could feel it. The way she acts and the way she does things. She's been here seven years and all the kids I've talked to that have had her before say, "Oooh! You have Ms. G.!" Just like that.
Interviewer:	But a teacher who really cares, how do they act?
Nichole:	Like Mr. P. He really cares about his students. He's helping me a lot and he tells me, "I'm not angry with you, I just care about you." He's real caring and he does teach me when he cares. (Kramer & Colvin, 1991, p. 13)

Interviews can provide valuable insights into both students' and teachers' thoughts.

Observations have also been used in descriptive research. Perhaps the most significant has been the work done by Jean Piaget (1952, 1959), a pioneer in the study of cognitive development (one of the cornerstones of education psychology). Piaget studied the way learners' thinking develops by making detailed observations of his own children. Based on his observations, and a great deal of research conducted by others, we realize that 10-year-olds don't simply know more than 5-year-olds; they think in ways that are qualitatively different. For instance, look at the accompanying "Family Circus" cartoon.

FAMILY CIRCUS By Bil Keane

8-26
© 1996 Bil Keane, Inc.
Dist. by Cowles Synd., Inc.

"This time try not to miss my bat."

From Dolly's perspective, it was her daddy's fault that she missed the previous pitch. A 10-year-old would realize that this isn't the case. We understand these differences in children's thinking because of Piaget's, and other researchers', systematic observations and descriptions. (We examine Piaget's work in detail in Chapter 2.)

Correlational Research

Consider the following questions:

Is there any relationship between

- Students' study time and their grades in school?
- Students' hair colors and their grades in school?
- Students' absences and their grades in school?

The answers are yes to the first and third questions and no to the second. A **correlation** *is a relationship between two or more variables*, and that relationship can be positive or negative. In our examples, the variables are *study time* and *grades, hair color* and *grades,* and *absences* and *grades.* In the first case, a *positive correlation* exists; in general, the more time students spend studying, the higher their grades will be. No correlation exists in the second; there is no relationship between hair color and achievement. In the third case, the variables are *negatively correlated*; the more school students miss, the lower their grades will be.

Correlational research *is the process of looking for relationships between two or more variables*, and much of what we know about learning and teaching is based on correlational studies.

A great deal of correlational research attempts to find relationships between teachers' actions and student achievement. For example, researchers found positive correlations between the amount of time teachers spend questioning and interacting with students and their students' achievement. They've also found negative correlations between achievement and the time teachers spend in noninstructional activities, such as taking roll, passing out papers, and explaining procedures (Brophy & Good, 1986).

Correlational research is valuable because it allows us to make predictions about one variable if we have information about the other. For instance, since a positive correlation exists between interaction and student achievement, we would predict that students will learn more in classrooms where teachers ask many questions than those where teachers primarily lecture. Correlational research is also valuable because it suggests variables to investigate in experimental studies.

Experimental Research

While correlational research looks for relationships in existing situations, **experimental research** *systematically manipulates variables in attempts to determine cause and effect*. Experimental studies are commonly built on and extend correlational research. For example, let's look again at the correlation between teachers' questioning and student achievement. In an extension of the correlational studies, researchers randomly assigned teachers to a treatment and a control group. **Random assignment** *means that an individual has an equal likelihood of being assigned to either group*, and it is used to ensure that the two groups are comparable. Teachers in the treatment group were trained to provide students with prompts and cues when students initially failed to answer a question; the

1.6 Consider student achievement in reading and student achievement in math. Would you predict that they are *positively correlated, uncorrelated* (not related), or *negatively correlated*? After selecting your choice, explain why.

1.7 Researchers have found that during the years 1980 to 1994 the number of Asian American students increased 100%, Hispanic students increased 46%, African American students increased 25%, and Caucasian students increased 10% (U.S. Bureau of the Census, 1996). Are these *descriptive research* results or *correlational research* results? Explain.

1.8 ▬

Research indicates that teachers who are high in *personal teaching efficacy*—the belief that they have an important positive effect on students—have students who achieve higher than teachers who are low in personal teaching efficacy (Bruning et al., 1999). Is this finding based on descriptive, correlational, or experimental research? Explain your response.

researchers attempted to consciously manipulate the variable, *frequency of teachers' prompts,* through training. Teachers in the control group were given no training; they taught as they normally did. Reading scores of the students in both groups were compared at the end of the year. Researchers found that students taught by teachers in the treatment group scored significantly higher on an achievement test than did students taught by teachers in the control group (L. Anderson, Evertson, & Brophy, 1979). In this case, researchers concluded that the ability to provide prompting questions and cues causes increases in achievement.

Research and the Development of Theory

As research accumulates, results are summarized, and patterns emerge. After making a great many observations, for instance, researchers have concluded that *the thinking of young children tends to be dominated by their perceptions.* For example, when first graders see an inverted cup of water with a card covering it, as we see in the accompanying picture, they commonly explain that the card doesn't fall because the water somehow holds it against the cup. They focus on the most perceptually obvious aspect of the object—the water—and ignore atmospheric pressure, which is the actual reason the card stays on the cup.

The statement "The thinking of young children tends to be dominated by perception" is a **principle** which *summarizes the results of large numbers of research studies with consistent results.* Some additional examples of research-based principles include the following:

▌ People strive for a state of order, balance, and predictability in the world.
▌ Behaviors that are rewarded some of the time, but not all of the time, persist longer than behaviors rewarded every time they occur.
▌ People tend to imitate behaviors they observe in others.

As additional research is conducted, related principles are formed, which in turn generate further studies. As knowledge accumulates, theories are gradually constructed. A **theory** is *a set of related principles derived from observations that, in turn, are used to explain additional observations.*

In the everyday world, the term *theory* is used more loosely. For instance, one person will make a point in a conversation, and a second will respond, "I have a theory on that." In this case, the person is merely offering an explanation for the point. In science, the notion of *theory* has a more precise, restricted definition.

Theories help teachers understand the complex world of classrooms and the connections between teacher actions and student learning.

Theories help organize research findings and can provide valuable guidance for teachers. Let's look at a brief example. One research-based principle indicates that reinforced behaviors increase in frequency, and as mentioned earlier, a related principle indicates that intermittently reinforced behaviors persist longer than those that are continuously reinforced (Baldwin & Baldwin, 1998; Skinner, 1957). Further, too much reinforcement can actually decrease its effectiveness (satiation). A classroom application of these principles occurs in learning activities. If students are praised for their attempts to answer questions (reinforced), they are likely to increase their efforts, but they will persist longer if they are praised for some, but not all, of their attempts (intermittently reinforced). If they are praised excessively, they may actually reduce their efforts—the result of satiation.

These related principles are part of the theory of *Behaviorism*, which studies the effects of experiences on observable behavior. Our illustration, of course, is only a tiny portion of the complete theory. (We examine Behaviorism in depth in Chapter 6.) The key feature of any theory is that a comprehensive body of information is formed when a number of principles are related to each other.

Theories are useful in at least two ways. First, they allow us to *explain* behaviors and events. For instance, look at the accompanying cartoon.

Piaget's theory of cognitive development, which includes the principle mentioned earlier ("the thinking of young children tends to be dominated by perception"), helps us explain why the child in the cartoon thinks the way he does. Using Piaget's theory, we can explain this behavior by saying that the boy can see only the water and the faucet, and because his thinking is dominated by his perception—what he can see—he concludes that all the water is in it. This is characteristic of the thinking of young children.

Similarly, using the theory of Behaviorism, we can explain why casino patrons persist in playing slot machines, though coins only seldom fall into the trays, by saying that they are being intermittently reinforced.

FAMILY CIRCUS

Copyright 1988
Cowles Syndicate, Inc

"How do they fit so much water in that little spigot?"

1.9

In the opening case study, how did Keith use reinforcement theory (behaviors that are reinforced will increase in frequency) to explain and predict Kelly's behavior?

Second, theories also allow us to *predict* behavior and events. For instance, attribution theory—a theory of motivation—allows us to predict that students who believe they are the ones who control how good their grades will be try harder than those who believe their grades are due primarily to luck or the whim of the teacher.

In all three instances—child development, behaviorism, and attribution theory—theories help us understand learning and teaching by allowing us to explain and predict people's actions.

Research and Teacher Decision Making

We've just seen how research and theory provide us with knowledge that we can use to guide our teaching. They don't answer all our questions, however. Just as medical research doesn't tell us exactly how many times a week people can safely eat fatty foods or how much exercise is necessary to maintain a healthy lifestyle, educational research and theory don't answer all our questions about the best classroom practice. For example, Jan cited research indicating that all students in classes should be called on as equally as possible, but the research doesn't specify who to call on at a particular moment or how to treat a shy and withdrawn student compared with an outgoing and assertive one. Research and theory help us understand patterns of student learning and effective teaching, but specific decisions are left to us.

Throughout this text, we'll make statements such as, "A teacher's careful judgment is required," "The specific decision will be left up to you," and "You must decide." Teaching includes a great deal of uncertainty and ambiguity. Careful professional judgment and personal decision making are essential for effective teaching.

Unfortunately, teacher decision making can sometimes be complicated by research results that appear contradictory. For example, one such dilemma exists related to waiting after asking a question—a practice that gives students time to think and results in increased learning.

> From Rowe's (1974) research on wait-time, for example, we learn the principle that longer wait-times produce higher levels of cognitive processing. Yet Kounin's (1970) research on classroom management warns the teacher against slowing the pace of the classroom too severely lest the frequency of discipline problems increase. How can the principle of longer wait-times and that of quicker pacing both be correct? (Shulman, 1986, p. 13)

Should we wait longer to give students time to think through a question fully, or will long pauses result in lessons that drag? Research doesn't provide a precise answer, so we must use our professional judgment and decide how long to wait and when to move the lesson along more quickly.

As another example of the need for teacher decision making, consider the following situation:

> April Sumner taught remedial English to a first-period class of inner-city high school students. Students were required to pass the class to graduate from high school, but motivation and attendance were problems.
>
> She liked the class, and because it was small, she knew all her students well. This closeness was rewarding, but the class was also frustrating; the students didn't bother to bring any materials to class. Daily reminders didn't seem to help, nor did threats of failure, because many students were repeating the class for the second or third time.

April talked with other teachers. Some said, "Let them sit"; others responded, "Lend them your own" but warned of logistical nightmares and economic disaster when the pencils disappeared and she ran out of paper.

April was hired to teach English, but first she had to solve the materials problem. What would you do?

Providing students with pencils reinforces their coming to class unprepared. However, if the teacher doesn't provide them, students can't participate, and research and theory both confirm the importance of student involvement in learning (Blumenfeld, 1992; Pratton & Hales, 1986).

It would obviously be easier if we could simply call up a research result, apply it as a rule, and get consistent, predictable results. However, neither the world nor teaching and learning work this way. So, to succeed, the ability to cope with uncertainty is necessary, and informed decision making is essential.

How should research be used in making decisions? Teachers need to think *critically, practically, and artistically* about the results of research (Gage & Berliner, 1989). When we do this, we do more than simply apply research; we personalize the results by selecting, modifying, and adapting the suggested applications to best meet the needs of our students. Let's look at these processes.

Critical Decision Making: The Role of Classroom Context

When using research results *critically*, teachers analyze their own situations and compare them with the settings that produced the results. For instance, in one study, researchers found that first graders called on in a predictable order—such as up and down rows—achieved higher in reading than students called on randomly (Ogden, Brophy, & Evertson, 1977). Does this imply that we should stop the intuitively sensible practice of calling on students at random? Certainly not, for at least three reasons. First, examining the results critically, we find that the study was conducted with first graders in small reading groups, a context very different from whole-group instruction.

Second, we should ask the question, "Did *the predictable order* cause higher achievement, or is some other explanation possible?" Additional research helps answer this question. This research indicates that everyone having a chance to participate equally is very important, and the predictable order may have been a mechanism for ensuring equal participation (Tierney, Readence, & Dishner, 1990). So, equal participation, rather than predictable order, is probably the cause for the higher achievement.

Third, the results with the first graders haven't been replicated in other settings, whereas additional research has consistently found that involving all students equally in learning activities increases learning (Brophy & Good, 1986; Kerman, 1979; McDougall & Granby, 1996), and better methods than predictable turns exist for ensuring equal participation.

The context in which decisions are made also helps us resolve the dilemma with wait-time that we cited earlier. For example, if a question is thought provoking, the lesson is moving smoothly, and the student "on the spot" is comfortable, we should probably wait. However, if the question calls for a fact, the lesson is dragging, other students are fidgety, or the target student appears uncomfortable, we should reduce the amount of wait-time. The context in which the question is asked helps us decide. Research assists in the process but does not substitute for sound teacher judgment.

We all periodically react with frustration because research seems inconsistent and uncertain, such as in the case with the first graders, described earlier. Unfortunately, this is reality, and it isn't unique to learning and teaching, or education in general. For instance, a number of studies caution against eating too many eggs, because of their high cholesterol content; others suggest that our bodies manufacture most of the cholesterol in our systems, and our diets have less to do with our cholesterol levels than previously believed.

All this suggests that individual research studies should be examined critically and interpreted with caution. They provide us with knowledge that we can use to make decisions, but the decisions are left up to us.

Practical Decision Making: The Need for Efficiency

Practicality is a second factor in making informed decisions. To be useful, research must be applied efficiently, with a minimum of disruption to the class or extra work for the teacher. Classrooms are complex and busy places; researchers estimate that elementary teachers have more than 500 exchanges with individual students in a day (W. Doyle, 1986). Many, if not most, of these require a split-second teacher decision. To be practical, research results must be applied efficiently.

For example, research suggesting that all students should be called on equally is practical. While it requires teachers skilled in questioning, the curriculum, classroom routines, and general patterns of instruction don't have to be radically altered. On the other hand, research also suggests that students taught in a one-to-one, personalized mode of instruction learn best (Bloom, 1984a; Slavin, Madden, Karweit, Dolan, & Wasik, 1992), but unfortunately, this isn't feasible.

April's dilemma illustrates the importance of practical teacher decisions and the role of research and theory in making them. As we said earlier, research indicates that students need to be involved in learning activities, so April can't let her students sit passively. She also can't repeatedly give students materials, because—based on her understanding of Behaviorism—doing so reinforces their irresponsibility (and she could spend a lot of money distributing pencils to students who consider the whole process a game).

At least two practical solutions to the problem exist. One teacher kept a box of short pencil stubs in his desk (Shulman, 1986). When a student forgot a pencil, the teacher gave the student the shortest stub he could find and required the student to complete the work with it and return it after class. Another teacher required a personal article, such as an earring, bracelet, or belt, as collateral, which she exchanged for the pencil at the end of class. These were simple, practical solutions that worked; students started bringing their materials to class.

1.10 ▬

Identify at least five decisions that Keith made in his attempts to deal with Kelly. On what basis did he make the decisions? Explain how they were practical.

Artistic Decision Making: Creativity in Teaching

The *artistic* element, the third dimension of informed decision making, asks teachers to apply the results of research in original and creative ways. Let's look at an example of creativity in teaching:

After three separate efforts to teach the principle of exposition, development, and recapitulation in music—each of which failed—the teacher was at wit's end. Having repeatedly reminded her students that composers like Wagner depended on the listeners' remembering earlier themes so as to recognize their later elaboration, she was determined to make her students understand musical form, no matter what it took.

The class had little trouble with simple variations and could easily identify themes that were repeated in a related key, but when it came to the development sections, the students' attention focused on the new detail to such an extent that they no longer "heard" the basic motif. For a week or two, the young teacher fretted over the problem.

Creative teachers design
activities that motivate
students to learn.

She discarded one idea after another as either too complicated or impractical. Older teachers advised her to go on with something else, suggesting that she was overly ambitious, and that such discrimination was impossible without formal music training. Still, the teacher searched for a solution.

One afternoon during the lunch hour, she noticed a group of students clustered in a corner of the yard. Several girls were swaying their bodies in a rhythmic cadence. Curious, she drew closer and found that the students were listening to a new rock hit. A boy in the center of the group held a tape recorder in his hand. A few moments later, as the teacher continued on her noon duty rounds, a sudden inspiration took hold.

The following day, when her music appreciation class arrived, she asked how many students had tape recorders. A dozen or so students immediately said, "I do." The teacher looked at her students pensively. "I have an idea," she said with sudden animation. "Maybe machines have better memories than people. What would you think," she said, "about trying an experiment? We could play Beethoven's 'Eroica' again, and one of you can record the theme of the second movement when it's first introduced. Then, later, when Beethoven gets into the development section, someone else can record that segment. Finally, when he comes to the recapitulation—the restatement—we'll have a third person record again. Of course," she added, "technically, it won't be a real recapitulation because we'll select passages in the same key. If," she finished triumphantly, "we can synchronize the timing, and start all three recorders at exactly the same instant, we'll play the three recordings together and see if they fit. What do you think?"

Her students looked at her in surprise. Suddenly, however, delight appeared on their faces.

"Neat," one boy exclaimed.

"We'll have to get three recorders with the same speed," another exclaimed. "I'll bring a timer."

And so it was arranged. They had difficulty starting the recorders simultaneously; there were slight variations in their pitch; and the tempo of the recorded passages was a bit uneven; but the sounds blended sufficiently for the students to recognize their commonality. (L. Rubin, *Artistry in Teaching*, 1985, McGraw-Hill, Inc., pp. 32–33 reproduced with permission of McGraw-Hill.)

This teacher capitalized on the principles suggesting that actively involving students and relating abstract ideas to their personal lives increases learning; artistic decision making applies these ideas to create meaningful lessons (Brophy, 1990). The teacher's instruction was artistic and informed by research.

1.11
Identify at least two important kinds of knowledge this music teacher possessed to develop her lesson as she did.

Reflection and Decision Making

Teaching involves making an enormous number of decisions, most of which can't be reduced to simple rules. How do teachers know whether their decisions are wise and valid? This is a tough question, because teachers receive little feedback about the effectiveness of their work. They are observed by administrators a few times a year at most and receive only vague, sketchy, and uncertain feedback from students and parents. In addition, they get virtually no feedback from their colleagues, unless the school has a peer coaching or mentoring program (Darling-Hammond, 1996, 1997). To improve, teachers must be able to assess their own classroom performance.

The ability to conduct this self-assessment can be developed, but it requires teachers to develop a disposition for critically examining what they're doing. This is the essence of a simple, yet powerful notion called **reflective teaching** (Cruickshank, 1987; Schon, 1983), which simply means *think about what you're doing*. Reflective teachers are thoughtful, analytical, even self-critical about their teaching. They plan lessons thoughtfully and take the time to analyze and critique them afterward.

Your study of educational psychology supports reflection by providing a research and theory base of knowledge that you can use in critiquing your teaching. In Keith's case, the fact that he knew, for instance, that students should be actively involved in the learning process and that problem solving is important to understanding helped him in his reflection. Had he been less well informed, he wouldn't have reacted as strongly when some of his students wanted to sit like "bumps on logs" and were unable or unwilling to go beyond "the plain old mechanics." He also recognized that the problem solving Jan suggested could improve both student motivation and understanding. His uneasiness about his students' progress and his openness to new ideas indicated a tendency to be reflective, and his knowledge base made the process more effective.

1.12 ▬

Identify a specific example in which Jan Davis demonstrated reflection in her teaching.

Reflective teachers analyze their teaching to ensure that learning activities meet the needs of all students.

Figure 1.1

Questions for reflective teaching

- Did I have a clear goal for the lesson? What was the specific goal?
- Was the goal important? How do I know?
- Was my learning activity consistent with the goal?
- What examples or representations would have made the lesson clearer for students?
- What could I have done to make the lesson more interesting for students?
- How do I know whether students understand what I taught? What would be a better way of finding out?
- Overall, what will I do differently to improve the lesson the next time I teach it?

Teachers can acquire the tendency to reflect by continually asking questions of themselves as they teach. Although the list in Figure 1.1 isn't exhaustive, some possibilities are shown.

More important than the questions themselves is the inclination to ask them. If teachers keep questions such as those shown in Figure 1.1 at the forefront of their thinking, they can avoid the trap of teaching in a certain way because they've always taught that way. Openness to change and the desire for improvement are two of the most important characteristics of professional growth, and careful reflection can have positive effects on the decisions teachers make.

Having introduced the different kinds of knowledge needed to develop as a teacher, we now briefly describe how this book is organized to help you acquire this knowledge.

Organization of This Book

Educational Psychology is organized into three parts, which are summarized in Table 1.1 .

Part I: The Learner

At the beginning of this chapter, we said that this is a book about learning and teaching, and knowledge of learners and learning is arguably the most important knowledge that teachers can have. Consistent with this idea, Part I examines the influence of student characteristics on learning. Chapter 2 describes the development of cognition and language. Personal, social, and moral development, and the development of self-concept are discussed in Chapter 3. In Chapter 4 we examine the influence of intelligence, culture and ethnicity, socioeconomic status, and gender on learning. The focus on learner differences continues in Chapter 5, where we discuss teaching students with exceptionalities.

Part II: Learning

In response to the need for knowledge of how students learn, Part II focuses in detail on learning processes. The two key questions that this section tries to answer are, "What is

Table 1.1

Organization of this book

Parts and Chapters	Goal
Part I: The Learner	
Chapter 2: The Development of Cognition and Language	To understand how learners' intellectual capacities and language abilities develop over time
Chapter 3: Personal, Social and Emotional Development	To understand how learners' personal characteristics, moral reasoning, and socialization develop over time
Chapter 4: Learner Differences	To understand how intelligence, culture, socioeconomic status, and gender affect learning
Chapter 5: Learners with Exceptionalities	To understand how learner exceptionalities affect learning
Part II: Learning	
Chapter 6: Behaviorism and Social Cognitive Theory	To understand learning from behaviorist and social cognitive perspectives
Chapter 7: Cognitive Views of Learning	To understand learning from cognitive perspectives
Chapter 8: Complex Cognitive Processes	To understand concept learning, problem solving, and the development of strategic learners
Chapter 9: Cognition in the Content Areas	To understand differences in the ways learning occurs in reading, writing, math, and science
Part III: Classroom Processes	
Chapter 10: Increasing Learner Motivation	To understand factors that affect students' motivation to learn
Chapter 11: Creative Productive Learning Environments	To understand how instruction and classroom management are related
Chapter 12: Teacher-Centered Approaches to Instruction	To understand instruction from a teacher-centered perspective
Chapter 13: Learner-Centered Approaches to Instruction	To understand instruction from a learner-centered perspective
Chapter 14: Assessing Classroom Learning	To understand how teachers assess student learning

learning?" and "What can teachers do to promote it?" We begin in Chapter 6, where the first section of the chapter discusses Behaviorism, one of the oldest and most developed theories of learning. The second part of the chapter analyzes Social Cognitive Theory, which extends behaviorism to consider individual, internal factors such as learners' beliefs and expectations and how they influence learning.

Cognitive views of learning are the focus of Chapter 7. The chapter begins with a discussion of Information Processing and continues with Constructivism, which is becoming increasingly influential in curriculum development, instruction, and assessment. Chapter 8 continues the discussion of cognitive learning to include concept learning, problem solving, the development of strategic learners, and the transfer of understanding. In Chapter 9 we examine learning in reading, writing, math, and science.

Part III: Classroom Processes

Part III considers relationships among learner motivation, classroom management, instruction, and assessment. Research indicates that the two biggest problems facing beginning teachers are classroom management and learner motivation (Veenman, 1984), and we examine them in this section. Chapter 10 begins with a discussion of motivation from behaviorist, cognitive, and humanistic perspectives and describes implications for classroom practice. A classroom model for promoting learner motivation, synthesized from theory and research, relates motivational theory to practice. Chapter 11 examines classroom management and the interdependence of orderly learning environments and effective instruction. Chapter 12 examines the research on teacher-centered approaches to instruction, and Chapter 13 complements Chapter 12 by describing the expanding body of research on learner-centered approaches, such as guided discovery, discussions, individualization, and cooperative learning.

The section is completed by considering assessment, an essential classroom process. Gathering information and assessing student progress are ongoing processes that have powerful effects on learning and instruction. Chapter 14 discusses the assessment process (including both traditional and alternative assessments), preparing students for assessments, and grading and reporting. The role of assessment as an integral part of the teaching–learning process is analyzed.

Using This Book

We've tried to make the information in this text not only current and accurate but also accessible to you as learners. To assist you in your study, we have included the following features in each chapter:

- **Chapter outlines** describe the major ideas in a chapter and how they're organized.
- **Case studies** open each chapter. The cases—all taken from actual classroom experiences—illustrate the content of the chapter, and we frequently refer to the case studies as we discuss the chapter's topics. The case studies reinforce our theme of application of educational psychology in the real world of classrooms.
- **Objectives** identify main concepts and ideas in each chapter. The objectives supplement the outlines and provide you with learning goals for each chapter.
- **Important concepts** identify major ideas in each chapter. They appear in bold type and are defined in italics in the body of the text. They are also listed by page number at the end of each chapter to help you as you review the content.
- **Margin questions** appear throughout each chapter. They encourage you to actively think about the content as you study. The margin questions are designed to stimulate your thinking and to help you form links among (a) topics you study and your personal life, (b) concepts from different chapters, and (c) concepts and their classroom applications. Answers to some of the questions can be found in the chapter itself; other questions require you to relate information from previous chapters. Some ask you to hypothesize, predict, explain, or apply. These processes are the foundation for your own analysis and reflection.
- **Classroom Connections** offer two types of suggestions for applying each chapter's topics to classrooms. The first helps you bridge the gap between theory and practice by offering classroom-tested suggestions for applying the chapter content to your own teaching. The second focuses specifically on ideas for adapting your teaching to the diverse learners in your classroom.

| **Windows on Classrooms** conclude each chapter with an additional case study for analysis and reflection. In many cases, the teaching described in the case could be improved, and you will be asked to make specific suggestions for improving it on the basis of chapter content. This slice of classroom life is an attempt to make the content of the text applicable to your future role in classrooms.

| **Integrated case studies** are a feature that doesn't exist in any other educational psychology text. The case study that introduces our discussion of constructivism in Chapter 7, the opening case studies in Chapters 8 and 13, and the case studies at the end of Chapters 2, 7, 8, and 13 are also available on videotape. These seven cases, in both written and video form, provide authentic, concrete examples taken from actual classrooms and further integrate the content of the book with the real world of teaching and learning.

| **Technology and Learning,** a new section in each chapter, links chapter content to issues in technology and describes how technology can be used to enhance student development and learning.

| An integrated **CD-ROM** provides you with concrete experiences related to topics in Chapters 2, 3, 7, and 9. These appear in the text in the sections called, "Using Technology in Your Study of Educational Psychology." The exercises on this CD-ROM allow you to experience first-hand, from a learner perspective, concepts that you've studied in the text.

| A **summary** integrating the chapter's main ideas appears at the end of each chapter. You may wish to review it before reading a chapter a second time.

Again, welcome to your study of educational psychology. We sincerely hope our book enhances both your personal and professional growth.

 **Important Concepts**

correlation (p. 15)

correlational research (p. 15)

descriptive research (p. 13)

educational psychology (p. 4)

experimental research (p. 15)

general pedagogical knowledge (p. 11)

pedagogical content knowledge (p. 9)

principle (p. 16)

random assignment (p. 15)

reflective teaching (p. 22)

research (p. 13)

theory (p. 16)

Part I The Classroom
The Learner

2
The Development of Cognition and Language

Karen Johnson, an eighth-grade physical science teacher, walked into the teachers' workroom with a clear plastic drinking cup filled with cotton balls.

"What are you up to?" asked Ken, one of her colleagues. "Drinking cotton these days?"

"I just had the greatest class," Karen exclaimed. "You know how I told you the other day that my third-period students didn't understand density? They would memorize the formula and solve problems but didn't really get it. I also found out they were confused about basic concepts such as mass, weight, size, volume . . . everything. To them, mass and weight were the same, and if something is bigger it's heavier, so it has more mass and also is more dense. It was a disaster."

"I thought you said they were your low class," Ken responded. "You said they're a little slow."

"They're not that bad," Karen said, shaking her head. "Their backgrounds are weak, but then they've never really had this material other than to memorize some definitions, so what do you expect? I kept thinking they could do better, so I decided to try something a little different, even if it seemed sort of elementary. See," she went on, compressing the cotton in the cup. "Now the cotton is more dense. . . . And now it's less dense," she pointed out, releasing the cotton.

"Then yesterday I made some different-sized wooden blocks out of the same wood, and we compared the densities of the large blocks with those of the small blocks. Some of the kids still wanted to say the density of a big block was greater, but after we weighed different-sized blocks and discussed the results, they started to understand that size is only one factor influencing density.

"Now, this morning," she said with increasing animation, "I had them put water and vegetable oil in little bottles that were the same volume on our balances, and when the balance tipped down on the water side, they saw that the mass of the water was greater, so water is more dense. I had asked them to predict which was more dense before we did the activity, and most of them said oil, so we talked about that, and they concluded the reason they predicted oil is the fact that it's thicker.

"Here's the good part," she continued, "Calvin—he hates science—remembered that oil floats on water, so it made sense to him that oil is less dense. He actually got excited about what we were doing.

"So we formed a principle that less dense materials float on more dense materials. Then, even better, Donelle wanted to know what would happen if the materials mixed together, you know, like water and alcohol. You could almost see the wheels turning. So we discussed that and thought about more examples where that might be the case. We even got into population density and how a door screen with the wires close together compared with one with the wires farther apart, and how that related to what we were studying. It was exciting. I really felt as if I was teaching and the students were really into learning for a change, instead of poking each other. A day like that now and then keeps you going."

As you began your study of teaching and learning, one of the first principles you probably heard was "You must begin where the learner is." If we expect to teach as effectively as possible, the need to understand our learners is obvious. One part of this understanding is knowing about human development—how students think, feel, and act at different ages and what factors influence their thoughts and actions. In this book we examine three important aspects of this process: **personal development**, which *includes an understanding of who we are, including our emotional and moral growth*; **social development**, which *examines our changing abilities to relate to each other; and cognitive development*, which *describes changes in the way we think and process information.* We study cognitive development in this chapter and then turn to personal and social development in Chapter 3.

After you've completed your study of this chapter, you should be able to meet the following objectives:

▌ Explain how cognitive development is influenced by learning, experience, and maturation.
▌ Describe basic concepts in Piaget's theory of cognitive development.
▌ Explain the role of language, activity, and social interaction in Vygotsky's theory of cognitive development.
▌ Describe the implications of constructivism for teaching.
▌ Explain how language development contributes to other aspects of development.

In the opening case study, Karen described a problem typical for many teachers. In working with her students, she found they had only a superficial understanding of an important concept. Her students' reactions were also typical; in their efforts to cope, they memorized a formula, plugged in numbers, and got answers that had little meaning for them.

Why are some concepts, such as *density*, so hard for students to understand? It would be easy to think of these students as being a little slow, as Ken suggested, and let it go at that. This leads nowhere, however. Even if these aren't the most able students, they're often capable of achieving much more than they demonstrate. Other, more useful explanations are needed.

Development: A Definition

Theories of development help us understand learners by systematically describing changes in the ways they think, feel, act, and relate to others. For instance, these theories help us understand why older children can perform in ways that younger ones cannot, and they also help us understand factors that cause these changes in an individual. The better we understand learner development, the better able we are to meet each student's needs.

Let's look at an example.

Mike began playing the trumpet as a sixth grader in his middle school band. Evenings were filled with odd sounds coming from his bedroom, and even Chews, his devoted dog, retreated to the relative sanctuary of the living room. As an eighth grader, however, practicing his part in the piece that he and two friends were playing for a concert, he produced very different sounds. Now, after listening to his son play his last concert as a high school senior, Mike's dad is convinced that Mike could play in a professional orchestra.

Several factors influenced Mike's success. First, he practiced and worked and practiced some more. In the process, he learned much about playing the trumpet. In addition, he simply became stronger and more physically capable as a high schooler than he was earlier; he matured. We use this example to illustrate the concept of **development**, *the orderly, durable changes in a learner resulting from a combination of learning, experience, and maturation*. It begins for all of us at birth and continues until we die. Figure 2.1 illustrates the relationship between development and experience, learning, and maturation.

In Mike's case, his musical ability developed. Athletes develop their physical skills; all of us try to develop our social skills. In this chapter, we focus on the ways that learners' thinking, reasoning, and intellectual abilities develop. As you study, keep these questions in mind, "How is the thinking of young children different from the thinking of older learners and adults?" and "How do learners' thinking patterns change as they get older?"

2.1
A first grader tries to imitate her brother shooting baskets on the basketball court but has neither the strength nor the skill. She practices, receives tips from her brother, gets bigger and stronger, and by the fourth grade is making baskets consistently. Identify the experiential, the learning, and the maturation parts of development in this example.

Figure 2.1

Factors influencing human
intellectual development

Principles of Development

Though development is complex, some general principles exist that apply to all children and all forms of development: physical, social, emotional, and cognitive.

- Development is influenced by **maturation**, *the biological changes in individuals that result from the interaction of their genetic makeup and the environment*. A 5-year-old will not be able to run as fast as she can when she's 10, for example, and a first grader can't solve problems a seventh grader can solve. In extreme cases, such as malnutrition or severe sensory deprivation, the environment can retard normal maturation. In most cases, genes and the environment interact to produce normal growth.

- Learning contributes to development. Learning refers to increased understanding or the acquisition of distinct abilities, and development occurs when understanding or abilities are appropriately incorporated in the context of a complex activity (Bredo, 1997). For instance, you will *learn* specific questioning skills in your teacher-training program, and when you're able to use them appropriately in the context of a variety of lessons, your teaching will have *developed*.

- Experience enhances development. Children who are read and talked to at home are more successful in school than those who aren't, for example. Children exposed to music, physical activities, and social experiences become more capable in these areas than those having less experience.

- Development is continuous and relatively orderly. As people mature, learn, and gather experience, their development continually advances. They don't suddenly "jump" from one set of abilities to another (Berk, 1997). Rather, development builds upon itself.

- Individuals develop at different rates. A middle school girl will be a young woman, for example, towering head and shoulders over her slower developing classmate. In another case, two fourth graders will vary significantly in their ability to benefit from a learning activity. These different rates of development have important implications for teaching, as you'll see in this and the next chapter.

With these principles in mind, we now want to focus on *cognitive development* and consider current research on the role of the brain in it, a topic that is receiving increasing attention in education.

The Human Brain and Cognitive Development

Should young children be taught a second language at the same time they are learning their first? Is there a critical period during early childhood when artistic and musical abilities are best nur-

Concrete learning experiences contribute to development by encouraging learners to apply and adjust existing schemes.

Figure 2.2

Brain physiology and functions

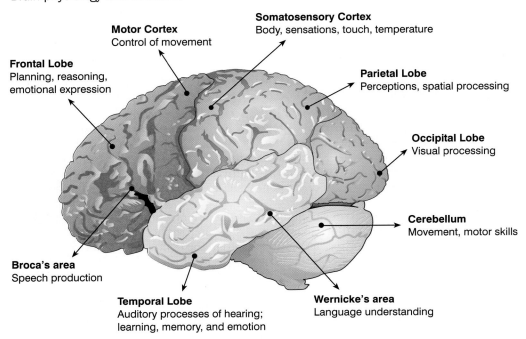

Motor Cortex
Control of movement

Somatosensory Cortex
Body, sensations, touch, temperature

Frontal Lobe
Planning, reasoning,
emotional expression

Parietal Lobe
Perceptions, spatial processing

Occipital Lobe
Visual processing

Cerebellum
Movement, motor skills

Broca's area
Speech production

Temporal Lobe
Auditory processes of hearing;
learning, memory, and emotion

Wernicke's area
Language understanding

tured and developed? Some educators believe the answers to these questions can be found in research on the brain.

Educators and researchers have increasingly turned to neuroscientific or brain research in their efforts to understand and shape cognitive development, and discussions of brain development have appeared in respected academic journals; the entire December, 1998, issue of *Educational Psychology Review,* for example, was devoted to the topic. Some educators hope to create direct links between research on the physiological development of the brain and educational practice (Wolfe & Brandt, 1998). Areas of the brain and their functions are illustrated in Figure 2.2.

Research on Brain Development

Educators trying to create links between brain development and educational practice point to three major findings from the neuroscience research (Bruer, 1997, 1998, 1999). These educators interpret the findings to suggest that

▌ Rapid brain growth occurs during early stages of development.
▌ Rapid brain growth results in critical periods of development for central processes like language and perception.
▌ Enriched environments can result in increased brain growth and development.

Let's consider these findings in more detail.

Early Brain Development.   The human brain has between 100 and 200 billion neurons (nerve cells), and the connections between them, called synapses, determine to a large extent the direction and extent of cognitive growth. Scientists have found that the rate of synapse formation peaks around age 4, resulting in synaptic density levels that are 50% higher than adults. In addition, blood sugar utilization in the brains of 4-year-olds is twice that of adults, indicating increased brain activity (Bruer, 1999). This increased neural activity suggests that this might be an optimal time for cognitive growth and development, and this information is a major reason educators have become interested in brain development.

Critical Periods.   If periods of increased brain activity exist, what happens to the brain if it doesn't receive adequate stimulation during these periods? **Critical periods** *are time spans that are optimal for certain capacities in the brain to develop* (Berk, 1997). If environmental stimulation occurs, development proceeds naturally; if not, development is retarded.

Evidence for critical periods in brain development comes from both human and animal research. For example, the brains of young kittens deprived of light for 3 or 4 days degenerate, and longer periods of stimulus deprivation can result in permanent brain damage (Berk, 1997). Research also indicates that after early childhood, it is extremely difficult to learn to speak a foreign language without an accent. After that time, adults can learn vocabulary and grammar, but their ability to form accent-free speech is hampered. At the extreme, the critical period concept suggests "use it or lose it."

Optimal Environments.   If critical periods exist, some educators believe that enriched environments during those periods should enhance cognitive development. Support for this conclusion comes from research with rats indicating that animals reared in complex environments have 25% more synapses per neuron in the visual areas of their brains than rats raised in isolation (Bruer, 1998).

Putting Brain Research Into Perspective

It is tempting to extrapolate from the neuroscience research to educational applications. In essence, we should capitalize on critical or active periods of brain growth by providing enriched environments for cognitive development. However, much of the research on brain development has been done with laboratory animals, and experts are cautious about direct applications with humans (Bruer, 1998). Though critical periods probably do occur in humans, our brains retain an enormous ability to benefit from environmental stimulation throughout our lives. In addition, there is no evidence indicating that critical periods exist for traditional academic subjects such as reading or math (Geary, 1998). Also, brain research isn't specific, and it doesn't provide educators with suggestions about when and how to capitalize on surges in brain growth.

Obviously, we should try to provide the best possible environments for growth and development, but the reasons for doing so can be better found in cognitive research on learning and development. Bruer (1997) summarizes this position in saying,

> Educational applications of brain science may come eventually, but as of now neuroscience has little to offer teachers in terms of informing classroom practice. There is, however, a science of mind, cognitive science, that can serve as a basic science for the development of an applied science of learning and instruction. Practical, well-founded examples of putting cognitive science into practice already exist in numerous schools and classrooms. Teachers would be better off looking at these examples than at speculative applications of neuroscience. (p. 4)

This is the reason you're studying educational psychology and reading this text.

With this advice in mind, we turn to Piaget's efforts to describe the course of human cognitive development.

2.2
To which of the three influences on development—*experience, learning,* or *maturation*—is the concept of critical period most closely related? Explain.

Piaget's Theory of Intellectual Development

Jean Piaget (1896–1990) was an unlikely influence on American education. His initial work was in biology, rather than psychology or education, and his writing had to be translated from French into English. He wasn't even interested in education, instead being fascinated by *genetic epistemology*, or the study of the growth of knowledge in people. He formed the beginnings of his theory by observing his own three children. His research method—intensively observing small numbers of subjects—was very different from the behaviorist tradition so dominant in the United States at the time and, as a result, his work wasn't initially accepted. As additional research verified and expanded his findings, however, his work has had an increasing impact on our views of development and learning, and on education in the United States. Let's look now at his theory, beginning with its cornerstone, the drive for equilibrium.

The Drive for Equilibrium

Think about some of your everyday experiences. Are you bothered when something doesn't make sense? Do you want the world to be predictable? Are you more comfortable in classes when the instructor specifies the requirements, schedules the classes, and outlines the grading practices? Does your life in general follow patterns more than random experiences? Most people's do.

According to Piaget (1952, 1959), people have an innate need to understand how the world works and to find order, structure, and predictability in their existence. He calls this need the drive for **equilibrium,** or *a state of cognitive balance between our understanding of the world and our experiences.*

Equilibration, *the act of searching for order or balance, involves testing one's understanding against the real world.* When our understandings can explain the events we observe, the world makes sense, and we are at equilibrium. When they can't, disequilibrium occurs, and we are motivated to search for better explanations. Disequilibrium is the energizing force in development.

Organization and Adaptation: The Creation of Schemes

The drive for equilibrium is the cornerstone of Piaget's theory (Piaget, 1952, 1959). We are all motivated by a need to understand the world, and, as we acquire experiences, we try to fit them into what we already know. For example, when you first went off to college, you probably based your expectations on your high school experiences. When you were able to understand your college experiences, you remained at equilibrium. When you couldn't, disequilibrium occurred, and you changed your thinking.

In response to the need for equilibrium, people organize their experiences into coherent patterns, which Piaget calls schemes. **Organization** is *the process of forming these **schemes,** which are mental patterns, operations, and systems that people use as their basis for understanding the world.* Schemes are the building blocks of thinking.

The importance of different learner schemes varies with age. Very young children use psychomotor schemes such as reaching for and holding an object; school-age children have more abstract schemes such as classification or proportional reasoning. As you learned to operate a car, you developed a *driving scheme* to start the car, shift gears, maneuver in traffic, obey traffic signals and laws, and make routine decisions about your speed.

2.3
Identify at least two schemes that you should have formed by now in your study of this chapter.

Piaget used the concept of schemes to refer to a narrow range of abstract operations, such as infants' object permanence scheme (the idea that an object is still there even when we can't see it) or young children's conservation of volume scheme (the idea that the amount of liquid doesn't change if it is poured into a different-shaped container) (Piaget, 1952). However, teachers and some researchers (e.g., Wadsworth, 1996) find it useful to extend Piaget's idea to include content-related schemes when adapting instruction to meet the developmental needs of their students. We use this expanded view in our description of Piaget's work.

The formation of schemes abounds in school. For example, we want young learners to understand that number is something that can be applied to a variety of objects varying from cookies to toys, and the number of objects doesn't change with their spacing or arrangement. Older learners use a classification scheme in science when they decide if crabs or snakes are vertebrates and in math if they're asked to determine if integers are rational numbers. From a content perspective, all the concepts, principles, rules, and procedures that students learn in school are organized into schemes that allow them to make sense of the world.

Adapting Schemes

As we acquire experiences, our existing schemes often become inadequate, and we are forced to adapt to function effectively. **Adaptation** is *the process of adjusting schemes and experiences to each other to maintain equilibrium*. For example, if we have learned to drive a car with an automatic transmission and we buy one with a stick shift, we must adapt our driving scheme accordingly.

Adaptation consists of two reciprocal processes: accommodation and assimilation. **Accommodation** is a *form of adaptation in which an existing scheme is modified and a new one is created in response to experience*, such as learning to drive with the stick shift. The driving scheme has been modified, and a driving-with-a-stick-shift scheme is created. Accommodation functions with its counterpart process, **assimilation**, which is *a form of adaptation in which an experience in the environment is incorporated into an existing scheme*. For instance, a child who has formed a "doggy" scheme encounters a Chihuahua and a German shepherd. Although the dogs are obviously very different from each other, she classifies them both as dogs. The child ignores characteristics such as size and color and focuses on the critical ones—those that make each a dog. This is adaptation through the process of assimilation. In contrast, in response to seeing a bear, the child says, "Doggy," but hears her father say, "No, that's not a dog. That's a bear. See how big it is. Listen to it growl." The child in this case has to modify her "doggy" scheme so that bears are not included and has to form a new "bear" scheme. Modifying her existing scheme and creating the new one is an example of accommodation. The relationship between assimilation and accommodation is illustrated in Figure 2.3.

Both assimilation and accommodation are required to maintain equilibrium. If new knowledge is only assimilated into existing schemes, the schemes don't change and development doesn't occur. "Flat-earthers," people who cling to the belief that

Figure 2.3

Maintaining equilibrium through the process of adaptation

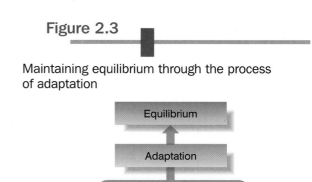

Figure 2.4

Illustration of growth in math depending on existing schemes

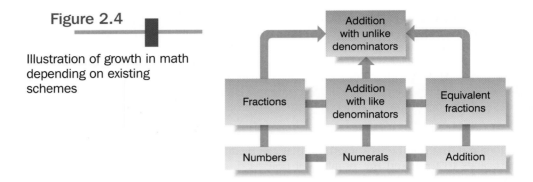

2.4

A young child believes that all short-haired people are male and long-haired ones are female. This classification system works until she encounters a long-haired male married to a short-haired female. This causes her to reconsider her original classification system. Identify where *assimilation* occurs for the child and where *accommodation* occurs. Explain how her experiences lead to development.

Earth is flat, are an extreme example. On the other hand, if existing schemes never work, a person is in a constant state of disequilibrium. *Culture shock*—the uneasy feeling people have when they visit a new country and must quickly adjust to different customs, food, and language—is an example. The amount of accommodation required can be overwhelming.

The drive for equilibrium, together with the processes of assimilation and accommodation, combine to promote cognitive development in people. As we consider these processes, however, keep in mind an important principle: *All growth depends on existing schemes*; a scheme is never formed in isolation. For example, a math student's ability to add fractions with unlike denominators develops from an understanding of adding fractions with like denominators, which was based on an understanding of fractions themselves, which began with an understanding of numbers and numerals. This principle, one of the most important contributions of Piaget's developmental theory, is illustrated in Figure 2.4.

This principle suggests that teachers should provide learning experiences for students by selecting and presenting topics that build on learners' current understanding and disrupt equilibrium enough to be motivating but not overwhelming. If new information is presented at the same level as existing understanding, it is simply assimilated and no growth occurs. On the other hand, if it is too different from present understanding, learners will be incapable of linking it to what they already know, and they will maintain equilibrium by discarding the experience rather than accommodating their present schemes.

Let's look at these ideas in more detail.

Factors Influencing Development

We saw earlier that development, in general, results from the combination of maturation, learning, and experience, and we've already discussed maturation. We now want to consider Piaget's emphasis on the role of experience in more detail.

In comparison with the general descriptions of development we discussed earlier, Piaget tends to subsume the role of *learning* under a more general description of *experience*. In addition, he separates the roles of *experience with the physical world* and *social experiences* in their influence on development (Piaget, 1970).

Experience with the Physical World

Carol Barnhart was working with her students on map-reading skills in social studies. She wanted them to understand how the scale on a map relates to real distances.

She began by saying, "Look at the map of Ohio in front of you. How far is it from Cleveland to Columbus? . . . Antonio?"

"I . . . I don't know . . . About 4 inches," Antonio shrugged.

Carol could tell from the silence and embarrassed giggles that met Antonio's answer that most of her students didn't have a clue about the scale on their map and how it worked.

She was about to launch into a minilecture on *scale* when she thought better of it, saying instead, "Okay everyone, let's try something. . . . Each of you take out a sheet of paper and a ruler. We're going to make a map of our classroom."

She then organized the students into pairs and had each pair use rulers to measure the room and draw pictures of what they found. When they finished, she reconvened the class and led a discussion on the problem of scale. Some groups made larger drawings by taping their sheets together, giving her an opportunity to discuss different kinds of scale. During their lunch break, she paced off approximate dimensions of the outside of the school, and, after lunch, the class again constructed a map and discussed the problems of scale.

The next day she returned to the map of Ohio and related the map to their activities of the day before. As they compared the map they had constructed to the map of Ohio, she could see that their understanding was much improved.

According to Piaget, experience influences the formation of schemes. Carol applied this principle by using the classroom as the focus of the learning activity, which allowed students to capitalize on their own background knowledge and provided them with direct, concrete experiences with the concept of *scale*. She could have merely written the definition of scale on the chalkboard and had students memorize it, which would have taken less time and effort but wouldn't have resulted in her students developing a meaningful understanding. We've all had the experience of memorizing definitions that we don't understand and promptly forgetting them.

Piaget's principle of *direct experience* has resulted in the emphasis on hands-on activities that we see in schools. For example, using sticks, blocks, and shapes helps children understand how abstract math concepts and operations relate to their everyday lives (Ball, 1992; Hartnett & Gelman, 1998). In our opening case study, Karen's eighth graders didn't understand *density*, so they memorized and mechanically applied the formula with little comprehension. Karen attempted to address this problem by providing direct, concrete experiences that allowed them to develop more effective schemes. Now, because they better understand the concept of *density*, they're equipped to incorporate that understanding into explanations about weather fronts, hot-air balloons, why people float more easily in the ocean than in lakes, and many others. Their ability to understand and cope with the outside world has expanded; development has occurred.

2.5
A middle school science teacher starts discussing the principles behind sundials and realizes that most of the class is confused because they aren't familiar with how shadows are affected by the different positions of the sun. Describe what the teacher can do to help remedy the situation.

Social Experience

Piaget also emphasizes the role of social experience in development (DeVries, 1997). Social experience allows learners to test their schemes against those of others. When their schemes are comparable, they remain at equilibrium; when they aren't, equilibrium is disrupted, learners are motivated to adapt their schemes, and development occurs.

Recognizing the importance of social interaction has strongly influenced education and child-rearing practice. Parents, for example, organize play groups for their young children, cooperative learning is emphasized in schools, and students are encouraged to get involved in service clubs and extracurricular activities. The positive influence of these activities illustrates the value of social interaction.

Social interaction encourages learners to examine their own schemes and compare them to others.

Stages of Development

Perhaps the most widely known elements of Piaget's theory are his descriptions of stages of development. Piaget's stages describe the ways children at different ages use information and think about the world. Progress from one stage to another represents qualitative changes in children's thinking, that is, changes in the *kind* of thinking rather than the *amount* (Siegler, 1991). These changes are more like the transformation of a caterpillar to a butterfly than the accumulation of bricks to make a house. For example, kindergartners' thinking is essentially limited to their perceptions, a conceptual "what you see is what you get." They typically don't reason systematically or logically. A fourth grader, in comparison, can think logically but requires concrete objects as reference points. More advanced students can think logically and hypothetically about abstract ideas. The differences in the ways learners at different ages think have important implications for teaching.

As you study the characteristics of each stage, keep three ideas in mind:

▌ Children develop steadily and gradually, and experiences in one stage form the foundation for movement to the next (Berk, 1997).

▌ Although approximate chronological ages are attached to the stages, the rate at which individual children pass through them differs widely, depending on maturation rates, experience, and culture (Papalia & Wendkos-Olds, 1996). While our students are usually grouped by chronological age, their developmental levels may differ significantly (Weinert & Helmke, 1998).

▌ Although rates vary, all people pass through each stage before progressing into a later one. No one skips any stage. This means that older children and even adults, if they lack experience in an area, will process information in ways that are characteristic of young children.

Piaget's stages of development are summarized in Table 2.1.

Table 2.1

Piaget's stages and characteristics

Stage	Characteristics	Example
Sensorimotor (0–2)	Goal-directed behavior	Makes jack-in-the-box pop up
	Object permanence (Represents objects in memory)	Searches for object behind parent's back
Preoperational (2–7)	Rapid increase in language ability with overgeneralized language	"We goed to the store."
	Symbolic thought	Points out car window and says, "Truck!"
	Dominated by perception	Concludes that all the water in a sink came out of the faucet (the first cartoon in chapter 1)
Concrete Operational (7–11)	Operates logically with concrete materials	Concludes that two objects on a "balanced" balance have the same mass even though one is larger than the other
	Classifies and serial orders	Orders containers according to decreasing volume
Formal Operational (11–Adult)	Solves abstract and hypothetical problems	Considers outcome of WW II if the Battle of Britain had been lost
	Thinks combinatorially	Systematically determines how many different sandwiches can be made from three different kinds of meat, cheese, and bread

Sensorimotor Stage (0 to 2 Years)

In the **sensorimotor stage**, *children use their sensory and motor capacities to make sense of the world.* The schemes they develop are based on physically interacting with their environments, such as using eye–hand coordination to grab objects and bring them to their mouths.

Initially, children in the sensorimotor stage don't mentally represent objects; for these children, it is "out of sight, out of mind." Later in the stage, however, they acquire **object permanence,** *the ability to represent objects in memory.* Children in this stage also develop the ability to imitate, an important skill that forms the basis for later observational learning.

Preoperational Stage (2 to 7 Years)

The **preoperational stage** is *characterized by perceptual dominance.* The name of this stage comes from the idea of operation or mental activity. A child who can classify different animals as dogs, cats, and bears, for example, is performing a mental operation.

In one sense, use of the term *preoperational* is unfortunate, because it suggests an incomplete stage of development. In fact, many dramatic changes occur in children as they pass through the preoperational stage, and a child at the end of the stage is very different from one at the beginning. For example, enormous progress in language development occurs, reflecting growth in symbolic thought and conceptual ability (Miller, 1993).

Children at this stage also learn a huge number of concepts. For example, a child will point animatedly and say, "Truck," "Horse," and "Tree," delighting in exercising these

2.6
A small child has not acquired *object permanence*. His mother takes a stuffed toy the child can see and puts it behind her back. What is the child likely to do? What will the child do after object permanence is acquired?

newly formed ideas. These concepts are concrete, however; the horse, truck, and tree are physically present or associated with the current situation. Children in this stage have limited notions of abstract ideas like *fairness, truth, democracy,* and *energy*.

The powerful effect of perceptual dominance is also seen in other aspects of preoperational thinking: *egocentrism, centration,* and lack of *transformation, reversibility,* and *systematic reasoning*.

Egocentrism.   **Egocentrism** is *the inability to interpret an event from someone else's point of view*.

> Two 3-year-olds were playing in the same area. They were both talking enthusiastically but weren't the least bit concerned that each conversation was independent of the other. A toy truck sat between the children, and at the moment neither was playing with it. When Sean began to play with the truck, Gail grabbed it away from him, saying, "My truck!" Gail's mother reprimanded her with an admonition to share. For Gail, however, the mother's reproof was incomprehensible, and she only reluctantly gave up the truck.

From the 3-year-old's perspective, the truck *was* hers; she saw it, wanted it, and believed she should have it. Later, through accommodation, the child's egocentric thinking expands to consider others' perspectives.

> **2.7**   ▬
>
> Which factor affecting development—*experience with the physical world, social experience,* or *maturation*—is probably most important for reducing egocentrism? Why?

Centration.   **Centration,** or centering, is *the tendency to focus on one perceptual aspect of an object or event to the exclusion of all others* (Ackerman, 1998). For instance, 5-year-olds are shown two rows of nickels such as the following:

When asked whether the number of coins in each row is the same, the children will say it is. However, when one row is lengthened right in front of the children, like this,

the children typically conclude that the bottom row has more coins. They *center* on the length of the bottom row, which is more perceptually obvious than the more abstract idea of number.

Centering is common, even in adults, and merchants, magicians, and others capitalize on it. For instance, we see gasoline prices written as 1.34^9 or an item of clothing priced at $69.95. We tend to center on the $1.34 and the $69, which makes the items seem less expensive to us. Magicians realize that we tend to focus on the most perceptually obvious aspect of their trick, so we miss the sleight-of-hand that makes the trick "magic."

Transformation.   **Transformation** is *the ability to mentally record the process of changing from one state to another*. Preoperational children have a difficult time with the

A nonconserver is influenced by appearances, believing that the flat pieces of clay have different amounts than the balls of clay even though they were initially the same size.

process of change and typically cannot transform. For instance, the children in the example with the coins cannot *mentally represent the process of lengthening the row*, even though they directly observe it; they focus instead only on the beginning and ending state. They see it as a different row, rather than as the earlier one lengthened.

Reversibility.   **Reversibility** is *the ability to mentally trace a line of reasoning back to its beginning*. Again with the coins, the children cannot *mentally* "reverse" the lengthening process. They don't mentally represent lengthening the row, can't mentally reverse it, and center on the length—which is more perceptually obvious than the number. It's easy to see why they conclude that the bottom row is longer.

Systematic Reasoning.   Preoperational children also don't systematically use inductive or deductive reasoning. In this regard, the term pre*logical* could be substituted for pre*operational.* For instance, a child reasoning deductively—albeit unconsciously—would conclude that the number of coins in the two rows remains the same, because they were initially the same and no coin has been added or taken away. A fourth grader given the problem would simply say something such as, "You just made the row longer," or, "You just spread the coins apart," reflecting systematic reasoning about the event.

Conservation

> As he's taking an order, the waiter at the pizza place asks, "Do you want that pizza cut into four or eight pieces?"
> The customer replies, "You'd better make it four; I couldn't eat eight all by myself!"

This joke illustrates a widely publicized feature of Piaget's work: his concept of conservation. **Conservation** is *the idea that the "amount" of some substance stays the same regardless of its shape or the number of pieces into which it is divided.*

The ability to conserve can be determined by a number of tasks. One was illustrated in the example with the coins. A second, involving conservation of mass, is illustrated by the following:

A child is given two balls of clay, as shown.

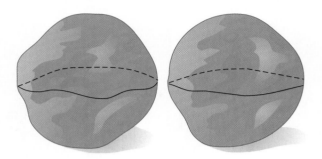

The child is asked which ball has more clay, and she concludes that they have the same amount. (If she believes they have different amounts, she is asked to remove clay from one and put it on the other until she says they're equal.) The experimenter then rolls out one of the balls, as shown here:

The child is asked if she now has the same amount of clay. The nonconserver concludes that the amounts are unequal; the conserver notes that the shape has changed but that the amounts are the same.

Preoperational children don't think about the world in the same way adults do. Their thinking is dominated by perception, their mental representations are limited to concrete objects, and they have difficulty mentally representing the process of change. They've made huge strides from the sensorimotor stage, however; they have a much greater ability to use symbols and words to think about their world.

2.8

Use the concepts *egocentrism, centration, transformation,* and *reversibility* to explain why preoperational children don't "conserve" in the clay problem.

2.9

Describe the "logic" in the fourth grader's thinking.

Concrete Operational Stage (7 to 11 Years)

The **concrete operational stage,** which is *characterized by the ability to think logically about concrete objects,* marks another important advance in children's thinking (Flavell, Miller, & Muller, 1993). The fourth grader who concluded that the number of coins in the two rows was the same because all the experimenter did was "spread the coins apart" was thinking logically, for example. As another case, consider the following:

We have three sticks. We see 1 and 2 as shown:

1   2

Now we see 1 and 3, as follows (Stick 2 is no longer visible):

1   3

We're then asked, "What do we know about the relationship between Sticks 2 and 3?"

A preoperational thinker cannot deal with the problem. A concrete operational thinker would conclude that 2 is longer than 3, reasoning that, since 2 is longer than 1 and 1 is longer than 3, 2 must be longer than 3. This is a logical operation.

Seriation and Classification.   Seriation and classification are two logical operations that develop during this stage (Piaget, 1977); both are essential for understanding number concepts (Siegler, 1991). **Seriation** is *the ability to order objects according to increasing or decreasing length, weight, or volume.* Piaget's research indicates that this ability gradually evolves until it is finally acquired at about age 7 or 8.

Classification *involves grouping objects on the basis of a common characteristic.* Before age 5, children can form simple groups, such as putting white circles in one and black circles in another. When a black square is added, however, they typically include it with the black circles, instead of forming subclasses of black circles and black squares. By age 7, they can form subclasses, but they still have problems with more complex classification systems. For example, when shown 10 black and 3 white cardboard circles, they conclude that the circles are all cardboard, with 10 black and 3 white. When asked if there are more cardboard or more black circles, however, 6-year-olds typically say there are more black, suggesting that they *center* on the colors, ignoring the larger class of cardboard circles and the subclass of black cardboard circles.

Teaching the Concrete Operational Student.   Although concrete operational thinkers have made important developmental strides, their thinking is still tied to available experiences; they need to solve problems, such as the one with the three sticks, with concrete objects. Let's see how one third-grade teacher does this.

> Lucy Amato introduced the concept of graphing to her third graders by having each student plant bean seeds in a pot. Each day after the seeds sprouted, the students measured them with a piece of paper and glued the actual length of paper on a graph. As the plants grew, the lines on the graph also got longer, and students could see the link between the actual plant growth and the graph.

Lucy taught graphing by using concrete objects: the pieces of paper and actual plants. Her lesson demonstrates how teachers of young children can increase understanding by using concrete materials to illustrate abstract ideas.

Because concrete experiences are needed, manipulatives are emphasized to teach concepts such as *place value, borrowing,* and *carrying* in math, and hands-on experiences are encouraged in science. As students use the materials, they acquire experiences that lay the foundation for more advanced thinking. Examples with other topics are shown in Table 2.2.

Concrete Materials and Language.   Teachers often mistakenly believe that if their students are using manipulatives, then learning is taking place. This is not always the case, however (Ball, 1992). Unless connections between manipulatives and the abstract con-

Table 2.2

The use of concrete examples in teaching

Topic	Example
Geography: Longitude and latitude	A teacher draws longitude and latitude lines around a beach ball to illustrate that latitude lines are parallel and longitude lines intersect.
Elementary Science: Air takes up space	A first-grade teacher places an inverted cup into a fishbowl of water. To demonstrate that air keeps the water out of the cup, she tips it slightly to let some bubbles escape.
Chemistry: Charles's law (when pressure is constant, an increase in temperature causes an increase in the volume of a gas.)	A teacher places one balloon into ice water, a second, equally inflated balloon, into room-temperature water, and a third into hot water. She asks the students to compare the final volumes of each.
History: Mercantilism	A teacher writes short case studies illustrating England and France trading raw materials from their colonies with manufactured products, forbidding trade with others, and requiring their ships for transport.

cepts and symbols that represent them are specifically made, students are left uncertain and may even view using the manipulatives and the descriptions of the concepts and symbols as two different lessons. Let's see how a second-grade teacher attempts to help her students make these connections:

> Kristen Michler was teaching her students about place value. She began by putting the students in pairs and had them make three groups of 10 interlocking cubes and then gather 4 separate cubes beside the groups.
>
> After the groups were finished, Kristen asked, "Look at what you've made. What do we have there? . . . Jason?"
>
> "Cubes."
>
> "What have we done with the cubes? . . . Lonnie?"
>
> "Put them together."
>
> "All of them?"
>
> " . . . No, not these" (pointing at the four separate ones).
>
> "When we put them together, how many do we have in each group? . . . Jianna?"
>
> " . . . 10."
>
> "How many groups of 10?"
>
> " . . . Three."
>
> "Good," Kristen smiled. "What else do we have? . . . Trang?"
>
> " . . . These" (pointing to the four separate ones).
>
> "Good. So, we have three groups of 10 and four separate ones. Now, look up here."

Kristen then wrote 34 on the chalkboard.

"Look at the number I've just written. What do you suppose the 3 is?" she asked, pointing at the 3. . . . Yolanda?"

" . . . "

"Look at your cubes. How many groups of 10 do you have?"

" . . . Three."

"Yes, good! So, what is this 3?"

" . . . It's . . . these."

"Yes," Kristen smiled encouragingly. "Go ahead and say it."

" . . . "

"It is the number of groups of . . . ," Yolanda continued, " . . . 10."

"Yes, excellent. We have made three groups of ten, and this 3," again pointing at the 3 on the chalkboard, "is the number of groups of 10 that we have."

Kristen then continued by asking the students about the 4 on the chalkboard. Next, she had the groups make two groups of 10 cubes and 6 separate cubes, discussing that example just as she did the first one.

As we see, students don't automatically form links between concrete materials and abstract numerals (Ball, 1992). An essential part of Kristen's lesson was her questioning, which led students to think about the *relationship* between the cubes and the numerals. Seeing the relationship is difficult for students, but it's critical if they are to understand the connection between the abstractions we want them to learn and the experiences we provide. If this link is missing, learning will be incomplete, with manipulatives and abstract concepts remaining unrelated in students' minds.

> **2.10**
> Think again about Karen Johnson's work with her students. Describe a series of questions that she would need to ask to help her students link the abstract formula for density (density = mass/volume) to her demonstration with the cotton.

Formal Operational Stage (Age 11 to Adult)

Although concrete thinkers are capable of logic, their thinking is tied to the real and tangible. Formal thinkers, in contrast, can think logically about the hypothetical—and even the impossible—as well as the real. During the **formal operational stage**, *the learner can examine abstract problems systematically and generalize about the results.* These abilities open a whole range of possibilities for thinking about the world that were unavailable to learners at the earlier stages.

Characteristics of Formal Thought. Formal thinking has three characteristics (Flavell, 1985):

- Thinking abstractly
- Thinking systematically
- Thinking hypothetically and deductively

Differences between concrete and formal operational thinkers on these dimensions are illustrated in Figure 2.5.

As shown in Figure 2.5, the formal operational learner can consider the abstract and hypothetical, as in the question about laws. This ability makes the study of courses such as algebra, in which letters and symbols stand for numbers, meaningful on a different level. To the concrete operational child, $x + 2x = 9$ is made meaningful only by representing it as a concrete problem, such as

> *Dave ate a certain number of cookies. His sister ate twice as many. Together they ate nine. How many did each one eat?*

Formal operational learners can think logically about abstract and hypothetical ideas.

Figure 2.5

A comparison of concrete and formal operational thinking

FLAVELL'S CHARACTERISTICS OF FORMAL THOUGHT	FORMAL OPERATIONAL THINKER	CONCRETE OPERATIONAL THINKER
ABSTRACT THINKING	Can describe the meaning of abstract ideas, such as "make hay while the sun shines" to conclude something such as, "take an opportunity when it's given."	Tends to view ideas concretely and literally, such as concluding, "you need to harvest hay during the daylight hours."
SYSTEMATIC STRATEGIES	Systematically examines the possible influence of the length, weight, and height on the frequency of a simple pendulum.	Changes more than one variable at a time, such as changing both the length and the weight in trying to see what affects the frequency.
HYPOTHETICAL AND DEDUCTIVE THINKING	Can consider questions like "What if we lived in a country without laws?" to make conclusions, such as, "People would have autonomy, but, . . ."	Hypothetical ideas tend to be confusing, such as, "I don't understand what you want. We *do* have laws."

Formal operational learners, in contrast, can think about the equation as a general idea, just as they would in describing the problem with the sticks by saying, "If *A* is greater than *B*, and if *B* is greater than *C*, then *A* is greater than *C*." In doing so, formal thinkers are operating in the abstract, an ability that allows them to use the solution for a variety of problems.

Formal thinkers also think systematically and recognize the need to isolate and control variables in forming conclusions. For example, a girl hearing her father say, "I've got to stop drinking so much coffee. I've been sleeping terribly the last few nights," responds, "But, Dad, maybe that's not it. You've also been bringing work home every night, and you didn't do that before." She recognizes that her father's sleeplessness may be caused by extra work, rather than by the coffee and that they can't tell until they isolate each variable. This is an example of systematic thinking.

Because much of the content of middle, junior high, and high school curricula is abstract, the transition to formal thinking is very important. For instance, in American history, considering what might have happened if the British had won the Revolutionary War requires hypothetical and deductive thinking. Biology students are asked to consider the results of crossing different combinations of dominant and recessive genes. Art students must imagine multiple perspectives and light sources when they create drawings. In the study of literature, students are asked to consider the viewpoints of different characters in the stories they read. Middle and high school curricula are filled with experiences requiring formal operational thought.

The difficulty Karen Johnson's students had in understanding the concept of density further illustrates the need for formal thinking. When students cannot think abstractly and solve abstract problems, they revert to memorizing what they can or, in frustration, give up altogether.

Stages of Development: Research on Student Thinking

We've just seen that much of the middle, junior high, and particularly the high school curriculum is geared toward formal operational thinking, and a strict application of Piaget's work suggests that this is appropriate.

This can create a dilemma, however, because research indicates that *most middle, junior high, and high school students are still concrete operational in their thinking* (Karplus, Karplus, Formisano, & Paulsen, 1979; Lawson & Snitgren, 1982; Thornton & Fuller, 1981).

Additional research indicates that even college students are unlikely to reason formally in areas outside their majors (De Lisi & Straudt, 1980), and similar patterns have been found in adults.

> Formal operations, like the concrete reasoning that preceded it, seems to be a gradual rather than abrupt development. And rather than emerging in all contexts at once, it is specific to situation and task. All normal adults are capable of abstract thought, but they are likely to demonstrate it only in areas in which they have achieved considerable mastery. (Berk, 1996, p. 552)

If older students lack concrete experiences in a particular area, they may even be preoperational in their thinking. As an example, consider the following problem. Seventh graders observed a balance with blocks on it, as shown in Figure 2.6, and were then asked to judge the accuracy of the following propositions:

▌ The volume of A is greater than the volume of B.
▌ The mass of A is greater than the mass of B.
▌ The density of A is greater than the density of B.

2.11 ▬
What is the most likely reason middle, junior high, high school, and university students are concrete operational in their thinking?

Figure 2.6

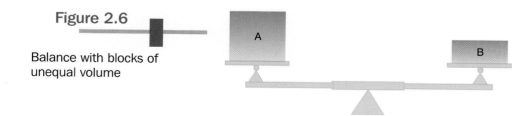

Balance with blocks of unequal volume

The reasoning involved can be described as follows:

We can see that the volume of A is greater than the volume of B. The balance is level, so the masses are equal. Because the masses are equal but A's volume is greater, its density is less than B's.

2.12
What preoperational characteristic explains why the students would conclude that the bigger box had more mass, even though the balance was balanced? Explain using that characteristic.

The problem occurs in the present and is tangible; it requires concrete operational thinking. The seventh graders, typically 12 or 13 years old, were chronologically at the formal operational stage; they should have been able to solve the problem with ease. Researchers found, however, that more than three fourths of the students concluded that both the mass and density of A were greater than the mass and density of B. The students were still dominated by perceptions, concluding that because A is larger, it must have more mass and also be more dense (Eggen & McDonald, 1987). *Their reasoning was preoperational.*

These findings have important implications for teachers, particularly those in middle schools, junior highs, and high schools (and even universities). Many students come to these learning settings without the concrete experiences needed to think at the level of abstraction often required. Wise teachers realize this and provide concrete experiences for them, as Karen Johnson did with her eighth graders. Otherwise, students will revert to whatever it takes for them to survive—in most cases, memorization without understanding.

We've seen that much of the junior high and high school curricula require formal thought, yet most students at these ages remain concrete operational, which poses a major dilemma. What can be done to bridge this gap?

Technology and Learning: Using Technology to Develop Formal Thinking

Laboratory experiences in science can be one solution to the problem of the discrepancy between the demands of junior high and high school curricula and the developmental stage of most of these students. Designed properly, they simultaneously provide concrete experiences while requiring students to think logically, systematically, and hypothetically—

Computer simulations allow learners to test hypotheses, control variables, and develop their formal thinking abilities.

characteristics of formal operational learners (Lawson, 1995). Effective lab experiments give learners practice in designing, implementing, and evaluating experiments in which the values of variables are systematically changed and controlled.

Lab experiments are effective because the implementation and results of the experiments are concrete, yet they require logical, systematic, and hypothetical thought, helping learners make the transition from concrete to formal operations. Unfortunately hands-on labs are often expensive, time-consuming, logistically difficult to implement, and sometimes even dangerous, which discourages many teachers from using them. Technology provides a viable alternative.

Laboratory Simulations

Researchers have been working to create laboratory simulations that allow students to design experiments using computer technology (Fisher, 1997; Weller, 1997). The simulations present realistic situations in which students can systematically investigate and control variables. For example, in one simulation, students design experiments investigating the effects of heat on different objects (e.g., "How does the size of a swimming pool influence cooling and evaporation?") (Friedler, Nachmias, & Songer, 1989, 1990). In another, students investigate the effects of different DNA combinations on genetics (Lundeberg et al., 1999).

> 2.13 ▬
> Identify at least one advantage and one disadvantage of using a computer simulation examining the effects of heat on different objects, compared to conducting the experiment with the concrete materials.

Research on the use of these simulations indicates they can be effective in helping learners develop formal thinking. For example, students unable to control variables before their involvement in the simulation were able to do so after their experience, indicating that the simulation provided the experience needed to make the transition to systematic reasoning, one attribute of formal thinking (Friedler et al., 1990). In addition, technology-based simulations have also increased students' interest and confidence in science, as well as their ability to interpret data (Lundeberg et al., 1999).

Technology-based simulations won't work automatically, however, and careful thought and planning are needed to implement them effectively. The following suggestions can help in making decisions about using them in our classes:

▌ Ensure that learners have adequate background knowledge before beginning the simulation. If background knowledge is lacking, provide examples and representations of the content to develop it.

▌ Be as certain as possible that the students understand the procedures involved in the simulation by reviewing them before having the students complete the activity.

▌ Make the logic behind operations visible by carefully debriefing the experience after the students have completed it.

▌ Require that students apply the ideas they learn in the simulations to other, real-world problems.

If carefully planned, implemented, and monitored, technology simulations can provide valuable educational experiences for students. They won't work magic, however. As with all aspects of teaching, they're only as effective as the teacher who uses them.

Putting Piaget's Theory Into Perspective

As with virtually all theories, Piaget's work isn't perfect, and it doesn't offer a complete description of cognitive development. In an effort to put his work into perspective, we examine some common criticisms, as well as the strengths of his theory.

Using Technology in Your Study of Educational Psychology

Examining Cognitive Development

You've just read about laboratory simulations that provide students with experiences in designing, implementing, and evaluating simulated lab experiments. Using the CD-ROM that accompanies this book, you can now design one of your own. This simulation will give you some direct experience in using the CD to examine your own thinking as well as the thinking of students who have completed the experiment in an actual lab setting. To complete the activity do the following:

- Open the CD and click on the "Pendulum Experiment." (Your instructor will show you how to access the information on the CD.)
- Complete the activities involved in the "Pendulum Experiment."
- After completing the activities, answer the following questions:

1. With respect to the pendulum experiment, was your thinking *concrete operational* or was it *formal operational*? What, specifically, did you do in conducting the experiments that indicated your thinking was either *concrete* or *formal operational*?

_____

_____

_____

2. Suppose your thinking in this experiment was concrete operational. (It may or may not have been, and if it was, it isn't any negative reflection on your ability.) What is the most likely reason your thinking was concrete operational?

_____

_____

_____

3. Now, let's examine the thinking of students who conducted this same experiment in an actual lab setting. Read the case study at the beginning of Chapter 13. (You may also watch a video of this same case study. Your instructor can make the video available to you if he or she chooses to do so.) Based on what you read in the written case study or saw in the video case study, decide if the thinking of the students was *concrete operational* or *formal operational*. What, specifically, did the students do that indicated that their thinking was *concrete* or *formal operational*?

_____

_____

_____

Your instructor will provide you with feedback with respect to these three questions, and he or she may ask you to complete some of the additional exercises on the CD.

Some of the most common criticisms of Piaget's work include the following:

- Piaget underestimated the abilities of young children. Abstract directions and requirements cause children to fail at tasks they can do under simpler conditions (Gelman, Meck, & Merkin, 1986). When 3-year-olds are given a simplified conservation-of-number task, for example, such as with three instead of six or seven items, they respond correctly (Berk, 1997).
- Piaget overestimated the abilities of older learners, and this can cause a problem for both learners and teachers. For example, middle and junior high teachers interpreting Piaget's work literally will assume that their students can think logically in the abstract, yet, as we saw earlier, this often isn't the case. Learners needing, but lacking, concrete experiences then usually revert to memorizing, forgetting it soon afterward.
- Piaget's description of broad developmental stages that affect all types of tasks isn't valid (Siegler, 1991). For example, the progression to concrete operational thinking begins with conservation of mass and ends with conservation of volume (Bee, 1989).
- Children's logical abilities depend more strongly on experience and knowledge in a specific area than Piaget suggested (Marini & Case, 1994; Siegler & Ellis, 1996). For example, if students are given adequate experiences, they can solve proportional reasoning problems, but without the experiences, they cannot.
- Piaget's work fails to adequately consider the influence of culture on development (Berk, 1997). Cultures determine the kinds of experiences children have, the values they develop, the language they use, and the way they interact with adults and each other (Rogoff & Chavajay, 1995). (We examine the role of culture in development in the next section, discussing the work of Lev Vygotsky.)

On the other hand, the influence of Piaget's work on education is so pervasive that we may forget there was a time when teaching and curriculum were different. For example, in part because of Piaget's work, teachers no longer believe that having students memorize rules, such as the algorithm for subtracting one two-digit number from another, will help them understand and apply the rule (Porter, 1989). Piaget has also been instrumental in changing the way learning is viewed; educators now see it as an active process in which learners construct their own understanding of how the world works (we discuss constructivism in more detail later in this chapter and in Chapter 7).

Piaget's work has also influenced the curriculum. Lessons are now organized with concrete experiences presented first, followed by more abstract and detailed ideas (Ackerman, 1998). We see elementary math teachers armed with beans glued to craft sticks and boxes filled with cubes (National Council of Teachers of Mathematics, 1989), and "hands-on" experiences are emphasized in science (American Association for the Advancement of Science, 1993). "Language experience" and "whole language" focus on developing children's reading and writing abilities by building on their experience and naturally developing language instead of requiring memorized words and definitions (Tompkins, 1997). The social studies curriculum begins with a study of children's homes and families and then becomes more abstract as it moves to their neighborhoods, cities, states, and finally to a study of their culture and those of other nations (Brophy, 1990).

In summary, some of the specifics of Piaget's theory are now subject to criticism, but his emphasis on experience and the learner as active in the learning process are unquestioned. He continues to have an enormous influence on teaching in this country.

Classroom Connections

Applying an Understanding of Piaget's Views of Development in Your Classroom

1. Provide concrete and personalized examples, particularly when abstract concepts are first introduced.
   - A kindergarten teacher begins her unit on animals by taking her students to the zoo. She plans for most of the time to be spent with hands-on activities in the petting zoo.
   - A high school social-studies teacher involves his students in a simulated trial to help them understand the American court system. After the trial is over, he has participants discuss the process from their different perspectives.
2. To assess students' present levels of development, ask students questions and involve them in discussions.
   - A kindergarten teacher is discussing geometric shapes with his students. Using a flannel board and shapes of different colors and sizes, he asks the students to group them in different ways. After each grouping, he asks the class, "Does that make sense? Are there other ways to group these together?" At the conclusion of his lesson, he emphasizes that there are many ways to group objects.
   - Before beginning a unit on light, reflection, and refraction, a science teacher asks students to explain different phenomena using a flashlight, mirrors, prisms, and lenses. As students explain different phenomena, such as shadows and rainbows,

she asks, "Does that make sense?" and encourages other students to ask questions.
3. Use student interaction to expose students to the thought processes of more advanced students.
   - A high school math teacher talks about problems at the chalkboard, helping students see how he solves each one. He then encourages students to demonstrate different solutions and asks questions that elicit their thinking in the process.
   - A junior-high science teacher gives her students a brief pretest at the beginning of the year on formal operational tasks such as controlling variables and doing proportional thinking. She uses this information to group students for cooperative learning projects, placing some formal operational and some concrete operational students in the same groups. She encourages students to think aloud when they solve problems and does the same herself at the chalkboard.
4. Provide practice in hypothetical reasoning for upper-elementary, middle, and junior high school students.
   - An eighth-grade algebra teacher is working with factoring polynomials and has the students factor the expression: $m^2 + 2m + 1$. She then asks, "What if no 2 appeared in the middle term, would it still be factorable?"
   - A history class concludes that people often emigrate for economic reasons. The teacher asks, "Consider a family named Fishwiera, who are upper-class Lebanese. What is the likelihood of their immigrating to the United States?"

A Sociocultural View of Development: The Work of Lev Vygotsky

Piaget (1952) viewed developing children as individuals—busy, self-motivated explorers of their environments who, on their own, form ideas and test them against the world. Lev Vygotsky (1896–1934), a Russian psychologist, provides an alternative view that emphasizes social influences on the child's developing mind (Rogoff & Chavajay, 1995).

As a boy, Vygotsky was instructed by private tutors who used Socratic dialogue—a question and answer approach that challenges current ideas to promote higher levels of understanding—to teach him (Kozulin, 1990). These sessions, combined with his study of literature and experience as a teacher, convinced him of the importance of two factors in human development: social interaction and language (Vygotsky, 1978, 1986). This is the source of the term, a *sociocultural* view of development.

Let's look at some examples and see how they relate to Vygotsky's work.

Suzanne was reading *The Little Engine That Could* to her 4-year-old daughter, Perri, as Perri sat on her lap. "I think I can, I think I can," she read enthusiastically from the story.

"Why do you think the little engine kept saying, 'I think I can, I think I can'?" she smiled at Perri as they talked about the events in the story.

" . . . We need to try . . . and . . . try and try," Perri finally said after some hesitation and prompting from Suzanne.

Sometime later, Perri was in school and working on a project with two of her classmates. "I don't get this," her friend Dana complained. "It's too hard."

"No, we can do this if we hang in," Perri countered. "We need to try a little harder."

Monique was struggling with the process of solving simultaneous equations in algebra.

"Look at these equations," Mrs. Castillo directed.

$$2x + 4y = 9$$
$$3x - 4y = 6$$

"Suppose we add them together. What will we have?"

"$5x = 15$," Monique responded.

"Yes, good," Mrs. Castillo smiled. "What might we do now to find the value of x?"

"We can . . . divide both sides by 5."

"Good, . . . and what will we get?"

"We . . . have . . . x equal to 3."

After a considerable amount of practice, Monique was working on the following problem:

A company's inventory of oil reserves has been lost because of a computer glitch. Through manipulating several of their inventory programs, however, they do know that they have 1,000 M (an M is one million barrels) in Houston, and they have three times as much 30-weight as 10–30-weight oil. They've also been able to determine that the ratio of 30 to 10–30 is 2 to 3 in New Orleans and that they have 900 M in New Orleans.

"I can write this as $3x + y = 1000$, and $2x + 3y = 900$," she said to herself after carefully thinking about the problem. She then struggled but solved the problem, finding that the company has 900 M of 30 and 100 M of 10–30 in Houston, and 600 M of 30 and 300 M of 10–30 in New Orleans.

Limok and his father looked out and saw a fresh blanket of snow on the ground.

"Ahh, beautiful," his father observed enthusiastically. "Iblik, the best kind of snow for hunting, especially when it's sunny."

"What is *iblik*? Limok wondered.

"It is the soft, new snow; . . . no crystals," his father responded, picking up a handful and demonstrating how it slid easily through his fingers.

"The seals like it," said his father. "They come out and sun themselves in it. Then, we only need the spear. Our hunting will be good today."

Sometime later, as Limok and his friend Osool hiked across the ice, Limok saw a fresh blanket of snow covering the landscape.

"Let's go back and get our spears," Limok said eagerly, "The seals will be out and easy to find today."

These examples have the following in common:

▌ Learning took place in the context of a social situation that was culturally bound and facilitated by language.
▌ The learners developed understanding that they wouldn't have been able to acquire on their own.
▌ A "more knowledgeable other" guided the learners' developing understanding.
▌ The learners were able to benefit from the experience.
▌ Development occurred as the learning was later integrated into the context of a broader experience (Bredo, 1997).

Social Interaction, Language, and Culture

In each of the preceding cases, learning took place in the context of a social experience; Perri learned about perseverance as her mother read and talked to her, Monique learned how to apply algebraic equations to real-world problems under Mrs. Castillo's guidance, and Limok learned about the conditions conducive to hunting as he interacted with his father. "Vygotsky argued that higher mental functions develop through participation in social activities; hence, the social context of learning is critical" (Bredo, 1997, p. 34).

Also, the children were exposed to ideas they wouldn't understand on their own, or it would take a great deal of time to develop on their own. In contrast with Piaget, who sees children as individual explorers of the world, Vygotsky's view of development suggests that children need not, and should not, reinvent the knowledge of a culture on their own. This knowledge has been built up over thousands of years and should be *appropriated* (internalized) through the process of social interaction (Leont'ev, 1981).

Adults—particularly parents, other caregivers, and teachers—as well as peers play an important role in the process of appropriation, and the preceding examples illustrated their roles. Adults explain, give directions, provide feedback, and guide communication (Rogoff, 1990). Children use conversation to collaborate when solving problems—both in play and in the classroom. This interaction allows the exchange of information and provides feedback about the validity of existing ideas.

Language was the medium that allowed the children to learn in each of the examples, and it is central to Vygotsky's theory of development. Language allows learners to access knowledge others already have, and it provides learners with cognitive tools that allow them to think about the world and solve problems.

When children learn language, they aren't just learning words; they also are learning the ideas connected with those words. When Limok learned *iblik*, he didn't just learn the word and how to pronounce it; he also learned that it is snow that is soft, fresh, crystal free, and that increases the likelihood of a successful hunt.

As we just saw, these ideas are culturally bound. For example, *iblik* is neither a term nor an idea that most Americans use; it is unique to Limok's culture. Language becomes a cultural tool kit that children carry around in their heads to help them make sense of the world.

The Role of Activity in Social Interaction

The concept of *activity* is another important element of Vygotsky's theory. Children learn by doing—by becoming involved in meaningful activities with more knowledgeable peo-

2.14 ▬
In mainstream American culture, the concept of *snow* is a relatively simple idea, whereas the Inuit people have many terms for the concept *snow*. What idea (discussed in this section) does this difference illustrate?

ple. Perri, Monique, and Limok didn't passively listen to the adults; they were actively involved in the discussions.

Activity provides a framework in which dialogue can occur. Through dialogue driven by activity, ideas are exchanged and development occurs.

2.15
Some educators believe that non-native English-speaking students should be immersed in "English-only" programs as soon as possible. On the basis of the information in this section, how effective are those programs likely to be? Explain.

Social Interaction, Learning, and Development

At the beginning of the chapter, we said that "learning contributes to development" was one of the principles of learner development. Let's see how learning and development are related in the context of Vygotsky's work.

According to Vygotsky, learning occurs when learners acquire specific understanding or develop distinct abilities, and development progresses when this specific understanding is incorporated into a larger, more complex context (Bredo, 1997). Each of the children in our examples, because of their experience with adults, learned something specific; Perri learned the value of perseverance, Monique learned how to solve algebraic equations, and Limok learned about the conditions for good hunting. Then, later, each of the children incorporated what they had learned into the context of a different and more complex context. Perri, for example, in her interaction with Dana—who wanted to give up—exhorted her to continue making an effort; Perri's behavior indicated an advanced level of development. Monique and Limok had similar experiences. Monique was able to solve a complex algebra problem on her own, and Limok recognized the conditions for good hunting when he and Osool were merely hiking across the ice.

These descriptions illustrate that learning is necessary for development, development is stimulated by learning, and learning and development both occur in the context of a social situation mediated by language (Bredo, 1997).

Language: A Tool for Self-Regulation and Reflection

Language is essential as a medium for social interaction, but it also serves an individual function; it gives us a means for regulating and reflecting on our own thinking.

> Every function in the child's cultural development appears twice: first, on the social level, and later, on the individual level; first, between people (interpsychological), and then inside the child (intrapsychological). This applies equally to voluntary attention, to logical memory, and to the formation of concepts. (Vygotsky, 1978, p. 57)

We all talk to ourselves. For example, we grumble when we're frustrated or angry: "Now where did I put those x%#* keys?" or when we're in uncertain situations, "Oh no, a flat tire. Now what? The jack is in the trunk. Yeah. I'd better loosen the nuts before I jack up the car."

Children also talk to themselves; walk into a preschool or kindergarten during free play and you'll hear muttering that appears to have no specific audience. If you listen more closely, you'll hear learners talking to themselves as they attempt tasks: "Hmm, which button goes where? . . . I better start at the bottom and put the first button down there." Vygotsky believed that this free-floating external speech is the precursor of internalized, private speech.

Private speech is *self-talk that guides thinking and action*. Piaget (1926) observed it in young children and termed it "egocentric speech," reflecting his belief that it was a by-product of the preoperational child's inability to consider the perspectives of others.

Vygotsky interpreted private speech differently. He believed that these seemingly targetless mutterings indicated a beginning in the development of self-regulation. Private speech, first muttered aloud and then internalized, forms the foundation for complex cognitive skills such as sustaining attention ("I better pay attention now. This is important."), memorizing new information ("If I repeat the number, I'll be able to remember it."), and problem solving ("Hmm, what kind of answer is the problem asking for?"). We saw private speech illustrated when Monique said to herself, "I can write this as $3x + y = 1,000$, and $2x + 3y = 900$," as she attempted to solve the algebra problems on her own.

Research supports Vygotsky's functional view of private speech. Children use more of it when tasks are difficult, such as we saw with Monique, or when they are confused about how to proceed (Berk, 1997). In addition, children who use private speech during problem-solving tasks are more attentive and goal oriented and show more improvement than their less talkative peers (Behrend, Rosengren, & Perlmutter, 1992). Finally, as Vygotsky predicted, private speech becomes internalized with age, changing from overt mutterings to whispers and lip movements.

2.16

You have assigned your second graders a series of word problems in math. As they work, you hear audible muttering about the problems. What might you infer on the basis of these mutterings? Would you expect similar mutterings if you were teaching sixth graders?

Vygotsky's Work: Instructional Applications

As we've seen, Vygotsky emphasizes the importance of social interaction and language in development. By using language in social situations, more knowledgeable partners share their expertise about the world. Instructional strategies based on Vygotsky's theory place students in situations where the topics and skills discussed are within the developmental grasp of the learner, an area called the zone of proximal development.

Zone of Proximal Development

In the preceding examples, the children all benefited from the experience of interacting with the adults; they were in the **zone of proximal development**, which is *a range of tasks that a child cannot yet do alone but can accomplish when assisted by a more skilled partner*. The zone represents a learning situation in which knowledgeable partners, working with students, can promote development (Walsh, 1991). For learners, there is a zone of proximal development for each task they are expected to master. When learners are in the zone, they can benefit from assistance. For example, Perri would have benefited little from a story about the French Revolution, and Monique probably would have been unable to understand calculus; these children were below a zone of proximal development for these activities.

Let's look at an example of the zone of proximal development in a classroom.

> Jeff Malone, a student intern, was working with a small group of students on percentage problems in math. He began by presenting the three students with a sample percentage problem and observing their work. Sandra zipped through the problem in no time; Javier struggled, muttering to himself; Stewart gave up and sat with his arms folded, a frown on his face.
>
> Instead of explaining the procedure to Javier and Stewart, as he had done in the past when students had difficulty, Jeff tried a different approach.
>
> "Let's talk about how we compute percentages in problems like this. Sandra, why don't you explain to us how you did the first problem? The rest of us will follow along, and then I'll ask someone else to do the next one."
>
> Sandra started, "Okay, the problem asks what percentage of the video games are on sale. Now, when I see a problem like this, I think, how can I make a fraction? After I make a fraction, then I make a decimal out of it and then make a percent. Yeah, that's what I do, so here's what I do first."
>
> As she continued to think aloud, Stewart and Javier followed along.

On the next problem, Jeff involved the two who were having problems. "Javier and Stewart, follow along with me and help me solve this problem: *'Joseph raised gerbils to sell to the pet store. He had 12 gerbils and sold 9 to the pet store. What percentage did he sell?'*

"The first thing," Jeff continued, "I need to find out is what fraction he sold. Now, why do I need to find a fraction? . . .   Javier?"

"To . . . then . . . if . . . once we get a fraction, we can make a decimal and then a percent."

"Good," Jeff smiled. "What fraction did he sell?"

" . . . 9 . . . 12ths."

"Excellent, Javier. Now, Stewart, how might we make a decimal out of the fraction?"

" . . . "

"Look again at the fraction. What is it?"

" . . . 9/12ths."

"Good. So, to find a decimal, we divide the 12 into what number? Go ahead and give it a try."

As Jeff watched, he saw that Javier quickly got .75. Stewart, however, began hesitantly, appearing confused by dividing a large number into a smaller one.

This learning experience relates to Vygotsky's theory in several ways:

▌ The learners were at different developmental levels; Sandra was beyond the zone, Javier was in the zone (he benefited from the experience), and Stewart was below the zone.

▌ Javier's learning took place in the context of a social situation. Javier acquired understanding that he wouldn't have been able to achieve on his own.

▌ Jeff, as a "more knowledgeable other," guided Javier's increasing understanding.

▌ Language was the medium used to promote Javier's understanding, both in the interaction and by having Sandra think aloud as she solved the problem. This made her tacit problem-solving procedures observable and provided a model the other students could follow.

▌ When Javier can incorporate his increased understanding into a different, complex context, his development will have advanced. For Stewart, Jeff will have to adapt his instruction to identify Stewart's zone of proximal development for this problem, so he will benefit from future social interaction.

> **2.17** ▬
> You are unsuccessfully trying to learn a new word processing program on your computer. A friend comes over. You're fine with her help, but after she leaves you again run into problems. Are you below, in, or beyond the zone of proximal development? In which of these three areas is your friend?

Applying the Zone of Proximal Development to Teaching

Applying the zone of proximal development to teaching involves three tasks: *assessing current understanding, selecting learning activities,* and *providing instructional support* to help students move through the zone successfully. Let's look at them.

First, assessment allows the teacher to determine students' current level of development. Jeff, for example, *gauged his students' abilities to understand a realistic problem*, a process called **dynamic assessment** (Spector, 1992). Reasoning ability, background knowledge, and motivation all influence a learner's zone of proximal development (Winn, 1992), and Jeff was able to assess each as he worked with the students.

Second, teachers must adapt learning tasks to the developmental levels of their students. Jeff, for example, needs to simplify the task for Stewart and increase the challenge for Sandra as he continues to work with them.

In addition to selecting tasks, the teacher must design them to create shared understanding. **Shared understanding** *occurs when the teacher and students have a common view of the task.* Shared understanding is important because it marks a beginning point for development through joint problem solving.

Teachers can ensure shared understanding in at least two ways. First, embed the task in a meaningful context. Instead of presenting math problems in the abstract, for example, the teacher relates them to students' lives; rather than teaching writing as disengaged communication, a teacher has students write letters to friends and relatives and compose stories about their own experiences. Second, shared understanding can be accomplished through dialogue that helps students understand and analyze the problems they face. Jeff used teacher and student think-alouds and questioning to help students see how percentage problems could be solved using a fraction algorithm.

A special form of dialogue that provides instructional support is called *scaffolding*. Let's look at this concept.

Scaffolding: Interactive Instructional Support

> A toddler was learning to walk. As she took her first tentative steps, her father walked behind her, holding both hands above her head as she lurched forward with uncertain steps. As she gained confidence, the father held only one hand, walking to the side, keeping an eye out for toys and other objects that could trip her. After awhile, he let go but continued at his daughter's side to catch her if she fell. When the child became tired or the terrain got bumpy, Dad grabbed her hand to make sure she didn't fall and skin a knee. Eventually, his daughter both walked and ran on her own. (Adapted from Cazden, 1988)

Parents provide scaffolding for their children as they learn to walk. In an educational setting, **scaffolding** is *assistance that allows students to complete tasks they cannot complete independently* (Wood, Bruner, & Ross, 1976). Scaffolding helps learners move through the zone of proximal development by enabling them to eventually complete tasks independently. Suzanne provided scaffolding for Perri by helping her understand that "I think I can, I think I can," suggests that we should persevere in life's tasks; Mrs. Castillo provided scaffolding by using questioning to guide Monique through the solution; and Limok's father provided scaffolding by demonstrating the characteristics of the snow that made it ideal for hunting.

Teachers provide individualized scaffolding for students through their numerous personal interactions during the day.

Table 2.3

Types of instructional scaffolds

Type of scaffolding	Example
Modeling	An art teacher demonstrates drawing with two-point perspective before asking students to try a new drawing on their own.
Think aloud	A physics teacher verbalizes her thinking as she solves momentum problems at the chalkboard.
Questions	After modeling and thinking aloud, the same physics teacher "walks" students through several problems, asking them questions at critical junctures.
Adapting instructional materials	An elementary physical education teacher lowers the basket while teaching shooting techniques and then raises it as students become proficient.
Prompts and cues	Preschoolers are taught "The bunny goes around the hole and then jumps into it" as they learn to tie their shoelaces.

Effective scaffolding is responsive to learners' needs; it adjusts instructional requirements to the learners' capabilities and level of performance (Rosenshine & Meister, 1992). When learners need more help, the teacher steps in; when less is required, the teacher steps back to allow learners to progress on their own.

Instructional scaffolding is a metaphor for the scaffolding that workers use as they construct a building. An instructional scaffold provides support to the learner. In the example of learning to walk, the father provided both literal and figurative support to his daughter. In classrooms, teachers provide scaffolding by breaking content into manageable pieces, modeling skills, providing practice and examples with prompts, and letting go when the student is ready. The scaffold functions as a tool for students, helping them learn new skills, much as an actual scaffold supports workers as they paint or plaster. Scaffolding extends the range of learners, allowing them to accomplish tasks otherwise impossible. If children were faced with learning to walk with no intermediate props, such as a parent or even furniture to pull themselves up on, their development would be delayed because of a lack of scaffolding. Similarly, some classroom tasks are so formidable that they cannot be accomplished without a teacher's guidance and support. Different types of instructional scaffolding are outlined in Table 2.3.

2.18 ▬
Explain how the father accomplished the three instructional tasks—assessing, adapting, providing support—as he helped his toddler daughter progress through the zone of proximal development.

2.19 ▬
The distinction between scaffolding and simply explaining is subtle but important. What is the key characteristic of scaffolding that makes it different from simple explaining?

Constructivism: A Developmentally Based View of Teaching and Learning

Development, and the related areas of learning and teaching, are undergoing something close to a revolution, and the learner is at the center of this change. **Constructivism** is *a*

view of learning and development that emphasizes the active role of the learner in building understanding and making sense of the world.

> Constructivists believe that knowledge results from individual constructions of reality. From their perspective, learning occurs through the continual creation of rules and hypotheses to explain what is observed. The need to create new rules and formulate new hypotheses occurs when students' present conceptions of reality are thrown out of balance by disparities between those conceptions and new observations. (Brooks, 1990, p. 68)

Constructivism emphasizes active learners, the linking of new knowledge to knowledge learners already possess, and the application of understanding to authentic situations. Experience, interaction between teachers and students, and students' interacting with each other are instructional tools for constructivists.

Piaget's and Vygotsky's Views of Knowledge Construction

Although they disagreed on some points, Piaget and Vygotsky were both constructivist in their orientation (Fowler, 1994). Similarities and differences between the two are outlined in Table 2.4.

2.20

Which view of constructivism provides for a more prominent role for teachers?

As shown in Table 2.4, Piaget more strongly emphasized individual learners' creation of new knowledge, whereas Vygotsky focused on the transmission of the tools of knowledge—namely, culture and language (Fowler, 1994; Rogoff, 1990). Regardless of philosophical differences, however, all views of constructivism recommend that teachers go beyond lecturing and telling as teaching methods and move toward "structuring reflective discussions of the meanings and implications of content and providing opportunities for

Table 2.4

A comparison of Piaget's and Vygotsky's views of knowledge construction

	Piaget	Vygotsky
Basic question	How is new knowledge created in all cultures?	How are the tools of knowledge transmitted in a specific culture?
Role of language	Aids in developing symbolic thought; It does not qualitatively raise the level of intellectual functioning. (The level of functioning is raised by action.)	Is an essential mechanism for thinking, cultural transmission, and self-regulation. Qualitatively raises the level of intellectual functioning.
Social interaction	Provides a way to test and validate schemes.	Provides an avenue for acquiring language and the cultural exchange of ideas.
View of learners	Active in manipulating objects and ideas.	Active in social contexts and interactions.
Instructional implications	Design experiences to disrupt equilibrium.	Provide scaffolding. Guide interaction.

students to use the content as they engage in inquiry, problem solving, or decision making" (Good & Brophy, 1997, pp. 398–399).

Applying Constructivist Ideas to Teaching

To illustrate these ideas, let's look at a teacher using constructivist concepts to guide her teaching.

Tracey Stoddart began her unit on heat by innocently asking, "What is heat?" Her students, confident of their 9 years of experience with the world, were more than willing to share their knowledge of the sun, bonfires, radiators, and other sources of heat.

Everything was going smoothly until Nick shared his belief that heat came from clothes such as sweaters and coats. The rest of the class nodded in agreement. Tracey was momentarily at a loss for words. How should she deal with this situation? We have all had the experience of being "cold," putting on a sweater, and "warming up."

After thinking for a few moments, she set aside her plans for the day and continued by asking, "Which do you think produces more heat, a sweater or a coat?"

"A coat!" the class unanimously agreed.

"What about a sweater and a jacket? Which one makes more heat?"

Students weren't so sure about this one. Some of them had heavy wool sweaters that they said kept them warmer than jackets; others thought they felt warmer in jackets.

"How could we find out for sure?" Tracey wondered aloud.

"How about, we put a thermometer in a coat?" Brad suggested.

"Yeah, and we can put another one in a sweater, and see which one gets hotter," Sonja added.

"Very good ideas," Tracey smiled. After more discussion, the class divided into seven groups of three and two groups of four. Three groups dug out thermometers from the file cabinet, read and recorded the temperature, and carefully wrapped them in coats. Three other groups did the same with sweaters, and the final three with jackets. They then went to lunch.

They returned, read the temperatures, and again recorded them on the chalkboard.

		Before	After
Coat	1.	72	72
	2.	73	72
	3.	72	73
Sweater	1.	74	73
	2.	74	74
	3.	73	73
Jacket	1.	71	72
	2.	72	71
	3.	72	73

As they looked at the information, the students began mumbling and commenting that the numbers didn't seem to make sense.

"None of them got hot," Brad said with uncertainty in his voice.

"About three of them got colder," Anne added in bewilderment.

"Yeah, but the sweaters and coats weren't the same," Anthony countered.

"That doesn't matter," Greta responded. "They shoulda still got hot."

"Maybe we didn't do it long enough," Gary suggested.

"When I was up in the attic with my mom, it was terrible hot 'cause air couldn't get in there," Suzanne added. "I think we should put plastic around them."

Several additional suggestions were made, and the groups went back to work on additional experiments. To the students' amazement, the results were the same, and finally, most of the students were willing to consider the possibility that coats and sweaters don't actually generate heat.

"If that's the case, how do they keep us warm?" Tracey wondered aloud. After additional discussion, Tracey asked what the class would expect if they wrapped a book with a sweater. Would the book warm up? How about a piece of metal? A pencil?

Opinions varied. The class did additional experiments to check and confirm their ideas. Finally, Tracey asked the students for some important differences between them and the book, pencil, and piece of metal.

"We're big, and they're little."

"The book is square, sort of."

"The pencil is skinny."

"We're alive; they aren't."

After several additional comments, Sonja noted, "The iron is cold."

"Do you think that's important?" Tracey queried.

" . . . Maybe. We're not cold."

" . . . Maybe if we're warm, a coat just keeps us warm," Andrew added after several seconds.

They then considered and discussed the idea that clothing merely traps heat rather than generates it. As the discussion came to a close, most of the students suggested that this was probably a more sensible idea.

The process had taken more time, but the time was well spent. (Adapted from Watson & Konecek, 1990)

Let's compare Tracey's experience with Karen Johnson's at the beginning of the chapter. In both instances, the teachers found that their students had a limited—in some cases inaccurate—understanding of the topic. For example, most of Karen's students believed, on the basis of their experience with the "thickness" of oil, that vegetable oil is more dense than water, and Tracey's students thought coats and sweaters produced heat. Both teachers adapted their lessons to learners' existing conceptions and provided the concrete experiences that Piaget stresses to help learners construct more accurate and valid concepts. In addition, both teachers used the Vygotskyan idea of social interaction to assist students in evaluating old and constructing new ideas. The evolving nature of constructed understanding was illustrated as Karen's students, on the basis of the experiences she provided for them, linked population density and the "density" of a screen to their understanding of the density of cotton, water, oil, and wood. Tracey used the experiments with coats and sweaters to help her students revise and refine their ideas about heat.

Constructivism is a powerful idea. It helps teachers apply Piaget's and Vygotsky's work to classroom learning and development. It suggests that teachers provide experiences, guide discussions, and assume a supportive role in assisting students' attempts at developing understanding.

Teaching based on constructivist principles is demanding and requires a great deal of expertise (A. Brown, 1994). For instance, both teachers had to be alert and flexible enough in their own thinking to capitalize on students' thoughts and insights when they surfaced in discussions. Less alert teachers might have missed opportunities to help their students move through their zones of proximal development. Worse yet, less effective teachers might ignore or even disapprove of student's reactions. With effort and practice, however, teachers can learn to guide student learning and help develop both the thinking and the deep understanding of content you saw in these classrooms. We return to constructivism in later chapters to discuss specific implications for instruction, motivation, and assessment.

2.21
Describe one approach to teaching that would be consistent and another approach that would be inconsistent with constructivism.

Classroom Connections

Applying Vygotsky's Descriptions of Development in Your Classroom

1. Use meaningful activity as an organizing theme for your curriculum.
   - A third-grade teacher structures a unit on weather around a daily recording of the weather conditions at her school. Each day, students observe the temperature, clouds, and precipitation, record the data on a calendar, graph it by using strips of paper, and compare it to the weather report in the paper.
   - A middle school social studies teacher tries to help his students understand political polls and the election process. Prior to a national election, he has students poll their parents and peers. Students then have a class election and compare their results with national results.

2. Use scaffolding to help students progress through the zone of proximal development.
   - When her students are first learning to print, a primary teacher initially provides dotted outlines of letters for the students and half lines to help them gauge size. Gradually, these aids are removed.
   - A middle school teacher helps her students learn to prepare lab reports by doing a lab with the whole class and writing it up as a class activity. Later, she provides only an outline with the essential categories in it. Finally, she only reminds them to follow the proper format.

Applying an Understanding of Constructivism in Your Classroom

3. Provide experiences that allow students to construct their own understanding.

- An art teacher begins a unit on perspective by showing slides, displaying works from other students, and sharing her own work. As students turn in their products, she shares them with the class and asks the class to discuss how perspective contributed to each drawing.
- To help his students understand the "process" of history, a history teacher asks them to write a "history" of some local event or phenomenon. He asks the students to find primary sources, interview people, and present their findings in writing.

4. Embed important concepts in authentic learning tasks.
   - A second-grade teacher teaches graphing by having the students graph class attendance. Information is recorded for both boys and girls, the figures are kept for several weeks, and patterns are discussed.
   - Students in a high school biology class adopt a local stream as a project for a study of ecology. They study stream conditions and identify local polluters. They share this information by writing to local newspapers and politicians.

5. Structure classroom tasks to encourage student interaction.
   - After students complete an experiment, their fourth-grade teacher has them verbally describe their observations and conclusions. When they disagree, she encourages detailed discussion of the differences and guides them to valid explanations.
   - An English teacher uses cooperative learning groups to discuss the literature the class is studying. The teacher asks each group to respond to a list of prepared questions and to share their conclusions with the class.

Language Development

A miracle occurs in the time from birth to 5 years of age. Born with a limited ability to communicate, the young child enters kindergarten with an impressive command of the language spoken at home. Kindergartners have vocabularies of thousands of words and can carry on conversations in complex sentences with adults and peers.

How does this language ability develop, and how does it contribute to cognitive development? The answers to these questions are the topics of this section.

Understanding language development is important for several reasons:

■ As shown in the preceding discussions of Vygotsky and Piaget, language is a catalyst for developmental change. As children interact with peers and adults, they construct increasingly complex and accurate schemes and ideas about the world.

■ Language development facilitates learning in general (Berk, 1997). As students' develop their capacity to communicate, they also increase their ability to learn about abstract ideas and concepts.

■ The development of language is closely tied to learning to read and write (Adams, 1990). As you'll see in Chapter 9, these processes provide learners with essential learning and communication tools.

Theories of Language Acquisition

Psychologists who study the growth and development of human language have differing views of how language is acquired. We discuss four of those theories in this section: behaviorist, social cognitive, psycholinguistic, and constructivist.

Behaviorist Theory

Behaviorism is a theory of learning that focuses on how reinforcers and punishers shape observable behavior. (Reinforcers increase behavior, and punishers decrease it. We examine behaviorism in detail in Chapter 6.) Behaviorists suggest that language learning is the acquisition of sounds and words resulting from reinforcement (Moerk, 1992; Skinner, 1953, 1957). For instance,

A 2-year-old picked up a ball and said, "Baa."
Mom smiled broadly and said, "Good boy! Ball."
The little boy repeated, "Baa."
Mom responded, "Very good."
Mom's "Good boy! Ball," and "Very good," reinforced the child's efforts and, over time, language developed.

Social Cognitive Theory

Social cognitive theory emphasizes the role of modeling, the child's imitation of adult speech, adult reinforcement, and corrective feedback (Bandura, 1977, 1986). (We also examine social cognitive theory in detail in Chapter 6.)

"Give Daddy some cookie."
"Cookie, Dad."
"Good. Giselle gives Daddy some cookie."

Here, Giselle's father modeled an expression, she attempted to imitate it, and he praised her for her efforts.

Both behaviorism and social cognitive theory make intuitive sense. Children probably do learn certain aspects of language by observing and listening to others, trying it out themselves, and being reinforced. Scientists who study the development of languages in different cultures, however, believe something else is occurring.

2.22 ■
Children who grow up in bilingual families typically learn to speak both languages. Which approach—behaviorism or social cognitive theory—better explains this phenomenon? Why?

Nativist Theory

A parent listened one morning at breakfast while her 6- and 3-year-olds were discussing the relative dangers of forgetting to feed the goldfish versus overfeeding the goldfish:

six-year-old: It's worse to forget to feed them.
three-year-old: No, it's badder to feed them too much.

six-year-old:	You don't say badder, you say worser.
three-year-old:	But it's baddest to give them too much food.
six-year-old:	No it's not. It's worsest to forget to feed them.
	(Bee, 1989, p. 276)

Virtually all humans learn to speak, and, despite diversity, all languages share basic structures, such as a subject–verb sequence at the beginning of sentences, called language universals (Pinker, 1994). In addition, children pass through basically the same age-related stages when learning these diverse languages.

Nativist theory asserts that all humans are genetically "wired" to learn language and that exposure to language triggers this development. Noam Chomsky (1972, 1976), the father of nativist theory, hypothesized that an innate, genetically driven language acquisition device predisposes children to learn a new language. According to Chomsky, the **language acquisition device (LAD)** is *a genetic set of language-processing skills that enables children to understand the rules governing others' speech and to use these in their own speech*. When children are exposed to language, this program analyzes speech patterns for the rules of grammar—such as the subject after a verb when asking a question—that govern a language. The LAD explains why children are so good at producing sentences they have never heard before. For example, our young fish caretakers used "badder," "baddest," "worser," and "worsest." Both behaviorists and social cognitive theorists have trouble explaining these original constructions.

Chomsky's position also has its critics, however (Tomasello, 1995). Most developmental psychologists believe that language is learned through a combination of factors that include both an inborn predisposition, as Chomsky proposed, and environmental factors that shape the specific form of the language. These environmental factors explain how different languages and dialects are learned, as well as why some home environments are better for language growth than others (D. Walker, Greenwood, Hart, & Carta, 1994). In addition, increased emphasis is being placed on the child as an active participant in language learning (Genishi, 1992). This constructivist view of language learning emphasizes the importance of experience and interaction with others in a child's language development. Let's look at this view.

A Constructivist View of Language Development

As you saw earlier, language is central to Vygotsky's theory of cognitive development. It provides a vehicle for social interaction, the transmission of culture, and the internal regulation of thinking. Vygotsky's theory also provides insights into the process of language development itself.

As we also saw, activity is central to Vygotsky's theory of development, and language is no exception. Children learn language by practicing it in their interactions with adults and peers. Language development appears effortless because it is embedded in everyday activities and the process of communication.

In helping young children develop their language, adults adjust their speech to operate within the children's zones of proximal development (Bruner, 1985). Baby talk and "motherese" use simple words, short sentences, and voice inflections to simplify and highlight important aspects of a message (Baringa, 1997). These alterations provide a form of linguistic scaffolding that facilitates communication and language development.

Let's see how this linguistic scaffolding works. Children use language to express needs and desires. Parents adapt language to fit the capabilities of the child and then raise the ante by using bigger words and more complex sentences as the child's language skills develop. Teachers and other adults promote language development through interactions that encourage children's use of language and feedback that helps correct and refine language (Arnold, Lonigan, Whitehurst, & Epstein, 1994).

2.23 ▬
Which of the three theories of language acquisition best supports the fact that virtually all children reach school able to speak a language? Which theory best explains the fact that some children have better language backgrounds than others?

2.24 ▬
Describe specifically how constructivist views of language development are different from each of the other three views that have been discussed. Which of the other three views is most closely related to constructivist views?

Stages of Language Acquisition

Children pass through a series of stages as they learn to talk. In the process, they make errors, and their speech is an imperfect version of adult language. Most important, however, are the huge strides they make. Understanding this progress helps teachers promote language growth through their interactions with learners.

Early Language: Building the Foundation

Learning to speak actually begins in the cradle when adults use "Ooh" and "Aah" and "Such a smart baby!" to encourage the infant's gurgling and cooing. These interactions lay the foundation for future language development by teaching the child that language is a process human beings use to communicate.

The first words occur between ages 1 and 2 when the child uses **holophrases**, *one- and two-word utterances that carry as much meaning for the child as complete sentences,* to convey meaning. For example,

"Momma car."	That's Momma's car.
"Banana."	I want a banana.
"No go!"	Don't leave me alone with this scary baby sitter!

During this stage, the child also learns to use intonation to convey meaning. For example, the same word said differently has a very different message for the parent:

"Cookie."	That's a cookie.
"Cookie!"	I want a cookie.

This intonation is significant; it indicates that the child is beginning to understand and use language as a functional tool.

Two patterns creep into speech at this stage and stay with the child through the other stages. **Overgeneralization** *occurs when a child uses a word to refer to a broader class of objects than is appropriate* (Naigles & Gelman, 1995), such as using the word *car* to refer to buses, trucks and trains, as well as cars.

Undergeneralization, which is harder to detect, *occurs when a child uses a word too narrowly*, such as *kitty* used only for a child's cat but not for cats in general. Both overgeneralization and undergeneralization are normal aspects of language development, and in most instances are corrected through normal listening and talking. A parent or other adult may intervene, saying something, such as "No, that's a truck. See, it has more wheels and a big box on it."

Notice how closely language development parallels the development of schemes in children. Overgeneralization occurs when children inappropriately assimilate new information into an already-existing structure; undergeneralization occurs when they overaccommodate. Concrete experiences and interactions with adults and peers help young children fine-tune their language.

2.25 ▬
Sometimes a child will call all men "Daddy." What is this an example of? How could it be remedied?

Fine-Tuning Language

During the "twos," children elaborate and fine-tune their initial speech (Berk, 1996, 1997). The present tense is elaborated to include verb forms such as

Present progressive:	I eating.
Past regular:	He looked.

| Past irregular: | Jimmy went. |
| Third person irregular: | She does it. |

One problem that surfaces in this stage is overgeneralization of grammatical rules, for example, "badder," "worsest," and "He goed home." Piaget's work helps explain this tendency. "He goed home" uses an existing scheme, which allows the child to remain at equilibrium, whereas "He went home" requires accommodation, or the creation of a new scheme.

Increasing Language Complexity

At about age 3, a child learns to use sentences more strategically. Subjects and verbs are reversed to form questions, and positive statements are modified to form negative statements. For instance, "He hit him" is changed to "He didn't hit him" and "Did he hit him?" The idea that the form of language is determined by its function begins to develop more fully in this stage.

Simple declarative sentences with subject-verb-object evolve into more complex forms during this stage. Two separate but related ideas that earlier appeared as distinct sentences now become one. For example, "The boy ran too fast" and "The boy fell down" can now be combined to produce "The boy ran too fast and fell down." Notice how the increasingly complex sentence structure also reflects more complex thinking.

The introduction of more complex sentence forms happens at around age 6 and parallels other aspects of cognitive development. For instance, "Jackie paid the bill" and "She had asked him out" become "Jackie paid the bill because she had asked him out." The ability to form and use more complex sentences reflects the child's developing understanding of cause-and-effect relationships.

The typical child brings to school a healthy and confident grasp of the powers of language and how it can be used to communicate with others and think about the world. The importance of this language foundation for reading and writing instruction as well as learning in general is difficult to overstate (Berk, 1996, 1997; Tompkins, 1997). We'll return to this topic in Chapter 9 when we describe learning to read and write.

Classroom Connections

Applying an Understanding of Language Development in Your Classroom

1. Begin language development and concept learning activities with tangible experiences.
   - A second-grade teacher stops whenever an unfamiliar word is used in a reading passage or discussion and asks for an example of it. He keeps a list of new words, writes them on cards, and displays them next to objects around the classroom. If the objects don't exist in the room, he gathers pictures and displays the words and pictures together.
   - A third-grade teacher begins a unit on bones and muscles by having the students feel their own legs, arms, ribs, and heads. As they do this, she identifies the bones on a skeleton in front of the classroom.
2. Use open-ended questions to encourage the development of language.

- The third-grade teacher doing the unit on bones and muscles begins her discussion by having the students simply describe what they feel when they squeeze their arms and legs and poke their ribs and heads. She writes these descriptions on the chalkboard and uses them to frame her discussion.
- A fifth-grade teacher, in a unit on fractions, has the students fold pieces of paper into halves, thirds, fourths, and eighths. She then has them shade different sections of the folded papers, describe what they've done, and compare the sections.

3. Focus on meaning, rather than on pronunciation and mechanics in reading comprehension activities. Model standard pronunciation for students.
   - A first-grade teacher asks students to discuss stories, including what they think would happen in a different situation, why the characters behaved as they did, and what a good summary of the story would be. She accepts each response without correction and paraphrases the responses by using standard English when necessary.

4. Provide for differences in language proficiency in your classroom.
   - At the beginning of the school year, a junior high social studies teacher finds out which of his students have limited abilities in English. He pairs these students with student volunteers who sit next to the students, answer questions, and generally help with the course. The teacher has discovered that tutors not only enjoy their task, but also benefit from it cognitively.
   - A second-grade teacher enlists the aid of older students to tutor her students in reading. When possible, the tutors speak the same native language as her second graders and provide assistance in both English and the native tongue.

Language Diversity

As we've just seen, language plays a central role in cognitive development and is a powerful tool for acquiring new knowledge. Increasingly, however, our students are bringing different languages to school, and their facility with English varies greatly (Fashola, Slavin, Calderon, & Duran, 1997; Walton, Kuhlman, & Cortez, 1998). We examine this diversity in this section and discuss its implications for teaching.

English Dialects: Research Findings

Anyone who has traveled in the United States can confirm the fact that our country has many regional and ethnic dialects. A **dialect** is a *variation of standard English that is distinct in vocabulary, grammar, or pronunciation.* Everyone in the United States speaks a dialect; people merely react to those different from their own (Wolfram, 1991). Some dialects are accepted more than others, however, and language plays a central role in what Delpit (1995) calls "codes of power," the cultural and linguistic conventions that control access to opportunity in our society. What does research say about these dialects?

Research indicates that use of nonstandard English results in lowered teacher expectations for student performance (Bowie & Bond, 1994), lowered assessments of students' work, and the students themselves (Taylor, 1983). Teachers often confuse nonstandard English with mistakes during oral reading (Washington & Miller-Jones, 1989), and some critics argue that dialects, such as black English, are substandard. Linguists, however, argue that these variations are just as rich and semantically complex as standard English (Labov, 1972; Rickford, 1997).

A controversy over ebonics—a term created by combining *ebony* and *phonics* and used to describe an African American dialect—erupted in California when the Oakland

2.26

How would behaviorism explain the development of dialects? How would social cognitive theory explain them?

school board wanted to use ebonics as an interim scaffold to help children learn standard English (McMillen, 1997). Proponents claimed that ebonics would help African American students form a bridge between home and school cultures and better understand instruction. Critics contended that the move was political, would isolate African American children, and would "dumb-down" the curriculum.

Dialects in the Classroom: Implications for Teachers.   Culturally responsive teaching begins with accepting and valuing learner differences, and this is particularly important when responding to learners with nonstandard dialects. Dialects are both functional and valued in the culture of students' neighborhoods, and requiring that they be eliminated communicates that differences are neither accepted nor valued.

Standard English allows access to other educational and economic opportunities, which is the primary reason for teaching it. Students realize this when they interview for their first job or when they plan for post-high school education. So, what should teachers do when a student says, "I ain't got no pencil" or brings some other nonstandard dialect into the classroom? Opinions vary from "rejection and correction" to complete acceptance. The approach most consistent with culturally responsive teaching is, first, to accept the dialect and then build on it (Speidel, 1987). For example, when the student says, "I ain't got no pencil," the teacher (or adult) might say, "Oh, you don't have a pencil. What should you do, then?" Although results won't be apparent immediately, the long-range benefits—both for language development and attitudes toward school—will be worthwhile.

Language differences don't have to form barriers between home and school. **Bidialecticism,** *the ability to switch back and forth between a dialect and standard English,* allows access to both (Gollnick & Chinn, 1994). For example, one teacher explicitly taught differences between standard and black English, analyzing the strengths of each and specifying respective places for their use. The teacher read a series of poems by Langston Hughes, the African American poet, focusing on the ability of black English to create vivid images. The class discussed contrasts with standard English and ways in which differences between the two languages could be used to accomplish different communication goals (Shields & Shaver, 1990).

> **2.27** ▬
> State one disadvantage and one advantage of the *rejection and correction* approach. State an advantage and a disadvantage of the *complete acceptance* approach.

English as a Second Language

In an urban fourth-grade class composed of 11 Asian and 17 Black children, Sokhom, age 10, has recently been promoted to the on-grade-level reading group and is doing well. Instead of being "pulled out" of her regular classroom for special instruction in English, she now spends her whole day in the mainstream classroom. At home, she pulls out a well-worn English–Khmer dictionary that she says her father bought at great expense in the refugee camp in the Philippines. She recounts that when she first came to the United States and was in second grade, she used to look up English words there and ask her father or her brother to read the Cambodian word to her; then she would know what the English word was. Today, in addition to her intense motivation to know English ("I like to talk in English. I like to read in English, and I like to write in English."), Sokhom wants to learn to read and write in Khmer and, in fact, has taught herself a little via English.

In another urban public school across the city, Maria, a fifth-grader who has been in a two-way maintenance bilingual education program since pre-kindergarten, has both Spanish and English reading every morning for 1¼ hours each, with Ms. Torres and Mrs. Dittmar, respectively. Today, Mrs. Dittmar is reviewing the vocabulary for the story the students are reading about Charles Drew, a Black American doctor. She explains that "influenza" is what Charles's little sister died of. Maria comments that "you say it [influenza] in Spanish the same way you write it [in English]."

In the same Puerto Rican community, in a new bilingual middle school a few blocks away, Elizabeth, a graduate of the two-way maintenance bilingual program mentioned above, hears a Career Day speaker from the community tell her that of two people applying for a job, one bilingual and one not, the bilingual has an advantage. Yet Elizabeth's daily program of classes provides little opportunity for her to continue to develop literacy in Spanish; the bilingual program at this school is primarily transitional. (Hornberger, 1989, pp. 271–272)

As a result of rapidly increasing immigration (more than 7 million people a decade during the 1970s and 1980s and nearly as many in the 1990s), increasing numbers of students with limited backgrounds in English are entering U.S. classrooms. Coming with their families from places such as Southeast Asia, the Middle East, Haiti, and Mexico, the number of non-English-speaking and limited-English students increased by more than 50% between 1985 and 1991, and between 1991 and 1993, the language minority population increased 12.6% versus an increase of only 1.02% in the general population (Weaver & Padron, 1997).

The diversity is staggering. Currently, more than 3.2 million students who are limited English proficient (LEP) are in U.S. schools (U.S. Department of Education, 1998); California has 1.4 million of these, comprising nearly 40% of the student population (Office of Bilingual Education and Minority Language Affair, 1999; Stoddart, 1999). Nationwide, the number of students whose primary language is not English is expected to triple during the next 30 years. The most common language groups for students who are LEP are Spanish (73%), Vietnamese (4%), Hmong (1.8%), Cantonese (1.7%), and Cambodian (1.6%).

This language diversity is a challenge for teachers because most of our instruction is verbal. How should schools respond to this linguistic challenge? Bilingual programs offer one solution.

Types of Bilingual Programs

True bilingual programs offer instruction to non-native English speakers in both English and their primary language. They attempt to maintain and enhance the native language while building on it to teach English. The term *bilingual,* however, has been expanded to refer to a range of second-language programs (Echevarria & Graves, 1998; Peregoy & Boyle, 1997). We look at three of them:

- Maintenance bilingual programs
- Transitional bilingual programs
- English as a second language (ESL) programs

> **2.28** ▬
> Using Piaget's concepts of equilibrium, assimilation, and accommodation, describe the process of second-language learning in maintenance programs.

Maintenance Bilingual Programs.   Maintenance bilingual programs *maintain and build on students' native language by teaching in both the native language and English* (Peregoy & Boyle, 1997). Also called "two-way" bilingual programs because of the interaction between the two languages (Ovando, 1997), maintenance programs are found primarily at the elementary level, with the goal of developing students who can truly speak two languages. Maria, the fifth grader in the preceding example, had both a Spanish- and an English-speaking teacher to help her develop proficiency in both languages. Maintenance programs have the advantage of retaining and building on students' heritage, language, and culture, but they are difficult to implement because they require groups of students with the same native language and bilingual teachers or teacher teams in which one member speaks the heritage language.

Transitional Bilingual Programs.   Transitional bilingual programs *use the native language as an instructional aid until English becomes proficient.* Transitional programs

Effective bilingual programs teach English while building on and enriching student's native language.

begin with the first language and gradually develop learners' English proficiency. The transition period is often too short, however, leaving students inadequately prepared for learning in English (Gersten & Woodward, 1995). In addition, loss of the first language and lack of emphasis on the home culture can result in communication gaps between children who no longer speak the first language and parents who don't speak English.

English as a Second Language Programs.   Although, technically, all bilingual programs fit this category because mastery of English is a goal, **English as a second language (ESL) programs** *focus explicitly on the mastery of English.* Unlike the other programs, they emphasize learning English and mainstreaming students into regular classrooms. Sokhom, the Cambodian student in the preceding example, was initially in a pull-out ESL program until she could function in an English-only environment. Pulling students out of the regular classroom, however, disrupts the continuity of their instruction, and cultural discontinuities similar to those associated with transitional programs can result. ESL programs are common when classes contain students who speak a variety of languages, making maintenance or transitional programs difficult to implement.

When they work with students from ESL programs, teachers should be careful not to overestimate their students' English proficiency. After about 2 years in a language-rich environment, students develop **basic interpersonal communication skills**, a *level that allows students to interact conversationally with their peers* (Cummins, 1991), but students may need an additional 5 to 7 years to develop **cognitive academic language proficiency**, a *level that allows students to handle demanding learning tasks in an abstract curriculum.*

Evaluating Bilingual Programs

In comparing bilingual with English-only programs, researchers have found that students in bilingual programs achieve higher in math and reading and have more positive attitudes toward school and themselves (Arias & Casanova, 1993; Diaz, 1983). Also, because of their exposure to two languages, they better understand the role of language in communication (Diaz, 1990).

These findings make sense. Programs that use a student's native language not only build on an existing foundation but also say to the student, "To do well in school, you don't have to forget the culture of your home and neighborhood."

2.29
Identify at least one similarity and one difference between maintenance and transitional programs. From an economic perspective, with the current emphasis on a move to a global economy, which approach would be preferable? Explain.

2.30
Describe an ESL program based on behaviorist principles. Describe one based on social cognitive theory.

2.31
Use the concept of *zone of proximal development* to explain the difference between successful and unsuccessful bilingual programs.

Teaching Bilingual Students

Teachers are crucial to the success of bilingual programs.

> Tina Wharton had read about diversity in her education classes, but she wasn't expecting what she encountered when she took a job in a suburb of Los Angeles. Her first-grade class of 29 students had 9 who spoke Spanish as their first language. In working with them, she knew that building communication skills would need to be a top priority in her class.
>
> At the suggestion of other teachers, she wrote to each of the parents—in Spanish—and asked for their help. With the aid of Spanish-speaking teachers, she labeled all the objects in the room with both Spanish and English names and encouraged students to learn to read both. Her class made frequent field trips to local parks, a nearby food-processing plant, and the airport. After they returned, they talked about their trips, and students drew pictures and wrote about their visits. She enlisted the aid of several parents and had these stories transcribed into both Spanish and English.
>
> Six blocks down the street, Jim Harrison taught the brothers and sisters of Tina's students in his middle school science class. He had attended a workshop on the problems that students who are LEP might encounter in different content areas and adjusted his classes accordingly. He used hands-on activities, de-emphasized reading, and paired students who were LEP with other students to discuss and write about the experiments. At the beginning of each unit, he used demonstrations, concrete examples, pictures, and diagrams to introduce new vocabulary and abstract ideas.

It is likely that you will teach students whose first language is not English, and you can use a number of strategies to help students who are LEP learn both English and academic content. These strategies begin with awareness and move on to language- and concept-development strategies.

Awareness.   Research indicates that a surprising number of teachers are unaware of the home languages that students bring to school; one study found that teachers recognized only 27% of the non-native English speakers in one sample of Asian students (Schmidt, 1992). Teachers can't adjust their teaching to meet the needs of students who are LEP if they aren't aware that these students exist. Also, many teachers believe that learning a second language depends on losing the first (Weaver & Padron, 1997). Instead, research suggests that effective ESL teachers build on both the language and background experiences of their ESL students (Gersten, 1996). Talking with counselors, administrators, other teachers, the students themselves, and their parents can help teachers understand their learners' backgrounds. Then teachers can communicate through actions and words that they respect and value this diversity.

Facilitating Language and Concept Development.   Students learn English by using it in their day-to-day lives. In large part, language is a skill, and students in general—LEP students in particular—need to spend as much time as possible literally "practicing the language" (Fitzgerald, 1995; Ravetta & Brunn, 1995). Teacher-centered instruction, in which the teacher does most of the talking while students listen passively, should be avoided (Hernandez, 1997; Peregoy & Boyle, 1997). Instead, students should be provided with concrete experiences and opportunities to talk, write, and read about them. Open-ended questions that allow students to respond without the pressure of giving specific answers are valuable tools for eliciting student responses (Echevarria & Graves, 1998). Let's see what this looks like in the classroom.

> Felicia Marquez had a group of 8 non-native English speakers in her second-grade class of 24 students. She had been reading a story to her class from a book liberally illustrated

with pictures depicting the events in the story. As she read, she showed the pictures and had the students identify the object or event being illustrated, such as a cave in the woods that the boy and girl in the story decided to explore.

After she finished reading the story, she continued by discussing the events in it.

"Please tell us something you remember about the story. . . . Carmela?" she began.

" . . . A boy and a girl," Carmela responded hesitantly.

"Yes, good, Carmela," Felicia smiled. "The story is about a boy and a girl," and she pointed again to the picture of the boy and girl.

"Tell us something about the boy and girl. . . . Segundo."

" . . . Lost . . . cave."

"Yes," Felicia nodded encouragingly. "The boy and girl were exploring a cave and they got lost," again pointing to the pictures in the book. "What do you think exploring means? . . . Anyone?"

Felicia employed at least three simple, but effective, strategies to promote language and concept development in her students (Ovando, 1997). First, she used pictures to provide concrete reference points for the vocabulary she was developing. Second, she used open-ended questions to allow Carmela and Segundo to "practice" using English without the pressure of having to give a specific answer. Third, she modeled elaborated descriptions such as, "The boy and girl were exploring a cave and they got lost," in response to Segundo's " . . . Lost . . . cave." The strategies took little preparation; all she needed was the book with pictures. These same strategies can be used in content areas as well. When consistently used, they can do much to help students develop their language while simultaneously learning concepts.

Other strategies proven effective with ESL students include the following:

▌ Modify speech by slowing down and simplifying vocabulary and supplementing words with gestures and pictures.
▌ Use small-group activities to provide opportunities for interaction.
▌ Supplement verbal instruction with visuals such as charts and diagrams.
▌ Relate new vocabulary to native terms.
▌ Encourage writing and reading through creative and interactive tasks (Ovando, 1997; Weaver & Padron, 1997).

These strategies not only help ESL learners but also enrich instruction for all students.

Classroom Connections

Capitalizing on Language Diversity in Your Classroom

1. Accept and value the language diversity in your classroom.
   • As they use variations of standard English, a fifth-grade teacher asks his students to describe the meanings of vocabulary and phrases and where they originated. He describes the explanations as interesting and paraphrases them in standard English.

2. Use instructional strategies that accommodate diversity.
   • A physical education teacher uses the "buddy system" to help students with limited English skills participate in class. She asks bilingual students with well-developed English skills to pair with less-proficient students to explain rules and concepts during instruction and games.

- A second-grade teacher enlists the aid of older students to come into her classroom to tutor her students in reading. When possible, the tutors speak the same native language as her second graders and provide assistance in both English and the native tongue.

3. Use concrete examples and open-ended questions to help learners acquire experiences and reference points for language.
    - A first-grade teacher working in a low-socioeconomic status classroom begins her lessons with demonstrations, concrete examples, or hands-on experiences. She begins discussions by asking individual students to describe what they see in the examples. On the basis of their observations, she guides them to an understanding of the topics.

4. Provide students with opportunities to actively use language.
    - A first-grade teacher places students of differing language abilities into groups to work on their assignments. She structures this group work so that students explain their answers to each other and encourages stronger students to help the others.
    - A middle school social studies teacher has students prepare oral reports in groups. After practicing the reports in their groups, everyone is asked to give a part of each report. The teacher then meets with each student to provide specific feedback about strengths and areas needing work.

Windows on Classrooms

At the beginning of the chapter, you saw how Karen Johnson used her understanding of student development to help her students learn about density. In studying the chapter, you've seen how concrete and personalized examples and high levels of interaction facilitate learning and development. In addition, you've seen how an understanding of students' developmental needs can affect the effectiveness of instruction.

Let's look now at another teacher who is working with a group of first-grade students. As you read the case study, analyze the teacher's approach in terms of the ideas you've studied in the chapter.

Jenny Newhall gathered her first graders around her on the rug in front of a small table to begin her science lesson. After they were settled, she announced, "Today, we are going to be scientists. Scientists use their senses to find out about the world."

She then reviewed the five senses by asking students for examples as she proceeded, and then she asked, "How do you know if something is real? . . . Jessica?"

When Jessica failed to respond, Jenny continued by holding up a spoon and asking, "Jessica, is this real?"

Jessica nodded, and Jenny continued, "How do you know?"

" . . . "

"What is it?"

" . . . A tablespoon."

"How do you know it's a spoon?" Jenny prompted.

After some thought, students agreed they could touch it, see it, and even taste it. Jenny then asked, "Is air real? . . . Anthony?"

Anthony offered, "Yes, because you can breathe it."

Jenny probed further, "Can we see it?"

Her students thought for a moment and shook their heads, indicating no.

"Let's think about air for a while," Jenny said as she turned to a large fishbowl filled with water.

"What do you see?" she asked, pointing to the fishbowl.

"A tank with water in it," one student volunteered.

"What is this?" Jenny continued, holding up an empty water glass.

After spending a few minutes asking them to use their sense of sight to describe various features of the glass, Jenny said, "I'm going to put this glass in the water upside down. What's going to happen? What do you think? . . . Michelle?"

" . . . Water will go in the glass."

"No, it'll stay dry," Samantha countered.

To address this difference of opinion, Jenny asked, "Raise your hand if you think it will get water in it. . . . Okay," she said, surveying the room. "Raise your hand if you think it'll remain dry. . . . How many aren't sure? . . . Well, let's see if we can find out.

"First, we have to be sure it's dry. Terry, because you're not sure, I want you to help me by feeling the inside of the glass. How does it feel? Is it dry?"

"Yeah," replied Terry after putting his hand into the glass.

Then Jenny asked the students to watch carefully as she pushed the inverted glass under the water, as shown in the following drawing.

"Is the glass all the way under?" she asked, with her hand under the water.

The class agreed that it was.

Terry then offered, "There's water inside it. I can see the water inside."

"Then what will it feel like when I pull it out?" Jenny asked.

"Wet," Terry responded.

After pulling it carefully out of the water, she then asked Terry to check the inside of the glass.

"How does it feel?"

"Wet."

Jenny was momentarily taken aback. For the demonstration to work and for students to begin to understand that air takes up space, the inside of the glass was supposed to be dry. After pausing a second, she said, "Samantha, come up here and tell us what you feel."

As Samantha placed her hand up the glass she said, "It's wet on the outside, but dry on the inside."

"It's wet!" Terry asserted.

With a look of concern, Jenny said, "Uh, oh! We have two differing opinions. We've got to find out how to solve this problem."

After a short pause, she continued, "Let's dry this glass off and start again. Only this time, we're going to put a paper towel in the glass. Now if water goes in the glass, what is the paper towel going to look like?"

The class agreed it would be wet and soggy.

Then she held up the glass for the class to see. "Okay, it's dry. The paper towel is up in there. We're going to put it in the water again and see what happens."

The class watched carefully as Jenny put the glass into the water again, and after a few moments, she pulled it out.

"Okay, Marisse, come up here and check the paper towel and tell us whether it's wet or dry."

Marisse felt the towel, thought for a moment, and said, "Dry."

"Why did it stay dry? Raise your hand if you can tell us why it stayed dry. What do you think, Jessica?"

"'Cause it's inside and the water is outside?"

"But why didn't the water go into the glass? What kept the water out? . . . Anthony?"

"A water seal."

"A water seal. Hmm, . . . There's all that water on the outside. How come it didn't go inside? How can the towel stay dry?"

A quiet voice volunteered, "Because there's air in there."

"Air! Is that what kept the water out?" Jenny asked with enthusiasm.

"Well, earlier Samantha said that when she was swimming in a pool and put a glass under some water, it stayed dry, but when she tipped it, it got wet inside. Now what do you think will happen if I put the glass under the water and tip it? What do you think . . . Devon?"

"It'll get wet."

"Let's see. Now watch very carefully. What is happening?" Jenny asked as she slowly tipped the inverted glass, allowing some of the bubbles to escape. " . . . Andrea?"

"There were bubbles."

"Andrea, what were those bubbles made of?"

"They're air bubbles."

"Now look at the glass. What do you see?" Jenny asked, pointing to the half-empty glass upside down in the water. "In the bottom half is water. What's in the top half?"

"It's dry."

"What's up in there?"

"Air."

"Air is up there. Well, how can I get that air out?"

"Tip it over some more," several students responded. When Jenny did that, additional bubbles floated to the surface.

"Samantha, how does that work? When I tip it over, what's pushing the air out?"

" . . . The water," Samantha offered hesitantly.

"So, when I tip it this way (tipping it until more bubbles came out), what's pushing the air out?"

"Water," several of the class answered in unison.

Jenny then changed the direction of the lesson by saying, "Now I have something else for you," showing the students a glass full of water. "What do you think will happen if I tip this glass over?"

Jenny continued by covering the glass with a card and again asked what they thought would happen. This time there were disagreements, some suggesting that the water would spill, but others believing that the water would stay in the glass.

Jenny then held the card on the glass, tipped the glass over, and the students saw that the water didn't spill. Jenny asked for explanations, and one of the students suggested that the water acted like "super glue" to keep the card on the glass.

After some additional discussion, one of the children suggested that air kept the card next to the glass. They discussed this possibility a bit further, and Jenny then switched to small-group work.

She divided the class into groups of four or five, and students then used tubs of water, glasses, cards, and paper towels to experiment on their own. After each student had a chance to try the activities, Jenny again called the children together, and they reviewed and summarized what they had found.

Questions for Discussion and Analysis

Analyze Jenny's lesson in the context of the information in this chapter. In doing your analysis, consider the following questions. In each case, be specific and take information directly from the case study.

1. At what level of cognitive development were Jenny's students likely to be? Was her instruction effective for that level? Explain.

2. Why was the medium of water important for Jenny's lesson? How does this relate to Piaget's levels of development?

3. How well did Jenny follow constructivist guidelines? What could she have done differently to make the lesson more constructivist?

4. When Samantha and Terry disagreed about the condition of the inside of the glass, how did Jenny respond? What other alternatives might she have pursued? What are the advantages and disadvantages of these alternatives?

5. Were Jenny's students in the zone of proximal development for the lesson she was teaching? What forms of scaffolding did Jenny provide? How effective was the scaffolding?

6. How did Jenny use social interaction in her lesson? What instructional functions did this social interaction perform?

7. On the basis of this chapter's content, what suggestions do you have to improve the instruction in this lesson?

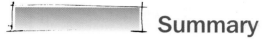

Summary

Now go to our Companion Website to assess your understanding of chapter content with the Student Self-Assessment, apply comprehension in the Online Casebook, and broaden your knowledge base with links to important Educational Psychology World Wide Web sites.

Development: A Definition

Development, the orderly, durable changes that occur over a lifetime, results from the interaction of the environment and heredity. Though it proceeds in a relatively orderly fashion, individuals can vary considerably in the ways and rates at which they develop. Brain research attempts to forge links between descriptions of how the brain physically grows and cognitive development.

Piaget's Theory of Intellectual Development

Piaget suggests that development is an orderly process that occurs in stages. The quality of experiences in the physical and social world, together with the drive for equilibrium, combine to influence development. Intellectually, developing children organize their experiences into schemes that help them understand the world. Compatible experiences are assimilated into existing schemes. Incongruent experiences require an accommodation of these schemes to reestablish equilibrium.

As children develop, they progress through stages characterized by unique ways of understanding the world. During the sensorimotor stage, young children develop eye–hand coordination schemes and object permanence. The preoperational stage includes the growth of symbolic thought, as evidenced by increased use of language. During the concrete operational stage, children can perform basic operations such as classification and serial ordering on concrete objects. In the final stage, formal operations, students develop the ability to think abstractly, reason hypothetically, and think about thinking. Computer-based simulations can provide learners with valuable experiences in controlling variables and systematically analyzing data.

Piaget's work has influenced curriculum and instruction, as evidenced by the emphasis on manipulatives, language experience, hands-on activities, and discovery-oriented instruction.

Vygotsky's Description of Development

Lev Vygotsky offers an alternate view of development. His description focuses heavily on language and social interaction, and the role they play in helping learners acquire an understanding of the culture in which they live. Language is the tool people use for cultural transmission, communication, and reflection on their own thinking.

Vygotsky's work has begun to exert influence in classrooms. Teachers are encouraged to engage students in meaningful learning tasks that involve language and social interaction. Those learners who can benefit from assistance are in what Vygotsky calls the zone of proximal development. Learners within this zone can profit from instructional scaffolding in the form of modeling, questions, prompts, and cues.

Constructivism

Constructivism suggests that learners develop their own understanding of the way the world works, rather than have that understanding delivered to them. Piaget and Vygotsky, both constructivists, agree that active learners and social interaction are important for development, but they differ in their reasons why. Piaget focuses on manipulation of objects and ideas, together with the validation of schemes; Vygotsky emphasizes participation in verbal cultural exchange.

Constructivism suggests that learners should be active participants in learning activities, that learning should be guided rather than presented by teachers, and that interaction and discussion are critical components in the learning process.

Language Development

All views of development are closely linked to language and its uses. Behaviorism, social cognitive theory, and psycholinguistic theory explain language development differently; each probably forms part of the explanation. Children progress from one- and two-word utterances to elaborate language that involves complex sentence structures by the time they reach school.

Language diversity poses new challenges for teachers. Schools respond to this challenge with bilingual and ESL programs that use differing strategies to teach English.

 **Important Concepts**

accommodation (p. 35)

adaptation (p. 35)

assimilation (p. 35)

basic interpersonal communication skills (p. 71)

bidialecticism (p. 69)

centration (p. 40)

classification (p. 43)

cognitive academic language proficiency (p. 71)

cognitive development (p. 29)

concrete operational stage (p. 42)

conservation (p. 41)

constructivism (p. 59)

critical periods (p. 33)

development (p. 30)

dialect (p. 68)

dynamic assessment (p. 57)

egocentrism (p. 40)

English as a second language (ESL) programs (p. 71)

equilibration (p. 34)

equilibrium (p. 34)

formal operational stage (p. 45)

holophrases (p. 66)

language acquisition device (LAD) (p. 65)

maintenance bilingual programs (p. 70)

maturation (p. 31)

object permanence (p. 39)

organization (p. 34)

overgeneralization (p. 66)

preoperational stage (p. 39)

personal development (p. 29)

private speech (p. 55)

reversibility (p. 41)

scaffolding (p. 58)

schemes (p. 34)

sensorimotor stage (p. 39)

seriation (p. 43)

shared understanding (p. 57)

social development (p. 29)

transformation (p. 40)

transitional bilingual programs (p. 70)

undergeneralization (p. 66)

zone of proximal development (p. 56)

The Classroom

Part I The Learner

3

Personal, Social, and Emotional Development

"Ahh," Anne Dillard, an eighth-grade English teacher, sighed wearily as she slumped into a chair in the faculty lounge.

"Tough day?" her friend Beth asked.

"Yes. It's Sean again," Anne explained, straightening up. "I just can't seem to get through to him. He won't do his work, and he has a bad attitude about school in general. I talked with his mother, and she said he's been a handful since birth. He can't get along with the other students, and when I try to talk with him about it, he always says they're picking on him for no reason. I don't know what's going to become of him. The funny thing is, I get the feeling that he knows he's out of line, but he just can't seem to change."

"I know what you mean," Beth responded. "I had him for English last year. He was a tough one—very distant. He lost his dad in a messy divorce; his mother got custody of him, and his father just split. Every once in a while, he'd open up to me, but then the wall would go up again. . . . and his younger brother seems so different. He's eager and cooperative, and he seems to get along with everyone. . . . Same home, same situation."

"Sean's a bright boy, too," Anne continued, "but he seems to prefer avoiding work to doing it. If I could just help him get his act together, I think he'd do all right. If . . . ?"

In Chapter 2, we studied theories that describe the cognitive development of students and, as a result, we know that younger students think in ways that are qualitatively different from those of older students and adults. We now want to examine the personal, social, and moral development of these students.

Since some argue that schools should focus solely on academic subjects, why should teachers study these topics? The answer is simple; our students' personal, social, and moral development influence their motivation and learning in school, and how successfully they cope with life, both during and after the formal school years. The better teachers understand this development, the better equipped they are to promote learning and help students grow into capable citizens. The need for this understanding grows ever greater as modern life becomes more complex and students are faced with challenges in the form of alcohol and other drugs, sex, and potential violence.

After you've completed your study of this chapter, you should be able to meet the following objectives:

▌ Identify factors that influence personal development.
▌ Describe factors influencing social development.
▌ Explain the implications of Erikson's theory for teaching.
▌ Explain the relationships between self-concept and academic achievement, and what teachers can do to influence each.
▌ Identify different stages of moral reasoning and how they apply to classroom practice.

Personal Development

Think about the people you know. Some are very comfortable with themselves, new situations, and people in general, but others tend to be shy and uneasy. We all know people who are trusting and see the best in everything, and we also see individuals who are wary, distrustful, and almost paranoid.

How did they get that way? What causes differences in people's personalities? What factors have influenced our own development, resulting in us interacting with others and our environments in the ways we do? We try to answer these questions in this chapter.

Personal development describes *the growth of relatively enduring personality traits that influence the way individuals interact with their physical and social environments.* The primary causes of this development are heredity and the environmental influences of parents, other adults, and peers. These factors are outlined in Figure 3.1 and discussed in the sections that follow.

Heredity

People differ in temperament, virtually from birth. They vary in traits such as happiness, confidence, irritability, and adventurousness, and these differences persist over time (Caspi & Silva, 1995). Siblings raised in the same environments can develop very different personalities, such as what we saw in Sean's mother's comment about him being a "handful since birth," and the apparent differences between Sean and his brother. These examples illustrate the influence of heredity on personal development.

Parents and Other Adults

Parents also exert a major influence on children's personal development (Grolnick, Kourowski, & Gurland, 1999). This intuitively sensible and widely accepted factor isn't surprising, given the amount of time children, and especially young children, spend with their parents.

Figure 3.1

Influences on personal development

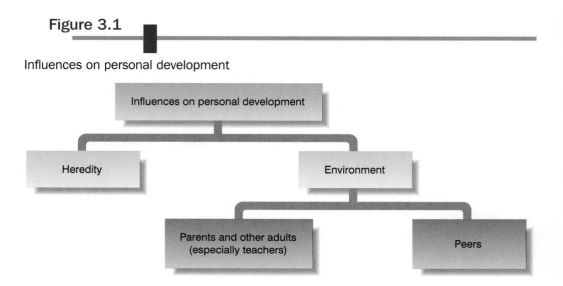

Research indicates that certain parenting styles promote more healthy personal development than others (Baumrind, 1991), and the effects of healthy parenting can last into the college years, influencing students' grades, motivation, and relationships with teachers (Strage & Brandt, 1999). Researchers have found two important differences among parents in the ways they relate to their children: their *expectations* and their *responsiveness*. For example, some parents set high expectations for their children and insist that these expectations are met, whereas others expect little of their children and rarely try to influence them.

High expectations aren't as simple as they appear on the surface, however; they interact with, and are strongly influenced by, parental responsiveness. Responsive parents accept their children and interact with them frequently; unresponsive parents tend to be rejecting or negative. If parents are unresponsive, children often rebel when faced with high expectations, viewing them as unfair or intrusive.

Using expectations and responsiveness as a framework, researchers have identified four parenting styles and patterns of personal development associated with them. These styles and patterns are summarized in Table 3.1.

As we see from Table 3.1, an authoritative parenting style—one that combines high expectations and responsiveness—is most effective for promoting healthy personal development. Children need challenge, structure, and support in their lives, and authoritative parents provide these.

Each of the other parenting styles can result in development problems. Authoritarian parents are rigid, and they seem unable to communicate caring to their children; permissive parents are emotionally responsive but fail to communicate and maintain high expectations; uninvolved parents are laissez-faire, providing neither structure nor emotional support.

The quality of parent–child relationships promotes personal development by helping children acquire a healthy sense of autonomy, competency, and belonging (Grolnick et al., 1999; Wentzel, 1999). Healthy parent–child relationships also support the development of personal responsibility—the ability to control one's own actions based on developing values and goals.

> **3.1**
> Identify two characteristics of an authoritarian parenting style that could result in children failing to develop social skills. Identify one characteristic of a permissive parenting style that could lead to children being unable to set long-term goals.

Table 3.1

Parenting styles and patterns of personal development

Interaction Style	Parental Characteristics	Child Characteristics
Authoritative	Are firm but caring. Explain reasons for rules, and are consistent. Have high expectations.	High self-esteem. Confident and secure. Willing to take risks, and are successful in school.
Authoritarian	Stress conformity. Are detached, don't explain rules, and do not encourage verbal give-and-take.	Withdrawn. Worry more about pleasing parent than solving problems. Defiant, and lack social skills.
Permissive	Give children total freedom. Have limited expectations, and make few demands on children.	Immature, and lack self-control. Impulsive. Unmotivated.
Uninvolved	Have little interest in their child's life. Hold few expectations.	Lack self-control and long-term goals. Easily frustrated and disobedient.

Other adults—most commonly teachers—also influence personal development. Teachers' interaction styles are similar to those for parents, and the description of authoritative parenting strongly parallels the management practices of effective teachers (W. Doyle, 1986). As you'll see in Chapter 11, effective teachers are clear about classroom rules and procedures and take the time to explain why they are necessary. They have high expectations for their students, but they're simultaneously warm and supportive. When a disruption occurs, they quickly intervene, eliminate the problem, and return just as quickly to the learning activity. Like authoritative parents, they are firm but caring, they establish rules and limits, and they expect students to exert self-control. Research indicates that this kind of teacher support leads to increased student motivation and enhanced self-concept (Wentzel, 1999). Though the time they spend with children may be limited, teachers can exert an important influence on learners' personal development.

Peers

Peers are the third major contributor to personal development, influencing it in two primary ways. First, through forming friendships, young people practice their social skills. Students who are socially accepted and have the support of peers are happier, more motivated, achieve higher, and have healthier self-concepts than those receiving less support (Wentzel, 1999). At the other extreme, being rejected can lead to loneliness and isolation, poor academic work, and dropping out of school. We all want to be liked and valued by others; children's abilities to form healthy peer relationships influence their happiness and performance in schools and their general sense of satisfaction with life.

A second way peers influence development is through the transmission of attitudes and values, most commonly in their day-to-day interactions. Unfortunately, these influences can be negative, such as the impact of gang membership and other school subcultures that reject academic achievement. In examining adolescent friendships, researchers have found that a student's choice of friends predicts grades, disruptive behaviors, and teachers' ratings of involvement (Berndt & Keefe, 1995). When students selected academically oriented friends, their grades improved; when they chose disruptive friends, their grades declined and behavioral problems increased.

The influence of peers has also been linked to ethnicity (Steinberg, Brown, & Dornbusch, 1996). For example,

> One clear reason for Asian students' success is that Asian students are far more likely to have friends who place a great deal of emphasis on academic achievement. Asian-American students are, in general, significantly more likely to say that their friends believe that it is important to do well in school, and significantly less likely than other students to say that their friends place a premium on having an active social life. Not surprisingly, Asian students are the most likely to say that they work hard in school to keep up with their friends. (Steinberg et al., 1996, p. 44)

Unfortunately, the opposite is also true. In some minority groups, academic success is viewed as "selling out" or "becoming white." Media messages sometimes portray successful minority youth as being hip, tough, or cool, but not academically oriented. To combat these messages, minority youth need role models who can demonstrate that being a minority and academically successful are compatible (Berndt, 1999).

In this section, we've seen how peers influence personal development and that the ability to establish healthy peer relationships is important in this process. Let's examine social development more closely.

3.2 ▬

The influence of peers on academic success can be interpreted in different ways. One is selection; for example, low achievers seek out other low achievers. Offer one alternative interpretation based on the information in this section.

Social Development

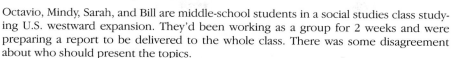

Octavio, Mindy, Sarah, and Bill are middle-school students in a social studies class studying U.S. westward expansion. They'd been working as a group for 2 weeks and were preparing a report to be delivered to the whole class. There was some disagreement about who should present the topics.

"So what should we do?" Mindy asked looking at the other members of the group. "Octavio, Sarah, and Bill all want to report on the Pony Express."

"I thought of it first," Octavio argued.

"But everyone knows I like horses," Sarah countered.

"Why don't we compromise?" Mindy asked. "Octavio, didn't you say that you were kind of interested in railroads because your grandfather worked on them? Couldn't you talk to him and get some information for the report? And Sarah, I know you like horses. Couldn't you report on horses and the Plains Indians? . . . And Bill, what about you?"

"I don't care . . . whatever," Bill replied, folding his arms and peering angrily at the group.

People are social beings, and classrooms are social places that require students and teachers working together cooperatively. **Social development** describes *the advances young people make in their ability to interact and get along with other people.*

Understanding social development is important because increased understanding helps us guide our students in their attempts to become effective social beings. As students' social skills advance, their abilities to work effectively in groups improve, increasing both how much they learn and their satisfaction with the learning situations. As we saw in the last section, the ability to make and keep friends contributes to students' sense of belonging and their overall attitudes toward school.

Next we examine two dimensions of social development—perspective taking and social problem solving—because they are keys to effective interpersonal relations.

Perspective Taking

Perspective taking is *the ability to think about and understand the thoughts and feelings of others.* When Mindy suggested that Octavio and Sarah switch assignments because of their interest in alternate topics, she was demonstrating perspective taking.

Research indicates that perspective taking develops slowly and is related to Piaget's stages of cognitive development (Berk, 1997). To measure children's perspective-taking abilities, researchers present children with scenarios similar to the one at the beginning of the section and ask them to describe what different people are thinking and why. Young children, such as those from about ages 3 through 8, typically don't understand Bill's angry response or why Octavio might be happy reporting on railroads. As they develop, the ability to understand other peoples' motives and see the world from another person's perspective grows.

Perspective taking is important because it helps children understand and work effectively with other people. Effective perspective takers are better at handling difficult social situations, are more likely to display empathy and compassion, and tend to be better liked by their peers (Berk, 1997). Children who are poor at perspective taking often mistrust others and tend to resolve conflicts by arguing or fighting without experiencing the guilt or remorse of hurting another person's feelings. In addition, they are more likely to misinterpret the intentions of others as hostile, which can lead to aggressive or antisocial acts (Dodge & Price, 1994).

> **3.3**
> Using Piaget's theory as a basis, explain why young children are unlikely to be effective at perspective taking. What factor influencing development helps them improve their perspective-taking abilities?

Perspective taking and problem solving are important components in learners' social development.

Social Problem Solving

Social problem solving, *the ability to resolve conflicts in ways that are beneficial both to oneself and others,* is closely related to perspective taking. Mindy demonstrated social problem-solving skills when she tried to incorporate the wants and desires of other students into a compromise that would satisfy each.

Research on the development of social problem solving suggests that it is similar to problem solving in general (we examine problem solving in detail in Chapter 8) and can be described in a series of sequential steps:

▌ Observing and interpreting social cues ("Bill seems upset. He's probably angry because he's not getting his first choice.")
▌ Identifying social goals ("If this group is going to finish this project, everyone must contribute.")
▌ Generating strategies ("Can we find alternative topics that will satisfy everyone?")
▌ Implement and evaluate a strategy ("This will work if everyone agrees to shift their topic slightly.")

Understanding and being able to implement these steps provides learners with powerful social tools. Students who are good at social problem solving have more friends and fight less. Less competent students have fewer friends, fight more, and work less effectively in groups (Crick & Dodge, 1994).

Research indicates that, like perspective taking, social problem solving develops gradually. Young children, for example, are not adept at reading social cues; over time, they improve in their ability to understand the needs and desires of others. Young children also have difficulty with identifying goals and generating alternate strategies; they tend to create simplistic approaches that satisfy them but not others. Older children realize that persuasion and compromise can result in solutions that are beneficial to all, and they're better at adapting when initial efforts aren't successful.

3.4
Which step of social problem solving is most closely related to perspective taking? Explain. What can teachers do to develop this ability in students?

Programs designed to teach young children social problem-solving skills have decreased aggression, substituting peaceful alternatives to force (Goodman, Gravitt, & Kaslow, 1995). Kindergartners and preschoolers are presented with social dilemmas in the form of puppet skits, which they analyze, discuss, and try to solve; older children are asked to analyze and define problems, such as the one at the beginning of this section, and generate strategies to solve them. Students in these programs have improved in both their ability to talk about and analyze social problems and in their classroom behavior (Gettinger, Doll, & Salman, 1994).

Technology and Learning: Using the Internet to Promote Social Development

Technology is changing both the way we live and the way we communicate. In this section, we look at the Internet, how it's changing the ways students communicate with each other, and what we as teachers can do to capitalize on it to promote social development.

How the Internet Influences Communication

Researchers examining differences between face-to-face and Internet communications have identified both advantages and disadvantages of the Internet (Fabos & Young, 1999; Jehng, 1998; Johnson & Johnson, 1996). Internet technologies can connect students all over the world, allowing them access to others' thinking and perspectives that would be impossible to obtain in any other way. This access, together with some of the personal relationships that are formed, can strongly influence social growth. One such relationship was so powerful that it was profiled by *National Public Radio* in 1999 in a feature called "Letters from Kosovo." The following is a partial transcript of an interchange, via e-mail, between two students.

> Because this Kosovo teenager is living in such a dangerous place, she's using a pseudonym, Adona, and her letters are being read aloud by someone else (a person named Belia Mayeno Choy). The California student she's writing to is Finnegan Hamill, who heard about Adona at a church meeting. She's exactly his age, 16, and cares about some of the things he does: rock music, dating, and what to do after high school. But, says Finnegan, Adona's concerns are far more serious these days.

> HAMILL: From the beginning of my correspondence with Adona, I've wanted to somehow make a difference in her life. One of her biggest fears is that she is slipping behind in her education, and if the war is ever over, it will be too late for her to have a career in journalism or whatever field she chooses.
>
> "ADONA" (CHOY): Dear Fini, thank you that you offered to help me find a scholarship. I've been trying to do that for weeks now. I'm looking at the Web sites through Yahoo! of different high schools and colleges, but I haven't found anything yet. I know I cannot go forward if I stay here, which is towards a disaster. People aren't thinking much about school and ambitions, but I am trying to keep my head somehow in a distance from this catastrophe. . . . I'll tell you more about my life and me. I love having fun and doing crazy things. I used to hang out with my friends until 11:00 in the evening. We were never safe in the street, but now

we're not safe in our homes. I never take my ID card with me when I go out, because if I'm stopped by the police or somebody similar to them, I just start talking in Serbian and avoid troubles. It always works out. Tell me, what do you think about aliens? Write to me soon. (National Public Radio, 1999)

The power, feeling, and emotion elicited by this correspondence would be difficult to capture in any other form, including face-to-face. Both Fini's and Adona's lives were almost certainly changed by this relationship, an experience impossible without the use of technology.

Internet interactions also can be more equitable, since extraneous factors such as attractiveness, prestige, and material possessions are eliminated. In addition, communicating on the Internet gives students time to form and present more complete thoughts, interconnect ideas, and think and reflect. These are important advantages.

Disadvantages also exist, however. For instance, Internet communication uses only one channel—the written word—which doesn't help students learn to read nonverbal social cues, such as facial expressions and eye contact, or vocal signals like emphasis and intonation. Communications research suggests a large part (some estimates are as high as 90%) of a message's credibility is communicated through nonverbal channels (Mehrabian & Ferris, 1967), so learning to read nonverbal behavior is an important part of social development. Further, spending a great deal of time in front of computers reduces the time students spend in face-to-face social experiences, which some experts believe impairs social development (Kuh & Vesper, 1999).

Technology can provide an effective vehicle to develop perspective taking and social problem solving.

Because Internet communication uses only one channel, writers may be out of touch with their audiences, feeling a sense of anonymity. This can be helpful when it encourages students to disagree or express opinions but can also lead to insensitivity and treating others like objects rather than people.

Finally, some experts warn that, while a great many claims have been offered about the positive effect of Internet communication for the development of writing skill and preparation for a global workforce in addition to social development, well-designed research documenting these claims is still sparse (Fabos & Young, 1999).

With these cautions in mind, we offer some suggestions for effective Internet communication in the next section.

> **3.5** ▬
> *Flaming*, the practice of name calling and using epithets on the Internet, is sometimes a problem. Explain why a person would be more likely to behave inappropriately on the Internet than in person.

Using the Internet to Promote Social Development

While the majority of social development still results from day-to-day contacts with parents, teachers, and peers, Internet communication is becoming increasingly common, and students need to be socially skilled in using it (Roblyer & Edwards, 2000). Like face-to-face social skills, Internet communication skills can be developed through modeling, practice, and feedback.

Developing both the ability and inclination to consider the perspective of our receivers is most important in this process. Since we don't have access to the immediate feedback available in face-to-face communication, the impression that's left from our messages will have a lingering effect. The following include some guidelines to help students make Internet communication positive and open:

- Greet the person you're addressing. A simple, "Hello, Cindy" or "Hi, Leroy" creates a very different impression than simply beginning the communication with the text of your message.
- End the message cordially. A closing such as "Thanks," "The Best," or a similar ending together with your name leaves a similar positive impression.
- Describe the reasons for writing at the beginning of the message. Remember, you're getting no feedback to help you determine whether or not you're communicating clearly, and people often don't carefully read what they're sent.
- Use correct grammar, spelling, and punctuation. As with any communication, what you send on the Internet creates an impression, and people seem to tacitly feel that an Internet communication doesn't have to be as "clean" as a letter. This isn't true.
- Avoid insults, sarcasm, and inappropriate language. Nothing leaves a worse impression on the reader, and this impression won't change without a face-to-face encounter.
- Ask specific questions in responding to another's message to clarify points and eliminate ambiguities.
- Acknowledge other persons' ideas, and clearly identify areas of agreement or disagreement.

There is no doubt that the influence of the Internet on our lives will continue to grow, and being able to communicate effectively on it will become increasingly important. Many of the characteristics of effective face-to-face communication apply to Internet communication as well, and some aspects of social development are even more important when using it.

Classroom Connections

Applying an Understanding of Personal Development in Your Classroom

1. Enlist the help of parents in promoting learners' personal development.
   - A sixth-grade teacher sends a letter home at the beginning of the year giving parents specific suggestions for working with their children on both academic and personal tasks.
   - A second-grade teacher sends a weekly report home to parents, asks them to sign and return the report, and holds the children accountable for returning the report.

2. Discuss peer relationships and personal responsibility with students.
   - A first-grade teacher conducts a daily "meeting" just before dismissing the students, during which they discuss the ways they should treat their classmates and other issues related to personal responsibility.
   - An eighth-grade teacher spends some time each week discussing friendship, the need to be personally responsible, and the effort everyone should make to try and influence friends in positive ways.

Encouraging Social Development in Your Classroom.

3. Encourage students to consider the perspectives of others.
   - A fourth-grade language arts teacher has her students analyze different characters' motives and feelings when they discuss a story they've read. Her questions include: "How does he or she feel? Why do they feel that way? How would you feel if you were them?"
   - A high school social studies teacher always encourages her students to consider point of view when they read reports of historical events. For example, when studying the Civil War, she constantly reminds her students that both sides thought they were fighting on the side of the right by asking questions like, "Well how did the other side interpret the Emancipation Proclamation?" and "Why was states' rights such a controversial topic?"

4. Provide opportunities for students to engage in active social problem solving.
   - A middle school teacher purposefully leaves individual task assignments vague and open-ended when she uses cooperative learning groups, so that students can learn to solve their own problems. When disagreements occur, she waits to intervene and then facilitates the process rather than solving the problem herself. If the problem is widespread, she calls a class meeting to discuss the problem with the whole group.
   - A second-grade teacher occasionally uses student pairs to check math homework. She passes out two answer sheets to each group to decide how to proceed. When she sees unequal responsibilities, she will intervene, asking how the process could be made more equitable.

5. Encourage students to think about and analyze social problems.
   - Second-grade participants in a scuffle on the playground are allowed to give each of their own personal perspectives on the problem. Then the teacher requires them to describe the problem from the others' perspective. Finally, the teacher asks them to suggest alternatives to fighting.
   - Students in a middle school art class frequently argue about access to materials and supplies. When this happens, the teacher requires the students to come up with a compromise that satisfies both parties.

Erikson's Theory of Personal and Social Development

Having looked at both personal and social development, we turn now to the work of Erik Erikson (1902–1994), who developed a comprehensive theory describing individuals' development in these areas throughout their life span (Erikson, 1968).

Erikson's background, like Piaget's and Vygotsky's (see Chapter 2), provides insights into his work. He dropped out of high school and spent time traveling in Europe and studying art. In the process, he met Sigmund Freud and studied under Freud's daughter, Anna. As he studied young people in different cultures, Erikson became interested in how they acquire a personal identity and how society helps shape it. Because his theory *integrates personal, emotional, and social development,* it is often called a **psychosocial theory**.

Erikson's work is based on five important ideas:

▌ People, in general, have the same basic needs.
▌ Personal development occurs in response to these needs.
▌ Development proceeds in stages.
▌ Movement through the stages reflects changes in an individual's motivation.
▌ Each stage is characterized by a psychosocial challenge that presents opportunities for development.

Erikson described *the time that an individual experiences a psychological challenge* as a **crisis**, and the challenge is closely tied to social relationships. A positive resolution of a crisis means that a favorable ratio of positive to negative psychosocial traits emerges. For example, Erikson describes the first psychosocial challenge (crisis) as *trust vs. mistrust* (Erikson's stages are outlined in Table 3.2). If this crisis is successfully resolved, individuals grow up trusting themselves and others and having a relaxed, optimistic, and generous attitude about life. A negative resolution results in individuals seeing the world as unpredictable and threatening. This doesn't mean that people who successfully resolve the crisis never have negative thoughts or distrust another person. In general, however, they see the best in others and have a positive orientation toward life.

Although a crisis is never permanently resolved, healthy resolution of the crisis at each stage leads to positive personal development, an accurate perception of self in the larger society, and an integration of the two. A negative resolution can retard development at later stages and leave the personality impaired.

Here we see an important difference between Piaget's and Erikson's theories (Erikson, 1968; Piaget, 1952). Piaget's stages are hierarchical, and progression to formal operations, for example, depends on concrete operations. Erikson's stages, in contrast, are not hierarchical. They are influenced by, but don't directly depend on, development at earlier stages.

> **3.6** ▬
> Is the statement "Motivation is an important part of Erikson's theory, but it isn't a part of Piaget's work" true or false? Explain your answer.

Erikson's Stages of Psychosocial Development

Descriptions of Erikson's developmental stages are outlined in Table 3.2. Notice how each stage involves a crisis that the person resolves through interaction with others.

Trust Versus Mistrust (Birth to 1 Year)

Developing a sense of **trust**, or *confidence in the honesty and justice of others*, is the first psychological challenge facing all people, and resolving the crisis begins at birth. An infant who receives consistently good care from parents develops a sense of trust; an infant who

Table 3.2

Erikson's stages of psychosocial development

Stage	Approximate Age	Characteristics
Trust vs. Mistrust	Infancy (0–1 year)	Trust in the world is developed through consistent and continuous love and support.
Autonomy vs. Shame and Doubt	Toddler (1–3 years)	Independence is fostered by successful experiences formed by support and structure.
Initiative vs. Guilt	Early Childhood (3–6 years)	An exploratory and investigative attitude results from meeting and accepting challenges.
Industry vs. Inferiority	Middle Childhood (6–12 years)	Enjoyment of mastery and competence comes through success and recognition of accomplishment.
Identity vs. Confusion	Adolescence (12–18 years)	Personal, social, sexual, and occupational identity comes from success in school and experimentation with different roles.
Intimacy vs. Isolation	Young Adulthood	Openness to others and the development of intimate relationships result from interaction with others.
Generativity vs. Stagnation	Middle Adulthood	Productivity, creativity, and concern for the next generation are achieved through success on the job and a growing sense of social responsibilities.
Integrity vs. Despair	Old Age	Acceptance of one's life is achieved by an understanding of a person's place in the life cycle.

Source: Adapted from *Identity, Youth and Crisis* by Erik E. Erikson, by permission of W. W. Norton & Company, Inc. Copyright 1968 by W. W. Norton & Company, Inc.

is left to cry or who receives unpredictable care can develop basic mistrust that leads to fear and suspicion of other people and the world in general. These ideas are supported by studies of bonding, or the social attachment between babies and their primary caregivers, usually parents (Isabella & Belsky, 1991). Although we have no evidence about the care Sean (the student in the introductory case study) received as an infant, his behavior suggests that he didn't successfully resolve the trust–mistrust crisis. His perception that the other students are "picking on him for no reason" and his inability to communicate with his teachers may be indicators of this problem.

Autonomy Versus Shame and Doubt (Ages 1 to 3)

Securely attached children next face the challenge of **autonomy**, or *doing things on their own*. They learn to feed and dress themselves, and toilet training begins. As you recall from studying cognitive development, children at that age demonstrate goal-directed behavior and begin to communicate verbally. They no longer want to depend totally on others. At this point, parents need to encourage and reassure children who try to put their shoes on, for example, and express confidence in the child's ability, even though it would be easier to do the task for them. Overly restrictive parents or those who punish minor accidents, such as bedwetting or spills while eating, can lead children to doubt their own abilities or to have a sense of shame about their bodies. Erikson believed this leads to a lack of confidence in their power to deal with and control their world.

Initiative Versus Guilt (Ages 3 to 6)

Initiative is *characterized by an exploratory and investigative attitude that results from meeting and accepting challenges.* At the beginning of this stage, children are likely to be found upside-down in the drawer with the pots and pans—"into everything." Having developed a sense of autonomy, children are now ready to explore and respond to their curiosity. At this stage, children make enormous cognitive leaps, and those developing abilities provide the impetus for exploration in all areas of their lives. When a child offers to "help" his mother make cookies, for example, he needs the assurance that his contributions are welcome and valued. Parents who criticize or punish initiative cause children to feel guilty about their self-initiated activities. Sean's withdrawal and lack of personal initiative at school suggest problems at this stage.

School and the Development of Initiative.   As children enter preschool and kindergarten, they are moving forward, taking on more tasks, and searching eagerly for more experiences. "I can do it!" and "Let me try," are signs of this initiative. They are interacting more with their peers, and their play is becoming more complex and interdependent. As children go through these changes, parents and teachers can do much to help them develop into happy and healthy children.

> "Good, Felipe. I see you've used a lot of colors to draw your bird. That's a very pretty bird."
> "Nice, Taeko. Those are really bright colors. They make me feel happy."
> "Look what Raymond did. He cut out his picture when he was done. That's a nice job of cutting."

Teachers play an important role in students' developing independence and initiative. Felipe and Taeko made their own decisions about coloring, and Raymond decided on his own to cut out the picture when he was finished. The kind of support children receive influences their future sense of initiative and competence. Criticism of this initiative detracts from the feeling of independence and, in extreme cases, leads to guilt and dependency. Simple tasks, such as buttoning clothes and putting away toys, form the concrete challenges that children use to estimate their own competence and self-worth. A child's performance on a task isn't as important as an adult's response to it. Children at this age are taking initiative and trying to be independent, but adult affirmation is still very important. Supportive and encouraging teachers play an essential role in learners' growing sense of initiative.

> **3.7** ▬
> Given what we know about young children's personal growth, is competition a generally healthy or generally unhealthy component of the early school curriculum? Explain.

Industry Versus Inferiority (Ages 6 to 12)

Students' efforts to resolve the crisis at the industry versus inferiority stage also have important implications for teachers. The challenge is to develop a sense of **industry**, *the enjoyment of mastery and competence through success and recognition of accomplishment.* Because children spend large amounts of time and energy at school, the influence of teachers and peers is very important. If challenges are too difficult or result in failure, the child may develop a sense of inferiority, or if accomplishments involve only trivial tasks, industry fails to develop.

In a longitudinal study of development, researchers found that of *intelligence, family background,* and *industry*, a healthy sense of industry was the most significant factor in later personal adjustment, economic success, and interpersonal relationships (Vaillant & Vaillant, 1990). This finding is very encouraging; if teachers can help students respond to challenges and develop a sense of industry, they can overcome many obstacles later in life.

As you study Erikson's work, keep in mind that children may not necessarily recognize the need to develop a sense of industry, competence, and success at the time they are going through the stage. It might appear, for example, that peer relationships are most important to them at this point in their lives. Erikson asserts, however, that during this

> **3.8** ▬
> Using the information in this section, explain the likely effect on learners' resolution of the industry versus inferiority crisis if students are consistently given schoolwork that they can complete with little effort. Explain the effect of schoolwork that is too difficult.

Early childhood and elementary classrooms should provide opportunities for students to develop personal independence and initiative.

period their main psychosocial task is to develop a sense of competence and purpose. Teachers assist in this process by providing a challenging menu of learning experiences and helping learners meet them.

Identity Versus Confusion (Ages 12 to 18)

During adolescence, middle and junior high school youngsters experience major physical, intellectual, and emotional changes. Many go through growth spurts, and their coordination doesn't keep up with their bodies. The magnitude of physical change in early adolescence is surpassed only during infancy. Adolescents experience new sexual feelings, and, not quite knowing how to respond, they're frequently confused. They are concerned with what others think of them and are preoccupied with their looks. They are caught in the awkward position of wanting to assert their independence, yet longing for the stability of structure and discipline. They want to rebel, but they want something solid to rebel against. They write "Ms. Smith is a b_____" on the bathroom wall on Wednesday, but on Thursday they decide they really like her. Further, they would feel terrible if they thought she didn't like them.

During this period, youngsters are wrestling with the **identity** question *Who am I?* These changes and struggles don't imply that all teenagers are doomed to a period of distress and uncertainty, however. Most negotiate adolescence successfully, and most maintain positive relationships with their parents and other adults. Erikson, who coined the term **identity crisis**—*the feeling of uncertainty about who one is*—suggests that youngsters who have a basic sense of trust, can function on their own, aren't afraid to take initiative, and feel competent to effectively overcome the uncertainty of adolescence and develop a firm notion of who they are and what their role in society should be.

Some contemporary theorists reject the term *crisis*, arguing that it suggests a sudden, intense upheaval of the self. They prefer the term *exploration*, because in their view it better reflects day-to-day experimentation with different roles and people (Berk, 1996).

Failure to form a viable identity results in role confusion, which prolongs adolescent characteristics and inhibits successful functioning as adults. We've all heard remarks such as, "He never grew up," or, "She still behaves like an adolescent." These descriptions typify people who have failed to resolve the identity–confusion crisis. Teachers can help in the process by providing the authoritative interaction style we discussed in the first section of the chapter.

3.9 ■
Explain specifically how an authoritative interaction style can contribute to an adolescent's sense of identity.

Stages of Identity Development.

Four seniors were talking about their after high school plans.

> "I'm not sure what I want to do," Sandy commented. "I've thought about veterinary medicine, and I've also thought about teaching. I've been working at the vet clinic, and I really like it, but I'm not sure about doing it forever. I guess I should take some kind of interest inventory or something. I don't know."
>
> "I wish I could do that," Ramon replied. "But I'm off to the university full-time in the fall. I'm going to be a lawyer. At least that's what my parents think. It's not a bad job, and they make good money."
>
> "How can you just do that, Ramon?" Nancy wondered aloud. "You don't really want to be a lawyer; you've said that before. Me, I'm not going to decide for a while. I'm only 18. I'm good in biology. I've thought about trying premed, and I'm going to take some more courses in biology-oriented stuff, but I'm not sure I'm ready for that many years of school. I'm going to think hard about it for a while. How about you, Taylor?"
>
> "I'm going into nursing," Taylor answered. "I've been working part-time at the hospital, and it feels really good. I thought I wanted to be a doctor at one time, but I don't think I can handle all the pressures. I've talked with the counselors, and I think I can do the chem and other science. I guess we'll see."

Conversations with caring adults provide opportunities for adolescents to think about and refine their developing personal identities.

The process of identity formation isn't smooth and uniform; it takes different paths, like a railroad train. Sometimes it's sitting on a holding spur beside the main track; at others it's chugging full speed ahead (Marcia, 1980).

Researchers have studied identity resolution by interviewing adolescents and asking them about their occupational, religious, and political choices (Marcia, 1980). The researchers found that young people's commitments tend to cluster around one of four positions, outlined in Table 3.3 (Marcia, 1987).

The descriptions in Table 3.3 show that identity moratorium and identity achievement are healthy positions on the path to identity formation. With identity diffusion and identity foreclosure—less healthy positions—adolescents fail to wrestle with choices that will have important consequences for them throughout life.

Research helps in understanding this process. In a synthesis of eight studies, Waterman (1985) found that—in contrast with the predictions of Erikson's theory—identity achievement more often occurs after, than during, high school. This finding was especially true for college students, who had more time to consider what they wanted to do with their lives. These results suggest that the uncertainty of adolescence is more related to increasing independence than to career or gender identity resolution. Conflict with parents, teachers, and other adults peaks in early adolescence and then declines as teenagers accept responsibility and adults learn how to deal with the new relationships (Offer, Ostrov, & Howard, 1989). This helps explain why teaching junior high or middle school students can be particularly challenging.

Helping Adolescents Grow.

Understanding emotionally developing adolescents helps a teacher better respond to their sometimes capricious behavior. Fads and bizarre clothing and hairstyles, for example, reflect teenagers' urges to identify with groups while simultaneously searching for their individuality. If their behaviors don't interfere with learning or the

3.10
Research indicates that for American youngsters, identity resolution and formation are postponed until the post-high school years. Why do these processes occur later for American youth than for youth in other countries?

Table 3.3

Positions in identity development

Position	Description and Example
Identity diffusion	Occurs when individuals fail to make clear choices. Confusion is common. Choices may be difficult, or individuals aren't developmentally ready to make choices. This state is illustrated by Sandy's comments in the case study.
Identity foreclosure	Occurs when individuals prematurely adopt ready-made positions of others, such as parents. This is an undesirable position, because decisions are based on the identities of others. Ramon's comments suggest this state.
Identity moratorium	Occurs when individuals pause and remain in a holding pattern. Long-range commitment is delayed. Nancy appears to be in this state.
Identity achievement	Occurs after individuals experience a period of crises and decision making. Identity achievement reflects a commitment to a goal or direction. Taylor's comments indicate that he has made this commitment.

rights and comfort of others, they shouldn't be major issues. A teacher can help by spending time discussing students' concerns and simply talking with them openly and honestly. This is the best advice we can give teachers struggling to reach students like Sean.

Perhaps more significant is the sensitivity both Anne and Beth demonstrated in their efforts to reach him. Students, particularly at the middle and junior high levels, need firm, caring teachers—teachers who empathize with them, while providing the security of clear limits for acceptable behavior. They don't need a teacher who is a buddy. They need a solid adult who can guide their intellectual and emotional growth (Emmer, Evertson, Clements, & Worsham, 2000).

Intimacy Versus Isolation (Young Adulthood)

During Erikson's sixth stage, individuals wrestle with personal relationships. A person with a firm sense of identity is prepared for **intimacy**, or *giving the self over to another,* based on something other than a basic need. Giving for the sake of giving, without expecting something in return, characterizes a positive resolution of the crisis at this stage. In contrast, people who fail to resolve the crisis remain emotionally isolated, unable to give and receive love freely.

Generativity Versus Stagnation (Middle Adulthood)

The key characteristics of **generativity** are *creativity, productivity, and concern for and commitment to guiding the next generation* (Erikson, 1980). Generative adults try to contribute to the betterment of society by working for principles such as a clean physical environment, a safe and drug-free social world, and adherence to the principles of freedom and dignity for individuals. Teachers who genuinely care about students and their learning exemplify people who have positively resolved the crisis at this stage. An unhealthy resolution leads to apathy, pseudointimacy, or self-absorption.

Integrity Versus Despair (Old Age)

Erikson describes people who *accept themselves, conclude that they have only one life to live, live it about as well as possible, and have few regrets* as having **integrity**. They accept responsibility for the way they've lived and accept the finality of death. A person filled with regret for things done or left undone, worried that there is no turning back and that time is running out, experiences despair.

Putting Erikson's Work Into Perspective

Having read the descriptions of Erikson's eight stages, you probably have some questions about his theory. Maybe you wonder "When a crisis at a particular stage isn't resolved, what happens later? Does the person not go on to the next stage?" Let's look at Sean and his development to begin answering these questions.

The evidence in our case study suggests that Sean didn't fully resolve the trust–mistrust crisis. However, this doesn't mean that it prevented him from wrestling with autonomy or initiative (although some evidence indicates that he also lacked initiative). Rather, it has left him with a personality "glitch" that keeps him from functioning as fully as he might.

Sean's behavior also suggests that he is having problems resolving the identity–confusion crisis. His father's absence leaves him without an important male role model to help him in this process. This confusion, Erikson notes, can result in a negative identity, which rejects productive roles and substitutes negative ones. Sean may well grow up to be a successful adult, however.

No one knows for sure what the long-range ramifications of any personality imperfections might be. People who don't resolve the autonomy–doubt crisis, for example, may be less successful than their ability would indicate because they are afraid to move forward on their own. On the other hand, they may find satisfying careers in a support role.

Rather than being absolute causes of behavior, "glitches" are simply that—personality imperfections that we all have in some form. Erikson's theory doesn't give specific answers, such as precisely when a problem causes a person to be dysfunctional, but neither do other theories.

Because of its descriptive nature, Erikson's theory is difficult to document with empirical research. This is typical of personality theories; few have an extensive body of experimental data supporting them (Mischel, 1993). Erikson's work, however, is intuitively sensible, and it helps us understand learners' personal development. We've all met people we admire because of their openness, drive, and enthusiasm. They seem to be comfortable around other people, have a good understanding of their own strengths and weaknesses, enjoy their work, and feel committed to contributing to society. However, we've also seen those who believe that others are trying to take advantage of them or are somehow inherently evil. We see good minds sliding into lethargy as the result of apathy or even substance abuse. We are frustrated by people who are apathetic or lack a zest for living. Erikson's work helps us understand these problems.

3.11
You are teaching ninth graders, and you have a student whom you can't "get going." He will do what is required of him and no more. He does a good job on his required work, however, and he seems to be quite happy. Explain his behavior on the basis of Erikson's work.

As teachers, we gain some insight from Erikson's theory into the personalities of our students and how they can be nurtured and strengthened. Further, we can see implications for ourselves in working with students at all school levels. It reminds us that we are there to do much more than help students learn to make subjects and verbs agree or to solve algebraic equations. We are also there to help them develop as individuals and relate productively to others.

Classroom Connections

Applying Erikson's Work in Your Classroom

1. Help students achieve a high degree of success, especially in the elementary school.
   - A sixth-grade teacher develops a grading system based partially on improvement so that each student can succeed by improving performance.
   - A second-grade teacher carefully covers each topic and provides precise directions before making seat-work assignments. He conducts "monitored practice" with the first few items to be sure all students get started correctly.

2. Be tolerant of honest mistakes when dealing with students at all levels.
   - A prealgebra teacher, working with a student on simplifying expressions involving signed numbers, sees a student repeat a mistake explained only moments before. The teacher patiently reminds the student of the rule and then models the solution to the problem.
   - A kindergarten student responsible for watering the classroom plants knocks one over and spills the water. The teacher says evenly, "It looks like we have a problem. What needs to be done?" She pauses and continues, "Sweep up the dirt and use the paper towels to wipe up the water."

3. In a middle or junior high school, provide the security of structure while allowing freedom of expression.
   - An eighth-grade history teacher consistently enforces her classroom rules and procedures. She also uses a few minutes of home room each day to discuss issues with students. They may say anything they wish other than criticizing people in the school by name.
   - A life science teacher jokes with her students as they enter the classroom. When the bell rings, however, the students are settled and ready to begin working.

4. Know the emotional needs of young people, and use that knowledge as an umbrella under which you conduct your instruction.
   - A junior high earth science teacher pays little attention to the attire and slang of his students as long as offensive language isn't used, the rights of others are recognized, and learning occurs.
   - After school, a seventh-grade geography teacher listens sympathetically as a girl talks about an incident in which her feelings were hurt as a result of an encounter with some of her friends.

5. Be a role model for students, both professionally and personally. With elementary students, model industry; with older students, also model the professionalism and individual dignity helpful in identity formation.
   - A fourth-grade teacher arranges his classroom procedures so that everyone—including himself—is given responsibilities, including homework. He discusses the work that he takes home at night, stressing its importance for teaching and learning.
   - A tenth-grade English teacher stresses that discourtesy and mistreatment of others are mortal sins in her class. She pledges her own courtesy and preservation of everyone's individual dignity.

The Development of Self-Concept

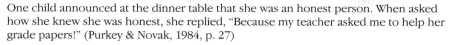

One child announced at the dinner table that she was an honest person. When asked how she knew she was honest, she replied, "Because my teacher asked me to help her grade papers!" (Purkey & Novak, 1984, p. 27)

"I'll never forget my seventh-grade teacher. At that time I was overweight and wore braces on my teeth. Our teacher asked us to turn in a paper of different types of sentences. To demonstrate an exaggeration, I wrote, 'I am the most beautiful girl in the world.' The teacher wrote back: 'This is an exaggeration?' He'll never know how good he made me feel." (Purkey & Novak, 1984, p. 28)

As children develop, they grow not only in size, knowledge, and skills but also in their awareness and views of themselves as learners and as people. These views are positive when students enter school but, unfortunately, often become less positive over time (Stipek, 1998). This is especially true for students who experience learning problems (Heward, 1996).

Self-Concept and Self-Esteem

The terms *self-concept* and *self-esteem* are commonly used to describe learners' views of themselves. They are often used interchangeably but in fact are quite distinct. **Self-concept** is *a cognitive appraisal of our physical, social, and academic competence*. In comparison, **self-esteem**, or **self-worth**, is *an affective or emotional reaction to the self* (Pintrich & Schunk, 1996). Self-esteem is significant because researchers have found that learners with high self-esteem are confident, curious, independent, and motivated and do well in school. In contrast, low self-esteem has been linked to substance abuse, antisocial acts, adolescent pregnancy, suicide, and other self-destructive behaviors (Beane, 1991). We examine self-esteem in more detail later in the chapter.

Sources of Self-Concept

As children develop, several factors influence their self-concepts. Young children's (3- to 5-year-old's) self-concepts are concrete, focusing on tangible things like appearance, possessions, and everyday behaviors (Berk, 1996). This is consistent with Piaget's observation that young children's developing schemes depend heavily on direct experience with their environment.

As children grow older, interactions with others become increasingly influential (Hay, Ashman, van Kraayenoord, & Stewart, 1999). Initially, the most significant interactions are with parents, and during early school years, teachers are important as well. Even young children sense whether adults have low or high expectations for them, and these expectations influence achievement (Phillips, 1990). As students progress through school, the influence of peers and friends increases, but adults remain important (Berk, 1997).

Self-Concept and Achievement

The relationship between general self-concept and achievement is positive but weak (Walberg, 1984). In attempting to understand why, researchers have found that self-concept has at least three subcomponents—academic, social, and physical (Marsh, 1989)—with social and physical self-concepts being virtually unrelated to academic achievement (Byrne

3.12

What parts of the total school experience most influence the development of social and physical self-concepts? What does this suggest about the importance of a total school program?

& Gavin, 1996). This makes sense; we've all known socially withdrawn students who are happy as academic isolates, and we've also known popular students who are only average in schoolwork.

Academic Self-Concept

For teachers, **academic self-concept**, *the component of general self-concept that deals with students' perception of their competence as learners,* is most important. Academic self-concept and school performance strongly interact. Children enter school expecting to learn and do well (Stipek, 1998), but as they progress, this expectation is altered by their accomplishments (Harter & Connell, 1984). When learning experiences are positive, self-concept is enhanced; when they're negative, it suffers.

Subject Matter Specificity.   Although researchers find a moderate relationship between academic self-concept and achievement, the strongest correlations exist between specific academic self-concepts and their corresponding subject matter areas. For example, people with positive self-concepts of ability in math perform better on mathematical tests (and vice versa). Researchers have also found that concepts of ability in different subjects, such as math and English, become more distinct over time, and students become better able to differentiate between their performances in different areas (Marsh, 1992). Unfortunately, we've all heard people make statements such as, "I'm okay in English, but I'm no good in math." Some evidence suggests that comments such as these are based more on perceived ability resulting from lowered societal expectations of others than from actual ability (American Association of University Women, 1992).

The relationships between different components of self-concept and achievement are illustrated in Figure 3.2.

> **3.13** ▬
>
> What, specifically, is the primary source of information students use to develop their academic self-concepts? Describe what you as a teacher can do to help low achievers form positive self-concepts.

Figure 3.2 ▬

The relationships among the dimensions of self-concept and achievement

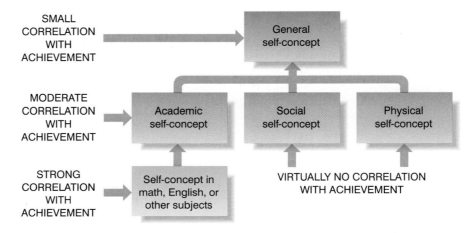

Improving Learner Self-Concept

The connections among self-concept, academic performance, and students' attitudes toward school have prompted efforts to improve the way students view themselves. These efforts have used two distinct approaches: (a) attempts to improve self-concept directly, and (b) attempts to improve self-concept through increased academic success.

The first approach involves varied strategies, such as using multicultural learning materials with minority students, establishing residential summer camps, and implementing support groups and sensitivity training (Beane, 1991); the second focuses on achievement (Stipek, 1998).

These approaches were tested in a federally funded, primary-grade program. The program that tried to improve self-concept directly stressed a learning environment of support and trust, with students selecting from a variety of stimulating materials. Program components were designed specifically to enhance participants' self-concepts. The program that attempted to increase self-concept as a result of academic success featured structured learning activities with positive reinforcement.

Research examining the two approaches indicated that students in the second group not only learned more but also had more positive self-concepts. This study, and later corroborating research, suggests that efforts to improve academic achievement through self-concept intervention alone are misguided and naive (Skaalvik & Valas, 1999). Learners are active, thinking people. Without genuine, observable accomplishment, they're unlikely to develop positive feelings about their competence (Hay et al., 1999).

Children form their academic self-concepts on the basis of the concrete experiences and feedback they receive in school.

Self-Concept: Instructional Implications

The implications for teachers are clear. We must design learning activities so that students succeed; if we do, self-concepts are likely to improve. Berliner (1987) summarizes this position:

> It is now thought likely that a high level of success in a learning environment causes students to develop an enhanced self-concept as a learner. Thus, to build a positive self-concept, a teacher needs to design environments and make assignments so that students can have experience in attaining high levels of success. (p. 100)

This process isn't as simple as it appears on the surface, however. For self-concepts to improve, students must perceive learning activities as challenging and worthwhile (Ames, 1990; Clifford, 1990). Success on trivial tasks does little to increase learners' self-concepts.

Classroom climate and grading practices also influence self-concept (Beane, 1991). High expectations communicate that all students can and will learn; democratic classrooms—where students participate in decision making—foster initiative, self-direction, and self-concept. Teachers who emphasize effort and individual improvement in their grading practices, in contrast with those who emphasize competition and social comparisons, enhance self-concept by recognizing genuine progress (Cohen, 1991).

Ethnic Pride: Promoting Positive
Self-Esteem and Ethnic Identity

Maria Robles squeezed her mother's hand tightly as they entered the busy doors of her new school. Her mother could tell she was nervous as she anxiously eyed the bigger boys and girls walking down the hallway.

As they stopped in front of the doorway marked Kindergarten, Room 3, Mrs. Avilla, a woman with a smiling face, came out to greet them.

"Hola. ¿Cómo te llamas, niña?" (Hello. What is your name, little one?)

Maria was still uneasy but, as she looked at her mother's face, she felt relieved.

"Dile tu nombre" (Tell her your name), her mother prompted, squeezing her hand and smiling.

" . . . Maria," she offered hesitantly.

Her mother added quickly, "Maria Robles. Yo soy su madre." (I am her mother.)

Mrs. Avilla looked on her list, found Maria's name, and checked it off. Then she invited them, in Spanish, to come into the room and meet the other boys and girls. Music could be heard in the background. Maria recognized some of her friends who were playing with toys in one corner of the room.

"Maria, ven aquí y juega con nosotros." (Maria, come here and play with us.)

Maria hesitated for a moment and looked up at her mother to see whether it was all right. When her mother smiled and nodded, Maria ran over to join her friends.

Self-Esteem and Ethnicity

We all wonder about our self-worth. Will others like us? Are we worthy of their love? Are we perceived by others as smart? beautiful? handsome? As you saw at the beginning of this chapter, our interactions with others help shape our beliefs, and schools play an important role in this process. This applies to both self-concept and self-esteem.

Research suggests that culture plays an important role in the development of self-esteem in minority youth, and researchers have found that the self-esteem of minorities includes both a personal and a collective component (Wright & Taylor, 1995).

Collective self-esteem refers to *children's perceptions of the relative worth of the groups to which they belong.* For all of us, families and peer and ethnic groups contribute to our sense of self-worth. When we (and others) perceive these groups as valued and having status, our self-esteem is enhanced. The opposite is also true.

Children as young as Maria Robles know they are part of an ethnic minority, and research dating back to the 1930s indicates that minority children such as African Americans (Clark & Clark, 1939), Mexican Americans (Weiland & Coughlin, 1979), and Chinese Americans (Aboud & Skerry, 1984) evaluate their ethnic reference groups lower than the white majority. These findings suggest that simply being part of a minority group can make students feel less confident and less good about themselves; this is a disturbing problem for teachers since we want each student to develop a healthy self-esteem.

What can teachers do to combat this problem? We can make every effort to communicate to students that their ethnic heritage and language are both recognized and valued. In a test of this idea, researchers taught elementary native Canadian children in either their native (heritage) language or in a second language, such as French (Wright & Taylor, 1995). Children educated in their heritage language showed a substantial increase in their personal self-esteem, whereas children educated in the nonheritage second language did not. The researchers concluded that "early heritage language education can have a positive impact on the personal and collective self-esteem of minority language students" (p. 251).

3.14 ■
What data do ethnic minority children use in forming these lower evaluations? How does this process compare with the process that occurs in forming personal self-esteem and self-concept?

Teachers can help students develop ethnic pride and positive self-esteem by actively acknowledging and valuing the ethnic and cultural strengths different students bring to school.

Students who hear their home language used in the classroom learn that the language and the culture in which it is embedded are valued. Stories such as Maria Robles's occur frequently. Many students come to school wondering if they will be welcome and questioning whether the knowledge they bring with them will be valued (Jackson, 1999). The way a teacher reacts to these students influences their sense of self-worth.

Ethnic Pride and Identity Formation

Membership in an ethnic group also affects identity formation (Jones, 1999). Sometimes the messages teenagers receive about their ethnic identities are mixed or even negative. An African American journalist reported, "If you were black, you didn't quite measure up. . . . You didn't see any black people doing certain things. . . . Well, it must mean that white people are better than we are" (Monroe, Goldman, & Smith, 1988, pp. 88–99). Similar problems with ethnic identity formation have been documented with Mexican American (Matute-Bianchi, 1986) and Asian American teenagers (Wong-Fillmore, 1992).

On a more positive note, research indicates that students who are encouraged and helped to explore their ethnic identities and who have adopted values from both the dominant culture and their own tend to have a clearer sense of their identity (Nieto, 1999). They also achieve higher, like school more, have higher self-esteem, and have a more positive view of their ability to cope with their environments (Hood, 1999; Jackson, 1999).

The research reveals consistent patterns. Minority students need to know that their cultures are valued and that the languages they bring to school are assets rather than obstacles or liabilities (Wilson, 1998). Teachers play a crucial role in making every student feel wanted and welcomed by the overt and implicit messages they send through their teaching.

3.15
Explain how positive ethnic role models can assist in identity-resolution tasks, such as independence, career decision making, sexual adjustment, and peer group relations.

Classroom Connections

Developing Positive Self-Concepts in Your Classroom

1. Make students feel wanted and valued in your class.
   - A fourth-grade teacher starts the school year by having students write autobiographical sketches and bring in pictures of themselves taken when they were preschoolers. They list their strengths and weaknesses and describe what they want to be when they grow up.
   - A high school teacher begins each school year by announcing that everyone is important in her classes and that she expects everyone to learn. She structures her classrooms around success, minimizing competition. She also stays in her room every day after school and invites any students who are having problems to come by for help.

2. Provide learning experiences that promote success.
   - A fifth-grade teacher allows students to drop their lowest quiz grade, and he gives bonus points if students show consistent improvement.
   - A sixth-grade teacher has students keep portfolios of products they create in art, music, science, and social studies. She shares the portfolios with parents and encourages parents to take the portfolios home and discuss them with their children.

Capitalizing on Diversity in Your Classroom

3. Build on students' cultures and ethnic backgrounds to develop positive self-esteem.

   - A first-grade teacher discovered that three different native languages were spoken in the homes of her students. With the help of other teachers and parent volunteers, she constructed a chart of common nouns and phrases (e.g., chair, table, mother, hello) in the different languages. She used the chart to explain to her students differences in the languages and to establish commonalities between them.
   - A social studies teacher teaching in an ethnically diverse school encourages her students to do reports on the country from which their ancestors came. Students place the information they discover on a poster and bring in things from home, such as clothes and food, to illustrate the culture of the ancestral country.

4. Use ethnic role models as a foundation for the development of students' personal identities.
   - A middle school teacher in a career exploration unit makes a special effort to bring in minorities in different occupations and professions. He encourages them to talk openly about the challenges and satisfactions they encountered in pursuing their careers.
   - A social studies teacher makes a special effort to emphasize the contributions of ethnic minorities and women to American society. As contemporary newspapers and magazines report the accomplishments of different ethnic groups, she brings these in to share with her students.

Development of Morality, Social Responsibility, and Self-Control

"Listen, everyone. . . . I need to go to the office for a moment," Mrs. Kellinger said as her students were completing a seat-work assignment. "You all have work to do, so work quietly on it until I get back."

The quiet shuffling of pencils and papers could be heard for a few moments, and then Gary whispered, "Psst, what math problems are we supposed to do?"

"Shh! No talking," Talitha said, pointing to the rules posted on the chalkboard.

"But he needs to know so he can do his homework," Krystal put in. "It's the evens on page 79."

"Who cares?" Dwain growled. "She's not here. She won't catch us."

What do students think about classroom rules? Perhaps more important, how do they think about the laws and conventions that govern our society? What influences their interpretations of rules, and how do they learn to follow and modify them? In this section, we continue our discussion of student development, examining changes in children's thinking about issues of right, wrong, fairness, and justice.

Increased Interest in Moral Education and Development

In recent years, interest in moral education and how it should be used to promote moral development has increased markedly (Wynne, 1997). In the popular media, *Newsweek* and *Time* have devoted cover articles to the topic, and the cover of the November 22, 1999, issue of *U.S. News* addressed the issue of cheating, saying "A new epidemic of fraud is sweeping through our schools." Within education, periodicals such as *Educational Leadership* and *Clearinghouse* have also addressed the issue of moral development.

Part of the reason for this growing interest in moral development is the perception that adolescents are being bombarded by a number of risk factors with moral undertones. For example, alcohol and drug abuse remain persistent problems among youth (Kuther & Higgins-D'Alessandra, 1997). Out-of-wedlock births to white adolescent females are at historical highs, as are homicide and suicide rates for white adolescent males (U.S. Department of Health and Human Services, 1998). The U.S. public is increasingly looking to moral education for solutions to problems such as these.

The need for moral education has also been voiced within the teaching profession (Goodlad, Soder, & Sirotnik, 1990; Tom, 1984). Some argue that teaching is an inherently moral activity, with value decisions around every instructional corner. This view separates the morality of teaching (e.g., who gets called on, and who receives extra help) from the teaching of morality (e.g., how should we treat each other, and why we have classroom rules) (Buzzelli & Johnston, 1997). On a broader level, some argue that value conflicts and the decisions that follow are an integral part of applying knowledge within any profession (D. Stern, 1997).

Moral issues are also embedded in the curriculum. Social studies are not a mere chronology of events; they are the study of humans' responses to situation-specific moral dilemmas, such as war and peace and justice and equality (Sunai & Haas, 1993). Ethical issues have also been commonly used in literature designed for young people. For instance, Charlotte in *Charlotte's Web* was faced with the dilemma of saving Wilbur the pig at the loss of her own life. Old Yeller's master was faced with losing his dog or allowing the potential health menace of rabies. Students commonly study books such as *The Yearling* and *A Tale of Two Cities* not only because they are good literature but also because they introduce moral problems with no clear answers.

Most importantly, moral education is an essential and integral part of learner development. To become healthy socially and emotionally, learners must acquire the moral compass that values provide and the thinking capacities to apply these values in intelligent ways. Further, research indicates that the moral atmosphere of a school (e.g., democratic and prosocial versus authoritarian) can influence motivation and the value students place on school (Binfet, Schonert-Reicht, & McDougal, 1997; Grolnick et al., 1999). Moral development theory can help us understand these issues.

Piaget's Description of Moral Development

Although most people think of Piaget primarily in the context of cognitive development, he examined the development of ethics and morals as well (1932/1965). He studied cognitive and moral development in much the same way; he presented children with problems and tasks, listened to their reactions, and asked questions to gain insight into their thinking.

Piaget found that children's responses to moral problems could be divided into two broad stages of development on the basis of a principle he labeled *internalization* (1932/1965). **Internalization** refers to *the source of control for children's thoughts and actions.* In the first stage, which Piaget called **external morality**, *children view rules as fixed and permanent and externally enforced by authority figures.* External morality lasts to about age 10. In the preceding case, Talitha, with her reference to the rules, demonstrated thinking at this stage. It didn't matter that Gary was only asking about the homework assignment; rules are rules. Dwain, who responded, "Who cares? She's not here. She won't catch us," was also responding at this level; he was focusing on the fact that no authority figure was there to enforce the rule. Piaget believed that parents and teachers who stress unquestioning adherence to adult authority retard moral development and encourage students to remain at this level (DeVries & Zan, 1995).

At the second stage, called **autonomous morality**, *children develop rational ideas of fairness and see justice as a reciprocal process of treating others as they would want to be treated.* Children at this stage begin to rely on themselves instead of others to regulate moral behavior. Krystal's comment, "But he needs to know so he can do his homework," is characteristic of thinking at this stage; she views Gary's whispering as an honest request for assistance, rather than a rule infraction.

3.16 ▬
Use the concept of *egocentrism* from our discussion of Piaget's work in Chapter 2 to explain the difference between *external* and *autonomous* morality. Describe what you as a teacher can do to help students progress from one stage to the next.

Kohlberg's Theory of Moral Development

> Steve, a high school senior, was working at a night job to help support his mother, a single parent of three. Steve was a conscientious student who worked hard in his classes, but he didn't have enough time to study.
>
> History wasn't Steve's favorite course, and because of his night work, he had a marginal D average. If he failed the final exam, he would fail the course and wouldn't graduate. He arranged to be off work the night before the exam so that he could study extra hard, but early in the evening, his boss called, desperate to have Steve come in and replace another employee who called in sick at the last moment. His boss pressured him heavily, so Steve went to work reluctantly at 8:00 P.M. and came home exhausted at 2:00 A.M. He tried to study but fell asleep on the couch, with his book in his lap. His mother woke him for school at 6:30 A.M.
>
> Steve went to his history class, looked at the test, and went blank. Everything seemed like a jumble. Clarice, one of the best students in the class, happened to have her answer sheet positioned so that he could clearly see every answer by barely moving his eyes.

From what you've read here, is Steve justified in cheating on the test? You've just experienced a **moral dilemma**, which is *an ambiguous situation that requires a person to make a moral decision.* Steve was caught in a position that had no clear course of action; any decision had both positive and negative consequences. Students' responses to moral dilemmas provide insight into their moral development (Rest, Thoma, Narvaez, & Bebeau, 1997).

Influenced by the work of Piaget and John Dewey, Lawrence Kohlberg (1929–1987), a Harvard educator and psychologist, used dilemmas to study moral reasoning. While work-

Cheating is a persistent problem in classrooms. How students think about this problem and how teachers should respond to it depend on students' levels of moral development.

ing with teenagers, he found that moral reasoning was developmental, and, on the basis of research conducted in cities and villages in Great Britain, Malaysia, Mexico, Taiwan, and Turkey, Kohlberg concluded that the development of moral reasoning is similar across cultures. Using responses to hypothetical moral dilemmas such as the one you just read, Kohlberg (1963, 1969, 1981, 1984) developed a theory of moral development that extended Piaget's earlier work. Like Piaget, he concluded that morality develops in stages, and all people pass through all the stages in the same order but at different rates.

Kohlberg originally described moral development as existing in three levels consisting of two stages each. These levels represent the perspectives people take as they wrestle with moral dilemmas or problems. The levels and stages are outlined in Table 3.4.

As you read the following descriptions, remember that the specific response to a moral dilemma isn't the critical issue; level and stage are determined by the *reasons* a person gives for making the decision.

Level I: Preconventional Ethics

The preconventional level is an egocentric orientation focusing on moral consequences for the self. As you might predict, on the basis of their egocentrism, young children reason at this level.

The level consists of two stages: *punishment–obedience* and *market exchange*. Some research indicates that 15% to 20% of the U.S. teenage population still reason at this level (Turiel, 1973).

Stage 1: Punishment–Obedience. People reasoning at the **punishment–obedience stage** *make moral decisions based on their chances of getting caught and being punished.* They determine right or wrong by the consequences of an action. For example, if a child is punished, the act was morally wrong; if not, the act was right. People encountering an unguarded purse and not taking it because they fear getting caught are operating at this stage. The same principle applies in a classroom. A person who argues that Steve is justified in cheating because he could see every answer on Clarice's paper by barely moving his eyes, and so he probably won't get caught, is reasoning at Stage 1.

Table 3.4

Kohlberg's stages of moral reasoning

Level I Preconventional Ethics	The ethics of egocentrism. Typical of children up to about age 10. Called preconventional because children typically don't fully understand rules set down by others.
Stage 1: Punishment-Obedience	Consequences of acts determine whether they're good or bad. Individuals make moral decisions without considering the needs or feelings of others.
Stage 2: Market Exchange	The ethics of "What's in it for me?" Obeying rules and exchanging favors are judged in terms of the benefit to the individual.
Level II Conventional Ethics	The ethics of others. Typical of 10- to 20-year-olds. The name comes from conformity to the rules and conventions of society.
Stage 3: Interpersonal Harmony	Ethical decisions are based on concern for or the opinions of others. What pleases, helps, or is approved of by others characterizes this stage.
Stage 4: Law and Order	The ethics of laws, rules, and societal order. Rules and laws are inflexible and are obeyed for their own sake.
Level III Postconventional Ethics	The ethics of principle. Rarely reached before age 20 and only by a small portion of the population. The focus is on the principles underlying society's rules.
Stage 5: Social Contract	Rules and laws represent agreements among people about behavior that benefits society. Rules can be changed when they no longer meet society's needs.
Stage 6: Universal Principles	Rarely encountered in life. Ethics are determined by abstract and general principles that transcend societal rules.

Stage 2: Market Exchange.   At the **market exchange stage**, *people focus on the consequences of an action for themselves, but reciprocity is involved.* "An eye for an eye and a tooth for a tooth" or "Don't bite the hand that feeds you" reflect morality at this stage, and "You do something for me and I'll do something for you" is a key characteristic. A naive hedonism is used to judge the rightness or wrongness of an action.

Aspects of the political system exist at this stage. Political patronage, the tendency of successful office seekers to give their supporters "cushy" jobs regardless of qualifications, is an example of Stage 2 ethics.

Cheating is a common problem in classrooms. A person reasoning at Stage 2 might argue that Steve should go ahead and cheat because if he doesn't, he'll have to repeat the course and quit his job. From this perspective, "The right thing to do is what makes me the happiest." This reasoning again focuses on the self.

Level II: Conventional Ethics

As egocentrism declines and development progresses, students become better able to see the world from others' points of view. Moral reasoning no longer depends on the consequences for the individual but instead becomes linked to the perspectives of, and concerns for, others. Values such as loyalty, others' approval, family expectations, obeying the law, and social order become prominent. Stages 3 and 4 reflect this orientation, and it is how the bulk of the population reasons.

Stage 3: Interpersonal Harmony.   Individuals reasoning at Stage 3 do not manipulate people to reach their goals, as they might at Stage 2. Rather, the **interpersonal harmony stage** is *characterized by conventions, loyalty, and living up to the expectations of others*. The Stage 3 person is oriented toward maintaining the affection and approval of friends and relatives by being a "good" person. This is sometimes called the "nice girl/good boy" stage, such as a teenager on a date who meets a curfew because she doesn't want to worry her parents.

A person reasoning at Stage 3 might offer at least two different perspectives on Steve's dilemma. One could argue that he needed to work to help his family, and therefore he was justified in cheating. A contrasting view, still at Stage 3, would suggest that he should not cheat, because people would think badly of him if they knew about it.

Reasoning at Stage 3 includes the danger of being caught up in the majority opinion. Accepting that cheating on one's income taxes is okay because "everybody cheats" is an example. We might call Stage 3 the "ethics of adolescence" because of the influence peers have on young people's thinking at this age.

Stage 4: Law and Order.   A person reasoning at Stage 4 would argue that Steve should not cheat, because "It's against the rules to cheat." The focus at this stage is on adherence to laws and rules for their own sake, rather than on pleasing particular people, as in Stage 3. According to the ethics of the **law and order stage**, *laws and rules exist to guide behavior and should be followed uniformly*.

Concern for the orderliness of society is also characteristic of this stage, such as a person arguing that Steve should not cheat, because "What would our country be like if everybody cheated under those same conditions?" Concern for others is still the focus, but rules and order are key criteria. People reasoning at Stage 4 don't care whether the rest of the world cheats on their income taxes; they pay theirs because the law says they should.

Level III: Postconventional Ethics

A person reasoning at Level III has transcended both the individual and societal levels and makes moral decisions based on principles. People operating at this level, also called *principled morality*, follow rules but also see that, at times, rules need to be changed or ignored. Only a small portion of the population attains this level, and most don't reach it until their mid- to late 20s.

Some of the great figures in history have sacrificed their lives in the name of principle. Sir Thomas More, who knew that he was, in effect, ending his own life by refusing to

3.17 What teacher behaviors contribute to students continuing to reason at the preconventional level? What can teachers do to help students move to higher levels?

3.18 Heavy traffic is moving on an interstate highway at a speed limit of 65. A sign appears that says, "Speed Limit 55." The flow of traffic continues as before. How might a driver at Stage 3 reason, compared with a driver reasoning at Stage 4?

acknowledge King Henry VIII as the head of the Church of England, nevertheless stood on a principle. Mohandas K. Gandhi chose jail rather than adhere to England's laws as he applied the principle of nonviolent noncooperation; his work, as well, ultimately led to his death.

Stage 5: Social Contract.   The person reasoning according to **social contract** *understands that a society of rational people needs socially agreed-on laws in order to function.* The laws are not accepted blindly or for their own sake; rather, they are based on the principle of utility, or "the greatest good for the greatest number," and are followed because they adhere to rights such as life, liberty, and the dignity of the individual.

Stage 5 is the official ethic of the United States. The constitutional Bill of Rights is an example of a cultural social contract; for example, Americans agree *in principle* that people have the right to free speech (The First Amendment to the Constitution), and the legal profession is conceptually committed to interpreting the laws in this light. In addition, the American legal system has provisions for changing or amending laws in the light of new values or conditions. A person reasoning at Stage 5 would say that Steve's cheating is wrong because teachers and learners agree on principle that grades should reflect achievement. Cheating violates the agreement.

Stage 6: Universal Principles.   At the **universal principles** stage, the individual's *moral reasoning is based on abstract and general principles above society's rules.* People at this stage define rightness in terms of internalized universal standards that go beyond concrete laws. "The Golden Rule" is a commonly cited example. Because very few people operate at this stage, and questions have been raised about the existence of "universal" principles, Kohlberg de-emphasized this stage in his later writings (Kohlberg, 1984).

Putting Kohlberg's Theory Into Perspective

As with most theories, Kohlberg's has both proponents and critics. In this section, we examine both research that has investigated the theory and criticisms claiming it contains inherent gender biases.

Research on Kohlberg's Work.   Kohlberg's work has been widely researched, and this research has led to the following conclusions (Berk, 1997; Taylor, 1987):

- Every person's moral reasoning passes through the same stages in the same order.
- People pass through the stages at different rates.
- Development is gradual and continuous, rather than sudden and discrete.
- Once a stage is attained, a person continues to reason at that stage and rarely regresses to a lower stage.
- Intervention usually results in moving only to the next higher stage of moral reasoning.

These results are generally consistent with what Kohlberg's theory would predict. Despite this support, however, there have been questions and criticisms of his work.

Criticisms of Kohlberg's Work.   Kohlberg's original work has been criticized because of a lack of cross-cultural validation, the small number of people who reason at the postconventional level, and the uncertain connection between moral thought and moral behavior. Kohlberg contended that the moral dilemmas faced by individuals in all societies are similar and, therefore, the stages are the same across cultures. Cross-cultural research indi-

3.19 ■
Describe the reasoning of a person at Stage 5 in responding to the problem of people cheating on their income tax.

3.20 ■
All the conclusions we see here, but one, are similar to Piaget's descriptions of cognitive development. Which one is different? Explain how it's different.

cates that the stages do exist for people in other cultures and that children pass through these stages in the same sequence as they do in Western cultures. The rate and end point of moral development may vary, however, with the extent to which different societies encourage moral problem solving, dialogue, and debate about moral issues (Berk, 1997). Social constructivist theory suggests that social interaction is a critical component of moral development.

Though Kohlberg attempted to make his levels content free, research indicates that thinking about moral dilemmas, like problem solving in general, is influenced by domain-specific knowledge (Bebeau, Rest, & Narvaez, 1999; Bech, 1996). For example, a medical doctor asked to deliberate about an educational dilemma or a teacher asked to resolve a medical dilemma may be hampered by their lack of knowledge of the issues involved.

The problem of content also surfaces in cross-cultural studies; postconventional reasoning appears to be biased in favor of Western cultures (Vine, 1986). In describing Stage 5, for example, we used the phrase "rights such as life, liberty, and the dignity of the individual." The "dignity of the individual" certainly reflects Western values. Other cultures, such as the Amish and Native Americans, de-emphasize individuality, placing greater value on cooperation and collaboration. A person from a more group-oriented culture, for example, might respond to the cheating dilemma by saying, "He shouldn't have been placed in a situation like that. Other people—his mother, his teacher, and peers—should be helping him so that he wouldn't be forced into such a dilemma." Teachers should be sensitive to interpretations of morality that people from different cultures may carry with them.

Kohlberg's data-gathering methods—interviews in which the study participants describe their thinking—have also been questioned, with researchers arguing that self-reported explanations of thought processes have severe limitations. "Using interview data assumes that participants can verbally explain the workings of their minds. In recent years, this assumption has been questioned, more and more" (Rest, Narvaez, Bebeau, & Thoma, 1999, p. 295).

If subjects are unable to accurately describe their thinking, as the critics assert, the focus on moral reasoning rather than moral behavior becomes even more problematic. People may reason at one stage and behave at another. However, Kohlberg (1975) found that only 15% of students reasoning at the postconventional level cheated when given the opportunity to do so, but 55% of those reasoning at the conventional level, and 70% of those reasoning at the preconventional level cheated. In addition, adolescents reasoning at the lower stages are likely to be generally less honest and to engage in more antisocial behavior, such as delinquency and drug use (Gregg, Gibbs, & Basinger, 1994). In contrast, reasoning at the higher levels is associated with altruistic behaviors, such as defending free speech, victims of injustice, and the rights of minorities (Berk, 1997; Kuther & Higgins-D'Alessandra, 1997).

Gender Differences: The Morality of Caring.   Early research examining Kohlberg's theory identified differences in the ways men and women responded to moral dilemmas (Gilligan, 1982; Gilligan & Attanucci, 1988). Men were more likely to base their judgments on abstract concepts, such as justice, rules, individual rights, and obligations. Women, in contrast, were more likely to base their moral decisions on personal relationships, interpersonal connections, and attending to human needs.

These findings resulted in females' responses being scored lower, suggesting a lower stage of moral development (Holstein, 1976). Gilligan (1982) argued that the findings, instead, indicate an "ethic of care" in women that is not inferior; rather, Kohlberg's stage descriptions don't adequately represent the complexity of female thinking. Caring appears to be more central to females' sense of identity and, when asked to identify moral dilem-

3.21   ▬
Using Gilligan's arguments, how might a woman respond to the problem of the student not knowing his assignment, presented in the case study at the beginning of this section? How might her response be different from that of a man?

Using Technology in Your Study of Educational Psychology

Assessing Moral Thinking

You've studied Kohlberg's theory of moral development, and now, using the CD-ROM that accompanies this book, you have a chance to personally experience dilemmas similar to those that Kohlberg used to study and measure moral development. To complete the activity, do the following:

- Open the CD, and click on "Assessing Moral Development." (Your instructor will show you how to access the information on the CD.)
- Complete the activities involved in "Assessing Moral Development."
- After completing the activities, answer the following questions:

1. Did any of the following factors influence your responses to the different moral dilemmas? If so, explain how.

   - The gender of the person involved
   - The focus of the dilemma (i.e., whether it involved a teacher and schooling or a life-saving drug)
   - Whether your response was positive or negative

   _____

   _____

   _____

2. What do your responses to these questions tell you about assessing moral development?

   _____

   _____

   _____

3. In reacting to the moral dilemmas, did you always respond at the same stage? What does this tell you about assessing moral development?

   _____

   _____

   _____

4. What advantages and disadvantages are there in open-ended versus multiple-choice responses to moral dilemmas? Which would be most effective in assessing an individual's level of moral development? A group's?

_____

_____

_____

Your instructor will provide you with feedback with respect to these questions, and he or she may ask you to complete some of the additional exercises on the CD.

mas, they are more likely than males to choose interpersonal problems of real life rather than abstract and impersonal problems (Skoe & Dressner, 1994).

More recent research on gender differences is mixed, with some studies finding differences and others not (Leon, Lynn, McLean, & Perri, 1997). Like cross-cultural studies, Gilligan's research reminds us of the complexity of the issues involved in moral development.

The Moral Education Versus Character Education Debate

Over the years, debate over the proper place of values and moral education in the curriculum has continued. At present, people generally agree that moral education is needed, but they disagree about the form it should take. This disagreement has become polarized with *character education* at one extreme and *moral education* at the other. (Bebeau et al., 1999; Wynne, 1997).

Character education *emphasizes the transmission of moral values, such as honesty and citizenship, and the translation of these values into character traits or behaviors.* Instruction in character education emphasizes the study of values, practicing these values both in school and out, and rewarding displays of these values (Benninga & Wynne, 1998; Lickona, 1998).

Moral education, by contrast, is *more value free, emphasizing instead the development of students' moral reasoning.* Moral education uses moral dilemmas and classroom discussions to teach problem solving and to bring about changes in the way learners think with respect to moral issues.

These positions also differ in their views of learners' and teachers' roles. Learners are viewed by character educators as unsocialized at best, potentially evil at worst, and in need of moral guidance. A character education teacher serves as a lecturer/advocate, explaining and modeling appropriate values and reinforcing learners for displaying desirable behaviors.

Moral educators view learners as undeveloped, needing cognitive stimulation to construct better and more comprehensive moral perspectives (Bebeau et al., 1999). A teacher using a moral education approach acts as a problem poser and facilitator, helping students grapple with complex moral problems. These differences are summarized in Table 3.5.

Critics of character education argue that it emphasizes indoctrination instead of education, it ignores the issue of transfer to new situations, and its theoretical underpinnings

Table 3.5

A comparison of character and moral education

	Character Education	Moral Education
Goals	Transmission of moral values	Development of moral reasoning capacities
	Translation of values into behavior	Decision making about moral issues
Instruction	Reading about and analyzing values	Moral dilemmas serve as the focus for problem solving
	Practicing and rewarding good values	Discussions provide opportunities to share moral perspectives and analyze others
Role of a Teacher	Lecturer/advocate Role model	Problem poser Facilitator
View of Learner	Unsocialized citizen of the community needing moral direction and guidance	Undeveloped Uses information to construct increasingly complex moral structures

focus on behavior instead of learner thinking (Kohn, 1997, 1998). Critics of moral education assert that it has a relativistic view of morals, with no right or wrong answers, and they further criticize the use of hypothetical and decontextualized dilemmas that are removed from real classroom life (Wynne, 1997).

Perhaps the greatest strength of the character education perspective is its willingness to identify and promote core values. For instance, honesty, caring, and respect for others should undergird the way we structure our classrooms, interact with students, and expect them to treat each other. On the other hand, emphasizing student thinking and decision making is important as well, and this is the focus of the moral education perspective.

Moral Development and Classroom Structure

Studying moral development is valuable for teachers because it helps us understand that the way we structure our classrooms and interact with students influences their moral growth. If our goal is self-regulation, with students who understand and appreciate the need for orderly classrooms, we must explain the reasons for rules and involve students in the rule-setting process (Brantlinger, Morton, & Washburn, 1999). This emphasis on explanation and involvement changes the classroom culture from one in which there is an adherence to rules because punishment is threatened—an external form of regulation—to one in which rules are followed because students realize they're necessary—self-regulation.

Research suggests that moral development is enhanced in an atmosphere where a spirit of cooperation exists and adults are verbal, rational, and supportive (Berk, 1997; Boyes & Allen, 1993). Research also indicates that teachers who reason at higher stages are more democratic and promote student development to a greater extent than those reasoning at lower levels (Strom, 1989). The opposite is also true. Students working in an

3.22

Explain why teachers reasoning at higher levels would likely be more democratic and involve students more in classroom discussions than teachers reasoning at lower levels.

environment where punishment or the threat of punishment is emphasized will obey rules, but growth in self-control and regulation suffers. (We discuss these ideas further in Chapter 11 when we study classroom management.)

Promoting Moral Development Through Peer Interaction

Teachers can also promote moral development by consciously creating opportunities for students to share and analyze their views. Here's an example:

> "We've been reading an interesting story, and now I'd like to focus on a particular incident in it. Let's talk a bit about the boy in the story who found the wallet. Would it be wrong for him to keep the money? . . . Okay, I see a lot of heads nodding. . . . Why? . . . Jolene?"
>
> "Because it didn't belong to him."
>
> "Helena?"
>
> "Because it was a lot of money, and his parents would probably make him give it back anyway."
>
> "Todd?"
>
> "Why not keep it? It wasn't his fault that the person lost it."
>
> "Juan?"
>
> "But what if the person who lost the money really needed it?"
>
> "Okay. Those are all good reasons. We'll return to them in a moment, but there are a lot of other interesting questions to consider. First, put yourself in his shoes. Would you keep the money? What else might the boy have done, rather than keep the money? If he gives the wallet back, does he have the right to expect a reward? What do you think?"

Research indicates that moral development can be enhanced through classroom discussions that allow students to examine their own moral thinking and to compare it to others (Kuther & Higgins-D'Alessandra, 1997; Thoma & Rest, 1996). Interaction among peers is particularly effective because it encourages active listening and analysis of different moral positions (Kruger, 1992). Exposure to more complex ways of reasoning about moral dilemmas helps students reevaluate their own thinking by examining it in relation to others. These comparisons can disrupt a person's equilibrium and promote development.

Some guidelines for effective discussions about moral dilemmas follow:

▌ Focus on concrete moral conflicts and different ways of resolving them.
▌ Encourage students to consider the perspectives of others.
▌ Ask students to make personal choices in responding to dilemmas and to justify their choices.
▌ Analyze different courses of action by discussing the advantages and disadvantages of each.

In addition to systematically comparing different moral positions, the range of those positions also influences whether or not development will occur (Narvaez, 1998; Thoma & Rest, 1996). An optimal mix is one stage beyond learners' present reasoning; if learners are exposed to moral positions too far beyond their present level, they have trouble relating the positions to their existing background knowledge and experience.

3.23
Using Piaget's theory, predict what stage of cognitive development would be necessary for a learner to reason at the *conventional level*. What stage of cognitive development would be required for *postconventional reasoning*?

Moral Framework of Schools

Kohlberg's work (1984) also reminds us that much of what teachers do in schools is grounded in moral decisions. When teachers emphasize student responsibility, make rules that prevent students from ridiculing each other, emphasize industry, and advocate hon-

Discussing moral dilemmas provides students opportunities to analyze and evaluate their own moral views.

3.24
Write a specific statement describing how you would respond to parents who strongly express the opinion that the teaching of morals belongs in the home and that teachers should not deal with the subject.

esty, they are teaching about morality. Laws that apply to schools also promote these values. For example, Public Law 94-142, which requires that students with learning exceptionalities be placed in the least restrictive environment possible, is based on an ethical issue. It says that it is not fair to deny a student with an exceptionality access to the mainstream learning environment. (We examine PL 94-142 in detail in Chapter 5.)

Arguments that schools shouldn't teach morals are naive. Values are involved every time a teacher emphasizes one topic over another, and morals reflect the values of individuals as well as cultural groups. A more realistic approach is to become as well informed as possible. This allows you as a teacher to make sensitive and considered decisions based on your judgment and understanding.

Classroom Connections

Applying Moral Principles in Your Classroom

1. Openly discuss ethical dilemmas when they arise.
   - A high school teacher's students view cheating as a game, seeing what they can get away with. The teacher addresses the issue by saying, "Because you feel this way about cheating, I'm going to decide who gets what grade without a test. I'll grade you on how smart I think you are." This statement forms the basis for a discussion on fairness and cheating.
   - The day before a new student joins the class, a first-grade teacher discusses with the class how they would feel if they were new, how new students should be treated, and how they should treat each other in general.

2. Make and enforce rules requiring ethical treatment of each other.
   - A seventh-grade teacher has a classroom rule that students may not laugh, snicker, or make remarks of any kind when one of their classmates is trying to answer a question. In introducing the rule, she has the students discuss the reasons for it.
   - A second-grade teacher is explaining classroom rules at the beginning of the school year. One of them is "Respect other students' property." In the discussion, the teacher encourages students to think about the importance of the rule from other students' perspectives.

3. Model ethical behavior for students.
   - A science teacher makes a commitment to students to have all their tests and quizzes graded by the following day. One day, he is asked, "Do you have our tests ready?" "Of course," he responds. "I made an agreement, and people can't go back on their agreements."
   - A group of tenth graders finishes a field trip sooner than expected. "If we just hang around a little longer, we don't have to go back to school," someone comments. "Yes, but that would be a lie, wouldn't it?" the teacher counters. "We said we'd be back as soon as we finished."

Windows on Classrooms

As you've studied this chapter, you've seen how the characteristics of preschool and primary-age learners, elementary students, and adolescents affect the ways they feel about themselves and the way they learn. You've seen how an environment that combines structure with opportunities for autonomy and decision making and teachers who are sensitive to their students promote personal, social, and emotional development.

Let's look now at another teacher working with a group of middle school students. As you read the case study, compare the teacher's approach to the suggestions you've studied in the chapter.

"Gee, this is frustrating," Helen Sharman, a seventh-grade teacher, mumbled as she was scoring a set of quizzes in the teachers' workroom after school.

"What's up?" her friend Natasha asked.

"Look," Helen directed, pointing to Item 6 on the quiz that read:
"Theirs were the first items to be loaded."

"These students just won't think at all," Helen continued. "Three quarters of them put an apostrophe between the *r* and the *s* in *their*s. The

quiz was on using apostrophes in possessives. I warned them I was going to put some questions on the quiz that would make them think and that some of them would have trouble if they weren't on their toes. I should have saved my breath. . . . Not only that, but I had given them practice problems to work that were just like those on the quiz. We had one almost exactly like Number 6, and they still missed it. . . . And I explained it so carefully," she mumbled, shaking her head.

Helen returned to scoring her papers.

Hearing Helen mumble some more, Natasha asked, "Not getting any better?"

"No," Helen said firmly. "Maybe worse."

"What are you going to do?"

"What's really discouraging is that some of the students won't even try. Look at this one. Half of the quiz is blank. This isn't the first time Kim has done this either. When I confronted him about it last time, he said, 'But I'm no good at English.' I replied,

"But you're doing fine in science and math." He thought about that for a while and said, 'But, that's different.' I wish I knew how to motivate him. You should see him on the basketball floor—poetry in motion—but when he gets in here, nothing."

"That can be discouraging. I've got a few like that myself," Natasha replied empathetically.

"What's worse, I'm almost sure some of the students cheated. I left the room to go to the office, and when I returned, several of them were talking and had guilt written all over their faces."

"Why do you suppose they did it?" Natasha returned.

"I'm not sure; part of it might be grade pressure. I grade on the curve, and they complain like crazy, but how else am I going to motivate them? Some just don't see any problem with cheating. If they don't get caught, fine. I really am discouraged."

"Well," Natasha shrugged, "hang in there."

The next morning, Helen returned the quizzes.

"We need to review the rules again," she commented as she finished. "You did so poorly on the quiz, and I explained everything so carefully. You must not have studied very hard."

"Let's take another look," she went on. "What's the rule for singular possessives?"

" . . . Apostrophe s," Felice volunteered.

"That's right, Felice. Good. Now, how about plurals?"

"S apostrophe," Scott answered.

"All right. But what if the plural form of the noun doesn't end in s? . . . Russell?"

"Then it's like singular. . . . It's apostrophe s."

"Good. And how about pronouns?"

"You don't do anything," Connie put in.

"Yes, that's all correct," Helen nodded. "Why didn't you do that on the quiz?"

" . . . "

"Okay, look at Number 3 on the quiz."

It appeared as follows: *"The books belonging to the lady were lost."*

"It should be written like this," Helen explained, and she wrote "The lady's books were lost" on the chalkboard.

"Ms. Sharman," Nathan called from the back of the room. "Why is it apostrophe s?"

"Nathan," Helen said evenly. "Remember my first rule?"

"Yes, Ma'am," Nathan said quietly.

"Good. That's the second time today. If you speak without permission again, it's a half hour after school."

"Now, to answer your question, it's singular. So that's why it's apostrophe s.

"Now look at Number 6." Helen waited a few seconds and then continued, "You were supposed to correctly punctuate it. But it's correct already because *theirs* is already possessive. Now, that one was a little tricky, but you know I'm going to put a few on each quiz to make you think. You'd have gotten it if you were on your toes."

Helen identified three more items that were commonly missed. She then gave the students a review sheet for some additional practice.

"Now, these are just like the quiz," she said. "Practice hard on them, and we'll have another quiz on Thursday. Let's all do better. Please don't let me down again.

"And one more thing. I believe there was some cheating on this test. If I catch anyone cheating on Thursday, I'll tear up your quiz and give you a failing grade. Now, go to work."

The students then worked on the practice exercises as Helen walked among them, offering periodic suggestions.

Questions for Discussion and Analysis

Analyze Helen's lesson in the context of the information in this chapter. In doing your analysis, you may want to consider the following questions. In each case, be specific and take information directly from the case study in answering these questions.

1. How might Erikson explain Kim's behavior in Helen's class?
2. Using findings from the research on self-concept, explain Kim's behavior.
3. Using concepts from Kohlberg's theory, analyze Helen's cheating problem. From Kohlberg's perspective, how well did she handle this problem?
4. If you think Helen's teaching could have been improved on the basis of the information in Chapter 3, what suggestions would you make? Again, be specific.

 # Summary

Now go to our Companion Website to assess your understanding of chapter content with the Student Self-Assessment, apply comprehension in the Online Casebook, and broaden your knowledge base with links to important Educational Psychology World Wide Web sites.

Personal Development

Personal development is influenced by heredity, parents and other adults, and peers. Parents can positively influence development by providing a structured environment that is both demanding and responsive to children's affective needs. Peers influence development by providing opportunities for social skill development and by influencing the formation of values and attitudes.

Social Development

Social development influences children's ability to make and interact with friends and their ability to learn cooperatively in school. Perspective taking allows students to consider problems and issues from others' points of view. Social problem solving includes the ability to read social cues, generate strategies, and implement and evaluate these strategies.

Erikson's Theory of Personal and Social Development

Erikson's psychosocial theory, an effort to integrate personal and social development, is based on the assumption that development of self is a response to needs. This development occurs in stages, each marked by a psychosocial challenge called a crisis. As people develop, the challenges change.

  According to Erikson, positive resolution of the crisis in each stage results in an inclination to be trusting, autonomous, willing to take initiative, and industrious, from the period of birth through approximately the elementary school years. Continued resolution of crises leaves people with a firm identity, the ability to achieve intimacy, desire for generativity, and finally, a sense of integrity as life's end nears. As teachers work with students they should keep these developmental challenges in mind and structure their classrooms and interactions with students to facilitate growth in these areas.

The Development of Self-Concept

Self-concept, based largely on personal experiences, describes people's cognitive assessments of their physical, social, and academic competence. Academic self-concept, particularly in specific content areas, is correlated with achievement, but achievement and physical and social self-concepts are essentially unrelated.

  Attempts to improve students' self-concepts by direct intervention have been largely unsuccessful. In contrast, attempts to improve self-concept as an outcome of increased success and achievement have been quite successful. This suggests that when teachers direct their efforts toward improving students' effort and achievement, then self-concept will improve as well.

Development of Morality, Social Responsibility, and Self-Control

Piaget is identified with cognitive development, but he studied moral development as well. He suggests that individuals progress from the stage of external morality, where rules are enforced by authority figures, to the stage of autonomous morality, where individuals see morality as rational and reciprocal.

  Lawrence Kohlberg's theory of moral development was influenced by Piaget's work. Kohlberg presented people with moral dilemmas—problems requiring moral decisions—

and, on the basis of their responses to the dilemmas, developed a classification system for the description of moral reasoning. At the preconventional level people make egocentric moral decisions; at the conventional level moral reasoning focuses on the consequences for others; and at the postconventional level moral reasoning is based on principle. Kohlberg suggested that conventional reasoning requires concrete operational thinking and that postconventional reasoning requires formal operational thinking.

Character education advocates emphasize the study, practice, and reinforcement of moral values. In contrast, moral education proponents emphasize the development of moral reasoning and students' thinking about moral issues.

Teachers can promote moral development in their classrooms by emphasizing personal responsibility and the functional nature of rules designed to protect the rights of others. Students should be encouraged to think about topics such as honesty, respect for others, and basic principles of human conduct. As teachers interact with students, they should recognize the powerful influence they have in encouraging the moral development of their students.

 **Important Concepts**

academic self-concept
  (p. 100)

autonomous morality
  (p. 106)

autonomy (p. 92)

character education
  (p. 113)

collective self-esteem
  (p. 102)

crisis (p. 91)

external morality (p. 106)

generativity (p. 96)

identity (p. 94)

identity crisis (p. 94)

industry (p. 93)

initiative (p. 93)

integrity (p. 97)

internalization (p. 106)

interpersonal harmony
  stage (p. 109)

intimacy (p. 96)

law and order stage (p. 109)

market exchange stage
  (p. 108)

moral dilemma (p. 106)

moral education (p. 113)

personal development
  (p. 82)

perspective taking (p. 85)

psychosocial theory
  (p. 91)

punishment-obedience
  stage (p. 107)

self-concept (p. 99)

self-esteem (p. 99)

self-worth (p. 99)

social contract stage
  (p. 110)

social development
  (p. 85)

social problem solving
  (p. 86)

trust (p. 91)

universal principles stage
  (p. 110)

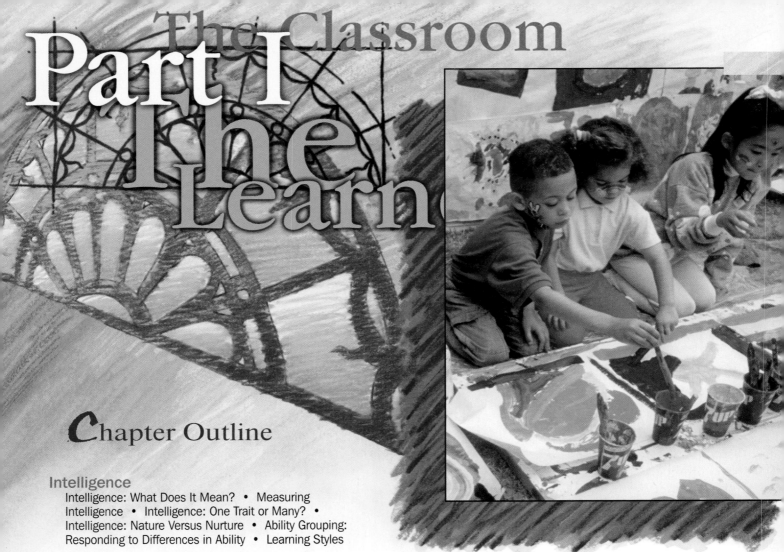

4

Learner Differences

Chapter Outline

Tim Wilkinson was a fifth-grade teacher in a large urban elementary school. He had 29 students: 16 girls and 13 boys. His group included 10 African Americans, 3 students of Hispanic descent, and 2 Asian Americans. Most of his students come from low-income families.

He smiled as he watched the students, bent over their desks, busy with seat work. As Tim walked among his students, he glanced at Selena's work. As usual, it was nearly perfect. Everything was easy for her, and she seemed to be a happy, well-adjusted child.

He smiled as he walked by Helen's desk. She was his "special project," and she had begun to blossom in response to his attention and effort. The quality of her work had improved dramatically since the beginning of the year.

As he stepped past Juan, Tim's glow turned to concern. Juan had been quiet from the first day of school, and he was easily offended by perceived slights from his classmates. Because his parents were migrant workers, the family moved constantly, and he had repeated the first grade. Now his parents were separated, and his mother had settled in this area so that the children could stay in the same school.

Juan had to struggle to keep up with the rest of the class. Spanish was his first language, and Tim wasn't sure how much of his instruction Juan understood. What seemed certain, however, was that Juan was falling farther and farther behind, and Tim didn't know what to do. Not knowing where else to turn, he consulted Jeanne Morton, the school psychologist.

After talking with Tim and meeting with Juan, Jeanne contacted Juan's mother and suggested several tests. One of these was an individually administered intelligence test. On the basis of the tests, Jeanne eliminated aptitude as a potential source of Juan's problem. "Juan is definitely capable of doing better work," she commented to Tim. They agreed to meet again to consider other alternatives.

When we enter our classrooms for the first time, a sea of faces appears before us. In some ways, our students seem very much alike; they are nearly the same age, they have similar interests, and they study common subjects. A closer look, however, reveals many differences. Almost certainly, we have both boys and girls in our classes, and their ethnic and cultural backgrounds differ. From your study of Chapters 2 and 3, you know that your students develop at different rates. Learning is nearly effortless for some; others struggle with even basic ideas. A few have affluent parents; others' parents barely eke out a living. Unfortunately, demographic combinations put some of our students at risk of not being able to fully benefit from the educational system.

Suddenly, our sea of faces turns into 30 individuals! In this chapter, we examine these differences and their implications for our teaching.

After you've completed your study of this chapter, you should be able to meet the following objectives:

▌ Explain how different views of intelligence influence your teaching.
▌ Define socioeconomic status, and explain how it may affect school performance.
▌ Explain the role culture plays in learning.
▌ Describe the influence of gender on different aspects of school success.
▌ Describe ways that schools and classrooms can be adapted to meet the needs of students placed at risk.

As you saw in the opening case, Tim's concerns for Juan are important. In a perfect world, all learning would be as easy as it is for Selena, and teaching would be a continuous pleasure. Teachers know, however, that students vary in ability and in other important ways. They truly are individuals, and teachers must keep this in mind when they make professional decisions. Figure 4.1 illustrates some of these sources of individuality.

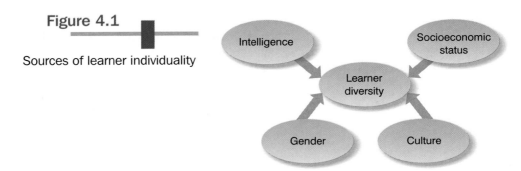

Figure 4.1

Sources of learner individuality

Intelligence

Everyone, including teachers, has an intuitive notion of intelligence; it's how "sharp" people are, or how much they know, how quickly and easily they learn, and how perceptive and sensitive they are. We react to people—and teachers respond to students—based on these intuitions, but how accurate are they? We try to answer this question in the next section.

Intelligence: What Does It Mean?

Many experts define **intelligence** as three dimensional: *(a) the capacity to acquire knowledge, (b) the ability to think and reason in the abstract, and (c) the capability for solving novel problems* (Snyderman & Rothman, 1987; Sternberg, 1986). The capacity to acquire knowledge is also called *aptitude*, and some learning theorists equate it with the time and quality of instruction students need to master a subject (Bloom, 1981; Carrol, 1963). In this view, learners with high aptitude need less time and instruction than those whose aptitude is lower. In seeing Juan falling farther and farther behind, Tim was intuitively reacting to this dimension.

From another perspective, intelligence is simply defined as the attributes that intelligence tests measure. Let's examine some of them.

Measuring Intelligence

Following are some items commonly found on intelligence tests:

1. Cave:Hole::Bag: _____ (Cave is to hole as bag is to _____ ?)
    a. paper   b. container   c. box   d. brown
2. Sharon had x amount of money, and this could buy eight apples. How much money would it take to buy four apples?
    a. $8x$ b. $2x$ c. $x/2$ d. xX
3. Inspect the following list of numbers for 5 seconds:
       9 7 4 6 2 1 8 3 9
    Now cover them and name the digits in order from memory.

Items like these have been used on standardized intelligence tests, and people's intelligence is inferred from their performance on such a test.

In looking at these items, one aspect of the tests is clear; experience is an important factor in test performance (Perkins, 1995). The first item, for example, requires both vocabulary and an understanding of analogies, and experience with analogies would certainly improve performance. The second item requires background in math, and even the third, a seemingly simple memory task, can be improved with experience and training (Brown, Bransford, Ferrara, & Campione, 1983).

The impact of experience on intelligence test performance corroborates Piaget's work. In Chapter 2, we saw that experience is an important factor in cognitive development, and children who have the advantage of rich experiences consistently perform better than their less-experienced peers. Clearly, intelligence tests measure more than innate ability.

Intelligence: One Trait or Many?

Because scores on different measures of intelligence, such as verbal ability and abstract reasoning, were highly correlated, early researchers believed intelligence to be a single trait. Charles Spearman (1927), an early intelligence researcher, described it as "g," or general intelligence. Since then the concept has been expanded, and more specific kinds of intelligence, such as verbal, mathematical, spatial, and perceptual, have been proposed (Jensen, 1987). Contemporary researchers have further extended the idea that intelligence is composed of several abilities (Woodcock, 1995). We look at three of them:

- Guilford's structure of intellect
- Gardner's multiple intelligences
- Sternberg's triarchic theory of intelligence

Guilford's Structure of Intellect

J. P. Guilford (1967) believed that intelligence depends on what people think about *(content)*, their *mental operations*, and the *products* of these operations. He developed a *structure of intellect (SOI)* model that describes intelligence as the intersection of four content areas, five mental operations, and six products. For example, remembering a telephone number requires a memory operation in a symbolic content area to produce a single product—the number (Perkins, 1995).

When analyzed using the Guilford model, school curricula disproportionately emphasize limited aspects of intelligence, such as memorizing facts, while virtually ignoring others, such as searching for relationships (Goodlad, 1984). Proposed changes in curricula, particularly in math and science, are attempting to address this imbalance by increasing the emphasis on problem solving and processes such as hypothesizing and analyzing (American Association for the Advancement of Science [AAAS], 1993; National Council of Teachers of Mathematics [NCTM], 1991). We discuss these changes in Chapter 9.

Guilford's pioneering work is valuable because it encouraged researchers and educators to broaden their concept of intelligence, but the complexity of the model makes it difficult to apply in classrooms.

Gardner's Theory of Multiple Intelligences

Influenced by Guilford's original work, Howard Gardner (1983, 1999b) describes a theory of multiple intelligences (MI) that has eight relatively independent dimensions of intelligence and makes a persuasive argument for the idea of multiple talents.

Gardner originally described seven intelligences but later expanded his theory to include an eighth, called "naturalist intelligence," which is the ability to recognize patterns

4.1
How does experience influence a person's aptitude, or "capacity to acquire knowledge"? Explain your answer with a specific example.

4.2
Describe an important implication that Guilford's model would have for intelligence testing.

Table 4.1

Gardner's theory of multiple intelligences

Dimension	Example
Linguistic intelligence: Sensitivity to the meaning and order of words and the varied uses of language	Poet, journalist
Logical-mathematical intelligence: The ability to handle long chains of reasoning and to recognize patterns and order in the world	Scientist, mathematician
Musical intelligence: Sensitivity to pitch, melody, and tone	Composer, violinist
Spatial intelligence: The ability to perceive the visual world accurately, and to re-create, transform, or modify aspects of the world on the basis of one's perceptions	Sculptor, navigator
Bodily-kinesthetic intelligence: A fine-tuned ability to use the body and to handle objects	Dancer, athlete
Interpersonal intelligence: The ability to notice and make distinctions among others	Therapist, salesperson
Intrapersonal intelligence: Access to one's own "feeling life"	Self-aware individual
Naturalist Intelligence: The ability to recognize similarities and differences in the physical world	Naturalist, biologist, anthropologist

Source: Adapted from H. Gardner and Hatch (1989) and Chekley, 1997.

in nature, identify and classify plants, animals, and minerals, and use this information in applied activities such as farming or landscaping. He is also considering a ninth dimension, existential intelligence, reflecting a person's ability to think about fundamental questions about life such as "Who are we?" and "Where do we come from?" (Gardner, 1999c). Table 4.1 outlines these eight dimensions.

Gardner's Theory: Educational Applications.   Gardner's argument for multiple intelligences derives from three sources (Krechevsky & Seidel, 1998). The first is research on people with brain damage, which suggests that neural functioning is specific to a single domain, such as speech or aesthetic ability. The second is the variety of skills found in modern society. For example, many people are not high in verbal or logical dimensions but excel in others, such as spatial ability (artists and architects) and interpersonal skills (effective counselors and empathetic teachers). A third is the existence of prodigies, savants, and other people who are exceptionally talented in specific domains.

The concept of multiple intelligences makes sense. For example, we all know people who don't seem particularly "sharp" analytically but who excel in getting along with others. This ability serves them well, and in some instances, they're more successful than

---

4.3 ▬

On which of Gardner's eight intelligences does the typical school curriculum focus most strongly? On which report card—an elementary or a secondary—are more of the intelligences evaluated? Why is this the case?

Spatial intelligence includes the ability to perceive and re-create physical relations in the world.

Bodily-kinesthetic intelligence allows dancers and athletes to use their bodies in effective and creative ways.

their "brighter" counterparts. Others seem very self-aware and can capitalize on their strengths and minimize their weaknesses. According to Gardner's theory, these people are high in interpersonal and intrapersonal intelligence, respectively.

The idea of representing content in different ways is central to MI theory, and Gardner (1999a) has identified six: *narration, logical analysis, hands-on experience, artistic exploration, philosophical examination,* and *participatory experience.* For example, students studying the theory of evolution could employ any or all of the following:

- Read about Darwin's voyage on the Beagle (narration)
- Analyze the results of genetic crosses of dominant and recessive genes (logical analysis)
- Breed peas or fruit flies to investigate the role of dominant and recessive genes (hands-on experience)
- Present the results of these experiments in interesting and compelling ways (artistic exploration)
- Address fundamental questions, such as what evolution suggests about the past history and future of the human race (philosophical examination)
- Work together on a project where students assume different roles (participatory experience)

These avenues address different students' strengths and provide various paths for making meaningful connections in memory. (We examine memory processes in Chapter 7.)

Table 4.2 presents additional applications of Gardner's theory. He warns, however, that not all ideas or subjects can be approached with each intelligence. "There is no point in assuming that every topic can be effectively approached in [multiple] ways, and it is a waste of effort and time to attempt to do this" (Gardner, 1995b, p. 206). In addition, other researchers caution that Gardner's theory and its applications, while intuitively sensible, still need to be validated by research (Berk, 1997).

Table 4.2

Instructional applications of Gardner's multiple intelligences

Dimension	Application
Linguistic	How can I get students to talk or write about the idea?
Logical/Mathematical	How can I bring in number, logic, and classification to encourage students to quantify or clarify the idea?
Spatial	What can I do to help students visualize, draw, or conceptualize the idea spatially?
Musical	How can I help students use environmental sounds, or set ideas into rhythm or melody?
Bodily Kinesthetic	What can I do to help students involve the whole body or to use hands-on experience?
Interpersonal	How can peer, cross-age, or cooperative learning be used to help students develop their interactive skills?
Intrapersonal	How can I get students to think about their capacities and feelings to make them more aware of themselves as persons and learners?
Naturalist	How can I provide experiences that require students to classify different types of objects and analyze their classification schemes?

Sternberg's Triarchic Theory of Intelligence

Robert Sternberg (1988, 1990), another multitrait theorist, views intelligence as consisting of three parts: (a) processing components—skills used in problem solving—(b) contextual components—links between intelligence and the environment—and (c) experiential components—mechanisms for modifying intelligence through experience. These components and their features are illustrated in Figure 4.2 and discussed next.

Processing Components.   The most basic parts of Sternberg's model are the processing components that learners use to solve problems: a *metacomponent,* a *knowledge acquisition component,* and a *performance component.* Sternberg describes them as analogous to management, trainees, and labor in a company (Sternberg, 1988). For example, suppose a student is faced with the problem of writing a term paper. Metacomponents (management) decide on a topic, plan the paper, and monitor progress as it's written. Knowledge acquisition components (trainees) gather facts and combine them into related ideas, and performance components (labor) do the actual writing. The three work together to produce a final product.

Contextual Components: Intelligence and the Environment.   Contextual components explain how intelligence affects the way we operate in the everyday world. To reach goals, intelligent people adapt to the environment, change it, or select out of it when necessary. For example, in an attempt to succeed in a college course, a student adjusts her study strategies in response to a professor's testing procedures (adapts). She can't clearly hear

4.4
Illustrate the three processing components with an example such as buying a car.

Figure 4.2

Sternberg's triarchic model of intelligence

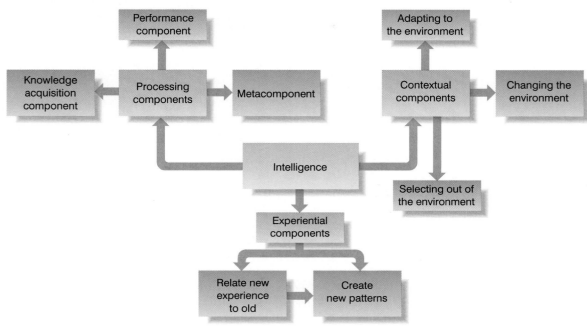

Source: Sternberg (1988, 1990)

his presentations, so she moves to the front of the class (changes the environment). Despite these efforts, she isn't succeeding, so she drops the class (selects out of the environment). In each case, the student is sensitive to the effect that environment is having on her learning. Contextual components help us apply our intelligences to the solution of everyday problems.

Experiential Components: Modifying Intelligence Through Experience.   The third aspect of Sternberg's (1988, 1990) theory relates intelligence to experience. In Sternberg's view, intelligent behavior includes (a) the ability to effectively deal with novel experiences and (b) the ability to solve problems efficiently and automatically. An intelligent person relates new experiences to old and forms patterns that can be used automatically and efficiently. For example:

> A beginning reader encountered the word *she*. The teacher said, "Shheee."
>
> Then the reader encountered the word *show*. The teacher said, "This word sounds like 'Shho.'"
>
> Next, the student saw the word *ship*. He tried pronouncing it himself: "Shhip." He now had a rule to decode future words. When *s* and *h* are together, they go "shh."

According to Sternberg, an intelligent child recognizes patterns quickly and soon can use rules automatically. The ability to analyze data and find patterns increases with age and makes older children more efficient problem solvers. This ability to process information efficiently is a cornerstone of increased intellectual functioning (Sternberg, 1998a, 1998b).

4.5
Consider Sternberg's strategies for dealing with the environment—adapting to it, changing it, and selecting out of it. Which do schools emphasize the most? Which *should* they emphasize most? least?

4.6
Identify at least two ways in which Sternberg's and Piaget's theories are similar. Identify an important implication that these similarities have for schools.

Intelligence can be enhanced by learning activities that emphasize abstract reasoning and problem solving.

Analytic, Creative, and Practical Intelligence.   In more recent work, Sternberg emphasizes three types of intelligence: *analytic*, which involves comparing, contrasting, critiquing, judging, and evaluating; *creative*, including inventing, discovering, imagining, and supposing; and *practical,* which involves implementing, applying, using, and seeking relevance (Sternberg, 1998a, 1998b; Sternberg, Torff, & Grigorenko, 1998a, 1998b). These abilities allow students to process information in different ways and capitalize on individual strengths (Sternberg et al., 1998a, 1998b). Applications of these types of intelligence are shown in Table 4.3 (Sternberg, 1998a, 1998b).

Sternberg claims that research supports the application of his theory in classrooms. In two studies involving third and eighth graders, instruction based on the three types of intelligence was more effective than both traditional, memory-based, and critical thinking approaches (Sternberg, 1998a). He attributes these results to students learning material in more than one way, enabling them to capitalize on their strengths and to compensate for their weaknesses (Sternberg et al., 1998b).

Improving Intelligence.   According to Sternberg, intelligence consists of subcomponents that can be improved, and students should be given experiences that require them to relate new to existing ideas (Sternberg, 1998a). For example, if the ability to solve analogies is an indicator of intelligence (and measurable on intelligence tests), then it should be possible to improve intelligence and intelligence test performance by giving students experience with analogies. This issue—the extent to which intelligence can be modified—is the focal point of the next section.

Intelligence: Nature Versus Nurture

No aspect of intelligence has been more hotly debated than the issue of heredity versus environment. The extreme **nature view of intelligence** asserts that *intelligence is solely determined by genetics;* the **nurture view of intelligence** emphasizes *the influence of the environment.* Differences between these positions are very controversial when race or ethnicity are considered. For example, research indicates that some cultural minority groups collectively score lower on intelligence tests than American white children (McLoyd, 1998). People who emphasize the nurture view explain this finding by arguing that minority children have fewer stimulating experiences while they are developing.

4.7
Identify at least one similarity and one difference between Sternberg's analytic, creative, and practical intelligence and Gardner's multiple intelligences.

Table 4.3

Applying analytic, creative, and practical thinking in different content areas

Content Area	Analytic	Creative	Practical
Math	Express the number 44 in base 2.	Write a test question that measures understanding of the Pythagorean theorem.	How might geometry be useful in the construction area?
Language Arts	Why is *Romeo and Juliet* considered a tragedy?	Write an alternative ending to *Romeo and Juliet* to make it a comedy.	Write a TV ad for the school's production of *Romeo and Juliet*.
Social Studies	In what ways were the Korean War and the Vietnam War similar and different?	In hindsight, what could the United States have done differently in these two wars?	What lessons can we take away from these two wars?
Art	Compare and contrast the artistic style of Van Gogh and Monet.	What would the Statue of Liberty look like if it were created by Picasso?	Create a poster for the student art show using the style of one of the artists studied.

People adhering to the nature view argue that heredity is the more important factor. In the highly controversial book, *The Bell Curve*, Hernnstein and Murray (1994) concluded that the contribution of heredity outweighed environmental factors in minority populations, especially African Americans. Methodological problems, such as inferring causation from correlational data, caused other researchers to reject this position (Jacoby & Glauberman, 1995; Marks, 1995).

Most experts take a position somewhere in the middle, believing that a person's intelligence is influenced by both heredity and the environment (Weinberg, 1989; Yee, 1995). In this view, a person's genes provide the potential for intelligence, and stimulating environments make the most of the raw material.

Unfortunately, the opposite is also true; most learning environments do not provide enough stimulation to allow people to reach their full potential (Ceci, 1990). For example, researchers tracked children born of low-income parents but adopted as infants into high-income families. The enriched environments resulted in children who scored an average of 14 points higher on intelligence tests than did their comparable siblings (Schiff, Duyme, Dumaret, & Tomkiewicz, 1982). School experiences also produce consistent gains on intelligence test scores (Ceci & Williams, 1997).

Intelligence also changes over time. One review found IQ changes of 28 points from early childhood to adolescence; one seventh of the students had changes of more than 40 points (McCall, Appelbaum, & Hogarty, 1973). Although some testing error is likely, in many cases intelligence itself was probably altered because of changes in an individual's environment and others' expectations (Perkins, 1995).

Efforts to improve intelligence have also been fruitful. Attempts to directly teach the cognitive skills tapped by intelligence tests have been successful with preschool and elementary students (Sprigle & Schoefer, 1985), adults (Whimbey, 1980), and students with learning disabilities (A. Brown & Campione, 1986). A longitudinal study of disadvantaged, inner-city children also indicated that early stimulation can have lasting effects on IQ (Garber, 1988).

4.8
Describe specifically what kinds of experiences children—and particularly disadvantaged children— need to increase their scores on intelligence tests.

Ability Grouping: Responding to Differences in Ability

Although other adaptations exist (we discuss them in detail in Chapter 5), the most common way schools have responded to differences in learner ability is by **ability grouping**, which *places students of similar abilities together and attempts to match instruction to the needs of different groups.* Because ability grouping is so common, yet controversial and politically charged, we examine it in this section.

Types of Ability Grouping

Ability grouping in elementary schools is popular, and it typically exists in three forms, described and illustrated in Table 4.4. Many teachers of elementary students endorse ability grouping, particularly in reading and math.

In middle, junior high, and high schools, ability grouping goes further, with high-ability students studying advanced and college preparatory courses and their low-ability counterparts receiving vocational or work-related instruction. In some cases, students are grouped only in certain areas, such as English or math; in other cases, it exists across all content areas—a practice called **tracking**, which *places students in different classes or curricula on the basis of ability.* Some form of tracking exists in most middle, junior high, and high schools (Braddock, 1990), and tracking has its most negative effects on minorities in the lower tracks (Davenport et al., 1998; Mickelson & Heath, 1999).

Ability Grouping: Research Results

Why is ability grouping so pervasive? Advocates argue that it enhances instruction by allowing teachers to adjust the rate, methods, and materials to better meet students' needs. Because pace and assessments are similar for a particular group, instruction is easier for the teacher.

Table 4.4

Types of ability grouping in elementary schools

Type	Description	Example
Between-class grouping	Divides students at a certain grade into levels, such as high, average, and low	A school with 75 third graders divides them into one class of high achievers, one of average, and one of low.
Within-class grouping	Divides students in a class into subgroups based on reading or math scores	A fourth-grade teacher has three reading groups based on reading ability.
Joplin plan	Regroups across grade levels	Teachers from different grade levels place students in the same reading class.

Critics counter these arguments and cite several problems with all forms of ability grouping. Some of these follow:

4.9
Explain how being placed in a low-ability group might adversely affect students' self-esteem and motivation.

- Within-class grouping creates logistical problems, because different lessons and assignments are required, and monitoring students in different tasks is difficult (Good & Brophy, 1997; Oakes, 1992).
- Improper placements occur, and placement tends to become permanent. Cultural minorities are underrepresented in high-ability classes (Grant & Rothenberg, 1986; Oakes, 1992).
- Low groups are stigmatized. The self-esteem and motivation of low groups suffer (Hallinan, 1984).
- Homogeneously grouped low-ability students achieve less than heterogeneously grouped students of similar ability (Good & Brophy, 1997).

Negative Effects of Grouping: Possible Explanations

Negative effects of grouping are related, in part, to the quality of instruction. Presentations to low groups are more fragmented and vague than those to high groups; they focus more on memorizing than on understanding, problem solving, and "active learning." Students in low-ability classes are often taught by teachers who lack enthusiasm and stress conformity versus autonomy and the development of self-regulation (Good & Brophy, 1997; Ross, Smith, Loks, & McNelie, 1994).

Grouping also affects the students themselves. In addition to lowered self-esteem and motivation to learn, absentee rates tend to increase. One study found that absenteeism increased from 8% to 26% after transition to a tracked junior high (Slavin & Karweit, 1982), and most of the truants were students in the low-level classes. Tracking can also result in racial or cultural segregation of students, making social development and the ability to form friendships across cultural groups difficult (Oakes, 1992).

Grouping: Implications for Teachers

Suggestions for dealing with the problems of grouping vary. At one extreme, critics argue that the negative effects of grouping are so pernicious that the practice should be abolished completely.

> We suggest . . . that there is a fundamental conflict between the practice of ability grouping and public schools' avowed goal of providing equal opportunity to all students. More equitable alternatives must be sought, even if they involve major changes in classroom organization. (Grant & Rothenberg, 1986, p. 47)

A more moderate position suggests that grouping may be appropriate in some areas, such as reading and math, where learning is more hierarchical and sequential (Good & Brophy, 1997), but that every effort should be made to deemphasize groups in other content areas. Researchers have found that use of the **Joplin plan**, which *uses homogeneous grouping in reading, combined with heterogeneous grouping in other areas,* can have positive effects on reading achievement without negative side effects (Slavin, 1987). At the junior and senior high levels, between-class grouping should be limited to the basic academic areas, with heterogeneous grouping in others.

When grouping is necessary, specific measures to reduce its negative effects should be taken. Summaries of some suggestions are presented in Figure 4.3. These suggestions are demanding; teachers must constantly monitor both the cognitive and affective progress of their students and make careful decisions about group placements. The need

Figure 4.3

Suggestions for reducing the negative effects of grouping

1. Keep group composition flexible, and reassign students to other groups when their rate of learning warrants it.
2. Make every effort to ensure that the quality of instruction is as high for low-ability students as it is for high-ability students.
3. Treat student characteristics as dynamic rather than static; teach low-ability students appropriate learning strategies and behaviors.
4. Avoid assigning negative labels to lower groups.
5. Constantly be aware of the possible negative consequences of ability grouping.

to maintain high expectations and instructional flexibility in this process cannot be overemphasized (Bixby, 1997).

Efforts to reverse the negative effects of tracking have been positive but require instructional adaptations within classrooms (Nyberg et al, 1997; Tomlinson, Callahan, & Moon, 1998). When teaching students whose backgrounds vary, effective teachers adapt their instruction in a number of ways, including the following:

- Give students who need it more time to complete assignments.
- Provide peer tutors for students requiring extra help.
- Use small group work.
- Provide options on some assignments, such as giving students the choice of presenting a report orally or in writing.
- Break large assignments into smaller ones, and provide additional scaffolding and support for those who need it.

Effective teachers need to adapt instruction to meet the needs of all students, and this need is especially acute at the upper and lower extremes of the ability continuum (Tomlinson, 1995; Tomlinson et al., 1998).

Classroom Connections

Applying an Understanding of Ability Differences in Your Classroom

1. Remember that intelligence test scores are just one indicator of school ability.
   - In deciding whether to place a student in a special education class, a team of teachers and the guidance counselor consider grades, work samples, and teacher observations, in addition to intelligence test scores.

2. Be cautious when using intelligence test scores to make educational decisions about cultural minorities.
   - A first-grade teacher working in an inner-city school consults with the school psychologist in interpreting intelligence test scores. She reminds herself of the effect that language and experience can have on test performance.

3. Use instructional strategies that minimize narrow definitions of aptitude and maximize student interest and effort.
   • A math teacher allows students two opportunities to pass his quizzes. When they need extra help, he uses peer tutoring and special small-group work as additional aids.
   • An English teacher makes two types of assignments: required and optional. Seventy percent of the assignments are required for everyone; the other 30% provide students with choices, and the students negotiate with the teacher on the specific assignments.

4. Consider the implications of MI for teaching and learning.
   • In a unit on the Revolutionary War, a teacher has all students take a test on basic information but bases 25% of the unit grade on special projects. Groups of students research topics such as the music and art of the times and present their information to the class on poster boards, in videotape and audiotape recordings, or in replicas of battle sites.

Using Grouping Appropriately in Classrooms

5. View group composition as flexible, and reassign students to other groups when warranted by their learning progress.
   • A team of four first-grade teachers meets at the end of each grading period to reexamine groups and to move students when appropriate.

6. Use heterogeneous grouping whenever possible.
   • A second-grade teacher uses different ability groups in his reading instruction but uses whole-class instruction when he does units on poetry and American folktales.

7. When using ability groups, make every effort to ensure that the quality of instruction is the same for each ability level.
   • A teacher has a colleague observe and monitor her questioning strategies during a series of language arts lessons. She asks the colleague to record her questions and to whom they're addressed to ensure that each ability group receives the same amount of active teaching and appropriate mix of high- and low-level questions.

Learning Styles

One thing Nate Crowder remembered from his teacher preparation experience was that variety is important in promoting learning and motivation. In social studies, he tended to mostly use large-group discussions because many of the students seemed to respond well. Others, however, appeared disinterested, and their attention often wandered.

In an effort to involve all his students, he decided to try some small-group work focusing on problem solving. This fit nicely in a unit on cities and the problems they face.

He organized the groups and assigned each a problem. As he watched the group members interact, he was struck by the fact that some of the quietest, most withdrawn students in whole-class discussions were leaders in the small groups.

"Great!" he thought. But at the same time, he saw that some of his typically more active students were sitting back, uninvolved.

Historically, psychologists have used intelligence tests to measure mental abilities, and concepts such as *introvert* and *extrovert* to describe different personality types. Researchers who think about the interface between the two areas study **learning styles**, *students' approaches to learning, problem solving, and processing information* (Snow, Corno, & Jackson, 1996). Some researchers distinguish between the concepts *learning style* and *cognitive style* (Beaty, 1995), whereas others do not (Snow et al., 1996).

4.10 ■

What are the most likely causes of differences in learning style? Are the causes similar or different from the causes of differences in intelligence? Explain.

One of the most common descriptions of learning style distinguishes between deep and surface approaches to processing information in learning situations (Snow et al., 1996). Students who use deep processing approaches view the information they're studying, or the problem they're attempting to solve, as a means to understanding the content; they attempt to link the information to a larger conceptual framework. Those who use a surface approach view the information itself as the content to be learned without attempting to link it to bigger ideas. For instance, as you studied the concept of *centration* in Chapter 2, did you note that it is part of Piaget's theory and relate it to other concepts, such as *egocentricity, conservation*, and *preoperational thinking?* Did you also relate it to the fact that adults often *center* in spite of the fact that it's associated with the thinking of young children? If so, you were using a deep processing approach. On the other hand, if you memorized the definition and identified one or two examples of centering, you were using a surface approach.

As you might expect, deep processing approaches result in higher achievement if tests focus on understanding, but surface approaches can be successful if tests tend to emphasize fact learning and memorization. Deep approaches have also been linked to learning goals, intrinsic motivation—engaging in a learning activity for its own sake—and self-regulated learning. Surface approaches are associated with performance goals and extrinsic motivation—engaging in an activity as a means to an end (Pintrich & Schrauben, 1992; Snow et al., 1996). (We examine goals and intrinsic and extrinsic motivation in detail in Chapter 10.)

Learning Preferences: Research Results

The concept *learning style* is widely used, and many inservice workshops for teachers have been designed around it. However, while the term *learning style* is often used, the focus typically differs from the way we described it in the last section. In these workshops, the term *preferences* is probably more accurate, because they tend to focus on environmental factors such as room lighting, whether or not music is playing, and where and with whom students want to sit. Workshop leaders then emphasize matching classroom environments to students' preferences.

Research on the effectiveness of this matching is mixed. Some claim the match results in increased achievement and improved attitudes (Carbo, 1997; Dunn & Griggs, 1995). However, the validity of the tests used to measure learning styles (preferences) has been questioned (Snider, 1990; Stahl, 1999), and additional research has found that attempts to match learning environments to learning preferences have resulted in no increases, and in some cases, even decreases in learning (Curry, 1990; Knight, Halpen, & Halpen, 1992; Snow, 1992; Stahl, 1999). In comparing learning preference results to those found in studies of careful curricular alignment—congruence between goals, instruction, and assessment—researchers found no effects due to learning style alone (S. Cohen, Human, Ashcroft, & Loveless, 1989). In other words, increases in learning came from instruction and assessments that are matched to goals, not from pairing the learning environment to learning preferences.

Learning Styles: Implications for Teachers

Unquestionably, students come to us with different preferences and different ways of attacking learning tasks. The key question is, "What should we as teachers do in response to these differences?" and perhaps more realistically, "What *can* we do about these differences?"

We believe the concept of learning style has at least three implications for us as teachers. First, learning styles remind us that we need to vary our instruction, and this need is corroborated by research (Shuell, 1996). Alternatives such as individual projects, small-group discussions, cooperative learning, and learning centers provide flexibility in meeting individual differences.

Second, the concept of learning style reminds us of the need to help students become aware of the ways they most effectively learn. (*Metacognition* is the concept that describes learners' awareness of and control over their thinking and learning. We examine metacognition in depth in Chapter 7.) We also saw earlier that Sternberg (1998a) links learner self-awareness to intelligent behavior.

Third, the concept of learning style reminds us that our students are different and increases our sensitivity to those differences. With increased sensitivity, we are more likely to respond to our students as individuals. The classroom becomes a model of tolerance, and classroom climate improves.

A sensible compromise in thinking about learning styles is offered by Snider (1990).

> People are different, and it is good practice to recognize and accommodate individual differences. It is also good practice to present information in a variety of ways through more than one modality, but it is not wise to categorize learners and prescribe methods solely on the basis of tests with questionable technical qualities. . . . The idea of learning style is appealing, but a critical examination of this approach should cause educators to be skeptical. (p. 153)

Socioeconomic Status

One of the most powerful factors related to school performance is **socioeconomic status (SES)**, *the combination of parents' incomes, occupations, and levels of education* (see Figure 4.4). SES consistently predicts intelligence and achievement test scores, grades, truancy, and dropout and suspension rates (Macionis, 1997). For example, dropout rates for students from the poorest families in our country exceed 50%, and, when compared with students whose families are in the highest income quartile, students in the lowest quartile are 2½ times less likely to enroll in college and 8 times less likely to graduate (Levine & Nediffer, 1996; Young & Smith, 1999). The pervasive influence of SES on learning is attested to by the following conclusion reached in a review of this area, "the relationship between test scores and SES is one of the most widely replicated findings in the social sciences" (Konstantopoulas, 1997, p. 5).

Why is SES important to teachers? Consider the following statistics:

Figure 4.4

Sources of learner individuality:
Socioeconomic status

▌ Between 1979 and 1997, the number of children under age 6 living in poverty increased from 3.5 million to 5.2 million.

▌ In 1995, the poverty rate for children was 20%, but varied considerably for different populations in the United States; for African Americans it was 42%, for Hispanics 39%, for Whites 16%.

▌ The proportion of children living in single-parent homes has more than doubled since 1970, averaging 25% for all families, with much higher rates for African American (60%) and Hispanic families (29%).

Parents promote both cognitive and language development by discussing ideas and experiences with their children.

 ▌ Children under age 6 living with a single mother were 5 times more likely to be poor than those living with both parents (56% compared to 11%).
 ▌ The poverty rate for parents with less than a high school education was 62.5% (National Center for Children in Poverty, 1999; Young & Smith, 1999).

Influence of SES on Learning

In what ways does SES influence learning, and what are the mechanisms behind these influences? Researchers have identified three areas in which SES plays a role in learning: (a) basic needs and experiences, (b) parental involvement, and (c) attitudes and values. We examine them in the following sections.

Basic Needs and Experiences

The first influence SES has on learning is in the area of basic needs. Some families lack adequate medical care, and children may come to school without proper nourishment (L. Miller, 1995). In addition, homelessness is a major problem; experts estimate that families now account for almost 40% of all homeless, and that the number of homeless children is higher than any time since the Great Depression (Homes for Homeless, 1999).

Economic problems can lead to family and marital conflicts, which result in less stable and nurturant homes (McLoyd, 1998). Children of poverty may come to school without a sense of safety and security, so they are less equipped to tackle school-related tasks.

Children of poverty also move more than their peers. For example, researchers examining student mobility in one urban school system found that only 38% of sixth graders attended the same school throughout their elementary years, and the average elementary school in the system had a 50% turnover rate every 3 years (Kerbow, 1996). These frequent moves are a source of stress for students and a problem for teachers attempting to create nurturant, caring relationships with them (Fisher & Mathews, 1999; Nakagawa, 1999).

SES also influences children's background experiences (McLoyd, 1998; Trawick-Smith, 1997). High-SES parents are more likely to provide their children with educational activities outside school, like visits to art and science museums, concerts, and travel. They also have more learning materials in the home, such as computers, encyclopedias, and news magazines, and they provide more formal training outside of school, such as music and dance lessons. These activities complement classroom learning by providing an experiential base for school activities (Peng & Lee, 1992). Some researchers call these experiences "cultural capital" that forms a foundation for the concepts young children bring to school (Ballantine, 1989). In studying Piaget's work in Chapter 2, we saw that experience is essential for intellectual development. Bloom (1981) estimated that 80% of human potential intelligence is developed by age 8; this high percentage underscores the importance of early, family-based experiences.

> 4.11 ◼
> Look ahead in your text to Chapter 10, where Maslow's hierarchy of needs is described. Read this section and then explain, on the basis of Maslow's work, why children of poverty might be ill-equipped for learning.

Involvement in Their Children's Lives

SES also influences learning through parental involvement in their children's activities and parent–child interaction patterns (Hess & McDevitt, 1984). High-SES parents tend to be more involved in their children's extracurricular activities, which provides a focal point for parent–child interactions (Peng & Lee, 1992). One mother commented, "When she sees me at her games, when she sees me going to open house, when I attend her Interscholastic League contests, she knows I am interested in her activities. Plus, we have more to talk about" (Young & Scribner, 1997, p. 12).

In general, high-SES parents talk to their children more and differently than do low-SES parents. High-SES parents explain the causes of events and provide reasons for rules, their language is more elaborate, their directions are clearer, and they are more likely to encourage problem solving. In addition, high-SES parents are more likely to ask *"wh"* questions (*who, what, when, where,* and *why*), which promote language development and prepare their children for the kind of verbal interaction found in schools. Sometimes called "the curriculum of the home," these rich interaction patterns, together with the experiences described in the last section, provide a foundation for reading and vocabulary development (Walberg, 1991).

Attitudes and Values

The impact of SES is also transmitted through parental attitudes and values. For example, high-SES parents value and emphasize autonomy, individual responsibility, and self-control; low-SES parents place greater emphasis on conformity and obedience (Ballantine, 1989).

Values are also communicated by example. For instance, adults who have books, newspapers, and magazines around the home and who read themselves communicate that reading and learning are important. As a result, their children are more likely to read, and students who read at home show higher reading achievement than those who don't (M. Adams, 1990).

High-SES parents are also better at playing the "schooling game," being more likely to monitor their children's learning progress and to contact schools for information (Marks, 1995). For example, researchers documented the ways that high-SES parents "managed" the system, "steering" their sons and daughters into advanced high school courses (D. Baker & Stevenson, 1986), which reflects their expectations. They tend to have high expectations for their children, and children who are expected to graduate from high school and attend college achieve much more than children of parents with lower aspirations (Trusty & Pirtle, 1998).

4.12   ▬

Of the three characteristics of SES—*occupation, income,* and *level of edu-cation*—researchers have found the last to be most influential in school perfor-mance. Explain why this is the case.

Low-SES parents tend to have lower aspirations, allowing their children to "drift" into classes, and relying on the decisions of others. Students can get lost in the shuffle, ending up in inappropriate or less challenging classes and tracks.

SES: Some Cautions and Implications for Teachers

As with all sources of diversity, the research we've cited is in the form of generalizations, which means many exceptions to the patterns exist. Obviously, for example, many low SES parents read to their children, talk to them, encourage their involvement in extracurricular activities, and attend school events. They take their children to museums and zoos and have high expectations for their learning. None of these factors is restricted to high-SES parents. In fact, both of your authors come from low-SES families.

Remembering that many low-income families provide both a rich learning environ-ment and a strong system of parental support can help prevent inappropriately lowered expectations for students from low-income families. Teachers can tap into and use this sys-tem to promote learning for these children.

Work with minority populations documents the untapped potential of family and home resources (Halle, Kurtze-Costes, & Mahoney, 1997). Researchers found "funds of knowledge," informal networks of information that low-SES, minority families can access. For example, fathers who work in construction have knowledge and skills about different ways that math can be applied in the real world (Moll, 1992). Teachers can use these funds of knowledge to make connections with students' homes and help students use and develop pride in the family and community resources available to them.

Teachers can also support learning for all students by providing safe and structured learning environments, using high-quality examples and representations, relating content to students' lives, and promoting high levels of interaction in learning activities. These are effective for all students; for those from low-SES backgrounds, they're essential.

Culture

Think about the way you dress, the music you like, the foods you eat, how you spend time with your friends, and what you do for recreation. These and other factors, such as reli-gion, family structure, and values, are all part of your culture.

Culture refers to *the attitudes, values, customs, and behavior patterns that charac-terize a social group* (Banks, 1997). Its enormous impact on even the most basic aspects of our lives is illustrated by its influence on our eating habits.

4.13   ▬

Think back to your study of development in Chapter 2. Which theorist—Piaget or Vygotsky—places more emphasis on culture? Explain.

> Culture not only helps to determine what foods we eat, but it also influences when we eat (for example, one, three, or five meals and at what time of the day); with whom we eat (that is, only with the same sex, with children or with the extended family); how we eat (for example, at a table or on the floor; with chopsticks, silverware, or the fingers); and the ritual of eating (for example, in which hand the fork is held, asking for or being offered seconds, and belching to show appreciation of a good meal). These eating pat-terns are habits of the culture. (Gollnick & Chinn, 1986, pp. 6–7)

Like SES, culture influences school success through the attitudes, values, and ways of view-ing the world that are held and transmitted by it (see Figure 4.5).

Figure 4.5

Sources of learner individuality: Culture

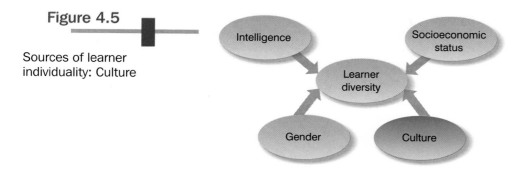

Ethnicity

An important part of culture is a person's ethnic background. **Ethnicity** refers to *a person's ancestry; the way individuals identify themselves with the nation from which they or their ancestors came* (deMarrais & LeCompte, 1999). Members of an ethnic group have a common history, language (although sometimes not spoken), customs and traditions, and value system.

More than 7 million people immigrated to the United States during the 1970s, and another 7 million came during the 1980s. Between 1980 and 1994, the number of Asian American students increased by almost 100%, Hispanic students increased by 46%, African American students increased by 25%, and Caucasian students increased by only 10% (U.S. Bureau of Census, 1996). Experts estimate that by the year 2020 the white student population will decrease by 11%, with dramatic increases in African American (between 15% and 20%), Hispanic (between 47% and 61%) and Asian/Pacific Islander/American Indian/Alaskan Native (between 67% and 73%) student populations (Young & Smith, 1999). Each of these groups brings a distinct set of values and traditions that influences student learning.

Culture and Schooling

A second-grade class in Albuquerque, New Mexico, was reading *The Boxcar Children* and was about to start a new chapter. The teacher said, "Look at the illustration at the beginning of the chapter and tell me what you think is going to happen." A few students raised their hands. The teacher called on a boy in the back row.

He said, "I think the boy is going to meet his grandfather."

The teacher asked, "Based on what you know, how does the boy feel about meeting his grandfather?"

Trying to involve the whole class, the teacher called on another student—one of four Native Americans in the group—even though she had not raised her hand. When she didn't answer, the teacher tried rephrasing the question, but again the student sat in silence.

Feeling exasperated, the teacher wondered if there was something in the way the lesson was being conducted that made it difficult for the student to respond. She sensed that the student she had called on understood the story and was enjoying it. Why, then, wouldn't she answer what appeared to be a simple question?

The teacher recalled that this was not the first time this had happened, and that, in fact, the other Native American students in the class rarely answered questions in class discussions. She wanted to involve them, wanted them to participate in class, but could not think of ways to get them to talk. (Villegas, 1991, p. 3)

Why do students respond differently to instruction, and how does culture influence these differences? In this section, we examine these questions, focusing on the relationships between culture and:

▍ Attitudes and values
▍ Adult–child interactions
▍ Classroom organization
▍ School communication

Attitudes and Values

Our students come to us with a long learning history. In their homes, they've learned to talk, dress, care for themselves, and function as family members. On their streets and playgrounds, they have learned to interact with their peers, make friends, and solve interpersonal problems. Through these experiences, they develop attitudes and values that can either complement or detract from school learning. Research helps us understand how.

Ogbu (1992, 1999b) divides minority cultures in the United States into two broad categories. *Voluntary minorities*, such as recent Chinese, Vietnamese, and Indian immigrants, came to the United States seeking a better life, whereas some *involuntary minorities*, such as African Americans, were brought here against their will, and others, such as Native Americans, Hawaiians, and early Hispanics in the Southwest were conquered.

Ogbu suggests that these two minority groups approach assimilation and integration into U.S. culture (and schooling) in different ways. Voluntary minorities see school as an opportunity for quick assimilation and integration into the economic and social mainstream, and schooling and hard work are strongly valued. Involuntary minorities, because of a long history of separatism and low status, defend themselves through **cultural inversion**, which is *"the tendency for involuntary minorities to regard certain forms of behavior, events, symbols, and meanings as inappropriate for them because these are characteristic of white Americans"* (Ogbu, 1992, p. 8). To adopt these values and ways of behaving is to reject their own culture.

Language and school success are examples. Students from involuntary minorities are hesitant to drop the use of nonstandard English dialects in favor of "school English" because it would alienate their peers and distance their families (Ogbu, 1999a). These students may interpret school success as rejecting their native culture; to become a good student is to become "white"—adopting white cultural values and rejecting their own. Students who study and become actively involved in school risk losing the friendship and respect of their peers. Ogbu believes that in many schools peer values either don't support school learning or actually oppose it; students form what he calls "resistance cultures" (Ogbu & Simons, 1998). Low grades, management and motivation problems, truancy, and high dropout rates are symptoms of this conflict.

Ogbu encourages teachers to help minority students adapt to the dominant culture (including schools) without losing their cultural identity, a process he calls "accommodation without assimilation." Others use the term "alternation"—the ability to comfortably function in both cultures (Hamm & Coleman, 1997). The challenge for teachers is to help students learn about the "culture of schooling"—the norms, procedures, and expectations necessary for success in school—while honoring the value and integrity of the students' home cultures.

Minority role models are especially powerful in helping minority youth understand how they can succeed without losing their ethnic or cultural heritage. One student commented,

It all started in the second grade. One faithful (sic) Career day at Jensen Scholastic Academy in my teacher Mrs. F.'s room an M.D. came to speak to the class about his career as

---

4.14 ▬

Is the concept *accommodation without assimilation* consistent or inconsistent with the idea of America as a "melting pot"? Explain.

a doctor. Reluctantly I can't remember his name but from that day forward I knew I was destined to be a doctor. From that point on I began to take my work seriously, because I knew to become a doctor grades were very important. Throughout my elementary career I received honors. In the seventh grade I really became fascinated with science, which I owe all to my teacher Mr. H. He made learning fun and interesting. I started to read science books even when it wasn't necessary, or I found myself watching the different specials on Channel 11 about operations they showed doctors performing. When I entered Kenwood Academy I decided to take Honors Biology which was very helpful. I wanted to be in a medical program at U.I.C. but I received a B second semester so I did not get chosen. That incident did not discourage me one bit. Through high school I continued my science classes. (Smokowski, 1997, p. 13)

Role models provide minority learners with evidence that they can succeed and success can be accomplished without sacrificing their cultural identity.

Cultural Differences in Adult–Child Interactions

Children from different cultures also learn to interact with adults in different ways; sometimes it complements communication in schools, and sometimes it doesn't. This phenomenon can be illustrated by one of your authors' personal experiences:

I was a Chicago-raised person living in the South for the first time. I soon developed a warm relationship with a family having three children, ages 3, 7, and 10. I reacted when the children would always call me "Dr. Kauchak" and my fiancee "Miss Lake," rather than "Don" and "Kathy," as we preferred. We thought these addresses were formal, but quaint. The parents also referred to us in this way, so we didn't press the issue. As we worked in schools, we noticed that middle-class children said, "Yes, ma'am," and, "No, ma'am," when talking with teachers. We came to realize that these formal (to us) ways of addressing adults were expected by both middle-class families and the teachers who came from these families. To encourage these children to call us by our first names would have been inappropriate in social situations and in conflict with accepted behavior in the schools.

Although the previous case reflects a minor (and positive) cultural difference, others can result in misunderstanding or even conflict. An experience described by a principal working with Pacific Island students is an example. The principal had been invited to a community awards ceremony at a local church that was to honor students from her school. She gladly accepted, arrived a few minutes early, and was ushered to a seat of honor on the stage. After an uncomfortable (to her) wait of over an hour, the ceremony began, and the students proudly filed to the stage to receive their awards. Each was acknowledged, given an award, and applauded. After this part of the ceremony, she had an eye-opening experience.

The children all went back and sat down in the audience again, and the meeting continued on to several more items on the agenda. Well, the kids were fine for a while, but as you might imagine, they got bored fast and started to fidget. Fidgeting and whispering turned into poking, prodding, and open chatting. I became a little anxious at the disruption, but none of the other adults appeared to even notice, so I ignored it, too. Pretty soon several of the children were up and out of their seats, strolling about the back and sides of the auditorium. All adult faces continued looking serenely up at the speaker on the stage. Then the kids started playing tag, running circles around the seating area and yelling gleefully. No adult response—I was amazed, and struggled to resist the urge to quiet the children. Then some of the kids got up onto the stage, running around the speaker, flicking the lights on and off, and opening and closing the curtain! Still nothing from the Islander parents! It was not my place, and I shouldn't have done it, but I was so beyond my comfort zone that with eye contact and a pantomimed shush, I got the kids to settle down.

Minority role models help
minority youth understand how
they can succeed without
losing their ethnic or
cultural heritage.

4.15
Implementing the concept
of *accommodation without
assimilation* requires considerable teacher judg-
ment and tact to imple-
ment. Explain specifically
how you would deal with
the Pacific Island chil-
dren's concept of time and
their spirited behavior in
your classroom.

> I suddenly realized then that when these children . . . come to school late, it does-
> n't mean that they or their parents don't care about learning . . . that's just how all the
> adults in their world operate. When they squirm under desks and run around the class-
> room, they aren't trying to be disrespectful or defiant, they're just doing what they do
> everywhere else. (Winitzky, 1994, pp. 147–148)

This experience gave the principal insights into the ways (and reasons) her students
often acted as they did. Students bring with them ways of acting and interacting with
adults that may differ from the traditional teacher-as-authority-figure role. (We discuss the
difficult question of what to do about these differences later in the chapter.)

Classroom Organization: Working with and Against Students' Cultures

In most classrooms, emphasis is placed on individual initiative and responsibility, which
are often reinforced by grades and competition. Competition demands successes and failures, and the success of one student is often tied to the failure of another (Cushner,
McClelland, & Safford, 1992).

Contrast this orientation with the learning styles of the Hmong, a mountain tribe from
Laos that immigrated to the United States after the Vietnam War. The Hmong culture
emphasizes cooperation, and Hmong students constantly monitor the learning progress of
their peers, offering help and assistance. Individual achievement is deemphasized in favor of
group success. A researcher working with the Hmong described her classroom in this way:

> When Mee Hang has difficulty with an alphabetization lesson, Pang Lor explains, in
> Hmong, how to proceed. Chia Ying listens in to Pang's explanation and nods her head.
> Pang goes back to work on her own paper, keeping an eye on Mee Hang. When she
> sees Mee looking confused, Pang leaves her seat and leans over Mee's shoulder. She
> writes the first letter of each word on the line, indicating to Mee that these letters are in
> alphabetical order and that Mee should fill in the rest of each word. This gives Mee the
> help she needs and she is able to finish on her own. Mee, in turn, writes the first letter
> of each word on the line for Chia Ying, passing on Pang Lor's explanation.
>
> Classroom achievement is never personal but always considered to be the result of
> cooperative effort. Not only is there no competition in the classroom, there is constant
> denial of individual ability. When individuals are praised by the teacher, they generally
> shake their heads and appear hesitant to be singled out as being more able than their
> peers. (Hvitfeldt, 1986, p. 70)

Consider how well these students would learn if instruction were competitive and teacher centered, with few opportunities for student help and collaboration.

Native Americans and other cultures, including Mexican American, Southeast Asian, and Pacific Islander students, experience similar difficulties in competitive classrooms (Greenfield, 1994; Triandes, 1995). Their cultures teach them that cooperation is important; they view competition as silly, if not distasteful. When they come to school and are asked to compete, they experience cultural conflict. Getting good grades at the expense of their fellow students is both strange and offensive. Raising hands and jousting for the right to give the correct answer isn't congruent with the ways they interact at home. If they're forced to choose between two cultures, they may conclude that schools are not for them. (We examine competitive classroom structures and their impact on motivation in Chapter 10.)

School–Culture Matches and Mismatches

Some cultural patterns strongly support schooling. In a cross-cultural study comparing Chinese, Japanese, and American child-raising practices, researchers found significant differences in parental support for schooling (Stevenson, Lee, & Stigler, 1986). Over 95% of native Chinese and Japanese fifth graders had desks and quiet study areas at home; only 63% of the American sample did. Also, 57% of the Chinese and Japanese parents supplemented their fifth graders' schoolwork with additional math workbooks, as compared with only 28% of the American parents. Finally, 51% of the Chinese parents and 29% of the Japanese parents supplemented their children's science curriculum with additional work, compared with only 1% of the American parents.

Additional research has examined the phenomenal successes of Vietnamese and Laotian refugee children in U.S. classrooms. In spite of being in the United States less than 4 years, these students earned better than B averages in school, and scores on standardized achievement tests corroborated the grades. This occurred in spite of vast language differences and very different cultures (Caplan, Choy, & Whitmore, 1992).

In attempting to explain these encouraging patterns of school acculturation and progress, the researchers looked to the families. They found heavy emphasis on the importance of hard work, autonomy, perseverance, and pride. These values were reinforced with a nightly ritual of family homework in which both parents and older siblings helped younger members of the family. Indo-Chinese high schoolers spent an average of 3 hours a day on homework; junior high and elementary students spent an average of 2½ hours and 2 hours, respectively, compared with the 1½ hours a day U.S. junior and senior high students spend on homework (Caplan et al., 1992).

In other cases, mismatches occur (Owens, 1996). A study of differences in language patterns between white and African American students illustrates this possibility (Heath, 1989). For example, teachers would say, "Let's put the scissors away now." White students, accustomed to this indirect way of speaking, interpreted this as a command; African Americans did not. Failure to obey was then viewed as either a management or motivation problem—a result of the mismatch between home and school cultures.

Similar disparities caused problems during instruction. From their home experience, white children were accustomed to using language to explore abstract relationships and were asked questions requiring specific answers, such as, "Where did the puppy go?" and "What's this story about?". African American children were accustomed to questions that were more "open-ended, story-starter" types that didn't have single answers. African American children "were not viewed as information-givers in their interactions with adults, nor were they considered appropriate conversation partners and thus they did not learn to act as such" (Heath, 1982, p. 119). When these children went to school, they were unprepared for the verbal give-and-take of fast-paced, convergent questioning.

Made aware of these differences, teachers incorporated more open-ended questions in their lessons, and worded commands more directly, such as "Put your scissors away now." They also helped African American students become more comfortable with answering factual questions. In this way, bridges were built between African American students' natural learning styles and the schools.

Culture and Learning: Deficit or Difference?

In the previous sections, we've seen how cultural differences can affect school success. Efforts have been made to synthesize this information into theories to further explain the relationship between school learning and culture.

Cultural deficit theories *suggest that "the linguistic, social or cultural backgrounds of minority children prevent them from doing well academically"* (Villegas, 1991, p. 5). These theories have at least three weaknesses. First, they don't account for the many successes of different cultural groups. Second, because of their negative orientation, they result in lowered expectations for minority students. Third, they can't explain why the longer some minorities are in school, the farther behind they fall. If deficit theories were valid, the gap should be greatest when students first enter school and should gradually narrow over time (Villegas, 1991).

Cultural difference theories *emphasize the strengths of different cultures and look for ways that instructional practice can recognize and build on those strengths* (Villegas, 1991). They begin with the premise that different cultural groups have unique ways of learning and that no single way of teaching is most effective for all. They then attempt to understand different cultural groups and to adapt instruction to best meet these groups' learning needs. Evidence supports their premise, and we discuss implications for teaching cultural minorities on the basis of this concept.

4.16
Using Ogbu's concept of cultural inversion, explain why some minorities might fall farther and farther behind.

Culturally Responsive Teaching

Culturally responsive teaching *acknowledges cultural diversity in classrooms and accommodates this diversity in instruction* (Gay, 1997). It does this in at least three ways, which are illustrated in Figure 4.6.

Figure 4.6

Characteristics of culturally responsive teaching

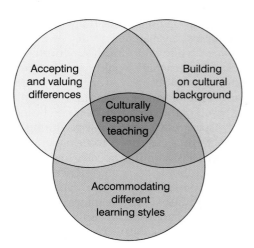

Accepting and Valuing Differences

By recognizing and accepting student diversity, teachers communicate that all students are welcome and valued. This notion is particularly important for cultural minorities, who sometimes feel alienated from school. Teachers must try to communicate with minority students and help them understand that school success and belonging to their minority culture are not in conflict.

Genuine caring is the essential element in the process; students quickly see through artificial attempts to communicate caring, and lip service to minorities will be seen as superficial. This is difficult, of course, because we can never be sure that our intentions are accurately perceived. We can take the following actions, however, which are rarely misperceived:

- Give students time: Giving your time is one of the most effective ways to communicate caring.
- Demonstrate personal interest: All people react positively to someone taking an interest in their personal lives.
- Involve all students in learning activities: Teachers who try to involve all students equally in classroom activities communicate that everyone is important and that each student's contributions to learning activities are valued.

Accommodating Different Cultural Learning Styles

Teachers who are sensitive to possible differences between home and school patterns are in a position to adapt their instruction to best meet their students' needs. For example, we saw earlier that the values of Native Americans may clash with typical classroom practice. Recognizing that these students don't learn effectively in competitive learning environments, teachers can use techniques such as cooperative learning to complement teacher-centered approaches (we describe cooperative learning in Chapter 13). These adaptations can increase learning for all students (Slavin, 1995).

Culturally responsive teachers build on the strengths that different students bring to school.

Another example illustrates how teachers can accommodate different cultural learning styles. When the teacher learned that her Asian American students were overwhelmed by the hustle and bustle of American schools, she tried to keep her classroom quiet and orderly (Park, 1997). In another case, knowing that Asian Americans are sometimes shy and reluctant to speak in class, the teacher promoted participation with open-ended questioning, giving them more time, and gently encouraging them to speak a bit louder (Shields & Shaver, 1990).

Building on Students' Cultural Backgrounds

Effective teachers also learn about their students' cultures and use this information to promote personal pride and motivation in their students, as the following illustration demonstrates:

> In one third-grade classroom with a predominately Central American student population, youngsters are greeted most mornings with the sound of salsa music in the background, instruction takes place in both English and Spanish, magazines and games in both languages are available throughout the classroom, maps of both the United States and Latin America line one wall with pins noting each student's origin, and every afternoon there is a Spanish reading lesson to ensure that students learn to read and write in Spanish as well as English. . . . The teacher argues very clearly that a positive instructional environment for these students must be tailored to the home cultures. (Shields & Shaver, 1990, p. 9)

4.17

Identify at least three advantages, to all students, of learning about different students' cultural backgrounds.

The benefits of this approach are felt in both the classroom and the home. In addition to increases in student achievement, parents are more positive about school, which in turn enhances student motivation (Shumow & Harris, 1998). Students bring to school a wealth of experiences embedded in their home cultures. Sensitive teachers build on these experiences, and all students benefit.

Classroom
Connections

Using SES and Culture as Tools to Understand Your Students

1. Communicate with students about who they are and who you are.
   - On the first day of class, a sixth-grade teacher has students write essays about themselves. He has them include a description of their favorite activities and foods, the kind of music they like, and any information they want to include about parents, caregivers, or other close relatives. He asks them to include, if they would like, anything about school that worries them or that they don't like. He writes an essay of his own and shares it with his students.

   - A math teacher makes an effort to get to know each of his students. He tries to learn something personal about each and refers to this information in one-on-one conversations.

2. Make an attempt to learn about the cultures of the students you are teaching.
   - A third-grade teacher asks her students about their after-school activities and their holiday customs. She designs classroom "festivals" that focus on different cultures and invites parents and other caregivers to help celebrate and contribute to enriching them.
   - A high school teacher in an inner-city school makes himself available before and after school. Although

the focus in these sessions is on academics, the conversations often turn to students' lives and the problems they encounter in school.

3. Make students aware of the values and accomplishments of ethnic minorities.
   - A second-grade teacher emphasizes values, such as courtesy and respect, that cross all cultures. He has students discuss the ways values, such as respect for others, are displayed differently in various cultures.
   - An art teacher decorates the room with pictures of Native American art and discusses its quality and contributions to the general field of art.

- An inner-city American history teacher displays pictures of prominent African Americans and discusses the contributions they made to the American way of life. She emphasizes that many history books often underrepresent the contributions of minorities and women.
- A teacher with many Hispanic students in her classroom points out the accomplishments of Americans of Latin heritage, such as the Cuban population in Miami and prominent Hispanic politicians around the country.

Gender

What Marti Banes saw on her first day of teaching advanced-placement chemistry was both surprising and disturbing. Of the 26 students watching her, only 5 were girls, and they sat quietly in class, responding only when she asked them direct questions. One reason that she had gone into teaching was to share her interest in science with girls, but this situation gave her little chance to do so.

The fact that some of our students are boys and others are girls is so obvious that we sometimes miss this important difference. When we're reminded, we of course notice that boys and girls look different and often act and think differently. These differences are natural—even desirable, but problems can occur if societal or school forces limit the academic performance of either girls or boys. In this section, we examine gender-related student differences and their implications for our teaching (Figure 4.7).

Males and females *are* different (Feingold, 1995). In general, women are more extroverted, anxious, trusting, less assertive, and have slightly lower self-esteem than their male counterparts. Differences also exist in boys' and girls' developmental rates; girls develop faster, with differences in verbal and motor skills appearing at an earlier age. Girls tend to play with dolls and other girls and gravitate toward activities such as make-believe and dress-up. Boys play with blocks, cars, dinosaurs, and other boys. These differences, together with societal expectations, result in **gender role identity** differences, *beliefs about appropriate characteristics and behaviors of the two sexes.*

Why do these gender differences exist? Like the nature–nurture argument with respect to intelligence, this question continues to be controversial and, again as with intelligence, evidence suggests that the differences result from an

Figure 4.7

Sources of learner individuality: Gender

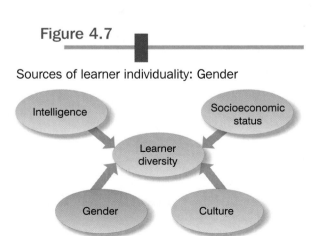

interaction between genetics and environment. Genetics result in physical differences such as size and growth rate and probably also influence differences in temperament, aggressiveness, and early verbal and exploratory behaviors (Berk, 1996). On the other hand, girls and boys are treated differently by parents, peers, and teachers, and this treatment also influences what they ultimately become.

What should teachers do? Again, the suggestions are controversial, with some people believing that most differences between boys and girls are natural, and little intervention is necessary, whereas others believe that every attempt should be made to minimize any perceptions of difference.

Research sheds light on the issue, and some suggests that schools are not meeting girls' needs.

- In the early grades, girls score as high or higher than boys on almost every standardized measure of achievement and psychological well-being. By the time they graduate from high school or college, they have fallen behind boys.
- In high school, girls score lower on the SAT and ACT, which are important for college admission. The greatest gender gaps are in science and math.
- Women score lower on all sections of the Graduate Record Exam, the Medical College Admissions Test, and admission tests for law, dental, and optometry schools (Sadker, Sadker, & Long, 1997).

Other research suggests that schools also fail to meet the learning needs of boys.

- Boys outnumber girls in remedial English and math classes, are held back in grade more often, and are two to three times more likely to be placed in special education classes.
- Boys consistently receive lower grades than girls and score lower than girls on both direct and indirect measures of writing ability.
- The proportion of both bachelor's and master's degrees earned favors women by a ratio of 53 to 47. (Willingham & Cole, 1997)

Differences in the Behavior of Boys and Girls

Historically, boys have participated in learning activities to a greater extent than girls. They are more likely to ask questions and make comments about ideas being discussed in class, and teachers have called on them more often (Sadker, Sadker, & Klein, 1991), probably because boys are more verbally aggressive (Altermatt, Jovanovic, & Perry, 1998).

These differences are particularly pronounced in science and math. In one study, researchers found that 79% of a teacher's science demonstrations were carried out by boys. At the third-grade level, 51% of boys reported experiences with microscopes compared to 37% of girls. In an 11th-grade sample, 49% of boys, but only 17% of girls, reported experiences with electrical equipment (Sadker et al., 1991). These hands-on experiences are important because they influence girls' attitudes toward and their perceptions of their ability to do science (Jovanovic & King, 1998).

Differences in participation become greater as students move through school, with an especially significant decrease in girls' participation during the middle school years. In the seventh grade, they initiated 41% of the student–teacher interactions, but by eighth grade, this number had decreased to 30% (Sadker et al., 1991).

This decrease appears during the time girls are wrestling with gender-role identities. In spite of increased sensitivity to girls' needs, our society still commonly views female roles as submissive and conforming, and middle school girls often feel uncomfortable asserting themselves in classes.

4.18 ▬
Explain gender differences from both "nature" and "nurture" perspectives. Then explain these differences from an interactionist position.

4.19 ▬
Explain girls' participation in math and science, using Erikson's stage of identity versus confusion as the basis for your explanation.

On the other hand, a considerable amount of boys' behavior is disconcerting and counterproductive. They cut class more often than girls, hold more part-time jobs out of school, read less for pleasure, do less homework, and are less likely to take college preparatory classes. In college they party and watch TV more than girls (Riordan, 1996). The long-term consequences of these patterns for learning and achievement, both at the K–12 and college level, is troublesome.

While the troublesome areas are different, evidence suggests that our schools aren't serving the needs of either boys or girls particularly well.

Gender Stereotypes and Perceptions

Increased national attention has focused on the problem of gender stereotyping (Riordan, 1996). For example, in 1993, Mattel attempted to market a new "Teen Talk Barbie" which—when you pressed her tummy—said, "I like shopping," "I like boys," and "Math class is tough."

This marketing attempt was significant for two reasons. First, the fact that it immediately caused a storm of protest (and was quickly pulled from the market) indicates heightened sensitivity to gender issues, and second, it illustrates how pervasive male and female stereotypes can be.

Perceptions of Male and Female Domains

Both society and parents—most likely unconsciously—sometimes communicate different expectations for their sons and daughters. For example, researchers found that mothers' gender-stereotyped attitudes toward girls' ability in math adversely influenced their daughters' achievement in math and reinforced their beliefs that math is a male domain (Campbell & Beaudry, 1998).

The perception that certain areas, such as math, science, and computer science, are male domains is having a powerful effect on career choices. For instance, while achievement differences between boys and girls at the K–12 level are small and declining (Willingham & Cole, 1997), girls are less than half as likely as boys to pursue careers in engineering and physical and computer sciences (American Association of University Women, 1998). The percentage of female doctors (20%), lawyers (21%), and engineers (8%) as well as professors in science-related fields (36%), also remains low (U.S. Bureau of the Census,

Science activities that actively involve female students in designing and carrying out science experiments help combat gender stereotypes that the sciences are a male domain.

1996; U.S. Department of Education, 1998), and the problem of gender stereotypic views of math- and science-related careers seems to be especially acute for minority females (O'Brien, Kopola, & Martinez-Pons, 1999). These trends are troubling because the perception of these fields being male domains is limiting the career options for females as well as the pool for future scientists and mathematicians (Campbell & Beaudry, 1998).

Single-Gender Classrooms and Schools

One response to these perceptions has been the creation of single-gender classes and schools (Mael, 1998). One study found girls more likely to ask and answer questions in a girls-only middle school math class than in coeducational classes (Streitmatter, 1997). Girls also preferred this environment, saying that it enhanced their ability to learn math and their view of themselves as mathematicians.

Research on single-gender schools has found similar positive effects for both girls and boys. Girls who attend single-gender schools are more apt to adopt leadership roles, take more math and science courses, have higher self-esteem, and have an increased perception of being in control of their own learning. Advocates of all-boy schools claim that they promote male character development and are especially effective with boys from low-income and minority families (Datnow, Hubbard, & Conchas, 1999).

Although research shows generally positive effects of single-gender schooling for both general achievement and achievement in stereotyped fields, like math and science, it raises other issues (Mael, 1998). For example, these environments tend to reinforce stereotypical attitudes toward the opposite sex, and they don't prepare students for the real world in which men and women work together (Datnow et al., 1999). More research is needed that examines the long-term effects of these experiments and the impact they have on the development of both boys and girls.

Gender Differences: Implications for Teachers

Teachers can play an important role in helping reverse the negative impact of gender stereotyping in education (Brantlinger, Morton, & Washburn, 1998). As with many aspects of individual differences, the first step is awareness. Teachers who know they may unconsciously treat boys and girls differently are more sensitive to their own behavior. The next step is to make every effort to treat boys and girls as equally as possible and to expect and encourage the same academic behaviors in both.

"Academic" behavior is a key idea. No one is suggesting that boys and girls are the same in every way, and we're not asking them to be. We are, however, suggesting that, academically, boys and girls should be given the same opportunities and encouragement, just as students from different cultures and socioeconomic backgrounds would be. We have four suggestions for teachers:

1. *Communicate openly with students.* Simply telling your students that teachers often treat boys and girls differently and that you're going to try to treat them equally is a positive step.
2. *Make an effort to call on boys and girls as equally as possible in learning activities* (Altermatt, Jovanovic, & Perry, 1997). Knowing that girls are less aggressive than boys reminds us to make an extra effort to call on girls, particularly in math and science classes, where they're even more reluctant to respond.
3. *Present our students with nonstereotypical role models.* For example, inviting female engineers and male nurses to our classes to demonstrate that they are

growing and evolving occupations can do a great deal to change stereotyped attitudes.

4. *Take a personal interest in all our students.* Some informal, personal counseling
with a boy who comes to class chronically tired might encourage him to work
fewer hours. Willingness to listen to the personal concerns of adolescent boys and
girls can do a great deal to help both boys and girls develop as fully as possible.

Classroom Connections

Eliminating Gender Bias in Your Classroom

1. Be sensitive to the possibilities of unconscious gender bias.
   - A junior high teacher checks her interaction with her students by periodically videotaping one of her classes. She checks the tape to ensure that boys and girls are called on equally, are asked the same number of high-level questions, and receive the same quality of feedback.
   - A first-grade teacher consciously deemphasizes sex roles and differences in her classroom. She has boys and girls share equally in chores, and she eliminates gender-related activities, such as competition between boys and girls and forming lines by gender.

2. Actively attack gender bias in your teaching.
   - At the beginning of the school year, a social studies teacher explains how gender bias hurts both sexes, and he forbids sexist comments in his classes. As classes study historical topics, he emphasizes the contributions of women and how they have been ignored by historians, and he points out the changes in views of gender over time.
   - A second-grade teacher selects stories and clippings from newspapers and magazines that portray women in nontraditional roles. She matter-of-factly talks about nontraditional careers with the students in reference to "when you grow up."

Students Placed at Risk

I was told that "the class was all right, but some children were pretty hopeless." I was
also told that the children were used to working through their arithmetic book and
were tested at the end of each week. After receiving the first test papers in long division,
most of which were disastrous, I did not know what to do. Nothing in my training had
prepared me for a class where some children failed because they did not understand
the meaning of zero, some because they had not learned how to carry over numbers
from one stage to another; others seemed to have very little understanding of division
and would try to divide the smaller number by the larger one, while some children
seemed confused and unable to make any sense of the set number work.

I subsequently divided the papers into small groups according to the main errors
they revealed, and spent my next lunch breaks working with the children on their own
specific difficulties. I soon realized that some of the "hopeless" children were pretty
bright, but for different reasons had lost confidence in their ability to cope with their
schoolwork. However, I found out that when each child was helped to understand the

specific problem in arithmetic that had been holding him back, his progress was not only remarkable, but also quite out of proportion to the effort I invested. (Butler-Por, 1987, p. 3)

The school population is changing. Increasing numbers of students come from households where both parents work, and the likelihood of being in a single-parent family is increasing (Macionis, 1997). Compared to the past, today's students are more academically and linguistically diverse, many of them receive less care, and some aren't as ready to profit from schools. This presents an enormous challenge for schools and teachers.

Students Placed at Risk: A Definition

Let's look again at Juan in our case study at the beginning of the chapter. He is a member of a cultural minority from a low-SES background, he missed a great deal of school, and he was retained in the first grade. His tendency to be easily offended suggests low self-esteem. Juan exhibits several characteristics of students placed at risk (see Table 4.5).

Students placed at risk are *those in danger of failing to complete their education with the skills necessary to survive in a modern technological society* (Slavin, Karweit, & Madden, 1989). The term became widely used after the National Commission on Excellence in Education proclaimed the United States a "nation at risk" (National Commission on Excellence in Education, 1983). The report emphasized the connection between education and success and economic well-being in a modern technological society. Since that time, increased attention has been given to problems and issues relating to students placed at risk. It is a virtual certainty that you will have some of these students in your classes.

Table 4.5

Characteristics of students placed at risk

Background Factors	
Low SES	Minority
Inner city	Non-native English speaker
Male	Divorced families
Transient	

Educational Problems	
High dropout rate	Management problems
Low grades	Low self-esteem
Retention in grade	High criminal activity rates
Low achievement	Low test scores
Low involvement in extracurricular activities	Dissatisfaction with and lack of interest in school
Low motivation	High suspension rates
Poor attendance	
High rates of drug use	

Students placed at risk have learning problems and adjustment difficulties, and they often fail, even though they can succeed. These students used to be called underachievers, but the term *at-risk* describes the long-term consequences of school failure more clearly. A male high school dropout, for example, will earn a quarter of a million dollars less over a lifetime than a high school graduate. Families whose primary breadwinners lack high school diplomas earn 30% less than those with a high school education (Mishel & Frankel, 1991). Many jobs requiring few specialized skills no longer exist, and others are becoming increasingly rare in our technological society.

We see from Table 4.5 that students placed at risk suffer from a variety of academic, social, and emotional problems. The presence of "male" as a background factor needs clarification. Though research indicates that males are more likely to experience difficulties in school and drop out, many low-SES female students who either leave school before graduation or graduate with inadequate survival skills are more likely to live in poverty than male dropouts (American Association of University Women, 1992). In addition, many girls who drop out are pregnant and are left with the burden of single parenting on a below-the-poverty-level income. Being at risk is a problem facing both male and female students.

A note of caution before continuing. We use the term *students placed at risk* rather than *at-risk students* for two reasons. First, the phrase *students placed at risk* emphasizes that these are students first, deserving our full energies to help them learn. Second, many educators worry that use of the term *at-risk* causes low expectations for success and low achievement (Franklin, 1997). We must guard against negative stereotyping as we work with these students and continually ask ourselves, "Am I providing every opportunity for success for all students?" The following sections offer suggestions to help ensure that this occurs.

Students Placed at Risk: Promoting Resilience

Research on students placed at risk has focused on the concept of resilience. **Resilience** *results in a heightened likelihood of success in school and in other aspects of life, despite environmental adversities* (Wang, Haertel, & Walberg, 1995). Educators have become interested in resilience for both theoretical and practical reasons. Theoretically, the study

4.20
Why are students who are placed at risk increasingly seen as both educational and economic problems? Will this trend increase or decrease? Why?

Resilient children come from homes and classrooms that are supportive but demanding and where caring adults provide nurturant challenge.

of resilience helps us understand the larger process of development, especially as it occurs in youth who are placed at risk for school failure. Practically, the study of resilient youth offers the possibility of identifying practices that result in academically successful learners.

Research on resilience focuses on youth who have survived and even prospered despite obstacles such as poverty, poor health care, and fragmented services. Resilient children have well-developed self-systems, including high self-esteem, optimism, and feelings that they are in control of their destinies (Jew, Green, Millard, & Posillico, 1999). They are good at setting personal goals, possess good interpersonal skills, and have positive expectations for success (Benard, 1993; Wang et al., 1995). These strengths pay off in higher academic achievement, motivation, and satisfaction with school (Waxman & Huang, 1996).

How do these skills develop? Resilient children come from families and communities that are nurturant and caring (Jew et al., 1999; Stull, 1998). Their families provide structure and hold high moral and academic expectations for their children. Resilient youth also come from schools that are both demanding and supportive; in many instances schools serve as a home away from home (Haynes & Comer, 1995). Let's look more closely at the connections between school experiences and the development of resiliency.

4.21
Identify two of Gardner's multiple intelligences that are particularly important for resilient children.

Effective Schools for Students Placed at Risk

Important research has been conducted on schools that are effective in developing student resilience (Wang et al., 1995). In these schools, students and teachers treat each other with respect, and personal responsibility and cooperation are stressed (Kim, Solomon, & Roberts, 1995; Roberts, Horn, & Battistich, 1995). The meaning and purpose of rules are stressed, and mastery of content and quality of work, rather than passive attendance and merely completing assignments, are emphasized (Corbett, Wilson, & Williams, 1999). High expectations for student learning permeate both the school and classrooms (Glidden, 1999).

Interestingly, these same characteristics seem to apply to other countries and cultures; a study done with similar students in Israel arrived at the same conclusions (Gaziel, 1997). The characteristics of these schools are summarized in Figure 4.8.

Effective Teachers for Students Placed at Risk

Research studying students placed at risk consistently finds alienation from school as a problem for them (Goodenow, 1992a; Yazejian, 1999). Boredom, lack of involvement, and

Figure 4.8

Characteristics of effective schools for students placed at risk

- Safe, orderly school climate
- Concentration on academic objectives
- Positive teacher attitudes and high expectations for all students
- Continuous monitoring of student performance
- Emphasis on the development of cooperation, a sense of community, and prosocial values
- Emphasis on student responsibility and self-regulation; decreased emphasis on external controls
- Strong parental involvement

feelings of not belonging keep them on the fringe, prevent them from participating in school experiences, and inhibit their motivation.

While well-organized and academically focused schools are important, they are not—in themselves—able to overcome these problems. Success with these students ultimately depends on teachers; in other words, schools are no more effective than the teachers who work in them (Waxman, Huang, Anderson, & Weinstein, 1997). What makes an effective teacher for students placed at risk? How do teachers help students develop resilience and make connections between their lives and the classroom? Let's see what research has to say.

One series of studies used the terms *high impact* and *low impact* to describe differences in teachers' abilities to reach students placed at risk (Kramer-Schlosser, 1992). High-impact teachers talked frequently with students, found out about their families, and shared their own lives. They maintained high expectations, used a variety of teaching strategies, and emphasized success and mastery of content. They motivated students through personal contacts, instructional support, and attempts to link school to students' lives.

Low-impact teachers, in contrast, were less interactive and more authoritarian. They distanced themselves from students and placed primary responsibility for learning on them. They viewed instructional help as "babying the student" or "holding the student's hand." Instruction was teacher centered and lecture oriented, and primary responsibility for motivation was the student's. Students thought of low-impact teachers as adversaries, to be avoided if possible, tolerated if not. In contrast, they sought out high-impact teachers, both in class and out.

Let's look now at what students have to say about these two kinds of teachers:

Well it's like you're family, you know. Like regular days like at home, we argue sometimes, and then it's like we're all brothers and sisters and the teachers are like our guardians or something.

And the teachers really get on you until they try to make you think of what's in the future and all that. It's good. I mean it makes you think, you know, if every school was like that I don't think there would be a lot of people that would drop out. (Greenleaf, 1995, p. 2)

[This teacher is] always ready to help you. When I first came to this school, I didn't like her, 'til I realized that the only thing she was trying to do was help me.
Student, *Accelerated Academics Academy*,
Flint, Michigan

The teachers stay on you . . . they'll keep staying on you until you get your goals.
Student, *Project ACCEL*, Newark, New Jersey

[The teachers] believe you can do the work, and you don't want to let them down.
Student, *Up With Literacy Program*,
Long Beach, California

There's this teacher [over at the regular school] . . . you can put anything down and he'll give you a check mark for it. He doesn't check it. He just gives you a mark and says, 'OK, you did your work.' How you gonna learn from that? You ain't gonna learn nothing.
Student, *JFY Academy*,
Boston, Massachusetts

(Dynarski & Gleason, 1999, p. 13)

Caring combined with high expectations are the themes we see in this research; effective teachers for students placed at risk care about their students as people, commu-

4.22 ▬

In Margin Note 4.11, we referred to Maslow's hierarchy of needs, outlined in Chapter 10. Again using this hierarchy, explain why caring teachers are so important for students placed at risk.

nicate this caring through their actions, and accept nothing less than consistent effort and quality work (Freese, 1999). Personalized, caring learning environments are important for all students; for students placed at risk, they're essential.

But beyond this human element, what else can teachers do? We consider this question in the next section.

Effective Instruction for Students Placed at Risk: Structure and Support

> When students entered the classroom, they saw a review assignment written on the chalkboard. As Mrs. Higby took roll and prepared for the lesson, they routinely started on the assignment.
>
> At exactly 9:05, Mrs. Higby began with a brief review of the previous day's lesson. Both the pace and accuracy of the answers convinced her that the class knew the content and was ready to move on.
>
> As she introduced two-column subtraction, she explained the new idea, guided the students through the steps by using manipulatives, and used questioning to link the manipulatives to the written numerals. Then she had students solve problems on their own minichalkboards and hold them up to allow her to check their solutions. Whenever mistakes occurred, she stopped, analyzed the errors, and helped students correct them.
>
> When 90% of the class was correctly solving the problems, the teacher started the students on seat-work, which they checked in pairs when they were done. As they worked, she gave some extra help to those still having difficulty, periodically getting up to respond to pairs who disagreed with each other or had questions.

How should regular classroom teachers adapt their instruction to meet the needs of students placed at risk? In a review of the research in this area, Brophy (1986) concluded that "research has turned up very little evidence suggesting the need for qualitatively different forms of instruction for students who differ in aptitude, achievement level, socioeconomic status, ethnicity or learning style" (p. 122).

In short, teachers of students placed at risk don't need to teach in fundamentally different ways; they need to provide sufficient structure and instructional support to ensure student success while at the same time teaching students strategies that allow them to take control of their own learning.

4.23 ▬

Earlier, we found that students placed at risk often have poorer motivation than their more advantaged peers. How do *structure and support, frequent feedback,* and *active teaching* address this problem?

Interactive teaching methods are essential. In a comparison of more and less effective urban elementary teachers, researchers found that less effective teachers interacted with students only 47% of the time versus 70% of the time for their more effective counterparts (Waxman et al., 1997). Interactive teaching is characteristic of good instruction in general; its importance with students placed at risk is crucial (Gladney & Greene, 1997; Hundley, 1998; Wang et al., 1995).

Effective strategies for students placed at risk are outlined in Table 4.6.

Effective Instruction for Students Placed at Risk: The Need for Challenge

All the increased structure and support just described still aren't enough, however. One study found many of the effective instructional practices outlined in Table 4.6 being implemented, but they also found that expectations for students were low, higher-level thinking and problem solving were deemphasized in favor of low-level worksheets, and students were bored and apathetic (S. Miller, Leinhardt, & Zigmond, 1988). The increased structure and support had resulted in a remedial program that lacked rigor and stimulation.

Table 4.6

Effective instruction for students placed at risk

Characteristic	Description
Greater structure and support	Course expectations need to be clearly laid out, and assignments and grades need to be designed to encourage achievement.
Active teaching	The teacher needs to carry the content to students personally through interactive teaching rather than depend on curricular materials, such as the text or workbooks.
Instruction emphasizing student engagement	Interactive teaching with high questioning levels invites students to participate in lessons. Open-ended questions allow successful responses and give students a chance to explain their thinking.
More frequent feedback	Student progress should be monitored frequently through classroom questions, quizzes, and assignments.
Higher success rates	Classroom questions, assignments, and quizzes should be designed to maximize opportunities for success.
High expectations	Teachers should assume that all students can learn and emphasize higher order thinking in all classes.
Emphasis on learning strategies	Teachers teach and model learning strategies, emphasizing how they contribute to effective learning.
Emphasis on student motivation and self-regulation	Teachers stress the importance of student control over their own learning; teachers demonstrate and model how learning tasks can be accomplished through proactive planning, monitoring and self-assessment.

Several programs have been developed to provide challenge for students placed at risk. The *Accelerated Schools Program* builds on student strengths by combining high expectations with an enriched curriculum focusing on a language-based approach in all academic areas (Levin, 1988; Rothman, 1991). The *Higher Order Thinking Skills Program* (HOTS) focuses on teaching students skills such as inferencing and generalizing to help them realize the importance of critical thinking in learning (Pogrow, 1990).

Results from both programs have been encouraging. One Accelerated Schools site in San Francisco registered the highest achievement gains on standardized test scores in the city, and spring-to-spring comparisons of achievement gains in one HOTS program showed students were 67% above the national average in reading and 123% higher in math (Rothman, 1991).

Common to both programs are high expectations, emphasis on enrichment versus remediation, and the teaching of higher-order thinking and learning strategies. These strategies are integrated into the regular curriculum so that students can see their usefulness in different content areas (Means & Knapp, 1991).

The dilemma in working with students placed at risk is how to be structured and responsive while still presenting a challenging intellectual menu. It isn't an easy task, but it can be done. It requires a caring environment, effective instruction, and administrative support. Admittedly, it requires a great deal of effort from teachers. However, seeing students who were previously unsuccessful and apathetic succeed and meet challenges is enormously rewarding.

Classroom Connections

Using Effective Teaching Practices for Students Placed at Risk in Your Classroom

1. Communicate positive expectations by carefully specifying procedures and requirements for your class.
   - A fourth-grade teacher spends the first 2 weeks of school teaching her students her classroom procedures. She makes short assignments, carefully monitors students to be certain the assignments are turned in, and immediately calls parents if an assignment is missing. This positive beginning lays the foundation for the rest of the year.
   - A junior high math teacher takes extra time explaining his course procedures to his basic math classes. He explains how homework and quizzes contribute to learning and the overall grade. He emphasizes the importance of attendance and effort and expects all to pass his course. He makes himself available before and after school for help sessions.

2. Make active attempts to involve parents or other caregivers in your classroom.
   - An English teacher sends home a description of his class expectations at the beginning of the school year. He makes this letter upbeat and positive and carefully explains student work requirements and grading practices. He enlists the aid of students to translate the letter for parents whose first language is not English and asks parents to sign the letter, indicating they have read it. He also invites questions and comments from parents or other caregivers.
   - An inner-city elementary teacher makes a special effort to make parents welcome at parent–teacher conferences. She mails a letter of invitation a week before the conference and sends home an addi-

tional reminder with students. So that parents feel comfortable, she puts a welcome sign on the door in all of the students' home languages, and provides light refreshments in the waiting area.

3. Maintain high levels of student involvement in your teaching.
   - A sixth-grade teacher arranges the seating in her classroom so that minority and nonminority students are mixed. She combines small-group and whole-class instruction and, when she uses group work, she arranges the groups so they include high and low achievers, minorities and nonminorities, and boys and girls.
   - In language-arts activities, a teacher builds her teaching around questioning and examples. She comments, "My goal is to call on each student in the class at least twice during the course of a lesson. I also use a lot of repetition and reinforcement as we cover the examples."

4. Give frequent quizzes and return them the following day to provide continual feedback.
   - An earth science teacher gives students a short quiz of one or two questions every day. It is discussed at the beginning of the following day, and students calculate their own averages each day during the grading period.

5. Use grading practices that promote success and encourage effort and achievement.
   - An eighth-grade math teacher computes students' averages after the third week of the grading period, shares them with students, and, from that point on awards bonus points for improvement on tests and quizzes. She writes a brief note on the paper every time students improve, praising them for their effort and achievement.

Technology and Learning: Equity Issues

At one time, technology was viewed as the great equalizer, minimizing learning gaps between the rich and poor, minority and nonminority, and male and female students. Unfortunately, recent research suggests a growing "digital divide" involving access to technology for these different groups (National Telecommunications and Information Administration, 1999).

Ethnicity and Computer Use

As shown in Table 4.7, ethnicity plays a major role in access to and use of computers, especially in home use. For example, at the elementary level, while 54% of white students used computers at home, only 21% of African American and 19% of Hispanics used them. Disparities were even greater at the high school level.

Income and Computer Use

Similar disparities occur in terms of parents' incomes. As shown in Table 4.8, in comparing students from families with household incomes ranging from about the poverty level to those above $75,000, huge differences occur in computer use at home and significant differences occur at school. If students are expected to work on computers at home to complete assignments, access is a serious problem.

Table 4.7

Ethnicity and computer use

Ethnicity	School Use of Computer		Home Use of Computer	
	Grades 1–8	Grades 9–12	Grades 1–8	Grades 9–12
White	84%	72%	54%	61%
African American	72%	73%	21%	21%
Hispanic	68%	63%	19%	22%

Source: U.S. Department of Commerce, 1998

Table 4.8

Household income and computer use

Household Income	School Use of Computer		Home Use of Computer	
	Grades 1–8	Grades 9–12	Grades 1–8	Grades 9–12
$15,000–$20,000	75%	67%	16%	21%
$35,000–$40,000	80%	70%	44%	46%
$75,000 or more	86%	72%	80%	81%

Source: U.S. Department of Commerce, 1998

Teachers can help ensure equal access to technology through strategically assigning central roles to girls and minorities.

In addition to computers themselves, access to the Internet is also a problem. Schools serving high percentages of cultural minorities, and schools located in communities with high poverty rates tend to have older, lower quality computers without CD-ROM capability or Pentium or Power Mac processors (Bracey, 1999).

Access to the Internet is also influenced by the percentage of economically disadvantaged students in a school; those with the most disadvantaged students (71% or more) had 17 students per Internet-linked computer versus 10 students per computer for schools with fewer than 11% disadvantaged students (U.S. Department of Education, 1998).

Gender Divides

Gender also influences computer access and use. Boys are three times more likely to enroll in computer clubs and summer classes, and only 15% of users in cyberspace are female (Hale, 1998). At the Massachusetts Institute of Technology, one of the premier science and technology universities in the country, one third of all graduates are women, but only 15% of computer science graduates are women; in comparison, 60% of the graduates in chemistry are women, and 52% in biology are women (Hale, 1998). At the high school level, only 17% of students taking the College Board Advanced Placement Test in computer science were women (American Association of University Women, 1998).

Implications for Teachers

Unquestionably, technology will become increasingly important in our society, and technology can be a powerful learning tool for students. But what can teachers do to ensure that access to the benefits of technology will be distributed equitably to all students? Some suggestions include

▍ *Broaden school access to computers.* Since many students don't have computers at home, take steps to increase access in school, such as allowing students ample

162

time to finish assignments in class, working with administrators to make school computer labs available before and after school and during lunch, and informing students of places where they can access computers like public libraries.

▌ *Use positive role models.* Teachers, especially female, can be effective role models for students by describing how they use technology in their teaching. Teachers can also bring in minority and female members from different professions, such as architecture and construction, to describe how they use technology in their work.

▌ *Stress equity in group assignments.* When students work on computers in groups, openly discuss the need for students to share responsibilities. Also, assign specific roles to female and minority students. Monitor groups so that equitable participation is occurring.

With awareness and effort teachers can do much to ensure that all students benefit from the potential of technology.

Windows on Classrooms

Throughout this chapter, we've seen how sources of individuality—intelligence, SES, culture, and gender—can influence learning. We also saw how some unfortunate combinations of these factors can place students at risk. Further, we've examined the implications these factors have for teachers: sensitivity to differences, building on students' backgrounds, structure and support, active teaching, frequent feedback, and high success rates with appropriate challenge.

Now read the following case study, and assess the teacher's effectiveness in the context of the information you've studied:

Diane Smith was a fifth-grade teacher at Oneida Elementary, a school in a lower-middle-class section of the city. The school was crowded, and Diane had 33 students, 14 of whom were ethnic minorities, in a classroom built for 25. The students sat facing each other across an aisle as shown in the outline of her classroom. Her desk, with a filing cabinet behind it, was on one side of the screen—the chalkboard was behind the screen—with an area for the students to file papers on the opposite side of the screen, next to the door. A worktable was at the back of the room, and the pencil sharpener (ps) was near the door.

In language arts, scheduled from 12:35 to 1:45, Diane had covered adjectives with her students and now wanted to cover the comparative and superlative forms of adjectives.

At 12:33, the students were filing into the room from their lunch break. As they came into the room, they looked at the screen and saw a series of 10 sentences on the overhead with directions stating, "Number your paper from 1 to 10, write down the adjective in each of the sentences, and identify the noun that it modifies."

Her students moved to their desks, took out paper, and began working on the exercises.

At 12:35, all students were seated and busy. As the students were working, Diane surveyed the room, identifying students who had pencils of different lengths and students whose hair colors varied. Deciding that she would use these as examples for her lesson, rather than the pencils and colored pieces of paper she brought with her, she put the pencils and paper back into her filing cabinet.

The students finished at 12:45, and Diane began, "It looks like we're in good shape on these exercises, but let's go over them just to be sure."

Diane reviewed each exercise, identifying both the adjective and the noun in each case.

At 1:05 they finished, and Diane announced, "Okay, very good, everyone. Now put your materials away, and we'll move on to today's lesson."

At 1:06, the students had their papers in their desks, and Diane began, "Calesha and Daniel, hold your pencils up high so that everyone can see. What do you notice about the pencils? . . . Naitia?"

" . . . Calesha's is red and Daniel's is blue."

"Okay. What else?" Diane smiled, " . . . Sheila?"

"You write with them."

"Indeed you do!" Diane nodded and smiled again. "What else, Kevin?" she asked quickly.

"Calesha's is longer."

"That's true," Diane confirmed. "Does everyone see that? Hold them up again," she directed energetically.

Calesha and Daniel held their pencils up again, and Diane moved to the chalkboard and wrote:

Calesha has a long pencil.
Calesha has a longer pencil
than does Daniel.

"Now, let's look at Matt and Leroy. What do you notice about their hair? . . . Judy?" Diane asked as she walked down the aisle.

As she walked back to the front of the room, Diane took a note Elaine had been writing to Maria, folded it so that Elaine saw she didn't read it, and said quietly, "Please pay attention. You can have this back after school."

"Leroy's is black, and Matt's is brown," Randy responded.

"Okay. Good, Randy. So who has darker hair?"

"LEROY!" several in the class blurt out.

"Okay, everyone. I understand your eagerness, and I think it's good," Diane waved at the class. "Just as a reminder, what is one of our most important rules in here? . . . Todd?"

"We wait until you call on us before we answer."

"Okay. Excellent, everyone. You've all done very well with this. We just need a little reminder now and then.

"Now, let's see where we are. What did we say about Leroy's and Matt's hair? . . . Vicki?"

"Leroy's is darker."

"Good!" and Diane then wrote three more sentences on the chalkboard, and they appeared as follows:

Calesha has a long pencil.
Calesha has a longer pencil
than does Daniel.
Leroy has black hair.
Matt has brown hair.
Leroy has darker hair than
does Matt.

"Now, let's look at the adjectives in the sentences and compare them with each other. How do they compare? . . . Heather?"

" . . . The adjectives in the bottom sentences have an -er on the end of them," Heather responded hesitantly.

"Yes, good," Diane smiled reassuringly.

"So, what are we doing in each of the sentences? . . . Jason?" Diane continued.

"We're comparing two things to each other."

"Very good, Jason! And what are we comparing in the first sentence? . . . Lawsikia?"

"The length of the pencils."

"And how about the second sentence? . . . Jana?"

"The color of Leroy's and Matt's hair."

"Good! Now, Calesha and Daniel, hold your pencils up again, and Kerri and David, you hold yours up too. Now, what do you notice? . . . Tom?"

"Kerri's pencil is longer than any of the others."

"Good, Tom. We can see that it is. Now, look at Teresa's hair. What do you notice about it? . . . Angie?"

"It's blonde."

"Yes, it is," Diane nodded, and she then wrote the following three more sentences on the chalkboard:

Calesha has a long pencil.
Calesha has a longer pencil
than does Daniel.
Kerri has the longest pencil.
Leroy has black hair.

Matt has brown hair.
Teresa has blonde hair.
Leroy has darker hair than
does Matt.
Leroy has the darkest hair.

"Now, what do you notice about the adjectives in the third set of sentences? . . . Sean?"

Sean suddenly looked up at the sound of his name, " . . . Could you repeat the question?"

"What do you notice about the adjectives in the third set of sentences?" Diane repeated.

" . . . They have -est on the end of them," Sean said hesitantly.

"Okay. Good, Sean. And what did we do in each of those cases? . . . Spence?"

"We compared the pencils and the hair."

"How many pencils? . . . Steve?"
"Four."
"And how many people's hair? . . . Debbie?"
"Three."
"So, how do we write adjectives if we compare two things? . . . Todd?"

"We put an -er on the end of them."

"And suppose we have three or more things. Then what? . . . Sara?"

"We put an -est on them."

"Very good, everyone. In describing nouns, if we're comparing two, we use the comparative form of the adjective, which has an -er on the end, and if we have three or more, we have an -est on the end of the adjective.

"Now, look," Diane continued, and she reached back and took a tennis ball and a golf ball from her desk. "Write a sentence that tells us about the size of the two balls."

The students then took out paper and began writing their sentences. As they worked, Diane walked up and down the rows, looking at each student's work.

"Now let's look at some sentences," Diane began after a few minutes. "Someone volunteer a sentence, and I'll write it on the chalkboard. . . . Okay, Rashad?"

"The tennis ball is bigger than the golf ball," Rashad volunteered.

"Very good, Rashad. And why did you write bigger with an er in your sentence?"

"We're comparing the size of two balls."

"That's excellent. Now, I want you to write a paragraph that has in it at least two examples that use the comparative form of adjectives and at least two other examples that use the superlative form of the adjectives. Underline the adjectives in each case."

The students then begin writing their paragraphs. As they worked, Diane circulated among them, periodically stopping for a few seconds to comment on a student's work and to offer suggestions.

At 1:40, Diane announced, "All right, everyone. Please turn in your paragraphs; we're going to get ready for social studies."

The students then passed their papers forward. By 1:45, the students had turned in their papers and had their social studies books out and waiting.

Questions for Discussion and Analysis

Analyze Diane's teaching. In conducting your analysis, consider the following questions. In each case, be specific and take information directly from the case study to defend your assessment.

1. Describe how Diane provided structure and support in her teaching. How effective was this structure and support?

2. Did Diane demonstrate active teaching? Cite specific examples to support your answer.

3. To what extent was Diane's teaching designed to emphasize active engagement of the students? Again, cite specific examples.

4. How did Diane attempt to ensure success in her teaching?

5. Most of Diane's students are from relatively low SES backgrounds. Overall, how effective was her teaching for these students?

6. To what extent did Diane display culturally responsive teaching in her lesson?

7. To what extent did Diane's teaching reflect sensitivity to gender issues?

8. How effective was Diane's teaching for students placed at risk?

Now go to our Companion Website to assess your understanding of chapter content with the Student Self-Assessment, apply comprehension in the Online Casebook, and broaden your knowledge base with links to important Educational Psychology World Wide Web sites.

 # Summary

Students differ in intelligence, socioeconomic status (SES), culture, and gender, each of which influences learning. Certain combinations of these factors place students at risk of not being able to take full advantage of their educational experience.

Intelligence

Intelligence is the ability to think and reason abstractly, to solve problems, and to acquire new knowledge. Some theories suggest that intelligence is a single entity; others describe intelligence as existing in several forms.

Experts disagree about the contributions of heredity and environment on the development of intelligence. Nature advocates argue that intelligence is genetically determined; nurture proponents contend that it is influenced primarily by a child's cumulative experiences. Most theorists believe that intelligence is determined by a combination of the two.

The most common response to differences in ability has been to group students according to those differences. Within- and between-class ability grouping is common in elementary schools; tracking is prevalent in middle and secondary schools. Ability grouping can lower performance and stigmatize students in low-ability classes.

Socioeconomic Status

Socioeconomic status (SES) includes parents' income, occupation, and level of education. SES can strongly influence student attitudes, values, background experiences, and school success.

Culture

Culture helps determine the attitudes, values, customs, and behavior patterns a child brings to school. The match between a child's culture and the school has a powerful influence on school success. Culturally responsive teaching creates links between a student's culture and classroom instruction.

Gender

Gender differences in aptitude or intelligence are minor and are caused primarily by different treatment of boys and girls. Teachers can minimize the negative effects of gender differences by treating boys and girls equally and by actively combating negative stereotypes in their teaching.

Students Placed at Risk

Students placed at risk are more likely to exit school with subminimal learning skills. Effective schools for students placed at risk stress high expectations, an academic focus, continuous monitoring of progress, and strong parent involvement. Effective teachers hold high expectations for academic success, use a variety of instructional and motivational strategies, and demonstrate caring through sincere interest in students' lives. Effective instruction for students placed at risk provides greater structure and support, more active teaching, greater student engagement, and more feedback with higher success rates.

 **Important Concepts**

ability grouping (p. 132)

cultural deficit theories
(p. 146)

cultural difference theories
(p. 146)

cultural inversion (p. 142)

culturally responsive
teaching (p. 146)

culture (p. 140)

ethnicity (p. 141)

gender role identity
(p. 149)

intelligence (p. 124)

Joplin plan (p. 133)

learning styles (p. 135)

nature view of intelligence
(p. 130)

nurture view of
intelligence (p. 130)

resilience (p. 155)

socioeconomic status
(SES) (p. 137)

students placed at risk
(p. 154)

tracking (p. 132)

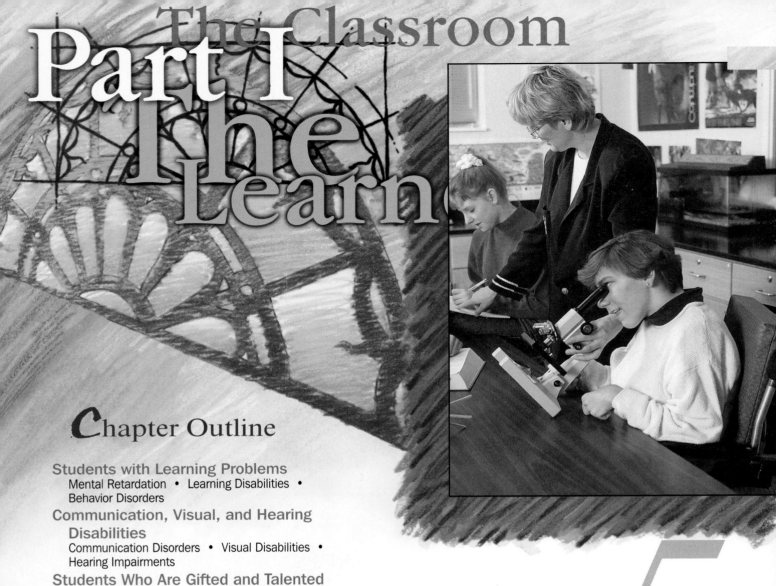

The Classroom

Part I
The Learner

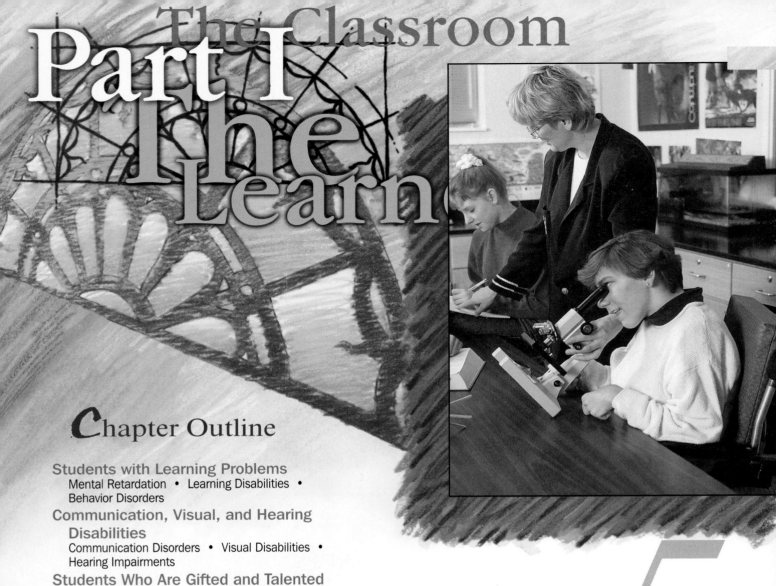

Chapter Outline

Students with Learning Problems
Mental Retardation • Learning Disabilities •
Behavior Disorders

**Communication, Visual, and Hearing
Disabilities**
Communication Disorders • Visual Disabilities •
Hearing Impairments

Students Who Are Gifted and Talented
Creativity: What Is It? • Identifying Students Who Are Gifted
and Talented • Programs for the Gifted: More and Faster or
Deeper and Different?

**Changes in the Way Teachers Help Students
with Exceptionalities**
Federal Laws Redefine Special Education • The Evolution
Toward Inclusion • Putting Inclusion Into Perspective

**A Legal Framework for Working with Students
Who Have Exceptionalities**
Due Process Through Parental Involvement • Protection
Against Discrimination in Testing • Least Restrictive
Environment • Individualized Education Program • Recent
Changes in the Individuals with Disabilities Education Act

The Teacher's Role in Inclusive Classrooms
Identifying Students with Exceptionalities • Teaching
Students with Exceptionalities • Technology and Learning:
Assistive Technology • Strategies for Social Integration
and Growth

5

Learners
with
Exceptionalities

Sabrina Curtis was a beginning first-grade teacher in a large inner-city school district. She survived the hectic first weeks of school and was beginning to feel comfortable as she worked her way into the routines of teaching. At the same time, something bothered her.

"It's kind of frustrating," she admitted, sandwich in hand as she shared her half-hour lunch break with Clarisse, a "veteran" of 3 years who had become her friend and confidant. "I'm teaching the students, but some of them just don't seem to get it."

"Maybe you're being too hard on yourself," Clarisse responded. "Students are different. Remember some of the stuff you studied in college? One thing they emphasized was that we should be trying our best to treat students as individuals."

"Well, . . . yes, . . . I understand that, but that seems almost too pat. I still have this feeling. For instance, there's Rodney. You've seen him on the playground. He's a cute boy, but his engine is stuck on fast," she smiled, rolling her eyes up. "I can barely get him to sit in his seat, much less work.

"When he sits down to do an assignment, he's all over his desk, squirming and wiggling. It takes just the smallest distraction to set him off. He can usually do the work when he sticks to it, but that's a major challenge for him. I've spoken with his mother, and he's the same way at home. I wonder if he has some type of learning disability.

"Then there's Amelia; she's so sweet, but she simply doesn't get it. I've tried everything under the sun with her. I explain it, and the next time, it's as if it's all brand new again. I feel sorry for her, because I know she gets frustrated because she can't keep up with the other kids. What she seems to lack are basic learning strategies like paying attention and keeping track of her assignments. When I work with her individually, it seems to help, but I wish I had more time to spend with her. I just see her falling farther and farther behind."

"Maybe it's not your fault. You're supposed to be bright and energetic and do your best, but you're going to burn yourself out if you keep this up," Clarisse encouraged. "Check with the Teacher Assistance Team. Maybe these students need some extra help."

As you saw in Chapter 4, students differ in several ways, and effective teachers consider these differences when they plan and teach. In some cases, *the differences are such that special help and resources are needed for students to reach their full potential.* In these cases, the students are said to have **exceptionalities**.

Special education refers to *instruction designed to meet the unique needs of students with exceptionalities.* In the past, special education often meant separate classrooms for these students. Today, the practice of inclusion attempts to integrate students with exceptionalities into the regular flow of school and classroom life, and it requires teachers in regular classrooms to play an ever-increasing role in this practice. This chapter is designed to help you prepare for that role.

After you've completed your study of this chapter, you should be able to meet the following objectives:

▌ Explain the role of classroom teachers in working with students with exceptionalities.
▌ Explain how different exceptionalities—mental retardation, learning disabilities, behavior disorders, communication disorders, and visual and hearing impairments—affect learning.
▌ Describe different methods of identifying and teaching students who are gifted and talented.
▌ Explain how instructional strategies can be adapted to meet the needs of students with exceptionalities.

Incidents like those in the opening case study are not uncommon. Although we can't be certain from the brief descriptions, Rodney and Amelia may have problems that prevent them from taking full advantage of their educational opportunities. As teachers, we all work with students who, despite our best efforts, fail to learn as their classmates do.

 # Students with Learning Problems

The terms *children with exceptionalities, special education students, children with handicaps, students with special needs,* and *individuals with disabilities* have all been used to describe students needing additional help to reach their full potential. Currently, the term *students with disabilities* is often preferred because it emphasizes that disabilities can be altered and that they don't necessarily result in handicapped performance (Hallahan & Kauffman, 1997).

A **disability** is *a functional limitation or an inability to do something specific, such as hear or walk.* A **handicap** is *a limitation that an individual experiences in a particular environment,* such as a person in a wheelchair attempting to enter a building. Some disabilities, but not all, lead to handicaps. For example, a student with a visual disability can wear glasses or sit in the front of the classroom to function effectively; if not severe, it isn't a handicap. A challenge for teachers is to try and prevent disabilities from becoming learning handicaps.

About 5 million students are enrolled in special programs, two-thirds of them for relatively minor problems (Heward, 1996). Approximately 10% of students in a typical school receive special education services, and the kinds of disabilities they have range from mild learning problems to physical impairments such as deafness and blindness (U.S. Department of Education, 1997). Federal legislation has created categories to identify specific learning problems, and educators use these categories in developing programs to meet the needs of each type of student.

The use of categories and the labeling that results are controversial (King-Sears, 1997). Advocates argue that categories provide a common language for professionals and encourage specialized instruction that meets the specific needs of all students (Heward, 1996). Opponents claim that categories are arbitrary, many differences exist within the categories, and categorizing encourages educators to treat students as labels rather than as people. Despite the controversy, these categories are widely used, so teachers need to be familiar with the terms and the implications they have for working with students.

Figure 5.1 presents the percentage of students in each of the categories commonly used in education (U.S. Department of Education, 1997). The figure shows that three categories—mental retardation, learning disabilities, and behavior disorders—make up a large majority of the total population (over 70%) of students with disabilities, and they are ones you will most likely encounter in your classroom.

Mental Retardation

Gail Toomey watched her first-grade class as they worked on their reading assignment. Most of the class was working quietly, with occasional whispers and giggles. Stacy, in contrast, was out of her seat for the third time, supposedly sharpening her pencil. Gail had reminded her once to sit down and this time went over to see what the problem was.

"I can't do this! I don't get it!" Stacy responded in frustration when Gail asked her why she hadn't started her work.

Figure 5.1

The exceptional student population

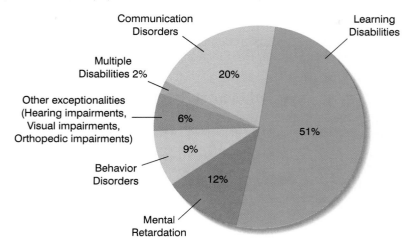

Communication Disorders

Learning Disabilities

Multiple Disabilities 2%

20%

Other exceptionalities (Hearing impairments, Visual impairments, Orthopedic impairments)

6%

51%

9%

Behavior Disorders

12%

Mental Retardation

Source: U.S. Department of Education (1997)

After helping her calm down, Gail worked with Stacy for a few moments, but she could tell by Stacy's responses and her facial expression that she truly didn't "get" the assignment. Gail made a note to herself to talk to a special educator about Stacy.

All first-grade teachers have had experiences similar to Gail's. Stacy, like Amelia in our opening case study, seems to be slower than others and may be frustrated because she can't keep up with her peers. Unfortunately, this problem often isn't identified until students are well into their school experience—sometimes several years. Many of these students have mild mental retardation. (You may also encounter the terms *educationally* or *intellectually handicapped,* which some educators prefer.)

The American Association on Mental Retardation (AAMR) defines **mental retardation** as follows:

> *Mental retardation refers to substantial limitations in present functioning. It is characterized by significantly subaverage intellectual functioning, existing concurrently with related limitations in two or more of the following applicable adaptive skill areas: communication, self-care, home living, social skills, community use, self-direction, health and safety, functional academics, leisure, and work. Mental retardation manifests before age 18.* (italics added) (AAMR Ad Hoc Committee on Terminology and Classification, 1992, p. 5)

This definition emphasizes two important characteristics (Turnbull, Turnbull, Shank, & Leal, 1999). The first identifies limitations in intellectual functioning, as indicated by difficulties in learning; the second focuses on adaptive skills, such as communication, self-care, and social ability. The characteristics suggest the need for support that shifts the focus from the person's limitations to an array of services designed to meet the student's needs.

Before the 1960s, definitions of mental retardation were based primarily on below-average scores on intelligence tests, but this approach had at least three problems. First,

5.1   ▬

In Chapter 4, intelligence was defined as "the capacity to acquire knowledge, the ability to think and reason in the abstract, and the capability for solving novel problems." To which of these is *adaptive behavior* most closely related? Least related?

any test has built-in error, which sometimes resulted in misdiagnoses. Second, disproportionate numbers of minorities and non-English-speaking students were identified as mentally retarded and placed in inappropriate educational settings (Hallahan & Kauffman, 1997; Hardman, Drew, & Egan, 1999). Third, individuals with the same IQ scores varied widely in their ability to cope with the real world, and the differences couldn't be explained based on the tests alone (Heward, 1996). Because of these limitations, adaptive functioning became a central concept in defining mental retardation. Classroom teachers' input is essential in determining adaptive functioning.

Levels of Mental Retardation

Educators describe mental retardation as having four levels, and each relates to the amount of support needed (Turnbull et al., 1999):

- Intermittent: Support on an as-needed basis
- Limited: Support consistently needed over time
- Extensive: Regular (e.g., daily) support required
- Pervasive: High-intensity, potentially life-sustaining support required

This classification system replaces the one based on IQ scores alone. That system categorized people as having either mild (50 to 70 IQ), moderate (35 to 50 IQ), or severe and profound (IQ below 35) mental retardation. The transition from the older, IQ-anchored system to the new one is not complete, so you might encounter both in your work.

Programs for Students with Mental Retardation

Programs for students who have intermittent (mild) mental retardation focus on creating support systems to augment existing instruction. These students are often placed in regular classrooms where teaching is adapted to meet their special needs, and attempts are made to help students fit in socially and academically.

Research indicates that these students often fail to acquire basic learning strategies—such as maintaining attention, organizing new material, and studying for tests—that regular students pick up naturally (Choate, 1997; Heward, 1996). Amelia, in our opening case study, is an example of a student who needs additional help to function successfully in school. Sabrina recognized this need and attempted to provide support by working with her one-on-one.

Learning Disabilities

Tammy Fuller, a middle school social studies teacher, was surprised as she scored Adam's test. He seemed to be doing so well. He was rarely absent, paid attention, and participated willingly and intelligently. Why was his test score so low? Tammy made a mental note to watch him more closely, because his classroom behavior and his test performance were inconsistent.

In her second unit, Tammy emphasized both independent and cooperative work, so she prepared study guide questions and had students work in groups to study the material. As she circulated around the room, she noticed that Adam's sheet was empty; when she asked him about it, he mumbled something about not having time the night before. Because the success of the unit depended on students coming to class prepared, Tammy asked Adam to come in after school to complete his work.

Adam arrived promptly at 3:10 and opened his book to the chapter. When Tammy stopped to check on his progress 15 minutes later, his page was blank; in another 15 minutes, it was still virtually empty.

As she sat down to talk with him, he appeared embarrassed and evasive. When they started to work on the questions together, she discovered that he couldn't read the text.

Some students, such as Adam, have average or above average intelligence but, despite their teachers' best efforts, have a difficult time learning. These are students with **learning disabilities (LDs)**, *difficulties in acquiring and using listening, speaking, reading, writing, reasoning, or mathematical abilities* (The National Joint Committee on Learning Disabilities, 1994). Problems with reading, writing, and listening are most common. Learning disabilities are assumed to be due to central nervous system dysfunction, and they may exist along with, but are not caused by, other disabilities such as sensory impairments or attention problems.

Students with learning disabilities are the largest group of students with exceptionalities—approximately 4% of the total school-age population. The category first became widely used in the early 1960s, and the number of school-age children diagnosed as having learning disabilities has continually increased, now consisting of more than half of all children with disabilities (U.S. Department of Education, 1997).

Although it is probable that every classroom will have students with learning disabilities, they are often overlooked because learning disabilities are difficult to identify.

Characteristics of Students with Learning Disabilities

5.2
Identify at least one similarity and one difference between *learning disabilities* and *mental retardation*.

Students with learning disabilities have problems such as those outlined in Table 5.1. However, each student with a learning disability is unique, and educational adaptations should be individualized.

Some of the characteristics shown in Table 5.1 are typical of general learning problems or immaturity. Unlike developmental lags, however, problems associated with learning disabilities often increase over time instead of disappearing. Students fall farther behind in achievement, management problems increase, and self-esteem decreases (Hardman et al., 1999; Heward, 1996). Lowered achievement and reduced self-esteem exacerbate each other and result in major learning problems.

Rodney, in the case study at the beginning of this chapter, may have a learning disability. He's hyperactive, easily distracted, and has difficulties focusing his attention. His teacher is wise in seeking additional help for him. But before she does, she should examine how well her instruction and the learning environment meet Rodney's specific learning needs. For example, teachers often find that moving a student like Rodney to a quieter part of the room can eliminate distractions and help him focus on learning tasks. The characteristics he displays may suggest either a learning disability or attention deficit/hyperactivity disorder, but his teacher should explore other possibilities before seeking outside help.

Table 5.1

Characteristics of students with learning disabilities

General Patterns
Hyperactivity and fidgeting
Lack of coordination and balance
Attention deficits
Disorganization and tendency toward distraction
Lack of follow-through and completion of assignments
Uneven performance (e.g., capable in one area, extremely weak in others)

Academic Performance	
Reading	Lacks reading fluency
	Reverses words (e.g., *saw* for *was*)
	Frequently loses place
Writing	Makes jerky and poorly formed letters
	Has difficulty staying on line
	Is slow in completing work
	Has difficulty in copying from chalkboard
Math	Has difficulty remembering math facts
	Mixes columns (e.g., 10s and 1s) in computing
	Has trouble with story problems

Attention Deficit/Hyperactivity Disorder

Attention deficit/hyperactivity disorder (AD/HD) is *a learning problem characterized by high rates of purposeless movement and students' inability to focus their attention on the learning task at hand*. Attention problems and hyperactivity are often connected with a learning disability; estimates indicate that at least a third of students with learning disabilities also have attention problems (Hallahan & Kauffman, 1997). Teachers should use caution in applying this term because high levels of activity and inability to focus attention are often characteristics of developmental lags, especially in young boys.

Characteristics of AD/HD include:

▮ Difficulty in concentrating and failure to finish tasks
▮ Inattention and distractibility
▮ Forgetfulness and inordinate need for supervision
▮ Impulsiveness (e.g., acting before thinking, frequent calling out in class, and difficulty awaiting turns)

These characteristics suggest that AD/HD students have difficulty controlling their responses to the stimuli around them (Barkley, 1994; Davies, Luflig, & Witte, 1999). It's easy to see why students with AD/HD have difficulties adjusting to the "sit-down" pace of school life, where many activities are done quietly at a desk (Nahmias, 1995).

AD/HD usually appears early (at age 2 or 3 years), and three to nine times as many boys as girls are identified (American Psychiatric Association, 1994). Treatments range from medication (e.g., the controversial drug Ritalin) to reinforcement programs and structured teaching environments (described later in this chapter). Diagnosis and treatment of AD/HD are usually done in consultation with medical experts.

> **5.3** ▬
> Explain the high ratio of boys to girls with AD/HD from a genetic, or nature, position; from an environmental, or nurture, position; and from an interactionist position.

Identifying and Working with Students Who Have Learning Disabilities

As with all exceptionalities, identification is the first step, and it must be done early to prevent damaging effects from accumulating. Although early identification is essential, at least two factors complicate the process. First, uneven rates of development can easily be mistaken for learning disabilities, and second, classroom management issues can complicate identification. Students with learning disabilities frequently display inappropriate classroom behavior, and misbehaving students are referred as having learning disabilities at a much higher rate than those who behave appropriately (Gottleib & Weinberg, 1999). On the other hand, students with learning disabilities who comply with rules and complete assignments on time are often passed over for referral. These patterns can be gender related; more boys than girls are identified because boys tend to act out, whereas girls tend to be quiet (Heward, 1996).

Using Classroom-Based Information for Identification.   The teacher plays an important role in identifying and working with a learning disability (Mamlin & Harris, 1998). Information taken from teachers' assessments of behavior, anecdotal records, direct observation, and curriculum-based measurements are combined with test scores. Often, a discrepancy model, which looks for differences in three areas, will be used to diagnose the problem (Turnbull et al., 1999):

1. Differences between intelligence and achievement test performance
2. Differences between intelligence test scores and school achievement
3. Large differences between subtests on either intelligence or achievement tests

The rationale is that performance in one area, such as an intelligence test, should predict performance in others; when the two are not comparable, a learning disability may be the cause.

Earlier, we mentioned the problem of labeling. Critics contend that *learning disability* is a catch-all term for students who have learning problems (Spear-Swerling & Sternberg, 1998). Part of this criticism results from the rapid growth of the category—nonexistent in the early 1960s to the largest category of exceptionality at present. Before using the learning disability label, teachers should examine their own instruction to ensure it meets the needs of different students.

Adaptive Instruction.   Students with learning disabilities require modified instruction and teacher support. Because learning disabilities have different causes, the most effective strategies are tailored to meet each student's needs. One study of 25 college students with learning disabilities illustrates the range of modifications that increase success (Cowan, 1988). These students budgeted their time carefully, attended class regularly, and completed all work on time. To compensate for reading deficits, they always read in a quiet environment, subvocalized (read aloud to themselves), and even purchased previously highlighted books. In writing, they used a dictionary, frequently substituted an easier word if they had trouble spelling one, and asked other people to proofread their papers. Other strategies included using taped textbooks, tape-recording lectures to compensate for poor note taking, and asking for extra time on tests or for someone to help them read through test questions.

Behavior Disorders

> Kyle came in from recess sweaty and disheveled, crossed his arms, and looked at the teacher defiantly. The playground monitor had reported another scuffle. Kyle had a history of these disturbances and was a difficult student. He struggled at his studies but could handle them if provided with enough structure. When he became frustrated, he sometimes acted out, often ignoring the feelings and rights of others.
>
> Ben, who sat next to Kyle, was so quiet that the teacher almost forgot he was there. He never caused problems. In fact, he seldom participated in class. He had few friends and walked around at recess by himself, appearing to consciously avoid other children.

Although their behaviors are very different, these two students both display symptoms of a behavior disorder. This term is often used interchangeably with *emotional disturbance, emotional disability,* or *emotional handicap*, and you may encounter any of these terms in your work. The term *behaviorally disordered* is preferred because it focuses on overt behavior instead of internal causes.

Students with **behavior disorders (BDs)** *display serious and persistent age-inappropriate behaviors that result in social conflict, personal unhappiness, and school failure*. In this definition, the terms *serious* and *persistent* are important. Many children occasionally fight with their peers, and all children go through periods when they want to be alone. When these patterns are chronic and interfere with normal development and school performance, however, a behavior disorder may exist.

Prevalence of Behavior Disorders

Estimates of the frequency of behavior disorders vary (Hardman et al., 1999). Some suggest that about 1% of the total school population and about 9% of the special education population have the problem (U.S. Department of Education, 1997), whereas others suggest that it's closer to 6% to 10% of the total population (Hallahan & Kauffman, 1997). Identification is a problem because the characteristics are elusive, making diagnosis difficult (Turnbull et al., 1999).

Kinds of Behavior Disorders

Behavior disorders can be *externalizing* or *internalizing* (Hallahan & Kauffman, 1997). Students like Kyle fall into the first category, exhibiting characteristics such as hyperactivity, defiance, hostility, and even cruelty. Males are three times more likely to be labeled as having an externalizing behavior disorder than females, and a higher incidence of this category exists in low-socioeconomic status and minority students. Evidence suggests that some aggressive behaviors are learned from aggressive parents and peers (Hallahan & Kauffman, 1997). Externalizing children often don't respond to typical rules and consequences.

Internalized behavior disorders are characterized by social withdrawal, guilt, depression, and anxiety. Like Ben, these children lack self-confidence and are often shy, timid, and depressed—sometimes suicidal. They have few friends and are isolated and withdrawn (H. Walker & Bullis, 1991). Because they don't have the high profile of the acting-

Students with behavior disorders fall into two major categories: externalizing, characterized by acting out, and internalizing, characterized by social withdrawal and anxiety.

out student, many go unnoticed, so a teacher's sensitivity and awareness are crucial in identifying these students.

Students with behavior disorders often have academic problems, some of which are connected with learning disabilities. The combination of these problems results in a dropout rate of 40%, the highest of any group of students with special needs (U.S. Department of Education, 1999).

Teaching Students with Behavior Disorders

Since students with behavior disorders have problems monitoring and controlling their behaviors, a classroom environment that invites participation and success while providing structure through clearly stated and uniformly enforced rules and expectations is essential.

Behavior Management Strategies.   Behavioral management strategies are commonly used (Alberto & Troutman, 1999). Some include:

- *Positive reinforcement:*   Identifying and rewarding positive behaviors (e.g., negotiating for a wanted toy)
- *Replacement:*   Teaching appropriate behaviors that substitute for inappropriate ones (e.g., expressing personal feelings versus verbal aggression toward another student)
- *Extinction:*   Ignoring disruptive behaviors
- *Time out:*   Removing the child from opportunities for reward for brief periods of time
- *Overcorrection:*   Requiring restitution beyond the damaging effects of the immediate behavior (e.g., requiring a child to return one of his own cookies in addition to the one he took from another student)

5.4

Identify at least one similarity and one difference between students with *learning disabilities* and those with *behavior disorders*.

5.5

Which behavioral management strategy would likely be *least* effective in working with Kyle, the student at the beginning of this section? Explain.

Self-Management Skills.   Teaching self-management skills can also be effective (Heward, 1996). For instance, students might be helped to identify behaviors they want to increase (such as making eye contact with the teacher) or decrease (such as finger snapping or playing with a pencil). They are then taught to evaluate their behaviors when a timer goes off at their desks. By counting and graphing the results, students monitor their own behavior over the course of the day. The teacher also meets with them—frequently at first—to reinforce progress and to set new goals. This strategy has succeeded in increasing desired behaviors such as paying attention, as well as decreasing other behaviors, like talking out and leaving seats without permission (Alberto & Troutman, 1999).

Teacher Flexibility and Sensitivity.   Students with behavior disorders can be difficult to teach, and frustrated teachers sometimes forget that they have unique needs. A school psychologist describes an encounter that illustrates this point.

The psychologist was testing a 4-year-old boy who had been referred to her for aggressive behaviors and acting "out of control." The psychologist found the young boy to be friendly, polite, and cooperative, and the session went smoothly until the child announced he was done. When the psychologist tried to get him to continue, an outburst followed with screaming, kicking, and shoving and the boy running out of the room.

> I assumed the testing phase of the evaluation was over and started writing a few notes. . . . A few minutes later, however, the little boy returned . . . and said that he was ready to continue. After another 10 minutes or so . . . the child again said, "I'm done now," to which I replied, "That's fine." The child calmly got out of his chair, walked around the room for a minute, and then sat down to resume testing. This pattern was repeated. . . .
>
> It was easy to see in a one-to-one testing situation that this child recognized the limits of his concentration and coped with increasing frustration by briefly removing himself. . . . It is equally easy to see, however, how this behavior created problems in the classroom. By wandering around, he would be disrupting the learning of other children. When the teacher tried to make him sit back down, she was increasing his frustration by removing from him the one method he had developed for coping. (Griffith, 1992, p. 34)

But how do teachers deal with behavior like this in the regular classroom? The psychologist suggested marking an area in the back of the room where the child could go when he became frustrated. With this safety valve in place, the teacher could return to her teaching and work with the boy on other, long-term coping strategies. By attempting to understand the acting-out child as an individual, the teacher was able to continue with her instructional agenda while meeting the needs of the student.

Classroom Connections

Teaching Students with Exceptionalities in Your Classroom

1. Identify resources that are available for working with students with exceptionalities.
   - A beginning teacher talks with other teachers about their past experiences in working with students with exceptionalities: What approaches work for them? Who in the school is especially helpful in working with these students? Who do they turn to when they needed help?
   - A first-year teacher talks with the principal about programs and personnel available in the building

and the school district. She makes an effort to introduce herself to the special education team in the building and find out how the referral process works.

2. Use a variety of data sources for help in identifying and understanding the students with exceptionalities in your classroom.
   - A third-grade teacher starts the school year by giving her students diagnostic work sheets in all the subject matter areas. Each assignment is arranged in order of difficulty. After the teacher has a complete battery from each student, she spends a weekend reviewing the worksheets and identifying each student's strengths and weaknesses.
   - A junior high teacher is having trouble with one student. After talking with the student's other teachers, he looks over her past records and discusses the problem with the guidance counselor. Then he calls the student in and talks with her about the problem directly.

3. Work to create a positive classroom learning environment for students with exceptionalities who are in your classroom.
   - At the beginning of the school year, a first-grade teacher explains to the class where resource students go and why. He explains that all people are different and that some people learn in different ways.
   - A sixth-grade teacher sits with his pull-out students in one-to-one sessions to voice his support for the program and to explain that any assignments they miss will be written on assignment sheets for them. He also sends a letter home to parents, explaining these procedures and inviting their questions or comments.

Communication, Visual, and Hearing Disabilities

Communication, visual, and hearing impairments are exceptionalities that also detract from learning. In addition to spoken words, teachers use overheads, chalkboards, maps, and diagrams to illustrate ideas and connections between concepts. A disability can prevent students from capitalizing on these instructional aids.

Communication Disorders

Communication disorders *interfere with students' abilities to receive and understand information from others and express their own ideas or questions.* They exist in two forms. **Speech or expressive disorders** *involve problems in forming and sequencing sounds.* Examples are stuttering and mispronouncing words, such as saying, "I taw it" for "I saw it." **Language or receptive disorders** *include problems with understanding language or in using language to express ideas.* Language disorders are often connected to other problems, such as a hearing impairment, learning disability, or mental retardation.

As shown in Table 5.2, there are three kinds of speech disorders. If they are chronic, a therapist is usually required, but sensitive teachers can help students cope with the emotional and social problems that are often associated with them.

Language disorders are more serious than speech disorders and involve more than the production of sounds. The vast majority of students learn to communicate quite well by the time they start school, but a small percentage (less than 1%) experience problems expressing themselves verbally.

Table 5.2

Kinds of speech disorders

Disorder	Description	Example
Articulation disorders	Difficulty in producing certain sounds, including substituting, distorting, and omitting	'Wabbit' for rabbit 'Thit' for sit 'Only' for lonely
Fluency disorders	Repetition of the first sound of a word (stuttering)	'Y, Y, Y, Yes'
Voice disorders	Problems with the larynx or air passageways in the nose or throat	High-pitched or nasal voice

Symptoms of a language disorder include:

▌ Seldom speaking, even during play
▌ Using few words or very short sentences
▌ Overrelying on gestures to communicate

The causes of language disorders include hearing loss, brain damage, learning disabilities, mental retardation, severe emotional problems, and inadequate developmental experiences in a child's early years. If teachers suspect a communication disorder, they should keep cultural diversity in mind. As you saw in Chapter 4, English is not the primary language for many students. The difficulties involved in learning both content and a second language should not be confused with communication disorders. These students will respond to an enriched language environment and teacher patience and understanding. Students with language disorders require the help of a language specialist.

Helping Students with Communication Disorders

Primary tasks for the teacher working with students who have communication disorders are identification, acceptance, and follow-through on classroom instruction. As with other exceptionalities, teachers play an important role in identification because they are in the best position to assess students' performances in classroom settings. Modeling and encouraging acceptance are crucial because teasing and social rejection can cause lasting emotional damage. It is not easy being a student who talks differently. In communicating with these students, a teacher should be patient and refrain from correcting their speech, which calls attention to the problem. Also, cooperative and small-group activities provide opportunities for students to practice their language skills in informal and less threatening settings.

Visual Disabilities

One in ten students enters school with some type of visual impairment (Kirk & Gallagher, 1989). Fortunately, most can be corrected with glasses, surgery, or therapy. In some situations, though—approximately 1 child in 1,000—the impairment cannot be corrected. People with this condition have a **visual disability**, *an uncorrectable impairment that interferes with learning.*

Figure 5.2

Symptoms of potential visual problems

1. Holding the head in an awkward position when reading, or holding the book too close or too far away.
2. Squinting and frequently rubbing the eyes.
3. Tuning out when information is presented on the chalkboard.
4. Constantly asking about classroom procedures, especially when information is on the board
5. Complaining of headaches, dizziness, or nausea.
6. Having redness, crusting, or swelling of the eyes.
7. Losing place on the line or page and confusing letters.
8. Using poor spacing in writing or having difficulty in staying on the line.

Source: Hallahan and Kauffman (1994)

Nearly two thirds of visual impairments exist at birth, and most children are screened for visual problems when they enter elementary school. Some visual impairments, however, do appear during the school years as a result of growth spurts, and teachers should remain alert to the possibility of an unscreened visual impairment in students. Some symptoms of vision problems are outlined in Figure 5.2.

Research on people with visual disabilities reveals little or no lag in intellectual development (Kirk & Gallagher, 1989), but word meanings in language development may not be as rich or elaborated because of the students' lack of visual experience with the world. As a result, hands-on experiences are even more important for students with visual disabilities than they are for other learners.

5.6
Who, Piaget or Vygotsky (from your study of Chapter 2), would more strongly favor instructional modifications emphasizing hands-on experiences for visually disabled students? Explain how they would differ in their suggestions for using the materials.

Adaptive instructional devices—such as machines and books with large print, Braille printers, and books in Braille—allow students with visual disabilities to integrate into the regular classroom.

Working with Students Who Have Visual Disabilities

Suggestions for working with visually disabled students include seating them near chalkboards and overheads, verbalizing while writing on the board, and ensuring that duplicated handouts are dark and clear (Heward, 1996). Large-print books and magnifying aids also help adapt instructional materials. Peer tutors can provide assistance in explaining and clarifying assignments and procedures.

Lowered self-esteem and learned helplessness are two possible side effects of a visual disability. Learned helplessness results from teachers and other students overreacting to the disability and doing for the student what the student, with training, can do alone. This can result in an unhealthy dependence on others and can compound self-esteem problems (Hallahan & Kauffman, 1997).

Hearing Impairments

Hearing impairments can be divided into two categories. A student who has a **partial hearing impairment** *uses a hearing aid and hears well enough to be taught through auditory channels*. A student who is **deaf** *has hearing that is impaired enough so that other senses, usually sight, are used to communicate*. Only about 1 student in 1,000 is deaf; 3 to 4 in 1,000 are severely hard of hearing (Kirk & Gallagher, 1989).

Hearing impairments result from rubella, or German measles, during pregnancy, heredity, complications during birth or pregnancy, meningitis, and other childhood diseases (Kirk & Gallagher, 1989). Unfortunately, in almost 40% of cases involving hearing loss, the cause is unknown; this makes prevention and remediation more difficult.

A trained audiologist working in a school screening program is the best method of identifying students with hearing problems, but these programs don't exist everywhere, and students can be overlooked because of transfers or absences. When such an omission happens, the classroom teacher's awareness of the signs of hearing difficulties is essential. These are outlined in Figure 5.3.

Figure 5.3

Indicators of hearing impairment

1. Favoring one ear by cocking the head toward the speaker or cupping a hand behind the ear.
2. Misunderstanding or not following directions, and exhibiting nonverbal cues (e.g., frowns or puzzled looks) when directions are given.
3. Being distracted or seeming disoriented at times.
4. Asking people to repeat what they have just said.
5. Poorly articulating words, especially consonants.
6. Turning the volume up loud when listening to cassette recorders, radio, or television.
7. Showing reluctance to participate in oral activities.
8. Having frequent earaches or complaining of discomfort or buzzing in the ears.

Source: Adapted from Kirk and Gallagher (1989)

Working with Students Who Have Hearing Impairments

Lack of proficiency in speech and language are learning problems that result from hearing impairments. These problems affect learning that relies on reading, writing, and listening. Teachers should remember that these language deficits don't mean learners are unintelligent; students with hearing impairment can learn if appropriately helped.

Programs for students with hearing impairment combine regular classroom instruction with supplementary classes; 92% of students who are deaf are in full- or part-time special education classes, and about half of these are mainstreamed in regular classes (Kirk & Gallagher, 1989). Supplementary programs for students who are deaf include using whatever hearing there is together with lipreading, sign language, and finger spelling. Total communication, which uses the simultaneous presentation of manual approaches (signing and finger spelling) and speech (through speech reading and residual hearing), is becoming more popular (Heward, 1996).

Students Who Are Gifted and Talented

What is it like to be gifted in a regular classroom? Here are the thoughts of one 9-year-old:

> Oh what a bore to sit and listen,
> To stuff we already know.
> Do everything we've done and done again,
> But we still must sit and listen.
> Over and over read one more page
> Oh bore, oh bore, oh bore.
> Sometimes I feel if we do one more page
> My head will explode with boreness rage
> I wish I could get up right there and march right out the door.
> (Delisle, 1984, p. 72)

While we don't think of gifted and talented students as having an exceptionality, they also are often unable to reach their full potential in the regular classroom. **Students who are gifted and talented** are *those at the upper end of the ability continuum who need supplemental help to realize their full potential*. At one time, the term *gifted* was used to identify these students, but the category has been enlarged to include both students who do well on IQ tests (typically 130 and above) and those who demonstrate above-average talents in such diverse areas as math, creative writing, and music (G. Davis & Rimm, 1993; Subotnik, 1997).

The history of gifted and talented education in the United States began with a longitudinal study of gifted students by Louis Terman and his colleagues (Terman, Baldwin, & Bronson, 1925; Terman & Oden, 1947, 1959). Using teacher recommendations and IQ test scores, he identified 1,500 gifted individuals to track over a lifetime of development (the study is projected to run until 2010). In addition to finding that these students did better academically, the researchers found that they:

- Were better adjusted as children and adults
- Were better achievers and learned more easily
- Had more hobbies
- Read more books
- Were healthier

This and more current research have done much to dispel the stereotype of gifted students as maladjusted and narrow "brains" (Moon, Zentall, Grskovic, Hall, & Stormont-Spurgin, 1997).

Enrichment activities provide opportunities for gifted students to explore alternative areas of the curriculum.

5.7

Identify at least one similarity between the Congressional definition of giftedness and Gardner's (1983, 1995) description of intelligence.

Present views of gifted and talented students see them as possessing diverse abilities and needs. The current definition used by the federal government identifies them as possessing demonstrated or potential abilities that give evidence of high performance capability in areas such as intellectual, creative, specific academic or leadership ability, or in the performing and visual arts, and who by reason thereof require services or activities not ordinarily provided by the school. (U.S. Congress, Educational Amendment of 1978 [PL 95-561, IX(A)])

Another popular definition uses three criteria (Renzulli, 1986):

1. Above-average ability
2. High levels of motivation and task commitment
3. High levels of creativity

According to this definition, not only are gifted people "smart," but they also use this ability in focused and creative ways.

More recent work in the area of gifted education has shifted from a general notion of giftedness to giftedness or talent in specific areas. For example, John Feldhusen's (1998) *Talent Identification and Development in Education* (TIDE) program seeks to identify talents in specific domains and match instruction to those areas. In a similar way the *Levels of Service* (LOS) approach adapts instruction on the basis of specific student strengths (Treffinger, 1998). Like intelligence, the area of gifted education is focusing more on multiple forms of giftedness, attempting to develop each student's unique talents and strengths (Black, 1998).

Creativity: What Is It?

Creativity is *the ability to identify or prepare original and divergent solutions to problems.* Creativity and IQ are related but not identical (Sternberg, 1989; Torrance, 1995); intellectual ability that is at least average is a necessary, but not sufficient, component of creativity. People who score low on IQ tests typically don't score high on measures of creativity; people who score high on IQ tests may or may not score high on measures of creativity. Like intelligence, it is probably influenced by both genetics and the environment.

Research suggests that creativity uses three kinds of intelligence: *Synthetic intelligence*, which helps a creative person to see a problem in a new way; *analytic intelligence*, which allows a person to recognize productive ideas and allocate resources to solve problems; and *practical intelligence*, which helps a creative person use feedback to promote ideas. In all three, the emphasis is on problem solving in real-world settings.

Divergent thinking, or the ability to generate a variety of original answers to questions or problems, is a central component in many definitions of creativity (Guilford, 1988). Divergent thinking has three dimensions:

- Fluency—the ability to produce many ideas relevant to a problem
- Flexibility—being able to break from an established set to generate new perspectives
- Originality—the facility for generating new and different ideas

To illustrate each, let's consider a social studies class discussing the problem of world hunger. Fluency would result in many solutions to the problem, such as growing food in domes in deserts, altering humans' genetic makeup so that they require less food, and growing food on the moon; flexibility would cast the problem in a new light (e.g., from economic or political rather than traditional perspectives); and originality would produce new and creative solutions to the problem (e.g., superpower cooperation).

More recently, Howard Gardner (1993) (see Chapter 4) defined the creative person as one "who regularly solves problems, fashions products, or defines new questions in a domain in a way that is initially considered novel but that ultimately becomes accepted" (p. 35). Here creativity is viewed as a recurring trait, rather than as a one-time event. Also, creativity typically occurs within, rather than across, domains, such as within art or music but not both. As with most aspects of learning, creativity requires background knowledge (Shaughnessy, 1998; Sternberg & Lubart, 1995). Knowledge makes a person aware of what has gone before—prevents "reinventing the wheel"—and allows a person to concentrate on new ideas instead of existing ones.

Teachers play an important role in developing students' creativity (Esquival, 1995; Shaughnessy, 1998). Their attitudes, the learning environments they create, and the way they interact with students all communicate whether or not they value creativity.

> **5.8** ▬
> A science class is discussing the problem of pollution and the environment. Explain how the creative elements of fluency, flexibility, and originality might be applied to the solution of this problem.

Measuring Creativity

Creativity is usually measured by giving students a verbal or pictorial stimulus and asking them to generate as many responses as they can, such as listing as many uses as possible for a brick (e.g., doorstop, bookshelf, paperweight, weapon, building block) or suggesting ways to improve a common object such as a chair (G. Davis, 1989). Pictorial tasks involve turning an ambiguous partial sketch into an interesting picture. Responses are then evaluated in terms of fluency, flexibility, and originality. Current ways of measuring creativity are controversial, with critics charging that existing tests are too narrow and fail to capture its different aspects (Sternberg, 1989; Ward, Ward, Landrum, & Patton, 1992).

Identifying Students Who Are Gifted and Talented

Meeting the needs of gifted and talented students requires early identification. Failure to do so can result in gifted underachievers with social and emotional problems linked to boredom and unmotivating school experiences (Clinkenbeard, 1992; Dai, Moon, & Feldhusen, 1998). Current identification practices often miss students who are gifted and talented because they rely heavily on standardized test scores and teacher nominations (G. Davis & Rimm, 1993; Gallagher, 1998). Experts recommend more flexible and less culturally dependent methods, such as creativity measures and peer and parent nominations in addition to teacher recommendations (G. Davis & Rimm, 1993).

Minorities are underrepresented in gifted programs, and the reasons include limited definitions of giftedness, lack of culturally sensitive means of assessing potential, and over-reliance on standardized tests (Strom, 1990; Tomlinson, Callahan, & Lelli, 1997). For example, standardized tests are usually verbal and in English. Students for whom English is a second language have two challenges—the test itself and understanding and responding in English. Minority students also may not understand the "classroom game" as well as other students, which teachers interpret as lack of ability or potential (Subotnik, 1997). In addition, minority youth may lack gifted role models, or mentors, who have succeeded in school or in work (Pleiss & Feldhusen, 1995; Tomlinson et al., 1997).

As with all exceptionalities, teachers' roles are crucial in identifying gifted and talented learners because they work with these students and can identify strengths that tests miss. However, research indicates that teachers often confuse conformity, neatness, and good behavior with being gifted and talented (G. Davis & Rimm, 1993).

What should teachers look for in attempting to identify gifted and talented students? Experts have identified the following characteristics (G. Davis & Rimm, 1993):

- Likes to work alone
- Is imaginative, enjoys pretending
- Is highly verbal and flexible in thinking
- Is persistent, stays with a task
- Goes beyond assignments
- Is often bored with routine tasks
- Is sometimes impulsive, with little interest in details

Working with these students can be challenging; their giftedness places unique demands on teachers, and the flexibility of teachers' responses can make school a happy or an unhappy experience for these students.

Programs for the Gifted: More and Faster or Deeper and Different?

Programs for the gifted and talented are typically based on either **acceleration**, which *keeps the curriculum the same but allows students to move through it more quickly,* or **enrichment**, which *provides richer and varied content through strategies that supplement usual grade-level work.* Table 5.3 offers examples of each.

Time for acceleration or enrichment can be generated through a process called **curriculum compacting**, which *is an approach to individualization that identifies mastered content, concentrates on content not yet mastered, and uses the time saved for acceleration or enrichment* (Reis, 1992). For example, a primary teacher might pretest math skills at the beginning of a new unit and then focus on unmet objectives, freeing students to pursue additional math topics or content in other areas. The practice evolved from research indicating that gifted students are often asked to spend time on content they already understand (Reis & Purcell, 1992).

Which is better? Critics of enrichment call it busywork and irrelevant, contending that students should be provided a healthy menu of regular academic fare. Critics of accel-

5.9

Explain why curriculum compacting is most easily adopted in areas such as math and reading.

Table 5.3

Options in enrichment and acceleration programs

Enrichment Options	Acceleration Options
1. Independent study and independent projects	1. Early admission to kindergarten and first grade
2. Learning centers	2. Grade skipping
3. Field trips	3. Subject skipping
4. Saturday programs	4. Credit by exam
5. Summer programs	5. College courses in high school
6. Mentors and mentorships	6. Correspondence courses
7. Simulations and games	7. Early admission to college
8. Small-group investigations	
9. Academic competitions	

eration point to the narrowness of the regular curriculum, the dangers of pushing students too fast, and possible social mismatches when younger students are thrown together with older students. One research study found that accelerated students surpassed by nearly one grade level the achievement of nonaccelerated students of equal age and intelligence (Kulik & Kulik, 1984). These students were also equivalent in achievement to older, talented, but nonaccelerated students. No affective differences, such as attitudes toward school or self-concept, were found. A 10-year longitudinal study also found no negative effects resulting from acceleration (Swialth & Benbow, 1991).

Supporters point to these studies as evidence for the superiority of acceleration (Feldhusen, 1989). Critics counter that the comparison is unfair because the outcomes of enrichment, such as creativity and problem solving, are not easily measured on standardized achievement tests. The question remains unanswered, and the debate is likely to continue.

Classroom Connections

Teaching Students with Disabilities in Your Classroom

1. Work closely with parents and other professionals to understand the special needs of students with physical disabilities.
   - A second-grade teacher, knowing a student with hearing impairment will be in her class, talks with the student's previous teacher and discusses strategies that work for him. She also meets with the special education teacher, who gives her materials on working with those who have hearing impairment. She also makes a special effort to communicate with the student's parents about the student's strengths and needs.
   - A high school math teacher works with parents and the special education specialist in his school to

adapt his instruction for a student with partial vision. He seats her at the front of the room, consciously uses the front chalkboard, and makes a special effort to write clearly, using large numbers and letters. He also repeats written information aloud. If the print on quizzes and assignments is too small, he asks other students to help copy problems.

2. Help other students understand the disability and enlist their aid in supporting the student.
   • Before a blind student is transferred into a sixth-grade teacher's class, the teacher holds a class meeting to discuss the new student's disability and asks the other students to think of ways to make the classroom a positive learning environment.
   • A junior high teacher notices nervous shuffling and muffled laughter when a quiet boy stutters during the first week of class. The next day, the teacher sends the student to the office on an assignment and discusses the problem with the rest of the class. She explains how everyone stutters when nervous and how important it is to give each student a chance to participate. In the next few days, she makes a special effort to call on the student, especially when she thinks he knows the answer. When the student responds, she is careful to make eye contact and not interrupt or complete sentences for the boy.

Teaching Students Who Are Gifted and Talented in Your Classroom

3. Prevent boredom in the classroom by providing supplementary activities.
   • A sixth-grade teacher confers with her students who are gifted and talented at the beginning of each grading period to identify areas of interest and to outline projects. After students have finished their regular work, they are free to read books and work on their projects.
   • A junior high math teacher pretests students at the beginning of each unit. Whenever a student has mastered the concepts and objectives of the unit, he or she receives an honor pass to work on an alternative activity in the school media center. The activities may be extensions or applications of the concepts taught in the unit, or they may involve learning about mathematical principles or math history not usually taught in the regular classroom.

4. Integrate activities that require creativity and critical thinking in the classroom.
   • A high school social studies teacher caps off every unit with a hypothetical problem (e.g., "What would the United States be like today if Great Britain had won the Revolutionary War?"). Students work in groups to address the question.
   • A junior high science teacher begins every unit with a problem or question (e.g., "How are birds and airplanes similar?"). She leaves the question unanswered and returns to it for discussion at the end of the unit.

Changes in the Way Teachers Help Students with Exceptionalities

In the past, students with exceptionalities were separated from their peers and placed in segregated classrooms or schools. However, instruction in these situations was often inferior, achievement was no better than in regular classrooms, and students didn't learn social and life skills needed to live in the real world (D. Bradley & Switlick, 1997). Educators looked for other ways to help these students.

Federal Laws Redefine Special Education

In 1975, the U.S. Congress passed Public Law 94-142, the *Individuals With Disabilities Education Act (IDEA)*, which is intended to ensure a free and public education for all students with exceptionalities. IDEA, combined with more recent amendments, provides the following guidelines for working with students having exceptionalities:

- Identify the needs of students with exceptionalities by nondiscriminatory assessment.
- Involve parents in developing each child's educational program.
- Create an environment that is minimally restrictive.
- Develop an individualized education program (IEP) of study for each student.

IDEA has affected every school in the United States and has changed the roles of regular and special educators.

The Evolution Toward Inclusion

As educators realized that segregated classes and services were not meeting the needs of students with exceptionalities, they wrestled with alternatives. One of the first was **mainstreaming**, *the practice of moving students with exceptionalities from segregated settings into regular classrooms*. Popular in the 1970s, mainstreaming had advantages and disadvantages (Hardman et al., 1999). It began the move away from segregated services and allowed students with exceptionalities and other students to interact. Unfortunately, however, students with exceptionalities were often placed into classrooms without the necessary support and services.

As educators grappled with these problems, they developed the concept of the **least restrictive environment (LRE)**, *one that places students in as normal an educational*

The least restrictive environment provides students with opportunities to develop to their fullest potential.

setting as possible while still meeting their special academic, social, and physical needs. Broader than the concept of *mainstreaming*, the LRE can consist of a continuum of services, ranging from mainstreaming to placement in separate facilities. Mainstreaming occurs only if parents and educators decide it best meets the child's needs.

Central to the LRE is the concept of **adaptive fit**, *the degree to which a student is able to cope with the requirements of a school setting and the extent to which the school accommodates the student's special needs* (Hardman et al., 1999). Adaptive fit requires an individualized approach to dealing with students having exceptionalities; it can only be determined after an analysis of a student's specific learning needs. As educators considered mainstreaming, LRE, and adaptive fit, they gradually developed the concept of *inclusion.*

Inclusion is *a comprehensive approach to educating students with exceptionalities that advocates a total, systematic, and coordinated web of services.* Inclusion has three components:

1. Include students with special needs in a regular school campus
2. Place students with special needs in age- and grade-appropriate classrooms.
3. Provide special education support within the regular classroom.

Initially, inclusion was thought of as additive; students with exceptionalities received additional services to help them function in regular school settings (Turnbull et al., 1999). Gradually, the concept of coordination replaced addition. Special and regular educators collaborated closely to ensure that the experiences of students with exceptionalities were coordinated and integrated. For example, rather than having a special educator come into the classroom to offer supplementary instruction, the special educator would plan with the regular classroom teacher to ensure that the additional instruction was integrated with ongoing classroom activities.

Putting Inclusion Into Perspective

The practice of inclusion is controversial, with criticisms coming from parents, regular classroom teachers, and special educators themselves (Turnbull et al., 1999). Parents, concerned that their children might be lost in the busy shuffle of school life, wonder whether their children might receive more effective help in special classrooms. Regular classroom teachers, faced with individualizing instruction without adequate assistance, question the educational benefits of inclusion for all students.

Members of the special education community also disagree. Advocates of full inclusion contend that placement in a regular classroom is the only way to eliminate the negative effects of segregation (Stainback & Stainback, 1992). Opponents contend that the child's needs must be determined before an inclusion decision can be made (Fuchs & Fuchs, 1994). They argue that inclusion is not for everyone and that some students are better served in special classes for parts of the day.

As a regular classroom teacher, you will be asked to implement inclusion in your school and classroom. Effective inclusion makes all educators responsible for creating supportive learning environments. Its thrust is to include students with exceptionalities in regular classrooms whenever possible, but it also allows for delivering services in other places (D. Bradley & Switlick, 1997; Larrivee, Semmel, & Gerber, 1997).

Where inclusion works, regular teachers and special educators collaborate extensively to make sure that placements and services meet the needs of all students (Larrivee et al., 1997). Without this collaboration, full inclusion isn't effective.

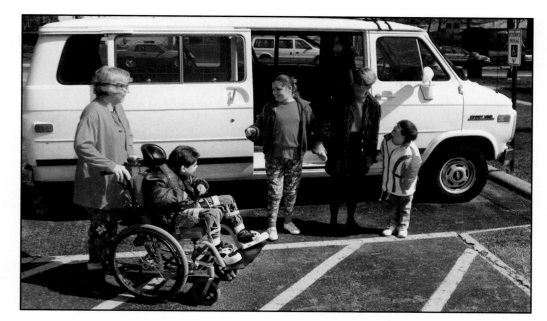

Inclusion creates a web of services to integrate students with exceptionalities into the educational system.

A Legal Framework for Working with Students Who Have Exceptionalities

Kevin had mild retardation and had been going to a resource program for an hour a day during his elementary school years. The resource teacher worked closely with the regular teacher to ensure that Kevin's work in each classroom was consistent. Through their combined efforts, they were able to help him learn in the regular classroom, even though his achievement test scores were well below his grade level.

The move to junior high posed new challenges for Kevin. He would have five teachers instead of one, and the prospect of moving from one class to the next was frightening. Before school started, Mr. Endo, Kevin's resource teacher in the junior high, called a meeting of Kevin's parents and teachers. They discussed Kevin's strengths and weaknesses and what kinds of teaching strategies had worked at his old school. He liked science and art, and a special effort was made to provide him with some additional science materials. Out of this meeting came an IEP that provided short- and long-term goals and additional teaching strategies to use with him. The IEP would take effect with the start of his next semester and would guide teachers during the next year, after which it would be reviewed and revised. The group shared the IEP with Kevin, who was more at ease knowing that he was being looked after.

As you saw in the previous section, IDEA fundamentally changed the way schools educate students with exceptionalities. This change occurred through specific provisions that require:

▌ Due process through parental involvement
▌ Protection against discrimination in testing
▌ The LRE
▌ An IEP

Teachers and other professionals meet with parents to design an IEP that meets a student's individual learning needs.

Due Process Through Parental Involvement

Due process guarantees parents' involvement in identifying and placing their children in special programs, access to school records, and the opportunity for an independent evaluation if they're not satisfied with the initial one. Legal safeguards are also in place if parents don't speak English; they have the right to an interpreter, and their rights must be read to them in their native language. Involving Kevin's parents in developing his IEP is one facet of due process.

Protection Against Discrimination in Testing

5.10
You suspect that a Hispanic student in your class, who speaks understandable English, has a learning disability in math. Because he speaks understandable English, can he be given the diagnostic test written in English? Explain.

The law requires that any testing used in the placement process be conducted in a student's native language by qualified personnel, and that no single instrument, such as an intelligence test, can be used as the sole basis for placement. In response to a court decision (*Larry P. v. Riles,* 1979), California severely restricted the use of standardized intelligence tests in identifying minority children with disabilities. In recent years, increased emphasis has been placed on a student's classroom performance and general adaptive behavior (Heward, 1996).

Least Restrictive Environment

The LRE is intended to provide an environment that best promotes the academic and social growth of all students with exceptionalities. These students are taken out of the regular classroom only when regular classes combined with supplementary help cannot meet their needs.

The LRE provision means that *you will have students with exceptionalities in your classroom,* and you will be asked to work with special educators to design and implement programs for these students. The LRE means that students with exceptionalities should participate as much as possible in the regular school agenda, including academics, recess, lunch in the cafeteria, regular school assemblies, and extracurricular activities. The form of these programs varies with the nature of the problem and the capabilities of the students. Figure 5.4 presents a continuum, or cascade, of services for implementing the LRE, starting with the least confining at the top and moving to the most confining at the bottom.

Figure 5.4

Educational service options for implementing the LRE

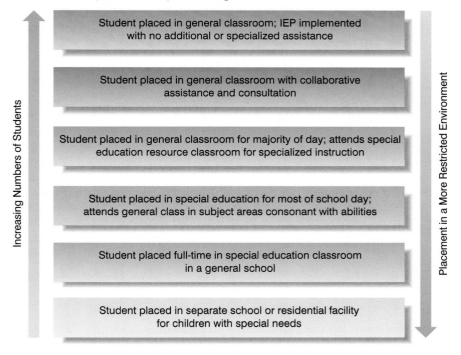

Source: *To Assure the Free Appropriate Public Education of All Children with Disabilities: Eighteenth Annual Report to Congress on the Implementation of the Individuals with Disabilities Education Act*, by U.S. Department of Education, 1996, Washington, DC: U.S. Department of Education.

Special educators use the word *cascade* to label the connectedness of levels; if students can't succeed at one level, they are moved to the next.

These placement options represent a continuum from greater to lesser involvement in the regular classroom. The goal of inclusion is to identify the point on the continuum that best meets the student's needs.

Individualized Education Program

To ensure that inclusion works and learners with exceptionalities don't get lost in the regular classroom, an **individualized education program (IEP)**—*an individually prescribed instructional plan devised by special education and classroom teachers, other resource professionals, and parents*—is prepared. It specifies the following:

- An assessment of the student's current level of performance
- Long- and short-term objectives
- Services or strategies to be used
- Schedules for implementing the plan
- Criteria to be used in evaluating the plan's success

5.11 ▬
Explain specifically how an IEP addresses the previously discussed concepts of *due process, parental involvement,* and *least restrictive environment.*

Teachers and other professionals meet with parents to design an IEP that meets a student's individual learning needs. A sample is illustrated in Figure 5.5. It has three important features. First, the initials of all participants indicate that its development was a cooperative effort. Second, the specific information in Columns 3, 4, 5, and 6 and in Section 7 guides the classroom teacher and special education personnel when they implement it. Third, the parent's signature indicates that they were involved in developing the plan and agree with its details.

Functions of the IEP

The IEP performs at least four functions. First, it provides support for the classroom teacher, who may be uncertain about dealing with students with special needs. Second, it creates a link between the regular classroom and the resource team. Third, it helps parents monitor their child's educational progress. Fourth, and most important, it provides a program to meet the individual needs of the student.

IEPs sometimes provide for work in settings outside the regular classroom, such as a resource room; at other times, they focus exclusively on adaptations in the regular classroom. They are most effective when the two are coordinated, such as when a classroom teacher working on word problems in math asks the resource teacher to focus on the same type of problems (Choate, 1997).

Recent Changes in the Individuals with Disabilities Education Act

In 1997 Congress amended the Individuals With Disabilities Education Act to ensure that all children with disabilities were provided with a free appropriate public education (FAPE) that emphasizes special education and related services designed to meet their unique needs and to prepare them for employment and independent living (Huefner, 1999; Lewis & Doorlag, 1999). The IDEA was also amended to ensure that the legal rights of children with disabilities are protected. Key provisions of the amended law include

- *Child find.*   The IDEA creates an affirmative duty for states to locate children with disabilities that require services.
- *Nondiscriminatory assessment.*   The amendment reaffirms the importance of assessment that does not penalize students for their native language, race, culture or disability.
- *Due process.*   If school officials or the parents of a student with disabilities are not satisfied with the existing educational program, an impartial due process hearing can be requested.
- *IEP.*   A copy of the IEP must be provided to parents, and they may bring to IEP meetings a person with knowledge or special expertise regarding their child.
- *Confidentiality.*   Districts must keep confidential records of each child, protect the confidentiality of these records, and share them with parents on request.

The major thrust of the 1997 amendments was to clarify and extend the quality of services to students with disabilities rather than significantly change them.

One of the most controversial aspects of this new law has been in the area of disciplinary suspensions (Sach, 1999). It establishes procedural safeguards for students while maintaining the right of districts to suspend students if necessary.

Figure 5.5

Individualized education program (IEP)

INDIVIDUAL EDUCATION PROGRAM

Date ___3-1-00___

(1) Student

Name: Joe S.
School: Adams
Grade: 5
Current Placement: Regular Class/Resource Room

Date of Birth: 10-1-88   **Age:** 11-5

(2) Committee

		Initial
Mrs. Wrens	Principal	*D.Q.W.*
Mrs. Snow	Regular Teacher	*AS*
Mr. LaJoie	Counselor	*SLJ*
Mr. Thomas	Resource Teacher	*M.T.*
Mr. Ryan	School Psychologist	*H.R.R.*
Mrs. S.	Parent	*J.S.*
Joe S.	Student	*Joe S.*

EP from __3-15-00__ to __3-15-01__

(3) Present Level of Educational Functioning	(4) Annual Goal Statements	(5) Instructional Objectives	(6) Objective Criteria and Evaluation
MATH Strengths 1. Can successfully compute addition and subtraction problems to two places with regrouping and zeros. 2. Knows 100 basic multiplication facts. Weaknesses 1. Frequently makes computational errors on problems with which he has had experience. 2. Does not complete seatwork. Key Math total score of 2.1 Grade Equivalent.	Joe will apply knowledge of regrouping in addition and renaming in subtraction to four-digit numbers.	1. When presented with 20 addition problems of 3-digit numbers requiring two renamings, the student will compute answers at a rate of one problem per minute and an accuracy of 90%. 2. When presented with 20 subtraction problems of 3-digit numbers requiring two renamings, the student will compute answers at the rate of one problem per minute with 90% accuracy. 3. When presented with 20 addition problems of 4-digit numbers requiring three renamings, the student will compute answers at a rate of one problem per minute and an accuracy of 90%. 4. When presented with 20 subtraction problems of 4-digit numbers requiring three renamings, the student will compute answers at a rate of one problem per minute with 90% accuracy.	Teacher-made tests (weekly) Teacher-made tests (weekly) Teacher-made tests (weekly)

(7) Educational Services to be provided

Services Required	Date initiated	Duration of Service	Individual Responsible for the Service
Regular reading-adapted	3-15-00	3-15-01	Reading Improvement Specialist and Special Education Teacher
Resource room	3-15-00	3-15-01	Special Education Teacher
Counselor consultant	3-15-00	3-15-01	Counselor
Monitoring diet and general health	3-15-00	3-15-01	School Health Nurse

Extent of time in the regular education program: 60% increasing to 80%
Justification of the educational placement:

It is felt that the structure of the resource room can best meet the goals stated for Joe; especially when coordinated with the regular classroom.

It is also felt that Joe could profit enormously from talking with a counselor. He needs someone with whom to talk and with whom he can share his feelings.

(8) I have had the opportunity to participate in the development of the Individual Education Program.

     I agree with Individual Education Program   (✓)
     I disagree with the Individual Education Program ( )

Parent's Signature ___*Mrs S.*___

Source: Adapted from *Developing and Implementing Individualized Education Programs* (3rd ed.) (pp. 308, 326) by B. B. Strickland and A. P. Turnbull, 1990, New York: Macmillan. Adapted by permission.

The Teacher's Role in Inclusive Classrooms

Earlier in this chapter, we examined different kinds of disabilities, how they affect the students you teach, and how views of special education have changed over time. We now turn to strategies regular classroom teachers use to help these students reach their potential. In this process, they perform three roles:

▮ Help identify students with exceptionalities.
▮ Teach students with exceptionalities in the regular classroom.
▮ Foster other students' acceptance of students with exceptionalities.

Identifying Students with Exceptionalities

Because regular classroom teachers work with these students every day, they are in the best position to help identify students with exceptionalities. Identification often begins by simply monitoring a student's learning progress on typical classroom tasks. In doing so, teachers should remember that a disproportionate number of males and cultural minorities tend to be identified (Hardman et al., 1999). This imbalance suggests that you should ask yourself, for example, whether a difficulty truly indicates a *learning* problem or if some other factor might be operating. This is the dilemma that Sabrina Curtis faced in our opening case study as she worked with Rodney and Amelia.

Prereferral Strategies: Gathering Data
for Instructional Problem Solving

Current approaches to identification use a team-based problem-solving model with the teacher as the key member. The process begins when a learning problem is suspected; the teacher's first step is to diagnose the problem and try different instructional strategies. If this fails, other educators are called in and additional data are gathered, including standardized test scores, classroom performance, and interviews with parents and other teachers.

    If the data warrant additional help, a "prereferral team" is formed, often consisting of a school psychologist, a special educator, and the classroom teacher. The team further evaluates the problem, suggests ways that classroom procedures could be modified to create a better adaptive fit, and assists the classroom teacher in modifying instruction. Prereferral interventions might identify classroom, instructional, home, or schoolwide changes responsive to the needs of the student (Mamlin & Harris, 1998). Teachers will be expected to document the strategies attempted in solving the problem (Hallahan & Kauffman, 1997). Specifically, the teacher should describe:

▮ The nature of the problem
▮ How it affects classroom performance
▮ Dates, places, and time the problem has occurred
▮ Strategies the teacher has tried
▮ Evidence of the strategies' successes

    Before a referral is made, the classroom teacher should also check the student's records to see if the student has had a previous evaluation, has any physical problems, has been included in other special programs, or is qualified for special services (Hallahan & Kauffman, 1997).

    Teachers should also communicate with parents before initiating a process. Parents need to be informed and involved for at least three reasons:

5.12 ▬

Why are tests, quizzes, papers, and other work samples important in the referral process? Are they more or less important than standardized test results? Explain.

1. Due process legally requires their involvement.
2. They can provide valuable information about the student's educational and medical history.
3. Involving parents is a professional courtesy.

When considering a referral, the teacher should check with school administrators or the school psychologist to learn about the school's policy. If the referral results in a recommendation for special services, an IEP is then prepared.

Teaching Students with Exceptionalities

Almost certainly, some of your students will have exceptionalities, and you will be expected to teach them as effectively as possible. Fortunately, changes that you'll need to make are more in how than in what you teach (Choate, 1997). One teacher working in an inclusive classroom commented, "I wasn't sure that I knew what to do for special ed kids. And now I think I do know what to do for special ed kids and it's not a whole lot different than . . . what I've always done for regular ed kids" (Oka, Kolar, Rau, & Stahl, 1997, p. 10).

Also, special educators should be available to you—*resource teachers* who can help you modify instruction for your students with exceptionalities, the *prereferral teacher assistance teams* we discussed earlier, and site-based or *collaborative consultation teams*—as resources.

Curriculum-Based Assessment

To help both the classroom teacher and the special education assistance teams, educators are placing increased emphasis on **curriculum-based assessment**, *which attempts to measure learners' performance in specific areas of the curriculum* (Meltzer & Reid, 1994). As opposed to broader measures, such as standardized achievement tests, curriculum-based measurement identifies specific areas in which students need help, such as finding the main idea in reading or knowing multiplication facts. Identifying these areas helps the team design more effective IEPs.

Effective Teaching for Inclusive Classrooms

Most modifications that work with students having exceptionalities are based on principles of effective teaching that work with all students, such as managing a classroom effectively, matching learning tasks to student abilities, and providing frequent and specific practice and feedback (Mercer & Mercer, 1993; Swanson & Hoskyn, 1998). This is encouraging because it means the knowledge and effective strategies that teachers use with regular students need to be only adapted, not fundamentally changed. Table 5.4 outlines these effective teaching practices.

As described in Table 5.4, teachers need to structure their time so that students have meaningful learning tasks and opportunities to learn important content. The classroom should be emotionally warm and supportive, and students must believe that they can and will learn. Management reinforces instruction, with disruptions minimized. Tasks should be designed so that students have high rates of success on classwork and homework. Finally, effective feedback reinforces instruction and provides learning correctives. These teaching strategies are effective for students in general and are particularly important for students with exceptionalities.

Table 5.4

Effective teaching practices for inclusion

Practice	Description
Effective use of time	• High rates of on-task behavior • Minimal losses of instructional time to transitions and disruptions
Warm academic climate	• Supportive responses to *all* students—particularly those mainstreamed • Supportive responses when problems occur (e.g., "I know we can learn this if we try.")
Effective classroom management	• Structured and orderly classroom • Minimal use of punishment • Minimal loss of instructional time to manage misbehavior
High success rates	• Correct answers to most teacher questions • Success rate of 80%–90% on seat work and homework assignments
Effective feedback	• Feedback that is immediate • Feedback that provides information (e.g., "Good, Sarah. You remembered to borrow from the tens column.") • Feedback that includes no criticism

Of the five areas, the most challenging is adapting instruction to ensure high success rates. This often means spending more time with individual learners and providing more opportunities for practice and feedback. Teachers may need to shorten assignments, giving 10 instead of 15 problems, for example, or a teacher might break an assignment of 15 problems into three groups of 5, with opportunities for teacher, peer, or self-checking after each group.

Adapting Instruction.   To help students overcome a history of failure and frustration and to convince them that renewed effort will work, teachers often have to adapt their methods. Peer tutoring has been used effectively, and much of the benefit comes from doing the actual tutoring (Miller, Barbetta, & Heron, 1994). Home-based tutoring programs that involve parents can also be effective (Barbetta & Heron, 1991). You can set up a home-based tutoring program by contacting parents and explaining specifically what they can do in working with their youngster. Additional adaptations are outlined in Table 5.5.

A Successful Homework Program.   Increased structure and support are essential characteristics of successful adaptive instruction. Students with learning problems need to be taught in small steps, with every effort to promote success. Inappropriate assignments, or homework that is too difficult, can be frustrating for the regular student; for students with learning problems, it can be devastating.

Table 5.5

Instructional adaptations for students with exceptionalities

Skill Area	Adaptations
Math	• Model correct solutions on the chalkboard. • Use peer tutors to explain problems. • Break long assignments into several shorter ones. • Encourage the use of calculators and other manipulative aids.
Reading	• Use old textbooks and other alternative reading materials at the appropriate level. • Use study guides that identify key concepts. • Preteach difficult concept before presenting a reading passage. • Encourage group assignments in which students assist each other.
Spelling	• Avoid spelling as a grading criterion. • Focus on spelling words used in science, social studies, and other areas. • Stress mastery of several short spelling lists, rather than one long list. • Encourage students to proofread papers, circling words of which they're uncertain.
Writing	• Increase time allotted for writing assignments. • Allow assignments to be typed, rather than handwritten. • Allow reports to be taped or dictated to others. • Encourage daily writing through the use of short, creative assignments.

Source: Dolgins, Myers, Flynn, and Moore (1984).

One successful homework program made a concerted effort to ensure student success (Rosenberg, 1989). Homework was an extension of seat work successfully completed in class. Parents' assistance was solicited; they orally administered a quiz each night on material being studied, and confirmed the completion of the homework and quiz with their signatures.

The signature was both concrete and symbolic; it was a concrete indicator that parents were participating in their child's homework, and, symbolically, it provided a link between home and school. To reinforce students, points were used; students received some points for doing homework and additional ones for doing both homework and the quiz. The program was demanding, but positive results indicated the time and energy were well spent.

Adapting Reading Materials.   Reading poses particular instructional problems because the special texts students need are usually unavailable. However, teachers can supplement the available materials through the following strategies:

> ▌ Set goals at the beginning of an assignment.
> ▌ Use advance organizers that structure or summarize passages.

5.13 ▬
According to research, most modifications for mainstreamed students are more of "degree" than of "kind." What does this mean? Explain this statement using Rosenberg's (1989) homework study as a focus.

❙ Introduce key concepts and terms before students read the text.
❙ Create study guides with questions that focus attention on important information.
❙ Ask students to summarize information in the text. (Graham & Johnson, 1989)

These strategies increase reading comprehension with regular learners (Dole, Duffy, Roehler, & Pearson, 1991), and using them with mainstreamed students provides an additional level of support.

Strategy Training: Learning How to Learn

Strategy training is one of the most promising approaches to helping students with learning problems (Swanson & Hoskyn, 1998). A strategy is a plan for accomplishing a learning goal. Let's see how a strategy might be applied when encountering a task such as learning a list of 10 spelling words. For example, a student might say to himself,

> "Okay, . . . 10 words for the quiz on Friday. That shouldn't be too hard. I have 2 days to learn them.
> "Let's see. These are all about airports. Which of these do I already know—airplane, taxi, apron, and jet? No problem. Hmmm . . . Some of these aren't so easy, like causeway and tarmac. I don't even know what a 'tarmac' is. I'll look it up. . . . Oh, that makes sense. It's the runway. I'd better spend more time on these words. I'll cover them up and try to write them down and then check 'em. Tonight, I can get Mom to give me a quiz, and then I'll know which ones to study extra tomorrow."

This student was strategic in at least three ways. First, separating the words he already knew from those he didn't, spending extra time on the difficult ones, and looking up *tarmac* in the dictionary indicate the presence of clear goals. Second, he took a deliberate approach to the task, allocating more time to the words he didn't know and skipping the ones he did. Third, he monitored his progress through quiz-like exercises (Palincsar & Brown, 1987).

Students with learning difficulties often approach learning tasks in a "strategically inactive" manner, either approaching a learning task passively or using the same strategy for all goals (Montague, 1990). For example, they might approach a task like the one above by merely reading the words, instead of trying to actually spell them. They also continue to spend time on the words they already know and make little effort to test themselves to receive feedback.

In contrast with most students, who learn strategies naturally as they progress through school, students with learning problems often have to be explicitly taught them. Teacher modeling and explanation, together with opportunities for practice and feedback, are essential (De La Paz, Swanson, & Graham, 1998; G. Miller, 1990).

5.14 ❙
Describe specifically how a teacher might instruct students to more strategically attack the spelling list in the example.

Collaborative Consultation: Help for the Classroom Teacher

Collaboration between regular and special educators is essential if inclusion is to work. In the *consulting teacher model*, a special education expert assists the classroom teacher in meeting the classroom needs of students requiring special help (Hardman et al., 1999). In working with the classroom teacher, the consulting teacher can perform a number of valuable functions:

❙ Assist in collecting assessment information.
❙ Maintain students' records.
❙ Develop special curriculum materials.
❙ Coordinate the efforts of team members in implementing the IEP.

❙ Work with parents.
❙ Assist the regular teacher in adapting instruction.

Perhaps most important is helping the regular teacher adapt instruction. One way to do so is through team teaching, which allows efficient use of special education resources and a reduction of the stigma of pull-out programs. Research on team teaching is encouraging, indicating that learning environments improve and resources and instructional variety increase (Pugach & Wesson, 1995).

Technology and Learning: Assistive Technology

Technology is changing the ways we teach and the ways students learn. **Assistive technology**, which *includes adaptive tools that help students use computers and other types of technologies,* is having a particularly important impact on students with exceptionalities. Some, such as those who are blind or who have severe physical impairments, cannot interact with a standard computer unless adaptations are made. These changes occur either through alternative input or output devices (Lewis & Doorlag, 1999).

Adaptations to Computer Input Devices

To use computers effectively, students must be able to input their words and ideas. This can be difficult if not impossible for nonreaders or those with visual or other physical disabilities that don't allow standard keyboarding.

One adaptation includes devices that enhance the keyboard, such as making it larger and easier to see, arranging the letters alphabetically to make them easier to find, or using pictures for nonreaders. In addition, keyboards can be adapted to allow vision-impaired students to type in Braille (Zorfass, Corley, & Remz, 1994). Additional adaptations completely bypass the keyboard. For example, students with physical disabilities that don't allow them to use their hands to input information can use switches activated by a body movement, such as a head nod, to interact with the computer. Touch screens allow students to go directly to the monitor screen to indicate their responses.

Adaptations to Output Devices

Adaptations to the standard computer monitor either bypass visual displays or increase their size. Size enhancement can be accomplished by using a special large-screen monitor or by using a magnification device that increases screen size. For students who are blind, speech synthesizers can read words and translate them into sounds, or Braille adapters can convert regular print into Braille (Zorfass et al., 1994).

These technologies are important because they prevent disabilities from becoming handicaps. Their importance to students with exceptionalities is likely to increase as technology becomes a more integral part of classroom instruction.

Technology can be used to provide students who have exceptionalities with opportunities for practice with frequent and specific feedback.

Strategies for Social Integration and Growth

Among the most difficult obstacles that students with exceptionalities face are the negative attitudes of others and the impact of these attitudes on their confidence and self-esteem (Moon et al., 1997; Pearl et al., 1998). Often, a student who has a disability and is labeled as different is neither well understood nor accepted by other students.

In addition, these students are often behind in their academic work, frequently act out in class, and sometimes lack social skills. Further, being pulled out for extra help calls attention to their differences (Hallahan & Kauffman, 1997). Special efforts are needed to promote their acceptance in regular classrooms.

Attempts to foster acceptance focus on three approaches:

- Help regular students understand and accept students with exceptionalities.
- Help students with exceptionalities behave acceptably.
- Use strategies that encourage social interaction and cooperation.

Helping Regular Students Understand and Accept Students with Exceptionalities

Regular students often have negative attitudes toward students with exceptionalities because they don't understand the disabilities. The first approach attempts to change that. Providing information about disabilities and promoting interaction between regular and mainstreamed students can help (Heward, 1996). Some successful strategies follow:

- Use people who have overcome disabilities as models.
- Discuss disabilities, including their causes.

Creative teachers design learning activities that allow students of differing abilities to interact and learn about each other.

▌ Use literature and videos to explore the struggles and triumphs of people with disabilities.
▌ Teach students the manual alphabet.

In addition, teachers can promote acceptance by calling on all students—including those with exceptionalities—regularly, using cooperative learning that puts learners with exceptionalities into direct contact with other students, and identifying areas of interest or strength (e.g., art or science) in which these students can excel. Above all, teachers communicate through their language and actions that they value these students as individuals, expect them to learn, and want to have them in their classrooms.

Helping Students with Exceptionalities Behave Acceptably

A second approach attempts to improve the social skills of students with exceptionalities, who often misbehave, acting out because of frustration or learned inappropriate behaviors (Pearl et al., 1998). Ways of changing these behaviors include modeling, contracts that specify appropriate behavior in advance, and individual or group reward systems that allow individuals or the whole class to receive tokens or points for desired behavior.

Students with disabilities often avoid contact with regular students because they lack the social skills needed to make friends (Choi & Heckenlaible-Gotto, 1998). Teachers can help by modeling and coaching. For example, a teacher says, "Barnell's over there on the playground. I think I'll say, 'Hi, Barnell! Want to play ball with me?' Now you try it, and I'll watch." Another strategy is to teach social problem solving; for instance, a teacher comments, "Hmm . . . Mary has a toy that I want to play with. What could I do to make her want to share that toy?" Direct approaches have proved successful in teaching social skills such as empathy, perspective taking, negotiation, and assertiveness (Choi & Heckenlaible-Gotto, 1998; Vaughn, McIntosh, Spencer, & Rowe, 1990).

5.15
Of the "students with learning problems" discussed in the first section of the chapter, which type—mentally retarded, learning disabled, behaviorally disordered—would be most likely to have problems with social integration and growth? Explain.

Using Strategies That Encourage Social Interaction and Cooperation

One obstacle to social integration is the classroom itself. Students often work alone, and grades are based on competition rather than cooperation. Peer tutoring and cooperative learning can help break down these barriers (D. Bradley & Switlick, 1997).

Peer Tutoring.   Peer tutoring places students in groups of two or three and provides them with structured learning activities, including practice and feedback. For example, after introducing a new concept in math, the teacher assigns students in pairs to work on practice exercises. Students take turns tutoring and being tutored, one doing the sample problems and the other checking the answers and providing feedback. Various combinations have been used: high and low ability, students with and without exceptionalities, and students with exceptionalities tutoring each other. All have proved successful in teaching content (Fuchs, Fuchs, Mathes, & Simmons, 1997), while also promoting social interaction and improved attitudes toward those with exceptionalities (Elbaum, Vaugn, Hughes, & Moody, 1999). For both cognitive and affective gains to be maximized, it is important that students with exceptionalities have opportunities to tutor and be tutored.

Training for the tutors is essential, however; research indicates that the quality of the instruction during peer tutoring can be improved markedly by teaching students to be more interactive and task oriented in their feedback (Fuchs, Fuchs, Bentz, Phillips, & Hamlett, 1994).

Cooperative learning activities encourage students to interact as they learn content and depend on each other for mutual help and support.

Cross-age tutoring, in which older students tutor younger ones, appears to be an especially promising practice for students with exceptionalities. In one study, upper elementary students categorized as having either a learning disability or behavior disorder served as tutors for first-graders (Top & Osgthorpe, 1987). After 12 weeks of tutoring, both the tutors and those tutored showed significant learning gains. In addition, tutors increased in their perceptions of their general academic ability and their reading/spelling ability. Anyone who has taught something successfully knows how fulfilling it can be. Successful tutoring appears to provide feelings of competence and satisfaction that can improve self-concept.

Cooperative Learning.   Cooperative learning strategies place students in teams and encourage them to work toward common goals. Students are rewarded for helping and encouraging other students. Cooperative learning strategies have been used effectively at all grade levels and in all content areas. They have been found to increase achievement, improve attitudes toward minorities and those with disabilities, and increase inclusion in mainstream classroom activities (Slavin, 1995). We discuss cooperative learning in detail in Chapter 13.

Classroom Connections

Teaching Students with Exceptionalities in the Regular Classroom

1. Adapt regular instruction to meet the unique needs of students with exceptionalities.
   - A third-grade teacher circulates around the room after an assignment is given, making sure his mainstreamed students understand the directions. If necessary, he gathers them together in a small group or works with them one-on-one to go over the directions again.
   - A junior high math teacher has organized a buddy system in which his abler students are paired with mainstreamed students. A short training program teaches students how to assist with homework assignments and helps them understand the difference between academic and nonacademic help.

2. Teach students with exceptionalities learning strategies they can use in the classroom.
   - An English teacher teaches and models strategies step-by-step. A unit on writing one-paragraph essays taught students to use five steps: (a) Write a topic sentence. (b) Give two reasons why they believe it is a good topic sentence. (c) Write sentences that support the topic sentence. (d) Add a summary sentence. (e) Reread and edit it.
   - An elementary math teacher teaches problem-solving strategies by thinking aloud at the chalkboard while she's working through a problem. She breaks word problems into the following steps: (a) Read: What is the question? (b) Reread: What information do I need? (c) Stop and think: What do I need to do—add, subtract, multiply, or divide? (d) Compute: Put the correct numbers in and solve. (e) Label and check: What answer did I get? Does it make sense?

Fostering Acceptance of All Students in Your Classroom

3. Emphasize the value of diversity in the classroom.
   - A first-grade teacher begins a unit on diversity with a discussion of how all students in the class are similar. The next day, he focuses on diversity, both physical and cultural. Students draw pictures of themselves, and the teacher helps each student point out on the pictures, "I'm me because . . . "
   - A junior high homeroom teacher begins the school year by asking students to fill out an autobiographical fact sheet that asks them to think about their favorites (e.g., food, hobby, movie), as well as their strengths and weaknesses. The teacher, too, fills out a fact sheet and puts them all up on the bulletin board. The teacher discusses these in the first few weeks to get to know students and to introduce the idea "Different is great."

4. Deal with the subject of exceptionalities in an open and straightforward manner.
   - An elementary teacher uses role playing and modeling to discuss problems such as teasing and laughing at others, and she specifically emphasizes treating students who look or act different with the same respect that other students receive.
   - A junior high school English teacher uses literature, such as *Summer of the Swans,* by Betsy Byars (1970), as a springboard for talking about individual differences. Students are encouraged to reflect on their own individuality and how important this is to them.

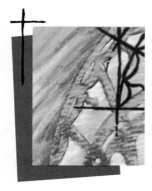

Windows on Classrooms

As you've studied this chapter, you've examined characteristics of students with exceptionalities, and you've learned that they all can learn if you adapt your instruction to meet their needs. Efficient use of time, a supportive academic climate, effective classroom management, high success rates, and frequent and informative feedback are important in helping students with exceptionalities achieve their maximum potential.

Read the following case study, and assess the teacher's effectiveness in the context of the information you've been studying:

Mike Sheppard is a math teacher at Landrom Junior High School. Yesterday Mike introduced his seventh-grade prealgebra class to a procedure for solving word problems, and he modeled the solution of some examples by using the procedure. He then assigned five problems for homework.

Mike had 28 students in his second-period class, which included five students with exceptionalities: Herchel, Marcus, and Gwenn, who had learning disabilities, and Todd and Horace, who had behavior disorders. Herchel, Marcus, and Gwenn each had problems with decoding words, reading comprehension, and writing. Other teachers described Todd as verbally abusive, aggressive, and lacking in self-discipline. He was extremely active and had a difficult time sitting through a class period. Horace was just the opposite: a very shy, timid, and withdrawn boy.

At 10:07, Herchel, Marcus, and Gwenn were among the first of Mike's students to file into class. As the students entered, they looked in anticipation at the screen in the front of the room. Mike typically displayed one or more problems on the overhead for the students as warm-up exercises, which they completed while he took roll and finished other beginning-of-class routines.

Mike watched and, as soon as Herchel, Marcus, and Gwenn were in their seats, he slowly read the displayed problem: "On Saturday, the Trebek family drove 17 miles from Henderson to Newton, stopped for 10 minutes to get gas, and then drove 22.5 miles from Newton through Council Rock to Gildford. The trip took 1 hour and 5 minutes, including the stop. On the way back, they took the same route but stopped in Council Rock for lunch. Council Rock is 9.5 miles from Gildford. How much farther will they have to drive to get back to Henderson?"

As Mike read, he pointed to each displayed word. "Okay," he smiled after he finished reading. "Do you know what the problem is asking you?"

"Could you read the last part again, Mr. Sheppard?" Gwenn asked.

"Sure," Mike nodded and repeated the part of the problem that described the return trip, again pointing to the words as he read.

"All right, jump on it. Be ready because I'm calling on one of you first today," he again smiled and touched each of them on the shoulder.

The students were in their seats, and most were studying the screen as the bell rang at 10:10. Mike quickly took roll and then moved back to Todd's desk.

"Let's take a look at your chart," he said. "You've improved a lot, haven't you?"

"Yeah, look," Todd responded, proudly displaying the following chart.

	2/9–2/13	2/16–2/20	2/23–2/27
Talking out	ЖЖ ЖЖ ЖЖ ЖЖ	ЖЖ IIII ЖЖ	ЖЖ II
Swearing	ЖЖ ЖЖ	ЖЖ II	IIII
Hitting/touching	ЖЖ III	ЖЖ IIII	III
Out of seat	ЖЖ ЖЖ ЖЖ III	ЖЖ ЖЖ ЖЖ IIII	ЖЖ ЖЖ ЖЖ III
Being friendly	II	IIII	ЖЖ II

"That's terrific," Mike whispered to Todd as he leaned over the boy's desk. "You're doing much better. We need some more work on 'out-of-seat,' don't we? I don't like getting after you about it, and I know you don't like it either," he went on. "Stop by after class. I have an idea for you. I think it will help. Don't forget to stop. I'll give you a pass to your next class if you're late. . . . Okay. Get to work on the problem." Mike then gives Todd a light thump on the back and returns to the front of the room.

"Okay, everyone. How did you do on the problem?"

Amid a mix of "Okay," "Terrible," "Fine," "Too hard," some nods, and a few nonresponses, Mike began, "Let's review for a minute. . . . What's the first thing we do whenever we have a word problem like this?"

He then looked knowingly at Marcus, remembering his pledge to call on one of them first. . . . Marcus?"

"Read it over at least twice."

"Good. . . . That's what our problem-solving plan says," Mike continued, pointing to a chart hanging from the top of the chalkboard that had the following information on it:

PLAN FOR SOLVING WORD PROBLEMS

1. Read the problem at least twice.
2. Ask the following questions:
   What is asked for?
   What facts are given?
   What information is needed that we don't have?
   Are unnecessary facts given? What are they?
3. Make a drawing.
4. Solve the problem.
5. Check to see whether the answer makes sense.

"Then what do we do? . . . Melissa?"

"See what the problem asks for."

"Very good. What is the problem asking for? . . . Rachel?"

" . . . How much farther they will have to drive."

"Excellent. Now, think about this. Suppose I solved the problem and decided that they had 39½ miles left to drive. Would that make sense? Why or why not? Everybody think about it for a moment."

Mike hesitated for several seconds and then said, "Okay. What do you think? . . . Herchel?"

" . . . I . . . I . . . don't know."

"Oh, yes you do," Mike encouraged. "Let's look. . . . How far from Henderson to Gildford altogether?"

"Thir . . . " Rico began until Mike put his hand up, stopping him in midword. He then waited a few seconds as Herchel studied the sketch on his paper that appeared as follows:

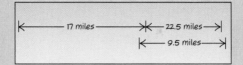

" . . . 39 and ½ miles," Herchel said uncertainly. "Oh! . . . The whole trip was only that far, so they couldn't still have that far to go."

"Excellent thinking, Herchel. See, I told you that you knew. That's very good.

"Now go ahead, Rico. How far do they still have to go?"

"Thirty miles," Rico, one of the higher achievers in the class, responded quickly.

"Good," Mike nodded. "Someone explain carefully how Rico might have gotten that. . . . Go ahead, Brenda."

" . . . The total distance is 39½ miles over, . . . and they came back 9½, . . . so, 39½ minus 9½ is 30."

"Good, Brenda, that's a good, clear description.

"Now," Mike continued, "is there any unnecessary information in the problem?"

"Yes!" several students responded at once.

"Okay. Like what? . . . Horace?" Mike asked, lowering his tone of voice slightly and moving toward Horace's desk.

" . . . "

"Look at the problem," Mike encouraged softly.

" . . . "

"How long did the trip take?"

" . . . An hour and 5 minutes."

"And again, what does the problem ask us for?" Mike continued, nodding to Horace.

" . . . How much farther they had to drive."

"Excellent, so the amount of time they took is irrelevant," Mike smiled, raising his tone of voice and turning back to the front of the room.

Mike guided the class toward identifying other items of unnecessary information in the problem, and then asked students to raise their hands, holding up three fingers if they had solved it correctly, two fingers if they had solved it but got an incorrect answer, and one finger if they had gotten no solution.

Seeing about a third of the class holding up three fingers, he thought wryly, "We're going to need some extra work on this material.

"Okay. Not too bad for the first time through," he continued cheerfully. "Let's take a look at your homework."

Mike then reviewed each homework problem just as he did the first one, asking students to relate each problem's parts to the steps in the problem-solving plan, drawing a sketch on the chalkboard, and calling on a variety of students to supply specific answers and describe their thinking as they worked their way to the solutions.

With 20 minutes left in the period, he assigned 10 more problems for seatwork/homework, and the students began working.

Once the class was working quietly, Mike nodded to Herchel, Marcus, and Gwenn, and the three of them quietly got up from their desks and moved to a table at the back of the room.

"How'd you do on the homework when we went over it?" Mike asked. "Do you think you get it?"

"Sort of," Gwenn responded, and the other two nodded.

"Good," Mike smiled. "Now, let's see what we've got, but before we start," he continued, "I noticed your drawing on our practice problem," he said to Herchel. "Let's take another look at it. . . . Go ahead and get it out."

Herchel then got out the following sketch:

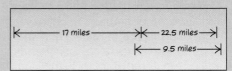

"Take a good look at it," Mike directed. "What looks funny? . . . Gwenn, you and Marcus look too."

"The 9½ miles is longer than the 22½ miles," Gwenn answered after looking at the sketch for a few seconds.

"Exactly," Mike nodded. "Now remember, this has to make sense. We know that 22½ is longer than 9½, and also we know that 22½ is longer than 17. So, when you make your sketches, be sure they make sense. Now, you all can do this work. So, I want to see good work from each of you. Okay? Good," he finished, nodding encouragingly.

"Okay. Go ahead and read the first problem, Gwenn."

"Ramon b . . . b . . . "

"Bought," Mike interjected.

"Bought," Gwenn continued, " . . . bought a CD for $13.95." She finished reading the problem, haltingly, and with Mike's help.

"Okay. What are we trying to find in this problem?"

"How much more the first CD cost than the cassette?" Marcus answered.

"Good. You all understand the problem?"

The three nodded.

"Okay. Let's look at the next one. . . . Go ahead and read it, Marcus."

Mike reviewed each of the problems with the three students to be sure they could read the problems and comprehend the information in each. As they worked, other students periodically came to the table and briefly asked questions. Mike then momentarily stopped his work with Marcus, Herchel, and Gwenn to answer the question and then returned to working with them. He also stopped briefly to go over and speak to Connie and Pamela, who were whispering.

After he returned, he said, "There are about five minutes left in the period. Run back to your desks now and see whether you can get one or two of them done before the bell rings."

Mike then watched as the students worked until the bell rang.

As the students filed out of the room, Mike caught Todd's eye, Todd stopped, and Mike lead him to a small area in the back of the room, partially enclosed but facing the front of the class.

"Here's what we'll do," Mike directed. "When you have the urge to get out of your seat, you quietly get up and move back here for a few minutes. Stay as long as you want, but be sure you pay attention to what we're doing. When you think you're ready to move back to your seat, go ahead. All I'm asking is that you move back and forth quietly and not bother the class. . . . Okay? . . . What do you think?"

Todd nodded, and Mike then put his arm around him and said, "You're doing so well on everything else; this will help, I think. You're a good student. You hang in there. . . . Now, get out of here," Mike smiled, giving Todd a little push. "Here's a pass into Mrs. Miller's class."

Questions for Discussion and Analysis

Now analyze Mike's teaching. In conducting your analysis, you may want to consider the following questions. In each case, be specific and take information directly from the case study to defend your assessment.

1. Describe Mike's use of time. How efficiently did he use it?

2. How did he create a warm academic climate for his students? Cite specific evidence from the case study.

3. How effective was Mike's classroom management? Again cite specific evidence.

4. How did Mike attempt to ensure success in his teaching?

5. What did Mike do to alter instruction for his students with learning disabilities? How effective were these modifications?

6. What did Mike do to meet the needs of his students with behavior disorders? How effective were these interventions?

7. Give Mike's teaching an overall assessment, using the information in this chapter as a basis for your conclusions. You may also want to consider your answers to Items 1 through 6 in making your analysis.

 # Summary

Students with Learning Problems

Many students with exceptionalities have mild learning problems that interfere with classroom performance but do not require separate instructional settings. These exceptionalities include mental retardation, learning disabilities, and behavior disorders. Teachers play an integral part in identifying these students and adapting instruction to meet their needs.

Communication, Visual, and Hearing Disabilities

Communication disorders include speech or expressive disorders and language or receptive disorders. Care should be taken to differentiate language disorders from culturally influenced difficulties encountered in learning English as a second language.

Other disabilities include visual and hearing disorders, which are serious because of their adverse influence on communication channels that affect learning. In both instances, teachers can adapt instruction to meet the special needs of these students.

Students Who Are Gifted and Talented

Gifted and talented students are at the upper end of the ability continuum and display unique talents in specific domains. Acceleration moves these students through the regular curriculum faster; enrichment provides alternative instruction to encourage student exploration.

Changes in the Way Teachers Help Students with Exceptionalities

In the past, students with exceptionalities were often segregated from the regular classroom. Mainstreaming placed them in the regular classroom. Inclusion attempts to take the process a step further by creating a web of services that ensures student success. Inclusion works best when special education services are matched to the unique needs of each child.

A Legal Framework for Working with Students Who Have Exceptionalities

A series of federal laws has changed the way teachers work with students who have exceptionalities. These laws require that students with exceptionalities be taught in the LRE, guaranteed due process through parental involvement, protected against discrimination in testing, and provided with IEPs. Recent changes in the IDEA reinforce parents' rights in helping their children.

The Teacher's Role in Inclusive Classrooms

Teachers perform three roles in inclusive classrooms: identification, instruction, and social integration and growth.

Teachers are crucial in identification because they have direct experience with students. Before making a referral, teachers should document the nature of the problem and different strategies attempted.

Effective instruction for students with exceptionalities uses basic principles of effective teaching, such as effective management and high success rates, as a foundation. In addition, strategy instruction teaches students to approach learning tasks by setting and monitoring progress toward goals.

Now go to our Companion Website to assess your understanding of chapter content with the Student Self-Assessment, apply comprehension in the Online Casebook, and broaden your knowledge base with links to important Educational Psychology World Wide Web sites.

Social acceptance for students with exceptionalities can be promoted through modeling, practice, and feedback. Attitudes of other students can be improved through instructional approaches focusing on increased understanding and through strategies such as peer tutoring and cooperative learning, which provide students with opportunities to interact in productive ways.

 **Important Concepts**

acceleration (p. 186)

adaptive fit (p. 190)

assistive technology (p. 201)

attention deficit/hyperactivity disorder (AD/HD) (p. 174)

behavior disorders (BDs) (p. 176)

communication disorder (p. 179)

creativity (p. 184)

curriculum-based assessment (p. 197)

curriculum compacting (p. 186)

deaf (p. 182)

disability (p. 170)

enrichment (p. 186)

exceptionalities (p. 169)

handicap (p. 170)

inclusion (p. 190)

individualized education program (IEP) (p. 193)

language or receptive disorders (p. 179)

learning disabilities (LDs) (p. 173)

least restrictive environment (LRE) (p. 189)

mainstreaming (p. 189)

mental retardation (p. 171)

partial hearing impairment (p. 182)

special education (p. 169)

speech or expressive disorders (p. 179)

students who are gifted and talented (p. 183)

visual disability (p. 180)

The Classroom

Learning Part II

Chapter Outline

Behaviorist Views of Learning
Contiguity • Classical Conditioning • Operant
Conditioning • Putting Behaviorism Into Perspective

Social Cognitive Theory
Comparing Behaviorism and Social Cognitive Theory •
Modeling • Vicarious Learning • Effects of Modeling
on Behavior • Technology and Learning: The Impact of
Symbolic Modeling on Behavior • Learning from Models:
The Processes Involved • Effectiveness of Models •
Self-Regulation • Putting Social Cognitive Theory
Into Perspective

**Dealing with Diversity: Behaviorism and
Social Cognitive Theory**
Classical Conditioning: Learning to Like and Dislike
School • Motivating Hesitant Learners

6

Behaviorism
and Social
Cognitive Theory

Tim, a 10th grader, was taking Algebra II and had been doing fairly well—getting a few Cs but mostly Bs on the weekly tests. In fact, he had become fairly confident about his ability to do algebra until the last test, when something inexplicably went wrong. For some reason, he became confused, got solutions mixed up, seemed to "blank out," panicked, and badly failed the test. Even with his parents' sympathy and support, he was devastated. On the next test, he was so anxious and nervous that when he started, the first few answers he circled on his problems had wiggly lines around them from his shaking hand.

"What if I flunk again? . . . I still don't get this stuff. . . . What am I doing in here?" he thought as he struggled with the problems. Although he did better than he had on the previous test, he still barely passed it.

"I'm not sure I can do this," he concluded.

After making only a halfhearted effort on the next test and again barely passing it, he thought, "Maybe I should drop algebra."

He was also more nervous when he took chemistry tests than he had been previously, even though he hadn't done poorly on any chemistry exam. Fortunately, he still did fine in his English and world history classes.

Mrs. Lovisolo, his Algebra II teacher, talked with him, exhorting him to remember that he had only failed one test and hadn't been making his usual effort as he studied.

"Thanks, Mrs. Lovisolo," Tim said, on the brink of tears, "but math . . . is so hard for me. I don't know. Maybe geometry is as far as I can go."

"I don't want to hear those words," she said with a supportive smile. "Now, I want you to relax. You can do this work. I'm going to keep an eye on you in class, and if you're having trouble, just let me know, and we'll work together after school. Okay?"

" . . . Okay," Tim said and, although he remained unconvinced, he vowed to redouble his efforts.

Tim's friend Susan sat directly in front of him in Algebra II. He talked with her about his uneasiness. She always did so well on the tests. "I think they're tough," Susan commented, "so I really study for them. How about if we get together and study?" Susan added.

"Okay," Tim responded uncertainly, but he decided to go ahead. So on Thursday, the night before the next test, he went to Susan's home to study with her. In the process, he saw how she selected problems from the book and solved them completely in writing, rather than just reading over the sample problems and explanations. As she began working on her third problem, he asked her why she was doing another one.

"I try to do as many different kinds as I can, to be sure I don't get fooled on the test," she explained.

"That way, I'm more confident when I go into the test.

" . . . See, this one is different," she continued. "The first thing I look for is how it's different. Then I try it.

"I sometimes even make . . . a little chart. I try to do at least three problems of each type we study, and then I check 'em off as I do them. It's sort of fun. . . . I can see I'm making some progress. If I get all of them right, I treat myself with a bowl of ice cream."

" . . . Good idea," Tim nodded. "I usually do one, maybe two and if I'm okay on them, I quit," he shrugged.

Tim now had a goal to do three problems of each type, selecting the odd problems so that he could check the correct answers in the back of the book. Also, when Mrs. Lovisolo used a term in class that he didn't understand, he wrote it down, together with the definition, and then studied it so that he immediately understood what she meant when she used it in her explanations.

Tim did much better on the next test. "Whew, what a relief," he said to himself.

He was still somewhat nervous for the following week's test, but his effort had paid off, and he did very well; in fact, his score was the highest for the year.

"Maybe I can do this after all," he concluded with an inward smile.

Learning is at the core of any study of educational psychology, and a primary focus of this text is on what teachers can do to promote learning in all students. This chapter is the first of four devoted to theoretical descriptions of the topic.

We begin by examining behaviorism, a view of learning that, in spite of controversy, continues to be widely applied in classrooms, especially in the area of classroom management (Reynolds, Sinatra, & Jetton, 1996). We then turn to social cognitive theory, a view of learning with historical roots in behaviorism but that goes beyond it to examine processes, such as learners' beliefs and expectations, that behaviorists don't consider. In Chapters 7 through 9, we extend this discussion to examine cognitive learning in greater detail.

After you've completed your study of this chapter, you should be able to meet the following objectives:

- Explain how classical conditioning can influence student learning.
- Explain student behavior by using concepts such as reinforcement, punishment, generalization, discrimination, satiation, and extinction.
- Describe the influence of different reinforcement schedules on student behavior.
- Identify examples of modeling and vicarious learning in classroom situations.
- Describe how self-regulation influences student learning.

Behaviorist Views of Learning

Tim's experience in the opening case illustrates the theme of this section. The incident involved learning, and here we examine learning from a behaviorist point of view. According to this view, **learning** is *a relatively enduring change in observable behavior that occurs as a result of experience* (Skinner, 1953; J. Walker, 1996). Notice that this definition focuses on observable behaviors; behaviorism doesn't consider ideas, insights, goals, or needs that are "in learners' heads."

Consider our definition again. It says that the change in behavior is relatively enduring. We all have seen or experienced temporary changes in behavior resulting from illness, injury, or emotional distress. These changes would not be classified as learning.

In addition, changes in behavior resulting from maturation are not considered learning. For example, a 15-year-old can carry a large bag of groceries that his 6-year-old brother can't even lift. He is bigger and stronger as a result of maturation. Parents say with excitement that their small child has "learned" to walk, but, although some experience with crawling is certainly a factor, walking depends more on maturation than on learning.

Let's look again at Tim's situation. He makes wiggly lines around his problems. This behavior is observable, and based on the example, it was relatively enduring. His making wiggly lines was a result of his experience on the earlier test. We would say that these wiggly lines are "learned" behaviors. Other learned behaviors are illustrated in the case study as well, and we discuss them later in the chapter.

In this section, we examine three types of learning according to behaviorism. They are outlined in Figure 6.1.

6.1 ▬
Identify two other types of enduring behaviors that wouldn't be called learning. Give an example of each type.

Contiguity

Someone asks you, "What is 7 times 8?" and you immediately respond, "56." Your response is the result of learning that occurs through **contiguity**, or *the simple pairing of stimuli and responses, so that if they occur together often enough, experiencing one causes the*

Figure 6.1

Types of learning in behaviorism

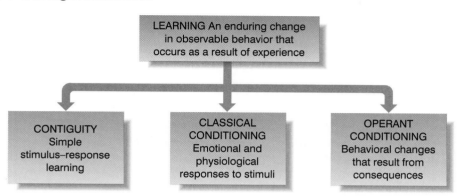

LEARNING An enduring change in observable behavior that occurs as a result of experience

| CONTIGUITY Simple stimulus–response learning | CLASSICAL CONDITIONING Emotional and physiological responses to stimuli | OPERANT CONDITIONING Behavioral changes that result from consequences |

Flash cards and drill-and-practice help students learn through contiguity.

other (Catania, 1998; Guthrie, 1952). **Stimuli** are *all the sights, sounds, smells, and other influences the senses receive from the environment.* **Responses** are *the behaviors that result from the association.* If you pair 7 × 8 with 56 often enough, you respond "56" when you hear "What is 7 times 8?" Hearing "What is 7 times 8?" is the stimulus, and "56" is the response. Contiguity occurs in classrooms in activities such as drill-and-practice with flash cards. Tim was applying the principle of contiguity when he wrote new terms and definitions and practiced them.

Classical Conditioning

Although stimulus–response pairings can be used to explain fact learning and other simple behaviors, most learning is more complex. This complexity was originally described by Ivan Pavlov, a Russian physiologist who won a Nobel Prize in 1904 for his work on digestion. As a part of his research, he had his assistants feed dogs meat powder, so that their rates of salivation could be measured. As the research progressed, however, the dogs began to salivate at the sight of the assistants, even when they weren't carrying meat powder with them (Pavlov, 1928). This startling phenomenon resulted in a turn in Pavlov's work and opened a new field of study called **classical conditioning**, or *respondent learning, because the learner is responding to the environment.*

In Pavlov's experiments, a dog's initial salivation was an **unconditioned response**, *a reflexive (unlearned), involuntary response induced by the meat powder,* which was an **unconditioned stimulus**, *the original stimulus that produces an unconditioned response.*

Now the process becomes a bit more complex. Initially, Pavlov's dogs didn't react one way or another to the lab assistants; they were **neutral stimuli**, *stimuli that don't produce any response.* In time, however, the lab assistants became *associated* with the meat powder, and they caused salivation all by themselves. The lab assistants became **conditioned stimuli**, which are *stimuli that become associated with unconditioned stimuli* and produce **conditioned responses**, *responses identical or similar to the unconditioned responses.*

<table>
<tr><td>

6.2 ━

Identify the unconditioned and conditioned stimuli and the unconditioned and conditioned responses in Tim's case.

</td></tr>
</table>

Let's see how Tim *learned* to fear tests, based on these ideas. Initially, he didn't react to tests one way or another; they were neutral stimuli. Then he failed a test and was devastated by his failure. Subsequent tests became *associated* with his initial failure, resulting in his nervousness, as evidenced by the wiggly lines around his answers.

Our examples illustrate the following essential characteristics of classical conditioning:

 ▌ Classical conditioning is a form of learning. Tim's behavior underwent an enduring change as a result of his experience: He learned to be nervous in tests, just as Pavlov's dogs learned to salivate at the sight of the lab assistants.
 ▌ Classically conditioned responses are emotional or physiological and involuntary (Baldwin & Baldwin, 1998). Tim's nervousness was a learned, emotional response, and it was out of his control; he didn't choose to be nervous when he took Algebra II tests.
 ▌ Conditioned and unconditioned stimuli, which are initially unrelated, became *associated.* Pavlov's assistants and the meat powder, which weren't related in any way, became associated, and Tim's tests became associated with failure.
 ▌ Conditioned and unconditioned responses are identical or similar. In Pavlov's experiments, they were identical. In Tim's case, devastation and nervousness are related emotions.

Classical conditioning helps teachers understand how supportive classroom environments and warm and caring teachers result in positive feelings toward schools and learning.

Classical Conditioning in the Classroom

Classroom examples of classical conditioning are actually quite common. For example, many students experience test anxiety (Pintrich & Schunk, 1996). It's not uncommon for some young children to become physically ill in anticipation of school, and some parents are reluctant to attend school functions or respond to teacher requests because of past unpleasant school experiences. Classical conditioning helps us explain these problems.

It can also help us explain positive feelings toward school and can help sensitize teachers to the importance of a positive emotional climate in their classrooms. Some researchers, in fact, suggest that the emotional reactions associated with the topics they study are the most meaningful experiences learners take away from schools (Gentile, 1996). For example, suppose students—often uneasy about a new school, class, or topic, such as a difficult idea in math—are treated with warmth, caring, and encouragement by their teachers. Learners respond positively to these displays of genuine warmth and encouragement. If teachers are consistently caring and encouraging, students will begin to associate school and studying with the teacher's encouragement, and the school will elicit comfortable and safe feelings in students. These relationships are outlined in Table 6.1.

Generalization and Discrimination

Let's look once more at our opening case study. In addition to his nervousness when he took his Algebra II tests, Tim became nervous when he took chemistry tests, even though he hadn't done poorly on any of them. His fears had generalized to chemistry. **Generalization** *occurs when a stimulus similar to the conditioned stimulus elicits the conditioned response all by itself.* The physical sciences are somewhat similar to algebra, so chemistry tests are stimuli similar to the algebra tests, and they elicited the conditioned response—nervousness—by themselves.

The process can also work in a positive way. Students who associate school with the caring of one teacher may, through generalization, have similar reactions to other classes, club activities, and school-related functions.

6.3

Using concepts from classical conditioning, explain a child becoming ill in anticipation of school, and explain why a parent might be reluctant to attend school functions.

6.4

One of this text's authors gets a funny feeling when he enters a dentist's office. This doesn't happen when he goes to see a medical doctor. Using the concepts of generalization and discrimination, explain the feeling.

Table 6.1

Promoting positive classroom climate

Unconditional Stimuli	Unconditional Responses
Teacher displays caring and encouraging behaviors	Learner's feelings of comfort
Conditional Stimuli	**Conditional Responses**
Classrooms and topics (that have become associated with the teacher's manner)	Learner's feelings of comfort

The opposite of generalization is discrimination. **Discrimination** is *the ability to give different responses to related but not identical stimuli.* For example, Tim is nervous during chemistry tests but not during those in English and history. He discriminates between English and algebra, as well as between history and algebra.

Extinction

In our case study, we saw that Tim has been doing better since he started working with Susan and changed his study habits. In time, if he continues to succeed, his nervousness will disappear, or the conditioned response will become extinct. **Extinction** *occurs when the conditioned stimulus occurs repeatedly in the absence of the unconditioned stimulus* (Baldwin & Baldwin, 1998). Eventually, the conditioned stimulus no longer elicits the conditioned response. In Tim's case, repeated test taking (the conditioned stimulus) occurring without failure (the unconditioned stimulus) will, in time, no longer result in nervousness (the conditioned response).

Effective teachers use concrete examples to encourage students to generalize and discriminate when learning concepts.

Classroom Connections

Applying Contiguity in Your Classroom

1. Carefully consider the forms of fact learning for which students will be responsible. Provide frequent review and drill to cement the contiguous links between the facts.
   - An elementary teacher takes a few minutes each morning to review difficult multiplication facts in a simple drill-and-practice activity.
   - A history teacher wants students to remember several important dates. She identifies the dates and their significance on a handout and tells students they're responsible for knowing the information. She reviews the material with them periodically before they are tested.

Applying Classical Conditioning in Your Classroom

2. Provide a safe and warm environment so that the classroom will elicit positive emotions.
   - A first-grade teacher greets each of her students with a smile when they come into the room in the morning. She makes an attempt to periodically ask each of them about their family, a pet, or some other personal part of their lives.
   - A junior high teacher makes a point of establishing and enforcing rules that forbid students to ridicule each other in any way, particularly when they're involved in class discussions or responding to teacher questions. He makes respect for each other a high priority in his classroom.

3. When questioning students, put them in safe situations and arrange the results to ensure a positive outcome.
   - A fourth-grade inner-city teacher tries to get all his students to participate by doing the following:
     a. When calling on reluctant responders or low-achieving students, he begins with open-ended questions such as, "What do you notice about the problem?" and "How would you compare the two examples?" These are questions for which virtually any answer is appropriate.
     b. When students are unable or unwilling to respond, he prompts them until they give an acceptable answer. (Effective prompting techniques are discussed in Chapter 11.)
     c. He calls on all students in his class, so that being in his class becomes associated with responding and making an effort.
   - A senior high math teacher deals with test anxiety by specifying precisely what information students are accountable for on tests. He gives them sample items to practice on and provides ample opportunity to go over problem areas before the test.
   - When a middle school social studies teacher encounters students who are anxious about making a presentation to the whole class, she has them come in and make their presentations to her alone so that they can practice and she can provide reassurance and support.

Operant Conditioning

So far, we've progressed from simple stimulus–response pairings, which apply to fact learning (contiguity), to more complex stimulus–response relationships (classical conditioning), and we've used these relationships to help explain involuntary emotional and physiological reactions to classroom activities and other events. However, we observe a great deal of behavior in our everyday experiences that we're unable to explain on the basis of either simple contiguity or classical conditioning because people often initiate behaviors, rather than merely respond to stimuli. In other words, people "operate" on their environments, which is the source of the term *operant conditioning*.

6.5 ▬
A child approaches a dog and is bitten. From that point on, the child is filled with fear and runs away whenever a dog approaches. Describe the classically conditioned aspect of this example, and also describe the operantly conditioned aspect of this example.

This leads us to the work of B. F. Skinner (1904–1990), a behavioral psychologist whose influence was so great that heads of psychology departments late in the 1960s identified him as the most influential psychologist of the 20th century (Myers, 1970). Skinner argued that instead of merely responding to stimuli, learners' actions are more controlled by the consequences of the behavior than by events preceding the behavior. A **consequence** is *an outcome (stimulus) occurring after the behavior, that influences future behaviors.* For example, a teacher's praise after a student answers is a consequence. Being stopped by the highway patrol and fined for speeding is also a consequence. Test results and grades are consequences, as are recognition for outstanding work and reprimands for inappropriate behavior.

Operant and classical conditioning are often confused. To help clarify the differences, a comparison of the two is presented in Table 6.2. We see that learning occurs as a result of experience for both classical and operant conditioning, but the type of behavior is different, and the behavior and stimulus occur in the opposite order for the two.

We said in the introduction to the chapter that behaviorism, while controversial, is widely used as a tool for managing student behavior in classrooms (Reynolds et al., 1996). Operant conditioning, in particular, is used in this area. (We consider classroom management in depth in Chapter 11.)

Let's turn now to a detailed discussion of operant conditioning and the different consequences of behavior as they are presented in Figure 6.2.

Reinforcement

Imagine that during a class discussion you make a comment, and your instructor responds, "That was a very insightful idea. Good thinking." The likelihood that you'll try to make another comment in the future increases. The instructor's comment is a **reinforcer**, *a consequence that increases the frequency or duration of a behavior. The process of applying reinforcers to increase behavior* is called **reinforcement**, and it exists in two forms: positive and negative.

Table 6.2 ▬

A comparison of operant and classical conditioning

	Classical Conditioning	Operant Conditioning
Behavior	Involuntary (Person does not have control of behavior) Emotional Physiological	Voluntary (Person has control of behavior)
Order	Behavior follows stimulus	Behavior precedes stimulus (consequence)
How learning occurs	Neutral stimuli become associated with unconditioned stimuli	Consequences of behaviors influence subsequent behaviors
Example	Learners associate classrooms (initially neutral) with the warmth of teachers, so classrooms elicit positive emotions.	Learners attempt to answer questions and are praised, so their attempts to answer increase.
Key researcher	Pavlov	Skinner

Figure 6.2

Consequences of behavior

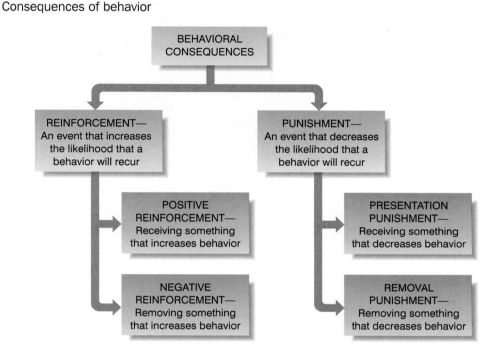

Positive Reinforcement.   **Positive reinforcement** is *the process of increasing the frequency or duration of a behavior as the result of presenting a reinforcer.* In classrooms, we typically think of a positive reinforcer as something desired or valued, such as your instructor's comment, but an increase in student horseplay following a reprimand can also be a case of positive reinforcement. It's positive reinforcement because the behavior—horseplay—has (strangely enough) increased as a result of being presented with a consequence—the reprimand.

Teacher praise in all its forms is perhaps the most common positive reinforcer in classrooms. High test scores, "happy faces" for young children, tokens that can be cashed in for privileges, and stars on the bulletin board all can act as positive reinforcers for students. Likewise, attentive looks from students, student questions, high student test scores, and compliments from students or their parents are positive reinforcers for teachers.

6.6
Praise, though well intended, isn't always a positive reinforcer. How do we know when it isn't?

The Premack Principle

> Don Zentz's jazz band students loved playing modern, upbeat jazz–rock compositions but were less enthusiastic about some of the standards.
>
> "No, not 'Mood Indigo' again," they protested when he held up the sheet music for the Duke Ellington classic.
>
> "A good job one time through it, and we'll do 'Watermelon Man,'" he countered.
>
> "All right! Let's do it!" they shouted.

In this example, Mr. Zentz employed the Premack principle, named after David Premack (1965). Also called "Grandma's rule" ("First eat your vegetables, and then you can

Frequent graded assignments
provide opportunities for both
practice and feedback.

have dessert"), the **Premack principle** says that *a more preferred activity can be used as a positive reinforcer for a less preferred activity*. Don's students preferred playing "Watermelon Man" to "Mood Indigo," so he used being given permission to play it as a reinforcer for playing the less preferred piece.

6.7

Judy is off-task in your class, and you admonish her for her misbehavior. However, in a few moments she's off-task again. What concept from operant conditioning does this situation illustrate? Explain.

Negative Reinforcement.   You've just completed a strenuous workout, and your body is "achy," so you decide to take aspirin or ibuprofen to get some relief and help you sleep better. It works, and the next time you work out, you take the aspirin again. In fact, some times you take the aspirin before you work out to avoid the aches and pains.

These examples illustrate the concept of **negative reinforcement**, which is *the process of removing or avoiding a stimulus to increase behavior* (Skinner, 1953). Notice that although the term *negative* appears in the label, negative reinforcement results in an *increase,* not a *decrease* in behavior.

Think of the term *negative,* in negative reinforcement, mathematically, not emotionally. In our example, the "achy" muscles were the stimuli that were *removed* (or subtracted) when you took the pain killer, so your behavior increased; you took it more readily the next time. You also *avoided* the achy muscles on another occasion by taking the aspirin before you worked out. In both cases, you were negatively reinforced for taking the aspirin.

As another example, suppose on Monday you have a student who chronically misbehaves, so in frustration, you send her to the dean of students. However, on Tuesday, her misbehavior occurs even sooner than it did Monday, and you send her out again. Your intent was to stop the misbehavior but, in fact, you *negatively reinforced* her.

How do we know? First, we know her behavior has been reinforced because she misbehaved sooner on Tuesday than she did on Monday; her behavior is increasing. Second, the stimulus—the classroom environment—has been removed (subtracted) by sending her out of the room.

Notice that when negative reinforcement is applied, one of two circumstances exists:

▌ Learners are in the situation before they demonstrate the behavior. Your muscles ached before you took the pain killer, and the student was in the classroom before she was sent to the dean.

▌ Learners can avoid a consequence (you took the pain killer to avoid the achy muscles).

Punishment

Positive and negative reinforcers are consequences that strengthen or increase behavior. Some consequences, however, *weaken behaviors or decrease their frequency. These consequences are called* **punishers,** and *the process of using these consequences to decrease behavior* is called **punishment.**

Presentation Punishment.   As shown in Figure 6.2, **presentation punishment** *occurs when a learner's behavior decreases as a result of being presented with a punisher.* Presentation punishment is intended when students have to pick up lunchroom trash because they were rowdy or when teachers verbally reprimand students for misbehavior. Picking up the trash and the reprimands are intended as punishers designed to decrease the rowdiness or the talking.

Removal Punishment.   Two kinds of punishment are illustrated in Figure 6.2. Whereas presentation punishment is the process of weakening a behavior by *presenting* a punisher, *decreasing behavior by removing a stimulus or the inability to get positive reinforcement* is **removal punishment**. As with negative reinforcement, the learner is in the situation before the consequence; but unlike negative reinforcement, removal punishment reduces rather than increases behavior.

A fairly common and somewhat controversial application of removal punishment in elementary classrooms is called *time-out*. A misbehaving student is removed from the class and physically isolated behind filing cabinets or some other barrier. The rationale is that removal from the class eliminates the student's chances to get positive reinforcement, so isolation acts as a form of removal punishment.

In middle and high school classrooms, after-school detention is quite commonly used in an attempt to use removal punishment to decrease unwanted behaviors. When in detention, the student's free time and opportunity to interact with classmates is taken away. If they're not used excessively, both can be effective management techniques (Skiba & Raison, 1990; White & Bailey, 1990).

Let's consider another teacher's application of removal punishment:

> Bette Ponce was having management problems with her second-grade class. To try to solve these problems, she handed each of her second graders a small packet containing three slips of paper every morning when they came into the room. Each time a student broke one of her classroom rules, Bette took a slip of paper from that student's packet. Bette then called the parents of any students who lost all three slips during the course of the day. Losing all three slips for a second day resulted in half an hour of detention.
>
> Bette also combined positive reinforcement with the program. Any student who had 10 or more slips left in his or her packet by the end of the week could trade the slips for free time and other rewards.

Bette's system is sometimes called **response cost**, *the application of removal punishment by taking away reinforcers already given.* Bette's students were given the slips of paper, which they lost for infractions of the rules. Traffic fines, revoked drivers' licenses,

---

6.8 ▬
Picking up the trash and reprimands are *intended* as punishers. How would we know if they actually are punishers? What would indicate to us that they are reinforcers instead?

6.9 ▬
Explain how allowing students to talk with each other during detention or even allowing them to finish their homework might defeat its purpose.

backing up 10 yards for holding in football games, and loss of free classroom time previously earned are all additional examples of response cost.

Using Punishers: Research Results.   What long-range impact does the use of punishment have on learners? Is it effective? Does it work? Should it ever be used?

Research has identified several problems associated with using punishment:

▮ Physical punishment can teach aggression. Punished individuals often demonstrate similar behaviors at a later time (Bandura, 1986).

▮ Punishment causes more vigorous responding. Students who have learned to defy authority figures, for example, are likely to be even more defiant after receiving punishers (Nilsson & Archer, 1989).

▮ Punishment only temporarily suppresses behavior. Punishment is only a temporary solution to the problem of misbehavior, unless the person administering the punishers is willing to continually use them (Walters & Grusec, 1977).

▮ Punishment causes an individual to avoid both the punishers and the person administering them. A punished individual may learn more sophisticated ways to avoid getting caught, and students avoid teachers who use punishment frequently (Cressey, 1978).

▮ Punishment causes negative emotions. Through classical conditioning, learners begin to associate the classroom with being punished, so classrooms become conditioned stimuli that produce negative emotions (Baldwin & Baldwin, 1998), and they may generalize their aversion to their assignments, other teachers, and the school (Jenson, Sloane, & Young, 1988).

Some critics of behaviorism argue that behavioral techniques in general, and punishers in particular, are undesirable and shouldn't be used (Kohn, 1996). Others emphasize positive reinforcement as an alternative to punishment. For example, everyone's heard the maxim "Catch 'em being good." Research indicates that systems focusing on positive behaviors are vastly superior to those emphasizing a decrease in inappropriate behaviors (R. Williams, 1987).

Focusing exclusively on positive behaviors isn't a panacea, however. If all punishers are eliminated, some students actually become more disruptive (Pfiffer, Rosen, & O'Leary, 1985; Rosen, O'Leary, Joyce, Conway, & Pfiffer, 1984). It's unrealistic to think that punishment can be totally avoided; it is probably necessary in some cases (Axelrod & Apsche, 1983; Maccoby, 1992). For example, chronically or severely disruptive students don't have the right to destroy the learning environment for students who want to learn, and if the only alternative is removing them from the classroom, this action is appropriate. Remember, however, that punishers only suppress undesirable behaviors; students must still be taught how to behave appropriately.

Sensitivity and good judgment are required in using punishers. The most effective solution is a combination of clear classroom rules with consequences that are administered fairly and consistently. We examine these issues in detail in Chapter 11 when we discuss classroom management.

Operant Conditioning: Applications

Generalization and Discrimination.   We examined generalization and discrimination when we discussed classical conditioning, and now we consider them from an operant perspective. As an example, suppose kindergarten students see shapes such as those in Figure 6.3a and respond with "square." Similarly, after dissecting a shark or frog, biology

Figure 6.3

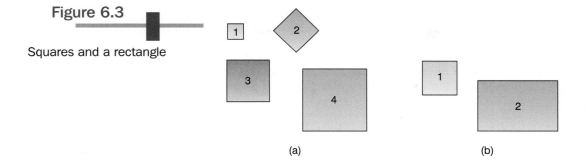

Squares and a rectangle

(a)   (b)

students recognize the heart in each case. Both the squares and the hearts are similar but not identical. The squares differ in size and orientation, and a shark's heart is two-chambered, whereas a frog's is three-chambered. Nevertheless, students learn that they are all squares or hearts despite these differences. They have generalized.

Like in classical conditioning, **generalization** is *giving the same response to similar but not identical stimuli.* The responses are voluntary, however, rather than involuntary—as they are in the case of classical conditioning—and result from reinforcers. For example, children are reinforced for saying the first shape in Figure 6.3b is a square, but they are told, "No, it's a rectangle," when they say the second shape is a square. This feedback helps them learn **discrimination**—*to give different responses to similar, but not identical, stimuli*—between the two shapes. Likewise, the biology student who recognizes the difference between the frog's heart and its liver is also discriminating, as is the child who recognizes the difference between *p* and *q* or *b* and *d*.

> 6.10
> Identify two differences between generalization and discrimination in the context of operant conditioning, compared with generalization and discrimination in the context of classical conditioning.

Shaping.   Positive reinforcement can also be used to change or shape behavior as we'll see in the following episode:

> "I start out praising every answer even if it's only partially right," Maria Brugera commented. "I also praise them for trying even if they can't give me an answer. Then as they improve, I praise them only for better, more complete answers, until finally they have to give well thought-out explanations before I'll say anything."
>
> "I don't," Greg Jordan responded. "I like to give a lot of praise, but I think praising every answer takes too much time. I also think if you do too much, you lose your credibility, so I start right off praising them only when they give me a really good answer."

According to Maria, her students aren't always able to give her the answers she is after, so she praises partial answers and even effort. Gradually, she raises her expectations, so they have to give more complete responses to earn her praise. Maria is applying the concept of **shaping**, *the process of reinforcing successive approximations of a desired behavior.* Although Maria was obviously after the correct answer, student effort was a beginning step, and a partially correct response was a close approximation of the desired behavior. By reinforcing each step, she hoped to eventually get complete and thoughtful answers from her students.

Reinforcement Schedules.   Even though you may not have played them, you likely understand how slot machines work. You insert a coin, pull the handle, and hope for some coins in return. Sometimes a few coins drop into the tray; many times they don't. The coins you receive are reinforcers, and if you continue to receive them, you're likely to continue playing. Since you only periodically receive the coins, you're on an **intermittent**

reinforcement schedule, which is *the process of reinforcing a behavior only periodically.* If you received coins every time you pulled the handle, you would be on a **continuous reinforcement schedule**, which *occurs when every response is reinforced.* These two basic types illustrate **reinforcement schedules**, which describe *patterns in the frequency and predictability of reinforcers.* By praising every student answer, Maria initially used a continuous schedule in her shaping process, whereas Greg used an intermittent schedule.

There are two types of intermittent schedules. **Interval schedules** *distribute reinforcers based on time;* **ratio schedules** *base reinforcers on the number of responses.* Teachers use a **fixed-interval schedule** when they *reinforce learners on a predictable time interval,* such as every 3 minutes or every day. A **variable-interval schedule** *changes the amount of time between reinforcers in an unpredictable way.*

Greg praised students on the basis of responses, rather than time, and he praised using his judgment of the answer's quality, rather than every fifth answer, for example. He was using a **variable-ratio schedule**, which is *a schedule that reinforces students in an unpredictable way based on the number of responses.* If he had chosen to praise every third or fifth or some other numbered answer, he would have been using a **fixed-ratio schedule**, which is *a schedule that reinforces students in a predictable way based on the number of responses.*

These relationships are illustrated in Figure 6.4, and additional classroom examples are outlined in Table 6.3.

These different schedules are important to teachers because each has advantages and disadvantages. A continuous schedule yields the fastest rates of initial learning, so it can be effective, for example, when students are initially learning new content such as how

6.11 ━

To encourage on-task behaviors, a teacher has a classroom beeper that periodically makes a noise. If students are on-task when the beeper goes off, the class gets points toward a party. What reinforcement schedule is the teacher using? Explain.

Figure 6.4 ▮

Schedules of reinforcement

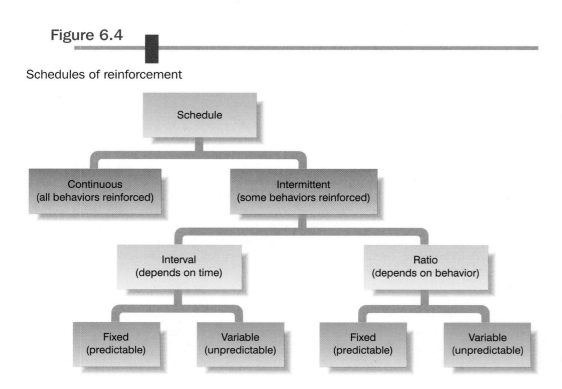

Table 6.3

Reinforcement schedules and examples

Schedule	Example
Continuous	A teacher "walks students through" the steps for solving simultaneous equations. They are liberally praised at each step as they first learn the solution.
Fixed-ratio	The algebra teacher announces, "As soon as you've done two problems in a row correctly, you may start on your homework assignment so that you'll be able to finish by the end of class."
Variable-ratio	Students volunteer to answer questions by raising their hands and are called on at random.
Fixed-interval	Students are given a quiz every Friday.
Variable-interval	Students are given unannounced quizzes.

to solve simultaneous equations. On the other hand, these behaviors are less persistent; that is, learners quickly stop displaying the behaviors when the reinforcers are removed.

Fixed schedules also have disadvantages: Behavior increases rapidly just before the reinforcer is given and then decreases rapidly and remains low until just before the next reinforcer is given. For instance, if you give a quiz every Friday—a fixed-interval schedule—students may study diligently on Thursday and then not study again until the following Thursday.

This might suggest using a variable-interval schedule, such as giving "pop" quizzes. This strategy, however, has its own disadvantages. It can cause high anxiety in students and detract from their motivation to learn. The best compromise is probably brief, frequent, announced quizzes once a week or even more often (Eggen, 1997; Kika, McLaughlin, & Dixon, 1992).

Potency and Satiation. As you would expect, reinforcers vary in their effectiveness. Behaviorists use the term **potency** to refer to *a reinforcer's ability to strengthen behaviors.* Reinforcement potency depends on at least three factors:

- The learners themselves. High test scores and recognition, for example, are effective reinforcers for some students but not for others.
- The source of reinforcers. For instance, compliments are more potent reinforcers when they come from respected teachers than from those less respected.
- The frequency of reinforcers. A simple "Excellent!" written beside a response on a test paper can be a potent reinforcer, but if it appears too often or is written on every student's paper, it can lose its potency.

When a reinforcer occurs so frequently that it loses its potency, **satiation** results. Greg Jordan demonstrated that he was aware of the possibility of satiation when he chose to be judicious in his use of praise.

Satiation can be used to eliminate the power of a reinforcer. For example, we've all heard the tale of the father who catches his son smoking behind the barn and then forces the boy to smoke the rest of the pack of cigarettes. Although we wouldn't recommend the

6.12
With what kind of a reinforcement schedule—continuous or intermittent—would satiation occur first? What implication does this have for your teaching?

father's technique, classroom applications of satiation have been used successfully. Let's look at an example:

> Isabelle Ortega was having a problem with chronic note passing in her seventh-grade English class, so she developed the following plan. After identifying the culprits, she required them to write a long personal note to a friend near the end of class while the other students began their homework. The note could not be related to classwork, nor could it be copied, and she required it to be a full handwritten page. She didn't read any of the notes but did inspect them to be certain they were of proper length. If they weren't, she demanded that the students continue writing until the page was full or until the period ended.
>
> By the end of the second day, several of the students asked whether they could stop writing notes and work on their homework, and by the end of the third day, Isabelle stopped the process. She did not have problems with note writing in her class since that time.

This example also illustrates the importance of teacher sensitivity and professional judgment. For instance, Isabelle made a point of not reading any of the notes, so she didn't embarrass the students or violate their privacy, and she required that the topic be a personal note so that note writing became the aversive behavior. Had she allowed them to write about a class topic, the topic or writing itself could have become aversive instead.

Isabelle was also respected by the students as a teacher who was strict but fair. She cared about her students and communicated that she expected them to learn. Had these factors not existed, her application of satiation might not have succeeded.

Extinction.   You saw in our opening case study that Tim's nervousness decreased with each test and that, in time, it could be eliminated. This was an example of extinction with classical conditioning.

Operantly conditioned behaviors can also become extinct, as illustrated in the following example:

> Renita, a tenth-grader, enjoyed school and liked to respond in her classes. She was attentive and raised her hand, eager to answer most teachers' questions. She said she could "stay awake better when the teacher asks questions."
>
> Mr. Frank, her world history teacher, asked a few questions but usually lectured. Renita raised her hand when he did ask a question, but someone would usually blurt out the answer before she could respond.
>
> Renita rarely raises her hand now and often catches herself daydreaming in world history.

This situation demonstrates how operantly conditioned behaviors can become extinct and, further, how important the way we teach is in promoting student attention and learning. For Renita, being called on by the teacher reinforced both her attempts to respond and her attention. Because she wasn't called on or allowed to respond, she wasn't reinforced, and her behaviors were becoming extinct. **Extinction**, from an operant perspective, is *the elimination of a response as a result of nonreinforcement*.

Often, teachers don't interact enough with their students; this is unfortunate because classroom interaction and learning are closely related (Good & Brophy, 1997; McCarthy, 1994). Renita's experience illustrates one aspect of this relationship, and our study of behaviorism helps us understand why classroom interaction and learning are so closely related. (We discuss the role of interaction in detail—both teacher to student and student to student—in Chapters 11 to 13.)

Cues: Antecedents to Behavior.   In our discussion, we have emphasized the consequences of behavior. What do teachers do, however, when they identify behaviors that

---

6.13 ▬

Explain specifically the difference between extinction in the context of operant conditioning and extinction in the context of classical conditioning. What key feature is similar in both?

6.14 ▬

Identify one characteristic that satiation, extinction, and punishment have in common. Describe the specific differences in each.

Teacher questions act as effective cues to elicit responses
from a number of students.

they want to reinforce but can't because students don't demonstrate the behaviors? For instance, teachers ask questions and want to reinforce students' answers, but often, students don't answer or answer incorrectly. Unfortunately, this situation commonly occurs with the very kind of student—low achieving or poorly motivated—teachers are trying to involve in the first place.

Teachers can provide **cues**, *antecedent stimuli that prompt the learner to display the desired behavior*. For example:

Alicia Wendt was working with her fourth graders on adverbs. She wrote this sentence on the chalkboard:

"John quickly jerked his head when he heard his name called."

Then she asked, "What is the adverb in the sentence? . . . Wendy?"
" . . . "
"Look at the sentence. What did John do?"
" . . . He . . . er . . . jerked . . . his head."
"How did he jerk it?"
" . . . Ahh . . . quickly."
"So what is the adverb?"
" . . . Is . . . it . . . *quickly*?"
Alicia smiled, "Yes! Well done, Wendy."
Alicia provided cues that allowed Wendy to produce the desired behavior, which
Alicia then reinforced.

Cues come in other forms as well. When a teacher moves to the front of the class, turns off the light switch, or walks among the students as they do seat work, she is cuing them to turn their attention toward her, become quiet, or remain on task. In each case, the desired behavior can then be reinforced. Expert teachers use both verbal and nonverbal cues to develop routines that result in smoothly running classrooms (Cazden, 1986; W. Doyle, 1986).

Implications of Behaviorism for Instruction.   What do the applications you've studied in this section suggest for the way students learn and the way we should teach? Think about how you learned many of the grammar rules you use in your writing. Most of us completed many exercises similar to "Juanita and (I, me) went to the football game." The assumption is that being able to complete exercises such as these will ultimately result in us becoming skilled writers. This type of exercise is so common that we may not realize it is based on principles of behaviorism.

According to behaviorism, information must be broken down into small, specific items. This allows learners to display and teachers to focus on observable behaviors; teachers can see whether the learner identifies the "I" or the "me" in the sentence on the previous page, for example. If learners demonstrate the behaviors, they're reinforced; if not, they receive corrective feedback until they do. This tactic promotes generalization and discrimination.

The teacher's role is to present information in highly organized and tightly sequenced segments that help learners demonstrate the desired behaviors. Learners are viewed as passive recipients of the information, and learning is described as hierarchical, with prerequisite skills mastered before more advanced ones are tackled. In addition, behaviorism has given teachers a powerful tool to modify individual behaviors as we'll see in the next section.

Applied Behavioral Analysis

To begin this section, let's look back at the case study in Chapter 5 with Mike Sheppard and his class (p. 205). Todd, one of Mike's 28 students, was described by other teachers as verbally abusive, aggressive, and lacking in self-discipline. Mike found him to be extremely active and having a difficult time sitting through a class period.

As a result Mike worked with Todd in an effort to help him learn to control his behavior. After 3 weeks of the process, he saw the following results:

	2/9–2/13	2/16–2/20	2/23–2/27
Talking out	ЖЖ ЖЖ ЖЖ ЖЖ ЖЖ	ЖЖ IIII ЖЖ	ЖЖ II
Swearing	ЖЖ ЖЖ	ЖЖ II	IIII
Hitting/ touching	ЖЖ III	ЖЖ IIII	III
Out of seat	ЖЖ ЖЖ ЖЖ III	ЖЖ ЖЖ ЖЖ IIII	ЖЖ ЖЖ ЖЖ III
Being friendly	II	IIII	ЖЖ II

What does this mean, and how was Mike able to accomplish these results? He was *systematically applying behaviorist principles in an effort to change specific behaviors in an individual*, a process called **applied behavior analysis** (Baldwin & Baldwin, 1998). (It is also called *behavior modification*, but this term has a negative connotation for some people, so experts prefer the term we use here.) Applied behavior analysis has been used successfully to increase physical fitness, overcome fears and panic attacks, learn social skills, and stop smoking (Gould & Clum, 1995; Green & Reed, 1996). It is widely used in working with students having exceptionalities (Werts, Caldwell, & Wolery, 1996), and this was the case in Mike's class, since Todd was a student with a behavior disorder.

Applied behavior analysis is an application of the basic principles of operant conditioning—any behavior that isn't reinforced or is punished will decrease, and behaviors that are reinforced will increase. Applying these principles typically includes the following steps:

▌ Identify target behaviors.
▌ Establish a baseline for the target behaviors.
▌ Choose reinforcers and punishers (if necessary).

- Measure changes in the target behaviors.
- Gradually reduce the frequency of reinforcers as behavior improves.

Identify Target Behaviors.   The first step in the process is to identify specific behaviors that the teacher wants to change and measure their frequency. Mike identified five target behaviors; *talking out, swearing, hitting/touching* other students, *out-of-seat,* and *being friendly*. Some experts might argue that Mike included too many target behaviors and might further suggest that "being friendly" isn't specific enough. As with virtually all teaching/learning applications, these decisions are a matter of professional judgment.

Establish a Baseline.   Establishing a baseline for the target behaviors simply means measuring their frequency to establish a reference point for comparison. For instance, during the baseline period (the week of 2/9 to 2/13) Todd talked out in class 20 times, he swore 10 times, hit or touched another student 8 times, was out of his seat 18 times, and was friendly to other students only twice. This baseline allowed both Mike and Todd to see what changes would occur in each of the target behaviors.

Applied behavioral analysis provides teachers with the tools to help students change their own behavior.

Choose Reinforcers and Punishers.   Ideally, an applied behavior analysis system is based on reinforcers instead of punishers, and this is what Mike used with Todd. In some cases, however, punishers may be necessary, and if they are, they should also be established in advance.

Mike used personal attention and praise as his primary reinforcers, and their effectiveness is indicated by the changes we see in Todd's behavior. If the undesirable target behaviors hadn't decreased, Mike would have modified his system; he would have identified some additional reinforcers and might have included some punishers as well.

A second factor increased the effectiveness of Mike's system. Since Mike made Todd responsible for monitoring his own behavior, Todd saw concrete evidence of his improvement; he could see, for example, that the frequency of talking out dropped from 20 to 14 incidents by the end of the second week. This improvement, in itself, is reinforcing.

> 6.15   ▬
> We saw no evidence of punishment in Mike's work with Todd. Using behaviorism as a basis, explain why Todd's undesirable behaviors decreased (such as *talking out* decreasing from 20 to 14 incidents in the second compared to the first week).

Measure Changes in Behavior.   After establishing a baseline and determining possible reinforcers and punishers, the target behaviors are measured for specified periods to see if changes occur. For example, Todd talked out six fewer times in the second week than in the first. Except for "out of seat," improvement occurred for each of the other behaviors during the 3-week period.

Since both Mike and Todd had concrete evidence for each of the target behaviors, Mike was able to design an additional intervention to help Todd cope with his tendency to get out of his seat without permission. This is why he prepared a place where Todd could go when the urge to get out of his seat became overwhelming.

Reduce Frequency of Reinforcers.   While not illustrated in the case study, Mike would gradually reduce the frequency of his reinforcers as Todd's behavior improved. Initially, a teacher might use a continuous, or nearly continuous schedule, and later, the schedule

6.16 ▄

What intermittent schedule would likely be most effective and easiest to use, once the target behaviors begin to improve? Explain.

would become more intermittent. Reducing the frequency of reinforcers helps maintain the desired behaviors and increases the likelihood that they will generalize to other classrooms and to behaviors out of school.

Like all interventions, applied behavior analysis isn't a panacea, it won't work magic, and its application can be labor intensive. In most cases, for example, teachers can't assume that a student will accurately measure each of the target behaviors, so they will have to monitor those behaviors as well. This makes managing an already-busy classroom even more complex.

Also, personal attention and praise were effective reinforcers in Todd's case, but if they hadn't been, Mike would have needed others. If he chose to give Todd free time for improvement, for example, what would he do for the rest of the students who are already behaving appropriately? This question doesn't have an easy answer.

On the other hand, in the case of a severely or chronically disruptive student, applied behavior analysis gives teachers an additional tool that can be used when conventional methods, such as a basic system of rules and procedures, don't work. The decision about using it, and its effectiveness, depends on the teacher's professional judgment and skill.

Putting Behaviorism Into Perspective

Like any theory, behaviorism has both proponents and critics. In this section, we examine some of the arguments related to behaviorism.

Criticisms of behaviorism include:

▌ Assuming learners are passive, as behaviorists do, isn't valid. Teachers can attest to the misconceptions and sometimes "off-the-wall" ideas students bring to the classroom. They don't acquire these ideas through reinforcement; instead, they are actively trying to make sense of the world, and, to them, these idiosyncratic and sometimes bizarre notions make sense.

▌ Behaviorism cannot adequately explain higher-order functions, such as language. For instance, Chomsky and Miller (1958) demonstrated that even people with small vocabularies would have to learn sentences at a rate faster then one per second throughout their lifetimes if their learning was based on responses and reinforcers.

▌ Much of what we learn is not effectively acquired through reinforcement of specific, decontextualized items of information. For example, we learn to write effectively by practicing writing in meaningful contexts, not by responding to exercises such as "Juanita and (I, me) went to the football game."

▌ Offering reinforcers for engaging in intrinsically motivating activities can decrease interest in the tasks (Deci & Ryan, 1987; Kohn, 1993). The use of rewards may detract from intrinsic interest in learning.

Finally, some criticisms of behaviorism are philosophical, with critics arguing that schools should attempt to promote learning for its own sake rather than learning to receive rewards (Anderman & Maehr, 1994). Other critics argue that behaviorism is essentially a means for controlling people, rather than helping students learn to control their own behavior (Kohn, 1993).

On the other hand, we all know that our experiences undeniably influence the ways we behave, and the influence of experience on behavior is at the core of behaviorism. For example, virtually all teachers understand that a timely, genuine compliment can exert a powerful influence on students' motivations as well as how they feel about themselves.

Also, how many of us would continue working if we stopped receiving paychecks, and do we lose interest in our work merely because we get paid for it?

Further, research indicates that reinforcing appropriate classroom behaviors, such as paying attention and treating classmates well, decreases misbehavior (Elliot & Busse, 1991), and behaviorist classroom management techniques are often effective when others are not (Maccoby, 1992).

Finally, proponents argue, if reinforcers enhance learning, such as learning a mathematical operation, the students have still acquired the ability, and the ability won't disappear merely because praise or some other reinforcer has been removed (Chance, 1993).

Behaviorism isn't a complete explanation for learning and behavior, and it is neither a panacea nor a totally ineffective view of learning. As with most of what we know about teaching and learning, effective application of behaviorism requires the careful judgment of an intelligent teacher.

Classroom Connections

Applying Operant Conditioning in Your Classroom

1. When using behavioral methods, use reinforcement rather than punishment if possible. When punishment is necessary, use removal punishment rather than presentation punishment.
   - After giving an assignment, a first-grade teacher circulates around the room and gives tickets to students who are working quietly. The tickets may be exchanged for opportunities to play games and work at learning centers.
   - A fifth-grade teacher gives students "behavior points" at the beginning of the week. If they break a rule, they lose a point. At the end of the week, a specified number of remaining points may be traded for free time.

2. Carefully select reinforcers for their potency.
   - A seventh-grade teacher asks students what they would like as rewards. (They typically suggest watching videos or being given free time to visit.) Then she tries to use their suggestions, so they feel as though they have influence over their environment.
   - A math teacher increases the potency of grades as reinforcers by awarding bonus points for improvement. After an average for each student is determined, she offers them incentive points for scoring higher than their averages.

3. Promote generalization and discrimination by encouraging students to make comparisons among examples and other information.
   - A life science teacher, in a unit on deciduous and coniferous trees, asks students to compare a pine and an oak tree. He helps them identify the essential differences between the trees by asking specific questions.
   - A teacher praises a third grader who, on her own, notices that frogs and toads are not the same and that frogs climb trees but toads don't.

4. Use appropriate schedules of reinforcement.
   - At the beginning of the school year, a first-grade teacher plans activities that all students can do. She praises liberally and rewards frequently. As students get used to first-grade work, she requires more effort.
   - A second-grade teacher is careful to provide compliments on an intermittent basis for consistent work and effort. She knows that students who do steady, average to above-average work and are not disruptive tend to be taken for granted and are often "lost in the shuffle."
   - An algebra teacher gives frequent announced quizzes to prevent the decline in effort that can occur after reinforcement with a fixed-interval schedule.

5. Provide clear, informative feedback on student work.
   - A sixth-grade teacher has students do sample math problems that are similar to their homework, the class goes over the problems, and the teacher answers any questions they have before having them work independently.
   - A high school history teacher uses essay items to teach, not just to assess. With each essay question, she provides written feedback to each student, giving a concrete explanation for the grade. If this is too time-consuming, she prepares an "ideal" response to the item and shares it with the class, specifically explaining grading criteria.

6. Shape desired behaviors.
   - A language arts teacher begins a unit on paragraph writing by assigning a written paragraph from each student. As she scores them, she is initially gener-

ous with positive comments, but she becomes more critical as time goes on and the students' work improves.
   - A second-grade teacher openly praises a student whose behavior is improving. With continued improvement, she requires longer periods of acceptable behavior to earn the praise.

7. Provide cues for appropriate behavior.
   - After completing a lesson and assigning seat work, a seventh-grade English teacher circulates around the room, reminding students both verbally and nonverbally to begin working.
   - Before students line up for lunch, a first-grade teacher reminds them to stand quietly while waiting to be dismissed. When they're standing quietly, she compliments them on their good behavior and lets them go to lunch.

Social Cognitive Theory

"What are you doing?" Jason asked Kelly as he came around the corner and caught her in the act of swinging her arms back and forth.

"I was sort of practicing my batting swing," Kelly responded with a red face. "I was watching a game on TV last night, and noticed the way those guys swing. It always looks so easy, but they hit it so hard. It just seems like I should be able to do that. It was running through my head, so I just had to try it."

Three-year-old Jimmy crawled up on his dad's lap with a book. "I read too, Dad," he said as his father put down his own book to help Jimmy up on his lap.

"Wait a minute," Jeanna Edwards said as she saw Joanne struggling with the microscope. "Let me show you once more. . . . Now, watch closely as I adjust the microscope. This is important because these slides crack easily and are expensive. The first thing I think about is getting the slide in place. Otherwise, I might not be able to find what I'm looking for in the microscope. Then I want to be sure I don't crack the slide while I lower the objective lens, so I watch from the side. Finally, I slowly raise the objective lens until I have the object in focus. You were trying to focus as you lowered it. It's easier and safer if you try to focus as you raise it. Now go ahead. You try it."

What do these have in common? Although they involve three distinct situations—a girl practicing her softball swing, a child wanting to be like his father, and a girl learning a laboratory technique—they all involve learning by observing the behavior of others.

Researchers have become interested in what happens as people learn by watching others and have found that the process is more complex than the simple imitation of others' behaviors. This line of inquiry, pioneered by Albert Bandura (1925–), is called social cognitive theory. **Social cognitive theory** *examines the processes involved as people learn* *from observing others and gradually acquire control over their own behavior* (Bandura, 1986, 1997). Social cognitive theory has its historical roots in behaviorism but goes well beyond it. Let's examine the relationships between the two.

Comparing Behaviorism and Social Cognitive Theory

At this point you might be asking yourself, "Since behaviorists focus on observable behavior (as opposed to thinking and other processes 'in learners' heads'), and the term *cognitive* implies memory, thinking, and knowing, why is a *cognitive* learning theory being included in the same chapter with behaviorism?"

Here's why. First, we said earlier that social cognitive theory has its historical roots in behaviorism. Second, many authors continue to include aspects of social cognitive theory in books focusing on behavioral principles (e.g., Baldwin & Baldwin, 1998), and some people still prefer the terms *observational learning* or *social learning theory* to social *cognitive* theory. However, social cognitive theory is the preferred label by leaders in the field (Bandura, 1986; Bruning, Schraw, & Ronning, 1999; Schunk, 2000).

Third, at least three similarities exist between the two theories:

▎ They agree that experience is an important cause of learning (as do other cognitive descriptions, such as Piaget's and Vygotsky's work).
▎ They both include the concepts of reinforcement and punishment in their explanations of behavior.
▎ They agree that feedback is important in promoting learning.

However, social cognitive theory differs from behaviorism in at least three ways: (a) the way learning is viewed, (b) the way interactions among behavior, the environment, and personal factors are described, and (c) the way reinforcement and punishment are interpreted. We examine these differences in the following sections.

Views of Learning

As we described at the beginning of the chapter, behaviorism defines learning as a change in observable behavior. Social cognitive theorists, however, view **learning** as *an internal process that may or may not result in immediate behavioral change.* Looking at the preceding examples, we begin to see why the term *cognitive* appears in it. Kelly, for example, didn't try to imitate the baseball swing until the next day; therefore, her observations of the players on television had to be stored in her memory. Also, her comment, "It just seems like I should be able to do that," suggests a *belief* or *expectation* about her ability that influenced her behavior. Beliefs and expectations are internal processes that behaviorists don't consider.

Interactions Among Behavior, the Environment, and Personal Factors

Behaviorism suggests a "one-way" relationship between the environment and behavior; the environment directly causes behavior. Social cognitive theory's explanation is more complex, suggesting that behavior, the environment, and personal factors, such as beliefs and expectations, all influence each other. For instance, Tim's low score on his algebra test (an environmental factor) influenced his belief (a personal factor) about his ability to do algebra. His belief, in turn, influenced his behavior (he adapted his study habits), and his behavior influenced the environment (he went to Susan's home to study). Social cognitive theorists call these mutual influences *reciprocal causation*.

Interpretations of Reinforcement and Punishment

Behaviorists and social cognitive theorists agree that *reinforcement* and *punishment* are important concepts, but they interpret the influence of these concepts differently. For behaviorists, reinforcers and punishers are direct causes of behavior; for social cognitive theorists, reinforcers and punishers cause *expectations* instead. For example, if you study hard and do well on a test, you *expect* to do well on a second test by studying the same way. If you see someone being reinforced for a certain behavior, you expect to be reinforced for a similar behavior. Like beliefs, expectations are mental processes, occurring within learners, that influence their behavior.

The fact that people form expectations means they're aware of which behaviors will be reinforced. This is important because, according to social cognitive theory, reinforcement only changes behavior when learners know what behaviors are being reinforced (Bandura, 1986). Tim believed that his changed study habits were the cause of his improved scores, so he maintained those habits. If he had believed that some other strategy was more effective, he would have used that strategy. He wasn't passively responding to reinforcers; he was actively assessing the effectiveness of his strategy.

The importance of student cognitions has two implications for teachers. First, they should explain what behaviors will be reinforced, so students can adapt their behavior accordingly, and second, learners need feedback so they know what behaviors have been reinforced. For instance, if a student gets full credit for an essay item on a test but doesn't know why the credit was given, she may not know how to respond correctly the next time.

Nonoccurrence of Expected Consequences.   Social cognitive theory also helps explain behavior when expectations aren't met. For example, suppose your instructor gives you a homework assignment, you work hard on it, but she doesn't collect it. The nonoccurrence of the expected reinforcer (credit for the assignment) can act as a punisher; you will probably be less inclined to work hard for the next assignment.

Just as the nonoccurrence of an expected reinforcer can act as a punisher, the nonoccurrence of an expected punisher can act as a reinforcer (Bandura, 1986). A student who breaks a classroom rule, for example, and isn't reprimanded (punished) is more likely to break the rule in the future.

Modeling

Modeling, which refers to *changes in people that result from observing the actions of others*, is a central concept of social cognitive theory. Tim, for example, observed that Susan was successful in her approach to studying for exams. As a result, he imitated her behavior; direct imitation of behavior is one form of modeling.

The importance of modeling in our everyday lives is difficult to overstate. Modeling helps explain the powerful influence of culture on student learning, which we described in Chapter 4. Parents are urged to use correct grammar and pronunciation in talking to their infants, in hopes of promoting language development. Studies of disadvantaged youth indicate that a lack of effective adult role models is one reason they have difficulty handling the problems they encounter (Ogbu, 1987, 1999b).

In addition to direct modeling (as illustrated by Tim's imitation of Susan's behavior or children imitating their parents), at least two other forms of modeling exist: symbolic

---

6.17 ■

Tenille commented, "I seem to have a feel for math," as she began her homework. Her teacher complimented her on her conscientiousness, and her efforts continually increased. How would behaviorists explain her continuing effort? How would social cognitive theorists explain it?

6.18 ■

A teacher showed her students a videotape of Dr. Martin Luther King, Jr.'s, famous "I Have a Dream" speech. What form of modeling is illustrated in the speech?

Students are able to learn a wide range of complex behaviors through modeling.

and synthesized (Bandura, 1986). They are described in Table 6.4. Common to each is the fact that people learn by observing the actions of others.

Cognitive Modeling

An application of modeling that is increasingly emphasized in instruction is called cognitive modeling. **Cognitive modeling** *involves modeled demonstrations, together with verbal descriptions of the model's thoughts and actions* (Pintrich & Schunk, 1996). As Jeanna

Table 6.4

Different forms of modeling

Type	Description	Example
Direct modeling	Simply attempting to imitate the model's behavior	Tim imitates Susan in studying for exams. A first grader forms letters in the same way a teacher forms them.
Symbolic modeling	Imitating behaviors displayed by characters in books, plays, movies, or television	Teenagers begin to dress like characters on a popular television show oriented toward teens.
Synthesized modeling	Developing behaviors by combining portions of observed acts	A child uses a chair to get up and open the cupboard door after seeing her brother use a chair to get a book from a shelf and seeing her mother open the cupboard door.

Edwards demonstrated how to use the microscope, for example, she also described her thinking, "The first thing I think about is getting the slide in place. Otherwise, I might not be able to find what I'm looking for in the microscope. Then I want to be sure I don't crack the slide while I lower the objective lens, so I watch from the side."

Cognitive modeling allows learners to benefit from the thinking of experts. When teachers describe their thinking out loud, or when they encourage other students to explain their thinking, they provide all learners with specific, concrete examples of how to think about and solve problems. Students have the opportunity to imitate both their behaviors and their thinking.

Vicarious Learning

Although merely observing the actions of other people can affect a learner, the effects are amplified if the learner also observes the consequences of those actions. This is called **vicarious learning**, and it occurs *when people observe the consequences of another person's behavior and adjust their own behavior accordingly* (Schunk, 2000). For example, Tim saw how well Susan did on tests with her approach to studying, so he was *vicariously reinforced* through her success. When students hear a teacher say, "I really like the way Jimmy is working so quietly," they are being vicariously reinforced, and when a student receives a verbal reprimand for leaving his seat without permission, other students in the class are *vicariously punished.* Modeling and vicarious learning work together to affect behavior in several ways.

Effects of Modeling on Behavior

Modeling can affect behavior in at least four ways:

- Learning new behaviors
- Facilitating existing behaviors
- Changing inhibitions
- Arousing emotions

Learning New Behaviors

Through modeling, people can acquire behaviors they weren't able to display before observing the model. Examples include being able to properly swing a forehand after seeing a tennis instructor demonstrate it or being able to factor a trinomial after watching a teacher execute the procedure.

Facilitating Existing Behaviors

You're attending a concert, and at the end of one of the numbers, someone stands and begins to applaud. Others notice and, after hesitating briefly, join in to create a standing ovation. Obviously, people already know how to stand and clap. The person "facilitated" your and others' behaviors through modeling.

We saw this demonstrated in Tim's behavior. He practiced solving problems before tests, but by his own admission, "I usually do one, maybe two, and if I'm okay on them, I quit." After observing Susan, he modified his behavior and increased his efforts.

Changing Inhibitions

An **inhibition** is *a self-imposed restriction on one's behavior,* and modeling can either strengthen or weaken the inhibition. Unlike facilitating existing behaviors, inhibitions involve *socially unacceptable* behaviors, such as breaking classroom rules (Pintrich & Schunk, 1996).

For example, pedestrians who've stopped at a red light are more likely to obey or disregard that red light if they see others doing the same. If a teacher has a classroom rule requiring students to raise their hands before speaking, students are less likely to break the rule if they see one of their peers reprimanded for doing so. The inhibition against speaking without permission is strengthened. Kounin (1971), one of the pioneer researchers in the area of classroom management, called this phenomenon the ripple effect. On the other hand, if a student speaks without permission and isn't reprimanded, other students are more likely to do the same. The inhibition is weakened.

Arousing Emotions

Finally, a person's emotional reaction can be changed by observing a model's display of emotions. For example, observing the uneasiness of a diver on a high board may cause an observer to become more fearful of the board as well. If you see a couple having a heated argument at a party, you may find yourself feeling awkward and embarrassed. Notice here that the emotions modeled aren't necessarily the same ones aroused in others. You see anger modeled, but your emotions are more likely to be embarrassment or uneasiness.

On the positive side, the emotional arousal effect of modeling is a strong endorsement for teacher enthusiasm. Observing teachers genuinely enjoying themselves as they discuss a topic can help generate similar excitement in students.

From these examples, we see that modeling can result in behavioral, cognitive, and even affective outcomes. Behavioral outcomes occur when behaviors are learned or facilitated; cognitive outcomes result from observing the consequences of others' actions, such as the example in which a student broke a classroom rule, and affective outcomes are the result of modeling emotions.

> **6.19** ▬
> Research indicates that teachers who model persistence in problem-solving tasks have students who persist longer than teachers who don't (Zimmerman & Blotner, 1979). What form of modeling is illustrated in this case? Which modeling effect is best illustrated in this research finding? Explain.

Technology and Learning: The Impact of Symbolic Modeling on Behavior

Our concept of technology is so closely linked to computers that we tend to forget that it exists in a number of other forms, including videotape, videodisc, digital video, and even television. Television and other forms of video are significant with respect to social cognitive theory because of the impact of symbolic modeling on behavior and the almost universal exposure to television.

Hundreds of studies done over nearly four decades have produced a number of disconcerting findings with respect to television viewing (Berk, 1997). For example, children with lower measured intelligence and those who come from low-income families watch more television than their more advantaged counterparts (Huston, Watkins, & Kunkel, 1989), and excessive television viewing is associated with adjustment problems, including difficulties with family and peer relations (Liebert, 1986).

Symbolic Modeling and Television Viewing

Literally thousands of studies have consistently confirmed that symbolic modeling influences behavior. This research began with Bandura's classic studies in the 1960s indicating that children who watched aggressive models either on film or depicted as cartoon characters behaved more aggressively in free play than those who saw no models (Bandura, Ross, & Ross, 1963).

Television can have both positive and negative effects on learners through the role models it provides.

Since then, research—carefully controlled for factors such as intelligence, socioeconomic status, school achievement, and child-rearing practices—consistently indicates that exposure to violence on television increases mean-spirited and hostile behavior in young people (Donnerstein, Slaby, & Eron, 1994). It has been described as "an extensive how-to course in aggression" (Slaby, Roedell, Arezzo, & Hendrix, 1995, p. 163), and it tends to "harden" children to aggression, making them more willing to tolerate it in others (Drabman & Thomas, 1976).

Televised violence also has an emotional arousal effect. Heavy viewers of televised violence tend to see the world as a scary place where aggression is widespread and hostility is an acceptable means for solving problems (Donnerstein et al., 1994).

Finally, research indicates that television tends to reinforce stereotypes. For example, cultural minorities are underrepresented, and when they do appear, they tend to be depicted as villains or victims of violence (Graves, 1993). Women tend to be cast as victims and in stereotypically feminine roles, such as wife, mother, teacher, or secretary (Signorielli, 1993). Since this research was done, efforts have been made to counter these stereotypes, but progress is slow and wavering. For example, NBC was strongly criticized in its 1999 programming for underrepresenting African Americans, so much so that it was a frequent topic of jokes on talk shows, such as *The Tonight Show with Jay Leno*.

Television and Symbolic Modeling: Guidelines for Teachers and Parents

The message from research on television viewing and behavior is clear and consistent. Excessive exposure to television, and particularly televised violence, is harmful. As teachers, we should work with parents, encouraging and helping them to promote healthy television viewing. Some suggestions for parents include:

> *Limit TV viewing.* Make and stick to clear rules for television viewing, limit what children can watch, and avoid using television as a babysitter.

■ *Avoid using TV as a consequence.* Don't use television to reward or punish behavior; it makes it even more attractive.

■ *Model healthy viewing.* When possible, watch TV with your children, discuss the content, and express disapproval when it's inappropriate. Watch programs with children that are informative and prosocial.

■ *Use authoritative child-rearing.* Counter the negative effects of television by using the characteristics of authoritative child-rearing practices discussed in Chapter 3: firm but caring, providing reasons for rules, behaving consistently, and holding high expectations (Slaby et al., 1995).

As teachers, we can also encourage our students to watch informative and prosocial programming, and model these behaviors ourselves. While frequently criticized, television also has the potential to be a positive force for learning and behavior.

Learning from Models: The Processes Involved

Modeling can result in learning and facilitating behaviors, changing inhibitions, and arousing emotions. How do these effects occur, and what mechanisms are involved?

Learning from models involves four processes: *attention, retention, reproduction,* and *motivation* (Bandura, 1986). They're illustrated in Figure 6.5 and summarized as follows:

■ *Attention:*   A learner's attention is drawn to the critical aspects of the modeled behavior, such as Tim paying attention to Susan's study strategies.

■ *Retention:*   The modeled behaviors are transferred to memory by mentally verbalizing or visually representing them; Tim mentally recorded Susan's behaviors.

■ *Reproduction:*   Learners reproduce the behaviors that have been stored in memory. Tim imitated Susan's study habits.

■ *Motivation:*   Learners are motivated by the expectation of reinforcement for reproducing the modeled behaviors. Tim was motivated to imitate Susan's behaviors because he expected to be reinforced for doing so.

Figure 6.5

Processes involved in learning from models

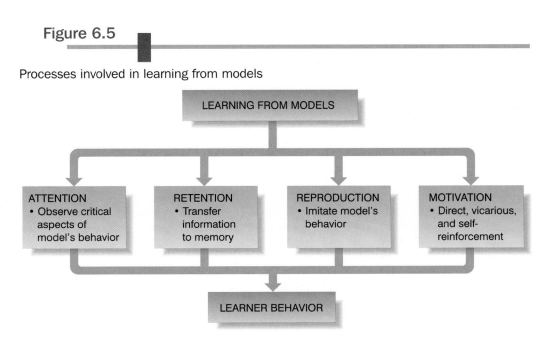

Two aspects of these processes are important for teachers. First, to learn from models, the learner's attention must be drawn to the critical aspects of the modeled behavior (Bandura, 1986). For example, preservice teachers often go into schools and observe veteran teachers in action. If they don't know what they're looking for, the observations don't result in a great deal of learning. As teachers, we need to call attention to the important aspects of the skill or procedures we're modeling.

Second, attending to the modeled behaviors and, presumably, recording them in memory, doesn't ensure that learners will be able to reproduce them. Additional scaffolding and feedback will often be required. Let's look at a teacher who has modeled the procedure for solving simultaneous equations but whose students are having difficulty.

> "Look up here," Sally Hernandez commented after seeing that several of her students were struggling with problems she had assigned for seat work. "We're having a little difficulty, so let's look at another example.
>
> "Try this one," she said, writing on the chalkboard:
>
> $$4a + 6b = 24$$
> $$5a - 6b = 3$$
>
> "What's one way of solving this problem? . . . Alfino?"
>
> " . . . By addition."
>
> Sally nodded. "How do we know that will work?"
>
> "There's a *6b* in the first equation and a negative *6b* in the second equation," Kim volunteered.
>
> "Yes. Good, Kim. That's the key that determines whether you can use addition. Let's go on. What do we do first? . . . Lakesha?"
>
> " . . . We add the two equations together."
>
> "And we get? . . . Hue?"
>
> " . . . Nine *a* plus zero *b* equals 27."
>
> "Okay," Sally smiled. "And what is the value of *a*? . . . Chris?"
>
> " . . . Three."
>
> "Good! That's right. Now let's find the value of *b*. What should we do first? . . . Mitchell?"

6.20 ■
As Sally questioned, she first asked the question, paused briefly, and then called on a student. By pausing in this way, Sally implemented what concept from behaviorism discussed earlier in the chapter?

Through questioning and feedback, Sally helped her students reproduce the behaviors she had modeled, and the importance of her guidance has been confirmed by research (Rosenshine, 1983). Not all students pay close attention to teachers' presentations, and learners may not accurately represent the modeled behaviors in memory. As a result, the retention phase fails to become an effective foundation for reproducing the behavior. Sally helped overcome those difficulties by guiding students' initial reproductions as a group process. This tactic allowed her to provide immediate feedback in the case of incorrect answers and cues when students were unable to answer. Sally's strategy is sometimes described as *controlled practice* (Murphy, Weil, & McGreal, 1986).

Effectiveness of Models

As you might expect, not all models are equally effective, and learners are more likely to imitate some models than others. A model's effectiveness depends primarily on three factors: (a) perceived similarity, (b) perceived competence, and (c) perceived status.

Perceived Similarity

When we observe a model's behavior, we are more likely to imitate it if we perceive the model as similar to us (Schunk, 1987). In addition, several models are more effective than a single model, or even a few, because the likelihood of finding a model perceived as similar increases as the number of models increases.

This helps us understand why nontraditional career models and presenting the contributions of women and minorities are important. For example, while learners will imitate models of either gender, girls are more likely to believe that engineering is a viable career choice if they observe the work of a female rather than a male engineer. Similarly, a Hispanic student is more likely to believe he can accomplish challenging goals if he sees the accomplishments of a successful Hispanic adult than if the adult is a nonminority.

Perceived Competence

Perception of a model's competence interacts with perceptions of similarity. People are more likely to imitate models perceived as competent than those perceived as less competent, regardless of similarity. Although Susan and Tim were similar, since they were classmates, it is unlikely he would have imitated her behaviors had she not been a successful student.

Perceived Status

Individuals acquire social status by distinguishing themselves from others in their fields, and people tend to imitate these individuals more often than others. Professional athletes, popular rock stars, and world leaders are all high-status models. At the school level, athletes, cheerleaders, and in some cases even gang leaders have high status for many students. Teachers are also influential models. Despite concerns expressed by educational reformers and teachers themselves, they remain and will continue as powerful influences on students.

Status has a spill-over effect; high-status models are often tacitly credited for competence outside their own areas of expertise. This is the reason you see professional basketball players (instead of nutritionists) endorsing breakfast cereal, and actors (instead of engineers) endorsing automobiles and motor oil.

Self-Regulation

Earlier, we saw that learners' beliefs and expectations can influence both behavior and the environment. This is accomplished through the process of **self-regulation**, *students using their own thoughts and actions to reach academic learning goals.* Self-regulated learners identify goals and adopt and maintain strategies for reaching these goals.

For example, Tim chose to go to Susan's home to study, and he developed a pattern of changed study strategies, which he monitored himself. Behaviorists are unable to explain why Tim initially went to Susan's house; he hadn't gone before, so he couldn't have been reinforced for doing so. Behaviorists also can't explain why Tim changed and continued his efforts without reinforcement; he was reinforced only after he made the conscious choice to change, monitor, and sustain his study strategies. To behave as he did, Tim had to be self-regulated; the consequences of his actions existed too far in the future to affect his behavior in the present (Bandura, 1986). If he hadn't been self-regulated, he wouldn't have maintained the behavior until it could be reinforced.

Cognitive Behavior Modification

The emphasis on self-regulation represents a trend toward increasing learners' roles in the learning process (Stipek, 1996; Zimmerman & Schunk, 1989), and a number of programs

6.21
One group of students watched teachers successfully solve math problems, a second group watched peers do the same, and a third group saw no models. Which group successfully solved the most math problems, and which group solved the fewest? Explain the results on the basis of the information in this section.

have been developed over the years to teach self-regulation. Common to these programs is the combination of cognitive self-management strategies with the targeting of specific behaviors (Alberto & Troutman, 1999). One such program is **cognitive behavior modification**, which has been defined as *"the modification of overt behavior through the manipulation of covert thought processes"* (Hallahan & Sapona, 1983, p. 616). It includes aspects of behaviorism because it assumes that the basic principles of reinforcement are operating, but it differs from behaviorism in that it emphasizes using a person's cognitive operations to achieve a change in behavior (Stipek, 1996).

Cognitive behavior modification requires that students take more responsibility for their own learning by doing the following:

- Set their own goals.
- Monitor their own behavior.
- Assess their behavior.
- Administer their own rewards. (Ainly, 1993; Meichenbaum, 1977; Pintrich & Schrauben, 1992)

6.22

Think about your work in this class. Identify at least two goals that you could use to increase your learning. Based on information from the text, explain why you believe the goals are effective.

Goal Setting.   Goals provide direction for a person's actions and provide ways for measuring progress. Susan, in our opening case study, set the goal of working at least three of each type of problem, and Tim imitated her behavior by setting goals of his own.

Challenging but realistic goals and goals set by students themselves are more effective than those imposed by the teacher (Schunk, 1994; Spaulding, 1992). An important role for teachers is to help students learn to set effective goals.

Self-Observation.   Once goals have been set, self-regulated learners monitor their progress. Susan, for example, said, "I sometimes even make a little chart. I try to do at least three problems of each type we study, and then I check them off as I do them." Self-observation allowed Susan to monitor her own progress.

6.23

Think about one of the goals you identified in Note 6.22. Now describe a simple form of self-observation that you could use to monitor your progress toward the goal.

Students can be taught to monitor a variety of behaviors. For example, they can keep a chart and make a check every time they catch themselves "drifting off" during an hour of study, the number of times they go off-task during seat work, the number of times they blurt out answers in class, or, on the positive side, the number of times they use a desired social skill (Alberto & Troutman, 1999).

Self-observation combined with appropriate goals can change student behavior, sometimes dramatically (Mace, Belfiore, & Shea, 1989). With effort and teacher support, study habits and concentration can be improved and social interactions can be made more positive and productive.

Self-Assessment.   Schools historically have been places where a person's performance is judged by someone else. Although teachers can provide valuable feedback in assessing student performance, they don't have to be the sole judges; students can learn to assess their own work (Stiggins, 1997). For example, students can assess the quality of their solutions to word problems by learning to ask themselves whether their answers make sense and to compare their answers with estimates. Tim was involved in a form of self-assessment when he checked his answers against those given at the back of the book.

Developing self-assessment skills takes time, and students won't automatically be good at it. The best way to help students develop these skills is to be sure their goals are specific and quantitative, as were Susan's and Tim's. Helping students make valid self-assessments based on accurate self-observations is one of the most important instructional tasks teachers face.

Self-Reinforcement.   We all feel good when we accomplish a goal, and we often feel guilty when we don't, vowing to do better in the future (Bandura, 1989). As learners become self-regulated, they learn to reinforce or punish themselves for meeting or failing to meet their goals.

Self-reinforcers and self-punishers can be an internal pat on the back, or they can be something more tangible, such as Susan's, "If I get all of them right, I treat myself with a bowl of ice cream." A powerful form of self-reinforcement is the feeling of accomplishment that can result from setting and meeting challenging goals.

Self-reinforcement is somewhat controversial. Some researchers argue that it is unnecessary; goals, self-observation, and self-assessment should be sufficient in themselves (Hayes et al., 1985). Others argue that self-reinforcement can be a powerful strategy, particularly for low achievers. In one study, low-achieving students were taught to award themselves points, which they could use to buy privileges when they did well on their assignments. Within a few weeks, the low achievers were achieving as well as their classmates (Stevenson & Fantuzzo, 1986). Bandura (1986) argues that rewarding oneself for good work can lead to higher performance than goals and self-monitoring alone.

Cognitive behavior modification isn't without problems. For instance, research indicates that learners tend to set very lenient goals (Wall, 1983), and they sometimes cheat when allowed to reinforce themselves (Speidel & Tharp, 1980). Researchers emphasize that learners need guidance in setting goals, and they need to be monitored for cheating. Though effective, cognitive behavior modification strategies are not always easy to implement (Stipek, 1996).

Putting Social Cognitive Theory Into Perspective

Like all descriptions of learning and behavior, social cognitive theory has its strengths. For example, the influence of modeling as both a tool for learning and an influence on behavior is difficult to overstate, and social cognitive theory overcomes some of the limitations of behaviorism by helping us understand the importance of learner cognitions, in the form of beliefs and expectation, on their actions.

However, like any theory, social cognitive theory has limitations. Some of them follow:

- It cannot explain why learners attend to and imitate some modeled behaviors but not others.
- It doesn't account for the learning of complex tasks, such as learning to write (beyond mere mechanics).
- It cannot explain the role of context and social interaction in complex learning environments. For example, research indicates that student interaction in small groups facilitates learning (Greeno, Collins, & Resnick, 1996; Shuell, 1996). The processes involved extend well beyond modeling and imitation.

We identify these limitations as a reminder that every theory of learning is incomplete, able to explain some aspects of learning but not others. This is why it's important for teachers to understand different views of learning together with their strengths and limitations.

Classroom Connections

Applying Social Cognitive Theory in Your Classroom

1. Act as a role model for your students.
   - A school committee charged with improving the quality of instruction develops the following guidelines to encourage teachers to be good role models: (a) Treat students with respect and courtesy. Avoid criticism and any form of sarcasm. (b) Require that students respect you and each other. Enforce this rule consistently. (c) Communicate your interest in reading and studying. (d) Approach the topics you teach with enthusiasm, energy, and effort.

2. As you model the skills you teach, use think-alouds to verbally illustrate your thinking.
   - A kindergarten teacher helping students form letters says, "I start with my pencil here and make a straight line down," as she begins to form a *b*.
   - A physics teacher solving acceleration problems involving friction writes $F = ma$ on the chalkboard and says, "First, I think about finding the net force on the object. Let's see what the problem tells me."

3. As students are learning to reproduce skills, provide group practice by walking them through examples before having them practice on their own.
   - A sixth-grade teacher has his class adding fractions with unlike denominators. He displays the problem $\frac{1}{4} + \frac{2}{3} = ?$ and then begins, "What do we need to do first? . . . Karen?" He continues until the class works through the problem and then does a second example the same way.

4. Use vicarious reinforcement to increase the effectiveness of modeling.

- As one reading group moves back to their desks, a first-grade teacher comments loud enough for the class to hear, "I like the way this group is returning to their desks. Karen, Vicki, Ali, and David each get a star because they have gone so quickly and quietly."
- An art teacher hands back students' pottery projects. She then displays several excellent pieces and comments, "Look at these, everyone. These are excellent. Let's see why. . . . " This art teacher accomplished three things. First, the students whose pottery was displayed were directly reinforced, but they weren't put on the spot because the teacher didn't identify them. Second, the class was vicariously reinforced. Third, the teacher gave the class feedback and provided a model for future imitation.

5. Have high-status students model behaviors for others.
   - A choral director has one of his most popular and talented singers demonstrate the timing on a difficult concert piece.
   - An English teacher has one of the better writers in the class describe his thoughts as he organized a persuasive essay.

6. Promote self-regulation in your students.
   - A geography teacher helps her students set individual goals by asking each to write a study plan. She returns to the plan at the end of the unit and has each student assess his or her progress.
   - A fifth-grade teacher works with students to design a checklist for monitoring desired social skills in cooperative learning groups. They use the checklist to assess their interaction skills at the end of each cooperative learning session.

Dealing with Diversity:
Behaviorism and Social Cognitive Theory

As Carlos entered his second-grade classroom early Tuesday morning, he heard salsa music in the background. Donna Evans sometimes played it as she prepared her classroom for the day. The walls were decorated with colorful prints from Mexico and Central America, and vocabulary cards in both Spanish and English were hung around the room, near the blinds, chalkboard, clock, file cabinet, and other objects in the room.

"Buenos días, Carlos. How are you today?" Donna asked. "You're here very early."

" . . . Buenos días. . . . I'm fine," Carlos responded, smiling as he went to his desk to take out his homework from the night before.

Donna watched Carlos for a few moments as he worked in the empty room. Then she walked over to him, put her hand on his shoulder, and asked, "What are we working on today, Carlos? . . . Math?"

"I cannot do it! I do not understand," Carlos replied in his halting English, frustration in his voice.

As Donna looked over his shoulder at the 12 problems she had assigned for homework, she noticed that he had done the first two correctly, but then had forgotten to borrow on the next three, and had left the last seven undone.

"Carlos, look," she said, kneeling down so that she was at eye level with him. "You did the first two just fine. Then you forgot an important step. Look here. . . . How is this problem different from this one?" she asked, pointing to the two following problems:

$$
\begin{array}{r} 36 \\ -14 \\ \hline \end{array}
\qquad
\begin{array}{r} 45 \\ -19 \\ \hline \end{array}
$$

" . . . The numbers . . . are different."

"Okay," she smiled. "What else?"

" . . . This one . . . is bigger," he said, pointing to the 45 and then to the 36.

"How about the 9 and the 5? . . . Which is bigger?"

" . . . This," pointing at the 9.

"Good, and how about the 6 and the 4?"

" . . . Here," referring to the 6.

"And where is the bigger one in each case?"

" . . . There," Carlos said, pointing to the 6 in the first problem, " . . . and there," pointing to the 9 in the second.

"Very good, Carlos. It is very important to know where the bigger number is," she continued. "Now, let's work this one together. . . . Watch what I do."

Donna worked with Carlos as they solved the next two problems, carefully discussing her thinking and what they were doing as they went along, comparing problems that require regrouping to those that don't.

"Now try the next three on your own," she said, "and I'll be back in a few minutes to see how you're doing. Remember what Juanita's father said about becoming a scientist when he came and visited our class. You have to study very hard and do your math. I know you can do it, especially because you already did it on the first two. . . . Now go ahead."

Carlos nodded and then bent over his work and was finishing the last of the three problems as the other students entered into the classroom. Donna went to him, checked his work, and commented, "Very good, Carlos. You got two of them right. Now check this one. You have just enough time before we start."

In another elementary school in the same city, Roberto shuffled into class and hid behind the big girl in front of him. If he was lucky, his teacher wouldn't discover that he hadn't done his homework—12 problems! How could he ever do that many? Besides, he wasn't good at math.

Roberto hated school. He was very uncomfortable. It seemed so strange and foreign. His teacher would sometimes frown when he spoke because his English wasn't as good as most of the other students'. Sometimes when the teacher talked, he couldn't understand what she was saying.

Even lunch wasn't much fun. If his friend Raul wasn't there, he would eat alone. One time when he sat with some other students, they started laughing at the way he talked, and they asked what he was eating when he had tortillas for lunch. He couldn't wait to go home.

Learning theories help teachers understand how their classrooms influence learners from diverse backgrounds differently.

As we saw in Chapter 4, students from different cultures sometimes feel that they aren't welcome and don't belong in their classes. Schools seem strange and cold, and classrooms are threatening. School tasks are difficult, and failure is all too common. Behaviorism and social cognitive theory can help teachers understand why schools aren't friendlier places for these students and what can be done about this problem.

Classical Conditioning: Learning to Like and Dislike School

You learned earlier in the chapter that classical conditioning occurs when neutral stimuli become associated with unconditioned stimuli. Although you may have heard about schools from your parents or siblings, schools are essentially neutral stimuli when you first enter them, and initial experiences influence your emotional reactions to them (Gentile, 1996).

6.24

Using the terms *unconditioned stimulus, unconditioned response, conditioned stimulus,* and *conditioned response,* explain how Donna Evans's room made Carlos feel good about being there.

We respond instinctively to warmth and support, as Carlos did to Donna's manner. In time, school becomes associated with a teacher like Donna, and the school and class elicit positive emotions similar to those Donna caused with her behavior. We can all create warm and supportive learning environments for our students by the way we interact with them and the rules and procedures we establish.

Unfortunately, the opposite can also be true, as it was in Roberto's case. School was not associated with positive feelings for him, and he didn't feel wanted, safe, or comfortable.

Motivating Hesitant Learners

When students are struggling, how can modeling and appropriate use of reinforcers enhance their efforts? The answer to this question both influences initial learning and affects lifelong views of competence.

Let's look again at Donna's work with Carlos:

▌ She reinforced him for the problems he had done correctly.

▌ She provided corrective feedback to help him understand where he had made mistakes.

▌ She reduced the task to three problems to ensure that the reinforcement schedule would be motivating.

▌ She used both direct and cognitive modeling to show him the correct procedures for solving the problems.

▌ She helped Carlos increase his sense of accomplishment by encouraging him and by providing only enough assistance so that he could do the problems on his own.

In her work with Carlos, Donna supported his efforts by applying concepts from both behaviorism and social cognitive theory. This support can increase learner motivation as well as increase opportunities for success.

Roberto: A Study in Contrasts

Let's compare Roberto's experience to Carlos's. To Roberto, the classroom was a strange and unfriendly place. His teacher didn't greet him, and nothing in the classroom made him feel welcome. When the problems seemed impossible, no one came to help. He had already "learned" that he wasn't "good" at math.

In Chapter 4, we examined the ways students from different backgrounds and cultures respond to schooling. In this chapter, behaviorism and social cognitive theory help us understand how factors such as caring, reinforcement, modeling, and feedback can be used to help all students learn successfully.

Classroom Connections

Capitalizing on Diversity in Your Classroom

1. Make your classroom a place that welcomes all students.
   - An elementary teacher invites students to bring in posters and pictures to decorate their room. On Friday afternoons during earned free time, she allows them to bring in and play music.
   - An inner-city social studies teacher displays pictures of historical minority figures around her room. Throughout the year, she refers to these people and emphasizes that American history is the story of all people.

2. Provide instructional support to ensure as much success as possible.

- An English teacher assigns a research paper at the beginning of the term. He breaks the assignment into parts, such as doing a literature search, making an outline, and writing a first draft before the final paper is finished. He meets with students each week to check their progress and give them feedback.

- A fifth-grade teacher uses student graders to provide immediate feedback on math assignments. Two students are chosen each week and are provided with answers for each day's assignment. After students have completed their work, they have it checked immediately; if their scores are below 80%, they see the teacher for help.

Windows on Classrooms

From reading this chapter, you've seen how contiguity, classical and operant conditioning, modeling, vicarious learning, and self-regulation can be used to explain the behavior of students.

Let's look now at a case study describing a teacher working with his middle school students. As you read the case study, analyze the teacher's effectiveness in applying the behavioral and social cognitive principles described in the chapter.

Warren Rose was a seventh-grade math teacher involved in a unit on decimals and percents. He was beginning class on Thursday of the third week of the grading period.

"Here are your tests from last Thursday," Warren said as he handed the students their papers. "The ones you missed have a check by them. Your grades are at the top of your paper."

He paused briefly and continued, "Be sure you write your grade in your notebook." He waited for a few minutes as the students looked over their tests, and then directed, "Okay. Pass the tests back in. . . . Remember now, the next test is at the end of next week, so you need to work hard to be ready for it."

The students passed their test papers forward, and as he picked up the last one, he began, "All right, everyone, let's look up here at the problems on the chalkboard. . . . I realize that percents and decimals aren't your favorite topic, and I'm not wild about them either, but we have no choice, so we might as well buckle down and learn them.

"Let me show you a few more examples," he continued, displaying the following problem on the overhead:

You have gone to the mall, shopping for a jacket. You see one that

looks great, originally priced at $84, marked 25% off. You recently got a check for $65 from the fast-food restaurant where you work. Can you afford the jacket?

"Now, . . . the first thing I think about when I see a problem like this one is, 'What does the jacket cost now?' I have to figure out the price, and to do that I will take 25% of the $84. . . . That means I first convert the 25% to a decimal. I know when I see 25% that the decimal is understood to be just to the right of the 5, so I move it two places to the left. Then I can multiply .25 times 84."

Warren demonstrated the process as he spoke, working the problem through to completion. He had his students work one at their desks and discussed their solutions and then asked, "Okay, do you all understand?"

Hearing no response, he continued, "Okay, for homework, do the odd problems on page 113. The answers are at the back of the book."

"Do we have to do all six of them . . . the word problems?" Robbie asked.

"Why not?" Warren answered after looking at the problems he had assigned.

"Aww, . . . gee, Mr. Rose," Will put in, "they're so terrible hard."

"Uh hunh," Ginny added. "I can't ever do 'em."

" . . . Yeah, and they take so long," Mark added. "All I ever do is math . . . I get so sick of it."

Several other students chimed in, arguing that six word problems were too many.

"Wait, . . . people, please," Warren held up his hands. "All right. You only have to do the first four word problems . . . but! . . . you have to promise not to complain if I give you homework over the weekend."

"Yeah!" the class shouted.

"All right, Mr. Rose," Matt nodded. "You've got a deal."

"Yikes, Friday," Helen commented to Jenny as they walked into Warren's room Friday morning.

"I . . . like . . . blanked out last week. I get so nervous when he makes us go up to the board, and everybody's . . . like staring at us. If he calls me up today, I'll die."

Warren had the students exchange their papers, score the homework, and pass their papers forward. He then turned to the day's work by saying, "Let's look at this problem on the chalkboard."

A bicycle selling for $145 was marked down 15%. What is the new selling price?

"First, let's estimate so that we can see whether our answer makes sense. About what should the new selling price be? . . . Helen?"

". . . I . . . You . . . I'm not sure," Helen stammered.

"Callie, what do you think?"

". . . I . . . think it would be about $120."

"Good thinking. Describe for everyone how you arrived at that."

". . . I . . . Well, 10% . . . would be $14.50, . . . so 15% would be about another $7, . . . well, about another $7, . . . so that would be about $21, and $21 off would be a little over $120."

"Good," Warren nodded. "Now, let's go ahead and solve it. What do we do first? . . . David?"

". . . We . . . er . . . we make the 15% into a decimal."

"Good, David. Now, what next? . . . Leslie?"

"Take the .15 times the 145."

"Okay. Do that everybody. . . . What did you get? . . . Someone?"

". . . $200.17," Cris volunteered. ". . . Whoops, . . . that . . . can't be right. . . . That's more than the bicycle cost to start with. . . . Wait, . . . $21.75."

"Good," Warren smiled. "That's what we're trying to do. We are all going to make mistakes, but if we catch ourselves, we're making progress. Keep it up. You can do these problems. Now what do we do?" he continued.

". . . Subtract," Matt volunteered.

"All right, go ahead," Warren directed.

". . . $142.83," Molly answered.

"Now, think about that for a second. What was our estimate?"

"What? . . . Oh, yeah, . . . No, . . . wait, . . . $123.25."

"What did you do the first time?" Warren queried.

". . . Wrong decimal point."

"Okay, good work. Now, let's look at another one," Warren responded, and then he displayed the following problem:

Christy has a job working at a novelty store, making $5.25 an hour. After 4 months on the job, her boss gave her an 8% raise. What does she make now?

"Let's see who can solve this one. . . . Go ahead, Helen."

". . . I . . . I don't know," Helen said after looking at the problem briefly.

"Shannon?"

". . . Make . . . a decimal out of the 8% and . . . times it by $5.25," Shannon responded.

"Good, Shannon. Let's do it, everybody." Warren then watched as the students solved the problem, and the class worked two more examples together. Then he said, "For homework, do the problems on page 116, and look, only four word problems."

The class began the problems, and Warren circulated around the room as they worked. Seeing Kevin had the wrong answer on the second word problem, he commented, "Look at this one again, Kevin. I know you can figure it out. Try it again. I'll be around to check on you in a few minutes."

As he continued his monitoring, he saw that Helen was just staring at her paper. "How are you doing?" he smiled.

". . . I'm lost. . . . I don't know what I'm doing," she shrugged in frustration, pointing at the second word problem.

"Here, let me show you," Warren said encouragingly. "I know that math is a little tough for you. Watch what I do."

Warren then solved the problem while Helen watched.

"There, you see. Not so bad. Now, you try the next one."

Warren again circulated among the students, making occasional comments and suggestions.

"How're you coming?" he said as he walked by Kevin. "Very good, I see you figured it out. That's super.

"Let's look at the next one," he said to Helen, seeing that she had gotten the third one wrong.

"First, remember that you have to change the percent to a decimal, and then the problem says that the value increased by 30%. You subtracted, and you didn't change the percent to a decimal. Here, let me show you." He then carefully solved the problem and left the solution with Helen.

Warren continued monitoring the students until 2 minutes were left in the period. "All right, everyone, the bell will ring in 2 minutes. Get everything cleaned up around your desks and get ready to go."

Questions for Discussion and Analysis

Analyze Warren's teaching in the context of the information in this chapter. In conducting your analysis, you may want to consider the following questions. In each case, be specific and take information directly from the case study in conducting your analysis.

1. How well did Warren apply an understanding of classical conditioning in working with his students? Provide a specific example that illustrates classical conditioning.

2. Describe specifically how operant conditioning affected the behavior of both Warren and the students. What might Warren have done to change the effect?

3. Identify at least two examples in the case study where Warren (perhaps inadvertently) negatively reinforced student behaviors that detracted from student's learning.

4. How well did Warren apply an understanding of reinforcement schedules in his teaching (and particularly in his testing)? Provide a specific explanation based on your understanding of reinforcement schedules and information taken from the case study.

5. Assess Warren's use of feedback and praise in the lesson. Describe specifically what he might have done to improve it. Be sure to refer directly to the case study in making your assessment.

6. How effectively did Warren provide cues to elicit behaviors that he could then reinforce?

7. Assess Warren's modeling in his lesson. Identify at least one positive and one negative example.

8. What could Warren have done to increase his students' self-regulation? Be specific in your response.

Now go to our Companion Website to assess your understanding of chapter content with the Student Self-Assessment, apply comprehension in the Online Casebook, and broaden your knowledge base with links to important Educational Psychology World Wide Web sites.

Summary

Behaviorist Views of Learning

Contiguity and Classical Conditioning: Contiguity helps explain the learning of simple memorized information through the pairing of stimuli and responses. Classical conditioning occurs when a formerly neutral stimulus becomes associated with a naturally occurring (unconditioned) stimulus to produce a response similar to an instinctive or reflexive response. Classical conditioning helps teachers understand emotional reactions such as test anxiety and how students learn to be comfortable in school environments.

Operant Conditioning: Operant conditioning focuses on overt, voluntary responses that are influenced by consequences. Praise, high test scores, and good grades are consequences that increase behavior and are called *reinforcers*, whereas reprimands are consequences that decrease behavior and are called *punishers*. The schedule of reinforcers influences both the rate of initial learning and the persistence of the behavior.

Applied behavior analysis systematically uses the principles of operant conditioning to change severe or chronic misbehavior. It is used quite commonly with students having exceptionalities.

Social Cognitive Theory

Social cognitive theory extends behaviorism and focuses on the influence that observing others has on behavior. It considers, in addition to behavior and the environment, learners' beliefs and expectations. Social cognitive theory suggests that reinforcement and punishment affect learners' motivation, rather than directly cause behavior.

Modeling lies at the core of social cognitive theory. Modeling can be direct (from live models), symbolic (from books, movies, and television), or synthesized (combining the acts of different models). It can cause new behaviors, facilitate existing behaviors, change inhibitions, and arouse emotions. In learning from models, observers go through the processes of attention (observation), retention in memory, reproduction of the observed behavior, and motivation to produce the behavior in the future.

Learners become self-regulated when they set learning goals on their own, monitor their progress toward the goals, and assess the effectiveness of their efforts.

 **Important Concepts**

applied behavior analysis
  (p. 230)

classical conditioning
  (p. 216)

cognitive behavior
  modification (p. 244)

cognitive modeling
  (p. 237)

conditioned responses
  (p. 216)

conditioned stimuli
  (p. 216)

consequence (p. 220)

contiguity (p. 214)

continuous reinforcement
  schedule (p. 226)

cues (p. 229)

discrimination
  (pp. 218, 225)

extinction (pp. 218, 228)

fixed-interval schedule
  (p. 226)

fixed-ratio schedule
  (p. 226)

generalization
  (pp. 217, 225)

inhibition (p. 238)

intermittent reinforcement
  schedule (pp. 225–226)

interval schedules (p. 226)

learning (pp. 214, 235)

modeling (p. 236)

negative reinforcement
  (p. 222)

neutral stimuli (p. 216)

positive reinforcement
  (p. 221)

potency (p. 227)

Premack principle (p. 222)

presentation punishment
  (p. 223)

punishers (p. 223)

punishment (p. 223)

ratio schedules (p. 226)

reinforcement (p. 220)

reinforcement schedules
  (p. 226)

reinforcer (p. 220)

removal punishment
  (p. 223)

response cost (p. 223)

responses (p. 216)

satiation (p. 227)

self-regulation (p. 243)

shaping (p. 225)

social cognitive theory
  (p. 234)

stimuli (p. 216)

unconditioned response
  (p. 216)

unconditioned stimulus
  (p. 216)

variable-interval schedule
  (p. 226)

variable-ratio schedule
  (p. 226)

vicarious learning (p. 238)

The Classroom

Learning

Part II

Chapter Outline

7

Cognitive
Views of
Learning

David Shelton was preparing a unit on the solar system for his ninth-grade earth science class. From his filing cabinet, he retrieved a color transparency showing the sun throwing off globs of gases into space. He assembled a large model of the solar system to illustrate the planets in their orbital planes and their relative distances from the sun. Finally, he prepared a large matrix, made from a roll of chart paper, and taped it to the back wall of the room.

David began his unit on Monday by saying, "We're getting ready to study the solar system for the next several days, so I've prepared some things to help us get started. Take a look at the chart I made," he said, pointing to the back of the room.

"This chart is going to help us learn about the solar system. . . . But first, we need information to fill in the chart. . . . So, I want you to work in your groups to gather the information. Think about it for a moment, and decide which planet you want. If more than one group wants a planet, you'll have to negotiate to see which one gets its first choice."

The students turned to their groups, talked briefly, and quickly made their choices, compromising in a few cases.

David listed the groups' choices on the chalkboard and then directed the students to books, videos, computer software, and other resources in the room. The students spent the rest of Monday's class gathering their information and putting it on the chart with marking pens.

At the beginning of Tuesday's class, David displayed and briefly discussed the color transparency showing the sun throwing off globs of gases into space. He also referred to the model of the solar system he had assembled and suspended from the ceiling after school on Monday. He reminded the class that it might serve as a frame of reference for their study. The students then spent the rest of Tuesday's class continuing to put information into the chart.

On Wednesday, David began, "Let's review what we've found out so far. Then I'm going to do a little demonstration, and I want you to think about how it relates to what you've been doing."

After completing his review, David tied a pair of athletic socks to a 3-foot piece of string, another pair to a 5-foot piece of string, and whirled the two around his head simultaneously to demonstrate that the planets revolve around the sun on the same plane and in the same direction.

After the students made a number of observations about what they saw, he continued, "Now our job gets a bit more challenging. Each group should identify a piece of information from the chart that might explain or provide evidence about how the solar system was formed. . . . Let me give you an example. . . . For instance, when we look at Pluto, we see that the plane of its orbit differs from the plane of all the other planets.

"Tanya, Juan, and Randy—who are studying Pluto—must figure out why Pluto is different," he said, pointing to the orbital plane cell for Pluto on the chart, "and explain to the rest of the class why they think that's the case. Use any of the information you have—the demonstration I just did, the transparency, the model we have hanging from the ceiling—and anything else."

"Let me give you one more example," he continued. "Here," referring to the diameter and gravity cells for Saturn. "Saturn is much bigger than Earth, but its gravity is about the same as Earth's. Now why might that be the case? . . . Karen, Jack, and Karl will have to explain that to the rest of us. . . . Okay, see what I mean? . . . If you get totally stuck, let me know, and I'll come around and help you. Any questions? . . . Go ahead."

The room was again quickly filled with the buzz of voices as the

	Mercury	Venus	Earth	Mars	Jupiter	Saturn	Uranus	Neptune	Pluto
Orbital plane									
Diameter									
Distance from sun									
Length of year									
Length of day									
Average surface temperature									
Gravity (compared to earth)									

students prepared for the discussion to follow. As they worked, David moved from group to group, offering periodic comments, suggestions, and compliments to groups that were working hard.

"Pluto wasn't part of the solar system to begin with," Juan commented to Randy and Tanya as they started their work.

"What do you mean?" Randy responded.

"I was watching 'Nova' with my mom, and the narrator said that scientists think Pluto was an asteroid floating around and the sun kinda grabbed it. . . . See, when Mr. Shelton did that thing with the socks, the socks stayed sorta level," he continued, moving his hand back and forth to demonstrate a flat plane.

"What's that got to do with it?" Randy asked, still confused.

"Well, look," said Juan, pointing to the model.

"Oh, I get it! Pluto isn't level with the rest of them," Tanya interrupted.

"Gee, I didn't even notice that," Randy lamented.

"Yeah, and look there," Tanya added, pointing to the chart. "See how little Pluto is? It's the littlest one, so it would be sorta easy to capture."

"And it's the last one," Randy added, beginning to warm to the task. "I better write some of this stuff down, or I'll never remember it."

David listened as the students talked, and then he suggested, "I think you're doing a super job, but you might be forgetting something. Take another look at the transparency, and see how it relates to what you're talking about. . . . Look at how the globs are coming off the sun,

and look at the title of the transparency."

The students studied the transparency for a moment, and Juan finally said, "Look, all those globs are even, too, you know, level, like the socks. . . . And it says, 'One Theory of the Formation of the Solar System.' So, that's how the planets were made."

"Now, what was that again about Pluto being the littlest?" Randy wondered. "What's that got to do with anything?"

"If it was really big and floating around out there, the sun's gravity might not be strong enough to grab it," Juan offered.

"But it's easier to grab if it's little," Tanya added.

The students continued their work for a few more minutes, and then David called the class together. "Now, let's see what we've got. Are you all ready? . . . Which group wants to go first?"

"We will," Tanya offered after several seconds.

"Go ahead."

"We can explain why Pluto isn't on the same plane with the other planets," she continued, pleased with her group's accomplishments. "It wasn't part of the solar system when it was first made."

"Now, the rest of you should be asking for what . . . what else do you need to know?" David probed.

" . . . "

"You should be asking for evidence," David continued after hearing no response. "Each group needs to provide evidence that makes sense to the rest of us. . . . Go ahead, Tanya, or Juan, or Randy."

Juan and Randy motioned for Tanya to continue. "It's the littlest one, and it's way out there," motioning to the end of the model.

"Does that support or contradict what the group said?" David queried.

"Supports," Lori volunteered.

"How?" David nodded, gesturing for her to continue.

"If it were captured from somewhere else, it makes sense that it would be the last one."

"Wait, Mr. Shelton, you're going too fast. I'm getting lost. What is this about supporting the theory?" Alfredo asked.

"That's a good question, Alfredo. Let's think about that one, everyone. What do you think?"

" . . . If the rest of the solar system were already in place, and if Pluto came by and was snagged by the sun's gravity, then it would be the farthest one out," Dena offered.

"I see that, but what if Pluto was snagged first? Then how could it be the farthest out?" Alfredo continued.

" . . . Yes, but we found out that the planets weren't snagged; they spun off as molten stuff . . . globs. So Pluto, if it was caught by the sun, would be the last one," Dena replied.

"What do you think, Alfredo?" David gestured.

" . . . Yeah, I see what she means. . . . I guess it makes sense."

"And, also, it isn't in line with the others," Juan added, motioning with his hand to indicate that its orbital plane was different from the others, "And its path is funny, too. Sometimes it's actually inside Neptune's."

"And what did we call the paths?" David probed.

"Orbits," several of the students responded in unison.

"Excellent, everyone. See how this relates to what Dena said a minute ago? When I think of location and orbit, the first thing that pops in my mind is 'origin.' I relate the location and orbit to their origins," David continued, thinking aloud for the students.

The groups continued to present their information and explanations until David saw the period was nearing an end. "Okay, everyone.

We'll continue tomorrow. You've done an excellent job of gathering and relating items of information about the solar system. Now, to check on us, I have a short assignment. For tonight's homework, I want you to write a paragraph summarizing how Earth became a member of the solar system and compare that to how Pluto became a member. Use all the information we have and today's discussion to help you. This should take less than a page."

"Just a reminder in passing," he added as he pointed to the overhead. "This is just one theory of how the solar system was formed. There are others, but we're focusing on this one for now. Also remember," David emphasized, "the information must be in a paragraph. Don't just write down isolated sentences."

As the students began their summaries, David circulated around the room, answering questions and offering suggestions.

In Chapter 6 we examined behaviorism and its emphasis on experience and observable behavior. We then turned to social cognitive theory and demonstrated that, although it has behavioral roots, it marked a transition from behaviorism to more cognitively oriented learning theories. We expand our discussion of cognitive learning theories in this chapter, and in Chapters 8 and 9 where we discuss information processing and constructivism, two of the most prominent cognitive theories.

After you've completed your study of this chapter, you should be able to meet the following objectives:

▌ Describe the components of information processing, including sensory memory, working memory, and long-term memory.
▌ Explain the role of cognitive processes in learning.
▌ Explain how teachers can help students develop metacognitive abilities.
▌ Identify the essential elements of constructivist views of learning.
▌ Describe the implications of constructivism for teaching.

As you saw in Chapter 6, behaviorists describe learning as a change in observable behavior that occurs as a result of experience. In contrast, **cognitive learning theories** *explain learning by focusing on changes in mental processes that people use in their efforts to make sense of the world.* These processes are used to complete tasks as simple as remembering a phone number and as complex as solving detailed math problems. The influence of cognitive learning theories on education has increased steadily since the 1960s (Greeno, Collins, & Resnick, 1996; Mayer, 1996).

From a cognitive perspective, **learning** is *a change in a person's mental structures that provides the capacity to demonstrate different behaviors.* These "mental structures" include schemas, beliefs, goals, expectations, and other components "in the learner's head." In David's lesson, for example, Randy consciously thought about his need to take notes; and Tanya, Randy, and Juan all used higher-order reasoning to relate information from the chart, transparency, model, and demonstration. Cognitive learning theories stress the importance of mental processes and focus on what is happening in the learner. These processes allow learners to actively interpret and organize information, an underlying principle of all cognitive theories.

7.1
In our study of behaviorism, we didn't discuss any internal mental processes. Why not?

Information Processing

Cognitive psychology is eclectic, meaning there isn't *one* but rather a number of cognitive theories of learning. We begin by examining information processing, one of the first and most influential of these theories.

   Information processing is *a cognitive theory that examines the way knowledge enters and is stored in and retrieved from memory.* It was the most prominent cognitive theory during the 20th century and has important implications for teaching (Mayer, 1996).

Models: Aids to Understanding

7.2

There is an important difference between the model of the atom and the model of Earth. What is this difference? The information processing model is more like which of the two? Explain.

Think back for a moment to courses you've taken during your schooling. You probably studied geography, perhaps chemistry, and now you're taking educational psychology. In geography, you examined the face and makeup of the earth, and in chemistry, you studied the structure of the atom. Because you can only directly experience a small portion of the earth, you doubtless made frequent use of maps and globes. The globe is a miniature representation of the earth, faithful in shape and proportion; it's a *model.* Likewise, in chemistry we cannot directly observe the atom with all its individual parts, so scientists created a model, such as the one in Figure 7.1, to help people visualize it. In this case, the **model** is *a representation that allows learners to visualize what they can't observe directly.*

   We encounter a similar situation when we try to visualize what occurs during information processing. We can't directly observe the structures that operate when we process information, so we use a model to help understand this process. The model in Figure 7.2 represents a current view of how cognitive psychologists think the mind processes information (Atkinson & Shiffrin, 1968; Leahey & Harris, 1997).

Models allow students to visualize abstract relationships that are often difficult to understand.

Figure 7.1

Model of an oxygen atom

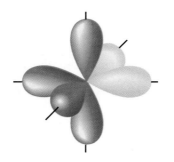

Figure 7.2

An information processing model

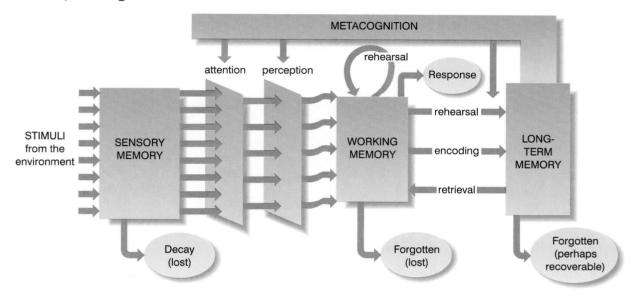

The computer is often used as an analogy for information processing. For example, both computers and humans acquire, store, and retrieve knowledge and make decisions. Computers take symbols as input, apply operators to them, and produce output; humans do, as well (Mayer, 1996). For example, when we're faced with a math problem, we use symbols in the form of numbers and written language (input), we work on the problem (operate on it), and we produce a solution (output). A computer's symbols are electronic; ours are written and spoken language and numbers.

The information processing model has three major components:

- Information stores
- Cognitive processes
- Metacognition

Information stores are *repositories that hold information,* analogous to a computer's main memory and hard drive. The information stores in the information processing model are *sensory memory, working memory,* and *long-term memory.*

Cognitive processes—*intellectual actions that transform information and move it from one store to another*—include *attention, perception, rehearsal, encoding,* and *retrieval.* They're analogous to the programs that direct and transform information in computers.

The third component of the information processing model is **metacognition,** *which is knowing about and having control over cognitive processes* (Hiebert & Raphael, 1996). When Randy decided to take notes because he realized that note taking would help him pay attention better, he was demonstrating knowledge of and control over his attention, one of the cognitive processes. Metacognition is a form of self-regulation; it controls and directs the processes that move information from one store to another. (We discuss self-regulation in detail in Chapter 10.)

7.3
In the model in Figure 7.2, fewer lines connect "attention" and "perception" than connect "sensory memory" and "attention." What is this intended to help us understand?

Working memory is the "workbench" where students think about and solve problems.

Next we examine the information stores, then the cognitive processes that move information from one store to another, and last the metacognitive abilities that regulate those processes.

Sensory Memory

We are constantly bombarded with stimuli from our environment. The sound of a lawn-mower, the smell of car exhaust, a teacher's voice, words on a book page, and other students shuffling in their seats are all stimuli. These stimuli are what people "process" when they learn and remember, and this processing begins with the senses.

Hold your finger in front of you, and rapidly wiggle it. Do you notice a faint "shadow" that trails behind your finger as it moves? Or, someone says, "That's an oxymoron," and you respond, "Ox see what?" as you repeat part of the word without understanding it. The "shadow" and the fact that you're able to repeat the word even though it's meaningless are both representations of stimuli that are retained in your sensory memory.

Sensory memory is *the information store that briefly holds stimuli from the environment until they can be attended to and further processed* (Neisser, 1967). The material in sensory memory is "thought to be completely unorganized, basically a perceptual copy of objects and events in the world" (Leahey & Harris, 1997, p. 106). Sensory memory is nearly unlimited in capacity, but if processing doesn't begin almost immediately, the memory trace quickly fades away. Estimates vary from about .1 to 1 second for vision and 2 to 4 seconds for hearing (Leahey & Harris, 1997; Pashler & Carrier, 1996).

Sensory memory is critical to further processing. In trying to read, for example, if the words at the beginning of a sentence were lost from your sensory memory before you got to the end, it would be impossible to get any meaning from the sentence. The same is true for spoken language. Sensory memory allows you to hold information long enough to transfer it to working memory, the next store.

Working Memory

Working memory, historically called *short-term memory*, is *the store that holds informa-tion as a person works with it*. Working memory can be equated with consciousness; it is where deliberate thinking takes place (Sweller, van Merrienboer, & Paas, 1998). We aren't aware of the contents of either sensory memory or long-term memory until they're pulled into working memory.

Limitations of Working Memory

The most striking feature of working memory is its limitations. It can hold only about seven items of information at a time (G. Miller, 1956) and holds the information for a rela-tively short period (about 10 to 20 seconds for adults), particularly when new information is being received (Greene, 1992). More importantly, selecting, comparing, organizing, and otherwise processing information also takes up working memory space, so the number of items that can be dealt with is much less than the seven that can be simply held in working memory; "humans are probably only able to deal with two or three items of information simultaneously when required to process rather than merely hold information" (Sweller et al., 1998; p. 252).

The characteristics of working memory are summarized in Figure 7.3.

> **7.4**
> In the lesson, Randy asked, "Now, what was that again about Pluto being the littlest?" His question tells us that he had lost the relationship between size and origin. Based on the information in this section, explain why this information was lost.

Figure 7.3

Characteristics of working memory

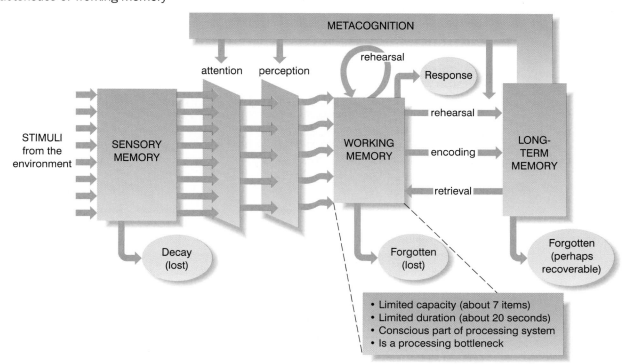

Cognitive Load Theory:
Overcoming the Limitations of Working Memory

When we encounter new information, our learning is influenced by some factors that are out of our control, such as the complexity of the material. On the other hand, as teachers and learners, we can control other factors, such as the way we design instruction and the strategies we use to make information understandable. **Cognitive load theory** *recognizes the limitations of working memory and emphasizes instruction that can influence that capacity* (Sweller et al., 1998).

Cognitive load theory recognizes at least three factors that can help accommodate the limitations of working memory:

- Chunking
- Automaticity
- Dual Processing

Chunking.   **Chunking** is *the process of combining separate items into larger, more meaningful units* (G. Miller, 1956). To illustrate, try this simple exercise. Look at the following row of letters for 5 seconds:

A E E E G G I I I I L N N N N R R S S T T

Now cover them up, and try to write down all 21 letters in any order. How did you do? Most people cannot remember the entire list, even though the letters are presented in alphabetical order, all but two are repeated and grouped together, and you're told that there are 21 letters in all. The capacities of their working memories have been exceeded.

Now look at the same letters presented as follows:

LEARNING IS INTERESTING

Now you have no trouble remembering the letters because they have been "chunked" into three meaningful words (three units) and into a meaningful sentence (one unit).

Table 7.1 presents other examples of chunking. In each case, you can see that remembering the chunk requires less working memory space than the individual items because you can remember the chunked information as a single unit.

Automaticity.   A second way of overcoming the limitations of working memory is to make the mental processes involved in a task automatic. **Automaticity** *refers to mental operations that can be performed with little awareness or conscious effort* (Healy et al., 1993; Schneider & Shiffrin, 1977).

7.5

Why would a health club prefer to advertise its telephone number as 2HEALTH rather than 243-2584?

Table 7.1

Saving working memory space through chunking

Information Unchunked	Information Chunked
u, n, r	run
2492520	24 9 25 20
I, v, o, I, o, u, e, y	I love you
seeletsthiswhyworks	Let's see why this works.

Driving a car and working at a keyboard are examples. After learning these tasks to automaticity, people can drive, talk, listen (and sometimes shave or put on makeup) at the same time. As people's keyboarding skills develop, they don't 'think about' what their fingers are doing; they devote their mental resources to what they're composing.

Automaticity is essential for developing higher-level cognitive skills (Stanovich, 1990). For example, decoding words in reading must be automatic, so that working memory space is left for comprehension (Samuels, 1988). The same applies in math, where basic operations such as addition and multiplication must be automatic, to allow working memory to be used for problem solving. If learners must think about the product of 7×9, for example, not enough working memory space will be left to think about the solution to the problem.

Dual Processing.   **Dual processing** *describes working memory as composed of two parts: a visual and an auditory working memory* (Baddeley, 1992). While each is limited in capacity, they work independently and somewhat additively, and we can capitalize on their independent processing capabilities by presenting information in both visual and verbal forms (Mayer, 1997, 1998; Sweller et al., 1998). The verbal processor supplements the auditory processor and vice versa.

To understand how dual processing works in the classroom, let's think back to David Shelton and how he represented information for his students. He used a *model* of the solar system, a color *transparency* showing 'globs' thrown off from the sun, and a *matrix* with information about the planets. David capitalized on the dual processing capabilities of working memory by combining these visual representations with considerable explanation and discussion. It is important that the visual and verbal presentations occur together, however. For example, presenting and simultaneously discussing the model of the solar system is more effective than presenting the model and then discussing it sometime later, or vice versa (Mayer, 1997).

These findings have implications for teaching. A great deal of instruction is conducted verbally; teachers often use words alone to explain ideas to students. Dual processing suggests that students will learn more if these explanations are supplemented with visual representations, as David did in his lesson (Mayer & Moreno, 1998).

Long-Term Memory

Long-term memory is *our permanent information store*. In a sense, it's like a library with millions of entries and a network that allows them to be retrieved for reference and use. It differs from working memory in both capacity and duration. Whereas working memory is limited to approximately seven items of information for a matter of seconds, long-term memory's capacity is vast and durable. Some experts suggest that information in it remains virtually forever (Pashler & Carrier, 1996). For example, people will often recall personal events they haven't thought of in years (Schab, 1991). Information taught in schools can also be remembered for long periods of time, depending on the quality of initial learning (Ellis, Semb, & Cole, 1998). Although the information hasn't been used or examined in a very long time, it has been stored in long-term memory.

Let's consider how information is stored in this vast repository. One of the most widely accepted descriptions uses the concepts *declarative* and *procedural* knowledge (J. Anderson, 1990). **Declarative knowledge** is *knowledge of facts, definitions, procedures, and rules,*

> **7.6** ▬
> Two students are about equal in general ability, but one is a better algebra student than the other. Using the information in this section, explain why the better algebra student would likely be more successful in physics than the other student.

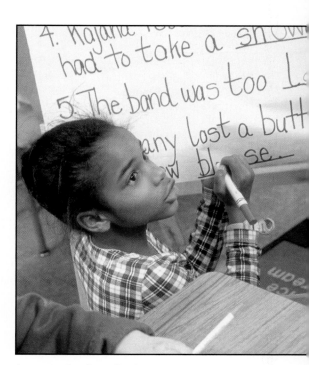

Learners develop effective procedural knowledge by actively applying concepts and ideas in different contexts.

7.7

David said to his students, "For tonight's homework I want you to write a paragraph summarizing how the Earth became a member of the solar system and compare that to how Pluto became a member." Does writing the paragraph primarily require declarative knowledge or procedural knowledge? Explain.

whereas **procedural knowledge** is *knowledge of how to perform tasks*. For example, a learner who says, "To add fractions, you must first have like denominators," knows the rule for adding fractions but might not be able to actually perform the task of adding the fractions. Knowing the rule is a form of declarative knowledge; being able to add the fractions requires procedural knowledge. Declarative knowledge can be determined directly from a person's comments, whereas we infer procedural knowledge from the person's performance. Next we'll look at each in more detail.

Representing Declarative Knowledge in Memory: Schemas

All of us hold a great deal of knowledge in our memories. How is this information stored? What form does it take? How is new information added and old information retrieved? We begin to answer these questions in this section.

Many researchers believe that declarative knowledge is mentally stored in the form of **schemas** (also called *schemata*), which are *complex networks of connected information* (J. Anderson, 1990; Hiebert & Raphael, 1996; Voss & Wiley, 1995). Schemas combine simpler forms of information, such as propositions, linear orderings, and images (Gagne, Yekovich, & Yekovich, 1993). For instance, "Pluto is a planet" is a proposition; it is the smallest bit of information that can be judged true or false. Linear orderings rank information according to some dimension, such as the planets in their order from the sun, and images store physical characteristics as mental pictures, such as visualizing the globs in David's transparency.

Schemas are individually constructed, dynamic, and contextual (Wigfield, Eccles, & Pintrich, 1996). As a way of visualizing them, look at Figure 7.4, which illustrates Randy's schema for the solar system.

Though it doesn't capture any imagery that Randy may have used, this illustration helps us see how his ideas are organized. He has linked Pluto, the solar system, and the Earth to the sun. His understanding of the relationship between the sun, the globs, the orbital plane, and the origins is uncertain, however, because they are not linked to the rest of the information.

7.8

How would Juan's schema look if he simply memorized the information about the planets' names, their order from the sun, and their orbital planes?

In comparison, Figure 7.5 illustrates the way Juan's understanding is organized. He sees how the origins of the solar system, the orbital plane, the location of Earth, and Pluto's size and distance from the sun are all related, as indicated by the links between the items in Figure 7.5. These links have important implications for learning, as we'll discuss shortly.

Schemas as Scripts.   Schemas can also guide our actions. For example, when you first go into a university class, you may ask questions such as:

Figure 7.4

Schema illustrating Randy's understanding

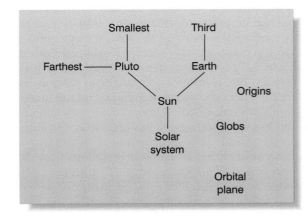

Figure 7.5

Schema for Juan's
understanding

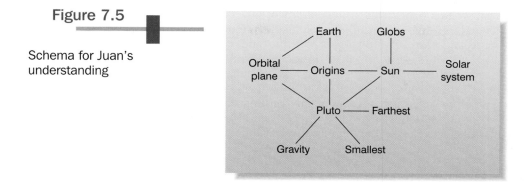

- What are the instructor's expectations?
- What are the course requirements?
- How should I prepare for quizzes and other assessments?
- How will I interact with my peers?

Answers often come from your understanding of the proper way to operate in university classes. These are called **scripts**, which are *"schema representations for events"* (Bruning, Schraw, & Ronning, 1999, p. 60). They can also be thought of as plans for action in particular situations. For example, your script guides your behavior as you prepare for, attend, and participate in your class. In this regard, scripts contain some procedural knowledge, as well as propositions about ways to interact with other students, images of past classes, and linear orderings about what tasks to complete first.

Schemas: Implications for Teaching and Learning.   Schemas are very important for teaching and learning for at least two reasons. First, they help us understand why background knowledge and the way it's organized are so important (Nuthall, 1999). To illustrate, consider some of the dialogue from David's lesson:

Juan:	Pluto wasn't part of the solar system to begin with.
Randy:	What do you mean?
Juan:	I was watching 'Nova' with my mom, and the narrator said that scientists think Pluto was an asteroid floating around and the sun kinda grabbed it. . . . See, when Mr. Shelton did that thing with the socks, the socks stayed sorta level.
Randy:	What's that got to do with it?
Juan:	Well, look. (pointing to the model)
Tanya:	Oh, I get it! Pluto isn't level with the rest of them.
Randy:	Gee, I didn't even notice that.

To help us see why Juan's and Randy's comments were so different, look again at Figures 7.4 and 7.5. We see that each has 10 individual items of information in it. However, Randy's schema has 6 links in it, compared to Juan's, which has 12. Because the items in his schema were more interrelated, Juan could relate David's demonstration to both a television documentary and information in the unit. Since his schema wasn't as well developed, Randy initially didn't even notice one of the relationships. Understanding schemas helps us explain why Juan's and Randy's experiences were different.

Schemas also help reduce the load on working memory. We saw earlier that working memory capacity is limited. However, "although the number of elements is limited, the size, complexity, and sophistication of elements [are] not" (Sweller et al., 1998, p. 256). We see this illustrated in Juan's and Randy's schemas. Because all the items in Juan's are connected, his schema behaves as a single entity; it takes up only one working memory slot. Because Randy's is less well connected, it takes up four slots: one for the seven interconnected items and one each for "origins," "globs," and "orbital plane." In thinking about the origins of our solar system, the load on Randy's working memory will be much greater than the load on Juan's.

The organization of information in long-term memory and the reduced load on working memory suggest that teaching and learning should focus on relationships among the items of information we expect students to learn. Learning information in isolated bits is clearly less effective than learning that stresses links and connections.

7.9
Research indicates that students from high socioeconomic status (SES) backgrounds are generally more successful in school than students from low SES homes. Using the information in this section, explain this research result.

Using Technology in Your Study of Educational Psychology

The Importance of Background Knowledge

You've just read about schema theory and how schemas influence the way learners perceive, encode new information, and retrieve old information from long-term memory. Using the CD-ROM that accompanies this book, you have an opportunity to experience first-hand how schemas influence learning. To complete the activity, do the following:

- Open the CD, and click on "Bartlett's Ghosts." (Your instructor will show you how to access information on the CD.)
- Complete the activities involved in "Bartlett's Ghosts."
- After completing the activities, answer the following questions:

1. What did the relative number of omissions, transformations, and additions tell you about your schema for the information contained in "Bartlett's Ghosts"?

   _____

   _____

   _____

2. From a classroom perspective, which are most problematic: omissions, transformations, or additions? What can teachers do to minimize these different kinds of schema errors?

   _____

   _____

   _____

3. How would your memory for the information contained in "Bartlett's Ghosts" be influenced by increased knowledge in the following areas?

   Boats and canoes

   _____

   _____

   _____

■ Native American burial customs

_____

_____

_____

■ Previous exposure to this story

_____

_____

_____

4. What implications do your responses to these questions have for instruction?

_____

_____

_____

Your instructor will provide you with feedback with respect to these four questions, and he or she may ask you to complete some of the additional exercises on the CD.

Representing Procedural Knowledge in Memory: Conditions and Actions

Earlier, we said that procedural knowledge involves knowing "how to perform tasks." In implementing procedural knowledge, learners need to adapt to changing *conditions* and then *act* according to these conditions. Using our earlier example with adding fractions, if the denominators are the same, we merely add the numerators. If they differ, we must find a common denominator and then add the numerators. The conditions for adding fractions differ depending on the denominators, and the ability to add them correctly depends on recognizing these conditions and acting appropriately.

Procedural knowledge also depends on declarative knowledge; you must first know the rule to adapt to the different conditions and correctly perform the addition.

Acquiring Procedural Knowledge.   Procedural knowledge is developed in three stages (J. Anderson, 1995; Gagne et al., 1993). In the *declarative stage*, learners acquire declarative knowledge about the procedure, such as understanding where to place the fingers on a keyboard to begin the process of typing, or stating rules for adding fractions. They are unable to perform the action at this stage.

During the *associative stage*, learners can perform the procedure but must think about what they are doing, and their thoughts occupy most of their working memory (J. Anderson, 1990). For example, novice typists focus most of their energies on correctly using the keyboard during this stage. With additional practice, learners finally move to the *automatic stage*, when they can perform the process with little conscious thought or

7.10 ■
You are given a problem that asks, "How much pizza have you eaten if you eat a piece from a pizza cut into six pieces and another piece from an identical pizza cut into eight pieces?" What are the conditions, and what are the actions required in this problem? What declarative knowledge is required in solving the problem?

effort, freeing much of their working memory for other activities. Typists at this stage are devoting their working memories to what they're composing, giving little thought to the ways their fingers are moving on the keyboard.

The limitations of working memory and developing procedural knowledge to the point of automaticity have important implications for teaching. Research indicates that reaching the automatic stage can take a great deal of time and practice, so students must be provided with as many opportunities to practice as possible. Research also indicates that complex procedural knowledge, such as the ability to speak and write a foreign language, continues to improve even after thousands of hours of practice (Bruning et al., 1999).

This also helps us understand the interdependence of declarative and procedural knowledge. Learners must practice to acquire procedural knowledge, but the efficiency of this practice depends on declarative knowledge being organized into well-developed schemas. For instance, as you move through your teacher preparation program, you will practice both classroom management and questioning skills, but you must understand the principles of sound management and the characteristics of effective questioning, or you won't know how to practice most efficiently. This interdependence with declarative knowledge exists for all procedural knowledge.

Importance of Context in Acquiring Procedural Knowledge.   Accurately applying procedural knowledge first requires that learners identify conditions in a learning situation

Figure 7.6

Characteristics of long-term memory

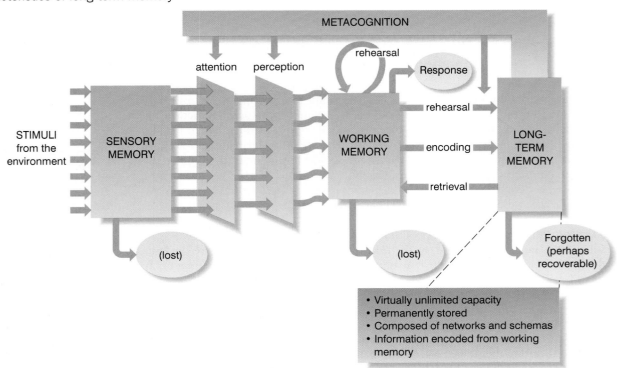

before they can appropriately apply procedures. To become proficient, students should practice using procedural knowledge in a variety of **contexts**, which *involves embedding problems and exercises in a variety of realistic settings*. This helps them learn to identify different conditions for individual problems, yet appropriately generalize on the procedures. This means that students should be solving realistic word problems in math as soon as possible and in a variety of different contexts. For example, when learning how to add, they should be given practice with a variety of addition problems so they can see that addition works with a variety of objects ranging from balls to cookies to kittens.

In a similar way, when learning to apply grammar and punctuation rules, learners should practice those rules in a variety of contexts, including their own writing, rather than in isolated sentences. Having students complete decontextualized exercises, such as commonly occur in worksheets, doesn't provide them with opportunities to identify conditions and apply the appropriate actions. (We examine the role of context again later in this chapter and again in Chapter 8.)

As a review, take a moment now to examine Figure 7.6, which summarizes the characteristics of long-term memory.

Classroom Connections

Applying an Understanding of Sensory Memory in Your Classroom

1. As information is presented, give students time to process it before changing the stimulus.
   - A third-grade teacher displays problems on the overhead projector and waits until the students have copied the problems before she starts talking.
   - In a social studies lesson, a teacher puts a map on the overhead and says, "Look at the map of the neighborhood where our school is located. I'll stop for a second to give you an opportunity to examine it. Then we'll go on."

2. Ask only one question at a time. Otherwise, the memory trace for succeeding questions may be lost before students can attend to them.
   - A first-grade teacher gives students directions for seat work by presenting them slowly and one at a time. She asks different students to repeat the directions before she has them begin.

Applying an Understanding of Working Memory in Your Classroom

3. Keep descriptions short to prevent overloading students' working memories. Use questions to encourage transfer to long-term memory.
   - A teacher in a high school woodworking class begins by saying, "The hardness and density of wood from the same kind of tree vary, depending on the amount of rainfall the tree has received and how fast it grows." He waits a moment, holds up two pieces of wood, and says, "Look at these wood pieces. What do you notice about the rings on them?"

4. To develop automaticity, provide frequent practice and review in basic skills.
   - A first-grade teacher begins language arts each morning by having students write one or two sentences about some event that occurred the night before. She selects samples to review the basic structure of sentences.

5. Encourage organization by identifying and highlighting key points in your presentation and writing them on the chalkboard or overhead.
   - A 10th-grade history teacher prepares an outline of the events that led up to the Revolutionary War. As he presents the information, he refers to the outline for each important point and encourages students to use the outline to organize their note taking.

Applying an Understanding of Long-Term Memory in Your Classroom

6. Encourage students to explore relationships among ideas to help in developing complex networks and schemas.
   - During story time, a first-grade teacher asks the students to explain how the events in a story contribute to the conclusion.
   - A third-grade teacher presents examples of writing in which facts, inference, and opinions are embedded and asks students to explain how fact, inference, and opinion are each similar to and different from each other.

7. Connect new ideas to previous learning.
   - In developing the rules for multiplying fractions, a math teacher asks the class, "How does this process compare to what we did when we added fractions? What do we do differently? Why?"

8. Encourage meaningful learning by presenting topics in a variety of contexts.
   - An English teacher presents the rules for singular and plural possessives in the context of a passage about the school. She guides students into an understanding of the rules by using the passage.
   - A sixth-grade math teacher reviews percentages by bringing in newspaper ads and having students compute the percentages saved on CDs and tapes on sale.

Cognitive Processes

Let's return to our model. Having examined the information stores and seen how information is stored in long-term memory, let's shift our attention to the processes that move information from one store to another: *attention, perception, rehearsal, encoding,* and *retrieval*. They're highlighted in Figure 7.7 and discussed in the sections that follow.

Attention: The Beginning of Information Processing

Consider the room you're in right now. A myriad of stimuli exists—pictures, furniture, other people moving and talking, the whisper of an air conditioner—even though you're not aware of some of them. Others, however, attract your **attention**, which is *the process of consciously focusing on a stimulus or stimuli*.

Reexamine the model in Figure 7.7. "Attention" appears next to "sensory memory" and is where processing begins. All additional processing depends on whether and how well learners attend to appropriate stimuli in their learning environment.

7.11 ▬

Research indicates that teacher enthusiasm improves student learning and motivation. Explain why this would be the case, using information processing as the basis for your explanation. Explain the positive effects of enthusiasm based on social cognitive theory.

Attracting and Maintaining Student Attention.   Since attention is where learning begins, attracting and maintaining student attention are crucial first steps in teaching. Teachers should plan their lessons so students attend to what is being taught and ignore outside noises and other stimuli irrelevant to the learning experience (Brophy & Good, 1986; Rosenshine & Stevens, 1986). If a teacher pulls a live, dripping, wriggling crab out of a cooler to begin a lesson on crustaceans, for example, even the most disinterested student is likely to pay attention.

Teachers attract students' attention in a variety of ways. Demonstrations, displays on transparencies, pictures, maps, graphs, thought-provoking questions, and even the chalkboard can attract students' attention. Enthusiastic teachers move around the classroom, change their rate, pitch, and intensity of speech, and use gestures and other energetic movements to maintain attention. Additional examples of attention-getting strategies are presented in Table 7.2.

Figure 7.7

Cognitive processes in the information processing model

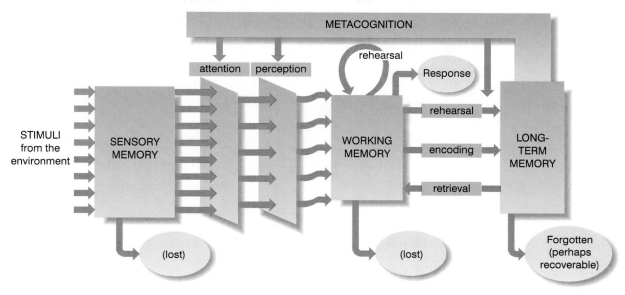

Table 7.2

Strategies for attracting attention

Type	Example
Demonstrations	A physical science teacher pulls a student in a chair across the room to demonstrate force and work in a physical science class.
Discrepant events	A world history teacher who usually dresses conservatively comes to class in a sheet, makeshift sandals, and a crown to begin a discussion of ancient Greece.
Visual displays	A health teacher displays a chart showing the high fat content of some popular foods.
Thought-provoking questions	A history teacher begins a discussion of World War II with the question, "Suppose Germany had won the war. How might the world be different now?"
Emphasis	A teacher says, "Pay careful attention now. The next two items are very important."
Student names	In her question and answer session, a teacher always asks her question, pauses briefly, and then calls on a student *by name* to answer.

Effective teachers use a variety of visual aids to attract and maintain students' attention.

Let's see how David attempted to attract his students' attention. Perhaps most significant was his demonstration with the strings and socks, but his model, transparency, and matrix were effective as well. The use of students' names is also a powerful attention getter. Effective teachers direct their questions to individual students, rather than the class as a whole, and when this becomes a pattern, attention and achievement increase (Kauchak & Eggen, 1998; Kerman, 1979).

Perception: Finding Meaning in Stimuli

Perception is *the process by which people attach meaning to experiences*. After people attend to certain stimuli in their sensory memories, processing continues with perception. Perception is critical because it influences the information that enters working memory. Information in working memory is in the form of "perceived reality" rather than "true reality." If students misperceive the teacher's examples, the information that enters working memory will be invalid, as will the information they transfer to long-term memory.

Background Knowledge Affects Perception.   Background knowledge in the form of schemas affects perception and subsequent learning. This explains why Randy didn't "notice" that Pluto's plane differed from that of the other planets. His perception of the model and demonstration was affected by his lack of background knowledge.

As another example, science students are studying the formation of calcium deposits from hard water and see the following on the chalkboard:

$$CaCO_3 + CO_2 + H_2O \rightarrow Ca + 2HCO_3$$

For learning to be effective, students must accurately perceive several aspects of this equation, such as

- A symbol without a subscript implies one atom of the element in the compound.
- Some elements have two letters in their symbols; others have only one.
- The subscript indicates the number of atoms of the element.

Accurate perceptions of these features depend on students' background knowledge with respect to chemical equations.

An effective way of checking students' perceptions is to review by asking open-ended questions (Kauchak & Eggen, 1998). For example, after writing the equation on the chalkboard, the science teacher might ask, "Look at the equation. What do you notice about it?" If students can't identify essential information, such as the elements involved, the numbers of each in the compounds, and what the arrow means, the teacher knows

7.12
Based on the information in this section, we would predict that Juan is more likely to accurately perceive the information in David's lesson than is Randy. Why?

272

that their perceptions are inaccurate or incomplete, and she can then adjust her review to cover these features.

Rehearsal: Retaining Information Through Practice

You want to dial a phone number, so you look it up, and repeat it to yourself a few times until you dial it. You have *rehearsed* the number to keep it in working memory until you're finished with it. **Rehearsal** is *the process of repeating information over and over, either aloud or mentally, without altering its form*. It is analogous to rehearsing a piece of music. When people do so, they play the music over and over as written; they don't alter it or change its form.

While rehearsal is primarily used to retain information in working memory until it is used, if rehearsed enough, it can sometimes be transferred to long-term memory (Atkinson & Shiffrin, 1968). This is an inefficient method of transferring information, however, and not surprisingly, it's one of the first memory strategies that develops in young children (Berk, 1997).

Meaningful Encoding:
Making Connections in Long-Term Memory

Encoding is *the process of placing information in long-term memory* (Bruning et al., 1999); it is perhaps the most critical cognitive process in the information processing model.

When encoding information, our goal is for it to be *meaningful*. **Meaningfulness** *describes the number of connections or associations between an idea and other ideas in long-term memory* (Gagne et al., 1993). For example, we saw earlier that Randy had 6 links in his schema, whereas Juan had 12. Juan's was much more meaningful.

The concept of meaningfulness helps us understand why background knowledge and an understanding of schemas are important. The more background information that exists, and the more interrelated that knowledge is, the more locations a learner has to connect the new information and the more likely it is to be meaningfully encoded.

Meaningful encoding can be enhanced in at least three ways:

▌ Organization
▌ Elaboration
▌ Activity

They are outlined in Figure 7.8 and discussed in the sections that follow.

7.13
In the last section, we said that if information is rehearsed enough, it can sometimes be transferred to long-term memory. Under these conditions, is rehearsal a form of encoding? Yes or no? Explain.

Figure 7.8

Making information meaningful

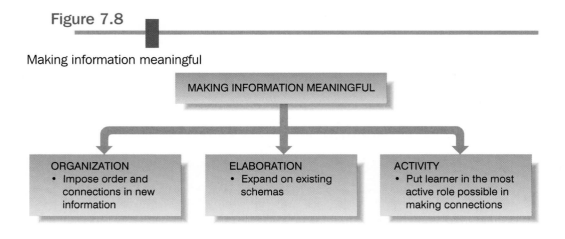

7.14   ▬

Research indicates that students commonly think green plants get their food from the environment, as animals do, rather than make their own. Does this research finding imply that the information is not organized for these students? Explain.

Organization.   We know that information in long-term memory is stored in the form of schemas, and schemas are important because they organize information and make it meaningful. **Organization** is *the process of clustering related items of content into categories or patterns that illustrate relationships*. David's model of the solar system displayed the sun, the relative distances of the planets, and the orbital plane; it helped students see the relationships among the different parts. Research in reading (Eggen, Kauchak, & Kirk, 1978), memory (Bower, Clark, Lesgold, & Winzenz, 1969), and classroom instruction (Mayer, 1997; Nuthall, 1999) confirms the value of organization in promoting learning.

Information can be organized in several ways. Among them are

- *Charts and matrices:*   Useful for organizing large amounts of information into meaningful patterns. David used a matrix in his lesson to help his students organize their thoughts about the planets. Table 7.3 contains an additional example from American history.
- *Hierarchies:*   Effective when new information can be subsumed under existing ideas. We made frequent use of hierarchies in our discussion of behaviorism in

Table 7.3   ▬

Chart used to organize information about immigration

	Italians	**Chinese**
Reasons for coming	Small farms that couldn't support families	Overpopulation
	Population increase	Fixed status
	Poor land, poor equipment	Inefficient warlords
	Few factories and plants in which to work	High taxes
	Heavy taxes	Crop failures and famine
	Stories of wealth in America	Active recruitment—promise of high wages
Characteristics	Lower socioeconomic class	Originally coolie laborers
	Large families	Tight family structure
	Tight family structure	Low literacy rate in English
	Low literacy rate in English	Laborers' jobs
	Quick to learn English	Slow to learn English
Assimilation	First generation: very religious, little outside contact	Settlement in Western U.S.
	Second generation: increased intermarriage	Togetherness
	Third generation: "Americanized"	Establishment of "Chinatowns"
		Preservation of Chinese customs

Source: Strategies for Teachers: Teaching Content and Thinking Skills, 3rd ed., by P. Eggen and D. Kauchak, 1996, Needham Heights, MA: Allyn & Bacon. Copyright 1996 by Allyn & Bacon. Adapted with permission.

Figure 7.9

Organizational hierarchy
in English

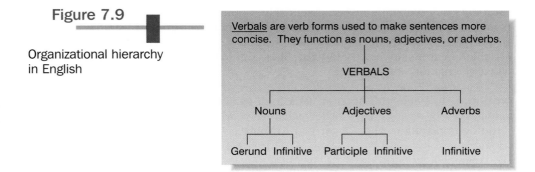

<u>Verbals</u> are verb forms used to make sentences more
concise. They function as nouns, adjectives, or adverbs.

VERBALS

Nouns   Adjectives   Adverbs

Gerund Infinitive   Participle Infinitive   Infinitive

Chapter 6 (such as in "Behavioral Consequences in Operant Conditioning," on
p. 221). Figure 7.9 contains an additional example from English.

▮ *Models:*   Helpful for representing relationships that cannot be observed directly.
David's model of the solar system and the models in this chapter that illustrate the
different aspects of information processing are examples.

▮ *Outlines:*   Useful for representing the organizational structure in a body of written
material. The outlines at the beginning of each chapter in this book are examples.

Other types of organization include graphs, tables, flowcharts, and maps. Each is
intended to make information meaningful by illustrating relationships among the different
parts (Mayer, 1997). Learners should be encouraged to adapt these forms of organization
as personal study strategies to help them in their efforts to encode information.

Keep in mind that, although organizing content is important, it doesn't ensure that
students will learn. If the organizational structure doesn't make sense to learners, they will
(mentally) reorganize the information in a way that does make sense to them, they will
memorize snippets of it, or they will reject or ignore it. For organization to be effective,
students must understand the relationships in the information.

Interaction is crucial to this process. David, for example, not only used his model,
demonstration, and matrix but also guided his students' developing understanding
through questioning and class discussion. Organization combined with high levels of interaction helps make information meaningful to students.

Dual-Coding Theory: Imagery in Long-Term Memory.   Organizers—such as charts, hierarchies, maps, and models—can also be used to capitalize on **imagery,** *the process of forming mental pictures* (Schwartz, Ellsworth, Graham, & Knight, 1998). **Dual-coding theory**
*describes long-term memory as consisting of two distinct memory systems: one for verbal
information and one that stores images* (Paivio, 1986, 1991). For instance, as we study
information processing, we can visualize the model (see Figure 7.2): We see that working
memory is smaller than sensory and long-term memory, and the lines emerging from perception are curved, which reminds us that working memory has limited capacity and that
people perceive information differently. The fact that we can both read about and create
an image of working memory helps us capitalize on the dual-coding capacity of long-term
memory. The model is more meaningfully encoded than it would be if we had to rely on
words alone (Clark & Paivio, 1991, Willoughby, Porter, Belsito, & Yearsley, 1999). This again
reminds us of the importance of supplementing our verbal presentations with visual supplements such as pictures, outlines, charts, and maps.

Research shows that imagery can also facilitate problem solving (Kozhevnikov,
Hegarty, & Mayer, 1999). Visualizing abstract relationships between problem components

7.15 ▬

Research indicates that a word like *car* is much easier to remember than one like *truth* (Sadoski & Goetz, 1998). Using the information in this section, explain why this is the case.

helps students differentiate between essential and nonessential information in problems. For example, if students are attempting to solve area problems involving irregularly shaped polygons, instructing them to visually impose a grid over the figure encourages them to think in area dimensions and also filters out irrelevant information like the color or physical orientation of the shape.

Elaboration.   To begin this section, let's look again at David's lesson. He began his Wednesday class by saying, "Let's review what we've found out so far. Then I'm going to do a little demonstration, and I want you to think about how it relates to what you've been doing."

By having students review their current understanding and expanding on it with his demonstration, David capitalized on **elaboration**, which is *the process of making information meaningful by forming additional links in existing knowledge or adding new knowledge* (Willoughby, Wood, & Khan, 1994). It occurs in a noisy party, for example, when you miss some of a conversation; you fill in details, trying to make sense of the message. You do the same when you read or listen to a lecture. You expand on (and sometimes distort) information to make it fit your expectations and current understanding.

Elaboration can enhance meaningfulness in one or both of two ways. For example, when Tanya said, "Oh, I get it! Pluto isn't level with the rest of them," she formed an additional link in her schema without adding any new information. This is one type of elaboration.

7.16 ▬

You're a language arts teacher and have discussed direct objects. Describe specifically how you would begin a lesson on indirect objects to capitalize on elaboration.

David's review capitalized on a second type. It reactivated his students' schemas (organized background knowledge), to which the information from Wednesday's lesson would be attached (O'Reilly, Symons, & Macleish-Gaudet, 1998). Teacher questioning, such as David's, can be a powerful tool to encourage student elaboration (Seifert, 1993; Simpson, Olejnik, Tam, & Suprattathum, 1994).

In addition to questioning, teachers can promote elaboration by using three additional strategies:

▌**Examples**:   *specific instances or cases that illustrate ideas*
▌**Analogies**:   *comparisons in which similarities are created between otherwise dissimilar ideas* (Mayer & Wittrock, 1996)
▌**Mnemonic devices**:   *strategies that promote meaningfulness by forming associations between items or ideas that don't exist naturally in the content* (Leahey & Harris, 1997)

We begin with constructing, or finding, examples because it is perhaps the most powerful elaboration strategy (Cassady, 1999). Whenever learners can generate or find a new example of an idea, they elaborate their understanding of that idea. We obviously believe very strongly in this strategy because we have tried to use examples extensively throughout this book, and we encourage you to focus on the examples to increase your understanding of the topics you're studying.

When topics don't lend themselves to examples, or examples aren't available, using analogies can be an effective elaboration strategy. For instance, in an attempt to make information processing more meaningful to you, we presented an analogy between it and a computer. As another example, consider the following analogy from science:

Our circulatory system is like a pumping system that carries the blood around our bodies. The veins and vessels are the pipes, and the heart is the pump.

In this case, the circulatory system (the new information) is linked to pipes and a pump (familiar ideas). As a result, links between the new information and old information stored in long-term memory are created.

Mnemonic devices typically pair knowledge to be learned with familiar information to make it more meaningful (Bruning et al., 1999). Acronyms, such as HOMES (Huron, Ontario, Michigan, Erie, and Superior) and SCUBA (self-contained underwater breathing apparatus) are examples, as are phrases like "Every good boy does fine," for E, G, B, D, and F—the names of the notes in the treble clef, and rhymes such as "*i* before *e* except after *c*" as spelling aids. Mnemonics are used to help remember vocabulary, names, rules, lists, and other kinds of factual knowledge. As these devices are used to recall information, learners remember the mnemonic and then link it to the items it represents. Table 7.4 lists some additional examples.

7.17

What is an important limitation in the classroom use of mnemonics?

Activity.   Active student participation in learning is at the heart of cognitive learning theories. You first saw activity emphasized in our study of Piaget and Vygotsky in Chapter 2, and our discussion of information processing emphasized cognitively active learners. Active learning facilitates meaningful encoding by providing a variety of ways to organize and remember information (Nuthall, 1999). For example, students who measure geometric shapes such as triangles and rectangles, who use their measurements in problem solving, and who discuss the logic behind their strategies are more likely to solve complex problems effectively than students who are provided with explanations, regardless of how clear the explanations are.

Table 7.4

Types and examples of mnemonic devices

Mnemonic	Description	Example
Method of loci	Learner combines imagery with specific locations in a familiar environment, such as the chair, sofa, lamp, and end table in a living room.	Student wanting to remember the first seven elements in order visualizes hydrogen at the chair, helium at the sofa, lithium at the lamp, and so on.
Peg-word method	Learner memorizes a series of "pegs" such as a simple rhyme like "one is bun" and "two is shoe," on which to-be-remembered information is hung.	A learner wanting to remember to get pickles and carrots at the grocery visualizes a pickle in a bun and carrot stuck in a shoe.
Link method	Learner visually links items to be remembered.	A learner visualizes *homework* stuck in a *notebook* which is bound to her *textbook, pencil,* and *pen* with a rubber band to remember to take the (italicized) items to class.
Key-word method	Learner uses imagery and rhyming words to remember unfamiliar words.	A learner remembers that *trigo* (which rhymes with tree) is the Spanish word for wheat by visualizing a sheaf of wheat sticking out of a tree.
First-letter method	Learner creates a word from the first letter of items to be remembered.	A student creates the word *Wajmma* to remember the first six presidents in order: Washington, Adams, Jefferson, Madison, Monroe, and Adams.

"Activity" isn't as simple as it appears on the surface, however. For instance, since hands-on activities are strongly encouraged in science instruction, if learners are working with materials, such as magnets and objects, teachers often assume that learning is taking place. This isn't necessarily the case. If the goal isn't clear, or if students aren't encouraged to describe connections between what they're doing and information they already understand, learning may not be happening. "Hands-on" activities don't guarantee "minds-on" activities.

The same is true with manipulatives in math (Ball, 1992), cooperative learning, or any other strategy that is intended to promote active learner participation. Because learners are physically active, or are talking, we assume that learning is taking place. This may not be the case.

Activity can also be deceiving at an individual level. For example, consider two chemistry students who use the worked examples in their text to help them understand the material in the chapter.

> Selena reads the sample problem and then carefully reads through the solution provided by the text's authors. Gretchen covers up the solution, first trying to work the problem on her own and then comparing the solution in the book to hers.

At a casual glance, both girls appeared to be actively studying. However, Gretchen was in a more mentally "active" mode than Selena. By preparing a solution that she could compare to the one provided, she was forming links between the problems and information in long-term memory. Selena was simply passively reading the information.

The following are some suggestions for encouraging active learning:

- Put content in the form of problems to solve, instead of information to be memorized.
- Employ questions that require students to analyze, rather than recall, information.
- Require students to provide evidence for conclusions, instead of merely form conclusions.
- Develop lessons around examples and applications, instead of definitions.
- Use tests, quizzes, and homework that require application, rather than rote memory.

In each of these strategies, students are cognitively active, the activity is purposeful, and connections and deep processing are required.

7.18 ■
One student highlights entire paragraphs of her text, whereas another highlights only sentences and small sections. Which of the two is likely to be the more "active" in her study? Explain.

Active learning encourages students to encode information in meaningful ways.

Levels of Processing:
An Alternate View of Meaningful Encoding

Think again about David Shelton and the matrix he used to organize information about the solar system. To guide his students as they processed the information, he could have asked

"Which planet is the fourth one from the sun?"

"Why do you suppose Mercury is so hot on one side and so cold on the other?"

"What patterns can you find in the information in the chart?"

Which of these questions would result in the most learning?

Levels of processing is *a view of learning that suggests that the more deeply information is processed, the more meaningful it becomes*. Although originally proposed as an alternative to the three-store information processing model that we've been studying (Craik & Lockhart, 1972), more recent views describe it as a way of processing information into long-term memory (Cermak & Craik, 1979).

For instance, asking students to explain why the temperature on Mercury varies so much requires them to understand that Mercury is a small planet, without enough gravity to hold an atmosphere (which helps prevent extreme temperatures), and that its periods of rotation and revolution are the same, so the same side of the planet always faces the sun, making it very hot, while leaving the opposite side cold. Being able to answer the question requires students to link all this information in a meaningful, deep level of processing.

The same is true for finding patterns in the information in the chart, whereas merely identifying Mars as the fourth planet requires few meaningful connections; it is a "shallow" form of processing. Teachers should continually ask students to search for relationships in the information they're studying, which will result in deeper, more meaningful processing.

 # Classroom
Connections

Applying an Understanding of Attention in Your Classroom

1. Use examples in your teaching that attract students' attention.
   - A teacher introducing the concept of pressure to her science students has them stand by their desks, first on both feet and then on one foot. They then discuss the force and pressure on the floor in both cases.
   - A ninth-grade economics teacher introduces the concept of opportunity cost by saying, "You could spend your after-school time at a job, or you could socialize with your friends. If you work, what happens?" She then guides them to the idea that the opportunity cost for the job is the amount of time they don't get to spend with their friends.

2. Call on all students equally and by name to capitalize on this attention-arousing element.
   - A ninth-grade teacher calls on all students, including those who don't have their hands up. He tells them in advance what he is going to do and explains why it is important.
   - A third-grade teacher mentally keeps track of who she has called on. She periodically asks, "Who have I not called on lately?" to be sure students are treated as equally as possible.

3. Use emphasis to ensure that students attend to important information in the lesson.
   - An earth science teacher emphasizes, "Class, listen carefully now, because the idea of volcanism is important to the way landforms are created."

Applying an Understanding of Perception in Your Classroom

4. Check to be certain that students are perceiving your examples accurately.
   - A geography teacher, when teaching about landforms, shows her class a series of colored slides. After displaying each one, she asks students to describe the slide before she moves on to the next.

Using Organization in Your Classroom

5. Carefully organize the information you present to your students.
   - A biology teacher displays an outline of the topics covered to that point in the unit and then highlights the topics to be covered in the current day's lesson.
   - A math teacher presents a flowchart with a series of questions students are encouraged to ask themselves as they solve word problems. She then models the process, using the flowchart as a guide.

Using Imagery in Your Classroom

6. Whenever possible, encourage students to form images of the topics they study.
   - A geography teacher encourages her students to visualize flat parallel lines on the globe as they think about latitude and vertical lines coming together at the North and South Poles as they think about longitude.
   - A language arts teacher asks students to imagine the appearance of the characters in the books they read. She asks them to describe the characters in detail, including their facial features, the way they wear their hair, how they're dressed, and how they act.

Applying Elaboration in Your Classroom

7. Relate new information to previously learned material.
   - A health teacher states, "We've been studying the digestive system. We're turning now to the circulatory system. As we study the circulatory system, think about aspects of it that are similar to or different from the digestive system."
   - An art teacher begins, "Color is one way to give pictures depth. Perspective is another. As we study perspective, keep in mind how both it and color interact to give the perception of depth."

8. Ask questions requiring students to make comparisons, find relationships, and search for patterns.
   - A science teacher asks, "We've just examined physical changes. How does this compare with chemical changes? Can you give me an example of each?"
   - A high school English class studying Shakespeare is asked, "How are the plot and the setting related in Macbeth?"
   - A math teacher asks, "Why are the units for volume cubic centimeters, whereas the units for area are square centimeters?"

9. Review at the beginning and end of each class period.
   - A class studying American literature is asked, "We started our discussion of Hemingway's *The Sun Also Rises* yesterday. What were the key ideas we discussed?"
   - A math teacher summarizes by saying, "Our class period is nearly over, so let's review what we've learned today. We know some new formulas. Who can tell me how we would find the volume of this box?"

10. Ask for and use examples to illustrate abstract ideas.
    - A third-grade teacher demonstrates that heat causes expansion by placing a balloon-covered soft drink bottle in a pot of hot water. He supplements the demonstration with a drawing simulating the spacing and motion of the air molecules.
    - A junior high English teacher dealing with the concept of internal conflict in literature displays the following on the overhead: "Joanne didn't know what to do. She was looking forward to the class trip, but if she went, she wouldn't be able to take the scholarship-qualifying test."

Applying an Understanding of Activity in Your Classroom

11. Actively involve students in the learning process.
    - When discussing word problems, a math teacher asks individual students to explain how they arrived at their solutions and why they chose a particular process.
    - A history teacher begins new topics with a description of a historical event and asks students why they think the event occurred. The unit is then developed around the students' search for an explanation.

Forgetting

No discussion of memory would be complete without considering **forgetting**, which is *the loss of, or inability to retrieve, information from memory*. Forgetting is both a very real part of people's everyday lives ("Now, where did I put those car keys?") and an important factor in school learning.

Let's look again at the information processing model first presented in Figure 7.2. There you see that information can be lost from the memory stores in different ways. If a person doesn't quickly attend to the information in sensory memory, it is lost and cannot be retrieved. Information can be retained in working memory if it is rehearsed; otherwise, it is also lost and can't be recovered. In the case of long-term memory, however, information has been encoded. Why can't the learner find it or use it?

Forgetting as Interference. One view of forgetting uses the concept of **interference**, which is *the loss of information because something else learned either before or after detracts from the learning* (M. Anderson & Neely, 1996; Schunk, 1996). When we examine topics commonly taught in schools, we can see how interference occurs. For example, students learn that possessives are formed by adding an apostrophe *s* to singular nouns. They also study plural possessives and contractions, and they find that the apostrophe is used differently; it comes after the *s* in some cases, it appears before the *s* in the case of plural nouns such as *women* and *children*, and it comes between letters in the case of contractions. Students' understanding of plural possessives and contractions can interfere with their understanding of singular possessives and vice versa.

Interference increases when breadth of content coverage is emphasized over understanding in depth—a common problem in today's schools (Dempster & Corkill, 1999). Textbooks that include a myriad of topics pose particular problems for learners attempting to relate and differentiate ideas.

One solution to the problem of interference is instruction that emphasizes explicit relationships between ideas using review and comparison. After a new topic is introduced, teachers should compare it with closely related information that students have already studied, identifying easily confused similarities. Doing so elaborates on the original schema, reducing interference.

A second solution is to teach closely related ideas together—for example, adjective and adverb phrases, longitude and latitude, and adding and subtracting fractions with similar and different denominators (Hamilton, 1997). As teachers present related ideas together, they need to highlight relationships for students, emphasize differences, and identify areas that are easily confused.

Forgetting as Retrieval Failure. A second view of forgetting ties it to individuals' inability to retrieve information from long-term memory.

> This test is a bear. Maybe I should have studied more last night. Oh, well, almost done.
>   Now for the fill-in-the-blanks section. First question: Landing site for the Allied invasion of France? I know that. I remember reading it in the text and seeing it in my notes.
>   Paris? No, that's inland. We talked about Calais. No, that was a diversion to trick Germany. . . . I know that I know it. . . . Why can't I think of the name?

Unless learners can **retrieve** information—*pull it from long-term memory into working memory again for further processing*—it's useless. It's like putting information into a file folder and then trying to figure out where the folder is stored; the information is there but can't be found. Many researchers believe that learners don't literally "lose" information when they forget; rather, they can't retrieve it (Ashcraft, 1989).

7.19 ▬
In which case would interference be most likely to occur: when studying similes and metaphors, or when studying figures of speech and parts of speech? Explain.

7.20

Explain why encoding specificity might be harmful in classroom learning. What can teachers do to help learners cope with its effects?

The Role of Context in Retrieval.   You saw earlier that context is important in acquiring procedural knowledge, and it is also important for encoding and retrieval. For instance, you know a person at work or school, but you can't remember her name when you see her at a party. Her name is stored in your long-term memory, but you can't put your mental "finger" on it. Researchers call this the "tip-of-the-tongue" phenomenon (R. Brown & McNeill, 1966; Burke, MacKay, Worthley, & Wade, 1991), and it is often related to context; the party is a different context from the one in which her name was encoded. *This contextual influence on retrieval* is sometimes called the **encoding specificity hypothesis** (Tulving, 1979).

David Shelton capitalized on the impact of context when he presented his information about Pluto in different ways. He didn't merely say that the first eight planets had one origin and that Pluto had another. Instead, he presented the information in the context of the planets' orbital planes, their direction of revolution, and the origin of the solar system. The more detailed and interconnected knowledge is in long-term memory, the easier it is to retrieve (Nutthal, 1999).

Meaningfulness is the key to retrieval. By encouraging his students to learn and connect the new information in a variety of ways, David increased the likelihood that it would be meaningful, which increased the chance of later retrieval (Martin, 1993).

Metacognition: Knowledge and Control of Cognitive Processes

We have now examined the first two parts of the information processing model. We've studied the memory stores—*sensory memory, working memory,* and *long-term memory*—and the cognitive processes—*attention, perception, rehearsal, encoding,* and *retrieval*—that move information from one store to the next.

The cognitive processes are not simple mechanisms that merely turn on or off, however. To be useful, they must be integrated so they can be used strategically. Metacognition serves this function. (We examine the relationships between learner motivation, metacognition, and self-regulation in depth in Chapter 10.)

Earlier in the chapter, we said **metacognition** is *knowing about and having control over our cognitive processes.* The metacognitive components of the information processing model are illustrated in Figure 7.10.

Metacognition operates from the beginning of the learning process, starting with attention. If you choose to sit near the front of the class so you don't drift off, for example, you are demonstrating **meta-attention**, which is *knowledge of and control over attention.* You *know about* your attention, and you exercise *control over it,* by moving to the front of the room.

Metacognition can play a role in perception as well. Being aware of the possibility of misperceiving something and consciously reserving judgment until you have additional information demonstrate awareness of and control over perception.

Metacognition also helps regulate the flow of information through working memory. For example, we've all been in situations where we've had to remember a phone number. If we're going to dial the number immediately, we simply rehearse; if we're going to call later, we'll probably write the number down. Each decision is strategic, influenced by our goal and the awareness and control over our memories. This is an example of **metamemory**, which is *knowledge of and control over our memory strategies* (Schraw & Moshman, 1995). Alfredo, in David's lesson, demonstrated metamemory when he said, "Wait, Mr. Shelton, you're going too fast. I'm getting lost. What is this about supporting the theory?"

Figure 7.10

Metacognition in the information processing model

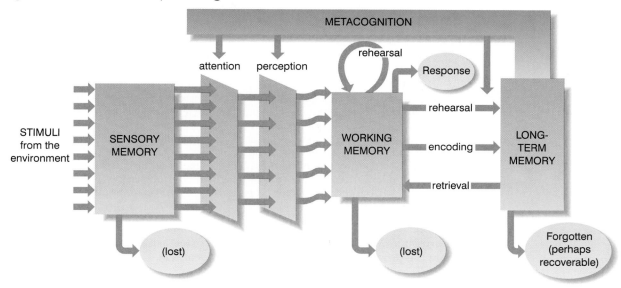

He was aware that he was missing some of the information, and he demonstrated control over his memory by asking David to slow down and explain the information about Pluto. The ability to monitor the processing of information in working memory is crucial because of its limited capacity (Wilson & Swanson, 1999).

Finally, metacognition involves awareness and control of long-term memory and encoding. For example, knowing that you tend to associate items of information in long-term memory rather than store them in isolation can help you consciously look for relationships in the topics you study. Being aware of the way you store information and making a conscious effort to look for relationships make up another form of metacognition.

The Development of Metacognition

As students develop their metacognitive abilities, they learn to effectively use **strategies**— *plans for accomplishing learning goals* (Berk, 1997). For instance, summarizing would be an effective strategy for increasing comprehension of a written passage, or a mnemonic could be a strategy to remember lists of words such as the names of the Great Lakes.

Young learners are often passive; they don't realize that they can influence the learning process. As they develop, however, they acquire an increasing number of strategies, their strategies become more efficient, and their strategies are used more selectively (Berk, 1997).

Meta-Attention: Development of Attention Strategies.   As mentioned, meta-attention is knowledge of and control over attention. Research indicates that older children are more aware of the role of attention in learning than their younger counterparts, are better at directing their attention toward important information in a learning task, and are better at ignoring distracting or irrelevant stimuli (Berk, 1997).

Although meta-attention develops naturally during the school years, efforts by teachers can enhance it.

> Connie Mahera began working with her first graders by saying, "We know how important it is to pay attention." She then modeled attention by focusing on a sample seat work assignment, working carefully, and keeping her eyes on the paper.
>
> Then she had Mrs. Morton, her parent volunteer, talk, and she listened intently to Mrs. Morton, maintaining eye contact and keeping her hands and body still. She next modeled inattention in both an interactive and a seat work situation.
>
> She then asked, "Now, am I paying attention?" as she modeled inattention to seat work by gazing out the window and playing with objects on her desk. She demonstrated several more examples, had the students classify them as attention or inattention, and then told the students, "I am going to click the cricket, and if you're paying attention each time I click it, make an X in a box." She showed students a sheet of paper with several boxes drawn on it and passed each student a sheet. She went on, "Each time you hear a click, put an X in the next box if you're paying attention."
>
> The next morning and for several consecutive mornings, Connie demonstrated and had students demonstrate attentive and inattentive behaviors as part of the class routine. As time went on, students' attention improved markedly. (based on Hallahan et al., 1983).

Young children often don't realize that they're inattentive, and this awareness needs to be developed. With time and teacher assistance, meta-attention increases, and students can begin the process of becoming self-regulated learners.

Metamemory: Development of Memory Strategies.   An 8-year-old described her strategy for remembering a telephone number:

> Say the number is 663-8854. Then what I'd do is say that my number is 663, so I won't have to remember that really. And then I would think now I've got to remember 88. Now I'm eight years old, so I can remember, say my age two times. Then I say how old my brother is, and how old he was last year. And that's how I'd usually remember that phone number. [Interviewer: Is that how you would most often remember a phone number?] Well, usually I write it down. (Kreutzer, Leonard, & Flavell, 1975, p. 11)

Researchers have found developmental differences in children's use of metamemory strategies. This 8-year-old used a sophisticated strategy, linking the numbers to information that was already encoded in her memory.

Older children and adults are much better than young children at using strategies for remembering information (Short, Schatschneider, & Friebert, 1993). For example, nursery school students given a list of objects to memorize in order didn't use rehearsal as a strategy. Fourth graders, in contrast, both rehearsed aloud and anticipated succeeding items by naming them before they were shown by the experimenter (Flavell, Friedrichs, & Hoyt, 1970). Similar patterns have been found with categorizing and imagery as strategies; kindergartners don't use them, whereas fourth graders can and do (Berk, 1997).

Besides using different and more effective strategies, older learners are more aware of their memory limitations (Everson & Tobias, 1998; Sternberg, 1998b). For example, when asked to predict how many objects, such as a shoe or ball, they could remember from a list, nursery school students predicted 7; when tested, they remembered fewer than 4 (Flavell et al., 1970). Adults given the same task predicted an average of 5.9 and actually remembered 5.5 (Yussen & Levy, 1975). These examples illustrate differences in memory capacities as well as students' awareness of them.

The example with Connie Mahera and her first graders demonstrated how instruction can help children develop their meta-attention. Instruction can also help students

---

7.21 ▬

Most college and university students take notes as a strategy. Does note taking better illustrate meta-attention or metamemory? Explain.

improve in the area of metamemory, by making them aware of their memory capacities and the importance of matching strategies to task demands. For routine tasks, such as remembering a class assignment, a simple strategy like writing it down is enough. For more complex tasks, like understanding written material, more sophisticated strategies such as summarizing or self-questioning are required. The goal for teachers at all levels should be the development of students who take responsibility for their own learning.

Classroom Connections

Applying an Understanding of Interference in Your Classroom

1. Teach closely related ideas together, stressing similarities and differences.
   - A life science teacher combines the topics of reptiles and amphibians in the same unit, stressing the features that make them different.

2. Carefully review and compare closely related topics after they're covered.
   - A teacher presenting a unit on verbals states, "We've finished our discussion of participles now. Yesterday, we covered gerunds. Tell me the key difference between the two, and give us an example of each."

Applying an Understanding of Retrieval in Your Classroom

3. Present information in enriched contexts.
   - A life science teacher begins a unit on arteries and veins by saying, "We've all heard of hardening of the arteries, but we haven't heard of 'hardening of the veins.' Why not? Are we using the term *artery* to mean both, or is there a difference? Why is hardening of the arteries bad for people? I'm going to write these questions down so that we keep them in mind as we study arteries, veins, and capillaries."

Applying an Understanding of Metacognition in Your Classroom

4. Consciously teach students about the role of attention in learning.

   - A fourth-grade teacher plays an attention game with his students. During a lesson, he holds up a card with the sentence "If you're paying attention, raise your hand." He then acknowledges those who are and encourages them to share their strategies for maintaining attention during class.
   - A social studies teacher tries to teach attention-monitoring skills by saying, "Suppose you're reading, and the book states that there are three important differences between capitalism and socialism. What should you do?"

5. Teach students the importance of listening carefully.
   - To encourage students to listen to each other, a middle school teacher periodically has the class write down what a student has just said in answering a question. She has them monitor their listening and try to continually improve.

6. Model metacognitive abilities for your students.
   - A ninth-grade economics teacher says, "Whenever I read something new, I always ask myself, 'How does this relate to what I've been studying?' For example, how is the liberal economic agenda different from the conservative economic agenda?"
   - A chemistry teacher, in trying to help his students remember the symbols for elements in the periodic table, asks students to volunteer any mnemonic devices and images they use.

Impact of Diversity on Information Processing

As a warm-up activity for his world geography class, Mike Havland asked his students to turn to page 267 of their text, on which was a "modern" map of Europe.

As Carl looked at the map, he thought it looked familiar. "Yeah," he thought, "there's England, France, Germany, and Russia. Hey, there's Yugoslavia. That's where Goran's grandparents came from."

Next to him, Celeena, whose father was a career military man with whom she had traveled all over Europe, was also looking at the map, but with a look of disbelief. "How old is this book?" she thought. "Look at Yugoslavia. It doesn't exist anymore. It's been torn apart. Hmm, where's Barcelona? . . . Oh yeah. Down there on the coast of Spain. We saw it when we went to the Olympics several years ago."

After a few minutes, Mike began. "Okay, everyone. It's important to have some idea of the geography of Europe, because the geography reflects an important idea that we'll return to again and again." With that, he wrote on the chalkboard: "The history of Europe reflects the tension between nationalism and intercountry cooperation like the European Common Market."

He continued by saying, "As you've already noticed, the face of Europe is continually changing, reflecting the ebbs and flows of nationalistic fervor and efforts to reduce cultural and trade barriers."

As he was talking, he noticed a few nods but more blank looks. Celeena sat knowingly, while Carl thought, "What's he talking about? nationalism? cultural and trade barriers? What is this?"

Not knowing what to do about the blank looks, Mike continued with his planned lecture.

Teachers know that background knowledge is a powerful influence on perception and encoding. Students come to class with widely varying experiences, and dealing with this diversity is one of the biggest challenges facing all teachers (Veenman, 1984).

Diversity and Perception

Background knowledge resulting from experience strongly influences perception. As you saw in Mike's lesson, what students perceive from something complex, such as a map, largely depends on what they already know. This notion has been verified in areas as varied as chess, reading, math, and physics (Glover, Ronning, & Bruning, 1990).

Experience affects both what and how much students learn. For example, one student seeing a movie on the Vietnam conflict interprets the war as an effort to stop the spread of communism, whereas another perceives it as the imposition of American values on a distant country. When Carl viewed the map of Europe, he perceived an accurate representation; when Celeena viewed it, she perceived it as an antiquated document. Learners' schemas influence the way they perceive information.

Diversity, Encoding, and Retrieval

Just as learners' background knowledge influences their perception, it also influences how effectively they encode new information. Celeena, for example, has a richer geography background than Carl. As a result, the statement "The history of Europe reflects the tension between nationalism and intercountry cooperation" was meaningful to her, whereas it meant little to Carl; he had little in his background to which ideas such as "nationalism" and "intercountry cooperation" could be linked.

We've all been in situations when a presentation or passage in a book doesn't make sense, and we've all been in conversations in which we're not connecting with the other

7.22 ■

Consider the following two statements: "Many students have less well-developed schemas than other students" and "Many students have different schemas than other students." On the basis of the information in this section, which is the more accurate statement? Explain.

The diverse experiential backgrounds of students can be used to enrich the learning experiences of all students.

person. In each case, we may lack the background to which new information can be linked, so meaningful encoding doesn't occur.

Instructional Adaptations for Background Diversity

What can teachers do when lack of encoding happens in the classroom? Research suggests several strategies (Brenner et al. 1997; Nuthall, 1999):

- Begin lessons by asking students what they know about the topic you're planning to teach.
- Provide background experiences with rich examples and representations of the content you're teaching.
- Use open-ended questions to assess student perceptions of your examples and representations.
- Use the experiences of students in the class to augment the backgrounds of those lacking the experiences.

For instance, it would have been easy for Mike to say, "Celeena, you lived in Europe. What do people in Europe say about the conflict in the former Yugoslavia?" Also, because nationalism was an organizing idea for much of what followed, Mike could have asked, "What does nationalism mean? Give an example of strong and weak nationalism." If students couldn't respond, he should have altered his plans to focus on the concept, laying the groundwork for subsequent learning. For example, he could have used the school as context for his discussion of nationalism by describing school spirit, pride in the school, and the school's traditions as analogies for the feelings of nationalism in European countries. The analogies would make the notion of nationalism more meaningful for students, and subsequent encoding and retrieval would be improved (Zook, 1991). The ability to adapt lessons in this way is one characteristic of teaching expertise.

Classroom Connections

Capitalizing on Diversity in Your Classroom

1. Assess students' backgrounds before lessons.
   - A second-grade teacher begins a unit on communities by requesting, "Tell us what you know about the community we live in." He encourages a number of students to respond so that he can get an accurate idea of what students know.
   - An art teacher begins a unit on perspective by asking students to sketch a three-dimensional scene. He has students put their names on the back of the sketches and then discusses the sketches during the following class period.

2. Use open-ended questioning to assess students' perceptions.
   - A fourth-grade teacher begins a unit on the North and South before the Civil War by preparing a matrix comparing the economy, geography, and climate of the North and South. He displays the matrix and says, "Now, tell us what you see in the first column on the chart. . . . Anything you notice or observe there?"
   - An English teacher puts a sonnet on the overhead and says, "Someone describe what's on the overhead." In the discussion that follows, he relates characteristics of sonnets to the students' observations.

3. Have students with different backgrounds share their experiences and ideas.
   - A sixth-grade teacher beginning a study of plants says to a student whose parents own a greenhouse, "Melinda, you've had some interesting experiences working with plants and crops. Tell us about the kinds of plants your parents grow, what they're used for, and anything else about plants you think might be interesting."

4. Provide concrete experiences to develop learners' background knowledge.
   - As an introduction to the study of refraction, a science teacher has students put coins in opaque dishes and then back up until they can't see the coins. She then has a partner pour water into the dish until the coin becomes visible. Finally, she shows a model illustrating how the light rays are bent when they enter and leave the water.
   - Before beginning a unit on geometric shapes, a kindergarten teacher has his students draw, color, and cut out squares, triangles, rectangles, and circles. He then has students identify examples of the shapes around the classroom.

Putting Information Processing Into Perspective

Information processing was the most influential cognitive theory of learning in the 20th century (Mayer, 1996). It offered a workable alternative to behaviorism and provided both teachers and researchers with useful concepts that helped them better understand learning.

Like virtually all theories, however, information processing has its critics (Derry, 1992; Mayer, 1996). For example, learners enter our classrooms with a variety of emotions, beliefs, expectations, and personal goals, all of which influence learning. Information processing has been criticized for ignoring these factors.

In addition, critics argue that information processing fails to take into account the social context in which learning occurs, tacitly assuming that learning is learning, no matter where it occurs. Research indicates, however, that the social environment strongly affects what is learned and how it transfers to other settings (Greeno et al. 1996).

Finally, critics contend that information processing doesn't adequately emphasize the extent to which learners actively construct their own understanding (Derry, 1992). (In the next section we examine constructivism, a cognitive learning theory that addresses this criticism.)

On the other hand, most cognitive descriptions of learning—including descriptions that endorse the principle that learners construct understanding—accept the architecture of information processing (Mayer, 1998). These descriptions include the idea of a human sensory memory, a limited-capacity working memory, a long-term memory, cognitive processes that move the information from one store to the other, and the regulatory mechanisms of metacognition (Metcalfe, 1996; Pashler & Carrier, 1996; Sternberg, 1998a).

Keep these perspectives in mind as you read the following discussion of constructivism.

Constructivism

Jenny Newhall, a fourth-grade teacher, wanted her 29 students to develop their math problem-solving skills, learn to work collaboratively in groups, and learn that a balance beam balances when the weight times the distance on one side equals the weight times the distance on the other. She began the lesson by giving each group of students a balance beam and directing them to place weights on it, as shown in the following drawing:

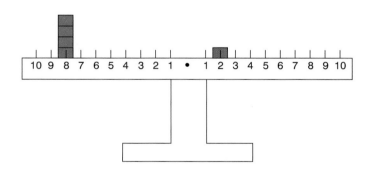

The students' task was to make the beam balance by adding more weights, without moving any of the existing weights. To encourage individual problem solving, she first asked each student to write down a possible solution. Then the individuals would share their solutions with their teammates, and the groups would discuss the validity of each solution, deciding which solution to try first.

One of the groups—Molly, Suzie, Tad, and Drexel—was explaining their strategies:

"I think we should put 3 on 10, because 4 and 8 is the same as 32—like 32 on one side. And since we only have 2 on the other side, we need to make them equal. So 3 on 10 would equal 30 and so we'd have 32 on both sides," Molly offered first.

"I did a short one," Drexel added. "4 times 8 is 32 and 1 times 2 is 2. 6 times 5 is 30 and 30 plus 2 is 32."

Suzie then offered hers, "There are 4 on the 8 and 1 on the 2. I want to put 3 on the 10 so there will be 4 on each side."

As Jenny joined the group, she listened to the different solutions and asked Tad if he had a solution to add. When he hesitated, she asked if he wanted to think about the ones already offered.

Tad replied, "These three, I guess."

Jenny then encouraged each of them to explain and defend their solutions and decide which they wanted to try first on the balance beam.

Suzie began by asserting, "See, if 4 is on each side, that'll make 8, which is even and it'll even out."

"Drexel's will work, too," Molly interjected. "Let's try it second," (after the 3 on the 10), "'cause we may not be able to fit five weights on the balance . . . Do you agree? . . . Yes or no? . . . Okay? . . . Tad, what's your prediction?"

"I never had time to write it," Tad replied, shrugging.

Suzie suggested an alternate solution. "Put 2 weights on the 10 and 1 on the 6."

The group considered this suggestion until Jenny returned to the group and asked, "Why did you decide to try the 3 on 10 as your first choice?"

"'Cause it would make 4 here and 4 there," Suzie offered.

"Also, if you times that, it'll be 32, and it'll also equal 32 on this side. So it'll make it equal. 4 times 8 is 32 and 3 times 10 is 30 plus two is 32," Molly added.

"Your second choice was 5 on 6?" Jenny interjected.

"I think we should make it third, 'cause it may not work [physically], and mine may," Molly continued.

"Suzie, why do you think yours should be second?" Jenny asked.

"'Cause 5 tiles won't fit on there."

"Molly, why do you think 5 on 6 should still be second?" Jenny asked.

"Because I think it's the second best that will work."

"Why?" Jenny probed.

"What was yours again, Suzie?" Jenny asked.

"Put 2 on 10 and 1 on 6."

"See, 2 on 10 is 20, and 1 on 6 will only make it 26," Molly countered.

Jenny asked, "When you do the multiplying, they need to be the same on both sides? Is that what you're telling me? And you think that what you have down for the third one is not going to be heavy enough, and so that's why you want Drexel's idea to be second? Well, you guys need to decide that. Talk it over and decide."

As Jenny circulated around the room, the group discussed the different options.

When Jenny returned, Suzie volunteered, "We've decided to keep the same order" (to try the 6 on 5 solution second).

"What made you decide to keep it as it is?" Jenny asked.

"Because mine. . . . It kind of sunk in what she said when we add them up—it won't be even. It kind of sunk in."

"And that was a good compromise. She gave her point of view and you could see the rationality of it," Jenny offered.

They then add 3 to the 10 spot and wait for the balance to stop jiggling.

"That one has more weight," Tad asserted as the beam tipped to the side where they added weights.

After a few moments, it balanced, and Suzie cried out, "It's perfect! It works!"

Jenny then called the whole class together to discuss the solutions different groups formed. Allison suggested the 3 on 10 strategy. Jenny asked for a volunteer to draw and explain this solution and Danielle—another of the students in the class—drew the following diagram on the chalkboard:

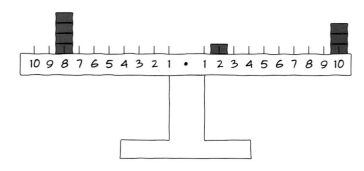

"Danielle, can you explain why that works?" Jenny asked.

"Because there are 4 tiles on each side and so that makes it equal."

Paraphrasing, Jenny added, "So there are 4 tiles on this side and 4 on the other, and that made it work. Does anyone else have another explanation why that worked? Can someone tell us why that works in a different way? Mavrin? Can you go up to the board and explain it a different way? Can you write something to show us why it works?"

Mavrin then wrote the following under the balance beam on the board:

$$8 \times 4 = 32 \;=\; (10 \times 3) + 2 = 32$$

"Do you see what he's done?" Jenny asked. "He has a number sentence on both sides. Over on this side, he came up with 8 times 4, which is 32. When he started out with just a 2 over here, what do you think Mavrin thought to himself to figure this problem out? Blair?"

"He needed something to add to 2 to make it 32."

"And since we already have 2, now he needs something to add up to . . . Blair?"

"30."

"And that's why he had to put the 3 on the 10," Jenny added. "Now, Becky, you had a different solution. Would you go up and do the one you had?"

Becky erased Mavrin's answer and put the following on the board:

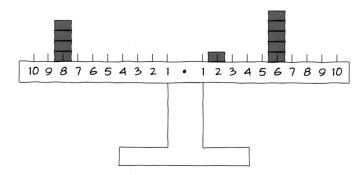

"Now, can you write a number sentence underneath to show us how that works?" Jenny encouraged. After Becky wrote a number equation on the board, Jenny explained Becky's solution, referring to both the balance beam on the board and the number sentence underneath it. She then gave the groups the following problem to solve:

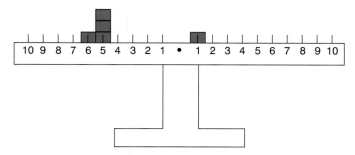

Again, Jenny encouraged students in each group to come up with their own individual solutions. When Jenny called the class back together, she asked Suzie to share her answer. Suzie drew the following on the chalkboard:

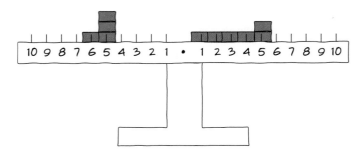

With Jenny's help, Suzie wrote the following number sentence on the board:

$$(3 \times 5) + 6 = 21 = 1 + 2 + 3 + 4 + 5 + 5$$

"Add that up and see what you get," Jenny directed Suzie. "You boys and girls at your seats could be adding this up to see if it comes up to 21."

Suzie concluded that the numbers added up to 22, and Jenny responded, "Does anyone else have a different answer?" The lesson continued with other students offering and explaining additional possible solutions.

After the lesson, we interviewed Molly, Suzie, Tad, and Drexel to determine their understanding of balance beam problems. Molly and Drexel thoroughly understood the principle, but Tad and Suzie initially did not. As the interview progressed, both Suzie and Tad learned to solve balance beam problems, but this occurred only after additional discussion and experimentation with the balance beam.

Emerging Role of Constructivism in Education

You first encountered the idea of knowledge construction in Chapter 2, when you saw that, instead of recording understanding delivered from others, learners "construct" their understanding of the topics they study. We now consider this view of learning in more detail.

The idea that learners construct understanding is now widely accepted (Bruning et al., 1999; Lambert & McCombs, 1998; Mayer, 1998; Phye, 1997). For example, instruction in writing (McCarthy, 1994), math (National Council of Teachers of Mathematics, 1989), science (American Association for the Advancement of Science, 1993), and early childhood education (Pfannenstiel & Schattgen, 1997) are increasingly grounded in constructivist views of learning, as are modern K–12 textbooks (e.g., Boehm, Armstrong, & Hunkins, 1998). The influence of constructivism can be seen across the school curriculum.

Different Views of Constructivism

As with cognitive learning theory in general, there is no single, unified view of constructivism (Bruning et al., 1999; Greeno et al., 1996). Constructivists disagree on the nature of knowledge and the importance of different elements in the knowledge construction process, particularly social interaction. We'll look at two positions.

The first, based largely on Piaget's work, is called **cognitive constructivism**, which *focuses on individual, internal constructions of knowledge* (Cobb, 1994; Greeno et al., 1996). In this view, social interaction is important, but only as a catalyst for individual cognitive conflict (Fowler, 1994). When one child suggests an idea that causes disequilibrium in another, for example, the second child resolves the disequilibrium by individually constructing, or reconstructing, his or her understanding. As an example, let's look at some dialogue between two children on a playground:

Devon:	Look at the bugs. (Holding a beetle between his fingers and pointing at a spider.)
Gino:	Yech . . . Put that thing down. Besides, that's not a bug. It's a spider. (Gesturing to the spider.)
Devon:	What do you mean? A bug is a bug. They look the same.
Gino:	Nope. Bugs have six legs. See. (Touching the legs of the beetle.) He has eight legs. . . . Look. (Pointing to the spider.)
Devon:	So, . . . bugs . . . have . . . six legs, and spiders have eight.

Cognitive constructivists would interpret this episode by saying that Devon's equilibrium was disrupted by the discussion since he saw evidence that the beetle and spider were different, and—individually—he resolved the problem by reconstructing his thinking to accommodate the evidence.

Cognitive constructivists emphasize learning activities that are child-centered and discovery-oriented. For instance, they would argue that children learn math facts more effectively if they discover these facts based on what they already know, rather than have them presented by a teacher or other expert (Pressley, Harris, & Marks, 1992).

Cognitive constructivism poses dilemmas for educators. One interpretation of Piaget's work is that it "fundamentally distrusted all attempts to instruct directly" (Resnick & Klopfer, 1989, p. 3). A second interpretation suggests that teacher–student interaction is important for learner growth, but that teachers need to guard against imposing their thoughts and values on developing learners (DeVries, 1997). Both minimize the role of the teacher in directly instructing students. So, other than providing materials and a supportive learning environment, what is the teacher's role in this process? This question hasn't been satisfactorily answered for classroom teachers (Airasian & Walsh, 1997; Greeno et al., 1996).

A second position, strongly influenced by Vygotsky's (1978) work, is called **social constructivism**, which *suggests that knowledge exists in a social context and is initially shared with others instead of being represented solely in the mind of an individual* (Bruning et al., 1999; Cole, 1991; Turner, 1995).

According to social constructivists, the *process* of sharing results in learners refining their own ideas and helping shape the ideas of others (Greeno et al., 1996). For example, social constructivists, instead of concluding that Devon individually reconstructed his

Social interaction in small-group work provides opportunities for students to refine their own ideas as they shape the ideas of others.

understanding of insects and spiders in an effort to re-establish equilibrium, would argue that Devon's understanding was increased as a direct result of the exchange with Gino. They would also assert that the dialogue between the two—in and of itself—played an important role in helping Devon arrive at a clearer understanding of insects and spiders.

This interpretation has important implications for instruction and helps resolve the cognitive constructivists' dilemma. It "does not suggest that educators get out of the way so children can do their natural work, as Piagetian theory often seemed to imply" (Resnick & Klopfer, 1989, p. 4). Unlike the Piagetian-based downplaying of the role of the social environment, social constructivism highlights that role and suggests that teachers consider all the traditional questions of teaching: how to organize and implement learning activities, how to motivate students, and how to assess learning. It answers these questions, however, with a focus on students' own constructions of understanding within a community of learners (Greeno et al., 1996; Shuell, 1996).

Characteristics of Constructivism

Despite their differences, most constructivists agree on four characteristics that influence learning, as outlined in Figure 7.11 (Bruning et al., 1999; Mayer, 1996).

Learners Construct Understanding

Learners are not tape recorders; they don't record and store in memory an exact copy of what they hear or read. Rather, they interpret stimuli on the basis of what they already know, and they construct understandings that make sense to them. This is the basic principle of constructivism. Brophy (1992) summarizes this position,

> Current research, while building on the findings indicating the vital role teachers play in stimulating student learning, also focuses on the role of the student. It recognizes that students do not passively receive or copy input from teachers, but instead actively mediate it by trying to make sense of it and to relate it to what they already know (or think they know) about the topic. Thus, students develop new knowledge through the process of active construction (p. 5).

We saw the process of "knowledge construction" in Jenny's students. Suzie and Tad struggled with the idea that length times weight on one side of the fulcrum equals length times weight on the other. Suzie, especially, characterized this struggle. At first she believed that four weights on each side were all that were needed to balance the beam. Then she reconsidered, commenting, "It kind of sunk in what she [Molly] said when we add them up—it won't be even." But this understanding remained fragile, and she rejected it when the balance didn't work with the "6 on 5" solution. In spite of repeated explanations and much discussion, she didn't understand the principle until she participated in the interview after the lesson.

7.23 ■

What concept from Piaget's theory best illustrates Suzie's thinking when she concluded that to balance the beam the number of weights on each side of the balance needed to be equal?

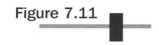

Figure 7.11

Characteristics of constructivism

- Learners construct their own understanding.
- New learning depends on current understanding.
- Learning is facilitated by social interaction.
- Meaningful learning occurs within authentic learning tasks.

We see from the students' comments that they didn't listen to others' explanations and record understanding. Rather, they conducted experiments, discussed the problem, and finally constructed their own meaning.

New Learning Depends on Current Understanding

We described the role of current understanding (background knowledge) when we discussed the importance of making information meaningful in information processing. Constructivists go even farther, emphasizing that new learning is interpreted in the immediate context of current understanding; it isn't first learned as isolated information, which is later connected to existing knowledge.

This principle was illustrated in David's lesson. Juan had more background knowledge than did Randy, so David's model, transparency, and matrix were more meaningful to him. He was able to learn more in the lesson.

7.24 ▬
Research indicates that learners are often very reluctant to modify their existing understanding of the way the world works. Using Piaget's work as a basis, explain this reluctance.

Learning Is Facilitated by Social Interaction

Jenny's lesson also underscores the importance of social interaction in learning. Discussion in the group allowed Molly and Drexel to share their correct solutions and provided opportunities for Suzie to share hers. This resulted in continued dialogue that helped both Suzie and Tad move in the direction of a clearer understanding. Social interaction provides opportunities for students to articulate their own ideas, compare them to others, and change them if necessary (Mason, 1998; Olsen, 1999).

To emphasize the importance of social interaction, researchers have called for the creation of "communities of learners" within classrooms (A. Brown & Campione, 1994). Learning communities encourage students to take responsibility for their own learning through cooperative ventures. Both Jenny and David attempted to create learning communities by forming groups that were responsible for problem solving. As students worked on problems, both teachers facilitated the process by offering only enough guidance to ensure they were making progress and by encouraging students to listen to the solutions of their peers.

Meaningful Learning Occurs Within Authentic Learning Tasks

Think about Jenny's lesson again. She used concrete materials to help students advance their current understanding of balance beams. The lesson used an **authentic task**, which is *a classroom learning activity that requires understanding similar to understanding that would be used in the world outside the classroom.* Her students experimented on their own to investigate how their ideas would work in the real world.

Authentic tasks simulate real-world problem situations and provide students with practice in thinking in realistic, lifelike situations (Needels & Knapp, 1994). Teachers provide this practice by posing problems that are embedded in realistic situations. Authentic situations also increase students' motivation to learn, and as their motivation increases, so does further learning.

Implications of Constructivism for Teaching

Understanding that learners construct—instead of record—understanding has important implications for the way we teach. In this section, we outline four of them. As teachers, we should:

Social interaction embedded within authentic learning tasks provides opportunities for learners to share ideas and analyze and refine their own thinking.

▌ Provide learners with a variety of examples and representations of content.
▌ Promote high levels of interaction in our teaching.
▌ Connect content to the real world.
▌ Be skeptical about the effectiveness of verbal explanations.

Provide a Variety of Examples

The way topics are represented for learners is essential for constructing understanding. The importance of examples as content representations is difficult to overstate; examples are what learners use to construct their understanding (Cassady, 1999; Spiro, Feltovich, Jacobson, & Coulson, 1992). One of the most basic questions teachers can ask when attempting to teach based on constructivist views of learning is, *"What can I show the students or have them do that will illustrate this topic?"* It is perhaps the most fundamental planning question that teachers can ask. David showed his students his demonstration, model, transparency, and the matrix, which included a variety of information about the planets. Similarly, Jenny's students had different balance beam problems that they used to construct understanding of the principle.

Table 7.5 includes some additional illustrations of different ways teachers that you've studied in this text have represented their topics.

Promote High Levels of Interaction

Constructivists generally agree that social interaction facilitates learning, and we saw the role of interaction in Jenny's lesson. In spite of seeing at least three different solutions, Suzie remained uncertain about the principle until the interview after the lesson, illustrating that examples and other representations, alone, won't necessarily result in learning. Constructing understanding requires a *combination* of knowledge representations *and*

Table 7.5

Teachers' representations of content

Teacher and Chapter	Goal	Representations
Jan Davis Chapter 1	Students will understand decimals	12-ounce soft drink can 16-ounce bottle Liter bottle 6-pack of soft drinks 12-pack of soft drinks 24-can pack
Karen Johnson Chapter 2	Students will understand density	Cotton balls in drink cup Wooden cubes Water and vegetable oil Population density Screen door screen
Jenny Newhall Chapter 2	Students will understand that air takes up space	Demonstration with drinking glass and paper towel Releasing air bubble Hands-on experiences
Diane Smith Chapter 4	For students to understand comparative and superlative adjectives	Three pencils of different lengths Three different hair colors

high levels of interaction. As an example, let's look again at some of the dialogue from Jenny's lesson. (They're discussing Suzie's suggestion.)

> *Jenny:* . . . What was yours again, Suzie?
> *Suzie:* Put 2 on 10 and 1 on 6.
> *Molly:* See, 2 on 10 is 20 and 1 on 6 will only make it 26.
> *Jenny:* When you do the multiplying, they need to be the same on both sides? Is that what you're telling me? And you think that what you have down for the third one is not going to be heavy enough, and so that's why you want Drexel's idea to be second? Well, you guys need to decide that. Talk it over and decide.

(Jenny circulated around the room, then returned to the group.)

> *Suzie:* We've decided to keep the same order. (To try the 6 on 5 solution second.)
> *Jenny:* What made you decide to keep it as it is?
> *Suzie:* Because mine. . . . It kind of sunk in what she said when we add them up—it won't be even. It kind of sunk in.
> *Jenny:* And that was a good compromise. She gave her point of view and you could see the rationality of it.

The importance of social interaction was also illustrated in the whole-group discussion. For example, Danielle's initial understanding, like Suzie's, was that keeping the number of weights equal on both sides of the balance was all that mattered. Without social interaction, it is unlikely that her understanding would have changed.

Jenny's guidance was critical in this process. She provided enough support with her questions to help students make progress, but not so much that she reduced their active role in the learning activity. Providing the appropriate amount of support is a very sophisticated process, requiring a great deal of teacher expertise (A. Brown, 1994).

The dialogue we've seen so far was teacher-facilitated. Let's look at an example of student–student dialogue from David's lesson.

Juan:	Pluto wasn't part of the solar system to begin with.
Randy:	What do you mean?
Juan:	I was watching 'Nova' with my mom, and the narrator said that scientists think Pluto was an asteroid floating around and the sun kinda grabbed it. . . . See, when Mr. Shelton did that thing with the socks, the socks stayed sorta level.
Randy:	What's that got to do with it?
Juan:	Well, look. (Pointing to the model.)
Tanya:	Oh, I get it! Pluto isn't level with the rest of them.
Randy:	Gee, I didn't even notice that.
Tanya:	Yeah, and look there. (Pointing to the chart.) See how little Pluto is. It's the littlest one, so it would be sorta easy to capture.
Randy:	And it's the last one.

Both forms of dialogue, teacher–student and student–student, are important (McCarthy, 1994). Combined with effective examples and representations, learners are provided opportunities to develop a clear understanding of the topics they're studying.

Connect Content to the Real World

Learners' constructions are most meaningful to them if they can connect what they study to the world outside the classroom. For example, Jenny could have enhanced the real-world nature of her task by asking the students to think about their prior experiences with teeter-totters and levers. This would have allowed them to use their background knowledge to attack their problem. Jan Davis (Chapter 1) used soft drink containers to illustrate how decimals can be used to determine the best buys in real-world examples. Karen Johnson (Chapter 2) used population density and screen door screens to further illustrate *density*. Other examples of real-world (authentic) tasks include identifying the longitude and latitude of their school (in geography), writing a persuasive essay for a school or class newspaper (in language arts), and conducting an ecological study of a stream or tract of land near a school (in science).

Be Skeptical About the Effectiveness of Explanations

7.25 ◼
We said, "In the extreme, explaining and lecturing treat learners as passive recipients of understanding." On what theory of learning is treating learners as 'passive recipients of understanding' based? Explain.

Teaching has historically been viewed as a process of transmitting information from either teachers, or written, or electronic, materials to learners. While cognitive learning theory in general, and constructivism in particular, attempt to dispel this notion, many teachers continue to believe that the way you help learners understand something is to explain it to them (Borko & Putnam, 1996).

In the extreme, explaining and lecturing treat learners as passive recipients of understanding, and they often don't work very well, as we saw concretely illustrated in Jenny's lesson. For example, in spite of hearing Molly's and Drexel's solutions in the small group, Mavrin's at the board, and Jenny's explanation, Suzie retained the view that the beam would balance if the number of weights on each side was the same. It wasn't until this understanding was directly confronted (in the interview) that she changed her view, finally concluding that the weight times the distance on each side had to be equal. This reluctance to give up current understandings helps us understand why merely telling or explaining to students—such as Jenny simply explaining the principle behind balance beams—isn't effective. Students must be provided with experiences that make sense to them, or current understandings are unlikely to mature or change.

This doesn't imply that teachers shouldn't explain content to students; it does suggest that we should be skeptical about how much understanding they develop on the basis of our explanations alone.

Technology and Learning: The Role of Technology in Knowledge Construction

Figure 7.12

Illustration of a falling ball

Research has identified a number of technology applications that are consistent with constructivist views of learning, including tutorials that support learners' reasoning (J. Anderson, Boyle, & Yost, 1985); problem-solving simulations in math, science, and social sciences (Cognition and Technology Group at Vanderbilt, 1996); and demonstrations to help learners build knowledge about new ideas (Lehrer, 1993; Spoeher, 1994). (We examine the role of technology in problem solving in Chapter 8.)

A pattern exists in these applications. In each case, technology was used to illustrate topics that are hard to represent with concrete materials or in actual situations, and we've already seen how important the representation of content is in the construction of understanding (Spiro et al., 1992). While useful in many areas, technology can be especially effective for illustrating topics that are difficult to represent in other ways.

Representing Topics with Technology

We can simply drop a paper clip and a ball of clay, for example, to demonstrate that objects of different weights fall at the same rate, but it's virtually impossible to illustrate the actual acceleration of a falling object. Here, technology can be a powerful tool because it allows us to represent this acceleration so that we can actually observe it. For example, Figure 7.12 illustrates the position of a falling ball at uniform time intervals. We see that the distance between the images is increasing, indicating that the ball is falling faster and faster. This presents a semiconcrete example of acceleration, which is virtually impossible to represent in any other way.

As another example, learners can use computer software to simulate a frog dissection, rather than cut up an actual frog. While the simulation has the disadvantage of not allowing students the hands-on experience, it has at least three advantages:

▌ It is less expensive, since it can be used over and over.
▌ It is more flexible because the frog can be "reassembled."
▌ The simulation avoids sacrificing a frog for science.

To examine these advantages, you may wish to visit the following websites:

▌ Interactive frog dissection:
curry.edschool.virginia.edu/go/frog
▌ Cow's eye dissection:
www.exploratorium.edu/learning_studio/cow_eye/index.html
▌ Virtual pig dissection
mail.fkchs.sad27.k12.me.us/fkchs/vpig).

Technology can be effective in helping learners visualize and understand hard-to-represent topics.

Other simulations give students a sense of what it would be like to walk on the moon or see how personnel work together in an emergency room (Roblyer & Edwards, 2000).

Representing topics with technology also helps capitalize on the effects of animation and the ability to combine the animation with text, which utilizes the dual-processing capability of working memory. For example, animations presented in *multimedia formats*—information delivered in two or more configurations, such as words and pictures (Mayer, 1997)—have been proven effective for helping students understand topics such as a car's braking system, the formation of lightning, the workings of a tire pump (Mayer, 1997, 1998), and the addition and subtraction of signed numbers (Moreno & Mayer, 1998).

Putting Constructivism Into Perspective

Like behaviorism and other cognitive theories, constructivism has its critics. In this section, we outline some of the controversies surrounding this view and consider some cautions that critics are suggesting.

Constructivist Controversies

In addition to differences between cognitive and social constructivist views of learning, constructivists also disagree about the kind of learning that occurs and the context in which it takes place. Situated learning is one of these controversies.

Situated Learning.   Most educational psychologists think of learning as something that occurs within the individual, and this learning can be transferred to other settings (Driscoll, 1994; Schunk, 1996). Proponents of **situated learning**, in contrast, *emphasize* *that much of what we learn is social in nature, context-bound, and tied to the specific situation in which it is learned* (Greeno, 1997; Putnam & Borko, 2000). For example, research indicates that sometimes people who can perform sophisticated mathematical operations in jobs such as selling merchandise or delivering milk cannot use the same operations to solve similar, classroom-based problems (J. Brown, Collins, & Duguid, 1989). Situated learning suggests a form of apprenticeship in which new members become enculturated into the language, customs, and beliefs of a learning community (Greeno, 1997).

At the extreme, however, situated learning asserts that learning is bound to the specific situation in which it occurs, making transfer virtually impossible (J. Anderson, Reder, & Simon, 1996). Transfer, however—while often difficult—can and does occur, and expert teachers design learning experiences that encourage this process.

The Nature of Knowledge.   A second controversy centers on the nature of knowledge itself. Does knowledge correspond to some external reality, or is it personally and idiosyncratically constructed? This latter view, called "radical constructivism," emphasizes that all knowledge is relative, individual, and different for each person (Derry, 1992; Phillips, 1995, 1996). In its extreme, it questions the existence of objective reality, suggesting that the only reality that exists is what an individual perceives and constructs.

This view is interesting at a philosophical level, but it both minimizes and confuses the role teachers and schools play in helping learners acquire the knowledge and cognitive tools that exist in cultures (Osborne, 1996).

Constructivist Cautions

Constructivism gives us important insights into the ways people learn. However, like any other theory of learning, it doesn't provide a complete picture of teaching and learning. Experts warn against the rejection of other theories of learning in favor of a full-scale adoption of constructivist ideas (Airasian & Walsh, 1997; J. Anderson et al., 1995, 1996).

For instance, discovery learning—commonly interpreted as the instructional approach most consistent with constructivism—has both advantages and disadvantages. While valuable for promoting learner involvement and motivation, it probably isn't the most effective way to learn complex strategies or develop automaticity (Anderson et al., 1995; Weinert & Helmke, 1995). Discovery also requires a great deal of teacher time, effort, and expertise (Airasian & Walsh, 1997). Teachers need to use a variety of approaches, both learner-centered and teacher-centered, to help students learn as much as possible. Chapters 12 and 13, which focus on teacher- and learner-centered instruction, analyze the strengths and weaknesses of different instructional strategies.

Finally, many of the controversies surrounding different views of learning may resolve themselves because at least some of their features are converging. For instance, information processing theorists accept the idea that learners construct understanding in their working memories, and the results of these constructions are what is stored in long-term memory. On the other hand, constructivists, as we pointed out at the beginning of this section, accept the existence of the information processing architecture. Further, information processing theorists believe that the information stored in long-term memory exists in the form of schemas, and researchers believe that these schemas are constructed. So, we see that information processing, schema theory, and constructivism are, in fact, very compatible theories. While we're not yet to the point of a comprehensive cognitive theory of learning, we see many convergent elements.

Classroom Connections

Applying Constructivism in Your Classroom

1. Develop learning activities around realistic problems.
   - In a unit on percent increase and decrease, a math teacher has students go to malls and find examples of clothes that have been marked down. He also brings in newspaper ads. The class discusses the examples and calculates the amount saved in each case.
   - An elementary social studies teacher has students describe their favorite forms of recreation and the way they're dressed while they participate in the activities. She also asks students who have moved to this area from other parts of the country to do the same for their previous locations. She then asks them to explain differences and guides a discussion of how climate and geography relate to lifestyle.

2. Teach new ideas in the context of current understandings.
   - A third-grade teacher beginning a unit on crustaceans, insects, and arachnids asks students to tell her as many things as they can think of about crabs, lobsters, and "bugs." She then presents examples of each and has the students compare the characteristics.
   - An English teacher has students describe what they know about writing persuasively. She then has them describe what they might want to know about this form of writing. She follows this discussion with examples of effective and ineffective persuasive essays.

3. Create a "learning community" environment in your classroom.
   - An English teacher discussing Hawthorne's *The Scarlet Letter* has the students share their individual perceptions of the characters, the events, and how those impressions were formed.
   - A science teacher discussing heat and expansion has the students articulate their understanding of a series of demonstrations that illustrate the relationship. Where students disagree in understanding, she encourages them to explain and defend their understanding to each other.

Windows on Classrooms

At the beginning of the chapter, David Shelton planned and conducted his lesson to make the information meaningful for his students and to help them construct their own understanding of the topic he was teaching. Then Jenny Newhall applied the characteristics of constructivism with her fourth graders.

In the following case, a teacher conducts a lesson with a group of high school students studying the novel *The Scarlet Letter*. As you read the case study, consider the extent to which the teacher applied the information you have studied in this chapter in her lesson.

Sue Southam, an English teacher at Highland High School, was discussing Nathaniel Hawthorne's *The Scarlet Letter*. This novel, set in Boston in the 1600s, describes a tragic and illicit love affair between the heroine (Hester Prynne) and a minister (Arthur Dimmesdale). The novel's title derives from the letter *A*, meaning "adulterer," which the Puritan community makes Hester wear as punishment for her adultery. The class had been discussing the book for several days; the focus for the current lesson was Reverend Dimmesdale's character.

After the class entered the room and quickly settled down, Sue briefly reviewed the novel's plot to date.

She then asked about Hester's illicit lover. After the class identified Dimmesdale as the baby's father, Sue challenged them by asking, "How do you know the baby is Dimmesdale's? What are the clues in the text in Chapter 3? . . . Nicole?"

"He acted very withdrawn. He doesn't want to look her in the face and doesn't want to be involved in the situation."

"Okay, anything else, any other clues?"

"The baby . . . it points at Reverend Dimmesdale."

"Good observation. That is a good clue and one of my favorite scenes from the novel," Sue added.

After several more comments, Sue paused and said, "Class, I'd like to read a passage to you from the text describing Dimmesdale. Listen carefully, and then I'd like you to do something with it."

After reading the paragraph, Sue continued, "In your logs, jot down some of the important characteristics in that description. If you were going to draw a portrait of him, what would he look like? Try to be as specific as possible. Try that now."

Sue gave the students a few minutes to write in their logs and then, with a questioning look, continued by asking, "If you were directing a film of *The Scarlet Letter,* what would Dimmesdale look like? . . . Mike?"

" . . . Thin, 5 feet 10, nervous, trembling lips," Mike offered.

"Yeah, and he's always mopping his brow with a handkerchief," Todd added, gesturing with his hands as if he were mopping his brow.

"What else?" Sue encouraged.

"Wire-framed glasses," Tamara contributed.

"With brown, melancholy eyes," Jeremy added.

After the class discussed additional characteristics, Sue shifted gears by asking, "What do these characteristics tell us about Dimmesdale as a person? . . . Anyone? . . . Sonya?"

"I think he's worried about getting caught."

" . . . Kasha?"

"I think he feels bad about what has happened to Hester. He feels guilty," Kasha added.

After a few additional comments, Sue said, "Let's see whether we can find out more about the Dimmesdale character through his actions. I'd like you to listen carefully while I read the speech by Reverend Dimmesdale in which he confronts Hester Prynne in front of the congregation and exhorts her to identify her secret lover and partner in sin. Think about both Dimmesdale's and Hester's thoughts while I'm reading."

She read Dimmesdale's speech, and after she finished, she divided the class into Dimmesdales and Hesters by counting "One, two" in front of different rows around the room.

Then she said, "Now I'd like you to role play; pretend you're either Hester or Dimmesdale during the speech. All the 'ones' are Dimmesdales, and all the 'twos' are Hesters. Dimmesdales, in your logs I want you to tell me what Dimmesdale is really thinking during this speech. Hesters, I want you to tell me what Hester is thinking while she listens to Dimmesdale's speech. Write in your logs in your own words the private thoughts of your character. Do that right now, and then we'll come back together in a few minutes."

As students wrote in their logs, Sue circulated around the room, clarifying the task and encouraging students to be creative in their perspectives.

After giving them a few minutes to write in their logs, she sorted them into groups of four, with each group

comprising two Hesters and two Dimmesdales. Once students were settled, she said, "In each group, I want you to start off by having Dimmesdale tell what he is thinking during the first line of the speech. Then I'd like a Hester to respond. Then continue with Dimmesdale's next line, and then Hester's reaction. Go ahead and share your thoughts in your groups."

After giving students about 5 minutes to share their perspectives, she reconvened the class with, "Okay, let's hear it. A Dimmesdale first. Just what was he thinking during his speech? . . . Mike?"

"The only thing I could think of was, 'Oh God, help me. I hope she doesn't say anything. If they find out it's me, I'll be ruined. . . . ' And then here comes Hester with her powerful speech," Mike concluded, turning to his partner in the group, Nicole.

With a nod, Sue acknowledged Mike's reply and gestured to Nicole. "Nicole, what do you think Hester is thinking during this speech?"

"I wrote, 'Good man, huh. So why don't you confess then? You know you're guilty. I've admitted my love, but you haven't. Why don't you just come out and say it?'"

"Interesting. . . . What else? How about another Hester? . . . Sarah?"

"I just put, 'No, I'll never tell. I still love you, and I'll keep your secret forever,'" Sarah offered.

Sue paused for a moment, looked around the room, and commented, "Notice how different the two views of Hester are. Nicole paints her as very angry, whereas Sarah views her as still loving him." Sue again paused to look for reactions. Karen raised her hand, and Sue nodded to her.

"I think the reason Hester doesn't say anything is that people won't believe her because he's a minister,"

Karen suggested. "She's getting her revenge just by being there reminding him of his guilt."

"But if she accuses him, won't people expect him to deny it?" Brad added, responding to Karen.

"Maybe he knows she won't accuse him because she still loves him," Julie offered.

"Wait a minute," Jeff interrupted, gesturing with his hands. "I don't think he's such a bad guy. I think he feels guilty about it all, but he just

doesn't have the courage to admit it in front of all of those people."

"I think he's really admitting it in his speech but is asking her secretly not to tell," Caroline added. "Maybe he's really talking to Hester and doesn't want the rest of the people to know."

The class continued, with students debating the hidden meaning in the speech and trying to decide whether Reverend Dimmesdale is really a villain or a tragic figure.

As the end of class neared, Sue said, "Interesting ideas . . . And who haven't we talked about yet? . . . Sherry?"

" . . . Hester Prynne's husband?"

" . . . Who's been missing for several years," Sue added.

"Tomorrow, I'd like you to read Chapter 4, in which we meet Hester's husband. That's all for today. Please put the desks back. . . . Thank you."

Questions for Discussion and Analysis

Analyze Sue's lesson in the context of the information in this chapter. In doing your analysis, you may want to consider the following questions. Be specific, and take information directly from the case study.

1. To what extent did Sue apply the information processing model in her teaching? Explain, using the concepts of attention, perception, working memory, encoding, and long-term memory, together with information taken directly from the case study.

2. To what extent did Sue help make the information meaningful for students? Explain, using the concepts of elaboration, organization, and activity, together with information taken from the case study.

3. To what extent did Sue apply the characteristics of constructivism in her lesson? Explain, using information taken directly from the case study.

4. Provide an overall assessment of the lesson. Provide evidence taken from the case study in making your assessment. What could Sue have done to make the lesson more effective? Be specific in your suggestions.

Now go to our Companion Website to assess your understanding of chapter content with the Student Self-Assessment, apply comprehension in the Online Casebook, and broaden your knowledge base with links to important Educational Psychology World Wide Web sites.

 Summary

Cognitive Views of Learning

Behaviorism and cognitive learning theories differ in that behaviorism treats learners as passively responding to the environment, whereas cognitive theories assume that learners are mentally active and construct their own understanding of the topics they study.

Cognitive theories emphasize internal, mental processes in attempting to understand learning. Cognitive theories were developed, in part, because behaviorism was unable to adequately explain both research results and everyday events, especially complex phenomena such as language learning and problem solving.

Information Processing

Information processing is a cognitive view of learning that compares human thinking to the way computers process information. Information stores—sensory memory, working memory, and long-term memory—hold information; cognitive processes, such as attention, perception, rehearsal, encoding, and retrieval, move the information from one store to another.

Information received by sensory memory is moved to working memory through the processes of attention and perception. Working memory, with its limited capacity, can easily be overloaded and become a bottleneck to subsequent processing. The capacity of working memory can, in effect, be increased through chunking, making aspects of processing automatic and capitalizing on its dual-processing capabilities.

Information processing theory assumes that knowledge is encoded in long-term memory in complex interrelationships (schemas) of declarative knowledge (which includes knowledge of facts, concepts, and other ideas) and procedural knowledge (which is knowledge of how to perform operations, such as writing an essay). Information processing is governed by metacognition—an awareness of and control over the processes that move information from one store to another. As metacognitive knowledge and skills improve, learners develop the capacity for self-regulation.

Information that is meaningful is interconnected with other information in memory, and an important goal in teaching is to help learners increase the number of connections between individual items of information. A teacher can make information meaningful by putting learners in active roles, encouraging visual imagery, organizing content in various ways, and encouraging learners to elaborate on their own understanding. Mnemonic devices help create connections in information where no natural connection exists.

Constructivism

Although all cognitive views of learning focus on learners being active, constructivism places more emphasis than other cognitive theories on learners constructing their own understanding. Constructivists disagree on the nature of knowledge, but they generally agree that learners construct their own understanding, that new learning exists in the context of prior understanding, that learning is enhanced by social activity, and that authentic tasks promote learning. Many constructivists suggest that teachers should create a learning community where teachers and students work together to solve problems.

 # Important Concepts

analogies (p. 276)

attention (p. 270)

authentic task (p. 295)

automaticity (p. 262)

chunking (p. 262)

cognitive constructivism
   (p. 292)

cognitive learning theories
   (p. 257)

cognitive load theory
   (p. 262)

cognitive processes
   (p. 259)

contexts (p. 269)

declarative knowledge
   (p. 263)

dual-coding theory
   (p. 275)

dual processing (p. 263)

elaboration (p. 276)

encoding (p. 273)

encoding specificity
   hypothesis (p. 282)

examples (p. 276)

forgetting (p. 281)

imagery (p. 275)

information processing
   (p. 258)

information stores (p. 259)

interference (p. 281)

learning (p. 257)

levels of processing
(p. 279)

long-term memory
(p. 263)

meaningfulness (p. 273)

meta-attention (p. 282)

metacognition (p. 259)

metamemory (p. 282)

mnemonic devices (p. 276)

model (p. 258)

organization (p. 274)

perception (p. 272)

procedural knowledge
(p. 264)

rehearsal (p. 273)

retrieve (p. 281)

schemas (p. 264)

script (p. 265)

sensory memory (p. 260)

situated learning (p. 300)

social constructivism
(p. 293)

strategies (p. 283)

working memory (p. 261)

The Classroom

Learning Part II

Chapter Outline

8

Complex Cognitive Processes

Laura Hunter, a fifth-grade teacher at Bennion Elementary School, was reading her notes as she planned for the following week's instruction. She kept a journal in which she wrote comments about units and lessons and referred to them when planning to teach the same topics later.

She reacted with a nod when she read a note from the previous year, "Seem to understand perimeter, but can't find area; don't know how to begin. Memorize." This note referred to a section on finding the area of irregularly shaped plane figures. Reflecting on her experience, Laura decided, "I'm going to try to make it more real for them this year. I need a real problem instead of that stuff in the book, something they can relate to."

After considering a series of possibilities, she thought, "Why not use the classroom? The carpeted area has an irregular shape."

After her beginning-of-class routines were completed the following Monday, she began by reviewing the concepts of *area* and *perimeter.*

"Okay," she began, "What kinds of things have we been talking about?"

"Area," the class responded in unison.

"Before that we talked about perimeter," Laura continued. "Can someone tell us what perimeter is? . . . Sam?"

"It's the length of the line going around the outside," Sam answered.

"Right, right, and what's the example we used? Like if we were

building a playground, it would be the . . . "

"Perimeter," several students mumbled.

"Fence," others said simultaneously.

"Right," Laura acknowledged. "It would be like the fence around it. . . . And then we talked about area. What's the area? . . . If you were going to build that same playground and you were going to cover it, with green stuff, . . . Elise what would that be?"

"The inside of the shape," Elise answered.

"The inside of the shape, . . . like how many squares of grass you would need to cover it," Laura responded.

"And here's the problem," she continued. "We're going to use this as a guide," displaying the following on the overhead:

"First, identify the problem," she said, referring to the overhead. . . . "Now here's the problem. . . . You

know how the first floor has blue carpeting. . . . The second floor will get carpeting too. But Mr. Garcia needs some help in determining what kind of carpeting to buy for this room. We know that it will be blue, but he doesn't know how much it will cost. . . . And we've made some changes. When the computers came in, they decided that, with kids sitting there so many times, moving their feet around, they want to put linoleum underneath where all the computers are. . . . So, your job is to figure out how much carpeting we need."

Laura paused for a moment to let the students think about what she had said, and then she broke the students into groups and had each decide what their problem was and how they would represent it.

The students worked together for several minutes, then Laura had each of the groups report their results to the class.

"Fred, what did your team decide you were supposed to do?" Laura began.

"Measure the area."

"Okay; Grant, can you give me some more details?"

"We decided we should measure the perimeter around and about 2 feet from the computers and the linoleum and measure all around."

"I'm writing 'remember the linoleum,' so you remember to go through that process," Laura noted, writing on the overhead.

"Okay, have we identified all the parts of the problem? . . . Paige, do you want to add anything?"

"Ahh . . . we could make a drawing of the outside of the room. Like on the graph paper like we did yesterday. Write the measurements on the side," Paige continued.

"Okay, outside measurements," Laura repeated as she wrote down what Paige said.

"Okay, who else? . . . Jamison?"

"We decided we had to get the perimeter before we could get the area. Everything else is the same."

"Okay," Laura commented, "so now we know what the problem is."

Laura then had students measure different parts of the room in their groups.

Using the information gathered from each group, Laura constructed a diagram of the room and distributed it. "I'll put one of these on each table," Laura said, changing the direction of the lesson.

"Now, on the side where the sink is, the L with a circle. Can you tell us what that means, the L word? . . . Kelly?" Laura began.

"Linoleum."

"Linoleum, right," and she then continued, "Everybody sees that the

distance across the front of the chalkboard is 30 feet," pointing to the diagram, "Okay, let's talk about the sink side. How many feet are there between the edge and the start of the counters?"

"Five feet," several students answered in unison.

"Five feet; that little symbol means feet. . . . and how many feet for the length of that counter?"

"Thirty-one," several students again said in unison.

"Okay, everybody see that? . . . Let's look back up here at our overhead. . . . Another way we can look at this map is to say it's representing the problem . . . I've heard it called a diagram. What you're looking at is a representation of the problem. . . . Okay, everybody look up here again. What's your job?"

"The problem" and "Solve the problem," several students said, after a brief pause.

"Do we want to add any more steps to this part?" Laura asked.

" . . . We did these things. We measured the area, we measured the perimeter. . . . Did we do all these things?"

"Yeah," most of the students replied in unison.

"Are we through?" Laura wondered.

"No," the students again answered in unison.

"We didn't measure the area. We still have the whole inside of the classroom. We just measured the perimeter," Nephi volunteered.

"Okay, you guys understand what Nephi's saying?" Laura queried.

"Yeah," several students respond.

"Okay," Laura nodded. "That's the part you're going to be working on with your team. . . . What I want you to do is select a strategy. You need to decide with your team what the best way is going to be to measure the area of this shape," she directed. "I only want to know right now the area of the carpet. I only want to know how much carpet I need to buy.

"You can go ahead and get started."

The students then turned back to their groups to try to decide how best to calculate the area.

As students attempted to solve the problem, they came up with two basic strategies. One was to find the area of the whole room and subtract the linoleum; the other was to find the area of an interior rectangle in the room and then add extra, irregularly shaped carpeted areas.

"Okay, let's look back up here at our diagram," Laura directed after the class had again reassembled. "In the select-your-strategies part, I saw a lot of different strategies as I was walking

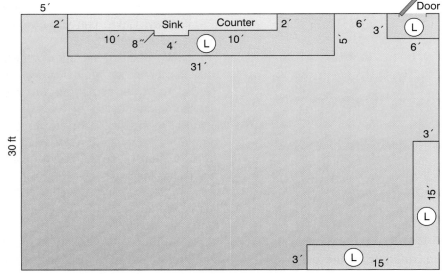

around. Raise your hand and tell me what one of the strategies was. . . . Yashoda."

"We figured out, . . . we multiplied the perimeter. And then we subtracted the places where the linoleum was."

"Okay, when you multiplied the perimeter, what does it give you?"

"1,440."

"Okay, that's called the . . . ?"

"Area," several students responded.

"Okay, and what was your next step?"

"We measured everything first, and then we subtracted where the linoleum was."

"Okay, raise your hand if your team tried that strategy," Laura directed.

Students from several groups raised their hands.

"Raise your hand if you tried a different strategy."

Several more students raised their hands.

"Matt, explain what your team did," Laura directed.

"We had two strategies. I'll do the first one that we tried. We took. . . . we squared it off, like covering up this," Matt responded, pointing to the diagram, "and then we multiplied the, then we got the middle, and then we were going to put the other pieces together . . . on it."

"Okay, I'm going to put 'found measurements and add area'. Is that okay?" Laura asked.

"Unh-huh," Matt answered.

After each team offered their strategies, Laura again changed the direction of the lesson, saying, "I have a green marker and a blue paper at each table.

"Here's your job. . . . The person with the green marker, your job is to draw lines on your diagram that illustrate how you solved the problem. . . . The person with the blue paper, your job is to write down three conclusions your team decided on about the problem."

After discussing the strategies they used to solve the problem, each group reported on their progress.

"One of our conclusions was, 'Put all the pieces together,'" Matt explained for his team. "We took all the extra pieces that we had, and we added them together."

After each group described their strategy, Laura put the diagrams and conclusions on a bulletin board to share with others.

She then continued, "Most of you said you took the 30, which is the width of the room, and the 48, which is the length of the room, and Sam already said the formula for that was 30 feet times 48 feet. . . . Would you say, as a strategy for solving a problem like this, that that would be a good place to start?

"Yeah," several students responded.

"Okay, and what was another step that most of you used to carry out the strategy? . . . Justin?"

"Subtract."

"Okay, and before you do that, you had to find the area of the linoleum, and then subtract it. . . . Were there other ways to solve this problem?

"Yeah," several students again responded.

"Did we get different answers? . . . Okay, tell me what the answer was that you got. How many square feet of carpet?" Laura asked one of the groups.

"1,173."

"Okay," and she nodded to another group.

"1,378."

"1,347," a third group reported.

"1,169," a fourth group added.

"1,600," the last group put in.

"Well, are you guys comfortable with that?"

Several students said "No," while a few said, "Yes."

"If you were the person purchasing the carpet, would you be comfortable with that?"

" . . . If you were the person estimating, would you be comfortable with that?" Laura continued.

Most of the class said they wouldn't be comfortable if they were the person purchasing the carpet but offered that they would be if they were merely estimating.

"If you were going to redo this tomorrow, what could we do to be more accurate? . . . Talk to your team for 30 seconds," Laura then directed.

The students talked to their teammates and offered some suggestions, such as remeasuring the room, rechecking to see if the strategy made sense, and even asking the janitor about the dimensions of the room.

Chuckling at the last suggestion, Laura said, "That's a strategy called 'Ask an expert,'" and she then had the students get ready for recess.

I n this chapter, we extend our study of cognitive theory to examine the complex cognitive processes we all use to learn concepts, solve problems, use our metacognitive abilities to be more strategic about what we learn, and transfer our understanding from one setting to another. As we examine these topics, we'll demonstrate how they're grounded in the cognitive learning theories you studied in Chapter 7.

After you've completed your study of this chapter, you should be able to meet the following objectives:

- Explain the application of concept learning to classroom activities.
- Apply problem-solving strategies to well-defined and ill-defined problems.
- Explain how critical thinking can be used in classroom learning activities.
- Describe how study strategies can be used to increase student learning.
- Discuss ways of increasing transfer of learning.

Teachers often encounter challenges similar to those Laura Hunter faced in the opening case study. Students struggle with certain topics, and teachers are often frustrated in their efforts to help. As a result, they approach a topic reluctantly the next time they teach it, or even skip it completely. Laura took a positive approach instead, knowing that her students had tried to "memorize their way through" the unit the year before, and she increased her efforts to make the information meaningful to them. She also recognized that the unit involved different types of learning, and she consciously directed her teaching to each. We examine these aspects of learning in this chapter, beginning with concepts.

Concept Learning

Think about some of the topics that you've studied in this book so far. A few, among many others in each chapter, include *development* and *equilibrium* in Chapter 2, *initiative* and *self-esteem* in Chapter 3, and *intelligence* and *socioeconomic status* in Chapter 4. Each is a *concept*. In this section, we'll look at the topic of *concepts* in detail.

Concepts: Categories That Simplify the World

Concepts represent a major portion of the school curriculum, and much of teachers' efforts are directed at teaching them (Klausmeier, 1992). **Concepts** are *mental structures that categorize sets of objects, events, or ideas*. For example, if learners saw the polygons in Figure 8.1, they would describe them all as triangles, even though the shapes vary in size and orientation. "Triangle" represents a mental structure into which all examples of triangles can be placed.

Figure 8.1

Triangles

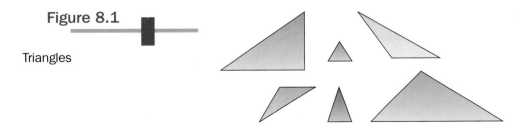

Table 8.1

Concepts in different content areas

Language Arts	Social Studies	Science	Math
Adjective	Culture	Acid	Prime number
Verb	Longitude	Conifer	Equivalent fraction
Plot	Federalist	Element	Set
Simile	Democracy	Force	Addition
Infinitive	Immigrant	Inertia	Parabola

Concepts help us simplify the world. The concept *triangle*, for example, allows people to think and talk about the examples in Figure 8.1 as a group, instead of as specific objects. Having to remember each separately would make learning impossibly complex and unwieldy.

Although not the central focus, concepts were important in Laura's lesson. She began, for example, by reviewing the concept *perimeter*, and her students' ability to solve the problem depended on their having a clear concept of *area*. Significantly, both concepts were elaborated in the context of the lesson, rather than in isolation, and each time the students used them, their understanding evolved as the concepts were developed in new and richer contexts (J. Brown, Collins, & Duguid, 1989).

Additional examples of concepts in language arts, social studies, math, and science are listed in Table 8.1. This is only a brief list, and you can probably think of many more for each area. Students also study, for example, *major scale* and *tempo* in music, *perspective* and *balance* in art, and *aerobic exercise* and *isotonic exercise* in physical education. In addition, many other concepts exist that don't neatly fit into a particular content area such as *honesty, bias, love*, and *internal conflict*.

Theories of Concept Learning

Think again about concepts, such as *development* in Chapter 2 and *metacognition* in Chapter 7, or consider simple, common concepts like *perimeter, square*, or *bird*. How did you learn those concepts, and how do you use them?

Rule-Governed Theories of Concept Learning

Some concepts, such as *perimeter* in Laura's lesson, or *triangle* or *square*, have clear and precise **characteristics** (sometimes called *attributes* or *features*), which are *a concept's defining elements. Square*, for instance, has four characteristics—*closed, plane, equal sides,* and *equal angles*—and learners can identify examples of squares based on the rule saying that squares must have these attributes. Other characteristics, such as size, color, or orientation aren't essential, so learners don't have to consider them in making their classifications; they don't alter the concept.

Early concept learning research (e.g., Bruner, Goodenow, & Austin, 1956) found that learners quickly identify the essential characteristics of a concept and classify examples

8.1
Think about the concepts of *adjective* and *conifer* in Table 8.1. What are the characteristics of these concepts?

accordingly. Concepts are differentiated from one another on the basis of the rules for each (Bourne, 1982). For example, learners differentiate a square from a rectangle based on the rule for squares, compared to a rule for rectangles indicating that rectangles must be closed plane figures with equal angles, with opposite sides equal in length but not all sides equal.

More recent research emphasizes the *constructive* nature of the process. As you learned in Chapter 7, learners actively construct—rather than passively acquire—their understanding of concept rules (Confrey, 1990; Greeno, Collins, & Resnick, 1996).

Prototype Theories of Concept Learning

Now, let's look at another seemingly simple concept, such as *bird*. Characteristics commonly attributed to birds include *has feathers, flies,* and *lays eggs,* among others. However, penguins, ostriches, and emus are birds but don't fly, and many reptiles and even some mammals, such as the duck-billed platypus, lay eggs. So, what is the rule we follow for classifying animals as birds?

Prototype theories of concept learning don't assume a classification system based on a strict rule for inclusion as a member of the concept (Wattenmaker, Dewey, Murphy, & Medin, 1986). Rather, learners construct a **prototype**, which is *the best representative of its category* (Busmeyer & Myung, 1988; Nosofsky, 1988; B. Schwartz & Reisberg, 1991). For example, a robin might be a bird prototype for a person in this country. In many instances, a prototype isn't a specific, physical example, such as one particular robin. Rather, it is a mental composite constructed from encountering several examples.

Factors Influencing the Ease of Learning Concepts

The ease of learning a concept is directly related to the number of characteristics and how tangible and concrete they are (Tennyson & Cocchiarella, 1986). When a concept's characteristics are concrete and observable, concept learning is simplified. You saw this with *triangle, perimeter,* and *square*; the same is true for other concrete concepts, such as *adjective, latitude,* and *force*.

Others are much more difficult. Could you, for example, precisely describe what makes a democracy a democracy? For most people, our country is probably a prototype for the concept *democracy* (even though it's a republic and technically not a democracy), and people's prototypes will vary. *Democracy* is much harder to learn than a concept like *square*.

Concepts such as *justice, honesty,* and *bias* are still more difficult. The attributes of *justice,* for example, are extremely elusive, and constructing a prototype is also very difficult; it is a hard concept to understand (and teach).

Examples: The Key to Learning and Teaching Concepts

Regardless of the complexity of a concept, the key to effective concept teaching is a carefully selected set of **examples**, *instances illustrating what the concept is*, nonexamples, that indicate what the concept is not, and a definition (Tennyson & Cocchiarella, 1986). In teaching concepts, teachers may present the definition and then illustrate it with examples, or they may choose to present a sequence of examples and guide students as they construct the concept and its definition.

Regardless of the approach you choose, as you prepare to teach concepts, ask yourself, "What can I show the students, or what can I have them do that best illustrates the

8.2 ━━
Consider the concepts *noun* and *culture*. On the basis of the information in this section, which of the two should be easier to learn? Explain your answer.

8.3 ━━
In teaching a concept, should you first present an example, or should you first present a nonexample? Why? Would there ever be exceptions to this order?

concept?" The best examples are ones in which characteristics are observable or the example is the best prototype available. To illustrate this idea, look at the following examples of the concept *snurf*. Can you identify its characteristics?

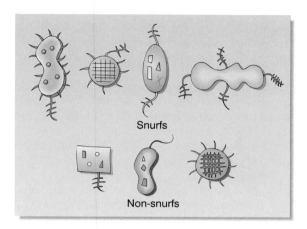

Snurfs

Non-snurfs

You can see that snurfs are curved shapes with cross-hatched tails. All other characteristics are irrelevant. You can also see nonexamples—cases that are not snurfs. When a concept can easily be confused with a closely related concept, nonexamples are particularly important (Tennyson & Cocchiarella, 1986). For example, if a teacher wants his students to understand the concept *reptile*, he might include a frog—an amphibian—as a nonexample, to be certain that students don't confuse reptiles and amphibians.

8.4
Which theory of concept learning–*rule driven* or *prototype*–best explains how we learned the concept *snurf*? Explain, based on that theory.

Effective teachers use concrete examples to help students learn concepts and relate them to the real world.

Concept Mapping: Embedding Concepts in Complex Schemas

Even though we grasp a concept based either on its attributes or a prototype, our understanding isn't complete until we see how the concept links to other, related concepts (Chmielewski & Dansereau, 1998; Hall, Hall, & Saling, 1999). **Concept mapping,** *in which the relationships among concepts are represented visually* (Linn, Songer, & Eylon, 1996), is a strategy designed to capitalize on the effects of organization, imagery, and the dual-processing capabilities of working memory—which we discussed in Chapter 7 (Robinson, Katayama, Dubois, & Devaney, 1998).

Concept maps can be effectively used in a number of ways (Calderhead, 1996; Novak & Musonda, 1991). First, teachers can use them as models of organization for students as they present new information. Second, learners can create their own concept maps after reading a chapter or listening to a teacher presentation, which requires them to think about and develop their understanding of the relationships among concepts (Hall et al.,1999). Finally, teachers can use the results of the students' efforts to diagnose the depth and complexity of their understanding.

Figure 8.2 illustrates a learner's understanding of the relationships among closed-plane figures. In looking at the map, we see that it doesn't include figures with more than four sides, or curved shapes other than circles (such as ellipses). Seeing the learner's incomplete understanding allows the teacher to intervene by providing and discussing examples of other closed, curved figures, as well as pentagons, hexagons, and other polygons.

The concepts in Figure 8.2 are organized hierarchically, but not all relationships among concepts are hierarchical, so other types of concept maps may be more appropriate (Wallace, West, Ware, & Dansereau, 1998). Figures 8.3 and 8.4 illustrate two students' understandings of the concept *novel* represented in a **network,** which is *a concept map illustrating nonhierarchical relationships among concepts.* The arrows and descriptions clarify the relationships.

The first student's concept of a novel is quite simplistic; it includes only the basic components of *plot, setting,* and *characters.* The second student's is more sophisticated;

8.5
In addition to promoting organization, which other processes that increase meaningfulness are learners using when they create their own concept maps? Explain.

8.6
Create a network for the concept *operant conditioning.*

Figure 8.2

Concept map for closed plane figures

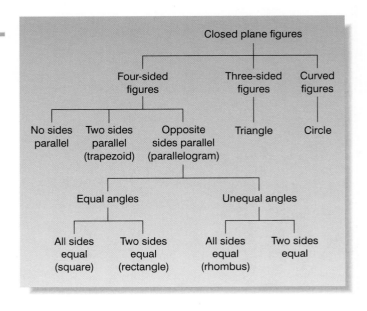

Figure 8.3

First learner's network for the concept *novel*

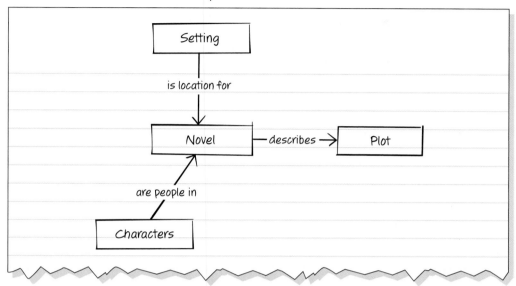

factors that influence the quality of a novel are also included. As with the example of closed plane figures, teachers can use information gathered from studying students' maps to further develop the concept.

The point in concept mapping is that teachers and students use the map to represent and construct relationships among concepts, which increase their meaningfulness. The form students use should be one that best illustrates these associations (Wallace et al., 1998). Hierarchies often work best in math and science; in other areas, such as reading, social studies, and literature, a network may be more effective.

Concept Learning: Misconceptions and Conceptual Change

The effect of background knowledge on learning was a theme emphasized in Chapter 7 when we considered general cognitive theories of learning, and it is important for concept learning as well (Greeno et al., 1996). While learners construct understanding of concepts on the basis of examples and nonexamples, their background knowledge, expectations, beliefs, and emotions also influence their thinking (Dole & Sinatra, 1998). Learners develop many intuitive understandings of the topics they study, and once formed, these understandings are extremely resistant to change (Leander & Brown, 1999; Shuell, 1996).

An example from educational psychology is the concept *negative reinforcement*. We emphasized that negative reinforcement is a process that *increases* behavior by removing or avoiding a consequence, and we carefully illustrated the concept with examples. In spite of these efforts, however, many learners continue to view negative reinforcement as a process that *decreases* behavior, inappropriately equating it with punishment. Similar examples can be found in many areas. For instance, science students often confuse rep-

8.7
Which of the concepts from Piaget's work discussed in Chapter 2 best help you understand why students' understandings are so resistant to change? Explain, based on this concept.

Figure 8.4

Second learner's network for the concept *novel*

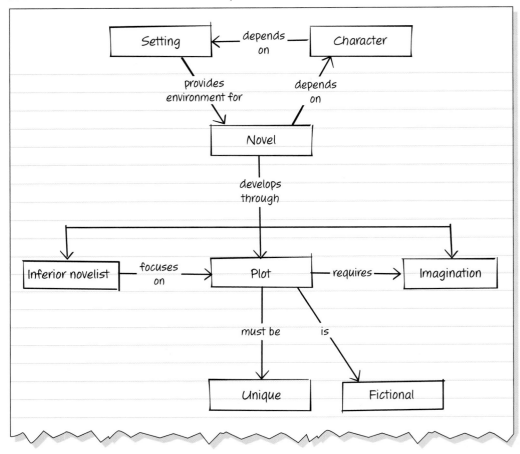

tiles with amphibians and spiders with insects, geography students have problems with longitude and latitude, and language arts students have difficulty differentiating between figures of speech such as simile, metaphor, and personification.

To develop more valid understandings, researchers have found that learners must become uncomfortable with their present understanding, and a new conception must be understandable and more capable of explaining learners' experiences than were their original ideas (Dole & Sinatra, 1998; Nissani & Hoefler-Nissani, 1992). This can only be accomplished if learners' intuitive understandings are directly confronted (Chinn & Brewer, 1993).

> Elaine Madison has been working with her middle-school students on basic science concepts and has defined force as any push or pull and work as the combination of force and movement. She knows that students often incorrectly think that work is done if effort is expended, regardless of whether movement occurs.
>
> To try to eliminate these misconceptions, she suggested, "Kari, stand up and hold up the chair."

Kari stood, lifted the chair that was at the side of the room, and remained standing motionless.

"Now," Elaine continued. "Is Kari doing any work?"

"Yes," Jared volunteered.

"What did we say the definition of work is?" Elaine probed.

"The combination of force and movement," Natalie offered.

"Okay, is Kari doing any work?" Elaine went on.

"If she stands there for a while, she'll get tired, and you get tired when you work," Jared persisted.

"But she's not moving," Kathy added. "For work to be done, there has to be movement."

"That doesn't make sense," Jared continued. "That means you can get tired without doing any work."

"What actually makes you tired?" Elaine queried.

"Holding up the chair."

"Sure. So, the effort of holding up the chair would make any of us tired. Effort is the force we're exerting, and exerting a force can make us tired."

The class continued to discuss the example, noting that Kari actually did do work when she first lifted the chair. They then discussed additional examples, noting that because of their day-to-day experience, they tend to equate effort, work, and being tired. As a result of this discussion, Jared finally concluded that the idea that work requires movement makes sense.

This example illustrates how difficult it is to change misconceptions. They exist because they make sense to us, and changing them requires restructuring our schemas. It's also possible that a student like Jared will revert back to his earlier thinking—work equals effort—even though he accepted the definition; additional examples and discussion will be required for him to restructure his ideas. Alert teachers are aware of this possibility and provide additional experiences.

Classroom Connections

Applying Concept Learning in Your Classroom

1. Use examples that include all the information learners need to understand the concept.
   - A physical education teacher is helping her students learn to serve a tennis ball. She videotapes several people, some with good serves and others with poor ones. During the next class period, she shows the class the videotapes and discusses the differences before having them practice their own serves.
   - A fourth-grade teacher's students are having difficulty understanding the concept of *ecosystem*. She delves into her stack of *National Geographics* and cuts out several pictures of different ecosystems—a jungle, a desert, and northern tundra. As she presents the pictures, she discusses them with her students and helps them identify essential characteristics of ecosystems in each.

2. Link essential characteristics to examples.
   - A kindergarten teacher wants her class to understand the concept *living things*. She displays and discusses examples, such as themselves, their pets, grass near the school grounds, and plants in their classroom. They identify "the ability to grow and change" and "the need for food and water" as two characteristics the examples had in common.

- A language arts teacher, working with her class on *summary sentences*, displays paragraphs on the overhead. With her guidance, the class analyzes the summary sentences in each paragraph, determining which are good and poor, explaining why in each case.

3. Link new concepts to related concepts.
   - The term *cultural revolution* comes up in a social studies lesson. The teacher asks the students to compare cultural revolutions to other revolutions they have studied, such as the Industrial Revolution and the American Revolution, pointing out similarities and differences in each case.
   - An earth science class is learning about "old" and "new" geologic formations. The teacher shows slides of the two kinds of formations, with examples of *young mountains* and *young rivers* serving as the nonexamples for the *old mountains* and *old rivers*. The class then relates "old" and "new" mountains and rivers to climate, weathering, and erosion, which have been discussed in earlier lessons.

4. Illustrate relationships among concepts.
   - A science teacher, wanting his students to understand the relationship between the *length* of a vibrating column and its *pitch*, has students lay rulers on their desks, extend different lengths of the rulers over the edge, and snap the rulers to hear differences in pitch.

5. Have students apply relationships to new situations.
   - The science teacher working with length and pitch puts different amounts of water into three identical soft-drink bottles and asks students to predict how the amount of water would affect pitch. He then has students blow across the bottle openings to make sounds and asks them to relate the different pitches to the differing amounts of space and water in each bottle.

Adaptive Instruction: Dealing with Diversity in Students' Thinking

Jody Curtis was a third-grade teacher in an ethnically diverse school. Of her 27 students, more than a third were non-native English speakers. They came from a variety of backgrounds and had widely varying experiences.

Jody was beginning a unit on reptiles. She prepared by gathering colored pictures from magazines and other sources. She knew that her class had studied amphibians in the second grade, and she planned to build on their knowledge by comparing reptiles to amphibians.

As she showed each picture, she called on different students to describe and discuss what they observed. Disagreements began to emerge almost immediately.

"They're sort of worms, except they have eyes," Sarina suggested. "They wiggle when they move."

"No, they got bones," Miguel countered.

"Yeah, I saw a skeleton once," Bryan added. "It looked funny, but it had bones."

When the discussion turned to reproduction, there was more disagreement.

"They lay eggs in a nest like birds," Monica said.

"Uh-huh," Jamille agreed. "In the water."

"No, they have babies like dogs and cats," Manuel retorted, arguing that the young were born alive.

They even disagreed about basic features.

"They're yucky and slimy," Sanra asserted.

"Gross," Lucia added. "All slippery and gross."

"What makes you say that?" Jody wondered aloud.

" . . . Uhh."

"No," Muhammed interjected. "My brother has a snake, and I felt it. It was dry, not slimy. It was smooth and clean," he added, reacting to the skeptical looks on his classmates' faces.

"What's your reaction to what Muhammed said?" Jody turned to Lucia, trying to reinvolve her in the discussion.

"I . . . I . . . What do you mean, reaction?"

"I mean, how does Muhammed's experience compare to what you said?"

" . . . I . . . don't know."

"Tell us about your experience with snakes," Jody encouraged.

" . . . My brother caught one in a pond, and he was holding it up by its head, . . . and I was so scared, and finally I touched it, . . . and it was all wet and slimy."

Jody and her students continued the discussion for the remainder of the science period.

As she reflected on it, Jody was struck by two aspects of the lesson. First, students' experiences with reptiles varied widely, and as a result, they had very different preconceptions about reptiles.

Second, the way the students responded to the interaction in the lesson also varied. Some were confident, whereas others were less comfortable, perhaps even confused. For example, when Jody asked Lucia, a non-native English speaker of Hispanic background, "What makes you say that?" Lucia was uncertain about how to respond. Jody was asking her to provide evidence for her conclusion that snakes are slippery and gross, but Lucia didn't realize that this is what the question called for. A similar thing happened when Jody asked her, "What's your reaction to what Muhammed said?" and her effort to clarify the question by asking, "I mean, how does Muhammed's experience compare to what you said?" still didn't help. Until she simply asked Lucia to describe her experience with snakes, Jody had little insight into Lucia's understanding.

Differences in learners' background experiences and patterns of interaction require two kinds of instructional adaptations: accommodating differences in background experiences and in patterns of interaction.

> **8.8**
> What factor in Piaget's description of development best explains why the students came to the lesson with strong preconceptions about reptiles? What other factor from Piaget's work is critical in helping a student change preconceptions if they're invalid? Explain.

Accommodating Differences in Background Experiences

To begin this section, let's look at what Jody did to follow up with her students:

> To deal with the differences in the students' experiences, Jody arranged to have several reptiles brought to class. She had Muhammed bring his brother's snake, and she went to a pet store and talked the owners into letting her borrow a turtle and a lizard.
>
> The next day, as students observed and handled the animals, they realized that snakes do have bones and that reptiles have dry, clean skin. Using additional photos, Jody showed how some reptiles laid their eggs in the ground, whereas others are born alive. On the basis of their new experiences, even Sanra and Lucia reluctantly agreed that reptiles' skins are dry and clean.

Because Jody provided concrete experiences for the students, their concepts of *reptile* were clarified and enriched. Providing these experiences can be demanding—Jody had to go to a pet store to get a live turtle and lizard, for example—but the results are worth the effort. Merely explaining that snakes are usually dry and clean would have been unconvincing for students such as Sanra and Lucia.

Although Jody's was a science lesson, similar approaches can be used in other content areas. If students are consistently misspelling the same types of words, for example, teaching rules that directly address the errors allows students to restructure their understanding (Hall, Gerber, & Stricker, 1989). When adapting their instruction, teachers design their lessons to build on students' current understandings. This is congruent with both information processing and constructivist views of learning.

Accommodating Differences in Patterns of Interaction

Although accommodating differences in background is challenging, dealing with differences in patterns of interaction can be even more difficult because these differences are easy to miss. A teacher less sensitive than Jody, for example, might not have persisted with Lucia, concluding instead that the girl didn't understand the topic, was uninterested, or a generally weak student.

In Chapter 4, we addressed the issue of discontinuities between the home and the school, and this might explain Lucia's reluctance to answer. Her reasoning wasn't faulty, and her misconception about snakes was sensible. On the basis of her experience, snakes *are* slippery and gross. It's also likely that her home experience didn't prepare her for questions such as "What makes you say that?" "What's your reaction to what Muhammed said?" and " . . . how does Muhammed's experience compare to what you said?" When Jody persisted and asked her about her experience with snakes, the basis for Lucia's comment was revealed. Had Lucia been familiar with the questioning patterns in the class, she would have responded to Jody's first question by simply saying something such as, "I felt a snake once, and it was slippery and gross."

Helping students learn to interact effectively in school is an important teacher task. "The key challenge for schools is to introduce and enculturate students into these school-based discourses without denigrating their culturally specific values and ways of using language" (Michaels & O'Connor, 1990, p. 18).

Teachers can help students acquire these school-effective ways of interacting in at least three ways (Michaels & O'Connor, 1990). First, they can provide and lead discussions that build on common experiences, such as having the students observe, describe, and discuss the reptiles Jody brought to class.

Second, during the discussions, they can introduce new kinds of talk, such as Jody's questions that asked for evidence. Because the new talk was related to concrete and familiar experiences—snakes and Muhammed's comments in Jody's lesson—the questions gradually become meaningful.

8.9 ▬
What concept from Chapter 7 best helps you understand why the way students respond to your questioning and other aspects of instruction varies so much?

By designing activities that encourage student involvement and group problem solving, teachers help students acquire and understand classroom-effective ways of interacting.

Third, teachers can discuss the new talk explicitly. For instance, Jody could discuss the intent of questions such as "What makes you say that?" with students and model responses for them. As students become familiar with patterns of classroom questioning and discussion, and they see that teachers are *explicitly* trying to involve them, they learn that their contributions are valued.

As teachers work with their students, they should monitor their own communication and realize that students' inability to respond may indicate miscommunication rather than lack of understanding, as was illustrated in the example with Lucia. Asking open-ended questions, as Jody did when she asked Lucia to describe her experience with snakes, is an excellent way to informally assess learners' current understanding.

Classroom Connections

Capitalizing on Diversity in Your Classroom

1. Assess students' background knowledge related to the topics you plan to teach.
   - A health teacher beginning a study of nutrition and eating habits asks her students to describe what they believe to be a good meal.
   - A math teacher beginning a unit on percentage increase and percentage decrease preassesses students by giving them several problems that require changing fractions to decimals and decimals to percentages.

2. Adapt instruction to students' different backgrounds.
   - A middle school English teacher finds that several of his students don't use Standard English in speaking and writing. He regularly assigns them short essays and encourages them to express themselves in whatever way they're comfortable. He then builds on the students' thinking and helps them learn to rephrase their writing to conform to standard practice by providing examples of correctly written passages and pairing students who act as peer editors for each other's work.
   - A sixth-grade teacher beginning a unit on Central America asks his students to describe their lives in their neighborhoods. He reminds them that this is their local "culture" and to use it as a comparison when they study the different cultures in Central America.

3. Provide examples that are meaningful for all the students in the class.
   - To illustrate the concept *adverb*, a fifth-grade teacher has a student walk quickly across the front of the room, asks students to describe how the student walked, and writes on the chalkboard: "Brenda walked quickly across the front of the room." As students discuss the sentence, the teacher leads them to conclude that quickly tells how Brenda walked, so it describes the verb in the sentence.
   - A third-grade teacher demonstrates the process of multiplication by having students make four groups of seven interlocking cubes, then three groups of eight interlocking cubes, and six groups of eight interlocking cubes. She then writes on the chalkboard

$$4 \times 7 = 28$$
$$3 \times 8 = 24$$
$$6 \times 8 = 48$$

and leads the class in a discussion of what the numerals mean in each case, carefully linking the numeral to the sets of cubes.

Problem Solving

As an introduction to this section, think about the following:

▌ You want to write a greeting card to a friend who has moved to New York, but you don't know her home address.

▌ You're planning to paint your living room. To determine how much paint you should buy, you need to know the area of the ceiling and walls.

▌ You're a teacher, and your seventh-graders resist thinking on their own. They expect to find the answer to every question specifically stated in the textbook.

8.10

You don't know the meaning of a word, so you look it up in a dictionary. Under these conditions, is not knowing the meaning of the word a problem? Explain.

What do the three incidents have in common? Although they look different, each can be described as a problem. A **problem** *exists when you're in a state that differs from a desired end state and there is some uncertainty about reaching the end state* (Bransford & Stein, 1984). "In short, a problem occurs when a problem solver has a goal but lacks an obvious way of achieving the goal" (Mayer & Wittrock, 1996, p. 47). In the preceding cases, for example, our goals are finding the address, knowing the area of the ceiling and walls, and having students think on their own.

Thinking of problems more broadly is beneficial in at least two ways. First, it recognizes the pervasiveness of problem solving in our everyday lives, and second, it allows people to apply general strategies to solve different kinds of problems (Bruning, Schraw, & Ronning, 1999).

Problem Solving: Theoretical Perspectives

Problem solving is grounded in both information processing and constructivist views of learning. For example, both emphasize the role of background knowledge as the foundation on which additional learning is based, and expert problem solvers have a great deal of well-organized background knowledge. In addition, expert problem solvers are strategic in their approaches to solving problems, they have well-developed metacognitive abilities, they organize their understanding in ways that overcome the limitations of working memory, and they develop their expertise through practice and experience. Each characteristic is grounded in information processing.

In addition, you will see that problem solving is facilitated by social interaction, and authentic problems are more effective than less meaningful problems. These are constructivist notions. Keep both of these views in mind as you study the following sections.

Well-Defined and Ill-Defined Problems

Experts on problem solving find it useful to distinguish between well-defined and ill-defined problems (Eysenck & Keane, 1990; H. Simon, 1978). A **well-defined problem** *has only one correct solution, and a certain method for finding it exists* (Bruning et al., 1999), whereas an **ill-defined problem** *has more than one acceptable solution and no generally agreed-on strategy for solving it; the goal is ambiguous* (Dunkle, Schraw, & Bendixon, 1995; Mayer & Wittrock, 1996). Our first two examples are well defined; your friend has only one home address, the area of the ceiling and walls of your living room is specific, and straightforward strategies for finding each exist. Many problems in math, physics, and chemistry are well defined, such as this example:

> *Roger and Diana were selling lemonade. The lemonade mix was $.40*
> *for a package that made 2 quarts. They sold the lemonade at $.10 for*

an 8-ounce glass and sold a total of 15 quarts. How much money did
they make on each glass they sold?

Although students often have difficulty solving this type of problem, its goal is clear, specific strategies exist for solving it, and there is only one correct answer.

In contrast, students' not wanting to think for themselves is an ill-defined problem. The goal state isn't clear: teachers are often not even sure what "thinking," means and a readily agreed-on strategy for getting students to "think" doesn't exist. The problem can be solved with several strategies, and several "right" answers can be found.

As teachers, we have an ill-defined problem of our own. Research indicates that our students are not very good at solving problems (Bruer, 1993; Mayer & Wittrock, 1996), and our goal is obviously for them to be better at it. In attempting to get a handle on this problem, we can identify at least two subproblems. First, most of learners' experiences in schools focus on well-defined problems, such as the example with the lemonade, but the majority of the problems we encounter in life are ill-defined. For instance, you're encountering an ill-defined problem as you study this book. Your goal is to understand the content and do well in the class, but "understanding" is ambiguous, and a variety of paths to understanding exist. Taking careful notes, studying with classmates, highlighting appropriate parts of the text, and completing the exercises in the student study guide are all possibilities.

Our second subproblem is the fact that the problem-solving process is personal (Mayer & Wittrock, 1996), and a well-defined problem for one learner is ill-defined for another. Further, solving well-defined and ill-defined problems requires different abilities (N. Hong & Jonassen, 1999).

As an example, let's look again at Laura's lesson. Finding the amount of carpeting necessary appears to be well-defined, and for an expert, it is; simply determine the total area of the floor, and subtract the area covered by linoleum. Only one answer exists, and the solution is straightforward. For Laura's students, however, the problem was ill-defined. Their understanding of the goal wasn't clear, some of them were uncertain about the difference between area and perimeter—as an interview after the lesson revealed—and they used a variety of strategies to reach the goal. Evidence of their uncertainty is indicated in the range of answers. No group got 1,186 square feet, the actual amount of carpeting required, and one group got 1,600 square feet, more than the total area of the room.

We've seen that our students are not very good at solving problems, and helping them become better problem solvers is one of the biggest challenges teachers face. In an attempt to solve our problem, we offer four strategies:

- Discuss with students a general problem-solving model that can be applied in a variety of domains.
- Describe for students the characteristics of expert problem solvers that might be used as models for novices.
- Present a specific set of suggestions for helping students improve their problem-solving abilities.
- Use technology to help learners become better problem solvers.

A General Problem-Solving Model

Some experts believe that one solution to our students' lack of problem-solving abilities is to develop general approaches to problem solving that can be applied in a variety of domains. Since the 1950s, computer scientists and cognitive psychologists have worked in this area, and their efforts have led to the problem-solving model illustrated in Figure 8.5 and discussed in the sections that follow (based on work by Bransford & Stein, 1984).

> **8.11**
> You're involved in a relationship with a member of the opposite sex, but the relationship isn't as satisfying as you would hope. Is this a well-defined or an ill-defined problem? Explain.

Figure 8.5

A general problem-solving model

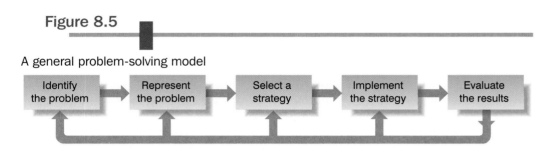

Identifying the Problem

Question: There are 26 sheep and 10 goats on a ship. How old is the captain?

Amazingly, in one study, 75% of the second graders who were asked this question answered 36 (cited in Prawat, 1989)! Obviously, they had difficulty understanding what the problem was asking.

At first glance, it appears that identifying a problem is simple and straightforward, but in fact, it is one of the most difficult aspects of problem solving. It requires patience and a willingness to avoid committing to a solution too soon (J. Hayes, 1988).

Obstacles to effectively identifying problems include

▌ Lack of experience in defining problems
▌ The tendency to rush toward a solution before the problem has been clearly defined
▌ The tendency to think convergently
▌ Lack of domain-specific knowledge (Bruning et al., 1999)

Lack of Experience in Defining Problems.   As you saw in the last section, most school-related experiences with problem solving involve well-defined problems presented by teachers or textbooks; in the elementary schools, the problems are usually in math, and in the middle and secondary schools, they're commonly limited to math, chemistry, and physics. Students often go through 13 or more years of formal schooling and acquire virtually no experience in defining problems.

Laura's lesson was an attempt to respond to this issue. On one hand, the lesson might appear unproductive since none of the groups got a correct answer. On the other, the students acquired valuable experience in defining problems, experience that is rare in schools but much needed in life.

8.12
What is the most effective thing a teacher can do to prevent students from rushing toward a solution before they fully understand the problem? Explain.

Tendency to Rush Toward a Solution.   Novice problem solvers tend to "jump" into a solution before they've clearly identified the problem (Lan, Repman, & Chyung, 1998; Van Leuvan, Wang, & Hildebrandt, 1990). The second graders who added sheep and goats to get the age of the captain illustrate this tendency. Even university students will quickly select and persist with a strategy despite the fact that it isn't working or making sense (Schoenfeld, 1989).

Research from a variety of domains indicates that time spent planning and defining problems results in more effective problem solving. For example, researchers found that experienced teachers spent much more time planning than did novices, and they generated more solutions to potential classroom problems (Moore, 1990). Similar results have been found in areas varying as widely as art (Getzels & Czikszentmihalyi, 1976) and mathematics (Schoenfeld, 1983).

Tendency to Think Convergently.   In contrast with **convergent thinking**, which is *thinking that tends to focus on one solution to a problem*, **divergent thinking** *occurs when problem solvers consider solutions that are novel or even seemingly inconsistent* with what appears to be the original problem. An example follows:

> Paula Waites, a second-year teacher, was having classroom management problems. Her students were inattentive and disruptive, and despite clearly stated rules and an effort to enforce them consistently, the behaviors persisted.
>
> "I'm not sure what to do," Paula confided to her friend, Linda, an 8-year veteran. "I know I'm supposed to be consistent, and I'm trying. I told them I mean business, and I wrote several referrals last week, but it isn't helping that much. I guess I'll just have to get tougher, but I hate coming down on them all the time. I've thought and thought about it, and that's all I can come up with."
>
> "I'm not sure," Linda responded, "but maybe you ought to try something a little different."
>
> "I don't know what you mean."
>
> "Maybe try working up a few really interesting activities, even if it takes some extra work. If the students like them, maybe they'll behave better. . . . Whenever my students are acting up, I ask myself if I'm doing a good job of motivating and involving them in my lessons. I mean, that isn't always the case, but it's often a factor in their behavior."
>
> "Gee, I guess I never actually thought about approaching it that way. I admit that most of what I do is lead discussions about what they've read or were supposed to read in the book."
>
> A week later, Paula reported that she had been experimenting with different motivational strategies and that her students were behaving much better.

In this case, Linda prompted Paula to look at her problem in a different way. What on the surface appeared to be a management problem was actually a problem with student motivation caused by unimaginative instruction. Paula was so focused on management that she was unable to see the problem in another way until Linda prompted her.

Learning to think divergently results from having a variety of experiences requiring divergent thinking. This suggests a crucial role for teachers. As they guide students' discussions of problems, they can ask questions that encourage thinking about the problems in different ways. As students acquire experience, they gradually develop their abilities to think divergently.

Lack of Domain-Specific Knowledge.   In Chapter 7, we emphasized the importance of schemas in organizing learners' background knowledge, and background knowledge is no less important in problem solving (Mayer, 1998a; Tuovinen, & Sweller, 1999). Teachers can help students access background knowledge by encouraging them to analyze and discuss problems before attempting to identify solutions (Bernardo, 1994; M. Lawson & Chinnappan, 1994).

Unfortunately, this isn't as easy as it appears. As we saw in Laura's lesson, the students reviewed area and perimeter, and they spent a considerable amount of time analyzing the problem. In spite of this discussion, her students weren't able to find the area of a nonroutine problem—the carpeted portion of the room—and many of them didn't have a clear understanding of *area* and *perimeter*. This lack of background knowledge is the most probable reason the students got different answers to the problem, reminding us again that the importance of background knowledge is difficult to overstate.

Teachers can help students learn general problem-solving strategies by focusing their attention on specific strategies, such as identifying and representing the problem during their problem-solving efforts.

Representing the Problem

The second step of the general problem-solving model involves representing the problem. Using a visual or written representation of the problem, such as the diagram that Laura's students used to represent their problem, is useful for at least two reasons: First, it puts the problem in a larger context and connects it to learners' existing background (Lovett & Anderson, 1994; Mevarech, 1999).

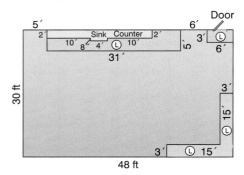

Second, putting problems on paper reduces the load on working memory. Working memory's capacity is limited (see Chapter 7), and many problems are so complex that working memory can easily be overloaded. A drawing, such as Laura's students used, helps identify important aspects of the problem. Without it, their working memories could easily be overloaded.

Selecting a Strategy: Algorithms and Heuristics

After the problem has been identified and represented, a strategy for solving it must be selected. This is the third step in the model.

Let's look at another problem:

A coat costing $90 is marked 25% off. What is the sale price of the coat?

For most of us, this is a well-defined problem. We simply take 25% of 90, subtract the result from $90, and get $67.50 as the sale price. We used an **algorithm**, or *specified set of steps*, in solving the problem. Algorithms vary widely in their complexity. For instance, when we subtract whole numbers with regrouping, add fractions with unlike denominators, and solve algebraic equations, we are using simple algorithms. On the other hand, computer experts, for example, use complex algorithms to solve sophisticated programming problems.

Many problems can't be solved with algorithms, however. They don't exist for ill-defined problems, and many well-defined problems also lack algorithms. In those cases, problem solvers use **heuristics**, which are *general, widely applicable problem-solving strategies* (Mayer & Wittrock, 1996). Three common heuristics include (a) trial and error, (b) means–ends analysis, and (c) drawing analogies.

Trial and Error.   The use of trial and error is obviously an inefficient strategy, but it is one that problem solvers often try first when faced with unfamiliar problems. Trial and error can be valuable, however, because it allows learners to explore the specifics of new problems, and experience is one of the most important factors in acquiring expertise (J. Hayes, 1988; Wagner & Sternberg, 1985). As learners gain experience, they switch to more efficient strategies.

Means–Ends Analysis.   Means–ends analysis is *a heuristic in which the problem solver attempts to break the problem into subgoals and works successively on each.* Some of Laura's students used means–ends analysis in solving their problem. For example, one of the strategies they used was (a) find the area of the whole room; (b) find the area of the floor covered by linoleum; and (c) subtract the areas covered by linoleum from the total area of the room. In this way they used their understanding of a well-defined problem (finding the areas of rectangles) to solve a problem that was, for them, ill-defined (finding the area of an irregular shape).

Means–ends analysis is one of the most effective strategies for solving ill-defined problems. Because ill-defined problems have ambiguous goals, identifying subgoals that can be operationally defined helps problem solvers "get a handle" on the problem. In the case of the seventh graders who don't want to "think," for example, we might operationally define "thinking" as an inclination to search for relationships in the topics they study, to make conclusions on the basis of evidence, and to remain open-minded. We can then design learning activities that provide experiences for them in these areas.

8.13 Think again about the ill-defined problem of a personal relationship that is less satisfying than you would like it to be. Describe a means–ends analysis that might be used to "solve" the problem.

Drawing Analogies.   Drawing analogies is *an attempt to solve unfamiliar problems by comparing them with familiar ones that have already been solved* (Mayer, 1992). While it is potentially a very effective strategy, at least two difficulties with using it commonly occur (Mayer & Wittrock, 1996). First, learners often can't find problems in their memories analogous to the one they want to solve, and second, even when they do find a similar problem, they often don't make appropriate connections between base and target problem. For example, in an interview after Laura's lesson, students were given the following problem:

> *How much carpet will be needed to cover the floor of the closet shown in the following drawing?*

This problem (the target) is directly analogous to the problem the students were given in the lesson (the base problem), and they recognized that the two were similar. In spite of recognizing the close similarity, however, they were initially unable to abstract the strategy of subtracting parts from the total area of the rectangle. Only with considerable scaffolding from the interviewer were they able to use the strategy.

Key factors in situations such as this are background knowledge and experience. The more background knowledge learners have with the analogy, the more effective it will be for helping learners solve the unfamiliar problem. This is true for both teacher-generated and learner-generated analogies (Pittman & Beth-Halachmy, 1997). Laura's students need a great deal of practice in solving problems involving the area of irregularly shaped plane figures.

Implementing the Strategy

The key to successfully implementing the strategy is clearly defining and representing the problem and selecting an appropriate algorithm or heuristic. If these processes have been effective, implementing the strategy is essentially routine. If learners cannot implement a strategy, they should rethink the original problem or the strategy they've selected.

This was the difficulty Laura's students had. Their understanding of *area* and *perimeter* was uncertain, and they lacked experience in defining problems, which made selecting an effective strategy hard for them. Their difficulties occurred well before they were to implement their strategies.

Evaluating the Results

Evaluating results is the final step in problem solving. Although this step seems basic, it is often a challenge for learners. For example,

> One boy, quite a good student, was working on the problem "If you have six jugs, and you want to put two thirds of a pint of lemonade into each jug, how much lemonade will you need?" His answer was 18 pints. I (Holt) said, "How much in each jug?" "Two thirds of a pint." I said, "Is that more or less than a pint?" "Less." I said, "How many jugs are there?" "Six." I said, "But that doesn't make any sense." He shrugged his shoulders and said, "Well, that's the way the system worked out." (Holt, 1964, p. 18)

This case illustrates a common occurrence in classrooms. Getting an answer, regardless of whether or not it makes sense, is typically the students' goal. Young children in particular have trouble at this stage, wanting to rush through, get on to the next problem, and finish the assignment (Schunk, 1994). This occurred in Laura's class, where several of her students were satisfied with widely discrepant answers.

When students learn to evaluate their results, their problem-solving abilities greatly improve (L. Baker, 1989; Zimmerman, 1990). Teachers can help in this process, particularly in math, by having students estimate answers before they begin. Estimates require thought, and when answers and estimates are far apart, questions are raised. The habit of estimating is an important disposition that teachers should try to help students develop.

Expert–Novice Differences in Problem-Solving Ability

Having described a general problem-solving model, we now look at characteristics of people who are good at solving problems. An **expert** is an *"individual who is highly skilled or knowledgeable in a given domain"* (Bruer, 1993, p. 12). A **novice** *isn't knowledgeable or skilled*. Research has identified four important differences between experts and novices in problem-solving ability (Bruning et al., 1999; Glaser & Chi, 1988). They're outlined in Table 8.2 and discussed in the paragraphs that follow.

Table 8.2

Expert–novice differences in problem-solving ability

Area	Experts	Novices
Representing problems	Search for context and relationships in problems.	See problems in isolated pieces.
Problem-solving efficiency	Solve problems rapidly and possess much knowledge that is automatic.	Solve problems slowly, and focus on mechanics.
Planning for problem solving	Plan carefully before attempting solutions to unfamiliar problems.	Plan briefly when attempting solutions to unfamiliar problems; quickly adopt and try solutions.
Monitoring problem solving	Demonstrate well-developed metacognitive abilities; abandon inefficient strategies.	Demonstrate limited metacognition; persevere with unproductive strategies.

8.14
The tendency of students to accept solutions that don't make sense is a common problem for teachers attempting to help their students become better problem solvers. Is this a well-defined or an ill-defined instructional problem? Explain. Describe specifically what you might do to help the boy in the lemonade problem arrive at a valid solution.

In looking at the differences in Table 8.2, we see a pattern; experts better overcome the limitations of working memory than do novices. First, for example, experts represent problems more effectively because their complex schemas allow them to recognize patterns and "chunk" large amounts of information into smaller units that don't exceed working memory's capacity.

Second, because much of experts' knowledge is automatic, they have working memory space available to focus on the overall problem instead of specific mechanics (Bruer, 1993). The combination of seeing patterns and automaticity also leaves working memory space that can be allocated to metacognition, so experts can monitor their progress and assess the validity of their solutions.

How do experts acquire these characteristics? The answer is simple. Experts possess a great deal of both domain-specific and general knowledge, and they have acquired much experience. Because of their experience, they can use heuristics, such as *drawing analogies,* effectively. "Specific experiences are represented in memory as 'cases' that are indexed and searched so that they can be applied analogically to new problems that occur" (Bransford, 1993, p. 4).

For example, expert teachers have experience; they possess a wide range of general knowledge; and they have a broad and deep understanding of learning, student characteristics, and the content they teach (Bruning et al., 1999). The same is true for experts in physics, computer science, history, music, and all others. No simple path to expertise exists, and some researchers estimate that it takes up to 10,000 hours to develop true expertise in a domain, such as teaching or computer science (Ericsson, 1996).

What implications does our understanding of expertise have for helping learners become better problem solvers? Let's take a look.

Developing Expertise: Role of Deliberate Practice

Research on the development of expertise is clear; if learners are to become expert in any area, they must have in-depth experiences with and learn a great deal about the area. If students are to develop their mathematical problem-solving skills, for example, they have to solve a lot of problems—nonroutine, ill-defined problems, not simple, drill-and-practice problems that require the application of memorized algorithms.

Recognizing this need, researchers have become interested in the concept of *deliberate practice* and its role in the acquisition of expertise (Ericsson, 1996; Ericsson, Krampe, & Tesch-Romer, 1993). Their research has identified four characteristics of deliberate practice:

- Learner motivation to attend to the task and exert effort
- Instruction that takes learners' background knowledge into account
- Feedback to learners about errors and how to improve performance
- Opportunities for learners to repeatedly perform similar (but not identical) tasks

In addition, researchers have found that deliberate, extensive practice is more important than native ability. They state emphatically,

> In summary, our review has uncovered essentially no support for the fixed innate characteristics that would correspond to general or specific natural ability (in the development of expertise), and, in fact, has uncovered findings inconsistent with such models. (Ericsson et al., 1993, p. 399)

This doesn't imply that native ability is irrelevant; acquiring expertise will be easier for some than for others. It does mean, however, that if we're willing to work hard enough and long enough, expertise can be ours as well as our students. In the vast majority of cases, talent doesn't block our road to competence. This is an encouraging finding.

8.15

Experts represent problems more effectively because their complex schemas allow them to recognize patterns and "chunk" large amounts of information into smaller units that don't exceed working memory's capacity. What implications does this have for the way you study for this or any other course? Be specific in your response.

8.16

Which heuristic is deliberate practice likely to help students' effectively use most: *trial and error, means–ends analysis,* or *drawing analogies?* Explain.

Acquiring Expertise: The Importance of Motivation

The research we've discussed has important implications for us as teachers. Practicing and sustaining effort requires motivated students. This isn't easy; students often complain about and try to avoid word problems in math, for example, because they are difficult and require thinking. Unless we consciously plan for learner motivation in our efforts to improve problem solving, we are likely to have limited success with all but the most successful and highly motivated students (Pintrich, Marx, & Boyle, 1993).

We've now discussed a general problem-solving model and the characteristics of expert performance, two of the strategies we identified for improving our students' problem-solving abilities. We turn now to the third strategy: specific suggestions for improving their skills.

Helping Learners Become Better Problem Solvers

Problem-solving ability requires a great deal of background knowledge in the form of schemas, expert problem solvers monitor their progress (they're metacognitive), and expert problem solvers have a great deal of automatic procedural knowledge. These are concepts grounded in information processing.

In addition, researchers generally agree that learners construct understanding, and the process of constructing is facilitated by social interaction and authentic, or real-world, tasks. These theoretical notions, suggesting that problem solving is a *cognitive process,* are confirmed by research (Mayer & Wittrock, 1996).

We now want to apply these ideas to some specific suggestions for improving learners' abilities to solve problems. They're outlined in Figure 8.6 and discussed in the sections that follow.

Capitalize on Social Interaction

Research indicates that encouraging students to discuss and analyze problems increases understanding and promotes transfer (Mevarech, 1999; E. Stern, 1993). Teachers can apply this research by arranging learning activities that encourage students to think about their problem-solving strategies and to share their thoughts with others. Laura, for example, had her students work cooperatively to both gather information and attempt solutions to problems, and she also involved the whole class in discussion when they explained their strategies and evaluated results.

Present Problems in Meaningful Contexts

In looking at Laura's lesson again, we can see she attempted to reach her goal of finding the areas of irregular plane figures by embedding her learning activity in a problem involv-

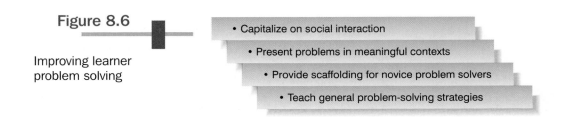

Figure 8.6

Improving learner problem solving

- Capitalize on social interaction
- Present problems in meaningful contexts
- Provide scaffolding for novice problem solvers
- Teach general problem-solving strategies

Social interaction in small groups provides opportunities for students to learn new problem-solving strategies from others.

ing carpeting her classroom, which was an "authentic task." Embedding problems in concrete contexts can significantly improve problem-solving ability as well as transfer (Bransford & Schwartz, 1999; Mayer, 1992).

Information processing supports the importance of practice and experience in developing expertise. One way of acquiring experience is to solve a wide variety of examples embedded in different contexts. For example, to extend their learning, Laura's students need to solve other area problems, such as the surface areas of objects in the room or in their homes. A variety of contextualized problem-solving experiences provides opportunities for students to embed specific solutions in larger conceptual frameworks, which increases the chances for transfer (Reed, Willis, & Guarino, 1994). In addition, presenting problems in meaningful contexts can increase learner motivation, which is essential if learners are to persist long enough to develop problem-solving expertise.

8.17
You saw in Chapter 7 that context is important in helping students develop procedural knowledge. Explain why this is the case. Describe the declarative and procedural knowledge that Laura's students needed in order to solve the "carpeting the room" problem.

Provide Scaffolding for Novice Problem Solvers

Social constructivism, grounded in Vygotsky's views, emphasizes the importance of scaffolding in assisting learning. As learners attempt to solve problems, teachers provide enough scaffolding to ensure that learners make progress on their own, but not so much guidance that learners' active roles in the process are reduced. A painter's scaffold supports the painter, but the painter does the painting; the teacher provides support, but the students solve the problems.

Three forms of scaffolding can be particularly helpful: analyzing worked examples, visually representing problems, and cognitive apprenticeships.

Analyzing Worked Examples.   In traditional problem-solving instruction, teachers typically display one or more problems and model the solutions, which students then try to imitate, often with little understanding.

In contrast, an expanding body of research confirms that analyzing worked examples, discussing them in detail, and relating the completed solutions to the problems makes the entire process much more meaningful (Mwangi & Sweller, 1998; Renkl, Stark,

Gruber, & Mandl, 1998). These results have been found with learners ranging from lower elementary to university students.

Analyzing worked examples has at least three advantages over traditional explanations. First, immediate achievement is higher; students using worked examples made fewer errors, completed the work more rapidly, and required less assistance from the teacher than students who received traditional explanations, and they even outperformed students who received individualized instruction. Second, analyzing worked examples increases learners' understanding of the broader problem-solving principles involved (Reed et al., 1994; Tuovinen & Sweller, 1999). Third, analyzing worked examples is motivating; learners prefer the analysis of worked examples to traditional instruction (Renkl et al., 1998).

The combination of the worked examples *with discussion* makes the learning experience especially meaningful for students. Worked examples alone are insufficient; without discussion, learners often miss important aspects of the process and are likely to try to memorize the steps in it instead of developing a meaningful understanding (Chi, Bassok, Lewis, Reiman, & Glaser, 1989).

Visually Representing Problems.   We know from our study of information processing that the limitations of working memory are obstacles we all face when trying to solve problems. This obstacle is particularly important for novices because they represent problems less efficiently than experts. Putting as much information as possible on paper helps reduce this load and improves problem-solving efficiency. Drawings and diagrams are particularly helpful because they often result in reconceptualizing the problem and they encourage the use of analogies as a strategy. As Laura's students worked, they used the diagram they had prepared, and this diagram guided their problem-solving efforts.

Cognitive Apprenticeship.   One form of scaffolding is **cognitive apprenticeship**, which *occurs when a less skilled learner works at the side of an expert* (Collins, Brown, & Holum, 1991; Collins, Brown, & Newman, 1989). Cognitive apprenticeship involves modeling, teacher think-alouds, teacher questions to promote active student involvement, coaching, and gradually removing support as the apprentice becomes proficient. (We discuss think-alouds and coaching in more detail in the next section.) In an apprenticeship model, teachers embed tasks in realistic and authentic contexts to build on the motivation and meaningfulness that are characteristic of work situated in out-of-school settings (Good & Brophy, 1997).

Teach General Problem-Solving Strategies

Research indicates that although general strategies in the absence of domain-specific knowledge are of limited value, within specific domains, such as mathematics, they can increase problem-solving abilities (Higgins, 1997; Mayer, 1992).

Teachers can help learners think in terms of general strategies by modeling the thinking involved. Thinking aloud provides a model for students and also allows those less confident to see that it's alright to take risks and make mistakes. As with all forms of teaching, an accepting teacher attitude is essential. By inviting alternative solutions, teachers emphasize thinking and the general problem-solving process rather than getting the right answer to a specific problem.

Teachers can also help students acquire general problem-solving skills through explicit instruction in the form of "coaching" (Collins et al., 1989; Mayer, 1998a). For example, as students work in small groups to solve problems, the teacher can ask questions to help the students develop an awareness of the problem-solving process:

8.18
Using constructivism as a basis, explain why discussion is so important to developing problem-solving expertise.

8.19
What elements of cognitive apprenticeship did Laura Hunter incorporate in her lesson?

8.20
Explain why general problem-solving strategies would be more effective within a particular domain, such as social studies or science, than across domains.

What (exactly) are you doing? (Can you describe it precisely?)

Why are you doing it? (How does it fit into the solution?)

How does it help you? (What will you do with the outcome when you obtain it?)
(Shoenfeld, 1989, p. 98)

In time and with practice, students begin to think in terms of general problem-solving strategies, and their problem-solving skills improve.

Technology and Learning:
Using Technology to Improve Problem-Solving Ability

We said earlier that developing problem-solving abilities requires that learners practice and acquire experience in solving problems, which requires motivated learners. They're more likely to be motivated if the problems they're expected to solve are realistic and interesting. Technology can be an effective tool in helping to meet this need. Here's an example:

> Jasper Woodbury sees an ad for a boat docked at Cedar Creek and decides to take a look. His dock is at mile 132.6, and in looking at his navigational map, he guesses it will take him about 2 hours to get to Cedar Creek in his boat, the Sweetie $\frac{1}{4}$. On the radio, he hears that the temperature is 91, the sunset will be at 7:52 P.M., and the wind is from the west at 4 mph.
>
> Jasper goes to Larry's to get gas, which is $1.29^9 with 4¢ off per gallon for cash. Jasper provides a pint of his own oil, which he adds to the tank before Larry puts the fuel in. When Larry looks at the pump, he sees that Jasper has gotten 5.0 gallons for a total of $6.30. Larry says to Jasper, "You can't put much more than 5 gallons in a 5-gallon tank, now can you?" Larry gives Jasper change from a 20-dollar bill, which is all the cash Jasper has.
>
> After a minor repair on his boat, costing $8.25, Jasper continues to Cedar Creek, which is at mile 156.6. He makes it all the way on one tank of gas.
>
> Jasper looks at an advertised boat and decides to buy it. The gas tank holds 12 gallons, and the boat burns about 5 gallons per hour at a cruising speed of 7½ mph. Sal, the previous owner, warns him that the running lights don't work, so she always gets home before the sun goes down.
>
> They settle on a price for Sal's boat, and Jasper pays her with his last check.
>
> Jasper looks at his watch and sees that it's 2:35 P.M.

Challenge:

When should Jasper leave for home?

Can he make it without running out of fuel?

The problem you just read is an abbreviated "story summary" of the episode "Journey to Cedar Creek," taken from the problem-solving series called *The Adventures of Jasper Woodbury* (Cognition and Technology Group at Vanderbilt, 1997). (The complete story summary, together with other problems, solutions, and extension problems are available at the Internet address shown in the reference list.) The series consists of 12 problems, three each in *trip planning, statistics and business, geometry,* and *algebra.* Each begins with a 15- to 20-minute video episode that illustrates a challenge to the characters in the episode.

Researchers developed the video-based episodes because many of the problems students are expected to solve don't capture the realism and complexity of life-related applications (S. Williams, Bareiss, & Reiser, 1996). The problems in each episode are purpose-

8.21 ▬
While each of the steps in the general problem-solving model are important, which one will be crucial for learners attempting to solve Jasper's problem? Explain why it will be so crucial.

Technology can provide learners with complex problems to solve in realistic contexts.

fully left ill-defined so students are given practice in problem finding and separating relevant from irrelevant information. The problems also provide the students with experiences in using means–ends analysis and identifying subgoals, such as finding out how much money Jasper has left.

Students work collaboratively over several class periods to solve the problems, during which they share their suggested solutions and receive feedback from the teacher and their classmates.

Research indicates that middle school students using the Jasper series were more successful than students in traditional programs in solving problems, planning for problem solving, and generating subgoals. They also understood basic math concepts as well as traditional students, and they had more positive attitudes toward math (Cognition and Technology Group at Vanderbilt, 1992). Teachers' comments corroborated these results.

> The kids would go home so excited and [the parents would say] "I've got to find out about this Jasper. It is all my kids would talk about. . . . " and "If you have any way of getting to (my) kids in high school, you'll find that they remember those four Jasper episodes. They may not remember anything else that we did that year but they'll remember. . . . those episodes because it did hit them and it did make an impact on them this year. (Cognition and Technology Group at Vanderbilt, 1992, p. 308)

Classroom Connections

Teaching Problem Solving in Your Classroom

1. Teach students general problem-solving strategies.
   - A third-grade math teacher spends time at the beginning of the school year teaching her students to break down problems into subgoals; she uses categories such as "We know" and "We need to know." She provides practice and spends considerable class time discussing general approaches to problem solving.

2. Make problems as concrete as possible, and discuss them qualitatively before attempting to solve them.
   - A middle-school math teacher teaches the first stage of problem solving by having his students practice putting problems into their own words. He asks them to replace the variables in an equation by using a concrete description, such as a person's age or a number.

3. Put problems into meaningful contexts.
   - A second-grade teacher has a "problem of the week" activity. Each student in the class is required to bring in at least one "real-world" problem each week. She selects from among them, and the class works on them in groups. She is careful to ensure that each student has a problem selected during the year.

4. Provide students with practice in problem finding.
   - A second-grade teacher begins a lesson on graphing by asking students how they might determine what people's favorite jelly beans are. She helps them identify a problem and guides their discussion of how to represent and solve it.

5. Teach students to evaluate the products of their problem solving.
   - A middle-school math teacher requires his students to write down an estimate of the answer before actually solving the problem. After the problem is solved, he requires students to compare the two answers.
   - A science teacher requires her students to underline the part of the word problem that suggests or requests units, such as square centimeters and meters per second. After students solve the problem, they have to draw a line from their answer to the underlined part.

The Strategic Learner

As you begin this section, think about the way you study for the courses you're taking. Do you highlight large portions of the book, or make note cards with terms and definitions on them? As a general pattern, do you think about the way you study and periodically ask yourself if your efforts and the way you spend your time are as effective as possible? Do you adapt to different conditions, such as skimming if you only want an overview of the content, or summarizing if you want a deeper understanding?

You should. And in the following discussion, you'll see why.

Metacognition: The Foundation of Strategic Learning

One principle of effective studying is *Learners who are aware of the way they study and learn, and consciously take steps to improve both, learn more than those who are less aware.* Strategic learners, learners who use strategies effectively, are metacognitive about their learning (C. Weinstein, 1994). They consciously match a particular strategy (e.g., summarizing, note taking) to a specific learning goal.

In Chapter 7, we defined **strategies** as *plans for accomplishing learning goals.* A large and consistent body of research documents the effectiveness of strategies in increasing learning (Rosenshine, 1997).

When you take notes, for example, you're using a strategy. Your note taking is a plan you're using to reach the goal of better understanding the content, and note taking involves operations that go beyond simply reading a passage or listening to an instructor. As you use this strategy, ask yourself questions such as:

▮ Am I taking enough notes, or am I taking too many?
▮ Am I writing down important ideas in my notes, or are my notes filled with unimportant details?

▌ Am I simply reading my notes when I study, or do I attempt to elaborate on them with examples?

▌ Am I using my notes together with the text, or am I studying each independently?

8.22   ▬

Which theory of learning—*behaviorism, social cognitive theory, information processing,* or *constructivism*—best supports the value of strategy use for increasing learning? Explain.

These are metacognitive questions, questions a strategic learner would ask. If you highlight parts of the text or reorganize your notes after class, you should ask similar questions because they are also strategies.

Although most strategy research has focused on reading (Bruning et al., 1999), other studies examined strategy use in a variety of areas, including problem solving in math and science, writing, and study skills (Rosenshine, 1997). This research indicates that effective strategy users, in addition to being metacognitive about their learning, have at least two other characteristics: (a) a broad background of knowledge and (b) a repertoire of strategies.

Broad Background Knowledge

The importance of a broad knowledge base has been emphasized repeatedly in both this chapter and Chapter 7. It is no less important for effective strategy use (Alao & Guthrie, 1999). Trying to encode information and represent it in memory without a strong knowledge base as an anchor makes strategy use difficult, if not impossible (Alexander, Graham, & Harris, 1998). Research underscores this point in a study in which reciprocal teaching (discussed in Chapter 9) was used with science students. Researchers found that without sufficient background knowledge students used the strategy to "predict trivia, to summarize details, and to clarify big words" (C. Anderson & Roth, 1989, p. 300). Additional research indicates that students with extensive background knowledge were able to use deep processing strategies to generate questions, create images, and use analogical thinking (Chinn, 1997). Implementing strategies across the curriculum requires adequate student background knowledge and instructional scaffolding that activates this knowledge.

8.23   ▬

Concepts are a form of *declarative knowledge,* while using strategies requires *procedural knowledge.* Explain the implications of these differences for teaching students concepts and teaching them to use strategies.

A Repertoire of Strategies

Just as effective problem solvers have wide experience in solving problems, effective strategy users have a variety of strategies from which to choose. For instance, they can take notes, skim, use outlines, take advantage of bold and italicized print, and capitalize on examples. They can use heuristics, such as means–ends analysis to break ill-defined problems into manageable parts. Without a repertoire of strategies, learners cannot match strategies to different contexts and goals.

Becoming a strategic learner takes time and effort. Research indicates that most students use primitive strategies, such as simple repetition, regardless of the difficulty of the material, in spite of being aware of more sophisticated strategies. Unfortunately, rarely do students receive strategy instruction before high school (E. Wood, Motz, & Willoughby, 1998).

Study Strategies

Students use **study strategies** when they attempt to *increase their understanding of written materials and teacher presentations.* In this section, we examine different study strategies, beginning with basic study skills.

Basic Study Skills

Basic study skills are simple, commonly used strategies, such as highlighting and taking notes. The effectiveness of study strategies depends on the thought involved in making decisions about what is important enough to highlight, include in notes, or use in organizing ideas (Moreland, Dansereau, & Chmielewiski, 1997; J. Wiley & Voss, 1999).

Again we see how effective strategy use is grounded in metacognition. The decision-making thoughts are metacognitive, and engaging in metacognitive thought is the most difficult part of the process. Some students avoid these decisions by highlighting entire sections, for example, tacitly feeling like they're studying when, in fact, the process is little more than the combined acts of reading and physically marking the text. These students are metacognitively "inert"; they're studying passively instead of actively.

Students often have difficulty making decisions about what information is most important. They tend to focus on the first sentence of paragraphs; items that stand out, such as those in boldface or italics (Mayer, 1984); or items that are intrinsically interesting, missing important ideas embedded in the body of a passage (Garner, Alexander, Gillingham, Kulikowich, & Brown, 1991).

Note taking is similar to highlighting; its effectiveness depends on the learner's decisions about what is important enough to write down. As with highlighting, some students take notes passively—even though they write furiously—by attempting to write down everything the teacher says, thereby avoiding decisions about what is important and how ideas are interconnected.

> **8.24**
> Using information processing as a basis, explain why students have the tendency to avoid making the decision about what is important, focusing instead on the first sentence of paragraphs, items that stand out, or information that is intrinsically interesting.

Comprehension Monitoring

Comprehension monitoring is *the process of periodically checking to see whether you understand the material you're reading or hearing* (Palincsar & Brown, 1984). It is an advanced study strategy, and it obviously requires well-developed metacognitive abilities. Low achievers and others who aren't inclined to be metacognitive seldom check themselves and fail to take action when they don't understand what they're reading or hearing (L. Baker & Brown, 1984).

Let's look at two important comprehension monitoring strategies: summarizing and self-questioning.

Summarizing.   Learning to **summarize**, or *prepare a concise statement of the essential meaning of a verbal or written passage*, is a powerful comprehension-monitoring strategy. Teaching students to summarize takes time and requires training, but upper elementary students and higher can become skilled with it (Pressley, Johnson, Symons, McGoldrick, & Kurita, 1989). Training usually consists of walking students through a passage and helping them identify and delete unimportant information, construct general descriptions for lists of items, and construct a topic sentence for each paragraph. Although time-consuming, training results in increased comprehension (T. Anderson & Armbruster, 1984; A. Brown & Palincsar, 1987). We examine summarizing in more depth in Chapter 9 when we focus on cognition in reading.

Self-Questioning.   A second effective way of learning to monitor comprehension is through self-questioning (Dole, Duffy, Roehler, & Pearson, 1991). It occurs when students stop periodi-

Study strategies such as note taking and outlining are effectively learned through teacher modeling, think-alouds, and discussion.

cally as they read and ask themselves questions about the material. **Elaborative questioning**—which is *the process of drawing inferences, identifying relationships, citing examples, or identifying implications of the material being studied*—is a particularly effective form of self-questioning (E. Wood, Willoughby, McDermott, Motz, Kaspar, & Ducharme, 1999). You saw in Chapter 7 that elaboration is one way to promote meaningfulness, and students can also use the process as an effective comprehension-monitoring strategy. Three elaborative questions are especially effective:

▌ What is an additional example of this idea?
▌ How is this topic similar to or different from the one in the previous section?
▌ What is this a part of?

To illustrate these strategies, consider your own study of this chapter. As you were studying the section on problem solving, you could have asked yourself questions, such as

What is another example of a well-defined problem in this class? What is another example of an ill-defined problem?

What makes the first well-defined and the second ill-defined?

How are problem-solving and learning strategies similar? How are they different?

Could concept learning ever be problem solving? Why or why not?

Elaborative self-questioning creates links between new information and knowledge in long-term memory, improving both comprehension and learning.

8.25

Give an example of a self-question that would *not* be classified as elaborative questioning. Explain why it wouldn't be considered an elaborative question.

Advanced Comprehension-Monitoring Strategies

In an effort to help learners improve their comprehension-monitoring, researchers have developed complex study systems specifically focusing on those abilities, and because of their complexity, these systems require extensive training. We describe two of these strategies in this section.

SQ4R.   One of the oldest study systems, SQ4R (Survey, Question, Read, Reflect, Recite, Review) teaches students to attack a text and monitor comprehension in a series of sequential steps (Thomas & Robinson, 1972). A descendant of an earlier system called SQ3R (the additional R is for reflect), SQ4R has proven effective for both learning and retention (A. Adams, Carnine, & Gersten, 1982). The steps in SQ4R are outlined in Figure 8.7.

Figure 8.7

The steps in SQ4R

S	Survey	Skim material. Use headings as guides.
Q	Question	Construct questions about material.
R	Read	Read, using questions as guides.
R	Reflect	Think about what has been read. Relate ideas to what is already known.
R	Recite	Answer questions. Relate information to headings.
R	Review	Organize information. Restudy difficult material.

Source: Improving Reading in Every Class: A Sourcebook for Teachers by E. Thomas and H. Robinson, 1972, Boston: Allyn & Bacon. Copyright 1972 by Allyn & Bacon. Adapted by permission of the publisher and the author.

Figure 8.8

Sequential steps in MURDER

M	Mood	Plan for study. Schedule time. Monitor concentration.
U	Understanding	Identify important and difficult ideas.
R	Recall	Paraphrase content. Map key concepts.
D	Digest	Reflect. Identify key points and trouble spots.
E	Expand	Ask how information is applied.
R	Review	Analyze errors on quizzes. Modify study methods.

Source: "Learning Strategy Research" by D. Dansereau. In J Segal, S. Chipman, and R. Glaser (Eds.), *Thinking and Learning Skills* (Vol. I), 1985. Hillsdale, NJ: Erlbaum. Copyright 1985 by Lawrence Erlbaum. Reprinted by permission.

MURDER.   A more recent comprehension-monitoring system uses a mnemonic aid to help students remember the steps (Dansereau, 1985). The MURDER (Mood, Understanding, Recall, Digest, Expand, Review) system is more specific than the SQ4R system. The steps are outlined in Figure 8.8.

Research done with college students supports the effectiveness of the MURDER system. Trained students scored more than 30% higher than those in a control group on post-tests and also reported favorable attitudes toward the system. Three-month follow-up questionnaires revealed continued use and favorable attitudes (Dansereau, 1985).

> 8.26 ▬
> You're studying a topic in biology, such as *genetics* or *DNA*. Which of the strategies—SQ4R or MURDER—is probably better for helping you understand the content? Explain your answer, referring to the specific characteristics of each strategy.

Helping Students Become Effective Strategy Users

Teachers can help learners become more effective strategy users by encouraging them to think about and discuss when and why a specific strategy is effective, modeling for students the process and the thinking involved, and having students practice with specific topics (Carpenter, Levi, Fennema, Ansell, & Franke, 1995; Rickards, Fajen, Sullivan, & Gillespie, 1997). The teacher then provides instructional scaffolding as learners practice applying it, gradually withdrawing support as they become more competent (Rosenshine, 1997; Rosenshine & Meister, 1994). Let's look at an example:

> Donna Evans, a middle-school geography teacher, began a lesson by saying, "We need to read the section of our text that describes the low-latitude climates, middle-latitude climates, and high-latitude climates. Let's talk for a few minutes about how we can help ourselves remember and understand what we've read.
>
> "One way to help us be more effective readers is to summarize the information we read into a few short statements. This is a very useful reading skill. First, it makes the information easier to remember, and second, it helps us compare one climate region with another. We can use this skill whenever we're studying a specific topic, such as climates, and later when we study culture and economics. You can do the same thing when you study different classes of animals in biology or parts of the court system in your government class.
>
> "Now go ahead and read the passage, and see if you can decide what makes a low-latitude climate a low-latitude climate," she said.
>
> After giving the class a few minutes to read the section, Donna continued, "As I was reading, I kept asking myself what makes the low-latitude climates what they are. . . . Here's how I thought about it. I read the section, and I saw that the low latitudes could

be either hot and wet or hot and dry. Close to the equator, the humid tropical climate is hot and wet all year. A little farther away, it has wet summers and dry winters. For the dry tropical climate, high-pressure zones cause deserts, like the Sahara.

"Now, let's all give it a try with the section on the middle-latitude climates. Go ahead and read the section, and see whether you can summarize it the way I did."

The class read the passage, and after they finished, Donna began, "Okay. Give me a summary, someone. . . . Go ahead, Dana."

Dana offered her summary, and Donna and other class members responded, adding information and comments to what Dana said. They then practiced again with the section on the high-latitude climates.

In this episode, Donna demonstrated at least four characteristics of effective strategy instruction:

▌ She explicitly taught the skill, explaining how it worked and why it was important. (She modified the skill slightly, focusing on the characteristics of the climate regions, rather than merely identifying a topic sentence and supporting details. In this way, it better fit her content area.)

▌ She attempted to increase students' metacognitive awareness of the skill by identifying where it is useful, both in geography and in other parts of the curriculum.

▌ She modeled the skill, including her thinking, with the students.

▌ She had students practice the skill, providing feedback in the process.

Notice also that although Donna focused explicitly on summarizing, she also modeled self-questioning when she said, "I kept asking myself, 'What makes the low-latitude climates what they are?'" Helping students see the larger picture by combining strategies in this way makes strategy instruction even more effective (G. Duffy, 1992).

Critical Thinking

The term **critical thinking** has been defined in a variety of ways, but the definitions generally refer to a person's *ability and inclination to make and assess conclusions based on evidence*. For example, an advertisement says, "Doctors recommend . . . more often," touting a pain reliever or other health product. A person thinking critically is wary because the advertisement provides no evidence for its claims. Similarly, a person thinking critically listens to another person's argument with skepticism because people often have unconscious biases. Critical thinkers are irritated with the directive to "take these [pills] with meals" if they aren't told why.

The development of learners who think critically is at the core of cognitive approaches to teaching and, as with the development of problem-solving skills, expertise, learning strategies, and any other objective, it takes practice (Halpern, 1995). If learners are to take responsibility for their own learning, they must be given opportunities to practice analyzing and evaluating ideas, weighing opinions, assessing evidence, and constructing solutions to problems. A classroom climate that values different perspectives and high levels of discussion is essential. Reasons for answers are as important as the answers themselves.

Interest in critical thinking has grown over the years because of several factors, some of which are outlined in Table 8.3 (based on work by Bransford et al., 1991).

Although critical thinking is related to using study skills, the two differ in scope. Study skills focus on learning from teacher presentations and written materials. Critical thinking is broader; it's used to process information from multiple sources in a general sense (Beach, 1999; E. Jones, 1995). For example, reading a column in the editorial section

---

8.27

Explain specifically one way in which Donna's approach was an application of information processing, and also explain one way in which her approach was an application of social cognitive theory.

Table 8.3

Factors contributing to the interest in teaching critical thinking

Factor	Description
Poor test scores	American students score poorly on tests that require thinking (e.g., writing persuasive essays, solving word problems in math, using formal and informal reasoning).
Concerns of business leaders	Business leaders believe that high school and college graduates cannot speak and write effectively, learn on the job, and use quantitative skills.
Increased need for thinking in the future	Many future jobs will require complex learning skills and the ability to adapt to rapid change. Thinking will no longer be the domain of a select few.
National needs and personal rights	The primary weapon against being exploited by selfish leaders is the ability to think. A major impediment to peace in the world is irrational behavior (Nickerson, 1986).

of a newspaper, you might ask a question or summarize the passage to increase your comprehension of it. When you go beyond comprehension of the passage, however, to look for evidence for the author's position or to question whether the author is justified in taking the position he or she does, you are thinking critically.

Teaching Thinking: Within or Outside the Regular Curriculum?

Over the years, many programs have been developed to teach different aspects of thinking outside traditional content courses. Among them are the CoRT Thinking Program (de Bono, 1976), Philosophy for Children (Lipman, Sharp, & Oscanyan, 1980), and Project Intelligence/Odyssey (Herrnstein, Nickerson, Sanchez, & Swets, 1986). The problem with these programs has been that the skills have rarely transferred to the regular curriculum (Bransford et al., 1991).

A trend that began in the 1980s and continues today is the explicit teaching of thinking within the context of the regular curriculum. Emphasis on either without the other is likely to be less effective than combining the two. Nickerson (1988) summarizes this position:

> On the one hand, it is important to treat the skills, strategies, attitudes, and other targeted aspects of thinking in such a way that students come to understand their independence from specific domains and their applicability to many; on the other, it seems equally important to demonstrate their application in meaningful contexts, so students witness their genuine usefulness. (p. 34)

Current approaches to teaching critical thinking skills vary but are generally organized around four basic elements, illustrated in Figure 8.9 (adapted from Nickerson, 1988).

Basic Processes

Basic processes are *the fundamental components or "tools" of thinking*. With some variation from one source to another (Beyer, 1988; Halpern, 1998), most experts include the processes summarized in Table 8.4.

8.28
What is the most likely reason that efforts to teach thinking outside the context of the regular curriculum have been unsuccessful?

Figure 8.9

Elements of critical thinking

Source: Adapted from Nickerson, 1988

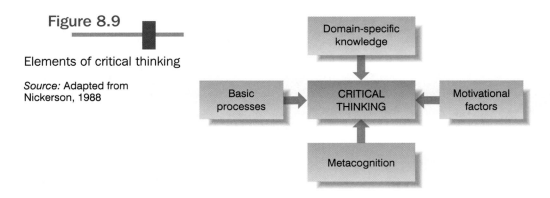

Table 8.4

Basic processes in thinking

Process	Subprocesses
Observing	Recalling Recognizing
Finding patterns and generalizing	Comparing and contrasting Classifying Identifying relevant and irrelevant information
Forming conclusions based on patterns	Inferring Predicting Hypothesizing Applying
Assessing conclusions based on observation	Checking consistency Identifying bias, stereotypes, clichés, and propaganda Identifying unstated assumptions Recognizing overgeneralizations or undergeneralizations Confirming conclusions with facts

8.29
Which of the basic processes in thinking could a *preoperational* learner use? What processes would require *concrete operational thinking? Formal operational thinking*? Explain in each case.

You can think of these processes as the basic building blocks of thinking. By focusing on these processes and subprocesses, we attempt to break the complex phenomenon of thinking into teachable and learnable parts.

Laura emphasized these processes when she had her students compare the strategies they used to solve their problem. The comparisons helped her students see patterns in their thinking. David Shelton, in his astronomy lesson in Chapter 7, also emphasized these processes when he encouraged his students to explain different characteristics related to planets on the basis of the information students had available to them.

Research on the teaching of critical thinking skills supports the idea of focusing on basic processes, which are specifically described, modeled, and practiced with feedback (Beyer, 1984; Sternberg, 1998b, 1998c). By integrating critical thinking into the regular school curriculum, teachers not only teach thinking but also help their students process information in a deeper, more meaningful way (Bransford et al., 1991; Van Leuvan et al., 1990).

Domain-Specific Knowledge

Like the other aspects of cognitive learning discussed in this chapter and in Chapter 7, domain-specific knowledge is critical to the teaching of thinking. To think, a person must think about something; domain-specific knowledge is the content in a given area about which a person thinks critically. "The importance of domain-specific knowledge to thinking is not really debatable. To think effectively in any domain one must know something about the domain and, in general, the more one knows the better" (Nickerson, 1988, p. 13).

Metacognition

We emphasize metacognition throughout this text. In the context of critical thinking, metacognition means that the learner knows when to use the basic processes, how they relate to domain-specific knowledge, and why they're used. Effective thinkers not only find patterns and form conclusions based on evidence, for example, but also are keenly aware of what they're doing. Explicitly teaching and talking about thinking as it occurs in the classroom are effective ways to develop students' metacognitive abilities (M. Adams, 1989; Butler, 1998). Explicitly focusing on and discussing metacognitive skills increases both reading comprehension and mathematical problem solving (Mayer & Wittrock, 1996).

Motivational Factors

Experts are becoming increasingly aware of the role motivation plays in thinking (Pintrich & Schunk, 1996; Resnick, 1987). Learner motivation determines the attitudes and dispositions students bring to their learning experiences, and attitudes are an essential component of thinking, influencing how and when thinking skills will be used. Examples include:

▎ The inclination to rely on evidence in making conclusions
▎ The willingness to respect opinions that differ from your own
▎ A sense of curiosity, inquisitiveness, and a desire to be informed

Asking students to compare, contrast, analyze, and make predictions encourages them to use and develop higher level cognitive processes.

▌ A tendency to reflect before acting

▌ The willingness to "let go" of previous ideas, beliefs, and assumptions (Bransford & Schwartz, 1999; Nickerson, 1988; Tishman, Perkins, & Jay, 1995)

Each of these influences students' inclinations to think critically.

Much of a teacher's effort in teaching thinking is directed toward helping learners develop these inclinations. For example, we want our students to ask themselves, "Where is the author coming from?" when they read a political commentary, knowing that political orientation will slant the author's opinion. In school, we want learners to be skeptical about the truth of rumors, and in classroom settings, we want them to constantly wonder, "What does this relate to?" and, "How do we know?"

Attitudes and dispositions often can't be taught directly. They're learned primarily by modeling; students disposed to think critically and accurately usually have teachers who demonstrate and set this tone for them.

This completes our discussion of critical thinking, the second major category of cognitive strategies emphasized in U.S. schools. We now turn our attention to transfer, a variable that influences how successfully concept learning, problem solving, and strategy use are applied in future learning situations.

Classroom Connections

Teaching Cognitive Strategies in Your Classroom

1. Teach study strategies across the curriculum.
   - A sixth-grade teacher introduces note taking as a listening skill and then provides note-taking practice in science and social studies by using a skeletal outline to organize his presentations and by requiring students to take notes from his presentations.
   - A home economics teacher introduces outlining at the beginning of the school year. Later, she collects students' outline notes of her lectures and gives them feedback on the quality of the notes.

2. Teach students to analyze their study strategies and to match them to learning tasks.
   - A biology teacher reviews for a unit test by surveying the important concepts and then describing the types of items on the test, such as essay and multiple choice. Then he asks for volunteers to share ways of studying that they have found effective.

Teaching Critical Thinking in Your Classroom

3. Plan and conduct lessons to promote thinking.
   - A first-grade teacher recaps every field trip by asking students to list things they saw on the trip.

   Then the class categorizes items and thinks of names for the categories.
   - A social studies teacher develops much of the content in her units with charts, graphs, and tables. She begins the units by asking her students to first make observations, then comparisons, then conclusions based on the comparisons. Finally, they generalize whenever possible and analyze their thinking to see whether they have over- or under-generalized.

4. Use questioning to promote thinking.
   - A fifth-grade teacher makes an effort to ask questions that promote thinking in his students. He has a list he calls "The Big Five" and looks for opportunities to ask them whenever he can: (a) What do you see? notice? observe? (b) How are these alike? How are they different? (c) Why? (d) What would happen if . . . ? (e) How do you know?
   - An English teacher attempts to help his students analyze literature. As they talk about a work, he constantly asks, "Why do you say that?" and, "What in the story supports your idea?"

Transfer of Learning

Consider the following situation:

> *You get into your car, insert the key into the ignition, and the seat belt buzzer goes off. You quickly buckle the belt. Or anticipating the buzzer, you buckle the belt before you insert the key.*

Think now for a moment before reading further. What concept from behaviorism does your behavior—buckling the seat belt—best illustrate? Behaviorists would describe this as an example of *negative reinforcement*. If you identified it as such, you have demonstrated **transfer**, which *"occurs when a person's prior experience and knowledge affect learning or problem solving in a new situation"* (emphasis added, Mayer & Wittrock, 1996, p. 48). You have applied your understanding of the concept *negative reinforcement* to the situation with the seat belt.

> Transfer makes survival possible by allowing humans to adapt to new situations. Schools are not able to teach students everything they will need to know, but rather must equip students with the ability to transfer—to use what they have learned to solve new problems successfully or to learn quickly in new situations. (Mayer & Wittrock, 1996, p. 49)

Merely recalling information, however, doesn't involve transfer. If, for example, your instructor has previously discussed buckling the seat belt as an example of negative reinforcement and if you later identify it as such, there is no transfer. You merely remembered the information.

With respect to problem solving, transfer occurs when students can solve problems they haven't previously encountered, and, in the case of study skills, transfer occurs when students use self-questioning, for example, in areas other than reading.

> **8.30** ■
> One learner transfers understanding of a topic to a new situation, whereas another learner does not. Describe possible differences in the two learners' schemas.

Positive and Negative Transfer

Positive transfer occurs when learning in one situation *facilitates* performance in another, whereas *negative* transfer occurs when one situation hinders performance in another (Mayer & Wittrock, 1996). As a simple example, if students know that a mammal nurses its young and breathes through lungs and then, using these characteristics, conclude that a whale is a mammal, they demonstrate positive transfer. On the other hand, if they believe that a fish is an animal that lives in the sea and then conclude that a whale is a fish, negative transfer occurs.

General and Specific Transfer

At one time, educators believed that taking courses such as Latin, Greek, and mathematics were valuable not only for learning Latin, Greek, and math, per se but also to "discipline" the mind. The hope was these courses would strengthen learners' general thinking ability. If these beliefs had been confirmed, they would involve **general transfer**, which is *the ability to take knowledge or skills learned in one situation and apply them in a broad range of different situations*. For example, if becoming an expert chess player would help a person learn math more easily because both require logic, general transfer would occur. **Specific transfer** is *the ability to use information in a setting similar to the one in which the information is originally learned*. If having learned that photos means "light" in Greek results in a learner better understanding words such as photography and photosynthesis, specific transfer occurs.

Unfortunately, as researchers found more than 80 years ago and have since confirmed repeatedly, transfer is quite specific (Driscoll, 1994; Perkins & Salomon, 1989; E. Thorndike, 1924). Studying Latin, for example, results in learners' acquiring expertise in Latin and perhaps specific transfer to the Latin roots of English words; it does little to improve thinking in general. Teachers can, however, significantly increase their students' ability to transfer.

Factors Affecting the Transfer of Learning

At least six factors affect students' ability to transfer:

- Similarity between the two learning situations
- Depth of learners' original understanding
- Quality of learning experiences
- Context for learners' experiences
- Variety of learning experiences
- Emphasis on metacognition

Similarity Between the Two Learning Situations

As our discussion of general and specific transfer implies, the more closely the two learning situations are related, the more likely transfer is to occur. For instance, if students have encountered examples of mammals such as dogs, cats, horses, and deer, they are likely to identify a cow as a mammal because cows are similar to the other examples. By comparison, learners are less likely to transfer the concept *mammal* to bats because bats aren't as closely related to the original examples.

With respect to problem solving, when first graders are given the following problem,

> *Angi has two pieces of candy. Kim gives her three more pieces of candy. How many pieces does Angi have now?*

they do well on this one:

> *Bruce had three pencils. His friend Orlando gave him two more. How many pencils does Bruce have now?*

When they're given the problem about Angi and Kim followed by this problem,

> *Sophie has three cookies. Flavio has four cookies. How many do they have together?*

they perform less well (Riley, Greeno, & Heller, 1982). The first two problems are more closely related than the first and third. These results demonstrate how specific transfer can be.

Depth of Original Understanding

Transfer requires a high level of original understanding (Bransford & Schwartz, 1999). While this seems obvious, research indicates that students often fail to transfer because they don't understand the topic in the first place (A. Lee, 1998; A. Lee & Pennington, 1993).

8.31 ▬

Assess the level of Laura's students' understanding after the lesson, but before the interview in which their ability to transfer understanding was measured. Provide evidence for your assessment.

The more time learners spend studying a topic, the more likely they'll understand it, and the more likely transfer will occur (Bransford & Schwartz, 1999; Gick & Holyoak, 1987). The key is depth of understanding versus breadth. "Schools should pick the most important concepts and skills to emphasize so that they can concentrate on the quality of understanding rather than on the quantity of information presented" (Rutherford & Algren, 1990, p. 185).

Student discussion also facilitates understanding and transfer; as students share ideas and identify relationships in the topics they're studying, they gain insights into the ways ideas apply in different settings (Vanderstoep & Seifert, 1994).

Quality of Learning Experiences

Quality refers to the extent that the content representations that the students study contain the information that students need in order to understand the topic. For example, Karen Johnson's compressed cotton (in the opening case of Chapter 2) was a high-quality example because *the students could see the essential characteristic* of density in the example. Similarly, Diane's Smith's pencils (in the closing case for Chapter 4) were high-quality examples because the students *could see* that one was longer than another. Karen's and Diane's examples were also effective because they were concrete, and research indicates that concrete examples are particularly meaningful for learners (Bransford & Schwartz, 1999).

With respect to problem solving, high-quality problem-solving experiences have real-world applications, are meaningful to students' lives, and emphasize meaning over procedures (Rittle-Johnson, & Alibali, 1999). Problems that students identify or generate themselves are particularly powerful. Laura capitalized on the value of real-world applications in guiding her students as they found the area of the classroom carpet.

Context for Learners' Experiences

In Chapter 7, we saw that learners encode both the information they're learning and the context in which that information exists (J. Brown et al., 1989). This is important because contextualized information is more meaningful than information learned in the abstract. An example follows:

Shaleena Adams was working with her students on their writing skills, and found that they had difficulty with correctly forming plural nouns. In an attempt to make the skill more meaningful for them, she presented the following passage:

Jefferson, one rural **county** among several **counties**, has six **schools**—one high **school**, two elementary **schools**, and one middle **school**. Five of the **schools** are in Brookesville, the largest city in Jefferson **county. Schools** in the three **cities** nearest Brookesville are Brookesville's biggest rivals. The **schools** in all the cities hold an annual athletic and scholastic competition.

The two **women** advisors of the debate team and the **woman** who coached the softball team were proud of both the performance of the **students** from Big Tree High School and their appearance. (The school is named after a 600-year-old **tree** that stands prominently in a grove of oak **trees** near the school grounds.) One **student** took all-around honors, and four other **students** won medals. One **girl** and one **boy** were honored for their work in math, and two **boys** and two **girls** wrote exemplary essays.

8.32
Shaleena's example was in context, but it was also high *quality*. Explain why it was high quality, referring directly to the passage in making your explanation.

> One essay was voted top of the competition. It described a **child** and how she helped several other **children** learn to cope with difficulty.
>
> The **students** all looked the part of **ladies** and **gentlemen**. Each young **gentleman** wore a shirt and tie, and each young **lady** wore a dress or pant suit.

> Shaleena guided the students' discussion of the passage, helping them identify the reasons for the different spellings of the plural nouns.

In general, *context* refers to real-world application. In the real world, students read passages, not decontextualized sentences, for example, and their understanding of spelling rules is more likely to transfer if they learn the rules in the context of a passage, such as Shaleena's. Similarly, students' understanding of the law of inertia is more likely to transfer if they study it in the context of real-world applications, such as why we wear seatbelts and why cars sometimes "miss" curves.

Context is a double-edged sword, however. While contextualized concepts and problems are more meaningful than those presented in the abstract, overly contextualized information can impede transfer because learners' understanding is tied too tightly to the original context (Bransford & Schwartz, 1999). We saw this illustrated in Laura's lesson. She embedded her entire problem-solving experience in the context of a practical problem that her students could directly relate to. As the interview after the lesson revealed, however, students had difficulty transferring their understanding of the classroom area problem to the context of other irregularly shaped objects.

Variety of Learning Experiences

For transfer to occur, knowledge and skills learned in one context must be applied in others. This means that concepts and problems must be presented in a variety of contexts (Cognition and Technology Group at Vanderbilt, 1997). Variety of contexts is perhaps the most important factor affecting the transfer of understanding.

Variety also means that a topic has been covered in several ways from a number of perspectives and is sometimes called "multiple knowledge representations" (Brenner et al., 1997; Spiro, Feltovich, Jacobson, & Coulson, 1992). As learners construct understanding that prepares for transfer, each case or example adds connections that others miss.

One way of visualizing this variety of examples is to think of "criss-crossing" a conceptual landscape (Spiro et al., 1992). For instance, if the topic is *reptiles*, adequate variety means that examples of snakes, alligators, turtles, and lizards are included to help students understand the breadth and depth of the concept. Inadequate variety results in students' undergeneralizing and forming an incomplete concept. The same applies to problem solving and cognitive strategies; the greater the variety of applications, the greater the likelihood that students' understanding will transfer (Sternberg & Frensch, 1993).

Emphasis on Metacognition

Research indicates that an emphasis on metacognition—encouraging students to monitor, reflect upon, and improve their learning strategies and problem solving—also increases transfer (Renkl et al., 1998; Tobias & Everson, 1998).

Evidence also indicates that dispositions can transfer in a general sense (Prawat, 1989). The inclination to be open-minded, to reserve judgment, to search for facts to support conclusions, and to take personal responsibility for learning is a general disposition. Domain-specific knowledge is required for understanding the conclusion and the relevant facts, but the disposition is a general orientation. Schoenfeld (1989), after acknowledging that much learning and problem solving is domain-specific, concludes:

> At the level of self-regulation, however, the issues appear to be the same across subject-matter boundaries. Are things going well as you perform a complex task? If yes, then leave well enough alone. If not, then there might be things you can do—and here, the details might be domain-specific. (p. 95)

Teachers encourage transfer of these dispositions through modeling across disciplines and by the day-in and day-out message that learning is a meaningful activity facilitated by metacognition.

Classroom Connections

Promoting Transfer in Your Classroom

1. Provide a wide range of examples and applications for the content you teach.
   - A fifth-grade teacher provides practice in writing paragraphs by requiring students to report their science experiments in paragraph form. She also requires appropriate paragraph structure in social studies reports and letters to foreign pen pals. Before each assignment, she reminds students of key points in paragraph structure before they begin their writing.
   - A geometry teacher illustrates applications of course content with examples from architecture. He also uses photographs from magazines and slides to illustrate how math concepts relate to the real world.

2. Plan representations that provide the information students need for understanding the topics they study.
   - A history teacher writes short cases to illustrate concepts, such as mercantilism, that are hard to understand from text alone. He guides students' analyses of the cases, helping them identify the essential characteristics of the concepts.
   - An English teacher prepares a matrix illustrating the characters, setting, and themes for several of Shakespeare's plays. Students use the information in summarizing and drawing conclusions about Shakespeare's works.

3. Embed information in meaningful contexts.
   - A fifth-grade teacher selects samples of student writing to teach grammar and punctuation rules. She copies samples onto overheads and uses the samples as the basis for her instruction.
   - A science teacher begins a discussion of light refraction by asking students why they can see better with their glasses on than they can without them. He tries to begin each new topic with a problem presented in a personalized way.

4. Use regular reviews to strengthen ideas and to provide practice with broad applications.
   - A chemistry teacher includes at least one problem from the previous topic on every new problem sheet. During the week before the grading period ends, she gives an assignment sheet containing problems from each topic covered during the grading period.
   - A fourth-grade social studies teacher caps each unit with the following questions:
     What have we learned in this unit?
     Why is it important?
     What does it have to do with our world today?

Windows on Classrooms

At the beginning of this chapter, you saw how Laura Hunter planned and conducted her lesson in an effort to promote thinking and problem solving in her students. Let's look now at a teacher with a group of second graders involved in a lesson on graphing. As you read the case study, consider the extent to which the teacher applied the information in this chapter in her lesson.

Suzanne Brush, a second-grade teacher at Webster Elementary School, had her students involved in a unit on graphing.

She began, "I'm planning a party for us, and a question came to my mind. I thought maybe you could help me solve it today. I need to know how I can figure out the class's favorite kind of jelly bean. If you can help me out with that, raise your hand."

Several students offered suggestions and, after considerable discussion, they finally settled on giving each student a variety of jelly beans and having them indicate which one was their favorite.

"It just so happens," Suzanne smiled as they decided on the idea, "that I did bring in some jelly beans today, and you'll be able to taste the jelly beans and vote for your favorite flavor."

She then handed out a baggy with seven different-flavored jelly beans in it to each student. After Suzanne directed the students to taste all the jelly beans before they chose their favorite, the students opened the bags and began tasting them as Suzanne monitored the process.

"Okay," she started when everyone was done tasting. "Right now, I need your help. . . . Raise your hand, please, if you can tell me what we can do now that we have this information. . . . How can we organize it

so that we can look at it as a whole group? We want the favorite-flavor jelly bean. . . . Jacinta?"

"See how much people like the same one, and see how much people like other ones," Jacinta responded.

"Okay. . . . Can you add to that? . . . Josh?"

"You can like write their names down and see how many . . . like black," Josh answered uncertainly.

"That was right in line with what Jacinta said," Suzanne smiled and nodded. "Here's what we're going to do. Stacey and someone else, when we first started off, mentioned that we could graph the information, and we have an empty graph up in the front of the room," she continued, moving to the front of the room and

displaying the outline of a graph that appears at the bottom of this page.

"Yes, Justin," she nodded in response to his raised hand.

"See like which ones like, like red, get the people that like red and write it down; get all the colors and like red and like yellow, green, orange, black, yellow, white," he suggested haltingly, as Suzanne carefully monitored the attention of the rest of the students while Justin made his suggestion.

"That's a great idea," she smiled. "We're going to do that," explaining that she had a series of cut-out cardboard pieces that matched the colors for the graph. She directed individual students to come to the front of the room and paste the color of the piece that represented their favorite color on

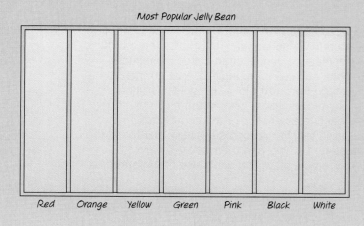

Most Popular Jelly Bean

Red   Orange   Yellow   Green   Pink   Black   White

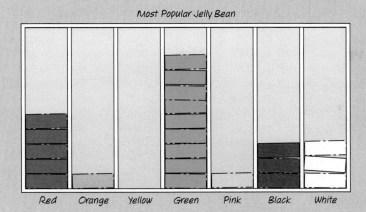

Most Popular Jelly Bean

Red Orange Yellow Green Pink Black White

the graph. After all the groups were done, the graph appeared as above.

"I need your attention back up here, please, for just a moment," she continued. "We collected the information and organized the information up here on the graph. Now we need to look at and analyze the information. I need you to tell me what we know by looking at the graph up here. . . . What do we know? Please look at the graph up front. . . . Candice, what do we know?" she asked as she walked toward the middle of the room.

"People like green," Candice answered.

"Candice said most people like the green jelly beans. . . . Candice, how many people like green?"

". . . Nine."

"Nine people like green. . . . And how did you find that out? Can you go up there and show us how you read the graph?"

Candice went up to the graph and moved her hand up from the bottom, counting the green squares as she went.

"What else do we know by just looking at the graph? . . . Justin?"

"There's three people that like black and three people that like white."

"Three people like black and three people like white," Suzanne repeated, pointing to the black and white columns on the graph. "Let's let Stacey add some more to that."

"No one liked yellow," Stacey answered.

"Nobody picked yellow," Suzanne repeated. "Okay, here we go. . . . How many more people liked green than red?" she asked, changing the direction of the questioning. "How many more people liked the green jelly beans than the red? Look up at the graph. Try to find out the information, set up the problem, and then we'll see what you come out with. You have to have a problem set up on your paper."

Suzanne watched as the students looked at the graph and began setting up the problem. She commented, "Quite a few hands, and a few people are still thinking," as she moved across the room. She stopped briefly to offer Carlos some help, continued watching the students as they finished, and then said, "I'm looking for a volunteer to share an answer with us. . . . Dominique?"

"Nine plus 5 is 14," Dominique answered.

"Dominique says 9 plus 5 is 14. Let's test it out," Suzanne said, asking Dominique to go up to the graph and show the class how she arrived at her answer.

Dominique went to the front of the room as Suzanne said, "We want to know the difference. . . . How many more people liked green than red, and you say 14 people, . . . 14 more people liked green. Does that work?" Suzanne said, pointing at the graph.

Dominique looked at the graph for a moment and then said, "I mean 9 take away 5."

"She got up here and she changed her mind," Suzanne said with a smile to the rest of the class after Dominique made her comment. "Tell them."

"Nine take away 5 is 4," Dominique said.

"Nine take away 5 is 4," Suzanne continued, "so how many more people liked green than red? . . . Carlos?"

"Four," Carlos responded.

"Four, good, four," she smiled at him warmly. "The key was, you had to find the difference between the two numbers.

"Raise your hand," she then continued, "if you can make up a problem like that, as I just set up and asked the whole class. . . . Okay, Jacinta."

"We could take pieces of paper and get all the students different colors . . ." Jacinta began.

"Oh, I see. . . . You're giving me a different example of something that we could collect information on and graph. . . . Let's look at the one we have up there, though. Could you just think of another problem that we could ask everyone to figure out?"

"How many more reds there are? . . . How many more people like red than black?" Jacinta responded haltingly.

"How many more people liked red than black?" Suzanne repeated. "Go ahead and do it," she said to the class.

She watched as students solved the problem, and responding to Timmy energetically waving his hand, she nodded for him to answer.

"Two," he said.

"And how did you get your answer? What problem did you set up?"

"Five take away 3," Timmy explained.

Suzanne then continued, "I have one more question, and then we'll switch gears a little bit. How many people participated in this voting? How many people took part or participated in this voting?"

Suzanne watched as students turned to the problem and then said, "Matt? . . . How many people?" she said as she saw that students were finished and several had their hands raised.

"Twenty-four," Matt answered.

"Matt said 24. Did anyone get a different answer? So we'll compare . . . Robert?"

"Twenty-two."

"How did you solve the problem?" she asked, walking past the table and motioning to Robert. "That's the most important thing."

"Nine plus 5 plus 3 plus 3 plus 1 plus 1 equals 22," he answered quickly.

"Where'd you get all those numbers?"

"There," he said, pointing to the graph.

"He went from the highest to the lowest, and the answer was 22."

" . . . Okay, I need your attention," she said, changing the direction of the discussion, "so that I can explain to you six fun and exciting centers that you're going to be working at this morning. I'll explain the centers very quickly, and then you will break up into those groups and begin working."

The students then moved to the centers. In one, students attempted to flip a penny into a cup and fill in a bar graph comparing their attempts to their successful tries. In another, they tallied the number of students who had birthdays each month and entered the information on a bar graph. In a third, they used pictures to make a graph of the type of transportation each student used to get to school. In a fourth, they looked at a videotape of children at play, and measured and graphed their times in different activities. A fifth group went out of the classroom, interviewing people about their favorite soft drinks, tallying the results in a graph. A sixth group called four pizza delivery places, priced the cost of comparable pizzas, entered the information on a

graph, and explained why they would choose a particular pizza place.

As time for lunch neared, Suzanne called the groups back together. After the students were settled, she said, "Raise your hand if you can tell me what you learned this morning in math."

"How to bar graph," Jenny responded.

"How to bar graph," Suzanne repeated. "More important, when we set up a problem, what do we have to do to solve the problem. . . . Timmy?"

"Add or subtract."

"Okay, but we have to decide what, before we add or subtract?"

"The numbers."

"So, we have to collect the information, then we have to organize it, and we organized it by setting up a bar graph, something that we can look at and talk about and decide what we need to do with the information. And we set up some problems, and we solved them. It's a nice way to look at information and make decisions about certain things, and at your centers too. . . . Do you have any questions about your centers?" she asked as she ended the lesson.

Questions for Discussion and Analysis

Analyze Suzanne's lesson now in the context of the information in this chapter. In doing your analysis, you may want to consider the following questions. In each case, be specific and take information directly from the case study.

1. How effectively did Suzanne teach problem solving in her lesson? To what extent did she apply the suggestions for helping students become better problem solvers? Explain, using information taken directly from the case study.

2. To what extent did Suzanne encourage critical thinking in her lesson? What could she have done to give students more practice in developing critical thinking abilities? Explain.

3. How effective would Suzanne's lesson have been for promoting transfer? Explain, using information taken directly from the case.

4. Offer an overall assessment of Suzanne's lesson, based on the content of this chapter. What could she have done to improve the lesson? Be specific in any suggestions you make.

 ## Summary

Concept Learning

Concepts help people make sense of the world by allowing them to categorize stimuli. Rule-driven theories of concept learning suggest that learners construct an understanding of concepts based on their common characteristics. Prototype theories suggest that concepts are constructed on the basis of the best representative of its class.

Concepts with few concrete characteristics are easier to learn than those with many characteristics or characteristics that are more abstract. Learners construct an understanding of concepts by analyzing a wide variety of examples in which the characteristics are observable or which are the best prototypes available.

Problem Solving

Problems describe situations in which individuals have goals but lack obvious ways of achieving them. Well-defined problems have clear goals and clear paths for achieving them; ill-defined problems have ambiguous goals and no clear means of achieving them.

Experts in any domain have thorough knowledge backgrounds organized into complex schemas that allow them to represent problems as relationships in context, to process problems quickly and in some cases automatically, and to monitor their problem-solving efforts effectively. Novices have schemas that are less well developed, often represent problems in isolated pieces, and don't monitor their efforts effectively. Experts spend more time thinking about and planning for problem solving than novices. Teachers can help students become better problem solvers by helping them understand and acquire the problem-solving strategies of experts.

The Strategic Learner

A strategy is a plan for achieving a specific learning goal. Metacognition is the key to effective strategy use. In addition, strategic learners have broad background knowledge and a repertoire of strategies to choose from in reaching their goals.

Study skills are strategies used to increase comprehension of information in teacher presentations and written text. Comprehensive strategies (like SQ4R and MURDER) as well as specific strategies (like summarizing and self-questioning) are effective in monitoring and improving comprehension.

Critical thinking includes reflective strategies designed to improve understanding and decision making. Critical thinking requires thorough domain-specific knowledge, the ability to use basic cognitive processes, well-developed metacognitive ability, and dispositions for open-mindedness and a respect for evidence. Research indicates that critical thinking is most effectively developed in the context of specific topics.

Now go to our Companion Website to assess your understanding of chapter content with the Student Self-Assessment, apply comprehension in the Online Casebook, and broaden your knowledge base with links to important Educational Psychology World Wide Web sites.

Transfer of Learning

Transfer occurs when learners are able to apply previously learned information to a new setting. Specific transfer involves an application in a situation closely related to the original; general transfer occurs when two learning situations are quite different. Transfer also depends on the amount of time and practice that learners spend on a topic, the quality and variety of the representations they study, and the context in which learning experiences are embedded. Research indicates that transfer tends to be specific. Metacognitive and self-regulatory skills, however, may transfer across domains.

 **Important Concepts**

algorithm (p. 328)

basic processes (p. 343)

characteristics (p. 313)

cognitive apprenticeship (p. 334)

comprehension monitoring (p. 339)

concepts (p. 312)

concept mapping (p. 316)

convergent thinking (p. 327)

critical thinking (p. 342)

divergent thinking (p. 327)

drawing analogies (p. 329)

elaborative questioning (p. 340)

examples (p. 314)

expert (p. 330)

general transfer (p. 347)

heuristics (p. 328)

ill-defined problem (p. 324)

means–ends analysis (p. 329)

network (p. 316)

novice (p. 330)

problem (p. 324)

prototype (p. 314)

specific transfer (p. 347)

strategies (p. 337)

study strategies (p. 338)

summarize (p. 339)

transfer (p. 347)

well-defined problem (p. 324)

The Classroom

Learning
Part II

9

Cognition
in the Content
Areas

Carla Thompson, a fifth grader in Hannah Brown's class, sat looking out the window.

She thought to herself, "Man, this is hard. . . . I'm supposed to make a report on Michigan, and I have to write about 'agricultural products,' and I'm not even really sure what that means. Now what? . . . I'll look in the book. Where was this stuff? Yeah, here it is. Yikes! Three pages. How am I gonna get this down to three paragraphs? I better write something down. . . . Let's see, I'll list everything, like cherries and dairy products, and then see if any things go together. . . . At least that's a start," she shrugged.

Suddenly, Carla's work was interrupted by Hannah's voice. "Okay, everyone, you need to put away your social studies writing assignment and get ready for math," she said.

When the shuffling subsided, Hannah continued, "Class, you'll remember we've been working on how to spend the money the class earned for winning the city's environmental education poster contest. We have $50 and lots of ideas about how to spend it," Hannah continued, pointing to the board where items like pizza party, trip to the zoo, and software games for the room were listed.

"You remember yesterday we asked everyone to identify their first, second, and third choices. Now we need to figure out what to do with the information we collected, which I've put on this sheet that I'm handing out. I'd like you to get into your groups and discuss what to do next."

As Carla slid her desk next to Carlos, Shelly, and Tran, she whispered, "What are we supposed to do?"

"Easy, just tell Mrs. Brown what's our favorite way to spend the money," Carlos replied. "We just need to see which things got the most votes."

"But what about the second and third choices?" Shelly asked. "If you don't get your first choice, shouldn't your second and third ones count?"

"But how do we do that?" Tran wondered as he studied the sheet in front of them.

As different groups discussed the problem, Hannah circulated around the room asking questions and encouraging students to represent their ideas in some form of graph.

After lunch, Carla returned from the playground and fanned herself while Hannah got out the supplies she needed for her science lesson. These included a basketball, tennis and golf balls, and a flashlight.

She began by asking, "Who remembers what we've been talking about? . . . Sarina?"

"The solar system?"

"And what have we found out about our solar system? Nadia?"

"Well, the sun's in the middle of it."

After reviewing additional information about the sun and the planets, Hannah continued, "Anybody notice what the moon looked like last night? . . . Dwayne?"

"Umm, it was only a piece, kind of like almost a half."

"Good, Dwayne. Yes, it was almost a half moon. What makes the moon look like that? . . . Anyone? . . . Look at these pictures [holding up several pictures of the moon in different phases]. Why is the moon completely round sometimes, a half moon at others, and just a crescent at other times? Any ideas? . . . Kira?"

" . . . Clouds?"

"Tyrone?"

" . . . The atmosphere?"

"Kevin?"

" . . . It might have something to do with the sun, like solar flare-ups . . . or whatever."

"Those are all interesting ideas. Let's see if we can figure this question out. First, I need some volunteers up here to hold the sun, the moon, and the earth. Let me see. . . . "

tudents learn a great deal in schools. They study math, science, reading, social studies, art, music, and other disciplines. The way students learn the content in these areas is similar in many ways, and we used examples from each in our discussion of learning theories in Chapters 6 to 8.

However, a growing body of research suggests that the way we learn some forms of content differs from the ways we learn others (Bruning, Schraw, & Ronning, 1999; Mansilla

& Gardner, 1997). In this chapter, we examine the unique aspects of learning in four areas: reading, writing, math, and science.

After you've completed your study of this chapter, you should be able to meet the following objectives:

▌ Explain the developmental process of learning to read and how teachers can implement strategies to help students learn to read.

▌ Analyze cognitive factors influencing the process of learning to write, and explain how teachers can facilitate students in this process.

▌ Describe current views of learning in mathematics, and explain implications for instruction in math.

▌ Explain how students' conceptions of science content influence learning in that area and describe instructional strategies to confront those conceptions.

Learning to Read and Teaching Reading

What is reading? What does it mean to learn to read, and how can teachers help learners in the process? These questions guide us in this first section of the chapter.

We've organized this section into two parts, learning to read, which is emphasized in the lower elementary grades, and reading to learn, which occurs when students develop enough expertise to use reading as a learning tool. The importance of learning to read can't be overstated; it opens educational and occupational doors that no other form of learning can. Let's try to understand this process.

Learning to Read

Read the following passage:

> We see that two high-energy phosphate groups, one from ATP and one from GRP, each yielding -7.3 kcal/mole under standard conditions, must be expended to phosphorylate one molecule of pyruvate from phosphoenolpyruvate, which requires input of 14.8 kcal/mol under standard conditions. In contrast, when phosphoenolpyruvate is converted in pyruvate during glycolysis, only one ATP is generated from ADP. Although the standard free-energy change G of the net reaction learning to phosphoenolpyruvate synthesis is +0.2 kcal/mol, the actual free-energy change G under intracellular conditions is very strongly negative, about -6.0 kcal; it is thus essentially irreversible.

Did you understand what you "read"? Were you able to pronounce most of the words? If you had difficulties, you can see why students who are not good readers struggle with textbooks. You can also begin to appreciate the developmental process young students go through in figuring out how written language works.

Reading is *the translation of symbols or letters into thoughts or speech* (Bruning et al., 1999). The purpose in reading is to obtain meaning from what we read. Learning to read is a developmental process that builds on **background knowledge**—*general declarative knowledge about the world*—and **linguistic knowledge**—*a person's understanding of the different dimensions of language*. Children acquire linguistic and background knowledge as they interact with the world and other people.

Reading as a Developmental Process

Learning to read begins at birth. Stimuli in the home, walks around the neighborhood, trips to the supermarket, and many other experiences provide background for forming concepts about the world. The richer these experiences, the greater the wealth of background knowledge beginning readers bring to the classroom.

Experiences with language also influence linguistic knowledge. Conversations with adults and peers provide opportunities to learn vocabulary and the way language works. Exposure to books and other print media, such as cereal boxes, stop signs, and billboards helps children understand that symbols correspond to both sounds and meaning. Sitting on someone's lap and talking and thinking about books help children understand what words and books are about and motivate them to learn to read.

This view of language learning, called **emergent literacy**, *emphasizes that learning to read and write is a natural, gradual process that develops over time* (Whitehurst, Crone, Zevenbergen, & Schultz, 1999). It also parallels and depends on learning to communicate orally (Peregoy & Boyle, 1997). If children are immersed in a world of words, they begin to understand and appreciate the powerful role played by spoken and printed words in communication (Morrow & Young, 1997; Saracho & Spodek, 1999). Background and linguistic knowledge interact to influence the process of learning to read, as you'll see in the following sections.

9.1 Explain specifically how a trip to the zoo could help learners develop both *background* and *linguistic* knowledge.

Background Knowledge

When learners enter first grade, they bring with them an impressive store of background knowledge and a vocabulary of between 5,000 and 6,000 words (Chall, Jacobs, & Baldwin, 1990). As discussed in Chapter 7, this background knowledge is stored as schemas—organized networks of connected information—in long-term memory. These schemas influence both perception and encoding. Next we'll explore how background knowledge lays a foundation for reading.

What is happening in the following passage?

Toby wanted to get a birthday present for Chris. He went to his piggy bank. He shook it. There was nothing in it. (Adapted from Bruning et al., 1999)

Why did Toby go to the piggy bank? What did he think was in it? How did he know it was empty? Answering these questions (and making sense of the passage) requires background knowledge, as did the passage about energy at the beginning of this section. The information that students extract from text can be categorized as either *text explicit* (Toby wanted to get Chris a birthday present) or *text implicit* (Toby expected money in his piggy bank) (Raphael & Pearson, 1985). The background knowledge learners bring to a reading passage strongly influences how meaningful it is by allowing them to make text-implicit inferences.

9.2 In Chapter 7 knowledge in long-term memory was described as *declarative* and *procedural*. Which did you use to make sense of the passage about the piggy bank? In what form is this knowledge stored?

Linguistic Knowledge

The importance of linguistic knowledge is illustrated by the following passage:

Once upon a time a wimmy Wuggen zonked into the grabbet. Zhe was grolling for poft because zhe was very blongby.

What kind of wuggen was it? What was the wuggen doing and why? Successful answers to these questions require linguistic knowledge, an understanding of the different aspects of language. The aspect of linguistic knowledge that you used to make sense of the wuggen passage was *syntax,* the way words in larger units make sense. For example, we know what kind of wuggen it was (a wimmy one) because, in English, adjectives precede nouns.

Other aspects of linguistic knowledge that influence learning to read include:

▌ Print awareness—understanding that letters and symbols, such as McDonald's golden arches and a child's name on his door, mean something.
▌ Graphic awareness—recognizing that letters have different shapes or configurations (e.g., *d* and *p*) and that words include letters.
▌ Phonemic awareness—understanding that speech incorporates a series of individual sounds.
▌ Syntactic awareness—understanding how sentence-level patterns influence both meaning (e.g., "He did go." versus "Did he go?") and pronunciation (e.g., "read" in "He read the book." versus "Let's read a book.") (Hiebert & Raphael, 1996; Tompkins, 1997; Whitehurst et al., 1999).

Reading educators disagree about the relative importance of background and linguistic knowledge in learning to read, as discussed in the next section (Hempenstall, 1997).

9.3 ▬
How is linguistic knowledge similar to background knowledge? How is it different? Explain.

Conflicting Conceptions of Learning to Read

More disagreements probably exist in reading instruction than in any other area of education. Jeanne Chall, in her 1967 landmark book, *Learning to Read: The Great Debate,* divided reading methods into two categories, *meaning-emphasis* and *code-emphasis* approaches. Though understanding is the goal for both, they use different strategies to help learners reach that goal.

Meaning-Emphasis Approaches.   **Meaning-emphasis approaches** *focus on general comprehension by stressing the functional nature of printed words.* Two prominent meaning-emphasis approaches include language experience and whole language.

Language experience *uses children's oral language, based on their everyday experiences, as the basis for dictated stories that become texts for learning to read.* Language experience advocates stress the importance of individual students' background experiences in making reading meaningful. Language experience is consistent with information processing theory because the stories that learners dictate depend on information stored in long-term memory; constructivists explain the effectiveness of language experience by arguing that creating and subsequently reading a story based on prior knowledge and experiences is an authentic task for each learner.

A more recent meaning-emphasis approach, called **whole language**, *integrates reading into the total literacy process (i.e., learning to speak, listen, write, and read)* (Stahl, 1999a). Most whole-language classrooms use literature as the foundation of the reading process. Books, projects, tapes, and videos are used to discover connections between vocabulary and concepts related to a topic. Whole language has three essential characteristics:

▌ It uses language to think about and describe experiences, and it links spoken and written language.
▌ It emphasizes using language to communicate with others.
▌ It links different content areas by emphasizing language across the curriculum.

Let's see how a teacher attempts to implement whole language in the classroom.

Samantha Taylor's third-grade classroom was a beehive of activity. One corner was decorated with a giant paper spider web with drawings and students' written descriptions comparing spiders' eight legs with insects' six. These came from books and video-tapes the students had been studying and from a field trip to a park near the school. Students were taking turns reading descriptions of different insects and spiders, matching them to the drawings, and checking their answers with a key on the back.

Several students were at their desks, writing about a visit from one of the parents, an amateur entomologist, who had brought a mounted insect collection to class. The rest of the students would later read these descriptions of the visit. In a third corner, students were manipulating multiples of 6 and 8 in math to find patterns and were discussing their thinking and answers with each other.

Samantha had the rest of the class in a half circle in front of her. She was reading *The Very Quiet Cricket* by Eric Carle (1990), about a cricket who could not find another cricket to talk to among the insects it encountered in a field. When she neared the end, she stopped and asked each student to create an ending for the story and to share it with the group. Later in the day, students compared their story endings to the book's.

Samantha capitalized on the first characteristic of whole-language instruction by having students write about things they had experienced—insects, the field trip, and the visit from the parent. Second, by having students write and have other students read what they wrote, her instruction complemented children's natural tendency to communicate with others. In time, learners see how reading, speaking, and writing are interrelated, and they learn to communicate more clearly (Needels & Knapp, 1994).

Third, whole-language instruction emphasizes the use of language across the curriculum. Teachers will use science, for example, as an opportunity to both practice language and study science concepts. Samantha capitalized on this dimension by having her students write about insects and discuss their thinking and answers in their math activity.

Because of its emphasis on concrete experiences, whole language is consistent with both cognitive views of learning and development. Its emphasis on dialogue and communication also makes it compatible with Vygotsky's social constructivism.

Code-Emphasis Approaches.   **Code-emphasis approaches** to reading *stress learning the correspondence between letters and sounds.* Advocates claim that, once learned, decoding strategies can be used both to recognize words learners already know and to learn new words (Stahl, Duffy-Hester, & Stahl, 1998). **Phonics**, *the most prominent code-emphasis approach, stresses learning basic letter–sound patterns and rules for sounding out words.* Phonics emphasizes two processes: *phonemic awareness* and *decoding.*

Code-emphasis approaches to reading stress letter–sound connections in language.

As shown earlier, **phonemic awareness** involves *understanding that speech incorporates a series of individual sounds.* For instance, the word *cat* has three sounds, *k, aa,* and *tuh*. Dividing words into individual sounds can be difficult for young children because they think of words as carrying meaning; focusing on the sounds of individual letters and words requires a different and sometimes more abstract way of thinking (Tompkins, 1997).

Researchers measure learners' phonemic awareness by asking them to perform tasks such as the following:

- Segment words (What are the two sounds in *go*?).
- Identify first and last sounds in a word (What sound does *hat* begin with? End with?).
- Delete first or last sounds (What would *ham* sound like without the *h*?).
- Substitute first and last sounds ("Say *ball*. Now instead of *b*, begin the word with a *t*.") (M. Adams, Foorman, Lundeberg, & Beeler, 1998).

9.4
Is phonemic awareness declarative knowledge, or is it procedural knowledge? Explain. What are the implications for instruction?

The value of phonemic awareness is confirmed by research (M. Adams et al., 1998; Bus & van Ijzendoorn, 1999; Troia, 1999). For example, older poor readers scored lower on phonemic awareness than did younger good readers, in spite of the fact that the older readers had exposure to more words (Pennington, Groisser, & Welsh, 1993). Also, young children taught phonemic awareness were more skilled in reading individual words, scored higher on standardized reading tests, and spelled words more accurately than comparable students who did not receive the same training (L. Bradley & Bryant, 1991; Spector, 1995). Significantly, these differences on standardized reading test scores lasted up to 5 years.

Code-emphasis approaches also emphasize the process of **decoding**, which is *the translation of sounds into words*. To illustrate, try to read these imaginary words:

kigt

phrend

blud

nale

Most people read these words as *kite, friend, blood,* and *nail*. How do we do this? The answer is based on the structure of American English, which includes about 40 sounds, or phonemes (M. Adams, 1990; Tompkins, 1997). These include:

- consonants (e.g., *d, b, t*).
- vowels—both long and short (e.g., *hat* and *hate*).
- blends (e.g., *bl, st, tr*).
- digraphs (e.g., *sh, ch, th*).
- diphthongs (e.g., *oi, oy, ou, ow, ar, er, ir, or, ur*).

9.5
Describe the phonetic generalizations that allow us to decode the *ph* in *phrend* and the *ale* in *nale*.

Phonics emphasizes that these sounds are represented by a fixed number of letters or letter combinations and that, once learned, these sounds are used to sound out any new word. Unfortunately, exact one-to-one correspondence between letters or letter combinations and sounds doesn't exist (e.g., the *c* in *cent* and the *c* in *cat*, and the *ch* in *change, chaos,* and *chiffon*). However, a number of generalizations such as, When *c* is followed by an *a, o,* or *u*, it makes a '*k*' sound and when followed by an *i, e,* or *y* it makes an '*s*' sound, work often enough, so we can use them quite effectively in sounding out new words (Stahl et al., 1998).

Advocates argue that, once learned, decoding strategies allow readers to decipher words automatically and that "as less attention is required for decoding, more attention becomes available for comprehension" (Samuels, 1979, p. 405). To test this hypothesis, researchers trained second- through fifth-grade poor readers to rapidly decode words by using flashcards with single words or phrases on them (Tan & Nicholson, 1997). On a comprehension task in which the target words were embedded in longer passages, the trained group performed better than students who didn't receive training. Researchers suggested that learning words to the point of automaticity helped reduce the load on learners' working memories.

Putting the Reading Debate Into Perspective.   The meaning-emphasis and the code-emphasis camps are deeply divided, each asserting that their approach is superior (Flippo, 1997; Joyce, 1999). In 1995, California adopted two statutes called the *ABC Laws*, which require code-based approaches in the schools because leaders there believed that low reading test scores resulted from sole reliance on meaning-emphasis approaches (Halford, 1997).

What does research evidence suggest? Most reading experts believe that decoding is an essential part of successful reading (M. Adams, 1990; Freppon & Dahl, 1998). On the other hand, these same experts stress that additional comprehension strategies are necessary if students are to become skilled readers. Further, the researchers cited in the last section emphasized that the instruction was effective not only because decoding was practiced to automaticity but also because it included emphasis on the meanings of the words (Tan & Nicholson, 1997).

This suggests that both camps have some valid points. Neither meaning-emphasis nor code-emphasis approaches alone are likely to be effective. Students must have decoding skills, but comprehension must also be emphasized (Armbruster & Osborn, 1999; Wharton-McDonald, Pressley, & Hampston, 1998). This makes sense, and this likely was the problem in California. In focusing solely on meaning, teachers went too far in deemphasizing phonemic awareness and decoding skills. On the other hand, exclusive focus on these processes, in the absence of meaning, is equally inappropriate. Both are necessary.

> **9.6**
> Using the piggy bank passage as an example, explain how both code-emphasis and meaning-emphasis approaches are necessary for comprehension.

Reading to Learn

During the middle grades, the emphasis changes from learning-to-read to reading-to-learn (Stevens, Hammann, & Balliett, 1999). The same controversies persist, however. In reading to learn, **data-driven models** *stress decoding and view reading as a sequential, letter-by-letter, word-by-word analysis of text* (Bruning, et al., 1999). **Conceptually driven views** *suggest that the meaning learners take from text is determined by individual expectations and prior knowledge.* Most experts advocate a combination of the two, in which automatized decoding is guided by background knowledge and strategies (Freppon & Dahl, 1998; Neuman, 1999). In this section, we examine different ways students use these processes to construct meaning from text.

Components of Comprehension

As discussed in Chapter 8, strategic learners have broad background knowledge, a repertoire of strategies (particularly comprehension strategies), and well-developed metacognitive abilities. These characteristics are essential in comprehending written text (Mayer, 1999). They are illustrated in Figure 9.1 and discussed in the sections that follow.

Figure 9.1

Characteristics of effective strategy users

Have broad background knowledge

Have a repertoire of comprehension strategies

Have well-developed metacognitive abilities

Background Knowledge.   As mentioned earlier, the background knowledge that we bring to text influences both comprehension and attention. It tells us what to look for and how to make sense of ambiguities. Our ability to understand the energy and piggy bank passages, for instance, depended on our background knowledge in these areas.

As another example, read the following passage:

> The procedure is actually quite simple. First you arrange items into different groups. Of course one pile may be sufficient depending on how much there is to do. If you have to go somewhere else due to lack of facilities that is the next step; otherwise, you are pretty well set. It is important not to overdo things.
>
> That is, it is better to do too few things at once than too many. In the short run this may not seem important but first, the whole procedure will seem complicated. Soon, however, it will become just another facet of life. It is difficult to foresee any end to the necessity for this task in the immediate future, but then, one never can tell. After the procedure is completed, one arranges the materials into different groups again. Then they can be put into their appropriate places. Eventually they will be used once more and the whole cycle will then have to be repeated. However, that is part of life. (Bransford & Johnson, 1972, p. 722)

Did you realize that the passage was about washing clothes? If you didn't, don't worry. One group of college students was told beforehand that the paragraph was about washing clothes; a second group wasn't. The students who were told judged the passage twice as comprehensible and remembered twice as much information from it (Bransford & Johnson, 1972). Because their background knowledge was activated, their comprehension increased.

Background knowledge also influences attention and perception during reading. Students were asked to read the following passage from one of two perspectives: as a prospective home buyer or as a thief. Take one of these perspectives, and note what you remember from the passage.

> The two boys ran until they came to the driveway.
>
> "See, I told you today was good for skipping school," Mark asserted. "Mom is never home on Thursday."
>
> Tall hedges hid the house from the road so the pair strolled across the finely landscaped yard.
>
> "I never knew your place was so big," Pete said.
>
> "Yeah, but it's nicer now since Dad had the new stone siding put on and added the fireplace."
>
> There were front and back doors and a side door, which led to the two-car garage, empty now except for three 10-speed bikes.
>
> They went in the side door, Mark explaining that it was always open in case his younger sisters got home earlier than their mother.
>
> Pete wanted to see the house, so Mark started with the living room. It, like the rest of the downstairs, was newly painted.
>
> Mark turned on the stereo, the noise of which worried Pete. "Don't worry, the nearest house is a quarter of a mile away," Mark shouted.
>
> Pete felt more comfortable, observing that no houses could be seen in any direction beyond the huge yard. (Adapted from Pichert & Anderson, 1977)

If you read from a burglar's perspective, you probably noted that the house was unlocked, isolated, shielded from view, and full of expensive items like stereos and bikes. A home-buyer's perspective might focus on the size of the lot, stone siding and fireplace, and two-car garage. This is exactly what the researchers found; the perspective taken influenced what readers attended to and remembered from the text (Pichert & Anderson, 1977).

9.7 ▬

The text makes the statement, "Because their background knowledge was activated, their comprehension increased." Explain this statement, based on information processing views of learning.

In both the clothes washing and house examples, background knowledge in the form of schemas guided attention, perception, and comprehension. Schemas influence reading comprehension in at least three ways:

⬛ They guide attention by helping us differentiate between important and unimportant information.
⬛ They help us search our memories to provide "slots" for assimilating new information.
⬛ They allow us to make predictions and inferences, filling in gaps and making connections that aren't apparent in what we read. (Bruning et al., 1999)

Teachers can increase comprehension by helping learners access relevant background knowledge and by providing missing background information before reading difficult passages.

Comprehension Strategies.   Comprehension strategies allow us to actively attack print, making sense of passages that aren't clear (Hiebert & Raphael, 1996). In Chapter 8, you learned that two strategies in particular are effective for promoting comprehension–summarizing and self-questioning.

Summarizing may be the most powerful comprehension strategy. One review concluded that "the evidence to date in favor of this strategy as a facilitator of comprehension and memory is so striking that we recommend the procedure without hesitation" (Pressley, Johnson, Symons, McGoldrick, & Kurita, 1989, p. 9). Summarizing is effective because it encourages learners to:

⬛ Read for meaning.
⬛ Identify important information.
⬛ Describe content in their own words.

Identifying important information in what we read is an essential skill. Without it, learners can't allocate their study efforts strategically.

The background knowledge learners bring with them to the reading process facilitates comprehension.

Comprehension strategies allow learners to attack reading passages and construct meaning from text.

9.8

What are at least two features of this text that help you identify important information?

This ability develops over time. Researchers found, for example, that third and fifth graders couldn't differentiate between more and less important ideas, seventh graders were beginning to develop some proficiency, and high school students were quite good at it (A. Brown & Smiley, 1977). Further, when given extra time to study a passage, fifth graders' recall of important information didn't improve, seventh graders' recall improved slightly, and high school students improved significantly (Brown & Smiley, 1978). The high school students allocated their effort more strategically than their younger counterparts.

Learning to summarize takes time and effort. Students initially tend to take words and phrases verbatim from the original text instead of putting ideas into their own words. Teachers can help them move beyond this tendency in several ways, including the following:

▋ Focus on specific paragraphs and help students identify the main ideas in them.
▋ Encourage students to describe main ideas in their own words.
▋ Use modeling and think-alouds to demonstrate how strategies like outlining and concept mapping can be used to illustrate connections in longer passages.
▋ Require students to apply summarizing strategies across the curriculum.

9.9

Middle school students taught outlining strategies improved both their recall and comprehension scores (B. Taylor & Beach, 1984). Using the information in this section, explain how outlining can improve comprehension.

Self-questioning can also be a powerful strategy, and one of its most important components is the ability to draw inferences from the material being studied. For example, what is happening here?

The driver started the car and entered traffic.

Was a key involved in the process?

Was the car in neutral when the engine started?

Did the driver check the traffic flow before entering it?

Did this take place in the city or the country?

Your ability to answer these questions depends on your ability to make text-implicit inferences. Research indicates that good readers are better at this process than poor readers, and teaching readers to make inferences improves comprehension (Fielding & Pearson, 1994).

Metacognition.   As discussed in Chapter 7, metacognition involves students' knowledge and control of their cognitive processes. As we read, metacognition helps monitor our comprehension, telling us when text makes sense and when it doesn't. For example, read the following passage:

> Many fish live at the bottom of the ocean, where no light can reach. Fish need light to see and find their favorite food, which is a red fungus that grows at the bottom of the deepest parts of the ocean. Being able to find this fungus is very important because a closely related one, which is green, is poisonous. (Adapted from Markman, 1979)

Something is wrong here. How can the fish differentiate red from green fungus if there is no light at the bottom of the ocean? When similar inconsistent or contradictory passages were either read to or by younger and older readers, researchers found the following:

▋ Most sixth graders can explain why they reread an unclear passage; second graders can't (M. Myers & Paris, 1978).
▋ Young readers have problems identifying inconsistencies in text (Markman, 1979).
▋ When students were told to look for inconsistencies, sixth graders' performance increased but third graders' didn't (Markman, 1979).
▋ Children as young as third grade can learn to identify inconsistencies when provided with examples (Markman & Gorin, 1981).
▋ Skilled readers allocate more of their processing time to inconsistent than to consistent parts of passages (L. Baker & Anderson, 1982).

9.10

Explain why rereading a passage is an example of metacognition. In your answer, identify differences between younger and older students.

Figure 9.2

Comprehension-monitoring steps in reciprocal teaching

1.	Summarize	the paragraph for the main idea.
2.	Construct a text question	that captures the essence of the passage.
3.	Clarify	any points in the passage that are not clear.
4.	Predict	what the author is going to say in the next paragraph.

Reciprocal Teaching of Comprehension Strategies: A Natural History of One Program for Enhancing Learning by A. Brown and A. Palincsar, 1985, University of Illinois, Champaign-Urbana, The Center for the Study of Reading. Copyright 1985 by The Center for the Study of Reading. Reprinted by permission.

Metacognition in reading develops over time, but the process can be taught to young and low-achieving readers (Hiebert & Raphael, 1996). **Reciprocal teaching** is *a teaching strategy specifically designed to help students learn to monitor their comprehension* (Palincsar & Brown, 1984; Palincsar, Brown, & Martin, 1987). When using this strategy, students take turns leading dialogues that combine clarifying, summarizing, and predicting into logical sequences. These steps, which students apply to each paragraph they read, are outlined in Figure 9.2. By first seeing the strategies modeled by the teacher, and then having opportunities to practice, students gradually internalize the strategies to the point where they become automatic.

Researchers emphasize the importance of explicitly teaching the strategy. In doing so, the teacher first describes and models each step, and students then practice the skill and receive feedback. As they gradually learn the process, additional responsibility is transferred to them by having them assume the role of the teacher when new passages are read and discussed.

Let's look at an example of the strategy in use with a group of students who have read a section of a story about aquanauts. The discussion begins with a student question:

Student 1:	(Question) My question is, what does the aquanaut need when he goes under water?
Student 2:	A watch.
Student 3:	Flippers.
Student 4:	A belt.
Student 1:	Those are all good answers.
Teacher:	(Question) Nice job! I have a question too. Why does the aquanaut wear a belt? What is so special about it?
Student 3:	It's a heavy belt and keeps him from floating to the top again.
Teacher:	Good for you. Now how about a summary for the paragraph?
Student 1:	(Summary) For my summary: This paragraph was about what aquanauts need to take when they go under the water.
Student 5:	(Summary) And also why they need that gear.
Student 3:	(Clarify) I think we need to clarify *gear.*
Student 6:	That's the special things they need.
Teacher:	What's another word for *gear?*
Student 5:	In this story it might be *equipment,* the equipment that makes it easier for the aquanauts to do their job.
Student 1:	I don't think I have a prediction to make.
Teacher:	(Prediction) Well, in the story they tell us that there are "many strange and wonderful creatures" that the aquanauts see as they do their work. My prediction is that they'll describe some of

---

9.11 ▬
Explain specifically how the teacher provided instructional scaffolding during this reciprocal teaching lesson.

these creatures. What are some of the strange creatures you already know about that live in the ocean?

Student 6:   Octopuses.
Student 3:   Whales?
Student 5:   Sharks? (Palincsar & Brown, 1986, pp. 771-772)

Reciprocal teaching has been thoroughly researched, and it has been successfully used with both high and low achievers (Kelly, Moore, & Tuck, 1994; Rosenshine & Meister, 1994). However, it is designed to be used with groups of six to eight students, which makes it difficult to implement with whole classes. In addition, parts of the strategy are difficult to implement in different content areas. For example, Brady (1990) found that clarifying and predicting were difficult with social studies texts because of the structure and density of the material. The benefits of generating questions and summarizing, however, are well documented (Rosenshine & Meister, 1994).

Classroom Connections

Helping Students Learn to Read

1. Create a literacy-rich classroom learning environment.
   - A kindergarten teacher labels common objects around the room like clocks, doors, windows, and chairs. She also puts a sign on each student's desk and chair that says "Maria's desk" and "Antonio's chair."
   - A first-grade teacher creates a number of literacy-focused learning centers. In one, students can read along with big-print books while they listen on tape. Another contains games where learners match words to pictures. In a third, parent volunteers help students create their own stories.

2. Provide a balanced approach that includes both code- and meaning-emphasis components.
   - A first-grade teacher incorporates phonics as one important part of learning to read. During the first part of the year, he uses word families (e.g., cat, bat, hat) to illustrate letter–sound correspondence. Later, he encourages students to read predictable books (that repeat the same sentences over and over) to develop reading fluency. He uses students' own writing to forge links between spoken, written, and read words.
   - When second graders encounter a word that they don't know, they are encouraged to use two strategies: (1) what does context tell you about the meaning of the word, and (2) sound it out and see if it makes sense.

Helping Students Read to Learn

3. Teach students to activate prior knowledge before reading.
   - A middle school teacher uses the KWL strategy (What do I **K**now?; What do I **W**ant to know?; What have I **L**earned?) to activate background knowledge (Ogle, 1986). Before reading a passage, she has them list and organize all the information they know about a topic and identify questions that need answering. After reading the passage, the class discusses what they learned from the passage and what additional information they want to know.
   - A fourth-grade teacher uses webbing and concept mapping to help students remember and organize background information before they read chapters in their science and social studies texts.

4. Actively teach comprehension strategies.
   - A middle school teacher found that her students had problems identifying the main idea in paragraphs. She used think-alouds and modeling to teach finding or constructing the main idea, then gave her students practice and feedback, using passages from different texts.
   - A teacher taught reciprocal teaching to her fifth graders in stages. During whole-group instruction, she modeled the strategy and then asked students to practice the steps while she provided feedback. Then she used one small group as the focus and asked the rest of the class to analyze and critique. Finally, she broke the whole class into small groups, monitoring them and providing feedback to the whole group at the end of the lesson.

Learning to Write and Teaching Writing

Learning to write is a complex cognitive task requiring thought and effort by learners and expertise by teachers. To help you better understand how we learn to write, we compare it to problem solving and consider what teachers can do to facilitate the process. Let's begin by looking at two sixth graders faced with a writing task.

Luis and Dave glanced at the blank page in front of them. Both appeared deep in thought. On the board their teacher had written:

What is your favorite hobby or form of recreation? Why do you like to do this? What does it tell us about who you are?

The assignment was a beginning-of-the-year activity designed to build classroom community and help students get to know each other.

Luis looked at the blank page again and started thinking. He took out a second piece of paper and started jotting down some ideas. He circled some of these words and drew arrows connecting them. As he did, he periodically glanced at the board to remind himself of the task. As he drew on his paper, he said to himself, "Now, . . . why is Mrs. Greenleaf asking us to do this? . . . Oh, . . . yeah, to share something about ourselves with the class. What about myself would they be interested in? Stamp collecting—nah, too nerdy. How about soccer? Wonder if they know anything about soccer? I like to play soccer, but I'm not sure how to explain why. Hmm . . . why don't I start out by listing some of the things I like about soccer and see if they make sense."

Dave, in contrast, sat slouched at his desk, tapping his pencil against the desk and looking out the window.

"Hobby? Recreation? What does she mean? Favorite . . . I like to do all kinds of things. Why do I like them? I don't know. How long does this have to be? Lunch is only a half-hour away—if I can just finish it by then, I won't have to take it home. . . . Well, here goes. 'My favorite sport is soccer. I like to play soccer. I play sweeper on my team.'"

Writing as Problem Solving

Experts describe writing as a form of problem solving (R. Kellogg, 1994). When we face a writing task, we try to define and mentally represent it, just as we do in solving any problem.

Two factors influence this process. They are the *task environment* and *knowledge*—both domain-specific knowledge and discourse knowledge, which is knowledge of the way language is used for communication. Let's consider them.

The **task environment** *includes the writing assignment itself and available resources.* The task environment determines how complex defining the problem will be (J. Hayes & Flower, 1986). For example, if you're required to write an essay describing the implications of cognitive learning theory for teaching, you're likely to first consider the assignment itself, such as what it's about, how long it should be, who you're writing for (e.g., classmates or the instructor), and why you're writing the essay (e.g., for a grade, extra credit, learning exercise, or portfolio entry). Then you will want to know what resources you can use, such as collaborating with others, or referring to articles and papers. Accomplished writers consider elements of the task environment automatically; novices need help in considering resources. The components of the task environment are illustrated in Figure 9.3.

Knowledge is a second factor influencing writing. As discussed in Chapter 8, background knowledge is essential for problem solving, and it is equally important for writing (Ferrari, Bouffard, & Rainville, 1998; R. Kellogg, 1994). Writers need domain-specific

9.12 ■
The first three steps in the problem-solving model described in Chapter 8 were *identify the problem, represent the problem,* and *select a strategy.* Identify the differences in the ways Luis and Dave completed each of these steps.

Figure 9.3

Components of the writing task environment

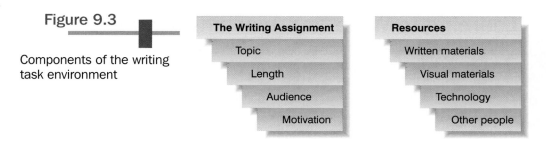

The Writing Assignment	Resources
Topic	Written materials
Length	Visual materials
Audience	Technology
Motivation	Other people

9.13
Linguistic knowledge was described in the section on learning to read, and now discourse knowledge is emphasized in learning to write. How are linguistic knowledge and discourse knowledge similar and different? What are the implications of their similarities for teaching?

knowledge, such as an understanding of cognitive learning theory in your assignment on its implications, and **discourse knowledge**, which is an *understanding of how language can be used to communicate.* We demonstrate discourse knowledge when we indent the beginnings of paragraphs, capitalize the first words of sentences, and use appropriate punctuation. Domain-specific knowledge is declarative, whereas discourse knowledge is procedural. Figure 9.4 illustrates these relationships.

The Writing Process

Armed with our understanding of the task environment, together with our conceptual and discourse knowledge, we're ready to begin writing. Or are we? Research examining learners' strategies as they face a writing task suggests that the writing process involves three stages:

1. Planning
2. Translating
3. Revising (J. Hayes, 1996; J. Hayes & Flower, 1986)

These stages are combined with the elements of the task environment and our knowledge to provide a model of the writing process, as seen in Figure 9.5.

Planning

During the **planning stage**, we *set goals and generate and organize ideas* (Mayer, 1999). Goal setting identifies the purpose for the product, and it can be as vague as filling up a page with words or as specific as trying to inform or persuade another person.

Goals are essential for good writing (Henning, 1999). They provide concrete targets for writers, motivation for them during the writing process, and standards to evaluate and revise the quality of written products (Page-Voth & Graham, 1999). Teachers can help students establish effective writing goals by providing concrete examples of exemplary writing and by modeling the processes themselves.

Figure 9.4

The influence of task environment and knowledge on the writing process

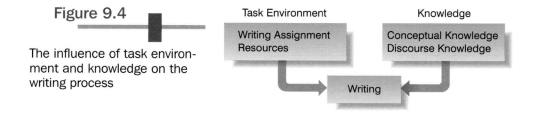

Task Environment	Knowledge
Writing Assignment	Conceptual Knowledge
Resources	Discourse Knowledge

Writing

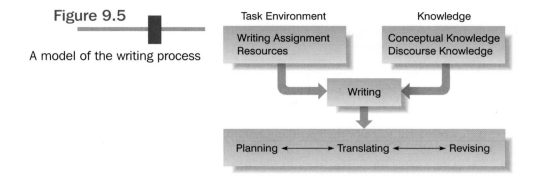

Figure 9.5

A model of the writing process

Task Environment	Knowledge
Writing Assignment Resources	Conceptual Knowledge Discourse Knowledge

Writing

Planning ⟷ Translating ⟷ Revising

Research suggests that teachers should emphasize both process goals, such as self-monitoring, and product goals, like a well-written persuasive essay, when they teach writing (Zimmerman & Kitsantas, 1999). Process goals increase motivation, and product goals provide criteria against which the written work can be judged.

After goals are set, generating ideas provides the raw material for our efforts. Internal processes (like brainstorming) and outside sources (such as books and journals, the Internet, notes, and other people) can be used to generate ideas. Once generated, techniques such as outlines, flow charts, and matrixes can be used to organize the information.

These processes are consistent with cognitive learning theory. For instance, constructivists view planning as the creation of new ideas based on learners' existing understanding, and they emphasize the importance of authentic writing tasks and scaffolding. Information-processing theorists emphasize the role of declarative and procedural knowledge (in the form of strategies) in long-term memory.

We saw these processes in Luis's efforts. His goal was to share something of himself with his classmates. He took a few moments to generate ideas and he organized his ideas by drawing arrows to connect them.

It was different with Dave. His goal was to get the job done by lunch. He started writing immediately, and any ideas he generated evolved as he wrote them. Because he didn't plan well, it is unlikely that he will generate a high-quality product.

Research confirms these differences. Good writers devote up to two thirds of their writing time to planning, focusing on factors such as the audience and how the final product holds together (Ferrari et al., 1998). Less effective writers start the process with little forethought, focusing their planning on specifics, such as how to begin, and adding sentences as they think of them. These differences parallel those of expert and novice problem solvers; when faced with unfamiliar problems, experts plan carefully before attempting solutions, whereas novices plan briefly or not at all before jumping into a solution.

Research has also identified developmental trends in planning (Bereiter & Scardamalia, 1987). Five- and six-year-olds, for example, have difficulties generating ideas, likely the result of their limited background knowledge (Caccamise, 1987). Eight- to twelve-year-olds can generate ideas but have trouble organizing and evaluating them. We saw this in Dave's writing, which was

Learning to write is a complex process that involves planning, translating, and revising.

9.14 ▬
Using an information-processing perspective, explain why poor writers are likely to jump into a writing task with inadequate planning.

9.15 ▬
Since we know our working memories are limited, identify at least two strategies we can use to overcome this limitation during the planning phase of writing.

primarily "knowledge telling"—presenting ideas essentially as they were generated. This results in short and disorganized final products (Ferrari et al, 1998).

Teaching planning strategies improves writing. For example, teaching college students to list ideas and organize them in outlines improves written products (R. Kellogg, 1987). We should emphasize, however, that simply listing ideas without organizing them or considering their relevance—as in brainstorming—does little to improve the product. If college students need instruction in writing strategies, younger learners need it even more.

The importance of planning can be explained using information processing (R. Kellogg, 1994). If writers fail to plan, their working memories will be overloaded during the next step—translation—because they will be trying to plan and translate simultaneously. Planning is also important because it requires that learners become metacognitive, which further guides the translating and revising stages.

Translating

In the **translation stage**, we *put our ideas on paper in an effort to communicate with others.* Though the products appear on paper, the tasks are organized in working memory, where ideas and words interact. This poses problems for young and inexperienced writers. Let's look again at the challenges Dave and Luis faced as they attempted to translate their ideas into words. Dave wrote:

> My favorite sport is soccer. I like to play soccer. I play sweeper on my team. Sweeper is import . . . ("Hmm, how do you spell important? . . . Oh well.") Playing sweeper is fun because we get to go after the ball a lot. Me and Luis are the best sweepers on the teem. Coach says we're import . . . because . . . Coach says he needs us to keep the other team from . . . scoring. That's why I like soccer. The end.

In the desk next to Dave, Luis is also translating his ideas into words.

> My favorite sport is soccer. I like playing on a team. There is lots of action, and when you work hard you can win. Teamwork is import . . . importund. Dave and I are both sweepers on the team. Our job is to stay in front of the goal. We make sure no clear shots are taken at the goal.
>
> When you are a sweeper there is lots of responsubility. People really depend on you when you're the sweeper. Sweepers help a team win.

We see that Dave and Luis both struggled with translating their ideas into meaningful sentences that obeyed spelling and grammar rules. They used invented spellings, wrote around words they didn't know how to spell, and used simple sentence structure.

There are important differences, however. Dave's essay is essentially a string of unconnected sentences. Luis's, in contrast, suggests some organization, and it also indicates effort to write to an audience. For instance, when he introduced the term *sweeper* he didn't assume the reader knew what it meant. Dave used the same term but didn't define it, and he also used the word "we" to refer to someone he hadn't yet discussed.

Developing writers, such as Dave in particular, have problems because they face several simultaneous challenges as they attempt to put their ideas on paper:

- Graphic challenges—writing legibly so that others can read what's written.
- Syntactic challenges—using appropriate grammar and punctuation.
- Semantic challenges—using ideas that make sense to readers.
- Textual challenges—creating sentences and paragraphs that form a cohesive whole.

Young writers often use so much working memory space on the first two that little is left for the others (Graham, Berninger, Weintraub, & Schafer, 1998; De La Paz & Graham,

1997). Significantly, instruction designed to improve first graders' handwriting skills improves general writing ability (Berninger et al., 1997; D. Jones & Christensen, 1999).

Attempts to consciously eliminate some of these hurdles have proven successful. For example, to bypass the graphic challenge, researchers allowed fourth and sixth graders to dictate rather than write their essays (Bereiter & Scardamalia, 1987), resulting in products that were twice as long and better in quality. To bypass the syntactic challenge, young writers can be allowed to initially make grammatical errors and use invented spellings, saving corrections for the revising stage (Graves, 1994). Too much initial emphasis on grammar and punctuation, as indicated by red-inked corrections all over an assignment, can discourage developing writers from taking risks.

Even simple words of encouragement can influence the amount young students write. For example, for both fourth and sixth graders, written cues to continue writing (e.g., "You're doing fine. Now what do you want to say next?") resulted in essays that were 50% longer than those for whom cues weren't given (Scardamalia, Bereiter, & Goel, 1982). Even short writing tasks can seem monumental to young writers, and teachers' support and encouragement are important emotional scaffolds for them (Pajares, Miller, & Johnston, 1999).

Revising

In the **revising stage**, we *reflect on what we've written and edit and improve our initial attempts.* Revising involves at least three tasks:

▌ Improve the overall organization of the piece.
▌ Ensure that the meaning of sentences and paragraphs is clear.
▌ Detect and correct errors in spelling and grammar. (J. Hayes & Flower, 1986)

Look back at Dave's essay again and see what he might do to improve it. The essay could be improved in at least three ways. First, the organization could be improved so it flows logically from beginning to end. For example, after saying that his favorite sport is soccer, he might write a sentence like, "I like it because I play sweeper, and sweepers get to go after the ball a lot." Second, he could consider his audience by defining *sweeper* and helping readers understand that the first *we* in the passage refers to himself and the other sweeper. Third, spelling and punctuation could be improved. Each of these aspects, while demanding, can be taught (Ferrari et al., 1998).

Research on the revision process has produced the following generalizations:

▌ As writers improve, they spend more time on organization and less on superficial issues like spelling and grammar.
▌ Expert writers spend a greater proportion of their total writing time on revising than do novices.
▌ Even skilled (and older) writers have problems detecting errors—especially their own. (Fitzgerald, 1987; J. Hayes & Flower, 1986)

Research indicates that revising greatly improves writing quality and that experts are better at this process than novices (J. Hayes & Flower, 1986; Henning, 1999). Information-processing theory explains this in two ways. First, the information in experts' long-term memories is better organized, and, second, their writing strategies are more developed.

Instruction can help learners improve these strategies. For example, sixth graders who were taught to add, delete, substitute, and rearrange their written products did significantly more revising, and their stories improved more than the stories written by students who did not receive strategy instruction (Fitzgerald & Markman, 1987).

9.16
Using information processing as a basis, describe what teachers can do—in addition to teaching writing strategies—to improve the revision process.

Helping Students Learn to Write

Writing instruction is changing (Galbraith & Rijlaarsdam, 1999; R. Kellogg, 1994; Mayer, 1999). Historically, writing was viewed as the process of creating a product by applying specific procedures, and transmitting information succinctly and accurately was emphasized. As we mentioned earlier, writing is now seen as a problem-solving process with the goal to communicate. These differences are summarized in Table 9.1.

Let's look at a classroom example that illustrates these differences:

> Jennifer Stevens, Luis and Dave's sixth-grade teacher, read their essays before putting them on the bulletin board to share with others.
>
> "Looks like we've got some work to do this year," she thought with a shake of her head as she finished stapling the last one on the board.
>
> The next day she began her language arts class by saying,
>
> "Class, this year we're going to practice our writing. I know all of you can write because I read the essays you wrote about yourselves. But, I think you can become better writers by doing a little more thinking about what you're doing. For instance, when we write something new, we need to think about what we're going to say before we put our ideas down on paper. I have a planning sheet that will help us in our thinking."
>
> With that, she shared an overhead (see Figure 9.6) with the class, and continued, "Let me show you what I mean, and let's use our planning sheet as a guide. Let's imagine that I need to write an essay about how to do something . . . like fix a flat on a bicycle tire. This is my topic. . . . Now, what's the first thing that I should think about? . . . Let's see what our planning guide says."
>
> The students agreed that they should think first about who they're writing the essay for.
>
> "Sure," Jennifer nodded, "it makes sense that the first thing I need to think about is, Who am I writing this paper for? Probably this person has ridden a bicycle and knows some names for the parts but maybe doesn't know how to fix a tire. That's why I'm writing this paper."
>
> Jennifer then asked the students what they knew about fixing a bike tire, they offered ideas, and she wrote their thoughts on the "What do I know?" part of the planning sheet.
>
> She went through the rest of the sheet and then gave the class a new topic—making a sandwich—and had each student go through the steps, first individually and then with a partner. Finally, she led a class discussion to summarize what they had learned.

As you saw earlier, learning to write is complex, but teachers can help with instruction that includes the following components:

- Teach writing strategies through modeling and think-alouds.
- Provide opportunities to practice strategies and receive feedback from both the teacher and peers.
- Embed strategies in the context of writing for a purpose.
- Create a community of writers where students share work and dialogue with their peers (Bruning et al., 1999; Mayer, 1999).

9.17

Identify an example in Jennifer's lesson of each of the features of present views of writing listed in Table 9.1.

Teach Writing Strategies

Writing instruction has moved away from a product-oriented, one-right-way approach toward one emphasizing strategies that can be used with different topics and audiences

Table 9.1

Changes in view of writing

	Previous View of Writing	Present View of Writing
Definition of writing	Writing as a product	Writing as a process
Goal of writing	Disseminate knowledge	Transform knowledge
View of the writing process	Composition	Communication
Learner task	Application of procedures	Solve problems

Figure 9.6

Planning sheet for a writing assignment

Planning to Write

Name _____   Date _____

TOPIC _____

Who: Whom am I writing for?

_____
_____
_____

Why: Why am I writing this?

_____
_____

What: What do I know? (Brainstorm)

1. _____
2. _____
3. _____
4. _____

How: How can I group my ideas?

_____   _____
_____   _____
_____   _____

How will I organize my ideas:

_____ Comparison/Contrast   _____ Problem/Solution
_____ Explanation   _____ Other

Source: Adapted from Englert & Raphael (1989)

(Graham & Harris, 1999). Since organization is a problem for developing writers, for example, teaching students strategies for organizing their topics, such as outlining or creating hierarchies, provides them with tools that they can use with a variety of writing tasks. Effective strategy instruction can result in improved planning, longer and better quality products, and more positive attitudes toward writing (Graham & Harris, 1999).

How much structure should we provide in teaching these strategies? This question was answered by a review that compared three strategies: teacher-centered expository approaches that focused on grammar, punctuation, and standard formats; "pure" discovery approaches that gave students ample opportunities to write but left them largely on their own; and guided-discovery approaches that were interactive.

The guided-discovery approaches were three times more effective than pure discovery and four times more effective than the expository approaches (Hillocks, 1984). Interaction—between the teacher and students and between the students under the watchful eye of the teacher—was the essential element that made the guided-discovery approaches more effective.

These results can be explained based on constructivist views of learning. Learners are constructing an understanding of the writing process, and interaction, together with guidance from the teacher, is crucial in helping them construct valid understandings.

Provide Opportunities for Practice and Feedback

The opportunity to practice strategies in a variety of settings and receive feedback is essential in helping students become effective strategy users (see Chapter 8). Learning to write is no different. Students need opportunities to learn strategies in one context and practice them in a variety of others to ensure transfer and retention (Bruning et al., 1999; Mayer, 1999).

Embed Strategies in Context

While learners need structure and guidance to learn specific writing strategies, these strategies should be embedded in the context of writing for a purpose. For example, opinions written to the editor of a school newspaper, inquiries to audiotape and CD catalogues, and letters to pen pals in other cities all provide opportunities to see how writing relates to the real world.

> Most importantly, the teaching–learning process must be contextualized and situated within the actual writing process, rather than talked about abstractly or removed from the process and reduced to a set of memorized writing principles, scripts, or rules. (Englert et al., 1991, p. 364)

These researchers found consistent results favoring contextualized strategies for both high- and low-ability students as well as those with learning disabilities.

Create a Community of Writers

When we write, we share both our ideas and ourselves, and this sharing involves taking risks. In the past, writing was a solitary task, and learning to write was viewed as something best done alone. As constructivist views of learning have become more prominent, this view has changed. Growth in the process requires a community of co-learners that we can become a part of and learn from. Just as learning communities support learning in reading (Palincsar & Brown, 1984; Saracho & Spodek, 1999), math (Forman, 1996), and

9.18   ■
How effectively did Jennifer implement each of the instructional components in her work with her students? Refer specifically to the case study in making your evaluation.

Creating a community of writers provides opportunities for developing writers to share their works and receive feedback from their peers.

science (Linn, Songer, & Eylon, 1996), they provide developing writers with support, differing perspectives, and feedback. Social interaction, which has proven to be effective in promoting learning in general (A. Brown, 1994; Rogoff, 1990), is also an essential ingredient in learning to write.

Technology and Learning:
Using Technology to Improve Students' Writing

Do you remember your first writing assignment? Your teacher emphasized that the draft copy was to be done in pencil, so you could erase your mistakes and write in corrections. When you were given approval to make a final copy, you took out a nice, clean sheet of white notebook paper and a new ball point pen. Using your best handwriting to copy the letter, you had the date, address, greeting, and first paragraph looking great when Bobby "accidentally" bumped your arm. Your pen slashed across the letter, ruining it. After yelling at Bobby, you pulled out another clean sheet of notebook paper and began again.

[It] looked great! Then your teacher reminded you to proofread your letter before turning it in. You thought it was a waste of time, but you did it anyway. To your dismay, you realized you had left out a complete sentence, so that the last paragraph did not make any sense. You reluctantly pulled out yet another clean sheet of notebook paper. All of the elation was gone. In fact, writing had become something that you did not like anymore. (Morrison, Lowther, & DeMuelle, 1999, p. 123)

Many of us have memories similar to these. However, technology is changing these experiences, making both writing and learning to write easier and more effective. In this section, we try to see why.

Technology supports learning to write in at least three ways. The first is the communication potential of e-mail, which helps create communities of writers by making drafts of students' work accessible for discussion and critique; the enormous access to information afforded by the Internet is the second; and third, word processing has the potential to revolutionize writing (Alexander et al., 1997).

Word processing is probably of greatest benefit in learning to write, and this benefit is especially important for young writers (Bruning et al., 1999; Mayer, 1999). It can improve student writing in several ways:

9.19 ▬

Using information processing as a basis, explain why eliminating handwriting is important for reducing the cognitive load on young writers.

▌ Eliminate the process of handwriting, so the cognitive load on young writers is reduced.
▌ Make it easy to enter new text, and cut and paste, so organizing, translating, and revising are more effective and less labor intensive.
▌ Make text legible, since it appears in typewritten form on a monitor.
▌ Increase the amount of text available for viewing at one time.
▌ Allow efficient storage and retrieval of ideas (Owston & Wideman, 1997; Roblyer & Edwards, 2000).

The capability of technology for storage, retrieval, and organization is powerful. To illustrate, let's look at a fourth-grade teacher's description of her work with an impulsive writer:

> Kevin's early drafts often had huge gaps of information. For example, his topic was Navajo rituals, and Kevin had written about the beginning of a naming ritual but had neglected to describe its end. After I discussed with him the importance of telling the whole ritual, he returned to his sources for more information and easily added it to his draft. At a later conference I pointed out that the three rituals he had written about were in an odd order: birth, death, and marriage. He agreed, and I showed him how to cut and paste text to reorganize the report. For Kevin, the word processing functioned as a bridge, narrowing the gap between his oral and written communication abilities. (Edinger, 1994, pp. 46–60)

Because Kevin's ideas were stored and easily accessible, his tendency—common with young writers—to come to premature closure was avoided.

Research on Word Processing

Though word processing has the potential to improve both writing and writing instruction, the results of research on its effects are mixed (Bangert-Drowns, 1993; Hawisher, 1989). Researchers have found that students who use word processing in their writing have the following characteristics (compared to their nonusing counterparts):

▌ They write more.
▌ They more effectively revise their drafts.
▌ They make fewer grammar and punctuation errors.
▌ They have more positive attitudes toward writing.

9.20 ▬

Using information processing as a basis, explain why the quality of writing decreases if the students lack experience in word processing skills.

However, they don't necessarily produce written products that are better organized or better in overall quality (Roblyer & Edwards, 2000). The age of the students, their writing experience, and their word processing skills all influence the ability of word processing to effect the quality of their products. One study found that word processing actually decreased writing performance when the writers were not experienced in word processing skills (Kellogg & Mueller, 1993).

Guidelines for Using Technology to Improve Writing

Experts are both optimistic and cautious about the potential of word processing technologies for improving writing instruction (Bruning et al., 1999; Roblyer & Edwards, 2000). For example, Roblyer and Edwards (2000) conclude, "Perhaps no other technology resource has had as great an impact on education as word processing" (p. 116). Technology can provide teachers with a powerful tool in helping implement effective writing programs. However, it cannot substitute for a well-planned program of writing instruction that provides both specific directions for writing strategically and scaffolding during the process.

Guidelines for using technology in writing instruction include:

▌ Teach—and have students practice—word processing skills to ensure that these skills become automatic.

▌ Use a developmental approach to integrating word processing and writing instruction by initially keeping writing tasks simple and gradually increasing their complexity.

▌ Emphasize the value of word processing for completing essential writing tasks, such as organizing and revising text.

▌ Use networking capabilities to create communities of writers, encouraging students to provide feedback to each other.

When used strategically, technology has the capability of dramatically changing the nature of writing instruction. It takes thought, planning, time, and effort, however. Merely putting students in front of computers won't work. As with all innovations, using technology to improve writing will be no more or less effective than the ability of the teacher guiding the instruction.

Classroom Connections

Helping Students Learn To Write

1. Teach specific strategies through modeling and think-alouds.

   • A third-grade teacher is trying to help students understand strategies to organize their writing. She begins by saying, "Let's brainstorm some ideas about pets for our writing assignment." After writing a number of ideas on the board, she asks them to connect related ideas through webbing.

   • To teach revision strategies, a high school teacher places an example of a short writing assignment with organization, clarity, grammar, and punctuation errors on an overhead. She asks, "Where should we start?" With input from the class, she systematically revises the essay, starting with clarity issues and then moving to grammar and punctuation problems.

2. Embed specific strategies in a context of writing with a purpose.

   • To help his students understand how audience influences the way persuasive letters are written, a middle school teacher allows his students to write letters to the school board and parents to try to convince these groups to oppose a proposed school-wide dress code. Before the class writes the letters, the teacher assigns students to groups, has them think of arguments that would persuade their audience, and discusses the ideas with the whole class.

   • A sixth-grade teacher reinforces her writing instruction by asking students to use planning and revision strategies in their social studies reports. She asks them to first turn in an outline, then a first draft to which other students respond, and, finally, a final revision.

3. Give students opportunities to practice strategies and receive feedback.
   - A fifth-grade teacher has students write in their journals the first 15 minutes of each day. She collects the journals each Friday and writes comments and questions in an effort to promote clarity.
   - A middle school teacher breaks students into groups and gives them an editing checklist to be used as a guide in providing feedback. The checklist asks students to evaluate organization, clarity, punctuation, and grammar. Students then revise their works based on the feedback.

4. Create a community of writers.
   - A high school teacher uses response groups as a way to provide peer feedback. Students read their works out loud, and others in the group comment on what was clear, what wasn't, and what they liked about the essays.
   - A second-grade teacher works with her students to write simple stories that they convert into books. Each child's book is bound by parent volunteers in the school publishing room. Students then take turns sitting in the author's chair and reading their books to the class.

 The Challenge of Diversity in Learning to Read and Write

As we've seen in the previous two sections, learning to read and write are cognitively challenging tasks for all learners. This is especially true for non-native English speakers and cultural minorities. Obstacles for these students include

- Background knowledge that differs from topics about which they're asked to read and write
- Lack of linguistic knowledge of English, including vocabulary and structure
- Lack of confidence in their ability to use English for reading and writing (Hernandez, 1997; Peregoy & Boyle, 1997)

Making Students Feel Welcome

Classrooms can be scary places for students, especially when they understand little of what goes on in them. Effective teachers of students from minorities and those who have limited proficiency in English make special efforts to explain the structure of the day and preview future learning activities.

> Ms. Reed meets with a group of seven English-language learners several times during the day for a variety of reasons (e.g., language arts instruction, one-on-one tutoring). One recurring theme in these meetings, which may last anywhere from 3 to 30 minutes, is to discuss and describe future events and activities. For example, Ms. Reed spent 15 minutes on activities and discussion that focused on an impending field trip to a nearby forest. During this meeting, she told the students about the forest, provided pictures of the terrain, and provided new vocabulary that they would be having to deal with in their interactions with the nature guides. During this interaction, she was able to address individual questions that students had about the forest and what they would be encountering there. (August & Pease-Alvarez, 1996, p. 39)

These discussions allowed the teacher to explain classroom procedures and assess and supplement learners' background knowledge, and they gave the students a chance to ask questions and practice using English.

Most important was Ms. Reed's willingness to take the time to work with these students, which communicates caring and a commitment to their learning. If cultural minorities feel welcome, their motivation to learn English and immerse themselves in the mainstream of the classroom and school can increase dramatically (Peregoy & Boyle, 1997).

9.21
Using cognitive learning theory as a basis, explain why classroom procedures might be confusing to minority or non-English-speaking students.

Providing Support in Literacy Activities

Teacher support in literacy activities is important for non-native English speakers. Teachers can support students in at least three ways:

- Supplementing background knowledge
- Providing linguistic scaffolds
- Making learning activities meaningful

Supplementing Background Knowledge

Gaps in background knowledge present barriers for both reading and writing. Comprehension depends on a range of cultural factors that may not be evident to the teacher. For example,

A middle-school text about an adolescent testing the limits of her personal freedom with her parents . . . may be largely incomprehensible to students from cultures that place more value on respecting parents and less on individuality—not because they fail to understand the words or even the sentences, but because they fail to grasp the cultural value Americans place on individuality. And it is this social factor that shapes the meaning of the text. (J. Williams & Snipper, 1990, p. 22)

As another example, when Ms. Reed was previewing the forest field trip, one of the students mistook the word *guide* for the word *guy* and asked, "How can the guys have names like Mary and Suzy?" Sensitive teachers discuss these ideas with their students, diagnosing and building on gaps in background knowledge.

Providing Linguistic Scaffolds

Effective instruction for minority students also provides linguistic scaffolds. In working with non-native English speakers, a strategy that can be effective is "accept and build upon." The following is a brief example of a teacher working with a young girl named Natalia, a native Russian speaker who had been in this country for only 4 months:

Natalia: I putting the marker on the points.
Teacher: Those are called dots. You're putting the marker on the dots.
Natalia: The dots. (Peregoy & Boyle, 1997, p. 52)

By focusing on the term *dots* and ignoring errors in grammar, such as "I putting," the teacher helped Natalia build her word knowledge and skills.

The same supportive scaffolding is effective when assessing students' written products. The following is a piece by a third grader named Jorge who was just learning to read and write in English. In his work he described the differences between two kinds of birds:

Tey are the same becaes the bofe of them haves two eggs and there head and there foot and they are not the same becaes they don't eat the same thing and ther beak and one place is the mountain and one is the valley. the end. (Peregoy & Boyle, 1997, p. 201)

9.22 ■
The ability to use invented spellings, such as Jorge created, reflects what kind of knowledge? (Consider again our discussion of learning to read.)

We see that Jorge's background knowledge with respect to the birds is quite good—he is able to identify similarities and differences in the birds' eggs, heads, beaks, food, and location—and he is able to use invented spellings to convey ideas. Building on these strengths, a teacher could help him develop spelling, grammar, and punctuation skills.

Making Learning Activities Meaningful

Perhaps the most important strategy in helping cultural minority and ESL students learn to read and write English is to contextualize literacy tasks within a meaningful framework. For example, the following is the opening passage of a 79-page book that Lynda Chittenden's fourth and fifth graders produced as a result of their study of the sea near their school:

> The sea is a radiant water galaxy. It's a world of its own in a special way. Under its foam created surface, there exists a universe of plant and animal life. With the tiniest microscopic beings to the most humungus creature that ever lived, the sea is alive! (Kids of Room 14, 1979, p. 1)

In preparing their book, the class took field trips to the sea, visited a seal rookery, observed gray whales migrating, observed dolphins in training, and had marine biologists visit their classroom. They recorded their experiences in learning logs. The following is one journal entry:

> Today I learned how important it is to have blubber. Our class went swimming in a 40 degree pool. I did learn that I COULD swim in that temperature. But, I couldn't even breathe the first time I jumped in. Gradually I got better. I could swim two laps without flippers. But I still don't see how a whale could live in 33 degree water, even with layers and layers of blubber. (Kids of Room 14, 1979, p. 16)

First-hand, concrete experiences made abstract ideas—such as relationships between water temperature and blubber—meaningful to students, which made reading and writing about them not only more meaningful but also easier. Integrated units such as these are especially effective for English language learners because they provide rich opportunities to use language in purposeful activities (Peregoy & Boyle, 1997).

Classroom Connections

Capitalizing on Diversity in Your Classroom

1. Use concrete experiences to develop learners' language skills.
   - A science teacher spends several minutes each class period having her students observe and describe the demonstrations and hands-on activities she uses. She records their observations on the board and refers specifically to the objects as she writes the descriptions.

2. Provide linguistic scaffolds for non-native-English speakers.
   - A geography teacher periodically stops a video and has the students verbally describe what they've seen in it. She carefully repeats what they say, using correct vocabulary and pronunciations.
   - A math teacher guides her students' descriptions of the different ways they solve problems. When they have difficulty articulating an idea, she supplies only enough information to help them continue their descriptions. She provides extra support for students who are just beginning to learn English.

3. Make learning activities meaningful.
   - Language arts students are writing a book about changes in the fall season. They begin soon after school starts and make entries each week. As they read their entries, the teacher has them describe the changes they've observed from week to week.

Learning and Teaching Mathematics

What does it mean to become proficient in mathematics? How important are basic facts and concepts to math thinking? What role should problem solving play in math learning and teaching? Questions like these have caused educators to rethink what it means to learn and teach math. These changes are the focus of this section of the chapter.

Gena Evans, a fifth grade teacher, walked casually to the front of the room holding a banana. As she began to peel it, she said pensively, "I wonder how much banana I'm actually getting for my money. . . . Look at that (pointing to the peel). Sure is a lot of peel. . . . I wonder how much I'm paying for peel."

"Same thing with oranges," Kevin interjected. "I had an orange this morning, and it was all peeling."

"That's an interesting idea," Gena nodded. "I wonder if we get more for our money with bananas or with oranges. . . . Any idea how we might figure that out. . . . Thinking about my banana again, if I paid 49 cents a pound for it, how much was I paying for the peel?

"Tell you what," she continued after a few seconds of silence. "I want you to work in your teams for a few minutes, and let's see if we can figure out how to determine which one, a banana or an orange, gives us more for our money."

Used to doing group work, Gena's students quickly went to work, while she circulated among them, listening to their discussions and making brief comments.

After a few moments, she called for their attention and asked for their ideas.

"We think we should put a banana peel down and also an orange peel, and see which is thicker," Andrea volunteered for her team.

"What if some bananas are thicker . . . I mean, if their skin is thicker?" Devon wondered.

"Good question," Gena nodded. "What do the rest of you think?"

"Maybe we could have a bunch of bananas and oranges too," Shelly offered. "Then they might sort of even out."

"What do you mean, 'even out'?" Gena wondered.

"Well, . . . you know, we could have a thick one and a thin one and some others, and then we even them out, sorta."

"You mean, find the average," Gena smiled.

"Yeah," Shelly nodded.

"How could we find the average?" Gena wondered.

After a few more comments, Gena saw that her students were uncertain about the concept of averaging, so she did an example using several of the children's heights. She then had them do some additional examples. First, they estimated the average weight of several students, calculated the average, and did the same with the lengths of their arms. This took up the remainder of their time, and Gena changed their homework assignment for the next day to problems that required them to find averages.

The next morning Gena had the children review what they had done, and then she asked, "So, where are we with the banana peel problem?"

"We think we oughta weigh the banana and orange . . . and then peel them . . . and then weigh them without the peels," Candice began.

"How about weigh the peelings too?" Brad wondered.

"Well, yeah, I . . . guess so."

"We should do a bunch of them and find the average," Latasha suggested, remembering yesterday's work.

The class generally agreed that weighing the bananas and oranges and peels was a good strategy. Some suggested that they should weigh the unpeeled and peeled bananas and oranges and compare them. Others suggested that they should weigh the unpeeled bananas and oranges and the peels and compare them. Still others thought it would be better if they did both.

Gena encouraged each of the strategies, commenting that often there isn't necessarily one best way to attack a problem. Then, over the next 3 days, the students tried their strategies, got results, and discussed and evaluated what they had done.

Changing Views of Learning Mathematics

Cognitive theories help us better understand the complexities of learning math, including the role that motivation, beliefs, expectations, and strategies play in determining how much students learn. To place this understanding in context, let's first look at the way learning and instruction in mathematics have historically been viewed.

Historical Views of Learning

Historically, math in this country has been taught in a highly proceduralized way (Woodward, Baxter, & Robinson, 1997). For example, students learned to convert fractions to percents (a) by dividing the numerator of the fraction by the denominator and (b) by moving the decimal point two places to the right.

> **9.23**
> Identify at least two similarities between the way math and the way writing were historically taught.

For instance, to convert ⅜ to a percent, we divide 3 by 8 = .375, and then moving the decimal results in 37.5%. Emphasis was on mastery of the algorithm and getting the correct answer.

This approach to math learning and teaching—though not always a conscious application of it—is consistent with behaviorism. The steps are specific and observable, and learners can be reinforced for demonstrating them or given corrective feedback if they don't.

This approach has at least two problems. First, students learn to perform the operations but may not understand why, so they do poorly on more complex tasks requiring them to adapt and use the operations. We can see how this might happen. For instance, other than simply accepting it because we're told to do so, why do we place a decimal point after the 3 when we divide it by 8? Also, we're told that ⅜, .375, and 37.5% are equivalent. On the surface, ⅜ and .375 appear unrelated, and what allows us to simply move the decimal point two places and then add the percent symbol? Understanding math requires more than the manipulation of symbols.

Second, learners often commit random and chronic errors and fail to question the validity of their answers. This is due to lack of understanding as well as confusion with the algorithms themselves; they forget or misapply some of the steps.

Culture of the Classroom

Classroom culture refers to *characteristics of the teaching/learning environment, including the values, expectations, language, learning experiences, unspoken rules, and conventions that guide day-to-day operations* (Tishman, Perkins, & Jay, 1995). Classroom culture influences learning in several ways, most prominently the beliefs students acquire and the strategies they use (Ginsburg-Block & Fantuzzi, 1998).

Beliefs About Learning Mathematics.   Research indicates that many American students hold negative and unproductive beliefs about learning mathematics. For example,

- The ability to do mathematics is innate; that is, some have it and some don't (Hess, Chih-Mei, & McDevitt, 1987; Stevenson, Lee, & Stigler, 1986).
- Math learned in school has nothing to do with the real world (Greer, 1993; Verschaffel, De Corte, & Lasure, 1994).

▌ Math consists primarily of rules and procedures to be memorized, there is only one right way to solve a problem, and the goal in doing mathematics is to get the right answer (Lampert, 1990; Schoenfeld, 1992b).

▌ Solving a math problem shouldn't take more than a few minutes. Problems that take longer are impossible to solve (Schoenfeld, 1988).

The sources of these beliefs are complex. Society as a whole and teachers in particular hold similar beliefs about mathematics (De Corte, Greer, & Verschaffel, 1996). As teachers interact with students and structure their math lessons, these beliefs become part of the classroom culture.

We see this culture reflected in the reactions of a group of veteran elementary teachers when asked to think about their own experiences in traditional math classes. The following are a few of their comments:

"Math was all taught in isolation from everything."
"It was straight arithmetic."
"Totally memorization."
"No higher-order-thinking or skills. It was a bunch of tricks."
"This is the one right way to do it. My thinking was not seen as useful or useable."
(O'Brien, 1999, p. 435)

Learner Strategies.   Classroom culture can also result in students' acquiring superficial strategies for solving problems (Mayer, 1999; Novick, 1998). A common one is looking for key words, such as *altogether*, which suggests that addition is the operation required, or *how many more,* which implies subtraction. Others include performing the operation most recently taught or looking at cues in chapter headings of the text.

Unfortunately, these strategies often bypass understanding completely yet can be quite successful (Schoenfeld, 1991). When they don't work, learners are often at a total loss, resulting in their accepting results that make no sense in the real world. For example, the following problem was given to a national sample of 13-year-olds (O'Brien, 1999):

An Army bus holds 36 soldiers. If 1,128 soldiers are being bused to their training site, how many buses are needed?

Unfortunately, only 23.9% of the 13-year-olds answered the problem correctly, and of those who tried, 46.4% simply dropped the remainder or reported 31⅓ buses.

In a problem such as this, learners commonly use the "key word" strategy, reacting to specific words in the problem, such as, "An Army bus holds . . . " and " . . . how many buses are needed?" They decide that division is the required operation, get an answer of 31⅓, and don't react to the fact that a third of a bus is meaningless.

9.24 ▬
Look again at the list of beliefs about learning mathematics. Which of the beliefs is most closely related to learners' tendencies to be satisfied with "31 and ⅓ buses" as an answer to the problem?

Learning Mathematics: Cognitive Perspectives

Cognitive learning theory, with its focus on thought and deep understanding, helps us understand why unproductive learner beliefs and superficial strategies detract from a meaningful understanding of mathematics.

These theoretical views are corroborated by research. American students tend to fare poorly in international measures of mathematics achievement, particularly compared to students in Japan (Calsyn, Gonzales, & Frase, 1999).

Researchers have identified at least three likely reasons for the achievement gap (Stigler, Gonzales, Kawanaka, Knoll, & Serrano, 1999):

▌ The content in Japanese classrooms requires more high-level thought than classes in the United States.

▌ U.S. math teachers' typical goals are to teach students how to do something, whereas Japanese teachers' goals are to help students understand mathematical concepts.

▌ Lessons are more coherent in Japan; explicit links and connections among different topics are emphasized.

Concerns about U.S. students' achievement have led to proposed reforms in the way math is taught in this country. We examine these next.

Reforms in Math Education

Grounded in cognitive views of learning, reform in the teaching of mathematics has been led by professional organizations, such as the National Council of Teachers of Mathematics, which published the *Curriculum and Evaluation Standards for School Mathematics* in 1989. The *NCTM Standards*, as they're commonly called, contain ambitious goals. At a societal level, they call for reform resulting in mathematically literate workers, increased participation of historically underrepresented groups in the study of mathematics, lifelong learners, and an informed electorate.

At the school and classroom levels, the *NCTM Standards* assert that

▌ Mathematics is a problem-solving activity, not the application of rules and procedures.

▌ Math involves reasoning (with heavy emphasis on estimation) more than memorization.

▌ Studying mathematics should make sense.

▌ Math is communication.

▌ Math should relate to the real world.

At the same time, the *NCTM Standards* deemphasize proceduralized aspects of instruction, such as memorizing facts and relationships, using clue words to determine which operation to use, performing paper-and-pencil computations, practicing routine problems and skills out of context, and teaching by telling.

Ironically, Japanese teachers, with their emphasis on understanding and the focus on links and connections among different topics, demonstrate instruction more consistent with the suggested reforms than do American teachers (Stigler et al., 1999). Specifically,

Effective mathematics instruction emphasizes learning strategies aimed at deep understanding.

high levels of interaction take place in Japanese lessons, and teachers guide learners' thinking rather than dispense information. Compared to American students, Japanese learners spend much less time doing seat work (Lappan & Ferrini-Mundy, 1993). Also, mathematics is more strongly related to students' lives than it is in this country (Stigler & Stevenson, 1991). Perhaps more ironically, most U.S. teachers report that they are familiar with reform recommendations, but relatively few apply the reforms in their classrooms (Stigler et al., 1999).

Characteristics of Effective Math Instruction

Gena Evans's work with her students in the preceding example reflects attempts to implement instruction consistent with the suggested reforms. Specifically, some characteristics of her work are

- A focus on problem solving
- Real-world application
- Emphasis on reasoning
- High levels of interaction

A Focus on Problem Solving.   Gena's lesson focused on problem solving, the activity took several days, and the problem required analytical and critical thinking. Like Laura Hunter's students in Chapter 8, Gena's students had to devise their own strategies for solving the problem, and the problem could be solved in different ways. No single strategy was necessarily better than others.

Real-World Application.   Gena's lesson also emphasized a concrete, real-world problem that provided a context for the lesson's concepts and procedures. For instance, the students acquired a concept of *average,* practiced finding averages, found the fraction or percentage of the fruits that were peel, and dealt with consumer issues. Each concept and procedure was more meaningful because it was studied in the context of a real-world problem (Bottge, 1999). Problems such as these can do much to dispel the unproductive beliefs previously described.

Emphasis on Reasoning.   Reasoning was at the heart of Gena's lesson. For instance, realizing that the peels from the fruits would vary in thickness and concluding that the students would need to average several samples required reasoning. Reasoning was also required to determine how much of the fruit was peel and what proportion of the total cost was paid for peel.

Gena promoted reasoning by guiding students as they discussed possible solutions instead of simply explaining how the problem should be solved and having students perform operations presented in the explanation.

High Levels of Interaction.   Gena also emphasized interaction as she guided students' progress. High levels of teacher–student and student–student interaction were used to analyze the problem.

Interaction is crucial to learning math, and cognitive learning theory helps us understand why (S. Williams, 1997). Interaction puts learners in active roles, and it allows students to describe their current understanding and compare it to others—activities consistent with constructivism.

In addition, a knowledge of students' thinking is essential if teachers are to provide the scaffolding necessary to guide learning. To understand students' thinking and guide

Problem-based learning helps students connect abstract math concepts to the real world.

them to valid understandings, we must interact with them and listen carefully as they talk about problems and interact with each other.

Cognitive Views of Learning: Experimental Programs

9.25 ■
Identify one other characteristic that the programs outlined in Table 9.2 have in common.

The emphasis on cognitive views of learning has resulted in a series of experimental math programs, all consistent with the positions taken by the NCTM. Four are outlined in Table 9.2. Each focuses on problem solving, all are based on the belief that mathematics should make sense, all emphasize real-world application, and in all, the teacher's role is to guide learning rather than to lecture and explain.

Research generally supports these approaches. For example, students in Cognitively Guided Instruction (CGI) classrooms (see Table 9.2) solved problems more effectively than students in control groups, they were more confident in their mathematical ability, and their computational skills were comparable (Villasenor & Kepner, 1993). Similar results have been found for students in anchored instruction (Van Haneghan, Barron, Young, Williams, Vye, & Bransford, 1992), heuristic problem solving (Schoenfeld, 1992a), and teaching for understanding (Lampert, 1992). Significantly, problem solving and peer interaction, two important features of suggested reforms, have also been effective with low-achieving, urban learners (Ginsburg-Block & Fantuzzo, 1998).

Putting Mathematics Reforms Into Perspective

Gena Evans's lesson was consistent with cognitive views of learning and the reforms suggested by the *NCTM Standards* (National Council of Teachers of Mathematics, 1989). But these approaches are demanding, and they have been criticized.

Table 9.2

Experimental approaches in the reform of mathematics

Experimental Approach	Characteristics
Cognitively Guided Instruction (CGI) (Fennema, Carpenter, & Peterson, 1989)	• Primary grades • Focus on solving word problems • Applications to students' lives • Strategy development • Guided discovery and modeling • Emphasis on understanding learner thinking as a route to teacher development
Teaching for Understanding (Lampert, 1989)	• Intermediate grades • Emphasis on processes, dialogue, relationships, and multiple methods • Involving learners in problems that matter to them • Teacher guides instruction
Anchored Instruction (Cognition and Technology Group at Vanderbilt, 1990, 1994)	• Emphasis on authentic problems • Problem situations presented in story form (instructional anchors) • All information needed to solve problems are embedded in the anchors • Supported by technology • Teacher guides and coaches learners
Heuristic Problem Solving (Schoenfeld, 1987, 1992a)	• Emphasis on real-world problems • Focus on strategic aspects of problem solving • Emphasis on metacognition • Teacher guides whole-class and small-group discussion

First, implementing reforms is difficult and won't happen quickly (Ball, 1996). Lessons like Gena's are time-consuming and require high levels of teacher expertise and organization. A great deal of content and pedagogical content knowledge is required—knowledge that teachers often lack (Lampert, 1989; M. Simon, 1993; Spillane & Zeuli, 1999). As we mentioned earlier, teachers report that they're familiar with reforms, but the reforms are rarely implemented (Stigler et al., 1999).

Reform efforts have also been criticized by conservative critics who assert that:

▌ Basic skills are being abandoned at the expense of "fuzzy" mathematics, where estimates replace right answers.
▌ The reform efforts are one more example of widespread "dumbing down" of the curriculum.
▌ The "new" math is a misguided attempt to promote self-esteem at the expense of learning (Battista, 1999; Schoen, Fey, Hirsch, & Coxford, 1999).

Three points put both the reforms and the criticisms into perspective: First, when teachers are faced with change, they sometimes tacitly believe that everything they've done to that point should be abandoned. For instance, since problem solving is being emphasized, teachers may conclude that they should deemphasize facts and basic skills. This isn't the case. Children need to know basic math facts, and most children won't learn the facts as incidental offshoots of problem solving; they must be practiced to automaticity (Weinert & Helmke, 1995). This is consistent with information processing theory, and reformers agree. They argue, instead, that the excessive amount of time students now spend in drill and seat work activities isn't the best way to produce meaningful learning.

Second, reformers aren't suggesting that learners be allowed to believe that any answer they get is as good as any other answer. "Anything goes" is a misinterpretation resulting from misconceptions about the reform efforts.

Third, the success of any reform depends on teachers; teacher knowledge is essential (J. Bay, Reys, & Reys, 1999; Spillane & Zeuli, 1999). Our goal in writing this chapter is to increase teachers' knowledge bases, so they can make decisions that result in the maximum learning for their students.

Classroom Connections

Helping Students Understand Mathematics

1. Embed operations and processes in the context of real-world problems.
   - A fourth-grade teacher, whose class is working on addition and subtraction of two-digit numbers, gives her students problems such as "You've gone to a convenience store, bought a soda for 79 cents, and a pack of gum for 35 cents. You give the clerk $2.00. He gives you back three quarters, a dime, and a penny. Was your change correct?"
   - A first-grade teacher has each of the children put 9 counters under one hand and, without looking, move 5 of them into view. She asks, "How could I figure out how many are left under my hand?"

2. Promote learner reasoning and emphasize that answers in mathematics must make sense.
   - The teacher who presented the problem with the convenience store purchases has students describe their thinking as they try to determine whether or not the clerk took advantage of them.
   - The first-grade teacher working with counters emphasizes "sense making" with questions such as, "How do we know that our answer will be less than 9?", "How do we know that our answer will be

more than 1?", and after they get an answer, "How do you know that your answer is correct?", and "How could we check to be sure our answer makes sense?"

3. Require students to provide estimates before they perform calculations.
   - A seventh-grade teacher working on percents and decimals has the students solve problems such as, "A jacket that sold for $40 is marked down 20%. How much is the sale price?" Before solving the problem, she requires an estimate, which they return to after they have solved the problem.

4. Promote high levels of interaction during math lessons.
   - The teacher who presented the problem with the convenience store purchase has the students work in groups for 5 minutes to discuss their solutions to the problem and their reasoning. She then guides a whole-group discussion of the problem.
   - The teacher who presented the problem with the jacket requires several students to explain how they arrived at their estimate. She also has them explain how they arrived at the discount price.

Learning and Teaching Science

To begin this section of the chapter, let's look again at Hannah Brown's students in the chapter's opening case. In response to her question about why the moon's shape changes, her students gave answers such as, "Clouds," "The atmosphere," and " . . . something to do with the sun, like solar flare-ups." Her students obviously had misconceptions about the moon's phases and what causes them.

To further illustrate the role of misconceptions in science, let's try a couple of simple exercises. Imagine that you're playing catch, and you've just thrown a baseball to your partner. The drawing below represents the path of the ball while it's in the air. Point A is just after the ball has left your hand, Point B is the top of the arc, and Point C is just before your friend catches it. Draw arrows at A, B, and C to illustrate the direction of the forces on the ball at each of these points. (Assume air resistance is negligible and can be ignored.)

As a second example, imagine that you have a tennis ball tied to a string, and you whirl the ball in a circular path around your head. Suppose you let go of the string. Which of the drawings below best illustrates the path of the ball after it's been released?

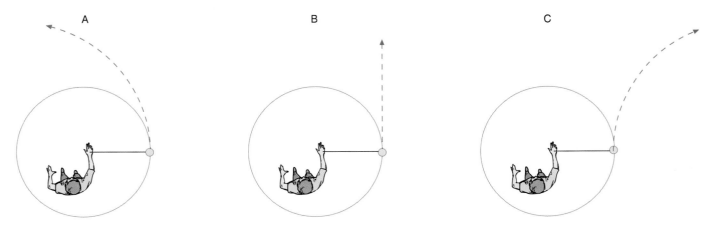

Now, let's see how you did. In the first activity, if air resistance is ignored, the only force acting on the baseball at each of the three points is gravity, which means you should have drawn one arrow pointing down at each of the points.

If you didn't respond this way, you're not alone. In tasks similar to yours, researchers found that more than two thirds of the participants failed to correctly describe the forces, including those who had taken a college physics course (Clement, 1983; R. Osborne & Freyberg, 1985).

In a task similar to the second activity, researchers found that a third of the college students in their study, again including those who had taken a physics course, selected Choice A, indicating that the ball would continue to travel in a curved path (McCloskey, Caramazza, & Green, 1980). Newton's law of inertia, however, states that a moving object continues moving *in a straight line* unless a force acts on it, so Choice B is most valid.

These examples suggest that many people have a number of misconceptions about the way the world works (Guzetti & Hynd, 1998). This was illustrated in the opening case in this chapter, in the students' thinking about the phases of the moon, and in the results we just saw. Why do learners think this way, and how does cognitive learning theory help us understand this thinking? We examine these questions in the sections that follow.

Using Technology in Your Study of Educational Psychology

Examining Thinking in Intuitive Physics

You've just seen that people often have misconceptions about natural events. Using the CD-ROM that accompanies this book, you can further examine this process by using a simulation to look at your thinking with respect to falling objects. To complete the activity, do the following:

- Open the CD, and click on "Intuitive Physics and Conceptual Change."
- Complete the activities involved in the simulation.
- After completing the activities, answer the following questions:

1. Which choice did you select in the *Cliff Problem*? Explain why you selected that choice.

_____

_____

_____

2. Which choice did you select in the *Conveyor Problem?* Explain why you selected that choice.

_____

_____

_____

3. Which choice did you select in the *Airplane Problem?* Explain why you selected that choice.

_____

_____

_____

4. Many people select a path in all three cases that is not the actual path. Why do you think they tend to do so?

_____

_____

_____

5. Now, consider your responses to each of the simulations, and people's tendencies to answer incorrectly. What implications do your answers and the answers of others have for teaching science? Be as specific as possible in your explanation.

_____

_____

_____

Your instructor will provide you with feedback with respect to these five questions and may ask you to complete some of the additional exercises on the CD-ROM.

Difficulties in Learning Science

Students often find science more difficult to learn than other subjects. This is true for at least three reasons. First, science courses typically introduce a great many new concepts very quickly. In fact, researchers found that middle and high school science texts introduce more new vocabulary per page than foreign language texts (Carey, 1986). More important, however, are two other factors:

▌ Life experiences often lead to naive theories and beliefs.
▌ The science curriculum and science instruction fail to confront learners' current understanding.

Life Experiences and Naive Theories

Let's look again at the activities that you did. In the first one, typical suggestions for the forces operating on the ball are illustrated in the following drawing:

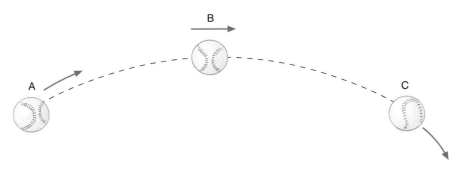

Intuitively, they make sense. For instance, at Point A the ball is traveling both up and forward, so it makes sense that there would be a force in this direction. The same applies at Points B and C.

In the second activity, since the ball is traveling in a circle, it also makes sense that it will continue in a curve once released. In fact, that probably makes more sense than concluding that the ball will suddenly begin to travel in a straight line. Once released, however, it does go straight. (The biblical story of David using his sling to slay Goliath, and many other examples, illustrate this principle.)

Naive theories are *intuitive understandings learners construct based on their day-to-day experiences* (C. Anderson & Roth, 1989; Glynn, Yeany, & Briton, 1991). Many well-documented examples exist. For instance, students commonly believe that green plants, rather than manufacturing their own food, get their food from outside sources, just as animals do. This makes intuitive sense. We feed ourselves and other animals. We water plants, and we even buy containers of "plant food" to sprinkle on them. So the misconception about green plants is sensible; in fact, probably more sensible than the idea that plants manufacture their own food.

Naive Theories: Theoretical Explanations.   Cognitive views of learning and development help us understand why learners form and retain naive theories. First, all cognitive theories view learners as actively trying to make sense of the world. This means that they don't passively respond to the environment as behaviorists assume, nor do they simply record information in the form it is presented. They construct understanding that makes sense to them and, as we mentioned in the previous section, some naive theories are more intuitively sensible than the accepted explanations (diSessa, 1999). So, naive theories allow learners to establish and maintain equilibrium, which, as you learned in Chapter 2, is the cornerstone of Piaget's theory.

Once formed, naive theories become schemas, which we described in Chapter 7 as organized networks of connected information. These schemas are stored in long-term memory and retrieved when needed to help learners understand new experiences. Changing a misconception requires that schemas be modified; that is, the network must be reor-

---

9.26 ▬

Some people believe that the reason summers in the northern hemisphere are warmer than winters is due to the earth being closer to the sun in the summer. In fact, the earth is slightly farther from the sun in summer. Identify at least one common life experience that could lead to this invalid conclusion.

Hands-on science activities allow learners to construct meaningful science concepts.

ganized. This reorganization is demanding and disrupts a learner's equilibrium; it's easier to simply retain the misconception. That's exactly what learners do unless a new conception is more sensible to them than their previous understanding.

Curriculum and Instruction That Don't Confront Naive Theories

Learners tend to interpret new experiences based on their existing understanding (recall our study of constructivism in Chapters 2, 7, and 8). They use any naive theories they have to interpret experiences, which means that additional understanding will be even further distorted.

Unfortunately, curriculum developers and teachers rarely confront learners' existing ideas. Information is commonly presented in general and imprecise terms, allowing learners to interpret new information on the basis of their naive theories (C. Anderson & Smith, 1987). For instance, in our example with the plants, science texts often discuss photosynthesis but don't directly confront the incorrect notion that plants "eat" food like animals do.

Teachers also fail to confront learners' existing conceptions, tending to fall into one of three categories, none being very successful in leading to valid and deep understanding of the topics being studied (E. Smith & Anderson, 1984):

| Activity-driven teachers focus on learner involvement in hands-on activities, assignments, and demonstrations. They tacitly assume that student engagement in the activity equals learning.
| Expository-directed teachers present information with their own naive belief that accurate presentation of content equals similarly accurate learner understanding.
| Discovery-oriented teachers allow students to continue interpreting new information on the basis of their existing ideas, even if those ideas aren't valid. Such teachers are often guided by the belief that teacher intervention in learning activities is inappropriate or ineffective.

Unfortunately, each of these approaches has shortcomings. In the first case, simply having students do a hands-on activity does little to change naive theories; learners simply interpret new experience based on their current understanding. "Hands-on" activities are not necessarily "minds-on" activities (see Chapter 7). Second, expository instruction is consistent with the view that learners record rather than construct understanding, a view of learning that is being increasingly discredited. Finally, research confirms that "pure" discovery is often inefficient and frustrating for learners (Bruning et al., 1999; Schauble, 1990).

So what can we do about learners' lack of understanding in science? Cognitive learning theory provides some answers.

Helping Learners Understand Science

Deeper learner understanding of science requires two essential changes (Anderson & Roth, 1989):

| Adapting the curriculum to emphasize depth over breadth
| Refocusing instruction to encourage meaningful learning

Adapting the Curriculum

Programs effective in increasing learners' understanding of science adapt the curriculum in two ways. First, they reduce technical vocabulary to those terms that are essential for

9.27 ■
Which view of learning—behaviorism, information processing, or constructivism—best explains why learner understanding varies dramatically, even though all learners in a class have heard the same accurate explanation of a topic?

explaining other ideas (Anderson & Roth, 1989). Second, they emphasize these topics in depth, something that American science courses haven't historically done. Program developers must make decisions about what topics are most important to teach, teach them thoroughly, and eliminate less important topics.

> Parsimony is essential in setting out educational goals. Schools should pick the most important concepts and skills to emphasize so that they can concentrate on the quality of understanding rather than on the quantity of information presented. (Rutherford & Algren, 1990, p. 185)

The National Research Council, in presenting its *National Science Education Standards* (1996), recommends less emphasis on "covering many science topics" and more emphasis on "studying a few fundamental science concepts" (p. 113).

This shift in emphasis has important implications for science teachers. Textbooks and curriculum guides are likely to present an overwhelming array of information. In using these materials, teachers must identify key topics to cover in depth, others to be examined less thoroughly, and still others to eliminate completely.

Refocusing Instruction

None of the traditional approaches to instruction—activity driven, expository directed, or discovery oriented—are very successful in promoting valid and deep understanding of science in students. So how can we refocus instruction to increase learning?

Fortunately, research provides some answers (Driver, Asoko, Leach, Mortimer, & Scott, 1994; Lederman, Schwartz, Abd-El-Khalick & Bell, 1999; Pintrich, Marx, & Boyle, 1993). Figure 9.7 summarizes these recommendations, which are discussed next.

9.28
Research indicates that naive theories must be directly confronted if learners are to develop more mature understanding. Using Piaget's work as a basis (see Chapter 2), explain why this is so.

Assessing Current Understanding.   To directly confront learners' naive theories and beliefs, we must first understand what they are. This means that we must assess learners' current understanding. To do so, lessons should—as often as possible—begin with a problem or demonstration that requires explanation. In the opening case, the teacher's question, "What makes the moon look like that?" was such a problem, and students' answers indicated that they had misconceptions about the phases of the moon. The questions we asked about the forces on a baseball in flight or the path of the tennis ball are also examples. Students reveal their present understanding as they offer their explanations, and teachers are then in a position to directly confront these understandings if they're invalid.

Representing Content.   Students use high-quality examples and representations to construct understanding, and representing problems is an essential step in successful problem solving (see Chapters 7 and 8). Promoting learning in science is consistent with these ideas; it also requires multiple, concrete representations of topics. For instance, suppose you're trying to understand Bernoulli's principle, which says that as the speed of air over a surface increases, the force the air exerts on the surface decreases (the principle that

Figure 9.7

A model for effective science instruction

Assessing current understanding

Representing content

Effective interaction

Real-world application

explains why airplanes can fly). At this point, the principle is probably not meaningful to you, so let's go on. Hold two pieces of paper as shown in the following drawing, lean over, blow between them, and observe what happens to the papers.

You likely saw that they came together at the bottom. Your blowing between the two pieces of paper and seeing them come together is a representation of Bernoulli's principle. It is a single, concrete representation, illustrating the second element of the model in Figure 9.7.

Learners can't typically construct a valid understanding of the principle based on this single representation, however, so additional representations are necessary (Brenner et al., 1997; Spiro, Feltovich, Jacobson, & Coulson, 1992). For instance, take one of the papers, hold it as shown in the following sketch, and blow vigorously over the top. This is a second, concrete representation. In this case, the paper rose up as you blew.

9.29
Based on the information in Figure 9.7, what is the first thing you would do after having students blow between the two pieces of paper? From an information processing perspective, what purpose does having the students blow between the papers serve?

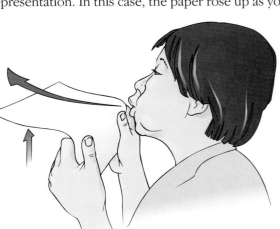

The two representations we just examined are concrete examples of Bernoulli's principle. While concrete representations are desirable beginning points—and should be used if available—other alternatives exist. Models, sketches, mathematical formulas, and even verbal descriptions can also serve as representations.

Effective Interaction.   Involvement in an activity, by itself, won't necessarily produce learning; neither will representations of content, by themselves. The combination of the two can, and you've seen throughout this book how important interaction is. Typical science instruction is often teacher-centered, however, and discussions between teachers and students and students with each other are often infrequent and inadequate (Dickinson, Abd-El-Khalick, & Lederman, 1999).

Interaction promotes meaningful science learning in several ways:

- It allows teachers to assess learners' current understandings.
- It helps create cognitive conflict.
- It promotes a community of learners.
- It allows teachers to provide scaffolding for students.
- It helps learners develop an understanding of the nature of science.

Cognitive Conflict.   Think again about the two pieces of paper, and, before reading further, write a brief description that explains why the papers came together at the bottom. Include a sketch with your explanation. The explanation and sketch will reflect your current understanding of Bernoulli's principle.

If your explanation is typical, you suggested that as you blew, the air curled around the papers at the bottom and pushed the pieces of paper together, as shown in the following diagram.

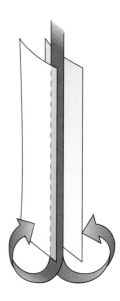

As we've emphasized repeatedly, one of the characteristics of constructivism is that new learning depends on current understanding. We've also said that science is sometimes difficult for learners because they bring naive theories and beliefs to the learning experience. This leads us to the role of cognitive conflict.

Cognitive conflict *occurs when learners are no longer satisfied with their existing understanding and consequently struggle to develop understanding that makes more sense to them.* In the absence of cognitive conflict, learners typically remain satisfied with what they currently know. Promoting learning in science requires identifying learners' current understandings, so naive theories and beliefs can be directly confronted (C. Anderson & Roth, 1989; Bruning et al., 1999). Confronting naive or incomplete conceptions is important because learners won't change their thinking until their current understandings are implausible to them.

Introducing cognitive conflict requires a teacher's skilled guidance in a supportive community of learners (C. Anderson & Roth, 1989). In a **community of learners**, *the teacher and students work together to develop understanding of the topics they're studying.* In a learning community, teachers introduce problems (such as why the two papers came together at the bottom), students offer explanations based on their current understandings, and the merits of these explanations are examined in small- and large-group discussions.

The teacher's role in these discussions is crucial. She must guide students so discussions don't wander unproductively, ask timely questions that cause students to reconsider their current thinking, and ultimately help students arrive at a valid understanding of the topic (diSessa, 1999). Simply explaining, or intervening too soon, robs learners of the chance to develop their own understandings. Not intervening soon enough can detract from learning because time is wasted and learners become uncertain and frustrated.

As an example of this process, let's look at how Clarice Torres, a fourth-grade teacher, guides her students toward an understanding of Bernoulli's principle.

Kathy:	I think air like curled around the bottom and then pushed the papers together.
Clarice:	What evidence do we have for that?
Kathy:	They went together. Something had to do it.
Clarice:	Does everyone agree . . . ?
Devon:	I . . . I'm not so sure. Why would the air just go around like that?
Kathy:	I dunno. . . . It just did.
Clarice:	(After waiting several seconds in which no one talked) What do any objects that are moving want to do? . . . Anyone?
Devon:	Go straight . . . They want to go straight.
Clarice:	So what does the air want to do?
Tiffany:	Go straight? It . . . wants to go straight, I guess.

As the discussion continues, Clarice asks students to analyze the forces on the papers and consider where the air is moving more rapidly. Gradually, they conclude that the faster-moving air (resulting from blowing) between the papers must have reduced the force between them, so the papers are pushed together by the slower-moving (still) air outside them.

This brief case illustrates several characteristics of effective interaction that we outlined earlier in this section. First, the discussion—together with students' direct experience—led to cognitive conflict. Their original thinking was challenged and became less plausible to them.

Second, Clarice didn't simply explain why the papers came together; instead, she guided students' thinking as their understanding evolved. This occurred within a supportive community of learners.

Third, Clarice's guidance provided a form of scaffolding. Without this scaffolding, it is unlikely that students—on their own—could have arrived at an understanding of the principle. Her scaffolding was an essential part of the process.

Social interaction allows learners to analyze and evaluate their own understanding of science concepts with other students.

Finally, as learners acquire experience in activities like this, they learn that conclusions are made on the basis of evidence, they figure out how to gather the best evidence possible, and also develop a tolerance for ambiguity. These are characteristic of science as a way of understanding the world.

Real-World Application.   Learning science can be intrinsically motivating because much of what students learn in science can be directly applied to the real world (A. Adams & Chiapetta, 1998; O. Lee & Fradd, 1999). For example, Bernoulli's principle helps us understand how airplanes can fly—a very real-world application. Examples could be given for nearly every topic learners study. As learners acquire experience, they come to believe that science is, in fact, an integral part of their lives.

Classroom Connections

Helping Learners Understand Science

1. Access learners' current understandings.
   - A first-grade teacher places two large, deflated balloons on a balance to demonstrate they have the same mass. Then, to demonstrate that air also has mass, she inflates one of the balloons and puts it back on the balance. When the children see that the side of the balance with the inflated balloon on it goes down, she asks them to explain why they think it happened.
   - To demonstrate convection as a method of heat transfer, a fifth-grade teacher places a covered baby food jar full of hot, colored water into a beaker of cold water. She pokes a hole in the cover, allowing a stream of colored water to rise from the baby food jar to the top of the cold water. She then asks the students to explain why they think the colored water rose to the top.

2. Provide as many concrete representations of topics as possible.
   - A third-grade teacher burns paper, puts vinegar into baking soda, and shows students a piece of rusted iron to demonstrate chemical changes. She contrasts these examples with crumpled and torn paper, melting ice, and brewing coffee to illustrate physical changes.
   - A chemistry teacher demonstrates Charles' law by putting one balloon in ice water and another in hot water to demonstrate changes in volume resulting from different temperatures. She links the demonstration to the relationship $T_1/V_1 = T_2/V_2$ and has the students solve problems using the equation.
   - A life science teacher illustrates the concept of camouflage by scattering different-colored toothpicks on measured areas of grass on the school grounds and has the students find as many as possible in 2 minutes. She also shows colored slides of snakes, insects, fish, and mammals in their natural habitats to illustrate how they are protected by their coloration.
   - A sixth-grade teacher helps her students understand adaptation by displaying a cactus (which has very small leaves—needles—to prevent loss of moisture) and a broad-leafed plant and by showing pictures of plants in their natural habitats. She also shows pictures of Arctic hares with small ears (so they won't lose too much heat) and Southwestern desert rabbits with large ears. She has the students consider why elephants have such large ears, why antelope have long legs, and why alligators' eyes are near the tops of their skulls—all to illustrate how organisms adapt to their environments.

3. Promote high levels of interaction in your teaching.
   - The fifth-grade teacher teaching convection has students explain why they think the colored water rose to the top of the cold water. During the discussion, she helps them see relationships between heat, expansion, density, and flotation, and she links each of these ideas to the concept of convection.
   - A sixth-grade teacher has her students work in groups to determine what factors would influence how fast aspirin tablets would dissolve. She monitors their work as they discuss and consider factors such as the volume and temperature of the liquids in which the aspirin are placed, the type of liquid, and whether or not the aspirin is left whole or is crushed. She then has the teams discuss their findings in a whole-group discussion.

4. Make tasks and problems as real-world as possible.
   - The chemistry teacher whose class is studying Charles' law presents problems such as, "You have this balloon here at room temperature, and we're going to put it in the freezer. In 4 hours, what will the volume of the balloon be?" To solve the problem, the students estimate the volume of the balloon and measure the temperature in the room and the freezer. They then calculate the balloon's volume in the freezer.
   - The teacher whose students examined the dissolving rates of aspirin has them discuss reasons why the experiment's results would provide useful knowledge, such as how quickly pain reliever would be absorbed into a person's system.

Looking Across the Content Areas

As we've seen in this chapter, there are unique aspects to learning to read, or write, or learn math or science. Despite these differences, some common issues exist across the disciplines. For example, the following elements influence learning in each of the content areas:

- Background knowledge
- Learning strategies
- Interaction and discussion
- Multiple representations of content

Background Knowledge

Students' background knowledge influences learning in all content areas, but it does so in different ways. It serves as a foundation for comprehension in reading and a storehouse of ideas in writing. Students' declarative and procedural knowledge help them identify and solve different types of problems in math, and naive conceptions often hamper learning in science. But in each content area, new understanding builds on what students already know.

Effective teachers assess students' background knowledge and use this information to adapt their instruction. Questioning, quizzes, short writing assignments, and other activities such as concept mapping can all be used to assess learners' current understandings (Winitzky, Kauchak, & Kelly, 1994).

Learning Strategies

All four content areas require active, strategic learners. Good readers attack text strategically, and effective writers frame their writing with goals. Math and science both require learners to become actively involved in making sense of new information.

Effective teachers provide explicit instruction in strategy use by explaining and modeling strategies (Rosenshine, 1997). They describe their thinking as they model, and they give learners many opportunities to practice strategies and receive feedback in a variety of contexts.

Interaction and Discussion

Sharing and comparing ideas through interaction and discussion are essential in all four content areas. The foundations of linguistic knowledge are found in dialogue, and student interaction is central to reciprocal teaching. The use of clear language is the central focus of writing, and both math and science learning are enhanced by opportunities to discuss and analyze our own and others' ideas.

Teachers promote interaction by creating supportive learning environments in which students are willing to talk and take risks. Effective teachers encourage learners to speculate, predict, share ideas, and analyze others' thinking in a supportive and nonthreatening way (Hiebert & Raphael, 1996). Teachers create these classrooms by establishing a classroom culture that accepts diverse views and opinions, modeling, promoting the involvement of all students through questioning, and encouraging learners to dialogue as they struggle with difficult ideas.

Multiple Representations of Content

Learning in all four content areas is enhanced when ideas are represented in a variety of ways and when tasks are embedded in real-world activities. Comprehension is increased when learners connect the printed word with real-life experiences and read from a variety of sources—books from different content areas, magazines, newspapers, and others. Writing improves when learners write about topics that are personally meaningful to them. Learning in math and science is most effective when linked to real-world applications and problems.

In all four areas, educators are moving away from abstract and detached teaching/learning, and toward functional and applied approaches. Creating meaningful and applied tasks benefits learning, motivation, and transfer (Pintrich & Schunk, 1996; Shuell, 1996; Mayer & Wittrock, 1996).

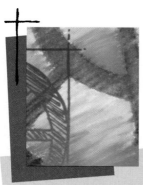

Windows on Classrooms

In the opening case, you saw how students in Hannah Brown's class dealt with learning experiences in the different content areas discussed in this chapter. Here's another example involving learning across the content areas.

Dan Metcalf was beginning an integrated unit in his sixth-grade class. The focus for the unit was a stream that passed within several blocks of his middle school. After working out safety and logistical problems with his principal, Dan took his class to the stream to begin their study.

For the science part of the project, the class was doing a study of the stream's ecology. Students measured stream flow, temperature, and even collected samples to send to the state's water testing division. As they discussed their findings, Dan realized that they believed the water in a river or stream flowed at a uniform rate. "Hmm," he thought, "they're going to have trouble understanding how sand bars form and why rivers and streams get more curved and convoluted if they don't understand that water flows faster on the outside of a curve and slower on the inside. "I better cover that very carefully."

For math, Dan asked his students to analyze the data they had gathered. To guide them, Dan wrote the following questions on the board:

1. How does water temperature change over the course of a day?
2. How does depth influence water temperature?
3. What happens to water temperature when rocks and logs form a pool in the stream?

Dan assigned students to groups to answer these questions and asked each group to share their answers in a graphic or pictorial form.

The reading part of the unit was Dan's biggest challenge. Most of the articles and chapters on stream ecology were written at the high school level or beyond. Dan had photocopied a number of articles for student use, but when he distributed them to the different groups, they stared at the materials, not knowing

what to do. Unfortunately, Dan was in the same boat.

The writing component of the unit wasn't as difficult. The class had decided at the beginning of the unit to "adopt" the stream they were studying. They agreed that it was a valuable community resource that many of them had played and fished in, and it ought to be protected. They agreed that the focus of their writing projects would be information dissemination and political activity. They wanted to write essays informing the public of the stream's fragile ecology and also write to local newspapers and politicians urging action to protect the stream.

Unfortunately, their missionary zeal outstripped their writing expertise. Their initial essays were disorganized, they ignored their audiences, and they failed to make convincing arguments. Dan didn't know where to begin.

Questions for Discussion and Analysis

Analyze Dan's instruction based on the content in this chapter. Whenever possible, take information directly from the case to support your answers.

1. How effective was Dan in countering students' naive theories about streams? What alternate strategies could he have used?
2. How well did Dan's math instruction implement the reforms suggested by the *NCTM Standards* (National Council of Teachers of Mathematics, 1989) and characteristics of effective math instruction?
3. What suggestions do you have to solve Dan's problem with reading?
4. What suggestions do you have to help Dan improve his students' writing ability?
5. Explain how learners' background knowledge, their learning strategies, interaction and discussion, multiple representations of content, and real-world application influenced the effectiveness of Dan's instruction.

Now go to our Companion Website to assess your understanding of chapter content with the Student Self-Assessment, apply comprehension in the Online Casebook, and broaden your knowledge base with links to important Educational Psychology World Wide Web sites.

Summary

Learning to Read and Teaching Reading

Learning to read occurs in two stages. The first emphasizes deriving meaning from symbols and requires background and linguistic knowledge. The second emphasizes the use of strategies to gain information from text.

Code-emphasis approaches target decoding skills, such as translating the sounds of letters into words. Phonics, a code-emphasis approach, stresses letter–sound relations and rules for sounding out words. Meaning-emphasis approaches stress the functional nature of printed words and reading as one element of the communication process.

In the middle elementary grades, the emphasis shifts to reading to learn. Through self-regulatory processes, such as summarizing and self-questioning, readers learn to monitor their comprehension and improve the amount they learn from reading.

Learning to Write and Teaching Writing

Learning to write requires understanding of task requirements and background and discourse knowledge. In the planning stage, writers generate and organize ideas. During translation, they put ideas on paper, and in the final stage—revising—they correct errors, clarify ideas, and restructure the piece to make it more organized and cohesive.

Writing instruction has shifted toward a process emphasis, where communication and problem solving are emphasized over rule-driven procedures. A cognitively oriented writing classroom emphasizes creating a community of writers and teaches writing strategies within the context of meaningful tasks.

The Challenge of Diversity in Learning to Read and Write

Different background knowledge, lack of linguistic knowledge in English, and lack of confidence in their ability to use English effectively are obstacles for cultural minorities. Teachers help overcome these obstacles by creating supportive and language-rich environments that include concrete experiences, linguistic scaffolds, and meaningful learning activities. Most important are caring teachers who welcome and embrace all students.

Learning and Teaching Mathematics

Learning mathematics requires a shift in emphasis away from mastery of procedures and rules to an understanding of the reasons behind these rules. Effective teachers create a classroom culture in which traditional beliefs about math are challenged and replaced with strategies that allow learners to attack problems in meaningful ways. Effective math instruction focuses on real-world problem solving, emphasizes multiple solutions to problems, and forges connections to other content areas.

Learning and Teaching Science

Learning and teaching science are complicated by the naive theories that learners bring to learning experiences. Based on life experiences, naive theories often conflict with accepted scientific explanations.

Increasing learner understanding requires change in both science curriculum and instruction. The curriculum needs to emphasize depth over breadth, focusing on key ideas. Instruction needs to represent content more effectively, encourage thoughtful dialogue about content, and apply content to real-world applications.

Looking Across the Content Areas

Despite content area differences, similarities across the different content areas also exist. Learning in all areas requires background knowledge and is enhanced when students assume a proactive strategic approach. Multiple representations of content help learners relate abstract ideas to the real world, and interaction and discussion provide opportunities for them to form, compare, and adapt ideas.

 **Important Concepts**

background knowledge
  (p. 360)

classroom culture (p. 386)

code-emphasis approaches
  (p. 363)

cognitive conflict (p. 401)

community of learners
  (p. 401)

conceptually driven views
  (p. 365)

data-driven models
  (p. 365)

decoding (p. 364)

discourse knowledge
  (p. 372)

emergent literacy (p. 361)

language experience
  (p. 362)

linguistic knowledge
  (p. 360)

meaning-emphasis
  approaches (p. 362)

naive theories (p. 396)

phonemic awareness
  (p. 364)

phonics (p. 363)

planning stage (p. 372)

reading (p. 360)

reciprocal teaching
  (p. 369)

revising stage (p. 375)

task environment (p. 371)

translation stage (p. 374)

whole language (p. 362)

Part III

The Classroom

Classroom Processes

10

Increasing Learner Motivation

"We better get moving," Susan urged Jim as they approached the door of Kathy Brewster's classroom. "The bell is gonna ring, and you know how Brewster is about this class. She thinks it's SO important."

"Did you finish your homework?" Jim asked and then stopped himself. "What am I talking about? You've done your homework in every class since I first knew you."

"I don't mind it that much. . . . It bothers me when I don't get something, and sometimes it's even fun. My dad helps me. He says he wants to keep up with the world," Susan responded with a laugh.

"In some classes, I just do enough to get a decent grade, but not in here," Jim responded. "I used to hate history, but Brewster sorta makes you think. It's actually interesting the way she's always telling us about the way we are because of something that happened a zillion years ago. . . . I never thought about this stuff in that way before."

"Gee, Mrs. Brewster, that assignment was impossible," Harvey grumbled as he walked in.

"That's good for you," Kathy smiled back. "I know it was a tough assignment, but you need to be challenged. It's hard for me, too, when I'm studying and trying to put together new ideas, but if I hang in, I feel like I can usually get it."

"Aw, c'mon, Mrs. Brewster. I thought you knew everything."

"I wish. I have to study every night to keep up with you people, and the harder I study, the smarter I get," Kathy continued with a smile. "And, . . . I feel good about myself when I do."

"But you make us work so hard," Harvey continued in feigned complaint.

"Yes, but look how good you're getting at writing," Kathy smiled again, pointing her finger at him. "I think you hit a personal best on your last one. You're becoming a very good writer."

"Yeh, yeh, I know," Harvey smiled on his way to his desk, " . . . and being good writers will help us in everything we do in life," repeating a rationale the students continually hear from Kathy.

Kathy turned to Jennifer as she walked in, and said quietly, "I pulled your desk over here, Jenny," motioning to a spot in the middle of the second row. "You've been a little quiet lately. . . . I almost considered calling your Mom, to see if everything's okay," and she touched Jennifer's arm, motioning her to the spot.

She finished taking roll and then pulled down a map in the front of the room. "Let's look again at the map and review for a moment to see where we are. We began our discussion of the Crusades yesterday. What was significant about them? . . . Greg?"

"You came in with pictures of Crusaders and asked us to imagine what it'd be like to be one of them . . . . Antonio said he didn't think he'd like iron underwear," Greg grinned as the rest of the class giggled.

"All right, that's true." Kathy smiled back. "Now, how did we start the lesson? . . . Kim?"

" . . . "

"Remember, we started by imagining that we all left Lincoln High School and that it was taken over by people who believed that all extracurricular activities should be eliminated. We then asked what we should do about it. What did we decide we should do?"

"We decided we'd talk to them . . . and try and change their minds," Kim responded hesitantly.

"Right. Exactly, Kim. Very good. We said that we would be on a 'crusade' to try to change their minds.

"Now, what were the actual Crusades all about? . . . Selena?"

" . . . The Christians wanted to get the Holy Land back from the Muslims."

"About when was this happening?"

"I . . . I'm not sure."

"Look up at our time line."

" . . . Oh, yeah, about 1100," Selena answered peering at the time line.

"Good, and why did they want them back? . . . Becky?"

"The . . . Holy Lands were important for the Christians. I suppose they just wanted them because of that."

"Yes. Good, Becky," Kathy smiled. "Indeed, that was a factor. What else? . . . Anyone?"

After surveying the class and seeing uncertainty on students' faces, Kathy said, "You might not see what I'm driving at. . . . Let's look at this," and she then displayed a map that illustrated the extent of Muslim influence in the Middle East, North Africa, and Europe.

"What do you see here? . . . Cynthia?"

Cynthia scanned the map for several seconds and then said, "It looks like the Muslims are getting more and more territory."

"Yes, very good. So, what implication did this have for the Europeans?"

"They probably were scared . . . like afraid the Muslims would take over their land," Scott volunteered.

"That's a good thought, Scott," Kathy responded. "They certainly were a military threat. In fact, the conflict that occurred in Kosovo is a present-day reminder of the clash between Christians and Muslims. How else might they have been threatening?"

"Maybe . . . economically," Brad added. "You're always telling us how economics rules the world."

"Brilliant, Brad," Kathy laughed. "Indeed, economics was a factor. In fact, this is a little ahead of where we are, but we'll see that the military and economic threats of the Muslims, together with the religious issue, were also factors that led to Columbus's voyage to the New World. . . . Think about that. The Muslims in 1000 A.D. have had an influence on us here today."

"Now," Kathy said, "let's get back on track. Why do we study the Crusades? 'Like, who cares, anyway?' . . . Toni?"

"They were important in Europe, . . . it affected its development in the Middle Ages, like fashion and war strategies, . . . all the way up to today. The Renaissance wouldn't have been the same without them."

"Excellent, Toni! Very good analysis. Now, for today's assignment, you were asked to write a paragraph answering the question, 'Were the Crusades a success or a failure?'

You could take either position. We want to learn how to make and defend an argument, so the quality of your paragraph depends on how you defended your position, not on the position itself. Remember, this is a skill that goes way beyond a specific topic like the Crusades. This applies in everything we do.

"So, let's see how we made out. Go ahead. . . . Nikki?"

"I said they were a failure. They didn't . . . "

"Wait a minute!" Joe interrupted. "How about the new fighting techniques they learned?"

"Joe," Kathy began firmly, "what is one of the principles we operate on in here?"

"We don't have to agree with someone . . . but we have to listen. . . . Sorry."

"Go on, Nikki," Kathy continued.

"That's okay," Nikki continued, nodding to Joe. "It seemed to me that militarily, at least, they failed because the Europeans didn't accomplish what they were after . . . to get the Holy Land back for Christianity," Nikki said. "There were several Crusades, and after only one did they get sort of a foothold, and it only lasted a short time, like about 50 years, I think."

"Okay. That's good, Nikki," Kathy responded. "You made your point and then supported it. That's what I wanted you to do in your paragraph."

"Now, go ahead, Joe. You were making a point," Kathy said, turning back to him.

"I said they were a success because the Europeans learned new military strategies that they used on the Natives," Joe responded, " . . . here, in the Americas, and they were

good at it. If it hadn't been for the Crusades, they probably wouldn't have learned the techniques, . . . at least not for a long time. Then, only the Japanese knew the attacking techniques the Crusaders learned when they went to the Middle East. It even changed our ideas about, like, guerrilla fighting."

"Also good, Joe," Kathy responded, nodding. "This is exactly what we're after. Nikki and Joe took opposite points of view in their paragraphs, but they each provided several details to support their positions. Again, we're more concerned with the support you provide than the actual position you take.

"Let's look at one more," she went on. "What was your position, Anita?"

"I said they . . . were a success," Anita responded. "Europe . . . Western Europe took a lot from their culture, their culture in the Middle East. Like, some of the spices we eat today first came to Europe then."

"Now isn't that interesting!" Kathy waved energetically. "See, here's another case where we see ourselves today finding a relationship to people who lived 1,000 or more years ago. That's what history is all about."

"Brewster loves this stuff," David whispered to Kelly, smiling slightly.

"Yeah," she replied. "History has never been my favorite subject, but some of this stuff is actually kind of neat."

"Okay. One more," Kathy continued, "and we'll move on."

The class reviewed another example, and then Kathy told the students to revise their paragraphs in light of what they had discussed that day and to turn in a final product the following day. "Remember, think about what you're doing when you make your revisions," she emphasized. "Read your paragraph after you write it, and ask yourself, 'do I actually have evidence here, or is it simply an opinion?' . . . The more aware you are when you write, the better your work will be."

When the period was nearly over, Kathy said, "Excuse me, but the bell is about to ring. Just a reminder, group presentations on the Renaissance are Wednesday and Thursday. You decide what groups will be on each day. For those who chose to write the paper on the Middle Ages, remember we agreed that they should be due next Friday."

In ideal classrooms, students pay attention, ask questions, and want to learn. They do their assignments without complaint and study without being coaxed or cajoled. But teachers don't teach in an ideal world. They often have students who are not motivated; more accurately, they don't seem motivated to work on the tasks their teachers set out for them.

Teachers contribute a great deal to students' desires to learn and to take responsibility for their learning. They aren't successful with every student, but with a positive approach to motivation, they can influence many (Stipek, 1996).

In this chapter we examine theory and research on student motivation, together with teacher characteristics, classroom climate variables, and instructional factors that can help increase students' desire to learn.

After you've completed your study of this chapter, you should be able to meet the following objectives:

▌ Explain learner motivation on the basis of behavioral, cognitive, and humanistic theories.
▌ Explain the role of motivation in developing self-regulation.
▌ Explain how teacher personal characteristics promote student motivation.
▌ Describe how classroom climate variables promote student motivation.
▌ Identify instructional factors that promote student motivation.

"Children's motivation to learn lies at the very core of achieving success in schooling. Given rapid technological advances, an ever-changing knowledge base, and shifting workplace needs, a continuing motivation to learn may well be the hallmark of individual accomplishment across the lifespan" (R. Weinstein, 1998, p. 81).

Motivation is *a force that energizes, sustains, and directs behavior toward a goal* (R. Baron, 1992; Pintrich & Schunk, 1996), and researchers have found a strong correlation between motivation and achievement (Wang, Haertel, & Walberg, 1993; R. Weinstein, 1998). In general, motivated students

▌ Have positive attitudes toward school and describe school as satisfying
▌ Persist on difficult tasks and cause few management problems
▌ Process information in depth and excel in classroom learning experiences (Stipek, 1996)

Not surprisingly, motivated students are a primary source of job satisfaction for teachers.

Motivation can be described in two broad categories. **Extrinsic motivation** refers to *motivation to engage in an activity as a means to an end*, whereas **intrinsic motivation** is *motivation to engage in an activity for its own sake* (Pintrich & Schunk, 1996). For example, extrinsically motivated learners may study hard for a test because they believe

Figure 10.1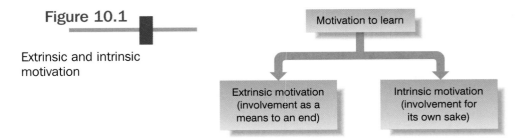

Extrinsic and intrinsic
motivation

studying will lead to high test scores, teacher compliments, or some other end; intrinsically motivated learners study because they view studying and learning as worthwhile in themselves. These relationships are illustrated in Figure 10.1.

Although we think of extrinsic and intrinsic motivation as two ends of a continuum (meaning the higher the extrinsic motivation, the lower the intrinsic motivation and vice versa), they are actually on separate continua (Pintrich & Schunk, 1996). For example, students might study hard both because a topic is interesting *and* because they want good grades in a class. Others might study only to receive the good grades. The first group is high in both extrinsic and intrinsic motivation, whereas the second is high in extrinsic motivation but low in intrinsic motivation.

Extrinsic and intrinsic motivation can also change over time and vary with the situation. Jim, in our opening case study, for example, appears to be extrinsically motivated in other classes ("In some classes, I just do enough to get a decent grade . . . "), but intrinsically motivated in Kathy's class ("I used to hate history, but Brewster sorta makes you think. It's actually interesting . . . ")

What might account for this difference? Researchers have identified at least four characteristics of intrinsically motivating activities:

10.1

On the basis of the information in the case study, would you describe Susan as being high in both extrinsic and intrinsic motivation, or high in one and low in another? Explain.

- Challenge—activities in which the goals are moderately difficult and success isn't guaranteed (Ryan & Deci, 1998; R. White, 1959)
- Control or autonomy—activities in which learners feel like they have some command or influence over their own learning (N. Perry, 1998; Ryan & Deci, 1998)
- Curiosity or novelty—experiences that are unique, surprising, or discrepant with learners' existing ideas (Lepper & Hodell, 1989)
- Aesthetic value—experiences that evoke emotional reactions, particularly those associated with beauty (Ryan & Deci, 1998)

Jim's comments, "Brewster sorta makes you think," and "I never thought about this stuff in that way before," suggests that Kathy capitalized on aspects of *challenge* as well as *novelty* in her teaching. This example demonstrates how important teachers can be in promoting intrinsic motivation, and research indicates that intrinsically motivated students achieve higher than those who are only extrinsically motivated (Gottfried, 1985). We examine ways that teachers can promote intrinsic motivation later in the chapter.

Theories of Motivation

In Chapters 6 to 8, we discussed different views of learning. These theories can also help us understand motivation, and, in fact, some researchers argue that learning and motivation are so interrelated that a person can't fully understand learning without considering motivation (Pintrich, Marx, & Boyle, 1993). We examine links between theories of learning and motivation in the following sections.

Behaviorism: Motivation as Reinforcement

In your study of behaviorism in Chapter 6, you learned that reinforcers increase behavior, with praise, high test scores, and grades being common reinforcers. Because they are ends that result from student effort, they are potential extrinsic motivators.

Using Rewards in Classrooms

Although the use of rewards is controversial (Harter & Jackson, 1992; Kohn, 1992, 1996), it is still common. (Rewards are intended reinforcers; we don't know if they actually reinforce behavior until we see if the behavior increases.) Some examples of rewards used in elementary classrooms include:

▌ Approval, such as teacher praise or being selected as a class monitor
▌ Consumable items, such as candy or popcorn
▌ Entertainment, like playing a computer game
▌ Competition, like being the first to finish a game or drill

In middle and secondary school classrooms, rewards include

▌ High test scores and good grades
▌ Teacher comments on papers, praising good work
▌ Teacher compliments delivered quietly and individually
▌ Phone calls to parents or other caregivers complimenting student work or attitudes
▌ Free time to talk to classmates

Criticisms of a Behavioral Approach to Motivation

As you saw in the last section, the use of rewards can be controversial. Some of the criticisms are philosophical; critics argue that schools should cultivate intrinsic motivation and believe that using rewards sends students the wrong message about learning (Anderman & Maehr, 1994).

Others contend that rewards decrease intrinsic motivation and cite research indicating that offering rewards for completing intrinsically motivating tasks decreases interest in the tasks (Deci & Ryan, 1987; Kohn, 1993; B. Schwartz, 1990).

Identifying effective reinforcers that are grade-level appropriate can increase student motivation.

Still others point to the logistical problems involved in using rewards. Administering them requires time and energy, and rewards given to some students may cause resentment in those who don't receive them. Further, when praise or rewards are overused, they lose their credibility with students, and their effectiveness as reinforcers is sharply reduced.

Finally, emphasizing rewards ignores students' thoughts and perceptions of the teacher's motives in giving them and their beliefs about what the rewards indicate. These cognitions influence learners' motivation. Next we'll look more closely at this issue.

Putting Rewards Into Perspective

While critics argue that rewards shouldn't be used in classrooms, eliminating them isn't realistic. For instance, they can be an effective way to encourage students to begin tasks that initially aren't motivating; once students become involved in these tasks, other factors like interest and challenge can influence motivation. Further, if they're used with thought and care, rewards not only don't detract from intrinsic motivation, they may actually increase it under the right conditions, such as when

- Rewards depend on the quality of the work instead of mere participation in the activity (Deci & Ryan, 1985, 1987)
- Rewards are indicators of increasing competence (Rosenfield, Folger, & Adelman, 1980)
- The task isn't initially interesting (Morgan, 1984)
- Rewards are social, such as praise, rather than material (J. Cameron & Pierce, 1994; Chance, 1992; A. Miller & Hom, 1990)

While rewards are less effective for underachievers and older students than with young children, sincere compliments and other rewards can be significant in increasing student effort. In addition to reinforcing learner behavior, they can communicate a human touch, which helps promote a positive classroom climate.

Cognitive Theories of Motivation

"C'mon, let's go," Melanie urged her friend Yelena as they were finishing a homework assignment.

"Just a sec," Yelena muttered. "I just can't seem to figure this out. I don't know why I missed this one. I thought I did the whole thing right, and it all made sense, but the answer turned out wrong."

"Let's work on it tonight. Everybody's leaving," Melanie urged.

"Go ahead, I'll catch up to you in a minute. I've gotta figure this out. . . . I just don't get it."

From this brief exchange, we see that we can't explain Yelena's behavior very well on the basis of behaviorism. Although getting the right answer would be reinforcing, it doesn't account for her efforts to understand why the problem made sense but still came out wrong. Behaviorism also doesn't help us understand why Yelena persisted in her efforts to solve the problem even though she was struggling with it.

Cognitive Theories: The Need to Understand

Cognitive theories of motivation *focus on learners' needs for order, predictability, and understanding.* "Children are seen as naturally motivated to learn when their experience is inconsistent with their current understanding or when they experience regularities in information that are not yet represented by their schemata" (Greeno, Collins, & Resnick, 1996, p. 25). For example, why do young children so eagerly explore their environments? Why is the "play" of puzzles completely engrossing for a 4-year-old (and many adults)? Why was Yelena unable to leave until she solved the problem? Cognitive theorists suggest that each is motivated by the need to understand and make sense of the world.

Piaget's concept of equilibrium (see Chapter 2), is an example of this need and is a cornerstone of his theory. When people cannot explain experiences with their existing schemes, they are motivated to modify the schemes, and this process results in development. Piaget (1952) also argued that humans are naturally inclined to practice their developing schemes. This inclination explains why young children open and close doors repeatedly with no apparent desire to examine the contents inside, and why they want the same story read so many times that their parents are on the verge of exasperation. Cognitive views of motivation also help explain a variety of other behaviors, such as:

▍ Why people are intrigued by brain teasers and other problems with no practical application
▍ Why people are curious when something occurs unexpectedly
▍ Why students ask questions about incidental and unrelated aspects of lessons
▍ Why people persevere on activities and then quit after they've mastered the task
▍ Why people want feedback about their performance, even if it's negative feedback

The items on the list all relate to a basic desire to simply understand the way the world works.

Humanistic Views of Motivation

Cognitive learning theory developed in the mid-1950s in response to the shortcomings of behaviorism (see Chapter 7). At about the same time, another movement called **humanistic psychology** began, which *views motivation as people's attempts to fulfill their total potential as human beings* (Hamachek, 1987). This perspective on motivation is still popular because it emphasizes learner growth and potential.

Humanistic Psychology: Development of the Whole Person

The first half of the 20th century was dominated by two major forces: behaviorism and psychoanalysis. As we know, behaviorism explains learning and motivation with concepts like reinforcers and punishers. Psychoanalysis, most heavily influenced by Sigmund Freud (1856–1939), focuses on unconscious drives and instincts, and has contributed familiar ideas such as the *id, ego,* and *superego.* Humanistic psychology is a reaction against the kind of thinking that reduces human behavior to responses to the environment or internal instincts; instead, it examines the total person—physical, emotional, interpersonal, and intellectual—and how these aspects interact to affect learning and motivation. It focuses on individuals' perceptions, responses to internal needs, and the drive for "self-actualization," or becoming all that one can be (Maslow, 1968, 1970). This orientation became known as a "third force" during the 1950s, alongside behaviorism and psychoanalysis.

Motivation as Growth

Humanistic views of motivation assume that learners seek fulfilling experiences. This view argues that people have an innate tendency to fully develop their inherited talents, and that learners are motivated to grow and enhance themselves (Graham & Weiner, 1996;

10.3 ▬
A father, reading his son a familiar story, sees that the child is getting sleepy, so he decides to skip a few pages. His son immediately corrects him and demands that all the pages be read. Explain the child's behavior on the basis of the information in this section.

10.4 ▬
Cognitive and humanistic views of motivation both have the notion of needs at their centers. Which of the two approaches views needs more broadly? Explain.

Maslow, 1971; C. Rogers, 1963). According to the humanistic view, there is no such thing as an unmotivated learner. The inattentive seventh grader who pokes the person in front of her is motivated; her motivation is just directed at nonacademic activities.

Promoting Growth: Implications for Teaching.   Humanistic views of motivation emphasize the personal and emotional side of learning and teaching. According to this view, learner motivation depends on how learners view themselves as people and how they see the school contributing to their growth. If classes are personally meaningful, students are motivated to learn; if not, they aren't. Good teaching is "the process of inviting students to see themselves as able, valuable, and self-directing, and of encouraging them to act in accordance with these self-perceptions" (W. Purkey & Novak, 1984, p. xiii).

Two elements of the teaching–learning process are essential to humanistic psychologists: the *student–teacher relationship* and *classroom climate* (Hamachek, 1987). Carl Rogers (1967), a prominent thinker in the humanistic movement, suggests that effective teachers have three qualities that promote student–teacher relationships:

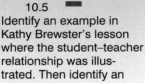

10.5
Identify an example in Kathy Brewster's lesson where the student–teacher relationship was illustrated. Then identify an example in which she promoted a positive classroom climate.

- They are genuine people, without personas or facades, who embrace their feelings as their own.
- They are accepting, viewing students as worthy individuals in their own right.
- They are empathetic, able to consider teaching–learning experiences from students' points of view.

Classroom climate is an outgrowth of student–teacher relationships that form over time. Humanistic classrooms are safe environments where students believe they can learn and are expected to do so. Standards remain high but attainable. All learners are valued because they are innately valuable human beings.

Classroom Connections

Using Rewards Effectively in Your Classroom

1. Reward students for genuine accomplishments and increasing competence, not for mere participation.
   - An English teacher underlines well-written passages in her students' essays, comments positively about them, and explains why the sections warrant the comments.
   - A middle school teacher quietly says to one of her students, "Tanya, you're getting very good at solving these problems. Keep it up."

2. Avoid punishers and threats of punishment in attempts to motivate students.
   - Positive example: A teacher comments to his class about an upcoming test, "Study hard for this test, everyone. The material we've been working on is very important, and your understanding will be a big help as we move on to the next topic."
   - Negative example: A teacher comments to his class about an upcoming test, "Study hard for this test. If you don't study, you might fail, and you could wind up back in this class again next year."

Applying Cognitive Approaches to Motivation in Your Classroom

3. Begin lessons with challenging questions and discrepant events.
   - A third-grade teacher drops an ice cube into a cup of clear alcohol (which the students initially think is water), and the ice cube drops to the bottom of the cup. "We know that ice floats on water," she says. "How can we explain what just happened?"

- A math teacher has a problem of the week that requires the students to bring in a challenging, everyday problem for the class to solve.

4. Explain the reasons for dealing with the topics being studied.
   - A teacher introducing a unit on body systems says, "Understanding each of our body systems can help us lead healthier lives, and being healthy allows us to enjoy things more than if we're sick or hurt."

5. Provide clear and prompt feedback on assignments and tests.
   - A math teacher returns all tests and quizzes the following day and discusses frequently missed problems.
   - An elementary teacher writes comments on students' papers, suggesting revisions. The originals and the revisions are then checked and placed in students' portfolios.

6. Establish clear expectations for your students.
   - A geography teacher writes a letter to parents at the beginning of the school year. The letter tells parents how learning activities will be conducted, describes the procedures for turning in work, and states that all students in her class are expected to be involved and successful.

Applying Humanistic Approaches to Motivation in Your Classroom

7. Create a supportive classroom climate for learners.
   - A fifth-grade teacher demands that all students treat each other with respect. Personal criticisms and sarcasm are forbidden. She carefully models these behaviors for students.
   - A first-grade teacher encourages and accepts all students' comments and questions. He tells students that mistakes are a part of learning and treats them that way in learning activities.

8. Display a caring and empathetic manner with students.
   - A math teacher spends time with students before and after school each day, helping students with problems and assignments.
   - A junior high teacher listens attentively when students talk about personal problems and uncertainties as they go through the emotional and physical changes characteristic of this time in their lives.

Motivation and Needs

A **need** is *a real or perceived lack of something necessary*. Needs can be obvious, such as the need for food as signaled by hunger, or they can be complex and abstract, such as the need for order and understanding—the foundation of cognitive theories of motivation. Here, eliminating uncertainty is the need; while not necessary for survival, it makes people feel more comfortable.

In this section, we examine needs from both humanistic and cognitive perspectives as we consider

- Maslow's hierarchy of needs
- Emotional and social needs
- Cognitive learning needs

Motivation as a Hierarchy of Needs: The Work of Maslow

Abraham Maslow (1968, 1970), the father of the humanistic movement, described needs as existing in two groups: the first consisting of basic needs, such as survival and safety, and the second based on the desire for self-fulfillment and self-actualization.

His work resulted in the hierarchy shown in Figure 10.2.

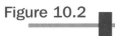

Figure 10.2

Maslow's hierarchy of needs

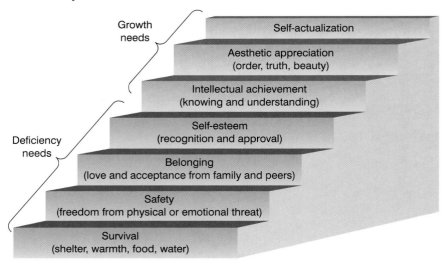

Adapted from *Motivation and Personality* 2nd Edition by Abraham H. Maslow. Copyright 1954 by Harper & Row, Publishers, Inc. Copyright © 1970 by Abraham H. Maslow. Reprinted by permission of HarperCollins Publishers Inc.

Deficiency and Growth Needs

The bottom four categories of Maslow's hierarchy are called **deficiency needs,** which *energize or move people to meet them when these needs are unfulfilled.* According to Maslow, people won't move to higher needs, intellectual achievement, for example, unless survival, safety, belonging, and self-esteem needs have all been met.

> **10.6** ▬
> On the basis of Maslow's work, would you conclude that people with a high need for aesthetic appreciation have high self-esteem? Have they met their need for intellectual achievement? Explain in each case.

If all deficiency needs are met, an individual can focus on the top three levels, which are called growth needs. According to Maslow, **growth needs** are *those that expand and increase as people have experiences with them.* In contrast with the deficiency needs, growth needs are never "met." For instance, as people's understanding of literature develops, their interest in studying literature actually increases, rather than decreases. This explains why some people seem to have an insatiable desire for learning and are constantly involved in growth activities, or why an individual never tires of quality art or music.

In an attempt to understand self-actualization, Maslow studied individuals he considered self-actualized, such as Eleanor Roosevelt, Thomas Jefferson, or Albert Einstein. As his work progressed, he began to see patterns in the characteristics of these people (see Figure 10.3). Although fewer than 1% of all people ever truly become self-actualized (Maslow, 1968), everyone strives for it, and Maslow concluded that it is reached by first satisfying deficiency needs so that one is free to reach for the growth needs.

Maslow's work has been criticized because his descriptions are imprecise and people don't always behave as would be predicted from the hierarchy. Michelangelo, for example, worked for years in enormous discomfort to create his masterpiece on the ceiling of the Sistine Chapel, a triumph of aesthetics at the expense of lower needs.

In Maslow's hierarchy, however, we see relationships among physical, personal, intellectual, and aesthetic needs; together, they illustrate the needs of the whole person, emphasized by humanistic thinkers.

Figure 10.3

Characteristics of self-actualized individuals

- They have a clear perception of reality.
- They accept themselves, others, and the world for what they are.
- The are spontaneous in act and thought.
- They are problem-centered rather than self-centered.
- They are autonomous and independent.
- They are sympathetic to the condition of other human beings and seek to promote the common welfare.
- They have a democratic perspective of the world.
- They are creative.
- They establish deep and meaningful relationships with a few people rather than superficial bonds with a large number of people.
- They have peak experiences that are marked by feelings of great excitement, happiness, and insight.

Implications of Maslow's Work for Teachers

Think about some of your day-to-day experiences. When you're shopping, your first reaction to salespeople is almost certainly an assessment of how helpful they are. When students talk about their teachers, and this includes university students, their first comments usually center on how "nice" they are. Maslow's work reminds us that we are all social and personal beings, and our needs in these areas precede intellectual ones. If our students believe that we genuinely care about them and are truly committed to their learning, their motivation increases. If not, it can decrease.

For example, in the opening case, Kathy was aware of these needs and consciously applied Maslow's work in her teaching. She attempted to increase Jennifer's feeling of belonging, for example, by moving her into the middle of the class. Also, by admonishing Joe for interrupting Nikki, she promoted an environment in which all students felt safe enough to offer their thoughts without fear of embarrassment. Students who work in safe and orderly environments are more motivated to learn and achieve higher than those whose learning situations are unsafe and disruptive (Blumenfeld, 1992; McCombs, 1998).

We also see applications of Maslow's work in school policy. To meet students' deficiency needs, many schools provide free or reduced lunch, for example, and teachers are now trained to identify evidence of child abuse so that counselors can respond immediately. Maslow's work helps us understand why these policies are necessary to promote learning and motivation.

Social and Emotional Needs

Maslow offered a comprehensive description of needs—physical, social, and personal, as well as intellectual and aesthetic. Other scholars have focused their research more narrowly, examining specific needs in detail. In this section, we focus on social and emotional needs, specifically considering the following:

    ▌ The need for relatedness
    ▌ The need for approval
    ▌ The need to reduce anxiety

The Need for Relatedness

> **10.7** ▬
>
> Which theory of motivation best explains people's need for relatedness? Provide a specific explanation for the need based on that theory.

Since the early 1990s, motivation researchers have been investigating the effects of learners' relationships with teachers and peers on their intrinsic motivation. They focused on the concept of **relatedness**, which is *the need to feel connected to others in a social environment and to feel worthy and capable of love and respect.* It is a basic need in all people, they argue (Connell & Wellborn, 1990). Research indicates that teachers who are available to students and who like, understand, and empathize with them, have learners who are more emotionally, cognitively, and behaviorally engaged in classroom activities than those rated lower in these areas (McCombs, 1998; E. Skinner & Belmont, 1993). Further, students who feel like they belong and perceive personal support from their teachers report more interest in their class work and describe it as more important than students whose teachers are more distant (Goodenow, 1993). Collectively, these findings suggest that an accepting and supportive classroom environment—where each student is valued regardless of academic ability or performance—is important for both learning and motivation (Stipek, 1996).

The Need for Approval

Andrea, Brad, Kevin, and Erika were searching the Internet for information about erosion on the earth and moon for a school project. Andrea, who was quite assertive, suggested that they download a picture of a lake in one of the national parks. Brad and Kevin appeared to agree. Erika, not seeing how the picture was relevant to the goals of the project, began, "What does this have to do? . . . " but quickly stopped when she saw a frown on Andrea's face.

Some researchers would explain Erika's behavior by saying that she has a strong desire for **approval**, which is *the need to secure acceptance and positive judgments from others* (Juvonen & Weiner, 1993; Urdan & Maehr, 1995). People with a high need for approval are overly concerned with pleasing others and, as we saw in Erika's behavior, tend to give in easily to group pressure, or perceptions of group pressure, for fear of being rejected (Wentzel & Wigfield, 1998).

These students are extrinsically motivated; engaging in learning activities is a means to being affirmed. As teachers, we can help them meet this need by using approval, both ours and others, to increase their motivation and learning.

We should be careful, however, for two reasons. First, we should praise them for evidence of increased understanding and effort to learn, not behaviors simply intended to secure our approval. Second, if other students disapprove of high achievers, they may consciously underachieve to secure the approval of their peers. We can reduce this tendency by avoiding competition among students and avoiding public displays of achievement. Telling a student outside of class something such as, "Your work over the last 2 weeks has been terrific. You're demonstrating a better and better understanding of. . . . Keep it up," can do much to increase motivation, while at the same time meeting a learner's need for approval.

The Need to Reduce Anxiety

Virtually all of us have been nervous and uncomfortable when anticipating a test or class presentation at some point in our school experiences. When it's extreme, our heart rates can increase, our mouths are dry, we have "butterflies," and we're worried about failing. We're experiencing **anxiety**, which is *a general uneasiness and feeling of tension*. It may also include a sense of foreboding.

The relationship between anxiety, motivation, and achievement is curvilinear; some is good, but too much can be damaging. For example, some anxiety can increase motivation and learning. It makes us work and study hard and develop competence. Relatively high anxiety improves performance on well-practiced tasks where our expertise is high (Covington & Omelich, 1987).

Too much anxiety, however, can decrease motivation and achievement. Its main source is fear of failure and with it the loss of self-esteem (K. Hill & Wigfield, 1984). Low achievers are particularly vulnerable, but high achievers, fearing they will do less well than expected, may also experience it.

Information processing helps us understand the debilitating effects of anxiety. First, highly anxious students can have difficulty concentrating, so they don't pay attention as well as they should. Second, because they worry about—and even expect—failure, they often misperceive the information they see and hear. Third, and perhaps most important, they waste working memory space on thoughts such as, "I'll never get this," leaving less space available for thinking about the task. As a result, their understanding of content is less thorough than it should be, further increasing their anxiety when required to perform on tests (Wolf, Smith, & Birnbaum, 1997).

We can help students cope with anxiety in several ways, including the following:

▌ Make expectations and standards clear and achievable.
▌ Model study strategies that increase understanding.
▌ Provide a variety of high-quality examples that illustrate the topics being taught.
▌ Require that all students are actively involved in learning activities.
▌ Provide specific feedback about learning progress.
▌ Be available for help outside of class.

Each of these suggestions is designed to help students increase their understanding of the topics they study. When understanding increases, failure decreases. In time, *fear* of failure will also decrease, and with it, anxiety.

> **10.8** ▬
> Using information processing as the basis, explain why relatively high anxiety *does not* detract from performance on well-practiced tasks.

Cognitive Learning Needs

As with research in social and emotional domains, scholars have also focused their efforts on specific cognitive needs. In this section, we examine those needs as we consider

▌ The need for autonomy
▌ The need to achieve
▌ The need to explain success and failure: attribution theory
▌ The need to protect self-worth

The Need for Autonomy

Autonomy—*being self-directed and in control of our environment* (together with challenge, novelty, and aesthetic value)—is a characteristic of intrinsic motivation. The need for autonomy makes sense; we all want to be in control of our destiny. Autonomy is especially important for adolescents as they attempt to develop a sense of independence.

The need for autonomy is well documented (deCharms, 1968; Deci & Ryan, 1985; Ryan & Deci, 1998), and one way of promoting autonomy is to give students choices

(Flowerday & Schraw, 1999; Reeve, Bolt, & Cai, 1999), such as Kathy did when she allowed her students to either make a class presentation or write a paper.

However, while intrinsic motivation is obviously an ideal, "most of the activities people do are not intrinsically motivated" (Ryan & Deci, 1998, p. 7). Since extrinsic motivation tends to decrease autonomy by using external controls, how can teachers balance extrinsic motivation and students' desire for autonomy? Deci and Ryan (1985) offer some suggestions by connecting *relatedness* (which we've already examined)*, competence,* and *autonomy*. Relatedness is a primary factor. A major reason learners are willing to engage in activities that aren't intrinsically motivating is if doing so is valued by others to whom they feel connected, such as family, peers, or teachers (Freese, 1999). If students feel respected and cared for by their teachers, they're more likely to involve themselves in learning activities than if they feel less connected (Ryan, Stiller, & Lynch, 1994). (This also helps us understand why parental involvement in their children's learning is so important.)

Learners are also more likely to commit to reaching a goal if they feel that it leads to increasing competence. R. White (1959), in a paper that has become a classic, argues that competence is an innate need in people. Increasing competence makes an individual more capable of coping with the environment, which is—in itself—motivating. For example, many people today are motivated to work with technology. Competence in this area allows them to gather a myriad of information from the Internet, communicate quickly and efficiently, and, in general, be more productive. According to White, this increasing capability is the source of competence motivation.

This leads to *autonomy*, which is closely linked to competence. Learners' feelings of competence increase when they clearly understand tasks, the tasks are challenging, and they succeed. As their perceptions of competence increase, so do their feelings of autonomy (Bruning, Shraw, & Ronning, 1999).

Teachers can do a great deal to promote a sense of autonomy in their students. In addition to giving students choices, which we discussed earlier, projects that involve them in decision making promote feelings of autonomy, by shifting responsibility from teachers to students (N. Perry, 1998). Student feelings of autonomy are also increased when teach-

---

10.9 ▬
Which theory of motivation best explains people's needs for competence? Provide a specific explanation based on that theory.

Teachers can increase learner autonomy and motivation by providing students with choices in terms of learning goals and activities.

ers make topics relevant, emphasize learning for it's own sake, and provide feedback that helps students grow and improve. Kathy's interaction with Harvey, as he walked into the classroom, is an example. She emphasized increasing competence when she said, "look how good you're getting at writing," to which he responded, "Yeh, yeh, I know . . . and being good writers will help us in everything we do in life," echoing Kathy's rationale. These factors are summarized in Table 10.1 (Bruning et al., 1999; Ryan & Deci, 1998).

The Need to Achieve

Student responses to the photograph on this page and questions in the caption are used to assess **achievement motivation**, which is *a need to excel in learning tasks and the capacity to experience pride in accomplishment* (Atkinson, 1980, 1983). Achievement motivation is important in classrooms because it both directs students toward accomplishments and reduces the need to avoid failure. (The need to avoid failure causes students to experience anxiety in testing situations and to avoid challenging tasks.)

To understand how achievement motivation operates, look again at the photograph and questions. A student with a high need to achieve might respond to the questions in this way:

> "He's concerned about the C. He knows he can do better and should have studied harder."

In contrast, a student with a high need to avoid failure might decide:

> "He's not very good at science, and it was a hard test. He maybe shouldn't have taken this class."

These responses indicate differences in the need to achieve and the need to avoid failure. Students with a high need for achievement have a mastery orientation; they're motivated by challenging assignments, high grading standards, explicit feedback, and opportunities to try again. In contrast, failure-avoiding students tend to shy away from challenging tasks and experience anxiety in testing situations (A. Elliot & Church, 1997). They're motivated by liberal reinforcement for success, small clear steps in assignments, easy grading, and protection from embarrassment for failure. Moving students from a failure-avoiding to an achievement orientation is one of the major challenges of teaching.

The Need to Understand Successes and Failures: Attribution Theory

Four students eagerly waited as their teacher handed back a test.

"How'd you do, Bob?" Anne asked.

"Terrible," Bob answered somewhat sheepishly. "I just can't do this stuff. I'm no good at writing the kind of essays she wants. . . . I'll never get it."

"I didn't do so good either," Anne replied, "but I knew I wouldn't. I just didn't study hard enough. I knew I was going to be in trouble. I won't let that happen again."

"Unbelievable!" Armondo added. "I didn't know what the heck was going on, and I got a B. I don't think she read mine."

"I got a C," Billy shrugged. "Not bad, considering how much I studied. I couldn't get into it for this test."

10.10 ▬
Research in the workforce indicates that workers on assembly lines experience more stress than do their supervisors. Explain these research results based on the information in this section.

10.11 ▬
Suppose a competitive diver was a failure-avoiding learner. How would this likely affect both her progress and her selection of dives to perform in competition?

Questions such as,"What is happening here?" "What happened in the past?" and "What is going to happen?" are used to measure students' acheivement motivation.

Table 10.1

Promoting autonomy in classrooms

Factor	Description
• Student choice	Students feel autonomous when they're given choices, such as allowing student input into classroom rules.
• Student involvement	Students who are actively involved in learning feel more autonomous than passive learners.
• Relevance	Relating topics to real-life experiences increases interest and achievement, and promotes autonomy.
• Feedback	Information-oriented (vs. performance-oriented) feedback increases a sense of autonomy, e.g., by emphasizing that testing is done to promote learning and improvement and by avoiding comparisons among students.
• Lesson-framing statements	Focusing on learning increases perceptions of autonomy, such as using statements like, "Study hard, so you will understand this material," versus "Study hard, so you will do well on the test."

We've seen that cognitive views of motivation assume people have a need for order and understanding. Based on this view, we would say that Bob, Anne, Armondo, and Billy have an innate desire to understand why they got the grades they did, so they created explanations (perceived causes) for their successes and failures, which are called attributions. Bob suggested he wasn't good enough (he lacked ability), Anne thought she hadn't tried hard enough (lack of effort), and Armondo wrote the issue off to luck. (We'll examine Billy's reaction in the next section.) In addition to ability, effort, and luck, learners may also attribute successes and failures to the difficulty of the task, effective or ineffective strategies, mood, help, interest, unfair teacher practices, clarity of instructions, or other factors. Ability, effort, luck, and task difficulty are most frequent (Weiner, 1990).

Attribution theory is *an attempt to systematically describe explanations for success and failure in classroom situations.* Attributions commonly occur on three dimensions (Weiner, 1992, 1994a, 1994b). The first is labeled *locus* (the location of the cause); it is either within or outside the learner. Ability and effort are within the learner, for example, whereas luck and task difficulty are outside. The second is *stability*, whether the cause stays the same or can change. Effort and luck are unstable because they can change, whereas ability stays the same. (Later in the chapter you'll see that young children and some adults believe that ability can change with effort.) The third is *control*—the extent to which students accept responsibility for their successes or failures, or are in control of the learning situation. Learners control their effort, for example, whereas they have no control over luck or task difficulty.

Impact of Attributions on Learners.   Attributions influence learners in several ways including their

- Emotional reactions to success and failure
- Expectations for future success
- Future effort
- Achievement

Let's see how students' attributions might affect these factors. For example, Anne did poorly, but she attributed it to lack of effort, for which she was responsible (she can control her effort). As a result, *guilt* was her *emotional reaction,* and she can *expect to be successful* in the future because effort is unstable. As a result, her *future effort* is likely to be greater, as indicated by her comment, "I won't let that happen again" and, with increased effort, her *achievement* will also increase. Attributing her results to lack of effort has the potential to increase both future motivation and achievement (Weiner, 1994a).

In contrast, Bob's *emotional reaction* was *shame* and *embarrassment* because he attributed his failure to lack of ability, which he viewed as uncontrollable. He *doesn't expect future success* ("I'll never get it"), and his *effort* and *achievement* are likely to decrease (Weiner, 1994a).

In general, when people attribute outcomes to controllable causes, motivation increases, whereas attributing them to uncontrollable causes decreases motivation. We saw this in both Anne's and Bob's reactions. If students attribute failure to lack of effort, poor strategies, or some other controllable cause, they usually focus on ways to do better the next time. This is a positive, adaptive approach that leads to increased achievement, pride, and a greater sense of autonomy (discussed earlier) (Ames, 1992).

Attributions can apply to teachers as well. For instance, if teachers believe that learners are succeeding as a result of their teaching efforts, they're likely to continue making the effort. On the other hand, if they believe learners are doing poorly because of causes beyond their control, such as students' lack of background, poor home lives, or some other cause, their teaching efforts often decrease.

Research indicates that people tend to attribute success to internal causes, such as hard work or high ability, and failures to external causes, such as bad luck or the behaviors of others (Marsh, 1990). When students do poorly, for example, they commonly attribute their failure to poor teaching, boring topics, tricky tests, or some other external cause. In contrast, they're likely to attribute success to working hard (effort), or high ability.

Bob is an exception to this tendency. Let's consider the ramifications of his attributions.

Learned Helplessness. We see that Bob attributed his failure to lack of ability, an internal, uncontrollable cause. In the extreme, Bob's attributions can lead to **learned helplessness**, *the feeling that no amount of effort can lead to success* (D. Seligman, 1975). This perspective leads to overwhelming feelings of shame and self-doubt that result in giving up without even trying.

Learned helplessness has both an affective and a cognitive component. Students with learned helplessness have low self-esteem and often suffer from anxiety and depression (Graham & Weiner, 1996). With respect to cognition, they expect to fail, so they don't take advantage of opportunities to increase understanding and develop skills, which results in low achievement and an even greater expectation for failure (Weiner, 1994a). Students placed at risk with histories of failure are particularly susceptible to learned helplessness.

In more recent work, M. Seligman (1995) recommends "immunizing" children against pessimism by providing them with successful mastery experiences, described next. Let's see how this might work.

Attribution Training. Research indicates that learners can improve the effectiveness of their attributions through training. In a pioneering study, Dweck (1975) provided students who demonstrated learned helplessness with successful and unsuccessful experiences. When the students were unsuccessful, the experimenter specifically stated that the failure was caused by lack of effort. Comparable students were given similar experiences but no training. After 25 sessions, the learners who were counseled about their lack of effort responded more appropriately to failure, persisted longer, and adapted their strategies

10.12
Explain Armondo's *emotional reaction, expectation for future success, future effort,* and *achievement,* based on his attributing his success to luck. If he had attributed his failure to a difficult task, how would you explain these characteristics?

more effectively. Subsequent research has corroborated Dweck's findings (Forsterling, 1985). Teachers need to help students see the crucial link between effort and learning. This is sometimes difficult because of students' need to protect their self-worth.

The Need to Protect Self-Worth

Let's return again to the four students in the last section. We saw Billy comment, "Not bad, considering how much I studied. I couldn't get into it for this test," emphasizing the fact that he *did not* study. The need to protect self-worth helps explain why he would behave this way.

According to Covington (1992), people have a compelling need to protect their self-worth; " . . . the search for self-acceptance is the highest human priority" (p. 74). Self-perceptions of ability exert the most influence on self-worth, particularly for older students (Snow, Corno, & Jackson, 1996). "Because society places such a high value on one's ability to achieve, self-worth theorists argue that students of all ages go to great lengths to protect a sense of their own ability" (Graham & Weiner, 1996, p. 73). (Self-worth and *self-esteem* are often used synonymously; Pintrich & Schunk, 1996).

Returning to the example of the students' reactions after their test, the effects of self-perceptions of ability on self-worth are demonstrated in Billy's behavior. By emphasizing that he didn't study, he was attempting to preserve the perception of high ability and, with it, his self-worth.

Effort can also be a source of self-worth, particularly in contexts where teachers model and emphasize a work ethic, but it's a double-edged sword. While making an effort can increase self-worth, the risk of failure exists. Failing after making an effort implies low ability, and with it the feelings of shame and embarrassment that we saw in our discussion of attribution theory. As a result, students often prefer to believe they achieve through ability rather than through effort (J. Brown & Weiner, 1984).

Researchers have identified several "self-handicapping" strategies that students use to protect their self-worth (Covington & Omelich, 1987; Mantzicopoulos, 1989; Pintrich & Schunk, 1996). These include setting unrealistically high goals, so failure can be attributed to task difficulty; procrastinating ("I could have done a lot better, but I didn't start studying until after midnight"); making excuses, such as suggesting that the teacher was poor or the tests were tricky; anxiety ("I understand the stuff, but I get nervous in tests"), or like Billy, making a point of not trying. "From the students' points of view, failure without effort doesn't reflect on their ability. What they have achieved is 'failure with honor'" (Ames, 1990, p. 413). These self-handicapping behaviors are most common among low achievers, who often choose to not seek help when it's needed (Middleton & Midgley, 1997).

While teachers can't completely eliminate learners' focus on ability, they can model and emphasize self-improvement, while deemphasizing competition and ability (Midgley, Arunkumar, & Urdan, 1996). Kathy's comment to Harvey in our opening case study is an example. She said, "the harder I study, the smarter I get . . . and I feel good about myself when I do." She consciously attempted to link self-worth to effort and improvement.

Kathy's comment also modeled a belief about the nature of *ability*, which leads us to our next topic.

10.13 ■
Research indicates that perceptions of ability exert a stronger influence on self-worth in older than in younger students. Using your understanding of learner development as a basis, explain why this is the case.

10.14 ■
Attribution theory has difficulty explaining why some students who attribute failure to lack of effort try harder in the future, whereas others who attribute failure to lack of effort give up. Use self-worth theory to explain why the first group tries harder and the second gives up.

10.15 ■
People tend to attribute success to internal causes, such as hard work or high ability, and failures to external causes, such as bad luck or the behaviors of others. Using self-worth theory as the basis, explain these research results.

Motivation and Beliefs

In the last section, we considered learners' needs: emotional, social, and cognitive. Now we discuss research examining learners' beliefs and see how they relate to learners' needs. We consider:

- Beliefs about ability
- Beliefs about capability: self-efficacy
- The influence of teachers on learners' beliefs

Beliefs About Ability

Attribution theory presents an **entity view of ability**, *the belief that ability is stable and uncontrollable*. Learners with a high need to avoid failure tend to have this view. Failure can imply low ability, and since ability is associated with self-worth, these learners can maintain self-worth by avoiding failure, which preserves the perception of high ability.

Other research indicates that young children (Nicholls & Miller, 1984) and some adults (Dweck & Bempechat, 1983) view ability as alterable and controllable. This **incremental view of ability** *holds that ability can be improved with effort*. This is what Kathy modeled when she said, "the harder I study, the smarter I get." Students with high need for achievement tend to view ability as incremental. Challenging tasks allow them to improve their skills, and improved skills mean they're "getting smarter," or more competent. Failure is less likely to threaten their self-worth because it merely means that more work is needed. This pattern leads to sustained, successful learning (McClelland, 1985).

10.16
How would a behaviorist explain an entity view of ability? An incremental view of ability? What are the implications for teachers?

Beliefs About Capability: Self-Efficacy

Social cognitive theory examines the relationships among behavior, the environment, and personal factors in the learner (see Chapter 6). With respect to motivation, social cognitive theorists focus on two personal factors: expectations and beliefs.

The role of expectations can be explained with **expectancy × value theories** (Atkinson, 1964; Brophy, 1999; Feather, 1982), which *suggest that learners are motivated to work on a task to the extent that they (a) expect to succeed and (b) value achievement on the task*. If both are present, learners may develop a sense of **self-efficacy**, which is *learners' beliefs about their capability of succeeding on specific tasks* (Schunk, 1994). *Self-efficacy* and *competence,* discussed earlier, are sometimes equated (Ryan & Deci, 1998; Pintrich & Schunk, 1996).

Self-efficacy and self-worth differ in three ways. First, self-efficacy is a cognitive appraisal of one's competence in a specific area, whereas self-worth is an affective reaction or evaluation of ourselves (Pintrich & Schunk, 1996). For example, a person may believe that she isn't a very good golfer, so she has low self-efficacy for golf, but this has no impact on her self-worth if golf isn't important to her.

Second, self-efficacy tends to be more focused and specific than self-worth. A person may have low self-efficacy in Spanish, for example, but have high self-efficacy in math.

Third, as we saw earlier, self-worth tends to be linked to perceptions of ability. Self-efficacy, in contrast, focuses on *capability,* as we saw in the definition. Learners may feel capable because they have high ability *or* because they have developed a high level of competence as a result of effort. Learners develop a sense of self-efficacy when they are making genuine progress toward a worthwhile goal, not succeeding on a trivial task, doing as well or better than others, or simply trying hard.

Self-efficacy is a positive emotional experience. It can be exhilarating, for example, to solve a difficult algebra problem on your own, to make it to the bottom of a ski slope for the first time without falling, or to repair your car. This feeling results in an eagerness to work on other problems, to try a more difficult slope, or to tackle another repair job. The effects of self-efficacy on learner behavior and cognition are summarized in Table 10.2 (Bandura, 1993; Schunk, 1994).

10.17
Research indicates that praising students for performance on an easy task can lower intrinsic motivation (Stipek, 1996). Using the concept of self-efficacy as the basis for your explanation, explain why this could happen.

Table 10.2

The influence of self-efficacy on behavior and cognition

	High Self-Efficacy Learners	Low Self-Efficacy Learners
Task orientation	Accept challenging tasks	Avoid challenging tasks
Effort	Expend high effort when faced with challenging tasks	Expend low effort when faced with challenging tasks
Persistence	Persist when goals aren't initially reached	Give up when goals aren't initially reached
Beliefs	Believe they will succeed	Focus on feelings of incompetence
	Control stress and anxiety when goals aren't met	Experience anxiety and depression when goals aren't met
	Believe they're in control of their environment	Believe they're not in control of their environment
Strategy use	Discard unproductive strategies	Persist with unproductive strategies
Performance	Perform higher than low-efficacy students of equal ability	Perform lower than high-efficacy students of equal ability

Factors Influencing Self-Efficacy

Four factors influence people's beliefs about their capability to perform (Bandura, 1986):

▌ Past performance
▌ Modeling
▌ Verbal persuasion
▌ Psychological state

Past performance on similar tasks is the most important factor. A history of success in giving oral reports, for example, increases a person's self-efficacy for giving future reports. Modeling, such as observing others deliver excellent reports, increases self-efficacy by raising expectations and providing information about how a skill is performed (Bandura, 1986).

Although limited in its effectiveness, verbal persuasion, such as a teacher commenting, "I know you will give a fine report," can also increase self-efficacy. It probably does so indirectly by encouraging students to engage in demanding tasks, and, if students succeed, efficacy increases.

Finally, factors such as fatigue or hunger can reduce efficacy even though they're unrelated to the task, and emotional states, such as anxiety, can reduce efficacy by filling working memory with thoughts of failure.

What can teachers do to help students increase their self-efficacy? Let's look at an example:

> Darren was a low achiever in Laura Cossey's seventh-grade math class. As Laura monitored the students during seat work, she saw that Darren had made little progress on the word problems.

"Come on, Darren. I know you can do this work," Laura whispered. "Read the problem carefully a few times. Then break the problem into parts, and try drawing a picture of each part. I'll be back here in a few minutes to see how you're doing."

In a few minutes, Laura returned, leaned over Darren, and said, "What do we have?"

Darren was still somewhat uncertain, but he obviously had gone over the problem and tried to get started. He pointed to the problem and said, "They want to know the percent decrease in the cost."

"Good," Laura smiled. "Now, what else do you know?"

As Darren began explaining his understanding of the problem, Laura asked only as many questions as necessary to keep him on the right track. Finally, as he arrived at a solution, she said, "That's excellent thinking, Darren. . . . Now, look at the problem again to see whether it all makes sense. I'll be back in a minute to see your final solution. You be ready to explain to me exactly how you did it. Okay?" She smiled and moved on to another student.

Let's consider what Laura did. First, she encouraged him to try working the problem (verbal persuasion). Second, although she offered a strategy, she provided only enough guidance to be sure that he made genuine progress toward the solution on his own. Most importantly, through her guidance, Darren saw evidence of his own learning progress.

This example illustrates how important teachers can be in the development of student self-efficacy. Suppose instead that she had simply explained how to do the problem while Darren looked on passively, had provided "false" success by praising minimal effort, or had said, "Here, I'll help you; I know this is hard for you." Though done in good faith, these attempts to be helpful would have decreased Darren's self-efficacy, leading him to conclude, "Mrs. Cossey doesn't think I can do this on my own," or, "She must not think I'm very smart if she compliments me for that."

The next section takes a more detailed look at this issue.

10.18
What concept from our study of learner development does "provided only enough guidance to be sure that he made genuine progress toward the solution on his own" best describe?

How Teachers Influence Learners' Self-Efficacy Beliefs

As you saw in the example with Laura and Darren, the way teachers respond to students strongly influences learners' beliefs about their capability. In this section, we consider four ways that this can happen:

- Attributional statements
- Praise and criticism
- Emotional displays
- Offers of help

Attributional Statements

Attributional statements are *comments teachers make about the causes of students' performances*, and they can influence students' beliefs about their competence. For instance, a teacher is talking to a student who is struggling with a problem. Which statement is more effective?

"That's a very good effort. I know that these problems are difficult for you."
"I believe if you tried a little harder, you'd be able to solve this problem."

Using attribution theory as a basis, the second is clearly better. The first attributes failure to lack of ability, and while the teacher may be concerned about the learner's feelings, it undermines beliefs about competence (Stipek, 1996). In contrast, attributing failure to lack of effort communicates that the learner has the ability to complete the task.

Student beliefs about their own ability as learners can be enhanced by experiences in which challenging tasks are successfully accomplished.

Now suppose the learner has succeeded in solving the problem. Which is more effective?

"You're getting very good at this."
"Well done. I see that you've been working hard on this."

Based on our discussion of self-worth, the first is better. While attributing failure to lack of effort is desirable, attributing success to effort can detract from beliefs about competence because learners tend to believe that success requiring high effort indicates low ability (Nicholls & Miller, 1984; Schunk, 1983).

Attributions of effort are further complicated by skill level. When learners are initially learning a skill, attributing progress to effort is desirable, but as their skills improve, they are likely to react better to attributions of ability. For example, in our opening case study, when Harvey complained, "But you make us work so hard," Kathy suggested that his hard work was increasing his competence, "Yes, but look how good you're getting at writing. . . . I think you hit a personal best on your last one. You're becoming a very good writer."

Praise and Criticism

Intuitively, using praise appears to be a straightforward motivational strategy; simply praise students for desired behavior. It isn't that simple, however. Older students may perceive praise as reward for effort, rather than for accomplishment, or they may interpret praise for performance on easy tasks as an indication that the teacher believes they have low ability (Graham, 1991; Stipek, 1996).

Criticism also appears to be straightforward; we should avoid it. However, research indicates that criticism can have a positive effect on learners' self-efficacy (Parsons, Kaczala, & Meece, 1982). Learners interpret criticism as an indication that the teacher believes they have high ability.

These interpretations are developmental. Learners younger than about age 11 are less likely to view effort and ability as inversely related (Barker & Graham, 1987).

Emotional Displays

Teachers' emotional reactions to learners' successes and failures can also affect their attributions. For example, when teachers express annoyance and frustration in response to learner failure, learners are likely to attribute their failure to lack of effort, whereas failing learners who receive sympathy from teachers are likely to attribute their failure to lack of ability (Graham, 1984). The teacher's expression of emotion influences learners' perceptions of the causes of their failures and their expectations for future success (Stipek, 1996).

Helping

Offering students unsolicited help can also be pernicious. For instance, researchers have found that children as young as 6 rated a student offered unsolicited help lower in ability than another offered no help (Graham & Barker, 1990). Further, learners who are offered help may feel negative emotions, such as incompetence, anger, worry, or anxiety (Meyer, 1982).

This research doesn't imply that teachers should avoid praising students, expressing sympathy, offering help, or encouraging effort. Rather, they remind us that we must be aware of how our actions will be interpreted by learners. As always, the way we respond to students requires sensitivity and careful judgment.

To this point in the chapter, we've examined theoretical views of motivation—behavioral, cognitive, and humanistic—as well as learners' needs and beliefs. In the next section, we describe practical applications of these elements synthesized into a classroom model for promoting student motivation.

> **10.19** ■
> You are supervising your students doing seat work, and one of them raises his hand and asks for help. Based on the information in this section, should you provide help? Is the student asking for help more likely to have a high or a low sense of self-worth? Explain.

Classroom Connections

Applying an Understanding of Motivation and Needs in Your Classroom

1. Attend to students' deficiency needs.
   - A seventh-grade teacher asks two of the more popular girls in her class to introduce a new girl to some of the other students and to take her under their wings until she gets acquainted.
   - A fifth-grade teacher calls on all students in her class to be certain they all feel that they're a part of the activity. She makes them feel safe by helping them respond correctly when they are initially unable to answer.

2. Model growth needs with your students.
   - A social studies teacher brings in a newspaper columnist's political opinion piece and asks students for their opinions on the issue.
   - An English teacher comments to his class on an interesting television special about environmental issues and asks students what they think could be done about some of them.

3. Promote feelings of autonomy by allowing students a voice in decision making.

   - A middle-school teacher has students suggest classroom rules. He makes it a point to include some of them on his list.
   - A geography teacher allows students to decide the order in which they will study different cultural units.

Applying an Understanding of Motivation and Beliefs in Your Classroom

4. Help students attribute initial achievement to effort and growing expertise to ability.
   - As they initially work on word problems, a second-grade teacher carefully monitors student effort in seat work. When she sees assignments that indicate effort, she makes comments to individual students, such as, "Your work is improving all the time" or "Your hard work is paying off, isn't it?"
   - As students' understanding of balancing equations increases, a chemistry teacher comments, "You people are getting smarter all the time. You've really gotten good at this stuff."

5. Describe ability as incremental.
   • A sixth-grade English teacher comments, "I wasn't good at grammar for a long time. But I kept trying, and I found that I can do it. I'm good at grammar and writing now. You can get better at it too, but you have to work at it."
6. Develop self-efficacy by giving students only as much help as they need to make progress on challenging goals.

• After displaying a problem, a fifth-grade teacher asks students to suggest ways of solving it. Each strategy offered is taken seriously and discussed.
• An English teacher returns students' essays with suggestions for improvement. After students make revisions, the essays are reviewed by peers, revised again, and turned in. The teacher makes comments identifying areas where the essays have been improved.

The Classroom: A Model for Promoting Learner Autonomy and Motivation

Before we begin, we caution you that the model presented in this section is not a set of rules to be applied without thinking, nor is it a list of teacher actions to be checked off. It is, instead, a conceptual framework that can guide your thinking as you make decisions in your teaching. It is thoroughly grounded in research and theory, and when implemented with care and professional judgment, can significantly increase student motivation. The model is presented in Figure 10.4.

Class Structure: Creating a Learning-Focused Environment for Motivation

To begin this section, let's review some of the things Kathy Brewster did in her lesson.

▮ She involved her students in the lesson, and she made the content relevant and personal by having a "crusade" to win back the school as context for her lesson.
▮ She promoted a climate of cooperation rather than competition, and she avoided comparisons of performance among her students.
▮ She demonstrated an incremental view of ability, as indicated by her comment to Harvey, "Yes, but look how good you're getting at writing. . . . You're becoming a very good writer."
▮ She promoted learner autonomy by giving her students the choice of making a group presentation or writing a paper.

10.20 ▬
A teacher says, "Excellent job on the last test, everyone. Over half the class got an A or a B." On the basis of the information in this section, how appropriate is this comment? Explain.

Through her actions, Kathy promoted a **learning-focused environment**, *one that emphasizes understanding, learner improvement, and mastery of tasks* (Patrick, Anderman, Ryan, Edelin, & Midgley, 1999; Pintrich & Garcia, 1991; Stipek, 1996). If, instead, she had displayed grade distributions on the chalkboard, made comments such as, "C'mon, there were only two A's on the last test," or "If some of you people don't get going, you'll be repeating this course next year," she would have promoted a **performance-oriented environment**, *one that focuses on ability, avoiding failure, and competition*. Emphasiz-

Figure 10.4

A model for promoting learner autonomy and motivation

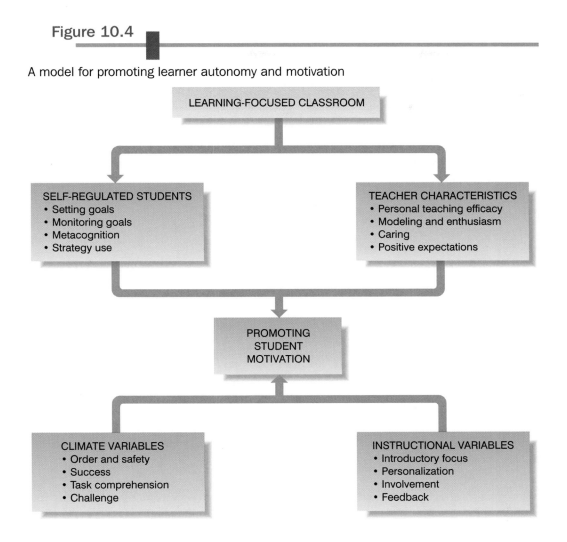

ing grades, comparing students' performances with each other, and attempting to motivate students with threats of failure characterize this orientation. These differences are summarized in Table 10.3.

Within this learning-oriented framework, the model for promoting student motivation has four parts:

1. Student attributes: Developing self-regulation
2. Teacher characteristics: Personal qualities that increase student motivation
3. Climate variables: Creating a motivating environment
4. Instructional variables: Developing interest in learning activities

Student Attributes: Developing Self-Regulation

Earlier in the chapter, you saw that autonomy is crucial for motivation, and teachers can promote learner autonomy in several ways. Teachers can also help students take responsi-

Table 10.3

Comparisons of learning-focused and performance-focused classrooms

	Learning-Focused	Performance-Focused
Definition of success	Improvement, progress, mastery	High grades, performance compared with that of others
Reasons for effort	Learn something new	High grades, demonstrate ability
Basis for satisfaction	Progress, challenge, mastery	Doing better than others, success with minimum effort
Evaluation criteria	Evidence of progress	Social comparisons
Interpretation of errors	Information, part of the learning process	Failure, lack of ability
Concept of ability	Incremental, improves with effort	Entity, fixed

Source: From *Transforming the School Culture to Enhance Motivation.* Paper presented at the Annual Meeting of the American Educational Research Association, San Francisco, April 1992. By M. Maehr. Adapted by permission.

bility for their own learning. We want them to become **self-regulated**, which is *learners' abilities to control all aspects of their learning* (see Chapter 6). Self-regulation involves four processes (Bruning et al., 1999):

▍ Setting goals
▍ Monitoring goals
▍ Metacognition
▍ Strategy use

Setting Goals

Self-regulation begins with goals, which have been widely used to motivate workers and improve performance in the business world (Locke & Latham, 1990). Learners who set goals experience high levels of autonomy, and as autonomy increases, so does motivation. Research indicates, however, that many learners—including university students—study without clear goals in mind (Alexander, Graham, & Harris, 1998; Rosenshine, 1997). Students copy and reorganize their notes, for example, but don't ask themselves if these tasks contribute to their understanding, seemingly thinking that spending time equals learning. After they are taught to set learning-focused goals, achievement increases.

Effective goals have three characteristics:

▍ Specific (vs. broad and general)
▍ Immediate or close at hand (vs. distant)
▍ Moderately difficult (vs. too easy or too hard) (Jagacinski, 1997; Schunk, 1994)

Assess the effectiveness of the following goals using these characteristics:

▍ Learn more in my classes.
▍ Get at least a B on my next essay.
▍ Score in the top fourth of the class on the next test.
▍ Answer and understand all the margin questions in each chapter.

The first goal is general and distant; it doesn't help us decide what our next step should be. The second and third are *performance goals,* and, as with a performance-oriented environment, they emphasize ability, avoiding failure, and competition. Performance goals can also lead to feelings of anxiety about success and failure, loss of self-worth after doing poorly (Dweck & Leggett, 1988), and an *ego orientation*, where students are less concerned with genuine understanding than with looking smarter or performing better than others (Nicholls, 1984).

The fourth goal is effective. It's specific, moderately difficult, and can be attacked immediately. In addition, it is a *learning goal*, a goal that focuses on understanding and mastery of a task (Pintrich & Garcia, 1991; Stipek, 1996). (We should point out that merely answering the questions isn't necessarily a learning goal. Answering *and understanding* is. This is a subtle but important distinction; Schunk, 1994.)

Research indicates that students who adopt learning goals develop a *task orientation*: They persist in the face of difficulty; attribute success to internal, controllable causes; take risks and accept academic challenges; and use deep processing strategies, such as self-questioning, summarizing, and elaboration (Alexander et al., 1998; Bruning et al., 1999). In addition, they don't worry about failure and comparisons with others (Nicholls, 1984). A task orientation leads to selecting more challenging activities and sustaining interest even after formal instruction has been completed.

For goals to work, learners must be committed to them (Pintrich & Schunk, 1996). The most effective way of increasing commitment is to guide students in setting their own goals, rather than imposing goals on them (Ridley, McCombs, & Taylor, 1994). In guiding students, however, it is important that they adopt learning instead of performance goals (Ames & Archer, 1988; Dweck, 1985).

> **10.21** ▬
> A person sets a goal, "to get in shape." Is this an effective or ineffective goal? Does it suggest an ego orientation or a task orientation? Explain. If it is an ineffective goal, rewrite it so it is more effective.

Monitoring Goals

Once goals are set, students take further responsibility by monitoring their progress. As an example, let's consider again our fourth goal in the preceding list. There are 31 questions in the margins of this chapter, so suppose on Monday you set the goal of answering all the questions by the end of the week. If on Wednesday, you've answered the first 15, and believe you understand them, you feel a sense of accomplishment. Because you have concrete evidence of your progress, your self-efficacy increases. In addition, setting and monitoring the goal has increased your sense of autonomy; you've taken responsibility for your own learning.

Self-monitoring can also increase motivation in a more general sense (Schunk, 1997; Wolters, 1997). For example, a student who monitors the amount of time spent "studying" may find that she is actually spending too much time on activities that don't contribute to learning, such as getting up and down to change the volume of the stereo, or reorganizing notes without actually learning from them. This realization can motivate her to shut the stereo off and look for relationships among the ideas in her notes instead of simply recopying them. If she believes her changed habits increases her learning, her motivation will be sustained (Schunk, 1997).

A learning-focused classroom capitalizes on learner involvement, cooperation, and improvement of skills.

Metacognition

Self-regulated learners are metacognitive. In other words, they're aware of the way they study and learn, they monitor the effectiveness of their efforts, and they adapt when necessary (Ridley et al., 1994). For example, the student in the last section, who monitors the amount of time she spends "studying," is demonstrating metacognition. She is aware of her study strategies, and she exercises control over them by eliminating distractions and changing the way she uses her notes.

Teachers can help learners become more metacognitive by modeling their own metacognition and by encouraging students to think about the way they study. The message that teachers want to communicate is that learning is conscious, intentional, and requires effort (Alexander et al., 1998). Kathy encouraged this awareness when she emphasized, "Remember . . . think about what you're doing when you make your revisions . . . Read your paragraph after you write it, and ask yourself, 'do I actually have evidence here, or is it simply an opinion?'. . . . The more aware you are when you write, the better your work will be."

10.22

Which theory of learning— *behaviorism, social cognitive theory, information processing,* or *constructivism*—best explains the importance of metacognition.

Strategy Use

Strategy use is a fourth component of self-regulation, and it requires broad background knowledge and a repertoire of strategies (Bruning et al., 1999). Without them, learners won't be able to adapt, even if they're aware of the need to do so. For example, skimming a passage is an effective strategy if the goal is to get an overview of the material, whereas summarizing is more effective if the goal is comprehension. That means that a strategic learner must be skilled at both skimming and summarizing.

Similarly, constructing examples of a topic is a powerful elaboration strategy that leads to deeper understanding, but without adequate background knowledge, students won't be able to construct, or find, the examples.

Having looked at elements of learner self-regulation, we now turn to teachers, the learning environments they create, and instruction that promotes motivation.

Teacher Characteristics: Personal Qualities That Increase Student Motivation and Learning

That teachers make a difference in student learning is a theme of this text, and it is certainly true for motivation as well. Teachers create learning environments, implement instruction, and establish learning-oriented or performance-oriented classrooms. None of the other components of the model are effective if the teacher characteristics—personal teaching efficacy, modeling and enthusiasm, caring, and positive expectations—are lacking. These characteristics are highlighted in Figure 10.5.

Personal Teaching Efficacy:
Beliefs About Teaching and Learning

Earlier, we saw that self-efficacy is an individual's beliefs about his or her capability of succeeding on specific tasks. **Personal teaching efficacy**, which is *the belief that teachers can have an important positive effect on students* (Bruning et al., 1999), is an extension of this concept; high-efficacy teachers believe that they can increase both motivation and achievement. They accept students and their ideas, use praise rather than criticism, persevere with low achievers, and use their time effectively. In contrast, low-efficacy teachers are less

Figure 10.5

Teacher characteristics in the model for promoting learner autonomy and motivation

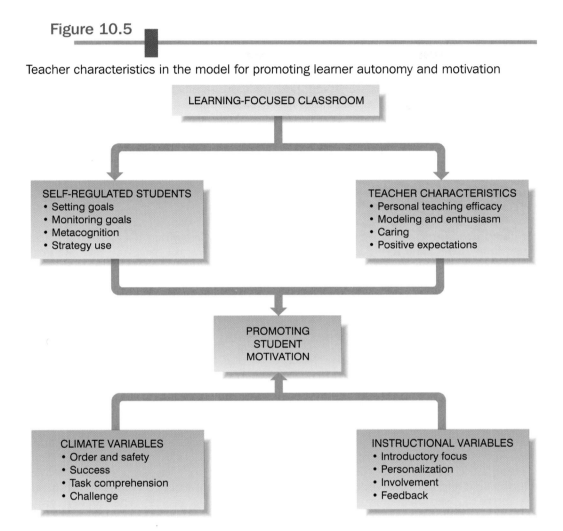

student-centered, spend less time on learning activities, "give up" on low achievers, and use criticism more than do high-efficacy teachers (Kagan, 1992). High-efficacy teachers also value and promote student autonomy more than do low-efficacy teachers (Woolfolk & Hoy, 1990).

Teacher Modeling and Enthusiasm:
Communicating Genuine Interest

Teachers' beliefs about teaching and learning are communicated through modeling. Student motivation is virtually impossible if teachers model distaste or lack of interest in the topics they teach. Statements such as the following are devastating for motivation:

"I know this stuff is boring, but we have to learn it."

"I know you hate proofs."

"This isn't my favorite topic either."

In contrast, even routine and potentially uninteresting topics are more motivating to students if teachers model interest in them. We saw evidence of this in the opening case when Kathy said, "Now isn't that interesting! . . . That's what history is all about." She modeled her own interest in the topic, and we saw how it impacted her students. David commented, "Brewster loves this stuff" and, perhaps more significantly, Kelly's reaction was, "History has never been my favorite subject, but some of this stuff is actually kind of neat."

> 10.23 ▬
> Which theory of learning—*behaviorism, social cognitive theory, information processing,* or *constructivism*—best explains the positive effects of enthusiasm? Explain on the basis of that theory.

Kathy's behavior captures the essence of *enthusiasm,* and research indicates that enthusiastic teachers increase learners' autonomy, self-efficacy, and achievement more than do less enthusiastic teachers (R. Perry, 1985; R. Perry, Magnusson, Parsonson, & Dickens, 1986). Teachers model enthusiasm, and the way they do so is to communicate their own genuine interest in the topic. It doesn't include pep talks, theatrics, or efforts to entertain students; rather, it is intended to induce in them the feeling that the information is valuable and worth learning (Good & Brophy, 1997).

Modeling affects motivation in other ways as well. For example, Kathy modeled effort attributions, an incremental view of ability and self-efficacy in saying, "It's hard for me, too, when I'm studying and trying to put together new ideas, but if I hang in, I feel like I can usually get it, . . . the harder I study, the smarter I get, . . . and I feel good about myself when I do." Other than direct experience, modeling is the most powerful factor affecting learners' self-efficacy (Bruning et al., 1999).

Teacher Caring: Meeting the Need for Relatedness

▍ A first grader calls her teacher "Mom."
▍ A fifth-grade teacher walks out on the playground during recess to talk with his students.
▍ A high school teacher makes a special effort to make sure that a new student feels welcome.

In our discussion of *relatedness,* we saw that a growing body of research confirms the importance of learners' relationships with their teachers in promoting motivation (Freese, 1999; Stipek, 1996). "Learners' natural motivation to learn can be elicited in safe, trusting, and supportive environments characterized by . . . quality relationships with caring adults that see their unique potential" (McCombs, 1998, p. 399). The teacher caring emphasized in humanistic views of motivation reminds us that we don't teach math, science, or language arts; we teach people. We should focus on the learner as a whole person, including emotional and social needs as well as intellectual ones.

Caring *refers to teachers' abilities to empathize with and invest in the protection and development of young people* (Chaskin & Rauner, 1995). It's more than warm, fuzzy feelings that make people kind. In addition to understanding how students feel, caring teachers are committed to their students' growth and competence. They attempt to do their very best for the people under their care (Noddings, 1995, 1999).

The importance of caring is captured in a fourth grader's comment, "If a teacher doesn't care about you, it affects your mind. You feel like you're a nobody, and it makes you want to drop out of school" (Noblit, Rogers, & McCadden, 1995, p. 683).

Communicating Caring.   How do teachers communicate caring to students? Although the ways are individual, research has identified several characteristics, which are outlined in Table 10.4 (Bosworth, 1995; Freese, 1999; Noddings, 1999).

The common thread in these characteristics is *time.* Everyone has 24 hours a day, and choosing to allocate some of that time to an individual student communicates caring

Table 10.4

Characteristics of caring teachers

Category	Description
Showing respect	Teachers are polite, treat students with respect, listen to their comments and questions, are patient when students make mistakes, and respond to legitimate needs for second chances and help.
Valuing individuality	Teachers know students as human beings, noticing and commenting on changes in dress, habits, and behavior.
Giving personal attention	Teachers listen to students and help them with school-work and extracurricular activities as well as personal relationships and other nonacademic problems.
Creating safe learning environments	Teachers have fair rules but do not apply them rigidly, and they encourage students to do their best and to freely express their thoughts and ideas without fear of embarrassment or ridicule.

better than any other single factor. We all react positively when someone is willing to spend time with us. Helping students who have problems with an assignment or calling a parent after school hours communicates that teachers care about student learning. Spending personal time to ask a question about a baby brother or compliment a new hairstyle communicates caring about a student as a human being.

Teacher Expectations: Increasing Learner Autonomy

"This is a new idea we've been working on, and it will be challenging, but I know you can all do the assignment. I want you to start right in while the ideas are still fresh in your mind. I'll be around in a moment to answer any questions. When you're done, you can choose a game until recess."

"This material is hard, but we've got to learn it. I want everyone to start right away, and no fooling around. Jesse, did you hear me? Some of you will have problems with this, and I'll be around as soon as I can to straighten things out. No messing around until I get there."

Teacher expectations for student behavior and achievement are communicated subtly (and not so subtly) every day. The first teacher acknowledged that the assignment was difficult, but she expected students to successfully complete it. The second, in contrast, implied that some students were less able than others and presented the entire assignment in a negative frame of reference.

How Teachers Form Expectations.   Research examining the ways teachers form expectations is controversial (Good & Brophy, 1997). Several studies indicate that test scores, information about ability grouping, physical appearance, socioeconomic status (SES), race, and gender can affect teacher expectations (Clifton, Perry, Parsonson, & Hryniuk, 1986; E. Jones, 1990; Jussim, 1989).

These studies were based on data from fictional student records, however; the teachers had no opportunity to interact with real students. Other research indicates that teachers' perceptions of students are based primarily on the students' participation in learning activities and their performance on assignments and tests, rather than physical appearance or status (Good & Brophy, 1997). These studies indicate that teachers' perceptions of students are quite accurate, sometimes more accurate than predications based on test data (Helmke & Schrader, 1987; G. Short, 1985).

How Expectations Affect Teacher Behavior.   The effects of expectations on the ways teachers treat students can be grouped into four categories: emotional support, teacher effort and demands, questioning, and feedback and evaluation. They are summarized in Table 10.5.

Table 10.5 shows that teachers can be discriminatory, treating students they perceive to be high achievers more favorably than those they perceive to be low achievers. Students are sensitive to this differential treatment, and children as young as first grade are aware of unequal treatment of high and low achievers (Stipek, 1996). In one study, researchers concluded that, "After ten seconds of seeing and/or hearing a teacher, even very young students could detect whether the teacher talked about or to an excellent or a weak student and could determine the extent to which that student was loved by the teacher" (Babad, Bernieri, & Rosenthal, 1991, p. 230).

Teacher Expectations: Implications for Motivation.   What does this research suggest to teachers? First, when teacher expectations are realistic, such as those based on student performance, they pose little problem. When they are based on something other than student performance, however, or are lower than past performance warrants, they can reduce both motivation and achievement.

Second, "Such low expectations can serve as **self-fulfilling prophecies**, that is, *the expression of low expectations by differential treatment can inadvertently lead children to confirm predictions about their abilities by exerting less effort and ultimately performing more poorly*" (R. Weinstein, 1998, p. 83)[emphasis added]. As a result, healthy attributions for both success and failure are harder to develop. High expectations, in con-

Table 10.5

Characteristics of differential teacher expectations

Characteristic	Teacher Behavior Favoring Perceived High Achievers
Emotional support	Have more interactions; interact more positively; give more smiles; make more eye contact; stand closer; orient body more directly; seat students closer to teacher
Teacher effort and demands	Give clearer and more thorough explanations; give more enthusiastic instruction; ask more follow-up questions; require more complete and accurate student answers
Questioning	Call on more often; allow more time to answer; give more encouragement; do more prompting
Feedback and evaluation	Give more praise; give less criticism; offer more complete and lengthier feedback and more conceptual evaluations

Source: Based on reviews by Good (1987a, 1987b) and Good and Brophy (1997)

trast, communicate that the teacher cares enough to make every possible effort on their behalf; ultimately, motivation and self-worth are enhanced.

The goal of this section is to increase awareness. Expectations are subtle and often out of teachers' conscious control. Teachers often don't realize that they hold different expectations for their students. With awareness and effort, teachers will do their best to treat all students as fairly and equitably as possible. We examine specific strategies to promote equitable treatment in Chapter 11.

Climate Variables: Creating a Motivating Environment

As students spend time in classrooms, they get feelings about whether they're safe and welcome and whether the classroom is a desirable place to learn. **Classroom climate** *refers to teacher and classroom characteristics that promote students' feelings of safety and security, together with a sense of success, challenge, and understanding* (see Figure 10.6).

Figure 10.6

Climate variables in the model for promoting student autonomy and motivation

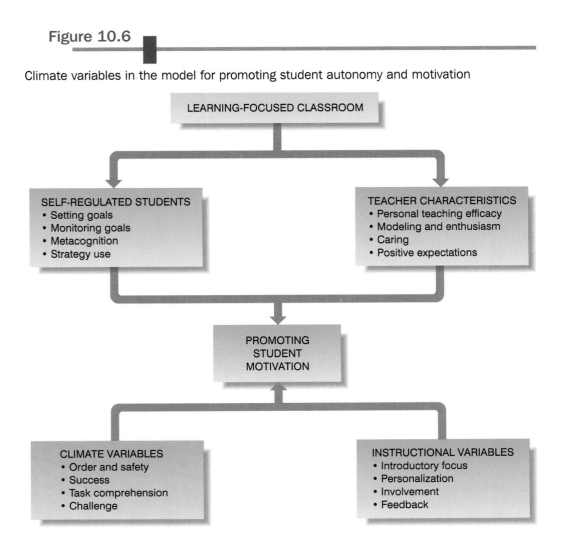

LEARNING-FOCUSED CLASSROOM

SELF-REGULATED STUDENTS
- Setting goals
- Monitoring goals
- Metacognition
- Strategy use

TEACHER CHARACTERISTICS
- Personal teaching efficacy
- Modeling and enthusiasm
- Caring
- Positive expectations

PROMOTING STUDENT MOTIVATION

CLIMATE VARIABLES
- Order and safety
- Success
- Task comprehension
- Challenge

INSTRUCTIONAL VARIABLES
- Introductory focus
- Personalization
- Involvement
- Feedback

In a healthy climate, students feel safe, and they're treated as competent people. They understand the requirements of learning tasks, perceive them as challenging, and believe they will succeed if they make reasonable effort (Brophy, 1987b; Clifford, 1990).

Safety and Order: Classrooms as Secure Places to Learn

> **10.24**
>
> A student is in a class environment where criticism and sarcasm are common. Explain why this environment is likely to detract from achievement using information processing as the basis for your explanation. (Hint: Think about our earlier discussion of anxiety.)

Research and theory both support the need for safety and order. Researchers have described effective schools as places of trust, order, cooperation, and high morale (Rutter, Maughn, Mortimore, Ouston, & Smith, 1979). The research-based Learner-Centered Psychological Principles (Alexander & Murphy, 1998; American Psychological Association Board of Educational Affairs, 1995) specifically address the need for emotional safety.

Both cognitive and humanistic views of motivation provide rationales for establishing safe and orderly learning environments. From a cognitive perspective, order helps create a sense of equilibrium in learners; from a humanistic view, Maslow's hierarchy addresses safety specifically as an important deficiency need (preceded only by survival).

How does this translate into practice? The teacher sets classroom tone by modeling respect and courtesy. "Teachers who . . . avoid such negative practices as criticism of student behavior, screaming, sarcasm, scolding, and ridicule facilitate student learning" (Murphy, Weil, & McGreal, 1986, p. 86). Students who are criticized for venturing personal or creative thoughts about a topic are unlikely to take the risk a second time.

Success: Developing Learner Self-Efficacy

Once a safe and orderly environment is established, student expectation for success is the most important climate variable. This is the expectancy component of expectancy–value theory. Note here that we're referring to learners' expectation for success, not teacher expectations as we discussed earlier.

Teachers promote positive student expectations by using instructional strategies that maximize opportunities for success:

- Begin lessons with open-ended questions and build on students' background knowledge.
- Use a variety of high-quality examples and representations that promote understanding.
- Prompt students when they have difficulty answering questions.
- Provide scaffolded practice before students are put on their own.

Success—like most aspects of teaching and learning—isn't as simple as it appears, however. Next we examine this idea further.

Challenge: Increasing the Value of Achievement

A long line of theory and research confirms the need not only for success but also for challenge. Challenge is one of the characteristics of intrinsically motivating activities. Expectancy–value theory says that learners will be motivated to engage in a task to the extent that they expect and value success on it. Research indicates that learners are more likely to value success if they perceive the task as challenging (Atkinson, 1964; Brehm & Self, 1989; Clifford, 1990). Challenge is necessary if students are to experience feelings of satisfaction, persistence, autonomy, and self-efficacy (J. Baron, 1998; Kloosterman, 1997; Schunk, 1994; Wasserstein, 1995). This helps us understand why children will persist in learning to ride a bicycle, for example, even though they fall repeatedly, and why intrinsic interest in a skill decreases after it's mastered.

For example, in the opening case, Kathy capitalized on the motivating features of challenge. She didn't limit her discussion of the Crusades to meaningless dates, times, and other facts, but instead focused on a thoughtful discussion of the Crusades' success or failure. Some students, like Harvey, initially perceived the assignment as difficult, but it was more satisfying than a hashing of the facts would have been. In pursuit of these challenging goals, Kathy provided enough scaffolding to ensure that her students could meet the challenge.

10.25
Explain specifically how *challenge* differs from *teacher expectations*.

Task Comprehension: Reasons for Effort

Challenge increases the "value" aspect of expectancy–value theory. Value is also enhanced when *students understand both what they're supposed to be learning and why they're learning it* (L. Anderson, 1989; Blumenfeld, 1992; Good & Brophy, 1997). This understanding is called **task comprehension**.

The "why they're learning it" aspect of task comprehension is essential for both teacher and learner. To provide an appropriate rationale for objectives and learning activities, teachers must think about what they want students to learn and why it is important. Motivation depends on students believing that what they're learning is worthwhile (Good & Brophy, 1997).

Understanding what they're learning and why is also important in the development of self-regulation. This understanding helps learners identify appropriate goals, select effective strategies, and maintain their effort in the face of difficulty.

Kathy focused explicitly on the reasons for studying the Crusades when she asked, "Why do we study the Crusades? Who cares, anyway?" Later, she commented, "We want to learn how to make and defend an argument, so the quality of your paragraph depends on how you defended your position, not on the position itself. Remember, this is a skill that goes way beyond a specific topic like the Crusades. This applies in everything we do." Then, when they do see a link between the Crusades and their lives today, they are likely to believe that what they're learning is worthwhile. This belief increases the "value" component of expectancy–value theory.

Compare Kathy's comments with the following statements, actually made by teachers:

"Today's lesson is nothing new if you've been here."

"Get your nose in the book; otherwise, I'll give you a writing assignment."

"This test is to see who the really smart ones are." (Brophy, 1987a, p. 204)

How motivated would you be if your teacher made those statements to you?

You can see how the climate variables are interdependent. Kathy's challenging assignment was an effective motivator because the other variables were present. If her classroom had been emotionally threatening or if students had been unable to succeed, the positive effects of challenge would have been lost. On the other hand, if her topic had been a dry coverage of facts or if students hadn't known why they were studying it, no level of success or safety would have motivated them.

10.26
Which theory of motivation best explains the need for *task comprehension*? Explain on the basis of that theory.

Instructional Variables: Developing Interest in Learning Activities

Teacher and climate variables form a general framework for motivation. Within this context, the teacher can do much in specific learning activities to enhance learner motivation. These factors are illustrated in Figure 10.7.

Figure 10.7

Instructional variables in the model for promoting learner autonomy and motivation

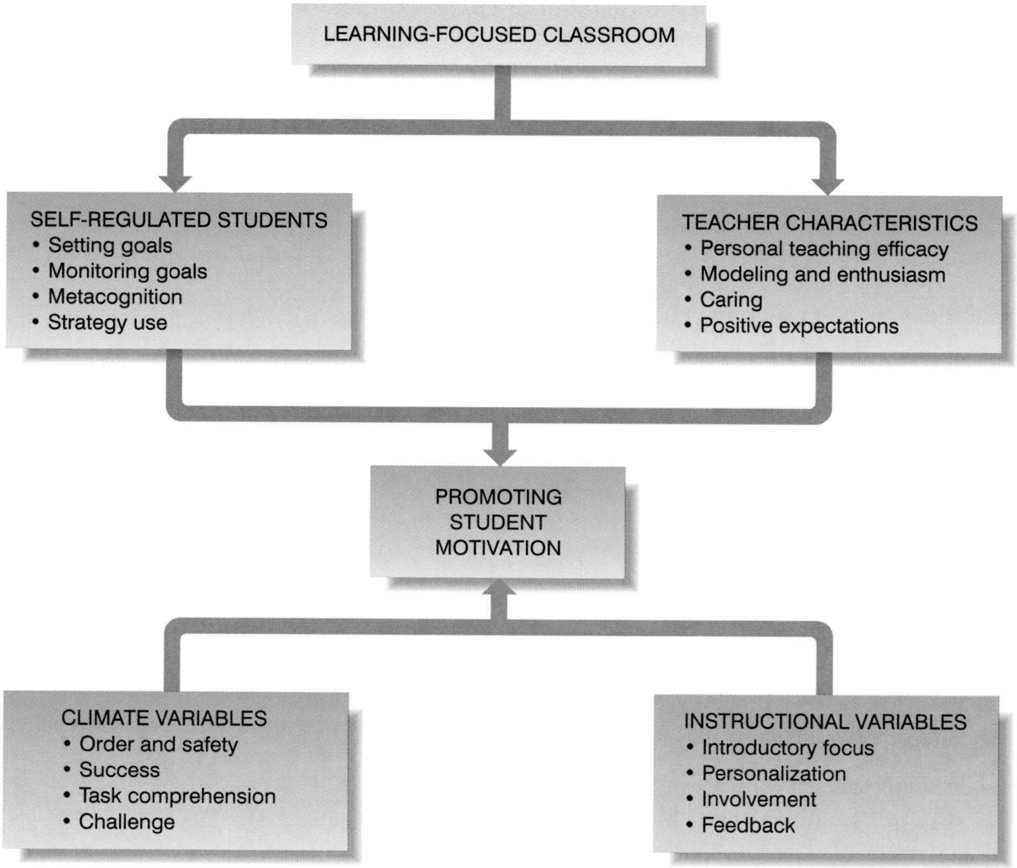

LEARNING-FOCUSED CLASSROOM

SELF-REGULATED STUDENTS
- Setting goals
- Monitoring goals
- Metacognition
- Strategy use

TEACHER CHARACTERISTICS
- Personal teaching efficacy
- Modeling and enthusiasm
- Caring
- Positive expectations

PROMOTING STUDENT MOTIVATION

CLIMATE VARIABLES
- Order and safety
- Success
- Task comprehension
- Challenge

INSTRUCTIONAL VARIABLES
- Introductory focus
- Personalization
- Involvement
- Feedback

From an instructional perspective, a motivated student can be viewed as "someone who is actively engaged in the learning process" (Stipek, 1996, p. 85). But how do we promote and maintain active engagement? Teachers often think about engagement using the concept of *interest* (Zahorik, 1996), and a body of research examining interest is beginning to emerge (Alexander & Murphy, 1998; Mayer, 1998a). Interest is important because it, like engagement, has been linked to learner attention, comprehension, and achievement (Krapp, Hidi, & Renninger, 1992; Mayer, 1998a).

Certain topics seem to be universally interesting to students—death, danger, chaos, power, money, sex, and romance for older students (Wade, 1992), and scary stories, humor, and animals for younger ones (Worthy, Moorman, & Turner, 1999). Unfortunately, little of the school curriculum focuses on these topics, leaving teachers with the question, "What can you do to increase learner interest?"

To increase interest, our goal is to initially capture students' attention and then maintain their involvement in the learning activity. The instructional variables in Figure 10.7 are intended to accomplish these goals.

Introductory Focus: Attracting Students' Attention

As an introduction to the topic of cities and their locations, a social studies teacher hands out a map of a fictitious island. On it are physical features such as lakes, rivers, mountains, and bays. Also included is information about altitude, rainfall, and average seasonal temperature. The teacher begins, "Our class has just been sent to this island to settle it. We have this information about its climate and physical features. Where should we make our first settlement?"

A science teacher passes a baseball and a golf ball around the room and has the students feel them. After confirming that the baseball feels heavier, he climbs up onto his desk, holds the two balls in front of him, and, as he prepares to drop them, says, "I'm going to drop these balls at the same time. What do you predict will happen?"

By beginning their lessons in these ways, the teachers were attempting to increase interest by capitalizing on **introductory focus**, which *attracts student attention and provides a framework for the lesson*. Introductory focus attempts to capitalize on the effects of novelty and curiosity, which are characteristics of intrinsically motivating activities.

Teachers can capitalize on curiosity motivation with unique problems, such as the teacher did in the example with the island; by asking paradoxical questions ("If Rome was such a powerful and advanced civilization, why did it fall apart?") or by using demonstrations with seemingly contradictory results (the two balls in the second example above will hit the floor at the same time). These events are designed to induce curiosity and pull students into the lesson.

Unfortunately, conscious planning for lesson introductions occurs infrequently; only 5% of teachers in one study made an explicit effort to draw students into the lesson (L. Anderson, Brubaker, Alleman-Brooks, & Duffy, 1984). Providing for effective introductory focus need not be difficult, however. All that is required is some conscious effort to con-

Effective teachers use introductory focus to draw students into their lessons.

Table 10.6

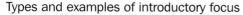

Types and examples of introductory focus

Type	Example
Problems and questions	A literature teacher shows a picture of Hemingway and says, "Here we see "Papa' in all his splendor. He seemed to have everything—fame, adventure, romance. Yet, he took his own life. Why would this happen?"
	A science teacher asks the students to explain why two pieces of paper come together at the bottom (rather than move apart) when students blow between them.
Inductive sequences	Students see the following sentences:
	"I had a ton of homework last night!"
	"That's the ugliest outfit ever!"
	"She's the most gorgeous girl in the world!"
	They find a pattern and develop a concept of *hyperbole*.
Attractive examples	A literature teacher shows the class pictures of Ernest Hemingway in a variety of settings.
	An elementary teacher begins a unit on amphibians by bringing in a live frog.
Objectives and rationales	A math teacher begins, "Today, we want to learn about unit pricing. This will help us decide which product is a better buy. It will help us all save money and be better consumers."

nect the content of the lesson to students' backgrounds and interest. Some examples are provided in Table 10.6.

Once learners are attracted to the lesson and a conceptual framework is provided, the lesson has to maintain their attention. This can be accomplished through personalization, involvement, and feedback.

Personalization: Links to Students' Lives

10.27
Look again at the example with Reeanne, Edward, and eye color. Explain how it might be used as an example of both introductory focus and personalization. Then describe how it might be used only as personalization.

One way to make learning tasks interesting is through personalization (Cordova & Lepper, 1996; Mayer, 1998a). Look again at Kathy's lesson. She said, "Remember, we started by imagining that we all left Lincoln High School and that it was taken over by people who believed that all extracurricular activities should be eliminated." She used this example as a framework for their study of the Crusades. Effective social studies teachers use personalization to help students see how events that happened long ago or far away relate to their own lives (Hallden, 1998). As another example, when introducing the topic of genetics, a teacher might say, "Once we understand genetics, we'll be able to figure out why Reeanne has blue eyes and Edward has brown."

These are both examples of **personalization**, which *attempts to make topics meaningful by using intellectually and/or emotionally relevant examples.* Kathy used her

school; she combined both intellectually and emotionally relevant examples. In the case with genetics, the teacher used two students in her class.

The value of personalization can be explained in several ways. First, Stipek (1996) suggests, "Most motivation theorists encourage the development of tasks that have some personal meaning for students" (p. 101). Second, relevance is one way of increasing learners' sense of autonomy. Third, meaningfulness enhances learning, and personalization is one way of increasing meaningfulness (see Chapter 7; Schunk, 2000). Fourth, anything people can relate to personally is more concrete for them than distant or abstract information (Mayer, 1998a); concrete experiences are an essential component of Piaget's work (see Chapter 2).

A survey of experienced teachers corroborates these views; they described personalization as one of the most important ways to promote student interest in learning activities (Zahorik, 1996).

Involvement: Increasing Intrinsic Motivation

Introductory focus and personalization pull students into lessons but, unless the topic is intriguing or timely, neither are likely to sustain motivation. The key to maintaining motivation is **involvement**, *students actively participating in the learning activity.*

> **10.28**
> Is the concept of involvement the same as the concept of activity as we discussed it in Chapter 7? If not, how are they different?

Think about your experience at lunch or a party. When you're talking and actively listening, you pay more attention to the conversation than you do when you're on its fringes. The same applies in classrooms. Conscious teacher efforts to promote involvement result in increased interest and learning (Blumenfeld, 1992). Let's look at two specific strategies for increasing student involvement: open-ended questioning and hands-on activities.

Using Open-Ended Questioning to Promote Involvement. Questioning is the most generally applicable tool teachers have for maintaining involvement. Student attention is at a peak when teachers ask questions but drops during teacher monologues (Lemke, 1982).

We discuss questioning in detail in Chapter 11, but we introduce one strategy here because it is particularly effective in improving involvement and motivation. This strategy is open-ended questioning (Kauchak & Eggen, 1998). **Open-ended questions** are *those for which a variety of answers are acceptable.*

For instance, in a lesson on amphibians, a teacher might begin by showing the students a frog or picture of a frog and asking, "Look at the frog. What do you see in the picture?"

In a lesson on Shakespeare's *Julius Caesar*, the teacher might ask,

"What has happened so far in the play?"

"What are some of the major events?"

"What is one thing you remember about the play?"

These ask for simple observations of the topic. A second type of open-ended question asks for comparisons. For instance,

"How is the frog similar to a lizard?"

"How are the frog and a toad similar or different?"

"How are Brutus and Marc Antony similar? How are they different?"

"How does the setting for Act I compare with that for Act II?"

Because many answers are acceptable, open-ended questions are safe and virtually ensure success—two of the climate variables we discussed earlier. By combining safety and success, even the most reluctant student can be encouraged to respond without risk or fear of embarrassment.

Also, because they can be asked and answered quickly by a number of students, open-ended questions can help solve the problem of involving 30 or more members of a class during a single lesson. Without the use of at least some open-ended questions, calling on reluctant responders often enough to increase their interest can be difficult.

Using Hands-On Activities to Promote Involvement.   Hands-on activities are another effective way of promoting involvement and student interest (Zahorik, 1996). When students are working with manipulatives in math or concrete materials in science, maps and globes in geography, or computers as they write essays, their level of interest increases significantly. In addition, hands-on activities add variety in learning activities, and variety has been found to create learner interest (Zahorik, 1996).

Additional ways of promoting involvement and interest are described in Table 10.7. Improvement drills add an element of game-like novelty to otherwise routine activities, and personal improvement can increase self-efficacy. Using chalkboards is similar to having students solve problems on paper at their desks, but the chalkboards allow sharing and discussion, and students often will use them even when they won't try if only paper is used.

Group work, in which students work together toward common learning goals, can also promote motivation (J. Baron, 1998; West, 1997). It provides opportunities for students to interact, share ideas, and compare their ideas with others. David Shelton, Jenny Newhall, and Sue Southam in Chapter 7 and Laura Hunter and Suzanne Brush in Chapter 8 all used group work to promote student involvement and interest.

Feedback: Meeting the Need to Understand

Returning to the opening case, Kathy gave students specific information about progress on their paragraphs. Research indicates that feedback that is intended to improve future performance has powerful motivational value (Clifford, 1990). In fact, the influence of feedback is so powerful that it could be called a basic principle of learning and motivation.

Table 10.7

Strategies to promote involvement

Technique	Example
Improvement drills	Students are given a list of 10 multiplication facts on a sheet. Students are scored on speed and accuracy, and points are given for individual improvement.
Games	The class is divided equally according to ability, and the two groups respond in a game format to teacher questions.
Individual work spaces	Students are given their own chalkboards on which they solve math problems and identify examples of concepts. They hold the chalkboards up when they've solved the problem or when they think an example illustrates a concept. They also write or draw their own examples on the chalkboards.
Student group work	Student pairs observe a science demonstration and write down as many observations of it as they can.

Feedback is particularly motivating when combined with clear student goals. Feedback gives learners information about the extent to which goals are being attained and, if they're falling short, they can try harder or use a different strategy. If they have met or exceeded the goal, they get a feeling of accomplishment and increased self-efficacy.

The need for feedback can be explained using cognitive theories of motivation. Not having a sense of how you're doing interferes with equilibrium, and a feeling of self-efficacy is impossible if you're not sure how you're performing. In our discussion of attribution theory, we also found that learners have a need to understand and explain why they are performing the way they are. Feedback helps them form accurate explanations.

When teachers provide feedback about performance, the emphasis should be on progress and mastery of the content, rather than on social comparisons (Crooks, 1988; Maehr, 1992; Schunk, 1994). This is especially important for less able students.

Combining Elements of the Model for Promoting Student Motivation

We have now examined the class structure and each of the 16 components of the model for promoting student motivation. We described them separately for the sake of clarity, but we want to emphasize the benefits of combining as many components as possible in your teaching. For instance, one middle school teacher did the following:

In beginning a unit on folktales, the teacher wrote three folktales about the school principal and two other teachers in the school. She began the lesson by telling the students that they would be given some brief stories and that they were to read them and find a pattern in them. The purpose was to give them some practice in becoming good thinkers. She then asked the students to make observations about the stories by comparing them and looking for characteristics they had in common.

This teacher capitalized on several elements of the model. She presented the folktales as a form of introductory focus, and her purpose and rationale for the lesson helped promote task comprehension. She used open-ended questioning to promote safety, success, and involvement, and her folktales capitalized on personalization. In this simple example, the teacher employed several features of the model, and it would have been easy to change the form of her introduction to increase the element of challenge. Assuming she has motivating personal characteristics, most of the model is employed in one simple yet creative lesson.

One of the most important messages we want to convey in this chapter is that *teachers' roles involve much more than simply delivering content.* One of those aspects is a conscious attempt to promote student motivation to learn.

Technology and Learning: Using Technology to Increase Learner Motivation

Technology is changing education, and nowhere is this impact more strongly felt than in the general domain of motivation (Barron, Hogarty, Kromrey, & Lenkway, 1999). Research has been done in at least four areas:

> **10.29** ▬
> On the basis of the information in this section, what should a teacher do after scoring a test and returning it to students?

Teacher feedback through interaction and discussion is essential for motivation and achievement.

Used properly, technology can be a tool for increasing learner motivation.

■ *Self-esteem and self-efficacy.*   Students using technology experience increased self-esteem, and beliefs about their capabilities improve (O'Connor & Brie, 1994). In addition, teachers who become proficient with technology increase in perceived self-efficacy (Kellenberger, 1996).

■ *Attendance.*   An 8-year study of one technology-implementation project found that student absenteeism dropped by nearly 50% after the project was put into place (Dwyer, 1994).

■ *Attitudes.*   Students participating in a technology-enriched program reported more positive attitudes toward school and more enjoyment of out-of-class activities (McKinnon, 1997).

■ *Involvement.*   Students in technology-supported programs were more willing to participate in school learning activities (Yang, 1991–1992).

The following comment gives a simple student perspective:

> *Interviewer:*   What do you think are the major advantages of using a computer to help you learn geometry?
>
> *Paul:*   If it's fun, it makes you want to learn something! It's fun! (Schofield, Eurich-Fulcer, & Britt, 1994, p. 602)

The Motivating Effects of Technology: Theoretical Explanations

Our understanding of learner needs and the characteristics of intrinsic motivation help us understand why technology can be motivating. Three aspects are significant: (a) the need for novelty and challenge, (b) the need for autonomy and personalization, and (c) the development of self-efficacy.

The Need for Novelty and Challenge.   Novelty is one characteristic of intrinsically motivating activities, and, when used strategically, technology can capitalize on this factor.

Technology provides one way to vary learning activities, while providing the practice with feedback needed to develop automaticity in basic skills. Skills must be developed to automaticity to free working memory space for higher-level tasks, such as problem solving (see Chapter 7). Extensive practice is required to develop expertise (see Chapter 8). Since a great deal of time is required to develop expertise, software programs can be used to vary learning activities and enhance student motivation (Bruning et al., 1999).

Challenge is a second factor. Even routine drill and practice activities are more motivating when students use software that can adapt the difficulty level of problems, decrease the time available as expertise develops, and provide immediate and customized feedback.

The Need for Autonomy and Personalization. People have an intrinsic need for autonomy and self-control, and computers allow students to control the pace of the activity and the kind and amount of help they receive. In addition, since computer assistance is private and personal, students experience less embarrassment and are more likely to seek help:

> *Interviewer:* How was getting help from the computer different from getting help from Mr. Adams?
>
> *Kim:* Well, some people, like when you have a teacher, man, you don't ask the teacher. You feel really *embarrassed*, you know. Sometimes I do. Like if you don't understand something. The computer—it's just a computer. It helps you and you wouldn't mind. (Schofield et al., 1994, p. 599)

Finally, authentic problems presented in realistic contexts (e.g., students are asked if Jasper can make it home without running out of fuel; see Chapter 8) are motivating (R. Davis, 1994). They capitalize on the intrinsically motivating effects of challenge and novelty, and solving real-world problems increases self-efficacy. Researchers investigating the effects of computer-based problem solving made the following observation:

> By the time the bell to start class rings, three fourths of the students in class today have problems on the screen and are working on them. The others (have all logged in and) appear to be waiting for their problems to appear. . . . I'm struck by the fact that the students have started their work without a word from the substitute teacher who is in charge of class today. (Schofield et al., 1994, p. 593)

The Development of Self-Efficacy. Technology can also increase learner self-efficacy (Schunk & Ertmer, 1999). It may, in fact, be unique in its ability to do so. The expertise that develops as students learn to compose on a keyboard, modify and manage files, use spreadsheets and databases, use the Internet, and communicate with others by e-mail, gives people a sense of personal satisfaction. As their expertise increases, students turn to more sophisticated activities, such as making technologically enhanced presentations, developing and improving their own Web sites, and creating their own simulations. Increased expertise with these activities is personally satisfying and can significantly increase self-efficacy.

Technology and Motivation: A Word of Caution

As with virtually all aspects of learning and teaching, using technology to increase motivation isn't as simple as it appears on the surface. First, if technology is to be used effectively, teachers must be very clear about the goals they expect to accomplish with it (Harrington-Lueker, 1997). Vague notions of "surfing the 'Net" or simply giving students access to computers aren't adequate. While students may, at least initially, enjoy the novelty, spending time in front of computers doesn't necessarily produce learning.

Second, while computers and other forms of technology may increase interest, researchers caution that the quality of software varies greatly (R. Davis, 1994), and merely being busy isn't an accurate indicator of student learning. Researchers have found that student engagement with computers can vary from superficial contacts with content to more productive and intense, goal-oriented interactions (Bangert-Drowns & Pyke, 1999).

Technology and Motivation: Guidelines for Teachers

With the research on technology and motivation in mind, the following are some guidelines for teachers:

- *Establish clear learning goals.*   Students should use computers and other forms of technology for clear learning purposes, such as developing automaticity with basic skills, or practicing solving complex problems.
- *Assess software before students work with it.*   The quality of instructional software varies greatly. It should be thoroughly examined to be sure that it is consistent with learning goals and compatible with learners' background knowledge.
- *Emphasize both process and product goals.*   Encourage students to reflect on their experiences in working with technology, both with respect to how technology works and also how it can be used as a learning tool. Ask students to explain why they are using a certain procedure, what they're trying to accomplish, and how they know that they're making progress.
- *Vary the uses of technology.*   Technology can be used to enhance learning in a number of ways including practice with feedback, problem solving, word processing, and locating information on the Internet. Provide students with opportunities to learn about technology and these different uses.

The kinds of software teachers choose and the way they present and monitor computer tasks can have important influences on learning. If study time isn't spent on activities related to clear, meaningful goals, or if software isn't matched to students' backgrounds, using technology may actually detract from learning (Bangert-Drowns & Pyke, 1999). EvaluTech offers a Web site in which teachers can review software:

www.evalutch.sreb.org

Classroom Connections

Promoting Learner Autonomy and Responsibility in Your Classroom

1. Promote learner responsibility with goal setting and self-monitoring.
   - An elementary language arts teacher conferences with students as they begin a writing project. She has each of them write down a schedule and time table for completing the project. She meets with each student again periodically to evaluate these goals and modify them if necessary.

2. Make students aware of the role of metacognition in their learning.
   - A junior high teacher says to her students, "It's very important to think about and be aware of the way you study. If you have your stereo on, ask yourself, 'Am I really learning what I'm studying, or am I distracted by the stereo?'"

3. Teach metacognition and strategy use.
   - An English teacher directs, "Let's read the next section in our books. After we've read it, we're going to stop and make a one-sentence summary of the passage. This is something each of you can do as you read on your own."
   - An elementary teacher says, "I make a list of everything I need to bring to school. Then, before I leave in the morning I check to see if I have everything on the list. Before you leave this afternoon, let's make a list of all the assignments and books you need to take home and use in planning your studying."

Demonstrating the Personal Characteristics of the Model for Promoting Student Motivation in Your Classroom

4. Show students you care by giving them your personal time.
   - A geography teacher calls parents as soon as he sees a student having even minor academic or personal problems. He solicits their help in monitoring the student and offers his assistance in solving the problem.

5. Model interest in the topics you're teaching.
   - During quiet reading time, a fourth-grade teacher comments on a book she's interested in and reads while the students are reading.
   - A science teacher brings in clippings from the local newspaper that relate to science and asks students to do the same. He discusses them at the beginning of class and pins them on a bulletin board for students to read.

6. Maintain appropriately high expectations for all students.
   - A second-grade teacher makes a conscious attempt to treat all students in her class as equally as possible, distributing her questions to them equally and demanding as much as she can from each.

Applying the Climate Variables of the Model for Promoting Student Motivation in Your Classroom

7. Carefully describe objectives and rationales for your assignments.

   - A junior high English teacher carefully describes his assignments and due dates and writes them on the board. Each time, he explains why the assignment is important.

8. Promote challenge and success in learning activities.
   - A fifth-grade teacher comments, "We're really getting good at percentages. I have a problem that is going to make us all think. It will be tough, but I think we can do it."
   - A language arts teacher always has the class practice three or four homework exercises as a whole group and discusses them before students begin to work independently.

Applying the Instructional Variables of the Model for Promoting Student Motivation in Your Classroom

9. Plan lesson introductions to attract students' attention and provide an umbrella for the lesson.
   - A middle school science teacher begins each class with a question or problem that leads into the lesson. She begins one lesson on local geology by asking students to imagine what their area looked like 1 million, 10 million, and 100 million years ago.
   - A fourth-grade teacher introduces a lesson on measuring by bringing in a cake recipe and ingredients that have to be modified if everyone in the class is going to get a piece. During the lesson, the class modifies the recipe, and during the lunch break, the teacher makes it up, arranges with the cafeteria to bake it, and brings it back in the afternoon to share with the class.

10. Promote involvement by eliciting responses from all students.
    - A language arts teacher randomly calls on all her students whether or not they raise their hands. At the beginning of the year, she explains that this is her practice, that her intent is to encourage participation, and that they will soon get over any uneasiness about being "put on the spot." Whenever students cannot answer, she gives them extra support in the form of cues and prompts.

11. Personalize content.
    - A history teacher begins a unit on World War II by commenting that many of the students' grandparents and great-grandparents were probably directly

involved in it either through serving in the armed forces or by rationing and working in factories. As an alternative assignment, he asks students to interview their grandparents about their memories of the war.

- A fifth-grade teacher begins a lesson on percentages by bringing in an advertisement for toys from a local newspaper. The ad says "10% to 25% off marked prices." After discussing how to compute percentage discounts, she returns to the ad and asks students to compute their savings on various items.

12. Provide prompt and informative feedback about student performance.
   - A fourth-grade teacher discussed the most frequently missed items on all her quizzes, asking students to explain why the correct answers are correct and considering the questions from different perspectives whenever possible.
   - A seventh-grade teacher writes on a student paper, "You have some very good ideas. Now you need to rework your essay so that it is grammatically correct. Look carefully at the notes I've made on your paper."

Motivation and Diversity

When we examine the research on the school success of minorities, we see a pattern. On most measures—achievement test scores, retention in grade, and dropout rates—many ethnic minorities in the United States perform less well than their majority counterparts (Macionis, 1997; Mullis, Dossey, Foertsh, Jones, & Gentile, 1991). Although some differences can be linked to socioeconomic status, disparities remain. Many minority students leave school unprepared for today's demanding world.

Educators have turned to motivational research in an attempt to address these problems, but the picture remains cloudy. For example, researchers have attempted to explain the lower-than-expected achievement of African American students by hypothesizing deficits in need for achievement, perceptions of autonomy, and self-efficacy. However, in a comprehensive review of this literature, Graham (1994) concluded that deficits don't exist in these areas and that African American students "maintain a belief in personal control, have high expectance, and enjoy positive self-regard" (p. 55). Researchers have also found that African American and Latina mothers are enthusiastic about education and hold high expectations for their children's future (Stevenson, Chen, & Uttal, 1990).

The picture is further complicated by the fact that motivation varies among communities, families, and peers within specific minority groups. For example, researchers have found that motivational issues in inner-city African American communities differ from those in suburban or rural ones (Graham, 1994; Slaughter-Defoe, Nakagawa, Takanashi, & Johnson, 1990), and some families approach the task of motivating their children differently than do others (Steinberg, Dornbusch, & Brown, 1992). Similar differences exist in Asian and Latino families. Peer groups sometimes complement school achievement and other times detract from it (Goodenow, 1992b; Steinberg et al., 1992).

Motivation Problems: Student Perspectives

In attempting to understand how schools influence minority students' motivation and achievement, researchers have focused on students' perceptions of their school experiences and have identified the following problems:

▌ Lack of connection between classroom content and students' lives
▌ Alienation from school
▌ Disengagement and lack of involvement in classes
▌ Distant and inflexible teachers

Students report feeling alienated from school, like outsiders at a party. This feeling results from factors such as cultural discontinuities, language barriers, and academic problems (Ogbu 1992; Wong-Fillmore, 1992). In one study, researchers asked about connections between school and students' personal happiness:

Interviewer:	What do you really like about school? What makes you happy?
Diane:	Nothing really. I just come because I have to. Because I don't want to grow up being stupid.
Interviewer:	There's nothing you look forward to?
Diane:	Ummm . . . (defiantly stares; challenges.) Getting an education?
Interviewer:	Do you think there's a way to get an education without coming to school?
Diane:	(shakes her head no)
Interviewer:	It has to be this way?
Diane:	(softly; no eye contact) Yeah. (Kramer & Colvin, 1991, p. 6)

Another student, who was discussing his decision to leave school at age 16, describes his alienation in this way:

Student:	I wouldn't go to nobody.
Interviewer:	Not even a counselor?
Student:	No.
Interviewer:	That seems funny. Don't you work in the office?
Student:	Yeah, but I don't *talk* to them [student emphasis]. (Kramer-Schlosser, 1992, p. 132)

Disengagement is another problem. Teachers report that students don't come to class or that when they do they are reluctant to participate.

They'll try to sit at the edges or the back of the classroom and they actually try to become less visible to me, or they'll act up so they get sent out of the classroom and there's less time, less chance I'll call on them or hold them accountable. . . . Usually they don't join the class. (Kramer & Colvin, 1991, p. 12)

Adding to these problems are student perceptions that teachers just don't care. One student described her teachers this way:

Nichole:	People here don't have many people to talk to. I don't. The teachers . . . some of them don't care about their students. They say, "They [administrators] want me to teach and I'm going to do it no matter what." I don't like that. I like them to say, "I'm here to teach and help you because I care." That's what I like. But a lot of them are just saying, "I'm here to teach so I'm gonna teach." I don't think that's right.
Interviewer:	Do they actually say that?
Nichole:	It's more an attitude, and they do say it. Like Ms. G. She's like . . . she never says it, but you know, she's just there and she just wants to teach, but she doesn't want to explain the whole deal.
Interviewer:	How do you know that?
Nichole:	I could feel it. The way she acts and the way she does things. She's been here seven years and all the kids I've talked to that have had her before say, "Oooh! You have Ms. G.!" Just like that.
Interviewer:	But a teacher who really cares, how do they act?

10.30 ▬
Consider again our earlier discussion of motivation and needs. Based on what you've read in this section, what two needs are not being met for cultural minorities? Explain.

Nichole: Like Mr. P. He really cares about his students. He's helping me a
lot and he tells me, "I'm not angry with you, I just care about
you." He's real caring and he does teach me when he cares.
(Kramer & Colvin, 1991, p. 13)

The pattern we see is a lack of connection to both school and classes. Students attend
school, sit in classes, but don't feel a part of them. They question whether anyone cares
about them, and, from their perspective, the classes have little meaning for their daily lives.

Motivation Problems: Possible Solutions

Research offers some possible solutions to the problem of student alienation and disengagement. Students must feel that they belong and can contribute to the classroom community. They need to value the classes they take and find them meaningful.

Teachers are critical to the success of this process. Research indicates that those who
are effective at motivating minority students and students placed at risk have the following
characteristics:

> 10.31 ▬
> Consider again the section
> on motivation and needs.
> Promoting high levels of
> involvement and making
> an effort to connect con-
> tent to students lives most
> closely relates to which of
> the needs discussed in
> that section? Explain.

- They are enthusiastic, supportive, and have high expectations for student achievement.
- They create learner-centered classrooms with high levels of student involvement.
- They make a special effort to connect classroom content to students' lives (Kramer & Colvin, 1991; Kramer-Schlosser, 1992).

Teachers need to make a special effort to make all students feel welcome and to
demonstrate that they sincerely care. They also need to communicate that they hold positive expectations and that they'll work with learners if students try. One teacher identified
as effective in working with minority and at-risk students described his efforts in this way:

> I believe that marginal students who begin the year poorly and improved did so because
> they knew I would do all I could to help them to be a success in school. I told them I
> would explain, and explain, and explain until they understood. They were worth every
> moment it would take. No one ever has to fail. (Kramer-Schlosser, 1992, p. 137)

Teacher characteristics such as caring, enthusiasm, and high expectations—important for all students—are critical for minority learners and students placed at risk. Other
motivational elements, such as order and safety, challenge, success, and feedback, make
classrooms accessible and inviting for students on the margins. Conscious attention to
these variables is important for all students and critical for motivating diverse learners.

Classroom
Connections

Capitalizing on Diversity in Your Classroom

1. Communicate positive expectations for student success through your words and teaching strategies.
   - A math teacher responsible for basic math classes stresses at the beginning of the school year that she expects all students to succeed. She collects and grades homework every day and talks with students and their parents when it isn't handed in.

She tests and quizzes frequently and gives detailed feedback to students about their performance.

2. Create learning environments that involve students in meaningful learning.
   - A social studies teacher supplements his units with student group projects. For example, in their study of the Civil Rights movement of the 1960s, he

asks students to interview older neighbors, relatives, and friends about their memories of the movement and has groups report on their findings on a class sharing day.

- An English teacher redesigned his writing class to address issues that were important to his students. At the beginning of the term, he spent some time identifying issues that students wanted to talk and write about (e.g., dress codes, cafeteria food, student clubs). He encouraged students to debate issues before writing about them and arranged with the school newspaper to publish some of the better ones in a pro and con editorial section.

3. Communicate caring by spending time with students, on both academic and personal topics.
   - A middle school science teacher in an inner-city school helps organize an after-school science club. Students work on projects, take field trips, and have different professionals in the scientific community come in to talk about their jobs. Whenever possible, she recruits minorities and women for these professional visits.
   - An elementary teacher regularly calls parents and other caregivers, both to discuss attendance or academic problems and to congratulate them on special achievements or improvements by their children.

Windows on Classrooms

At the beginning of the chapter, you saw how Kathy Brewster applied an understanding of student motivation in her teaching. She maintained high expectations for her students, accommodated their personal needs, promoted self-efficacy, and maintained a high level of student involvement in a safe and orderly learning environment.

We turn now to a case study that describes another teacher presenting the same topic to a different group of students. As you read this classroom episode, compare the approach with Kathy Brewster's work with her students.

"What are we up to today, Mr. Marcus?" Joe asked as he came into Damon Marcus's classroom Thursday morning.

"You'll see in a minute," Damon nodded and smiled. "Now, quickly, get to your seat so that we can get started."

Damon watched as students took their seats, and then announced, "Listen, everyone, I have your tests here from last Friday. Liora, Ivan, Lynn, and Segundo, super job on the test. They were the only A's in the class."

After handing back the tests, Damon moved to the chalkboard and wrote the following:

A-4
B-7
C-11
D-4
F-3

"You people down here better get moving," Damon commented, pointing to the D's and F's on the chalkboard. "This wasn't that hard a test.

Remember, we have another test in 2 weeks. We need some improvement. C'mon, now. I know you can do better. Let's give these four a run for their money.

"You can look over your papers, but be sure to turn them in by the end of the class period," Damon continued, as he turned to the day's lesson.

"Now let's get going. We have a lot to cover today. . . . As you'll recall from yesterday, we began talking about the Crusades and said that they were an attempt by the Christian powers of Western Europe to wrest control of the traditional holy lands of Christianity away from the Muslims. Now, when was the First Crusade?" Damon asked, looking over the classroom.

"About 1500, I think," Clifton volunteered.

"No, no," Damon shook his head. "Remember that Columbus sailed in 1492, which was before 1500, so that doesn't make sense. It was well before 1500. . . . Liora?"

"It was about 1100, I think."

"Excellent, Liora. Now, remember, everyone, you need to know these dates, or otherwise you'll get confused just as Clifton did here. I know that learning dates and places isn't the most pleasant stuff, but you might as well get used to it because that's what history is about and they'll be on the next test."

While this was going on, Brad whispered to Donna, "Let me look at your test a sec. I got 1 point on this one, and I don't get it." Donna handed Brad her test, and he carefully read her answer and then read his own again.

"I still don't get it," he whispered and shrugged as he handed back her paper.

"Ask him about it," Donna suggested.

Damon continued, "The First Crusade was in 1095, and it was called the 'People's Crusade.' There were actually seven Crusades in all, rang-ing from the one in 1095 to the point where enthusiasm for them ended by 1300."

"The Fourth Crusade was particularly notorious," he continued. "In it, the Crusaders sacked Constantinople in 1203, and the Greek Byzantine Church hated the Crusaders forever after that."

Damon continued, "The Crusades weren't just religiously motivated. The Muslim world was getting stronger and stronger, and it was posing a threat to Europe. For example, it had control of much of northern Africa, had expanded into southern Spain, and even was moving into other parts of southern Europe. So it was a threat economically and militarily, as well as religiously. This was also a factor in the Crusades."

Damon continued presenting information about the Crusades, and then, seeing that about 20 minutes were left in the period, he said, "Now, I want you to write a summary of the Crusades that outlines the major people and events and tells why they were important. You should be able to finish by the end of the class period. If you don't, turn them in tomorrow at the beginning of the class period. You may use your notes. Go ahead and get started while I come around and collect your tests."

As Damon started to collect the tests, Brad came up to his desk and said, "Mr. Marcus, I don't get this. I only got 1 out of 5 on this one. But Donna got a 4 and the answers say almost the same thing."

"Let me look at Donna's," Damon requested.

Brad went back and got Donna's test. Damon looked at both tests, and turned to Brad, "Donna's answer was better organized and clearer than yours."

He continued down the aisles, collecting students' tests. As he went by, he saw that Jeremy hadn't written anything on his summary paper. Damon finished collecting the papers and then went back to Jeremy's desk. Jeremy's paper was still blank.

"C'mon back here," Damon motioned to a table at the back of the room.

"Are you having trouble getting started?" Damon asked sympathetically. "I know you have a tough time with written assignments. Let me help you."

Damon then took a blank piece of paper and started writing as Jeremy watched. He wrote several sentences on the paper and then said, "See how easy that was? That's the kind of thing I want you to do. Go ahead—that's a start. Keep that so you can see what I'm looking for. Go back to your desk and give it another try."

Questions for Discussion and Analysis

Compare Damon's lesson with Kathy's. In making your comparison, consider the following questions. In each case, be specific and take information directly from the case studies.

1. Compare the two teachers' attempts to capitalize on the motivating effects of curiosity. How were they alike and different?
2. Would Damon's handling of the lesson likely appeal to students with a high need for achievement? How appealing would the lesson be for students with a high need to avoid failure? Explain in both cases.

3. Assess Damon's lesson in terms of Maslow's hierarchy. How well did he meet needs at each level?

4. Would Damon's teaching more likely promote learning goals or performance goals? A task orientation or an ego orientation? Explain.

5. On the basis of Damon's remarks as he turned back the test, describe some possible attributions for students who did well on the test and some possible attributions for students who did poorly on the test.

6. Assess the effectiveness of Damon's lesson for students from diverse backgrounds. Make specific suggestions for improvement in instances for which you believe his teaching could be improved.

7. Assess Damon's instruction on the basis of each element of the model for promoting student motivation. In instances in which you believe he could have improved, offer specific suggestions for improvement.

 ## Summary

Theories of Motivation

Behaviorism suggests that motivation results from using reinforcers effectively. Critics of behavioral approaches to motivation contend that reinforcers detract from intrinsic motivation and cause learners to focus on the reinforcers instead of learning. Used effectively, however, reinforcers can actually increase intrinsic motivation.

Cognitive views of motivation emphasize that people have an innate need for order and predictability. Closely related to Piaget's concept of equilibrium, cognitive theories suggest that learners are motivated to resolve cognitive conflict when experiences don't make sense to them.

Humanistic views of motivation focus on the learner as a whole person and examine the relationships among physical, emotional, intellectual, and aesthetic needs. Classroom climate and teacher–student relationships are central to this view.

Motivation and Needs

A need is a real or perceived lack of something necessary. From a humanistic perspective, Maslow described a hierarchy beginning with survival and safety needs, progressing through belonging and esteem needs, and ending with intellectual and aesthetic needs. Social and emotional needs include the need for relatedness, the need for approval, and the need to reduce anxiety.

Cognitive needs include needs for autonomy, achievement, and the need to understand why we succeed and fail, which is described in attribution theory. Because the ability to achieve is so strongly valued in our society, people's self-worth is strongly linked to their perceptions of their ability, and some learners will procrastinate, blame others, and engage in other self-handicapping behaviors to protect their perceptions of high ability.

Motivation and Beliefs

Some learners believe that ability is stable and uncontrollable, whereas others believe it can be improved with effort. Learners with a high need to avoid failure tend to have the first view, and those with a high need for achievement have the second.

Now go to our Companion Website to assess your understanding of chapter content with the Student Self-Assessment, apply comprehension in the Online Casebook, and broaden your knowledge base with links to important Educational Psychology World Wide Web sites.

Learners' beliefs about their capability to accomplish specific tasks describes their self-efficacy. It depends primarily on past success and modeling, but verbal persuasion and emotional state influence it as well. Self-efficacy influences learners' perceptions of autonomy as well as their effort, perseverance, strategy use, and achievement.

A Classroom Model for Promoting Student Motivation

Within a learning-focused rather than a performance-focused classroom, students take responsibility for their own learning by setting and monitoring goals, using metacognitive skills, and employing effective strategies. In addition, teacher characteristics—including personal teaching efficacy, modeling, caring, and high expectations—combine with classroom climate and instructional variables to enhance motivation.

Motivation is increased when students work in a safe and orderly classroom, experience success, understand tasks and the reasons for them, and experience optimal challenge. Teachers can increase motivation in their lessons by preparing attractive lesson beginnings, involving students, personalizing content, and providing informative feedback.

 # Important Concepts

achievement motivation
   (p. 423)

anxiety (p. 421)

approval (p. 420)

attribution theory (p. 424)

attributional statements
   (p. 429)

attributions (p. 424)

autonomy (p. 421)

caring (p. 438)

classroom climate (p. 441)

cognitive theories of
   motivation (p. 414)

deficiency needs (p. 418)

entity view of ability
   (p. 427)

expectancy–value theories
   (p. 427)

extrinsic motivation
   (p. 411)

growth needs (p. 418)

humanistic psychology
   (p. 415)

incremental view of ability
   (p. 427)

intrinsic motivation
   (p. 411)

introductory focus (p. 445)

involvement (p. 447)

learned helplessness
   (p. 425)

learning-focused
   environment (p. 432)

motivation (p. 411)

need (p. 417)

open-ended questions
   (p. 447)

performance-oriented
   environment (p. 432)

personalization (p. 446)

personal teaching efficacy
   (p. 436)

relatedness (p. 420)

self-efficacy (p. 427)

self-fulfilling prophecy
   (p. 440)

self-regulated (p. 434)

task comprehension
   (p. 443)

Chapter Outline

11
Creating
Productive
Learning
Environments

"What are you doing with those cake pans?" Jim Barton asked his wife, Shirley, as he saw her hard at work constructing some cardboard cake pans.

"What do you think?" she grinned at him. "Do they look like cake?" she asked, holding up rectangular cardboard pieces drawn to resemble two cakes cut into pieces.

"Actually, they almost do," he responded.

"My students didn't score as well as I would have liked on the fractions part of the Stanford Achievement Test last year, and I promised myself that they were going to do better this year."

"But you said the students aren't as sharp this year."

"That doesn't matter. I'm pushing them harder. I think I could have done a better job last year, so I swore I was really going to be ready for them this time."

Jim walked back into the living room with a smile on his face, mumbling something about thinking that teachers who have taught for 11 years were supposed to burn out.

The next day, Shirley met with her 28 fifth graders, and they began their day, which usually follows this schedule:

8:30–10:00	Language arts (spelling, writing, grammar)
10:00–10:55	Math
10:55–11:05	Break
11:05–11:35	Science
11:35–12:00	Lunch
12:00–1:30	Reading
1:30–2:00	Social Studies
2:00–3:00	Rotating subjects (art, music, P.E., computer)

As Shirley walked up and down the aisles, she put two pieces of paper on each student's desk and stopped periodically to comment on someone's work or offer reassurance as the class completed a writing assignment. When she glanced at her watch and saw that it was 9:58, she announced, "Quickly turn in your writing and get out your math homework. We're running a little late today." As she walked by Brad, she touched him on the arm and pointed to his folder, reminding him to return from his window gazing.

Her students stopped their writing and passed the papers forward, each putting his or her paper on top of the stack. Shirley collected them from the first person in each row and, as she walked by Shelli, she paused and asked, "How are you feeling today, Shelli? Is your cold better?"

"A lot better," Shelli replied.

Shirley put the papers into a folder and stepped to the chalkboard as she watched the students put their reading materials away and pull out their math books. She wrote the following problems on the chalkboard:

$$3/8 + 2/8 =$$
$$3/7 + 4/7 =$$
$$5/12 + 6/12 =$$

At 10:01, the students had their math books out and were waiting.

"Now," she began as she pulled out two drawings designed to look like pizzas, each cut into eight parts, "We've been adding fractions, so for a moment, let's look again at what we've been doing. What does the 8 mean in the first problem? . . . Dean?"

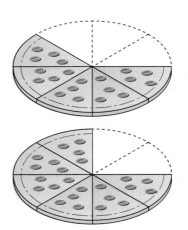

"We have eight parts of something altogether."

"Parts of what?"

" . . . Supposed to be pizza."

"And what kind of parts? . . . Emerson?"

" . . . "

"How do the parts compare with each other?"

" . . . They're all equal."

As soon as Shirley walked past him, Kevin stuck his foot across the aisle, tapping Alison on the leg with his shoe while he watched Shirley's back from the corner of his eye. "Stop it, Kevin," Alison muttered, swiping at him with her hand.

Shirley turned, came back up the aisle, and continued, "Good, Emerson," and standing next to Kevin, she asked, "How do we know they're equal? . . . Kevin?" looking directly at him.

" . . . I can see them. . . . they look equal."

"Okay. Good," Shirley smiled. "We have two pizzas, both cut into eight equal parts," and she then asked, "How much pizza did we eat altogether? . . . Gayle?"

"Five pieces."

"What part of a whole pizza did we eat?"

"I think . . . ⅝ of it."

"Good. And how did Gayle get that? . . . Estella?"

"She added them up."

"How might we prove that adding them up is the thing to do? . . . Anyone?"

After a short pause, Natasha said, "We have three pieces there (pointing to the first drawing), and if we had two more pieces, we would have five altogether, so it would be ⅜ and ⅖, which would be ⅝ altogether."

"What do the rest of you think about that?" Shirley queried.

"I don't think so," Adam shook his head. "It looks like 5/16 to me."

"No, look," Natasha countered, pointing to the drawing. "We have only eight pieces altogether."

"What about the other drawing?"

"We're not on the other drawing. We're on this one. I said put two more pieces on this one."

Shirley watched as other students joined the discussion; moved over to Sondra, who had been whispering and passing notes to Sherrill across the aisle; and said quietly, "Move up here," nodding to a desk at the front of the room.

"What did I do?" Sondra protested.

"When we talked about our rules at the beginning of the year, we agreed that it was important to listen when other people are talking," Shirley whispered to her.

"I was listening," Sondra protested.

"We don't learn as much when people aren't paying attention, and I'm uncomfortable when we don't

learn. Move quickly now," Shirley said evenly as she watched the progress of the discussion.

Her students continued discussing the pizza problem for a couple more minutes, finally agreeing that Natasha's "proof" seemed to make sense.

Shirley then continued with the second and third problems on the chalkboard and concluded by saying, as she tapped her knuckle on the chalkboard, "Now, let's think about these problems. What is similar about them? Like, pretend that they're all pizzas and we're adding pieces of them."

" . . . They all have the same pieces," Karen noted.

"I'm not sure what you mean," Shirley queried.

" . . . Like 8 and 8, 7 and 7, and 12 and 12."

"Ahh, I see," Shirley nodded. "Each of these problems has the same denominator." She pointed respectively to the 8s, the 7s, and the 12s. "Yes," she said raising her voice, "let's keep that in mind as we study some more problems.

"Now," she continued as she strode vigorously across the front of the room, "we're going to shift gears because I've got another, different kind of problem." She pulled out the two cardboard cake rectangles that she had made the night before, one divided into thirds and the other divided in half.

"Now we have cakes instead of pizza," she smiled, "and I'm still hungry, so I eat this piece," she said, pointing to the third. "Then I go sort of wild and eat this piece too," pointing to the half. "How much cake have I eaten?"

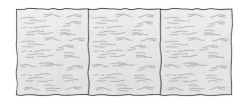

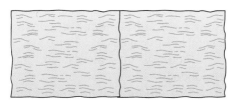

"A third of one and a half of the other," Tenisha volunteered.

"Makes sense, . . . but is that more than a whole cake, a whole cake, or what part of a cake?"

" . . . I'm pretty sure less," Adam offered, peering at the two cakes.

"How do you think we could find out for sure?" Shirley wondered. She paused and then said, "To help us, take two of the pieces of paper from the copying room that I put on your desks while you were working on your writing and carefully fold them like our cakes here."

The students quickly took the papers from their desks and began folding. Shirley helped some of them who had trouble folding their papers into thirds.

"Now we have two whole papers, which we'll pretend are our cakes. Let's think about our problem again. If we eat a third of one and a half of the other one, how much have we eaten altogether? . . . How can we figure that out?"

" . . . Let's lay one on top of the other," Jan suggested, after thinking for several seconds.

"Good idea. . . . Go ahead and try it."

" . . . It's less than a whole cake," Tanya offered after peering carefully at the papers.

"How much less?"

The students offered a few uncertain suggestions, and Shirley then asked, "Let's think about the work we've been doing. What did we just review?" pointing at the chalkboard.

"Adding up the pizzas," Juan offered.

"And what do we know about them?"

" . . . They weren't like the cakes," Bryan added.

"In what way?" Shirley asked with a quizzical shrug.

"They were the same. . . . They had the same-size parts, and these are different," he pointed to the cakes.

"Maybe we need to cut them different so they're the same," Enrico suggested.

This response prompted additional discussion, after which Shirley offered, "Let me make a suggestion how we can get them to be the same, using Enrico's idea."

She continued, "How much cake do we have here? . . . Tim?"

"A third."

"Fine," Shirley smiled. "Now, let's all fold our 'cakes' this way," and she folded a piece of paper so that it appeared as follows:

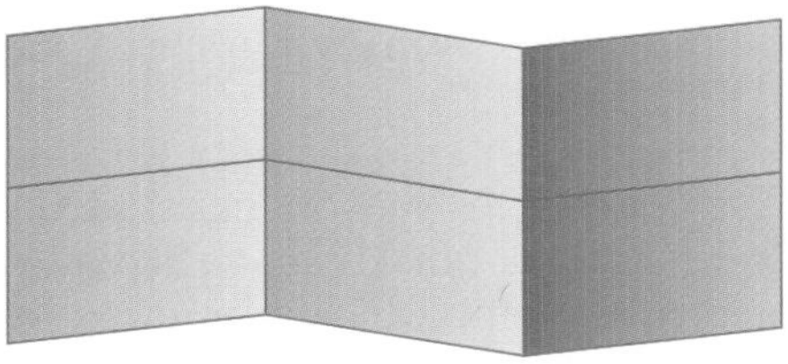

"How many pieces do I have altogether now? . . . Karen?"

" . . . It looks like six," she responded uncertainly.

"Yes. Good, Karen. I saw you actually counting them," Shirley noted and then counted the six squares again out loud. "So what portion is now shaded? . . . Jon?"

"Two sixths."

"Excellent, Jon!" and she moved to the chalkboard and wrote $\frac{1}{3}$ and $\frac{2}{6}$ alongside each other with an equal sign between.

"Now, how do we know that the $\frac{1}{3}$ and $\frac{2}{6}$ are equal?"

"It's the same amount of cake," Dan shrugged.

Shirley then continued by having the students fold the second 'cake' into thirds so that it appeared as follows:

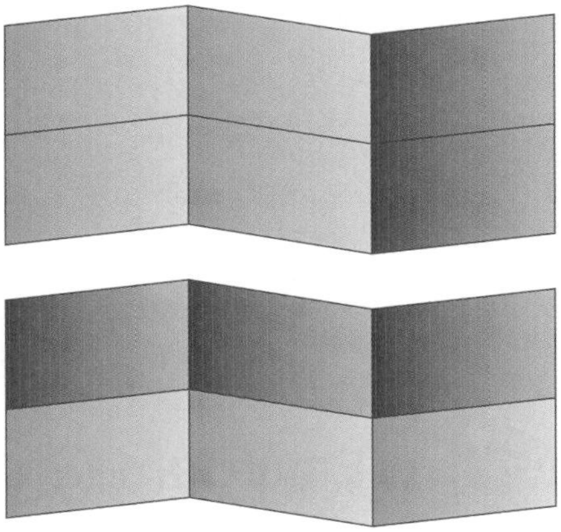

"Now, what do we see here?"

" . . . They both have the same number of pieces," Lorraine noted.

"And all the pieces are the same size," Crystal added.

"Ooh, ooh, I know!" Adam said excitedly. "We've eaten $\frac{5}{6}$ of the cake."

"That's an interesting thought, Adam. Would you explain that for us please?"

"It's like the pizza. We have two pieces there, and three pieces there, so it's $\frac{5}{6}$ of the pizza, ah cake."

"I don't get that," Mike shook his head.

"What if we cut them out, to see how many we have," Gail suggested.

"Good thought, Gail," Shirley nodded. "Let's do it. . . . Everybody cut out these pieces," she said, pointing to the marked pieces in the 'cake' on the top.

She watched as the students took out scissors from their desks and cut out the pieces.

"Now, go ahead and lay them over the other 'cake.' . . . What do you see there?"

"There are five pieces covered," John observed. "We ate $\frac{5}{6}$ of the cake alright."

"Now, let's think about what we did," Shirley continued. "What was our problem?"

" . . . We were trying to figure out how much cake we ate," Lakesha offered.

"Why was that a problem?"

"The pieces weren't the same size."

"So what did we do about it? . . . Karen?"

"We fixed them so they were the same size."

"And exactly how did we do that? . . . Bryan?"

" . . . We made the $\frac{1}{3}$ of a cake into $\frac{2}{6}$, and we made the $\frac{1}{2}$ a cake into $\frac{3}{6}$, and then we could just add them up."

Shirley then said with a grin, "You're all pretty clever. . . . Let's see how you do now," and she pulled out two more pieces of cardboard, one of which was divided into thirds and the other into fourths. She then guided the students' analysis of the second problem in the same way she had done with the first.

They then reviewed the problem as they did the first one, and Shirley said, "Tomorrow, I'll show you how we can figure out a little more quickly how to make the parts equal, so that we don't have to work as hard as we did with the ⅓ and ¼."

Finally, seeing that it was 10:52, Shirley said, "Yikes! It's nearly time for science. Put your math books and materials away, and we'll have our break."

Historically, both teachers and the public at large believe that creating an orderly classroom environment is essential for learning. For example, from 1968 until the present, national Gallup polls identified classroom management as one of the most important problems teachers face (Elam & Rose, 1995; Rose & Gallup, 1999), and as we've moved into the new millennium, concerns for safety and order have further increased in the wake of highly publicized incidents of school violence.

Although they receive enormous press coverage and arouse fear and concern in parents and students, incidents of violence in schools are rare; it's the day-to-day job of establishing and maintaining orderly, learning-focused classrooms that requires so much teacher effort.

Commonly overlooked in discussions of management and discipline is the role of effective instruction. Research indicates that it is virtually impossible to maintain an orderly classroom in the absence of good teaching and vice versa. In this chapter, we examine the results of this research and the relationship between effective instruction and classroom management.

After you've completed your study of this chapter, you should be able to meet the following objectives:

- Explain how instruction and classroom management contribute to productive learning environments.
- Identify essential teaching skills that help create productive learning environments.
- Explain how effective planning can prevent management problems.
- Identify differences between cognitive and behavioral approaches to management.
- Describe how effective intervention techniques can eliminate management problems.

Productive Environments and Learning-Focused Classrooms

Let's stop at this point and consider Shirley's classroom. It typifies conditions that many teachers face every day: She has too many students, they differ in many ways, and she never has enough time.

Despite her less-than-ideal conditions, Shirley created a classroom where learning could and did occur. She was well organized and effective in her instruction, her students were involved yet orderly, and she handled minor disruptions quickly and efficiently. Shirley created and maintained a **productive learning environment**, which is *orderly and focuses on learning*. In it students feel safe, both physically and emotionally, and the day-to-day routines—including the values, expectations, learning experiences, and both spoken and unspoken rules and conventions—are all designed to help students learn as much as possible (Tishman, Perkins, & Jay, 1995).

In productive learning environments, classroom order and effective instruction are interdependent (Doyle, 1986). As we said earlier, it is virtually impossible to maintain an orderly learning environment in the absence of effective instruction and vice versa.

Because instruction is so important in the creation of productive learning environments, we begin our discussion with it.

11.1 ▬
The need for students to feel physically and emotionally safe is emphasized as part of a productive learning environment. Using your study of motivation in Chapter 10 as a basis, explain why safety is so important.

Creating Productive Learning Environments: Effective Teaching

Imagine sitting in the back of any classroom, regardless of the grade level or the content students are learning. If the teacher is competent, what would you expect to see? Just as we're familiar with the basic skills in reading, writing, and math that all learners need, there are **essential teaching skills**, which are *the basic abilities that all teachers should have to promote order and learning, even in their first year of teaching.* Each of the essential teaching skills is correlated with increased student achievement and is derived from an extensive body of research that emerged in the 1970s and 1980s (Good & Brophy, 1986, 1997; Shuell, 1996). (Expert teachers go well beyond these essential skills as they create experiences that maximize learning for their students. We examine these approaches to instruction in Chapters 12 and 13.)

These essential teaching skills are outlined in Figure 11.1.

11.2 ▬
Figure 11.1 identifies questioning as one of the essential teaching skills. How would the questioning of an expert teacher differ from the questioning of a novice? Explain. (Hint: Think about the characteristics of expertise discussed in Chapter 8.)

Essential Teaching Skills

For the sake of clarity, we describe the essential teaching skills separately, but they are interdependent; none is as effective alone as it is in combination with the others. The interaction and integration of these skills are crucial.

Attitudes

Admittedly, "attitudes" are not skills, but we discuss them at the beginning of our coverage of essential teaching skills to emphasize that positive teacher attitudes are fundamental to effective teaching.

Teacher characteristics such as *personal teaching efficacy, modeling and enthusiasm, caring,* and *high expectations* promote learner motivation (see Chapter 10). These same characteristics are also associated with increased student achievement, which shouldn't be surprising since motivation and learning are so strongly linked (Bruning, Schraw, & Ronning, 1999; Noddings, 1999; Shuell, 1996).

In addition to these motivational characteristics, however, teachers who create productive learning environments have an additional attribute.

Democratic Teachers. Students in productive learning environments accept responsibility for their own learning and behav-

Figure 11.1 ▬

Essential teaching skills

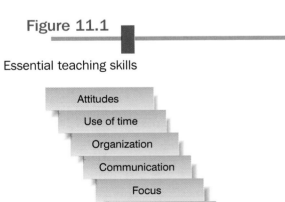

- Attitudes
- Use of time
- Organization
- Communication
- Focus
- Feedback
- Questioning
- Review and closure

ior, acquire learning strategies, and understand the reasons for classroom rules and procedures. This acceptance of responsibility for learning isn't innate; it's something students
learn, and it's best learned in a democratic environment (Slee, 1999).

Rudolph Dreikurs (1968), a psychiatrist known for his work with classroom management, argues that democratic teachers are both caring and firm. They listen and try to see
things from learners' perspectives, they create physically and emotionally safe classrooms,
and they help learners understand the reasons for classroom tasks and procedures (D.
Rogers, 1991). At the same time, they view students as responsible and hold them
accountable for their actions. Dreikurs argues that a teacher who doesn't stand firm when
a student breaks a rule communicates that the rule has no real purpose and actions don't
have consequences. These mixed messages confuse students who are trying to make
sense of the world.

11.3 ▬

What is the allocated time
for the class you're now
in? Of this time, how much
does your instructor typically devote to instruction?
Why is this an important
question?

Use of Time

In addition to having positive attitudes about students' capabilities and using democratic
practices to promote student responsibility, effective teachers increase learning by using
time effectively. Time is a valuable resource; efforts at reform have suggested lengthening
the school year, school day, and even the amount of time devoted to certain subjects (Karweit, 1989). However, improving learning through increased time isn't as simple as it
appears on the surface because, as shown in Table 11.1, different types of classroom time
influence learning in different ways.

As one moves from allocated time to academic learning time, the relationship with
learning becomes stronger (Nystrand & Gamoran, 1989). In classrooms where students
are engaged and successful, high levels of learning occur, and learners feel good about
themselves and the material they're learning (C. Fisher et al., 1980).

Unfortunately, teachers don't always use time effectively. Research indicates that a
great deal of class time is spent on noninstructional activities, often more than a third of
teachers' allocated time (Karweit, 1989). Further, some teachers seem unaware of the
value of time as a resource, thinking of it as something to be filled, or even "killed" rather
than as an opportunity to increase learning (Eggen, 1998; D. Wiley & Harnischfeger, 1974).

In our opening case, Shirley didn't fall victim to this tendency. Her students, for
instance, having made a quick and smooth transition from reading, had their math books

Table 11.1 ▬

Types of classroom time

Type	Description
Allocated time	The amount of time a teacher or school designates for a content area or topic
Instructional time	The amount left for teaching after routine management and administrative tasks are completed
Engaged time	The amount of time students are actively involved in learning activities
Academic learning time	The amount of time students are actively involved in learning activities *during which they're successful*

out and were waiting at 10:01. The class lost only 1 minute of their allocated time at the beginning of the class, and they continued until 10:52. Of the 55 minutes allocated to math, Shirley devoted 52 minutes to instruction.

The instructional ideal is to increase each of the other levels to the point where it's as close to allocated time as possible. When time is maximized, learning increases (Stallings, 1980).

Organization

Being well organized is one way of maximizing instructional time. How many times have you put something away and later can't locate it? Have you ever said, "I've simply got to get organized," or, "If he'd just get organized, he could be so effective"? Organization affects both our lives and our teaching. Teacher organization affects learning because it determines how efficiently time is used (S. Bennett, 1978; Rutter, Maughan, Mortimer, Ouston, & Smith, 1979).

Organization *includes the set of teacher actions that increase instructional time.* These characteristics are outlined in Table 11.2.

Shirley's organization allowed her to devote as much class time as possible to instruction, and, equally important, it saved her personal energy. Teachers who have their materials prepared and have established efficient routines can devote their physical energy and working memory space to thinking about and guiding student learning. This is essential for teachers as they conduct engaging and meaningful learning activities.

Organization is also important from learners' perspectives. Well-established routines are predictable and give learners a sense of order and equilibrium, all of which contribute to a productive learning environment.

Communication

The link between effective communication, student achievement, and student satisfaction with instruction is well established (Cruickshank, 1985; Snyder, et al., 1991). Also, research indicates that the way teachers interact with students influences their motivation and attitudes toward school (Pintrich & Schunk, 1996). Four aspects of effective communication are especially important for learning and motivation: (a) precise terminology, (b) connected discourse, (c) transition signals, and (d) emphasis.

Table 11.2

Characteristics of effective organization

Dimension	Example
Starting on time	Shirley's students had their math books out and were waiting by 10:01.
Preparing materials in advance	Shirley had her cardboard "cakes" prepared and waiting.
Established routines	At Shirley's signal, the students passed their papers forward without having to be told specifically to do so.

Effective organization allows teachers to make the best use of instructional time.

Precise Terminology: Using Clear Language.   **Precise terminology** *means that teachers eliminate vague terms (e.g.,* perhaps, maybe, might, and so on, *and* usually*) from their language*. When teachers use these seemingly innocuous terms in their explanations and responses to students' questions, students are left with a sense of uncertainty about the topics they're studying, and this uncertainty detracts from learning (L. Smith & Cotten, 1980). For example, suppose you asked, "What do high-efficacy teachers do that promotes learning?" and your instructor responded, "Usually, they use their time somewhat better and so on," in comparison with, "They believe they can increase learning, and one of their characteristics is the effective use of time." The first response is muddled and uncertain, whereas the second is clear and precise.

11.4 ▬
To which type of classroom time in Table 11.1 does precise terminology most closely relate? Explain. Does connected discourse imply that teachers should avoid interjecting additional material into lessons? Again, explain.

Connected Discourse: Making Relationships Clear.   **Connected discourse** *means the teacher's lesson is thematic and leads to a point*. If the point of the lesson isn't clear, if it is sequenced inappropriately, or if incidental information is interjected without indicating how it relates to the topic, classroom discourse becomes "disconnected" or "scrambled." Effective teachers keep their lessons on track, minimizing time on matters unrelated to the topic (Coker, Lorentz, & Coker, 1980; L. Smith & Cotten, 1980).

Transition Signals: Marking Changes in Topics.   **Transition signals** are *verbal statements indicating that one idea is ending and another is beginning*. For example, Shirley said, "Now, we're going to shift gears because I've got another, different kind of problem." An American government teacher might signal a transition by saying, "We've been talking about the Senate, which is one house of Congress. Now we'll turn to the House of Representatives." Because not all students are at the same place mentally, a transition signal alerts them that the lesson is making a conceptual shift—moving to a new topic—and allows them to adjust and prepare for it.

Emphasis: Signaling Important Ideas.   **Emphasis**, a fourth aspect of effective communication, *alerts students to important information in a lesson and is communicated* *through verbal and vocal cues and repetition.* Teachers influence what students learn by emphasizing it (Jetton & Alexander, 1997). For example, Shirley raised her voice—a form of vocal emphasis—in saying, "Let's keep that in mind as we study some more problems." When teachers say, "Now remember, everyone, this is very important . . . ," or, "Listen carefully now," they're using verbal emphasis.

Repeating a point—redundancy—is also a form of emphasis. For instance, "What did we say earlier that these problems had in common?" reminds students of an important feature in the problems and helps them link new to past information. Redundancy is particularly effective when reviewing abstract rules, principles, and concepts (Brophy & Good, 1986; Shuell, 1996).

Communication and Knowledge of Content: Implications for Teachers. Our discussion of communication has two implications for teachers. First, teachers should monitor their own speech to ensure that their presentations are as clear and logical as possible. Videotaping and reviewing lessons and developing lessons with many questions are simple and effective ways to improve clarity. Second, teachers must thoroughly understand the content they teach. If the content is unfamiliar, or if the teacher's own grasp of it is uncertain, the teacher should spend extra time studying and preparing. Teachers whose understanding of topics is thorough use clearer language, their discourse is more connected, and they provide better explanations than those whose background is weaker (Carlsen, 1987; Cruickshank, 1985).

Clear understanding is particularly important when teachers guide learners instead of lecturing to them. Guiding learning requires that teachers constantly keep their goals in mind, keep students involved, and ask appropriate questions at the right times. These are sophisticated abilities that require a deep and thorough understanding of the topics.

Focus: Attracting and Maintaining Attention

We saw in Chapter 10 that **introductory focus** *attracts students' attention and provides a framework for the lesson.* In addition to attracting attention, it can increase motivation by arousing curiosity and making lesson content interesting.

Shirley provided introductory focus for her students by showing them the two "cakes" and saying, " . . . I've got a problem," and, "How much cake have I eaten?" Her "cakes," together with her problem, attracted students' attention and provided a context for the rest of the lesson.

Shirley's "cakes" also acted as a form of **sensory focus**, which is *the use of stimuli—concrete objects, pictures, models, materials displayed on the overhead, and even information written on the chalkboard—to maintain attention.* Her "cakes" gave students something to focus on and provided a mental model to help them conceptualize an abstract idea. Jenny Newhall's demonstration with the cup and water in Chapter 2, her balances in Chapter 7, and Suzanne Brush's graph in Chapter 8 all provided different forms of sensory focus. Sensory focus serves as a continual reminder of the lesson's topic and direction.

Feedback

The importance of **feedback**—*information learners receive about the accuracy or appropriateness of a response*—in promoting learning is well documented (Weinert & Helmke, 1995). Feedback gives learners information about the validity of their knowledge constructions, and from both information processing and constructivist perspectives, feedback allows learners to assess the accuracy of their background knowledge. It also

11.5 Think about your study of Chapter 7. What concept is being illustrated when learners link new to past information or create new links in what they already understand?

11.6 Identify one important difference between introductory and sensory focus.

helps learners elaborate on their existing understanding. Feedback is also important for motivation (see Chapter 10) because it helps satisfy learners' intrinsic need to understand how they're progressing and why (Clifford, 1990).

Effective feedback has four essential characteristics:

| It is immediate.
| It is specific.
| It provides corrective information for the learner.
| It has a positive emotional tone. (Brophy & Good, 1986; Murphy, Weil, & McGreal, 1986)

To illustrate these characteristics, let's look at three examples.

Mr. Dole:	What kind of figure is shown on the overhead, Jo?
Jo:	A square.
Mr. Dole:	Not quite. Help her out, . . . Steve?
Ms. West:	What kind of figure is shown on the overhead, Jo?
Jo:	A square.
Ms. West:	No, it's a rectangle. What is the next figure, . . . Albert?
Ms. Baker:	What kind of figure is shown on the overhead, Jo?
Jo:	A square.
Ms. Baker:	No, remember we said that all sides have the same length in a square. What do you notice about the lengths of the sides in this figure?

We see that the feedback is *immediate* in each case, but Mr. Dole gave Jo no information about her answer other than it was incorrect; it was not *specific* and provided no *corrective information*. Ms. West's feedback was specific, but it gave Jo no corrective information. Ms. Baker, in contrast, provided specific, corrective information in her response to Jo.

The examples give us no information about the emotional tone of the teachers' responses. Positive emotional tone means that teachers are supportive in their responses to student answers. Harsh, critical, or sarcastic feedback detracts from both learning and student motivation (Pintrich & Schunk, 1996).

Praise.   Praise is probably the most common and adaptable form of teacher feedback. Research reveals some interesting patterns in teachers' use of praise:

| Praise is used less often than most teachers believe—less than five times per class.
| Praise for good behavior is quite rare, occurring once every 2 or more hours in the elementary grades and even less as students get older.
| Praise tends to depend as much on the type of student—high achieving, well behaved, and attentive—as on the quality of the student's response.
| Teachers praise students based on the answers they expect to receive as much as on those they actually hear. (Brophy, 1981)

Using praise effectively is complex and requires sound teacher judgment (see Figure 11.2). For example, it must be perceived as sincere to be credible, but effusive praise after every answer loses its credibility even if the teacher is sincere. This is particularly true with older students, who tend to discount praise they perceive as invalid and interpret praise given for easy tasks as indicating that the teacher thinks they're not intelligent (Emmer, 1988; Good, 1987a).

11.7 ▬

Research indicates that the emotional tone of feedback is important. On the basis of the model for promoting student motivation (in Chapter 10), explain why a positive emotional tone is important.

Figure 11.2

Characteristics of effective praise

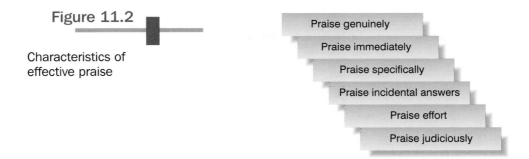

Praise genuinely
Praise immediately
Praise specifically
Praise incidental answers
Praise effort
Praise judiciously

11.8
What two concepts from Piaget's theory are being illustrated when young children tend to take praise at face value and bask openly in it in front of a class? Explain.

On the other hand, young children tend to take praise at face value and bask in praise given openly in front of a class, whereas junior high students may react better if it's given quietly and individually (Stipek, 1984). High-anxiety students and those from low-socioeconomic status (SES) backgrounds tend to react more positively to praise than their more confident and advantaged counterparts.

Finally, although research indicates that specific praise is more effective than general praise, if every desired answer is praised specifically, it begins to sound stilted and artificial, disrupting the flow of a lesson. You must judge the appropriate mix of specific and general praise.

Experts suggest that praise for student answers that are delivered with confidence should be simple and general (Rosenshine, 1987). In contrast, praise for student answers that are correct but tentative should be specific and provide additional or affirming information.

Written Feedback.   While much of the feedback students receive is verbal, teachers also provide valuable feedback through their notes and comments on student work. Because writing detailed comments is time-consuming, written feedback is often brief and sketchy, giving students little useful information (Bloom & Bourdon, 1980).

One solution to this problem is to provide model responses to written assignments. For instance, to help students evaluate their answers to essay items, teachers can write ideal answers and share them with the class, allowing students to compare their answers with the model. The model, combined with discussion and time available for individual help after school, provides valuable feedback yet is manageable for the teacher.

Questioning

As instruction has become more learner centered in response to the cognitive revolution in general and constructivism in particular, teachers are increasingly being asked to guide learning rather than to simply deliver information.

Questioning is the most important tool teachers have for guiding students as students construct their understanding (Wang, Haertel, & Walberg, 1993). A teacher skilled in questioning can assess student background knowledge, cause learners to rethink their ideas, help them form relationships, involve shy or reticent students, recapture students' wandering attention, promote success, and enhance self-esteem. Questioning can also be a tool to maintain the pace and momentum of a lesson, and research indicates that lesson momentum is an important factor in maintaining student engagement (Kounin, 1970).

Becoming skilled in questioning is difficult, but with effort and experience, teachers can and do become expert at it (Kerman, 1979; Rowe, 1986). To avoid overloading their

Questioning is an essential skill
for guiding students' learning.

own working memories, teachers need to practice questioning strategies to the point that they're essentially automatic, leaving working memory space available to monitor students' thinking and assess learning progress.

Effective questioning has four characteristics:

- Frequency
- Equitable distribution
- Prompting
- Wait time

Frequency.   Referring back to Shirley's lesson, she asked a large number of questions. In fact, she developed much of her lesson through questioning. **Questioning frequency** *refers to the number of questions teachers ask*, and research indicates that more effective teachers ask more questions (Morine-Dershimer, 1987). Questioning increases student involvement, which increases achievement (Lambert & McCombs, 1998), and increasing involvement also increases a learner's sense of autonomy and motivation (see Chapter 10).

Equitable Distribution.   Merely asking a lot of questions isn't enough, however. If the same students are answering all of the questions, others become inattentive, and overall achievement suffers. **Equitable distribution** *describes a questioning pattern in which all students in the class are called on as equally as possible* (Kerman, 1979). Research indicates that the majority of teacher questions are not directed to individuals (McGreal, 1985), so the highest achieving and most aggressive students answer most of them, and less vocal or less aggressive students fall into a pattern of not responding, becoming inattentive, with motivation and achievement suffering (Brophy & Evertson, 1974). "Teachers who restrict their questions primarily to a small group of active (and usually high-achieving) students are likely to communicate undesirable expectations . . . and generally to be less aware and less effective" (Good & Brophy, 1997, p. 378).

One solution is to call on all students as equally as possible, and *direct questions to students by name*. This promotes equitable distribution and prevents a vocal minority from dominating. Equitable distribution communicates to students that the teacher expects all students to be involved and participating. When this becomes a pattern, achievement and motivation improve for both high and low achievers, and classroom management problems decrease (McDougall & Granby, 1996; Shuell, 1996).

Shirley, at the beginning of the chapter, was effective in applying this research. For example, during her short review, she called on Dean, Emerson, Kevin, Gayle, and Estella; she continued this pattern of involving a broad array of students throughout the lesson; and her instruction never strayed from the lesson's goal.

This pattern is particularly important in teaching diverse learners. For example, by calling on all her students, Shirley communicated, "I don't care if you're African American, Latino, Asian, white, boy, or girl. I don't care if you're gifted or have a learning disability. I expect you to participate, and I expect you to learn." Nothing better communicates that the teacher and all the students are "in this together."

Equitable distribution is a simple idea but difficult to implement. It requires careful monitoring of students and a great deal of teacher energy. However, its effects can be very powerful for both learning and motivation, and we strongly encourage you to persevere and pursue it rigorously.

Prompting.   In attempting equitable distribution, an important question arises. What do you do when the student you call on doesn't answer or answers incorrectly? The answer is prompting. A **prompt** is *a teacher question or directive that elicits a student response after the student has failed to answer or has given an incorrect or incomplete answer,* and it's importance is well documented by research (Brophy & Good, 1986; Shuell, 1996). As an illustration, let's look again at Shirley's lesson:

Shirley:	What does the 8 mean in the first problem? . . . Dean?
Dean:	We have eight parts of something altogether.
Shirley:	Parts of what?
Dean:	Supposed to be pizza.
Shirley:	And what kind of parts? . . . Emerson?
Emerson:	. . .
Shirley:	How do the parts compare to each other?
Emerson:	. . . They're all equal.

This sequence illustrates a simple, but particularly effective technique in eliciting responses from students. Shirley combined an open-ended question—"How do the parts compare to each other?"—with something that the students could see, a form of sensory focus. **Open-ended questions** are *those for which a variety of answers are acceptable* (see Chapter 10), and Shirley used them effectively in involving Emerson in the lesson.

Wait-Time.   After asking a question, teachers need to wait a few seconds for an answer, giving students time to think. *This period of silence, both before and after a student responds*, is called **wait-time**, and research indicates that in most classrooms, it is too short, typically, less than 1 second (Rowe, 1986).

A more intuitively sensible label for wait-time might be "think-time" because in reality waiting actually gives the student time, ideally at least 3 to 5 seconds, to think. This practice has at least three benefits (Rowe, 1974, 1986):

11.9 ▬
Equitable distribution most directly applies to which *two* of the variables in the model for promoting student motivation, discussed in Chapter 10? Explain.

11.10 ▬
Most teachers, instead of prompting, turn the question to another student, and the student initially asked the question becomes even more reluctant to respond. What concept from behaviorism explains this increasing reluctance?

▌ Students give longer and better responses.
▌ Voluntary participation increases, and fewer students fail to respond.
▌ Equitable distribution improves, and responses from cultural minorities increase as teachers become more responsive to students.

Wait-time must be implemented judiciously, however. For example, if students are practicing basic skills, such as multiplication facts, quick answers are desirable, and wait-times should be short (Rosenshine & Stevens, 1986). Also, if a student appears uneasy, the teacher may choose to intervene earlier. However, students need time to respond to higher-level questions asking them to compare, apply, analyze, or evaluate information. In general, increasing wait-time reduces rather than increases student anxiety because a climate of positive expectations and support is established. All students are expected to participate, they're given time to think about their responses, and they know that the teacher will help them if they're unable to answer.

Cognitive Levels of Questions.   The kinds of questions teachers ask also influence learning. Which are better: low-level questions that require mere recall, or high-level questions that demand considerable student thought? The cognitive levels of teacher questions have been widely researched, but, surprisingly, the results are mixed. Both low-level questions (e.g., knowledge on Bloom's taxonomy; Bloom, Englehart, Furst, Hill, & Krathwohl, 1956) and high-level questions (e.g., application and synthesis in Bloom's taxonomy) correlate positively with achievement, depending on the teaching situation (Good & Brophy, 1997). (We discuss Bloom's taxonomy in Chapter 12.)

These seemingly contradictory results can be explained on the basis of teachers' goals. If the goal is automaticity with basic skills, low-level questions may be most effective. However, if the teacher wants students to analyze factors leading up to the Revolutionary War, for example, high-level questions are more effective. Teachers' first concerns should be what they are trying to accomplish—their goals—not the level of questions they choose to ask. When goals are clear, appropriate questions follow.

Review and Closure

Lessons are more coherent when review and closure are used to summarize and pull ideas together. **Review** *summarizes previous work and helps students link what has been learned to what is coming. It can occur at any point in a lesson,* although it is most common at the beginning and end. Effective reviews emphasize important points and encourage elaboration; in Shirley's lesson, students reviewed adding fractions with like denominators and then used this information to understand the need for making the pieces of "cake" equal, as a step toward learning to add fractions with unlike denominators. Effective reviews involve more than simple rehearsal; they shift the learner's attention away from verbatim details to deeper conceptual connections in the material being studied (Dempster, 1991).

Closure is *a form of review occurring at the end of a lesson; in it, topics are summarized and integrated.* The notion of closure is intuitively sensible; it pulls content together and signals the end of a lesson. When concepts are being taught, an effective form of closure is to have students state a definition of the concept or identify additional examples. This leaves them with the essence of the topic, providing a foundation for later lessons.

This completes our discussion of instructional factors that contribute to productive classroom learning environments. In the next section, we turn our attention to classroom management and how it influences those environments.

Classroom Connections

Demonstrating Professional Attitudes in Your Classroom

1. Have high expectations for all students, and show them you are committed to their learning.
   - A geometry teacher, knowing that her students initially have trouble with proofs, offers help sessions twice a week after school.
   - A third-grade teacher calls a student's parents and solicits their help as soon as the student fails to turn in an assignment or receives an unsatisfactory grade on a quiz or test.

2. Commit yourself to being a positive role model for students.
   - A seventh-grade teacher displays the statement "I will always try to behave in the way I expect you to behave in this class" on the bulletin board, and she uses it as a guiding principle in her class.

Maximizing Instructional Time in Your Classroom

3. Carefully plan and organize materials to maximize instructional time. Avoid spending class time gathering and displaying materials.
   - A first-grade teacher has several boxes filled with frequently used science materials, such as soft drink bottles, balloons, matches, baking soda, vinegar, funnels, and a hot plate. The night before a science demonstration, she spends a few minutes selecting her materials from the boxes and sets them on the shelf near her desk so that she'll have everything ready at the beginning of the lesson.

4. Begin lessons on time; give students a short assignment or problem while you conduct your beginning routines.
   - An English teacher displays a paragraph on the overhead at the beginning of the class period and asks students to identify and correct all the mechanical errors in it.

   - An algebra teacher gives students a problem that is slightly more difficult than their homework assignment and has them solve it while she takes roll.

Demonstrating Essential Teaching Skills in Your Classroom

5. Monitor your communication to make your presentations clear and concise.
   - A second-grade teacher videotapes a lesson she conducts with her students and then studies the tape to check her language and nonverbal communication.
   - A ninth-grade American government teacher asks colleagues to visit his class and check whether he clearly emphasizes the important points in the lesson, sequences the presentation logically, and communicates changes in topics.

6. Use problems, demonstrations, and displays to provide introductory and sensory focus during lessons.
   - A science teacher dealing with the concept of kindling temperature soaks a cloth in a water–alcohol mix, ignites it, and asks, "Why isn't the cloth burning?"
   - A life science teacher beginning a study of arthropods brings a live lobster to class and builds the lesson around the lobster's characteristics.

7. Begin and end each class with a short review.
   - An English teacher begins, "We studied pronoun–antecedent agreement yesterday. Give me an example that illustrates this idea, and explain why your example is correct."
   - A fifth-grade teacher whose class is studying different types of boundaries says, "We've looked at three kinds of boundaries between the states so far today. What are the three, and where do they occur?"

Technology and Learning: Increasing the Productivity of Learning Environments

Over the years, we've heard a great deal about basic skills—the abilities in reading, writing, and math that everyone must have in order to function effectively in today's world. The essential teaching skills that we described in the first section of the chapter, combined with orderly classrooms, are analogous to basic skills; *if students are to learn as much as possible, all classrooms must be productive learning environments.*

As we've moved into the new century, the ability to use technology has also become a basic skill, which means that productive learning environments will include technology.

But, how should this technology be integrated with curriculum and instruction? While definitive answers don't exist, and experts disagree on some of the issues, research gives us a start.

The Need for Clear Goals

As with all aspects of teaching, in thinking about technology, the first issue we should consider is our goals (Harrington-Lueker, 1997). As an example, a few years ago, the CBS news magazine *60 Minutes* reported that a large Midwestern school system—in an effort to increase student achievement—spent a great deal of money to place several computers in every classroom throughout the district. What followed this massive infusion of technology was a *decrease* in standardized test scores. Almost certainly, the reason test scores went down was that the district wasn't clear about their goals; they didn't know how the technology was to be used to increase the scores.

We should emphasize that raising standardized test scores is not the only appropriate goal that exists for using technology; this district's problem was that their thinking wasn't clear about their goals and about how they were going to use technology to reach those goals.

Effective teachers integrate technology into their classrooms by strategically using it to accomplish meaningful classroom goals.

In another case, our national leaders have said that all students should have access to the Internet. As teachers, we should be thinking and asking about the purposes in being on the Internet and what students will be doing with the information they gather. Simply "surfing the 'Net" for it's own sake isn't an effective goal.

Good and Bad Reasons for Using Technology

In viewing technology as a basic skill, we must ask questions about it that apply to all classrooms, just as basic skills apply to all learners and as essential teaching skills apply to all teachers. Using these ideas as the context for our thinking, at least two reasons exist for using technology: (a) the development of technological literacy and (b) increased learning and motivation (Roblyer & Edwards, 2000).

Technological Literacy.   Learning about technology in schools prepares students for life in a technological society. Learners now exist in a world that requires an understanding of technology, and the need for increased understanding is accelerating. We're at the point where all learners should have basic technology skills, such as word processing; communicating via e-mail; accessing the Internet; and the ability to create spreadsheets, databases, hypermedia, and use tools like PowerPoint (Roblyer & Edwards, 2000; Volker, 1992).

Perhaps more importantly, students need basic technology learning abilities. These are the abilities needed to adapt to technological change, which is occurring so rapidly that existing technology becomes dated almost before the discussion of it is complete. Nothing in our world is changing as fast.

Increased Learning and Motivation.   Increased learning and motivation is the obvious second reason for using technology. If teachers' goals are clear and appropriate, we can base our decisions on the following principle: *If students learn more or are more motivated to learn when technology is used than when it is not, then its use is desirable*. If learning and motivation are not positively affected, then the time, effort, and expense may not justify it.

Research provides some direction with respect to this principle. For instance, technology can be used to represent topics that are difficult to represent in traditional ways (see Chapter 7), and technology can be used to make problems more authentic and applied to the real world (see Chapter 8).

Research provides some additional perspectives. For instance, students often learn content more quickly in computer-based environments than they do with traditional instruction, and self-efficacy and involvement often increase and attitude improves in classes where technology is used (see Chapter 10) (Kulik, 1994; McKinnon, 1997).

Research also indicates that adding variety to learning activities increases student motivation (Brophy, 1986a), and technology can be effective for providing this variety. Using technology to create variety can be particularly effective in providing alternatives to page and pencil practice during seat work.

Bad Reasons for Using Technology.   You've seen how technology can become an integral part of a productive learning environment. However, if teachers' goals aren't clear, technology can be misused. For example, if competing with other teachers, keeping students busy, or impressing the principal or parents is the (tacit) goal, technology isn't being used effectively (Roblyer & Edwards, 2000).

Other misuses are more subtle. For instance, Van Horn (1997) reports a case where a number of teachers had access to software illustrating the characteristics of rainforests.

11.11

Research indicates that students using computers compose better quality essays than those who don't use computers only when their word processing skills are well developed. If their word processing skills are not well developed, they compose poorer quality essays. Using your understanding of information processing from Chapter 7 as a basis, explain why this is the case.

The schools where the teachers taught existed in rich natural ecosystems, yet the teachers had the students spend a great deal of time with the software instead of investigating their own environments. Using technology "because it's there," as these teachers did, is inappropriate, Van Horn argues.

Improving the Productivity of Learning Environments With Technology: Some Guidelines

Given the research just discussed, some guidelines can help us ensure that technology makes our learning environments more, rather than less, productive:

> ▌ *Set clear goals* (Harrington-Lueker, 1997; Van Horn, 1997). If goals aren't clear, technology is no more effective than any instruction in which a mismatch between goals and learning activities exists.
> ▌ *Be sure learners are using technology actively,* as in the problem-solving activities described in Chapter 8. If computers, for example, are little more than "electronic flashcard machines," (Carlson & Silverman, 1986), learners are involved in shallow information processing, they're relatively passive, and they're little better off than they would be without the computers.
> ▌ *Match technology to students' background knowledge* (Lambert & McCombs, 1998). A mismatch is no more effective when technology is used than it would be in the absence of technology.
> ▌ *Provide for social interaction* (Turner & Dipinto, 1997). Discussions between the teacher and students, and between students are as important when technology is used as they are without technology. (We examine the effectiveness of combining technology and cooperative learning in Chapter 13.)

Finally, technology doesn't replace teachers (Jerry & Ballator, 1999), and it isn't a panacea. Technology changes teachers' roles, but teachers remain the best judge of learning progress and what adaptations are necessary in learning activities.

Used properly, technology has enormous potential. Used improperly, it can detract from learning. It must be implemented with thought and care by expert teachers who understand its limitations.

11.12 ▬
Of the theories of learning you've studied so far, which best explains the need for social interaction? Explain why it is necessary using this theory.

Creating Productive Learning Environments: Classroom Management

Essential teaching skills describe the abilities that all teachers, regardless of topic taught or grade level, should possess. We now want to see how classroom management complements these skills to promote productive learning environments.

Classroom Management and Discipline

Some of the most basic research on classroom management was done by Jacob Kounin (1970), who concluded that the key to orderly classrooms is the teacher's ability to prevent behavior problems from occurring in the first place, rather than handling misbehavior once it happens. These findings have been consistently corroborated over the years (Freiberg, 1999).

Kounin's original research was important because it encouraged educators to separate the concepts of **classroom management**, which *refers to teachers' strategies that create and maintain an orderly learning environment*, and **discipline**, which *involves teacher responses to student misbehavior.* Management attempts to prevent problems; discipline deals with these problems when they occur.

The relationship between classroom management and learning is well documented. A comprehensive review of research on the topic concluded, "Effective classroom management has been shown to increase student engagement, decrease disruptive behaviors, and enhance use of instructional time, all of which results in improved student achievement" (Wang et al., 1993, p. 262). Additional research has identified well-managed classrooms as one of the characteristics of an effective school (S. Purkey & Smith, 1983).

Classroom management is also related to learner motivation (Radd, 1998). Order and safety are necessary to promote student motivation (see Chapter 10), and Brophy (1987a) identified classroom management as an "essential precondition for motivating students" (p. 208). Also, by seeking student input on instructional and management issues, teachers can increase learners' feelings of autonomy, which also increase motivation (see Chapter 10) (McLaughlin, 1994).

> **11.13** ▬
> Identify at least one way in which orderly classrooms contribute to learning. Identify at least one way in which orderly classrooms contribute to motivation. Explain in each case.

Cognitive Approaches to Management: Developing Learner Responsibility

Cognitive approaches to management focus on learner understanding, and emphasis is placed on the reasons for rules and procedures, not merely on obeying them because they exist. From an information processing perspective, classroom management can contribute to self-regulation by being "one vehicle for the enhancement of student self-understanding, self-evaluation, and the internalization of self-control" (McCaslin & Good, 1992, p. 8). These are metacognitive factors and metacognition plays an essential monitoring function in information processing (see Chapter 7).

From a constructivist perspective, learners construct their own understanding of rules and procedures, just as they construct understanding of concepts, principles, and other forms of content. During this process, they construct understanding of what it means to be responsible, why rules and procedures are necessary, and their role in contributing to a productive learning environment. This understanding evolves from discussions of reasons for rules and procedures and from examples of appropriate and inappropriate behavior (Blumenfeld, Pintrich, & Hamilton, 1987; Nelson, 1996).

Cognitive approaches to management are both sensible and practical. Learners are more likely to obey rules when they understand the reasons for them, one of which is to protect their rights and the rights of others. Research indicates that this responsibility orientation can also contribute to ethical development (DeVries & Zan, 1995; Kohn, 1996).

> **11.14** ▬
> Suppose a student accepts the responsibility for obeying a rule, reasoning that it is necessary to protect her and her peers' rights. At which of Kohlberg's stages of moral development is the student reasoning? (See Chapter 3.) Explain.

Planning for Effective Classroom Management

In some classrooms, the management system is nearly invisible. The atmosphere is calm but not rigid, movement and interaction are comfortable, and students work quietly. Teachers hardly seem concerned with management as an issue. They give few directions that focus on behavior, they reprimand students infrequently, and the reprimands they do give rarely intrude on learning. Are these ideal situations? Of course. Are they impossible to achieve? No.

Obviously, some classes are tougher to manage than others, and, in a few cases, it may be difficult to reach the ideals just described. In most instances, however, an orderly classroom is possible, but it doesn't happen by accident. It requires careful planning, and beginning teachers often underestimate the amount of time and energy it takes (Bullough, 1989; C. Weinstein, Woolfolk, Dittmeier, & Shankar, 1994).

The cornerstone of an effective management system is a well-conceived and well-administered set of rules and procedures (Emmer, Evertson, Clements, & Worsham, 2000; Evertson, Emmer, Clements, & Worsham, 2000). In planning rules and procedures, teachers must consider both the characteristics of their students and the physical environment of their classrooms. The relationship among these factors is illustrated in Figure 11.3.

Student Characteristics

Sam Cramer had completed his first semester's observation and tutoring in a high school, and it had been a terrific experience. He had taught several lessons, and, except for the occasional rough spot, they had gone well. Students were interested and responded when involved. Management was not a problem.

For his second semester, Sam moved to a middle school. It seemed like a different planet. Students were bubbling with excess energy. Giggling, whispering, and note passing were constant distractions. His first lesson was a disaster. They wouldn't let him teach!

From your study of development in Chapters 2 and 3, you know that students think, act, and feel differently at different stages of intellectual, psychosocial, and moral development. As Sam learned the hard way, students at different grade levels vary in the way they interpret and respond to rules and procedures, and teachers must anticipate these differences as they plan. Descriptions of developmental differences that influence management are outlined in Table 11.3.

Keep in mind that these are general characteristics and individual classrooms and students will vary. As a pattern, however, we see increasing independence and self-regulation as learners develop. Their reliance on and affection for teachers decreases, and they become more likely to question authority. The process peaks in early adolescence, when students' responses to their own physical, emotional, and intellectual changes are most uncertain. During the high school years, students begin to behave like young adults and respond well to being treated as such. Students of all ages, however, need the emotional security of knowing that their teachers are genuinely interested in them as people and sincerely care about their learning.

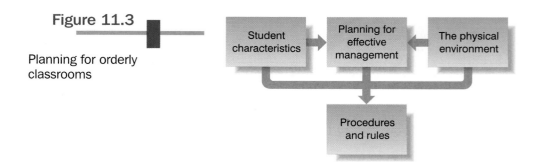

Figure 11.3

Planning for orderly classrooms

Table 11.3

Learner characteristics affecting classroom management

Stage	Student Characteristics
Stage 1: Kindergarten through grade 2	• Are compliant, eager to please teachers • Have short attention span, tire easily • Are restless, wander around room • Require close supervision • Break rules because they forget • Need rules and procedures to be explicitly taught, practiced, and reinforced
Stage 2: Grades 3 through 6	• Are increasingly independent, but still like attention and affection from teachers • Respond well to concrete incentives (e.g., stickers, free time), as well as praise and recognition • Understand need for rules and accept consequences; enjoy participating in rule-making process • Know how far they can push • Need rules to be reviewed and consistently and impartially enforced
Stage 3: Grades 7 through 9	• Attempt to test independence; are sometimes rebellious and capricious • Need firm foundation of stability; explicit boundaries and predictable outcomes are critical • Need rules clearly stated and administered
Stage 4: Grades 10 and above	• Behave more stably than in previous stage • Communicate effectively adult to adult • Respond to clear rationales for rules

Source: Learning From Teaching: A Developmental Perspective, by J. Brophy and C. Evertson, 1976, Boston: Allyn & Bacon. Copyright 1976 by Allyn & Bacon. Adapted with permission. Brophy, J., and Evertson, C. 1978. "Content Variables in Teaching," *Educational Psychologist, 12,* 310–316.

The Physical Environment

"I can't see the board."

"Fred tripped me."

"What? I can't hear."

Few classrooms are ideal. Classes are too large, storage space is limited, and, when used, maps or overhead projector screens cover the chalkboard. For many teachers, arranging desks and furnishings is a compromise between what they would like and what is possible.

Three aspects of the physical environment should be considered when teachers plan (Evertson, 1987):

‖ *Visibility.*   The room must be arranged so that all students can see the chalkboard, overhead projector, or other displays.

‖ *Accessibility.*   The room should be designed so that access to high-traffic areas, such as the pencil sharpener and places students put papers, are kept clear and separated from each other.

Teachers need to design their classrooms to ensure that the physical environment contributes to learning.

11.15 ▬

Beginning teachers' writing on the board is often too small for students—particularly those at the back of the room—to see, yet the teachers seem to be unaware of this possibility. Using your understanding of Chapter 7 as a basis, explain why beginning teachers may have this tendency.

▌ *Distractibility.* Desks should be arranged so that potential distractions, such as movement visible through doors and windows, are minimized.

Research indicates that no single arrangement works for all situations. One study found that behavior improved and quantity of work increased when learners were seated in rows (N. Bennett & Blundel, 1983), but another found that a semicircle was most effective for discussions (Rosenfield, Lambert, & Black, 1985). Teachers should think about the desk arrangement when they plan and then experiment to see what works best for them.

Establishing Procedures

Having considered the characteristics of your students and your classroom environment, you're ready to plan the procedures and rules for your classroom. **Procedures** *establish the routines students will follow in their daily activities,* such as how students pass in papers, sharpen their pencils, and make transitions from one activity to another.

As an example, let's look again at Shirley's class. When she told the students to turn in their writing, they passed the papers forward, each putting his or hers on top of the stack without being told to do so. It was a well-practiced procedure.

Expert teachers, to a much greater extent than novices, plan and teach procedures until they become routines that students follow automatically, and these routines provide a sense of regularity and equilibrium (Borko & Putnam, 1996). For example, teaching students what they are expected to do after completing assignments and how late or missing homework will be handled are essential procedures for all classrooms. These may seem minor, but they affect the efficiency of the classroom and communicate that learning is the primary purpose of school.

Creating Effective Rules

Rules *provide standards for acceptable behavior,* such as, "Listen when someone else is talking," and research confirms their value in creating an orderly environment (Emmer et al., 2000; Evertson et al., 2000); "Evidence exists indicating that clear, reasonable rules, fairly and consistently enforced, not only can reduce behavior problems that interfere with learning but also can promote a feeling of pride and responsibility in the school community" (S. Purkey & Smith, 1983, p. 445). Students in effective schools see rules and teachers as fair and necessary even if they don't like some individual rules and penalties (Wayson & Lasley, 1984).

The cornerstone of a cognitive approach to rules is learner understanding. Learners must understand the reasons behind rules if we expect them to accept responsibility for their own behavior. Some guidelines for establishing effective rules include (Evertson, 1987)

- *Provide rationales for rules.*   It's impossible for students to understand the importance of a rule if they haven't been given a reason for it's existence, and students who understand reasons for rules are more likely to obey them.
- *Allow student input.*   Cooperative rule setting promotes feelings of ownership and autonomy, increasing the likelihood that students will obey the rules, and it promotes moral development by treating students as moral thinkers (DeVries & Zan, 1995; Kohn, 1996).
- *Keep class and school rules consistent.*   This self-evident suggestion reminds teachers that they should review district and school rules before creating their own.
- *State rules positively.*   "Listen when someone else is talking" is preferable to "Don't interrupt," for example. Positively stated rules specify desired behavior; rules stated negatively only identify what students are not to do.
- *Keep the list short.*   For rules to be effective, students must be constantly aware of them and must instantly know when they break one. The most common reason students break rules is that they simply forget!

Table 11.4 contains some examples of different types of rules at the elementary, middle, and secondary levels.

You must decide what rules will work best for you. The basis for this decision is the kind of learning environment you want to create and the kind of relationship you want to have with your students.

> **11.16**
> We said students must instantly know when they break a rule. "Instantly knowing" relates to what concept from your study of information processing in Chapter 7?

Table 11.4

Examples of teachers' rules

First-Grade Teacher	Seventh-Grade Teacher	Tenth-Grade Teacher
• We raise our hands before speaking.	• Be in your seat and quiet when the bell rings.	• Be in your seat before the bell rings.
• We leave our seats only when given permission by the teacher.	• Follow directions the first time they're given.	• Stay in your seat at all times.
• We stand politely in line at all times.	• Bring covered textbooks, notebook, pen, pencils, and planner to class every day.	• Bring all materials daily. This includes your book, notebook, pen/pencil, and paper.
• We keep our hands to ourselves.	• Raise your hand for permission to speak or to leave your seat.	• Give your full attention to others in discussions, and wait your turn to speak.
• We listen when someone else is talking.	• Keep hands, feet, and objects to yourself.	• Leave when I dismiss you, not the bell.
	• Leave class only when dismissed by the teacher.	
	• Do all grooming outside of class.	

Classroom rules establish
standards for behavior that
allow learning to take place.

Making Rules and Procedures Work

So far, you've seen how instruction and classroom order are interdependent, effective teachers prevent rather than solve management problems whenever possible, and planning is important in this process. Now we turn to putting these plans into practice. We emphasize three important points:

- Behavior patterns are established in the first few days of school.
- Rules and procedures must be carefully taught.
- Rules and procedures must be constantly monitored.

Beginning the School Year

Research consistently supports the idea that the patterns of behavior for the year are established in the first few days of school (Doyle, 1986; Evertson et al., 2000).

> The first day of school has special significance for both teachers and students. At this time, rules, routines, and expectations are established. Students' first impressions about their classrooms, their teachers, and expected standards can have a lasting effect on their attitudes and on the ways they will engage in classroom tasks (Evertson, 1987, p. 69).

Effective teachers realize this and are ready to go from the first bell of the first day.

> Vicki Williams was organizing her handouts on the first day of class. Her eighth graders came into the room; some took their seats, while others milled around, talking in small groups. As the bell rang, she looked up and said over the hum of the students, "Everyone take your seats, please," and she turned back to finish organizing her materials.

> Donnell Alexander was waiting at the door for her eighth graders and had also prepared handouts. As the students came in, she said, "Take your seats quickly, please. You'll find your name on the desk. The bell is going to ring in less than a minute, and everyone must be at his or her desk and quiet when it does. Please read the handout while you're waiting." She was standing at the front of the room, surveying the class as the bell rang. When it stopped, Donnell began, "Good morning, everyone."

In these first few minutes, Vicki's and Donnell's students learned some important ideas about the way their classes would be run. From Vicki they learned, "Being in your seat at the beginning of the period isn't important," whereas Donnell's message was, "Be ready to start when the bell rings." Students quickly understand these differences and, unless Vicki changes her pattern, she will soon have problems—not dramatic perhaps, but chronic and low grade that, like nagging sniffles, won't go away. These kinds of problems cause more teacher stress and fatigue than any other.

Guidelines for beginning the first few days of school are summarized in Table 11.5.

Teaching Rules and Procedures

We've emphasized that cognitive approaches to classroom management focus on learner understanding. They treat procedures and rules as concepts and emphasize construction of understanding, just as learners construct understanding of any concept. Learners construct understanding from examples and discussions (see Chapter 7)(Cassady, 1999; Spiro, Feltovich, Jacobson, & Coulson, 1992). Let's see how Martha Oaks, a first-grade teacher, taught one of her procedures.

> I put each of their names, as well as my own, on a cubby hole in a storage place on the wall of my room. I did a very short worksheet myself and literally walked it over and put it in my storage spot, thinking aloud as I went. "Hmm, I'm finished with my worksheet. . . . What do I do now? . . . I need to put it in my cubby hole. If I don't put it there, my teacher can't check it, so it's very important. . . . Now, I start on the next assignment."

Table 11.5

Guidelines for beginning the school year

Guideline	Examples
Establish expectations	• Explain requirements and grading systems, particularly with older students.
	• Emphasize that learning and classroom order are interdependent.
Plan structured instruction	• Plan with extra care during this period.
	• Conduct eye-catching and motivating activities
	• Use the first few days to assess learners' skills and background knowledge
	• Use large- rather than small-group instruction.
	• Minimize transitions from one activity to another.
Teach rules and procedures	• Begin teaching rules and procedures the first day.
	• Frequently discuss and practice rules and procedures during the first few days.
	• Intervene and discuss every infraction of rules.
Begin communication with parents	• Send a letter to parents that states positive expectations for the year.
	• Call parents after the first or second day to nip potential problems in the bud.

Then, I gave each of them the worksheet, directing them to take it to their file, quietly and individually, as soon as they were finished. After we had done one, I asked them why we did that, and we spent a few minutes discussing the reasons for taking the finished work to their cubby hole immediately, not touching or talking to anyone as they move from and back to their desks, and starting right back to work. Then I gave them another, asked them what they were going to do and why, and had them do it. We then spent a few more minutes talking about what might happen if we didn't put papers where they belong. I asked them whether they had ever lost anything and how this was similar.

Now, we have a class meeting nearly every day, just before we leave for the day. During the meeting we give each other compliments, and offer suggestions for improving our classroom. Some people might be skeptical about whether or not first graders can handle meetings like this, but they can. This is also the way I help them keep the procedures fresh in their minds.

> **11.17** ■
> Based on our discussion of concept teaching in Chapter 8, explain specifically why the way Martha taught her procedures was effective.

Martha's approach to teaching procedures was consistent with cognitive views of learning in general and constructivism in particular. By modeling the procedure and having students practice it, she provided concrete examples for learners to use in constructing understanding, and she combined her examples with think-alouds and detailed discussions of the procedure and the reasons for it. Understanding procedures and rules is also an authentic task since they govern the way learners live and operate in classrooms.

Martha's use of classroom meetings is another process advocated by experts (Glasser, 1985; Nelson, Lott, & Glenn, 1997). These meetings are used to first establish, and then monitor and improve, classroom rules. The meetings are conducted in a problem-solving atmosphere, emphasize discussion and learner input, and focus on learner responsibility.

Let's see how a high school teacher uses a classroom meeting in an attempt to make her classroom learning environment more productive.

Deanna McDonald, a 10th-grade English teacher, conducted a class meeting the last 20 minutes in each of her classes on Fridays. She began one of her Friday meetings in her fourth-period class by displaying the following on the overhead,

Give your full attention to others in discussions and wait your turn to speak

and then saying, "We've been doing a generally good job in here, but we're going to begin our study of *Julius Caesar* next week, and we'll be involved in a lot of discussion, so this rule is extra important.

"Why," she continued, "do we have this rule in the first place? . . . Jonique?"

" . . . Well, first it's rude if we don't listen to each other, or interrupt when someone is talking."

"Of course," Deanna smiled. "What's another reason?"

Hearing no response after several seconds, Deanna went on, "Why are we here? . . . What's the purpose of school, period."

" . . . To learn stuff," Antonius volunteered.

"Absolutely, that's what school's all about. We're here to learn. You learn, I learn, we all learn, and we learn less if we don't listen.

"Plus," she added, "it's important to me that you all participate. Each of you has some important ideas to bring to the discussions, and I want you all to have a chance to share those ideas.

"And ultimately, what happens when you leave here?"

" . . . We're responsible for ourselves," Yolanda smiled knowingly. "You keep reminding us that no one can really make us do anything. . . . We're the one's in control of what we do."

"That's right, Yolanda," Deanna responded, nodding with emphasis. "And that, together with being here to learn, is really what we're all about. Out in the world it's up to us. That's the reason I don't want to hold a stick over your head. I don't want you to listen and be polite because you'll be punished if you aren't. I want you to believe it's important, and do it because we're all in this together.

"Now, work hard on this, and keep this idea in mind when we start discussing *Julius Caesar* on Monday."

Deanna's meeting took only a few minutes, and it focused on learning, appropriate behavior, and personal responsibility. The meeting also increased her students' feelings of autonomy, further increasing the likelihood that they will accept personal responsibility for following procedures and obeying rules.

Monitoring Rules and Procedures

No matter how good a job you do of "teaching" rules and procedures, monitoring and continuing to discuss them will be necessary over time (Emmer et al., 2000; Evertson et al., 2000). Effective teachers react to misbehavior immediately, refer students to the rule that was broken, and discuss the reasons why the rule is important and the behavior inappropriate. Shirley did this in stopping Sondra's whispering and note passing. It was an example of effective rule monitoring because she called Sondra's attention to the rule and reminded her of its rationale as she enforced it.

As their understanding of rules increases, students are more likely to obey them, regardless of consequences, because the rules make sense and the students have had a voice in their creation. It becomes a social contract—Stage 5 in Kohlberg's descriptions of moral reasoning (see Chapter 3). Other students will obey the rules because they know the teacher monitors them. Understanding, combined with the knowledge that rules are being monitored, prevents many off-task and disruptive behaviors.

> **11.18** ■
> Using your understanding of information processing as a basis, explain why—from a teacher's perspective—well-established rules and procedures are so important.

Communication with Parents

No classroom management system—or any other learning–teaching system—will be effective if parents are not involved in their children's education. Learning is a cooperative venture, and teachers, students, and parents are in it together. In a comprehensive review of factors affecting student learning, researchers concluded,

> Because of the importance of the home environment to school learning, teachers must also develop strategies to increase parent involvement in their children's academic life. This means teachers should go beyond traditional once-a-year parent/teacher conferences and work with parents to see that learning is valued in the home. Teachers should encourage parents to be involved with their children's academic pursuits on a day-to-day basis, helping them with homework, monitoring television viewing, reading to their young children, and simply expressing the expectation that their children will achieve academic success. (Wang et al., 1993, pp. 278-279)

Communication with parents or other primary caregivers is not an appendage to the teaching process; it is an integral part of teachers' jobs.

Benefits of Communication

Research indicates that students benefit from home–school cooperation in at least four ways:

■ Higher long-term academic achievement
■ More positive attitudes and behaviors

A home–school partnership leads to higher achievement and improved learner motivation.

   ▌ Better attendance rates
   ▌ Greater willingness to do homework (Cameron & Lee, 1997; López & Scribner, 1999)

These outcomes likely result from parents' increased participation in school activities, their higher expectations for their children's achievement, and teachers' increased understanding of learners' home environments (Weinstein & Mignano, 1993). Responding to a student's disruptive behavior is easier, for example, when his teachers learn that his mother or father has lost a job, his parents are going through a divorce, or there's a serious illness in the family. In addition, parents can help develop and reinforce behavior management plans. One teacher reported:

> I had this boy in my class who was extremely disruptive. He wouldn't work, kept "forgetting" his homework, distracted other children, wandered about the room. You name it; he did it. The three of us—the mother, the boy and I—talked about what we could do, and we decided to try a system of home rewards. We agreed that I would send a note home each day, reporting on the boy's behavior. For every week with at least three good notes, the mother added one Christmas present. In this way, what the child found under the tree on Christmas Day was directly dependent on his behavior. By Christmas, he had become so cooperative, I couldn't believe he was the same child! After Christmas, I observed some backsliding, so we all agreed to reverse the system: The mother took away one present each time a majority of the week's reports were negative. She didn't have to take many away! (Weinstein & Mignano, 1993, p. 226)

The most significant aspect of this incident is that it occurred as a result of parent and teacher collaboration. Collaborations like this can have long-term benefits that are hard to assess based on a single incident. For example, teachers who encourage parental involvement report more positive feelings about teaching and their school. They also rate parents higher in helpfulness and follow-through and have higher expectations for parents (Epstein, 1990).

11.19 ▬
What concept from behaviorism is illustrated by giving the child a present for three good notes? What concept is illustrated when the child gets good notes to avoid losing his presents? Explain in each case. Identify one advantage and one disadvantage of the system.

Strategies for Involving Parents

Virtually all schools have formal communication channels, such as *open houses* (usually occurring within the first 2 weeks of the year when teachers introduce themselves and describe general guidelines and procedures); *interim progress reports*, which tell parents about their youngster's achievement at the midpoint of each grading period; *parent–teacher conferences*; and, of course, *report cards*. Although these processes are schoolwide and necessary, as an individual teacher, you can enhance existing communication processes.

Early Communication. "Begin communication with parents" is one of the guidelines in Table 11.5, and this suggestion can hardly be overstated; parental involvement should start immediately and continue throughout the year. For example, one teacher worked with her students to create the letter that appears in Figure 11.4 and sent it home to parents the first week of school.

The letter is effective for several reasons:

- It was sent home within the first week of the school year.
- It expresses enthusiasm and positive expectations, and it reminds parents that the school cannot effectively promote learning without their help.
- It asks the parents to sign a contract committing to the support of their child's education.
- It specifies class rules (described as "guidelines"), and it also outlines procedures for homework, absences, and extra credit.
- It asks students to sign a contract committing them to following the guidelines.
- The letter was flawlessly written.

While a signature can't ensure that parents and students will totally honor the intent of the contract, the signatures symbolize a commitment to working with the teacher; they increase the likelihood that the parents and students will attempt to honor the contract (Katz, 1999). Also, because students had input into the content of the letter, they felt ownership of the process and encouraged their parents to work with them in completing their homework.

The last point on the list bears special mention. Although the need for error-free written communication should go without saying, teachers sometimes send home communications with spelling, grammar, or punctuation errors. *Don't do it.* First impressions are important and lasting. Parents' perceptions of the teacher will be based on this first letter, and a letter that contains errors detracts from a teacher's credibility, which may be necessary later in soliciting parental support.

Regardless of the approach, early and positive communication is essential. Don't wait until management problems arise to establish communication links with parents. The parents' support in the home will mean a better learning environment in the classroom.

Maintaining Communication. Early, positive communication helps get the year off to a good start, and continuing communication can help maintain the momentum. For example, many teachers send packets of students' work home each week, requiring that parents sign and return them. This maintains a tangible link between home and school and gives parents an ongoing record of their children's learning.

Calling Parents. One of the most powerful ways to maintain communication is to call parents. It is significant for at least two reasons. First, it strongly communicates caring. As we said in Chapter 10, everyone has 24 hours a day, and choosing to allocate some of a

11.20
Think about your study of motivation and needs in Chapter 10. For parents, which of the needs discussed in that chapter is most nearly met by a teacher's early and continuing communication? Explain.

Figure 11.4

Letter to parents

August 22, 2000

Dear Parents,

I am looking forward to a productive and exciting year, and I am writing this letter to encourage your involvement and support. You always have been and still are the most important people in your youngster's education. We cannot do the job without you.

For us to work together most effectively, some guidelines are necessary. With the students' help, we prepared the ones listed here. Please read this information carefully and sign where indicated. If you have any questions, please call me at Southside Junior High School (441-5935), or at home (221-8403) in the evenings.

Sincerely,

Joan Williams

AS A PARENT, I WILL TRY MY BEST TO DO THE FOLLOWING:

1. I will ask my youngsters about school every day. (Evening meal is a good time.) I will ask them about what they're studying and try to learn about it.
2. I will provide a quiet time and place each evening for homework. I will set an example by also working at that time or reading while my youngster is working.
3. Instead of asking if their homework is finished, I will ask to see it. I will have them explain some of the information to see if they understand it.

Parent's Signature _____

STUDENT SURVIVAL GUIDELINES:

1. I will be in class and seated when the bell rings.
2. I will follow directions the first time they are given.
3. I will bring covered textbook, notebook, paper, and two sharpened pencils to class each day.
4. I will raise my hand for permission to speak or leave my seat.
5. I will keep my hands, feet, and objects to myself.

HOMEWORK GUIDELINES:

1. Our motto is I WILL ALWAYS TRY. I WILL NEVER GIVE UP.
2. I will complete all assignments. If an assignment is not finished or ready when called for, I understand that I get no credit for it.
3. If I am absent, it is my responsibility to come in before school in the morning (8:15–8:45) to make it up.
4. I know that I get one day to make up a test or turn in my work for each day I'm absent.
5. I understand that extra credit work is not given. If I do all the required work, extra credit isn't necessary.

Student's Signature _____

teacher's personal time, usually in the evening, to calling a parent about an individual student communicates caring better than any other way.

Second, talking to a parent allows teachers to be specific in describing a student's needs and strengths, and it also gives the teacher the opportunity to further solicit parental support. For example, if a student is missing some assignments, the teacher can ask why, and also can encourage the parents to monitor their child's study habits more closely.

As with virtually all aspects of teaching, decisions about when to call parents is a matter of professional judgment. An effective guideline for making the decision rests in answering the question, "To what extent does this issue influence learning?" For instance, if a junior high student uses an occasional swear word in class, it's a problem best handled by the teacher. On the other hand, if the student's swearing or other behaviors are disrupting the learning environment, or if a student has failed to turn in several homework assignments, learning will be affected, and a call to parents is appropriate.

As it continues to expand, technology will provide another channel for improving communication. A voice mail system, for example, can result in improved quality and quantity of teacher–parent communication (Cameron & Lee, 1997), and as more people have e-mail capabilities, the opportunities for ongoing communication will increase.

Classroom Connections

Planning for Effective Classroom Management

1. Carefully plan and communicate your classroom procedures and rules before the year begins.
   - A third-grade teacher prepares a handout for his students and their parents that describes how papers should be prepared, how grades are determined, and procedures for making up work.
   - A seventh-grade math teacher prepares a written list of rules before she starts class on the first day. She then asks students to suggest additional rules that will help make the classroom a positive place to learn.

2. Consider the developmental level of your students in preparing and teaching rules and procedures.
   - A first-grade teacher takes a few minutes each day to review her procedures for entering class in the morning until the students can follow the procedure without directions.
   - At the beginning of the school year, an eighth-grade teacher tries to establish a positive classroom climate by conducting a daily review of the rule requiring students to speak to each other respectfully and by discussing the reasons for the rule.

3. Consider your physical environment in planning procedures and rules.
   - A sixth-grade teacher arranges students' desks so that they are facing away from the classroom window, which looks out on the physical education field.
   - A geometry teacher has the custodian move her projection screen into the corner of the room so that it doesn't cover the chalkboard.

Making Rules and Procedures Work

4. Be prepared for the first day of class.
   - A kindergarten teacher greets the children as they come to the door of her room. She takes each by the hand and walks with them to a seat at a table with the student's name on it. Crayons and other materials are waiting, and the students use these materials until everyone arrives.
   - An eighth-grade science teacher is standing at the door as the students file into the room on the first day. "Move to your seats quickly please," she says, "and begin reading the paper that's on your desk. We'll begin discussing it as soon as the bell rings."

5. Explain and have students practice your classroom procedures.
   - A first-grade teacher has his students practice his procedures several times in dry runs during the first few days of school. He has them continue to practice until they follow the procedures without being told.
   - An eighth-grade physical science teacher takes a full class period to describe and explain safe lab procedures. She distributes a handout describing them to each student, models correct procedures, and explains the reasons behind each.
   - A fifth-grade teacher goes through the rules one by one. She asks students to give her an example of following each rule and another example of not following the rule. In each case, she asks them why the rule is important, and they discuss the reasons.

Communicating Effectively with Parents

6. Establish communication links between school and home during the first few days of school.

- A kindergarten teacher makes a personal telephone call to the parents of each of her students during the first week of school. She tells the parents how happy she is to have their children in her class, encourages them to contact her at any time, and gives them her home phone number.

7. Maintain communication links throughout the year.
   - A fourth-grade teacher sends home a "class communicator" each month. It briefly describes the topics the students will be studying and gives suggestions parents might follow in helping their children. The students are required to write personal notes to their parents on the communicator, describing their efforts and progress.
   - A teacher calls a parent during the first week of school to report that her daughter didn't turn in her first two homework papers. "I want to catch these things early," she says on the phone. "Monica is a capable student, and I want her to get off to a good start."

Communication with Parents: Accommodating Learner Diversity

Classrooms with large numbers of cultural minorities present unique communication challenges. Research indicates that "characteristics associated with lower parent participation in school activities included being Hispanic, African American, or Asian American; being of lower-socioeconomic status; having a child enrolled in either special education or the English-as-a-second-language program" Griffith (1998, p. 53). In general, diversity tends to make encouraging parental involvement more challenging, and, as you saw in the previous section, this involvement is essential for learning.

What are the obstacles to greater parental involvement? Research identifies several barriers that can detract from the school involvement of minority and low-SES parents.

Economic Barriers.   Communication and involvement take time, and economic commitments often come first. For example, half the parents in one study indicated that their jobs prevented them from helping their youngsters with homework (S. Ellis, Dowdy, Graham, & Jones, 1992). Often parents lack economic resources (e.g., child care, transportation, and telephones) that would allow them to participate in school activities. Parents want to be involved in their children's schooling, but schools need to be flexible and provide help and encouragement (Epstein, 1990).

Cultural Barriers.   Discontinuities between home and school cultures can also create barriers to home–school cooperation (Delgado-Gaiton, 1992; Harry, 1992). Parents may have experienced schools that were very different from the ones their children attend. Some parents may have only gone through the elementary grades or may have had negative school experiences. One researcher described the problem as follows:

> Underneath most parents is a student—someone who went to school, sometimes happily, sometimes unhappily. What often happens when the parent-as-adult returns to school, or has dealings with teachers, is that the parent as child/student returns. Many parents still enter school buildings flooded with old memories, angers, and disappointments. Their stomachs churn and flutter with butterflies, not because of what is happening today with their own children, but because of outdated memories and past behaviors. (Rich, 1987, p. 24)

These parents require a great deal of encouragement and support to become involved.

Out of respect for teachers, many Asian and Latino parents hesitate to become involved in matters they believe are best handled by the school (Harry, 1992). This deference to authority implies, "You're the teacher; do what is best," but it can be misinterpreted as apathy by teachers.

Management style can also be a source of cultural conflict. A study of Puerto Rican families found that parents thought U.S. schools were too impersonal—that teachers didn't "worry about" their children enough. One parent explained, "In the U.S., the teachers care about the education of the child, but they don't care about the child himself and his problems" (Harry, 1992, p. 479). These parents wanted teachers to act more like parents, providing more warmth and structure for their children.

Language Barriers.   Language can be another potential barrier to home–school cooperation. Parents of bilingual students may not speak English, which leaves the child responsible for interpreting communications sent home by teachers. Homework poses a special problem because parents cannot interpret assignments or provide help (Delgado-Gaiton, 1992).

Schools compound the problem by using educational jargon when they send letters home. The problem is especially acute in special education, where legal and procedural safeguards can be bewildering. For example, studies indicate that parents often don't understand Individualized Education Program (IEPs) or even remember that they've signed one (Harry, 1992; Stein, 1983).

Involving Minority Parents.   Research indicates that many minority parents feel ill-prepared to assist their children with school-related tasks, but when teachers offer parents specific strategies for working with their children, the home–school gap is narrowed (Gorman & Balter, 1997; Porche & Ross, 1999). Let's look at an example.

> Nancy Collins, an eighth-grade English teacher, had students who spoke five different native languages in her class. During the first 2 days of school, she prepared a letter to parents, and with the help of her students, she translated it into each of their native languages. The letter began by describing how pleased she was to have students from varying backgrounds in her class, saying that these backgrounds would enrich all her students' educations.
>
> She continued with a short and simple list of procedures and encouraged the parents to support their children's efforts by
>
> 1.   Asking their children about school and school work each night
> 2.   Providing a quiet place to study for at least 90 minutes a night
> 3.   Limiting television until homework assignments are finished
> 4.   Asking to see samples of their children's work and grades they've received
>
> She told them that the school will have an open house, and a contest to see what class will have the highest attendance at it. She concluded the letter by reemphasizing

11.21 ■
Explain "stomachs churn and flutter with butterflies," using classical conditioning as the basis for your explanation.

that she was pleased to have so much diversity in her class. She asked parents to sign the letter and return it to the school.

The day before the open house, Nancy had each of her students compose a hand-written letter to their parents, asking them to attend the open house. Nancy wrote, "Hoping to see you there," at the bottom of each note and signed it.

Nancy's letter accomplished at least three things. First, the letter in the students' native languages communicated caring to her students and their parents. Second, the letter included specific suggestions for parents. Even if parents cannot read a homework assignment, for example, asking their children to show it to them and explain it communicates that the parents are working with teachers. Third, she strongly encouraged parents to attend the school's open house. This obviously doesn't ensure that they'll attend but does increase the likelihood. If they do attend, and the experience is a supportive atmosphere, their involvement is likely to increase.

The process of involving minority parents begins with awareness (A. Baker, Kessler-Sklar, Piotrkowski, & Parker, 1999). As we more fully realize that parents of cultural minorities, low SES, and learners with exceptionalities are often reluctant to become involved in school activities, we can redouble our efforts. Also, we can try to be as clear and specific as possible in our suggestions for parents as they work with their youngsters.

Finally, if parents speak English, calls are as effective as they are with nonminority parents. Some schools and teachers even conduct home visits. While these are very demanding and time consuming, nothing communicates a stronger commitment to a young person's education.

Classroom Connections

Communicating Effectively with Cultural Minorities

1. Send communications home in native languages.
   - At the beginning of each grading period, a sixth-grade teacher sends a letter home, in each student's native language, describing the topics that will be covered, the tests and the approximate times they will be given, and any special projects that are required for the period.

2. Communicate in straightforward language. Avoid technical terms and educational jargon.
   - A fifth-grade teacher goes over a letter to parents with her students. She has them explain to her what each part of the letter says, and she then asks the students to read and explain the letter to their parents.

3. Make specific suggestions to parents for working with their children.

   - A third-grade teachers asks all her parents to sign a contract agreeing that they will (a) Designate at least 1 hour an evening when the television is shut off and children do homework. (b) Ask their children to show them their homework assignments each day. (c) Attend the school's open house. (d) Look at, ask their children about, and sign the packet of papers that is sent home each week.

4. Take extra steps to make parents of minority children feel welcome in school.
   - A ninth-grade teacher calls parents if students miss 1 day of school or fail to turn in one homework assignment. She expresses concern and solicits parental support. She periodically calls parents to praise students for positive attitudes and good work.
   - A third-grade teacher sends personal handwritten notes home to parents commenting on students' work and inviting them to school functions.

Dealing with Misbehavior: Interventions

Our focus to this point has been on preventing management problems. We have emphasized the interdependence of instruction and classroom management, the importance of planning, and the role of carefully taught and monitored rules and procedures.

Despite teachers' best efforts, however, management problems occur, and teachers must intervene in cases of disruptive behavior or chronic inattention. In this section, we consider interventions, including

▍ General guidelines for successful interventions
▍ Cognitive approaches to intervention
▍ Behavioral approaches to intervention

Effective interventions require both clear verbal and congruent nonverbal communication.

Guidelines for Successful Intervention

Intervening when classroom management problems occur is never easy. If it were, classroom management wouldn't remain a chronic problem for teachers. As you work with your students, we recommend a blend of both cognitive and behavioral approaches to management. Cognitive perspectives emphasize understanding of rules and procedures; behaviorist approaches focus on establishing and maintaining order through rewards and consequences. Both have their place in the creation of productive learning environments.

Regardless of the theoretical orientation, some general guidelines increase the likelihood that your interventions will be successful. Let's look at these guidelines.

Withitness.   An essential component of successful interventions is a concept called **withitness**, which is *knowing what is going on in all parts of the classroom all the time and communicating this knowing verbally and nonverbally* (Kounin, 1970). Expert teachers describe withitness as "having eyes in the back of your head." Here's an example:

> Ron Ziers was explaining the procedure for finding percentages of numbers to his seventh graders. While Ron illustrated the procedure, Kareem, in the second desk from the front of the room, was periodically poking Katilyna, who sat across from him. She retaliated by kicking him in the leg. Bill, sitting behind Katilyna, poked her in the arm with his pencil. Ron didn't respond to the students' actions. After a second poke, Katilyna swung her arm back and caught Bill on the shoulder. "Katilyna!" Ron said sternly. "We keep our hands to ourselves! . . . Now, where were we?"
>
> Karl Wickes, a seventh-grade life science teacher in the same school, had the same group of students. He put a transparency displaying a flowering plant on the overhead. As the class discussed the information, he noticed Barry whispering something to Julie, and he saw Kareem poke Katilyna, who kicked him and loudly whispered, "Stop it." As Karl asked, "What is the part of the plant that produces fruit?" he moved to Kareem's desk, leaned over, and said quietly but firmly, "We keep our hands and materials to ourselves in here." He then moved to the front of the room, watched Kareem out of the corner of his eye, and said, "Barry, what other plant part do you see in the diagram?"

Karl demonstrated three features of withitness, which Ron lacked:

▍ Karl identified the misbehavior immediately, responding quickly to Kareem. Ron did nothing until the misbehavior had spread to other students.

11.22 ▬
Using your study of information processing in Chapter 7 as a basis, offer a likely reason for Ron's lack of withitness.

▌ He correctly identified the right student; he knew that Kareem was the original cause of the incident. Ron reprimanded Katilyna, leaving the students with a sense that the teacher didn't know what was going on.

▌ He saw two incidents of misbehavior, and he responded to the more serious infraction first. Since Kareem's poking was more disruptive than Barry's whispering, he first responded to Kareem, and he then simply called on Barry, which got him back into the activity, making further intervention unnecessary.

Withitness involves more than dealing with misbehavior. Teachers who are withit watch for evidence of inattention or confusion; they walk over to, or call on, inattentive students to bring them back into lessons; and they respond to quizzical looks with questions such as, "I see uncertain looks on some of your faces. Do you want me to rephrase that question?" Effective teachers are sensitive to students and make adjustments to ensure that they are as attentive and successful as possible (G. Duffy, Roehler, Meloth, & Vavrus, 1985; O'Keefe & Johnston, 1987).

Preserve Student Dignity.   Preserving a student's dignity is a basic principle of any intervention. Safety is essential for motivation (see Chapter 10), and earlier in this chapter, you saw that the emotional tone of feedback is also important. Loud public reprimands, public criticism, and sarcasm all detract from a sense of safety and a learning-focused classroom environment. For example,

> "Janet, what are you doing?"
> "Nothing."
> "Yes you were. Speak up so that everyone can hear."
> " . . . "
> "You were talking. What's the rule about talking without permission?"
> " . . . "
> "Let's hear it. I want to hear you say the rule."
> " . . . We don't talk until we're recognized."
> "That's right. Do you understand that?"
> " . . . Yes."

This prolonged encounter was unnecessary and unproductive. Janet understood what she was doing. Asking a student to state a rule makes sense, but the tone was negative, and Janet was forced into a humiliating position. Her only alternatives were to acquiesce or lash out; she loses either way, and she's likely to resent the teacher's abuse of power. Instead, the teacher could have had Janet identify the rule, asked or explained why it is important, enlisted compliance with it, and moved on with the lesson or spoken with the student privately (in the hall or after class).

Be Consistent.   "Be consistent" is recommended so often that it has become a cliché. The need for consistency is obvious, but achieving complete consistency in the real world of teaching is difficult, if not impossible. In fact, research indicates that our interventions should be individualized and contextualized; they depend on the specific student and situation (Doyle, 1986).

For example, most classrooms have a rule "Speak only when recognized by the teacher." You are monitoring seat work, and a student innocently asks a work-related question of another student then quickly turns back to work. Do you intervene, reminding her that talking is not allowed during seat work? Failing to do so is technically inconsistent, but you don't intervene, and you shouldn't. A student who repeatedly turns around and whispers, though, becomes a disruption, warranting an intervention.

11.23 ▬
Kounin (1970) describes a concept called **overlapping,** *which is a teacher's ability to attend to two incidents at the same time without focusing exclusively on either one.* Identify an example of overlapping in the examples with Karl Wickes.

11.24 ▬
What concept from Piaget's work in Chapter 2 most closely relates to the need for consistency? Explain how it is related.

Follow-Through.   Follow-through can be difficult, but it is essential. Without follow-through, a management system breaks down because students learn that teachers aren't fully committed to maintaining an orderly classroom environment. This confuses them, disrupting their equilibrium. This is another reason that the first few days of the school year are so important. If you follow through carefully during this period, management becomes much easier during the rest of the year.

Keep Interventions Brief.   Keep all interventions as brief as possible. Researchers have documented a negative relationship between time spent on discipline and student achievement; extended interventions break the flow of the lesson and detract from instructional time (Crocker & Brooker, 1986; Evertson, Anderson, Anderson, & Brophy, 1980).

In this chapter's opening case, Shirley applied this principle in her work with her fifth graders. She simply touched Brad on the arm, stopped Kevin by moving near him and giving him a look, and spoke quietly to Sondra when directing her to move. In each case, she kept the encounter short and kept the lesson moving.

> 11.25
> The statement, " . . . extended interventions break the flow of the lesson . . . " most closely relates to what concept discussed earlier in the chapter?

Avoid Arguments.   Finally, whenever possible, avoid arguing with students because teachers never "win" arguments. They can exercise their authority, but resentment is often the outcome, and the encounter may expand into a major incident. Shirley handled this problem skillfully in her encounter with Sondra. She simply referred to the rule, restated her request, and ensured that it was followed. In comparison, consider an alternative scenario:

> "I wasn't speaking."
> "You were whispering."
> "It doesn't say no whispering."
> "You know what the rule means. We've been over it again and again."
> "Well, it's not fair. I wasn't speaking. You don't make other students move when they whisper."
> "You were whispering, so move."

The student, of course, knew what the rule meant and was simply playing a game with the teacher, who allowed herself to be drawn into an argument. Shirley didn't, and the incident was disarmed almost immediately.

Having considered these general guidelines, we turn now to cognitive factors in interventions.

Cognitive Interventions

Learner cognitions are important in interpreting teachers' feedback and other responses to them (see Chapter 10). They are also important for management. For example, in the last section, you saw that achieving complete consistency in interventions is virtually impossible. A cognitive approach to intervention assumes that students can accommodate minor inconsistencies because they understand differences in situations. Learner understanding is at the core of cognitive approaches to management.

In this section, we examine four factors that influence the way learners understand and respond to our interventions:

▮ Verbal–nonverbal congruence
▮ I-messages
▮ Active listening
▮ Logical consequences

Verbal–Nonverbal Congruence.   If students are to develop understanding and responsibility, our classroom and the communication in it must make sense to them. For example:

> Karen Wilson's tenth graders were working on their next day's English homework as she circulated among them. She was helping Jasmine when Jeff and Mike begin whispering loudly behind her. "Jeff. Mike. Stop talking, and get started on your homework," she said, glancing over her shoulder.
>
> The two slowed their whispering, and Karen turned back to Jasmine. Soon, though, the boys were whispering as loudly as ever.
>
> "I thought I told you to stop talking," Karen said over her shoulder again, this time with irritation in her voice.
>
> The boys glanced at her and quickly resumed whispering.

> Isabel Rodriguez was in a similar situation with her ninth-grade algebra class. As she was helping Vicki, Ken and Lance began horsing around at the back of the room.
>
> Isabel quickly excused herself from Vicki, turned, and walked directly to the boys. Looking Lance in the eye, she said pleasantly but firmly, "Lance, we have plenty to do before lunch, and noise disrupts others' work. Begin your homework now," and then looking directly at Ken, she continued, "Ken, you, too. Quickly now. We have only so much time, and we don't want to waste it." She waited until they were working quietly, and then she returned to Vicki.

The teachers had similar intent, but their impact on the students was very different. Karen's communication was confusing; her words said one thing, but her body language said another, leaving students unable to make sense of her intent and how they were supposed to function in her classroom. When messages are inconsistent, people attribute more credibility to **nonverbal communication**, which includes *the tone of voice and body language people use to convey unspoken messages* (Mehrabian & Ferris, 1967).

In contrast, Isabel's communication was clear and consistent. She responded immediately, faced her students directly, emphasized the relationship between classroom order and learning, and made sure her students were on-task before she went back to Vicki. Isabel's verbal and nonverbal behaviors were consistent, so her communication made sense to the students. If we expect students to take responsibility for their own behavior, our messages must be consistent and understandable, or learner comprehension and compliance suffer.

Essential elements of nonverbal communication are outlined in Table 11.6.

Cognitive approaches to management emphasize learner understanding.

Table 11.6

Characteristics of nonverbal communication

Nonverbal Behavior	Example
Proximity	A teacher moves close to an inattentive student. In another case, a teacher moves to a student and touches her on the shoulder.
Eye contact	A teacher looks an off-task student directly in the eye when issuing a directive.
Body orientation	A teacher directs himself squarely to the learner, rather than over the shoulder or sideways.
Facial expression	A teacher frowns slightly at a disruption, brightens her face at a humorous incident, and smiles approvingly at a student's effort to help a classmate.
Gestures	A teacher puts her palm out (Stop!) to a student who interjects as another student is talking.
Vocal variation	A teacher varies the tone, pitch, and loudness of his voice for emphasis and displays energy and enthusiasm.

I-Messages.   The clarity and tone of our words as well as the messages contained within influence the effectiveness of our interventions. To illustrate, let's look again at Shirley's lesson.

> *Shirley:*   Move up here (quietly, in response to Sondra's whispering and note passing)
>
> *Sondra:*   What did I do?
>
> *Shirley:*   When we talked about our rules at the beginning of the year, we agreed that it was important to listen when other people are talking.
>
> *Sondra:*   I was listening.
>
> *Shirley:*   We don't learn as much when people aren't paying attention, and I'm uncomfortable when we don't learn. Move quickly now.

Shirley sent an **I-message**, which *addresses behavior rather than personal characteristics, describes the effects on the sender, and identifies feelings generated in the sender.*

The way Shirley talked to Sondra has both short- and long-term consequences for learners (Gordon, 1974). First, by referring to the rule, Shirley addressed Sondra's behavior rather than her character or personality. When teachers say, "You're driving me up the wall," they're blaming students and implying weaknesses in their characters. Focusing on the incident communicates that a student's intrinsic worth is valued, but the behavior is unacceptable. This approach takes learners' beliefs and needs into account.

Shirley then demonstrated the second and third parts of an I-message by saying, "We don't learn as much when people aren't paying attention, and I'm uncomfortable when we don't learn. . . . " This describes the effect on the sender and the feelings it generates. As with all cognitive approaches to management, the intent in the message is to help students understand, in this case, understand the effects their actions have on others—a step toward responsible behavior and self-regulation.

11.26
Look back at the section titled "Preserve Student Dignity," and describe an I-Message that would be appropriate for responding to Janet's talking without permission.

Active Listening.   "Communication is a two-way street" is another time-honored maxim. Teachers who effectively communicate with their students are also good listeners (Gordon, 1974). When students believe that teachers are listening rather than evaluating what they say, they begin to trust their teachers and feel free to communicate openly. For example,

> Gayle went to Mrs. Cortez after class and said, "Mrs. Cortez, I don't think I should have gotten a zero on that last assignment."
> Mrs. Cortez sat down, focused her attention on Gayle, and said evenly, "You don't think the grade was fair?"
> "No," Gayle said, squirming slightly.
> "Tell me why."
> "I was absent the day you assigned it, and I didn't know that it was due today."
> "I understand how you feel, Gayle," Mrs. Cortez responded, leaning forward. "I would feel bad, too, if I got a zero on an assignment. But our procedures say that assignments are due 2 days after you return, and when you're absent, you're responsible for finding out what those assignments are. I even gave you a break and reminded you that the assignment was due yesterday. In the future, I suggest that you write assignments down in your notebook so that you're less likely to forget them."

Mrs. Cortez sat down, *gave Gayle her full attention, and responded to both the intellectual and emotional content of the message.* These are the characteristics of **active listening** (Sokolove, Garrett, Sadker, & Sadker, 1990). Notice also that Mrs. Cortez didn't acquiesce to Gayle's implication of unfairness. Her response was consistent with her procedures, it was predictable, and it further contributed to Gayle's understanding of classroom rules and procedures.

Logical Consequences.   Logical consequences *treat misbehaviors as problems and help learners see a link between their actions and the consequence.* Here's an example:

> Allen, a rambunctious sixth grader, was running down the hall toward the lunch room.
> "Hold it, Allen," Doug Ramsay, who was monitoring the hall, said, as Allen ran by. "Go back to the door, start over, and walk back down this hall."
> "Aww."
> "Go on," Doug said firmly.
> Allen walked back to the door and then returned. As he approached, Doug again stopped him and said, "Now, why did I make you do that?"
> " . . . Cuz, we're not supposed to run."
> "Well, sure," Doug said pleasantly, "but more important, if people are running in the halls, somebody might get hurt, and of course, we don't want that to happen. . . . Plus, I want you to understand that, so the next time you'll realize that you don't want to hurt yourself, or anybody else, and you'll walk whether a teacher is here or not."

In this incident, Doug helped Allen see the link between his behavior and the consequence. The consequence, itself, isn't cognitive; an understanding of the link between the behavior and the consequence is. Again, the goal is the development of learner understanding. Research indicates that children who understand the effects of their actions on others become more altruistic and are more likely to take action to make up for their misbehavior (Berk, 1997).

Behaviorist Approaches to Intervention

While understanding and personal responsibility are worthy goals, we sometimes face situations in which learners either seem unable or unwilling to accept responsibility for their behavior. In addition, time or safety concerns may suggest more direct approaches to

11.27 ▬
A teacher sees a seventh grader spit on the door to the classroom. Based on the information in this section, which is the more appropriate response: putting the student in after-school detention (which is part of the school's management policy) or having the student wash the door? Explain.

management. In situations such as these, behavioral interventions can be effective (Reynolds, Sinatra, & Jetton, 1996).

> Cindy Daines's first-graders were sometimes frustrating. Although she tried alerting the groups and having the whole class make transitions at the same time, every transition took 4 minutes or more.
>
> To improve the situation, she made some "tickets" from construction paper, bought an assortment of small prizes, and displayed the items in a fishbowl on her desk the next day. She then explained, "We're going to play a little game to see how quiet we can be when we change lessons. . . . Whenever we change, such as from language arts to math, I'm going to give you 2 minutes, and then I'm going to ring this bell," she continued, ringing the bell as a demonstration. "Students who have their books out and are waiting quietly when I ring the bell will get one of these tickets. On Friday afternoon, you can turn these in for prizes you see in this fishbowl. The more tickets you have, the better the prize will be."
>
> During the next few days, Cindy moved around the room, handing out tickets and making comments such as, "I really like the way Merry is ready to work," "Ted already has his books out and is quiet," and "Thank you for moving to math so quickly."
>
> She knew it was working when she heard "Shh" and "Be quiet!" from the students, and she moved from the prizes to allowing the students to "buy" free time with their tickets, to finally giving them Friday afternoon parties as group rewards when the class had accumulated enough tickets. She gradually was able to space out the group rewards as the students' self-regulation developed.

Cindy's system was an application of concepts from both behaviorism and social cognitive theory. Her tickets, free time, and Friday afternoon parties were all intended as positive reinforcers for making quick and quiet transitions. In addition, comments such as, "I really like the way Merry is ready to work," and "Ted already has his books out and is quiet," were intended as vicarious reinforcers for the rest of the children. Research indicates that a behaviorist system such as Cindy's can be effective in initiating new behaviors (McCaslin & Good, 1992).

Systems focusing on reinforcement are preferable to those that use punishment (Alberto & Troutman, 1999), but focusing exclusively on positive behaviors won't always work (see Chapter 6). If all punishers are eliminated, some students actually become more disruptive (Pfiffer, Rosen, & O'Leary, 1985; Rosen, O'Leary, Joyce, Conway, & Pfiffer, 1984). It's unrealistic to think that punishment can be totally avoided; it is probably necessary in some cases (Axelrod & Apsche, 1983; Maccoby, 1992). Guidelines for using punishers are outlined in Figure 11.5.

> **11.28** ▬
> In this section, we said that systems focusing on desirable behaviors are preferable to those that use punishment, yet many teachers largely ignore positive behaviors and focus on undesirable ones. Offer at least two reasons for teachers' tendency to behave this way.

Figure 11.5 ▬

Guidelines for using punishers

- Use punishers as infrequently as possible to avoid negative emotional reactions.
- Apply punishers immediately and directly to the behavior.
- Apply punishers only severe enough to eliminate the behavior.
- Avoid using seat work as a punisher.
- Apply punishers logically, systematically, and dispassionately—never angrily.
- Explain and model appropriate alternative behaviors.

Approaches to management have been developed that systematically use reinforcers and punishers in attempts to promote desirable behaviors in classrooms. *Assertive discipline* is the best known of these systems.

Assertive Discipline: A Structured Approach to Consequences.　Assertive discipline *emphasizes carefully stating rules and specifically describing specific reinforcers and punishers* (Canter & Canter, 1992). For instance, look again at the examples of rules in Table 11.4. Teachers using an assertive discipline system would specify rules, such as "We raise our hands before speaking" (from the first-grade list), "Be in your seat and quiet when the bell rings," (from the seventh) and "Stay in your seat at all times" (from the tenth). Rules like this are recommended because they're specific and observable.

The system then describes specific reinforcers that are given for following the rules and punishers that are administered for breaking them. Sample sets of reinforcers and punishers are illustrated in Table 11.7.

Assertive discipline is controversial. Critics charge that it is punitive, pits teachers against students, and stresses obedience and conformity at the expense of learning and self-control (Curwin & Mendler, 1988; McLaughlin, 1994). Supporters disagree, contending that its emphasis on stated rules and positive reinforcement is proactive and effective (Canter, 1988).

Regardless of the controversy, the program has been widely used. It is difficult to find a school district in the country that hasn't had at least some exposure to assertive discipline; estimates suggest that more than 750,000 teachers have been trained in the program (D. Hill, 1990).

Designing and Maintaining a Behavioral Management System.　Designing a management system based on behaviorism typically involves the following steps:

▌ Prepare a list of specific rules. The rules should represent observable behaviors (e.g., "Speak only when recognized by the teacher").

Table 11.7

Sample consequences for following or breaking rules

Consequences for Breaking Rules	
First infraction	Name on list
Second infraction	Check by name
Third infraction	Second check by name
Fourth infraction	Half-hour detention
Fifth infraction	Call to parents

Consequences for Following Rules
A check is removed for each day that no infractions occur. If only a name remains, and no infractions occur, the name is removed.
All students without names on the list are given 45 minutes of free time Friday afternoon to do as they choose. The only restrictions are that they must stay in the classroom, and they must not disrupt the students who didn't earn the free time.

▮ Specify punishers for breaking rules and reinforcers for obeying each rule (e.g., the consequences in Table 11.7).
▮ Display the rules and procedures, and explain the consequences to the students.
▮ Consistently apply consequences.

A behavioral system doesn't preclude providing rationales or creating the rules with learner input, of course. The focus, however, is on the clear specifications of behavioral guidelines and application of consequences, in contrast with a cognitive system, which emphasizes learner understanding and responsibility.

In designing a comprehensive management system, you will likely use elements of both cognitive and behavioral approaches. Behavioral systems have the advantage of being immediately applicable, they're effective for initiating desired behaviors, particularly with young students, and they're useful for reducing chronic misbehavior. The results of cognitive systems take longer to appear, but they are more likely to develop learner responsibility.

Keeping both cognitive and behavioral approaches to management in mind, let's consider a series of intervention options.

An Intervention Continuum

Disruptions vary widely, from an isolated incident (such as a student briefly whispering to a neighbor during quiet time) to chronic infractions (such as someone repeatedly poking, tapping, or kicking other students). Because infractions vary, teachers' reactions should also vary. To maximize instructional time and minimize disruptions, our goal is to keep interventions as unobtrusive as possible. A continuum designed to reach this goal is described in Figure 11.6.

Praising Desired Behavior.   A principle of behaviorism is that reinforced behaviors increase and, since our goal in any classroom is to promote as much desirable behavior as possible, "praising desired behavior" is a sensible beginning point.

As you saw earlier in the chapter, praise occurs less often than might be expected, so efforts to "catch 'em being good," is a worthwhile goal, especially as a method of prevention. Elementary teachers praise openly and freely, and middle and secondary teachers quietly make comments such as the following to students: "I'm extremely pleased with your work this last week. You're getting better and better at this stuff. Keep it up." Making an effort to acknowledge desired behavior and good work can significantly contribute to a productive learning environment.

Figure 11.6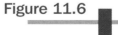

An intervention continuum

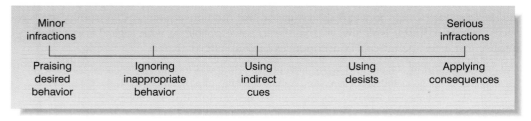

Ignoring Inappropriate Behavior.   A second principle of behaviorism says that behaviors that aren't reinforced become extinct, so one way of eliminating undesirable behaviors is to simply ignore them, which eliminates any reinforcer we as teachers might be inadvertently providing. This is appropriate, for example, if two students whisper to each other, but soon stop. Combining praise and ignoring misbehavior can be very effective with minor disruptions (Pfiffer et al., 1985; Rosen et al., 1984).

Using Indirect Cues.   Teacher can use **indirect cues**, such as *proximity, methods of redirecting attention,* and *vicarious reinforcers,* when students are displaying behaviors that can't be ignored but can be stopped or diverted without addressing them directly. For example, in the opening case, Shirley moved near Kevin and called on him after she heard Alison mutter. Her *proximity* stopped his foot tapping, and calling on him and looking directly at him *redirected his attention* back to the lesson.

Vicarious reinforcement can also be an effective management tool. Teachers, especially in the lower grades, use statements such as, "I really like the way Jimmy is working quietly," which are intended to use Jimmy as a model and vicariously reinforce the rest of the students for imitating his behavior.

Using Desists.   A desist *occurs when a teacher tells a student to stop a behavior* (Kounin, 1970). "Glenys, we don't leave our seat without permission," "Glenys!", a finger to the lips, or a stern facial expression are all desists and are the most common teacher reactions to misbehavior (Humphrey, 1979; Sieber, 1981).

Clarity and tone are important in the effectiveness of desists. For example, "Randy, what is the rule about touching other students in this class?" or, "Randy, how do you think that makes Willy feel?" are clearer than "Randy, stop that," because they link the behavior to a rule or the consequences of the behavior. Students react to these subtle differences, preferring rule and consequence reminders to teacher commands (Nucci, 1987).

The tone of desists should be firm but not angry. Research indicates that kindergarten students handled with rough desists actually became more disruptive, and older students were uncomfortable in classes where rough desists were used (Kounin, 1970). By contrast, gentle reprimands, together with the suggestion of alternative behaviors and effective questioning techniques, reduced time off-task by 20 minutes a day (Borg & Ascione, 1982).

Clear communication (including congruence between verbal and nonverbal behavior), an awareness of what's happening in the classroom (withitness), and the characteristics of effective instruction are essential in effectively using desists to stop misbehavior. However, even when these important elements are used, simple desists alone sometimes don't work.

Applying Consequences.   Careful planning and effective instruction will eliminate much misbehavior before it starts. Some minor incidents can be ignored, and simple desists will stop others. When these strategies don't stop disruptions, however, you must apply consequences that are related to the problem.

Logical consequences are preferable because they treat misbehaviors as problems and demonstrate a link between the behavior and the consequence. Classrooms are busy places, however, and it isn't always possible to solve problems with logical consequences. In these instances, behavioral consequences offer an alternative:

> Jason was an intelligent and active fifth grader. He loved to talk and seemed to know just how far he could go before Mrs. Aguilar became exasperated with him. He understood the rules and the reasons for them, but his interest in talking seemed to take

---

11.29 ▬

On the basis of your study of social cognitive theory in Chapter 6, explain why rough desists might result in students becoming more disruptive. What other explanations might there be?

precedence. Ignoring him wasn't working. A call to his parents helped for a while, but soon he was back to his usual behavior—never quite enough to require a drastic response, but always a thorn in Mrs. Aguilar's side.

Finally, she decided that she would give him one warning. At a second disruption, he was placed in time-out from regular instructional activities. She met with Jason and explained the new rules. The next day, he began to misbehave almost immediately.

"Jason," she warned, "you can't work while you're talking, and you're keeping others from finishing their work. Please get busy."

He stopped, but 5 minutes later, he was at it again. "Jason," she said quietly as she moved back to his desk, "I've warned you. Now please go back to the time-out area."

A week later, Jason was working quietly and comfortably with the rest of the class.

Jason's behavior is common, particularly in elementary and middle schools; it is precisely this type of behavior that drives teachers up the wall. Students like Jason cause more teacher stress and burnout than more publicized threats of violence and bodily harm. His behavior is disruptive so it can't be ignored; praise for good work helps to a certain extent, but much of his reinforcement comes from his buddies. Desists work briefly, but teachers burn out from constantly monitoring him. Mrs. Aguilar had little choice but to apply consequences.

The key to handling students like Jason is consistency. He understood what he was doing, and he was capable of controlling himself. When he could, with absolute certainty, predict the consequences of his behavior, he quit. He knew that his second infraction would result in time-out and, when it did, he quickly changed his behavior. There was no argument, little time was used, and the class wasn't disrupted.

11.30 Suppose Mrs. Aguilar has just begun implementing her system with Jason, and she saw him briefly talk to one of his buddies. Should she ignore the behavior or apply a consequence? Provide a rationale for your response.

Serious Management Problems: Violence and Aggression

Class is disrupted by a scuffle. You look up to see that Ron has left his seat and gone to Phil's desk, where he is punching and shouting at Phil. Phil is not so much fighting back as trying to protect himself. You don't know how this started, but you do know that Phil gets along well with other students and that Ron often starts fights and arguments without provocation. (Brophy & Rohrkemper, 1987, p. 60)

This morning several students excitedly tell you that on the way to school they saw Tom beating up Sam and taking his lunch money. Tom is the class bully and has done things like this many times. (Brophy & Rohrkemper, 1987, p. 53)

What would you do in these situations? What would be your immediate reaction? How would you follow through? What long-term strategies would you employ to try to prevent these problems from recurring? These questions were asked of teachers identified by their principals as effective in dealing with serious management problems (Brophy & McCaslin, 1992). In this section, we consider their responses, together with other research examining violence and aggression in schools.

Problems of violence and aggression require both immediate actions and long-term solutions.

Immediate Actions

Immediate actions involve three steps: (a) Stop the incident (if possible), (b) protect the victim, and (c) get help. For instance, in the case of the classroom scuffle, a loud noise, such as shouting, clapping, or slamming a chair against the floor will often surprise the students enough so they'll stop. At that point, you can begin to talk to them, check to see if Phil is all right, and then take them to the administration, where you can get help.

11.31 ▬

Where on the *intervention continuum* would immediate actions be? Why would other interventions be skipped?

If your interventions don't stop the fight, immediately rush a student to the main office for help. Unless you're sure that you can separate the students without danger to yourself, or them, attempting to do so is unwise.

You are legally required to intervene in the case of a fight. If you ignore a fight, even on the playground, parents can sue for *negligence*, on the grounds that you failed to protect a student from injury. However, the law doesn't say that you're required to physically break up the fight; immediately reporting it to the administration is an acceptable form of intervention.

Long-Term Solutions

Long-term, students must first be helped to understand the severity of their actions, that aggression will not be allowed, and that they're accountable for their behavior (Brophy, 1996; Limber, Flerx, Nation, & Melton, 1998). In the incident with the lunch money, for example, Tom must understand that his behavior will be reported; it's unacceptable and won't be tolerated.

11.32 ▬

Using Piaget's work as a basis, explain why aggressive youth might misperceive others' intentions.

As a preventive strategy, teachers must help students learn how to control their tempers, cope with frustration, and negotiate and talk, rather than fight. One approach uses problem-solving simulations to help aggressive youth understand the motives and intentions of other people. Research indicates that these youngsters often respond aggressively because they misperceive others' intentions as being hostile (Hudley, 1992). Following problem-solving sessions, aggressive students were less hostile in their interpretation of ambiguous situations and were rated as less aggressive by their teachers.

Other approaches to preventing aggression include teaching students to express anger verbally instead of physically and to solve conflicts through communication and negotiation rather than fighting (Burstyn & Stevens, 1999; J. Lee, Pulvino, & Perrone, 1998). One form of communication and negotiation is learning to make and defend a position—to argue effectively. Students taught to make effective arguments—emphasizing that arguing and verbal aggression are very different—become less combative when encountering others with whom they disagree. Learning to argue also has incidental benefits: skillful arguers of any age are seen by their peers as intelligent and credible.

Experts also suggest the involvement of parents and other school personnel (Brophy, 1996; Moles, 1992). Research indicates that a large majority of parents (88%) want to be notified immediately if school problems occur (Harris, Kagay, & Ross, 1987). In addition, school counselors, school psychologists, social workers, and principals have all been trained to deal with these problems and can provide advice and assistance. Experienced teachers can also provide a wealth of information about how they've handled similar problems. No teacher should face persistent or serious problems of violence or aggression alone.

In conclusion, we want to put problems of school violence and aggression into perspective. Though they are possibilities—and you should understand options for dealing with them—the majority of your management problems will revolve around issues of cooperation and motivation. Many can be prevented, others can be dealt with quickly, and some require individual attention. We all hear about students carrying guns to school and incidents of assault on teachers in the news. Statistically, however, considering the huge numbers of students that pass through schools each day, these incidents remain very infrequent.

Classroom Connections

Using Interventions Successfully in Your Classroom

1. In talking to students, be sure your verbal and non-verbal messages are congruent.
   - In response to an underachieving fourth grader's attempts to answer a question, the teacher orients her body directly toward him, looks directly at him, and nods reassuringly.
   - In directing two seventh graders to quit whispering and begin working, a teacher moves close to them, looks them in the eye, and remains standing in front of them until they comply.

2. Use problem-solving strategies and logical consequences to help students develop responsibility.
   - A second-grade teacher uses Friday afternoons to do classroom chores. Two students begin a tug-of-war over a cleaning rag and knock over a potted plant. The teacher talks to the students, and they agree that the mess should be cleaned up. They write a note to their parents explaining that they will be working in the classroom before school the next two mornings to pay for the cost of a new pot.

3. Use positive reinforcers to initiate and teach desirable behaviors.
   - A first-grade teacher, knowing that the times after recess and lunch are difficult for many students, institutes a system in which the class has 1 minute to settle down and get out their materials after a timer goes off. When the class meets the requirement, they earn points toward additional free-time activities.
   - To encourage students to clean up quickly after labs, a junior high science teacher offers them a free 5 minutes of talk in their seats if the lab is cleaned up in time. Students who don't clean up in time are required to finish in silence.

4. Keep discipline encounters with students brief, clear, and to the point. Hold discussions regarding fairness or equity after class and in private.
   - After having been asked to stop whispering for the second time in 10 minutes, a sixth grader protests that he was asking about the assigned seat work. The teacher reminds him of the two incidents in 10 minutes and that his whispering is disruptive. The teacher then removes a slip from his packet without further discussion. The teacher sits down with him after class to discuss the problem and work toward a solution.
   - A first-grade teacher tries to make interventions instructional. When she uses nonverbal cues to discipline, she points to the appropriate rule on the chalkboard. If students seem confused, she either bends down and talks to them quickly in private or makes a general reminder about the rule and its reason, such as "Class, there's too much noise in here, and I'm having trouble thinking."

5. Follow through consistently in cases of disruptive behavior.
   - A teacher separates two tenth graders who disrupt lessons with their talking, telling them the new seat assignments are theirs until further notice. The next day, they sit in their old seats as the bell is about to ring. "Do you know why I moved you two yesterday?" the teacher says immediately. After a momentary pause, both students nod. "Then move quickly now, and be certain you're in your new seats tomorrow. You come talk with me when you're ready to stop your talking."
   - An eleventh-grade teacher reminds students about being seated when the bell rings. As the bell rings the next day, two girls are standing, having a conversation. The teacher turns to them and says, "I'm sorry, but you must not have understood me yesterday. To be counted on time, you need to be in your seats when the bell rings. Please go to the office and get a late admit pass. Please do it now . . . and if you want to talk with me about this, come in after class. Now, class, yesterday we were talking about. . . . "

Windows on Classrooms

At the beginning of the chapter, you saw illustrated in Shirley Barton's lesson how instruction and classroom management are interdependent. The following case study illustrates two ninth-grade teachers working with their students on the same topic. As you read, look for similarities and differences in the two teachers' approaches to instruction and classroom management.

Judy Harris was a ninth-grade geography teacher whose class was involved in a cultural unit on the Middle East. She had 32 students in a room designed for 24, so the students sat within arm's reach across the aisles.

As Ginger entered the room, she saw a large map projected high on the screen at the front of the room. She quickly slid into her seat just as the bell stopped ringing. Most students had already begun studying the map and the accompanying directions on the chalkboard: "Identify the longitude and latitude of Cairo and Damascus."

Judy took roll and handed back a set of papers as students busied themselves with the task.

She waited a moment for students to finish, then pulled down a large map in the front of the classroom and began by saying, "We've been studying the Middle East, and you just identified Damascus here in Syria," she noted, pointing at the map. "Now, think for a moment and make a prediction about the climate in Damascus."

Judy paused, surveyed the class, and said, "Bernice?" as she walked down one of the rows.

" . . . Damascus is about 34 North latitude, I think."

As soon as Judy walked past him, Darren reached across the aisle, tapping Kendra on the shoulder with his

pencil while he watched Judy's back from the corner of his eye. "Stop it, Darren," Kendra muttered, swiping at him with her hand.

Judy turned, came back up the aisle, and continued, "Good, Bernice. It's very close to 34."

Standing next to Darren, she asked, "What would that indicate about its temperature at this time of the year? . . . Darren?" she asked, looking directly at him.

" . . . I'm not sure."

"Warmer or colder than here?"

" . . . Warmer, I think."

"Okay. Good prediction, Darren. And why might that be the case? . . . Jim?"

"Move up here," Judy said quietly to Rachel, who had been whispering and passing notes to Deborah across the aisle. Judy nodded to a desk at the front of the room as she waited for Jim to answer.

"What did I do?" Rachel protested.

Judy leaned over Rachel's desk and pointed to a rule displayed on a poster:

*LISTEN WHEN SOMEONE
ELSE IS TALKING.*

"Quickly, now." She motioned to the desk.

" . . . Damascus is south of us and also in a desert," Jim responded.

"I wasn't doing anything," Rachel protested.

"I get frustrated when I'm watching people who aren't paying attention. I'm uncomfortable when I'm frustrated. Please move," Judy said evenly, looking Rachel in the eye.

"Good analysis, Jim. Now let's look at Cairo," she continued as she watched Rachel move to the new desk.

Now, let's turn to another teacher, Janelle Powers. Like Judy's classroom, Janelle's room was crowded; she had 29 students.

Shiana came through the classroom doorway just as the tardy bell rang.

"Take your seat quickly, Shiana," Janelle directed. "You're just about late. All right. Listen up, everyone," she continued. "Ali?"

"Here."

"Gaelen?"

"Here."

"Chu?"

"Here."

Janelle finished taking the roll, and she then walked around the room and handed back a set of papers as she went.

"You did quite well on the assignment," she commented. "Let's keep up the good work. . . . Howard and Manny, please stop talking while I'm returning the papers. Can't you just sit quietly for 1 minute?"

The boys, who were whispering, turned back to the front of the room.

"Now," Janelle continued, after handing back the last paper and returning to the front of the room, "we've been studying the Middle East, so let's review for a moment. . . . Look at the map and identify the longitude and latitude of Cairo. Take a minute and figure it out right now."

The students began as Janelle went to her file cabinet to get out some transparencies.

"Stop it, Damon," she heard Leila blurt out behind her.

"Leila," Janelle responded sternly, "we don't talk out like that in class."

"He's poking me, Mrs. Powers."

"Are you poking her, Damon?"

" . . . "

"Well?"

" . . . Not really."

"You did, too," Leila complained.

"Both of you stop it," Janelle warned. "Another outburst like that, Leila, and your name goes on the chalkboard."

As the last students were finishing the problem, Janelle looked up from the materials on her desk to an example on the overhead and heard Howard and Manny talking and giggling at the back of the room.

"Are you boys finished?"

"Yes," Manny answered.

"Well, be quiet then until everyone is done," Janelle directed, and went back to rearranging her materials.

"Quiet, everyone," she again directed as she looked up once more in response to a hum of voices around the room. "Is everyone finished? . . . Good. Pass your papers forward. . . . Remember, put your paper on the top of the stack. . . . Roberto, wait until the papers come from behind you before you pass yours forward."

Janelle collected the papers, put them on her desk, and then began, "We've talked about the geography of the Middle East, and now we want to look at the climate a bit more. It varies somewhat. For example, Syria is extremely hot in the summer but is actually quite cool in the winter. In fact, it snows in some parts.

"Now, what did we find for the latitude of Cairo?"

" . . . 30 ," Miguel volunteered.

"North or south, Miguel? . . . Wait a minute. Howard? . . . Manny? . . . This is the third time this period that I've had to say something to you about your talking, and the period isn't even 20 minutes old yet. Get out your rules and read me the rule about talking without permission. . . . Howard?"

" . . . "

"It's supposed to be in the front of your notebook."

" . . . "

"Manny?"

" . . . 'No speaking without permission of the teacher,'" Manny read from the front page of his notebook.

"Howard, where are your rules?"

" . . . I don't know."

"Move up here," Janelle directed, pointing to an empty desk at the front of the room. "You've been bothering me all week. If you can't learn to be quiet, you will be up here for the rest of the year."

Howard got up and slowly moved to the desk Janelle had pointed out. After Howard was seated, Janelle began again, "Where were we before we were rudely interrupted? . . . Oh yes. What did you get for the latitude of Cairo?"

"30 North," Miguel responded.

"Okay, good. . . . Now, Egypt also has a hot climate in the summer, in fact, very hot. The summer temperatures will often go over 100 Fahrenheit. . . . Egypt is also mostly desert, so the people have trouble making a living. Their primary source of subsistence is the Nile River, which floods frequently. Most of the agriculture of the country is near the river."

Janelle continued presenting information to the students for the next several minutes.

"Andrew, are you listening to this?" Janelle interjected as she saw Andrew put his head down on his folded arms.

" . . . Yes," he responded, lifting up his head.

"I hope so, because all this will be on the next test, which is only a week away."

Janelle then continued with her presentation.

Questions for Discussion and Analysis

Compare Janelle's classroom environment to Judy's. In analyzing the two classes, you may want to consider the following questions. In each case, be specific, and take information directly from the case study in making your comparisons.

1. What might we infer about Janelle's planning for classroom management, compared with Judy's? What seemed to be different about the two?

2. Although you don't have a lot of specific evidence about either teacher's rules, how do they compare on the basis of the evidence you do have?

3. Compare the two teachers' application of essential teaching skills. Be sure to provide evidence when the presence or absence of the skill is inferred rather than observed.

4. Compare the way the teachers talked to their students when they intervened. Identify specific behaviors in the case study in making your comparison.

5. Using the information from this chapter as the basis for your assessment, assess Janelle Powers's overall management effectiveness. Consider your answers to Questions 1 through 4 as you make your analysis.

6. Like most classrooms, Janelle's class contains learners with diverse backgrounds. How effective would her management and instruction be for these students?

Now go to our Companion Website to assess your understanding of chapter content with the Student Self-Assessment, apply comprehension in the Online Casebook, and broaden your knowledge base with links to important Educational Psychology World Wide Web sites.

 # Summary

Productive Environments and Learning-Focused Classrooms

In productive learning environments, the classroom culture—which includes the language, values, and learning experiences—is focused on learning. In productive learning environments, classroom order and effective instruction are interdependent. It is very difficult to maintain an orderly classroom in the absence of effective teaching, and it is also impossible to teach effectively in a classroom that lacks order.

Creating Productive Learning Environments: Effective Teaching

Essential teaching skills are teaching behaviors that promote student learning and contribute to productive learning environments. Effective teachers are high in efficacy; they believe they are responsible for student learning and can increase it. They are caring and enthusiastic, they are good role models, and they have high expectations for their students.

Effective teachers are well organized, know what's going on in their classrooms, use their time well, and communicate clearly. They represent content in attention-getting ways, provide clear and informative feedback to students, and review important ideas.

Effective teachers use effective questioning strategies. They ask many questions, prompt students who don't answer successfully, employ equitable distribution, and give students time to think about their answers.

Creating Productive Learning Environments: Classroom Management

Well-planned rules and procedures help establish and maintain orderly classrooms. An effective list of rules should be short, clear, and positive and include reasons for the rules' existence. Allowing student input into rules promotes understanding, gives the students a sense of control, and contributes to responsibility and self-regulation.

Procedures organize daily classroom routines. Like any concept or skill, rules and procedures must be carefully taught, monitored, and reviewed.

Rules and procedures should be taught in the same way that any abstraction is taught: learners construct understanding of them as they see and discuss examples.

The first few days of the school year are critical in establishing expectations. Communication with parents should begin as soon as school opens and continue throughout the year.

Effective managers keep their interventions brief, preserve student dignity, and follow through consistently on management decisions. Focusing on positive behavior, ignoring misbehavior, and employing simple desists can eliminate minor disruptions. Logical consequences help students see the connection between their behaviors and the effects of their behaviors on others.

More lengthy interventions are sometimes necessary when misbehavior persists or occurs frequently. In cases of chronic or serious misbehavior, it is necessary to intervene immediately and hold students accountable.

Important Concepts

active listening (p. 502)

assertive discipline
    (p. 504)

classroom management
    (p. 481)

closure (p. 476)

connected discourse
    (p. 470)

desist (p. 506)

discipline (p. 481)

emphasis (p. 470)

equitable distribution
    (p. 474)

essential teaching skills
    (p. 467)

feedback (p. 471)

I-message (p. 501)

indirect cues (p. 506)

introductory focus (p. 471)

logical consequences
    (p. 502)

nonverbal communication
    (p. 500)

open-ended question
    (p. 475)

organization (p. 469)

overlapping (p. 498)

precise terminology
    (p. 470)

procedures (p. 484)

productive learning
    environment (p. 466)

prompt (p. 475)

questioning frequency
    (p. 474)

review (p. 476)

rules (p. 484)

sensory focus (p. 471)

transition signals (p. 470)

wait-time (p. 475)

withitness (p. 497)

Part III

The Classroom

Classroom Processes

Teacher-Centered Approaches to Instruction

12

Sam Barnett, a first-year second-grade teacher, was working with his students in a unit on addition. Because he was a beginning teacher and teaching a lesson on addition that he knew would be difficult for his second graders, he planned in detail. His plan for the next set of lessons appears at the bottom of this page.

With his plan on his desk, Sam began math by saying, "Okay, class, today we are going to go a step farther with our work in addition so that we'll be able to solve problems like this," displaying the following on the overhead.

Jana and Patti are friends. They were saving special soda cans to get a free compact disc. They can get the CD if they save 35 cans. Jana had 15 cans and Patti had 12. How many did they have together?

After pausing briefly to give students a chance to read the problem, Sam continued, "Now, why do you think it's important to know how many Jana and Patti have together?"

" . . . So, they can know how much they get, like . . . so they can get their CD," Devon answered haltingly.

"Sure," Sam smiled. "If they know how many they have, they'll

---

Unit: Addition of two-digit numbers
Objectives:
To understand addition of two-digit numbers:

1. Recognize that word problems require addition.
2. Add two-digit numbers that don't require regrouping.
3. Add two-digit numbers that require regrouping.

To understand place value:

1. Add numbers so places values are accurate.
2. Explain the difference between a numeral in the ones place and a numeral in the tens place.

Rationale: Being able to add two-digit numbers is a basic skill all students must possess. Understanding place value is critical for understanding all number operations.

Procedure:

1. Present problem requiring addition of two-digit numbers.
2. Explain that these problems are important and that we must be able to solve them quickly and easily.
3. Distribute beans and bean sticks to the students.
4. Review single-digit addition. Have students represent solutions with their materials.
5. Demonstrate the solution to a two-digit problem.
6. Have the students represent the solution with their materials.
7. Have the students explain the difference between a numeral in the tens place and a numeral in the ones place (such as 27 compared to 12).
8. Give practice problems and discuss them.
9. Assign problems on worksheet.

Assessment:
Give the students a series of word problems, some of which require two-digit addition, and have them solve the problems.

Materials:
Text, problem worksheet.

know how close they're coming to getting their CD. If they don't, they're stuck. That's why it's important."

"We'll come back to the problem in a minute," Sam continued, "but before we do, let's review. Everyone take out your bean sticks and beans and do this problem."

Sam then put the following on the chalkboard and watched as students used their sticks and beans to demonstrate their answer.

$$\begin{array}{r} 8 \\ +7 \\ \hline \end{array}$$

"Very good," Sam smiled as most of the students laid a stick with 10 beans glued on it and 5 more beans on the centers of their desks. Others laid out 15 beans, and Sam showed them how they could exchange 10 of them for a stick with 10 glued on it.

Sam had the students do two more problems with their counters and then continued, "Let's begin by looking at our problem again."

Turning on the overhead again, he said, "Everyone look up here. Good. Now what does the problem ask us? . . . Shalinda?"

"How many . . . they have together?" Shalinda responded hesitantly.

"And how many does Jana have? . . . Abdul?"

" . . . Fifteen?"

"Good, Abdul. And how many does Patti have? Celinda?"

"Twelve."

"Okay, so let's put the problem on the chalkboard like this," Sam continued, writing the following:

$$\begin{array}{r} 15 \\ +12 \\ \hline \end{array}$$

"Now, I'd like everyone to show me how to make a 15 at your desk by using your sticks and beans."

Sam paused as the class worked at their desks.

"Does everyone's look like this?" Sam asked as he demonstrated at the flannel board.

They did the same with the 12, and Sam continued, "Now, watch what I do here. . . . When I add 5 and 2, what do I get? Hmm, let me think about that . . . 5 and 2 are 7. Let's put a 7 up on the chalkboard," Sam said as he walked to the chalkboard and added a 7.

$$\begin{array}{r} 15 \\ +12 \\ \hline 7 \end{array}$$

"Now show me that with your beans," and he watched as the students combined 5 beans and 2 beans on their desks.

"Now, we still have to add the 10s. What do we get when we add two 10s? Hmm, that should be easy. One 10 and one 10 is two 10s. Now, look where I have to put the 2 up here. It is under the 10s column because the 2 means two 10s." With that, he wrote the following on the chalkboard:

$$\begin{array}{r} 15 \\ +12 \\ \hline 27 \end{array}$$

"So, how many cans did Jana and Patti have together? . . . Alesha?"

" . . . 27?"

"Good, Alesha. They had 27 altogether. Now, with your beans, what is this 7?" he asked, pointing to the 7 on the chalkboard. . . . Carol?"

" . . . It's this," she said, motioning to the seven beans on her desk.

"Good, yes it is. It's the seven individual beans. . . . Now, . . . what is this 2? . . . Jeremy?" Sam went on, pointing to the numeral on the chalkboard.

"It's . . . these," Jeremy answered, holding up the two sticks with the beans glued on them.

"Now, we saw that I added the 5 and the 2 before I added the two 1s. Why do you suppose I did that? . . . Anyone?"

"Maybe . . . you have to find out how many . . . ones you have to see if we can make a 10 . . . or something," Callie offered.

"That's excellent thinking, Callie. That's exactly right. We'll see why again tomorrow when we have some problems in which we'll have to regroup, and that will be just a little tougher, but for now let's remember what Callie said.

"Now, who can describe in words for us one more time what the 2 means. . . . Leroy?"

"It's . . . two, ah, two . . . bunches or something like that of 10 beans."

"Yes, that's correct, Leroy. It's two groups of 10 beans or, in the case of Jana and Patti, it's two groups of 10 soda cans.

"So let's look again. There is an important difference between this 2," pointing to the 10s column, "and this 2," pointing to the 2 in the 12. What is this difference? . . . Katrina?"

"That 2 . . . is two . . . groups of 10, and that one is just 2 . . . by itself."

"Yes, that's good thinking, Katrina. Good work, everyone. . . . Show me this 2," pointing to the 10s column.

The students held up two sticks with the beans glued on them.

"Good, and show me this 2," pointing to the 2 in the 12, and the students held up two beans.

"Great," Sam nodded. "Now, let's try another one," he continued, displaying the following on the chalkboard:

$$23$$
$$+12$$

Sam watched as students used their beans and sticks to make 35, and again they discussed the problem. They did two more, and then Sam gave the students an assignment of 10 more problems to do for homework.

*C*onducting high-quality instruction is at the heart of what teachers do. From the beginning of your study of learning and learners—starting in Chapter 1, you've learned that effective instruction requires a thorough understanding of content and how to represent it, the learning process, and the characteristics of learners. Using these elements as a framework, we turn now to two chapters examining instruction in depth. In this chapter we consider teacher-centered approaches, and in Chapter 13 we turn to instruction from a learner-centered perspective.

After you've completed your study of this chapter, you should be able to meet the following objectives:

▎ Describe characteristics of teacher-centered instruction.
▎ Identify goals and content for which teacher-centered instruction is most effective.
▎ Explain how teacher-centered planning occurs.
▎ Identify the phases of direct instruction
▎ Describe elements of effective lectures and lecture–discussions.

When Is Teacher-Centered Instruction Appropriate?

A great deal has been written about the advantages of learner-centered compared to teacher-centered approaches to instruction (e.g., Lambert & McCombs, 1998; Shuell, 1996). **Teacher-centered approaches** involve instruction *"in which the teacher's role is to present the knowledge to be learned and to direct, in a rather explicit manner, the learning process of the students"* (Shuell, 1996, p. 731), whereas **learner-centered approaches** include instruction *in which learners, with the teacher's guidance, are made responsible for constructing their own understanding.*

In our discussions of learning, we've emphasized the active involvement of students in learning, which is important for both their understanding and motivation. This might lead some to conclude that the only appropriate approaches to instruction are learner centered. This isn't true; for some goals teacher-centered approaches are more effective, and for others learner-centered approaches are superior (Shuell, 1996). In this chapter we examine topics for which teacher-centered approaches are more appropriate. This content typically has one or more of the following characteristics:

▎ It is content that is specific and well-defined. Adding one- and two-digit numbers, as Sam's students were doing, is an example.

▌ It is content that all students are expected to master. Sam's goal was for all his students to master the process of addition; it's a basic skill.

▌ It is content students would have difficulty obtaining on their own.

Making students responsible for constructing their own understanding of the procedure for adding two-digit numbers, as would be the case in learner-centered instruction, is inefficient and potentially confusing; for Sam's goals, a teacher-centered approach is more appropriate.

As you will see in Chapter 13, teacher-centered and learner-centered approaches can be very compatible. For instance, the basic skills Sam's students mastered with his teacher-centered approach are necessary for problem solving, and problem-solving abilities are often most effectively developed with learner-centered approaches. Similarly, teachers might use a well-organized lecture–discussion—a teacher-centered strategy—to help students acquire the background knowledge needed to carry on an effective discussion—a learner-centered process.

Characteristics of Teacher-Centered Instruction

To begin this section, let's look again at Sam's work with his second graders. As you saw earlier, Sam's goal was compatible with a teacher-centered approach; he was teaching well-defined content that all his students were expected to master. In addition, his instruction had the following characteristics:

▌ During his planning, Sam identified specific objectives for the lesson and designed learning activities to help students meet the objectives.

▌ The lesson remained focused on the objectives.

▌ Sam took primary responsibility for guiding the learning by modeling and explaining a specific procedure for the skill.

▌ Students practiced the skill with the goal of developing automaticity.

▌ The lesson was based on cognitive views of learning, particularly information processing.

Let's look at the last point in more detail.

Teacher-Centered Instruction: Theoretical Foundations

As cognitive views of learning have become more prominent, teacher-centered instruction has sometimes been criticized as ineffective and grounded in behaviorism (Marshall, 1992; Stoddart, Connell, Stofflett, & Peck, 1993). Done effectively, however, this isn't the case, and, in fact, teacher-centered instruction is well grounded in cognitive learning theory, particularly information processing.

To see how, let's look at Sam's lesson again. He began with a problem designed to *attract students' attention* and provide focus for the lesson. Then, he carefully reviewed what they had already done to help *access background knowledge from long-term memory*. He continued by carefully guiding students' understanding with questioning and modeling. He didn't focus on memorizing procedures or specific responses that he could reinforce; rather, he emphasized thought and understanding with questions and comments, such as

Effective teacher-centered instruction requires knowledge of learners and learning, understanding of content, and effective strategies to represent ideas to learners.

"Now, why do you think it's important to know how many Jana and Patti have together?"

"Now what does the problem ask us?"

"Why do you suppose I did that?"

"Yes, that's good thinking, Katrina," (in response to her identifying the 2 in 27 as 2 groups of 10, and the 2 in 12 as 2 units)

Finally, Sam had students practice, first under his guidance to help them *encode the procedure*, and then independently to *develop automaticity*. These relationships are outlined in Table 12.1.

Table 12.1

Teacher-centered instruction and information processing

Direct Instruction Step	Information Processing Element
Introduction and review	Attract and focus learner attention.
	Activate background knowledge.
Presentation	Input information into working memory.
Guided practice	Check perception.
	Begin encoding into long-term memory.
Independent practice	Complete encoding.
	Develop automaticity.

Having looked at the goals, characteristics, and theoretical foundation of teacher-centered instruction, let's turn to planning for teacher-centered lessons.

Planning for Teacher-Centered Instruction

On the surface, planning for instruction seems simple: specify objectives, design learning activities to help students reach them, and assess the extent to which the objectives have been reached. It isn't as simple as it appears on the surface, however, because planning and conducting effective lessons require extensive teacher knowledge and clear teacher thinking (Borko & Putnam, 1996).

Prerequisites to Effective Planning

The relationship between planning and instruction is complex and interconnected. Effective teachers possess at least four kinds of knowledge (see Chapter 1):

- Knowledge of content (Jetton & Alexander, 1997), such as a thorough understanding of mathematical skills, in the case of Sam's instruction.
- Pedagogical content knowledge (Shulman, 1986), such as a teacher's ability to represent the solutions to algebraic equations in concrete and understandable ways.
- General pedagogical knowledge (Borko & Putnam, 1996), such as understanding how to organize orderly classrooms, and use teaching strategies that involve students and lead to thorough understanding.
- Knowledge of learners and learning (Borko & Putnam, 1996), such as understanding that challenge and success are both necessary to help students develop a sense of self-efficacy about their math abilities.

12.1 ▬
Could teachers have thorough knowledge of content and inadequate pedagogical content knowledge? Could teachers have pedagogical content knowledge without knowledge of content? Explain in both cases.

Sam obviously understood addition, but more importantly, he demonstrated pedagogical content knowledge in helping his students represent two-digit numbers with their beans and sticks. The beans and sticks were concrete representations of the numbers, and he understood that these representations were essential in making abstract numbers and processes more meaningful for his second graders.

Sam also understood cognitive learning theory; he knew that students learn more when they're actively involved in learning, and he put them in active roles as they developed their skills. Further, he knew that second graders' thinking tends to be concrete operational, so he prepared concrete ways to represent *place value*. And, because he understood the central role language plays in learning and development, he provided scaffolding through questioning. Sam's knowledge of learners and learning guided his planning and the conduct of his lesson.

A Teacher-Centered Planning Model

The most common teacher-centered approach to planning is based on work done by Ralph Tyler and described in his book *Basic Principles of Curriculum and Instruction*, first published in 1950. This text is a classic; over the years, it has had more impact on the way teachers are taught to plan and organize instruction than any other work.

Tyler described the relationships between planning and instruction in four logical and sequential steps, outlined in Figure 12.1.

Figure 12.1

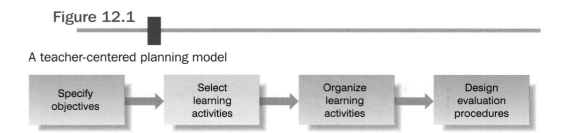

A teacher-centered planning model

Sam used this model in his planning, and this likely reflects his teacher-preparation experiences. Tyler's model was so influential that literally hundreds of thousands of teachers and educational leaders have been trained in its use. Let's look more closely at the components of the model.

Specifying Objectives

Planning begins when teachers identify objectives. According to Tyler, the most useful form for stating objectives is "to express them in terms which identify both the kind of behavior to be developed in the student and the content or area of life in which this behavior is to operate" (Tyler, 1950, p. 46). **Behavioral objectives**—*statements that specify learning outcomes in terms of observable student behaviors*—provide focus and direction for both teachers and learners.

Mager's Behavioral Objectives.   A second book that strongly influenced teaching was written by Robert Mager (1962), *Preparing Instructional Objectives*. Short and highly readable, Mager's book suggested that an objective ought to describe "what the student will be doing when demonstrating his achievement and how you will know he is doing it" (p. 53). Mager's behavioral objectives have three parts:

1. An observable behavior
2. The conditions under which the behavior will occur
3. Criteria for acceptable performance

Examples of objectives written according to Mager's format are listed in Table 12.2.

12.2 ▬
You want your students to understand the main ideas in a passage. Using Mager's format, write an objective that would reflect this goal.

Gronlund's Instructional Objectives.   A popular alternative to Mager's approach is suggested by Norman Gronlund (1995). **Gronlund's instructional objectives** *include a general objective, such as* know, understand, *or* apply, *followed by specific learning outcomes that operationally define what is meant by* knows, understands, *or* applies. Objectives written according to Gronlund's format are illustrated in Table 12.3.

Gronlund's objectives, in contrast with Mager's, don't include conditions and criteria. These two components "are especially useful for programmed instruction and for mastery testing in simple training programs. When used for regular classroom instruction, however, they result in long cumbersome lists that restrict the freedom of the teacher" (Gronlund, 1995, p. 10). Experience supports Gronlund's position. Teachers rarely specify conditions and criteria in their objectives, although thinking about them can help teachers design effective assessments. Mager's work is significant because of its historical impact, but most curriculum materials now use Gronlund's approach or a modification of it.

12.3 ▬
Using Gronlund's format, rewrite the objective you wrote for 12.2.

Objectives in the Cognitive Domain.   Let's look at three specific learning outcomes using Gronlund's format.

Table 12.2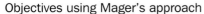

Objectives using Mager's approach

Objective	Condition	Performance	Criteria
Given a list of sentences, the student will identify the adjective in each.	given a list of sentences	identify	each
Given 10 problems involving subtraction with regrouping, the student will correctly solve 7.	given 10 problems	solve	7 of 10
Given a ruler and compass, the student will construct the bisector of an angle to within 1°.	given a ruler and compass	construct	within 1°

Table 12.3

Objectives using Gronlund's format

General Objective	Specific Learning Outcome
Understands concepts	1. Writes definitions of concepts 2. Identifies examples of concepts 3. Generates examples of concepts 4. Identifies coordinate concepts
Solves problems	1. Identifies information relevant to the problem 2. Describes problem qualitatively 3. Translates qualitative description into numerical symbols 4. Estimates answer 5. Generates solution to problem

▌ Defines adjectives
▌ Identifies adjectives in sentences
▌ Makes writing attractive by creatively using adjectives

Each has "understands adjectives" as the general objective, so they fit in the **cognitive domain**, which *focuses on knowledge and understanding of facts, concepts, principles, rules, skills, and problem solving.* The outcomes vary, however, in their demands on learners, how they should be taught, and how they would be assessed.

In response to these differences, researchers have developed a system to classify different kinds of learning outcomes and assessments (Bloom, Englehart, Furst, Hill, & Krath-

The different levels of the cognitive domain help teachers design learning activities that emphasize problem solving and critical thinking.

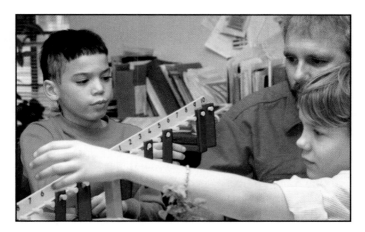

wohl, 1956). The results of this effort are referred to as **Bloom's taxonomy**, a *classification system developed to help teachers think about the objectives they write, the learning activities they design, and the assessments they prepare*. It has six levels ranging from memory to higher-order operations, which are outlined in Table 12.4.

The taxonomy reminds us that we want our students to do more than memorize knowledge about the topics we teach, and that we should design learning activities and assessments to help them reach the higher levels, such as application, analysis, synthesis, and evaluation. This goal is even more important now in the 21st century, as student thinking, decision making, and problem solving are increasingly emphasized.

12.4
Classify each of the three outcomes for the general objective "understands adjectives" into one of the levels of the taxonomy in Table 12.4.

Table 12.4

Levels, outcomes, and examples in the cognitive domain

Level	Outcome	Example
Knowledge	Knows terms, facts, rules, classifications, generalizations, principles, algorithms, and methods	States the definition of figurative language
Comprehension	Translates, interprets, predicts, generalizes, explains, identifies examples	Identifies statements that are similes and metaphors
Application	Applies rules, methods, and principles to unique situations	Rewrites a passage and increases expressiveness using figurative language
Analysis	Breaks communication into parts, determines point of view, recognizes bias, specifies implications, identifies theme	Identifies author intent in use of figurative language
Synthesis	Creates new products, methods, and patterns, from constituent elements	Creates an original work using figurative language
Evaluation	Judges on the basis of evidence and criteria	Assesses quality of a piece of writing in which the author has used figurative language

Source: Taxonomy of Education Objectives: Book 1: Cognitive Domain edited by Benjamin S. Bloom. Copyright © 1956, 1984 by Longman Publishing Group.

12.5 ▬

A science teacher says, "One of the things I'm after is for them to get over their fear of science. Otherwise, they'll take only what's required in high school." At what level in the affective taxonomy would this goal be classified?

12.6 ▬

Think back to your study of Chapter 10. Whose work, discussed there in particular, reminds us of the importance of affective factors in learning? Using his work, explain how these factors influence the amount that students learn.

Objectives in the Affective Domain.   While most of the focus in schools is on cognitive outcomes, teachers have many implicit objectives that don't fit in that domain. For example, science and math teachers want students to like these subjects and appreciate their importance in today's world, but they rarely write *liking* and *appreciating* as objectives. In these cases, teachers have goals that fit into the **affective domain**, which *focuses on attitudes and values and the development of students' personal and emotional growth.*

Objectives in the affective domain can also be classified into levels, and a taxonomy similar in structure to the one in the cognitive domain has been developed (Krathwohl, Bloom, & Masia, 1964). The guiding principle behind the affective domain is **internalization**, or *the extent to which an attitude or value has been incorporated into a student's total value structure.* The affective domain is outlined in Table 12.5 and illustrated with an example from science.

While much of teachers' focus in the affective domain is implicit, they sometimes concentrate on it deliberately. For example, many multicultural lessons have increased awareness of and appreciation for other cultures' values and customs as their goals. Similarly, learning about disabilities helps students develop more positive attitudes toward people with exceptionalities (Hardman, Drew, & Egan, 1999). The taxonomy reminds us that attitudes and emotions strongly affect learning, and that we should keep these factors in mind when we plan and teach.

Objectives in the Psychomotor Domain.   A third type of learning exists in the **psychomotor domain**, which *focuses on the development of students' physical abilities and skills.* It has historically received less emphasis than the cognitive or affective domains, except in physical education, and taxonomies for it weren't even developed until the 1970s (Harrow, 1972; E. Simpson, 1972). However, schools are increasing their emphasis on the psychomotor domain as its role in overall development becomes better understood. For instance, kindergarten children practice tying their shoes, and the ability to physically manipulate a pencil is considered in assessing a child's readiness for writing. Science requires using equipment such as microscopes and balances, geometry involves con-

Table 12.5 ▬

Levels, outcomes, and examples in the affective domain

Level	Outcome	Example
Receiving	Is willing to listen, open-minded	Pays attention in science class
Responding	Demonstrates new behavior, volunteers involvement	Volunteers answers, asks questions
Valuing	Shows commitment, maintains involvement	Reads ahead in text, watches science-oriented programs on television
Organizing	Integrates new value into personal structure	Chooses to take 4 years of science in high school because of interest in science
Characterizing by value	Gains open, firm, and long-range commitment to value	Chooses a branch of science as a career field

Source: Taxonomy of Educational Objectives: Handbook II: Affective Domain by D. Krathwohl, B. Bloom, and B. Masia, 1964, New York: David McKay. Copyright 1964 by David McKay. Adapted by permission.

Growth in the psychomotor domain contributes to healthy self-concepts and increases physical well-being in students.

structions with compasses and rulers, word processing and driver's training require physical skills, and fine motor movements are essential in art and music. These are all goals in the psychomotor domain.

Table 12.6 presents a description and illustrations of the psychomotor taxonomy using Harrow's (1972) conception as a framework.

The psychomotor domain provides us with a more complete picture of our students as human beings. In addition to helping them grow cognitively and affectively, we want them to develop healthy bodies that they can use throughout their lives.

Preparing Learning Activities

Once objectives have been specified, we next prepare learning activities designed to help learners reach them. For instance, Sam wanted his students to understand the addition of

Table 12.6

Levels, outcomes, and examples in the psychomotor domain

Level	Outcome	Examples
Reflex movements	Involuntary responses	Blinking, knee jerks
Basic fundamental movements	Innate movements, combinations of reflexes	Eating, running, physically tracking an object
Perceptual abilities	Movement following interpretation of stimuli	Walking a balance beam, skipping rope, writing p and q
Physical abilities	Endurance, strength, flexibility, agility	Pull-ups, toe touching, distance bicycling
Skilled movements	Efficiency in complex movement tasks	Hitting a tennis ball, jazz dancing
Nondiscursive communication	Communication with physical movement, body language	Pleasure, authority, warmth, and other emotions demonstrated with body language

Source: A Taxonomy of the Psychomotor Domain: A Guide for Developing Behavioral Objectives by A. Harrow, 1972. New York: David McKay. Copyright 1972 by David McKay. Adapted by permission.

two-digit numbers with and without grouping. He planned to help students reach this goal by demonstrating how to solve problems and by having students practice both with manipulatives and with paper and pencil. These were his learning activities.

Organizing Learning Activities

Merely selecting learning activities isn't enough. Activities must be organized and sequenced to be most effective. For instance, Sam began by reviewing single-digit addition, moved to the addition of two-digit numbers and, finally, discussed place value. This progression from simple to complex was intended to accommodate the developmental and learning needs of his students. Teachers consciously sequence and organize learning activities to help students reach higher-level objectives.

Task Analysis: A Planning Tool

Kelly Ryan stared at the second-grade math book and didn't know where to start. Her assignment in her methods class was to identify a topic in the area of math, plan a lesson, and teach it to a small group of second graders. She had met with Mrs. Ramirez, her cooperating teacher, and they had identified two-digit subtraction with regrouping as a topic that needed more work. Mrs. Ramirez had even given her some worksheets with subtraction problems:

$$98 \qquad 27 \qquad 25 \qquad 72 \qquad 45$$
$$-19 \qquad -18 \qquad -16 \qquad -13 \qquad -36$$

Kelly sat, a bit bewildered, not knowing where to begin.

Task analysis, which is *the process of breaking content down into its component parts* (Alberto & Troutman, 1999; Gardner, 1985), can be a helpful planning tool when teachers are uncertain about how to sequence parts of a topic. Breaking a complex skill into subskills helps teachers think about prerequisites and helps students by allowing them to practice simpler skills before moving to more complex ones. Basic steps in doing a task analysis are outlined in Figure 12.2.

Teachers begin a task analysis by specifying the terminal behavior—what students will be able to demonstrate when the lesson is finished. This is stated in the form of an objective, such as "converting fractions to decimals" or "solving two-digit subtraction problems that require regrouping."

Teachers then identify the prerequisite skills needed to reach the objective. For example, for performing two-digit subtraction with regrouping, they include

12.7 ▬

You want your first graders to improve their awareness of whether or not they're paying attention in lessons. Describe how you would prepare and organize learning activities to reach this objective.

Figure 12.2

Performing a task analysis

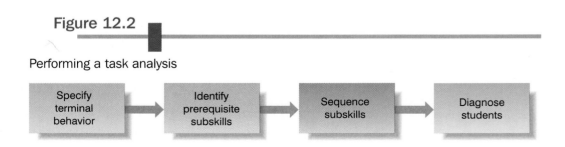

- Knowing basic subtraction facts (e.g., 7 – 5)
- Understanding place value (e.g., 15 is 1 ten plus 5 ones)
- Being able to do two-column subtraction with no regrouping when the bottom number is a single digit (e.g., 15 – 4)

Once identified, subskills must be sequenced from simple to complex. Gagne (1985) describes this process as a learning hierarchy and presents evidence that learning prerequisite skills facilitates learning more complex target skills (Gagne & Dick, 1983). The sequence in Kelly's case is straightforward: Students must first know basic facts and place value, then one-digit from two-digit subtraction, and two-digit from two-digit subtraction without regrouping before they can master subtraction with regrouping.

Having sequenced the skills, teachers determine which skills students lack, usually through a pretest at the beginning of a unit. Kelly's instruction will depend, for example, on whether or not her students understand subtraction without regrouping. If they don't, she will need to review or even formally reteach it before she moves to regrouping (Rosenshine & Stevens, 1986).

Task analysis can be very helpful in planning. By forcing teachers to think concretely about goals and specific outcomes, task analysis helps shift teachers' attention away from the content and toward students—what they already know and what kinds of learning activities can build on this knowledge.

> **12.8**
> You want your students to be able to write sentences using adverbs correctly. Design a brief task analysis for this skill.

Assessing Learner Understanding

The final phase of the Tyler model calls for specifying assessments. Sam followed the model by stating in his lesson plan how his students would be assessed. Specifying objectives during planning provides both a blueprint for learning activities and a focus for assessing learning. We discuss this process further in Chapter 14 when we describe assessment procedures in detail.

The Tyler model is a logical, sequential framework for planning instruction. It makes sense to first consider what you want students to learn, then to select ways of helping them learn it, and finally to determine whether or not the learning has taken place.

Instructional Alignment: A Key to Learning

One outcome of careful planning is **instructional alignment**, which is *the match between goals, learning activities, and assessments.* We saw alignment in Sam's planning. His objective was for his second graders to be able to add two-digit numbers, his learning activities focused on this skill, and his assessments were designed to determine the extent to which they could perform the skill.

Alignment is essential to effective teaching and maximal learning. However, it is surprisingly easy for instruction to be out of alignment. For instance, if a teacher's goal is for students to be

Assessment can be conducted in a variety of forms and provides teachers with information about whether or not objectives have been reached.

able to write effectively, yet instruction focuses on isolated grammar skills, the instruction is out of alignment, as is a teacher's instruction when the goal is for students to apply math concepts but the learning activities have students practicing computation problems. The question instructional alignment encourages us to ask is, "What does my goal (e.g., "apply math concepts") actually mean, and do my learning and assessment activities actually lead to the goal?"

Classroom Connections

Using Taxonomies to Effectively Select Objectives

1. Consciously plan for goals in different domains to provide a balanced educational experience.
   - A physics teacher plans her initial presentation of vector problems around soccer players kicking the ball and moving to it. "I want them to appreciate science and see that vectors apply to 'where they live,'" she says.
   - A music teacher dislikes rock music but plans to begin her unit on different musical forms with songs by prominent rock stars based on the classics. "Students appreciate the classics once they find out that a lot of rock stars first got their ideas from them," she notes.

2. In the cognitive domain, carefully consider the level of your instruction. Make an effort to focus your goals on meaningful activities that encourage student thinking.
   - A fourth-grade teacher comments after giving a quiz on body parts, "I give them a drawing and have them identify the parts in the drawing and explain their functions. It's much better than having them just memorize the definitions."
   - In a ninth-grade geography lesson, the teacher wants her students to understand how climate is influenced by the interaction of a number of vari-

ables. To reach her goal, she gives students a map of a fictitious island, together with longitude, latitude, topography, and wind direction. She then gears her instruction around the conclusions they can make about the climate of the island.

Using Instructional Alignment to Make Your Teaching Effective

3. Be sure that your goals, learning activities, and assessments are consistent. Keep the need for alignment in mind as you plan.
   - A geometry teacher wants her students to experience the intellectual rigor involved in geometric proofs. She then spends much of her planning time creating problems and examples to help students practice doing proofs and seeing the logic involved in them.
   - A middle school teacher wants her students to become persuasive writers. With this goal in mind, she has them write letters to local politicians and school board members taking positions on issues they feel strongly about, such as the building of a new park or a proposed student dress code. They discuss and analyze the letters before mailing them.

Types of Teacher-Centered Instruction

Having discussed planning for teacher-centered instruction, let's turn now to three teacher-centered approaches—direct instruction and two types of expository teaching, lectures and lecture–discussions.

Direct Instruction

At the beginning of the chapter, we said that teacher-centered instruction involves objectives and learning activities specified by the teacher, lessons that remain focused on the objectives, well-defined content, and teachers taking primary responsibility for guiding the learning. One teacher-centered approach, called **direct instruction**, is *a teacher-centered strategy designed to help students learn concepts and procedural skills.* Direct instruction is used when teachers want to ensure that all students master essential content (Gersten, Taylor, & Graves, 1999).

Procedural Skills

Procedural skills have three essential characteristics:

- *They have a specific set of identifiable operations or procedures* (which is why they're called procedural skills).
- *They can be illustrated with a large and varied number of examples.*
- *They are developed through practice* (Doyle, 1983).

Adding two-digit numbers, as we saw in Sam's lesson, is a procedural skill. Others include punctuating sentences, finding the longitude and latitude of cities, balancing chemical equations, and solving percent–mixture problems. Each has an unlimited number of examples, they follow specific procedures, and students develop facility through practice.

Models of Direct Instruction

A great deal of research was conducted in the 1970s and 1980s attempting to identify essential steps in effective direct instruction lessons (Good, Grouws, & Ebmeier, 1983; Hunter, 1982; Rosenshine & Stevens, 1986). Various authors describe the steps differently, but they are similar in all models. Table 12.7 illustrates the elements of three direct instruction models.

Steps in Direct Instruction

In analyzing the different models, we see that direct instruction occurs in four basic steps, illustrated in Figure 12.3 and discussed in the sections that follow.

Introduction and Review.   Direct instruction begins with a review of the previous day's work, including a discussion of students' homework (Gersten et al., 1999). The teacher then attempts to capture students' attention and motivate them to learn by describing the objective and explaining why studying the topic is important. Although this procedure may seem obvious, nearly a fourth of all skills lessons begin with little or no introduction (Brophy, 1982). Sam expanded this phase by asking students why they thought it was important, actively involving learners and allowing him to check their understanding of the problem.

> **12.9**
> The definition of direct instruction states that the strategy is designed to teach concepts and procedural skills. What are the similarities and differences between procedural skills and concepts (discussed in Chapter 8)?

> **12.10**
> Explain why review is important using information processing theory as a basis for your explanation. Also explain why introduction and review are important using motivation theory as a basis.

Table 12.7

Models of direct instruction

Teaching Functions (Rosenshine & Stevens, 1986)	Missouri Mathematics Program (Good, et al., 1983)	Hunter Mastery Teaching (Hunter, 1982)
Review Review homework, prior learning, prerequisite skills	**Opening** Review skills, collect homework	**Anticipatory set** Present problem or question to attract learners' attention; explain purpose of lesson
Presentation Specify goal; teach in small steps; use examples	**Development** Provide examples; model processes; rapid pace; high learner involvement	**Input and Modeling** Present information; provide examples; model processes
Guided Practice Practice problems; teacher questioning; high success; feedback; reteach if needed	**Seat work** Successful practice; student accountability	**Structured practice** Practice examples; check for learner understanding; provide feedback
Independent Practice Learners practice; teacher monitors work	**Homework** Homework every day but Friday; review problems each day	**Independent Practice** Learners practice; teacher monitors; provide feedback

Figure 12.3

Steps in direct instruction

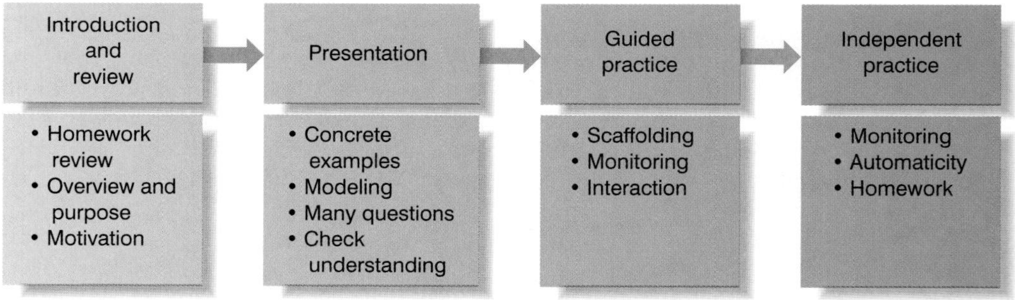

Presentation.   The second step in direct instruction involves presenting information so that it can be processed and encoded into long-term memory (Gersten et al., 1999; Stein & Carnine, 1999). Sam's presentation used both modeling and hands-on experiences to help students understand the procedure for adding two-digit numbers. Modeling provided a specific set of actions students could imitate, examples provided concrete experiences, and Sam proceeded in short steps to avoid overloading students' working memories.

Understanding that learners must be active, Sam also encouraged interaction in his lesson. He asked students to verbally explain what the 7 and 2 in 27 meant, he had them demonstrate each with their sticks and beans, and he also asked them to explain the difference between the 2 in 27 and the 2 in 12. Discussing and explaining the logic behind procedures is a very important part of learning activities and one that teachers frequently miss. The better students understand the reasons for specific steps, the more likely they are to use them correctly and transfer them to new situations (Rittle-Johnson, & Alibali, 1999). Teachers often involve learners in hands-on activities but then fail to make the connection between them and the abstractions—such as numerals written on the board—that they represent (Ball, 1992).

Guided Practice.   Guided practice applies the concept of scaffolding (see Chapters 2, 8, and 9) and helps learners encode information into long-term memory. After the initial presentation, students practice under the watchful eye of the teacher, who applies enough scaffolding to ensure success, but not so much that students' sense of challenge and accomplishment is reduced (Gersten et al, 1999; Rosenshine & Meister, 1992). Sam had his students work a problem, and they discussed it carefully while Sam monitored their progress. He had them work on their own only after he was sure they were ready.

Independent Practice.   In the independent practice phase, teacher support (scaffolding) is gradually reduced and responsibility is shifted to students. At this point, students are expected to perform the skill on their own—perhaps with some initial hesitancy, but later with ease and fluency. The goal is automaticity, intended to free working memory to focus on application, such as solving word problems (Sweller et al., 1998). Group work, where students work collaboratively on problem solutions, can be effective in helping students understand the logic behind procedures (Mevarech, 1999).

Teacher monitoring is still important during independent practice. Effective teachers carefully monitor students to be certain that they understand what they're doing; less effective teachers are more likely to merely check to see that students are on task (e.g., on the right page and following directions).

12.11
Which phase of direct instruction is most important in ensuring successful independent practice? Why?

Homework.   Homework is a common form of independent practice, and it significantly increases learning, especially when it is aligned with classroom work and when teachers grade and comment on it (Cooper, Lindsay, Nye, & Greathouse, 1998; Stein & Carnine, 1999). The effects of homework are especially strong at the junior high and high school levels (Cooper, Valentine, Nye, & Lindsay, 1999). Research also indicates that frequency is important. For example, five problems every night are more effective than 25 once a week. Effective homework has four essential characteristics, which are outlined in Table 12.8.

Table 12.8

Characteristics of effective homework

Characteristic	Rationale
Extension of classwork	The teacher teaches; homework reinforces.
High success rates	Success is motivating. Success leads to automaticity. No one is available to provide help if students encounter problems.
Part of class routines	Becomes a part of student expectations, increases likelihood of students completing assignments.
Graded	Increases accountability and provides feedback.

Source: Based on work by Berliner (1984) and Cooper (1989).

Instructional alignment—so important in all planning and teaching—is essential for homework. Homework should be an extension of instruction and, although grading homework can be time-consuming, some mechanism for providing feedback on it is crucial if students are to take it seriously and use it as a learning tool.

Research indicates that teachers should view homework as an integral part of an overall plan to teach students responsibility and self-regulation (Corno & Xu, 1998; Cooper et al., 1998), and teachers should solicit parents' support (Balli, Wedman & Demo, 1997). Homework requires that students take initiative and accept responsibility in several ways, such as remembering to take it home, finding a quiet place to work, actually doing it, and attempting to understand the topics. Parents can provide the at-home support that is so important for younger and less motivated students. Teachers can enlist their aid with notes, phone calls, and individual conferences.

> **12.12** ■
> Using social cognitive theory as a basis, explain why assigning but not collecting homework is ineffective practice.

Expository Teaching

Expository teaching *is designed to help students acquire information through structured teacher presentations.* It is based on David Ausubel's (1963, 1977) theory of meaningful verbal learning, which stresses the teacher's role in carefully structuring, sequencing, and presenting content. Ausubel believes that logical, organized presentations help learners effectively encode and later elaborate on new information. Schema theory and information processing both support the importance of organization in making information meaningful (Bruning et al., 1999).

The use of *advance organizers* is an important way that teachers help make information meaningful. **Advance organizers** are *brief statements that introduce, frame, and organize new material* (Ausubel, 1978; Corkill, 1992). For example, a lesson on the circulatory system might begin with the teacher presenting the following description:

> *The circulatory system is like the sanitary system of a city. In both there is a pumping station, pipelines that vary in size, a filtration plant, an exchange terminal, and a capacity for disposal of waste.*

A lesson introducing Spanish verbs might begin like this,

> *A Spanish verb is like a good mystery story. It tells who did it, how many were involved, and when.*

Advance organizers are most effective when they are concrete and familiar, and teachers frequently refer back to them during the lesson (Bruning et al., 1999).

Organized Bodies of Knowledge

An English teacher is involved in a unit on 19th-century novels, and she wants her students to understand the relationships among concepts such as *plot, character development,* and *symbolism* in *Moby Dick,* and she also wants them to conclude that "Authors' works are influenced by their personal experiences." Unlike procedural skills, which can be illustrated with examples and developed with practice, her topic doesn't have specific sets of characteristics, or procedures that can be practiced, and it can't be illustrated with precise examples.

The term **organized bodies of knowledge**—*topics that include facts, concepts, generalizations, and principles, and the relationships among them*—is commonly used to describe this type of content (Calfee, 1986; Rosenshine, 1986), and expository teaching is often used to help students understand them.

Because organized bodies of knowledge can't be illustrated with precise examples, practice and feedback—which are effective for learning skills—can't be used to help learners encode information and develop automaticity, so different instructional approaches are required. Most common among them are lectures and lecture–discussions.

Lectures

The prevalence of the lecture as a teaching method is paradoxical. Although it is, and historically has been, the most criticized of all teaching methods, it continues to be the most commonly used (Cuban, 1984). At least three reasons for its durability exist:

▌ Lectures are efficient for the teacher; planning time is limited to organizing content.
▌ Lectures are flexible; they can be applied to virtually any content area.
▌ Lectures are simple; all of teachers' working memory space can be devoted to organizing and presenting content.

Despite their widespread use, lectures have an important disadvantage; lecturing puts students in passive roles. Constructing understanding and encoding information into long-term memory require active learners. Lectures are especially problematic for young students because of their short attention spans and limited vocabularies, and they're also ineffective if higher-order thinking is our goal. In seven studies comparing lecture to discussion, discussion was superior in all seven on measures of retention and higher-order thinking. In addition, discussion was superior in seven of nine studies on measures of student attitude and motivation (McKeachie & Kulik, 1975).

However, lectures aren't always ineffective and, as with all aspects of instruction, the key to using them appropriately is clear goals. For example, Ausubel (1963) argued that lectures are effective if the goal is to provide students with information that would take them hours to find on their own. Lectures are also appropriate if the teacher's goals include

▌ Acquiring information not readily accessible in other ways
▌ Integrating information from a variety of sources
▌ Understanding different points of view (Henson, 1988; McMann, 1979)

If teachers are clear about their goals and if their goals can be met with lectures, their use can be appropriate.

Lecture–Discussions

One of the most effective ways to overcome the weaknesses of lectures is to use **lecture–discussions**, a *combination of short lectures supplemented with teacher questioning* (Kauchak & Eggen, 1998).

Lecture–discussions include three essential elements that occur in repeated cycles:

▌ *Presenting information.*   The teacher begins by providing the students with some information about the topic.
▌ *Comprehension monitoring.*   After a brief presentation, the teacher asks a series of questions designed to assess students' understanding of the information.
▌ *Integration.*   The teacher asks additional questions designed to help students identify conceptual links to other ideas in the content.

Let's look at an American history class using lecture–discussion:

Darren Anderson was discussing the events leading up to the American Revolutionary War. To introduce the topic, she pointed to a time line above the chalkboard and began, "About where are we now in our progress? . . . Anyone?"

12.13 ▬
Think about some of the case studies in other chapters in this text. Identify at least two in which an organized body of knowledge was being taught.

12.14 ▬
What concept from our discussion of *meaningful encoding* in Chapter 7 does "identify conceptual links to other ideas in the content" best illustrate? Explain.

Lecture–discussions involve short teacher presentations followed by questioning.

12.15 ▬

Which of the essential teaching skills that were discussed in Chapter 11 is best illustrated by Darren's description, "When we're finished today, we'll see . . . and even all the way to today?" Explain.

" . . . About there," Adam responded uncertainly, pointing to about the middle of the 1700s on the time line.

"Yes, good," Darren smiled. "That's about where we are. However, I would like for us to understand what happened before that time, so we're going to back up a ways. . . . Actually, all the way to the early 1600s. When we're finished today, we'll see that the Revolutionary War didn't just happen; there were events that led up to it that made it almost inevitable. . . . That's the fun part of history. To see how something that happened at one time affected events at another time, and even all the way to today . . . Okay, let's go.

"We know that the Jamestown Colony was established in 1607," she continued, "and it was founded by the British, but we haven't really looked that carefully at French expansion into the New World. Let's look again at the map," she went on, pulling a map down in the front of the room.

"Here we see Jamestown, . . . but at nearly the same time, a French explorer named Champlain came down the St. Lawrence River and formed Quebec City, here," again pointing to the map. "And, over the years, at least 35 of the 50 states were discovered or mapped by the French, and several of our big cities, such as Detroit, St. Louis, New Orleans, and Des Moines were founded by the French," she continued pointing to a series of locations she had marked on the map.

"Now, what do you notice about the location of the two groups . . . or what does it suggest to us?"

After thinking a few seconds, Alfredo offered, "The French had a lot of Canada, and . . . it looks like this country too," pointing to the north and west on the map.

"It looks like the east was, . . . British, and the west was . . . French," Troy added.

"Yes, and remember, this was all happening at about the same time," Darren continued. "Also, the French were more friendly with the Native Americans than the British were.

"Also, the French had what they called a seignorial system, where the settlers were given land if they would serve in the military. So, . . . what does this suggest about the military power of the French?"

" . . . Probably powerful," Josh suggested. "The people got land if they . . . went in the army."

"And the Native Americans probably helped, because . . . they were friendly with the French," Tenisha added.

"Now, what else do you notice here?" Darren asked moving her hand up and down the width of the map.

"Mountains?" Danielle answered uncertainly.

"Yes, exactly," Darren smiled. "Why are they important? What do mountains do? . . . Anyone?"

" . . . The British were sort of fenced in, and the French . . . they could expand and do as they pleased."

"Good. And now the plot thickens. The British needed land and wanted to expand. So they headed west over the mountains and guess who they ran into? . . . Sarah?"

"The French?" Sarah offered haltingly.

"And conflict broke out. Now, when the French and British were fighting, why do you suppose the French were initially more successful than the British? . . . What do you think? . . . Dan?"

"Well, . . . they had that seig . . . seignorial (struggling with the pronunciation) system, so they were more motivated to fight, because of the land and everything."

"Other thoughts? . . . Bette?"

" . . . I think that the Native Americans were part of it. The French got along better with them, so they helped the French."

"Okay, good thinking everyone, now let's think about the British. . . . Let's look at some of their advantages."

Let's stop now and take a look at Darren's work with her students. She began by trying to capture students' attention and increase their interest in the lesson by saying that events in the past influence the way we live today. She then presented information about Jamestown, Quebec, and French settlements in the present-day United States and, after this brief presentation, involved students in the lesson. Let's review a brief portion of the dialogue.

Darren:	Now, what do you notice about the location of the two groups . . . or what does it suggest to us?
Alfredo:	The French had a lot of Canada, and . . . it looks like this country too. (pointing to the north and west on the map)
Troy:	It looks like the east was, . . . British, and the west was . . . French.

Darren's question was intended to check students' understanding of the presentation to that point and to actively involve them in the lesson. After hearing their responses, she returned to presenting information when she said, "Yes, and remember, this was all happening at about the same time," and she continued by briefly describing the French seignorial system and pointing out that the French and Native Americans were friendly.

She then turned the lesson back to students a second time.

Darren:	So, . . . what does this suggest about the military power of the French?
Josh:	. . . Probably powerful. The people got land if they . . . went in the army.
Tenisha:	And the Native Americans probably helped, because . . . they were friendly with the French.

While the segments appear to be similar, there is an important difference between the two. In the first, by asking, "Now, what do you notice about the location of the two groups . . . or what does it suggest to us?" Darren asked students to paraphrase or summarize what she presented. Summarizing is a powerful form of comprehension monitoring (see Chapters 8 and 9).

In the second segment, Darren was attempting to promote deeper understanding of the topic by encouraging students to find links—integration—between the seignorial system, the relationship between the French and the Native Americans, and French military power. Darren's goal for the entire lesson was broad integration—an understanding of cause and effect relationships between the French and Indian Wars and the American Revolutionary War.

Lecture–Discussion: A Theoretical Analysis.   Earlier in the chapter, you saw that direct instruction is based on information processing theory. The same is true for lecture–discussion, and there are strong parallels between the two. For example, Darren began her lesson by trying to attract learners' attention, and material was transferred to her students' working memories when she *presented information*. In the *monitoring comprehension* phase, she actively involved students through questioning, allowing her to check their perceptions and helping them to effectively encode information into long-term memory. *Integration* extended the process of encoding and increased the meaningfulness of the content.

Teacher questioning is crucial to the effectiveness of lecture–discussions and consistent with four aspects of cognitive theories of learning:

▮ It allows teachers to assess student background knowledge.
▮ It encourages students to become actively involved in lessons.
▮ It promotes integration of ideas, which encourages meaningful encoding.
▮ It allows teachers to monitor learning progress and adapt accordingly.

Purely teacher-centered lectures provide none of these opportunities.

12.16 ▬
In addition to putting students in passive roles, lectures have an additional problem that directly relates to information processing theory. Identify this problem, and explain how teacher questioning overcomes it.

Classroom Connections

Using Direct Instruction Effectively in Your Classroom

1. Introduce lessons with a demonstration, question, or problem to promote student interest.
   - A fourth-grade teacher starting a lesson on possessives asked, "Class, how are these pairs of sentences different, and what makes them different?"
     The student's books were lost.
     The students' books were lost.
     Who can tell me the boy's story?
     Who can tell me the boys' stories?
   - A seventh-grade math teacher beginning a unit on percentages and decimals comments that the star quarterback for the state university completed 14 of 21 passes in the last game. "What does that mean? Is that good or bad? Was it better than the opposing quarterback who completed 12 of 17 passes?" she asks. "How can we figure these questions out?"

2. Maintain high levels of student involvement during the presentation phase of direct instruction lessons.
   - A ninth-grade geography teacher helps his students locate the longitude and latitude of a series of locations by "walking them through" the process, using a map and a series of specific questions.
   - A third-grade teacher helps her students understand the concept adjective by showing a paragraph with several italicized adjectives in it, explaining what adjectives do, and asking questions to help the students see how adjectives are used in sentences.

3. Provide guided practice to ensure students' successful transition from your presentation to independent practice.
   • A fifth-grade teacher, wanting students to understand similes and metaphors, makes the transition from teacher presentation to guided practice by saying, "Alright. Everyone write a sentence with at least one simile or metaphor in it." She then circulates around the class, examining students' sentences. She has several students share their sentences by writing them on the chalkboard. The class discusses whether these are similes or metaphors and then continues writing and sharing others until the teacher is sure the students can proceed on their own.

4. Monitor students during independent practice.
   • A first-grade teacher has assigned a series of problems involving addition and subtraction for homework. As students begin to work on the problems, he walks up and down the rows to check each student's progress. He periodically stops and offers suggestions as he checks their work.

Using Lecture–Discussions Effectively in Your Classroom

5. Incorporate as many examples as possible in the lesson, and relate these to students' experiences.
   • An American history teacher discussing immigration in the 19th and early 20th centuries compares these immigrant groups with the Cuban population in Miami, Florida, and Mexican immigrants in San Antonio, Texas. He examines the difficulties immigrants encounter when they first come to the United States.

6. Keep the presentation of information short, review frequently, and examine relationships among items of information.
   • A biology teacher is presenting information related to transport of liquids in and out of cells, identifying and illustrating several of the concepts in the process. About 5 minutes into the presentation, she stops and asks, "Suppose a cell is in a hypotonic solution in one case and a hypertonic solution in another. What's the difference between the two? What would happen to the cell in each case?"

Technology and Learning: Improving Teacher-Centered Instruction

A theme for this chapter has been the need for teachers to supplement their verbal presentations with examples, problems, figures, and diagrams that help learners see abstract ideas represented in concrete forms. Technology can be effective in helping teachers meet this need by supporting teacher-centered instruction in at least three ways. They include

> *Providing high-quality representations of topics.* Technology allows teachers to bring photos, film clips, and other relevant content representations into the classroom quickly and efficiently.

> *Illustrating hard-to-visualize relationships.* Technology can allow students to see physical phenomena in ways that make them understandable (e.g., seeing the acceleration of a falling object, as in Chapter 7).

> *Providing opportunities for practice with quality feedback.* Technology provides learners with opportunities to practice skills and receive immediate and responsive feedback about performance.

Let's examine these three uses.

Providing High-Quality Representations

An American history class is studying the Civil Rights movement in the United States. Because it occurred more than 30 years ago, it's hard for the class to understand the human struggle and sacrifice involved in this movement. To help them, the teacher brings in the videodisc *Martin Luther King*, which contains clips of civil rights marchers being attacked by water hoses and dogs, sit-in demonstrators being arrested, and the march on Washington, D.C., capped by Martin Luther King's "I Have a Dream" speech.

A biology class is studying mammals, and most characteristics like fur and live birth are easily identifiable. However, others, like a four-chambered heart, are harder to illustrate. The teacher uses a videodisc called *The Living Textbook* to help students visualize how a four-chambered heart appears and operates, and why it is more efficient than the three- and two-chambered hearts of reptiles, amphibians, and fish.

Technology can play an important role in helping teachers represent abstract ideas for learners. Videotape, computer simulations, and videodiscs all provide convenient ways to bring the outside world into the classroom. Videodiscs, with their capacity to store 108,000 razor-sharp images along with theater-quality sound, are especially powerful presentation tools (Forcier, 1999). For example, the *National Gallery of Art* videodisc, by Videodisc Publishing, contains a vast array of works by great artists, information that would be inaccessible in any other way. *Windows on Science*, a collection of still-life and moving images on CD, allows science teachers to illustrate hard-to-imagine ideas and structures. In addition to commercially prepared videodiscs, teachers can also construct their own, blending photographs, diagrams, and videotapes into high-quality images and sounds to supplement their presentations.

Illustrating Hard-to-Visualize Relationships

Many of the abstract topics we teach are difficult to represent, and this difficulty is what makes them hard to learn. For these topics, technologically based simulations have been found to be effective (Roblyer & Edwards, 2000). Using technology to illustrate the acceleration of a falling object (see Chapter 7) is an example.

In addition, software tools such as Microsoft *Power Point*, Adobe *Persuasion*, and Lotus *Freelance Graphics*, allow teachers to design their own presentations to illustrate difficult ideas. For example, students often have trouble understanding the logic behind the formula for finding the area of a parallelogram ($A = $ Base $\times$ Height). Software programs allow teachers to create illustrations like Figure 12.4 to illustrate why the equation works.

The effectiveness of juxtaposing the two parallelograms in the same figure can be explained using the concept of *spatial contiguity* (Moreno & Mayer, 1999). Researchers

Figure 12.4

The area of a parallelogram

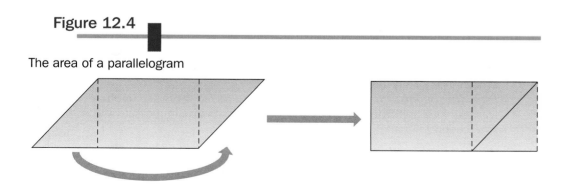

found that juxtaposing important information (placing them in a contiguous relationship) allows learners to visualize the relationships and integrate the ideas.

Providing Opportunities for Practice with Feedback

Technology is an effective medium for practicing skills because it adds variety to the process and provides students with immediate, personalized, and informative feedback. For example, students in a physical education class are videotaped as they practice tennis strokes, and the clips are reviewed and critiqued before they try again (Mohnsen, 1997). Slow motion and freeze-frame allow students to analyze their strokes at crucial moments.

As another example, computers are effective for helping students develop automaticity in math skills, and they're particularly effective for students with exceptionalities (Higgins & Boone, 1993; Okolo, 1992). For example, research indicates that students with mild learning disabilities depend heavily on finger counting in computing simple math problems, which creates a cognitive bottleneck when they move to more complex skills.

Computer programs can be used to remediate this problem. They pretest to determine students' entry skills, build on the skills by introducing new facts at a pace that ensures high success rates, and provide the answer and retest the fact when students answer incorrectly. To develop automaticity and discourage finger counting, presentation rates are increased as students' proficiency increases. Research indicates that students using these computer programs outperformed comparable students who didn't use them, performed almost as well as students without handicaps, and maintained their gains over a 4-month summer break (Hasselbring, Goin, & Bransford, 1988).

A similar program in language arts helps students with reading problems develop vocabulary, spelling, and comprehension skills (Hasselbring, Goin, Taylor, Bottge, & Daley, 1997). The program is especially effective with older students because it helps avoid embarrassment by allowing them to practice in private. One seventh-grade student made the following comments:

> I didn't know how to read. I said to myself, how can I do my work if I can't read? I was ashamed to ask for help.
>
> I was getting all F's on my report card. My mom was very disappointed at me. So I said, why come to school? And I missed half of the school year.
>
> In 7 grade I started going to this program. I started to realizing that this program started helping me. So I came to school and doing my work. Then I knew my life was chinging. I could read better. Now I wasn't ashamed to read to my classes. My grades was A, B, and C. My mom was impress of how I chinged. Now am getting rewards in all my classes. (Hasselbring et al., 1997, p. 32)

Technology is a powerful teaching tool because it allows students to practice reading skills in a private, nonthreatening environment.

Guidelines for Using Technology to Support Teacher-Centered Instruction

In using technology to support teacher-centered instruction, some guidelines are helpful. They include the following:

- Be sure that your goals are clear. As in nearly all the guidelines for using technology, we've emphasized the need for clear goals, and it is true in this case as well (Harrington-Lueker, 1997).
- Use technology to support learning that can't be accomplished effectively in other ways. For instance, technology is unique in its ability to provide practice with feedback in nonthreatening settings.

▌ Use technology to represent topics that can't be represented concretely. Technology is also unique in its ability to illustrate topics that are impossible to represent in other ways.

▌ Carefully monitor all uses of technology. Regardless of the activity—using technology, paper-and-pencil seat work, group activities, or hands-on experiences—teacher monitoring is essential if students are to learn as much as possible.

As with other innovations, technology can increase the effectiveness of teacher-centered instruction. However, it requires clear thinking and implementation, and it will be no more or less effective than the teacher who uses it.

Accommodating Learner Diversity: Classroom Interaction

Classroom interaction is central to all forms of effective teacher-centered instruction. Through questions and group interaction, teachers encourage students to think about ideas, link them to ideas that they already know, and compare their understanding with other students in the class. Since interaction is so important, understanding the interaction patterns of different learners is essential if teacher-centered lessons are to be effective.

Classroom Interaction: Research Findings

Classroom interaction patterns are amazingly homogeneous across the United States, both over time and across grade levels (Cazden, 1986; Cuban, 1984):

> [T]he dominant form of interaction is the teacher-directed lesson in which the instructor is in control, determining the topics of discussion, allocating turns at speaking, and deciding what qualifies as a correct response. Verbal participation is required of students. Implicitly, teaching and learning are equated with talking, and silence is interpreted as the absence of knowledge. Students are questioned in public and bid for the floor by raising their hands. They are expected to wait until the teacher awards the floor to one of them before answering. Speaking in turn is the rule, unless the teacher specifically asks for choral responses. Display questions prevail. Individual competition is preferred to group cooperation. Topics are normally introduced in small and carefully sequenced steps, with the overall picture emerging only at the end of the teaching sequence. (Villegas, 1991, p. 20)

Although this form of interaction works for some students, it is ineffective for others. Many students come from cultures in which adults and children interact in ways that differ from the patterns found in most American classrooms. Let's look at these differences and see how teachers might accommodate them.

Accommodating Diversity: Experimental Programs

KEEP: The Kamehameha Early Education Program

Teachers working with Native Hawaiian students have found that these learners don't interact effectively in environments like those described in the preceding quote. Often they don't participate at all, or they participate in disruptive ways, breaking in and inter-

---

12.17 ▬

What theory of learning is implied in this quote? Explain and document your explanation with information from the quote.

rupting other students (Au, 1992; Tharp, 1989). These patterns are associated with low-ered achievement and self-esteem.

Researchers, attempting to understand this problem, went into Hawaiian homes and observed the children interacting with adults, siblings, and peers. They discovered a con-versational style incompatible with traditional instruction. Typically, Hawaiian children jumped into conversations in their homes, contributing freely, as an adult or other child spoke. There were no clear turns marked by pauses; instead, several people talked at once, and overlapping speech was common. School felt strange to these children because teachers didn't allow them to join in whenever they wanted.

Working with these differences, researchers helped teachers adjust their questioning strategies to the Hawaiian students. Here's how one group reading lesson sounded. (The brackets indicate people speaking at the same time.)

Teacher: Why do you think the author wrote this story? What did he want—what did he want you to learn from it?
Chad: About moths
Teacher: About moths. What—what else?
Natasha: [Caterpillars
Kamalu: [You can't keep things in
you can't keep things [forever
Chad: [in jars
Kamalu: They have to come [like moths
Darralyn: [how to take care of it
Kamalu: [You can't keep them in a glass jar forever
Natasha: [You can keep a dog or cat forever
but like insects you cannot keep 'em [forever
Teacher: [Okay
Natasha: they have to be [free
Chad: [Hey, once
I kept one lizard forever
Keala: [Born to be free
Teacher: [Excuse me
Is there anything else that they were telling us?
[she was trying to tell us
Keala: [Yeah
Teacher: about? (Au, 1992, pp. 10–11)

Notice how the interaction patterns overlapped, with students joining in to con-tribute to each other's thoughts. Also, many interchanges were student-to-student. The teacher intervened only when necessary to clarify a point. These adjustments made the classroom interaction more like the conversation patterns in learners' homes and resulted in increased student achievement. "Hawaiian children in regular classrooms are among the lower achieving minorities in the United States; in Kamehameha School's KEEP classrooms, they approach national norms on standard achievement tests" (Tharp, 1989, p. 350).

Wait-Time: Working with Native American Students

Similar efforts to make questioning strategies compatible with Native American interaction patterns have also been successful (Tharp, 1989). Researchers noticed differences between the wait-times of Anglo and Navajo teachers. Anglo teachers interpreted pauses

12.18 ▬
Research with low-achiev-ing students in small read-ing groups found a posi-tive correlation between achievement and students being allowed to call-out answers. Explain both this finding and the results of the KEEP project. Base your explanation on cogni-tive learning theory.

12.19 ▬
What was described as a desirable amount of wait-time in Chapter 11? Based on the information in this section, would desirable wait-times with Native American students be longer or shorter than the length described in Chapter 11?

in a Navajo student's response as a sign of a completed answer, not realizing that long pauses (by Anglo standards) and silences were a regular part of Navajo conversation. Interrupted in this way, Navajo students felt unappreciated and uncomfortable and became less willing to participate. Adjusting wait-times produced expected results; in one study of Pueblo Indian children, students in longer wait-time classes participated twice as frequently as those in shorter wait-time classes (Winterton, 1977).

Learning About Student-Interaction Patterns

Research on Hawaiian and Native American interaction patterns is valuable because it reminds us that students come to class with varying interaction histories. It's impossible to understand all these patterns in advance, which means teachers must try to learn as much about their students as possible when beginning to work with them. Teachers can gather information about their students' interaction patterns in at least three ways:

▌ Listen to the way students interact when they're not influenced by academic expectations, such as extracurricular activities, nonacademic discussions outside of class, or during lunch.
▌ Listen to the way they talk as they participate in lessons and in small groups.
▌ See if any patterns exist in their reluctance to respond or in the way they behave when they cannot answer questions.

Opening lines of communication with parents and talking with colleagues from other cultures can also provide insights into ways to make our classroom interactions

Effective teachers adapt their questioning strategies to the interaction styles of their students.

more culturally compatible. These insights are important; research indicates that teachers who understand their students' speech patterns accept and use student responses more frequently than those who lack this understanding (Washington & Miller-Jones, 1989). Direct instruction and lecture–discussion both depend on student interaction for their success; understanding different patterns of interaction can increase their instructional effectiveness.

This understanding has an additional benefit. The better teachers understand their students' patterns, the more capable they are of helping students gradually acquire interaction patterns that can increase their school success.

> All of us, regardless of class or cultural background, have to acquire literacies that go beyond our home-based ways of making sense and using language. . . . The key challenge for schools is to introduce and enculturate students into these school-based discourses without denigrating their culturally specific values and ways of using language. (Michaels & O'Connor, 1990, p. 18)

This should be our goal, one that is consistent with Ogbu's (1987) concept of accommodation without assimilation.

Classroom Connections

Capitalizing on Diversity in Your Classroom

1. Be sensitive to different interaction patterns during instruction.
   - A fourth-grade teacher waits several seconds as a Native American student haltingly responds to a question. He admonishes other students who jump in and answer questions when the response is slow in coming.
   - A middle school teacher doesn't correct the language of his students, instead, offering substitute descriptions that build on students' responses.

2. Learn about the interaction patterns of your students.
   - A fourth-grade teacher invites the parents, guardians, or caregivers of her students to a special evening session of her class. She asks the students to introduce the adult with them and to tell something about each. In turn, she asks each adult to say something about the child in his or her care.
   - A junior high teacher volunteers to cosponsor a school club. He uses the club meetings to observe the way different students interact with each other.

3. Help learners develop school-based interaction patterns.
   - In learning activities, a first-grade teacher liberally praises students who listen to each other and wait their turn to speak. She reminds them that the way we talk and listen in class doesn't have to be the same as the way we talk and listen at home or on the playground.
   - A middle school teacher establishes the following rule at the beginning of the school year, "Listen respectfully while others have the floor." He discusses why the rule is important both from an interpersonal and learning perspective. He explains that he understands that everyone talks differently at lunch, in the halls and at home, but that his classroom is a place where everyone gets an opportunity to express themselves.

Putting Teacher-Centered Instruction Into Perspective

The prominence of constructivist views of learning and the increasing emphasis on learner-centered education has led to considerable criticism of teacher-centered instruction in general, and direct instruction in particular (Marshall, 1992; Stoddart et al., 1993). Critics argue that direct instruction focuses on lower-level objectives, emphasizes performance instead of understanding, and is based on behaviorism.

The following classroom example illustrates these criticisms:

> A teacher was attempting to teach place value to her third graders. On the basis of directions given in the teacher's manual, she began by putting 45 tally marks on the chalkboard and circled four groups of 10.

Teacher:	How many groups of 10 do we have there, boys and girls?
Children:	4.
Teacher:	We have 4 groups of 10, and how many left over?
Children:	5.
Teacher:	We had 4 tens and how many left over?
Beth:	4 tens.
Sarah:	5.
Teacher:	5. Now, can anybody tell me what number that could be? We have 4 tens and 5 ones. What is that number? Ann?
Ann:	(Remains silent)
Teacher:	If we have 4 tens and 5 ones, what is that number?
Ann:	9.
Teacher:	Look at how many we have there (points to the 4 groups of ten) and 5 ones. If we have 4 tens and 5 ones we have? (slight pause) 45.
Children:	45.
Teacher:	Very good. (Wood, Cobb, & Yackel, 1992, p. 180)

12.20
Describe specifically what the teacher might have done to increase students' understanding of place value in this lesson.

Unquestionably, Ann, and probably many others, didn't understand place value, and the teacher did little to increase their understanding. Once they gave the desired response, the teacher reinforced them with "Very good" and moved on.

Misconceptions About Teacher-Centered Instruction

This pattern of focusing on student verbalization or overt performance at the expense of understanding occurs in many classrooms (Goodlad, 1984; Stodolsky, 1988), and seeing that the instruction is teacher-centered, critics place the blame on the approach rather than ineffective teaching. This has resulted in several misconceptions about teacher-centered instruction in general and direct instruction in particular:

▮ Learners are passive.
▮ It is based on behaviorism.
▮ Content is delivered primarily through teacher-lecture and explanation.
▮ Student thinking is minimized.

When teacher-centered instruction is ineffective, as in the preceding example with place value, these criticisms are valid. The problem isn't with direct instruction itself, however, it is with the teacher's inability to implement it effectively.

When teacher-centered instruction is *effective,* none of these criticisms is true. Expert teacher-centered instruction puts learners in active roles and is based on cognitive views of learning. Teachers guide learners with questioning and emphasize understanding and thinking. You saw each of these elements in the opening case, in Sam's direct instruction lesson, and later, in Darren's lecture–discussion.

Those who defend teacher-centered instruction further argue that some criticisms of direct instruction are made on political grounds, direct instruction not being "politically correct or romantically correct" (Rosenshine, 1997, p. 2).

As with most instruction, it isn't the strategy, per se, that's to blame; it's that the strategy is overused, used inappropriately, or implemented ineffectively. No strategy, curriculum, program, or process is any better or worse than the expertise of the person implementing it. This is why educational psychology is so important. As your knowledge of learning and learners increases, your ability to implement and adapt teaching strategies that result in the maximum learning possible for all your students will improve, and your teaching effectiveness will grow.

Windows on Classrooms

Like Shirley Barton, in Chapter 11, Robin Voss is a fifth-grade teacher preparing for her next day's math lesson.

"What's up?" Darcie Towers, Robin's colleague from the next room, asked as she entered Robin's room.

"Just getting ready for tomorrow," Robin replied, looking up from her work.

"This class is so slow," Robin continued with a wry smile. "I love them to death, but it takes them forever to get anything. My kids last year were so sharp. What a pleasure they were."

"I know what you mean," Darcie smiled back. "When I take them for science, we struggle with some of the concepts. They eventually get the ideas, but it takes time."

"Yeah, if we only had more time . . . " Robin nodded. "My class is too big, and they aren't as well behaved as last year, besides not being as sharp. . . . Oh well. We do our best."

At 10 A.M., Robin looked up from her desk. "Time to put your language arts materials away," she announced. "Have your homework that you've been working on ready to turn in first thing tomorrow. Now you need to get out your math books and your assignment for today. Hurry now."

When they finished, she stood up and moved to the front of the room. "Ready to go?" she smiled at the class. "Tim? . . . Faye? You should have your math books on your desks by now."

"Everyone ready? . . . Good. I'm going to put some problems on the board, and I want you to solve them."

She moved to the board and wrote the following:

$$3/9 + 4/9 = ?$$
$$2/5 + 1/5 = ?$$
$$5/12 + 4/12 = ?$$

"We've been adding fractions, so let's review for a moment," she continued. "Joyce, what's the answer to the first problem?"

" . . . Seven ninths."

"Okay. Very good. And the second one. . . . John?"

"Three fifths."

"Excellent Kay, the third?"

"Nine . . . twenty . . . fours?" Kay responded hesitantly.

"No, no, sweetheart. What do we do when we add fractions?"

" . . . "

"What's our rule?"

" . . . "

"Gloria?"

"We add the numerators, . . . but the denominators stay the same."

"Very good, Gloria. Please repeat that, Kay."

"Add the numerators, but the denominators stay the same."

"Good, Kay, now remember that. . . . Remember that, everyone.

"Now, today we're going to look at some different kinds of problems. We're going to learn to add fractions when the denominators are not the same. Look back up here again," she said pointing at the review problems on the chalkboard. "See, these problems all have the same denominators, so that's why our rule of adding the numerators but leaving the denominators alone works. But when the denominators are not the same, we can't do that. That's what we're going to discuss today.

"Let me show you some examples," she continued, writing the following on the board:

$$1/3 + 1/6 = ? \quad 2/3 + 1/4 = ?$$
$$1/3 + 1/2 = ? \quad 1/6 + 4/9 = ?$$

"Here we see that the denominators in each problem are different. The 3 and 6 are different, the 3 and 4, the 3 and 2, and the 6 and 9," she noted, pointing to the respective problems. "So, what do you suppose we have to do with the problems? What do you think? Anyone?"

" . . . "

"I know this is tough, and you might not see it right off. We have to get the denominators to be the same. Then once they're the same we can do what? . . . Jianna?"

" . . . "

"What did we do in those problems?" she asked, pointing to the review problems.

" . . . Added."

"Added what?"

"Added . . . the top numbers," Jianna said quickly after remembering the rule.

"Good, Jianna. So, what can we do once we get the denominators to be the same?

"Add the top numbers."

"Yes! Super, Jianna. That's very good."

"And what is the top number in a fraction called?"

"Numerator," the class responded in unison. "And the bottom number?"

"DENOMINATOR!" they answered, anticipating the question.

"Good," Robin smiled. "So, let's review for a second. What are we going to do? . . . Quentin?"

" . . . "

"What did I just say a few minutes ago? . . . about the denominators being the same?"

"They're the same," Quentin nodded.

"Good. So, I'm going to show you how to get the denominators to be the same. Then, all we have to do is add the numerators the way we did before. Seems easy enough. What do you think . . . ?"

The students nodded, and Robin then wrote the following on the board:

1. See if one denominator will divide into the other. If it will, divide it and multiply the result by the numerator.
2. If one denominator won't divide into the other, find a number that both will go into. Then follow Step 1 for each number.

"Read Step 1 for us, . . . Neva," she directed after she finished writing.

Neva read the first step, and Robin then had Janelle read the second step.

"Now, let me show you how to follow the steps," she continued.

"Let's look at the first problem," she said, pointing at the board. "I'm looking at the denominators and seeing that the 3 will divide into the 6. . . . So, I will do that. Three into 6

is 2, and 2 times 1 is 2, so 1/3 equals 2/6," and she then wrote the 2/6 on the board, so it appeared as follows:

$$(2/6)=1/3 + 1/6 = ?$$

"The 1/3 and the 2/6 are equal, so we call them equivalent fractions," she continued, and she then wrote "equivalent fractions" on the board in large letters.

"Now, since they're equivalent, we can use the 2/6 in place of the 1/3 and ta da, we have fractions where the denominators are the same. . . . That's what we wanted," she finished with a wave of her hand.

She then erased the parentheses and the 1/3, so the problem appeared as follows:

$$2/6 + 1/6 = ?$$

"So, what is our answer now? . . . Horace?

" . . . "

"What do we do when we add fractions when the denominators are the same?"

"Add."

"Good. So, what's the answer?"

"Three . . . Tw . . . Sixths," Horace responded, changing when he saw Robin shaking her head as he started to say "twelfths."

"Excellent, Horace," Robin smiled, pleased that Horace gave the correct response.

"That's good, everyone," Robin added. "Now, let's look at the next one. What's a little funny about this one? . . . Anyone?"

" . . . "

"Look at the denominators."

" . . . "

"They're different," Alex volunteered.

"Well, yes, but what's more important than that?"

"We can't just add the numerators," Erin added.

"Yes, but we already know that, too. Come on, everybody, think. . . . Look at the steps on the board."

The students all looked at the board and read the two steps again.

"Okay," Robin said after giving the students a chance to finish. "We know that the 3 and 4 are different, and . . . " she paused emphasizing the *and,* "the 3 will not go into the 4. That's what I wanted you to realize. So, we need a number that both will go into. Give me a number that both 3 and 4 will go into . . . someone."

" . . . Eight," Marina offered.

"No, no. Will 3 go into 8? Think about it for a second."

"Twelve," Monica offered.

"Excellent, Monica. Yes, both 3 and 4 will go into 12. So, . . . now we do what we did with the first problem. Watch carefully . . . "

She then continued, "Three into 12 is 4, times 2 is 8, so, 2/3 is the same as 8/12. . . . What do we call 2/3 and 8/12?"

" . . . "

"What kind of fractions?"

" . . . "

"Look up here."

"EQUIVALENT FRACTIONS!" the class said in unison.

"Very good. . . . And, we do the same thing with the 1/4."

Robin then illustrated and described the process for finding the equivalent fraction for 1/4, writing on the board:

$$(8)/(12) = 2/3 + 1/4 = (3)/(12) = ?$$

"So, again we erase the 2/3 and the 1/4 . . . "

"Why did we do that, Mrs. Voss?" David asked from the middle of the room.

"Because they're equivalent fractions," Robin answered. "Eight twelfths and 2/3 are equivalent, and 1/4 and 3/12 are equivalent.

"So, what's the answer to the problem? . . . David?"

" . . . Eleven . . . Tw . . . Twelfths," David answered seeing Robin nodding as he began to say "Twelfths."

"Excellent, David. Good thinking," Robin smiled. "Yes, our answer is 11/12.

"Now, let's try the next one," Robin continued after hesitating for a few seconds. "Look again at the steps on the board for a second and think about what you should do."

Robin went through the next two problems as she had done with the others, then gave students two additional problems, discussed them with her students, and assigned 10 problems for homework.

"Are there any questions?" she asked. "Okay, good. Get started, and I'll be around to check on you after I've looked at your assignment for today."

Robin then began looking through the previous night's homework papers while students began their new homework.

"Good," she thought to herself as she scored them. "Most of them did okay. A few added both the numerators and the denominators, but they're the slowest ones in the class."

"Just a second," she smiled at Elliot, who had his hand raised as she glanced up from her desk. "Be patient for a moment, and I'll be right there."

She got out her grade book, opened it in preparation for recording the grades, and then went back to Elliot.

She continued this process—responding to students' questions and recording scores—until math class was over.

Questions for Discussion and Analysis

Analyze Robin's planning and conduct of her lesson. You may want to consider the following questions. In each case, be specific, and use information taken directly from the case study as evidence in responding to each question.

1. Robin's lesson was an application of direct instruction. How effectively did she implement the direct instruction model in her teaching?

2. As conducted, was Robin's application of direct instruction based more on an information processing view of learning or more on a behaviorist view of learning?

3. Consider the essential teaching skills that were discussed in Chapter 11. How effectively did Robin apply these skills in her teaching?

4. Shirley Barton at the beginning of Chapter 11, Sam Barnett at the beginning of this chapter, and Robin were all teaching procedural skills. Which of the three did the best job of helping students apply their understanding in the real world? Which did the poorest job?

5. As in most classrooms, Robin's class consists of learners with diverse backgrounds. How effective would the lesson be for these students?

6. What suggestions do you have for improving Robin's lesson based on the information in Chapter 12? Again, be specific.

Now go to our Companion Website to assess your understanding of chapter content with the Student Self-Assessment, apply comprehension in the Online Casebook, and broaden your knowledge base with links to important Educational Psychology World Wide Web sites.

 Summary

When Is Teacher-Centered Instruction Appropriate?

Teacher-centered approaches involve instruction where the teacher presents content in a direct way and takes responsibility for guiding students' learning. Teacher-centered instruction is appropriate for teaching well-defined content, content that all students are expected to master, and topics students have difficulty learning on their own.

Characteristics of Teacher-Centered Instruction

Teacher-centered instruction is based on information processing views of learning and is characterized by clearly specified objectives, lessons that remain focused on those objectives, teachers taking primary responsibility for teaching the content, and students practicing skills with the goal of developing automaticity.

Planning for Teacher-Centered Instruction

Teacher-centered approaches to planning involve identifying objectives, preparing and organizing learning activities consistent with the objectives, and designing assessments that match both the objectives and learning activities.

Types of Teacher-Centered Instruction

Direct instruction and expository teaching, which includes lectures and lecture–discussions, are types of teacher-centered instruction. Direct instruction is effective for teaching procedural skills, which are developed through practicing a set of specific steps on many and varied examples.

Because of their simplicity, lectures are widely used, in spite of evidence suggesting they are less than effective because they place students in passive learning roles. Lecture–discussions consist of teachers making short presentations followed by questions designed to monitor learners' comprehension and help learners integrate new with existing understanding. Lecture–discussions overcome the weaknesses in lectures by putting learners in active roles. Technology can enhance teacher-centered instruction by providing high-quality representations, illustrating hard-to-visualize relationships, and providing opportunities for practice with quality feedback.

Accommodating Learner Diversity: Classroom Interaction

Teacher–student and student–student interaction provide effective ways for students to share, compare, and evaluate ideas. To capitalize on classroom interaction, teachers need to understand learners' interaction patterns, which can both help them accommodate learner diversity in classroom activities and help learners develop effective classroom interaction capabilities.

Putting Teacher-Centered Instruction Into Perspective

Critics of teacher-centered instruction argue that it is based on a behavioral view of learning, focuses on low-level objectives, and emphasizes performance instead of understanding. More commonly, however, teacher-centered instruction isn't properly implemented; when conducted by expert teachers, teacher-centered instruction can be very effective. The effectiveness of any approach depends on the ability of the teacher to adapt it to the learning needs of students.

 **Important Concepts**

advance organizer (p. 532)

affective domain (p. 524)

behavioral objectives (p. 521)

Bloom's taxonomy (p. 523)

cognitive domain (p. 522)

direct instruction (p. 529)

expository teaching (p. 532)

Gronlund's instructional objectives (p. 521)

instructional alignment (p. 527)

internalization (p. 524)

learner-centered approaches (p. 517)

lecture–discussions (p. 533)

organized bodies of knowledge (p. 532)

procedural skills (p. 529)

psychomotor domain (p. 524)

task analysis (p. 526)

teacher-centered approaches (p. 517)

Classroom Processes

13

Learner-Centered Approaches to Instruction

Scott Sowell, a seventh-grade science teacher, sat at his desk planning for next week's classes. Looking at his notes, he thinks to himself, "Scientific method, experimenting, controlling variables. . . . They're still having problems with this stuff. . . . Funny, we did the plant experiment as a whole class, and they seemed to get it. I explained it so carefully. . . . Why are they still having trouble? . . . Maybe they just need some more practice. . . . Actually, I'm sure they need more practice. I think I'll have them do the pendulum problem."

The next Monday Scott began by demonstrating a simple pendulum, explaining frequency as the number of swings in a certain time period, and asking for some common examples. The students identified a metronome and a grandfather clock, and Scott then asked them what might affect the frequency of the pendulum. They offered length, weight, and angle of release as possibilities.

Scott continued, "Okay, your job as a group is to design your own experiment. Think of a way to test how each one of these affects the frequency of swing. Use the equipment at your desk to design and carry out the experiment. Go to it."

One group of four—Marina, Paige, Wensley, and Jonathan—tied a string to a ring stand and measured its length, as shown in the sketch at the top of the next column.

"49 centimeters," Wensley noted, measuring the string.

"The frequency is the seconds . . . and the what?" Marina turned to Scott as he came by the group.

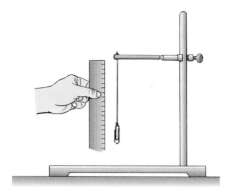

"The frequency is the number of swings in some time period. What time period are you using?" Scott responded.

The group agreed to use 15 seconds and then prepared to do their first test.

"Go," Jonathan said, as he began timing.

Wensley released the pendulum, and Marina counted for 15 seconds.

"Stop," Jonathan directed.

"21," Marina noted.

Scott again walked by the group, looked at Jonathan's results, and said, "Tell me exactly what you're doing right now. Explain to me what you're doing."

"We measured the length as 49. . . . The height was 25," Wensley explained.

"So you've done one test so far. . . . What are you going to do for your next test?"

"Make it heavier," "We could make it shorter," Wensley and Marina suggested almost simultaneously amid comments from Paige and Jonathan.

"I'm going to come back after your next test and look at it," Scott commented, moving on to another group.

"You want to make it shorter and add more weight?" Wensley wondered.

They briefly discussed whether the angle would be accurate since they were determining the angle by measuring the distance from the top of the table to the end of the pendulum, as shown in the following sketch:

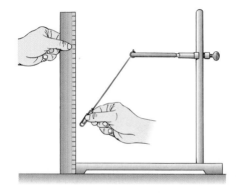

They then prepared to conduct their second test by shortening the string and adding a second paper clip to the end of the first one.

They again released the pendulum and counted the number of swings, this time getting 25 in 15 seconds.

Simultaneously, the students blurted out:

Marina:	The shorter it is, the longer it lasts.
Paige:	The faster.
Wensley:	The shorter, the shorter, the weight makes it go this way, it makes it go faster.
Jonathan:	Yeah, it makes it go faster.

"Mr. Sowell, we found out that the shorter it is and the heavier it is, the faster it goes," Marina reported to Scott as he returned to the group.

"So tell me how you found out that the length affected it," Scott asked as he knelt down in front of the group.

"We made it long, and then we shortened it a little more, and then we made it heavier, and that showed, . . . " Marina explained.

"So in Test 1, the length was 49, and the frequency was 21, and on the same test the weight was one paper clip?" Scott queried.

"And the height, . . . " Wensley began.

"The height was . . . ?" Scott repeated.

"The angle," Wensley broke in.

"Ohh, okay, the angle was 25, the weight was 1, your length was 49. . . . What did you change between Test 1 and Test 2?" Scott continued.

"The amount of paper clips," Marina explained.

"So you changed the weight? What else did you change?"

"The length," Wensley noted.

"The length, so you changed the weight and the length."

"And the angle," Marina added.

"So, you changed all three between the two tests. . . . Which caused that higher frequency?"

"The length," Paige responded.

"I think weight, the weight," Marina countered.

"What do you think?" Scott continued, looking at Wensley. "Marina thinks weight."

"Weight," Wensley answered.

"What do you think?" he asked, turning to Jonathan.

"The weight."

"What do you think, Paige?" Scott asked.

"The length."

"So, you think weight," pointing at Marina, "you think weight," turning to Jonathan, "you think weight," looking at Wensley, "and you think length," pointing at Paige. "Why can't you look at these two sets of data and decide? . . . Take a look at your two tests. This had one paper clip; this had two paper clips; this had 49 length; this had 27 length. . . . You should be able to look at these two and tell something. . . . Why can't you look at these numbers and come to a conclusion? Think about that."

"Well, like the length, and the height, and the weight was always changed. None of them ever stayed the same in any of them, so it has to be different," Marina offered.

"What was the first thing you said?"

"Everything changed," Wensley and Jonathan offered simultaneously.

"Think about that," Scott directed as he moved to another group.

"Everything needs to stay the same except for one thing," Jonathan offered as the group started back to work.

"Okay, I know," Paige suggested. "Add one more, like this one except keep the length 49 and . . . "

"Is that what the first one was, length was 49?" Wensley asked as he began measuring the string.

"So what are we going to keep the same, and what are we going to change?" Jonathan asked.

"We're going to change the paper clip weight," Wensley answered.

After measuring the string at 49, Wensley then attached a second paper clip to the end of the first one, as shown in the following sketch, pulled the paper clip to the side, and counted the swings.

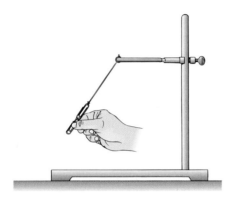

"21," Marina noted.

"One paper clip?" Jonathan asked.

"Two," Marina and Wensley replied simultaneously.

"Okay, and compare it to the second test now," Paige proposed.

"Okay, the same height, the same paper clips, except the length is different," Paige observed.

"Mr. Sowell?" Marina asked as Scott walked over to the group. "Okay, we did this test and we compared it to that test. . . . Everything was the same except for the length, and the shorter it is, the faster it goes. Do we need to test it again?"

"You need to come up with a conclusion about length, you need to come up with a conclusion about weight, and a conclusion about angle," Scott replied as he moved over to another group.

"Now we know that the shorter it is, the faster it goes," Marina concluded again.

The students discussed their results to this point and then decided to test the weight.

"We're going to keep the same height," Marina suggested.

"56," Paige offered.

"And the same length, 49," Wensley added.

"The weight will be . . . two?" Paige wondered.

"No, three," Marina responded.

Measuring the height to be 56, and adding three paper clips, they then conducted the next test.

"20," Marina counted after Jonathan said, "Stop."

"Have you done two tests on the weight?" Scott asked as he returned to the group.

"Okay, let's look at weight," he added.

"For both of them it's 20, but this is three and this is two," Paige noted.

"So what does that tell you about weight?" Scott asked, as he turned to another group.

As the group continued working on their experiment, Scott circulated around the room, finally announcing, "Let's take 3 or 4 more minutes, do one or two more tests, conclude the things you want to conclude, and then we're going to stop and talk."

The students briefly discussed their results, and then Marina said, "So now let's look at angle, I mean height . . . Make the height . . . "

"Taller or shorter?" Paige asked.

"How about . . . taller," Marina suggested.

"So the height is 62, no 63," Wensley said, measuring it with his meter stick.

"Go," Jonathan said, and they again counted the number of swings.

"21," Marina counted as Jonathan said, "Stop."

"It's the same as that one," Paige noted, observing that the frequencies were the same when the angles were different.

"It's the same because, remember, the weight changed," Marina responded, concluding that the difference in weight accounted for the frequency being the same when the angles were different. "The weight changed."

"What did you find out?" Scott asked as he returned to check on their progress.

Marina began, "Okay, Mr. Sowell, so this is what we did. . . . So, here we figured out that we changed the length. And the longer it is the shorter, the shorter the frequency is, . . . and for right here, the heavier it is the . . . the faster the frequency is. And then the height, . . . or the angle right here, so . . . it was the same as that one."

"This is good," Scott said, pointing to their paper. "Remember the problem we originally came up with. . . . "

"We only changed each time what we're testing," Paige broke in.

"Right, right," Scott confirmed. "But now when I look at these data, I see two different weights and two different heights."

"Yeah, but in the first one the height was 56 and the weight was 3, and it came out to 21, and in the second one, the height was higher and the weight was lower, so it was the same thing, so that's what we showed," Marina noted, again con-

cluding that the change in weight explains why the frequency was the same when the heights were different.

Scott prompted the students to think about the way they dealt with two different variables for an earlier test and to try to think about their present test in the same way.

"Okay, run another test, and then we're going to stop," he suggested, moving over to another group.

The group did two more tests, making the height greater in one and the weight greater in the next. Both come out to 21 swings, and the group concluded that the weight influenced the results in one and the height in the other. Scott returned and asked them to summarize their results.

"Let's do it out loud before you write it," Scott suggested as he listened to the students work. "Okay, talk to me about length."

"The lower it is, the lower the frequency," Marina responded.

"Rephrase that," Scott requested.

"The longer the string is, the slower the frequency is," Wensley added.

"The angle?" Scott asked.

"The higher the angle is, the faster the frequency is," Wensley continued.

"What about weight?"

"The heavier it is, the faster it goes," Marina added.

"I want to look at these again. . . . Write those down for me."

The students wrote their conclusions as Scott walked to the front of the room and rang a bell to call the class together.

"Okay, now, we've done the experiments, some groups maybe got further than others; that's fine. You've all come to some type of conclusion. You may not all have the same conclusions, and that's fine; you've used different methods, so you should expect different results.

"When I call your group, I want the speaker for your group to report your findings to the class," he continued to the class as a whole.

A spokesperson for each group then came to the front of the room to report their findings. In general, the groups concluded that each variable—the length, weight, and angle—affected the frequency.

Scott then asked the students to explain how they tested each of the variables. After they described their procedures, he asked them to offer reasons why the different groups' results varied and what they could do to improve the results.

Among their ideas was the suggestion that they do repeated tests.

Scott confirmed that their suggestions were good ones, and said, "Let's take a look at something here," as he took a ring stand and put it on his demonstration table. He

attached a paper clip, put the pendulum in motion, asked one of the students to count, added a second paper clip, and again had the students count, to demonstrate that weight doesn't affect the frequency. He had a student state the conclusion and write it on the board. Then he did a second demonstration to show that angle also has no effect on the frequency, and again asked a student to make a conclusion.

After the demonstrations, he said, "Now I want someone to give me a conclusion about what we learned about designing experiments and how we work our variables. . . . Who wants to talk about that? . . . Wensley? Tell me what we learned about how to set up an experiment. What did we learn from this?"

"Each time, you do a different part of the experiment, only change one of the variables," Wensley explained.

"Why is that?"

"You're only checking one thing at a time. If you do two, there might be an error in the experiment."

"Okay, . . . keep talking, . . . if you change more than one thing at one time, why would it be difficult?"

"Because, . . . because . . . ah, it's easy to do one thing, cuz that's the only thing you're doing, but if you do two things, you got to see, see the way it turns out to, because two things, two different things you can't work with as much as one."

"Good, okay, for example, if you were testing weight and length, your group had to finally decide that we can't change weight at the same time as we change length, because when we test it . . . "

"It came out, . . . it was different," Wensley interjected.

"Right, and what else, you couldn't, you couldn't tell what?"

"You couldn't compare them," Marina adds.

"Right, you couldn't compare them. You couldn't tell which one was causing it, could you? . . . It might go faster, but all of a sudden you'd say, well is it the weight or is it the length?"

"So, that's the two things we've learned, okay. Does anyone have any questions about anything we've done? . . . Okay!" Scott said as he dismissed the students.

As we better understand learning goals, we realize that some are better met with teacher-centered instruction; but for others, learner-centered approaches are more effective. We examined at content most effectively taught with teacher-centered approaches in Chapter 12, and now we're taking a similar look at learner-centered approaches.

After you've completed your study of this chapter, you should be able to meet the following objectives:

▌ Identify differences between teacher-centered and learner-centered approaches to planning.
▌ Describe the elements of learner-centered planning.
▌ Discuss the relationship between cognitive views of learning and learner-centered instruction.
▌ Describe features of different learner-centered approaches to instruction.

When Is Learner-Centered Instruction Appropriate?

We defined both teacher-centered and learner-centered approaches to instruction in Chapter 12. **Learner-centered approaches** include instruction *in which learners, with the teacher's guidance, are made responsible for constructing their own understanding.* Now we ask, "When is making students responsible for constructing their own understanding most appropriate?" To help answer this question, let's look again at Scott's lesson. He commented to himself, " . . . They're still having problems with this stuff [the scientific method, experimenting, and controlling variables] . . . Funny, we did the plant experiment as a whole class, and they seemed to get it. I explained it so carefully." By his own admission, in this case, explaining didn't work very well. His goal—for the students to understand experimenting and controlling variables—wasn't effectively reached with a teacher-centered approach; his students needed experience with experimenting on their own in order to understand it.

Goals that are most effectively reached through learner-centered strategies include the following:

- The development of inquiry and problem solving skills, such as in Scott's lesson.
- The development of deep understanding of topics, such as identifying relationships among Marco Polo's visit to the Orient, the Portuguese explorer's trips around the tip of Africa, and Columbus's discovery of the New World.
- The development of democratic processes, such as tolerance for dissenting views and the critical examination of our own and others' positions.

Learner-centered instruction actively involves learners in their quest for understanding.

These goals are complex, high level, and less able to be "mastered" in the same sense that Sam Barnett intended his students to master addition of two-digit numbers.

Keeping these goals in mind, let's look now at characteristics of learner-centered instruction.

Characteristics of Learner-Centered Instruction

In Scott's lesson, his instruction included the following features:

- He put his students at the center of the learning process by making them responsible for designing and conducting their own experiments.
- He guided the process and intervened only when necessary to prevent the students from heading down "blind alleys" or developing misconceptions.
- He emphasized a deep understanding of both the content and the processes involved.

These characteristics are illustrated in Figure 13.1 and described in the following sections.

Students at the Center of the Learning–Teaching Process

13.1

What two theories of motivation are most reflected in the learner-centered psychological principles? What theory of motivation is not reflected in the principles? Explain, citing evidence from the principles themselves.

The expanding influence of cognitive learning theory, research examining the thinking of experts, and criticisms of direct instruction have resulted in increased emphasis on the role of the student in learning. This emphasis has generated a number of learner-centered initiatives, among them the American Psychological Association's Learner-Centered Psychological Principles, which originally appeared in 1993 (Presidential Task Force on Psychology in Education, 1993) and have since been modified (American Psychological Association Board of Educational Affairs, 1995). These principles are outlined in Table 13.1.

Figure 13.1

Characteristics of learner-centered instruction

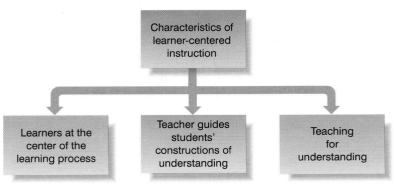

To make the list more manageable, researchers have distilled the principles into five generalizations about learning and teaching (Alexander & Murphy, 1998), which appear in Table 13.2.

The generalizations in Table 13.2 focus on the learner and remind us that we need to consider learners' background knowledge, their cognitive and affective thoughts, their development, and their social environment when we teach.

> **13.2** ■
> In Table 13.2 we see the statement, "The ability to reflect and regulate one's thoughts and behaviors is essential to learning and development." On what theory of learning is this statement most nearly based? Explain.

Table 13.1 ■

APA learner-centered psychological principles

Cognitive and Metacognitive Factors	
Principle	**Description**
1. Nature of the learning process	The learning of complex subject matter is most effective when it is an intentional process of constructing meaning from information and experience.
2. Goals of the learning process	The successful learner, over time and with support and instructional guidance, can create meaningful, coherent representations of knowledge.
3. Construction of knowledge	The successful learner can link new information with existing knowledge in meaningful ways.
4. Strategic thinking	The successful learner can create and use a repertoire of thinking and reasoning strategies to achieve complex learning goals.
5. Thinking about thinking	Higher-order strategies for selecting and monitoring mental operations facilitate creative and critical thinking.
6. Context of learning	Learning is influenced by environmental factors, including culture, technology, and instructional processes.
Motivational and Affective Factors	
Principle	**Description**
7. Motivational and affective influences on learning	What and how much is learned is influenced by the learner's motivation. Motivation to learn, in turn, is influenced by the individual's emotional states, beliefs, interests and goals, and habits of thinking.
8. Intrinsic motivation to learn	The learner's creativity, higher order thinking, and natural curiosity all contribute to motivation to learn. Intrinsic motivation is stimulated by tasks the learner perceives to be of optimal novelty and difficulty, relevant to personal interests and providing for personal choice and control.
9. Effects of motivation on effort	Acquisition of complex knowledge and skills requires extended learner effort and guided practice. Without learner's motivation to learn, the willingness to exert this effort is unlikely without coercion.

(continued)

Table 13.1 *continued*

Developmental and Social Factors	
Principle	**Description**
10. Developmental influences on learning	As individuals develop, there are different opportunities and constraints for learning. Learning is most effective when differential development within and across physical, intellectual, emotional, and social domains is taken into account.
11. Social influences on learning	Learning is influenced by social interactions, interpersonal relations, and communication with others.

Individual Differences	
Principle	**Description**
12. Individual differences in learning	Learners have different strategies, approaches, and capabilities for learning that are a function of prior experience and heredity.
13. Learning and diversity	Learning is most effective when differences in learners' linguistic, cultural, and social backgrounds are taken into account.
14. Standards and assessment	Setting appropriately high and challenging standards and assessing the learner as well as learning progress—including diagnostic, process, and outcome assessment—are integral parts of the learning process.

Source: American Psychological Association Board of Educational Affairs, 1995.

Table 13.2

Five statements summarizing the learner-centered principles

1.	The knowledge base	One's existing knowledge serves as the foundation of all future learning by guiding organization and representations, by serving as a basis of association with new information, and by coloring and filtering all new experiences.
2.	Strategic processing and control	The ability to reflect and regulate one's thoughts and behaviors is essential to learning and development.
3.	Motivation and affect	Motivational or affective factors, such as intrinsic motivation, attributions for learning, and personal goals, along with the motivational characteristics of learning tasks, play a significant role in the learning process.
4.	Development and individual differences	Learning, although ultimately a unique adventure for all, progresses through various common stages of development influenced by both inherited and experiential environmental factors.
5.	Situation or context	Learning is as much a socially shared undertaking as it is an individually constructed enterprise.

Source: Alexander and Murphy, 1998

Teachers Guide Learners

A second characteristic of learner-centered instruction is that teachers *guide* learners. To put this into perspective, return to Sam Barnett's work with his second graders in Chapter 12. In our discussion of Sam's lesson, we emphasized that "He continued by carefully *guiding* the students' understanding with questioning and modeling," so Sam was also *guiding* his students. There is an important difference between Sam's and Scott's approaches, however. Sam made *himself responsible* for students' learning by modeling and explaining a specific procedure for the skill and by being sure that students successfully followed it. Scott, in contrast, made the *students responsible* for their own learning by giving them a task and intervening only when they floundered. Because the teachers' goals were different, they placed different emphasis on student responsibility.

The role Scott played is very complex and demanding. For example, after his students conducted one test, they decided to make the pendulum both shorter and heavier, indicating that they didn't understand how to control variables. Let's see how Scott intervened.

Marina:	Mr. Sowell, we found out that the shorter it is and the heavier it is, the faster it goes.
Scott:	So, tell me how you found out that the length affected it.
Marina:	We made it long, and then we shortened it a little more, and then we made it heavier, and that showed . . .
Scott:	So, in Test 1, the length was 49, and the frequency was 21, and on the same test the weight was one paper clip? . . . Then you changed the weight? What else did you change?
Wensley:	The length.
Scott:	The length, so you changed the weight and the length.
Marina:	And the angle.
Scott:	So, you changed all three between the two tests. . . . Which caused that higher frequency?"
Paige:	The length.
Marina:	I think weight.
Scott:	What do you think? (looking at Wensley) Marina thinks weight.
Wensley:	Weight.
Scott:	What do you think? (looking at Jonathan)
Jonathan:	The weight.
Scott:	What do you think, Paige?
Paige:	The length.
Scott:	So, you think weight (pointing at Marina); you think weight (turning to Jonathan), you think weight (looking at Wensley), and you think length (pointing at Paige). Why can't you look at these two sets of data and decide? . . . Why can't you look at these numbers and come to a conclusion?"
Marina:	Well, like the length, and the height, and the weight was always changed. None of them ever stayed the same in any of them, so it has to be different.
Scott:	What was the first thing you said?
Wensley: *Jonathan:*	$\left[\begin{array}{l}\text{Everything changed.}\end{array}\right]$
Scott:	Think about that.

This dialogue illustrates the expertise and professional judgment teachers must have to effectively guide learning in learner-centered instruction. Scott didn't intervene so soon

13.3 ■
Think back to your study of information processing in Chapter 7. What characteristic of teachers' information processing systems makes learner-centered instruction difficult for teachers? What can be done to help overcome this difficulty? Explain.

that the students weren't allowed to struggle with the problem themselves, but he didn't wait so long that they became confused and frustrated.

This is very sophisticated instruction. Intervention is often necessary to help students make progress and prevent or eliminate misconceptions, but too much intervention prevents them from feeling problem ownership, developing initiative, and arriving at their own understanding. No rules exist to tell teachers whether or not they should intervene, or how extensive the intervention should be. And, when teachers work with one group, other groups may become confused or go off task, so they can't stay with any group too long.

The same cognitive balancing act occurs during whole-group discussions. When two students are talking to each other, others may not be understanding or even paying attention. If they aren't, the teacher must do something to involve them in the lesson.

With practice and effort, however, teachers can and do become expert with the process and, perhaps even more importantly, the satisfaction that we experience when we see a student understand something as a result of our guidance is difficult to overstate.

Teaching for Understanding

The phrase "teaching for understanding" seems like a paradox; no teacher consciously teaches for lack of understanding. As you saw in the example with place value at the end of Chapter 12, however, understanding doesn't always result from instruction, and "teaching for understanding" isn't as simple as it appears. Understanding involves thought-demanding processes such as explaining, finding evidence, justifying thinking, providing additional examples, generalizing, and relating parts to wholes (Knapp, Shields, & Turnbull, 1995; Perkins & Blythe, 1994). These elements were present in Scott's lesson.

By the end of Scott's lesson, how well did Paige, Marina, Wensley, and Jonathan grasp the idea of controlled variables? An interview following the lesson gives us some insight into their understanding.

The interviewer asked the students to write down three conclusions they made about the experiment, and they responded by saying that the length influenced the frequency, but that the angle and weight made no difference.

Interviewer:	Now I don't really believe that. I'm not sure about that business about the weight. Now, you told me that the weight doesn't matter, but I'm not convinced. Can you describe how we could test that, so I will believe you when you tell me that the weight doesn't matter?
Marina:	Okay, first you can do it with one or two [paper clips], it doesn't matter how many times you test frequency. . . .
Interviewer:	So, we're going to put on one paper clip (reaching for the end of the pendulum as shown in the following sketch). And then what are we going to do, Wensley?

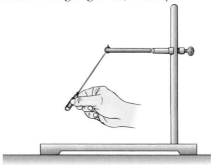

Wensley:	Set it at an angle that you want.
Interviewer:	Set it at some angle. What angle?
Wensley:	About here (pointing to what would be about a 45-degree angle).
Interviewer:	Okay, anything else I ought to do, Jonathan?
Jonathan:	Time how long we want to do it.

They decide to time the pendulum for 10 seconds, and they then conduct the test.

Interviewer:	So, it went back and forth 14 times in 10 seconds. So, what do we need to do now, Jonathan?
Jonathan:	Keep the same paper clip, but shorten it to see the difference.
Marina:	No, we're doing the weight.
Wensley:	We're doing the weight.
Jonathan:	Ohh, oh yeah, put two paper clips on.
Interviewer:	Put two paper clips on. (He then begins to attach a second paper clip to the end of the first one, in effect also changing the length of the pendulum.)
Marina:	No, no, inside the knot, inside the knot, inside the knot. If you put it there it changes the length.
Wensley:	No, you have to put it here (standing up and pointing to the knot).
Interviewer:	I can't do this?
All:	No!
Interviewer:	Now, explain to me why I can't do this. . . . Paige?
Paige:	When you do that, it's longer.
Interviewer:	Why do I care? We're testing the weight. We put on more weight. Why do I care if it's here (attached to the end of the first paper clip) or up here (in the knot)?
Wensley:	Because you can't have . . . it's easier to do one variable at a time.
Interviewer:	Now, what is the variable we're dealing with here?
All:	The weight.
Interviewer:	So, I don't want to do this? (Increase the length.) Tell me again why I don't want to do this, Wensley.
Wensley:	Cuz, your variables would change. You'd have two of them instead of only one. And you're only doing one variable, and that would be the weight.
Interviewer:	What other variable would I be changing by doing this?
Wensley:	The length.
Interviewer:	So, what do I need to do?
Marina:	Put the paper clip into the knot, next to the other one.
Interviewer:	So tell me one more time why we did this, Paige.
Paige:	So we could change the weight.
Interviewer:	So we could change the weight?
Paige:	But not make it longer.
Interviewer:	And not make it longer. So what is the word we use for the length. What are we doing with the length? We are . . .
Wensley:	Controlled variable?
Interviewer:	The length is a what?
Wensley:	Controlled variable.
Interviewer:	The length is a controlled variable. . . . So when you control a variable, what do you do?
Marina:	It doesn't change.

During the lesson, we saw confusion and uncertainty. But the interview suggests that the students understood the idea of controlled variables when they were finished. By focusing on understanding and placing students in the center of the process, teachers help students learn to take responsibility for constructing and verifying their own conclusions. Taking responsibility leads to self-regulated learning, a concept we've emphasized throughout this book.

Learner-Centered Instruction: Theoretical Foundations

13.4

Cite evidence from the first paragraph of the case study supporting the contention that "wisdom can't be told."

Learner-centered instruction is grounded in constructivism, and the characteristics of learner-centered teaching grow directly out of this view of learning. First, for example, *putting students at the center of the learning–teaching process* is a logical implication of the principle that *learners construct their own understanding. Teachers guiding learning* also makes sense based on the principle. Because of knowledge construction, each student's understanding is unique. Therefore, interaction is necessary to help students come to a common understanding, and guiding students requires high levels of interaction. As you've seen throughout your study of this book, "wisdom can't be told" (Bransford, 1993, p. 6). *Deep understanding* is the result of an evolving process that requires active learners and the guidance of skilled teachers.

Misconceptions About Learner-Centered Instruction

Teachers sometimes misinterpret learner-centered instruction when they attempt to apply it in their classrooms. Some misinterpretations include the following:

 ▌ Clear goals and careful preparation are less important in learner-centered than in teacher-centered approaches.
 ▌ If students are involved in discussions and other forms of interaction, learning automatically takes place.
 ▌ Teachers play less important roles in student-centered learning than in traditional instruction.

Because students are responsible for constructing their own understanding, teachers might infer that clear goals are less important when using learner-centered

In learner-centered instruction, teachers guide students through questions that help them see relationships in the content they're studying.

Clear goals allow teachers to design learning tasks that match students' needs.

approaches. Nothing could be further from the truth. Clear goals are as important—or even more important—with this approach because they give teachers focal points as they guide their students. Teachers may modify their goals as the lesson develops, but they begin with clear goals in mind. For example, Scott's students initially didn't know how to control variables, so he modified his original goal, helped them understand how to control variables, and then return to designing their experiments. He never lost sight of his original goal, however.

Concluding that discussions and other forms of social interaction automatically lead to learning is equally inaccurate. As you saw in Scott's lesson, teachers must carefully monitor discussions, and if students head down blind alleys or develop misunderstandings about the topic, teachers must intervene and redirect the discussion (A. Brown & Campione, 1994). We want students to become self-regulated and construct understandings that make sense to them, but their understandings must be valid. Allowing his students to continue experimenting without controlling variables would have been counterproductive in Scott's lesson, as would allowing students to conclude that both the weight and the angle influenced the frequency.

Finally, because teachers are not lecturing and explaining, it might appear that they have a less important role in learner-centered than in teacher-centered approaches. As we've already seen, their role is both more subtle and more sophisticated. If they understand a topic, most teachers can learn to adequately explain it. Guiding learners so they develop a deep understanding of the topic is much more difficult.

With these characteristics in mind, let's examine the planning process.

13.5

Think about Tracey Stoddart's lesson on heat with 9-year-olds (p. 61) in Chapter 2. Explain how she modified her goals during the course of her lesson.

Planning for Learner-Centered Instruction

Learner-centered planning is embedded in a planning model that considers the traditional questions of teaching (e.g., goals, learning activities, and assessment) but focuses on guiding learners' constructions of understanding and helping them monitor their own learning (Bransford, 1993; Resnick & Klopfer, 1989). These planning elements are illustrated in Figure 13.2 and discussed in the sections that follow.

Identifying Goals and Outcomes

As we've already said, in planning for learner-centered instruction, thinking about goals and outcomes is essential. However, because goals appropriately reached with learner-centered approaches are complex, stating them precisely can be difficult. Scott, for example, wasn't thinking of specific skills that must be practiced to mastery, such as Sam Barnett was when his second graders were working on subtraction (see Chapter 12). Instead, Scott wanted his students to understand how to design and conduct experiments. Reaching the goal required collaboration, discussion, and experience—perhaps even struggle—processes typically not part of a teacher-centered approach. (Similarly, in Chapter 12, Sam's goal was less appropriate for a learner-centered approach.) Teachers may modify their goals during the lesson, but they nevertheless begin with goals clearly in mind.

Learner-centered instruction attempts to increase students' awareness of and control over their own thinking as they work. This important goal is woven through all learning activities. Content outcomes are only part of our goal; the cognitive processes the students use to get there and the self-regulation of their own learning are equally important.

13.6

To what concept does students' self-regulation of their own learning refer? To what theory of learning does the concept most closely relate?

Designing and Organizing Learning Activities

Learner-centered instruction emphasizes learning activities that have two characteristics: authentic tasks and multiple representations of content.

Authentic Tasks

We saw in Chapter 7 that **authentic tasks** are *learning activities that require an understanding similar to the understanding that would be used in the world outside the classroom* (Needels & Knapp, 1994). As teachers plan, they embed learning activities in real-world tasks. This is both intuitively sensible and consistent with cognitive views of learning. Designing and conducting experiments, as we've discussed throughout this

Figure 13.2

A learner-centered planning model

Identifying goals and outcomes

Designing and organizing learning activities

Assessing current understanding

Planning for social interaction

Creating productive learning environments

Planning for assessment

chapter, requires real-world understanding. Tasks and understandings such as these are the focus of learner-centered activities.

Multiple Representations of Content

The need for a variety of examples and representations is one of the implications of constructivism (see Chapter 7), and this need also applies in transfer (see Chapter 8). Constructing understanding is a personal process, so individual understanding requires a variety of examples, or multiple representations of topics (Brenner, et al., 1997), described by some researchers as "criss-crossing a conceptual landscape" (Spiro, Feltovich, Jacobson, & Coulson, 1992). Certain ways of representing ideas will be meaningful to some students, and different representations will be meaningful to others. Providing an array of representations acknowledges the uniqueness of students and their background knowledge and provides multiple paths for making ideas meaningful.

Table 7.5 outlined the ways topics were represented by some of the teachers you had studied to that point. Table 13.3 provides some additional examples.

Preparing different ways of representing content is perhaps the most difficult planning task facing a teacher. It requires both a thorough knowledge of the topic and extensive pedagogical content knowledge.

> **13.7** ▬
> Consider the concept of transfer, which you studied in Chapter 8. To what feature of promoting transfer does the concept of *multiple representations of content* most closely relate? Explain.

Assessing Current Understanding

The influence of current understanding on new learning is at the core of all cognitive learning theories, and the third learner-centered principle (see Table 13.1) stresses the importance of linking new to existing information. This means teachers must plan to assess learners' current understanding.

Current understanding can be assessed in several ways. One is to give formal pretests related to the topic; another is to begin a lesson and informally assess under-

Table 13.3 ▬

Multiple representations of content

Teacher and Chapter	Goal	Representations
Jenny Newhall Chapter 7	Understand the relationship between length and weight on a balance beam Fourth grade	Manipulating a balance beam with a variety of lengths and weights
Suzanne Brush Chapter 8	Understand how data can be represented in graphics Second grade	Data from jelly bean survey Graphical representations Hands-on activities
Kathy Brewster Chapter 10	Understand the impact of the Crusades High school	School "crusade" Information from actual Crusades Learner essays
Shirley Barton Chapter 11	Understand equivalent fractions Fifth grade	Four concrete equivalent fractions Numerical examples
Scott Sowell Chapter 13	Understand controlled variables Seventh grade	Simple pendulums of different lengths, weights, and angles

Authentic learning tasks help students connect abstract ideas to the real world.

standing on the basis of students' comments and responses to questions. Scott, for example, assigned the task and observed students as they worked. In monitoring their efforts, he learned that they didn't know how to control variables. This process is sometimes called *dynamic assessment* (see Chapter 2), and it involves gathering information about students' understanding while they're involved in authentic learning tasks (Spector, 1992).

Planning for Social Interaction

Social interaction plays an important role in cognitive views of learning, and it is also emphasized in the eleventh learner-centered principle in Table 13.1. Social interaction encourages learners to think about and verbalize their ideas and share and compare them to other students'.

Too often, planning for social interaction simply means "put the students into groups." It isn't that simple, however. If group work/cooperative learning isn't carefully planned, it can result in confusion and wasted time. Effective group work requires specifying tasks clearly, teaching students how to work together effectively, and careful monitoring by the teacher. Scott's students worked well together, his task was clear, and he closely monitored their progress. (We discuss characteristics of effective group work later in the chapter.)

In whole-group activities, social interaction is facilitated by teacher questioning. The questioning skills we discussed in Chapter 11 are essential. If teachers don't have these skills, discussions tend to revert to minilectures, and the benefits of social interaction are lost.

The quality of the representations teachers use also influences student interaction. Effective representations provide students with the information they can use to construct understanding, so they give students reference points for discussing and exchanging ideas. This is why authentic learning tasks and multiple representations of content are so important. If the representations are ineffective, virtually no amount of teacher guidance will result in meaningful discussions.

13.8   ▬
Using constructivism as the basis, explain why social interaction is essential in learning activities.

Creating Productive Learning Environments

Productive learning environments are safe, orderly, and learning focused (see Chapter 11). A productive learning environment is crucial if learner-centered instruction is to succeed. This type of instruction requires that students feel free to offer conclusions, conjectures, and evidence without fear of criticism or embarrassment. It also requires students who are willing to listen to each other, wait their turn, and consider and reconsider their own ideas while others are talking. Students may not have these abilities or inclinations when learner-centered instruction is first introduced, so teachers need to help them learn to take responsibility for their own behavior. Conscious planning helps identify the specific skills to be developed and the strategies, such as modeling, that will be used to teach them.

Planning for Assessment

Learner-centered instruction also has implications for assessing learning. Rather than answer questions about abstract and isolated problems, students demonstrate their understanding in lifelike contexts. Scott's students, for example, could be asked to design an experiment to determine which type of dog food would make puppies grow better. In addition to assessing students' ability to apply the information they've learned, teachers can gather information about students' thinking in the process. (We discuss alternative assessments in detail in Chapter 14.)

In summary, when teachers plan for learner-centered instruction, they identify goals, organize and sequence learning activities, and assess learning, just as they would when using teacher-centered approaches. Learner-centered approaches, however, require more care in the way content is represented, as well as conscious planning for social interaction and the learning environment. In addition, teachers need to be more flexible in their thinking, adapting goals and strategies as instruction unfolds.

Classroom Connections

Planning for Effective Learner-Centered Instruction

1. Identify what you want your students to understand or be able to do after you're finished with a lesson or unit and have this guide your planning.
   - A social studies teacher is planning a unit on the Great Depression and how it influenced people's lives. She remains focused on the influence of the Depression on people as she plans the unit and gathers materials.
   - A third-grade teacher wants her students to understand the difference between physical and chemical changes. She keeps this goal in mind as she designs learning activities.

2. Prepare a variety of representations of the content you want students to understand.
   - The social studies teacher working on the Great Depression has students read excerpts from *The Grapes of Wrath,* finds a video of people standing in bread lines, finds statistics on the rash of suicides after the stock market crash, and selects descriptions of Franklin D. Roosevelt's back-to-work programs.
   - The third-grade teacher doing a unit on chemical and physical change plans to have the students melt ice, crumple paper, dissolve sugar, break toothpicks, and mix soft-drink powder to illustrate

physical change. She also plans to have them watch a laser disc that describes physical change. She plans to have them melt sugar, burn paper, pour vinegar into baking soda, and chew soda crackers to illustrate chemical change.

the United States plans to have students work in groups of three to identify similarities and differences in the regions. As students work in groups, they develop a chart comparing the different regions, and these charts form the basis for a whole-class discussion.

3. Plan for social interaction.
   • A geography teacher involved in a lesson on the geographies and economies of different regions in

Types of Learner-Centered Instruction

So far, we've determined when learner-centered instruction is appropriate, identified its characteristics, and discussed planning for learner-centered activities. We now want to examine the following learner-centered strategies:

- Discovery learning
- Problem-based learning and inquiry
- Discussions
- Cooperative learning
- Individualized instruction

Discovery Learning

Discovery learning is a *strategy that provides students with information they use to construct understanding.* Discovery learning was first made popular by Jerome Bruner (1960, 1966, 1971), who—in the 1960s and 1970s—argued persuasively for student autonomy and initiative. Many of his views about learning are similar to those held by constructivists today.

Types of Discovery

Discovery learning generated a body of research that helped clarify some of the issues involved, one of which is the distinction between unstructured and guided discovery (Keislar & Shulman, 1966). Pure, or **unstructured discovery**, occurs *in a natural setting where learners construct understanding on their own,* such as a scientist making a unique discovery in a research project. According to some, Piaget's work implies a pure discovery approach, suggesting that "educators get out of the way so that children can do their natural work" (Resnick & Klopfer, 1989, p. 4). **Guided discovery**, by contrast, occurs *when the teacher identifies a content goal, arranges information so that patterns can be found, and guides students to the goal.*

Research on Discovery Learning

Research indicates that unstructured discovery is less effective than guided approaches (Anastasiow, Bibley, Leonhardt, & Borish, 1970; Hardiman, Pollatsek, & Weil, 1986;

Schauble, 1990). In unstructured discovery activities, students often become lost and frustrated, and this confusion can lead to misconceptions (A. Brown & Campione, 1994). As a result, unstructured discovery isn't used as often in classrooms today, except in student projects and investigations.

Guided discovery is consistent with cognitive views of learning in general and constructivism in particular (Bransford, 1993; A. Brown & Campione, 1994), and it is supported by research. For example, a meta-analysis of studies examining writing instruction indicated that students taught with a guided-discovery approach showed three times more improvement than those taught through unstructured discovery and four times more improvement than those taught with a traditional, expository approach (Hillocks, 1984).

A more recent study found that guided discovery resulted in more transfer and greater long-term retention of science concepts and principles than did direct instruction (M. Bay, Staver, Bryan, & Hale, 1992). In comparing the two, researchers found that teachers spent less time lecturing and explaining and more time asking questions during guided discovery than during direct instruction. In addition, they found that students were more involved and had more opportunities to practice higher-order thinking—both important elements of learner-centered instruction (Alexander & Murphy, 1998; Marshall, 1997).

> **13.9**
> Figure 7.8 identified three ways of making information meaningful. Which of those three is most nearly illustrated by the information in this section?

Guided Discovery: An Application

Judy Nelson was beginning a study of longitude and latitude in social studies with her sixth graders. In preparation, she bought a beach ball, found an old tennis ball, and checked her wall maps and globes.

She began by having students identify where they live on the wall map and then said, "Suppose you were hiking in the wilderness and got lost and injured. You have a cellular phone, but you need to describe exactly where you are. How might you do that? You have a map of the area with you, but it's a topographic map showing rivers and mountains." As students discussed the problem, they realized that typical ways of locating themselves—such as cities and street signs—wouldn't work.

She continued, "It looks as if we have a problem. We want to be able to tell rescuers exactly where we are, but we don't have a way of doing it. Let's see whether we can figure this out."

She then held up the beach ball and globe and asked her students to observe and compare the two. In the process, they identified north, south, east, and west on the beach ball, and she drew a circle around the center of the ball, which they identified as the equator. They did the same with the tennis ball, which she then cut in half, allowing them to see that the ball was in two hemispheres.

Judy continued by drawing other horizontal lines on the beach ball and saying, "Now, compare the lines with each other."

" . . . They're all even," Kathy volunteered.

"Go ahead, Kathy. What do you mean by even?" Judy encouraged.

" . . . They don't cross each other," Kathy explained, motioning with her hands.

"Okay," Judy nodded, smiling.

Judy asked for and got additional comparisons, such as, "The lines all run east and west," and, "They get shorter as they move away from the equator." Judy wrote them on the chalkboard. After the class was done making comparisons, Judy introduced the term *latitude* to refer to the lines they'd been discussing.

Through guided discovery, teachers use constructivist learning principles to help students form concepts through hands-on experiences.

She continued by drawing vertical lines of longitude on the beach ball and identified them as shown below:

Discussion then followed:

Judy:	How do these lines compare with the lines of latitude?
Tricia:	. . . They go all around the ball.
Judy:	Good. And what else?
Elliot:	. . . Length, . . . they're all as long, long as each other, same length.
Thomas:	Lengths of what?
Elliot:	The up-and-down lines and the cross ones.
Judy:	What did we call the cross ones?
Elliot:	. . . Latitude.
Jime:	We said that they got shorter. . . . So how can they be the same length?
Tabatha:	I think those are longer (pointing to the longitude lines).
Judy:	How might we check to see about the lengths?
Jime:	. . . Measure them, the lines, like with a tape or string or something.
Judy:	What do you think of Jime's idea?

The students agreed that it seemed to be a good idea, so Judy helped hold pieces of string in place while Jime wrapped them around the ball at different points, and the class compared the lengths.

Chris:	They're the same (holding up two "longitude" strings).
Nicole:	Not these (holding two "latitude" strings).

After comparing the strings, Judy then asked students to work in pairs to summarize what they found. They made several conclusions, which Judy helped them rephrase. Then she wrote the following conclusions on the board:

Longitude lines are farthest apart at the equator; latitude lines are the same distance apart everywhere.

Lines of longitude are the same length; latitude lines get shorter north and south of the equator.

Lines of longitude intersect each other at the poles; lines of latitude and longitude intersect each other all over the globe.

Judy continued, asking, "Now, how does this help us solve our problem of identifying an exact location?" With some guidance from her, the class concluded that location can be pinpointed by where the lines cross. She noted that this is what they'll focus on the next day (Eggen & Kauchak, 2001, adapted with permission).

13.10 ▬

In the dialogue, Judy said, "It looks like we have a problem. We want to be able to tell rescuers exactly where we are, but we don't quite have a way of doing it. Let's see whether we can figure this out." What essential teaching skill from Chapter 11 does this statement best illustrate? Explain.

This guided discovery lesson illustrates the characteristics of learner-centered instruction. First, students were at the center of the learning process, and second, instead of simply explaining *longitude* and *latitude* to them, Judy guided their developing understanding. Third, she focused on deep understanding of the concepts instead of definitions or problems with little meaning for the students. Guided discovery provides teachers with one option in implementing learner-centered instruction.

We also see evidence of learner-centered planning in Judy's lesson. She used the beach ball, tennis ball, globe, and strings, and she planned to use maps the following day; she planned for multiple representations of content. Also, she planned for social interaction, both in the way she led the whole-group discussion and in planning to have the students work in pairs.

Several of the case studies you've already read used guided discovery to varying degrees, such as Jenny Newhall and Tracey Stoddart in Chapter 2, Diane Smith in Chapter 4, Suzanne Brush in Chapter 8, and Shirley Barton in Chapter 11. You may want to refer again to these case studies to further develop your understanding of guided discovery.

Problem-Based Learning and Inquiry

Problem-based learning is *a teaching strategy that uses problems as the focus for developing content, skills, and self-direction* (Krajcik, Blumenfeld, Marx, & Soloway, 1994). John Dewey (1910) first described the idea of using learners' natural curiosity as the starting point for instruction, and more recent advocates of problem-based learning see it as a way of teaching problem-solving skills while developing self-directed learning. Problem-based learning strategies typically have the following characteristics:

- Lessons begin with a problem or question, and solving the problem is the focus of the lesson (T. Duffy & Cunningham, 1996; Grabinger, 1996).
- Students are responsible for investigating the problem, designing strategies, and finding solutions (Slavin, Madden, Dolan, & Wasik, 1994).
- The teacher guides students' efforts through questioning and other forms of instructional scaffolding (Maxwell, Bellisimo, & Mergendoller, 1999; Stepien & Gallagher, 1993).

Goals of Problem-Based Learning

The goals of problem-based learning lessons are for students to (a) learn to systematically investigate questions and problems, (b) develop self-regulation and self-directed learning abilities, and (c) learn content.

Scott's lesson was aimed at these goals. First, his students were given practice in systematically investigating the problem of determining what influences the frequency of a simple pendulum. Second, the decisions and responsibility for conducting the investigation were theirs; Scott only intervened when necessary. Finally, he wanted them to understand that only the length influenced the frequency; neither the angle nor the weight had an effect.

The primary goals for problem-based learning activities are the development of problem-solving abilities and self-directed learning; learning content is less prominent. If learning content is a primary goal, strategies such as direct instruction, lecture–discussion, or guided discovery are probably more effective. However, some evidence indicates that content learned in problem-based lessons is retained longer and transfers better than content learned when other strategies are used (T. Duffy & Cunningham, 1996; Sternberg, 1998).

Inquiry

Inquiry is *a strategy in which facts and observations are used to answer questions and solve problems* (Kauchak & Eggen, 1998). Inquiry is a type or subset of problem-based learning, and it is also closely related to guided discovery. Inquiry typically includes the following steps:

▌ Identify a question or problem.
▌ Form a hypothesis to answer the question or solve the problem.
▌ Gather data to test the hypothesis.
▌ Draw conclusions from the data.
▌ Generalize on the basis of the conclusions.

Since inquiry is a subset of problem-based learning, their characteristics and goals are the same. The primary difference between general problem-based learning activities and inquiry is in the data gathering phase. Chapter 8 presented a problem-based activity with Jasper Woodbury (p. 335). In this case, all the information needed to solve the problem was provided for the students. In an inquiry activity, students gather the information needed to solve the problem.

Scott's students were involved in an inquiry activity. They were presented with the problem of determining how the length, weight, and angle affect the frequency of a simple pendulum. While the problem could have been presented more generally, such as, "What influences the frequency of a simple pendulum," Scott chose to narrow the problem to make it more manageable for the students.

In Scott's lesson, the students didn't form hypotheses; instead, they moved directly to gathering data. Understanding and applying the processes needed to gather meaningful data were the lesson's primary goals; understanding the relationships between length, weight, angle, and frequency were secondary. This emphasis on process is characteristic of inquiry activities specifically and problem-based learning in general (Eggen & Kauchak, 2001; Kauchak & Eggen, 1998).

Discussions

Discussions are *strategies designed to stimulate thinking, challenge attitudes and beliefs, and develop interpersonal skills* (Oser, 1986). These skills include

▌ Learning to listen to others
▌ Developing tolerance for dissenting views
▌ Learning democratic processes
▌ Critically examining one's understanding, attitudes, and values, as well as those of others

Like guided discovery and problem-based learning, discussions incorporate characteristics of learner-centered instruction; learners are at the center of the learning process, teachers guide students, and deep understanding of the topic is a goal. Discussions are consistent with cognitive views of learning since learners are active in developing their understanding, and social interaction is emphasized.

In Chapter 12, we said that teacher-centered and learner-centered instruction are compatible and can be used to complement each other. To see how, let's return to Darren Anderson and her work with her American History students in Chapter 12. She used lecture–discussion to help her students acquire background related to the conflicts between the French and British before the Revolutionary War. Then she wanted her students to further analyze certain aspects of the conflict.

Discussions provide opportunities for learners to share ideas and develop their interpersonal communication skills.

She began, "Today, we're going to pull together some ideas we've been thinking about related to the Revolutionary War. To do that, I'd like to present an idea and have us talk about it. Some historians, reviewing all the facts about the war, suggest that, on paper, the British 'should' have won. When they say this, they're not saying 'should' like 'ought' but rather that the British had important advantages but wasted them. What do you think? . . . Anyone? . . . Well, think about it while I put this statement on the board."

She then wrote

"The British advantages during the Revolutionary War should have ensured victory"

on the chalkboard.

"Okay," she went on. "Now that you've had time to think, does anyone want to take a stab at this? . . . Shirley, go ahead."

" . . . I agree," Shirley began. "They had lots of soldiers and guns and stuff, and equipment. They should have won."

"I agree too," Martha added. "They had more soldiers and they were . . . real soldiers. And . . . "

"But they, the soldiers, were in the wrong place most of the time," Hank interjected.

"Hold on a second, Hank. That's a good idea, but please give Martha a chance to finish," Darren admonished gently.

She continued, "Anything else, Martha?"

"Well, . . . I was just going to say that because they were real soldiers, they were better trained."

"Yeah, but the British started the war. You know, we talked about all the taxes, like on tea, and the people here, . . . in the colonies, got mad, because it wasn't fair," Ed added.

"Not really," Joan countered. "I think the Colonists started it. They shot first."

"That is an interesting issue," Darren smiled, "but what is the question we're examining here? Ken?"

" . . . If the British should have won the war or not."

"Yes, good, Ken. Let's keep that in mind, everyone. On the other hand, if you want to argue that the issue of who started the war is relevant, please go ahead."

After hesitating briefly, both Ed and Joan nodded that they didn't want to pursue the issue, so Darren continued.

"Now, Hank, what were you saying?"

"Well, even though they . . . the British, had more soldiers, it, it didn't always help them."

"Why do you say that, Hank?"

" . . . Well, like we talked about Saratoga, you know, you showed us on the map. That general . . . Burgoyne, sent a bunch of his soldiers to Philadelphia and wasted them, well at least sort of wasted them. He was supposed to go up, up to Albany. So, that's what I mean, they didn't seem to be too smart about the way they fought, or like they had bad strategy or something."

"That's an interesting thought, Hank. Jeremy, do you have something to add?"

"Also the British had, . . . those that were paid, were paid to fight . . . "

"Mercenaries," Darren added.

"Yeah, mercenaries, they were just being paid to fight, so they didn't fight very hard."

"So, what exactly are you saying?"

" . . . Well, having lots of soldiers isn't necessarily the most important. Like if they didn't really want to fight . . . that would matter. . . . The people in the colonies lived here, so they fought really hard, I think."

"Okay! Very good, everyone. Now, return to our question on the board. What other advantages or disadvantages did the British have that influenced the outcome of the war?"

Characteristics of Effective Discussions

Using Darren's lesson as context, let's look now at four characteristics of effective discussions:

- Student background knowledge
- Focus
- Emphasis on understanding
- Student–student interaction

13.11

When effectively done, direct instruction, lecture–discussion, guided discovery, and discussions have an important characteristic in common. What is this characteristic?

Student Background Knowledge.   Background knowledge is essential in discussions. Discussions should follow lessons in which background has been developed, such as the lecture–discussion we saw Darren conduct in Chapter 12. If students' backgrounds are insufficient, discussions are ineffective, disintegrating into random conjectures, uninformed opinions, and "pooled ignorance."

Focus.   Teachers provide focus in discussions by posing a question or problem, such as whether or not the British should have won the Revolutionary War, and they maintain this focus through their questions and comments (Krabbe & Polivka, 1990). Students have a tendency to wander and, without intervention, an animated discussion can develop over an irrelevant issue. The following excerpt from her lesson illustrates how Darren intervened.

Ed:	Yeah, but the British started the war. You know we talked about all the taxes, like on tea, and the people here, . . . in the colonies, got mad, because it wasn't fair.
Joan:	Not really. I think the Colonists started it. They shot first.
Darren:	That is an interesting issue, but what is the question we're examining here? Ken?

Ken: . . . If the British should have won the war or not.

Darren: Yes, good, Ken. Let's keep that in mind, everyone. On the other hand, if you want to argue that the issue of who started the war is relevant, please go ahead.

Keeping students focused and helping them recognize when they are making irrelevant arguments is an essential teacher role.

Emphasis on Understanding.   Discussions are best used to explore relationships, integrate ideas, and develop thinking and interpersonal skills. They're not effective for developing initial understanding. Successful discussions invite students to identify links between ideas and construct understanding that makes sense to them. Uncertainty, conjecture, and healthy disagreement are all part of this process. This is the reason background knowledge is so important.

Student–Student Interaction.   Student interaction is integral to discussions (Dillon, 1987; Krabbe & Polivka, 1990). Student–student interaction helps students learn to listen, to challenge others' thinking, explain and defend their own reasoning, respect others' opinions, wait their turn, and remain open-minded in the face of new evidence. Developing these communication skills is often as important as the content students are studying.

Research on effective discussions reveals that teachers have a difficult time shifting from an information-giving role to that of facilitator (Dillon, 1987). They tend to dominate discussions, turning them into minilectures (Cazden, 1986; Cuban, 1984). To be successful discussion leaders, teachers need to intervene only when necessary and ask questions that encourage students to think and interact with the content and each other, not with the teacher.

Cooperative Learning

Though much instruction is conducted in whole-class settings, teachers often have goals that can't be met in large groups, where it's easy for quiet or less confident students to go unnoticed. They learn that opportunities for participation are limited, some drift off, and individuals get few chances to present and defend their conclusions. To reach goals not effectively met in large groups and to encourage the involvement of all learners, cooperative learning provides an effective alternative.

Researchers don't agree on a single definition of cooperative learning. Most, however, agree that **cooperative learning** *consists of students working together in groups small enough so that everyone can participate in a clearly assigned task* (E. Cohen, 1994; Johnson & Johnson, 1994). They also agree that cooperative learning shares at least four common features:

- Students are placed in small groups (typically 2 to 5).
- Goals direct the groups' activities.
- Social interaction is emphasized.
- Learners must depend on each other to reach the goals.

The fourth characteristic is crucial and is called *positive interdependence* (Johnson & Johnson, 1994) or *reciprocal interdependence* (E. Cohen, 1994).

We saw these features in Scott's lesson. He placed his students in groups of four; their goal was to determine how length, weight, and angle affected the frequency of a simple pendulum; a great deal of interaction took place in the groups; and the students collaborated in designing, implementing, and interpreting the experiment.

Several of the teachers in the cases you've studied in earlier chapters used cooperative learning as a part of their instruction. In addition to Scott in this chapter, Jan Davis in Chapter 1, Jenny Newhall and Sue Southam in Chapter 7, and Laura Hunter and Suzanne Brush in Chapter 8 all used cooperative learning in their instruction.

Research documents the effectiveness of cooperative learning for developing problem-solving skills in various content areas and different grade levels (E. Cohen, 1994; O'Donnell & Dansereau, 1992; Quin, Johnson, & Johnson, 1995), and advocates argue that it is also consistent with constructivist views of learning. The benefits derive from the role of social interaction, proponents saying that learners co-construct more powerful understandings than individuals can construct alone (Lehman, Kauffman, White, Horn, & Bruning, 1999; M. Linn & Burbules, 1993; O'Donnell & O'Kelly, 1994). This position is grounded in Vygotsky's social constructivism (see Chapter 2).

Introducing Cooperative Learning

Effectively introducing students to cooperative learning requires careful planning and organization. Materials must be ready and quickly distributed to each group, and students must be able to get into and out of groups easily. If the process isn't well organized, instructional time is lost in transitions. Also, goals and directions must be clear to prevent activities from disintegrating into aimless "bull sessions."

Suggestions for initially planning and organizing cooperative learning activities include the following:

| Introduce your students to cooperative learning with short, simple tasks.
| Have students practice moving into and out of groups quickly. Group members can be seated together before the activity to make the transition from the whole-class activity to student groups and back again with little disruption.
| Give students a clear and specific task to accomplish in the groups.
| Specify the amount of time students have to accomplish the task (and keep it relatively short).
| Require that students produce a product as a result of the cooperative learning activity.
| Monitor the groups while they work.

These characteristics were illustrated in Scott's lesson. His students were used to working in groups, so they were able to work together effectively on a complex task. The groups were seated together, the task was clear and specific, he required that they write down their conclusions, and, perhaps most importantly, he carefully monitored the progress of the groups. Because the task was complex, they worked on it for most of the period.

Specific Approaches to Cooperative Learning

Different models of cooperative learning are designed to accomplish different goals. We look at two of them in this section.

Student Teams Achievement Divisions.   Created by Robert Slavin (1995), **Student Teams Achievement Divisions (STAD)** *implements cooperative learning by using a structured system of rewards to promote concept, skill, and fact learning.* The use of STAD is another illustration of the compatibility of teacher-centered and learner-centered instruction. It typically follows a direct instruction lesson, which is teacher-centered, but capitalizes on the advantages of student cooperation, which is learner-centered.

13.12

A teacher places her third graders in groups of three, gives each group magnets and a packet including a dime, spoon, aluminum foil, rubber band, wooden pencil, paper clip, and nails. She tells the groups to experiment with the magnets and items for 10 minutes and write their observations on paper. As they work, she answers questions and makes comments. The class as a whole group discusses the results. How effectively did the teacher introduce cooperative learning to her students? Cite evidence from the example to support your conclusion.

When STAD is used, solitary independent practice is replaced by *team study*. During team study, students complete exercises on teacher-prepared worksheets and compare their results with those of their teammates. The teacher intervenes only if team members are unable to resolve disagreements about answers. Team study is complete when all teammates understand and can explain the problems or exercises.

Team study is followed by quizzes, which are scored as they would be in any other situation. If individuals score higher on a quiz than their average to that point in the class, they are awarded improvement points, and individual improvement points contribute to team awards. Improvement points contributing to team awards is a mechanism designed to promote positive interdependence.

Two elements are essential to STAD: *individual accountability* and *group awards* (Slavin, 1995). Individuals are accountable because they take the quizzes alone, and they contribute to group awards if their quiz score is higher than their average at that point in the grading period. Although rewards are used with STAD, teams do not compete with each other; all groups can achieve the highest group awards if they improve enough or have high enough averages.

> **13.13** ▪
> Teachers sometimes give all students in a cooperative group the same grade. Based on the information in this section, is this effective practice?

Jigsaw II.   Jigsaw II is *a form of cooperative learning in which individual students become experts on subsections of a topic and teach that subsection to others.* In contrast with STAD, which is most effective for teaching procedural skills, Jigsaw II is designed to teach organized bodies of knowledge. In a unit on Central America, for instance, a social studies teacher may have one student from each team focus on the geography, another on the climate, a third on the economy, and a fourth on the political system of each country. Individuals study their topics and then attend "expert meetings," in which all students assigned to a particular topic (e.g., the climate) meet, compare notes, and clarify their understanding. "Experts" then teach the other members of their teams. Each member contributes a different piece of the knowledge puzzle, thus the name "Jigsaw." All members are held accountable for the content of each area.

Cooperative Learning: A Tool for Capitalizing on Diversity

Unfortunately, people tend to be somewhat wary of others who look or act differently than they do or of those who come from backgrounds that are different from their own. This tendency is common in social settings, and it is also occurs in schools. Students of a particular ethnic group tend to spend most of their time together, so they don't learn that all of us are much more alike than we are different.

As teachers, we can't mandate tolerance, trust, and friendship among students with different backgrounds. We need some additional tools, and cooperative learning can be one of them.

Research supports this idea. Students working in cooperative groups improve their social skills, increase their acceptance of students with exceptionalities, and develop friendships and positive attitudes with others who differ in achievement, ethnicity, and gender (Slavin, 1995).

One teacher reported the following:

> A special education student in the sixth grade was transferred to our classroom, a fifth/sixth grade. The classroom she was in has several special education students. The first—I'll call her Sara—was having behavior difficulties in her first classroom and was about to be expelled because of her unacceptable behavior with her peers. We offered her the opportunity to try our room with no special education students and with cooperative learning techniques being applied in various subjects along with TAI (coopera-

tive learning) math. Sara was welcomed by her new classmates. We added her to one of the TAI math learning teams, and the students taught her the program's routine. Sara worked very steadily and methodically trying to catch up academically and to fit in socially. She began to take more pride in her dress and grooming habits. I have been working with Sara on her basic facts in preparation for the weekly facts quizzes. Her attitude toward her schoolwork and her self-concept have blossomed within the length of time she has been in our classroom. (Nancy Chrest, Fifth/Sixth Grade Teacher, George C. Weimer Elementary School, St. Albans, WV, quoted in Slavin, 1995, p. 42)

These are impressive results, particularly when you consider that they were achieved with little additional teacher effort and without outside help.

The positive effects of cooperative learning on interpersonal attitudes likely stem from at least four factors:

- Opportunities for different types of students to work together on joint projects
- Equal-status roles for participants
- Opportunity for different types of students to learn about each other as individuals
- The teacher's implicit but unequivocal support for students with diverse backgrounds working together (Slavin, 1995)

Slavin speculates that cooperative learning's effects on intergroup relations result from opportunities for friendships and blurring of intergroup boundaries. As students work together, they develop friendships across cultural, gender, and ability lines, which tend to break down well-defined peer group boundaries that lead to cross-group friendships.

Let's see how Maria Sanchez, a third-grade teacher, attempted to accomplish these goals.

As Maria watched her third graders bent over their work, she was simultaneously pleased and uneasy. They had improved a great deal in their math and reading since the beginning of the year, but there was little mixing among her minority and nonminority students. She worried about the six from Costa Rica, who were struggling with English, and there were four students with exceptionalities who left her class every day for extra help.

Maria decided to try cooperative groups to see if she could help the class become more cohesive. Over the weekend, she used suggestions from their last year's teacher, test scores, and her own judgment to organize the students into groups of four, with equal numbers of high- and low-ability readers in each group. She also mixed the students by ethnicity and gender, and she put each student for whom English was a second language and each student with an exceptionality into a different group. Then she gathered the materials that she would use.

On Monday, she organized the groups and explained how they were to work together. She sat with one group and modeled cooperation and support for the rest of the students.

Then she sent each group to a different part of the room and had them work on specific tasks to help them become better acquainted. For example, one student from each group read a paragraph, and another asked questions of the other group members, using stems that Maria had provided. As they worked, Maria moved around the room, promoting cooperation, ensuring that all students were involved, and preventing individuals from dominating the groups.

After a demanding but fairly successful first session, Maria sent her students outside for recess.

"Phew," she thought to herself as she surveyed the classroom. "This isn't any easier, but it already seems a little better."

As you saw earlier, effective cooperative learning requires careful planning and monitoring, particularly when students are first introduced to the process. Groups need to be carefully organized, as Maria did, and trained to function effectively. Tasks must be structured to promote interaction, and group progress must be monitored (E. Cohen, 1994). Let's look at these elements.

Grouping.   As you saw in Maria's case, cooperative learning groups should have equal numbers of high- and low-ability students, boys and girls, ethnic minorities, and students with exceptionalities, particularly when the goal is to promote positive relationships among students.

Training.   Effective interaction doesn't just happen; it must be planned and taught. "Helping" behaviors can be learned, and these skills are especially valuable for minority students, who are often hesitant about seeking and giving help (Webb & Farivar, 1994). Guidelines for helpful interaction skills include:

> *Listening and questioning:*   Encourage other students to verbalize their understanding and listen to others' ideas without criticizing them.
> *Checking for understanding:*   Ask for elaboration when answers are incomplete.
> *Staying on-task:*   Make sure the discussion remains focused and time limits are met.
> *Emotional support:*   Offer supportive comments for incorrect answers (e.g., "That's okay. I don't always get it the first time either.")
> (S. Kagan, 1994; Webb & Farivar, 1994).

Role playing, teacher modeling, and videotapes of effective groups can all be used to help students learn these skills (Fitch & Semb, 1992).

Learning Tasks.   To succeed in promoting acceptance of diversity, tasks must require cooperation and communication (E. Cohen, 1994; Good, McCaslin, & Reys, 1992). Maria accomplished this by providing question stems for each group and by having students take turns reading paragraphs and asking and answering questions. By rotating students through these roles, she encouraged participation from all group members and helped prevent higher-status or more aggressive students from dominating the activity. Other tasks that can be used to encourage communication and cooperation include presenting and checking math problems, practicing spelling and grammar exercises in which students take turns as tutors, and providing open-ended problems (E. Cohen, 1994; Quin et al., 1995).

Monitoring.   As Maria found, groups need constant monitoring and support, especially initially. Student achievement is related to the amount and quality of interaction in groups, which also influences group cohesion and intragroup relations (E. Cohen, 1994). Teachers should deal with problems in individual groups. If the problems persist, they can reconvene the class for discussion, additional modeling, and role playing.

13.14
Provide a specific explanation for why students are more likely to develop positive attitudes toward students different from themselves in cooperative learning groups than in whole-group activities.

Teacher monitoring ensures that cooperative learning groups function effectively.

Classroom Connections

Capitalizing on Diversity in Your Classroom

1. Use the composition of cooperative learning groups to capitalize on the strengths of students with diverse backgrounds.
   - A second-grade teacher waits until several weeks into the school year to form cooperative learning groups. She uses this time to observe her students and gather data about student interests, talents, and friendships. She uses this information in making decisions about group membership.

2. Design learning tasks that require group interaction and cooperation.
   - A sixth-grade math teacher uses cooperative learning groups to provide practice and feedback in his class. When he assigns word problems, he asks students to work in pairs and compare and explain their answers to the other student in the pair. They may ask for help only when they're unable to resolve disagreements.
   - An English teacher uses cooperative learning as a way to provide student reactions and responses to each other's writing. Students in each group take turns reading and reacting to each other's works on the basis of style and clarity. They then make suggestions for revision.

3. Use warm-up, introductory, and team-building exercises to promote interaction within groups.
   - A social studies teacher encourages group solidarity by having members interview each other about such things as their favorite food, hobby, song, or vacation. Each interviewer then presents this information to other members of the group.

   - A high school teacher starts her cooperative learning activities with an icebreaker called "Truth and Lies." Each person in the group says four things about himself or herself, three of which are true and one of which is a lie. The others try to guess which one is the lie.

4. Provide feedback to students about their interactions within the group.
   - An English teacher monitors reader response sessions and joins in with students during the activities. Comments such as, "I really like the way you used examples from his writing to tell him what you liked," help students understand how to give constructive feedback.
   - A kindergarten teacher sometimes interrupts cooperative learning activities when she detects problems, such as students arguing about who gets to perform a certain task. She tells them they must learn to cooperatively solve their problem, and she models cooperation in simulations and think-alouds.

5. Evaluate cooperative learning groups to determine their effectiveness.
   - A fourth-grade teacher asks her students to fill out evaluation forms after cooperative group activities. On the half-sheet of paper, she asks students to tell her:
     a. What I learned
     b. What I liked about working in the group
     c. How the group could help me learn better

Technology and Learning: Integrating Cooperative Learning and Technology

Jim Daine, a middle school teacher, was attempting to integrate technology into his classroom:

> I had what I thought was a major problem. My room is quite small, so I don't know where I would have put all the computers, even if I could have gotten them. But really, the district didn't have the money to buy computers for every student in our classes anyway. I average 26 students a class, and they got me 12 computers. Actually, I'm luckier than most. Some of classrooms have only two or three.

Integrating cooperative learning and technology can capitalize on the best features of each.

So, I started talking to people and doing some reading, and I learned about combining cooperative learning while the kids work on the computers. I do quite a bit of cooperative work in my classes anyway, and the kids like it, but I just never thought about combining the two. I always thought, "One computer, one kid," and that's the way it had to be.

It was actually fairly simple. I assigned teams, so I had 10 pairs and two groups of three. When I first tried it, I let the kids pick their own partners, but that didn't work. So I ended up combining boys and girls, kids with different cultural backgrounds, and those whose computer skills were different. It took a lot of work and careful monitoring, but we've made a lot of progress, both in our technology skills and our ability to work together. Plus, it pretty much solved my problem with not enough computers.

Jim's comment, "One computer, one kid," is typical of prevailing thinking regarding the use of technology. "Many hardware and software designers (as well as teachers) automatically assume that all technology-assisted instruction should be structured individualistically. One student to a computer has been the usual assumption, and computer programs have been written accordingly" (Johnson & Johnson, 1996, p. 1018).

Cooperative Learning and Technology: Theory and Research

Some researchers believe that the technological infrastructure in schools has improved to the point that it is now capable of fundamentally changing the thinking of both students and teachers (Becker & Ravitz, 1999). However, in spite of the availability of hardware and improved software, students learn less if they aren't given opportunities to talk with others about their computer experiences.

Constructivism provides a theoretical framework that helps us understand why combining cooperative learning and technology should be effective, and an emerging body of research is examining the relationship. As would be expected, this research has identified both benefits and problems (Brush, 1997; Light & Mevarech, 1992; Turner & Dipinto, 1997).

Three benefits have been found:

▌ Reduced cost
▌ Enhanced social development
▌ Improved classroom climate

Reduced Cost.   Cost is obviously an important factor in the use of technology. Most teachers' classrooms have too few computers to be used effectively by individual students (Becker & Ravitz, 1999), and the problem is particularly acute for cash-strapped inner-city schools (National Telecommunications and Information Administration, 1999). Schools and households of poor and minority students have the lowest student-to-computer ratios (Gladieux & Swail, 1999). Designing instruction to combine cooperative learning with technology can increase access and reduce cost by half or more.

Enhanced Social Development.   Evidence also indicates that cooperative learning can aid learners' social development (Slavin, 1995), and additional research suggests that spending long periods in individual activities can increase boredom, frustration, anxiety, and the perception that learning is impersonal (Johnson & Johnson, 1996). Combining cooperative learning with technology can promote social development, while also eliminating the potentially negative aspects of working alone.

Improved Classroom Climate.   Combining cooperative learning and technology can also improve overall classroom climate. For example, students report they work better in a relaxed atmosphere, being able to help someone enhances their own sense of self-efficacy, and they can share interesting ideas when they work together. Teachers also report that classroom management problems decrease (Turner & Dipinto, 1997).

13.15 ▬
Using information processing as a basis, explain why the amount of content students learn decreases when students need high levels of computer skills.

Obstacles to Combining Cooperative Learning and Technology

As with any innovation, problems can exist. For example, combining cooperative learning and technology is obviously more complex than implementing either alone. To effectively combine the two, learners must have both technological skills and the abilities to work together. If students lack adequate technological skills, they are unable to participate or are forced to focus their cognitive energies on the mechanics of the technology, leaving less for understanding the content or working with each other. This problem is particularly acute with students placed at risk, who often lack both computer skills and school-related background knowledge (Lehman, et al., 1999). Similarly, if students lack social skills, interpersonal disagreements can detract from learning.

Cooperative Learning and Technology: Guidelines for Successful Implementation

Combining cooperative learning and technology is not a panacea (as teachers are sometimes led to believe); merely putting students together in front of computers doesn't guarantee learning (Johnson & Johnson, 1996).

Guidelines to ensure that learning does occur in these situations include the following:

▌ *Be certain that goals are appropriate.*   The software you're using must be consistent with your goals, and students must have adequate background knowledge to work with and learn from the software (Light & Mevarech, 1992). If learners lack the relevant background knowledge needed to attack a problem, neither cooperation nor the use of computers will help. This is a particularly important issue when dealing with students placed at risk (Kauffman, et al., 1999; Lehman, et al., 1999).

▪ *Carefully organize and monitor groups.*   When technology and cooperative learning are combined, group dynamics become more complex. Paired low-ability students stay on task less long than either high-ability pairs or pairs consisting of one high-ability and one low-ability student (Brush, 1997). However, high achievers sometimes express frustration at the amount of time required to help others in projects where technology is used (Turner & Dipinto, 1997).

▪ *Create a supportive classroom environment.*   Teach students how to disagree, and emphasize that differences of opinion are healthy and can contribute to learning. In groups with unequal status, some students may feel pressure to move along instead of offering dissenting views, and ideas from the highest-status or most dominant member of the group are often the ones accepted (M. Linn & Burbules, 1993). Monitor groups carefully, and intervene when necessary.

▪ *Maintain learning-focused interactions.*   When technology is used, learners can lose sight of the task and revert to a "video game" mentality. As with other forms of learning, the quality of interaction influences what is learned. Again, careful monitoring of the groups is important (Lehman et al., 1999).

▪ *Hold students accountable for what they're learning* (Slavin, 1995).   Accountability is crucial for all forms of cooperative learning, and it is equally important when technology is involved. Without individual accountability, one or two members of the group may do most of the work, while the others go along for the ride (E. Cohen, 1994; O'Donnell & O'Kelly, 1994; Slavin, 1995).

As with all aspects of instruction, effectively combining cooperative learning with technology isn't as simple as it appears on the surface; it requires careful thought and organization (which is true of all aspects of teaching). Further, it is likely to increase, not decrease, instructional and management demands on teachers. However, when carefully planned, implemented, and monitored, combining the two can capitalize on the best features of each.

Individualized Instruction

So far, we've examined guided discovery, discussions, and cooperative learning, which represent a trend from whole-group to small-group instruction. We continue the trend in this section with a discussion of individualization.

Individualization is *a form of instruction adapted to meet the specific learning needs of each student*. Three ways of individualizing are (a) varying time available for learning, (b) varying learning activities, and (c) varying instructional materials.

Varying Time Available for Learning

Learners differ in the amount of time needed to master a topic, with high-ability learners needing less time than low-ability learners (Slavin, 1987). Teachers often accommodate this difference by giving common assignments and then providing flexible time for students to finish their work.

In skill areas, a technique called *team-assisted individualization* (Slavin, 1985) keeps objectives constant but varies the time and resources available to students. In it, students work on individualized learning materials in mixed-ability teams. It differs from STAD primarily in that teachers provide direct instruction to small groups (but don't with STAD).

13.16 ▬
We saw earlier that "being able to help someone enhances their own sense of self-efficacy," but here we see that students providing help are sometimes frustrated at having to spend so much time helping others. Explain the apparent inconsistency in these two research results.

Varying Learning Activities

Varying learning activities provides a second way of individualizing. For instance, an English teacher might allow students to write a paper, give an oral report, or prepare a multimedia presentation about an author. A science teacher may allow students to prepare written reports or conduct an investigation. Allowing students choices in learning activities provides opportunities for students to pursue topics of individual interest and learn in different ways; both can greatly increase motivation.

Varying Instructional Materials

Individualization has become easier in recent years, with the increased availability of technology (audio- and videotaped instruction, films, and computer software) (Good & Brophy, 1997). If these materials are not available, reading passages can be made more accessible by providing study guides and by conducting prereading discussions that focus on key ideas (T. Anderson & Armbruster, 1984).

Research on Individualized Instruction

13.17

Based on the cognitive learning theories you've studied in this text, explain why individualization is not well suited to higher-order thinking and problem solving.

Research results examining individualized instruction are mixed. Individualization appears to be most effective when assessment is frequent and opportunities for student choice, self-regulation, and peer cooperation exist (Good & Brophy, 1997). Although acknowledging that some students need more time and instruction than others, Good and Brophy (1997) conclude, "It seems more appropriate to develop high-quality instructional materials and methods intended for all students than to set out from the beginning to develop different materials and methods for various students" (pp. 320–321). Further, they note, although individualization is well suited for practice on basic skills, it is not effective for developing higher-order thinking and problem solving.

Putting Learner-Centered Instruction Into Perspective

In Chapter 12, we attempted to present a balanced look at teacher-centered approaches to instruction, and we tried to do the same with learner-centered approaches in this chapter. We want to conclude our discussion with three reminders.

First, teachers should remember that all approaches to instruction are intended to help students reach goals; they are not goals in themselves. This statement seems self-evident, but strategies sometimes take on a life of their own: The strategy becomes the goal. For example, putting students into cooperative groups is not an appropriate goal. Helping students develop interpersonal skills is a desirable goal, and cooperative learning can be effective in reaching it. Cooperative learning for the sake of cooperative learning, however, is not appropriate.

Second, regardless of approach, effective instruction is clearly aligned. Teachers must be clear about their goals and design learning activities to reach them. Learner-centered approaches do not in any way reduce the need for instructional alignment. Scott began his lesson with a problem and used a hands-on, cooperative learning activity to help his students design and conduct experiments to understand the effect (or lack of effect) of length, weight, and angle on the frequency of a simple pendulum. He chose this approach because it was aligned with his goal. He didn't use a hands-on, cooperative learning approach for its own sake.

Third, as we said in Chapter 12, no strategy—teacher-centered or learner-centered—is more or less effective than the ability of the person implementing it. The crucial issue is not the effectiveness of direct instruction, guided discovery, or cooperative learning, for example; it is the expertise of the teacher using them.

In the past, experts and researchers tried to develop "teacher-proof" methods and curricula. They were unsuccessful. We would be better served trying to prepare teachers capable of exercising sound judgment, flexibility, and sensitivity (Michaels & O'Connor, 1990). This is why we believe that understanding learners and learning is so important. This is the understanding we hope you acquire by studying educational psychology.

Classroom Connections

Using Learner-Centered Approaches to Instruction in Your Classroom

1. Use a variety of examples and representations of the topics you teach.
   - A teacher beginning a unit on folktales writes a series of "folktales" about the school principal and other teachers. She also has students read folktales about characters such as Paul Bunyan and Pecos Bill and provides a matrix linking folktales to true historical events. She then discusses some contemporary figures who have been described in the media as "folk heroes" and how they may have achieved that status. Finally, she has the students write their own "folktales" about anyone they choose.

2. Use guided-discovery approaches to instruction to develop deep understanding of ideas.
   - A fourth-grade teacher embeds examples of possessive pronouns and singular and plural possessive nouns in the context of a paragraph. He then guides students' discussion as they develop explanations for why sentences (e.g., "The girls' and boys' accomplishments in the middle school were noteworthy, as were the children's feats in the elementary school") were punctuated the way they were.
   - A first-grade teacher begins a unit on reptiles by bringing a snake and turtle to class. She also includes colored pictures of lizards, alligators, and sea turtles. She has students describe the live animals and the pictures and then guides them to the essential characteristics of reptiles.

Conducting Effective Discussions in Your Classroom

3. Ensure that students have a solid background of information before conducting discussions.
   - A biology teacher is planning a discussion of global warming. Before the discussion, she presents information about the depletion of the Amazon rain forest, U.S. data on carbon dioxide emissions, and Eastern European countries' records on air emissions.

4. Begin discussions with a clear issue or problem, and keep the discussion focused on the issue.
   - A history teacher involved in a discussion of the efficacy of the U.S. involvement in Vietnam asks simply, "Considering the historical context, was America's decision to go into Vietnam a wise one?" He then keeps the students focused on America's initial decision to enter the conflict. When they discuss the war's outcome, he refocuses them on the original decision.

Using Cooperative Learning Effectively in Your Classroom

5. Introduce students to cooperative learning by using simple tasks.
   - A second-grade teacher begins the school year by having cooperative learning groups work on simple, convergent tasks. She keeps the time limits short and discusses group problems immediately. Later, she gives groups more complex and open-ended problems to solve.

Using Individualization Effectively in Your Classroom

6. Vary objectives and learning activities.
   • To increase students' interest in art, a kindergarten teacher provides watercolors and clay and allows students to work on individual projects with these different materials.

• A social studies teacher uses a unit on American immigrants to allow her students to explore their own cultural and ethnic backgrounds. After introducing the topic, she has students work individually or in groups, exploring the history of their ethnic group in the United States as well as their own family histories. At the end of the unit, students share their findings.

Windows on Classrooms

At the beginning of this chapter, you saw how Scott Sowell planned and conducted his lesson in an effort to actively involve his students in learning and to place them at the center of the learning process.

Let's look now at a teacher working with a class of ninth-grade geography students. As you read the case study, consider the extent to which the teacher applied the information you've studied in this chapter in her lesson.

Judy Holmquist, a ninth-grade geography teacher at Lakeside Junior High School, was involved in a unit on climate regions of the United States. To begin the unit, she divided the class into groups, and each group gathered information about the geography, economy, ethnic groups, and future issues in Florida, California, New York, and Alaska. She then put the information the students had gathered into a matrix. (See next page.)

Judy began the day's lesson by referring the class to information they had gathered and put on the chart and reminded them they would be looking for similarities and differences in the information.

Focusing their attention on the information in the first column, she began by saying, "What I want you to do is get with your partner and write down three differences and similarities on just the geography portion of the chart."

The groups began their work, and as Judy moved among the groups, offering help and answering questions, Chris raised his hand and said, "I don't understand exactly what we're supposed to do."

"Okay, take a look at the geography column. . . . You give me three things that are alike and three things that are different," Judy explained quietly.

"The temperature like in September in New York and California. Can I put that down as the same, cuz they're like 68 in California and 69 in New York?" Kiki asked as they were working.

"Yes," Judy nodded, "and you might think about why, too," reminding the class that they could use the climate and physical maps in their books as additional sources of information.

"Like for similarities, do they have to be alike in all of them?"

"Not necessarily, no. It could be in just two of them."

"Okay," Ann said brightly.

Judy continued to respond to questions as students worked, gave them another minute, and then called them back together.

"You look like you're doing a good job. . . . Okay, I think we're ready."

FLORIDA

Geography	Economy	Ethnic Groups	Future Issues
Coastal plain	Citrus industry	Native Americans	Population explosion
Florida uplands	Tourism	Spanish	Immigration problems
Hurricane season	Fishing	Cubans	Pollution
Warm ocean currents	Forestry	Haitians	Tax revisions
	Cattle	African American	Money for education

	Temp.	Moisture
Dec.	69	1.8
March	72	2.4
June	81	9.3
Sept	82	7.6

CALIFORNIA

Geography	Economy	Ethnic Groups	Future Issues
Coastal ranges	Citrus industry	Spanish	Earthquakes
Cascades	Wine/vineyards	Mexican	Deforestation
Sierra Nevadas	Fishing	Asian	Population explosion
Central Valley	Lumber	African American	Pollution
Desert	Television/Hollywood		Immigration problems
	Tourism		
	Computers		

	Temp.	Moisture
Dec.	54	2.5
March	57	2.8
June	66	T
Sept.	69	.3

NEW YORK

Geography	Economy	Ethnic Groups	Future Issues
Atlantic Coastal Plain	Vegetables	Dutch	Industrial decline
New England uplands	Fishing	Native Americans	Decaying urban areas
Appalachian Plateau	Apples	Italians	Waste disposal
Adirondack Mts.	Forestry	French	Crime
	Light manufacturing	Polish	Homelessness
	Entertainment/TV	Puerto Rican	Crowded schools
		African American	
		English	
		Irish	
		Russian	

	Temp.	Moisture
Dec.	37	3.9
March	42	4.1
June	72	3.7
Sept.	68	3.9

ALASKA

Geography	Economy	Ethnic Groups	Future Issues
Rocky Mountains	Mining	Eskimo (Inuit)	Unemployment
Brooks Range	Fishing	Native Americans	Cost of living
Panhandle area	Trapping	Russian	Oil spills
Plateaus between mountains	Lumbering/forestry		Pollution
Islands/treeless	Oil/pipeline		
Warm ocean currents	Tourism		

	Temp.	Moisture
Dec	−7	.9
March	11	.4
June	60	1.4
Sept.	46	1.0

"Give me a piece of information, Jackie, from the geography column," Judy began, pointing to the overhead.

"Mmm, they all have mountains except for Florida."

"Okay, they all have mountains except for Florida," Judy repeated and wrote it under "Similarities" on the chalkboard.

"Give me something else. . . . Jeff?"

"They all touch the oceans in places."

"Okay, what else? Give me something else. Go ahead, Todd."

"They're all in four corners."

"Okay, we have four corners."

"What else? . . . Missy?"

"New York and Florida both have coastal plains."

"New York and Florida both have coastal plains," she again repeated, writing the information on the chalkboard.

"Okay, you two in the back. I can hear you. Scott, give me something."

"They all have cold weather in December."

"Aha," Judy replied, "We're going to look at that one. Cold weather in December."

"Okay. . . . Tim?"

"All the summer temperatures are above 50% . . . er 50 degrees," Tim answered to some laughter from the rest of the class.

"What else can you tell me? How about some differences?" Judy encouraged. "Okay, Chris?"

"The temperature ranges a lot."

"All right. . . . John?"

"Different climate zones."

"Alaska gets below zero. It's the only one that gets below zero."

"It's the only one that gets below zero in winter. Is that what you said?" Judy asked to confirm Kiki's response, and Kiki nodded.

"Now, let's have a little bit more. I know you've got some more. I see it written on your papers."

"Carnisha, do you have anything to add?"

"All except Alaska have less than 4 inches of moisture in the winter," Carnisha offered.

"Okay, have we exhausted your lists? Anyone else have anything more to add?"

Judy waited a few seconds and then said, "Okay, now I want you to look at the economy, and I want you to write down three similarities and three differences in terms of the economy. You have 3 minutes."

As students again returned to their groups, Judy monitored them as she had earlier.

After they finished, she again called for and received a number of similarities and differences based on the information in the economy column.

She then shifted the direction of the lesson, saying, "Okay, great. . . . Now, let's see if we can link geography and economics. For example, why, in terms of a similarity, do they all have fishing?" she asked, waving her hand across the class as she walked toward the back of the room. "John?"

"They're all near the coast."

"Hmm, why do they all have forestry? . . . Okay, Jeremy?"

"They all have lots of trees," he answered to smiles from the rest of the class.

"Now, if they have lots of trees, what does this tell you about their climate?"

"It's warm enough for them to grow."

"But along with being warm enough, it has . . . ?"

"Fertile soil."

"And?"

"Moisture."

"Great."

"Now, let's look again at our chart. We have fruit in California and Florida. Why do they have the citrus industry there?"

"Jackie, good," she said, seeing Jackie's raised hand.

"Never mind."

"Oh, you know," Judy encouraged.

"No."

"Why can we grow oranges down here in Florida?"

"It's the climate."

"All right, because of the climate. Jackie says it's because of the climate. What kind of climate allows the citrus industry? . . . Tim?"

" . . . Humid subtropical."

"Okay, humid subtropical. Humid subtropical means that we have what? . . . Go ahead."

"Long humid summers, short mild winters," he replied.

"Now let's look at tourism. Why does each area have tourism?" Judy continued. "Okay, Lance?"

"Because they're all spread out. They're each at four corners, and they have different seasons that they're popular in."

Seeing that the period was nearing a close, Judy said, "Okay, let's deal with one issue. I want you to summarize . . . Listen up. I want to know what effect climate has on the economy of those regions."

She gave the class 1 minute to work again in their pairs, announcing that she expected to hear from as many people as possible.

"Let's see what you've got for an answer," she said after the minute had passed. "Braden, you had one. . . . I want to know what effect geography, which is climate and landforms, has on the economy," she said, pointing at Braden.

"If you have mountains in the area, you can't have farmland," he responded.

"Okay, what else? . . . Becky?"

"The climate affects like what's grown and like what's done inside the section."

"Okay, great. Climate affects what's grown, and what was the last part of that?"

"Like what's done," Becky repeated as the bell rang.

Judy waved, "Okay, great. Class dismissed," as students began gathering their materials to move to their next class period.

Questions for Discussion and Analysis

Analyze Judy's lesson in the context of the information in this chapter. In your analysis, you may want to consider the following questions. In each case, be specific and take information directly from the case study.

1. How effectively did Judy apply the characteristics of learner-centered instruction in her lesson? Explain, using information taken directly from the case study.

2. Of the learner-centered strategies described in the chapter, which did Judy use, or most nearly use? Explain.

3. How effectively did Judy use cooperative learning to meet the goals of her lesson? Assess her use of cooperative learning, using the following criteria: (a) clearly specified task, (b) concrete product, and (c) teacher monitoring.

4. Think back to the essential teaching skills discussed in Chapter 11. Which of these did Judy demonstrate in her lesson? Confirm your conclusions with information taken directly from the case study.

5. Provide an overall assessment of the lesson. Use evidence taken from the case study in making your assessment. What could Judy have done to make the lesson more effective? Be specific in making your suggestions.

Summary

When Is Learner-Centered Instruction Appropriate?

Learner-centered instruction is effective for goals that involve higher-level thinking, inquiry, and problem solving. It is less appropriate for goals, such as procedural skills, that all students are expected to master.

Characteristics of Learner-Centered Instruction

Learner-centered instruction, grounded in cognitive views of learning, places learners at the center of the learning process and emphasizes thought-demanding processes such as explaining, finding evidence, providing examples, and generalizing in an effort to acquire deep understanding of the topics being studied. Learner-centered instruction is based on learner-centered psychological principles, which view learners as intrinsically motivated, active seekers of knowledge who work with others to socially construct meaning.

Now go to our Companion Website to assess your understanding of chapter content with the Student Self-Assessment, apply comprehension in the Online Casebook, and broaden your knowledge base with links to important Educational Psychology World Wide Web sites.

Planning for Learner-Centered Instruction

Planning for learner-centered instruction involves identifying goals, designing learning activities to reach the goals, and constructing appropriate assessments. In addition, teachers planning for learner-centered activities consider how to make tasks authentic, represent content in a variety of ways, accommodate learners' current understanding, and social interaction, and create and maintain productive learning environments.

Types of Learner-Centered Instruction

Learner-centered approaches include guided discovery, inquiry, discussions, cooperative learning, individualization, and interactive applications of technology.

Teachers using guided discovery help learners reach goals by helping them identify patterns in information that has been provided. Inquiry helps students learn to solve problems by making and testing hypotheses with data. Discussions promote social and higher-order cognitive abilities by providing opportunities for learners to interact with each other. Cooperative learning develops thinking as well as collaborative social skills through structured small-group activities. Individualization tailors instruction to the unique needs of each student by varying time, learning activities, or instructional materials. Cooperative learning can be effectively combined with technology to capitalize on the beneficial effects of each.

Putting Learner-Centered Instruction Into Perspective

The approach to instruction that teachers use should depend on their goals. Effective teachers have clear goals and present learning activities that are aligned with them. Effective teachers remember that the approach to instruction is a means to reaching the goal; it isn't the goal itself.

 **Important Concepts**

authentic tasks (p. 564)

cooperative learning
(p. 575)

discovery learning (p. 568)

discussions (p. 572)

guided discovery (p. 568)

individualization (p. 583)

inquiry (p. 572)

Jigsaw II (p. 577)

learner-centered
approaches (p. 555)

problem-based learning
(p. 571)

Student Teams
Achievement Divisions
(STAD) (p. 576)

unstructured discovery
(p. 568)

14

Assessing
Classroom
Learning

Kathy Stevens walked among the desks of her seventh-graders as they worked on their seat work assignment. "Check that one again," she whispered as she passed Kim. Checking each student's work as she walked by, she continued this process for another 5 minutes. She then called for the students' attention.

"Let me hand back your quizzes," she announced. "You did fine on today's. You seem to understand when you explain your solutions, and you're doing okay on your homework, so we're going to have our test Thursday. We'll review a little more tomorrow to be sure you understand the word problems," she smiled.

"Now, let's take a look at several items that a few of you missed on the quiz," she continued as she handed the papers back to students.

Later, as Kathy worked on her test in the faculty lounge, Ken Allen, another math teacher, walked by. "How's your new system working?" he asked.

"Good," she replied. "Since I've been giving the short quiz every day, they're more conscientious about their homework, and they did better on the last test."

"Mmm. . . . Tell me again exactly what you're doing."

"I just give them a problem or two every day that's based on their homework. I score it while they begin the next day's assignment, and I hand it back at the end of the period. If we have an extra-tough topic, I don't get a quiz in every day, but they get at least three a week."

Quizzes, tests, and other assessments have a powerful effect on student learning. Despite its importance, teachers often feel ill-prepared to deal with the complexities of classroom assessment (Stiggins, 1997). Experienced teachers express concerns about their ability to write assessment items, to construct valid assessments, and to assign grades. Beginning teachers also express concerns about their ability to assess student progress (Lomax, 1994), ranking this problem fourth after classroom management, motivation, and dealing with individual differences (Veenman, 1984).

In this chapter, we address these concerns by examining the effects of assessment on learning and motivation, analyzing teachers' assessment patterns, and describing ways to design effective classroom assessments.

After you've completed your study of this chapter, you should be able to meet the following objectives:

▌ Explain basic assessment concepts.
▌ Describe classroom teachers' assessment patterns.
▌ Analyze assessment items for factors that detract from their validity.
▌ Construct alternative assessments in your content area or grade level.
▌ Apply effective assessment procedures in your own classroom.

Classroom Assessment

The case study at the beginning of the chapter illustrates the process of assessment, one of the most basic and difficult tasks teachers face in their work. **Classroom assessment** *includes all the processes involved in making decisions about students' learning progress* (Airasian, 1997). It includes observations of students' written work, their answers to questions in class, and performance on teacher-made and standardized tests. It includes performance assessments, such as watching first graders print or observing a word processing class type a letter. It also involves decisions, such as assigning grades or reteaching a topic. When combined, *these elements make up a teacher's* **assessment system**. In Kathy's case, her system included monitoring her students' learning progress by using their homework, her quizzes, and her tests.

Functions of Classroom Assessment

In addition to facilitating teacher decision making about learning progress through systematic information gathering, assessment accomplishes two other important goals: (a) increasing learning and (b) increasing motivation.

The relationship between learning and assessment is strong and robust. Students learn more in classes where assessment is an integral part of instruction than in those where it isn't, and brief assessments that provide frequent feedback about learning progress are more effective than long, infrequent ones, like once-a-term tests (Bangert-Drowns, Kulik, & Kulik, 1991; Dochy & McDowell, 1997).

Suggesting a link between testing and motivation is controversial because some critics argue that assessment detracts from motivation. Evidence runs counter to this argument, however (Brookhart, 1997; Eggen, 1997). Frequent assessment, linked to well-planned goals, encourages learners to pace themselves and keep up with their studies (Tuckman, 1998). Think about your own experiences. In which classes did you learn the most and for which did you study the hardest? For most students, they're the ones in which they're thoroughly assessed and given frequent feedback. Learners need to understand what they are supposed to learn, why they are learning it, and how they are progressing (see Chapter 10). Assessment gives them information about their progress, exerting a powerful influence on the amount and ways students study (Airasian, 1997; Stiggins, 1997).

14.1

How would a behaviorist explain the advantage of frequent, announced quizzes over those given infrequently? (Hint: Think about the concept of reinforcement schedules from Chapter 6.)

Measurement and Evaluation

Two basic processes are involved in assessment: **measurement**, which *includes all the information teachers gather as part of the assessment process*, and **evaluation**, which is *the process of making decisions on the basis of the measurements*.

Effective teachers use a range of measurement tools to capture different aspects of student learning. Some, as listed in Figure 14.1, use traditional paper-and-pencil formats, and others take advantage of alternative formats to assess critical thinking and problem-solving abilities.

14.2

Identify an important similarity and an important difference between traditional and alternative measurement formats. Also identify an advantage and a disadvantage of each.

Formal and Informal Measurement

Informal measurements are *measurements gathered incidentally*, such as listening to students' comments and answers to questions, noticing puzzled looks, or seeing that a

Figure 14.1

Traditional and alternative measurement formats

Traditional Measurement Formats	Alternative Measurement Formats
True–false	Specific performance task
Multiple choice	Timed trial
Matching	Exhibition of work
Fill in the blank	Reflective journal entry
Short, open-ended answer	Open-ended oral presentation
Paragraph response to specific question	Oral response to specific question
Paragraph response to open-ended question	Collaborative group project
Essay	Audiovisual presentation
	Debate
	Simulation

student isn't paying attention. In contrast, *the process of systematically gathering information* is called **formal measurement**. Tests and quizzes are formal measurements, as are performance assessments, such as a physical education teacher observing the number of sit-ups a student can do.

The Need for Systematic Assessment

Informal measurements are essential in helping teachers make the frequent instructional decisions required in every class. In the opening case, Kathy used them to help her decide when to stop seat work and when to schedule a test. Teachers also use informal measurements to decide how fast they can teach a topic, whom they should call on, and when they should stop one activity and move on to the next.

Informal measurements have a drawback, however. Because teachers don't obtain the same information from each student, they don't know about individual students' progress. Concluding that the whole class understands an idea on the basis of responses from only a few students is a mistake that teachers often make.

Without realizing it, teachers sometimes make decisions as important as assigning grades on the basis of informal measurements. Students who readily respond, have engaging personalities, and are physically attractive are often awarded higher grades than their less fortunate peers (Ritts, Patterson, & Tubbs, 1992). Gathering systematic information about each student's progress is one way to prevent these potential biases.

Systematic assessment is particularly important in the lower elementary grades, where teachers often rely on performance assessments, such as handwriting samples and verbal identification of written numerals, to make evaluation decisions. The question "Could I defend and document this decision to a parent if necessary?" is a helpful guideline in this process.

14.3
What would be an example of a systematic assessment in the class you're in now? What makes it systematic? What would be an example of an assessment that is not systematic?

Gathering systematic information about each student and keeping current records about students' learning progress help ensure accurate assessment.

Validity: Making Appropriate Evaluation Decisions

Validity *means that the assessment measures what it is supposed to measure*. It refers to "an evaluation of the adequacy and appropriateness of the interpretations and uses of assessment results" (R. Linn & Gronlund, 2000, p. 73).

Validity describes the link between the information gathered and the decisions made from that information (Shepard, 1993). In classroom practice, validity is the extent to which a measurement is congruent, or aligned, with the teacher's goals. For example, a classroom test measuring students' understanding of the Civil War that contains only factual items on names, dates, and places would be invalid because it failed to measure the connections between and significance of these facts.

The concept of validity is at the heart of many controversies in assessment. For example, critics argue that standardized tests are culturally biased and, as a result, are invalid for minority students (Helms, 1992). Other critics assert that questions measuring isolated and decontextualized skills—such as multiple-choice items on standardized tests—give an incomplete and therefore invalid picture of student understanding. This assertion has contributed to the movement toward "alternative" or "authentic" assessment (Herman, Aschbacher, & Winters, 1992; Moss, 1992). We examine alternative assessment in detail later in the chapter.

In classrooms, assessment decisions based on personality, appearance, or other factors unrelated to learning goals are also invalid. Teachers who give lower scores on essay items because of messy handwriting are using invalid criteria. In these cases, the actions are usually unconscious; without realizing it, teachers often base their assessments on appearance, rather than on substance.

None of this suggests, however, that teachers are doomed to use invalid assessments. Teachers who continually look for ways to improve their tests, quizzes, and other measures, analyze patterns in student responses, and conscientiously revise items, increase the validity of their assessment system. These actions are a part of the reflective attitude toward teaching that we emphasize throughout this text.

Reliability: Consistency in Measurement

Reliability, an intuitively sensible concept, *describes the extent to which measurements are consistent* (R. Linn & Gronlund, 2000). For instance, if your bathroom scale is reliable, and your weight doesn't change, the readings shouldn't vary from one day to the next. Similarly, if we could repeatedly give a student the same reliable test, the scores would all be the same, assuming no additional learning or forgetting occurred. Unreliable measurements cannot be valid, even if the measurements are congruent with the teacher's goals, because they give inconsistent information.

One way to think about the relationship between validity and reliability is to visualize a target and a person practicing shooting (R. Linn & Gronlund, 2000). A valid and reliable shooter consistently clusters shots in the target's bulls-eye. This is analogous to an assessment instrument that accurately and consistently measures the goals of instruction. A reliable but invalid shooter clusters shots, but the cluster is not in the bulls-eye. Assessment instruments that give teachers consistent scores but don't measure the prescribed goals of instruction are reliable but not valid. Finally, a shooter that scatters shots randomly over the target is analogous to an assessment instrument that is neither valid nor reliable. These relationships are illustrated in Figure 14.2.

The problem of scoring consistency can be illustrated with essay tests, which are often unreliable. Studies indicate that different instructors with similar backgrounds, ostensibly using the same criteria, have awarded grades ranging from excellent to failure on the same essay (Gronlund, 1993). When inconsistency in scoring occurs, lack of reliability makes the item invalid.

Informal measurements are often unreliable because not all students respond to the same question. Uncertainty on one student's face doesn't necessarily mean the other students are confused; likewise, a quick, confident answer from one student doesn't mean the entire class understands the topic. The solution is to use systematic assessments, which are more likely to be reliable.

14.4 ▬
A teacher gives her students the following writing assignment: "Describe a room in your home. Be sure your grammar and punctuation are correct." When she returns the papers, they have two grades, one for creativity and one for punctuation and grammar. Are both of these grades valid? Explain.

14.5 ▬
Research indicates that increasing the length of a test increases reliability, but studies of child development indicate that attention spans of young children are limited. Explain how teachers can reconcile these findings.

Figure 14.2 ▬

The relationships between validity and reliability

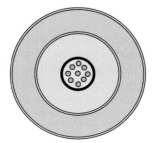
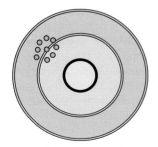
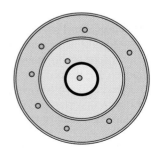

Valid and reliable measurements   Reliable but not valid measurements   Unreliable and invalid measurements

Adapted from R. Linn & Gronlund, 2000. Reprinted by permission.

Traditional Assessment

The way teachers have historically assessed learning, and a major way much of learning will continue to be assessed, is with teacher-made quizzes and tests. If well designed and constructed, these tests provide valid assessments of many aspects of student learning (R. Linn & Gronlund, 2000). In this section, we examine teachers' assessment patterns and discuss ways of constructing measurement items to make them as reliable and valid as possible.

Teachers' Assessment Patterns

Laura Brinson's second graders were working on subtracting one-digit from two-digit numbers with regrouping. She put a series of problems on the chalkboard, and her students were busily solving them as Laura circulated.

"Check this one again, Kelly," she said, seeing that Kelly had written

$$\begin{array}{r} 24 \\ -9 \\ \hline 25 \end{array}$$

on her paper.

"I think I'll take a grade on this one," Laura said to herself. She collected the papers after the students finished, scored them, and wrote "9" in her grade book for Kelly because she missed one of the 10 problems from the chalkboard.

Laura's on-the-spot decision to use the activity for grading is characteristic of elementary teachers, particularly at the primary level. They use informal measures more frequently than teachers at the higher levels, they rely on commercially prepared items, such as those that come with a textbook series, and they emphasize affective goals (McMillan, Workman, & Myran, 1999; Stiggins & Conklin, 1992). These patterns are summarized in Table 14.1.

Middle school and senior high teachers' assessment practices differ from those of elementary teachers in at least two ways. They depend more on traditional tests than on performance measures, and they more commonly prepare their own items instead of relying on published tests. Table 14.2 summarizes characteristics of these teacher-made items (Bol, Stephenson, O'Connell, & Nunnery, 1998; Stiggins & Conklin, 1992).

Several factors help explain the patterns in Table 14.2. First, teachers' jobs are complex and demanding, and teachers respond by simplifying their work. Reusing an item is simpler than revising it, for example. Essay items are easy to write but difficult and time-consuming to score; multiple-choice items are just the opposite. The simplest alternatives are the completion and matching formats, which are most popular with teachers. Further, knowledge and recall items are easy to construct, score, and defend.

In addition, teachers lack confidence in their ability to write good test items and use assessment to improve learning (Marso & Pigge, 1992; Plake & Impara, 1997). Because of inadequate training, teachers frequently have difficulty writing clear and precise test items at a level above knowledge and recall. These findings indicate a need for better quality assessments, particularly items that are unambiguous and require more of students than the simple recall of facts and information.

Designing Valid Test Items

We introduced the concept of validity earlier, and we reexamine it now, focusing on specific test items. Conceptually, item validity is simple; an item is valid if students who under-

Table 14.1

Elementary teachers' assessment patterns

Characteristic	Description
Performance measures	Primary teachers rely heavily on actual samples of student work (e.g., the ability to form letters or write numerals) to evaluate student learning (Marso & Pigge, 1992).
Informal measurements	Measurement is often informal, as was the case in Laura's class. She comments, "I take a grade a few times a week. I don't really have a regular schedule that I follow for grading." Further, teachers sometimes give social and background characteristics greater emphasis than ability (J. McMillan, Workman, & Myran, 1999).
Commercially prepared tests	When they do test, elementary teachers depend heavily on commercially prepared and published tests. Teachers in the primary grades rarely prepare their own formal tests, instead using informal assessments or using exercises from texts or teachers' editions (J. McMillan, Workman, & Myran, 1999).
Emphasis on affective goals	Primary teachers emphasize affective goals, such as "Gets along well with others." In one analysis of kindergarten progress reports sent home to parents, over a third of the categories were devoted to intrapersonal or interpersonal factors (Freeman & Hatch, 1989).

Table 14.2

Characteristics of teacher-made tests

1. Teachers commonly use test items containing many technical errors.
2. Teachers rarely use techniques such as item analysis and tables of specifications to improve the quality of their items. Once items are constructed, teachers tend to reuse them without revision.
3. Even though teachers state that higher order objectives are important, over three fourths of all items are written at the knowledge/recall level, and most of those above the knowledge level are in math and science. In other areas, 90% to 100% of the items are written at the knowledge level.
4. About 1% of all teacher-made test items use the essay format. This figure is higher in English classes.
5. The short-answer format is used most frequently, such as:

   a. Which two countries border on Mexico? _____

   _____

   b. Why does a cactus have needles, whereas an oak tree has broad leaves? _____

   _____

6. Matching items are common, for example:

   _____ A quadrilateral with one pair of opposite equal sides   a. Parallelogram

   _____ A three-sided plane figure with two sides equal in length   b. Pentagon

   _____ A quadrilateral with opposite sides equal in length   c. Rhombus

        d. Scalene triangle

        e. Square

        f. Isosceles triangle

stand the content answer it correctly and if those who don't understand it get the item wrong. For instance, if you have a multiple-choice item with *a* as the answer, but most of the class chooses *c*, the results may indicate a general misconception or a difficult idea, or the item may have been misleading. If a question is misleading, it's invalid; the other alternatives do not involve problems with validity.

If clues to the correct answer are included in the item, students may answer correctly without understanding the topic; this, too, makes the item invalid. Learners as young as fifth and sixth graders can use item clues to identify correct choices (Sudweeks, Baird, & Petersen, 1990). Teachers confess they have trouble writing effective items but believe many of these problems could be eliminated through increased teacher knowledge and understanding (Carter, 1986). Our goal for this section is to help you write better, more valid items.

The easiest and most effective way to evaluate an item is to discuss it with the class. In the case of a frequently missed item, for example, if missing it indicates a general misconception, the topic can be retaught. This is the primary purpose of assessment—to determine the extent to which students understand the content. On the other hand, if the item is misleading, it can be rewritten. In either case, discussing the students' responses to the item is important.

Using the concept of validity as our framework, we now turn to a discussion of specific item types. They can be classified as *selected-response* formats—multiple-choice, true–false, or matching—which require learners to choose the correct answer from a list of alternatives, or *supply* formats—completion and essay—which require learners to produce their own answers (Stiggins, 1997). Items can also be classified as objective, which are those on which equally competent learners get the same scores (e.g., multiple-choice), or subjective, where the scores are influenced by the judgment of the person doing the scoring, such as essay (R. Linn & Gronlund, 2000). Let's examine objective, selected-response formats first.

Multiple-Choice Items

The multiple-choice format can be one of the most effective for preparing valid and reliable items at different levels of thinking; most standardized tests use this format. Gronlund (1993) suggests that teachers should try writing multiple-choice items first and then switch to another format only if the objectives or content require it.

Multiple-choice items *contain a stem, which consists of a question or incomplete statement, and several choices; students choose the best one.* The incorrect alternatives are called **distracters** *because they are designed to distract students who don't understand the content being measured in the item.*

Items may be written so that only one choice is correct, or they may be in a "best-answer" form, in which more than one choice is partially correct but one is clearly better than the others. The best-answer form is more demanding, promotes higher-level thinking, and measures more complex achievement. Guidelines for preparing multiple-choice items are summarized in Table 14.3.

The Stem.   The stem should pose one question or problem for students to consider. With this guideline in mind, analyze the items in Figure 14.3.

The first item in Figure 14.3 is essentially a series of true–false statements linked only by the fact that they fall under the same stem. The second item presents two problems. Students selecting choice *b* may not know that veins are part of the circulatory system, or they may not realize that veins carry blood back to the heart rather than away

---

14.6 ■
You've found that most of the students in your class chose *d* on a multiple-choice item when the correct answer was *b*. In discussing the item with the class, you find that many of the students misinterpreted what you were asking for in the item. Is the item valid? Is it reliable? What should you do?

14.7 ■
What is the simplest and most effective way to correct Item 2 in Figure 14.3?

Table 14.3

Guidelines for preparing multiple-choice items

1. Present one clear problem in the stem of the item.
2. Make all distracters plausible and attractive to the uninformed.
3. Vary the position of the correct choice randomly. Be careful to avoid overusing choice *c*.
4. Avoid similar wording in the stem and the correct choice.
5. Avoid phrasing the correct choice in more technical terms than distracters.
6. Keep the correct answer and the distracters similar in length. A longer or shorter answer should usually be used as an incorrect choice.
7. Avoid using absolute terms (e.g., *always, never*) in the incorrect choices.
8. Keep the stem and distracters grammatically consistent.
9. Avoid using two distracters with the same meaning.
10. Emphasize *negative wording* by underlining if it is used.
11. Use "none of the above" with care, and avoid "all of the above" as a choice.

Source: How to Construct Achievement Tests, 4th ed., by N. Gronlund, 1988. Upper Saddle River, NJ: Prentice Hall. Copyright 1988 by Prentice Hall. Adapted by permission.

Figure 14.3

Multiple-choice items of differing quality

1. The circulatory system is the system that
   *a. transports blood throughout the body
   b. includes the lungs
   c. protects the vital organs of the body
   d. turns the food we eat into energy

2. Which of the following is a part and function of the circulatory system?
   *a. The blood vessels that carry food and oxygen to the body cells
   b. The blood veins that carry blood away from the heart
   c. The lungs that pump blood to all parts of the body
   d. The muscles that help move a person from one place to another

3. Which of the following describes the function of the circulatory system?
   *a. It moves blood from your heart to other parts of your body.
   b. It turns the sandwich you eat into energy you need to keep you going throughout the day.
   c. It removes solid and liquid waste materials from your body.
   d. It protects your heart, brain, and other body parts from being injured.

from it. The third item, presents a single, clearly stated problem, with the distracters providing possible alternatives.

Distracters.   Although carefully written stems are important, good distracters are essential for effective multiple-choice items. Distracters should address students' likely misconceptions so that these mistaken views can be identified and corrected. One way to generate effective distracters is to first include the stem on a test as a short answer or fill-in-the-blank item. As students respond, you can use incorrect answers as distracters for future tests (Stiggins, 1997).

Many problems with faulty multiple-choice items involve clues in distracters that allow students to answer the question correctly without knowing the content. Figure 14.4

Figure 14.4

Constructing distracters for multiple-choice items

1. Which of the following is a function of the circulatory system?
   a. to support the vital organs of the body
   *b. to circulate the blood throughout the body
   c. to transfer nerve impulses from the brain to the muscles
   d. to provide for the movement of the body's large muscles

2. Of the following, the definition of *population density* is
   a. the number of people who live in your city or town
   b. the number of people who voted in the last presidential election
   *c. the number of people per square mile in a country
   d. the number of people in cities compared to small towns

3. Of the following, the most significant cause of World War II was
   a. American aid to Great Britain
   b. Italy's conquering of Ethiopia.
   c. Japan's war on China
   *d. the devastation of the German economy as a result of the Treaty of Versailles.

4. Which of the following is the best description of an insect?
   a. It always has one pair of antennae on its head.
   *b. It has three body parts.
   c. None lives in water.
   d. It breathes through lungs.

5. The one of the following that is not a reptile is a
   a. alligator.
   b. lizard.
   *c. frog.
   d. turtle.

6. Which of the following illustrates a verb form used as a participle?
   a. Running is good exercise.
   *b. I saw a jumping frog contest on TV yesterday.
   c. Thinking is hard for many of us.
   d. All of the above.

contains six items with faulty distracters. See if you can identify features in them that are inconsistent with the guidelines. Then turn to the discussion that follows.

In Item 1 in Figure 14.4, forms of the term *circulate* appear in both the stem and the correct answer. In Item 2, the correct choice is written in more technical terms than the distracters. Teachers fall into this trap when they take the correct choice directly from the text and then make up the distracters. Their informal language appears in the distracters, whereas text language appears in the correct answer.

In Item 3, the correct choice is significantly longer than the incorrect choices; a similar clue is given when the correct choice is shorter than distracters. If one choice is significantly longer or shorter than others, it should be a distracter.

In Item 4, choices *a* and *c* are stated in absolute terms, which alerts test-wise students. Absolute terms, such as *all, always, none,* and *never*, are usually associated with incorrect answers. If used, they should be in the correct answer, such as "All algae contain chlorophyll."

The stem in Item 5 is stated in negative terms without this fact being emphasized. Also, choice *a* is grammatically inconsistent with the stem. One solution to the problem is to end the stem with a(n), so grammatical consistency is preserved.

In Item 6, choices *a* and *c* are automatically eliminated because both are gerunds and only one answer can be correct. Also, Item 6 uses "all of the above" as a choice; it can't be correct if *a* and *c* are eliminated. That makes *b* the only possible choice. A student could get the item right and have no idea what a participle is.

As you can see, preparing good multiple-choice items requires thought and care. With effort and practice, however, you can become skilled at it, and when you do, you have a powerful learning and measurement tool.

Measuring Higher-Level Learning.   Although most of the examples presented to this point measure low-level outcomes, the multiple-choice format can be effectively used to assess higher-order thinking as well. In an "interpretive exercise," students are presented with material similar to—but not identical to—information presented in class, and the distracters represent different analyses or "interpretations" of it (Gronlund, 1993). The material may be a graph, chart, table, map, picture, or case study. Figure 14.5 contains an example from science.

In this case, the teacher's goal was for science students to be able to apply information about heat, expansion, mass, volume, and density to a familiar but unique situation. This type of exercise promotes transfer, helps develop critical thinking, and can increase learner motivation.

14.8 ▬
Rewrite each of the six items in Figure 14.4 so they are consistent with the guidelines.

True–False Items

The **true–false format** *involves statements of varying complexity that learners have to judge as being correct or incorrect.* Because they usually measure lower-level outcomes, and because students have a 50–50 chance of guessing the correct answer, true–false items should be used sparingly (R. Linn & Gronlund, 2000). As with the multiple-choice format, guidelines can help teachers improve their effectiveness (see Figure 14.6).

Look at the examples presented next, and based on the guidelines, see if you can identify problems with the items. Then turn to the discussion that follows.

1. Mammals are animals with four-chambered hearts that bear live young.
2. Most protists have only one cell.
3. Negative wording should never be used when writing multiple-choice items.
4. All spiders have exoskeletons.

Figure 14.5

Interpretive exercise used with the multiple-choice format

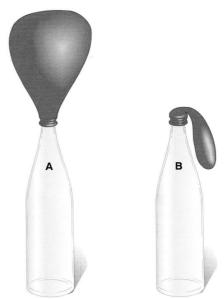

Look at the drawings above. They represent two identical soft drink bottles covered with identical balloons sitting side-by-side on a table. Bottle A was then heated. Which of the following is the most accurate statement?
  a. The density of the air in Bottle A is greater than the density of the air in Bottle B.
*b. The density of the air in Bottle A is less than the density of the air in Bottle B.
  c. The density of the air in Bottle A is equal to the density of the air in Bottle B.
  d. We don't have enough information to compare the density of the air in Bottle A to the density of the air in Bottle B.

Figure 14.6

Guidelines for preparing true–false items

1. When using the format, write slightly more false than true statements. (Teachers tend to write more true than false statements, and students tend to mark answers they're unsure of as "true.")
2. Make each item one clear statement.
3. Avoid clues that may allow students to answer correctly without fully understanding the content.

Item 1 contains two ideas: (a) mammals have four-chambered hearts, and (b) they bear live young. The first is true, but the second is not true in all cases; some mammals, such as the duck-billed platypus, are egg layers. Therefore, the item is false, and potentially confusing for students. If both ideas are important, they should be written in separate items.

In Item 2, we see the qualifying word *most*, which is a clue that the statement is true, and Item 3 uses the term *never*, which usually indicates a false statement. (As you saw in the previous section, negative wording should be used with caution in multiple-choice items, but to say *never* is false.) In general, true–false items should be free of qualifying terms such as *may, most, usually, possible,* and *often,* and absolutes such as *always, never, all,* and *none.* If qualifiers are used, they're most appropriate in false statements, and absolutes are most effective in true statements. For instance, Item 4 uses the absolute *all,* but the statement is true.

> **14.9**
> Recall our discussion of teachers' assessment patterns. Using this as a frame of reference, identify another problem common to the four sample items.

Matching Items

The **matching format** is *a variation on multiple-choice questions and is most effective when the same alternatives are used in a series of items* (Stiggins, 1997). For instance, consider the following items (asterisk indicates correct answer):

1. The statement, "Understanding is like a lightbulb coming on in your head" is an example of:
   * a. simile.
   b. metaphor.
   c. hyperbole.
   d. personification.
2. "That's the most brilliant comment ever made" is a statement of:
   a. simile.
   b. metaphor.
   * c. hyperbole.
   d. personification.

Combining the items into a single matching format is more efficient than writing a series of multiple-choice items, as the following example illustrates:

Match the following statements with the figures of speech by writing the letter of the appropriate figure of speech in the blank next to each statement. Each figure of speech may be used *once, more than once,* or *not at all.*

_____	1. Understanding is like a light-bulb coming on in your head.	a.	alliteration
_____	2. That's the most brilliant comment ever made.	b.	hyperbole
		c.	metaphor
_____	3. His oratory was a belch from the bowels of his soul.	d.	personification
_____	4. Appropriate attitudes are always advantageous.	e.	simile
_____	5. Her eyes are limpid pools of longing.		
_____	6. He stood as straight as a rod.		
_____	7. I'll never get this stuff, no matter what I do.		
_____	8. The colors of his shirt described the world in which he lived.		

14.10
Identify at least two other topics with homogeneous material that could be appropriately measured with the matching format.

At least four characteristics of effective matching items are illustrated in the example. First, the content is homogeneous; all the statements are figures of speech, and only figures of speech are given as alternatives. Other topics appropriate for matching items include persons and their achievements, historical events and dates, terms and definitions, authors and their works, and principles and their illustrations (R. Linn & Gronlund, 2000). Homogeneity is necessary to make all alternatives plausible.

Second, effective matching items have more statements than possible alternatives (to prevent getting the right answer by process of elimination). Third, the alternatives can be used more than once or not at all, and finally, the entire item fits on a single page. Items with more than 10 statements should be broken into two items, to prevent overloading learners' working memories.

Completion Items

1. What is an opinion _____?
2. What is the capital of Canada _____?

14.11
Completion formats have been described as supply-type items. Would you classify them as objective or subjective? When and why?

Completion items *include a question or an incomplete statement that requires the learner to supply appropriate words, numbers, or symbols.* As you saw earlier, the completion format is popular with teachers, probably because questions seem easy to construct. This advantage is misleading, however, because completion items have two serious disadvantages.

First, it is very difficult to phrase a question so that only one possible answer is correct. A number of defensible responses could be given to Question 1, for example. Overuse of the completion format puts students in the position of trying to guess the answer the teacher wants, rather than giving the one they think is most correct. Second, unless the question requires solving a problem, completion formats usually measure knowledge-level outcomes. Because of these weaknesses, completion formats should be used sparingly (Gronlund, 1993). Table 14.4 presents guidelines for preparing items using this format.

14.12
Rewrite the two sample completion items so that only one defensible response can be given.

Table 14.4

Guidelines for preparing completion items

Guideline	Rationale
1. Use only one blank, and relate it to the main point of the statement.	Several blanks are confusing, and one answer may depend on another.
2. Use complete sentences followed by a question mark or period, and place the blanks to the left of the question statements.	Complete sentences allow students to more nearly grasp the full meaning of the statement. Scoring is easier when all responses are to the left.
3. Keep blanks the same length. Use "a(an)" at the end of the statement or eliminate indefinite articles.	A long blank for a long word or a particular indefinite article commonly provides clues to the answer.
4. For numerical answers, indicate the degree of precision and the units desired.	Degree of precision and units clarify the task for students and prevent them from spending more time than necessary on an item.

Essay Items: Measuring Complex Outcomes

Essay items *require students to make extended written responses to questions or problems.* Essay questions are valuable for at least two reasons. First, the ability to organize ideas, make and defend an argument, or describe understanding in writing are important goals throughout the curriculum, and essay items are the only way these goals can be measured (Stiggins, 1997). Second, they can positively influence the way students study. If students know an essay format will be used, they are more likely to look for relationships in what they study and to organize information in a meaningful way (Foos, 1992).

Essay items also have two disadvantages. First, scoring them is time-consuming and sometimes unreliable, and second, scores on essay items are influenced by writing skill, including grammar, spelling, and handwriting (Airasian, 1997; McDaniel, 1994). If writing skill is a desired outcome, the influence is appropriate; if not, it detracts from the validity of the items.

Essay items appear easy to write, but they can be ambiguous, leaving students uncertain about how to respond. The result is that the student's ability to interpret the teacher's question is often the outcome measured. Table 14.5 presents guidelines for preparing and scoring essay items (Stiggins, 1997).

Improving the Scoring Reliability of Essays.   In addition to the suggestions that appear in Table 14.5, a valuable component in reliably scoring essays is to establish grading criteria in the form of a scoring rubric. A **rubric** is *a scoring tool that lists the criteria for grading* (Goodrich, 1996–1997). Criteria should be prepared before scoring and applied consistently through the process. Figure 14.7 contains an example that links points to criteria.

This rubric is content-free, referring to general, organizational criteria. Similar rubrics can be constructed that focus on specific concepts or topics. Using rubrics when scoring essays significantly increases reliability.

Table 14.5

Guidelines for preparing and scoring essay items

1. Elicit higher order thinking by using such terms as *explain* and *compare*. Have students defend their responses with facts.

2. Write a model answer for each item. This can be used both for scoring and for providing feedback.

3. Require all students to answer all items. Allowing students to select particular items prevents comparisons and detracts from reliability.

4. Prepare criteria for scoring in advance.

5. Score all students' answers to a single item before moving to the next item.

6. Score all responses to a single item in one sitting if possible. This increases reliability.

7. Score answers without knowing the identity of the student. This helps reduce the influence of past performance and expectations.

8. Develop a model answer complete with points, and compare a few students' responses to it, to see if any adjustments are needed in the scoring criteria.

Figure 14.7 ■

Rubric for scoring essay items

High Score	5	The response is clear, focused, and accurate. Relevant points are made with good support (derived from the content to be used, again as spelled out in the exercise). Good connections are drawn, and important insights are evident.
	3	The answer is clear and somewhat focused, but not compelling. Support of points made is limited. Connections are fuzzy and lead to few important insights.
Low Score	1	The response either misses the point, contains inaccurate information, or otherwise demonstrates a lack of mastery of the material. Points are unclear, support is missing, and/or no insights are included.

Source: Adapted from Stiggins (1997, p. 169).

Using Commercially Prepared Test Items

As you saw earlier, many teachers depend on the tests included in textbooks, teachers' guides, and other commercially prepared curriculum materials. Although using these tests obviously saves time, they should be used with caution for at least three reasons (Airasian, 1997):

> **14.13** ■
> Do the problems—goals, quality, and level—of commercially prepared items more commonly affect validity or reliability? Explain.

1. *Goals:*   The goals of the curriculum developers may not be the same as your goals. If items don't reflect the goals and instruction in your course, they are invalid.
2. *Quality:*   This factor is perhaps most important. Many commercially prepared tests are of low quality.
3. *Level:*   These items are commonly written at the knowledge level, measuring memorized information instead of higher-order thinking.

The time and labor saved using commercially prepared items are important advantages, and teachers can capitalize on these benefits by using the following guidelines:

▌ Download the items to your own computer to make them easy to edit.
▌ Think carefully about your goals before using these items.
▌ Select those items that are consistent with your goals, and put them into a test file.
▌ Modify items that need improvement, and add them to your file.
▌ Write your own test items, and gradually expand your file so you have a wide array of items that can be used to measure your students' understanding.

Remember, only you know what your goals are, and you are the best judge of the extent to which the items measure the goals.

Alternative Assessment

Traditional assessments, most commonly in the form of multiple-choice tests, have come under increasing criticism over the last several years (Herman et al., 1992; Reckase, 1997). In response to these criticisms, the use of alternative assessments, or "direct examination of student performance on significant tasks that are relevant to life outside of school" (Worthen, 1993, p. 445), is growing in importance. **Alternative assessments** *directly measure student performance through "real-life" tasks* (Wiggins, 1996–1997; Worthen, 1993). Examples include:

▌ Writing a persuasive essay
▌ Designing menus for a week's worth of nutritionally balanced meals
▌ Identifying and fixing the problems with a lawn mower engine that won't start

In addition to products, such as the essay, teachers using alternative assessments are also interested in students' thinking as they prepare the products, so higher-order thinking is strongly emphasized (Putnam & Borko, 2000). Insights into these processes provide teachers with opportunities to build on student knowledge and correct student misconceptions (Parke & Lane, 1996–1997). For example, a structured interview might be used to gain insight into students' thinking as they design science experiments.

Because of their emphasis on applied, higher-level tasks, alternative assessments have the potential to change both instruction and learning (Pomplun, Capps, & Sundbye, 1997). Alternative assessments are consistent with constructivist views of learning, which recognize that learning is holistic and should be contextualized within authentic tasks (Camp, 1992).

Let's look at two forms of alternative assessments: performance assessments and portfolios.

Performance Assessment

A middle school science teacher noticed that her students had difficulty applying scientific principles to everyday events. In an attempt to improve this ability, she focused on everyday problems, such as why an ice cube floats in one cup of clear liquid but sinks in another, which students had to solve in groups and discuss as a class. On Fridays, she presented another problem (e.g., why two clear liquids of the same volume, when put on a balance, don't have the same mass), and the students had to solve it in groups. As they worked, she circulated among them, taking notes that would be used for assessment and feedback.

A health teacher read in a professional journal that the biggest problem people have in applying first aid is not the mechanics per se, but knowing what to do and when. In an attempt to address this problem, the teacher periodically announced "catastrophe" days. Students entering the classroom encountered a catastrophe victim with an unspecified injury. In each case, they had to first diagnose the problem and then apply first-aid interventions.

These teachers are using performance assessments to gather information about students' abilities to apply information in realistic settings. **Performance assessments** *ask students to demonstrate their knowledge and skill by carrying out an activity or producing a product* (Airasian, 1997). In using performance assessments, teachers attempt to increase validity by placing students in as lifelike a situation as possible, evaluating their

14.14 ■
Are essay items performance assessments? Defend your answer, using the information from this section.

Performance assessments measure students' ability to demonstrate skills similar to those required in real-world settings.

performance against preset criteria (Feuer & Fulton, 1993). The term "performance assessment" originated in content areas such as science, where students were required to perform or demonstrate a skill in a hands-on situation rather than recognizing a correct answer on a teacher-made or standardized test (Hiebert & Raphael, 1996).

Designing Performance Assessments

Experts identify four steps in designing performance assessments (Gronlund, 1993): (a) specifying desired outcomes, (b) selecting the focus of evaluation, (c) structuring the evaluation setting, and (d) designing evaluation procedures.

Specifying Desired Outcomes.   The first step in designing any assessment is to develop a clear idea of what you're trying to measure. A clear description of the skill or process helps students understand what is required and assists the teacher in designing appropriate instruction. An example in the area of speech is outlined in Figure 14.8 (based on work by Gronlund, 1993).

Selecting the Focus of Evaluation.   Having specified performance outcomes, teachers next decide whether the assessment will focus on processes or products. Processes are often the initial focus, with a shift to products after procedures are mastered (Gronlund, 1993). Examples of both processes and products as components of performance assessments are shown in Table 14.6.

Structuring the Evaluation Setting.   The value of performance assessments lies in their link to realistic tasks; ultimately, teachers want students to apply the skill in the real world.

Figure 14.8

Performance outcomes
in speech

Oral Presentation

1. Stands naturally.
2. Maintains eye contact.
3. Uses gestures effectively.
4. Uses clear language.
5. Has adequate volume.
6. Speaks at an appropriate rate.
7. Topics are well organized.
8. Maintains interest of the group.

Time, expense, and safety may prevent realistic measurement procedures, however, and intermediate steps might be necessary.

For example, in driver education, the goal is to produce safe drivers. However, putting students in heavy traffic to assess how well they function behind the wheel is both unrealistic and dangerous. Figure 14.9 contains evaluation options ranging from low to high realism to assess driver education skills.

Simulations provide opportunities for teachers to measure performance with intermediate degrees of realism in cases in which high realism is impossible. For instance, a geography teacher wanting to measure students' understanding of the impact of climate and geography on the location of cities might display the information shown in Figure 14.10. Students would be asked to identify the best location for a city on the island and the criteria they used in determining the location. The criteria provide the teacher with additional insights into students' thinking.

Parents react positively to performance assessments, judging them to be a valuable source of information about their children's learning progress. They believe that performance assessment provides valuable insights into what students are understanding and that they encourage students to think (Shepard & Blum, 1995).

14.15
Explain how realism influences validity and reliability. Use the driver education example as a frame of reference.

Table 14.6

Processes and products as components of performance

Content Area	Product	Process
Math	Correct answer	Problem-solving steps leading to the correct solution
Music	Performance of a work on an instrument	Correct fingering and breathing that produces the performance
English Composition	Essay, term paper, or composition	Preparation of drafts and thought processes that produce the product
Word Processing	Letter or copy of final draft	Proper stroking and techniques for presenting the paper
Science	Explanation for the outcomes of a demonstration	Thought processes involved in preparing the explanation

Figure 14.9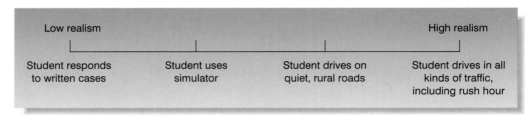

Continuum of realism on performance tasks

Low realism			High realism
Student responds to written cases	Student uses simulator	Student drives on quiet, rural roads	Student drives in all kinds of traffic, including rush hour

Figure 14.10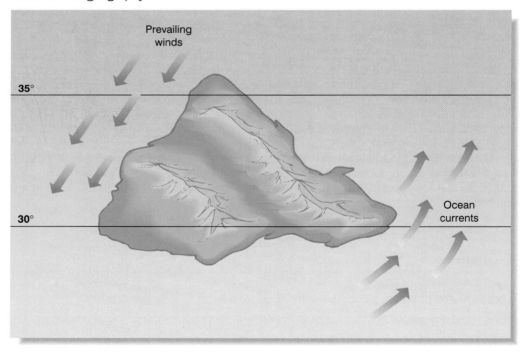

Simulation in geography

Designing Evaluation Procedures.   The final step in creating performance assessments is to design evaluation procedures. Reliability is a primary concern. Well-defined criteria in the form of scoring rubrics, similar to those used with essay items, increase both reliability and validity (Mabry, 1999; Stiggins, 1997). Clearly written criteria provide models of excellence and performance targets for students (McTighe, 1996–1997). Effective criteria have four elements (Herman et al., 1992; Messick, 1994b):

1. One or more dimensions that serve as a basis for assessing student performance
2. A description of each dimension

3. A scale of values on which each dimension is rated
4. Definitions of each value on the scale

Let's look now at three ways to evaluate learner performance: (a) systematic observation, (b) checklists, and (c) rating scales.

Ways of Evaluating Performance

Teachers observe students in classroom settings all the time. Observations typically are not systematic, however, and records are rarely kept. **Systematic observations** attempt to solve these problems by *encouraging teachers to specify criteria and take notes based on the criteria.* For example, a science teacher attempting to teach her students scientific problem-solving might establish the following criteria:

1. States problem or question
2. States hypotheses
3. Identifies independent, dependent, and controlled variables
4. Describes the way data will be gathered
5. Orders and displays data
6. Evaluates hypotheses based on the data

The teacher's observation notes would then refer directly to these criteria, making them consistent for all groups. The notes could be used to give learners feedback and provide information that could be used in future instructional planning.

Checklists extend systematic observation by specifying important aspects of performance and by sharing them with students. **Checklists** are *written descriptions of dimensions that must be present in an acceptable performance.* When checklists are used, the desired performances are typically "checked off" rather than described in notes, as they would be with systematic observation. For example, the science teacher wanting to assess scientific problem-solving ability might use a checklist like the one in Figure 14.11. Notes could be added to each dimension, to combine the best of checklists and systematic observations.

Systematic observation incorporating checklists and rating scales allows teachers to assess accurately and to provide valuable information to students about their performance.

Figure 14.11

Checklist for evaluating experimental technique

DIRECTIONS: Place a check in the blank for each step performed.

_____ 1. Writes problem at the top of the report.

_____ 2. States hypothesis(es).

_____ 3. Specifies values for controlled variables.

_____ 4. Makes at least two measurements of each value of the dependent variable.

_____ 5. Presents data in a chart.

_____ 6. Draws conclusions consistent with the data in the chart.

Checklists are useful when a criterion can be translated into a yes-or-no answer, such as "Specifies values for controlled variables," because students either did or did not specify the values. In other cases, however, such as "Draws conclusions consistent with the data in the chart," the results aren't cut-and-dried. Conclusions aren't entirely consistent or inconsistent with the data; some conclusions are more thorough or insightful than others. Rating scales address this problem.

Figure 14.12

Three rating scales for evaluating oral presentations

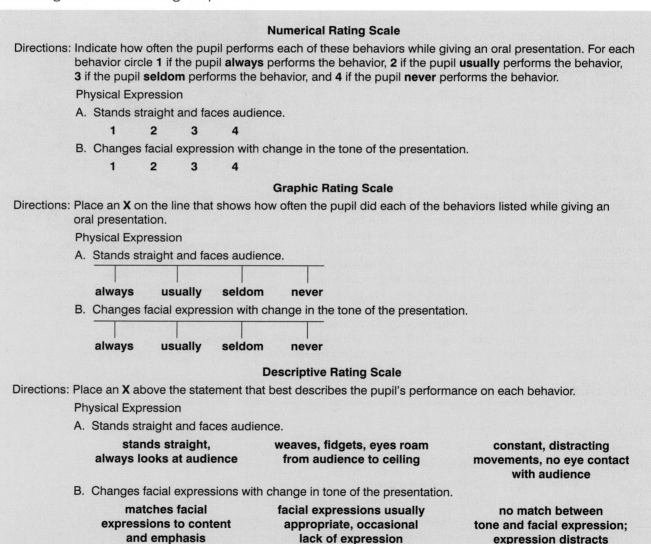

Numerical Rating Scale

Directions: Indicate how often the pupil performs each of these behaviors while giving an oral presentation. For each behavior circle **1** if the pupil **always** performs the behavior, **2** if the pupil **usually** performs the behavior, **3** if the pupil **seldom** performs the behavior, and **4** if the pupil **never** performs the behavior.

Physical Expression

A. Stands straight and faces audience.

    1   **2**   **3**   **4**

B. Changes facial expression with change in the tone of the presentation.

    1   **2**   **3**   **4**

Graphic Rating Scale

Directions: Place an **X** on the line that shows how often the pupil did each of the behaviors listed while giving an oral presentation.

Physical Expression

A. Stands straight and faces audience.

    always   **usually**   **seldom**   **never**

B. Changes facial expression with change in the tone of the presentation.

    always   **usually**   **seldom**   **never**

Descriptive Rating Scale

Directions: Place an **X** above the statement that best describes the pupil's performance on each behavior.

Physical Expression

A. Stands straight and faces audience.

| **stands straight, always looks at audience** | **weaves, fidgets, eyes roam from audience to ceiling** | **constant, distracting movements, no eye contact with audience** |

B. Changes facial expressions with change in tone of the presentation.

| **matches facial expressions to content and emphasis** | **facial expressions usually appropriate, occasional lack of expression** | **no match between tone and facial expression; expression distracts** |

Source: From P. Airasian, *Classroom Assessment,* p. 229. Copyright 1997 by McGraw-Hill Company. Reproduced with permission of the McGraw-Hill Company.

Rating scales are *written descriptions of evaluative dimensions and scales of values on which each dimension is rated.* Rating scales can be constructed in descriptive, graphic, or numerical formats, as shown in Figure 14.12. They allow more precise information to be gathered than is possible with checklists, and the increased detail gives the learner more specific feedback, which gives the teacher and class additional opportunities to evaluate and discuss the performance.

> **14.16** ■
> Create a rating scale that would allow you to assess someone's performance in creating high-quality multiple-choice test items.

Portfolios: Involving Students in Alternative Assessment

The use of portfolios, another form of alternative assessment, has the additional advantage of involving students in the design, collection, and evaluation of learning products. **Portfolios** are *purposeful collections of student work that are reviewed against preset criteria* (Stiggins, 1997). Because they are cumulative, connected, and occur over a period of time, they can provide a "motion picture" of learning progress versus the snapshots provided by disconnected tests and quizzes (Ziomek, 1997). The physical portfolio or collection of students' products, such as essays, journal entries, artwork, and videotapes is not the only assessment; the portfolio assessment also includes the students' and teacher's judgments of learning progress based on these products.

Two features distinguish portfolios from other forms of assessment. First, portfolios collect work samples over time, reflecting developmental changes, and second, portfolios involve students in design, collection, and evaluation. One eighth grader had the following comments about a piece she included in her writing portfolio:

> In **Ideas and Content** I gave myself a 5. I thought my ideas were clear, and I thought I created a vivid picture of an artist trying to keep his work alive.
>
> I would also give myself a 5 in **Organization**. My opening does a good job of leading the reader into my paper. . . .
>
> My **Voice** is not as strong as I would have liked it to be. It is hard to take on the voice of another person. I am pretending to be someone else, not myself. I guess I just haven't had enough practice at this. Also, my natural voice tends to be humorous, and

Portfolios foster self-regulation by providing opportunities for students to become actively involved in assessing their own learning progress.

clearly, this is the most serious of topics. Anyway, I just did not find quite the voice I wanted, and I gave myself a 4.

My **Sentence Fluency** is pretty strong. You will notice that I vary my sentence beginnings a lot. That's one of my strengths. It's smooth, whether you read it silently or aloud. I think a few sentences are a little short and choppy, though. Some sentence combining would help. So I rated myself a 4 on this trait. (Stiggins, 1997, p. 462)

Portfolios are intended to document and reflect student growth. For example, writing samples can document the changes that occur over a term or course. This documentation can then be used as a basis for communicating with parents and for helping students observe and reflect on their own progress.

Portfolios have been used in teacher education to help candidates reflect on their growth as professionals, identify strengths and weaknesses, and document professional skills during job seeking (Guillaume & Rudney, 1997). Significantly, teachers become more positive about the use of portfolios after using them to assess their own learning (Hootstein, 1999). Examples of portfolio assessments in different content areas are shown in Table 14.7.

At least three questions are involved when portfolio assessments are used. First, who decides what goes into the portfolio? Second, when and how often will student work be placed in portfolios? Finally, on what criteria will students' work be evaluated? Student involvement in selecting portfolio content gives students the chance to reflect on their learning progress. The following describes one teacher's experience:

I introduced the idea that their portfolios might present a broader picture—how students have changed or improved, what their particular interests are, and areas where they still have difficulties. This comment led my students to suggest including the following items: an early and a later piece of writing, a rewrite of something, examples of what they like and don't like, a list of books they like and don't, and reading logs that show how their thinking about books has changed. (Case, 1994, p. 46)

Criteria were also jointly established and included (a) how well students explained why they selected particular pieces, (b) the actual pieces, (c) clarity and completeness of the cover letter describing the contents, and (d) neatness and organization. As learners considered what to put in the portfolio, the issue of including only their best work versus pieces demonstrating growth came up. One student commented, "We could all just turn in the papers that got the best grades. But we already got those grades, so what would be the point of making a portfolio?" (Case, 1994, p. 46).

By involving students in these decisions, teachers promote self-regulation by helping them understand how to assess their own growth. Guidelines to make portfolios effective learning tools include the following:

- Provide examples of portfolios when introducing them to students.
- Involve students in the selection and evaluation of their work.
- Require students to provide an overview of each portfolio, a rationale for the inclusion of individual work, criteria they used to evaluate, and a summary of progress.
- Provide students with frequent and detailed feedback about their decisions.

Teachers have found student-led conferences to be an effective way to communicate with parents about portfolio achievements. Researchers found these conferences increased students' sense of responsibility and pride and improved both home–school cooperation and student–parent relationships. (Stiggins, 1997).

Time constraints and logistics are obstacles to full-scale implementation of student-led conferences, but the educational benefits of increased learner involvement and initiative balance these limitations.

Table 14.7

Portfolio samples in different content areas

Content Area	Example
Elementary Math	Homework, quizzes, tests, and projects completed over time.
Writing	Drafts of narrative, descriptive, and persuasive essays in various stages of development. Samples of poetry.
Art	Projects over the course of the year collected to show growth in an area like perspective or in a medium like painting.
Science	Lab reports, projects, classroom notes, quizzes, and tests compiled to provide an overview of learning progress.

Putting Traditional and Alternative Assessments Into Perspective

The idea of alternative assessments is not new (Worthen, 1993). Oral exams, art exhibits, performances in music, athletics, and business education, proficiency testing in language, and hands-on assessments in vocational areas have been used for years. Increased interest in alternative assessments is likely for at least three reasons.

First, traditional assessments have been increasingly criticized. These criticisms include the following:

- They focus on low-level knowledge and discrete,disconnected content and skills.
- Objective formats, such as multiple-choice, don't measure learners' ability to apply understanding in the real world.
- They measure only outcomes, providing no insight into the processes learners' use to arrive at their conclusions (Herman et al., 1992; Madaus & O'Dwyer, 1999).

Performance assessments and portfolios respond to these criticisms by attempting to tap higher-level thinking and problem-solving skills, emphasizing real-world applications, and focusing on the processes learners use to produce their products (Cizek, 1997; Newman, Secado, & Wehlage, 1995).

Second, critics argue that traditional formats are grounded in behaviorism; they "assume a theory of learning incompatible with current understanding—one that is componential, hierarchical, and unidimensional" (Camp, 1992, p. 243), whereas alternative assessment is more consistent with cognitive views of learning, which stress problem solving and self-regulation.

Third, designers of alternative assessments hope to increase access to higher education for learners with diverse backgrounds, particularly low-income students (Hiebert & Raphael, 1996).

As with many alternatives in education, problems and disadvantages also exist. First, little evidence indicates that access to higher education has been improved as the result of the alternative assessment movement (Haertel, 1999; Madaus, & O'Dwyer, 1999). In fact, some evidence suggests that alternative assessments may place additional demands on minorities, causing them to score as low as, if not lower than they would have, on traditional assessments (Worthen, 1993).

Second, implementing alternative assessments is difficult; without extensive staff development, teachers are unlikely to use them effectively (Hiebert & Raphael, 1996), and the process is very time-consuming, even with support (Valencia & Place, 1994). Further,

> 14.17 ■
> Explain specifically why performance assessments and portfolios are consistent with cognitive views of learning.

insufficient evidence exists to support claims that they do a better job than traditional assessments of measuring higher-order thinking (Terwilliger, 1997).

Finally, reliability remains an issue. Obtaining acceptable levels of reliability with alternative assessments is possible if care is taken (Nystrand et al., 1992), but in practice this has been a problem (Haertel, 1999; Stecher & Herman, 1997). For example, the state of Vermont, in a widely publicized movement, implemented a statewide Portfolio Assessment Program in 1992, but research on the program indicates that scorers assessing the same portfolio often gave very different ratings (Koretz, Stecher, & Diebert, 1993). Additional research on portfolios has identified similar problems (Herman & Winters, 1994).

At the classroom level, allowing students to determine portfolio content also raises the reliability issue. When students choose different items to place in their portfolio, cross-student comparisons are difficult, and reliability in assessing the portfolios suffers. Experts suggest supplementing portfolios with traditional measures to obtain the best of both processes (Reckase, 1997).

As with virtually all aspects of learning and teaching, assessment isn't as simple as it appears on the surface; effective measurement and evaluation require sensitive and intelligent teachers. A combination of traditional and authentic assessment—carefully considered and wisely implemented—is likely to be most effective (Terwilliger, 1997).

Classroom Connections

Creating Valid and Reliable Assessments in Your Classroom

1. Be sure objectives and tests are congruent.
   - A life science teacher compares items on his tests to the objectives in the curriculum guide and his unit plan to be sure all the appropriate objectives are covered.

2. Write individual test items soon after material has been presented. Make a special effort to write items above the knowledge/recall level.
   - A social studies teacher writes a draft of one test item at the end of each day to be certain the emphasis on her tests is consistent with her instruction. She reports that she can now write a good item in less than 5 minutes.

3. Analyze test items after they have been written to make sure they measure intended outcomes.
   - A fourth-grade teacher rereads the items she has written to eliminate wording that might be confusing or too advanced for her students.

4. Construct scoring rubrics for essay items. Score essays by using the rubric as the criterion.
   - Using a rubric, a high school economics teacher writes an "ideal" response to each essay item she prepares. She then awards points to students for each element of the model demonstrated in their answers.

5. Use commercially prepared items with caution.
   - A third-grade teacher comments, "I look at the tests they send with the book. I find the good items and use them. Then I either modify the rest to improve them or make up the rest of the items myself."

6. Use alternative assessments to increase validity.
   - A fifth-grade math teacher working on decimals and percentages assigns his students the task of going to three supermarkets and comparing prices on a list of five household items. They are required to determine which store provided the best bar-

gains and what the difference was among the stores on each item.

- A fourth-grade teacher uses portfolios to evaluate students' writing progress during the school year. Students are required to keep a weekly journal describing their work and noting accomplishments.

7. Use portfolios and performance assessments to develop learner self-regulation.

- A middle school language arts teacher uses portfolios as a central organizing theme for his curriculum. Students collect pieces of work over the course of the year and share and evaluate them with other members of their writing teams.

- A fifth-grade teacher asks each student to compile a portfolio of work and present it at parent–teacher conferences. Before the conference, the teacher meets with students and helps them identify individual strengths and weaknesses.

Effective Assessment Practices

In earlier sections, we examined both traditional and alternative assessment, and though good items and well-designed alternative measures are essential, there is more to effective assessment. To maximize learning, individual items must be combined into tests; alternative assessments must be planned; students need to be prepared; and assessments must be administered, scored, analyzed, and discussed. We look now at four components of effective assessment: (a) designing assessments, (b) preparing students, (c) administering assessments, and (d) analyzing results.

Designing Assessments

In designing assessments, the first task is to increase validity by ensuring they are consistent with your goals and instruction. This seems obvious, but, because tests are usually prepared some time after instruction is completed, it often doesn't occur. For example, a recent topic given little emphasis in class might have several items related to it, whereas another earlier topic, given much greater emphasis, is covered less thoroughly on the test. A topic may be discussed in class at the applied level, but test items occur at a knowledge level. A goal may call for student performance of some skill, but the assessment consists of multiple-choice questions. Each of these factors reduces the validity of a test.

Tables of Specifications: Increasing Validity Through Planning

One way to ensure that goals and tests are consistent is to prepare a **table of specifications**, *a matrix derived from the teacher's objectives that classifies topics measured on the test by cognitive level or specific outcomes.* For example, a geography teacher based her instruction in a unit on the Middle East on the following list of objectives:

Understands location of cities

1. States location
2. Identifies historical factors in settlement

14.18 ■
Two teachers are arguing about the best time to construct a table of specifications—during planning or after a unit has been taught. Describe the advantages and disadvantages of each. Explain.

Understands climate

1. Identifies major climate regions
2. Explains reasons for existing climates

Understands influence of physical features

1. Describes topography
2. Relates physical features to climate
3. Explains impact of physical features on location of cities
4. Analyzes impact of physical features on economy

Understands factors influencing economy

1. Describes economies of countries in the region
2. Identifies characteristics of each economy
3. Explains how economies relate to climate and physical features

14.19 ■
A teacher closely follows her curriculum guide, checks off objectives, and writes at least one test item related to each objective as soon as she's finished covering it with her students. Is she being consistent with the concept of tables of specifications by using this procedure? Why or why not?

Table 14.8 presents a table of specifications for a content-level matrix based on the objectives for a physical geography unit. The teacher has a mix of items, with greater emphasis on physical features than other items. This emphasis reflects the teacher's objectives, which stressed the influence of physical features on the location of cities, the climate, and the economy of the region. Also, this emphasis presumably also reflects the time and effort spent in class on each area. Ensuring this match among goals, instruction, and assessment is a primary function of a table of specifications.

For alternative assessments, establishing criteria—as discussed in the section on systematic observations, checklists, and rating scales—serves a function similar to that of tables of specifications. The criteria identify performance, determine emphasis, and attempt to ensure congruence between goals and assessments.

Preparing Students for Assessments

Tanya Erickson was preparing her students for an upcoming test. As she made the transition from reading to math, she stood in front of the room with a transparency in her hand.

Table 14.8 ■

Sample table of specifications

| Content | Outcomes | | |
	Knowledge	Comprehension	Higher-Order Thinking and Problem-Solving
Cities	4	2	2
Climate	4	2	2
Economy	2	2	
Physical features	4	9	7
Total items	14	15	11

"Also, get out your chalkboards and chalk," she reminded them, as students got out their math books, referring to small individual chalkboards she had made for each of them at the beginning of the year.

"Look up here at our front board," she began, pointing to the chalkboard at the front of the room. "I just want to remind you again that we're having a test tomorrow on finding equivalent fractions and adding fractions with unlike denominators, and we decided that the test will go in your math portfolios. On the test, you will have to add some fractions in which the denominators are the same and others in which the denominators are different. There will also be word problems in which you will need to do the same thing. I'll give the test back Friday, and if we all do well, we won't have any homework over the weekend."

"YEAH!" the students shouted in unison, as Tanya smiled at their response.

She held up her hand, they quieted down, and she continued. "I have some problems on the test that are going to make you think," she smiled. "But we've all been working hard, and we're getting so smart, we'll be able to do it. You're my team, and I know you'll come through," she said energetically.

"To be sure we're okay," she continued, "I have a few problems that are just like those on the test, so let's see how we do. Write these first two on your chalkboards."

$$1/3 + 1/4 = ? \qquad 2/7 + 4/7 = ?$$

Tanya watched as they worked on the problems and held their chalkboards up when they finished. Seeing that three of the students missed the first problem, she carefully reviewed it with the class, comparing it with the second problem.

She then displayed the following three problems:

$$2/3 + 1/6 = ? \qquad 4/9 + 1/6 = ? \qquad 2/9 + 4/9 = ?$$

Two students missed the second one, so again she reviewed this problem carefully.

"Now, let's try one more," she continued, displaying the following problem on the overhead:

You are at a pizza party with five other people, and you order two pizzas. The two pizzas are the same size, but one is cut into four pieces and the other is cut into eight pieces. You eat one piece from each pizza. How much pizza do you eat altogether?

Again, Tanya watched as students worked on the problem, discussed it, and reviewed the solution with them when they finished. In the process, she asked questions such as, "What information in the problem is particularly important, and how do we know?" "What do we see in the problem that's irrelevant?" and, "What should we do first in solving the problem?"

She displayed two more word problems for them and then said, "The problems on the test are like the ones we practiced in here today." She responded to additional questions from the students and concluded her review by saying,

"All right, when we take a test, what do we always do?"

"WE READ THE DIRECTIONS CAREFULLY!" the students shouted in unison.

"Okay, good," Tanya smiled. "Now, remember, what will you do if you get stuck on a problem?"

"Go on to the next one so we don't run out of time."

"And what will we be sure not to do?"

"We won't forget to go back to the one we skipped."

In preparing students for tests, teachers have both long- and short-term goals. Long term, they want students to understand test-taking procedures and strategies and to enter testing situations with a positive attitude and a minimum of anxiety. Short term, they want students to understand the test format and the content being tested. By preparing students, teachers increase the probability that test scores accurately reflect achievement, thus increasing validity.

Teaching Test-Taking Strategies

Teachers can improve students' test-taking strategies by helping them understand the importance of the following strategies:

> ▌ Use time efficiently and pace themselves.
> ▌ Read directions carefully.
> ▌ Identify the important information in questions.
> ▌ Understand the demands of different testing formats.
> ▌ Find out how questions will be scored.

To be most effective, these strategies should be emphasized throughout the school year, concrete examples should be linked to the strategies, and students should be given practice with a variety of formats and testing situations. Research indicates that strategy instruction significantly improves test-taking performance and that young, low-ability, and minority students who have limited test-taking experience benefit the most (Anastasi, 1988; S. Walton & Taylor, 1996–1997).

Reducing Test Anxiety

"'Listen my children and you shall hear. . . . Listen my children and you shall hear. . . . '
Rats! I knew it this morning in front of Mom."

Like this student, many of us have experienced the negative effects of anxiety in a testing situation. For most of us, the adverse effects of pressure are momentary and minor, with little impairment of performance. For a portion of the school population, however (estimates run as high as 10%), anxiety during testing situations is a serious problem (J. Williams, 1992).

Test anxiety is a *relatively stable, unpleasant reaction to testing situations that lowers performance.* Research on test anxiety suggests that it consists of two components (E. Hong, 1999; Pintrich & Schunk, 1996). Its *emotional component* can include physiological symptoms, such as increased pulse rate, dry mouth, and headache, as well as feelings of dread and helplessness and sometimes "going blank." Its *cognitive, or worry component,* involves thoughts, such as worrying about failure (e.g., parents being upset, having to retake the course) and being embarrassed by a low score. During tests, test-anxious students tend to be preoccupied with test difficulty and often cannot focus on the specific items.

Test anxiety is triggered by testing situations that (a) involve pressure to succeed, (b) are perceived as difficult, (c) impose time limits, and (d) contain unfamiliar items or formats (Wigfield & Eccles, 1989; Zohar, 1998). Unannounced or surprise tests, particularly, can trigger adverse amounts of test anxiety.

Teachers can do much to minimize test anxiety (Everson, Tobias, Hartman, & Gourgey, 1991), and the most successful of these efforts are usually aimed at the worry component (Pintrich & Schunk, 1996). Suggestions include the following:

> ▌ Use criterion-referenced measures to minimize the competitive aspects of tests.
> ▌ Avoid social comparisons, such as public displays of test scores and grades.
> ▌ Increase the frequency of quizzes and tests.

14.20 ▬
Describe at least two specific things Tanya did to develop test-taking skills in her students.

14.21 ▬
Using classical conditioning as a basis, explain the emotional component—such as feelings of dread—of test anxiety. Using information processing as a basis, explain how the cognitive component of test anxiety can lower test performance.

▌ Discuss test content and procedures before testing.

▌ Give clear directions, and ensure that students understand the test format and requirements.

▌ Teach students test-taking skills.

▌ Use a variety of measures, including authentic assessments, to measure students' understanding and skills.

▌ Provide students with ample time to take tests.

14.22 ▬
You have an extremely test-anxious student in your class. State specifically what you would do to reduce her anxiety. What should you do if you think her anxiety is a danger to her emotional health?

Specific Test-Preparation Procedures

Before any test, teachers want to ensure that learners understand test content and procedures and expect to succeed on the exam. In preparing students for her test, Tanya did three important things:

1. She specified precisely what would be on the test.
2. She gave students a chance to practice similar items under test-like conditions.
3. She established positive expectations in her students and encouraged them to link success and effort.

Clarifying test format and content establishes structure for students, and this structure reduces test anxiety. Research indicates that clarifying test content and formats leads to higher achievement for all students, particularly those of low ability (Carrier & Titus, 1981).

Merely specifying the content often isn't enough, however, particularly with young students, so Tanya actually gave students practice exercises and presented them in a way that paralleled the way they would appear on her test. In learning math skills, for instance, her students first practiced adding fractions with like denominators, then learned to find equivalent fractions, and finally added fractions with unlike denominators, each in separate lessons. On the test, however, the problems were mixed, and Tanya gave students a chance to practice integrating these skills before the test. The benefits of this practice are particularly important for young (Kalechstein, Kalechstein, & Doctor, 1981) and minority students (Dreisbach & Keogh, 1982).

Finally, Tanya clearly communicated that she expected students to do well on the test. The motivational benefits of establishing positive expectations have been confirmed by decades of research (Good, 1987b).

Tanya also encouraged attributions of effort and ability for success, and she modeled an incremental view of ability by saying, "But we've all been working hard, and we're getting so smart, we'll be able to do it." From your study of motivation in Chapter 10, you know that encouraging the belief that ability is incremental and can be improved through effort benefits both immediate performance and long-term motivation.

Administering Assessments

At 10:00 in her classroom the next morning, Tanya shut a classroom window because delivery trucks were driving back and forth outside. She'd considered rearranging the desks in the room but decided to wait until after the test.

"Okay, everyone," she called. "Let's get ready for our math test." With that, students put their books under their desks.

She waited a moment, saw that everyone's desk was clear, and said, "When you're finished with the test, turn it over, and I'll come and get it. Now, look at the chalkboard. After you're done, work on the assignment listed there until everyone else is finished. Then, we'll start reading." As she handed out the tests, she said, "If you get too warm, raise your hand, and I'll turn on the air conditioner. I shut the window because of the noise outside.

"Work carefully," she said after everyone had a copy of the test. "We've all been working hard, and I know you will do well. You have as much time as you need. Now go ahead and get started."

The students quickly began working, and Tanya stood near the door, watching their efforts.

After several minutes, she noticed Dean doodling at the top of his paper and periodically glancing around the room.

She went over to him, put an arm around his shoulders, and said, "It looks like you're doing fine on these problems," pointing to some near the top of the paper. "Now concentrate a little harder. I'll bet you can do most of the others." She smiled reassuringly and again stood near the door.

Tanya moved over to Abdul in response to his raised hand. "The lead on my pencil broke, Mrs. Erickson," he whispered.

"Take this one," Tanya responded, handing him one. "Come and get yours after the test."

As students finished, Tanya picked up their papers, and they began the assignment written on the chalkboard.

Let's look at Tanya's actions in administering the test. First, she arranged the environment to be comfortable, free from distractions, and similar to the way it was when students learned the content. Distractions can depress test performance, particularly in young or low-ability students.

Second, she gave precise directions about taking the test, collecting the papers, and spending their time afterward. These directions helped maintain order and prevented distractions for late-finishing students.

Finally, Tanya carefully monitored the test during the entire time students worked on it. This not only allowed her to encourage students who became lost or distracted but also discouraged cheating. In the real world, unfortunately, some students will cheat if given the opportunity. However, classroom climate, such as the emphasis on performance versus learning, and external factors, such as the teacher leaving the room, influence cheating more than whether students are inherently inclined to do so (Blackburn & Miller, 1999;

Monitoring student progress during assessment allows teachers to answer questions and clear up misunderstandings.

Newstead, Franklyn-Stokes, & Armstead, 1996). Teacher monitoring during tests also helps students learn to monitor their own test-taking behaviors.

In Tanya's case, monitoring was more a form of giving support than of being a watchdog. When she saw that Dean was distracted, she quickly intervened, offered him encouragement, and urged him to increase his concentration. This encouragement is particularly important for underachieving and test-anxious students, who tend to become distracted (Nottelman & Hill, 1977).

Analyzing Results

On Friday morning, Tanya handed back the tests.

"Do you have our tests finished, Mrs. Erickson?" the students asked as they got out their math books.

"Of course!" she smiled at them, handing back their papers.

"Overall, you did very well on the test, and I'm very proud of you. I knew all that hard work would pay off."

"There are a few items I want to go over, though," she continued. "We had a little trouble with Number 8, and you all made nearly the same mistake, so let's take a look at it."

She waited a moment while the students read the problem and then asked, "Now, what are we given in the problem? . . .

Hannah?"

"There's a drawing of two cakes. One is cut into 12 pieces, and the other is cut into 6 pieces."

"Okay. Good. And what else do we know? . . . Shareef?"

Tanya continued the discussion and explanation of the problem. She then carefully discussed two other problems that were frequently missed. In the process, she made notes at the top of her copy, identifying the problems that were difficult. She wrote "Ambiguous" by one problem and underlined some of the wording in it. By another, she wrote, "Teach them how to draw diagrams of the problem." Finally, she put her copy of the test in a file folder, laid it on her desk to be filed, and turned back to the class.

Tanya's assessment efforts didn't end with administering the test. She scored it and returned it the next day, discussed the results, and provided students with feedback as quickly as possible. This process is important for both achievement and motivation (Bangert-Drowns, Kulik, Kulik, & Morgan, 1991). Feedback allows learners to correct common misconceptions, and knowledge of results promotes student motivation (see Chapter 10). Virtually all teachers provide feedback after a test, and many take up to half a class period to do so (Haertel, 1986). Because student motivation is high, many teachers believe students learn more in these sessions than they do in the original instruction.

In addition, Tanya made positive comments about the performance of the class on the test. In a study examining this factor, students who were told they did well on a test performed better on a subsequent measure than those who were told they did poorly, even though the two groups did equally well on the first test (Bridgeman, 1974). Research also supports the benefits of individual feedback on tests; students who receive comments such as, "Excellent! Keep it up!" and, "Good work, keep at it!" do better on subsequent work (Page, 1992). The effects of these short, personalized comments justify the extra work involved.

Finally, Tanya made notes on her copy of the test before filing it. Her notes reminded her that the wording on one of her problems was misleading, so she could revise the problem before giving it again. This, plus other information taken from the test, will assist her in future planning for both instruction and assessment.

14.23

To keep his students informed about the amount of time remaining during a test, a teacher reminds them every 10 minutes. Is this a good idea? How will it affect test anxiety? If at all possible, what should teachers do in scheduling the amount of time students have to take a test?

Accommodating Diversity in Classrooms: Reducing Bias in Assessment

When teachers assess their students, they gather data to make decisions about student progress and improve their instruction. Learner diversity, however, often complicates this process. In this section, we examine strategies to accommodate this diversity.

Minority students may lack experience with general testing procedures, different test formats, and test-taking strategies, and they may not understand the purpose of assessments. Also, because most assessments are strongly language based, language may be another obstacle, so the effective testing practices we discussed in the previous section are particularly important for minority students (Land, 1997). In addition, teachers can respond to diversity in assessment in at least three other ways: (a) being careful with wording items, (b) making provisions for non-native English speakers, and (c) accommodating diversity in scoring.

Being Careful with Wording in Items

Content bias is always a possibility when assessing students with diverse backgrounds (Hanson et al., 1998). For example, minority learners can have difficulties with items containing information uncommon in their culture, such as transportation like cable cars, sports like American football, and musical instruments like the banjo (Cheng, 1987). In addition, holidays like Thanksgiving or U.S. historical figures such as Abraham Lincoln, which most people in American culture take for granted, may be unfamiliar to these students. When these types of terms and events are included in assessment items, teachers are measuring both the intended topic and students' understanding of American vocabulary and culture.

There is no easy solution to this problem, but teacher awareness and sensitivity are starting points. In addition, encouraging students to ask questions, and discussing tests thoroughly after they're given can help uncover unintended bias.

Making Provisions for Non-Native English Speakers

What would you do if your next exam in this class were presented in another language? This prospect gives you some idea of the problems facing non-native English-speaking students during tests. The most effective ways to help these students is to modify the test or the testing procedures. Some suggestions for doing so appear in Table 14.9, and of them, simplifying test language and providing extra time for students to use a glossary appear most promising (Abedi, 1999).

Accommodating Diversity in Scoring

Essay exams and alternative assessments can be effective for measuring students' ability to organize information, think analytically, and apply their understanding to real-world problems. However, they also place an extra burden on students who are wrestling with both content and language.

What can teachers do? Valid assessment often requires the use of essays and alternative formats, and teachers cannot ignore students' grammatical errors. One solution is to evaluate essays and performance assessments with two grades: one for content and another for grammar, spelling, and punctuation (Hamp-Lyons, 1992; Scarcella, 1990). **Multiple-trait scoring** *creates different criteria for different dimensions of a product.*

14.24

Is content bias more a problem with validity or reliability? Explain.

Table 14.9

Modifications to accommodate language diversity

Modifications of the Test	Modifications of the Test Procedures
Simplify test language.	Provide extra time to take the test.
Simplify test directions.	Allow students to use a glossary and dictionary.
Provide visual supports.	Read directions aloud (in the native language is even better).
Assess students in their native languages.	Read the test aloud, and clarify misunderstandings.

Source: Adapted from Butler and Stevens (1997).

For example, a question in science that asks students to propose a solution to the problem of water pollution might be scored using three criteria: (a) the solution to the problem, (b) the understanding of the content, and (c) the way the ideas are developed (Hamp-Lyons, 1992). Breaking the score into three areas allows the teacher to discriminate between understanding of content, problem solving, and ability to use language. These suggestions are designed to ensure, as much as possible, that test scores reflect differences in achievement and not cultural bias related to background knowledge, vocabulary, or testing sophistication.

Classroom Connections

Capitalizing on Diversity in Your Classroom

1. Be aware of the effect that diversity can have on assessment.
   - At the beginning of the school year, a math teacher in an inner-city school carefully explains her grading system and what it requires of students. She emphasizes that it is designed to promote learning.
   - A first-grade teacher takes extra time and effort during parent–teacher conferences to explain how she arrives at grades for her students. She saves students' work samples and shares them with the parents during the conferences.

2. Adapt testing procedures to meet the needs of all students.
   - A history teacher encourages her students to ask her about any terms on the test that they don't understand. Unless their understanding of the term is part of what she is measuring, she defines and illustrates the term for students.
   - A second-grade teacher adjusts her assessment procedures for her non-native English speakers. She arranges to give these students extra time, and she provides an older student to act as a translator for those whose command of English is still rudimentary.

3. Thoroughly discuss results after tests have been scored and returned.
   - A science teacher discusses all of the frequently missed items on his tests. He asks students why they responded as they did and what their thinking was. He writes notes during the discussion to revise items that may have been ambiguous or that required knowledge not all students should be expected to know.

Grading and Reporting: The Total Assessment System

To this point, we have discussed the preparation of traditional test items, the design of alternative assessments, and the assessment process itself, which includes preparing students, administering assessments, and analyzing results. Designing a total assessment system requires considering additional issues, such as

- How many tests and quizzes should be given
- How authentic assessments will be used
- How homework is counted
- How missed work is made up
- How affective dimensions, such as cooperation and effort, are reported in the overall assessment
- How performance is reported (e.g., letter grade, percentage, descriptive statement)

These decisions are the teacher's responsibility, and this is significant for beginning teachers, who have no experience to fall back on. Merely knowing that the decisions are the teacher's, however, removes some of the uncertainty in the process. We examine these decisions and offer some suggestions in the following sections.

Designing a Grading System

Designing a grading system is an important task, which influences both student learning and teacher workload. Some guidelines can help in this process:

- Your system should be clear and understandable and consistent with school and district policies.
- Your system should be designed to support learning and instruction by gathering frequent and systematic information from each student.
- Grading should be fair to all students regardless of gender, class, race, or socioeconomic status.
- You should be able to confidently defend the system to a parent or administrator if necessary (Loyd & Loyd, 1997).

With these guidelines in mind, let's look at elements of an effective system.

Formative and Summative Evaluation

The way a teacher uses quizzes and tests influences learning. Although we often think that the purpose of giving tests and quizzes is to assign grades, a more important function is to provide the teacher and students with feedback about learning progress. In some instances, quizzes and tests are given, scored, and discussed just as any other quiz or test would be, but they are not included in a grading decision. Using assessments in this way is called **formative evaluation** because it *is used only to provide feedback to students.* This feedback is important because it allows students to improve performance, which increases motivation to learn (Brookhart, 1997).

Tests, quizzes, homework, and authentic assessments used to make grading decisions, however, are part of the process called **summative evaluation**, which is *evaluation used for grading purposes.* Although summative evaluations are used as a basis for making decisions about grades, *they also provide feedback about learning progress,* and they

---

14.25 ▬

Think about the effects of formative evaluation on elementary, middle school, and high school students. With which group would formative evaluation be most important? least important? Explain why this would be the case.

should be discussed as thoroughly as any formative evaluation would be. In public schools, most assessments are used for summative evaluations, but, used properly, both formative and summative assessments can be useful in making instructional decisions and motivating students (Stipek, 1996).

Norm-Referenced and Criterion-Referenced Evaluation

Assigning value to students' work is an important part of assessment. This task is as varied as giving "smiley" faces, writing comments on papers, and assigning grades. Norm-referenced and criterion-referenced evaluations are two ways to assign value to student performance. **Norm referencing** means that *decisions about students' work are based on comparisons with their peers*; **criterion referencing** means that *a decision is made according to a predetermined standard*. Norm referencing gets its name from the normal curve (see Figure A.3 in the Appendix), and teachers using it would establish a grading curve such as the following:

A	Top 15% of students
B	Next 20% of students
C	Next 30% of students
D	Next 20% of students
F	Last 15% of students

In a criterion-referenced system, everyone who receives a score of 90 or above on quizzes, tests or assignments gets an A, for example, everyone above 80% a B, and so on. A comparison of norm and criterion referencing appears in Table 14.10.

Criterion-referenced evaluation has two important advantages. First, because it reflects the extent to which goals are met, it more effectively describes content mastery. Second, criterion referencing deemphasizes competition, which can discourage students from helping each other, threaten peer relationships, detract from intrinsic motivation, and encourage students to attribute success and failure to innate ability rather than to

> **14.26** ▬
> Is the assessment system for the class you're in norm referenced or criterion referenced? What makes it that way?

Table 14.10 ▪

A comparison of norm referencing and criterion referencing

	Examples	Characteristics
Norm referencing	Grading on the curve: 15% of students get A's 15% get B's 40% get C's 15% get D's 15% get F's	Compares students' performances to each other Creates a competitive environment
Criterion referencing	94–100 = A 86–93 = B Performance assessments (e.g., recognizes shapes, knows rhyming sounds, knows directions)	Reflects extent to which course goals are being met Reduces student competitiveness

effort (Ames, 1992; P. Black & William, 1998; Stipek, 1996). Although criterion referencing alone won't eliminate all these problems, it is usually preferable to norm referencing.

Tests and Quizzes

For teachers in upper-elementary, middle, and secondary schools, tests and quizzes are the cornerstone of a grading system. Some teachers add tests and quizzes together and count them as a certain percentage of the overall grade; others weigh them differently in assigning grades. However it is done, frequent monitoring of progress with feedback to students is important for both achievement and motivation (Dempster, 1991; Stipek, 1996).

Alternative Assessments

If you're using alternative assessments, they should be included in your grading system. To do otherwise communicates that they are less important than the traditional measures you're using. If you rate student performance on the basis of well-defined criteria, scoring will have acceptable reliability, and alternative assessments can then be an integral part of the total assessment system.

Homework

Properly designed homework contributes to learning (see Chapter 12). To be most effective, homework should be collected, scored, and included in the grading system (Cooper, 1989). Beyond this point, however, research provides little guidance as to how it should be managed. Accountability, feedback, and your own workload all influence this decision. Table 14.11 outlines some options.

14.27

Using social cognitive theory, explain why it is important that homework be scored and included in the grading system. What can you do about the possibility that students will copy their homework from others?

Table 14.11

Homework assessment options

Option	Advantages	Disadvantages
Grade it yourself	Promotes learning. Allows diagnosis of students. Increases student effort.	Is very demanding for the teacher.
Grade samples	Reduces teacher work, compared with first option.	Doesn't give the teacher a total picture of student performance.
Collect at random intervals	Reduces teacher workload.	Reduces student effort unless homework is frequently collected.
Change papers, students grade	Provides feedback with minimal teacher effort.	Consumes class time. Doesn't give students feedback on their own work.
Students score own papers	Is the same as changing papers. Lets students see their own mistakes.	Is inaccurate for purposes of evaluation. Lets students not do the work and copy in class as it's being discussed.
Students get credit for completing assignment	Gives students feedback on their work when it's discussed in class.	Reduces effort of unmotivated students.
No graded homework, frequent short quizzes	Is effective with older and motivated students.	Reduces effort of unmotivated students.

As you can see, each option has advantages and disadvantages. The best strategy is one that results in learners making the most consistent and conscientious effort on their homework without costing you an inordinate amount of time.

Assigning Grades: Increasing Learning and Motivation

Having made decisions about tests, quizzes, alternative assessments, and homework, you are now ready to design your total grading system. At this point, you must make two decisions: (a) what to include and (b) the weight to assign each component. Tests, quizzes, alternative assessments, and homework should each be included in most cases. Some teachers build in additional factors, such as effort, class participation, and attitude. This practice, though common in classrooms, is discouraged by assessment experts (R. Linn & Gronlund, 2000; J. McMillan, et al., 1999). Gathering systematic information about affective variables is difficult, and assessing them is highly subjective. In addition, a high grade based on effort suggests to both students and parents that important content was learned, when it may not have been. Factors such as effort, cooperation, preparedness, and class attendance should be reflected in a separate section of the report card.

The practice of inclusion, in which students with exceptionalities are placed in general education classrooms, presents special grading challenges for teachers. Research indicates that 60% to 70% of included students receive below-average grades in their general education classes (Munk & Bursuck, 1997–1998). The effects of these low grades can be devastating to students who already experience frustrations in attempting to learn and keep up with other students.

To prevent this, teachers often adapt their grading systems by grading on improvement, assigning separate grades for process and for product, and basing a grade on meeting the objectives of an individualized education program (IEP). The dilemma for teachers is how to motivate students while still providing an accurate assessment of learning progress. Experts suggest that districts develop comprehensive grading policies in this area to guide teacher efforts (Munk & Bursuck, 1997–1998).

Let's look now at two teachers' systems for assigning grades:

Sun Ngin		**Lea DeLong**	
(Middle School Science)		(High School Algebra)	
Tests and Quizzes	50%	Tests	45%
Homework	20%	Quizzes	45%
Observation	20%	Homework	10%
Projects	10%		

We see that the systems are quite different. Sun Ngin, an eighth-grade physical science teacher, emphasizes both homework and alternative assessments, which include projects and what he calls "observation." Traditional tests and quizzes count only 50% in his system. Lea DeLong emphasizes tests and quizzes much more heavily; they count 90% in her system. The rationale in each case is simple. Sun indicated that homework was important to student learning, and he believed that unless it was emphasized, students wouldn't do it. He also included projects as an important part of his grades, believing they involve his students in the study of science. He used systematic observation to chart their progress as they worked on the projects and other hands-on activities. Lea, a secondary Algebra II teacher, thought that students fully understood the need to do their homework in order to succeed on the tests and quizzes. She gave a weekly quiz and three tests during a 9-week grading period.

To be effective in promoting learning, your assessment system must be understood by students (Loyd & Loyd, 1997; Thorkildsen, 1996). Even young students can understand the relationship between effort and grades if they are quizzed frequently and if their homework is scored and returned promptly. On the other hand, even high school students have problems understanding a grading system if it is too complex (Evans & Engelberg, 1988).

Parents must also understand your assessment system if they are to become actively involved in their children's learning. Parents view parent–teacher conferences and graded examples of their child's work as most valuable in providing feedback about their children's learning progress, followed closely by report cards (Shepard & Blum, 1995). Standardized tests, which are given infrequently and often reported in technical language, tend to be rated less favorably by parents. Teachers' clients—both learners and their parents—need to be provided with frequent and clear information about learning progress.

Raw Points or Percentages?

In assigning scores to assignments, quizzes, or tests, teachers have two options. In a percentage system, teachers convert each score to a percentage and then average the percentages as the grading period progresses. In the other system, teachers accumulate raw points and convert them to a percentage only at the end of the period.

To illustrate these options, return to Laura Brinson's work with her second graders, first presented in our discussion of teachers' assessment patterns. Kelly, one of her students, missed 1 of 10 problems on a seat work assignment. As is typical of many teachers, Laura used a percentage system and, because 9 correct of 10 is 90%, she wrote 90 for Kelly on this assignment. This is a straightforward and simple process.

Suppose now that students are graded on another assignment; this time, it is five items long and Kelly gets three of the five correct. Her grade on this assignment would be 60. Teachers then typically average the assignments, meaning that Kelly's average at this point is 75 because the average of 90 and 60 is 75.

This process is flawed, however. By finding the percentage for each assignment and averaging the two, they are given equal weight. In fact, on the two assignments, Kelly has correctly responded to 12 of 15 problems. If Laura had recorded Kelly's raw points for each assignment, her average at that point would be 80 ($12/15 \times 100$), 5 points higher than the average obtained by using a percentage system.

If averaging percentages is flawed, why is it so common? The primary reason is simplicity. In addition to being simpler for teachers to manage, it is easier to communicate to students and parents. Many teachers, particularly those in the elementary and middle schools, have attempted point systems and later returned to percentage systems because of pressure from students, who better understand percentage systems.

Research indicates that computer grade-keeping programs facilitate the use of point systems (Feldman, Kropkf, & Alibrandi, 1996). These researchers also found that the use of a point system in which students are given points for turning in assignments and compiling projects can undermine intrinsic motivation by tacitly communicating that the goal in class is completing tasks and earning points (versus learning). To avoid this tendency, teachers need to grade on both quality and quantity and continually emphasize the role that instructional tasks play in learning.

As with most aspects of teaching, the option is your choice. A percentage system is fair if assignments are similar in length, tests are also similar in length, and tests are given more weight than quizzes and assignments. On the other hand, a point system can work if the teacher simply has the students keep a running total of their points and then communicates the number they must have for an A, a B, and so on at frequent, periodic points in the grading period.

Classroom Connections

Using Effective Assessment in Your Classroom

1. Be explicit about what will be covered on assessments.
   - A social studies teacher shares her table of specifications with her students before the test. In addition she explains, "On Thursday's test, you will be asked to explain in an essay question how the physical characteristics of the northern, middle, and southern colonies affected the economy of each region." The test the next day closely follows this blueprint.

2. Provide practice for your students under test-like conditions.
   - As she prepares her class for an essay exam, a social studies teacher displays the following question on the overhead: "The southern colonies were primarily agricultural rather than industrial. Using the physical characteristics of the region, explain why this would be the case." She gives students a few minutes to respond and then discusses the item and appropriate responses to it, reminding students that this is the type of question they will have on the test.

3. Prepare and keep a test-item file.
   - A fourth-grade teacher writes items for science and social studies and stores them in a computer file, classified according to topic. When he begins to prepare a test, he retrieves and reviews the items.

4. Do an analysis of test items.
   - After giving a test, a sixth-grade teacher surveys the distribution of student responses. She then revises items that are misleading or that have ineffective distracters. She stores the revisions in the computer for next time.

5. Hand back tests, discuss them, and collect them for later use.
   - A second-grade teacher discusses problems that a significant number of students missed on a math test and then asks the students to rework the problems and hand them back in.

6. Consider the effects of the total assessment system on learning and motivation.
   - A history teacher gives frequent quizzes between major tests. He notices a decrease in test anxiety, as well as an increase in the amount of time students spend studying for his classes.

Technology and Learning: Using Technology to Improve Assessment

The importance of frequent classroom assessment has been a theme for this chapter. Frequent assessment requires a great deal of teachers' time and effort, however, and it is here where technology can help.

Computers provide an efficient way to collect and store data gathered from these assessments, analyze them, and present them to students in an understandable way. These functions are summarized in Table 14.12 and discussed in the paragraphs that follow.

Because of its ability to store, manipulate, and process large amounts of data quickly, technology is proving to be especially valuable in classroom assessment. Technology, and particularly computers, can serve three important and time-saving assessment functions (Newby et al., 2000; Roblyer & Edwards, 2000):

- Planning and constructing tests
- Analyzing test data, especially data gathered from objective tests
- Maintaining student records

Table 14.12

Assessment functions performed by computers

Function	Examples
Planning and construction	Preparing objectives Writing, editing, and storing items Constructing tests Printing tests Organizing and storing student portfolios
Scoring and interpreting tests	Scoring tests Summarizing results Analyzing items
Maintaining student records	Recording results Developing a class summary Developing student profiles Reporting results to students Preparing grade reports

Planning and Constructing Tests

Software test generators have at least three advantages over standard word processing. First, they produce a standard layout; the teacher doesn't have to worry about spacing or format. Second, they automatically produce various forms of the test—helpful for makeup tests and preventing "wandering eyes." Third, they can be used with commercially prepared test banks, making it easier for teachers to combine the best of the commercially produced items together with the ones they've constructed. These time- and effort-saving features can make classroom assessment more effective and efficient.

A number of commercially prepared software programs can assist in this process, such as *Create a Test, Exam Builder, Test Writer, Test IT! Deluxe, Tests-Made-Easy, Quick Quiz,* and *Test Generator.* They can be used to:

- Develop a test file or item bank of multiple-choice, true–false, matching, and short-answer items that can be stored in the system. Within a file, items can be organized by topic, chapter, objective, or by difficulty.
- Select items from the created file bank either randomly, selectively, or by categories to generate multiple versions of a test.
- Modify items and integrate these into the total test.
- Produce student-ready copies and an answer key.

Analyzing Test Data

Technology can also assist in the process of scoring tests and reporting results, saving time for the teacher and providing students with more informative feedback. A number of software programs are available to machine-score tests (e.g., *Test Scorer, Quickscore,* and *Test Analysis*). These programs can perform the following functions:

- Score objective tests, and provide descriptive statistics such as test mean, median, mode, range, and standard deviation.

- Generate a list of items showing difficulty level, the percentage of students who selected each response, the percentage of students who didn't respond to an item, and the correlation of each item with the total test.
- Sort student responses by score, grade/age, or gender (Merrill et al., 1992).

The time and energy saved provide teachers with opportunities to analyze and improve individual items, as well as the entire test, thus improving student learning.

Maintaining Student Records

An effective assessment system frequently gathers information about student performance from a variety of sources. If this information is to be useful to the teacher, it must be stored in an easily accessible and useable form. Computers provide an efficient way of storing, analyzing, and reporting student assessments.

One teacher commented,

> I keep my grades in an electronic gradebook. By entering my grades into an electronic gradebook as I grade papers, I always know how my students are progressing and exactly where my students stand in relation to each other. It does take a little time to enter the grades, but it makes my job easier during reporting periods. All I have to do is open my disk and record my students' grades on the grade sheet. (Morrison, Lowther, & DeMuelle, 1999, p. 355)

Technology provides teachers with powerful tools to plan, construct, and analyze tests as well as maintain student records.

For teachers with some background in technology, general spreadsheet programs can be converted into individualized grade sheets (Forcier, 1999). Commercial software is also available, and most of the programs designed to analyze individual test score data also have the following capabilities:

- Begin a new class file for each class or subject. The files can be organized by name and/or student identification number.
- Average grades, create new grades, or change old ones, add extra credit.
- Compute descriptive statistics such as the mean, median, mode, and standard deviation for any test or set of scores.
- Weigh numerical or raw scores, and translate into letter grades.
- Record the type of activity and the point value for each activity.
- Average grades on a quarterly, semester, and/or yearly basis.

In addition to saving teachers time and energy, these programs are accurate and immediate. If the entered data are correct, teachers can accurately generate grades at the end of a grading period at the touch of a button. In addition, records are readily available at any time, providing students with instant and accurate feedback (Roblyer & Edwards, 2000). Some programs even have the capacity to print student reports in languages other than English (Forcier, 1999).

Technology and Portfolios

Technology can also be used to organize, store, and display student portfolios (Newby, Stepich, Lehman, & Russell, 2000; Stiggins, 1997). Electronic portfolios address problems of space and accessibility and improve usability because of being stored in a computer. One commercial program, Scholastic's *Electronic Portfolio,* allows schools to store parts of each student's portfolio from kindergarten through 12th grade, providing a developmental perspective on student growth. These programs are capable of storing standard text, graphs and charts, images, and videos, and portions can be transferred back onto VHS format for presentation to the whole class. Teachers who have dealt with the logistical problems involved in boxes upon boxes of student portfolios attest to the advantages of electronic storage.

Technology is revolutionizing the teaching–learning process. Nowhere is this impact more important than in the assessment process, and technology's capability of helping assessment contribute more strongly to learning is continually increasing.

Windows on Classrooms

At the beginning of the chapter, you saw how Kathy Stevens used her understanding of assessment to help increase both her students' achievement and motivation. In studying the chapter, you've seen how assessment, in both traditional and alternative forms, can help teachers make strategic decisions about their students' learning progress.

Let's look now at another teacher working with a group of students. As you read the case study, compare the teacher's approach with the ideas you've studied in the chapter.

In Ron Hawkins's third-period class on Monday, he began a unit on pronoun cases with one of his Standard English classes. The tardy bell rang at 9:10 as Ron began, "All right, listen, everyone. Today, we're going to begin a study of pronoun cases. Everybody turn to page 484 in your text. . . . We see at the top of the page that we're dealing with pronoun cases. This is important in our writing because we want to be able to write and use standard English correctly, and this is one of the places where people often get mixed up. So, when we're finished with our study here, you'll all be able to use pronouns correctly in your writing."

He then wrote the following on the chalkboard:

Pronouns use the nominative case when they're subjects and predicate nominatives.
Pronouns use the objective case when they're direct objects, indirect objects, or objects of prepositions.

"Let's review briefly," Ron continued. "Give me a sentence that has both a direct and indirect object in it. . . . Anyone?"

"Mr. Hawkins gives us too much homework," Amato offered jokingly.

Ron wrote the sentence on the chalkboard amid laughter from the students and then continued, smiling, "Okay, Amato. Good sentence, even though it's incorrect. I don't give you

enough work. . . . What's the subject in the sentence?"

" . . . "

"Go ahead, Amato."

"Mr. Hawkins?"

"Yes, good. Mr. Hawkins is the subject," Ron replied as he underlined "Mr. Hawkins" in the sentence.

"Now, what's the direct object? . . . Helen?"

" . . . Homework."

"All right, good. And what's the indirect object? . . . Anya?"

" . . . Us."

"Excellent, everybody." Ron then continued by reviewing predicate nominatives and objects of prepositions.

"Now let's look at some additional examples up here on the overhead," Ron continued.

He then displayed the following four sentences:

1. Did you get the card from Esteban and (I, me)?
2. Will Meg and (she, her) run the concession stand?
3. They treat (whoever, whomever) they hire very well.
4. I looked for someone (who, whom) could give me directions to the theater.

"Okay, look at the first one. Which is correct? . . . Omar?"

" . . . Me."

"Good, Omar. How about the second one? . . . Lonnie?"

" . . . Her."

"Not quite, Lonnie. Listen to this. Suppose I turn the sentence around a little and say, 'Meg and her will run the concession stand.' See, that doesn't sound right, does it? 'Meg and she' is a compound subject, and when we have a subject, we use the nominative case. Are you okay on that, Lonnie?"

Lonnie nodded and Ron continued, "Look at the third one. . . . Cheny."

" . . . I don't know. . . . whoever, I guess."

"This one is tricky all right," Ron nodded. "When we use *whoever* and *whomever, whoever* is the nominative case and *whomever* is the objective case. In this sentence, *whomever* is a direct object, so it is the correct form."

Ron then continued with the rest of the sentences as he had with the first four. After he finished, he gave the students another list of sentences in which they were to select the correct form of the pronoun.

On Tuesday, Ron first reviewed the exercises the students had completed for homework and then continued with some additional examples of using *who, whom, whoever,* and *whomever.* He then discussed the rules for pronoun–antecedent agreement (pronouns must agree with their antecedents in gender and number). Then he again had students work examples as he'd done with pronoun cases.

He continued with pronouns and their antecedents on Wednesday and began a discussion of indefinite pronouns as antecedents for personal pronouns—*anybody, either, each, one, someone*—and had students work examples as done before.

Near the end of class on Thursday, Ron announced, "Tomorrow, we're going to have a test on this material: pronoun cases, pronouns and their antecedents, and indefinite pronouns. You have your notes, so study hard . . . Are there any questions? . . . Good. I expect you all to do well. I'll see you tomorrow."

On Friday morning as students filed into class and the bell rang, Ron picked up a stack of tests from his desk. The test consisted of 30 sentences, 10 of which dealt with case, 10 with antecedents, and 10 with indefinite pronouns. The final part of the test directed the students to write a paragraph. The following are some sample items from the test:

For each of the items below, mark A on your answer sheet if the pronoun case is correct in the sentence, and mark B if it is incorrect. If it is incorrect, supply the correct pronoun.

1. Be careful *who* you tell.
2. Will Rennee and *I* be in the outfield?
3. My brother and *me* like water skiing.

Write the pronoun that correctly completes the sentence.

11. Arlene told us about _____ visit to the dentist to have braces put on.
12. The Wilsons planted a garden in _____ backyard.
13. Cal read the recipe and put _____ in the file.
14. Each of the girls on the team wore _____ school sweater to the game.
15. None of the brass has lost _____ shine yet.
16. Few of the boys on the team have taken _____ physicals yet.

The directions for the final part of the test were as follows:

Write a short paragraph that contains at least two examples of pronouns in the nominative case and two examples of pronouns in the objective case. (Circle and label these.) Include also at least two examples of pronouns that agree with their antecedents. Remember!! The paragraph must make sense. It cannot just be a series of sentences.

Ron watched as his students worked, and he periodically walked up and down the aisles. Seeing that 15 minutes remained in the period and that some students were only starting on their paragraphs, he announced, "You only have 15 minutes left. Watch your time and work quickly. You need to be finished by the end of the period."

He then continued monitoring students, again reminding them to work quickly when 10 minutes were left and again when 5 minutes were left.

Luis, Simao, Moy, and Rudy were hastily finishing the last few words of their tests as the bell rang. Luis finally turned in his paper as Ron's fourth-period students were filing into the room. "Here," Ron said. "This pass will get you into Mrs. Washington's class if you're late. . . . How did you do?"

"Okay, I think," Luis said over his shoulder as he scurried out of the room, "except for the last part. It was hard. I couldn't get started."

"I'll look at it," Ron said. "Scoot now."

On Monday, Ron returned the tests, saying, "Here are your papers. You did fine on the sentences, but your paragraphs need a lot of work. Why did you have so much trouble with them, when we had so much practice?"

"It was hard, Mr. Hawkins."

"Not enough time."

"I hate to write."

Ron listened patiently and then said, "Be sure you write your scores in your notebooks. . . . Okay. . . . You have them all written down? . . . Are there any questions?"

"Number 8," Enrique requested.

"Okay, let's look at 8. It says, 'I didn't know to (who, whom) to give the letter.' There, the pronoun is the object of a preposition, so it's *whom*.

"Any others?"

A sprinkling of questions came from around the room, and Ron responded, "We don't have time to go over all of them. I'll discuss three more."

He responded to the three students who seemed to be most urgent in waving their hands. He then collected the tests and began a discussion of adjective and adverb clauses.

Questions for Discussion and Analysis

Analyze Ron's actions in the context of the information in this chapter. In your analysis, consider the following questions. In each case, be specific and take information directly from the case study in making your comparison.

1. How well were Ron's curriculum and assessment aligned? Explain specifically. What could he have done to increase curricular alignment?

2. In the section on effective testing practices, we discussed preparing students for tests, administering tests, and analyzing results. How effectively did Ron perform each task? Describe specifically what he might have done to be more effective in these areas.

3. Like most classes, Ron's class is composed of learners with diverse backgrounds. How effective was his teaching and assessment for these students?

4. What were the primary strengths of Ron's teaching and assessment? What were the primary weaknesses? If you think Ron's teaching and assessment could have been improved on the basis of information in this chapter, what suggestions would you make? Be specific.

5. Was Ron's teaching primarily behaviorist in its orientation, or was it more cognitive? Explain. How might he change his orientation?

Now go to our Companion Website to assess your understanding of chapter content with the Student Self-Assessment, apply comprehension in the Online Casebook, and broaden your knowledge base with links to important Educational Psychology World Wide Web sites.

 # Summary

Classroom Assessment

Classroom assessment includes the data teachers gather through tests, quizzes, homework, and classroom observations, as well as the decisions teachers make about student progress. Effective assessment results in increased learning, as well as improved motivation.

Teachers informally measure student understanding during classroom activities and discussions. Formal measurements are attempts to systematically gather information for grading and reporting.

Validity involves the appropriateness of interpretations made from measurements. Reliability describes the extent to which measurements are consistently interpreted. Both concepts provide standards for effective assessment.

Traditional Assessment

Teachers in elementary schools rely on performance measures and commercially prepared items and focus on affective goals more than teachers of older students. Teachers of older students tend to use completion items more than other formats, and their assessments overemphasize memory and low-level outcomes.

Teachers can improve the effectiveness of their assessments by keeping validity and reliability issues in mind when they construct items. Multiple-choice, true–false, matching, completion, and essay items all have strengths and weaknesses that can be addressed through thoughtful item writing.

Alternative Assessment

Alternative assessments, including performance assessments and portfolios, ask students to perform complex tasks similar to those found in the real world. In designing alternative assessments, teachers attempt to place students in realistic settings, asking them to perform high-level tasks involving problem solving in various content areas. Portfolio assessment involves students in the construction of a collection of work samples that documents learning progress. The reliability of alternative assessments can be improved through careful application of predetermined criteria and the use of systematic observation, checklists, and rating scales to evaluate products.

Effective Assessment Practices

Effective assessments are congruent with goals and instruction, and effective teachers communicate what will be covered on assessments, allow students to practice on items similar to those that will appear on tests, teach test-taking skills, and express positive expectations for student performance. Increasing testing frequency, using criterion referencing, providing clear information about tests, and giving students ample time help reduce test anxiety.

Grading and Reporting: The Total Assessment System

Grading and reporting are important functions of an assessment system. Formative evaluation provides feedback about learning, whereas summative evaluations are used for grading purposes. Norm-referenced evaluation compares a learner's performance with that of peers, whereas criterion-referenced evaluation compares students' performance with a standard. Technology can assist teachers in planning, analyzing results, and maintaining student records.

 **Important Concepts**

alternative assessment (p. 609)

assessment system (p. 594)

checklists (p. 613)

classroom assessment (p. 594)

completion items (p. 606)

criterion referencing (p. 629)

distracters (p. 600)

essay items (p. 607)

evaluation (p. 594)

formal measurement (p. 595)

formative evaluation (p. 628)

informal measurements (p. 594)

matching format (p. 605)

measurement (p. 594)

multiple-choice items
(p. 600)

multiple-trait scoring
(p. 626)

norm referencing (p. 629)

performance assessment
(p. 609)

portfolios (p. 615)

rating scales (p. 615)

reliability (p. 597)

rubrics (p. 607)

summative evaluation
(p. 628)

systematic observations
(p. 613)

table of specifications
(p. 619)

test anxiety (p. 622)

true–false format (p. 603)

validity (p. 596)

Appendix

Standardized Tests

Teachers ask a number of questions about students' progress that are difficult to answer on the basis of teacher-made instruments alone. These include: How do the students in my class compare with students across the country? How well is our curriculum preparing students for college or future training? How does a particular student compare with other students of similar ability? **Standardized tests** are *assessment instruments given to large samples of students (in many cases, nationwide) under uniform conditions and scored according to uniform procedures*, and they are designed to answer those questions (Linn & Gronlund, 2000). The scores people make on a standardized test are compared with the scores of a **norming group**, who are *people similar in age, grade level, and background who have taken the same test*. A student's performance on the test is then reported in comparison with this norming group.

The influence of standardized testing can hardly be overstated. The fact that students in other industrialized countries, such as Japan and Germany, score higher than U.S. students on some of these tests has alarmed many in this country (Stedman, 1997). The "reform movement" that began in the early 1980s was largely a by-product of standardized test results. Few of the concerns voiced about students' learning progress have been made without information gathered from standardized tests. Standardized tests also influence individual students. "The results of a morning's testing often become a powerful factor in decisions about the future of each student" (Gardner, 1992, p. 77).

Standardized testing is also controversial. In a given year, 127 million students take state-mandated tests at a cost of between $725 million and $915 million annually (National Commission on Testing and Public Policy, 1990). In addition, standardized tests are often used to compare students' performance in different schools, districts, states, and even countries (Berliner & Biddle, 1997). Many teachers believe that standardized testing is overemphasized and adversely affects a balanced school curriculum (Herman, Abedi, & Golan, 1994; Urdan & Paris, 1991). To place these concerns in perspective, let's look at some uses of standardized tests.

Functions of Standardized Tests

Standardized tests serve several functions (Ansley, 1997; Stiggins, 1997). They can be used to gather information about learning progress, to diagnose an individual student's strengths and weaknesses, and to make selection and placement decisions in instructional programs. They also help school personnel in measuring the effectiveness of specific programs.

Student Assessment

The most common function of standardized testing is to provide an external, objective picture of student progress. Parents, teachers, and school administrators often want to know how individual students or groups of students compare with other students at their grade level. Standardized tests provide one means of comparison and, when combined with teacher-made assessments and other measures of classroom performance, they can help provide a complete picture of student progress.

Diagnosis

Standardized tests also help diagnose student strengths and weaknesses. For example, if a student scores low on the math section of an achievement test, a more detailed diagnostic test could be used to gather additional information about specific strengths and weaknesses in math.

Placement and Selection

Placing students and selecting students for programs where the number of available slots are limited are two other uses of standardized tests. For instance, a math faculty have students coming to their high school from "feeder" middle schools, private schools, and schools outside the district. Scores from the math section of a standardized test can help place students in classes that will best match their backgrounds and capabilities.

Standardized test results can also be used to place students in advanced programs, such as programs for the gifted, and they are used as one basis for university selection. Most of us, for instance, took either the *Scholastic Aptitude Test* (SAT) or the *American College Testing Program* (ACT) during our junior or senior year in high school. These are standardized tests, the results of which played an important part in determining whether we were accepted by the college of our choice. Because college students come from different parts of the country and because their backgrounds are diverse, these tests provide a basis for uniform comparison.

Program Evaluation and Improvement

Standardized tests can also provide valuable information about instructional programs. For example, an elementary school has moved from a traditional reading program to one that emphasizes writing and children's literature. To assess the effectiveness of this change, the faculty use teacher-made assessments, student work samples, and the perceptions of teachers and parents. However, the faculty still don't know how the students' performance compares with their performance when the old curriculum was in place or with the performance of peers in other reading programs. Standardized test results can help answer these questions.

Accountability

Increasingly, schools and teachers are being held responsible for student learning (Darling-Hammond & Snyder, 1992; Linn & Gronlund, 2000). Parents, school board members, state officials, and decision makers at the federal level are demanding evidence that tax dollars are being used efficiently. Standardized test scores provide one indicator of this effectiveness.

The accountability movement has resulted in the creation of a controversial testing program called the National Assessment of Educational Progress (L. Jones, 1996). Critics contend that misuse of standardized test scores can result in narrowing the curriculum and give an inaccurate picture of student learning (E. Baker, 1989). Proponents claim that standardized tests can provide valuable information about the relative performance of different states, districts, and schools.

Types of Standardized Tests

Achievement Tests

Achievement tests, the most widely used type of standardized tests, are *designed to measure and communicate how much students have learned in different content areas*. Although most common in reading and math, they also measure learning in science, social studies, computer literacy, and other content areas. Popular achievement tests include the *Iowa Test of Basic Skills*, the *California Achievement Test*, the *Stanford Achievement Test*, the *Comprehensive Test of Basic Skills*, and the *Metropolitan Achievement Test*, as well as individual state-designed assessments and minimum-level skills tests (Airasian, 1997; Stiggins, 1997).

Standardized achievement tests serve several purposes:

- Determine how well students have mastered a content area.
- Compare the performance of students with others across the country.
- Track student progress over time.
- Determine whether students have the background knowledge to begin instruction in particular areas.
- Identify learning problems.

Most standardized achievement tests come as batteries of specific tests administered over several days. These tests are intended to reflect a curriculum common to most schools and thus will assess some, but not all, of the goals of a specific school. This is both a strength and a weakness. Because they are designed for a range of schools, they can be used in a variety of locations. On the other hand, this "one size fits all" approach may not accurately measure achievement for a specific curriculum. For example, one study found that only 47% to 71% of the math content measured on commonly used standardized achievement batteries was the same as content covered in popular elementary math textbooks (Berliner, 1984). In a worst-case scenario, this means that students might have had opportunity to learn less than half the content measured on the test.

Schools and teachers should be cautious in selecting and interpreting standardized achievement tests for their students. When selecting a test, it is important to go beyond the name and to examine the specific contents described in the testing manual's table of specifications. Comparing the content of the test with your curriculum objectives helps determine whether the test is valid for your use.

Diagnostic Tests

Whereas achievement tests measure students' progress in a variety of curriculum areas, **diagnostic tests** *provide a detailed description of learners' strengths and weaknesses in specific skill areas*. They are common in the primary grades, where instruction is designed to match the developmental level of the child, especially in the areas of math and reading. Diagnostic tests are usually administered individually and, compared to achievement tests, they include a larger number of items, use more subtests, and report scores in more specific areas (Linn & Gronlund, 2000). A diagnostic test in reading, for example, might target letter recognition, word analysis skills, sight vocabulary, vocabulary in context, and reading comprehension. Commonly used diagnostic tests include the *Metropolitan Achievement Tests*, the *Detroit Test of Learning Aptitude*, the *Durrell Analysis of Reading Difficulty*, and the *Stanford Diagnostic Reading Test* (Linn & Gronlund, 2000).

Intelligence Tests

In Chapter 4, we discussed **intelligence** in the context of individual differences and defined it as *the capacity to acquire knowledge, the ability to think and reason in the abstract, and the capability for solving problems.* **Intelligence tests** are designed to measure those abilities. Attempts to measure intelligence in a valid and reliable way were among the first standardized tests.

A Short History of Intelligence Tests.   Standardized intelligence tests originated in the early 1900s when Alfred Binet was asked by the French minister of public instruction to assist in developing an instrument to be used in the education of students with mental disabilities. He selected a number of school-related skills, such as defining words and making change, and with his partner, Theodore Simon, Binet developed a series of tests based on these skills. They gave the tests to heterogeneous groups of children, eliminating items so difficult that no students passed or so easy that all did. The result was an objective instrument, essentially independent of social class or the person administering the test, that could be passed by the average child of a given age.

Although intelligence tests were first developed to measure the capabilities of learners with disabilities, they were later broadened to describe the performance of a broad spectrum of people. Initially, performance was described as a mental age; for example, a child succeeding on tasks designed for a typical 8-year-old had a mental age of 8 years.

To overcome problems with older populations—describing a 20-year-old as functioning like a 30-year-old wasn't meaningful, for example—the mental age (M.A.) was divided by the chronological age (C.A.) and multiplied by 100, resulting in the familiar ratio IQ (intelligence quotient). For example, a 6-year-old with an M.A. of an 8-year-old would have an IQ of 133 ($8/6 = 1.33 \times 100 = 133$).

The importance of Binet and Simon's pioneering work is hard to overstate. For the first time, educators had an objective way of predicting school success; students who performed well on the test usually did well in school and vice versa. The predictions weren't perfect, but they were a vast improvement over people's subjective intuitions. The test was translated and brought to the United States by Lewis Terman, a professor at Stanford, and it then became the famous Stanford-Binet. The updated version is one of the two most widely used intelligence tests in schools today.

The Stanford-Binet—Fourth Edition.   The Stanford-Binet is an individually administered instrument with subtests, much like Binet's original. It comes in a kit that includes a box of standard toy objects for young children, booklets of printed cards for older students, a large picture of unisex and multicultural dolls to be used in asking questions, a recording booklet, and a test manual. Earlier versions heavily emphasized verbal tasks, but the most recent edition is more diverse, including 15 subtests, a number of which contain items not requiring verbal skills (Linn & Gronlund, 2000; R. Thorndike, Hagen, & Sattler, 1986). Table A.1 contains descriptions of some sample subtests in the latest revision.

The Stanford-Binet is a technically sound instrument second only to the Wechsler scales (described in the next section) in popularity. It has been revised and renormed a number of times over the years, most recently in 1986, using 5,000 schoolchildren in 47

Table A.1

Sample subtests from the revised Stanford-Binet

Subtest	Example/Description
Comprehension (Verbal reasoning)	Students are asked to explain facets of everyday life (e.g., "Why do people wear sunglasses?" or "Why do we go to the doctor?"). This subtest measures the ability to use and reason with words.
Number series (Quantitative reasoning)	Students are presented with a numerical sequence such as 1, 4, 7 and are expected to provide the next number. This subtest measures students' ability to find abstract patterns in numbers.
Abstract/visual reasoning (Copying)	Pictures of block designs are shown to students, and they are asked to copy them either with blocks (young children) or with paper and pencil (older children). This subtest measures students' ability to visualize and reproduce abstract patterns.

Source: Adapted with permission of The Riverside Publishing Company from *Stanford-Binet Intelligence Scale Technical Manual: Fourth Edition* by R. L. Thorndike, E. P. Hagen, and J. M. Sattler. The Riverside Publishing Company, 8420 W. Bryn Mawr Avenue, Chicago, IL 60631. Copyright 1986.

states and in grades 3 through 12, stratified by economic status, geographic region, and community size. Members of the white, African American, Hispanic, Asian, and Asian/Pacific Islander subcultures were all represented in proportion to their membership in the total U.S. population. Teachers should consider the norming population for a test because similarities between that population and their own influences test validity.

The Wechsler Scales.   Developed by David Wechsler over a period of 40 years, the Wechsler scales are the most popular intelligence tests in use today (Salvia & Ysseldyke, 1988). The three Wechsler tests, aimed at preschool–primary, elementary, and adult populations, have two main parts: verbal and performance. The Wechsler Intelligence Scale for Children—Third Edition (WISC-III; Wechsler, 1991) is an individually administered intelligence test with 13 subtests, of which six are verbal and seven performance (Table A.2 presents some sample subtests). The performance sections were added because of dissatisfaction with the strong verbal emphasis of earlier intelligence tests. Like the Stanford-Binet, the Wechsler scales are technically sound (Anastasi, 1988; Kaplan & Saccuzzo, 1993).

The Wechsler's two subtests, yielding separate verbal and performance scores, are an asset. For example, a substantially higher score on the performance compared with the verbal subtest could indicate a language problem related to poor reading or language-based cultural differences (Kaplan & Saccuzzo, 1993). Because performance subtests demand a minimum of verbal ability, these tasks are helpful in studying students who resist school-like tasks, learners with disabilities, and persons with limited education (Maller, 1994).

Individual Versus Group Intelligence Tests.   Individually administered intelligence tests have significant advantages over group ones. Because both the directions and responses are oral, they eliminate errors on answer sheets, and the test administrator can seek clarification of uncertain answers and spot signs of fatigue, worry, or anxiety. Also, by observing carefully, the test administrator can often determine why the student gave the answer he

Table A.2

Sample items from the WISC–III

Verbal Section	
Subtest	**Description/Examples**
Information	This subtest taps general knowledge common to American culture: a. How many minutes are there in an hour? b. Who was the first president of the United States?
Arithmetic	This subtest is a test of basic mathematical knowledge and skills, including counting and addition through division: a. Ted had three cookies but gave one to his friend. How many did he have then? b. There were six balls to play with and two teams. How many balls could each team have?
Similarities	This subtest is designed to measure abstract and logical thinking through use of analogies: a. How are a dog and a tree alike? b. How are books and newspapers alike?

Performance Section	
Subtest	**Description/Examples**
Picture completion	Students are shown a picture with elements missing, which they are required to identify. This subtest measures general knowledge as well as visual comprehension.
Block design	This subtest focuses on a number of abstract figures. Designed to measure visual-motor coordination, it requires students to match patterns displayed by the examiner.

Top

Left face

Right face

Front and back face

Bottom

Student given blocks
of this configuration

or she did. These factors are important in interpreting a student's score. Experts emphasize that attentiveness, motivation, and anxiety can all have powerful effects on intelligence test performance (Snyderman & Rothman, 1987).

In contrast with individually administered tests, group tests are heavily weighted toward verbal skills and are susceptible to motivational, test-taking, and language problems. Because test data are so important in decision making and because individual tests are clearly superior, the use of group intelligence tests for individual diagnosis and placement is questionable.

Aptitude Tests

Although *aptitude* and *intelligence* are often used synonymously, aptitude is only one characteristic of intelligence—the capacity to acquire knowledge. **Aptitude tests** *are designed to predict the potential for future learning and to measure general abilities developed over long periods of time*. Aptitude tests are commonly used in selection, placement, and assessment decisions, and they correlate highly with achievement tests (Linn & Gronlund, 2000; W. Popham, 1995). The concept of aptitude is intuitively sensible; for example, people will say, "I just don't have any aptitude for math," implying that their potential for learning math is limited.

The two most common aptitude tests at the high school level are the SAT and the ACT. They are designed to measure a student's potential for success in college. This potential is heavily influenced by previous experience, however; classroom-related knowledge, particularly in language and mathematics, is essential for success on the tests. But because the tests are objective and reliable, they eliminate teacher bias and the unevenness of grades from different teachers and different schools. In this regard, they add valuable additional information in predicting future success.

The SAT I is a revised version of the original Scholastic Aptitude Test (SAT) containing six subsections: three verbal and three math. The verbal subtests include analogies, sentence completion (vocabulary and sentence structure), and critical reasoning; math subtests include standard computation, estimation, and student-produced response questions. Calculators are now allowed for use during the test.

The American College Testing Program (ACT) consists of tests in four areas: English, math, reading, and science reasoning. The total test takes about 3 hours, and calculators are not allowed.

Evaluating Standardized Tests: Validity Revisited

Wendy Klopman was a little nervous. She had been asked to serve on a district-wide committee to select a new standardized achievement test battery for the elementary grades. Her task was to get feedback from the faculty at her school about two options, the Stanford Achievement Test and the California Achievement Test.

After giving a brief overview of the two tests during a faculty meeting, Wendy opened the floor to questions.

"How much do the two tests cover problem solving?" a fifth-grade teacher asked.

"We're moving our language arts curriculum more in the direction of writing. How do the tests cover this topic?" a first grade teacher wondered.

As the discussion continued, a confused and exasperated colleague asked, "Which one is better? That's really the bottom line. How about a simple answer?"

Wendy couldn't offer a simple answer, not because she was unprepared, but because she was asked to make a judgment about validity.

Appendix

In Chapter 14, you saw that validity involves "an evaluation of the adequacy and appropriateness of the interpretations and uses of assessment results" (Linn & Gronlund, 2000, p. 73), and we emphasized the importance of matching assessments and goals. For teacher-made tests, validity is influenced by the kinds of assessments teachers construct and how the assessments are used.

In the case of standardized tests, determining validity is different because the tests have already been constructed. Here, the teacher is asked to judge the suitability of a test for a specific purpose. Validity resides in the appropriate use of a test, not in the test itself (Messick, 1989; Shepard, 1993).

Experts describe three kinds of validity: (a) content, (b) predictive, and (c) construct, and each provides a different perspective on the issue of appropriate use.

Content Validity

Content validity *represents the overlap between what is taught and what is tested*. Content validity is determined by comparing test content with curriculum objectives and is a primary concern when considering standardized achievement tests. The questions Wendy was asked about which test was "better" and whether they covered problem solving and writing addressed content validity. The "better" test is the one with the closer match between a school's goals and the content of the test (J. Popham, 1998).

Predictive Validity

Often, educators use standardized tests to predict how students will do in a future course or program of study. **Predictive validity** is *an indicator of a test's ability to gauge future performance*. It is central to the SAT and the ACT; these tests are designed to measure a student's potential to do college work. Predictive validity is also the focus of tests that gauge students' readiness for academic tasks in kindergarten and first grade.

Predictive validity is usually quantified by correlating a test and some other criterion, such as grades. A perfect correspondence or correlation between two variables would be 1.0; in testing, most correlations are substantially less than that. For example, a correlation of .42 exists between the SAT and college grades (Shepard, 1993). High school grades are the only better predictor (a correlation of .48).

Why isn't the correlation between tests and college performance higher? The primary reason is that the SAT is designed to predict "general readiness" for college; other factors, such as motivation, study habits, and specific content background, also affect performance.

Construct Validity

Construct validity is *an indicator of the logical connection between a test and what it is designed to measure*. It is somewhat abstract but important in understanding the total concept of validity (Messick, 1989; Shepard, 1993). It answers the question, Do these items actually measure the ideas the test is designed to measure? For instance, in examining the SAT, many of the items do indeed tap the ability to do abstract thinking about words and numbers—tasks that students are likely to face in their college experience. Because of this, the test has construct validity.

Understanding and Interpreting Standardized Test Scores

We said earlier that standardized tests are given to literally thousands of students. To deal with the vast amounts of information gathered and to describe individuals' performances compared with others', statistical methods are used in summarizing test information.

Descriptive Statistics

To understand the use of statistics in summarizing information, examine Table A.3, which contains scores made by two classes of 31 students on a 50-item test. (As you examine this information, keep in mind that a standardized test would have a sample much larger than 31 and would probably contain a larger number of items. We use a class-size example here for the sake of illustration.)

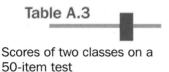

Table A.3

Scores of two classes on a 50-item test

Class #1	Class #2
50	48
49	47
49	46
48	46
47	45
47	45
46	44 ⎤
46	44
45	44 mode
45	44
45	44 ⎦
44 ⎤	43
44 mode	43
44	43
44 ⎦	43
43— median	42— median & mean
42— mean	42
41	42
41	42
40	41
40	41
39	41
39	40
38	40
37	39
37	39
36	38
35	38
34	37
34	36
33	35

The scores for the two classes are ranked from the highest to the lowest score and also include the mean, median, and mode. (We discuss the mean, median, and mode in the sections that follow.) As you can see, the simple array of scores can be cumbersome and uninformative, even when scores are ranked. An efficient way of summarizing information is needed.

Frequency Distributions

One way of summarizing test data is to simply count the number of people who obtained each score; this is called a **frequency distribution**, which can be represented as a graph with the possible scores on the horizontal (x) axis and the frequency, or the number of students who got each score, on the vertical (y) axis. The frequency distributions for the two classes are shown in Figure A.1.

This information is still in rough form, but we can already begin to see differences between the two classes. For instance, the scores from the first class are spread out over a wider range than the second class, and there is a greater grouping of scores near the middle of the second distribution. Beyond this qualitative description, however, the frequency distribution isn't particularly helpful. A more quantitative summary of the information is needed.

Measures of Central Tendency

Measures of central tendency—*the mean, median, and mode— are quantitative descriptions of how the group performed as a whole*. The **mean** is *the average score*, the **median** is *the middle score in the distribution*, and the **mode** is *the most frequent score*.

To obtain a mean, simply add the scores and divide by the number of scores. As it turns out, both distributions have 1,302/31 = 42. The class average or mean of 42 is one indicator of how each group performed as a whole.

The median for the first distribution is 43 because half the scores (15) fall equal to or above 43, and the other half are equal to or below 43. Using the same process, we can find that the median for the second distribution is 42.

Figure A.1

Frequency distributions for two classes on a 50-item test

Class 1

														X						
														X	X					
				X			X		X	X	X			X	X	X	X		X	
			X	X	X	X	X	X	X	X	X	X	X	X	X	X	X	X	X	X
30	31	32	33	34	35	36	37	38	39	40	41	42	43	44	45	46	47	48	49	50

Class 2

														X						
												X	X	X						
											X	X	X	X						
								X	X	X	X	X	X	X	X	X				
					X	X	X	X	X	X	X	X	X	X	X	X	X	X		
30	31	32	33	34	35	36	37	38	39	40	41	42	43	44	45	46	47	48	49	50

The median is useful when extremely high or low scores skew the mean and give a false picture of the sample. For example, you commonly hear or read demographic statistics such as "The median income for families of four in this country went from . . . in 1990 to . . . in 2000." The *median* income is used because just a few people like Bill Gates would make the average (mean) income quite high and give an artificial indicator of a typical family's standard of living. The median, in contrast, is not affected by these extremes and gives a more realistic picture of the typical American family's economic status.

Looking once more at the two samples, you can see that the most frequent score for each is 44, which is the mode. Small samples, such as here, often have more than one mode, resulting in "bimodal" or even "trimodal" distributions.

Using our measures of central tendency, you can see that the two samples are very much alike: the same mean, nearly the same median, and the same mode. As you saw from examining the frequency distribution, however, this doesn't give a complete picture of the two. A measure of their variability or "spread" is also needed.

Measures of Variability

To get a more accurate picture of the samples, you need to find out how much the scores in the sample vary, or what the spread is. One measure of variability is the **range**—*the distance between the top and bottom scores*. In the first class, the range is 17; in the second class, the range is 13. This finding confirms what you saw earlier in the frequency distribution. Although simple to compute, the range suffers from the problem of being overly influenced by one or more extreme scores. Another measure of variability that minimizes this problem is the **standard deviation**, which is *a statistical measure of the spread of scores*. With the use of computers, teachers rarely have to calculate a standard deviation manually, but we describe the procedure here to help you understand the concept. To find the standard deviation

1. Calculate the mean.
2. Subtract the mean from each of the individual scores.
3. Square each of these values. (This eliminates negative numbers.)
4. Add the squared values.
5. Divide by the total number of scores (31 in our samples).
6. Take the square root.

In our samples, the standard deviations are 4.8 and 3.1, respectively. We saw from merely observing the two distributions that the first was more spread out; the standard deviation gives a quantitative measure of that spread.

Normal Distribution

Standardized tests are administered to large (in the thousands) samples of students, and the distribution of scores often approximates a normal distribution. To understand this concept, look again at our two distributions of scores and then focus specifically on the second one. If you drew a line over the top of the frequency distribution, it would appear as shown in Figure A.2.

Now imagine a very large sample of scores, such as you would find from a typical standardized test. The curve would approximate the one shown in Figure A.3. This is a **normal distribution,** which is a *distribution of scores in which the mean, median, and mode are all the same score, and the scores distribute themselves in a bell-shaped curve.* Many large samples of human characteristics, such as height and weight, tend to distribute themselves in this way, as do the large samples of most standardized tests.

Figure A.2

Frequency distribution for the second class

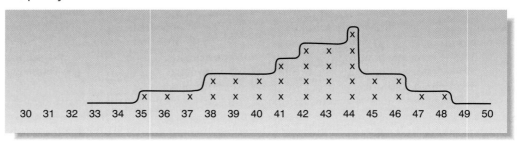

Our classroom sample has both a mean and median of 42 but a mode of 44, so its measures of central tendency don't quite fit the normal curve. Also, as you can see from Figure A.3, 68% of all the scores fall within 1 standard deviation from the mean, but in our distribution, about 71% of the scores are within 1 standard deviation above and below the mean. You can see from these illustrations that the samples aren't quite normal distributions; this is typical of smaller samples found in most classrooms.

Interpreting Standardized Test Results

Using our two small samples, we have illustrated techniques to summarize standardized test score results. Again, keep in mind that data gathered from standardized tests come from literally thousands of students, rather than from the small number we used in our illustrations. A goal for standardized test users is to compare individual students with other students from around a state, the nation, or even the world. To make these comparisons, test makers use raw scores, percentiles, stanines, and grade equivalents. Some of these scores are illustrated in Figure A.4 on a Stanford Achievement Test Report.

Raw Scores

All standardized tests begin with and are based on raw scores. A **raw score** is simply *the number of items the individual answered correctly*. For example, in Figure A.4, you can see that David's raw score for reading comprehension was 43: Of a possible 54 items, David answered 43 of them correctly. But what does this mean? Was the test easy or difficult? How did he do, compared with others taking the exam? As you can see, this score doesn't tell us much until we compare it with others. Percentiles, stanines, grade equivalents, and standard scores help us do that.

Percentiles

Percentile is one of the most commonly reported scores on standardized tests. The **percentile rank (PR)** is *a ranking that compares an individual's score with the scores of all the others who have taken the test*. For instance, David's raw score of 43 in reading comprehension placed him in the 72nd percentile nationally and the 80th percentile locally. That means his score was as high or higher than 72% of the scores of people who took the test across the nation and 80% of the scores of students who took the test in his district.

Figure A.3

Normal distribution

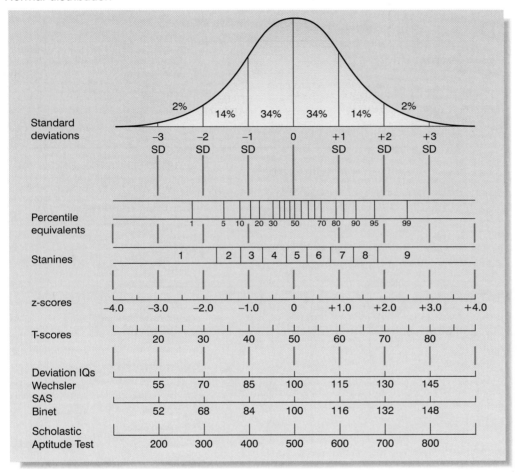

Parents and students often confuse percentiles with percentages. Percentages reflect the number correct compared with the total number possible. Percentile rank, in contrast, tells how a student did in comparison with other students taking the test.

Percentiles are used because they are simple and straightforward. However, they have a major weakness: they're rankings, and differences between the ranks are not equal (Linn & Gronlund, 2000). For instance, in our first distribution of 31 students, a score of 48 would be in the 90th percentile, 46 in the 80th, 44 in the 60th, and 43 in the 50th percentile. You can see that the difference between the 90th and 80th percentiles is twice as great (2 points) in our sample as the difference between the 60th and 50th percentiles (1 point). With large samples, this difference can be even more pronounced. Students who score at the extremes in the sample vary more from their counterparts than do those who score near the middle of the distribution. This finding is confirmed in Figure A.3, where you can see that the range of scores from the 50th to the 60th percentile is much smaller than the range from the 90th to the 99th percentile.

Figure A.4

Stanford Achievement Test Report

STANFORD

ACHIEVEMENT TEST SERIES, EIGHTH EDITION

TEACHER:	DANNY CHAVEZ		1988 NORMS: SPRING	STANFORD GRADE 4 NATIONAL INTER 1	OLSAT GRADE 4 NATIONAL E
SCHOOL:	LAKESIDE ELEMENTARY	GRADE: 4 TEST DATE:	LEVEL:		
DISTRICT:	NEWTOWN	9/2000	FORM:	J	1

STUDENT SKILLS ANALYSIS FOR DAVID PALMER

TESTS	NO. OF ITEMS	RAW SCORE	NATL PR-S	LOCAL PR-S	GRADE EQUIV	NATIONAL GRADE PERCENTILE BANDS
Total Reading	94	70	65–6	75–6	5.6	
Vocabulary	40	27	54–5	59–5	5.0	
Reading Comp.	54	43	72–6	80–7	6.7	
Total Math	118	58	28–4	29–4	4.2	
Concepts of No.	34	14	20–3	21–3	3.6	
Computation	44	22	28–4	29–4	4.0	
Applications	40	22	37–4	38–4	4.3	
Total Language	60	47	64–6	60–6	5.8	
Lang. Mechanics	30	21	41–5	38–4	4.4	
Lang. Expression	30	26	80–7	75–6	9.7	
Spelling	40	22	37–4	37–4	4.2	
Study Skills	30	21	53–5	55–5	5.2	
Science	50	31	60–6	80–7	5.5	
Social Science	50	42	88–7	90–8	8.7	
Listening	45	25	34–4	35–4	3.9	
Using Information	70	35	24–4	25–4	3.5	
Thinking Skills	101	45	27–4	30–4	3.5	
Basic Battery	387	243	44–5	45–5	4.6	
Complete Battery	487	316	52–5	55–5	5.1	

(National Grade Percentile Bands scale: 1 10 30 50 70 90 99)

AGE 10 YRS 2 MOS	READING GROUP	LANGUAGE ARTS GROUP	MATHEMATICS GROUP	COMMUNICATIONS GROUP
(H) REGULAR INSTRUCTION		SPELLING	CONCEPTS	LISTENING

COPY XX

PROCESS NO. X–(SSAI)–X REVISED 09/29/89

(Ψ) THE PSYCHOLOGICAL CORPORATION
HARCOURT BRACE JOVANOVICH, INC.

Percentile bands *describe standardized test score performance in percentile ranges, rather than as precise percentiles.* Their advantage is they acknowledge the possibility of measurement error by presenting a range of percentile scores (Lyman, 1991). In this respect, percentile bands function somewhat like stanines.

Stanines

The stanine is another score that can be used to describe David's achievement test results. For example, his reading comprehension score placed him in Stanine 6 nationally and Stanine 7 locally. We obtained these by comparing his percentile scores to the stanine ranges in Figure A.3. The **stanine (s)**, or **standard nine**, *describes a range of scores.* Stanine 5 is in the center of the distribution and includes all the scores within one fourth of a standard deviation on either side of the mean (see Figure A.3). Stanines 4, 3, and 2 are each a band of scores half a standard deviation in width extending below Stanine 5, and Stanines 6 to 8 are also a half standard deviation in width extending above Stanine 5. Stanines 1 and 9 cover the tails of the distribution. A student with a score that falls 1 standard deviation above the mean will have a stanine score of 7, and a score 2 standard deviations above the mean will have a stanine score of 9.

The stanine is widely used because it is simple and because it encourages teachers and parents to interpret scores based on a range instead of fine distinctions that may be artificial. For instance, a score in the 57th percentile may be the result of 1 or 2 extra points on a subtest, compared with a score in the 52nd percentile, and the student may have guessed the answer correctly, so the difference between the two wouldn't be meaningful. Both scores would fall in Stanine 5, which is probably a more realistic indicator of performance. Reducing scores to a simple 9-point band, however, sacrifices considerable information. For instance, in our first distribution, with a standard deviation of 4.8, a score of 40 would be in Stanine 4 because 40 is slightly more than one-fourth standard deviation below the mean. A score of 44 would be in Stanine 6 because it is slightly more than one-fourth standard deviation above the mean. However, a 40 is at the 35th percentile, and a 44 is at the 65th, a considerable difference. It is important to keep the advantages and disadvantages of stanines in mind as you help parents and students interpret standardized test scores.

Grade Equivalents

A third commonly reported score is called the grade equivalent. **Grade equivalents** *compare an individual's score with those of a particular age group.* For example, David's grade equivalent for total reading is 5.6. This means he scored as well on the test as the average score for those students taking the test who are in the sixth month of the fifth grade.

Reporting results in this way can be misleading because it oversimplifies results and suggests comparisons that are not necessarily valid. Grade equivalents say that David is somewhat advanced in reading. They do not suggest that he should be promoted to fifth grade, nor do they suggest that he should be reading with fifth graders. Other factors, such as maturity, psychosocial development, and motivation, must be considered in making decisions about students. Because of these limitations and the possibility for misinterpretation, grade equivalents should be used cautiously and never in isolation from other measures (Mehrens & Lehmann, 1987).

Standard Scores

As you saw in our discussion of percentiles, differences in raw scores don't result in comparable differences in the percentile rank. For instance, you saw that it took only 1 raw score point difference—43, compared with 42—to move from the 50th to the 60th percentile but that it took a 2-point difference—48, compared with 46—to move from the 80th to the 90th percentile in the first distribution in Figure A.2. To deal with this discrepancy, standard scores were developed.

Standard scores *express test performance in standard deviation units* (Linn & Gronlund, 2000). Standardized test makers use the mean and standard deviation to report standard scores.

One type of standard score is the **z-score**, which is *the number of standard deviation units from the mean*. A z-score of 2 is 2 standard deviations above the mean, for example, and a z-score of –1 is 1 standard deviation below the mean. The **T-score**, *with the mean defined as 50 and the standard deviation defined as 10, is another standard score*. A T-score of 70 is 2 standard deviations above the mean and corresponds to a z-score of 2. The SAT has a mean defined as 500 and a standard deviation defined as 100. A score of 550 on the verbal part means that you scored one-half deviation above the mean, or at the 68th percentile for this subtest.

Standard scores are useful because they make comparisons convenient. Because they are based on equal units of measurement throughout the distribution, intergroup and intertest comparisons are possible (Lyman, 1991).

Standard Error of Measurement

Although standardized tests are technically sophisticated, they still contain measurement error; scores only reflect an approximation of a student's "true" score. If we gave a student the same test over and over, for example, the scores would vary. If you averaged those scores, you would have a good estimate of the student's "true" score. Although it's impractical to give a person the same test repeatedly, you can get an estimate of the true score by using the **standard error of measurement**, which *describes a range of scores within which a person's true score is likely to fall*. This range is sometimes termed the confidence interval, score band, or profile band. For example, suppose Ben has a raw score of 46 and Kim has a raw score of 52 on a test with a standard error of 4. This means that Ben's true score is between 42 and 50 and that Kim's is between 48 and 56. At first glance, Kim appears to have scored significantly higher than Ben, but considering the standard error, their scores may be equal, or Ben's true score may even be higher than Kim's. Understanding the concept of standard error is important when you make decisions based on standardized tests. For instance, it would be unwise to place Ben and Kim in different ability groups solely on the basis of the results illustrated here.

References

Abedi, J. (1999, spring). CRESST report points to test accommodations for English language learning students. *The CRESST Line,* pp. 6–7.

Aboud, F., & Skerry, S. (1984). The development of ethnic identity: A critical review. *Journal of Cross-Cultural Psychology, 15,* 3–34.

Ackerman, E. (1998). New trends in cognitive development: Theoretical and empirical contributions. *Learning and Instruction, 8*(4), 375–385.

Adams, A., Carnine, D., & Gersten, R. (1982). Instructional strategies for studying content area texts in the intermediate grades. *Reading Research Quarterly, 18,* 27–53.

Adams, A., & Chiapetta, E. (1998, April). *Students' beliefs, attitudes, and conceptual change in a traditional high school physics classroom.* Paper presented at the annual meeting of the American Educational Research Association, San Diego.

Adams, M. (1989). Thinking skills curricula. *Educational Psychologist, 24,* 25–77.

Adams, M. (1990). *Beginning to read.* Cambridge, MA: MIT Press.

Adams, M., Foorman, B., Lundeberg, I., & Beeler, T. (1998). The elusive phoneme: Why phonemic awareness is so important and how to help children develop it. *American Educator, Spring/Summer,* 18–22.

Ainly, M. (1993). Styles of engagement with learning: Multidimensional assessment of the relationship with strategy use and school achievement. *Journal of Educational Psychology, 85,* 395–405.

Airasian, P. (1997). *Classroom assessment* (3rd ed.). New York: McGraw-Hill.

Airasian, P., & Walsh, M. (1997). Constructivist cautions. *Phi Delta Kappan, 78*(6), 444–449.

Alao, S., & Guthrie, J. (1999). Predicting conceptual understanding with cognitive and motivational variables. *Journal of Educational Research, 92*(4), 243–254.

Alberto, P., & Troutman, A. (1999). *Applied behavior analysis for teachers* (4th ed.). Upper Saddle River, NJ: Merrill/Prentice Hall.

Alessi, S., & Trollip, S. (1991). *Computer-based instruction: Methods and development.* Upper Saddle River, NJ: Prentice Hall.

Alexander, B., Crowley, J., Lundin, D., Murdy, V., Palmer, S., & Rabkin, E. (1997). E-Comp: A few words about teaching writing with computers. *T.H.E. Journal, 25, September,* 66–67.

Alexander, P., & Murphy, P. (1998). The research base for APA's learner-centered psychological principles. In N. Lambert & B. McCombs (Eds.), *How students learn: Reforming schools through learner-centered education* (pp. 25–60). Washington, DC: American Psychological Association.

Alexander, P., Graham, S., & Harris, K. (1998). A perspective on strategy research: Progress and prospects. *Educational Psychology Review, 10*(2), 129–153.

Allen, V. (1992). Teaching bilingual and ESL children. In J. Flood, J. J. Jensen, D. Lapp, & J. Squire (Eds.), *Handbook of research on teaching the English language arts* (pp. 356–364). New York: Macmillan.

Altermatt, E., Jovanovic, J., & Perry, M. (1997, March). *Bias or responsivity? Sex and achievement-level effects on*

teachers' classroom questioning practices. Paper presented at the annual meeting of the American Education Research Association, Chicago.

Altermatt, E., Jovanovic, J., & Perry, M. (1998). Bias or responsivity? Sex and achievement-level effects on teachers' classroom questioning practices. *Journal of Educational Psychology, 90*(3), 516–527.

American Association for the Advancement of Science (AAAS). (1993). *Benchmarks for science literacy.* Washington, DC: Author.

American Association of University Women. (1992). *How schools shortchange girls.* Annapolis Junction, MD: Author.

American Association of University Women. (1998). *Gender gaps: Where schools still fail our children.* Annapolis Junction, MD: Author.

American Association on Mental Retardation Ad Hoc Committee on Terminology and Classification. (1992). *Mental retardation: Definition, classification, and systems of support* (9th ed.). Washington, DC: American Association on Mental Retardation.

American Psychiatric Association. (1994). *Diagnostic and statistical manual of mental disorders.* Washington DC: Author.

American Psychological Association Board of Educational Affairs. (1995). Learner-centered psychological principles: A framework for school redesign and reform [On-line]. Available: http://www.apa.org/ed/lcp.html

Ames, C. (1990). Motivation: What teachers need to know. *Teachers College Record*, *91*, 409–421.

Ames, C. (1992). Classrooms: Goals, structures, and student motivation. *Journal of Educational Psychology*, *84*(3), 261–271.

Ames, C., & Archer, J. (1988). Achievement goals in the classroom: Students' learning strategies and motivation processes. *Journal of Educational Psychology*, *80*, 260–267.

Anastasi, A. (1988). *Psychological testing* (6th ed.). New York: Macmillan.

Anastasiow, N., Bibley, S., Leonhardt, T., & Borish, G. (1970). A comparison of guided discovery, discovery, and didactic teaching of math to kindergarten poverty children. *American Educational Research Journal*, *7*, 493–510.

Anderman, E., & Maehr, M. (1994). Motivation and schooling in the middle grades. *Review of Educational Research*, *64*, 287–309.

Anderson, C., & Roth, K. (1989). Teaching for meaningful and self-regulated learning in science. In J. Brophy (Ed.), *Advances in research on teaching* (Vol. 1, pp. 265–309). Greenwich, CT: JAI Press.

Anderson, C., & Smith, E. (1987). Teaching science. In V. Richardson-Koehler (Ed.), *Educators' handbook*. New York: Longman.

Anderson, J. (1990). *Cognitive psychology and its implications* (3rd ed.). New York: Freeman.

Anderson, J. (1995). *Cognitive psychology and its implications* (4th ed.). New York: Freeman.

Anderson, J., Boyle, C., & Yost, G. (1985). The geometry tutor. In *Proceedings of the International Joint Conference on Artificial Intelligence* (pp. 1–7). Los Angeles: IJCAI.

Anderson, J., Reder, L., & Simon, H. (1995). *Applications and misapplications of cognitive psychology to mathematics education*. Unpublished manuscript [On-line]. Available: http://www.psy.cmu,edu/ ~mm4b/misapplied.html

Anderson, J., Reder, L., & Simon, H. (1996). Situated learning and education. *Educational Researcher*, *25*(4), 5–10.

Anderson, L. (1989). Learners and learning. In M. Reynolds (Ed.), *Knowledge base for the beginning teacher* (pp. 85–100). New York: Pergamon Press.

Anderson, L., Brubaker, N., Alleman-Brooks, J., & Duffy, G. (1984). *Making seatwork work* (Research Series No. 142). East Lansing: Michigan State University, Institute for Research on Teaching.

Anderson, L., Evertson, C., & Brophy, J. (1979). An experimental study of effective teaching in first-grade reading groups. *Elementary School Journal*, *79*, 193–223.

Anderson, M., & Neely, J. (1996). Interference and inhibition in memory retrieval. In E. Bjork & R. Bjork (Eds.), *Memory* (pp. 237–313). San Diego: Academic Press.

Anderson, T., & Armbruster, B. (1984). Studying. In D. Pearson (Ed.), *Handbook of reading research* (pp. 657–679). White Plains, NY: Longman.

Ansley, T. (1997). Assessment during the preschool years. In G. Phye (Ed.), *Handbook of classroom assessment* (pp. 265–286). San Diego: Academic Press.

Applebee, A., Langer, J., Mullis, I., & Jenkins, L. (1990). *The writing report card, 1984–88: Findings from the Nation's Report Card*. Washington, DC: U.S. Department of Education, Office of Educational Research and Improvement.

Arias, M., & Casanova, U. (Eds.). (1993). Bilingual education: Politics, practice, and research. *Ninety-second yearbook of the National Society for the Study of Education, Part 2*. Chicago: University of Chicago Press.

Armbruster, B., & Osborn, J. (1999). Reading instruction in American classrooms: Practice and research. In R. Stevens (Ed.), *Teaching in American schools* (pp. 173–194). Upper Saddle River, NJ: Merrill/Prentice Hall.

Armstrong, T. (1994). Multiple intelligences: Seven ways to approach curriculum. *Educational Leadership*, *52*(3), 26–27.

Arnold, D., Lonigan, C., Whitehurst, G., & Epstein, J. (1994). Accelerating language development through picture book reading: Replication and extension to a videotape learning format. *Journal of Educational Psychology*, *86*(2), 235–243.

Arnone, M., & Grabowski, B. (1991). *Effects of variations in learner control on children's curiosity and learning from interactive video*. Proceedings of selected research presentations at the annual conventions of the AECT (ERIC Document Reproduction No. ED 334972).

Ashcraft, M. (1989). *Human memory and cognition*. Glenview, IL: Scott, Foresman.

Atkinson, J. (1964). *An introduction to motivation*. Princeton, NJ: Van Nostrand.

Atkinson, J. (1980). Motivational effects in so-called tests of ability and educational achievement. In L. Fyans (Ed.), *Achievement motivation: Recent trends in theory and research*. New York: Plenum Press.

Atkinson, J. (1983). *Personality, motivation, and action*. New York: Praeger.

Atkinson, R., & Shiffrin, R. (1968). Human memory: A proposed system and its control processes. In K. Spence & J. Spence (Eds.), *The psychology of learning and motivation: Advances in research and theory (Vol. 2)*. San Diego: Academic Press.

Atwell, N. (1987). *In the middle: Writing, reading and thinking with adolescents*. Portsmouth, NH: Heinemann.

Au, K. (1992, April). *"There's almost a lesson here": Teacher and students' purposes in constructing the theme of a story*. Paper presented at the annual meeting of the American Educational Research Association, San Francisco.

August, D., & Pease-Alvarez, L. (1996). *Attributes of effective programs and classrooms serving English language learners*. University of California, Santa Cruz: National Center for Research on Cultural Diversity and Second Language Learning.

Ausubel, D. (1963). *The psychology of meaningful verbal learning*. New York: Grune & Stratton.

Ausubel, D. (1977). The facilitation of meaningful verbal learning in the classroom. *Educational Psychologist, 12,* 162–178.

Ausubel, D. (1978). In defense of advance organizers: A reply to the critics. *Review of Educational Research, 48,* 251–257.

Axelrod, S., & Apsche, J. (Eds.). (1983). *The effects of punishment on human behavior.* New York: Academic Press.

Babad, E., Bernieri, F., & Rosenthal, R. (1991). Students as judges of teachers' verbal and nonverbal behavior. *American Educational Research Journal, 28*(1), 211–234.

Baddeley, A. (1992). Working memory. *Science, 255,* 556–559.

Baker, A. Kessler-Sklar, S., Piotrkowski, C., Parker, F. (1999). Kindergarten and first-grade teachers' reported knowledge of parents' involvement in their children's education. *Elementary School Journal, 99*(4), 367–380.

Baker, D., & Stevenson, D. (1986). Mothers' strategies for children's school achievement: Managing the transition to high school. *Sociology of Education, 59,* 156–166.

Baker, E. (1989). Mandated tests: Educational reform or quality indicator? In B. Gifford (Ed.), *Test policy and test performance: Education, language, and culture* (pp. 3–23). Boston: Kluwer.

Baker, L. (1989). Metacognition, comprehension monitoring, and the adult reader. *Educational Psychology Review, 1,* 3–38.

Baker, L., & Anderson, R. (1982). Effects of inconsistent information on text processing: Evidence for comprehension monitoring. *Reading Research Quarterly, 17,* 281–293.

Baker, L., & Brown, A. (1984). Metacognitive skills of reading. In D. Pearson (Ed.), *Handbook of reading research*. White Plains, NY: Longman.

Baldwin, J., & Baldwin, J. (1998). *Behavior principles in everyday life* (3rd ed.). Upper Saddle River, NJ: Prentice Hall.

Ball, D. (1992, Summer). Magical hopes: Manipulatives and the reform of math education. *American Educator*, pp. 28–33.

Ball, D. (1996). Teacher learning and the mathematics reforms: What we think we know and what we need to learn. *Phi Delta Kappan, 77,* 500–508.

Ballantine, J. (1989). *The sociology of education*. Upper Saddle River, NJ: Prentice Hall.

Bandura, A. (1977). *Social learning theory.* Upper Saddle River, NJ: Prentice Hall.

Bandura, A. (1986). *Social foundations of thought and action: A social cognitive theory*. Upper Saddle River, NJ: Prentice Hall.

Bandura, A. (1989). Social cognitive theory. In R. Vasta (Ed.), *Annals of child development* (Vol. 6, pp. 1–60). Greenwich, CT: JAI Press.

Bandura, A. (1993). Perceived self-efficacy in cognitive development and functioning. *Educational Psychologist, 28*(2), 117–148.

Bandura, A. (1997). *Self-efficacy: The exercise of control.* New York: Freeman.

Bandura, A., Ross, D., & Ross, S. (1963). Imitation of film mediated aggressive models. *Journal of Abnormal and Social Psychology, 66,* 3–11.

Bangert-Drowns, R. (1993). The word processor as an instructional tool: A meta-analysis of word processing in writing instruction. *Review of Educational Research, 63*(1), 69–93.

Bangert-Drowns, R., Kulik, J., & Kulik, C. (1991). Effects of frequent classroom testing. *Journal of Educational Research, 85,* 89–99.

Bangert-Drowns, R., Kulik, C., Kulik, J., & Morgan, M. (1991). The instructional effect of feedback in test-like events. *Review of Educational Research, 61*(2), 213–238.

Bangert-Drowns, R., & Pyke, C. (1999, April). *Teacher ratings of student engagement with educational software.* Paper presented at the annual meeting of the American Educational Research Association, Montreal.

Banks, J. (1997). Multicultural education: Characteristics and goals. In J. Banks and C. Banks (Eds.), *Multicultural education: Issues and perspectives* (3rd ed., pp. 3–32). Boston: Allyn & Bacon.

Barbetta, P., & Heron, T. (1991). Project Shine: Summer home instruction and evaluation. *Intervention in School and Clinics, 26,* 276–281.

Baringa, M. (1997). New insights into how babies learn language. *Science, 277,* 641.

Barker, G., & Graham, S. (1987). Developmental study of praise and blame as attributional cues. *Journal of Educational Psychology, 79,* 62–66.

Barkley, R. (1994). Impaired delayed responding: A unified theory of attention-deficit hyperactivity disorder. In R. Barkley (Ed.), *Disruptive behavior disorders in children* (pp. 11–57). New York: Plenum.

Baron, J. (1998). Using learner-centered assessment on a large scale. In N. Lambert & B. McCombs (Eds.), *How students learn: Reforming schools through learner-centered education* (pp. 211–240). Washington, DC: American Psychological Association.

Baron, R. (1992). *Psychology* (2nd ed.). Needham Heights, MA: Allyn & Bacon.

Barron, A., Hogarty, K., Kromrey, J., & Lenkway, P. (1999). An examination of the relationships between student conduct and the number of computers per student in Florida schools. *Journal of Research on Computing in Education, 32,* 98–107.

Basili, P., & Sanford, J. (1991). Conceptual change strategies and cooperative group work in chemistry. *Journal of Research in Science Teaching, 28,* 293–304.

Battista, M. (1999). The mathematical miseducation of America's youth: Ignoring research and scientific study in education. *Phi Delta Kappan, 80*(6), 425–433.

Baumrind, D. (1971). Current patterns of parental authority. *Developmental Psychology Monograph, 4*(1, Pt. 2).

Baumrind, D. (1991). The influence of parenting style on adolescent competence and substance use. *Journal of Early Adolecence, 11,* 56–95.

Bay, J., Reys, B., & Reys, R. (1999). The top 10 elements that must be in place to implement standards-based mathematics curricula. *Phi Delta Kappan, 80*(7), 503–506.

Bay, M., Staver, J., Bryan, T., & Hale, J. (1992). Science instruction for the mildly handicapped: Direct instruction versus discovery teaching. *Journal of Research in Science Teaching, 29,* 555–570.

Beach, K. (1999). Consequential transitions: A sociocultural expedition beyond transfer in education. In A. Iran-Nejad & P. Pearson (Eds.), *Review of research in education* (Vol. 24, pp. 101–140). Washington, DC: American Educational Research Association.

Beane, J. (1991). Sorting out the self-esteem controversy. *Educational Leadership, 49*(1), 25–30.

Beaty, E. (1995). Study contracts and education orientations. In F. Marton, D. Hounsell, & N. Entwistle (Eds.), *The experience of learning* (2nd ed.). Edinburgh: Scottish Academic Press.

Bebeau, M., Rest, J., & Narvaez, D. (1999). Beyond the promise: A perspective on research in moral education. *Educational Researcher, 28*(4), 18–26.

Bech, K. (1996). *The segmentation of moral judgments of adolescent students in Germany: Findings and problems.* Paper presented at the annual meeting of the American Educational Research Association, New York.

Beck, J., & Zebb, B. (1994). Behavioral assessment and treatment of panic disorder: Current status, future directions. *Behavior Therapy, 25,* 581–611.

Becker, H., & Ravitz, J. (1999). The influence of computer and Internet use on teachers' pedagogical practices and perceptions. *Journal of Research on Computing in Education, 31,* 356–384.

Bee, H. (1989). *The developing child* (5th ed.). New York: Harper & Row.

Behrend, D., Rosengren, K., & Perlmutter, M. (1992). The relation between private speech and parental interactive style. In R. Diaz & L. Berk (Eds.), *Private speech: From social interaction to self-regulation* (pp. 85–100). Hillsdale, NJ: Erlbaum.

Benard, B. (1993). Fostering resilience in kids. *Educational Leadership, 51*(3), 44–48.

Benard, B. (1994). *Fostering resilience in urban schools.* San Francisco: Far West Laboratory.

Bennett, N., & Blundel, D. (1983). Quantity and quality of work in rows of classroom groups. *Educational Psychology, 3,* 93–105.

Bennett, S. (1978). Recent research on teaching: A dream, a belief, and a model. *British Journal of Educational Psychology, 48,* 27–147.

Benninga, J., & Wynne, E. (1998). Keeping in character: A time-tested solution. *Phi Delta Kappan, 79*(6), 439–448.

Bereiter, C., & Scardamalia, M. (1987). *The psychology of written composition.* Hillsdale, NJ: Erlbaum.

Berk, L. (1994). *Child development* (3rd ed.). Needham Heights, MA: Allyn & Bacon.

Berk, L. (1996). *Infants, children, and adolescents* (2nd ed.). Boston: Allyn & Bacon.

Berk, L. (1997). *Child development* (4th ed.). Needham Heights, MA: Allyn & Bacon.

Berliner, D. (1984). *Making our schools more effective: Proceedings of three state conferences.* San Francisco: Far West Laboratory.

Berliner, D. (1987). Simple views of effective teaching and a simple theory of classroom instruction. In D. Berliner & B. Rosenshine (Eds.), *Talks to teachers* (pp. 93–110). New York: Random House.

Berliner, D. (1988, February). *The development of expertise in pedagogy.* Paper presented at the annual meeting of the American Association of Colleges for Teacher Education, New Orleans.

Berliner, D., & Biddle, B. (1997). *The manufactured crisis: Myths, frauds, and the attack on America's public schools.* White Plains: Longman.

Bernardo, A. (1994). Problem-specific information and the development of problem-type schemata. *Journal of Experimental Psychology: Learning, Memory & Cognition, 20*(2), 379–395.

Berndt, T. (1999). Friends' influence on students' adjustment to school. *Educational Psychologist, 34,* 15–28.

Berndt, T., & Keefe, K. (1995). Friends' influence on adolescents' adjustment to school. *Child Development, 66,* 1312–1329.

Berninger, V., Vaughan, K., Abbott, R., Abbott, S., Rogan, L., Brooks, A., Reed, E., & Graham, S. (1997). Treatment of handwriting problems in beginning writers: Transfer from handwriting to composition. *Journal of Educational Psychology, 89,* 652–666.

Beyer, B. (1984). Improving thinking skills: A practical approach. *Phi Delta Kappan, 65,* 556–560.

Beyer, B. (1988). Developing a scope and sequence for thinking skills instruction. *Educational Leadership, 45*(7), 26–30.

Binfet, J., Schonert-Reicht, K., & McDougal, P. (1997, March). *Adolescents' perceptions of the moral atmosphere of school: Motivational, behavioral, and social correlates.* Paper presented at the annual meeting of the American Educational Research Association, Chicago.

Birch, S., & Ladd, G. (1996). Interpersonal relationships in the school environment and children's early school adjustment; the role of teacher and peers. In J. Juvonen & K. Wentzel (Eds.), *Social motivation: Understanding children's school adjustment* (pp. 199–225). New York: Cambridge.

Bixby, J. (1997, March). *School organization as context for white teachers' talk about race and student achievement.* Paper presented at the annual meeting of the American Educational Research Association, Chicago.

Black, P., & William, D. (1998). Inside the black box. *Phi Delta Kappan, 80*(2), 139–148.

Black, S. (1998, October). How are you smart? *American School Board Journal,* pp. 26–29.

Blackburn, M., & Miller, R. (1999, April). *Intrinsic motivation for cheating and optimal challenge: Some sources and some consequences.* Paper presented at the annual meeting of the American Educational Research Association, Montreal.

Bloom, B. (1981). *All our children learning.* New York: McGraw-Hill.

Bloom, B. (1984). The search for methods of group instruction as effective as one-to-one tutoring. *Educational Leadership, 41*(8), 4–17.

Bloom, B., & Bourdon, L. (1980). Types and frequencies of teachers' written instructional feedback. *Journal of Educational Research, 74,* 13–15.

Bloom, B., Englehart, M., Furst, E., Hill, W., & Krathwohl, O. (1956). *Taxonomy of educational objectives: The classification of educational goals: Handbook 1. The cognitive domain.* White Plains, NY: Longman.

Blumenfeld, P. (1992). Classroom learning and motivation: Clarifying and expanding goal theory. *Journal of Educational Psychology, 84*(3), 272–281.

Blumenfeld, P., Pintrich, P., & Hamilton, V. L. (1987). Teacher talk and students' reasoning about morals, conventions, and achievement. *Child Development, 58,* 1389–1401.

Boehm, R., Armstrong, D., & Hunkins, F. (1998). *Geography: The world and its people.* New York: Glencoe.

Bol, L., Stephenson, P., O'Connell, A., & Nunnery, J. (1998). Influence of experience, grade level, and subject area on teachers' assessment practices. *Journal of Educational Research, 91*(8), 323–330.

Borg, W., & Ascione, F. (1982). Classroom management in elementary mainstreaming classrooms. *Journal of Educational Psychology, 74,* 85–95.

Borko, H., & Putnam, R. (1996). Learning to teach. In D. Berliner & R. Calfee (Eds.), *Handbook of educational psychology* (pp. 673–708). New York: Simon & Schuster.

Bosworth, K. (1995). Caring for others and being cared for: Students talk about caring in school. *Phi Delta Kappan, 76,* 686–693.

Bottge, B. (1999). *Performance of average- and under-achieving students on contextualized math tasks.* Paper presented at the annual meeting of the American Educational Research Association, Montreal.

Bourne, L. (1982). Typicality effects in logically defined categories. *Memory & Cognition, 10,* 3–9.

Bower, G., Clark, M., Lesgold, A., & Winzenz, D. (1969). Hierarchical retrieval schemes in recall of categorized word lists. *Journal of Verbal Learning and Verbal Behavior, 8,* 323–343.

Bowie, R., & Bond, C. (1994). Influencing future teachers' attitudes toward Black English: Are we making a difference? *Journal of Teacher Education, 45*(2), 112–118.

Boyes, M., & Allen, S. (1993). Styles of parent–child interaction and moral reasoning in adolescence. *Merrill-Palmer Quarterly, 39,* 551–570.

Bracey, G. (1999). Research: The growing divide. *Phi Delta Kappan, 81*(1), 90.

Braddock, J. (1990). Tracking the middle grades: National patterns of grouping for instruction. *Phi Delta Kappan, 71*(6), 445–449.

Bradley, D., & Switlick, D. (1997). The past and future of special education. In D. Bradley, M. King-Sears, & D. Tessier-Switlick (Eds.), *Teaching students in inclusive settings* (pp. 1–20). Boston: Allyn & Bacon.

Bradley, L., & Bryant, P. (1991). Phonological skills before and after learning to read. In S. Brady, & D. Shankweiler (Eds.), *Phonological processes in literacy* (pp. 37–45). Hillsdale: NJ: Erlbaum.

Bradsher, M., & Hagan, L. (1995). The kids network: Student-scientists pool resources. *Educational Leadership, 53*(2), 38–43.

Brady, P. (1990). *Improving the reading comprehension of middle school students through reciprocal teaching and semantic mapping strategies.* Unpublished doctoral dissertation, University of Oregon, Eugene.

Bransford, J. (1993). Who ya gonna call? Thoughts about teaching problem solving. In P. Hallinger, K. Leithwood, & J. Murphy (Eds.), *Cognitive perspectives on educational leadership* (pp. 2–30). New York: Teachers College Press.

Bransford, J., Goldman, S., & Vye, N. (1991). Making a difference in people's abilities to think: Reflections on a decade of work and some hopes for the future. In L. Okagaki & R. Sternberg (Eds.), *Directors of development* (pp. 147–180). Hillsdale, NJ: Erlbaum.

Bransford, J., & Johnson, M. (1972). Contextual prerequisites for understanding: Some investigations of comprehension and recall. *Journal of Verbal Learning and Verbal Behavior, 11,* 717–726.

Bransford, J., & Schwartz, D. (1999). Rethinking transfer: A simple proposal with multiple implications. In A. Iran-Nejad & P. Pearson (Eds.), *Review of research in education* (Vol. 24, pp. 61–100). Washington, DC: American Educational Research Association.

Bransford, J., & Stein, B. (1984). *The IDEAL problem solver.* New York: Freeman.

Brantlinger, E., Morton, M., & Washburn, S. (1999). Teachers' moral authority in classrooms: (Re)Structuring social interactions and gendered power. *Elementary School Journal, 99*(5), 500–504.

Bredo, E. (1997). The social construction of learning. In G. Phye (Ed.), *Handbook of academic learning:*

Construction of knowledge (pp. 3–45). San Diego: Academic Press.

Brehm, J., & Self, E. (1989). The intensity of motivation. *Annual Review of Psychology, 40,* 109–131.

Brenner, M., Mayer, R., Moseley, B., Brar, T., Durán, R., Reed, B., & Webb, D. (1997). Learning by understanding: The role of multiple representations in learning algebra. *American Education Research Journal, 34*(4), 663–689.

Bridgeman, B. (1974). Effects of test score feedback on immediately subsequent test performance. *Journal of Educational Psychology, 66,* 62–66.

Brody, N. (1992). *Intelligence* (2nd ed.). San Diego: Academic Press.

Brookhart, S. (1997). A theoretical framework for the role of classroom assessment in motivating student effort and achievement. *Applied Measurement in Education, 10*(2), 161–180.

Brooks, J. (1990). Teachers and students: Constructivists forging connections. *Educational Leadership, 47*(5), 68–71.

Brooks, L., & Dansereau, D. (1987). Transfer of information: An instructional perspective. In S. Cormier & J. Hagman (Eds.), *Transfer of learning: Contemporary research and applications.* San Diego: Academic Press.

Brophy, J. (1981). On praising effectively. *Elementary School Journal, 81,* 269–278.

Brophy, J. (1982). *Fostering student learning and motivation in the elementary school classroom.* East Lansing: Michigan State University, Institute for Research on Teaching.

Brophy, J. (1986a). Research linking teacher behavior to student achievement: Potential implications for instruction of Chapter 1 students. In B. Williams, P. Richmond, & B. Mason (Eds.), *Designs for Compensatory Education Conference proceedings and papers* (pp. IV-121–IV-179). Washington, DC: Research and Evaluation Associates.

Brophy, J. (1986b). *Socializing student motivation to learn* (Institute for Research Teaching Research Series No. 169). East Lansing, MI: Michigan State University.

Brophy, J. (1987a). On motivating students. In D. Berliner & B. Rosenshine (Eds.), *Talks to teachers* (pp. 201–245). New York: Random House.

Brophy, J. (1987b). Syntheses of research on strategies for motivating students to learn. *Educational Leadership, 45*(2), 40–48.

Brophy, J. (1990). Teaching social studies for understanding and higher order applications. *Elementary School Journal, 90,* 351–418.

Brophy, J. (1992). Probing the subtleties of subject-matter teaching. *Educational Leadership, 49*(7), 4–8.

Brophy, J. (1996). *Teaching problem students.* New York: Guilford Press.

Brophy, J. (1999). Toward a model of the value aspects of motivation in education: Developing appreciation for particular learning domains and activities. *Educational Psychologist, 34*(2), 75–86.

Brophy, J., & Evertson, C. (1974). *Texas teacher effectiveness project: Final report* (Research Rep. No. 74–4). Austin: University of Texas, Research and Development Center for Teacher Education.

Brophy, J., & Good, T. (1986). Teacher behavior and student achievement. In M. Wittrock (Ed.), *Handbook of research on teaching* (3rd ed., pp. 328–375). New York: Macmillan.

Brophy, J., & McCaslin, M. (1992). Teachers' reports of how they perceive and cope with problem students. *Elementary School Journal, 93*(1), 3–68.

Brophy, J., & Rohrkemper, M. (1987). *Teachers' strategies for coping with hostile-aggressive students.* East Lansing: Michigan State University, Institute for Research on Teaching.

Brown, A. (1994). The advancement of learning. *Educational Researcher, 23,* 4–12.

Brown, A., Bransford, J., Ferrara, R., & Campione, J. (1983). Learning, remembering, and understanding. In J. Flavell & E. Markman (Eds.), *Handbook of child psychology: Vol. 3. Cognitive development* (4th ed., pp. 77–166). New York: Wiley.

Brown, A., & Campione, J. (1986). Psychological theory and the study of learning disabilities. *American Psychologist, 41,* 1059–1068.

Brown, A., & Campione, J. (1994). Guided discovery in a community of learners. In K. McGilly (Ed.), *Classroom lessons: Integrating cognitive theory and classroom practice* (pp. 229–270). Cambridge: MIT Press.

Brown, A., & Palincsar, A. (1985). *Reciprocal teaching of comprehension strategies: A natural history of one program for enhancing learning.* Champaign-Urbana: The University of Illinois, The Center for the Study of Reading.

Brown, A., & Palincsar, A. (1987). Reciprocal teaching of comprehension strategies: A natural history of one program for enhancing learning. In J. Borkowski & J. Day (Eds.), *Cognition in special education: Comparative approaches to retardation, learning disabilities, and giftedness.* Norwood, NJ: Ablex.

Brown, A., & Smiley, S. (1977). Rating the importance of structural units of prose passages: A problem of metacognitive development. *Child Development, 48,* 1–8.

Brown, A., & Smiley, S. (1978). The development of strategies for studying texts. *Child Development, 49,* 1076–1088.

Brown, J., Collins, A., & Duguid, P. (1989). Situated cognition and the culture of learning. *Educational Researcher, 18,* 32–42.

Brown, J., & Weiner, B. (1984). Affective consequences of ability versus effort ascriptions: Controversies, resolutions, and quandaries. *Journal of Educational Psychology, 76,* 146–158.

Brown, R., & McNeill, D. (1966). The "tip-of-the-tongue" phenomenon. *Journal of Verbal Learning and Verbal Behavior, 5,* 325–337.

Bruer, J. (1993). *Schools for thought: A science of learning for the classroom.* Cambridge, MA: MIT Press.

Bruer, J. (1997). Education and the brain: A bridge too far. *Educational Researcher, 26*(8), 4–16.

Bruer, J. (1998). Brain science, brain fiction. *Educational Leadership, 56*(3), 14–18.

Bruer, J. (1999). In search of brain-based education. *Phi Delta Kappan, 89*(9), 649–657.

Bruner, J. (1960). *Process of education.* Cambridge, MA: Harvard University Press.

Bruner, J. (1966). *Toward a theory of instruction.* New York: W. W. Norton.

Bruner, J. (1971). *Relevance of education.* New York: W. W. Norton.

Bruner, J. (1985). Vygotsky: A historical and conceptual perspective. In J. Wertsch (Ed.), *Culture, communication, and cognition: Vygotskian perspectives* (pp. 21–34). New York: Cambridge University Press.

Bruner, J., Goodenow, J., & Austin, G. (1956). *A study of thinking.* New York: John Wiley.

Bruning, R., Schraw, G., & Ronning, R. (1999). *Cognitive psychology and instruction* (3rd ed.). Upper Saddle River, NJ: Prentice Hall.

Brush, T. (1997). The effects of group composition on achievement and time on task for students completing ILS activities in cooperative pairs. *Journal of Research on Computing in Education, 30,* 2–13.

Buchholz, W. (1991). *A learning activity for at-risk ninth through twelfth grade students in creating a computer-generated children's storybook design.* Master's thesis, New York Institute of Technology. (ERIC Document Reproduction No. ED 345695)

Bullough, R. (1989). *First-year teacher.* New York: Teachers College Press.

Burke, D., MacKay, D., Worthley, J., & Wade, E. (1991). On the tip of the tongue: What causes word finding failures in young and older adults? *Journal of Memory and Language, 30,* 542–579.

Burstyn, J., & Stevens, R. (1999, April). *Education in conflict resolution: Creating a whole school approach.* Paper presented at the annual meeting of the American Educational Research Association, Montreal.

Bus, A., & van Ijzendoorn, M. (1999). Phonological awareness and early reading: A meta-analysis of experimental training studies. *Journal of Educational Psychology, 91*(3), 403–414.

Busmeyer, J., & Myung, I. (1988). A new method for investigating prototype learning. *Journal of Experimental Psychology: Learning, Memory & Cognition, 14,* 1292–1302.

Butler, D. (1998). The strategic content learning approach to promoting self-regulated learning: A report of three studies. *Journal of Educational Psychology, 90*(4), 682–697.

Butler, F., & Stevens, R. (1997). Test accommodations: What are they? *CRESSTLINE, 2,* 8.

Butler-Por, N. (1987). *Underachievers in school: Issues and interventions.* New York: Wiley.

Buzzelli, C., & Johnston, B. (1997, March). *Expressive morality in a collaborative learning activity: The creation of moral meaning.* Paper presented at the annual meeting of the American Educational Research Association, Chicago.

Byars, B. (1970). *Summer of the swans.* New York: Viking.

Byrne, B., & Gavin, D. (1996). The Shavelson Model revisited: Testing for the structure of academic self-concept across pre, early, and late adolescents. *Journal of Educational Psychology, 88*(2), 215–228.

Caccamise, D. (1987). Ideas generation in writing. In A. Matsushashi (Ed.), *Writing in real time: Modeling production processes* (pp. 224–253). Norwood NJ: Ablex.

Calderhead, J. (1996). Teachers: Beliefs and knowledge. In D. Berliner & R. Calfee (Eds.), *Handbook of educational psychology* (pp. 709–725). New York: Macmillan.

Calfee, R. (1986, April). *Those who can explain teach.* Paper presented at the annual meeting of the American Educational Research Association, San Francisco.

Calsyn, C., Gonzales, P., & Frase, L. (1999). Highlights from TIMSS. Washington, DC: National Center for Educational Statistics.

Cameron, C., & Lee, K. (1997). Bridging the gap between home and school with voice-mail technology. *Journal of Educational Research, 90,* 182–190.

Cameron, J., & Pierce, D. (1994). Reinforcement, reward, and intrinsic motivation: A meta-analysis. *Review of Educational Research, 64,* 363–423.

Camp, R. (1992). Assessment in the context of schools and school change. In H. Marshall (Ed.), *Redefining student learning: Roots of educational change* (pp. 241–263). Norwood, NJ: Ablex.

Campbell, J., & Beaudry, J. (1998). Gender gap linked to differential socialization for high-achieving senior mathematics students. *Journal of Educational Research, 91*(3), 140–147.

Canter, L. (1988). Let the educator beware: A response to Curwin and Mendler. *Educational Leadership, 46*(2), 71–73.

Canter, L., & Canter, M. (1992). *Assertive discipline.* Santa Monica, CA: Lee Canter & Associates.

Caplan, N., Choy, M., & Whitmore, J. (1992). Indochinese refugee families and academic achievement. *Scientific American, 266*(2), 36–42.

Carbo, M. (1997). Reading styles times twenty. *Educational Leadership, 54,* 38–42.

Carey, S. (1986). Cognitive science and science education. *American Psychologist, 41,* 1123–1130.

Carle, E. (1990). *The very quiet cricket.* New York: Philomel.

Carlsen, W. (1987, April). *Why do you ask? The effects of science teacher subject-matter knowledge on teacher questioning and classroom discourse.* Paper presented at the annual meeting of the American Educational Research Association, Washington, DC.

Carlson, S., & Silverman, R. (1986). Microcomputers and computer assisted instruction in special classrooms: Do we need the teacher? *Learning Disability Quarterly, 9,* 105–110.

Carpenter, T., Levi, L., Fennema, E., Ansell, E., & Franke, M. (1995, April). *Discussing alternative strategies as a context for developing understanding in primary grade mathematics classrooms.* Paper presented at the annual meeting of the American Educational Research Association, San Francisco.

Carrier, C., & Titus, A. (1981). Effects of notetaking pretraining and text mode expectations on learning from lectures. *American Educational Research Journal, 18,* 385–397.

Carrol, J. (1963). A model of school learning. *Teachers College Record, 64,* 723–733.

Carrol, W. (1994). Using worked examples as an instructional support in the algebra classroom. *Journal of Educational Psychology, 86*(3), 360–367.

Carroll, A., Durkin, K., Hattie, J., & Houghton, S. (1997). Goal setting among adolescents: A comparison of delinquent, at-risk, and not-at-risk youth. *Journal of Educational Psychology, 89,* 441–450.

Carter, K. (1984). Do teachers understand the principles for writing tests? *Journal of Teacher Education, 35*(6), 57–60.

Carter, K. (1986). Test-wiseness for teachers and students. *Educational Measurement: Issues and Practice, 5*(6), 20–23.

Case, S. (1994). Will mandating portfolios undermine their value? *Educational Leadership, 52*(2), 46–47.

Caspi, A., & Silva, P. (1995). Temperamental qualities at age three predict personality traits in young adulthood: Longitudinal evidence from a birth cohort. *Child Development, 66,* 486–498.

Cassady, J. (1999, April). *The effects of examples as elaboration in text on memory and learning.* Paper presented at the annual meeting of the American Educational Research Association, Montreal.

Cassady, J., Mantzicopoulos, P., & Johnson, R. (1997, March). *Academic self-concept in first- and second-grade children: Relationships with external measures of ability.* Paper presented at the annual meeting of the American Educational Research Association, Chicago.

Catania, A. (1998). *Learning* (4th ed.). Upper Saddle River, NJ: Prentice Hall.

Cattell, R. (1963). Theory of fluid and crystallized intelligence: A critical experiment. *Journal of Educational Psychology, 54,* 1–22.

Cattell, R. (1971). *Abilities: Their structure, growth, and action.* Boston: Houghton Mifflin.

Cazden, C. (1986). Classroom discourse. In M. Wittrock (Ed.), *Handbook of research on teaching* (3rd ed., pp. 432–464). New York: Macmillan.

Cazden, C. (1988). *Classroom discourse.* Portsmouth, NH: Heinemann.

Ceci, S. (1990). *On intelligence . . . more or less.* Upper Saddle River, NJ: Prentice Hall.

Ceci, S., & Williams, W. (1997). Schooling, intelligence, and income. *American Psychologist, 53,* 185–204.

Cermak, L., & Craik, F. (1979). *Levels of processing in human memory.* Hillsdale, NJ: Erlbaum.

Chall, J. (1967). *Learning to read.* New York: McGraw-Hill.

Chall, J., Jacobs, V., & Baldwin, L. (1990). *The reading crisis: Why poor children fall behind.* Cambridge, MA: Harvard University Press.

Chance, P. (1992). The rewards of learning. *Phi Delta Kappan, 74*(3), 200–207.

Chance, P. (1993). Sticking up for rewards. *Phi Delta Kappan, 74,* 787–790.

Chandler, P., & Sweller, J. (1990). Cognitive load theory and the format of instruction. *Cognition and Instruction, 8,* 293–332.

Chaskin, R., & Rauner, D. (1995). Youth and caring: An introduction. *Phi Delta Kappan, 76,* 667–674.

Cheek, D. (1993). Plain talk about alternative assessment. *Middle School Journal, 25*(2), 6–10.

Chekles, K. (1997). The first seven . . . and the eighth. *Educational Leadership, 55,* 8–13.

Cheng, L. R. (1987). *Assessing Asian language performance.* Rockville, MD: Aspen.

Chi, M., Bassok, M., Lewis, M., Reimann, P., & Glaser, R. (1989). Self-explanations: How students study and use examples in learning to solve problems. *Cognitive Science, 5,* 121–152.

Chinn, C. (1997, March). *Learning strategies and the learner's approach to understanding some science concepts.* Paper presented at the annual meeting of the American Educational Research Association, Chicago.

Chinn, C., & Brewer, W. (1993). The role of anomalous data in knowledge acquisition: A theoretical framework and implications for science instruction. *Review of Educational Research, 63,* 1–49.

Chmielewski, T., & Dansereau, D. (1998). Enhancing the recall of text: Knowledge mapping training promotes implicit transfer. *Journal of Educational Psychology, 90,* 407–413.

Choate, J. (Ed.). (1997). *Successful inclusive teaching.* Boston: Allyn & Bacon.

Choi, H., & Heckenlaible-Gotto, M. (1998). Classroom-based social skills training: Impact on peer acceptance of first-grade students. *Journal of Educational Research, 91*(4), 209–214.

Chomsky, N. (1972). *Language and mind* (2nd ed.). Orlando, FL: Harcourt Brace.

Chomsky, N. (1976). *Reflections on language.* London: Temple Smith.

Chomsky, N., & Miller, G. (1958). Finite-state languages. *Information and Control, 1,* 91–112.

Cizek, G. (1997). Learning, achievement, and assessment: Constructs at a crossroads. In G. Phye (Ed.), *Handbook of classroom assessment* (pp. 1–31). San Diego: Academic Press.

Clark, J., & Paivio, A. (1991). Dual coding theory and education. *Educational Psychology Review, 3,* 149–210.

Clark, K., & Clark, M. (1939). The development of consciousness of self and the emergence of racial identification in Negro preschool children. *Journal of Social Psychology, 10,* 591–599.

Clement, J. (1983). A conceptual model discussed by Galileo and used intuitively by physics students. In D. Gentner & A. Stevens (Eds.), *Mental models* (pp. 206–251). Hillsdale, NJ: Erlbaum.

Clifford, M. (1990). Students need challenge, not easy success. *Educational Leadership, 48*(1), 22–26.

Clifton, R., Perry, R., Parsonson, K., & Hryniuk, S. (1986). Effects of ethnicity and sex on teachers' expectations of junior high school students. *Sociology of Education, 59,* 58–67.

Clinkenbeard, P. (1992, April). *Motivation and gifted adolescents: Learning from observing practice.* Paper presented at the annual meeting of the American Educational Research Association, San Francisco.

Cobb, P. (1994). Where is the mind? Constructivist and sociocultural perspectives on mathematical development. *Educational Researcher, 23,* 13–200.

Cochran, K., & Jones, L. (1998). The subject matter knowledge of preservice science teachers. In B. Fraser & K. Tobin (Eds.), *International handbook of science education.* Part II. Dordrecht, The Netherlands: Kluwer.

Cognition and Technology Group at Vanderbilt. (1990). Anchored instruction and its relationship to situated cognition. *Educational Researcher, 19,* 2–10.

Cognition and Technology Group at Vanderbilt. (1992). The Jasper Series as an example of anchored instruction: Theory, program description, and assessment data. *Educational Psychologist, 27,* 291–315.

Cognition and Technology Group at Vanderbilt. (1994). Multimedia environments for enhancing student learning in mathematics. In S. Vosniadu, E. De Corte, & H. Handl (Eds.), *Technology-based learning environments: Psychological and educational foundations (NATO ASI* Series F: Computers and Systems Sciences, Vol. 137, pp. 167–173). Berlin: Springer.

Cognition and Technology Group at Vanderbilt. (1996). A framework of understanding technology and educational research. In D. Berliner & R. Calfee (Eds.), *Handbook of educational psychology* (pp. 807–840). New York: Macmillan.

Cognition and Technology Group at Vanderbilt. (1997). *The Jasper Project: Lessons in curriculum, instruction, assessment, and professional development.* Mahwah, NJ: Erlbaum [On-line]. Available: http://peabody. vanderbilt.edu/projects/funded/jasper/ preview/JCCPreview.html

Cohen, E. (1991). Strategies for creating a multiability classroom. *Cooperative Learning, 12*(1), 4–7.

Cohen, E. (1994). Restructuring the classroom: Conditions for productive small groups. *Review of Educational Research, 64,* 1–35.

Cohen, M., & Riel, M. (1989). The effect of distant audiences on students' writing. *American Educational Research Journal, 26*(2), 143–459.

Cohen, S., Human, J., Ashcroft, L., & Loveless, D. (1989, April). *Mastery learning versus learning styles versus metacognition: What do we tell the practitioners?* Paper presented at the annual meeting of the American Educational Research Association: San Francisco.

Coker, H., Lorentz, C., & Coker, J. (1980, April). *Teacher behavior and student outcomes in the Georgia study.* Paper presented at the annual meeting of the American Educational Research Association, Boston.

Cole, M. (1991). Conclusion. In L. Resnick, J. Levine, & S. Teasley (Eds.), *Perspectives on socially shared cognition* (pp. 398–417). Washington, DC: American Psychological Association.

Collins, A., Brown, J., & Holum, A. (1991). Cognitive apprenticeship: Making thinking visible. *American Educator, 15,* 38–46.

Collins, A., Brown, J., & Newman, S. (1989). Cognitive apprenticeship: Teaching the crafts of reading, writing, and mathematics. In L. Resnick (Ed.), *Knowing, learning, and instruction: Essays in honor of Robert Glaser* (pp. 453–494). Hillsdale, NJ: Erlbaum.

Comstock, G. (1993). The medium and society: The role of television in American life. In G. Berry & J. Asamen (Eds.), *Children and television: Images in a changing sociocultural world* (pp. 117–131). Newbury Park, CA: Sage.

Confrey, J. (1990). A review of the research on student conceptions, in mathematics, science, and programming. In C. Cazden (Ed.), *Review of research in education, Vol. 1* (pp. 3–56). Washington, DC: American Educational Research Association.

Conger, R., Conger, K., Elder, G., Lorenz, F., Simons, R., & Whitbeck, L. (1992). A family process model of economic hardship and adjustment of early adolescent boys. *Child Development, 63,* 526–541.

Connell, J., & Wellborn, J. (1990). Competence, autonomy, and relatedness: A motivational analysis of self-system processes. In M. Gunnar & L. Sroufe (Eds.), *The Minnesota Symposia on Child Psychology* (Vol. 22, pp. 43–77). Hillsdale, NJ: Erlbaum.

Consortium for Longitudinal Studies. (1983). *As the twig is bent: Lasting effects of preschool programs.* Hillsdale, NJ: Erlbaum.

Corbett, D., Wilson, B., & Williams, B. (1999, April). *FY1998 Interim Report: The second year of the assumptions, actions, and student performance OERI field-initiated study.* Paper presented at the annual meeting of the American Educational Research Association, Montreal.

Cooper, H. (1989). Synthesis of research on homework. *Educational Leadership, 47*(3), 85–91.

Cooper, H., Lindsay, J., Nye, B., & Greathouse, S. (1998). Relationships among attitudes about homework, amount of homework assigned and completed, and student achievement. *Journal of Educational Psychology, 90*(1), 70–83.

Cooper, H., Valentine, J., Nye, B., & Lindsay, J. (1999). Relationships between five after-school activities and academic achievement. *Journal of Educational Psychology, 91*(2), 369–378.

Cordova, D., & Lepper, M. (1996). Intrinsic motivation and the process of learning: Beneficial effects of contextualization, personalization, and choice. *Journal of Educational Psychology, 88*(4), 715–730.

Corkill, A. (1992). Advance organizers: Facilitators of recall, *Educational Psychology Review, 4,* 33–67.

Corno, L., & Xu, J. (1998, April). *Homework and personal responsibility.* Paper presented at the annual meeting of the American Educational Research Association, San Diego.

Covington, M. (1984). The motive for self-worth. In R. Ames & C. Ames (Eds.), *Research on motivation in education* (Vol. 1, pp. 77–113). New York: Academic Press

Covington, M. (1992). *Making the grade: A self-worth perspective on motivation and school reform.* Cambridge, MA: Harvard University Press.

Covington, M., & Omelich, C. (1987). "I knew it cold before the exam": A test of the anxiety blockage hypothesis. *Journal of Educational Psychology, 79,* 393–400.

Cowan, S. (1988). Coping strategies of university students with learning disabilities. *Journal of Learning Disabilities, 21,* 161–164.

Craik, F., & Lockhart, R. (1972). Levels of processing: A framework for memory research. *Journal of Verbal Learning and Verbal Behavior, 11,* 671–680.

Cressy, D. (1978). White collar subversives. *The Center Magazine, 11,* 44–49.

Crick, N., & Dodge, K. (1994). A review and reformulation of social information-processing mechanisms in children's social adjustment. *Psychological Bulletin, 115,* 74–101.

Crocker, R., & Brooker, G. (1986). Classroom control and student outcomes in grades 2 and 5. *American Educational Research Journal, 23,* 1–11.

Crooks, T. (1988). The impact of classroom evaluation practices on students. *Review of Educational Research, 58,* 438–481.

Cruickshank, D. (1985). Applying research on teacher clarity. *Journal of Teacher Education, 35*(2), 44–48.

Cruickshank, D. (1987). *Reflective teaching: The preparation of students of teaching.* Reston, VA: Association of Teacher Educators.

Cuban, L. (1984). *How teachers taught: Constancy and change in American classrooms: 1890–1980.* White Plains, NY: Longman.

Cummins, J. (1991). Interdependence of first- and second-language proficiency in bilingual children. In E. Bialystol (Ed.), *Language processing in bilingual children* (pp. 70–89). Cambridge: Cambridge University Press.

Curry, L. (1990). A critique of research on learning styles. *Educational Leadership, 48*(2), 50–52, 54–56.

Curwin, R., & Mendler, A. (1988). Packaged discipline programs: Let the buyer beware. *Educational Leadership, 46*(2), 68–71.

Cushner, K., McClelland, A., & Safford, P. (1992). *Human diversity in education.* New York: McGraw-Hill.

Dai, D., Moon, S., & Feldhusen, J. (1998). Achievement motivation and gifted students: A social cognitive perspective. *Educational Psychologist, 33*(2/3), 45–63.

Dansereau, D. (1985). Learning strategy research. In J. Segal, S. Chipman, & R. Glaser (Eds.), *Thinking and learning skills* (Vol. 1, pp. 209–239). Hillsdale, NJ: Erlbaum.

Darling-Hammond, L. (1991). Inequality and access to knowledge. In J. Banks & C. Banks (Eds.), *Handbook of research on multicultural education.* New York: Macmillan.

Darling-Hammond, L. (1996). *What matters most: Teaching for America's future.* Washington, DC: National Commission on Teaching and America's Future.

Darling-Hammond, L. (1997). *The right to learn.* San Francisco: Jossey Bass.

Darling-Hammond, L., & Snyder, J. (1992). Reframing accountability: Creating learner-centered schools. In A. Lieberman (Ed.), *The changing contexts of teaching* (pp. 3–17). Chicago: University of Chicago Press.

Darling-Hammond, L., Wise, A., & Pease, S. (1983). Teacher evaluation in the organizational context: A review of the literature. *Review of Educational Research, 53,* 285–328.

Datnow, A., Hubbard, L., & Conchas, G. (1999, April). *How context mediates policy: The implementation of single gender public schooling in California.* Paper presented at the annual meeting of the American Educational Research Association, Montreal.

Davenport, E., Davison, M., Kuang, H., Ding, S., Kim, S., & Kwak, N. (1998). High school mathematics course-taking by gender and ethnicity. *American Educational Research Journal, 35*(3), 497–514.

Davies, S., Luftig, R., & Witte, R. (1999, April). *Self-management and peer-monitoring within a group contingency to decrease uncontrolled verbalizations of children with attention-deficit/hyperactivity disorder.* Paper presented at the annual meeting of the American Educational Research Association, Montreal.

Davis, G. (1989). Testing for creative potential. *Contemporary Educational Psychology, 14,* 257–274.

Davis, G., & Rimm, S. (1993). *Education of the gifted and talented* (3rd ed.). Upper Saddle River, NJ: Prentice Hall.

Davis, R. (1989). The culture of mathematics and the culture of schools. *Journal of Mathematical Behavior, 8,* 143–160.

Davis, R. (1994). The task of improving mathematics classrooms: A reply to Schofield, Eurich-Fulcer, and Britt. *American Educational Research Journal, 31*(3), 608–618.

de Bono, E. (1976). *Teaching thinking.* London: Temple Smith.

De Corte, E., Greer, B., & Verschaffel, L. (1996). Mathematics teaching and learning. In D. Berliner & R. Calfee (Eds.), *Handbook of educational psychology* (pp. 491–549). New York: Simon & Schuster.

De La Paz, S., & Graham, S. (1997). Effects of dictation and advanced planning instruction on the composing of students with writing and learning problems. *Journal of Educational Psychology, 89*(2), 203–222.

De La Paz, S., Swanson, P., & Graham, S. (1998). The contribution of executive control to the revising by students with writing and learning difficulties. *Journal of Educational Psychology, 90*(3), 448–460.

De Lisi, R., & Straudt, J. (1980). Individual differences in college students' performance on formal operations tasks. *Journal of Applied Developmental Psychology, 1,* 201–208.

deCharms, R. (1968). *Personal causation.* San Diego: Academic Press.

Deci, E. (1980). *The psychology of self-determination.* Lexington, MA: D. C. Heath.

Deci, E., & Ryan, R. (1985). *Intrinsic motivation and self-determination in human behavior.* New York: Plenum.

Deci, E., & Ryan, R. (1987). The support of autonomy and the control of behavior. *Journal of Personality and Social Psychology, 53,* 1024–1037.

Delgado-Gaiton, C. (1992). School matters in the Mexican American home: Socializing children to education. *American Educational Research Journal, 29*(3), 495–516.

Delisle, J. (1984). *Gifted children speak out.* New York: Walker.

Delpit, L. (1995). *Other people's children: Cultural conflict in the classroom.* New York: The New Press.

deMarrais, K., & LeCompte, M. (1999). *The way schools work* (3rd ed.). New York: Longman.

Dempster, F. (1991). Synthesis of research on reviews and tests. *Educational Leadership, 48*(7), 71–76.

Dempster, R., & Corkill, A. (1999). Interference and inhibition in cognition and behavior: Unifying themes for educational psychology. *Educational Psychology Review, 11*(1), 1–88.

Derry, S. (1992). Beyond symbolic processing: Expanding horizons for educational psychology. *Journal of Educational Psychology, 84,* 413–419.

DeVries, R. (1997). Piaget's social theory. *Educational Researcher, 26*(2), 4–18.

DeVries, R., & Zan, B. (1995, April). *The sociomoral atmosphere: The first principle of constructivist education.* Paper presented at the annual meeting of the American Educational Research Association, San Francisco.

Dewey, J. (1910). *How we think.* Boston: D. C. Heath.

Diaz, R. (1983). Thought and two languages: The impact of bilingualism. In Z. Gordon (Ed.), *Review of research in education* (Vol. 10). Washington, DC: American Educational Research Association.

Diaz, R. (1990). Bilingualism and cognitive ability: Theory, research, and controversy. In A. Barona & E. Garcia (Eds.), *Children at risk: Poverty, minority status, and other issues of educational equity* (pp. 91–102). Washington, DC: National Association of School Psychologists.

Dickinson, V., Abd-El-Khalick, F., & Lederman, N. (1999, April). *The influences of a reflective activity-based approach on elementary teachers' conceptions of the nature of science.* Paper presented at the annual meeting of the American Educational Research Association, Montreal.

Dillon, J. (1987). *Questioning and discussion: A multidisciplinary study.* Norwood, NJ: Ablex.

DiSessa, A. (1999). What do "just plain folk" know about physics? In D. Olson, & N. Torrance (Eds.), *Handbook of education and human development.* (pp.709–730). New York: Blackwell.

Dochy, F., & McDowell, L. (1997). Introduction: Assessment as a tool for learning. *Studies in Educational Evaluation, 23*(4), 279–298.

Dodge, K., & Price, N. (1994). On the relation between social information processing and socially competent behavior in early school-aged children. *Child Development, 65,* 1385–1397.

Dole, J., Duffy, G., Roehler, L., & Pearson, D. (1991). Moving from the old to the new: Research on reading comprehension instruction. *Review of Educational Research, 61,* 239–264.

Dole, J., & Sinatra, G. (1998). Reconceptualizing change in the cognitive construction of knowledge. *Educational Psychologist, 33*(2/3), 109–128.

Dolgins, J., Myers, M., Flynn, P., & Moore, J. (1984). How do we help the learning disabled? *Instructor, 93*(7), 29–36.

Donnerstein, E., Slaby, R., & Eron, L. (1994). The mass media and youth aggression. In L. Eron, J. Gentry, & P. Schlegel (Eds.), *Reason to hope: A psychosocial perspective on violence and youth* (pp. 219–250). Washington, DC: American Psychological Association.

Doyle, W. (1983). Academic work. *Review of Educational Research, 53,* 159–199.

Doyle, W. (1986). Classroom organization and management. In M. Wittrock (Ed.), *Handbook of research on teaching* (3rd ed., pp. 392–431). New York: Macmillan.

Drabman, R., & Thomas, M. (1976). Does watching violence on television cause apathy? *Pediatrics, 57,* 329–331.

Dreikurs, R. (1968). *Psychology in the classroom* (2nd ed.). New York: Harper & Row.

Dreisbach, M., & Keogh, B. (1982). Test-wiseness as a factor in readiness test performance of young Mexican American children. *Journal of Educational Psychology, 74,* 224–229.

Driscoll, M. (1994). *Psychology of learning for instruction.* Needham Heights, MA: Allyn & Bacon.

Driver, B., Asoko, H., Leach, J., Mortimer, E., & Scott, P. (1994). Constructing scientific knowledge in the classroom. *Educational Researcher, 23,* 5–12.

Duffy, G. (1992, April). *Learning from the study of practice: Where we must go with strategy instruction.* Paper presented at the annual meeting of the American Educational Research Association, San Francisco.

Duffy, G., Roehler, L., Meloth, M., & Vavrus, L. (1985, April). *Conceptualizing instructional explanation.* Paper presented at the annual meeting of the American Educational Research Association, Chicago.

Duffy, T., & Cunningham, D. (1996). Constructivism: Implications for the design and delivery of instruction. In D. Jonassen (Ed.), *Handbook of research for educational communications and technology* (pp. 170–195). New York: Macmillan.

Dunkle, M., Schraw, G., & Bendixon, L. (1995, April). *Cognitive processes in well-defined and ill-defined problem solving.* Paper presented at the annual meeting of the American Educational Research Association, San Francisco.

Dunn, R., & Griggs, S. (1995). *Multiculturalism and learning style: Teaching and counseling adolescents.* Westport, CT: Praeger.

Dunn, R., Griggs, S., Olson, J., Beasley, M., & Gorman, B. (1995). A meta-analytic validation of the Dunn and Dunn model of learning-style preferences. *Journal of Educational Research, 88*(6), 353–361.

Dweck, C. (1975). The role of expectations and attributions in the alleviation of learned helplessness. *Journal of Personality and Social Psychology, 31,* 674–685.

Dweck, C. (1985). Motivation. In R. Glaser & A. Lesgold (Eds.), *Handbook of psychology and education.* Hillsdale, NJ: Erlbaum.

Dweck, C., & Bempechat, J. (1983). Children's theories of intelligence: Consequences for learning. In S. Paris, G. Olson, & H. Stevenson (Eds.), *Learning and motivation in the classroom* (pp. 239–255). Hillsdale, NJ: Erlbaum.

Dweck, C., & Leggett, E. (1988). A social-cognitive approach to motivation and personality. *Psychological Review, 95,* 256–273.

Dwyer, D. (1994). Apple Classrooms of Tomorrow: What we've learned. *Educational Leadership, 51,* 4–10.

Dynarski, M., & Gleason, P. (1999, April). *How can we help? What we have learned from evaluations of federal dropout-prevention programs.* Paper presented at the annual meeting of the American Educational Research Association, Montreal.

Echevarria, J., & Graves, A. (1998). *Sheltered content instruction.* Upper Saddle River, NJ: Merrill/Prentice Hall.

Edinger, M. (1994). Empowering young writers with technology. *Educational Leadership, 51*(7), 58–61.

Eggen, P. (1997, March). *The impact of frequent assessment on achievement, satisfaction with instruction, and intrinsic motivation of undergraduate university students.* Paper presented at the annual meeting of the American Educational Research Association, Chicago.

Eggen, P. (1998, April). *A comparison of inner-city middle school teachers' classroom practices and their expressed beliefs about learning and effective instruction.* Paper presented at the annual meeting of the American Educational Research Association, San Diego.

Eggen, P., & Kauchak, D. (2001). *Strategies for teachers: Teaching content and thinking skills* (4th ed.). Needham Heights, MA: Allyn & Bacon.

Eggen, P., Kauchak, D., & Kirk, S. (1978). Hierarchical cues and the learning of concepts from prose materials. *Journal of Experimental Education, 46*(4), 7–10.

Eggen, P., & McDonald, S. (1987, April). *Student misconceptions of physical science concepts: Implications for science instruction.* Paper presented at the annual meeting of the National Association for Research in Science Teaching, Washington, DC.

Eisenberg, N., Martin, C., & Fabes, R. (1996). Gender development and gender effects. In D. Berliner, & R. Calfee (Eds.), *Handbook of educational psychology.* New York: Macmillan.

Elam, S., & Rose, L. (1995). The 27th annual Phi Delta Kappa/Gallup poll. *Phi Delta Kappan, 77*(1), 41–49.

Elbaum, B., Vaughn, S., Hughes, M., & Moody, S. (1999). Grouping practices and reading outcomes for students with disabilities. *Exceptional Children, 65*(3), 399–415.

Elliot, A., & Church, M. (1997). A hierarchical model of approach and avoidance achievement motivation. *Journal of Personality and Social Psychology, 72,* 218–232.

Elliot, S., & Busse, R. (1991). Social skills assessment and intervention with children and adolescents. *School Psychology International, 12,* 63–83.

Ellis, S., Dowdy, B., Graham, P., & Jones, R. (1992, April). *Parental support of planning skills in the context of homework and family demands.* Paper presented at the annual meeting of the American Educational Research Association, San Francisco.

Ellis, J., Semb, G., & Cole, B. (1998). Very long-term memory for information taught in school. *Contemporary Educational Psychology, 23,* 419–433.

Elton, L., & Laurillard, D. (1979). Trends in research on student learning. *Studies in Higher Education, 4,* 87–102.

Emmer, E. (1988). Praise and the instructional process. *Journal of Classroom Interaction, 23,* 32–39.

Emmer, E., Evertson, C., Clements, B., & Worsham, M. (2000). *Classroom management for secondary teachers* (5th ed.). Needham Heights, MA: Allyn & Bacon.

Englert, C., & Raphael, T. (1989). Developing successful writers through cognitive strategy instruction. In J. Brophy (Ed.), *Advances in research on teaching. Vol. I: Teaching for meaningful understanding and self-regulated learning.* Greenwich, CT: JAI.

Englert, C., Raphael, T., Anderson, L., Anthony, H., & Stevens, D. (1991). Making strategies and self-talk visible: Writing instruction in regular and special education classrooms. *American Educational Research Journal, 28*, 337–372.

Epstein, J. (1990). School and family connections: Theory, research, and implications for integrating sociologies of education and family. In D. Unger & M. Sussman (Eds.), *Families in community settings: Interdisciplinary perspectives* (pp. 99–126). New York: Haworth Press.

Ericsson, K. (1996). The acquisition of expert performance. In K. Ericsson (Ed.), *The road to excellence: The acquisition of expert performance in the arts, sciences, sports, and games* (pp. 1–50). Mahwah, NJ: Erlbaum.

Ericsson, K., Krampe, D., & Tesch-Romer, R. (1993). The role of deliberate practice in the acquisition of expert performance. *Psychological Review, 100*, 363–406.

Erikson, E. (1968). *Identity: Youth and crisis.* New York: Norton.

Erikson, E. (1980). *Identity and the life cycle* (2nd ed.). New York: Norton.

Esquival, G. (1995). Teacher behaviors that foster creativity. *Educational Psychological Review, 7*(2), 185–202.

Evans, E., & Engelberg, R. (1988). Student perceptions of school grading. *Journal of Research and Development in Education, 21*(2), 45–54.

Everson, H., & Tobias, S. (1998). The ability to estimate knowledge and performance in college: A metacognitive analysis. *Instructional Science, 26*(1–2), 65–79.

Everson, H., Tobias, S., Hartman, H., & Gourgey, A. (1991, April). *Text anxiety in different curricular areas: An exploratory analysis of the role of subject matter.* Paper presented at the annual meeting of the American Educational Research Association, Chicago.

Evertson, C. (1987). Managing classrooms: A framework for teachers. In D. Berliner & B. Rosenshine (Eds.), *Talks to teachers* (pp. 54–74). New York: Random House.

Evertson, C., Anderson, C., Anderson, L., & Brophy, J. (1980). Relationship between classroom behaviors and student outcomes in junior high mathematics and English classes. *American Educational Research Journal, 17,* 43–60.

Evertson, C., Emmer, E., Clements, B., & Worsham, M. (2000). *Classroom management for elementary teachers* (5th ed.). Needham Heights, MA: Allyn & Bacon.

Eysenck, M., & Keane, M. (1990). *Cognitive psychology: A student's handbook.* Hillsdale, NJ: Erlbaum.

Fabos, B., & Young, M. (1999). Telecommunication in the classroom: Rhetoric versus reality. *Review of Educational Research, 69,* 217–259.

Fan, X., Chen, M., & Matsumata, A. (1997). Gender difference in mathematics achievement: Findings from the National Education Longitudinal Study of 1988. *Journal of Experimental Education, 65*(3), 229–242.

Fashola, O., Slavin, R., Calderon, M., & Duran, R. (1997). *Effective programs for Latino students in elementary and middle schools.* Baltimore, MD: Center for Research on the Education of Students Placed At Risk.

Feather, N. (Ed.). (1982). *Expectations and actions.* Hillsdale, NJ: Erlbaum.

Feingold, A. (1995). Gender differences in personality: A meta-analysis. *Psychological Bulletin, 116,* 429–456.

Feis, C., & Simmons, C. (1985). Training preschool children in interpersonal cognitive problem-solving skills: A replication. *Prevention in Human Services, 3,* 59–70.

Feldhusen, J. (1998). Programs for the gifted few or talent development for the many? *Kappan, 79*(10), 735–738.

Feldhusen, J. (1989). Synthesis of research on gifted youth. *Educational Leadership, 46*(6), 6–11.

Feldman, A., Kropkf, A., & Alibrandi, M. (1996, April). *Making grades: How high school science teachers determine report card grades.* Paper presented at the annual meeting of the American Educational Research Association, New York.

Fennema, E. (1987). Sex-related differences in education: Myths, realities, and interventions. In V.

Richardson-Koehler (Ed.), *Educators' Handbook* (pp. 329–347). White Plains, NY: Longman.

Fennema, E., Carpenter, T., Jacobs, V., Franke, M., & Levi, L. (1998). A longitudinal study of gender differences in young children's mathematical thinking. *Educational Researcher, 27*(3), 6–11.

Fennema, E., Carpenter, T., & Peterson, P. (1989). Learning mathematics with understanding. In J. Brophy (Ed.), *Advances in research on teaching. Vol. 1: Teaching for meaningful understanding and self-regulated learning.* Greenwich, CT: JAI Press.

Fennema, E., & Koehler, M. (1983). Expectations and feelings about females' and males' achievement in mathematics. In E. Fennema (Ed.), *Research on relationship of spatial visualization and confidence of male/female achievement in grades 6–8* (Final Report, National Science Foundation Project No. SED78–17330). Washington, DC: National Science Foundation.

Fennema, E., & Peterson, P. (1987). Effective teaching for girls and boys: The same or different? In D. Berliner & B. Rosenshine (Eds.), *Talks to teachers* (pp. 111–125). New York: Random House.

Fernandez, C., Yoshida, M., & Stigler, J. (1992). Learning mathematics from classroom instruction: On relating lessons to pupils' interpretations. *Journal of the Learning Sciences, 2,* 333–365.

Ferrari, M., Bouffard, T., & Rainville, L. (1998). What makes a good writer? Differences in good and poor writers' self-regulation of writing. *Instructional Science, 26,* 473–488.

Feuer, M., & Fulton, K. (1993). The many faces of performance assessment. *Phi Delta Kappan, 74*(6), 478.

Fielding, L., & Pearson, P. (1994). Reading comprehension: What works. *Educational Leadership, 51*(5), 62–68.

Fisher, B. (1997). Computer modeling for thinking about and controlling variables. *School Science Review, 79*(287), 87–90.

Fisher, C., Berliner, D., Filby, N., Marliave, R., Cohen, K., & Dishaw, M. (1980). Teaching behaviors, academic learning time, and student achievement: An overview. In C. Denham & A. Lieberman (Eds.), *Time to learn* (pp. 7–32). Washington, DC: National Institute of Education.

Fisher, T., & Mathews, L. (1999, April). *Examining interventions for highly mobile students and their families.* Paper presented at the annual meeting of the American Educational Research Association, Montreal.

Fitch, M., & Semb, M. (1992, April). Peer teacher learning: A *comparison of role playing and video evaluation for effects on peer teacher outcomes.* Paper presented at the annual meeting of the American Educational Research Association, San Francisco.

Fitzgerald, J. (1987). Research on revision in writing. *Review of Educational Research, 57,* 481–506.

Fitzgerald, J. (1995). English-as-a-second-language learners' cognitive reading processes: A review of research in the United States. *Review of Educational Research, 65*(2), 145–190.

Fitzgerald, J., & Markman, L. (1987). Teaching children about revision in writing. *Cognition and Instruction, 41,* 3–24.

Flavell, J. (1985). *Cognitive development* (2nd ed.). Upper Saddle River, NJ: Prentice Hall.

Flavell, J., Friedrichs, A., & Hoyt, J. (1970). Developmental changes in memorization processes. *Cognitive Psychology, 1,* 324–340.

Flavell, J., Miller, P., & Miller, S. (1993). *Cognitive development* (3rd ed.). Upper Saddle River, NJ: Prentice Hall.

Flippo, R. (1997). Sensationalism, politics, and literacy: What's going on? *Phi Delta Kappan, 79*(4), 301–304.

Flowerday, T., & Schraw, G. (1999, April). *Teachers beliefs about instructional choice.* Paper presented at the annual meeting of the American Educational Research Association, Montreal.

Foos, P. (1992). Test performance as a function of expected form and difficulty. *Journal of Experimental Education, 60*(3), 205–211.

Forcier, R. (1999). *The computer as an educational tool* (2nd ed.). Upper Saddle River, NJ: Merrill/Prentice Hall.

Forman, E. (1996). Learning mathematics as participation in classroom practice: Implications of sociocultural theory for educational reform. In L. Steffe & P. Nesher (Eds.), *Theories of mathematics learning* (pp. 115–130). Mahwah, NJ: Erlbaum.

Forsterling, F. (1985). Attributional retraining: A Review. *Psychological Bulletin, 98,* 495–512.

Fowler, R. (1994, April). *Piagetian versus Vygotskian perspectives on development and education.* Paper presented at the annual meeting of the American Educational Research Association, New Orleans.

Frank, B. (1984). Effect of FID and study techniques and learning from a lecture. *American Educational Research Journal, 21,* 669–678.

Franklin, S. (1991). Breathing life into reluctant writers: The Seattle Public Schools laptop project. *Writing Notebook, 8,* 40–42.

Franklin, W. (1997, March). *African-American Youth at promise.* Paper presented at the annual meeting of the American Educational Research Association, Chicago.

Freeman, E., & Hatch, J. (1989). What schools expect young children to know: An analysis of kindergarten report cards. *Elementary School Journal 89,* 595–605.

Freese, S. (1999, April). *The relationship between teacher caring and student engagement in academic high school classes.* Paper presented at the annual meeting of the American Educational Research Association, Montreal.

Freiberg, H. (1999). Consistency mangagement & cooperative discipline: From tourists to citizens in the classroom. In H. Freiberg (Ed.), *Beyond behaviorism: Changing the classroom management paradigm* (pp. 75–97). Needham Heights, MA: Allyn & Bacon.

Freppon, P., & Dahl, K. (1998). Balanced instruction: Insights and considerations. *Reading Research Quarterly, 33*(2), 240–251.

Friedler, Y., Nachmias, R., & Songer, N. (1989). Teaching scientific reasoning skills: A case study of a microcomputer-based curriculum. *School Science and Mathematics, 89*(1), 58–67.

Friedrich-Cofer, L., Tucker, C., Norris-Baker, C., Farnsworth, J., Fisher, D., Hannington, C., & Hoxie, K. (1978). *Perceptions by adolescents of television heroines.* Paper presented at the annual meeting of the Southwestern Psychological Association, New Orleans.

Fuchs, D., & Fuchs, L. (1994). Inclusive schools movement and the radicalization of special education reform. *Exceptional Children, 60,* 294–309.

Fuchs, D., Fuchs, L., Mathes, P., & Simmons, D. (1997). Peer-assisted learning strategies: Making classrooms more responsive to diversity. *American Educational Research Journal, 34*(1), 174–206.

Fuchs, L., Fuchs, D., Bentz, J., Phillips, N., & Hamlett, C. (1994). The nature of student interactions during peer tutoring with and without prior training and experience. *American Educational Research Journal, 31*(1), 75–103.

Gage, N., & Berliner, D. (1989). Nurturing the critical, practical, and artistic thinking of teachers. *Phi Delta Kappan, 71,* 212–214.

Gagne, R. (1985). *The conditions of learning and a theory of instruction* (4th ed.). New York: Holt, Rinehart & Winston.

Gagne, R., & Dick, W. (1983). Instructional psychology. In M. Rosenzweig & L. Porter (Eds.), *Annual review of psychology.* Palo Alto, CA: Annual Reviews.

Gagne, E., Yekovich, C., & Yekovich, F. (1993). *The cognitive psychology of school learning* (2nd ed.). New York: HarperCollins.

Galbraith, D., & Rijlaarsdam, G. (1999). Effective strategies for the teaching and learning of writing. *Learning and Instruction, 9,* 83–108.

Gall, M. (1984). Synthesis of research on teachers' questioning. *Educational Leadership, 42*(3), 40–47.

Gallagher, J. (1998). Accountability for gifted students. *Kappan, 79*(10), 739–742.

Gambrell, L., & Marinak, B. (1997). Incentives and intrinsic motivation to read. In J. Guthrie & A. Wigfield (Eds.), *Reading engagement: Motivating readers through integrated instruction* (pp. 205–217). Newark, DE: International Reading Association.

Garber, H. (1988). *Milwaukee Project: Preventing mental retardation in children at risk.* Washington, DC: American Association on Mental Retardation.

Gardner, H. (1983). *Frames of mind: The theory of multiple intelligences.* New York: Basic Books.

Gardner, H. (1991). *The unschooled mind.* New York: Basic Books.

Gardner, H. (1992). Assessment in context: The alternative to standardized testing. In B. Gifford (Ed.), *Changing assessments: Alternate views of aptitude, achievement, and instruction* (pp. 77–119). Boston: Kluwer.

Gardner, H. (1993). *Creating minds: An anatomy of creativity seen through the lives of Freud, Einstein, Picasso, Stravinsky, Elliot, Graham, and Gandhi.* New York: Basic Books.

Gardner, H. (1995a). "Multiple intelligences" as a catalyst. *English Journal, 84*(8), 16–26.

Gardner, H. (1995b). Reflections on multiple intelligences: Myths and messages. *Phi Delta Kappan, 77,* 200–209.

Gardner, H. (1995c). *Where to draw the line: The perils of new paradigms.* Paper presented at the annual meeting of the American Educational Research Association, San Diego.

Gardner, H. (1999a). *The disciplined mind: What all students should understand.* New York: Simon & Schuster.

Gardner, H. (1999b). The understanding pathway. *Educational Leadership, 57*(3), November, 12–17.

Gardner, H. (1999c, April). *The well-disciplined mind: What all students should understand.* Paper presented at the annual meeting of the American Educational Research Association, Montreal.

Gardner, H., & Hatch, T. (1989). Multiple intelligences go to school. *Educational Researcher, 18*(8), 4–10.

Gardner, M. (1985). Cognitive psychological approaches to instructional task analysis. In E. Gordon (Ed.), *Review of research in education* (Vol. 12, pp. 157–195). Washington, DC: American Educational Research Association.

Garner, R., Alexander, P., Gillingham, M., Kulikowich, J., & Brown, R. (1991). Interest and learning from text. *American Educational Research Journal, 28,* 643–659.

Garner, R., Gillingham, M., & White, C. (1989). Effects of "seductive details" on macroprocessing in microprocessing in adults and children. *Cognition and Instruction, 6,* 41–57.

Gay, B. (1997). Educational equality for students of color. In J. Banks & C. Banks (Eds.) *Multicultural Education: Issues and Perspectives* (3rd ed., 195–228). Boston: Allyn & Bacon.

Gaziel, H. (1997). Impact of school culture on effectiveness of secondary schools with disadvantaged students. *Journal of Educational Research, 90*(5), 310–318.

Geary, D. (1998). What is the function of mind and brain? *Educational Psychology Review, 10,* 377–387.

Gelman, R., Meck, E., & Merkin, S. (1986). Young children's numerical competence. *Cognitive Development, 1,* 1–29.

Genishi, C. (1992, April). *Oral language and communicative competence.* Paper presented at the annual meeting of the American Educational Research Association, San Francisco.

Gentile, J. (1996). Setbacks in the "Advancement of learning?" *Educational Researcher, 25,* 37–39.

Gersten, R. (1996). The double demands of teaching English language learners. *Educational Leadership, 52*(5), 18–21.

Gersten, R., Taylor, R., & Graves, A. (1999). Direct instruction and diversity. In R. Stevens (Ed.), *Teaching in American schools* (pp. 81–106). Upper Saddle River, NJ: Merrill/Prentice Hall.

Gersten, R., & Woodward, J. (1995). A longitudinal study of transitional and immersion bilingual education programs in one district. *Elementary School Journal, 95*(3), 223–239.

Gettinger, M., Doll, B., & Salmon, D. (1994). Effects of social problem solving, goal setting, and parent training on children's peer relations. *Journal of Applied Developmental Psychology, 15,* 141–163.

Getzels, J., & Czikszentmihalyi, M. (1976). *The creative vision: A longitudinal study of problem finding in art.* New York: John Wiley.

Gick, M., & Holyoak, K. (1983). Schema induction and analogical transfer. *Cognitive Psychology, 15,* 1–38.

Gick, M., & Holyoak, K. (1987). The cognitive basis of knowledge transfer. In S. Cormier & J. Hagman (Eds.), *Transfer of learning: Contemporary research and applications.* San Diego: Academic Press.

Gilligan, C. (1982). *In a different voice: Psychological theory and women's development.* Cambridge, MA: Harvard University Press.

Gilligan, C., & Attanucci, J. (1988). Two moral orientations: Gender differences and similarities. *Merrill-Palmer Quarterly, 34,* 223–237.

Ginsburg-Block, M., & Fantuzzi, J. (1998). An evaluation of the relative effectiveness of NCTM standards-based interventions for low-achieving urban elementary students. *Journal of Educational Psychology, 90*(3), 560–569.

Gladieux, L., & Swail, W. (1999). *The virtual university and educational opportunity: Issues of equity and access for the next generation* [Online]. Available: http://www.collegeboard.org

Gladney, L., & Greene, B. (1997, March). *Descriptions of motivation among African American high school students for their favorite and least favorite classes.* Paper presented at the annual meeting of the American Educational Research Association, Chicago.

Glidden, H. (1999, April). *Breakthrough schools: What are the common characteristics of low income schools that perform as though they are high income schools?* Paper presented at the annual meeting of the American Educational Research Association, Montreal.

Glaser, R. (1984). Education and thinking: The role of knowledge. *American Psychologist, 39,* 93–104.

Glaser, R., & Chi, M. (1988). Overview. In M. Chi, R. Glaser, & M. Farr (Eds.), *The nature of expertise* (pp. xv-xxviii). Hillsdale, NJ: Erlbaum.

Glasser, W. (1985). *Control theory in the classroom.* New York: Perennial Library.

Glickman, C., & Bey, T. (1990). Supervision. In R. Houston (Ed.), *Handbook of research on teacher education* (pp. 549–568). New York: Macmillan.

Glover, J., Ronning, R., & Bruning, R. (1990). *Cognitive psychology for teachers.* New York: Macmillan.

Glynn, S., Yeany, R., & Briton, B. (Eds.). (1991). *The psychology of learning science.* Hillsdale, NJ: Erlbaum.

Gollnick, D., & Chinn, P. (1986). *Multicultural education in a pluralistic society* (2nd ed.). Upper Saddle River, NJ: Merrill/Prentice Hall.

Gollnick, D., & Chinn, P. (1994). *Multicultural education in a pluralistic society* (4th ed.). Upper Saddle River, NJ: Merrill/Prentice Hall.

Good, T. (1987a). Teacher expectations. In D. Berliner & B. Rosenshine (Eds.), *Talks to teachers* (pp. 159–200). New York: Random House.

Good, T. (1987b). Two decades of research on teacher expectations: Findings and future directions. *Journal of Teacher Education, 37*(4), 32–47.

Good, T., & Brophy, J. (1986). School effects. In M. Wittrock (Ed.), *Handbook of research on teaching* (3rd ed., pp. 570–604). New York: Macmillan.

Good, T., & Brophy, J. (1997). *Looking in classrooms* (7th ed.). New York: HarperCollins.

Good, T., Grouws, D., & Ebmeier, H. (1983). *Active mathematics teaching.* New York: Longman.

Good, T., & Marshall, S. (1984). Do students learn more in heterogeneous or homogeneous groups? In P. Peterson, L. Wilkinson, & M. Hallinan (Eds.), *The social context of instruction: Group organization and group process* (pp. 15–38). San Diego: Academic Press.

Good, T., McCaslin, M., & Reys, B. (1992). Investigating work groups to promote problem solving in mathematics. In J. Brophy (Ed.), *Advances in research on teaching* (Vol. 3, pp. 115–160). Greenwich, CT: JAI Press.

Goodenow, C. (1992a, April). *School motivation, engagement, and sense of belonging among urban adolescent students.* Paper presented at the annual meeting of the American Educational Research Association, San Francisco.

Goodenow, C. (1992b). Strengthening the links between educational psychology and the study of social contexts. *Educational Psychologist, 27*(2), 177–196.

Goodenow, C. (1993). Classroom belonging among early adolescent students: Relationships to motivation and achievement. *Journal of Early Adolescence, 13,* 21–43.

Goodlad, J. (1984). *A place called school.* New York: McGraw-Hill.

Goodlad, J., Soder, R., & Sirotnik, K. (Eds.). (1990). *The moral dimension of teaching.* San Francisco: Jossey-Bass.

Goodman, S., Gravitt, G., & Kaslow, N. (1995). Social problem solving: A moderator of the relation between negative life stresses and depression symptoms in children. *Journal of Abnormal Child Psychology, 23,* 473–485.

Goodrich, H. (1996–1997). Understanding rubrics. *Educational Leadership, 54*(4), 14–17.

Gordon, T. (1974). *Teacher effectiveness training.* New York: Wyden.

Gorman, J., & Balter, L. (1997). Culturally sensitive parent education: A critical review of quantitative research. *Review of Educational Research, 67,* 339–369.

Gottfried, A. (1985). Academic intrinsic motivation in elementary and junior high students. *Journal of Educational Psychology, 82,* 525–538.

Gottlieb, J., & Weinberg, S. (1999). Comparison of students referred and not referred for special education. *Elementary School Journal, 99*(3), 187–200.

Gould, R., & Clum, G. (1995). Self-help plus minimal therapist contact in the treatment of panic disorder: A replication and extension. *Behavior Therapy, 26,* 533–546.

Grabinger, R. (1996). Rich environments for active learning. In D. Jonassen (Ed.), *Handbook of research for educational communications and technology* (pp. 665–692). New York: Macmillan.

Graham, S. (1984). Communicating sympathy and anger to black and white children: The cognitive (attributional) consequences of affective cues. *Journal of Personality and Social Psychology, 47,* 14–28.

Graham, S. (1991). A review of attribution theory in achievement contexts. *Educational Psychology Review, 3*(1), 5–39.

Graham, S. (1994). Motivation in African Americans. *Review of Educational Research, 64*(1), 55–117.

Graham, S., & Barker, G. (1990). The downside of help: An attributional-developmental analysis of helping behavior as a low ability cue. *Journal of Educational Psychology, 82,* 7–14.

Graham, S., Berninger, V., Weintraub, N., & Schafer, W. (1998). Development of handwriting speed and legibility in grades 1–9. *Journal of Educational Research, 92*(1), 42–49.

Graham, S., & Harris, K. (1999, April). *Short-circuiting mindfulness when writing: Examples and possible solutions.* Paper presented at the annual meeting of the American

Educational Research Association, Montreal.

Graham, S., & Johnson, L. (1989). Teaching reading to learning disabled students: A review of research-supported procedures. *Focus on Exceptional Children, 21*(6), 1–9.

Graham, S., & Weiner, B. (1996). Theories and principles of motivation. In D. Berliner & R. Calfee (Eds.), *Handbook of educational psychology* (pp. 63–84). New York: Macmillan.

Grant, L., & Rothenberg, J. (1986). The social enhancement of ability differences: Teacher–student interactions in first- and second- grade reading groups. *Elementary School Journal, 87*, 29–49.

Graves, D. (1994). *A fresh look at writing.* Portsmouth, NH: Heinemann.

Graves, S. (1993). Television, the portrayal of African Americans and the development of children's attitudes. In G. Berry & J. Asamen (Eds.), *Children and television: Images in a changing sociocultural world* (pp. 179–190), Newbury Park, CA: Sage.

Green, C., & Reed, D. (1996). Defining, validating, and increasing indices of happiness among people with profound multiple disabilities. *Journal of Applied Behavior Analysis, 29*, 67–78.

Greene, R. (1992). *Human memory: Paradigms and paradoxes.* Mahwah, NJ: Erlbaum.

Greenfield, P. (1994). Independence and interdependence as developmental scripts: Implications for theory, research, and practice. In P. Greenfield, & R. Cocking (Eds.), *Cross-cultural roots of minority child development.* Hillsdale, NJ: Erlbaum.

Greenleaf, C. (1995, March). *You feel like you belong: Student perspectives on becoming a community of learners.* Paper presented at the annual meeting of the American Educational Research Association, San Francisco.

Greeno, J. (1997). On claims that answer the wrong questions. *Educational Researcher, 26*(1), 5–18.

Greeno, J., Collins, A., & Resnick, L. (1996). Cognition and learning. In D.

Berliner & R. Calfee (Eds.), *Handbook of educational psychology* (pp. 15–46). New York: Macmillan.

Greer, B. (1993). The mathematical modeling perspective on word problems. *Journal of Mathematical Behavior, 12,* 239–250.

Gregg, V., Gibbs, J., & Basinger, K. (1994). Patterns of developmental delay in moral judgment by male and female delinquents. *Merrill-Palmer Quarterly, 40*, 538–553.

Griffith, D. (1992, April). Prenatal exposure to cocaine and other drugs: Developmental and educational prognoses. *Phi Delta Kappan, 74*, 30–34.

Griffith, J. (1998). The relation of school structure and social environment to parent involvement in elementary schools. *Elementary School Journal, 99*, 53–80.

Grolnick, W., Kurowski, C., & Gurland, S. (1999). Family processes and the development of children's self-regulation. *Educational Psychologist, 34*(1), 3–14.

Gronlund, N. (1993). *How to make achievement tests and assessments.* Needham Heights, MA: Allyn & Bacon.

Gronlund, N. (1995). *How to write instructional objectives* (5th ed.). Upper Saddle River, NJ: Merrill/Prentice Hall.

Gronlund, N., & Linn, R. (1995). *Measurement and evaluation in teaching* (7th ed.). Upper Saddle River, NJ: Prentice Hall.

Guilford, J. (1967). *The nature of human intelligence.* New York: McGraw-Hill.

Guilford, J. (1988). Some changes in the structure-of-intellect model. *Educational and Psychological Measurement, 48,* 1–4.

Guillaume, A., & Rudney, G. (1997, March). *Stories of struggles and success: Implementing portfolio assessment across the disciplines.* Paper presented at the annual meeting of the National Educational Research Association, Chicago.

Guthrie, E. (1952). *The psychology of learning* (Rev. ed.). Gloucester, MA: Smith.

Guthrie, L., & Richardson, S. (1995). Turned on to language arts: Computer literacy in the primary grades. *Educational Leadership, 53*(2), 14–17.

Guzetti, B., & Hynd, C. (1998, April). *The influence of text structures on males' and females' conceptual change in science.* Paper presented at the annual meeting of the American Educational Research Association, San Diego.

Haan, N., Smith, M., & Block, J. (1968). Moral reasoning of young adults: Political-social behavior, family background, and personality correlates. *Journal of Personality and Social Psychology, 10*, 183–201.

Haertel, E. (1986, April). *Choosing and using classroom tests: Teachers' perspectives on assessment.* Paper presented at the annual meeting of the American Educational Research Association, San Francisco.

Haertel, E. (1999). Performance assessment and education reform. *Phi Delta Kappan, 80*(9), 662–666.

Hale, E. (1998, February 14). Cyber gap costs women at work. Gannett News Service. *Salt Lake City Tribune,* pp. A1, A4.

Halford, J. (1997). Reading instruction. *Infobrief, 10*, Sept. Alexandria, VA: Association for Supervision and Curriculum Development.

Hall, R. J., Gerber, M. M., & Stricker, A. G. (1989). Cognitive training: Implications for spelling instruction. In J. N. Hughes & R. J. Hall (Eds.), *Cognitive-behavioral psychology in the schools: A comprehensive handbook* (pp. 347–388). New York: Guilford Press.

Hall, R., Hall, M., & Saling, C. (1999). The effects of graphical postorganization strategies on learning from knowledge maps. *Journal of Experimental Education, 67*, 101–112.

Hallahan, D., Hall, R., Ianno, S., Kneedler, R., Lloyd, J., Loper, A., & Reeve, R. (1983). Summary of research findings at the University of Virginia Learning Disabilities Research Institute. *Exceptional Education Quarterly, 4*(1), 95–114.

Hallahan, D., & Kauffman, J. (1994). *Exceptional children* (6th ed.). Needham Heights, MA: Allyn & Bacon.

Hallahan, D., & Kauffman, J. (1997). *Exceptional children* (7th ed.). Needham Heights, MA: Allyn & Bacon.

Hallahan, D., & Sapona, R. (1983). Self-monitoring of attention with learning-disabled children: Past research and current issues. *Journal of Learning Disabilities, 16,* 616–620.

Hallden, O. (1998). Personalization in historical descriptions and explanations. *Learning and Instruction, 8*(2), 131–139.

Halle, T., Kurtz-Costes, B., & Mahoney, J. (1997). Family influences on school achievement in low-income, African American children. *Journal of Educational Psychology, 89*(3), 527–537.

Hallinan, M. (1984). Summary and implications. In P. Peterson, L. Wilkinson, & M. Hallinan (Eds.), *The social context of instruction: Group organization and group processes* (pp. 229–240). San Diego: Academic Press.

Halpern, D. (1995). *Thought and knowledge: An introduction to critical thinking* (3rd ed.). Hillsdale, NJ: Erlbaum.

Halpern, D. (1998). Teaching critical thinking for transfer across domains. *American Psychologist, 53,* 449–455.

Hamachek, D. (1987). Humanistic psychology: Theory, postulates, and implications for educational processes. In J. Glover & R. Ronning (Eds.), *Historical foundations of educational psychology* (pp. 159–182). New York: Plenum Press.

Hamilton, R. (1997). Effects of three types of elaboration on learning concepts from text. *Contemporary Education Psychology, 22,* 299–318.

Hamm, J., & Coleman, H. (1997, March). *Adolescent strategies for coping with cultural diversity: Variability and youth outcomes.* Paper presented at the annual meeting of the American Educational Research Association, Chicago.

Hamp-Lyons, L. (1992). Holistic writing assessment for L.E.P. students. In *Focus on evaluation and measurement* (Vol. 2, pp. 317–358). Washington, DC: U.S. Department of Education.

Hanson, M., Hayes, J., Schriver, K., LeMahieu, P., & Brown, P. (1998, April). *A plain language approach to the revision of test items.* Paper presented at the annual meeting of the American Educational Research Association, San Diego.

Hardiman, P., Pollatsek, A., & Weil, A. (1986). Learning to understand the balance beam. *Cognition and Instruction, 3,* 1–30.

Hardman, M., Drew, C., & Egan, W. (1999). *Human exceptionality* (6th ed.). Needham Heights, MA: Allyn & Bacon.

Harman, H. (1998). Metacognition in teaching and learning: An introduction. *Instructional Science, 26*(1–2), 1–8.

Harrington-Lueker, D. (1997). Technology works best when it serves clear educational goals. *Harvard Education Letter, 13,* 1–5.

Harris, L., Kagay, M., & Ross, J. (1987). *The Metropolitan Life survey of the American teacher: Strengthening links between home and school.* New York: Louis Harris & Associates.

Harrow, A. (1972). *A taxonomy of the psychomotor domain: A guide for developing behavioral objectives.* New York: McKay.

Harry, B. (1992). An ethnographic study of cross-cultural communication with Puerto Rican American families in the special education system. *American Educational Research Journal, 29*(3), 471–488.

Harter, S. (1990). Causes, correlates, and the functional role of global self-worth: A life-span perspective. In J. Kolligan and R. Sternberg (Eds.), *Competence considered: Perceptions.* New Haven, CT: Yale University Press.

Harter, S., & Connell, J. (1984). A comparison of alternative models of the relationships between academic achievement and children's perceptions of competence, control, and motivational orientation. In J. Nicholls (Ed.), *Development of achievement-related cognitions and behavior.* Greenwich, CT: JAI Press.

Harter, S., & Jackson, B. (1992). Trait versus nontrait conceptualizations of intrinsic/extrinsic motivational orientation. Special issue: Perspectives on intrinsic motivation. *Motivation and Emotion, 16,* 209–230.

Hartnett, P., & Gelman, R. (1998). Early understandings of numbers: Paths or barriers to the construction of new understandings. *Learning and Instruction, 8*(4), 341–374.

Hasselbring, T., Goin, L., & Bransford, J. (1988). Developing math automaticity in learning handicapped children: The role of computerized drill and practice. *Focus on Exceptional Children, 20,* 1–70.

Hasselbring, T., Goin, L., Taylor, R., Bottge, B., & Daley, P. (1997). The computer doesn't embarrass me. *Educational Leadership, 55*(3), 30–33.

Hawisher, G. (1989). Research and recommendations for computers and compositions. In G. Hawisher & C. Selfe (Eds.), *Critical perspectives on computers and composition instruction.* New York: Teachers' College Press.

Hay, I., Ashman, A., van Kraayenoord, C., & Stewart, A. (1999). Identification of self-verification in the formation fo children's academic self-concept. *Journal of Educational Psychology, 91*(2), 225–229.

Hayes, J. (1988). *The complete problem solver* (2nd ed.). Hillsdale, NJ: Erlbaum.

Hayes, J. (1996). A new framework for understanding cognition and affect in writing. In C. Levy & S. Ransdell (Eds.), *The science of writing* (pp. 1–28). Mahwah, NJ: Erlbaum.

Hayes, J., & Flower, L. (1986). Writing research and the writer. *American Psychologist, 41,* 1106–1113.

Hayes, S., Rosenfarb, I., Wulfert, E., Munt, E., Korn, Z., & Zettle, R. (1985). Self-reinforcement effects: An artifact of social standard setting? *Journal of Applied Behavior Analysis, 18,* 201–214.

Haynes, N., & Comer, J. (1995, March). *The School Development Program (SDP): Lessons from the past.* Paper presented at the annual meeting of the

American Educational Research Association, San Francisco.

Hawisher, G. (1989). Research and recommendations for computers and compositions. In G. Hawisher & C. Selfe (Eds.), *Critical perspectives on computers and composition instruction.* New York: Teachers' College Press.

Healy, A., Clawson, D., McNamara, D., Marmie, W., Schneider, V., Rickard, T., Crutcher, R., King, C., Ericsson, K., & Bourne, L. (1993). The long-term retention of knowledge and skills. In D. Medin (Ed.), *The psychology of learning and motivation: Advances in research and theory* (Vol. 30, pp. 135–164). New York: Academic Press.

Heath, S. (1982). Questioning at home and at school: A comparative study. In G. Spindler (Ed.), *Doing the ethnography of schooling.* New York: Holt, Rinehart & Winston.

Heath, S. (1989). Oral and literate traditions among black Americans living in poverty. *American Psychologist, 44,* 367–373.

Helmke, A., & Schrader, F. (1987). Interactional effects of instructional quality and teacher judgment accuracy on achievement. *Teaching and Teacher Education, 3,* 91–98.

Helms, J. (1992). Why is there no study of cultural equivalence in standardized cognitive ability testing? *American Psychologist, 47*(9), 1083–1101.

Hempenstall, K. (1997). The whole language-phonics controversy: An historical perspective. *Educational Psychology, 17,* 399–420.

Henning, J. (1999, April). *The expanding essay: Encouraging thinking in writing by explicitly teaching a complex text structure to 11th graders.* Paper presented at the annual meeting of the American Educational Research Association, Montreal.

Henson, K. (1988). *Methods and strategies for teaching in secondary and middle schools.* White Plains, NY: Longman.

Herman, J., Abedi, J., & Golan, S. (1994). Assessing the effects of standardized testing on schools. *Educational and Psychological Measurement, 54*(2), 471–482.

Herman, J., Aschbacher, P., & Winters, L. (1992). A *practical guide to alternative assessment.* Alexandria, VA: Association for Supervision and Curriculum Development.

Herman, J., & Winters, L. (1994). Portfolio research: A slim collection. *Educational Leadership, 52,* 48–55.

Hernandez, H. (1997). *Teaching in multilingual classrooms.* Upper Saddle River, NJ: Merrill/Prentice Hall.

Herrnstein, R., & Murray, C. (1994). *The bell curve.* New York: Free Press.

Herrnstein, R., Nickerson, R., Sanchez, M., & Swets, J. (1986). Teaching thinking skills. *American Psychologist, 41,* 1279–1289.

Hess, R., Chih-Mei, C., & McDevitt, T. (1987). Cultural variations in family beliefs about children's performance in mathematics: Comparisons among People's Republic of China, Chinese-American, and Caucasian-American families. *Journal of Educational Psychology, 79,* 179–188.

Hess, R., & McDevitt, T. (1984). Some cognitive consequences of maternal intervention techniques: A longitudinal study. *Child Development, 55,* 2017–2020.

Heward, W. (1996). *Exceptional children* (5th ed.). Upper Saddle River, NJ: Merrill/Prentice Hall.

Hidi, S., & Anderson, V. (1986). Producing written summaries: Task demands, cognitive operations, and implications for instruction. *Review of Educational Research, 56,* 473–493.

Hiebert, E., & Raphael, T. (1996). Psychological perspectives on literacy and extensions to educational practice. In D. Berliner & R. Calfee (Eds.), *Handbook of educational psychology* (pp. 550–602). New York: Macmillan.

Higgins, K. (1997). The effect of year-long instruction in mathematical problem-solving on middle-school students' attitudes, beliefs, and abilities. *Journal of Experimental Education, 66,* 5–28.

Higgins, K., & Boone, R. (1993). Technology as a tutor, tools, and agent for reading. *Journal of Special Education Technology, 12,* 28–37.

Hill, D. (1990). Order in the classroom. *Teacher, 1*(7), 70–77.

Hill, K., & Wigfield, A. (1984). Test anxiety: A major educational problem and what can be done about it. *Elementary School Journal, 85,* 105–126.

Hillocks, G. (1984). What works in teaching composition: A meta-analysis of experimental treatment studies. *American Journal of Education, 93,* 133–170.

Hodgkinson, H. (1991). Reform vs. reality. *Phi Delta Kappan, 73*(1), 8–16.

Holstein, C. (1976). Irreversible, stepwise sequence in the development of moral judgment: A longitudinal study of males and females. *Child Development, 47,* 51–61.

Holt, J. (1964). *How children fail.* New York: Putnam.

Homes for the Homeless. (1999). [Online]. Available: http://www.opendoor.com/hfh/

Hong, E. (1999, April). *Effects of gender, math ability, trait test anxiety, statistics course anxiety, statistics achievement, and perceived test difficulty on state test anxiety.* Paper presented at the annual meeting of American Educational Research Association, Montreal.

Hong, N., & Jonassen, D. (1999, April). *Well-structured and ill-structured problem-solving in multimedia simulation.* Paper presented at the annual meeting of the American Educational Research Association, Montreal.

Hood, D. (1999, April). *Racial identity attitudes and female African-American students' academic achievement, campus involvement, and academic satisfaction.* Paper presented at the annual meeting of the American Educational Research Association, Montreal.

Hootstein, E. (1999, April). *Implications of using portfolios with preservice social studies teachers.* Paper presented at the annual meeting of the American Educational Research Association, Montreal.

Hoover-Dempsey, K., Bassler, O., & Burow, R. (1995). Parents' reported involvement in students' homework: Strategies and practices. *Elementary School Journal, 95*(5), 435–449.

Hornberger, N. (1989). Continua of biliteracy. *Review of Educational Research, 59,* 271–296.

Hudley, C. (1992, April). *The reduction of peer-directed aggression among highly aggressive African American boys.* Paper presented at the annual meeting of the American Educational Research Association, San Francisco.

Hudley, C. (1998, April). *Urban minority adolescents' perceptions of classroom climate.* Paper presented at the annual meeting of the American Educational Research Association, San Diego.

Huefner, D. (1999, April). *Selected changes in IDEA regulations compared to the proposed regulations.* Paper presented at the annual meeting of the American Educational Research Association, Montreal.

Humphrey, F. (1979). *"Shh!" A sociolinguistic study of teachers' turn-taking sanctions in primary school lessons.* Unpublished doctoral dissertation, Georgetown University, Washington, DC.

Hunter, M. (1982). *Mastery teaching.* El Sugundo, CA: TIP Publications.

Huston, A., Watkins, B., & Kunkel, K. (1989). Public policy and children's television. *American Psychologist, 44,* 424–433.

Hvitfeldt, C. (1986). Traditional culture, perceptual style, and learning: The classroom behavior of Hmong adults. *Adult Education Quarterly, 36*(2), 65–77.

Individuals with Disabilities Education Act Amendments, Pub. L. No. 105–17, 1. (1997)

Isabella, R., & Belsky, J. (1991). Interactional synchrony and the origins of infant–mother attachment: A replication study. *Child Development, 62,* 373, 384.

Jackson, L. (1999, April). *"Doing" school: Examining the role of ethnic identity and school engagement in academic performance and goal attainment.* Paper presented at the annual meeting

of the American Educational Research Association, Montreal.

Jacoby, R., & Glauberman, N. (Eds.). (1995). *The bell curve debate: History, documents, opinions.* New York: Random House.

Jagacinski, C. (1997, March). *Effects of goal setting in an ego-involving context.* Paper presented at the annual meeting of the American Educational Research Association, Chicago.

Jale, E. (1998, Feburary 14). Cyber gap costs women at work. Gannett News Service. *Salt Lake City Tribune,* pp. A1, A4.

Jehng, J. (1997). The psycho-social processes and cognitive effects of peer-based collaborative interactions with computers. *Journal of Educational Computing Research, 17*(1), 19–46.

Jensen, A. (1987). Individual differences in mental ability. In J. Glover & R. Ronning (Eds.), *Historical foundations of educational psychology.* New York: Plenum Press.

Jenson, W., Sloane, H., & Young, K. (1988). *Applied behavior analysis in education.* Upper Saddle River, NJ: Prentice Hall.

Jerry, L., & Ballator, N. (1999). *The National Assessment of Educational Progress (NAEP) 1998 writing state reports* (Publication No. NCES 1999463). Washington, DC: National Center for Educational Statistics.

Jetton, T., & Alexander, P. (1997). Instruction importance: What teachers value and what students learn. *Reading Research Quarterly, 32,* 290–308.

Jew, C., Green, K., Millard, J., & Posillico, M. (1999, April). *Resiliency: An examination of related factors in a sample of students from an urban high school and a residential child care facility.* Paper presented at the annual meeting of the American Educational Research Association, Montreal.

Johnson, D., & Johnson, R. (1994). *Learning together and alone: Cooperation, competition, and individualization* (4th ed.). Needham Heights, MA: Allyn & Bacon.

Johnson, D., & Johnson, R. (1996). Cooperation and the use of technology. In D. Jonassen (Ed.), *Handbook of*

research for educational communications and technology (pp. 1017–1042). New York: Macmillan.

Jonassen, D., Carr, C., & Hsui-Ping, Y. (1998). Computers as MindTools for engaging learners in critical thinking. *Tech Trends, 43,* 24–32.

Jones, D., & Christensen, C. (1999). Relationship between automaticity in handwriting and students' ability to generate written text. *Journal of Educational Psychology, 91*(1), 44–49.

Jones, E. (1990). *Interpersonal perception.* New York: Freeman.

Jones, E. (1995, April). *Defining essential critical thinking skills for college students.* Paper presented at the annual meeting of the American Educational Research Association, San Francisco.

Jones, L. (1996). A history of the national assessment of educational progress and some questions about its future. *Educational Researcher, 25*(7), 15–20.

Jones, M. (1999, April). *Identity as strategy: Rethinking how African American students negotiate desegregated schooling.* Paper presented at the annual meeting of the American Educational Research Association, Montreal.

Jovanovic, J., & King, S. (1998). Boys and girls in the performance-based science classroom: Who's doing the performing? *American Educational Research Journal, 35*(3), 477–496.

Joyce, B. (1999). Reading about reading: Notes from a consumer to the scholars of literacy. *Reading Teacher, 52*(7), 662–671.

Jussim, L. (1989). Teacher expectations: Self-fulfilling prophecies, perceptual biases, and accuracy. *Journal of Personality and Social Psychology, 57,* 469–480.

Just, M., & Carpenter, P. (1987). *The psychology of reading and language comprehension.* Boston: Allyn & Bacon.

Juvonen, J., & Weiner, B. (1993). An attributional analysis of students' interactions: The social consequences of perceived responsibility. *Educational Psychology Review, 5,* 325–345.

Kagan, D. (1992). Implications of research on teacher beliefs. *Educational Psychologist, 27,* 65–90.

Kagan, S. (1994). *Cooperative learning.* San Juan Capistrano, CA: Resources for Teachers.

Kalechstein, P., Kalechstein, M., & Doctor, R. (1981). The effects of instruction on test-taking skills in second-grade black children. *Measurement and Evaluation in Guidance, 13,* 198–202.

Kaplan, R., & Saccuzzo, D. (1993). *Psychological testing* (3rd ed.). Pacific Grove, CA: Brooks/Cole.

Karabenick, S., Brackney, B., Dansky, J., Schippers, J., Smirth, S., Stephens, S., & Hicks, B. (1999, April). *Autobiographical narratives of important school events and college students' current academic engagement.* Paper presented at the annual meeting of the American Educational Research Association, Montreal.

Karplus, R., Karplus, E., Formisano, M., & Paulsen, A. (1979). Proportional reasoning and control of variables in seven countries. In J. Lockheed & M. Clements (Eds.), *Cognitive process instruction: Research on teaching thinking skills.* Philadelphia: Franklin Institute Press.

Karweit, N. (1989). Time and learning: A review. In R. Slavin (Ed.), *School and classroom organization.* Hillsdale, NJ: Erlbaum.

Katz, A. (1999, April). *Keepin' it real: Personalizing school experiences for diverse learners to create harmony instead of conflict.* Paper presented at the annual meeting of the American Educational Research Association, Montreal.

Kauchak, D., & Eggen, P. (1998). *Learning and teaching: Research-based methods* (3rd ed.). Needham Heights, MA: Allyn & Bacon.

Kauffman, D., Lehman, S., White, M., Barrett, K., Horn, C., Bruning, R., & Riesetter, M. (1999, April). *At-risk in cyberspace: How instructional designers, on-line teachers, and on-site facilitators can facilitate students at-risk in Web-based educational environments.* Paper presented at the annual meeting of the American Educational Research Association, Montreal.

Keislar, E., & Shulman, L. (Eds.). (1966). *Learning by discovery: A critical appraisal.* Chicago: Rand McNally.

Kellenberger, D. (1996). Preservice teachers' perceived computer self-efficacy based on achievement and value beliefs within a motivational framework. *Journal of Research on Computing in Education, 29*(2), 124–135.

Kellogg, J. (1988). Forces of change. *Phi Delta Kappan, 70,* 199–204.

Kellogg, R. (1987). Effects of topic knowledge on the allocation of processing time and cognitive effort to writing processes. *Memory and Cognition, 15,* 256–266.

Kellogg, R. (1994). *The psychology of writing.* New York: Oxford Press.

Kellogg, R., & Mueller, S. (1993). Performance amplification and process restructuring in computer-based writing. *International Journal of Man–Machine Studies, 39,* 33–49.

Kelly, M., Moore, D., & Tuck, B. (1994). Reciprocal teaching in a regular primary school classroom. *Journal of Educational Research, 88*(1), 53–59.

Kerbow, D. (1996). Patterns of urban student mobility and local school reform. *Journal of Education for Students Placed At Risk, 1*(2), 147–169.

Kerman, S. (1979). Teacher expectations and student achievement. *Phi Delta Kappan, 60,* 70–72.

Kreutzer, M., Leonard, C., & Flavell, J. (1975). An interview study of children's knowledge about memory. *Monographs of the Society for Research in Child Development, 40*(1, Serial No. 15).

Kerman, S. (1979). Teacher expectations and student achievement. *Phi Delta Kappan, 60,* 70–72.

Kher-Durlabhji, N., Lacina-Gifford, L., Jackson, L., Guillory, R., & Yandell, S. (1997, March). *Preservice teachers' knowledge of effective classroom management strategies.* Paper presented at the annual meeting of the American Educational Research Association, Chicago.

Kids of Room 14. (1979). *Our friends in the water.* Berkeley, CA: West Coast Print.

Kika, F., McLaughlin, T., & Dixon, J. (1992). Effects of frequent testing of secondary algebra students. *Journal of Educational Research, 85,* 159–162.

Kim, D., Solomon, D., & Roberts, W. (1995, March). *Classroom practices that enhance students' sense of community.* Paper presented at the annual meeting of the American Educational Research Association, San Francisco.

King-Sears, M. (1997). Disability: Legalities and labels. In D. Bradley, M. King-Sears, & D. Tessier-Switlick (Eds.), *Inclusive settings: From theory to practice* (pp. 21–55). Boston: Allyn & Bacon.

Kirk, S., & Gallagher, J. (1989). *Educating exceptional students* (6th ed.). Boston: Houghton Mifflin.

Klausmeier, H. (1992). Concept learning and concept thinking. *Educational Psychologist, 27,* 267–286.

Kloosterman, P. (1997, March). *Assessing student motivation in high school mathematics.* Paper presented at the annual meeting of the American Educational Research Association, Chicago.

Knapp, M., Shields, P., & Turnbull, B. (1995). Academic challenge in high-poverty classrooms. *Phi Delta Kappan, 76,* 770–776.

Knight, C., Halpen, G., & Halpen, G. (1992, April). *The effects of learning environment accommodations on the achievement of second graders.* Paper presented at the annual meeting of the American Educational Research Association, San Francisco.

Kochenberger-Stroeher, S. (1994). Sixteen kindergartners' gender-related views of careers. *Elementary School Journal, 95*(1), 95–103.

Kogan, N. (1994). Cognitive styles. In R. Sternberg (Ed.), *Encyclopedia of human intelligence.* New York: Macmillan.

Kohlberg, L. (1963). The development of children's orientation toward moral order: Sequence in the development of human thought. *Vita Humana, 6,* 11–33.

Kohlberg, L. (1969). Stage and sequence: The cognitive-developmental approach to socialization. In D. Goslin (Ed.), *Handbook of socialization theory and research*. Chicago: Rand McNally.

Kohlberg, L. (1975). The cognitive-developmental approach to moral education. *Phi Delta Kappan, 56,* 670–677.

Kohlberg, L. (1981). *Philosophy of moral development*. New York: Harper & Row.

Kohlberg, L. (1984). *Essays on moral development: Vol. 2. The psychology of moral development*. New York: Harper & Row.

Kohn, A. (1992). *No contest: The case against competition*. Boston: Houghton Mifflin.

Kohn, A. (1993). Why incentive plans cannot work. *Harvard Business Review, 71,* 54–63.

Kohn, A. (1996). *Beyond discipline: From compliance to community*. Alexandria, VA: Association for Supervision and Curriculum Development.

Kohn, A. (1997). How not to teach values. *Phi Delta Kappan, 78*(6), 429–439.

Kohn, A. (1998). Adventures in ethics versus behavior control: A reply to my critics. *Phi Delta Kappan, 79*(6), 455–460.

Konstantopoulos, S. (1997, March). *Hispanic–white differences in central tendency and proportions of high- and low-scoring individuals*. Paper presented at the annual meeting of the American Educational Research Association, Chicago.

Koretz, D., Stecher, B., & Diebert, E. (1993). *The reliability of scores from the 1992 Vermont Portfolio Assessment Program* (Tech. Rep. No. 355). Los Angeles: UCLA, Center for the Study of Evaluation.

Kounin, J. (1970). *Discipline and group management in classrooms*. New York: Holt, Rinehart & Winston.

Kounin, J. (1971). *Discipline and group management in classrooms*. New York: Holt, Rinehart & Winston.

Kozhevnikov, M., Hegarty, M., & Mayer, R. (1999, April). *Students' use of imagery in solving qualitative problems in kinematics*. Paper

presented at the annual meeting of the American Educational Research Association, Montreal.

Kozulin, A. (1990). *Vygotsky's psychology: A biography of ideas*. Cambridge, MA: Harvard University Press.

Krabbe, M., & Polivka, J. (1990, April). *An analysis of students' perceptions of effective teaching behaviors during discussion activity*. Paper presented at the annual meeting of the American Educational Research Association, Boston.

Krajcik, J., Blumenfeld, P., Marx, R., & Soloway, E. (1994). A collaborative model for helping middle grade science teachers learn project-based instruction. *Elementary School Journal, 94*(5), 483–497.

Kramer, L., & Colvin, C. (1991, April). *Rules, responsibilities, and respect: The school lives of marginal students*. Paper presented at the annual meeting of the American Educational Research Association, Chicago.

Kramer-Schlosser, L. (1992). Teacher distance and student disengagement: School lives on the margin. *Journal of Teacher Education, 43*(2), 128–140.

Krapp, A., Hidi, S., & Renninger, K. (1992). Interest, learning, and development. In K. Renninger, S. Hidi, & A. Krapp (Eds.), *The role of interest in learning and development* (pp. 3–26). Hillsdale, NJ: Erlbaum.

Krathwohl, D., Bloom, B., & Masia, B. (1964). *Taxonomy of educational objectives: The classification of educational goals: Handbook 2. Affective domain*. New York: McKay.

Krechevsky, M., & Seidel, S. (1998). Minds at work: Applying multiple intelligences in the classroom. In R. Sternberg, & W. Williams (Eds.), *Intelligence, instruction, and assessment* (pp. 17–42). Mahway, NJ: Erlbaum.

Kreutzer, M., Leonard, C., & Flavell, J. (1975). An interview study of children's knowledge about memory. *Monographs of the Society for Research in Child Development, 40*(1, Serial No. 15).

Kroger, J. (1993). Ego identity: An overview. In J. Kroger (Ed.), *Discussions on ego identity*. Hillsdale, NJ: Erlbaum.

Kruger, A. (1992). The effect of peer and adult–child transactive discussions on moral reasoning. *Merrill-Palmer Quarterly, 38*(2), 191–211.

Kuh, D., & Vesper, N. (1999, April). *Do computers enhance or detract from student learning?* Paper presented at the annual meeting of the American Educational Research Association, Montreal.

Kulik, J. (1994). Meta-analytic studies of finding on computer-based instruction. In E. Baker & H. O'Neil (Eds.), *Technology assessment in education and training* (pp. 9–33). Hillsdale, NJ: Erlbaum.

Kulik, J., & Kulik, C. (1984). Effects of accelerated instruction on students. *Review of Educational Research, 54,* 409–425.

Kuther, T., & Higgins-D'Alessandra, M. (1997, March). *Effects of a just community on moral development and adolescent engagement in risk*. Paper presented at the annual meeting of the American Educational Research Association, Chicago.

LaBerge, D., & Samuels, S. (1974). Toward a theory of automatic information processing in reading. *Cognitive Psychology, 6,* 293–323.

Labov, W. (1972). *Language in the inner city: Studies in the "Black" English vernacular*. Philadelphia: University of Pennsylvania Press.

Lambert, N., & McCombs, B. (1998). Introduction: Learner-centered schools and classrooms as a direction for school reform. In N. Lambert & B. McCombs (Eds.), *How students learn: Reforming schools through learner-centered education* (pp. 1–22). Washington, DC: American Psychological Association.

Lampert, M. (1989). Choosing and using mathematical tools in classroom discourse. In J. Brophy (Ed.), *Advances in research on teaching. Vol. 1: Teaching for meaningful understanding and self-regulated learning.* Greenwich, CT: JAI.

Lampert, M. (1990). When the problem is not the question and the solution is not the answer: Mathematical knowing and teaching. *American Educational Research Journal, 27,* 29–63.

Lampert, M. (1992). Practices and problems in teaching authentic mathematics. In F. Oser, A. Dick, & J. Patry (Eds.), *Effective and responsible teaching: The new synthesis* (pp. 295–314). San Francisco: Jossey-Bass.

Lan, W., Repman, J., & Chyung, S. (1998). Effects of practicing self-monitoring of mathematical problem-solving heuristics on impulsive and reflective college students' heuristics knowledge and problem-solving ability. *Journal of Experimental Education, 67*(1), 32–52.

Land, R. (1997). Moving up to complex assessment systems: Proceedings from the 1996 CRESST Conference. *Evaluation Comment, 7*(1), 1–21.

Langdon, C. (1996). The third Phi Delta Kappa Poll of teachers' attitudes toward the public schools. *Phi Delta Kappan, 78,* 244–250.

Lappan, G., & Ferrini-Mundy, J. (1993). Knowing and doing mathematics: A new vision for middle grades students. *Elementary School Journal, 93,* 625–641.

Larrivee, B., Semmel, M., & Gerber, M. (1997). Case studies of six schools varying in effectiveness for students with learning disabilities. *Elementary School Journal, 98*(1), 27–50.

Latham, A. (1998*).* Gender differences on assessments. *Educational Leadership, 55*(4), 88–89.

Lave, J. (1988). *Cognition in practice: Mind, mathematics, and culture in everyday life.* New York: Cambridge University Press.

Lawler-Prince, D., & Holloway, D. (1992). The family dynamics and characteristics of homeless children: Barriers to education. *National Forum of Teaching Education Journal, 2*(1), 49–53.

Lawson, A. (1995). *Science teaching and the development of thinking.* Belmont, CA: Wadsworth.

Lawson, A., & Snitgren, D. (1982). Teaching formal reasoning in a college biology course for preservice teachers. *Journal of Research in Science Teaching, 19,* 233–248.

Lawson, M., & Chinnappan, M. (1994). Generative activity during problem solving: Comparison of the performance of high-achieving and low-achieving high school students. *Cognition & Instruction, 12*(1), 61–93.

Leahey, T., & Harris, R. (1997). *Learning and cognition* (4th ed.). Upper Saddle River, NJ: Prentice Hall.

Leander, K., & Brown, D. (1999). "You understand, but you don't believe it": Tracing the stabilities and instabilities of interaction in a physics classroom through a multidimensional framework. *Cognition and Instruction, 17*(1), 93–135.

Lederman, N., Schwartz, R., Abd-El-Khalick F., & Bell, R. (1999, April). *Preservice teachers and their nature of science instruction: Factors that facilitate success.* Paper presented at the annual meeting of the National Association for Research in Science Teaching, Boston.

Lee, A. (1998). Transfer as a measure of intellectual functioning. In S. Soraci & W. McIlvane (Eds.), *Perspective on fundamental processes in intellectual functioning: A survey of research approaches* (Vol. 1, pp. 351–366). Stamford, CT: Ablex.

Lee, A., & Pennington, N. (1993). Learning computer programming: A route to general reasoning skills? In C. Cook, J. Scholtz, & J. Spohrer (Eds.), *Empirical studies of programmers: Fifth workshop* (pp. 113–136). Norwood, NJ: Ablex.

Lee, J., Pulvino, C., & Perrone, P. (1998). *Restoring harmony: A guide for managing conflicts in schools.* Upper Saddle River, NJ: Merrill/Prentice Hall.

Lee, O., & Fradd, S. (1999, April). *Instructional congruence to promote science learning and literacy and development.* Paper presented at the annual meeting of the American Educational Research Association, Montreal.

Lee, V., Burkam, D., & Smerdon, B. (1997, March). *Debunking the myths: Exploring common explanations for gender differences in high-school science achievement.* Paper presented at the annual meeting of the American Educational Research Association, Chicago.

Lehman, S., Kauffman, D., White, M., Horn, C., & Bruning, R. (1999, April). *Teacher interaction: Motivating at-risk students in Web-based high school courses.* Paper presented at the annual meeting of the American Educational Research Association, Montreal.

Lehrer, R. (1993). Authors of knowledge: Patterns of hypermedia design. In S. Lajoie & S. Derry, (Eds.), *Computers as cognitive tools* (pp. 197–227). Hillsdale, NJ: Erlbaum.

Leinhardt, G., & Greeno, J. (1986). The cognitive skill of teaching. *Journal of Educational Psychology, 78,* 75–95.

Lemke, J. (1982, April). *Classroom communication of science* (Final report to NSF/RISE). Washington, DC: National Science Foundation. (ERIC Document Reproduction Service No. ED 222 346).

Leon, M., Lynn, T., McLean, P., & Perri, L. (1997, March). *Age and gender trends in adults' normative moral reasoning.* Paper presented at the annual meeting of the American Educational Research Association, Chicago.

Leontíev, A. (1981). The problem of activity in psychology. In J. Wertsch (Ed.), *The concept of activity in Soviet psychology* (pp. 37–71). Armonk, NY: Sharpe.

Lepper, M., & Hodell, M. (1989). Intrinsic motivation in the classroom. In C. Ames & R. Ames (Eds.), *Research on motivation in education* (Vol. 3, pp. 73–105). San Diego: Academic Press.

Levin, H. (1988, March). *Structuring schools for greater effectiveness with educationally disadvantaged or at-risk students.* Paper presented at the annual meeting of the American Educational Research Association, San Francisco.

Levine, A., & Nediffer, J. (1996). *Beating the odds: How the poor get to college.* San Francisco: Jossey Bass.

Levitt, M., Levitt, J., Bustos, G., Crooks, N., Santos, J., Telan, P, & Silver, M. (1999, April). *The social ecology of achievement in pre-adolescents: Social support and school attitudes.* Paper presented at the annual meeting of the American Educational Research Association, Montreal.

Lewis, R., & Doorlag, D. (1999). *Teaching special students in general education classrooms.* Upper Saddle River, NJ: Merrill/Prentice Hall.

Lickona, T. (1998). A more complex analysis is needed. *Phi Delta Kappan, 79*(6), 449–454.

Liebert, R. (1986). Effects of television on children and adolescents. *Developmental and Behavioral Pediatrics, 7,* 43–48.

Liebert, R., & Sprafkin, J. (1988). *The early window: Effects of television on children and youth* (3rd ed.). New York: Pergamon.

Light, P., & Mevarech, Z. (1992). Cooperative learning with computers: An introduction. *Learning and Instruction, 2,* 155–159.

Limber, S., Flerx, V., Nation, M., & Melton, G. (1998). Bullying among school children in the United States. In M. Watts (Ed.), *Cross-cultural perspectives on youth and violence.* Stamford, CT: J. I. Press.

Lin, X., Bransford, J., Kantor, R., Hmelo, C., Hickey, D., Secules, T., Goldman, S., Petrosino, A., & the Cognition and Technology Group at Vanderbilt. (1995). Instructional design and the development of learning communities: An invitation to a dialogue. *Educational Technology, 35,* 53–63.

Linn, M., & Burbules, N. (1993). Construction of knowledge and group learning. In K. Tobin (Ed.), *The practice of construction in science education* (pp. 91–119). Washington, DC: American Association for the Advancement of Science.

Linn, M., & Hyde, J. (1989). Gender, mathematics, and science. *Educational Researcher, 18*(8), 17–19, 22–27.

Linn, M., Songer, N., & Eylon, B. (1996). Shifts and convergences in science learning and instruction. In D. Berliner & R Calfee (Eds.), *Handbook of educational psychology* (pp. 438–490). New York: Macmillan.

Linn, R. (1990). Essentials of student assessment: From accountability to instructional aid. *Teachers College Record, 91,* 422–436.

Linn, R., & Gronlund, N. (2000). *Measurement and assessment in teaching* (8th ed.). Upper Saddle River, NJ: Merrill/Prentice Hall.

Lipman, M., Sharp, A., & Oscanyan, F. (1980). *Philosophy in the classroom.* Philadelphia: Temple University Press.

Locke, E., & Latham, G. (1990). *A theory of goal setting and performance.* Upper Saddle River, NJ: Prentice Hall.

Loehlin, J. (1989). Partitioning environmental and genetic contributions to behavioral development. *American Psychologist, 44,* 1285–1292.

Lomax, R. (1994, April). *On becoming assessment literate. Preservice teachers' beliefs and practices.* Paper presented at the annual meeting of the American Educational Research Association, New Orleans.

López, G., & Scribner, J. (1999, April). *Discourses of involvement: A critical review of parent involvement research.* Paper presented at the annual meeting of the American Educational Research Association, Montreal.

Lovett, M., & Anderson, J. (1994). Effects of solving related proofs on memory and transfer in geometry problem solving. *Journal of Experimental Psychology, 20*(2), 366–378.

Loyd, B., & Loyd, D. (1997). Kindergarten through grade 12 standards: A philosophy of grading. In G. Phye (Ed.), *Handbook of classroom assessment,* (pp. 481–490). San Diego: Academic Press.

Lundeberg, M., Bergland, M., Klyczek, K., Mogen, K., Johnson, D., & Harmes, N. (1999). *Increasing interest, confidence, and understanding of ethical issues in science through case-based instruction technologies.* Paper presented at the annual meeting of the American Educational Research Association, Montreal.

Lyman, H. (1991). *Test scores and what they mean* (5th ed.). Upper Saddle River, NJ: Prentice Hall.

Mabry, L. (1999). Writing to the rubric. *Phi Delta Kappan, 80*(9), 673–679.

Maccoby, E. (1992). The role of parents in the socialization of children: An historical overview. *Developmental Psychology, 28,* 1006–1017.

Maccoby, E., & Jacklin, C. (1974). *The psychology of sex differences.* Palo Alto, CA: Stanford University Press.

Mace, F., Belfiore, P., & Shea, M. (1989). Operant theory and research on self-regulation. In B. Zimmerman & D. Schunk (Eds.), *Self-regulated learning and academic achievement: Theory, research, and practice.* New York: Springer-Verlag.

Mace, F., & Kratochwill, T. (1988). Self-monitoring. In J. Witt, S. Elliot, & F. Gresham (Eds.), *Handbook of behavior therapy in education.* New York: Plenum Press.

Machado, L. (1980). *The right to be intelligent.* New York: Pergamon Press.

Macionis, J. (1994). *Sociology* (4th ed.). Upper Saddle River, NJ: Prentice Hall.

Macionis, J. (1997). *Sociology* (5th ed.). Upper Saddle River, NJ: Prentice Hall.

Madaus, G., & O'Dwyner, L. (1999). A short history of performance assessment. *Phi Delta Kappan, 80*(9), 688–695.

Maehr, M. (1976). Continuing motivation: An analysis of a seldom considered educational outcome. *Review of Educational Research, 46,* 443–462.

Maehr, M. (1992, April). *Transforming the school culture to enhance motivation.* Paper presented at the annual meeting of the American Educational Research Association, San Francisco.

Mael, F. (1998). Single-sex and coeducational schooling: Relationships to socioemotional and academic development. *Review of Educational Research, 68*(2), 101–129.

Mager, R. (1962). *Preparing instructional objectives.* Palo Alto, CA: Featon.

Maheady, L., Sacca, M., & Harper, G. (1987). Classwide student tutoring teams: The effects of peer-mediated instruction on the academic performance of secondary mainstreamed students. *Journal of Special Education, 21*(3), 107–121.

Maller, S. (1994, April). *Item bias in the WISC-III with deaf children.* Paper presented at the annual meeting of the National Educational Research Association, New Orleans.

Mamlin, N., & Harris, K. (1998). Elementary teachers' referral to special education in light of inclusion and prereferral: "Every child is here to learn . . . but some of these children are in real trouble." *Journal of Educational Psychology, 90*(3), 385–396.

Mansilla, V., & Gardner, H. (1997). Of kinds of disciplines and kinds of understanding. *Phi Delta Kappan, 78*(5), 381–386.

Mantzicopoulos, P. (1989, April). *Coping with school failure: The relationship of children's coping strategies to academic achievement, self-concept, behavior, and locus of control.* Paper presented at the annual meeting of the American Educational Research Association, San Francisco.

Marcia, J. (1980). Identity in adolescence. In J. Adelson (Ed.), *Handbook of adolescent psychology.* New York: Wiley.

Marcia, J. (1987). The identity status approach to the study of ego identity development. In T. Honess & K. Yardley (Eds.), *Self and identity: Perspectives across the life span.* London: Routledge & Kegan Paul.

Marini, Z., & Case, R. (1994). The development of abstract reasoning about the physical and social world. *Child Development, 65,* 147–159.

Markman, E. (1979). Realizing that you don't understand: Elementary school children's awareness of inconsistencies. *Child Development, 50,* 643–655.

Markman, E., & Gorin, L. (1981). Children's ability to adjust their standards for evaluating comprehension. *Journal of Educational Psychology, 73,* 320–325.

Marks, J. (1995). *Human biodiversity: Genes, race, and history.* New York: Aldine de Gruyter.

Marsh, H. (1989). Age and sex effects in multiple dimensions of self-concept: Preadolescence to early adulthood. *Journal of Educational Psychology, 81,* 417–430.

Marsh, H. (1990). Causal ordering of academic self-concept and academic achievement: A multiwave, longitudinal panel analysis. *Journal of Educational Psychology, 82,* 646–656.

Marsh, H. (1992). Content specificity of relations between academic achievement and academic self-concept. *Journal of Educational Psychology, 84*(1), 34–52.

Marsh, H., & Shavelson, R. (1985). Self-concept: Its multifaceted hierarchical structure. *Educational Psychologist, 20,* 107–123.

Marshall, H. (1992). Seeing, redefining, and supporting student learning. In H. Marshall (Ed.), *Redefining student learning: Roots of educational change* (pp. 1–32). Norwood, NJ: Ablex.

Marshall, H. (1997). Learner-centered psychological principles: Guidelines for teaching of educational psychology in teacher education programs. In N. Lambert & B. McCombs (Eds.), *How students learn: Reforming schools through learner-centered education.* Washington, DC: American Psychological Association.

Marshall, H. (1998). Teaching educational psychology: Learner-centered constructivist perspectives. In. N. Lambert & B. McCombs (Eds.), *How students learn: Reforming schools through learner-centered instruction* (pp. 449–474). Washington, DC: American Psychological Association.

Marso, R., & Pigge, F. (1992, April). *A summary of published research: Classroom teachers' knowledge and skills related to the development and use of teacher-made tests.* Paper presented at the annual meeting of the American Educational Research Association, San Francisco.

Martin, J. (1993). Episodic memory: A neglected phenomenon in the psychology of education. *Educational Psychologist, 28*(2), 169–183.

Maslow, A. (1968). *Toward a psychology of being* (2nd ed.). New York: Van Nostrand.

Maslow, A. (1970). *Motivation and personality* (2nd ed.). New York: Harper & Row. (Original work published 1954)

Maslow, A. (1971). *The farther reaches of human nature.* New York: Viking.

Mason, C., & Kahle, J. (1989). Student attitudes toward science and science-related careers: A program designed to promote a stimulating gender-free learning environment. *Journal of Research in Science Teaching, 26,* 25–40.

Mason, L. (1998). Sharing cognition to construct scientific knowledge in school context: The role of oral and written discourse. *Instructional Science 26,* 359–389.

Matsushashi, A. (1987). *Writing in real time: Modeling production processes.* Norwood, NJ: Ablex.

Matute-Bianchi, M. (1986). Ethnic identities and patterns of school success and failure among Mexican-descent and Japanese American students in a California high school: An ethnographic analysis. *American Journal of Education, 95,* 233–255.

Maxwell, N., Bellisimo, Y., & Mergendoller, J. (1999, April). *Matching the strategy to the students: Why we modified the medical school problem-based learning for high school economics.* Paper presented at the annual meeting of the American Educational Research Association, Montreal.

Mayer, R. (1984). Aids to text comprehension. *Educational Psychologist, 19,* 30–42.

Mayer, R. (1987). *Educational psychology: A cognitive approach.* Boston: Little, Brown.

Mayer, R. (1992). *Thinking, problem solving, cognition* (2nd ed.). New York: Freeman.

Mayer, R. (1996). Learners as information processors: Legacies and limitations of educational psychology's second metaphor. *Educational Psychologist, 31*(4), 151–161.

Mayer, R. (1997). Multimedia learning: Are we asking the right questions? *Educational Psychologist, 32*(1), 1–19.

Mayer, R. (1998a). Cognitive, metacognitive, and motivatinal aspects of problem solving. *Instructional Science, 26,* 49–63.

Mayer, R. (1998b). Cognitive theory for education: What teachers need to know. In N. Lambert & B. McCombs (Eds.), *How students learn: Reforming schools through learner-centered instruction* (pp. 353–378). Washington, DC: American Psychological Association.

Mayer, R. (1999). *The promise of educational psychology: Learning in the content areas.* Columbus OH: Merrill/Prentice Hall.

Mayer, R., & Moreno, R. (1998). A split-attention effect in multimedia learning: Evidence for dual processing systems in working memory. *Journal of Educational Psychology, 90*(2), 312–320.

Mayer, R., & Wittrock, M. (1996). Problem-solving transfer. In D. Berliner & R. Calfee (Eds.), *Handbook of educational psychology* (pp. 47–62). New York: Macmillan.

McCall, R., Appelbaum, M., & Hogarty, P. (1973). Developmental changes in mental performance. *Monographs of the Society for Research in Child Development, 38*(3, Serial No. 150).

McCarthy, S. (1994). Authors, text, and talk: The internalization of dialogue from social interaction during writing. *Reading Research Quarterly, 29,* 201–231.

McCaslin, M., & Good, T. (1992). Compliant cognition: The misalliance of management and instructional goals in current school reform. *Educational Researcher, 21*(3), 4–17.

McClelland, D. (1985). *Human motivation.* Glenview, IL: Scott, Foresman.

McCloskey, M., Caramazza, A., & Green, B. (1980). Curvilinear motion in the absence of external forces: Naive beliefs about the motion of objects. *Science, 210,* 1139–1141.

McCombs, B. (1998). Integrating metacognition, affect, and motivation in improving teacher education. In N. Lambert & B. McCombs (Eds.), *How students learn: Reforming schools through learner-centered education* (pp. 379–408). Washington, DC: American Psychological Association.

McDaniel, E. (1994). *Understanding educational measurement.* Madison, WI: Brown & Benchmark.

McDiarmid, G., Ball, D., & Anderson, C. (1989). Why staying ahead one chapter just won't work: Subject-specific pedagogy. In M. Reynolds (Ed.), *Knowledge base for the beginning teacher* (pp. 193–205). New York: Pergamon Press.

McDougall, D., & Granby, C. (1996). How expectation of questioning method affects undergraduates' preparation for class. *Journal of Experimental Education, 65,* 43–54.

McGreal, T. (1985, March). *Characteristics of effective teaching.* Paper presented at the first annual Intensive Training Symposium, Clearwater, Florida.

McKeachie, W., & Kulik, J. (1975). Effective college teaching. In F. Kerlinger (Ed.), *Review of research in education* (Vol. 3). Washington, DC: American Educational Research Association.

McKinnon, D. (1997, March). *Longitudinal case study of student attitudes, motivation, and performance.* Paper presented at the annual meeting of the American Education Research Association, Chicago. (ERIC No. Ed 408 350)

McLaughlin, H. J. (1994). From negation to negotiation: Moving away from the management metaphor. *Action in Teacher Education, 16*(1), 75–84.

McLoyd, V. (1998). Socioeconomic disadvantages and child development. *American Psychologist, 53,* 185–204.

McMann, R. (1979). In defense of lecture. *Social Studies, 70,* 270–274.

McMillan, J., Workman, D., & Myran, S. (1999, April). *Elementary teachers' classroom assessment and grading practices.* Paper presented at the annual meeting of the American Educational Research Association, Montreal.

McMillen, L. (1997, June 17). Linguists find the debate over "ebonics" uninformed. *Education Week, 43,* p. A16.

McTighe, J. (1996–1997). What happens between assessments? *Educational Leadership, 54*(4), 6–12.

Means, B. (1997). *Critical issue: Using technology to enhance engaged learning for at-risk students* [Online]. Available: http://www.ncrel.org/sdrs/areas/issues/students/atrisk/at400.htm

Means, B., & Knapp, M. (1991). Introduction: Rethinking teaching for disadvantaged students. In B. Means, C. Chelemer, & M. Knapp (Eds.), *Teaching advanced skills to at-risk students* (pp. 1–27). San Francisco: Jossey-Bass.

Mediascope, Inc. (1996). *National television violence study: Executive summary 1994–1995.* Studio City, CA: Author.

Mehrabian, A., & Ferris, S. (1967). Inference of attitude from nonverbal behavior in two channels. *Journal of Consulting Psychology, 31,* 248–252.

Mehrens, W., & Lehmann, I. (1987). *Using standardized tests in education* (4th ed.). White Plains, NY: Longman.

Meichenbaum, D. (1977). *Cognitive behavior modification: An integrative approach.* New York: Plenum Press.

Meltzer, L., & Reid, D. (1994). New directions in the assessment of students with special needs. *Journal of Special Education, 28,* 338–355.

Meng, K., & Patty, D. (1991). Field dependence and contextual organizers. *Journal of Educational Research, 84*(3), 183–190.

Mercer, C., & Mercer, A. (1993). *Teaching students with learning problems* (3rd ed.). New York: Macmillan.

Merrill, P., Hammons, K., Tolman, M., Christensen, L., Vincent, B., & Reynolds, P. (1992). *Computers in education.* Needham Heights, MA: Allyn & Bacon.

Messick, S. (1989). Validity. In R. Linn (Ed.), *Educational measurement* (3rd ed., pp. 13–103). New York: Macmillan.

Messick, S. (1994a). The matter of style: Manifestations of personality in cognition, learning, and teaching. *Educational Psychologist, 29,* 121–136.

Messick, S. (1994b). *Standards of validity and the validity of standards in performance assessment* (RM-94–17). Princeton, NJ: ETS.

Metcalfe, J. (1996). Metacognitive processes. In E. Bjork & R. Bjork (Eds.), *Memory* (pp. 381–407). San Diego: Academic Press.

Mevarech, Z. (1999). Effects of metacognitive training embedded in cooperative settings on mathematical problem solving. *Journal of Educational Research, 92*(4), 195–205.

Meyer, W. (1982). Indirect communications about perceived ability estimates. *Journal of Educational Psychology, 74,* 888–897.

Michaels, S., & O'Connor, M. (1990, Summer). *Literacy as reasoning within multiple discourses: Implications for policy and educational reform.* Paper presented at the Council of Chief State School Officers 1990 Summer Institute.

Mickelson, R., & Heath, D. (1999, April). *The effects of segregation and tracking on African American high school seniors' academic achievement, occupational aspirations, and interracial social networks in Charlotte, North Carolina.* Paper presented at the annual meeting of the American Educational Research Association, Montreal.

Middleton, M., & Midgley, C. (1997). Avoiding the demonstration of lack of ability: An underexplored aspect of goal theory. *Journal of Educational Psychology, 89,* 710–718.

Midgley, C., Arunkumar, R., & Urdan, T. (1996) "If I don't do well tomorrow, there's a reason": Predictors of adolescents' use of academic self-handicapping strategies. *Journal of Educational Psychology, 88*(3), 423–434.

Midgley, C., & Edelin, K. (1998). Middle school reform and early adolescent well-being: The good news and the bad. *Educational Psychologist, 33*(4), 195–206.

Miller, A., & Hom, Jr., H. (1990). Influence of extrinsic and ego incentive value on persistence after failure and continuing motivation. *Journal of Educational Psychology, 82,* 539–545.

Miller, D., Barbetta, P., & Heron, T. (1994). START tutoring: Designing, training, implementing, adapting, and evaluating tutoring programs for school and home settings. In R. Gardner, D. Sianato, J. Cooper, W. Heward, T. Heron, J. Eshleman, & T. Grossi (Eds.), *Behavior analysis in education: Focus on measurably superior instruction* (pp. 265–282). Pacific Grove, CA: Brooks/Cole.

Miller, G. (1956). Human memory and the storage of information. *IRE Transactions of Information Theory, 2–3,* 129–137.

Miller, G. (1990, April). *Critical factors in the design of successful self-instruction with disabled readers.* Paper presented at the annual meeting of the American Educational Research Association, Boston.

Miller, L. (1995). *An American imperative: Accelerating minority educational advancement.* New Haven, CT: Yale University Press.

Miller, P. (1993). *Theories of developmental psychology* (3rd ed.). New York: Freeman.

Miller, S., Leinhardt, G., & Zigmond, N. (1988). Influencing engagement through accommodation: An ethnographic study of at-risk students. *American Educational Research Journal, 25,* 465–487.

Miller, S., & Nelsen, E. (1999, April). *Convergence of possible selves and personal projects among urban high school students.* Paper presented at the annual meeting of the American Educational Research Association, Montreal.

Miserandino, M. (1996). Children who do well in school: Individual differences in perceived competence and autonomy in above-average children. *Journal of Educational Psychology, 88,* 203–214.

Mischel, W. (1993). *Introduction to personality* (5th ed.). Fort Worth, TX: Harcourt Brace Jovanovich.

Mishel, L., & Frankel, D. (1991). *The state of working America: 1990–1991 edition.* Armonk, NY: M. E. Sharpe.

Moerk, E. (1992). *A first language taught and learned.* Baltimore, MD: Paul H. Brookes.

Mohnsen, B. (1997). Stretching bodies and minds through technology. *Educational Leadership, 55*(3), 46–48.

Moles, O. (1992, April). *Parental contacts about classroom behavior problems.* Paper presented at the annual meeting of the American Educational Research Association, San Francisco.

Moll, L. (1992). Funds of knowledge for teaching; Using a qualitative approach to connect homes and classrooms. *Theory Into Practice, 3*(1), 132–141.

Moll, L. (1997, March). *Building bridges: Community curriculum and pedagogy.* Interactive symposium at the annual meeting of the American Educational Research Association: Chicago.

Monroe, S., Goldman, P., & Smith, U. (1988). *Brothers: Black and poor—A true story of courage and survivors.* New York: Morrow.

Montague, M. (1990, April). *Mathematical problem-solving characteristics of middle school students with learning disabilities.* Paper presented at the annual meeting of the American Educational Research Association, Boston.

Moon, S., Zentall, S., Grskovic, J., Hall, A., & Stormont-Spurgin, M. (1997, March). *Social/emotional characteristics of children with AD/HD and giftedness in school and family contexts.* Paper presented at the annual meeting of the American Educational Research Association, Chicago.

Moore, M. (1990). Problem finding and teacher experience. *Journal of Creative Behavior, 24,* 39–58.

Moreland, J., Dansereau, D., & Chmielewski, T. (1997). Recall of descriptive information: The roles of presentation format, annotation strategy, and individual differences. *Contemporary Educational Psychology, 22,* 521–533.

Moreno, R., & Mayer, R. (1998, April). *Learning from multiple representations in a multimedia environment.* Paper presented at the annual meeting of the American Educational Research Association, San Diego.

Moreno, R., & Mayer, R. (1999). Cognitive principles of multimedia learning: The role of modality and contiguity. *Journal of Educational Psychology, 91*(2) 358–368.

Morgan, M. (1984). Reward-induced decrements and increments in intrinsic motivation. *Review of Educational Research, 54,* 5–30.

Morgan, M. (1985). Self-monitoring of attained subgoals in private study. *Journal of Educational Psychology, 77,* 623–630.

Morgan, M. (1987). Self-monitoring and goal setting in private study. *Contemporary Educational Psychology, 12,* 1–6.

Morine-Dershimer, G. (1987). Can we talk? In D. Berliner & B. Rosenshine (Eds.), *Talks to teachers* (pp. 37–53). New York: Random House.

Morrison, G., Lowther, D., & DeMuelle, L. (1999). *Integrating technology into the classroom.* Upper Saddle River, NJ: Merrill/Prentice Hall.

Morrow, L., & Young, J. (1997). A family literacy program connecting school and home: Effects on attitude, motivation, and literacy achievement. *Journal of Educational Psychology, 89*(4), 736–742.

Moss, P. (1992, April). *Shifting conceptions of validity in educational measurement: Implications for performance assessment.* Paper presented at the annual meeting of the American Educational Research Association, San Francisco.

Mullis, I., Dossey, J., Foertsh, M., Jones, L., & Gentile, C. (1991). *Trends in academic progress.* Washington, DC: U.S. Department of Education,

National Center for Education Statistics.

Munk, D., & Bursuck, W. (1997–1998). Can grades be helpful and fair? *Educational Leadership, 55*(4), 44–47.

Murphy, J., Weil, M., & McGreal, T. (1986). The basic practice model of instruction. *Elementary School Journal, 87,* 83–95.

Mwangi, W., & Sweller, J. (1998). Learning to solve compare word problems: The effect of example format and generating self-explanations. *Cognition and Instruction, 16,* 173–199.

Myers, C. (1970). Journal citations and scientific eminence in contemporary psychology. *American Psychologist, 25,* 1041–1048.

Myers, M., & Paris, S. (1978). Children's metacognitive knowledge about reading. *Journal of Educational Psychology, 70,* 680–690.

Nagy-Jacklin, C. (1989). Female and male: Classes of gender. *American Psychologist, 44*(2), 127–133.

Nahmias, M. (1995). Including a child who has ADHD. *Early Childhood Today, 10*(1), 21–22.

Naigles, L., & Gelman, S. (1995). Overextensions in comprehension and production revisited: Preferential looking in a study of dog, cat and cow. *Journal of Child Language, 22,* 19–46.

Nakagawa, K. (1999, April). *Portraits of the schools and communities experiencing student mobility.* Paper presented at the annual meeting of the American Educational Research Association, Montreal.

Narvaez, D. (1998). The influence of moral schemas on the reconstruction of moral narratives in eighth graders and college students. *Journal of Educational Psychology, 90*(1), 13–24.

Narvaez, D., Gleason, T., Mitchell, C., & Bentley, J. (1999). Moral theme comprehension in children. *Journal of Educational Psychology, 91*(3), 477–487.

National Center for Children in Poverty. (1999). *Young children in poverty: A statistical update, June, 1999.*

Columbia University: Joseph Mailmon School of Public Health.

National Center for Educational Statistics. (1992). *Digest of education statistics.* Washington, DC: U.S. Department of Education.

National Center for Research on Teacher Learning. (1993). *Findings on learning to teach.* East Lansing: Michigan State University.

National Commission on Excellence in Education. (1983). *A nation at risk: The imperative for educational reform.* Washington, DC: Government Printing Office.

National Commission on Testing and Public Policy. (1990). *From gatekeeper to gateway.* Chestnut Hill, MA: Boston College Press.

National Council of Teachers of Mathematics. (1989). *Curriculum and evaluation standards for school mathematics.* Reston, VA: Author.

National Council of Teachers of Mathematics. (1991). *Professional standards for teaching mathematics.* Reston, VA: Author.

National Joint Committee on Learning Disabilities. (1994). Learning disabilities: Issues on definition. A position paper of the National Joint Committee on Learning Disabilities. In *Collective perspectives on issues affecting learning disability. Position papers and statements.* Austin, TX: Pro-Ed.

National Public Radio. (1999). *NPR morning edition* [On-line]. Available: http://www.npr.org/programs/morning/kosovo-transcript.031999.html

National Research Council. (1980). *Science and engineering doctorates in the United States.* Washington, DC: National Academy of Sciences.

National Research Council. (1996). *National science education standards.* Washington, DC: National Academy Press.

National Telecommunications and Information Administration. (1999). *Falling through the Net: Defining the digital divide* [Online]. Available: www:Hostname:ntia.doc.gov Directory: /ntiahome/fttn99/contents.html

Needels, M., & Knapp, M. (1994). Teaching writing to children who are underserved. *Journal of Educational Psychology, 86*(3), 339–349.

Neisser, U. (1967). *Cognitive psychology*. New York: Appleton-Century-Crofts.

Nelson, J., Lott, L., & Glenn, S. (1997). *Positive discipline in the classroom* (2nd ed.). New York: Ballantine Books.

Neuman, S. (1999). Learning to read and write: Developmentally appropriate practices for young children. *Reading Teacher, 52*(2), 193–216.

Newby, T., Stepich, D., Lehman, J., & Russell, J. (2000). *Instructional technology for teaching and learning. Designing instruction, integrating computers, and using media.* Upper Saddle River, NJ: Prentice Hall.

Newman, F., Secado, W., & Wehlage, G. (1995). A *guide to authentic instruction and assessment: Vision, standards & scoring.* Madison: University of Wisconsin Center for Education Research.

Newstead, J., Franklyn-Stokes, A., & Armstead, P. (1996) Individual differences in student cheating. *Journal of Educational Psychology, 88*(2), 229–241.

Nicholls, J. (1984). Achievement motivation: Conceptions of ability, subjective experience, task choice, and performance. *Psychological Review, 91,* 328–346.

Nicholls, J., & Miller, A. (1984). Conceptions of ability and achievement motivation. In R. Ames & C. Ames (Eds.)*, Research on motivation in education: Vol. 1. Student motivation* (pp. 39–73). New York: Academic Press.

Nickerson, R. (1986). Why teach thinking? In J. Baron & R. Sternberg (Eds.), *Teaching thinking skills theory and practice* (pp. 27–38). New York: Freeman.

Nickerson, R. (1988). On improving thinking through instruction. In E. Rothkopf (Ed.), *Review of research in education* (pp. 3–57). Washington, DC: American Educational Research Association.

Nieto, S. (1999, April). *Identity, personhood, and Puerto Rican students: Challenging paradigms of assimilation and authenticity*. Paper presented at the annual meeting of the American Educational Research Association, Montreal.

Nilsson, L., & Archer, T. (1989). Aversively motivated behavior: Which are the perspectives? In T. Archer & L. Nilsson (Eds.). *Aversion, avoidance and anxiety*. Hillsdale, NJ: Erlbaum.

Nissani, M., & Hoefler-Nissani, D. (1992). Experimental studies of belief dependence of observations and of resistance to conceptual change. *Cognition and Instruction, 9,* 97–111.

Noblit, G., Rogers, D., & McCadden, B. (1995). In the meantime: The possibilities of caring. *Phi Delta Kappan, 76,* 680–685.

Noddings, N. (1995). Teaching the themes of care. *Phi Delta Kappan, 76,* 675–679.

Noddings, N. (1999, April). *Competence and caring a central to teacher education*. Paper presented at the annual meeting of the American Educational Research Association, Montreal.

Nosofsky, R. (1988). Similarity, frequency, and category representations. *Journal of Experimental Psychology: Learning, Memory & Cognition, 14,* 54–65.

Nottelman, E., & Hill, K. (1977). Test anxiety and off-task behavior in evaluative situations. *Child Development, 48,* 225–231.

Novak, J. D., & Musonda, D. (1991). A twelve-year longitudinal study of science concept learning. *American Educational Research Journal, 28*(1), 117–153.

Novick, L. (1998, April). *Highly skilled problem solvers use example-based reasoning to support their superior performance*. Paper presented at the annual meeting of the American Educational Research Association, San Diego.

Nowell, A. (1997, March). *Trends in gender differences in academic achievement from 1960 to 1994: An analysis of mean differences, variance ratios, and differences in extreme scores*. Paper presented at the annual meeting of the American Educational Research Association, Chicago.

Nucci, L. (1987). Synthesis of research on moral development. *Educational Leadership, 44*(5), 86–92.

Nussbaum, J., & Novick, N. (1982). Alternative frameworks, conceptual conflict, and accommodation: Toward a principled teaching strategy. *Instructional Science, 11,* 183–200.

Nuthall, G. (1999). The way students learn: Acquiring knowledge from an integrated science and social studies unit. *Elementary School Journal, 99*(4), 303–342.

Nyberg, K., McMillin, J., O-Neill-Rood, N., & Florence, J. (1997). Ethnic differences in academic retracking: A four-year longitudinal study. *Journal of Educational Research, 91*(1), 33–41.

Nystrand, M. (1986). *The structure of written communication: Studies in reciprocity between writers and readers.* Orlando, FL: Academic Press.

Nystrand, M., Cohen, A., & Dowling, N. (1992, April). *Reliability of portfolio assessment for measuring verbal outcomes*. Paper presented at the annual meeting of the American Educational Research Association, San Francisco.

Nystrand, M., & Gamoran, A. (1989, March). *Instructional discourse and student engagement*. Paper presented at the annual meeting of the American Educational Research Association, San Francisco.

Oakes, J. (1992). Can tracking research inform practice? *Educational Researcher, 21*(4), 12–21.

O'Brien, T. (1999). Parrot math. *Phi Delta Kappan, 80*(6), 434–438.

O'Brien, V., Kopola, M., & Martinez-Pons, M. (1999). Mathematics self-efficacy, ethnic identity, gender, and career interests related to mathematics and science. *Journal of Educational Research, 92*(4), 231–235.

O'Connor, J., & Brie, R. (1994). Mathematics and science partnerships:

Products, people, performance and multimedia. *Computing Teacher, 22,* 27–30.

O'Donnell, A., & Dansereau, D. (1992). Scripted cooperation in student dyads: A method for analyzing and enhancing academic learning and performance. In R. Hertz-Lazarowitz & N. Miller (Eds.), *Interaction in cooperative groups: The theoretical anatomy of group learning.* Cambridge, MA: Harvard University Press.

O'Donnell, A., & O'Kelly, J. (1994). Learning from peers: Beyond the rhetoric of positive results. *Educational Psychology Review, 6,* 321–349.

Offer, D., Ostrov, E., & Howard, K. (1989). Adolescence: What is normal? *American Journal of Diseases of Children, 14*(3), 731–736.

Office of Bilingual Education and Minority Affairs. (1999). *Facts about limited English proficiency students.* Washington, DC: U.S. Department of Education. [On-line] Available: http://www.ed.gov/offices/OBEMLA/rileyfact.html

Ogbu, J. (1987). Variability in minority school performance: A problem in search of an explanation. *Anthropology and Education Quarterly, 18,* 312–334.

Ogbu, J. (1992). Understanding cultural diversity and learning. *Educational Researcher, 21*(8), 5–14.

Ogbu, J. (1999a). Beyond language: Ebonics, proper English, and identity in a Black-American speech community. *American Educational Research Journal, 36*(2), 147–184.

Ogbu, J. (1999b, April). *The significance of minority status.* Paper presented at the annual meeting of the American Educational Research Association, Montreal.

Ogbu, J., & Simons, H. (1998). Voluntary and involuntary minorities: A cultural-ecological theory of school performance with some implications for education. *Anthropology & Education Quarterly, 29*(2), 155–188.

Ogden, J., Brophy, J., & Evertson, C. (1977, April). *An experimental investigation of organization and management techniques in first-grade reading groups.* Paper presented at the annual meeting of the American Educational Research Association, New York.

Ogle, D. (1986). A teaching model that develops active reading of expository text. *Reading Teacher, 40,* 564–570.

Oka, E., Kolar, R., Rau, C., & Stahl, N. (1997, March). *The dynamic nature of collaboration and inclusion.* Paper presented at the annual meeting of the American Educational Research Association, Chicago.

O'Keefe, P., & Johnston, M. (1987, April). *Teachers' abilities to understand the perspectives of students: A case study of two teachers.* Paper presented at the annual meeting of the American Educational Research Association, Washington, DC.

Okolo, C. (1992). The effect of computer-assisted instruction format and initial attitude on the arithmetic facts proficiency and continuing motivation of students with learning disabilities. *Exceptionality: A Research Journal, 3,* 195–211.

Olsen, D. (1999, April). *Pedagogy that promotes student thinking in constructivist classrooms.* Paper presented at the annual conference of the American Educational Research Association, Montreal.

O'Reilly, T, Symons, S., & MacLatchy-Gaudet, H. (1998). A comparison of self-explanation and elaborative interrogation. *Contemporary Educational Psychology, 23,* 434–445.

Osborne, J. (1996). Beyond constructivism. *Science Education, 80,* 53–81.

Osborne, R., & Freyberg, R. (1985). *Learning science.* Portsmouth, NH: Heinemann.

Oser, F. (1986). Moral education and values education: The discourse perspective. In M. Wittrock (Ed.), *Handbook of research on teaching* (3rd ed., pp. 917–941). New York: Macmillan.

Ovando, C. (1997). Language diversity and education. In J. Banks & C. Banks (Eds.), *Multi-cultural education: Issues and perspectives* (3rd ed., pp. 272–296). Boston: Allyn & Bacon.

Owens, R. (1996). *Language development* (4th ed.). Boston: Allyn & Bacon.

Owston, R., & Wideman, H. (1997). Word processors and children's writing in a high-computer-access setting. *Journal of Research on Computing in Education, 30*(2), 202–217.

Page, E. (1992). Is the world an orderly place? A review of teacher comments and student achievement. *Journal of Experimental Education, 60*(2), 161–181.

Page-Voth, V., & Graham, S. (1999). Effects of goal setting and strategy use on the writing performance and self-efficacy of students with writing and learning problems. *Journal of Educational Psychology, 91*(2), 230–240.

Paivio, A. (1986). *Mental representations: A dual-coding approach.* New York: Oxford University.

Paivio, A. (1991). Dual coding theory: Retrospect and current status. *Canadian Journal of Psychology, 45,* 255–287.

Pajares, F., Miller, M., & Johnston, M. (1999). Gender differences in writing self-beliefs of elementary school students. *Journal of Educational Psychology, 91*(1), 50–61.

Palincsar, A. (1987, April). *Reciprocal teaching: Field evaluations in remedial and content area reading.* Paper presented at the annual meeting of the American Educational Research Association, Washington, DC.

Palincsar, A., & Brown, A. (1984). Reciprocal teaching of comprehension-fostering and comprehension-monitoring activities. *Cognition and Instruction, 2,* 117–175.

Palincsar, A., & Brown, A. (1986). Interactive teaching to promote individual learning from text. *Reading Teacher, 39,* 771–777.

Palincsar, A., & Brown, A. (1987). Advances in improving the cognitive performance of handicapped students. In M. Wang & H. Walberg (Eds.),

Adapting instruction to individual differences. Berkeley, CA: McCutchan.

Palincsar, A., Brown, A., & Martin, S. (1987). Peer interaction in reading comprehension instruction. *Educational Psychologist, 22,* 231–253.

Pallas, A., & Alexander, K. (1983). Sex differences in quantitative SAT performance: New evidence on the differential coursework hypothesis. *American Educational Research Journal, 20,* 165–182.

Pallas, A., Natriello, G., & McDill, E. (1989). The changing nature of the disadvantaged population: Current dimensions and future trends. *Educational Researcher, 18*(5), 16–22.

Papalia, D., & Wendkos-Olds, S. (1996). *A child's world: Infancy through adolescence* (7th ed.). New York: McGraw-Hill.

Paris, S., Wasik, B., & Turner, J. (1991). The development of strategic readers. In R. Barr, M. Kamil, P. Mosenthal, & P. Pearson (Eds.), *Handbook of reading research* (Vol. 2, pp. 609–640). New York: Longman.

Park, C. (1997, March). *A comparative study of learning style preferences: Asian-American and Anglo students in secondary schools.* Paper presented at the annual meeting of the American Educational Research Association, Chicago.

Parke, C., & Lane, S. (1996–1997). Learning from performance assessments in math. *Educational Leadership, 54*(4), 26–29.

Parsons, J., Kaczala, C., & Meece, J. (1982). Socialization of achievement attitudes and beliefs: Classroom influences. *Child Development, 53,* 322–339.

Pashler, H., & Carrier, M. (1996). Structures, processes, and the flow of information. In E. Bjork & R. Bjork (Eds.), *Memory* (pp. 3–29). San Diego: Academic Press.

Pask-McCartney, C. (1989). *A discussion about motivation.* Proceedings of Selected Research Presentations at the Annual Convention of the AECT. (ERIC Document Reproduction No. ED 308816)

Patrick, H., Anderman, L., Ryan, A., Edelin, K., & Midgley, C. (1999, April). *Messages teachers send: Communicating goal orientations in the classroom.* Paper presented at the annual meeting of the American Educational Research Association, Montreal.

Pavlov, I. (1928). *Lectures on conditioned reflexes* (W. Gantt, Trans.). New York: International Universities Press.

Pea, R., Tinker, R., Linn, M., Means, B., Bransford, J., Roschelle, J., Hsi, S., Brophy, S., & Songer, N. (1999). Toward a learning technologies knowledge network. *ETR&D, 47*(2),19–38.

Pearl, R., Farmer, T., Van Acker, R., Rodkin, P., Bost, K., Coe, M., &, Henley, W. (1998). The social integration of students with mild disabilities in general education classrooms: Peer group membership and peer-assessed social behavior. *Elementary School Journal, 99*(2), 167–185.

Peng, S., & Lee, R. (1992, April). *Home variables, parent-child activities, and academic achievement: A study of 1988 eighth graders.* Paper presented at the annual meeting of the American Educational Research Association, San Francisco.

Pennington, B., Groisser, D., & Welsh, M. (1993). Contrasting cognitive deficits in attention deficit disorder versus reading disability. *Developmental Psychology, 29,* 511–523.

Peregoy, S., & Boyle, O. (1997). *Reading, writing, and learning in ESL* (2nd ed.). New York: Longman.

Perkins, D. (1995). *Outsmarting IQ.* New York: Free Press.

Perkins, D., & Blythe, T. (1994). Putting understanding up front. *Educational Leadership, 51,* 4–7.

Perkins, D., & Salomon, G. (1989). Are cognitive skills context-bound? *Educational Researcher, 18,* 16–25.

Perry, M., Vanderstoep, S., & Yu, S. (1993). Asking questions in first-grade mathematics classes: Potential

influences on mathematical thought. *Journal of Educational Psychology, 85*(1), 31–40.

Perry, N. (1998). Young children's self-regulated learning and contexts that support it. *Journal of Educational Psychology, 90*(4), 715–729.

Perry, R. (1985). Instructor expressiveness: Implications for improving teaching. In J. Donald & A. Sullivan (Eds.), *Using research to improve teaching* (pp. 35–49). San Francisco: Jossey-Bass.

Perry, R., Magnusson, J., Parsonson, K., & Dickens, W. (1986). Perceived control in the college classroom: Limitations in instructor expressiveness due to noncontingent feedback and lecture content. *Journal of Educational Psychology, 78,* 96–107.

Peterson, P. (1988). Teachers' and students' cognitional knowledge for classroom teaching and learning. *Educational Research, 17,* 5–14.

Pfannenstiel, J., & Schattgen, S. (1997, March). *Evaluating the effects of pedagogy informed by constructivism: A comparison of student achievement across constructivist and traditional classrooms.* Paper presented at the annual meeting of the American Educational Research Association, Chicago.

Pfiffer, L., Rosen, L., & O'Leary, S. (1985). The efficacy of an all-positive approach to classroom management. *Journal of Applied Behavior Analysis, 18,* 257–261.

Phillips, D. (1990, April). *Parents' beliefs and beyond: Contributions to children's academic self-perceptions.* Paper presented at the annual meeting of the American Educational Research Association, Boston.

Phillips, D. (1995). The good, the bad and the ugly: The many faces of constructivism. *Educational Researcher, 24*(7), 5–12.

Phillips, D. (1996). Rejoinder: Response to Ernst von Glaserfeld. *Educational Researcher, 25*(6), 20.

Phinney, J., & Alipuria, L. (1990). Ethnic identity in college students from four ethnic groups. *Journal of Adolescence, 13,* 171–183.

Phye, G. (1997). Learning and remembering: The basis for personal knowledge construction. In G. Phye (Ed.), *Handbook of academic learning: Construction of knowledge* (pp. 47–64). San Diego: Academic Press.

Piaget, J. (1926). *The language and thought of the child.* New York: Harcourt, Brace & World.

Piaget, J. (1952). *Origins of intelligence in children.* New York: International Universities Press.

Piaget, J. (1959). *Language and thought of the child* (M. Grabain, Trans.). New York: Humanities Press.

Piaget, J. (1932/1965). *The moral judgment of the child.* New York: Free Press. (Original work published 1932)

Piaget, J. (1970). *The science of education and the psychology of the child.* New York: Orion Press.

Piaget, J. (1977). Problems in equilibration. In M. Appel & L. Goldberg (Eds.), *Topics in cognitive development: Vol. 1. Equilibration: Theory, research, and application* (pp. 3–13). New York: Plenum Press.

Pichert, J., & Anderson, R. (1977). Taking different perspectives on a story. *Journal of Educational Psychology, 69,* 309–315.

Pinker, S. (1994). *The language instinct: How the mind creates language.* New York: William Morrow.

Pintrich, P., & Garcia, T. (1991). Student goal orientation and self-regulation in the college classroom. In M. Maehr & P. Pintrich (Eds.), *Advances in motivation and achievement* (Vol. 7, pp. 371–402). Greenwich, CT: JAI Press.

Pintrich, P., Marx, R., & Boyle, R. (1993). Beyond cold conceptual change: The role of motivational beliefs and classroom contextual factors in the process of conceptual change. *Review of Educational Research, 63,* 167–199.

Pintrich, P., & Schrauben, B. (1992). Students' motivational beliefs and their cognitive engagement in academic tasks. In D. Schunk & J. Meece (Eds.),

Students' perceptions in the classroom: Causes and consequences (pp. 149–183). Hillsdale, NJ: Erlbaum.

Pintrich, P., & Schunk, D. (1996). *Motivation in education: Theory, research, and applications.* Upper Saddle River, NJ: Prentice Hall.

Pittman, K., & Beth-Halachmy, S. (1997, March). *The role of prior knowledge in analogy use.* Paper presented at the annual meeting of the American Educational Research Association, Chicago.

Plake, B., & Impara, J. (1997). Teacher assessment literacy: What do teachers know about assessment? In G. Phye (Ed.), *Handbook of classroom assessment,* (pp. 54–70). San Diego: Academic Press.

Pleiss, M., & Feldhusen, J. (1995). Mentors, role models, and heroes in the lives of gifted children. *Educational Psychologist, 30*(3), 159–169.

Pogrow, S. (1990). Challenging at-risk students: Findings from the HOTS Program. *Phi Delta Kappan, 71*(5), 389–397.

Pomplun, M., Capps, L., & Sundbye, N. (1997, March). *Criteria teachers use to score performance items.* Paper presented at the annual meeting of the National Educational Research Association, Chicago.

Popham, J. (1998, April). *Can instructionally focused low-stakes performance tests foster effective classroom instruction?* Paper presented at the annual meeting of the American Educational Research Association, San Diego.

Popham, W. (1995). *Classroom assessment: What teachers need to know.* Boston: Allyn & Bacon

Porche, M., & Ross, S. (1999, April). *Parent involvement in the early elementary grades: An analysis of mothers' practices and teachers' expectations.* Paper presented at the Annual Meeting of the American Educational Research Association, Montreal.

Porter, A. (1989). A curriculum out of balance. *Educational Researcher, 18*(5), 9–15.

Posner, G., Strike, K., Hewson, P., & Gertzog, W. (1982). Accommodation of a scientific conception: Toward a theory of conceptual change. *Science Education, 66,* 211–227.

Pratton, J., & Hales, L. (1986). The effects of active participation on student learning. *Journal of Educational Research, 79,* 210–215.

Prawat, R. (1989). Promoting access to knowledge, strategy, and disposition in students: A research synthesis. *Review of Educational Research, 59,* 1–41.

Premack, D. (1965). Reinforcement theory. In D. Levine (Ed.), Nebraska *Symposium on Motivation* (Vol. 13, pp. 3–41). Lincoln: University of Nebraska Press.

Presidential Task Force on Psychology in Education. (1993). *Learner-centered psychological principles: Guidelines for school redesign and reform.* Washington, DC: American Psychological Association.

Pressley, M., Borkowski, J., & Schneider, W. (1987). Cognitive strategies: Good strategies users coordinate metacognition and knowledge. In R. Vasta & G. Whitehurst (Eds.), *Annals of child development* (Vol. 5, pp. 89–129) Greenwich, CT: JAI Press.

Pressley, M., Harris, K., & Marks, M. (1992). But good strategy users are constructivists! *Educational Psychology Review, 4,* 3–31.

Pressley, M., Johnson, C., Symons, S., McGoldrick, J., & Kurita, J. (1989). Strategies that improve children's memory and comprehension of text. *Elementary School Journal, 90,* 3–31.

Pressley, M., Woloshyn, V., Lysynchuk, L., Martin, V., Wood, E., & Willoughby, T. (1990). A primer of research on cognitive strategy instruction: The important issues and how to address them. *Educational Psychology Review, 2,* 1–58.

Pugach, M., & Wesson, C. (1995). Teachers' and students' views of team teaching of general education and learning-disabled students in two fifth-grade classes. *Elementary School Journal, 95*(3), 279–295.

Pulos, S., & Linn, M. (1981). Generality of the controlling variable scheme in early adolescence. *Journal of Early Adolescence, 1,* 26–37.

Purkey, S., & Smith, M. (1983). Effective schools: A review. *Elementary School Journal, 83,* 427–452.

Purkey, W., & Novak, J. (1984). *Inviting school success* (2nd ed.). Belmont, CA: Wadsworth.

Putnam, R., & Borko, H. (2000). What do new views of knowledge and thinking have to say about research on teacher learning? *Educational Researcher, 29,* 4–15.

Putnam, R., Heaton, R., Prawat, R., & Remillard, J. (1992). Teaching mathematics for understanding: Discussing case studies of four fifth-grade teachers. *Elementary School Journal, 93,* 213–228.

Quin, Z., Johnson, D., & Johnson, R. (1995). Cooperative versus competitive efforts and problem *solving. Review of Educational Research, 65*(2), 129–143.

Radd, T. (1998). Developing an inviting classroom climate through a comprehensive behavior-management plan. *Journal of Invitational Theory and Practice, 5,* 19–30.

Raphael, T., & Pearson, D. (1985). Increasing students' awareness of sources of information for answering questions. *American Educational Research Journal, 22,* 217–236.

Ravetta, M., & Brunn, M. (1995, April). *Language learning, literacy, and cultural background: Second-language acquisition in a mainstreamed classroom.* Paper presented at the annual meeting of the American Educational Research Association, San Francisco.

Reckase, M. (1997, March). *Constructs assessed by portfolios: How do they differ from those assessed by other educational tests?* Paper presented at the annual meeting of the National Educational Research Association, Chicago.

Reed, S., Willis, D., & Guarino, J. (1994). Selecting examples for solving word problems. *Journal of Educational Psychology, 86*(3), 380–388.

Reeve, J., Bolt, E., & Cai, Y. (1999). Autonomy-supportive teachers: How they teach and motivate students. *Journal of Educational Psychology, 91*(3), 537–548.

Reis, S. (1992, April). *The curriculum compacting study.* Paper presented at the annual meeting of the American Educational Research Association, San Francisco.

Reis, S., & Purcell, J. (1992). *An analysis of content elimination and strategies used by elementary classroom teachers in the curriculum compacting process.* Storrs: University of Connecticut, National Research Center on the Gifted and Talented.

Relan, A. (1992). Motivational strategies in computer-based instruction: Some lessons from theories and models of motivation. In *Proceedings of selected research presentations at the annual convention of the AECT.* (ERIC Document Reproduction Service No. ED 348017)

Renkl, A., Stark, R., Gruber, H., & Mandl, H. (1998). Learning from worked-out examples: The effects of example variability and elicited self-explanations. *Contemporary Educational Psychology, 23,* 90–108.

Renzulli, J. (1986). The three-ring conception of giftedness: A developmental model for creative productivity. In R. Sternberg & J. Davidson (Eds.), *Conceptions of giftedness.* Cambridge, MA: Harvard University Press.

Resnick, L. (1987). *Education and learning to think.* Washington, DC: National Academy Press.

Resnick, L., & Klopfer, L. (1989). Toward the thinking curriculum: An overview. In L. Resnick & L. Klopfer (Eds.), *Toward the thinking curriculum: Current cognitive research* (pp. 1–18). Alexandria, VA: Association for Supervision and Curriculum Development.

Rest, J., Narvaez, D., Bebeau, M., & Thoma, S. (1999). A neo-Kohlbergian approach: The DIT and schema theory. *Educational Psychology Review, 11,* 291–324.

Rest, J., Thoma, S., Narvaez, D., & Bebeau, M. (1997). Alchemy and beyond: Indexing the defining issues test. *Journal of Educational Psychology, 89*(3), 498–507.

Reynolds, R., Sinatra, G., & Jetton, T. (1996). Views of knowledge acquisition and representation: A continuum from experience-centered to mind-centered. *Educational Psychologist, 31,* 93–194.

Rich, D. (1987). *Teachers and parents: An adult-to-adult approach.* Washington, DC: National Education Association.

Rickards, J., Fajen, B., Sullivan, J., & Gillespie, G. (1997). Signaling, notetaking, and field independence-dependence in text comprehension and recall. *Journal of Educational Psychology, 89*(3), 508–517.

Rickford, J. (1997). Suite for Ebony and phonics. *Discover, 18*(12), 82–87.

Ridley, D., McCombs, B., & Taylor, K. (1994). Walking the talk: Fostering self-regulated learning in the classroom. *Middle School Journal, 26*(2), 52–57.

Riley, M., Greeno, J., & Heller, J. (1982). The development of children's problem-solving ability in arithmetic. In H. Ginsburg (Ed.), *Development of mathematical thinking.* San Diego: Academic Press.

Riordan, C. (1996). *Equality and achievement: An introduction to the sociology of education.* New York: Longman.

Rittle-Johnson, B., & Alibali, M. (1999). Conceptual and procedural knowledge of mathematics: Does one lead to the other? *Journal of Educational Psychology, 91*(1), 175–189.

Ritts, V., Patterson, M., & Tubbs, M. (1992). Expectations, impressions, and judgments of physically attractive students: A review. *Review of Educational Research, 62,* 413–426.

Roberts, W., Horn, A., & Battistich, V. (1995, March). *Assessing students' and teachers' sense of the school as a caring community.* Paper presented at the annual meeting of the American Educational Research Association, San Francisco.

Robinson, D., Katayama, A., Dubois, N., & Devaney, T. (1998). Interactive effects of graphic organizers and delayed review on concept application. *Journal of Experimental Education, 67*(1), 17–31.

Roblyer, M., & Edwards, J. (2000). *Integrating technology into teaching* (2nd ed.). Upper Saddle River, NJ: Prentice Hall.

Roblyer, M., Edwards, J., & Havriluk, M. (1997). *Integrating technology into teaching.* Upper Saddle River, NJ: Prentice Hall.

Rogers, C. (1963). Actualizing tendency in relation to "motives" and to consciousness. In M. Jones (Ed.), *Nebraska symposium on motivation* (pp. 1–24). Lincoln: University of Nebraska Press.

Rogers, C. (1967). Learning to be free. In C. Rogers & B. Stevens (Eds.), *The problem of being human.* Lafayette, CA: Real People Press.

Rogers, D. (1991, April). *Conceptions of caring in a fourth-grade classroom.* Paper presented at the annual meeting of the American Educational Research Association, Chicago.

Rogoff, B. (1990). *Apprenticeship in thinking: Cognitive development in social context.* New York: Oxford University Press.

Rogoff, B., & Chavajay, P. (1995). What's become of the research on the cultural basis of cognitive development? *American Psychologist, 50,* 859–877.

Rose, L., & Gallup, A. (1999). The 31st annual Phi Delta Kappa/Gallup Poll of the public's attitudes toward the public schools. *Phi Delta Kappan, 81,* 41–56.

Rosen, L., O'Leary, S., Joyce, S., Conway, G., & Pfiffer, L. (1984). The importance of prudent negative consequences for maintaining the appropriate behavior of hyperactive students. *Journal of Abnormal Child Psychology, 12,* 581–604.

Rosenberg, M. (1989). The effects of daily homework assignments on the acquisition of basic skills by students with learning disabilities. *Journal of Learning Disabilities, 22,* 314–323.

Rosenfield, D., Folger, R., & Adelman, H. (1980). When rewards reflect

competence: A qualification of the overjustification effect. *Journal of Personality and Social Psychology, 39,* 368–376.

Rosenfield, P., Lambert, S., & Black, R. (1985). Desk arrangement effects on pupil classroom behavior. *Journal of Educational Psychology,* 77, 101–108.

Rosenshine, B. (1971). *Teaching behaviors and student achievement.* London: National Foundation for Educational Research.

Rosenshine, B. (1979). Content, time, and direct instruction. In P. Peterson & H. Walberg (Eds.), *Research on teaching: Concepts, findings, and implications* (pp. 28–56). Berkeley, CA: McCutchan.

Rosenshine, B. (1983). Teaching functions in instructional programs. *Elementary School Journal, 83,* 335–351.

Rosenshine, B. (1986). Synthesis of research on explicit teaching. *Educational Leadership, 43*(7), 60–69.

Rosenshine, B. (1987). Explicit teaching. In D. Berliner & B. Rosenshine (Eds.), *Talks to teachers.* New York: Random House.

Rosenshine, B. (1997, March). The *case for explicit, teacher-led, cognitive strategy instruction.* Paper presented at the annual meeting of the American Educational Research Association, Chicago.

Rosenshine, B., & Meister, C. (1992, April). *The use of scaffolds for teaching less structured academic tasks.* Paper presented at the annual meeting of the American Educational Research Association, San Francisco.

Rosenshine, B., & Meister, C. (1994). Reciprocal teaching: A review of the research. *Review of Educational Research, 64,* 479–530.

Rosenshine, B., & Stevens, R. (1986). Teaching functions. In M. Wittrock (Ed.), *Handbook of research on teaching* (3rd ed., pp. 376–391). New York: Macmillan.

Ross, S., Smith, L., Loks, L., & McNelie, M. (1994). Math and reading instruction in tracked first-grade

classes. *Elementary School Journal, 95*(2), 105–118.

Rothman, R. (1990). New study confirms income, education linked to parent involvement in schools. *Education Week, 9*(31), 10.

Rothman, R. (1991). Schools stress speeding up, not slowing down. *Education Week, 9*(1), 11, 15.

Rottier, K. (1995, October). If kids ruled the world: Icons. *Educational Leadership, 53*(2), 51–53.

Rowe, M. (1974). Wait-time and rewards as instructional variables, their influence on language, logic, and fate control: Part one—wait time. *Journal of Research in Science Teaching, 11,* 81–94.

Rowe, M. (1986). Wait-time: Slowing down may be a way of speeding up. *Journal of Teacher Education, 37*(1), 43–50.

Rubin, L. (1985). *Artistry in teaching.* New York: McGraw-Hill.

Rutherford, F., & Algren, A. (1990). *Science for all Americans.* New York: Oxford University Press.

Rutter, M., Maughan, B., Mortimore, P., Ouston, J., & Smith, A. (1979). *Fifteen thousand hours.* Cambridge, MA: Harvard University Press.

Ryan, R., & Deci, E. (1998, April). *Intrinsic and extrinsic motivations: Classic definitions and new directions.* Paper presented at the annual meeting of the American Educational Research Association, San Diego.

Ryan, R., Stiller, J., & Lynch, J. (1994). Representations of relationships to teacher, parents, and friends as predictors of academic motivation and self-esteem. *Journal of Early Adolescence, 14,* 226–249.

Sach, J. (1999, March 17). Department issues IDEA regulations. *Education Week, 18*(27), 1, 40.

Sadker, M., & Sadker, D. (1985, March). Sexism in the schoolroom of the 80's. *Psychology Today,* pp. 54–57.

Sadker, M., Sadker, D., & Klein, S. (1991). The issue of gender in elementary and secondary education.

In G. Grant (Ed.), *Review of research in education* (Vol. 17, pp. 269–334). Washington, DC: American Educational Research Association.

Sadker, M., Sadker, D., & Long, L. (1997). Gender and educational equality. In J. Banks & C. Banks (Eds.), *Multicultural education: Issues and perspectives* (3rd ed., pp. 131–149). Boston: Allyn & Bacon.

Sadoski, M., & Goetz, E. (1998). Concreteness effects and syntactic modification in written composition. *Scientific Studies of Reading, 2,* 341–352.

Salmon-Cox, L. (1981). Teachers and standardized achievement tests: What's really happening? *Phi Delta Kappan, 62,* 631–634.

Salomon, G., & Globerson, T. (1989). When teams do not function the way they ought to. *International Journal of Educational Research, 13,* 89–99.

Salvia, J., & Ysseldyke, J. (1988). *Assessment in special and remedial education* (4th ed.). Boston: Houghton Mifflin.

Samuels, S. (1979). The method of repeated readings. *Reading Teacher, 32,* 403–408.

Samuels, S. (1988). Decoding and automaticity: Helping poor readers become automatic at word recognition. *Reading Teacher, 41*(8), 756–760.

Sanders, M., & Jordan, W. (1997, March). *Breaking barriers to student success.* Paper presented at the annual meeting of the American Educational Research Association, Chicago.

Saracho, O., & Spodek, B. (1999). *Families' involvement in their children's literacy development.* Paper presented at the annual meeting of the American Educational Research Association, Montreal.

Scarcella, R. (1990). *Teaching language-minority students in the multicultural classroom.* Upper Saddle River, NJ: Prentice Hall.

Scardamalia, M., Bereiter, C., & Goel, H. (1982). The role of production factors in writing ability. In M. Nystrand (Ed.),

What writers know. New York: Academic Press.

Schab, F. (1991). Odors and remembrance of things past. *Journal of Experimental Psychology: Learning, Memory and Cognition, 17,* 648–655.

Schauble, L. (1990). Belief revision in children: The role of prior knowledge and strategies for generating evidence. *Journal of Experimental Child Psychology, 49,* 31–57.

Scheirer, M., & Kraut, R. (1979). Improving educational achievement via self-concept change. *Review of Educational Research, 49,* 131–150.

Schiff, M., Duyme, M., Dumaret, A., & Tomkiewicz, S. (1982). How much could we boost scholastic achievement and IQ scores? A direct answer from a French adoption agency. *Cognition, 12,* 165–192.

Schmidt, P. (1992). Gap cited in awareness of students' home languages. *Education Week, 11*(32), 11.

Schneider, W., & Shiffrin, R. (1977). Controlled and automatic human information processing: Detection, search, and attention. *Psychological Review, 84,* 1–66.

Schoen, H., Fey, J., Hirsch, C., & Coxford, A. (1999). Issues and options in the math wars. *Phi Delta Kappan, 80*(6), 444–453.

Schoenfeld, A. (1983). Beyond the purely cognitive: Belief systems, social cognitions, and metacognitions as driving forces in intellectual performance. *Cognitive Science, 7,* 329–363.

Schoenfeld, A. (1987). What's all the fuss about metacognition? In A. Schoenfeld (Ed.), *Cognitive science and mathematics education* (pp. 61–88). Hillsdale, NJ: Erlbaum.

Schoenfeld, A. (1988). When good teaching leads to bad results: The disasters of "well-taught" mathematics courses. *Educational Psychologist, 23,* 145–166.

Schoenfeld, A. (1989). Teaching mathematical thinking and problem solving. In L. Resnick & L. Klopfer

(Eds.), *Toward the thinking curriculum: Current cognitive research* (pp. 83–103). Alexandria, VA: Association for Supervision and Curriculum Development.

Schoenfeld, A. (1991). On mathematics as sense-making: An informal attack on the unfortunate divorce of formal and informal mathematics. In. J. Voss, D. Perkins, & J. Segal (Eds.), *Informal reasoning and education* (pp. 311–343). Hillsdale, NJ: Erlbaum.

Schoenfeld, A. (1992a). Learning to think mathematically: Problem solving, metacognition, and sense-making in mathematics. In D. Grouws (Ed.), *Handbook of research on mathematics teaching and learning* (pp. 334–370). New York: Macmillan.

Schoenfeld, A. (1992b). On paradigms and methods: What do you do when the ones you know don't do what you want them to? Issues in the analysis of data in the form of videotapes. *Journal of the Learning Sciences, 2,* 179–214.

Schofield, J., Eurich-Fulcer, R., & Britt, C. (1994). Teachers, computer tutors, and teaching: The artifically intelligent tutor as an agent for classroom change. *American Educational Research Journal, 31*(3), 579–607.

Schommer, M. (1994). An emerging conceptualization of epistemological beliefs and their role in learning. In R. Garner & P. Alexander (Eds.), *Beliefs about text and instruction with test.* Hillsdale, NJ: Earlbaum.

Schon, D. (1983). *The reflective practitioner: How professionals think in action.* New York: Basic Books.

Schraw, G., & Moshman, D. (1995). Metacognitive theories, *Educational Psychology Review, 7,* 351–371.

Schunk, D. (1983). Ability versus effort attributional feedback: Differential effects on self-efficacy and achievement. *Journal of Educational Psychology, 75,* 848–856.

Schunk, D. (1987). Peer models and children's behavioral change. *Review of Educational Research, 57,* 149–174.

Schunk, D. (1994, April). *Goal and self-evaluative influences during children's mathematical skill acquisition.* Paper presented at the annual meeting of the American Educational Research Association, New Orleans.

Schunk, D. (1996). *Learning theories* (2nd ed.). Englewood Cliffs, NJ: Prentice Hall.

Schunk, D. (1997, March). *Self-monitoring as a motivator during instruction with elementary school students.* Paper presented at the annual meeting of the American Educational Research Association, Chicago.

Schunk, D. (2000). *Learning theories* (3rd ed.). Upper Saddle River, NJ: Merrill/Prentice Hall.

Schunk, D., & Ertmer, P. (1999). Self-regulatory processes during computer skill acquisition: Goal and self-evaluative influences. *Journal of Educational Psychology, 91*(2), 251–260.

Schwartz, B. (1990). The creation and destruction of value. *American Psychologist, 45*, 7–15.

Schwartz, B., & Reisberg, D. (1991). *Learning and memory.* New York: Norton.

Schwartz, N., Ellsworth, L., Graham, L., & Knight, B. (1998). Accessing prior knowledge to remember text: A comparison of advance organizers and maps. *Contemporary Educational Psychology, 23*, 65–89.

Seifert, T. (1993). Effects of elaborative interrogation with prose passages. *Journal of Educational Psychology, 85*(4), 642–651.

Seligman, D. (1975). *Helplessness.* San Francisco: Freeman.

Seligman, M. (1995). *The optimistic child.* Boston: Houghton Mifflin.

Selman, R. (1980). *The growth of interpersonal understanding.* New York: Academic Press.

Shaughnessy, M. (1998). An interview with E. Paul Torrance: About creativity. *Educational Psychology Review, 10*(4), 441–452.

Sheldon, K., & Kasser, T. (1995). Coherence and congruence: Two

aspects of personality integration. *Journal of Personality and Social Psychology, 68*, 531–543.

Shepard, L. (1993). Evaluating test validity. In L. Darling-Hammond (Ed.), *Review of research in education* (Vol. 19, pp. 405–450). Washington, DC: American Educational Research Association.

Shepard, L., & Blum, C. (1995). Parents' think about standardized tests and performance assessments. *Educational Research, 24*(5), 25–32.

Sherman, L. (1988). A comparative study of cooperative and competitive achievement in two secondary biology classrooms: The group investigative model versus an individually competitive goal structure. *Journal of Research in Science Teaching, 26*, 55–64.

Shields, P., & Shaver, D. (1990, April). The *mismatch between the school and home cultures of academically at-risk students.* Paper presented at the annual meeting of the American Educational Research Association, Boston.

Short, E., Schatschneider, C., & Friebert, S. (1993). Relationship between memory and metamemory performance: A comparison of specific and general strategy knowledge. *Journal of Educational Psychology, 85*(3), 412–423.

Short, G. (1985). Teacher expectation and West Indian underachievement. *Educational Researcher, 63*, 95–101.

Shuell, T. (1996). Teaching and learning in a classroom context. In D. Berliner & R. Calfee (Eds.), *Handbook of educational psychology* (pp. 726–764). New York: Simon & Schuster.

Shulman, L. (1986). Those who understand: Knowledge growth in teaching. *Educational Researcher, 15*(2), 4–14.

Shulman, L. (1987). Knowledge and teaching: Foundations of the new reform. *Harvard Educational Review, 57*, 1–22.

Shumow, L., & Harris, W. (1998, April). *Teachers' thinking about home-school*

relations in low-income urban communities. Paper presented at the annual meeting of the American Educational Research Association, San Diego.

Sieber, R. (1981). Socialization implications of school discipline, or how first graders are taught to "listen." In R. Sieber & A. Gordon (Eds.), *Children and their organizations: Investigations in American culture* (pp. 18–43). Boston: G. K. Hall.

Siegler, R. (1991). *Children's thinking* (2nd ed.). Upper Saddle River, NJ: Prentice Hall.

Siegler, R., & Ellis, S. (1996). Piaget on childhood. *Psychological Science, 7*, 211–215.

Signorielli, N. (1993). Television, the protrayal of women, and children's attitude. In G. Berry & J. Asamen (Eds.), *Children and television: Images in a changing sociocultural world* (pp. 229–242). Newbury Park, CA: Sage.

Silver, E., Leung, S., & Cai, J. (1992). Solving a nonroutine mathematics problem: An analysis of U.S. students' solution strategies and modes of explanation and a comparison with Japanese students. In J. Becker (Ed.), Report *of US-Japan cross-national research on students' problem-solving behaviors* (pp. 3–23). Carbondale, IL: Southern Illinois University.

Simon, H. (1978). Information-processing theory of human problem solving. In W. Estes (Ed.), *Handbook of learning and cognitive processes: Vol. 5, Human information processing.* Hillsdale, NJ: Erlbaum.

Simon, M. (1993). Prospective elementary teachers' knowledge of division. *Journal for Research in Mathematics Education, 24*, 233–254.

Simpson, E. (1972). *The classification of educational objectives: Psychomotor domain.* Urbana: University of Illinois Press.

Simpson, J., Olejnik, S., Tam, A., & Suprattathum, S. (1994). Elaborative verbal rehearsals and college students' cognitive performance. *Journal of*

Educational Psychology, 86(2), 267–278.

Skaalvik, E., & Valas, H. (1999). Relations among achievement, self-concept, and motivation in mathematics and language arts: A longitudinal study. *Journal of Experimental Education, 67*(2), 135–149.

Skiba, R., & Raison, J. (1990). Relationship between the use of timeout and academic achievement. *Exceptional Children, 57,* 36–47.

Skinner, B. (1953). *Science and human behavior.* New York: Macmillan.

Skinner, B. (1957). *Verbal behavior.* Upper Saddle River, NJ: Prentice Hall.

Skinner, E., & Belmont, M. (1993). Motivation in the classroom: Reciprocal effects of teacher behavior and student engagement across the school year. *Journal of Educational Psychology, 85,* 571–581.

Skoe, E., & Dressner, R. (1994). Ethics of care, justice, identity, and gender: An extension and replication. *Merrill-Palmer Quarterly, 40*(2), 272–289.

Slaby, R., Roedell, W., Arezzo, D., & Hendrix, K. (1995). *Early violence prevention.* Washington, DC: National Association for the Education of Young Children.

Slaughter-Defoe, D., Nakagawa, K., Takanashi, R., & Johnson, D. (1990). Toward cultural/ecological perspectives on schooling and achievement in African and Asian American children. *Child Development,* pp. 363–383.

Slavin, R. (1985). Team-assisted individualization: A cooperative learning solution for adaptive instruction in mathematics. In M. Wang & H. Walberg (Eds.), *Adapting instruction to individual differences.* Berkeley, CA: McCutchan.

Slavin, R. (1987). Ability grouping and student achievement in elementary schools: A best-evidence synthesis. *Review of Educational Research, 57,* 293–336.

Slavin, R. (1995). *Cooperative learning: Theory, research, and practice* (2nd ed.). Needham Heights, MA: Allyn & Bacon.

Slavin, R., & Karweit, N. (1982, April). *School organizational vs. developmental effects on attendance among young adolescents.* Paper presented at the annual meeting of the American Psychological Association, Washington, DC.

Slavin, R., Karweit, N., & Madden, N. (Eds.). (1989). *Effective programs for students at risk.* Needham Heights, MA: Allyn & Bacon.

Slavin, R., Madden, N., Dolan, L., & Wasik, B. (1994). Roots and wings: Inspiring academic excellence. *Educational Leadership, 52,* 10–14.

Slavin, R., Madden, N., Karweit, N., Dolan, L., & Wasik, B. (1992). *Success for all: A relentless approach to prevention and early intervention in elementary schools.* Arlington, VA: Educational Research Service.

Slee, R. (1999). Theorizing discipline—Practical research implications for schools. In H. Freiberg (Ed.), *Beyond behaviorism: Changing the classroom management paradigm* (pp. 21–42). Needham Heights, MA: Allyn & Bacon.

Smith, E., & Anderson, L. (1984). *The planning and teaching intermediate science study: Final report.* East Lansing: Michigan State University Institute for Research on Teaching.

Smith, L., & Cotten, M. (1980). Effect of lesson vagueness and discontinuity on student achievement and attitude. *Journal of Educational Psychology, 72,* 670–675.

Smokowski, P. (1997, April). *What personal essays tell us about resiliency and protective factors in adolescence.* Paper presented at the annual meeting of the American Educational Research Association, Chicago.

Snider, V. (1990). What we know about learning styles from research in special education. *Educational Leadership, 48*(2), 53.

Snow, R. (1992). Aptitude theory: Yesterday, today, and tomorrow. *Educational Psychologist, 27*(1), 5–32.

Snow, R., Corno, L., & Jackson, D., III. (1996). Individual differences in affective and conative functions. In In

D. Berliner & R. Calfee (Eds.), *Handbook of educational psychology* (pp. 243–310). New York: Simon & Schuster Macmillan.

Snyder, S., Bushur, L., Hoeksema, P., Olson, M., Clark, S., & Snyder, J. (1991, April). *The effect of instructional clarity and concept structure on students' achievement and perception.* Paper presented at the annual meeting of the American Educational Research Association, Chicago.

Snyderman, M., & Rothman, S. (1987). Survey of expert opinion on intelligence and aptitude testing. *American Psychologist, 42,* 137–144.

Sokolove, S., Garrett, S., Sadker, M., & Sadker, D. (1990). Interpersonal communication skills. In J. Cooper (Ed.), *Classroom teaching skills* (pp. 185–228). Lexington, MA: Heath.

Spaulding, C. (1992). *Motivation in the classroom.* New York: McGraw-Hill.

Spear-Swerling, L., & Sternberg, R. (1998). Curing our "epidemic" of learning disabilities. *Phi Delta Kappan, 79*(5), 397–401.

Spearman, C. (1927). *The abilities of man: Their nature and measurement.* New York: Macmillan.

Spector, J. (1992). Predicting progress in beginning reading: Dynamic assessment of phonemic awareness. *Journal of Educational Psychology, 84*(3), 353–363.

Spector, J. (1995). Phonemic awareness training: Application of principles of direct instruction. *Reading and Writing Quarterly, 11,* 37–51.

Speidel, G. (1987). Conversation and language learning in the classroom. In K. Nelson & A. Van Kleeck (Eds.), *Children's language* (Vol. 6, pp. 99–135). Hillsdale, NJ: Erlbaum.

Speidel, G., & Tharp, R. (1980). What does self-reinforcement reinforce? An empirical analysis of the contingencies in self-determined reinforcement. *Child Behavior Therapy, 2,* 1–22.

Spillane, J., & Zeuli, J. (1999). Reform and teaching: Exploring patterns of practice in the context of national and

References

state mathematics reforms. *Educational Evaluation and Policy Analysis, 21*(1), 1–27.

Spiro, R., Feltovich, P., Jacobson, M., & Coulson, R. (1992). Knowledge representation, content specification, and the development of skill in situation-specific knowledge assembly: Some constructivist issues as they relate to cognitive flexibility theory and hypertext. In T. Duffy & D. Jonassen (Eds.), *Constructivism and the technology of instruction: A conversation* (pp. 121–127). Hillsdale, NJ: Erlbaum.

Spoeher, K. (1994). Enhancing the acquisition of conceptual structures through hypermedia. In K. McGilly (Ed.), *Classroom lessons: Integrating cognitive theory and classroom practice* (pp. 75–101). Cambridge, MA: MIT Press.

Sprigle, J., & Schoefer, L. (1985). Longitudinal evaluation of the effects of two compensatory preschool programs on fourth- through sixth-grade students. *Developmental Psychology, 21,* 702–708.

Stahl, S. (1999a, Fall). Different strokes for different folks: A critique of learning styles. *American Educator,* pp. 27–31.

Stahl, S. (1999b). Why innovations come and go (and mostly go): The case of whole language. *Educational Researcher, 28*(8), 13–22.

Stahl, S., Duffy-Hester, A., & Stahl, K. (1998). Everything you wanted to know about phonics (but were afraid to ask). *Reading Research Quarterly, 33*(3), 338–355.

Stainback, S, & Stainback, W. (Eds.). (1992). *Curriculum considerations in inclusive classrooms.* Baltimore: Broakes.

Stallings, J. (1980). Allocated academic learning time revisited, or beyond time on task. *Educational Researcher, 9,* 11–16.

Stanovich, K. (1990). Concepts in developmental theory of reading skill: Cognitive resources, automaticity, and modularity. *Developmental Review, 10,* 72–100.

Stecher, B., & Herman, J. (1997). Using portfolios for large-scale assessment. In G. Phye (Ed.), *Handbook of classroom assessment* (pp. 490–514). San Diego: Academic Press.

Stedman, L. (1997). International achievement differences: An assessment of a new perspective. *Educational Researcher, 26*(3), 4–15.

Stein, R. (1983). Hispanic parents' perspectives and participation in their children's special education program: Comparisons by program and race. *Learning Disability Quarterly, 6,* 432–439.

Stein, B. (1989). Memory and creativity. In J. Glover, R. Ronning, & C. Reynolds (Eds.), *Handbook of creativity.* New York: Plenum Press.

Stein, M., & Carnine, D. (1999). Designing and delivering effective mathematics instruction. In R. Stevens (Ed.), *Teaching in American schools* (pp. 245–270). Upper Saddle River, NJ: Merrill/Prentice Hall.

Steinberg, L. (1987). *Pubertal status, hormonal levels, and family relations: The distancing hypothesis.* Baltimore: Society for Research in Child Development.

Steinberg, L., Brown, B., & Dornbusch, S. (1996). Ethnicity and adolescent achievement. *American Education, 28–35,* 44–48.

Steinberg, L., Dornbusch, S., & Brown, B. (1992). Ethnic differences in adolescent achievement. *American Psychologist, 47*(6), 723–729.

Stepien, W., & Gallagher, S. (1993). Problem-based learning: As authentic as it gets. *Educational Leadership, 50*(7), 25–28.

Stern, D. (1997, March). *The role of values conflict in the development of professional attitudes.* Paper presented at the annual meeting of the American Educational Research Association, Chicago.

Stern, E. (1993). What makes certain arithmetic word problems involving the comparison of sets so difficult for children? *Journal of Educational Psychology, 85*(1), 7–23.

Sternberg, R. (1986). *Intelligence applied: Understanding and increasing your intellectual skills.* San Diego, CA: Harcourt Brace Jovanovich.

Sternberg, R. (1988). *The triarchic mind.* New York: Viking.

Sternberg, R. (1989). Intelligence, wisdom, and creativity: Their natures and interrelationships. In R. Linn (Ed.), *Intelligence: Measurement, theory, and public policy* (pp. 119–146). Chicago: University of Illinois Press.

Sternberg, R. (1990). *Metaphors of mind: Conceptions of the nature of intelligence.* New York: Cambridge University Press.

Sternberg, R. (1998a). Applying the triarchic theory of human intelligence in the classroom. In R. Sternberg & W. Williams (Eds.), *Intelligence, instruction, and assessment* (pp. 1–16). Mahway, NJ: Erlbaum.

Sternberg, R. (1998b). Metacognition, abilities, and developing expertise; What makes an expert student? *Instructional Science, 26*(1–2), 127–140.

Sternberg, R. (1998c). Principles of teaching for successful intelligence. *Educational Psychologist, 33*(2/3), 65–72.

Sternberg, R., & Frensch, P. (1993). Mechanisms of transfer. In D. Detterman & R. Sternberg (Eds.), *Transfer on trial: Intelligence, cognition, and instruction.* Norwood, NJ: Ablex.

Sternberg, R., & Grigorenko, E. (1997). Are cognitive styles still in style? *American Psychologist, 52,* 700–712.

Sternberg, R., & Lubart R. (1995). *Defying the crowd.* New York: Free Press.

Sternberg, R., Torff, B., & Grigorenko, E. (1998a). Teaching for successful intelligence raises school achievement. *Phi Delta Kappan, 79*(9), 667–669.

Sternberg, R., Torff, B., & Grigorenko, E. (1998b). Teaching triarchically improves school achievement. *Journal of Educational Psychology, 90*(3), 374–384.

Stevens, R., Hammann, L., & Balliett, T. (1999). Middle school literacy instruction. In R. Stevens (Ed.), *Teaching in American schools* (pp. 221–244). Upper Saddle River, NJ: Merrill/Prentice Hall.

Stevenson, H., Chen, C., & Uttal, D. (1990). Beliefs and achievements: A study of Black, White, and Hispanic children. *Child Development, 61,* 508–523.

Stevenson, H., & Fantuzzo, J. (1986). The generality and social validity of a competency-based self-control training intervention for underachieving students. *Journal of Applied Behavior Analysis, 19,* 269–276.

Stevenson, H., Lee, S., & Stigler, J. (1986). Mathematics achievement of Chinese, Japanese, and American children. *Science, 231,* 693–699.

Stiggins, R. (1997). *Student-centered classroom assessment* (2nd ed.). Upper Saddle River, NJ: Prentice Hall.

Stiggins, R., & Conklin, N. (1992). *In teachers' hands*. Albany: State University of New York Press.

Stiggins, R., Conklin, N., & Bridgeford, N. (1986). Classroom assessment: A key to effective education. *Educational Measurement: Issues and Practice, 5*(2), 5–17.

Stigler, J., Fernandez, C., & Yoshida, M. (1992, August). *Children's thinking during mathematics instruction in Japanese and American elementary school classrooms*. Paper presented at the Seventh International Congress on Mathematical Education, Quebec City, Canada.

Stigler, J., Gonzales, P., Kawanaka, T., Knoll, T., & Serrano, A. (1999). *The TIMSS videotape classroom study: Methods and finding from an exploratory research project on eighth-grade mathematics instruction in Germany, Japan, and the United States* (NCES 990074). Washington, DC: U.S. Department of Education, National Center for Educational Statistics.

Stigler, J., & Stevenson, H. (1991). How Asian teachers polish each lesson to perfection. *American Educator, 15,* 12–20, 43–47.

Stipek, D. (1984). The development of achievement motivation. In R. Ames & C. Ames (Eds.), *Research on motivation in education: Vol. 1. Student motivation*. San Diego: Academic Press.

Stipek, D. (1996). Motivation and instruction. In D. Berliner & R. Calfee (Eds.), *Handbook of Educational Psychology* (pp. 85–113). New York: Macmillan.

Stipek, D. (1998). *Motivation to learn* (3rd ed.). Needham Heights, MA: Allyn & Bacon.

Stipek, D., & Gralinski, H. (1991, April). *Gender differences in children's achievement-related beliefs and emotional responses to success and failure in math*. Paper presented at the annual meeting of the American Educational Research Association, Boston.

Stoddart, T. (1999, April). *Language acquisition through science inquiry*. Symposium presented at the annual meeting of the American Educational Research Association, Montreal.

Stoddart, T., Connell, M., Stofflett, R., & Peck, D. (1993). Reconstructing elementary teacher candidates' understanding of mathematics and science content. *Teaching and Teacher Education, 9,* 229–241.

Stodolsky, S. (1988). *The subject matters: Classroom activity in math and social studies*. Chicago: University of Chicago Press.

Stowe, C. (1992, April). *At-risk language-minority preschool children*. Paper presented at the annual meeting of the American Educational Research Association, San Francisco.

Strage, A., & Brandt, T. (1999). Authoritative parenting and college students' academic adjustment and success. *Journal of Educational Psychology, 91*(1), 146–156.

Streitmatter, J. (1997). An exploratory study of risk-taking and attitudes in a girls-only middle school math class. *Elementary School Journal, 98*(1), 15–26.

Strickland, B. B., & Turnbull, A. P. (1990). *Developing and implementing individualized education programs* (3rd ed.). Upper Saddle River, NJ: Merrill/Prentice Hall

Strom, B. (1990, April). *Teacher perceptions of talented and gifted minority children: An exploration*. Paper presented at the annual meeting of the American Educational Research Association, Boston.

Strom, S. (1989). The ethical dimension of teaching. In M. Reynolds (Ed.), *Knowledge base for the beginning teacher* (pp. 267–276). New York: Pergamon Press.

Stull, J. (1998, April). *Identification and analysis of school characteristics that are effective in fostering educational resilience in students*. Paper presented at the annual meeting of the American Educational Research Association, San Diego.

Subotnik, R. (1997). Teaching gifted students in a multicultural society. In J. Banks & C. Banks (Eds.), *Multicultural education: Issues and perspective* (3rd ed., pp. 361–382) Boston: Allyn & Bacon.

Sudweeks, R., Baird, J., & Petersen, G. (1990, April). *Test-wise responses of third-, fifth-, and sixth-grade students to clued and unclued multiple-choice science items*. Paper presented at the annual meeting of the American Educational Research Association, Boston.

Summers, J. (1990–1991). Effect of interactivity upon student achievement, completion intervals, and affective perceptions. *Journal of Educational Technology Systems, 19,* 53–57.

Sunai, C., & Haas, M. (1993). *Social studies and the elementary/middle school student*. New York, Harcourt Brace Jovanovich.

Swanson, H., & Hoskyn, M. (1998). Experimental intervention research on students with learning disabilities: A meta-analysis of treatment outcomes. *Review of Educational Research, 68*(3), 277–321.

Sweller, J., van Merrienboer, J., & Paas, F. (1998). Cognitive architecture and instructional design. *Educational Psychology Review, 10,* 251–196.

Swialth, M., & Benbow, C. (1991). Ten-year longitudinal follow-up of ability-match accelerated and unaccelerated gifted students. *Journal of Educational Psychology, 83*(4), 528–538.

Tan, A., & Nicholson, T. (1997). Flashcards revisited: Training poor readers to read words faster improves their comprehension of text. *Journal of Educational Psychology, 89*(2), 276–288.

Taylor, B., & Beach, R. (1984). The effects of text structure instruction on middle-grade students' comprehension and production of expository text. *Reading Research Quarterly, 19,* 134–146.

Taylor, J. (1983). Influence of speech variety on teachers' evaluation of reading comprehension. *Journal of Educational Psychology, 75,* 662–667.

Taylor, R. (1987, March). *Knowledge for critical thinking.* Paper presented at the meeting of the Near East South Asia Council for Overseas Schools, Nairobi, Kenya.

Tennyson, R., & Cocchiarella, M. (1986). An empirically based instructional design theory for teaching concepts. *Review of Educational Research, 56,* 40–71.

Terman, L., Baldwin, B., & Bronson, E. (1925). Mental and physical traits of a thousand gifted children. In L. Terman (Ed.), *Genetic studies of genius* (Vol. 1). Stanford, CA: Stanford University Press.

Terman, L., & Oden, M. (1947). The gifted child grows up. In L. Terman (Ed.), *Genetic studies of genius* (Vol. 4). Stanford, CA: Stanford University Press.

Terman, L., & Oden, M. (1959). The gifted group in mid-life. In L. Terman (Ed.), *Genetic studies of genius* (Vol. 5). Stanford, CA: Stanford University Press.

Terwilliger, J. (1997). Semantics, psychometrics, and assessment reform: A close look at "authentic assessments." *Educational Researcher, 26,* 24–27.

Tharp, R. (1989). Psychocultural variables and constants: Effects on teaching and learning in schools. *American Psychologist, 44*(2), 349–359.

Thoma, S., & Rest, J. (1996, April). *The relationship between moral decision-making and patterns of consolidation and transition in moral judgment development.* Paper presented at the annual meeting of the American Educational Research Association, New York.

Thomas, E., & Robinson, H. (1972). *Improving reading in every class: A source book for teachers.* Needham Heights, MA: Allyn & Bacon.

Thorkildsen, T. (1996, April). *The way tests teach: Children's theories of how much testing is fair in school.* Paper presented at the annual meeting of the National Educational Research Association, New York.

Thorndike, E. (1924). Mental discipline in high school studies. *Journal of Educational Psychology, 15,* 1–2, 83–98

Thorndike, R., Hagen, E., & Sattler, J. (1986). *The Stanford-Binet intelligence scale* (4th ed.). Chicago: Riverside.

Thornton, M., & Fuller, R. (1981). How do college students solve proportion problems? *Journal of Research in Science Teaching, 18,* 335–340.

Tierney, R., Readence, J., & Dishner, E. (1990). *Reading strategies and practices: A compendium* (3rd ed.). Boston: Allyn & Bacon.

Tingle, J., & Good, R. (1990). Effects of cooperative grouping on stoichiometric problem solving in high school chemistry. *Journal of Research in Science Teaching, 27,* 671–683.

Tishman, S., Perkins, D., & Jay, E. (1995). *The thinking classroom: Learning and teaching in a culture of thinking.* Needham Heights, MA: Allyn & Bacon.

Tobias, S., & Everson, H. (1998, April). *Research on the assessment of metacognitive knowledge monitoring.* Paper presented at the annual meeting of the American Educational Research Association, San Diego.

Tom, A. (1984). *Teaching as a moral craft.* London: Longman.

Tomasello, M. (1995). Language is not an instinct. *Cognitive Development, 10,* 131–156.

Tomlinson, C. (1995). Deciding to differentiate instruction in middle school: One school's journey. *Gifted Child Quarterly, 39*(2), 77–87,

Tomlinson, C., Callahan, C., & Lelli, K. (1997). Challenging expectations: Case studies of high-potential, culturally diverse young children. *Gifted Child Quarterly, 41*(2), 5–17.

Tomlinson, C., Callahan, C., & Moon, T. (1998, April). *Teachers learning to create environments responsive to academically diverse classroom populations.* Paper presented at the annual meeting of the American Educational Research Association, San Diego.

Tompkins, G. (1997). *Literacy for the twenty-first century.* Upper Saddle River, NJ: Merrill/Prentice Hall.

Top, B., & Osgthorpe, R. (1987). Reverse-role tutoring: The effects of handicapped students tutoring regular class students. *Elementary School Journal, 87*(4), 413–423.

Torrance, E. (1983). Status of creative women past, present, future. *Creative Child and Adult Quarterly, 8,* 135–144.

Torrance, E. (1995). Insights about creativity: Questioned, rejected, ridiculed, ignored. *Educational Psychology Review, 7*(3), 313–322.

Trawick-Smith, J. (1997). *Early childhood development: A multicultural perspective.* Upper Saddle River, NJ: Merrill/Prentice Hall.

Treffinger, D.(1998). From gifted education to programming for talent development. *Phi Delta Kappan, 79*(10), 752–756.

Triandis, H. (1995). *Individualism and collectivism.* Boulder, CO: Westview Press.

Troia, G. (1999). Phonological awareness intervention research: A critical review of the experiemental methodology. *Reading Research Quarterly, 34*(1), 28–52.

Trujillo, C. (1986). A comparative examination of classroom interactions between professors and minority and non-minority college students. *American Educational Research Journal, 23,* 629–642.

Trusty, J., & Pirtle, T. (1998). Parents' transmission of educational goals to their adolescent children. *Journal of Research and Development in Education, 32*(1), 53–65.

Tuckman, B. (1998). Using tests as an incentive to motivate procrastinators to study. *Journal of Experimental Education, 66*(2), 141–147.

Tulving, E. (1979). Relation between encoding specificity and level of processing. In L. Cermak & F. Craik (Eds.), *Levels of processing and human memory* (pp. 405–428). Hillsdale, NJ: Erlbaum.

Tuovinen, J., & Sweller, J. (1999). A comparison of cognitive load associated with discovery learning and worked examples. *Journal of Educational Psychology, 91*(2), 334–341.

Turiel, E. (1973). Stage transitions in moral development. In R. Travers (Ed.), *Second handbook of research on teaching* (pp. 732–758). Chicago: Rand McNally.

Turnbull, A., Turnbull, H. R., Shank, M., & Leal, D. (1999). *Exceptional lives* (2nd ed.). Upper Saddle River, NJ: Merrill/Prentice Hall.

Turner, J. (1995). The influence of classroom contexts on young children's motivation for literacy. *Reading Research Quarterly, 30,* 410–441.

Turner, S., & Dipinto, V. (1997). Peer collaboration in a hypermedia learning environment. *Journal of Research on Computing in Education, 29,* 392–407.

Tyler, R. (1950). *Basic principles of curriculum and instruction.* Chicago: University of Chicago Press.

U.S. Bureau of the Census. (1996). *Statistics.* Washington, DC: Author.

U.S. Congress. (1975). *Public Law 94–142, the Individuals With Disabilities Education Act IDEA* 1975.

U.S. Congress. (1978). *Educational Amendment of 1978, P.L. 95–561, IX(A).*

U.S. Department of Commerce. (1998). *Current population survey, 1997.* Washington, DC: Bureau of the Census.

U.S. Department of Education. (1993). *Fifteenth annual report to Congress on the implementation of the Individuals with Disabilities Act.* Washington, DC: Government Printing Office.

U.S. Department of Education. (1994). *Sixteenth annual report to Congress on the implementation of the Individ-uals with Disabilities Act.* Washington, DC: Government Printing Office.

U.S. Department of Education. (1996a). *Eighteenth annual report to Congress on the implementation of the Individuals with Disabilities Act.* Washington, DC: Government Printing Office.

U.S. Department of Education. (1996b). *To assure the free appropriate public education of all children with disabilities: Eighteenth annual report to Congress on the Implementation of the Individuals with Disabilities Education Act.* Washington, DC: U.S. Department of Education.

U.S. Department of Education. (1996c). *Youth indicators, 1996.* Washington, DC: National Center for Educational Statistics.

U.S. Department of Education. (1997). *Nineteenth annual report to Congress on the implementation of the Individuals with Disabilities Act.* Washington, DC: Government Printing Office.

U.S. Department of Education. (1998). *Advanced telecommunication in U.S.: Public school survey.* Washington, DC: National Center for Educational Statistics.

U.S. Department of Education. (1999). *Twentieth annual report to Congress on the implementation of the Individuals with Disabilities Act.* Washington, DC: Government Printing Office.

U.S. Department of Health and Human Services. (1998). *Annual vital statistics report.* Washington, DC: Author.

Urdan, T., & Maehr, M. (1995). Beyond a two-goal theory of motivation and achievement: A case for social goals. *Review of Educational Research, 65,* 213–243.

Urdan, T., & Paris, S. (1991). Teachers' perceptions of standardized achievement tests. *Educational Policy, 8*(2) 137–156.

Vaillant, B., & Vaillant, C. (1990). Natural history of male psychological health, XII: A 45–year study of predictors of successful aging. *American Journal of Psychiatry, 147,* 31–37.

Valencia, S., & Place, N. (1994). Literacy portfolios for teaching, learning, and accountability: The Bellevue Literacy assessment project. In S. Valencia, E. Hiebert, P. Afflerbach (Eds.), *Authentic reading assessment: Practices and possibilities* (pp. 134–156). Newark, DE: International Reading Association.

Vallerand, R., & Reid, G. (1984). On the causal effects of perceived competence on intrinsic motivation: A test of cognitive evaluation theory. *Journal of Sport Psychology, 6,* 94–102.

Vanderstoep, S., & Seifert, C. (1994). Problem solving, transfer, and thinking. In P. Pintrich, D. Brown, & C. Weinstein (Eds.), *Student motivation, cognition, and learning* (pp. 27–49). Hillsdale, NJ: Erlbaum.

Van Haneghan, J., Barron, L., Young, M., Williams, S., Vye, N., & Bransford, J. (1992). The Jasper series: An experiment with new ways to enhance mathematical thinking. In D. Halpern (Ed.), *Enhancing thinking skills in the sciences and mathematics* (pp. 15–38). Hillsdale, NJ: Erlbaum.

Van Horn, R. (1996). Kids, tools, and Ray Bradbury's basement. *Phi Delta Kappan, 78,* 97–98.

Van Horn, R. (1997). Bad ideas: Technology integration and job-entry skills. *Phi Delta Kappan, 78,* 417–418.

Van Leuvan, P., Wang, M., & Hildebrandt, L. (1990, April). *Students' use of self-instructive processes in the first and second grade.* Paper presented at the annual meeting of the American Educational Research Association, Boston.

Vaughn, S., McIntosh, R., Spencer, R., & Rowe, T. (1990, April). *Increasing peer acceptance with low-accepted LD students: An intervention model.* Paper presented at the annual meeting of the American Educational Research Association, Boston.

Veenman, S. (1984). Perceived problems of beginning teachers. *Review of Educational Research, 54,* 143–178.

Verschaffel, L., De Corte, E., & Lasure, S. (1994). Realistic considerations in mathematical modeling of school arithmetic word problems. *Learning and Instruction, 4,* 273–294.

Villasenor, A., & Kepner, H. (1993). Arithmetic from a problem-solving perspective: An urban implementation. *Journal of Research in Mathematics Education, 24,* 62–69.

Villegas, A. (1991). *Culturally responsive pedagogy for the 1990s and beyond.* Princeton, NJ: Educational Testing Service.

Vine, I. (1986). Moral maturity in socio-cultural perspective: Are Kohlberg's stages universal? In S. Modgil & C. Modgil (Eds.), *Lawrence Kohlberg: Consensus and controversy* (pp. 431–450). Philadelphia, Falmer Press.

Volker, R. (1992). *Applications of constructivist theory to the use of hypermedia. Proceedings of Selected Research Presentations at the Annual Convention of the AECT.* (ERIC Document Reproduction No. ED 348037)

Voss, J. (1987). Learning and transfer in subject-matter learning: A problem-solving model. *International Journal of Educational Research, 11,* 607–622.

Voss, J., & Wiley, J. (1995). Acquiring intellectual skills. *Annual Review of Psychology, 46,* 155–181.

Vygotsky, L. (1978). *Mind in society: The development of higher psychological processes* (M. Cole, V. John-Steiner, S. Scribner, & E. Souberman, Eds. & Trans.). Cambridge, MA: Harvard University Press.

Vygotsky, L. (1986). *Thought and language.* Cambridge: MIT Press.

Wade, S. (1992). How interest affects learning from text. In K. Renniger, S. Hidi, & A. Krapp (Eds.), *The role of interest in learning and development* (pp. 531–553). Hillsdale, NJ: Erlbaum.

Wade, S., Schraw, G., Buxton, W., & Hayes, M. (1993). Seduction of the strategic reader: Effects of interest on strategies and recall. *Reading Research Quarterly, 28,* 3–24.

Wadsworth, B. (1996). *Piaget's theory of cognitive and affective development* (5th ed.). White Plains, NY: Longman.

Wagner, R., & Sternberg, R. (1985). Practical intelligence in real-world pursuits: The role of tacit knowledge.

Journal of Personality and Social Psychology, 52, 1236–1247.

Walberg, H. (1984). Improving the productivity of America's schools. *Educational Leadership, 41*(8), 19–27.

Walberg, H. (1991). Improving school science in advanced and developing countries. *Review of Educational Research, 61,* 25–70.

Walberg, H., Paschal, R., & Weinstein, T. (1985). Homework's powerful effects on learning. *Educational Leadership, 42*(7), 76–79.

Walczyk, J., & Hall, V. (1989). Is the failure to monitor comprehension an instance of cognitive impulsivity? *Journal of Educational Psychology, 81,* 294–298.

Walker, D., Greenwood, C., Hart, B., & Carta, J. (1994). Prediction of school outcomes based on early language production and socioeconomic factors. *Child Development, 65,* 606–621.

Walker, H., & Bullis, M. (1991). Behavior disorder and the social context of regular class integration: A conceptual dilemma. In J. Lloyd, N. Singh, & A. Repp (Eds.), *The regular education initiative: Alternative perspectives on concepts, issues, and models* (pp. 75–94). Sycamore, IL: Sycamore

Walker, J. (1996). *The psychology of learning: Principles and processes.* Upper Saddle River, NJ: Prentice Hall.

Wall, S. (1983). Children's self-determination of standards in reinforcement contingencies: A re-examination. *Journal of School Psychology, 21,* 123–131.

Wallace, D., West, S., Ware, A., & Dansereau, D. (1998). The effect of knowledge maps that incorporate gestalt principles on learning. *Journal of Experimental Education, 67*(1), 5–16.

Walsh, D. (1991). Extending the discourse on developmental appropriateness: A developmental perspective. *Early Education and Development, 2*(2), 109–119.

Walters, G., & Grusec, J. (1977). *Punishment.* San Francisco: Freeman.

Walton, P., Kuhlman, N., & Cortez, J. (1998, April). *Preparing teachers for*

linguistically and culturally diverse learners: The case for developmental evaluation. Paper presented at the annual meeting of the American Educational Research Association, San Diego.

Walton, S., & Taylor, K. (1996–1997). How did you know the answer was boxcar? *Educational Leadership, 54*(4), 38–40.

Wang, M., Haertel, G., & Walberg, H. (1993). Toward a knowledge base for school learning. *Review of Educational Research, 63*(3), 249–294.

Wang, M., Haertel, G., & Walberg, H. (1995, April). *Educational resilience: An emerging construct.* Paper presented at the annual meeting of the American Educational Research Association, San Francisco.

Wapner, S., & Demick, J. (Eds.). (1991). *Field dependence–independence: Cognitive style across the life span.* Hillsdale, NJ: Erlbaum.

Ward, T., Ward, S., Landrum, M., & Patton, J. (1992, April). *Examination of a new protocol for the identification of at-risk gifted learners.* Paper presented at the annual meeting of the American Educational Research Association, San Francisco.

Washington, V., & Miller-Jones, D. (1989). Teacher interactions with non-Standard-English speakers during reading instruction. *Contemporary Child Psychology, 14,* 280–312.

Wasserstein, P. (1995). What middle schoolers say about their schoolwork. *Educational Leadership, 53*(1), 41–43.

Waterman, A. (1985). Identity in the context of adolescent psychology. *New Directions for Child Development, 30,* 5–24.

Watson, B., & Konicek, R. (1990). Teaching for conceptual change: Confronting children's experience. *Phi Delta Kappan, 71,* 680–685.

Wattenmaker, W., Dewey, G., Murphy, T., & Medin, D. (1986). Linear separability and concept learning: Context, relational properties, and concept naturalness. *Cognitive Psychology, 18,* 158–194.

Waxman, H., & Huang, S. (1996). Motivation and learning environment differences in inner-city middle school students. *Journal of Educational Research, 90*(2), 93–102.

Waxman, H., Huang, S., Anderson, L., & Weinstein, T. (1997). Classroom process differences in inner-city elementary schools. *Journal of Educational Research, 91*(1), 49–59.

Wayson, W., & Lasley, T. (1984). Climates for excellence: Schools that foster self-discipline. *Phi Delta Kappan, 65,* 419–421.

Weaver, L., & Padron, Y. (1997, March). *Mainstream classroom teachers' observations of ESL teachers' instruction.* Paper presented at the annual meeting of the American Educational Research Association, Chicago.

Webb, N. (1991). Task-related verbal interaction and mathematics learning in small groups. *Journal of Research in Mathematics Education, 22,* 366–389.

Webb, N., & Farivar, S. (1994). Promoting helping behavior in cooperative small groups in middle school mathematics, *American Educational Research Journal, 31*(2), 369–395.

Webb, N., & Palincsar, A. (1996). Group processes in the classroom. In D. Berliner & R. Calfee (Eds.), *Handbook of educational psychology* (pp. 841–876). New York: Macmillan.

Wechsler, D. (1991). The *Wechsler intelligence scale for children—Third edition—WISC-III.* San Antonio, TX: Psychological Corporation.

Weiland, A., & Coughlin, R. (1979). Self-identification and preferences: A comparison of White and Mexican American first and third graders. *Journal of Social Psychology, 10,* 356–365.

Weinberg, R. (1989). Intelligence and IQ. *American Psychologist, 44,* 98–104.

Weiner, B. (1990). History of motivational research in education. *Journal of Educational Psychology, 82,* 616–622.

Weiner, B. (1992). *Human motivation: Metaphors, theories, and research.* Newbury Park, CA: Sage.

Weiner, B. (1994a). Ability versus effort revisited: The moral determinants of achievement evaluation and achievement as a moral system. *Educational Psychologist, 29,* 163–172.

Weiner, B. (1994b). Integrating social and personal theories of achievement striving. *Review of Educational Research, 64,* 557–573.

Weinert, F., & Helmke, A. (1995). Interclassroom differences in instructional quality and interindividual differences in cognitive development. *Educational Psychologist, 30,* 15–20.

Weinert, F., & Helmke, A. (1998). The neglected role of individual differences in theoretical models of cognitive development. *Learning and Instruction, 8*(4), 309–324.

Weinstein, C. (1994). Strategic learning/strategic teaching: Flip sides of a coin. In P. Pintrich, D. Brown, & C. Weinstein (Eds.), *Student motivation, cognition, and learning* (pp. 257–273). Hillsdale, NJ: Erlbaum.

Weinstein, C., & Mignano, A. (1993). *Elementary classroom management.* New York: McGraw-Hill.

Weinstein, C., Woolfolk, A., Dittmeier, L., & Shankar, U. (1994). Protector or prison guard? Using metaphors and media to explore student teachers' thinking about classroom management. *Action in Teacher Education, 16*(1), 41–54.

Weinstein, R. (1998). Promoting positive expectations in schooling. In N. Lambert & B. McCombs (Eds.), *How students learn: Reforming schools through learner-centered education* (pp. 81–111). Washington, DC: American Psychological Association.

Weller, H. (1997, March). *What have we learned from 8 years of research on computer-based science learning? An analysis of 50 research papers.* Paper presented at the annual meeting of the American Educational Research Association, Chicago.

Wentzel, K. (1999). Social influences on school adjustment: Commentary. *Educational Psychologist, 34*(1), 59–69.

Wentzel, K., & Wigfield, A. (1998). Academic and social motivational influences on students' academic performance. *Educational Psychology Review, 10,* 155–175.

Werts, M., Caldwell, N., & Wolery, M. (1996). Peer modeling of response chains: Observational learning by students with disabilities. *Journal of Applied Behavior Analysis, 29,* 53–66.

West, J. (1997, March). *Motivation and access to help: The influence of status on one child's motivation for literacy learning.* Paper presented at the annual meeting of the American Educational Research Association, Chicago.

Wharton-McDonald, R., Pressley, M., & Hampston, J. (1998). Literacy instruction in nine first-grade classrooms: Teacher characteristics and student achievement. *Elementary School Journal, 99*(2), 101–128.

Whimbey, A. (1980). Students can learn to be better problem solvers. *Educational Leadership, 37,* 560–565.

White, A., & Bailey, J. (1990). Reducing disruptive behaviors of elementary physical education students with sit and watch. *Journal of Applied Behavior Analysis, 23,* 353–359.

White, R. (1959). Motivation reconsidered: The concept of competence. *Psychological Review, 66,* 297–333.

Whitehurst, G., Crone, D., Zevenbergen, A., & Schultz, M. (1999). Outcomes of an emergent literacy intervention from Head Start through second grade. *Journal of Educational Psychology, 91*(2), 261–272.

Wigfield, A., & Eccles, J. (1989). Test anxiety in elementary and secondary school students. *Educational Psychologist, 24,* 159–183.

Wigfield, A., Eccles, J., & Pintrich, P. (1996). Development between the ages of 11 and 25. In D. Berliner & R. Calfee (Eds.), *Handbook of educational psychology* (pp. 148–185). New York: Macmillan.

Wiggins, G. (1996–1997). Practicing what we preach in designing authentic assessment. *Educational Leadership, 54*(4), 18–25.

Wiley, D., & Harnischfeger, A. (1974). Explosion of a myth: Quantity of schooling and exposure to instruction, major education vehicles. *Education Researcher, 3,* 7–12.

Wiley, J., & Voss, J. (1999). Constructing arguments from multiple sources: Tasks that promote understanding and not just memory for text. *Journal of Educational Psychology, 91*(2), 301–311.

Williams, J., & Snipper, G. (1990). *Literacy and bilingualism.* New York: Longman.

Williams, J. (1992, April). *Effects of test anxiety and self-concept on performance across curricular areas.* Paper presented at the annual meeting of the American Educational Research Association, San Francisco.

Williams, R. (1987). Current issues in classroom behavior management. In J. Glover & R. Ronning (Eds.), *Historical foundations of educational psychology* (pp. 297–325). New York: Plenum Press.

Williams, S. (1997). Mathematics (Grades 7–12). In G. Phye (Ed.), *Handbook of academic learning: Construction of knowledge* (pp. 343–369). San Diego, CA: Academic Press.

Williams, S., Bareiss, R., & Reiser, B. (1996, April). *ASK Jasper: A multimedia publishing and performance support environment for design.* Paper presented at the annual meeting of the American Educational Research Association, New York.

Willingham, W., & Cole, N. (1997). *Gender and fair assessment.* Mahweh, NJ: Lawrence Erlbaum.

Willoughby, T., Porter, L., Belsito, L., & Yearsley, T. (1999). Use of elaboration strategies by students in grades two, four, and six. *Elementary School Journal, 99*(3), 221–232.

Willoughby, T., Wood, E., & Khan, M. (1994). Isolating variables that impact on or detract from the effectiveness of elaboration strategies. *Journal of*

Educational Psychology, 86(2), 279–289.

Wilson, B. (1998, April). *African American students' perceptions of their classroom climate and self-esteem.* Paper presented at the annual meeting of the American Educational Research Association, San Diego.

Wilson, K., & Swanson, H. (1999, April). *Individual and age-related differences in working memory and mathematics computation.* Paper presented at the annual conference of the American Educational Research Association, Montreal.

Wilson, S., Shulman, L., & Richert, A. (1987). 150 different ways of knowing: Representations of knowledge in teaching. In J. Calderhead (Ed.), *Exploring teacher thinking* (pp. 104–124). London: Cassel.

Winitzky, N. (1994). Multicultural and mainstreamed classrooms. In R. Arends, *Learning to teach* (3rd ed.), pp. 132–170). New York: McGraw-Hill.

Winitzky, N., Kauchak, D., & Kelly, M. (1994). Measuring teachers' structural knowledge. *Teaching and Teacher Education, 10*(2), 125–139.

Winn, J. (1992, April). *The promises and challenges of scaffolded instruction.* Paper presented at the annual meeting of the American Educational Research Association, San Francisco.

Winterton, W. A. (1977). *The effect of extended wait-time on selected verbal response characteristics of some Pueblo Indian children* (Doctoral dissertation, University of New Mexico, 1976). Dissertation Abstracts International, 38, 620–A. (University Microfilms No. 77–16, 130)

Wolf, L., Smith, J., & Birnbaum, M. (1997, March). *Measure-specific assessment of motivation and anxiety.* Paper presented at the annual meeting of the American Educational Research Association, Chicago.

Wolfe, P., & Brandt, R. (1998). What we know. *Educational Leadership, 56*(3), 8–13.

Wolfram, W. (1991). *Dialects and American English.* Upper Saddle River, NJ: Prentice Hall.

Wolters, C. (1997, March). *Self-regulated learning and college students' regulation of motivation.* Paper presented at the annual meeting of the American Educational Research Association, Chicago.

Wong-Fillmore, L. (1992). When learning a second language means losing the first. *Education, 6*(2), 4–11.

Wood, D., Bruner, J., & Ross, S. (1976). The role of tutoring in problem solving. *British Journal of Psychology, 66,* 181–196.

Wood, E., Motz, M., & Willoughby, T. (1998). Examining students' retrospective memories of strategy development. *Journal of Educational Psychology, 90,* 698–704.

Wood, E., Willoughby, T., McDermott, C., Motz, M., Kaspar, V., & Ducharme, M. (1999). Developmental differences in study behavior. *Journal of Educational Psychology, 91*(3), 527–536.

Wood, T., Cobb, P., & Yackel, E. (1992). Change in learning mathematics: Change in teaching mathematics. In H. Marshall (Ed.), *Redefining student learning: Roots of educational change* (pp. 177–205). Norwood, NJ: Ablex.

Woodcock, R. (1995, March). *Conceptualizations of intelligence and their implications for education.* Paper presented at the annual meeting of the American Educational Research Association, San Francisco.

Woodward, J., Baxter, J., & Robinson, R. (1997, March). *Rules and reasons: Decimal instruction for academically low achieving students.* Paper presented at the annual meeting of the American Educational Research Association, Chicago.

Woolfolk, A., & Hoy, W. (1990). Prospective teachers' sense of efficacy and beliefs about control. *Journal of Educational Psychology, 82,* 81–91.

Worthen, B. (1993). Critical issues that will determine the future of alternative assessment. *Phi Delta Kappan, 74,* 444–454.

Worthy, J., Moorman, M., & Turner, M. (1999). What Johnny likes to read is hard to find in school. *Reading Research Quarterly, 34*(1), 12–27.

Wright, S., & Taylor, D. (1995). Identity and the language of the classroom: Investigating the impact of heritage versus second-language instruction on personal and collective self-esteem. *Journal of Educational Psychology, 87*(2), 241–252.

Wynne, E. (1997, March). *Moral education and character education: A comparison/contrast.* Paper presented at the annual meeting of the American Educational Research Association, Chicago.

Yang, Y. (1991–1992). The effects of media on motivation and content recall: Comparison of computer and print-based instruction. *Journal of Education Technology Systems, 20,* 95–105.

Yazejian, N. (1999, April). *The relationship between school identification and dropping out of school.* Paper presented at the annual meeting of the American Educational Research Association, Montreal.

Yee, A. (1995). Evolution of the nature-nurture controversy: Response to J. Philipps Rushton. *Educational Psychology Review, 7*(4), 381–394.

Young, B., & Smith, T. (1999). *The condition of education, 1996: Issues in focus: The social context of education.* Washington, DC: U.S. Department of Education [On-line]. Available: http://NCES.ed.gov/pubs/ce/c9700.html

Young, M., & Scribner, J. (1997, March). *The synergy of parental involvement and student engagement at the secondary level: Relationships of consequence in Mexican-American communities.* Paper presented at the annual meeting of the American Educational Research Association, Chicago.

Yussen, S., & Levy, V. (1975). Developmental changes in predicting one's own span of short-term memory. *Journal of Experimental Child Psychology, 19,* 502–508.

Zahorik, J. (1996). Elementary and secondary teachers' reports of how they make learning interesting. *The Elementary School Journal, 96*(5), 551–564.

Zimmerman, B. (1990). Self-regulated academic learning and achievement: The emergence of a social cognitive perspective. *Educational Psychology Review, 2,* 173–201.

Zimmerman, B., & Blotner, R. (1979). Effect of model persistence and success on children's problem solving. *Journal of Educational Psychology, 71,* 508–513.

Zimmerman, B., & Kitsantas, A. (1999). Acquiring writing revision skill: Shifting from process to outcome self-regulatory goals. *Journal of Educational Psychology, 91*(2), 241–250.

Zimmerman, B., & Schunk, D. (Eds.). (1989). *Self-regulated learning and academic achievement: Theory, research, and practice.* New York: Springer.

Ziomek, R. (1997, March). *The concurrent validity of ACT's Passport Portfolio program: Initial validity results.* Paper presented at the annual meeting of the National Educational Research Association, Chicago.

Zohar, D. (1998). An additive model of test anxiety: Role of exam-specific expectations. *Journal of Educational Psychology, 90*(2), 330–340.

Zook, K. (1991). Effects of analogical processes on learning and misrepresentation. *Educational Psychology Review, 3,* 41–72.

Zorfass, J., Corley, P., & Remz, A. (1994). Helping students with disabilities become writers. *Educational Leadership, 51*(7), 62–66.

Author Index

Chambers, B., 598
Chance, P., 232, 414
Chaskin, R., 438
Chavajay, P., 51, 52
Chekley, K., 126
Chen, C., 454
Cheng, L. R., 626
Chi, M., 330, 334
Chiapetta, E., 402
Chih-Mei, C., 386
Chinn, C., 318, 338
Chinn, P., 69, 140
Chinnappan, M., 327
Chmielewski, T., 316, 339
Choate, J., 172, 194, 197
Choi, H., 203
Chomsky, N., 65, 232
Choy, M., 145
Christensen, C., 375
Church, M., 424
Chyung, S., 326
Cizek, G., 617
Clark, J., 275
Clark, K., 102
Clark, M., 102, 274
Clement, J., 393
Clements, B., 7, 96, 482
Clifford, M., 101, 442, 448, 472
Clifton, R., 439
Clinkenbeard, P., 186
Clum, G., 230
Cobb, P., 292, 544
Cocchiarella, M., 314, 315
Cochran, K., 8
Cognition and Technology Group at
    Vanderbilt, 299, 335, 336, 350, 391
Cohen, E., 101, 575, 576, 579, 583
Cohen, S., 136
Coker, H., 470
Coker, J., 470
Cole, B., 263
Cole, M., 293
Cole, N., 150, 151
Coleman, H., 142
Collins, A., 6, 245, 257, 301, 313, 314, 334,
    415
Colvin, C., 14, 455, 456
Comer, J., 156
Commerce, U.S. Department of, 161
Conchas, G., 152
Confrey, J., 314
Congress, U.S., 184
Conklin, N., 598

Connell, J., 100, 420
Connell, M., 518
Conway, G., 224, 503
Cooper, H., 531, 532, 630
Corbett, D., 156
Cordova, D., 446
Corkill, A., 281, 532
Corley, P., 201
Corno, L., 135, 426, 532
Cortez, J., 68
Cotten, M., 470
Coughlin, R., 102
Coulson, R., 296, 350, 399, 487, 565
Covington, M., 421, 426
Cowan, S., 175
Coxford, A., 391
Craik, F., 279
Cressy, D., 224
Crick, N., 86
Crocker, R., 499
Crone, D., 361
Crooks, T., 8, 449
Cruikshank, D., 22, 469, 471
Cuban, L., 533, 540, 575
Cunningham, D., 571
Curry, L., 136
Curwin, R., 504
Cushner, K., 144
Czikszentmihalyi, M., 326

Dahl, K., 365
Dai, D., 186
Daley, P., 539
Dansereau, D., 316, 339, 341, 576
Darling-Hammond, L., 642
Datnow, A., 152
Davenport, E., 132
Davies, S., 174
Davis, G., 183, 185, 186
Davis, R., 451, 452
De Bono, E., 343
DeCharms, R., 421
Deci, E., 232, 412, 413, 414, 421, 422, 423,
    427
De Corte, E., 386, 387
De La Paz, S., 200, 374
Delgado-Gaiton, C., 494, 495
De Lisi, 47
Delisle, J., 183
Delpit, L., 68
DeMarrais, K., 141
Dempster, F., 476, 630
Dempster, R., 281

DeMuelle, L., 379, 635
Derry, S., 288, 301
Devaney, T., 316
DeVries, R., 37, 106, 293, 481, 485
Dewey, G., 314
Dewey, J., 571
Diaz, R., 71
Dick, W., 527
Dickens, W., 438
Dickinson, V., 400
Diebert, E., 618
Dillon, J., 575
Dipinto, V., 480, 581, 582, 583
DiSessa, A., 396, 401
Dishner, E., 19
Dittmeier, L., 482
Dixon, J., 227
Dochy, F., 594
Doctor, R., 623
Dodge, K., 85, 86
Dolan, L., 20, 571
Dole, J., 200, 317, 318, 339
Dolgins, J., 199
Doll, B., 87
Donnerstein, E., 240
Doorlag, D., 194, 201
Dornbusch, S., 84, 454
Dossey, J., 454
Dowdy, B., 494
Doyle, W., 7, 12, 20, 84, 229, 467, 486, 498,
    529
Drabman, R., 240
Dreikurs, R., 468
Dreisbach, M., 623
Dressner, R., 113
Drew, C., 172, 524
Driscoll, M., 300, 348
Driver, B., 398
Dubois, N., 316
Ducharme, M., 340
Duffy, G., 200, 339, 342, 445, 498
Duffy, T., 571
Duffy-Hester, A., 363
Duguid, P., 301, 313
Dumaret, A., 131
Dunkle, M., 324
Dunn, R., 136
Duran, R., 68
Duyme, M., 131
Dweck, C., 425, 427, 435
Dwyer, D., 450
Dynarski, M., 157

Subject Index